1993 EDITION

FEDERAL INCOME TAXATION

1992 TAX RETURNS · 1993 TAX PLANNING

HAROLD Q. LANGENDERFER DBA, CPA
Peat, Marwick, Mitchell
Professor of Professional Accounting
University of North Carolina
Chapel Hill, North Carolina

WILLIS C. STEVENSON PhD, CPA
Professor of Business (Accounting)
University of Wisconsin-Madison
Madison, Wisconsin

HERBERT C. SIEG MAS, CPA
Associate Professor of Accounting
Illinois State University
Normal, Illinois

JAMES B. BOWER PhD, CPA
Professor Emeritus of Business (Accounting)
University of Wisconsin-Madison
Madison, Wisconsin

COLLEGE DIVISION South-Western Publishing Co.

Cincinnati Ohio

AG60CB
Copyright © 1993
by South-Western Publishing Co.
Cincinnati, Ohio

ISBN: 0-538-81616-3

1 2 DH 3 2

Printed in the United States of America

Sponsoring Editor: David L. Shaut, Sr.
Developmental Editor: Tom Bormann
Production Editor: Leslie Kauffman
Associate Editor/Production: Crystal Chapin, Michelle Cline
Forms Typist: Holly Knoechel
Cover Designer: Joseph M. Devine
Interior Designer: The Book Company
Consulting Editor: Audrey Smith
Marketing Manager: James Sheibley Enders

List of acronyms used:

ACRS—(Accelerated Cost Recovery System)
ADR—(Asset Depreciation Range)
ADS—(Alternate Depreciation System)
AEP—(Accumulated Earnings and Profits)
AGI—(Adjusted Gross Income)
AMT—(Alternative Minimum Tax)
AMTI—(Alternative Minimum Tax Income)
APR—(Annual Percentage Rate)
CEP—(Current Earnings & Profits)
E & P—(Earnings and Profits)
EIC—(Earned Income Credit)
EIN—(Employer Identification Number)
FICA—(Federal Insurance Contributions Act)
FMV—(Fair Market Value): The price at which the property would change hands between a buyer and a seller, neither being required to buy or sell, and both having reasonable knowledge of all necessary facts.

FUTA—(Federal Unemployment Tax Act)
HIP—(Hospital Insurance Program)
HOH—(Head Of Household)
IRA—(Individual Retirement Arrangement)
IRS—(Internal Revenue Service)
MACRS—(Modified Accelerated Cost Recovery System)
NOL—(Net Operating Loss)
OASDI—(Old Age, Survivors, and Disability Insurance)
PCM (Percentage-of-Completion Method)
PHC (Personal Holding Company)
SEP (Simplified Employer Pension Plan)
SSN (Social Security Number)
TIN (Taxpayer's Identification Number)

Preface

The 1993 edition of Federal Income Taxation continues to provide the best instruction in income tax preparation and reference for today's readers. The latest developments in tax law, clear explanations, and hands-on practice prepare readers to successfully complete tax returns for individuals, partnerships, or corporations. Many improvements are now combined with successful features from past editions to make this text truly the most important reference readers will need for completing 1992 Federal income tax returns.

Major Features

- The number of chapters was increased to 18 last year, which provided a more homogeneous group of topics in each chapter. The text can cover major topics in more depth, while still providing numerous illustrative examples of how to apply tax laws in given situations. This expanded format not only results in a better reference guide, but also appeals to the tax information user who wants a "hands-on" approach to preparing tax returns.
- An index of illustrated Federal tax forms, schedules, and worksheets located on the inside front cover, provides readers with an easy reference to the forms and schedules actually shown in the text.
- NEW "Your Rights As A Taxpayer" excerpts throughout the text, are taken from IRS Publication 1 to help readers become familiar with their rights as taxpayers.
- Shaded illustrations throughout every chapter clearly identify information which relates directly to particular forms or schedules.
- NEW reference boxes offer brief and specific tax facts and suggestions at key points within the text.

- A brief table of contents at the beginning of each chapter provides an overview and index of the chapter's contents so readers can quickly find specific information.
- Actual filled-in forms show readers where numbers should be placed and how items should be reported.
- NEW TurboTax® software (Headstart Edition), the leading commercial personal income taxation software, gives students hands-on experience with computerized tax preparation.

These characteristics combine with the text's clear, understandable language to make this book attractive as a teaching, learning, or reference tool.

Designed for Both Personal and Vocational Value

This text is designed to have both personal and vocational value. Readers will learn the latest tax information that is generally applicable to many taxpayers. This information will allow readers to prepare their own tax returns more intelligently and provide the necessary foundation for those who enter the vocation of preparing tax returns for others.

Based on Most Current Laws and Regulations

Since the tax laws change frequently, taxpayers need to maintain an awareness of any recent changes that affect their tax situation and the tax situations of their clients. The 1993 edition of this text includes the recent changes in the laws and regulations applicable to 1992 income tax returns. Also, tax planning issues for 1993 and later years are considered. The text also incorporates pertinent legislation passed up to the time the book went to press.

Income Tax Planning

Information provided in this text is significant to the average taxpayer, not only as the foundation for preparation of an income tax return, but also as background information for planning and controlling the income tax consequences of events yet to occur.

A substantial portion of the information reported on an income tax return can be altered through effective tax planning. A prudent taxpayer can often legally avoid income taxes. Avoidance consists of legal actions taken by a taxpayer to minimize the amount of tax owed. The text will also discuss the current penalties in effect that can be assessed for improper filing and tax evasion, which encompasses illegal actions to reduce the amount of tax paid. The goal is to help readers manage their financial affairs through effective income tax planning.

Structure of the Text

This text concentrates on concepts and procedures. Concepts are defined and discussed; then the procedures for tax reporting are discussed, and in many cases illustrated. This text includes many filled-in forms allowing readers hands-on experience in using the 1992 tax forms. Several forms were not available as we went to press; therefore we have either used an advance proof copy of the 1992 form or have used the 1991 form if no 1992 forms were available.

This edition starts with an overview of the reporting structure and presents a framework for understanding its elements and their interrelationships. Users who want to start with an overview of the payroll withholding structure should go to Chapter 14.

Chapters are designed to build on one another. Chapter 1 provides an overview of the income tax structure, including the basic calculation of taxable income and the amount of tax due. Chapter 2 goes into detail regarding tax withholdings and estimated tax payments and Forms 1040EZ and 1040A. Chapter 3 focuses on filing requirements of Form 1040. Chapter 4 covers gross income exclusions. Chapters 5 and 6 cover itemized deductions reported on Schedule A. Chapter 7 discusses other tax considerations such as additional taxes, extensions of time to file, underpayment of taxes, and tax penalties. Chapter 8 discusses business income and expenses reported on Schedule C by self-employed individuals. Chapter 9 follows up the discussion of business income by covering the deduction of depreciation and pension expenses. Chapter 10 focuses on real estate rentals and other passive activities that are reported on Schedule E. Chapters 11 and 12 cover the calculation of gain or loss on property transactions as being either capital gains or losses or ordinary income or loss. Chapter 13 deals with net operating losses, installment sales, long-term contracts, and the alternative minimum tax. Chapter 14 discusses tax withholding, estimated taxes, and payroll taxes. Finally, the last four chapters cover the tax treatment of partnerships and corporations. Chapter 15 focuses on partnerships, Chapter 16 on S corporations, Chapter 17 on C corporations, and Chapter 18 on special corporate situations, such as estimated taxes, controlled corporations, and consolidated tax returns.

The assignments for each chapter are located at the end of the chapter. There are short-answer questions, quantitative questions, and problems that require the completion of forms. Blank forms are provided for ease in completing the solutions. The assignments are generally designed to reinforce the text discussions. The last problem in some of the assignments presents a tax issue with an ethical dilemma that tax preparers can face and should be able to develop a strategy for how to cope with this dilemma. The 1992 Tax Table and the 1992 Tax Rate Schedules are located in the front of the text. These resources will be frequently referenced by readers.

The Highlights for 1992 and Beyond lists many of the new and pending tax laws and interpretations applicable to 1993. The 1993 edition continues the policy of including an available computer program to supplement the text.

Using the Text Effectively

To make the best use of this text, readers are encouraged to develop and overview of each chapter before delving into the details. A careful review of the chapter outline on the first page of each chapter and the Highlights for the chapter presented near the front of the text will provide insight as to the topics covered in the chapter. Then, a careful reading of the chapter will provide the reader with an appreciation of how each tax provision is applied. The best understanding of the tax provisions comes from working the problems and completing any applicable forms. Before working a particular problem or answering a question, the reader should first understand what tax provisions are involved in the problem or questions and then go back to the text to read about the tax provision in depth before attempting to solve the problem or answer the question. It should be noted that the solution to a particular problem often may be derived from a logical thought process involving a set of steps that is different from the way the information is presented on a tax form. A full understanding of a tax provision requires both a logical thinking process and an understanding of how the information is presented on the appropriate tax form. Also keep in mind that the purpose of this text is to provide a framework for the average taxpayer. Readers are referred to advanced tax texts if they are confronted with more complex issues than those presented in this text.

The authors are grateful for the feedback we receive each year from the users of the text. We would especially like to thank the following faculty:

David Bartram
Baker College

Terry Bill
Kaskaskia College

Verne Bryers
Fox Valley Technical College

Joseph M. Catalina
Hudson Valley Community College
Director of Revenue Opportunity Division
New York Department of Taxation and Finance

Skip Dent
Delta School of Business

Selwyn Glincher
Quincy College

James Joseph
Chabot College

Lucretia Mattson
University of Wisconsin Eau Claire

George McDaniel
Hocking Technical College

Robert Muir
Coastal Carolina Community College

John H. Palipchak
PSU-Beaver Campus

Bob Ripley
San Diego City College

Harold Royer
Miami Dade Community College

Vernon Schaller
Nicolet Area Technical College

Rick Sealscott
Northwest Technical College

Marlin Sekutera
Northeast Community College

Lois Slutsky
Broward Community College

Dana G. Thompson
National Business College

John Tiliakos
Advanced Software Analysis, Inc.

We welcome your comments and suggestions.

Harold Q. Langenderfer, DBA, CPA
Willis C. Stevenson, Ph.D, CPA
Herbert C. Sieg, MAS, CPA
James B. Bower, PhD, CPA

Contents

PART I INTRODUCTION TO FEDERAL INCOME TAXATION   1

CHAPTER 1 Overview of the Tax Structure 2

CHAPTER 2 Tax Determination 32

PART II GROSS INCOME   75

CHAPTER 3 Gross Income Inclusions 76

CHAPTER 4 Gross Income Exclusions and Adjustments to Income 112

PART III PERSONAL DEDUCTIONS AND OTHER TAX CONSIDERATIONS — 152

PART IV BUSINESS AND PROFESSIONAL RETURNS — 276

CHAPTER 9 Depreciation, Cost Recovery, Depletion, and Amortization 329

PART V PROPERTY TRANSACTIONS   358

CHAPTER 10 Supplemental Income Activities 359

CHAPTER 11 Property Transactions: Recognizing Gains and Losses 388

CHAPTER 12 Property Transactions: Tax Treatment of Gains and Losses 417

PART VI TAX CREDITS AND OTHER TAX SITUATIONS   445

CHAPTER 13 Tax Credits and Other Tax Situations 446

PART VII WITHHOLDING, PAYROLL, AND ESTIMATED TAXES 472

CHAPTER 14 Withholding, Payroll, and Estimated Taxes 473

PART VIII PARTNERSHIPS AND CORPORATIONS 512

CHAPTER 15 Partnerships 513

CHAPTER 16 S Corporations 555

CHAPTER 17 C Corporations 588

CHAPTER 18 Special Corporate Situations 628

Section 7.

1992 Tax Table

Use if your taxable income is less than $100,000.
If $100,000 or more, use the Tax Rate Schedules.

Example. Mr. and Mrs. Brown are filing a joint return. Their taxable income on line 37 of Form 1040 is $25,300. First, they find the $25,300–25,350 income line. Next, they find the column for married filing jointly and read down the column. The amount shown where the income line and filing status column meet is $3,799. This is the tax amount they must enter on line 38 of their Form 1040.

Sample Table

At least	But less than	Single	Married filing jointly *	Married filing separately	Head of a household
			Your tax is—		
25,200	25,250	4,275	3,784	4,736	3,784
25,250	25,300	4,289	3,791	4,750	3,791
25,300	25,350	4,303	(3,799)	4,764	3,799
25,350	25,400	4,317	3,805	4,778	3,806

If line 37 (taxable income) is— / And you are—

At least	But less than	Single	Married filing jointly *	Married filing separately	Head of a household
			Your tax is—		
0	5	0	0	0	0
5	15	2	2	2	2
15	25	3	3	3	3
25	50	6	6	6	6
50	75	9	9	9	9
75	100	13	13	13	13
100	125	17	17	17	17
125	150	21	21	21	21
150	175	24	24	24	24
175	200	28	28	28	28
200	225	32	32	32	32
225	250	36	36	36	36
250	275	39	39	39	39
275	300	43	43	43	43
300	325	47	47	47	47
325	350	51	51	51	51
350	375	54	54	54	54
375	400	58	58	58	58
400	425	62	62	62	62
425	450	66	66	66	66
450	475	69	69	69	69
475	500	73	73	73	73
500	525	77	77	77	77
525	550	81	81	81	81
550	575	84	84	84	84
575	600	88	88	88	88
600	625	92	92	92	92
625	650	96	96	96	96
650	675	99	99	99	99
675	700	103	103	103	103
700	725	107	107	107	107
725	750	111	111	111	111
750	775	114	114	114	114
775	800	118	118	118	118
800	825	122	122	122	122
825	850	126	126	126	126
850	875	129	129	129	129
875	900	133	133	133	133
900	925	137	137	137	137
925	950	141	141	141	141
950	975	144	144	144	144
975	1,000	148	148	148	148
1,000					
1,000	1,025	152	152	152	152
1,025	1,050	156	156	156	156
1,050	1,075	159	159	159	159
1,075	1,100	163	163	163	163
1,100	1,125	167	167	167	167
1,125	1,150	171	171	171	171
1,150	1,175	174	174	174	174
1,175	1,200	178	178	178	178
1,200	1,225	182	182	182	182
1,225	1,250	186	186	186	186
1,250	1,275	189	189	189	189
1,275	1,300	193	193	193	193
1,300	1,325	197	197	197	197
1,325	1,350	201	201	201	201
1,350	1,375	204	204	204	204
1,375	1,400	208	208	208	208
1,400	1,425	212	212	212	212
1,425	1,450	216	216	216	216
1,450	1,475	219	219	219	219
1,475	1,500	223	223	223	223
1,500	1,525	227	227	227	227
1,525	1,550	231	231	231	231
1,550	1,575	234	234	234	234
1,575	1,600	238	238	238	238
1,600	1,625	242	242	242	242
1,625	1,650	246	246	246	246
1,650	1,675	249	249	249	249
1,675	1,700	253	253	253	253
1,700	1,725	257	257	257	257
1,725	1,750	261	261	261	261
1,750	1,775	264	264	264	264
1,775	1,800	268	268	268	268
1,800	1,825	272	272	272	272
1,825	1,850	276	276	276	276
1,850	1,875	279	279	279	279
1,875	1,900	283	283	283	283
1,900	1,925	287	287	287	287
1,925	1,950	291	291	291	291
1,950	1,975	294	294	294	294
1,975	2,000	298	298	298	298
2,000					
2,000	2,025	302	302	302	302
2,025	2,050	306	306	306	306
2,050	2,075	309	309	309	309
2,075	2,100	313	313	313	313
2,100	2,125	317	317	317	317
2,125	2,150	321	321	321	321
2,150	2,175	324	324	324	324
2,175	2,200	328	328	328	328
2,200	2,225	332	332	332	332
2,225	2,250	336	336	336	336
2,250	2,275	339	339	339	339
2,275	2,300	343	343	343	343
2,300	2,325	347	347	347	347
2,325	2,350	351	351	351	351
2,350	2,375	354	354	354	354
2,375	2,400	358	358	358	358
2,400	2,425	362	362	362	362
2,425	2,450	366	366	366	366
2,450	2,475	369	369	369	369
2,475	2,500	373	373	373	373
2,500	2,525	377	377	377	377
2,525	2,550	381	381	381	381
2,550	2,575	384	384	384	384
2,575	2,600	388	388	388	388
2,600	2,625	392	392	392	392
2,625	2,650	396	396	396	396
2,650	2,675	399	399	399	399
2,675	2,700	403	403	403	403
2,700	2,725	407	407	407	407
2,725	2,750	411	411	411	411
2,750	2,775	414	414	414	414
2,775	2,800	418	418	418	418
2,800	2,825	422	422	422	422
2,825	2,850	426	426	426	426
2,850	2,875	429	429	429	429
2,875	2,900	433	433	433	433
2,900	2,925	437	437	437	437
2,925	2,950	441	441	441	441
2,950	2,975	444	444	444	444
2,975	3,000	448	448	448	448
3,000					
3,000	3,050	454	454	454	454
3,050	3,100	461	461	461	461
3,100	3,150	469	469	469	469
3,150	3,200	476	476	476	476
3,200	3,250	484	484	484	484
3,250	3,300	491	491	491	491
3,300	3,350	499	499	499	499
3,350	3,400	506	506	506	506
3,400	3,450	514	514	514	514
3,450	3,500	521	521	521	521
3,500	3,550	529	529	529	529
3,550	3,600	536	536	536	536
3,600	3,650	544	544	544	544
3,650	3,700	551	551	551	551
3,700	3,750	559	559	559	559
3,750	3,800	566	566	566	566
3,800	3,850	574	574	574	574
3,850	3,900	581	581	581	581
3,900	3,950	589	589	589	589
3,950	4,000	596	596	596	596
4,000					
4,000	4,050	604	604	604	604
4,050	4,100	611	611	611	611
4,100	4,150	619	619	619	619
4,150	4,200	626	626	626	626
4,200	4,250	634	634	634	634
4,250	4,300	641	641	641	641
4,300	4,350	649	649	649	649
4,350	4,400	656	656	656	656
4,400	4,450	664	664	664	664
4,450	4,500	671	671	671	671
4,500	4,550	679	679	679	679
4,550	4,600	686	686	686	686
4,600	4,650	694	694	694	694
4,650	4,700	701	701	701	701
4,700	4,750	709	709	709	709
4,750	4,800	716	716	716	716
4,800	4,850	724	724	724	724
4,850	4,900	731	731	731	731
4,900	4,950	739	739	739	739
4,950	5,000	746	746	746	746

* This column must also be used by a qualifying widow(er).

1992 Tax Table—*Continued*

If line 37 (taxable income) is— / And you are—

At least	But less than	Single	Married filing jointly *	Married filing separately	Head of a household
			Your tax is—		
5,000					
5,000	5,050	754	754	754	754
5,050	5,100	761	761	761	761
5,100	5,150	769	769	769	769
5,150	5,200	776	776	776	776
5,200	5,250	784	784	784	784
5,250	5,300	791	791	791	791
5,300	5,350	799	799	799	799
5,350	5,400	806	806	806	806
5,400	5,450	814	814	814	814
5,450	5,500	821	821	821	821
5,500	5,550	829	829	829	829
5,550	5,600	836	836	836	836
5,600	5,650	844	844	844	844
5,650	5,700	851	851	851	851
5,700	5,750	859	859	859	859
5,750	5,800	866	866	866	866
5,800	5,850	874	874	874	874
5,850	5,900	881	881	881	881
5,900	5,950	889	889	889	889
5,950	6,000	896	896	896	896
6,000					
6,000	6,050	904	904	904	904
6,050	6,100	911	911	911	911
6,100	6,150	919	919	919	919
6,150	6,200	926	926	926	926
6,200	6,250	934	934	934	934
6,250	6,300	941	941	941	941
6,300	6,350	949	949	949	949
6,350	6,400	956	956	956	956
6,400	6,450	964	964	964	964
6,450	6,500	971	971	971	971
6,500	6,550	979	979	979	979
6,550	6,600	986	986	986	986
6,600	6,650	994	994	994	994
6,650	6,700	1,001	1,001	1,001	1,001
6,700	6,750	1,009	1,009	1,009	1,009
6,750	6,800	1,016	1,016	1,016	1,016
6,800	6,850	1,024	1,024	1,024	1,024
6,850	6,900	1,031	1,031	1,031	1,031
6,900	6,950	1,039	1,039	1,039	1,039
6,950	7,000	1,046	1,046	1,046	1,046
7,000					
7,000	7,050	1,054	1,054	1,054	1,054
7,050	7,100	1,061	1,061	1,061	1,061
7,100	7,150	1,069	1,069	1,069	1,069
7,150	7,200	1,076	1,076	1,076	1,076
7,200	7,250	1,084	1,084	1,084	1,084
7,250	7,300	1,091	1,091	1,091	1,091
7,300	7,350	1,099	1,099	1,099	1,099
7,350	7,400	1,106	1,106	1,106	1,106
7,400	7,450	1,114	1,114	1,114	1,114
7,450	7,500	1,121	1,121	1,121	1,121
7,500	7,550	1,129	1,129	1,129	1,129
7,550	7,600	1,136	1,136	1,136	1,136
7,600	7,650	1,144	1,144	1,144	1,144
7,650	7,700	1,151	1,151	1,151	1,151
7,700	7,750	1,159	1,159	1,159	1,159
7,750	7,800	1,166	1,166	1,166	1,166
7,800	7,850	1,174	1,174	1,174	1,174
7,850	7,900	1,181	1,181	1,181	1,181
7,900	7,950	1,189	1,189	1,189	1,189
7,950	8,000	1,196	1,196	1,196	1,196
8,000					
8,000	8,050	1,204	1,204	1,204	1,204
8,050	8,100	1,211	1,211	1,211	1,211
8,100	8,150	1,219	1,219	1,219	1,219
8,150	8,200	1,226	1,226	1,226	1,226
8,200	8,250	1,234	1,234	1,234	1,234
8,250	8,300	1,241	1,241	1,241	1,241
8,300	8,350	1,249	1,249	1,249	1,249
8,350	8,400	1,256	1,256	1,256	1,256
8,400	8,450	1,264	1,264	1,264	1,264
8,450	8,500	1,271	1,271	1,271	1,271
8,500	8,550	1,279	1,279	1,279	1,279
8,550	8,600	1,286	1,286	1,286	1,286
8,600	8,650	1,294	1,294	1,294	1,294
8,650	8,700	1,301	1,301	1,301	1,301
8,700	8,750	1,309	1,309	1,309	1,309
8,750	8,800	1,316	1,316	1,316	1,316
8,800	8,850	1,324	1,324	1,324	1,324
8,850	8,900	1,331	1,331	1,331	1,331
8,900	8,950	1,339	1,339	1,339	1,339
8,950	9,000	1,346	1,346	1,346	1,346
9,000					
9,000	9,050	1,354	1,354	1,354	1,354
9,050	9,100	1,361	1,361	1,361	1,361
9,100	9,150	1,369	1,369	1,369	1,369
9,150	9,200	1,376	1,376	1,376	1,376
9,200	9,250	1,384	1,384	1,384	1,384
9,250	9,300	1,391	1,391	1,391	1,391
9,300	9,350	1,399	1,399	1,399	1,399
9,350	9,400	1,406	1,406	1,406	1,406
9,400	9,450	1,414	1,414	1,414	1,414
9,450	9,500	1,421	1,421	1,421	1,421
9,500	9,550	1,429	1,429	1,429	1,429
9,550	9,600	1,436	1,436	1,436	1,436
9,600	9,650	1,444	1,444	1,444	1,444
9,650	9,700	1,451	1,451	1,451	1,451
9,700	9,750	1,459	1,459	1,459	1,459
9,750	9,800	1,466	1,466	1,466	1,466
9,800	9,850	1,474	1,474	1,474	1,474
9,850	9,900	1,481	1,481	1,481	1,481
9,900	9,950	1,489	1,489	1,489	1,489
9,950	10,000	1,496	1,496	1,496	1,496
10,000					
10,000	10,050	1,504	1,504	1,504	1,504
10,050	10,100	1,511	1,511	1,511	1,511
10,100	10,150	1,519	1,519	1,519	1,519
10,150	10,200	1,526	1,526	1,526	1,526
10,200	10,250	1,534	1,534	1,534	1,534
10,250	10,300	1,541	1,541	1,541	1,541
10,300	10,350	1,549	1,549	1,549	1,549
10,350	10,400	1,556	1,556	1,556	1,556
10,400	10,450	1,564	1,564	1,564	1,564
10,450	10,500	1,571	1,571	1,571	1,571
10,500	10,550	1,579	1,579	1,579	1,579
10,550	10,600	1,586	1,586	1,586	1,586
10,600	10,650	1,594	1,594	1,594	1,594
10,650	10,700	1,601	1,601	1,601	1,601
10,700	10,750	1,609	1,609	1,609	1,609
10,750	10,800	1,616	1,616	1,616	1,616
10,800	10,850	1,624	1,624	1,624	1,624
10,850	10,900	1,631	1,631	1,631	1,631
10,900	10,950	1,639	1,639	1,639	1,639
10,950	11,000	1,646	1,646	1,646	1,646
11,000					
11,000	11,050	1,654	1,654	1,654	1,654
11,050	11,100	1,661	1,661	1,661	1,661
11,100	11,150	1,669	1,669	1,669	1,669
11,150	11,200	1,676	1,676	1,676	1,676
11,200	11,250	1,684	1,684	1,684	1,684
11,250	11,300	1,691	1,691	1,691	1,691
11,300	11,350	1,699	1,699	1,699	1,699
11,350	11,400	1,706	1,706	1,706	1,706
11,400	11,450	1,714	1,714	1,714	1,714
11,450	11,500	1,721	1,721	1,721	1,721
11,500	11,550	1,729	1,729	1,729	1,729
11,550	11,600	1,736	1,736	1,736	1,736
11,600	11,650	1,744	1,744	1,744	1,744
11,650	11,700	1,751	1,751	1,751	1,751
11,700	11,750	1,759	1,759	1,759	1,759
11,750	11,800	1,766	1,766	1,766	1,766
11,800	11,850	1,774	1,774	1,774	1,774
11,850	11,900	1,781	1,781	1,781	1,781
11,900	11,950	1,789	1,789	1,789	1,789
11,950	12,000	1,796	1,796	1,796	1,796
12,000					
12,000	12,050	1,804	1,804	1,804	1,804
12,050	12,100	1,811	1,811	1,811	1,811
12,100	12,150	1,819	1,819	1,819	1,819
12,150	12,200	1,826	1,826	1,826	1,826
12,200	12,250	1,834	1,834	1,834	1,834
12,250	12,300	1,841	1,841	1,841	1,841
12,300	12,350	1,849	1,849	1,849	1,849
12,350	12,400	1,856	1,856	1,856	1,856
12,400	12,450	1,864	1,864	1,864	1,864
12,450	12,500	1,871	1,871	1,871	1,871
12,500	12,550	1,879	1,879	1,879	1,879
12,550	12,600	1,886	1,886	1,886	1,886
12,600	12,650	1,894	1,894	1,894	1,894
12,650	12,700	1,901	1,901	1,901	1,901
12,700	12,750	1,909	1,909	1,909	1,909
12,750	12,800	1,916	1,916	1,916	1,916
12,800	12,850	1,924	1,924	1,924	1,924
12,850	12,900	1,931	1,931	1,931	1,931
12,900	12,950	1,939	1,939	1,939	1,939
12,950	13,000	1,946	1,946	1,946	1,946
13,000					
13,000	13,050	1,954	1,954	1,954	1,954
13,050	13,100	1,961	1,961	1,961	1,961
13,100	13,150	1,969	1,969	1,969	1,969
13,150	13,200	1,976	1,976	1,976	1,976
13,200	13,250	1,984	1,984	1,984	1,984
13,250	13,300	1,991	1,991	1,991	1,991
13,300	13,350	1,999	1,999	1,999	1,999
13,350	13,400	2,006	2,006	2,006	2,006
13,400	13,450	2,014	2,014	2,014	2,014
13,450	13,500	2,021	2,021	2,021	2,021
13,500	13,550	2,029	2,029	2,029	2,029
13,550	13,600	2,036	2,036	2,036	2,036
13,600	13,650	2,044	2,044	2,044	2,044
13,650	13,700	2,051	2,051	2,051	2,051
13,700	13,750	2,059	2,059	2,059	2,059
13,750	13,800	2,066	2,066	2,066	2,066
13,800	13,850	2,074	2,074	2,074	2,074
13,850	13,900	2,081	2,081	2,081	2,081
13,900	13,950	2,089	2,089	2,089	2,089
13,950	14,000	2,096	2,096	2,096	2,096

Continued on next page

* This column must also be used by a qualifying widow(er).

1992 Tax Table—Continued

If line 37 (taxable income) is— / And you are— / Your tax is—
 At least | But less than | Single | Married filing jointly* | Married filing separately | Head of a household

14,000

At least	But less than	Single	Married filing jointly*	Married filing separately	Head of a household
14,000	14,050	2,104	2,104	2,104	2,104
14,050	14,100	2,111	2,111	2,111	2,111
14,100	14,150	2,119	2,119	2,119	2,119
14,150	14,200	2,126	2,126	2,126	2,126
14,200	14,250	2,134	2,134	2,134	2,134
14,250	14,300	2,141	2,141	2,141	2,141
14,300	14,350	2,149	2,149	2,149	2,149
14,350	14,400	2,156	2,156	2,156	2,156
14,400	14,450	2,164	2,164	2,164	2,164
14,450	14,500	2,171	2,171	2,171	2,171
14,500	14,550	2,179	2,179	2,179	2,179
14,550	14,600	2,186	2,186	2,186	2,186
14,600	14,650	2,194	2,194	2,194	2,194
14,650	14,700	2,201	2,201	2,201	2,201
14,700	14,750	2,209	2,209	2,209	2,209
14,750	14,800	2,216	2,216	2,216	2,216
14,800	14,850	2,224	2,224	2,224	2,224
14,850	14,900	2,231	2,231	2,231	2,231
14,900	14,950	2,239	2,239	2,239	2,239
14,950	15,000	2,246	2,246	2,246	2,246

15,000

At least	But less than	Single	Married filing jointly*	Married filing separately	Head of a household
15,000	15,050	2,254	2,254	2,254	2,254
15,050	15,100	2,261	2,261	2,261	2,261
15,100	15,150	2,269	2,269	2,269	2,269
15,150	15,200	2,276	2,276	2,276	2,276
15,200	15,250	2,284	2,284	2,284	2,284
15,250	15,300	2,291	2,291	2,291	2,291
15,300	15,350	2,299	2,299	2,299	2,299
15,350	15,400	2,306	2,306	2,306	2,306
15,400	15,450	2,314	2,314	2,314	2,314
15,450	15,500	2,321	2,321	2,321	2,321
15,500	15,550	2,329	2,329	2,329	2,329
15,550	15,600	2,336	2,336	2,336	2,336
15,600	15,650	2,344	2,344	2,344	2,344
15,650	15,700	2,351	2,351	2,351	2,351
15,700	15,750	2,359	2,359	2,359	2,359
15,750	15,800	2,366	2,366	2,366	2,366
15,800	15,850	2,374	2,374	2,374	2,374
15,850	15,900	2,381	2,381	2,381	2,381
15,900	15,950	2,389	2,389	2,389	2,389
15,950	16,000	2,396	2,396	2,396	2,396

16,000

At least	But less than	Single	Married filing jointly*	Married filing separately	Head of a household
16,000	16,050	2,404	2,404	2,404	2,404
16,050	16,100	2,411	2,411	2,411	2,411
16,100	16,150	2,419	2,419	2,419	2,419
16,150	16,200	2,426	2,426	2,426	2,426
16,200	16,250	2,434	2,434	2,434	2,434
16,250	16,300	2,441	2,441	2,441	2,441
16,300	16,350	2,449	2,449	2,449	2,449
16,350	16,400	2,456	2,456	2,456	2,456
16,400	16,450	2,464	2,464	2,464	2,464
16,450	16,500	2,471	2,471	2,471	2,471
16,500	16,550	2,479	2,479	2,479	2,479
16,550	16,600	2,486	2,486	2,486	2,486
16,600	16,650	2,494	2,494	2,494	2,494
16,650	16,700	2,501	2,501	2,501	2,501
16,700	16,750	2,509	2,509	2,509	2,509
16,750	16,800	2,516	2,516	2,516	2,516
16,800	16,850	2,524	2,524	2,524	2,524
16,850	16,900	2,531	2,531	2,531	2,531
16,900	16,950	2,539	2,539	2,539	2,539
16,950	17,000	2,546	2,546	2,546	2,546

17,000

At least	But less than	Single	Married filing jointly*	Married filing separately	Head of a household
17,000	17,050	2,554	2,554	2,554	2,554
17,050	17,100	2,561	2,561	2,561	2,561
17,100	17,150	2,569	2,569	2,569	2,569
17,150	17,200	2,576	2,576	2,576	2,576
17,200	17,250	2,584	2,584	2,584	2,584
17,250	17,300	2,591	2,591	2,591	2,591
17,300	17,350	2,599	2,599	2,599	2,599
17,350	17,400	2,606	2,606	2,606	2,606
17,400	17,450	2,614	2,614	2,614	2,614
17,450	17,500	2,621	2,621	2,621	2,621
17,500	17,550	2,629	2,629	2,629	2,629
17,550	17,600	2,636	2,636	2,636	2,636
17,600	17,650	2,644	2,644	2,644	2,644
17,650	17,700	2,651	2,651	2,651	2,651
17,700	17,750	2,659	2,659	2,659	2,659
17,750	17,800	2,666	2,666	2,666	2,666
17,800	17,850	2,674	2,674	2,674	2,674
17,850	17,900	2,681	2,681	2,681	2,681
17,900	17,950	2,689	2,689	2,692	2,689
17,950	18,000	2,696	2,696	2,706	2,696

18,000

At least	But less than	Single	Married filing jointly*	Married filing separately	Head of a household
18,000	18,050	2,704	2,704	2,720	2,704
18,050	18,100	2,711	2,711	2,734	2,711
18,100	18,150	2,719	2,719	2,748	2,719
18,150	18,200	2,726	2,726	2,762	2,726
18,200	18,250	2,734	2,734	2,776	2,734
18,250	18,300	2,741	2,741	2,790	2,741
18,300	18,350	2,749	2,749	2,804	2,749
18,350	18,400	2,756	2,756	2,818	2,756
18,400	18,450	2,764	2,764	2,832	2,764
18,450	18,500	2,771	2,771	2,846	2,771
18,500	18,550	2,779	2,779	2,860	2,779
18,550	18,600	2,786	2,786	2,874	2,786
18,600	18,650	2,794	2,794	2,888	2,794
18,650	18,700	2,801	2,801	2,902	2,801
18,700	18,750	2,809	2,809	2,916	2,809
18,750	18,800	2,816	2,816	2,930	2,816
18,800	18,850	2,824	2,824	2,944	2,824
18,850	18,900	2,831	2,831	2,958	2,831
18,900	18,950	2,839	2,839	2,972	2,839
18,950	19,000	2,846	2,846	2,986	2,846

19,000

At least	But less than	Single	Married filing jointly*	Married filing separately	Head of a household
19,000	19,050	2,854	2,854	3,000	2,854
19,050	19,100	2,861	2,861	3,014	2,861
19,100	19,150	2,869	2,869	3,028	2,869
19,150	19,200	2,876	2,876	3,042	2,876
19,200	19,250	2,884	2,884	3,056	2,884
19,250	19,300	2,891	2,891	3,070	2,891
19,300	19,350	2,899	2,899	3,084	2,899
19,350	19,400	2,906	2,906	3,098	2,906
19,400	19,450	2,914	2,914	3,112	2,914
19,450	19,500	2,921	2,921	3,126	2,921
19,500	19,550	2,929	2,929	3,140	2,929
19,550	19,600	2,936	2,936	3,154	2,936
19,600	19,650	2,944	2,944	3,168	2,944
19,650	19,700	2,951	2,951	3,182	2,951
19,700	19,750	2,959	2,959	3,196	2,959
19,750	19,800	2,966	2,966	3,210	2,966
19,800	19,850	2,974	2,974	3,224	2,974
19,850	19,900	2,981	2,981	3,238	2,981
19,900	19,950	2,989	2,989	3,252	2,989
19,950	20,000	2,996	2,996	3,266	2,996

20,000

At least	But less than	Single	Married filing jointly*	Married filing separately	Head of a household
20,000	20,050	3,004	3,004	3,280	3,004
20,050	20,100	3,011	3,011	3,294	3,011
20,100	20,150	3,019	3,019	3,308	3,019
20,150	20,200	3,026	3,026	3,322	3,026
20,200	20,250	3,034	3,034	3,336	3,034
20,250	20,300	3,041	3,041	3,350	3,041
20,300	20,350	3,049	3,049	3,364	3,049
20,350	20,400	3,056	3,056	3,378	3,056
20,400	20,450	3,064	3,064	3,392	3,064
20,450	20,500	3,071	3,071	3,406	3,071
20,500	20,550	3,079	3,079	3,420	3,079
20,550	20,600	3,086	3,086	3,434	3,086
20,600	20,650	3,094	3,094	3,448	3,094
20,650	20,700	3,101	3,101	3,462	3,101
20,700	20,750	3,109	3,109	3,476	3,109
20,750	20,800	3,116	3,116	3,490	3,116
20,800	20,850	3,124	3,124	3,504	3,124
20,850	20,900	3,131	3,131	3,518	3,131
20,900	20,950	3,139	3,139	3,532	3,139
20,950	21,000	3,146	3,146	3,546	3,146

21,000

At least	But less than	Single	Married filing jointly*	Married filing separately	Head of a household
21,000	21,050	3,154	3,154	3,560	3,154
21,050	21,100	3,161	3,161	3,574	3,161
21,100	21,150	3,169	3,169	3,588	3,169
21,150	21,200	3,176	3,176	3,602	3,176
21,200	21,250	3,184	3,184	3,616	3,184
21,250	21,300	3,191	3,191	3,630	3,191
21,300	21,350	3,199	3,199	3,644	3,199
21,350	21,400	3,206	3,206	3,658	3,206
21,400	21,450	3,214	3,214	3,672	3,214
21,450	21,500	3,225	3,221	3,686	3,221
21,500	21,550	3,239	3,229	3,700	3,229
21,550	21,600	3,253	3,236	3,714	3,236
21,600	21,650	3,267	3,244	3,728	3,244
21,650	21,700	3,281	3,251	3,742	3,251
21,700	21,750	3,295	3,259	3,756	3,259
21,750	21,800	3,309	3,266	3,770	3,266
21,800	21,850	3,323	3,274	3,784	3,274
21,850	21,900	3,337	3,281	3,798	3,281
21,900	21,950	3,351	3,289	3,812	3,289
21,950	22,000	3,365	3,296	3,826	3,296

22,000

At least	But less than	Single	Married filing jointly*	Married filing separately	Head of a household
22,000	22,050	3,379	3,304	3,840	3,304
22,050	22,100	3,393	3,311	3,854	3,311
22,100	22,150	3,407	3,319	3,868	3,319
22,150	22,200	3,421	3,326	3,882	3,326
22,200	22,250	3,435	3,334	3,896	3,334
22,250	22,300	3,449	3,341	3,910	3,341
22,300	22,350	3,463	3,349	3,924	3,349
22,350	22,400	3,477	3,356	3,938	3,356
22,400	22,450	3,491	3,364	3,952	3,364
22,450	22,500	3,505	3,371	3,966	3,371
22,500	22,550	3,519	3,379	3,980	3,379
22,550	22,600	3,533	3,386	3,994	3,386
22,600	22,650	3,547	3,394	4,008	3,394
22,650	22,700	3,561	3,401	4,022	3,401
22,700	22,750	3,575	3,409	4,036	3,409
22,750	22,800	3,589	3,416	4,050	3,416
22,800	22,850	3,603	3,424	4,064	3,424
22,850	22,900	3,617	3,431	4,078	3,431
22,900	22,950	3,631	3,439	4,092	3,439
22,950	23,000	3,645	3,446	4,106	3,446

* This column must also be used by a qualifying widow(er).

Continued on next page

1992 Tax Table—Continued

If line 37 (taxable income) is— / And you are— / Your tax is—
 At least | But less than | Single | Married filing jointly* | Married filing separately | Head of a household

23,000

At least	But less than	Single	Married filing jointly*	Married filing separately	Head of a household
23,000	23,050	3,659	3,454	4,120	3,454
23,050	23,100	3,673	3,461	4,134	3,461
23,100	23,150	3,687	3,469	4,148	3,469
23,150	23,200	3,701	3,476	4,162	3,476
23,200	23,250	3,715	3,484	4,176	3,484
23,250	23,300	3,729	3,491	4,190	3,491
23,300	23,350	3,743	3,499	4,204	3,499
23,350	23,400	3,757	3,506	4,218	3,506
23,400	23,450	3,771	3,514	4,232	3,514
23,450	23,500	3,785	3,521	4,246	3,521
23,500	23,550	3,799	3,529	4,260	3,529
23,550	23,600	3,813	3,536	4,274	3,536
23,600	23,650	3,827	3,544	4,288	3,544
23,650	23,700	3,841	3,551	4,302	3,551
23,700	23,750	3,855	3,559	4,316	3,559
23,750	23,800	3,869	3,566	4,330	3,566
23,800	23,850	3,883	3,574	4,344	3,574
23,850	23,900	3,897	3,581	4,358	3,581
23,900	23,950	3,911	3,589	4,372	3,589
23,950	24,000	3,925	3,596	4,386	3,596

24,000

At least	But less than	Single	Married filing jointly*	Married filing separately	Head of a household
24,000	24,050	3,939	3,604	4,400	3,604
24,050	24,100	3,953	3,611	4,414	3,611
24,100	24,150	3,967	3,619	4,428	3,619
24,150	24,200	3,981	3,626	4,442	3,626
24,200	24,250	3,995	3,634	4,456	3,634
24,250	24,300	4,009	3,641	4,470	3,641
24,300	24,350	4,023	3,649	4,484	3,649
24,350	24,400	4,037	3,656	4,498	3,656
24,400	24,450	4,051	3,664	4,512	3,664
24,450	24,500	4,065	3,671	4,526	3,671
24,500	24,550	4,079	3,679	4,540	3,679
24,550	24,600	4,093	3,686	4,554	3,686
24,600	24,650	4,107	3,694	4,568	3,694
24,650	24,700	4,121	3,701	4,582	3,701
24,700	24,750	4,135	3,709	4,596	3,709
24,750	24,800	4,149	3,716	4,610	3,716
24,800	24,850	4,163	3,724	4,624	3,724
24,850	24,900	4,177	3,731	4,638	3,731
24,900	24,950	4,191	3,739	4,652	3,739
24,950	25,000	4,205	3,746	4,666	3,746

25,000

At least	But less than	Single	Married filing jointly*	Married filing separately	Head of a household
25,000	25,050	4,219	3,754	4,680	3,754
25,050	25,100	4,233	3,761	4,694	3,761
25,100	25,150	4,247	3,769	4,708	3,769
25,150	25,200	4,261	3,776	4,722	3,776
25,200	25,250	4,275	3,784	4,736	3,784
25,250	25,300	4,289	3,791	4,750	3,791
25,300	25,350	4,303	3,799	4,764	3,799
25,350	25,400	4,317	3,806	4,778	3,806
25,400	25,450	4,331	3,814	4,792	3,814
25,450	25,500	4,345	3,821	4,806	3,821
25,500	25,550	4,359	3,829	4,820	3,829
25,550	25,600	4,373	3,836	4,834	3,836
25,600	25,650	4,387	3,844	4,848	3,844
25,650	25,700	4,401	3,851	4,862	3,851
25,700	25,750	4,415	3,859	4,876	3,859
25,750	25,800	4,429	3,866	4,890	3,866
25,800	25,850	4,443	3,874	4,904	3,874
25,850	25,900	4,457	3,881	4,918	3,881
25,900	25,950	4,471	3,889	4,932	3,889
25,950	26,000	4,485	3,896	4,946	3,896

26,000

At least	But less than	Single	Married filing jointly*	Married filing separately	Head of a household
26,000	26,050	4,499	3,904	4,960	3,904
26,050	26,100	4,513	3,911	4,974	3,911
26,100	26,150	4,527	3,919	4,988	3,919
26,150	26,200	4,541	3,926	5,002	3,926
26,200	26,250	4,555	3,934	5,016	3,934
26,250	26,300	4,569	3,941	5,030	3,941
26,300	26,350	4,583	3,949	5,044	3,949
26,350	26,400	4,597	3,956	5,058	3,956
26,400	26,450	4,611	3,964	5,072	3,964
26,450	26,500	4,625	3,971	5,086	3,971
26,500	26,550	4,639	3,979	5,100	3,979
26,550	26,600	4,653	3,986	5,114	3,986
26,600	26,650	4,667	3,994	5,128	3,994
26,650	26,700	4,681	4,001	5,142	4,001
26,700	26,750	4,695	4,009	5,156	4,009
26,750	26,800	4,709	4,016	5,170	4,016
26,800	26,850	4,723	4,024	5,184	4,024
26,850	26,900	4,737	4,031	5,198	4,031
26,900	26,950	4,751	4,039	5,212	4,039
26,950	27,000	4,765	4,046	5,226	4,046

27,000

At least	But less than	Single	Married filing jointly*	Married filing separately	Head of a household
27,000	27,050	4,779	4,054	5,240	4,054
27,050	27,100	4,793	4,061	5,254	4,061
27,100	27,150	4,807	4,069	5,268	4,069
27,150	27,200	4,821	4,076	5,282	4,076
27,200	27,250	4,835	4,084	5,296	4,084
27,250	27,300	4,849	4,091	5,310	4,091
27,300	27,350	4,863	4,099	5,324	4,099
27,350	27,400	4,877	4,106	5,338	4,106
27,400	27,450	4,891	4,114	5,352	4,114
27,450	27,500	4,905	4,121	5,366	4,121
27,500	27,550	4,919	4,129	5,380	4,129
27,550	27,600	4,933	4,136	5,394	4,136
27,600	27,650	4,947	4,144	5,408	4,144
27,650	27,700	4,961	4,151	5,422	4,151
27,700	27,750	4,975	4,159	5,436	4,159
27,750	27,800	4,989	4,166	5,450	4,166
27,800	27,850	5,003	4,174	5,464	4,174
27,850	27,900	5,017	4,181	5,478	4,181
27,900	27,950	5,031	4,189	5,492	4,189
27,950	28,000	5,045	4,196	5,506	4,196

28,000

At least	But less than	Single	Married filing jointly*	Married filing separately	Head of a household
28,000	28,050	5,059	4,204	5,520	4,204
28,050	28,100	5,073	4,211	5,534	4,211
28,100	28,150	5,087	4,219	5,548	4,219
28,150	28,200	5,101	4,226	5,562	4,226
28,200	28,250	5,115	4,234	5,576	4,234
28,250	28,300	5,129	4,241	5,590	4,241
28,300	28,350	5,143	4,249	5,604	4,249
28,350	28,400	5,157	4,256	5,618	4,256
28,400	28,450	5,171	4,264	5,632	4,264
28,450	28,500	5,185	4,271	5,646	4,271
28,500	28,550	5,199	4,279	5,660	4,279
28,550	28,600	5,213	4,286	5,674	4,286
28,600	28,650	5,227	4,294	5,688	4,294
28,650	28,700	5,241	4,301	5,702	4,301
28,700	28,750	5,255	4,309	5,716	4,309
28,750	28,800	5,269	4,316	5,730	4,320
28,800	28,850	5,283	4,324	5,744	4,334
28,850	28,900	5,297	4,331	5,758	4,348
28,900	28,950	5,311	4,339	5,772	4,362
28,950	29,000	5,325	4,346	5,786	4,376

29,000

At least	But less than	Single	Married filing jointly*	Married filing separately	Head of a household
29,000	29,050	5,339	4,354	5,800	4,390
29,050	29,100	5,353	4,361	5,814	4,404
29,100	29,150	5,367	4,369	5,828	4,418
29,150	29,200	5,381	4,376	5,842	4,432
29,200	29,250	5,395	4,384	5,856	4,446
29,250	29,300	5,409	4,391	5,870	4,460
29,300	29,350	5,423	4,399	5,884	4,474
29,350	29,400	5,437	4,406	5,898	4,488
29,400	29,450	5,451	4,414	5,912	4,502
29,450	29,500	5,465	4,421	5,926	4,516
29,500	29,550	5,479	4,429	5,940	4,530
29,550	29,600	5,493	4,436	5,954	4,544
29,600	29,650	5,507	4,444	5,968	4,558
29,650	29,700	5,521	4,451	5,982	4,572
29,700	29,750	5,535	4,459	5,996	4,586
29,750	29,800	5,549	4,466	6,010	4,600
29,800	29,850	5,563	4,474	6,024	4,614
29,850	29,900	5,577	4,481	6,038	4,628
29,900	29,950	5,591	4,489	6,052	4,642
29,950	30,000	5,605	4,496	6,066	4,656

30,000

At least	But less than	Single	Married filing jointly*	Married filing separately	Head of a household
30,000	30,050	5,619	4,504	6,080	4,670
30,050	30,100	5,633	4,511	6,094	4,684
30,100	30,150	5,647	4,519	6,108	4,698
30,150	30,200	5,661	4,526	6,122	4,712
30,200	30,250	5,675	4,534	6,136	4,726
30,250	30,300	5,689	4,541	6,150	4,740
30,300	30,350	5,703	4,549	6,164	4,754
30,350	30,400	5,717	4,556	6,178	4,768
30,400	30,450	5,731	4,564	6,192	4,782
30,450	30,500	5,745	4,571	6,206	4,796
30,500	30,550	5,759	4,579	6,220	4,810
30,550	30,600	5,773	4,586	6,234	4,824
30,600	30,650	5,787	4,594	6,248	4,838
30,650	30,700	5,801	4,601	6,262	4,852
30,700	30,750	5,815	4,609	6,276	4,866
30,750	30,800	5,829	4,616	6,290	4,880
30,800	30,850	5,843	4,624	6,304	4,894
30,850	30,900	5,857	4,631	6,318	4,908
30,900	30,950	5,871	4,639	6,332	4,922
30,950	31,000	5,885	4,646	6,346	4,936

31,000

At least	But less than	Single	Married filing jointly*	Married filing separately	Head of a household
31,000	31,050	5,899	4,654	6,360	4,950
31,050	31,100	5,913	4,661	6,374	4,964
31,100	31,150	5,927	4,669	6,388	4,978
31,150	31,200	5,941	4,676	6,402	4,992
31,200	31,250	5,955	4,684	6,416	5,006
31,250	31,300	5,969	4,691	6,430	5,020
31,300	31,350	5,983	4,699	6,444	5,034
31,350	31,400	5,997	4,706	6,458	5,048
31,400	31,450	6,011	4,714	6,472	5,062
31,450	31,500	6,025	4,721	6,486	5,076
31,500	31,550	6,039	4,729	6,500	5,090
31,550	31,600	6,053	4,736	6,514	5,104
31,600	31,650	6,067	4,744	6,528	5,118
31,650	31,700	6,081	4,751	6,542	5,132
31,700	31,750	6,095	4,759	6,556	5,146
31,750	31,800	6,109	4,766	6,570	5,160
31,800	31,850	6,123	4,774	6,584	5,174
31,850	31,900	6,137	4,781	6,598	5,188
31,900	31,950	6,151	4,789	6,612	5,202
31,950	32,000	6,165	4,796	6,626	5,216

* This column must also be used by a qualifying widow(er).

Continued on next page

1992 Tax Table—*Continued*

If line 37 (taxable income) is— / And you are— / Your tax is—

Column headers for every block below: **At least | But less than | Single | Married filing jointly* | Married filing separately | Head of a household**

32,000

At least	But less than	Single	Married filing jointly*	Married filing separately	Head of a household
32,000	32,050	6,179	4,804	6,640	5,230
32,050	32,100	6,193	4,811	6,654	5,244
32,100	32,150	6,207	4,819	6,668	5,258
32,150	32,200	6,221	4,826	6,682	5,272
32,200	32,250	6,235	4,834	6,696	5,286
32,250	32,300	6,249	4,841	6,710	5,300
32,300	32,350	6,263	4,849	6,724	5,314
32,350	32,400	6,277	4,856	6,738	5,328
32,400	32,450	6,291	4,864	6,752	5,342
32,450	32,500	6,305	4,871	6,766	5,356
32,500	32,550	6,319	4,879	6,780	5,370
32,550	32,600	6,333	4,886	6,794	5,384
32,600	32,650	6,347	4,894	6,808	5,398
32,650	32,700	6,361	4,901	6,822	5,412
32,700	32,750	6,375	4,909	6,836	5,426
32,750	32,800	6,389	4,916	6,850	5,440
32,800	32,850	6,403	4,924	6,864	5,454
32,850	32,900	6,417	4,931	6,878	5,468
32,900	32,950	6,431	4,939	6,892	5,482
32,950	33,000	6,445	4,946	6,906	5,496

33,000

At least	But less than	Single	Married filing jointly*	Married filing separately	Head of a household
33,000	33,050	6,459	4,954	6,920	5,510
33,050	33,100	6,473	4,961	6,934	5,524
33,100	33,150	6,487	4,969	6,948	5,536
33,150	33,200	6,501	4,976	6,962	5,552
33,200	33,250	6,515	4,984	6,976	5,566
33,250	33,300	6,529	4,991	6,990	5,580
33,300	33,350	6,543	4,999	7,004	5,594
33,350	33,400	6,557	5,006	7,018	5,608
33,400	33,450	6,571	5,014	7,032	5,622
33,450	33,500	6,585	5,021	7,046	5,636
33,500	33,550	6,599	5,029	7,060	5,650
33,550	33,600	6,613	5,036	7,074	5,664
33,600	33,650	6,627	5,044	7,086	5,678
33,650	33,700	6,641	5,051	7,102	5,692
33,700	33,750	6,655	5,059	7,116	5,706
33,750	33,800	6,669	5,066	7,130	5,720
33,800	33,850	6,683	5,074	7,144	5,734
33,850	33,900	6,697	5,081	7,158	5,748
33,900	33,950	6,711	5,089	7,172	5,762
33,950	34,000	6,725	5,096	7,186	5,776

34,000

At least	But less than	Single	Married filing jointly*	Married filing separately	Head of a household
34,000	34,050	6,739	5,104	7,200	5,790
34,050	34,100	6,753	5,111	7,214	5,804
34,100	34,150	6,767	5,119	7,228	5,816
34,150	34,200	6,781	5,126	7,242	5,832
34,200	34,250	6,795	5,134	7,256	5,846
34,250	34,300	6,809	5,141	7,270	5,860
34,300	34,350	6,823	5,149	7,284	5,874
34,350	34,400	6,837	5,156	7,298	5,888
34,400	34,450	6,851	5,164	7,312	5,902
34,450	34,500	6,865	5,171	7,326	5,916
34,500	34,550	6,879	5,179	7,340	5,930
34,550	34,600	6,893	5,186	7,354	5,944
34,600	34,650	6,907	5,194	7,368	5,958
34,650	34,700	6,921	5,201	7,382	5,972
34,700	34,750	6,935	5,209	7,396	5,986
34,750	34,800	6,949	5,216	7,410	6,000
34,800	34,850	6,963	5,224	7,424	6,014
34,850	34,900	6,977	5,231	7,438	6,028
34,900	34,950	6,991	5,239	7,452	6,042
34,950	35,000	7,005	5,246	7,466	6,056

35,000

At least	But less than	Single	Married filing jointly*	Married filing separately	Head of a household
35,000	35,050	7,019	5,254	7,480	6,070
35,050	35,100	7,033	5,261	7,494	6,084
35,100	35,150	7,047	5,269	7,508	6,098
35,150	35,200	7,061	5,276	7,522	6,112
35,200	35,250	7,075	5,284	7,536	6,126
35,250	35,300	7,089	5,291	7,550	6,140
35,300	35,350	7,103	5,299	7,564	6,154
35,350	35,400	7,117	5,306	7,578	6,168
35,400	35,450	7,131	5,314	7,592	6,182
35,450	35,500	7,145	5,321	7,606	6,196
35,500	35,550	7,159	5,329	7,620	6,210
35,550	35,600	7,173	5,336	7,634	6,224
35,600	35,650	7,187	5,344	7,648	6,238
35,650	35,700	7,201	5,351	7,662	6,252
35,700	35,750	7,215	5,359	7,676	6,266
35,750	35,800	7,229	5,366	7,690	6,280
35,800	35,850	7,243	5,377	7,704	6,294
35,850	35,900	7,257	5,391	7,718	6,308
35,900	35,950	7,271	5,405	7,732	6,322
35,950	36,000	7,285	5,419	7,746	6,336

36,000

At least	But less than	Single	Married filing jointly*	Married filing separately	Head of a household
36,000	36,050	7,299	5,433	7,760	6,350
36,050	36,100	7,313	5,447	7,774	6,364
36,100	36,150	7,327	5,461	7,788	6,378
36,150	36,200	7,341	5,475	7,802	6,392
36,200	36,250	7,355	5,489	7,816	6,406
36,250	36,300	7,369	5,503	7,830	6,420
36,300	36,350	7,383	5,517	7,844	6,434
36,350	36,400	7,397	5,531	7,858	6,448
36,400	36,450	7,411	5,545	7,872	6,462
36,450	36,500	7,425	5,559	7,886	6,476
36,500	36,550	7,439	5,573	7,900	6,490
36,550	36,600	7,453	5,587	7,914	6,504
36,600	36,650	7,467	5,601	7,928	6,518
36,650	36,700	7,481	5,615	7,942	6,532
36,700	36,750	7,495	5,629	7,956	6,546
36,750	36,800	7,509	5,643	7,970	6,560
36,800	36,850	7,523	5,657	7,984	6,574
36,850	36,900	7,537	5,671	7,998	6,588
36,900	36,950	7,551	5,685	8,012	6,602
36,950	37,000	7,565	5,699	8,026	6,616

37,000

At least	But less than	Single	Married filing jointly*	Married filing separately	Head of a household
37,000	37,050	7,579	5,713	8,040	6,630
37,050	37,100	7,593	5,727	8,054	6,644
37,100	37,150	7,607	5,741	8,068	6,658
37,150	37,200	7,621	5,755	8,082	6,672
37,200	37,250	7,635	5,769	8,096	6,686
37,250	37,300	7,649	5,783	8,110	6,700
37,300	37,350	7,663	5,797	8,124	6,714
37,350	37,400	7,677	5,811	8,138	6,728
37,400	37,450	7,691	5,825	8,152	6,742
37,450	37,500	7,705	5,839	8,166	6,756
37,500	37,550	7,719	5,853	8,180	6,770
37,550	37,600	7,733	5,867	8,194	6,784
37,600	37,650	7,747	5,881	8,208	6,798
37,650	37,700	7,761	5,895	8,222	6,812
37,700	37,750	7,775	5,909	8,236	6,826
37,750	37,800	7,789	5,923	8,250	6,840
37,800	37,850	7,803	5,937	8,264	6,854
37,850	37,900	7,817	5,951	8,278	6,868
37,900	37,950	7,831	5,965	8,292	6,882
37,950	38,000	7,845	5,979	8,306	6,896

38,000

At least	But less than	Single	Married filing jointly*	Married filing separately	Head of a household
38,000	38,050	7,859	5,993	8,320	6,910
38,050	38,100	7,873	6,007	8,334	6,924
38,100	38,150	7,887	6,021	8,348	6,938
38,150	38,200	7,901	6,035	8,362	6,952
38,200	38,250	7,915	6,049	8,376	6,966
38,250	38,300	7,929	6,063	8,390	6,980
38,300	38,350	7,943	6,077	8,404	6,994
38,350	38,400	7,957	6,091	8,418	7,008
38,400	38,450	7,971	6,105	8,432	7,022
38,450	38,500	7,985	6,119	8,446	7,036
38,500	38,550	7,999	6,133	8,460	7,050
38,550	38,600	8,013	6,147	8,474	7,064
38,600	38,650	8,027	6,161	8,488	7,078
38,650	38,700	8,041	6,175	8,502	7,092
38,700	38,750	8,055	6,189	8,516	7,106
38,750	38,800	8,069	6,203	8,530	7,120
38,800	38,850	8,083	6,217	8,544	7,134
38,850	38,900	8,097	6,231	8,558	7,148
38,900	38,950	8,111	6,245	8,572	7,162
38,950	39,000	8,125	6,259	8,586	7,176

39,000

At least	But less than	Single	Married filing jointly*	Married filing separately	Head of a household
39,000	39,050	8,139	6,273	8,600	7,190
39,050	39,100	8,153	6,287	8,614	7,204
39,100	39,150	8,167	6,301	8,628	7,218
39,150	39,200	8,181	6,315	8,642	7,232
39,200	39,250	8,195	6,329	8,656	7,246
39,250	39,300	8,209	6,343	8,670	7,260
39,300	39,350	8,223	6,357	8,684	7,274
39,350	39,400	8,237	6,371	8,698	7,288
39,400	39,450	8,251	6,385	8,712	7,302
39,450	39,500	8,265	6,399	8,726	7,316
39,500	39,550	8,279	6,413	8,740	7,330
39,550	39,600	8,293	6,427	8,754	7,344
39,600	39,650	8,307	6,441	8,768	7,358
39,650	39,700	8,321	6,455	8,782	7,372
39,700	39,750	8,335	6,469	8,796	7,386
39,750	39,800	8,349	6,483	8,810	7,400
39,800	39,850	8,363	6,497	8,824	7,414
39,850	39,900	8,377	6,511	8,838	7,428
39,900	39,950	8,391	6,525	8,852	7,442
39,950	40,000	8,405	6,539	8,866	7,456

40,000

At least	But less than	Single	Married filing jointly*	Married filing separately	Head of a household
40,000	40,050	8,419	6,553	8,880	7,470
40,050	40,100	8,433	6,567	8,894	7,484
40,100	40,150	8,447	6,581	8,908	7,498
40,150	40,200	8,461	6,595	8,922	7,512
40,200	40,250	8,475	6,609	8,936	7,526
40,250	40,300	8,489	6,623	8,950	7,540
40,300	40,350	8,503	6,637	8,964	7,554
40,350	40,400	8,517	6,651	8,978	7,568
40,400	40,450	8,531	6,665	8,992	7,582
40,450	40,500	8,545	6,679	9,006	7,596
40,500	40,550	8,559	6,693	9,020	7,610
40,550	40,600	8,573	6,707	9,034	7,624
40,600	40,650	8,587	6,721	9,048	7,638
40,650	40,700	8,601	6,735	9,062	7,652
40,700	40,750	8,615	6,749	9,076	7,666
40,750	40,800	8,629	6,763	9,090	7,680
40,800	40,850	8,643	6,777	9,104	7,694
40,850	40,900	8,657	6,791	9,118	7,708
40,900	40,950	8,671	6,805	9,132	7,722
40,950	41,000	8,685	6,819	9,146	7,736

* This column must also be used by a qualifying widow(er).

Continued on next page

1992 Tax Table—*Continued*

41,000

At least	But less than	Single	Married filing jointly*	Married filing separately	Head of a household
41,000	41,050	8,699	6,833	9,160	7,750
41,050	41,100	8,713	6,847	9,174	7,764
41,100	41,150	8,727	6,861	9,188	7,778
41,150	41,200	8,741	6,875	9,202	7,792
41,200	41,250	8,755	6,889	9,216	7,806
41,250	41,300	8,769	6,903	9,230	7,820
41,300	41,350	8,783	6,917	9,244	7,834
41,350	41,400	8,797	6,931	9,258	7,848
41,400	41,450	8,811	6,945	9,272	7,862
41,450	41,500	8,825	6,959	9,286	7,876
41,500	41,550	8,839	6,973	9,300	7,890
41,550	41,600	8,853	6,987	9,314	7,904
41,600	41,650	8,867	7,001	9,328	7,918
41,650	41,700	8,881	7,015	9,342	7,932
41,700	41,750	8,895	7,029	9,356	7,946
41,750	41,800	8,909	7,043	9,370	7,960
41,800	41,850	8,923	7,057	9,384	7,974
41,850	41,900	8,937	7,071	9,398	7,988
41,900	41,950	8,951	7,085	9,412	8,002
41,950	42,000	8,965	7,099	9,426	8,016

42,000

At least	But less than	Single	Married filing jointly*	Married filing separately	Head of a household
42,000	42,050	8,979	7,113	9,440	8,030
42,050	42,100	8,993	7,127	9,454	8,044
42,100	42,150	9,007	7,141	9,468	8,058
42,150	42,200	9,021	7,155	9,482	8,072
42,200	42,250	9,035	7,169	9,496	8,086
42,250	42,300	9,049	7,183	9,510	8,100
42,300	42,350	9,063	7,197	9,524	8,114
42,350	42,400	9,077	7,211	9,538	8,128
42,400	42,450	9,091	7,225	9,552	8,142
42,450	42,500	9,105	7,239	9,566	8,156
42,500	42,550	9,119	7,253	9,580	8,170
42,550	42,600	9,133	7,267	9,594	8,184
42,600	42,650	9,147	7,281	9,608	8,198
42,650	42,700	9,161	7,295	9,622	8,212
42,700	42,750	9,175	7,309	9,636	8,226
42,750	42,800	9,189	7,323	9,650	8,240
42,800	42,850	9,203	7,337	9,664	8,254
42,850	42,900	9,217	7,351	9,678	8,268
42,900	42,950	9,231	7,365	9,692	8,282
42,950	43,000	9,245	7,379	9,706	8,296

43,000

At least	But less than	Single	Married filing jointly*	Married filing separately	Head of a household
43,000	43,050	9,259	7,393	9,720	8,310
43,050	43,100	9,273	7,407	9,734	8,324
43,100	43,150	9,287	7,421	9,748	8,338
43,150	43,200	9,301	7,435	9,762	8,352
43,200	43,250	9,315	7,449	9,776	8,366
43,250	43,300	9,329	7,463	9,791	8,380
43,300	43,350	9,343	7,477	9,806	8,394
43,350	43,400	9,357	7,491	9,822	8,408
43,400	43,450	9,371	7,505	9,837	8,422
43,450	43,500	9,385	7,519	9,853	8,436
43,500	43,550	9,399	7,533	9,868	8,450
43,550	43,600	9,413	7,547	9,884	8,464
43,600	43,650	9,427	7,561	9,899	8,478
43,650	43,700	9,441	7,575	9,915	8,492
43,700	43,750	9,455	7,589	9,930	8,506
43,750	43,800	9,469	7,603	9,946	8,520
43,800	43,850	9,483	7,617	9,961	8,534
43,850	43,900	9,497	7,631	9,977	8,548
43,900	43,950	9,511	7,645	9,992	8,562
43,950	44,000	9,525	7,659	10,008	8,576

44,000

At least	But less than	Single	Married filing jointly*	Married filing separately	Head of a household
44,000	44,050	9,539	7,673	10,023	8,590
44,050	44,100	9,553	7,687	10,039	8,604
44,100	44,150	9,567	7,701	10,054	8,618
44,150	44,200	9,581	7,715	10,070	8,632
44,200	44,250	9,595	7,729	10,085	8,646
44,250	44,300	9,609	7,743	10,101	8,660
44,300	44,350	9,623	7,757	10,116	8,674
44,350	44,400	9,637	7,771	10,132	8,688
44,400	44,450	9,651	7,785	10,147	8,702
44,450	44,500	9,665	7,799	10,163	8,716
44,500	44,550	9,679	7,813	10,178	8,730
44,550	44,600	9,693	7,827	10,194	8,744
44,600	44,650	9,707	7,841	10,209	8,758
44,650	44,700	9,721	7,855	10,225	8,772
44,700	44,750	9,735	7,869	10,240	8,786
44,750	44,800	9,749	7,883	10,256	8,800
44,800	44,850	9,763	7,897	10,271	8,814
44,850	44,900	9,777	7,911	10,287	8,828
44,900	44,950	9,791	7,925	10,302	8,842
44,950	45,000	9,805	7,939	10,318	8,856

45,000

At least	But less than	Single	Married filing jointly*	Married filing separately	Head of a household
45,000	45,050	9,819	7,953	10,333	8,870
45,050	45,100	9,833	7,967	10,349	8,884
45,100	45,150	9,847	7,981	10,364	8,898
45,150	45,200	9,861	7,995	10,380	8,912
45,200	45,250	9,875	8,009	10,395	8,926
45,250	45,300	9,889	8,023	10,411	8,940
45,300	45,350	9,903	8,037	10,426	8,954
45,350	45,400	9,917	8,051	10,442	8,968
45,400	45,450	9,931	8,065	10,457	8,982
45,450	45,500	9,945	8,079	10,473	8,996
45,500	45,550	9,959	8,093	10,488	9,010
45,550	45,600	9,973	8,107	10,504	9,024
45,600	45,650	9,987	8,121	10,519	9,038
45,650	45,700	10,001	8,135	10,535	9,052
45,700	45,750	10,015	8,149	10,550	9,066
45,750	45,800	10,029	8,163	10,566	9,080
45,800	45,850	10,043	8,177	10,581	9,094
45,850	45,900	10,057	8,191	10,597	9,108
45,900	45,950	10,071	8,205	10,612	9,122
45,950	46,000	10,085	8,219	10,628	9,136

46,000

At least	But less than	Single	Married filing jointly*	Married filing separately	Head of a household
46,000	46,050	10,099	8,233	10,643	9,150
46,050	46,100	10,113	8,247	10,659	9,164
46,100	46,150	10,127	8,261	10,674	9,178
46,150	46,200	10,141	8,275	10,690	9,192
46,200	46,250	10,155	8,289	10,705	9,206
46,250	46,300	10,169	8,303	10,721	9,220
46,300	46,350	10,183	8,317	10,736	9,234
46,350	46,400	10,197	8,331	10,752	9,248
46,400	46,450	10,211	8,345	10,767	9,262
46,450	46,500	10,225	8,359	10,783	9,276
46,500	46,550	10,239	8,373	10,798	9,290
46,550	46,600	10,253	8,387	10,814	9,304
46,600	46,650	10,267	8,401	10,829	9,318
46,650	46,700	10,281	8,415	10,845	9,332
46,700	46,750	10,295	8,429	10,860	9,346
46,750	46,800	10,309	8,443	10,876	9,360
46,800	46,850	10,323	8,457	10,891	9,374
46,850	46,900	10,337	8,471	10,907	9,388
46,900	46,950	10,351	8,485	10,922	9,402
46,950	47,000	10,365	8,499	10,938	9,416

47,000

At least	But less than	Single	Married filing jointly*	Married filing separately	Head of a household
47,000	47,050	10,379	8,513	10,953	9,430
47,050	47,100	10,393	8,527	10,969	9,444
47,100	47,150	10,407	8,541	10,984	9,458
47,150	47,200	10,421	8,555	11,000	9,472
47,200	47,250	10,435	8,569	11,015	9,486
47,250	47,300	10,449	8,583	11,031	9,500
47,300	47,350	10,463	8,597	11,046	9,514
47,350	47,400	10,477	8,611	11,062	9,528
47,400	47,450	10,491	8,625	11,077	9,542
47,450	47,500	10,505	8,639	11,093	9,556
47,500	47,550	10,519	8,653	11,108	9,570
47,550	47,600	10,533	8,667	11,124	9,584
47,600	47,650	10,547	8,681	11,139	9,598
47,650	47,700	10,561	8,695	11,155	9,612
47,700	47,750	10,575	8,709	11,170	9,626
47,750	47,800	10,589	8,723	11,186	9,640
47,800	47,850	10,603	8,737	11,201	9,654
47,850	47,900	10,617	8,751	11,217	9,668
47,900	47,950	10,631	8,765	11,232	9,682
47,950	48,000	10,645	8,779	11,248	9,696

48,000

At least	But less than	Single	Married filing jointly*	Married filing separately	Head of a household
48,000	48,050	10,659	8,793	11,263	9,710
48,050	48,100	10,673	8,807	11,279	9,724
48,100	48,150	10,687	8,821	11,294	9,738
48,150	48,200	10,701	8,835	11,310	9,752
48,200	48,250	10,715	8,849	11,325	9,766
48,250	48,300	10,729	8,863	11,341	9,780
48,300	48,350	10,743	8,877	11,356	9,794
48,350	48,400	10,757	8,891	11,372	9,808
48,400	48,450	10,771	8,905	11,387	9,822
48,450	48,500	10,785	8,919	11,403	9,836
48,500	48,550	10,799	8,933	11,418	9,850
48,550	48,600	10,813	8,947	11,434	9,864
48,600	48,650	10,827	8,961	11,449	9,878
48,650	48,700	10,841	8,975	11,465	9,892
48,700	48,750	10,855	8,989	11,480	9,906
48,750	48,800	10,869	9,003	11,496	9,920
48,800	48,850	10,883	9,017	11,511	9,934
48,850	48,900	10,897	9,031	11,527	9,948
48,900	48,950	10,911	9,045	11,542	9,962
48,950	49,000	10,925	9,059	11,558	9,976

49,000

At least	But less than	Single	Married filing jointly*	Married filing separately	Head of a household
49,000	49,050	10,939	9,073	11,573	9,990
49,050	49,100	10,953	9,087	11,589	10,004
49,100	49,150	10,967	9,101	11,604	10,018
49,150	49,200	10,981	9,115	11,620	10,032
49,200	49,250	10,995	9,129	11,635	10,046
49,250	49,300	11,009	9,143	11,651	10,060
49,300	49,350	11,023	9,157	11,666	10,074
49,350	49,400	11,037	9,171	11,682	10,088
49,400	49,450	11,051	9,185	11,697	10,102
49,450	49,500	11,065	9,199	11,713	10,116
49,500	49,550	11,079	9,213	11,728	10,130
49,550	49,600	11,093	9,227	11,744	10,144
49,600	49,650	11,107	9,241	11,759	10,158
49,650	49,700	11,121	9,255	11,775	10,172
49,700	49,750	11,135	9,269	11,790	10,186
49,750	49,800	11,149	9,283	11,806	10,200
49,800	49,850	11,163	9,297	11,821	10,214
49,850	49,900	11,177	9,311	11,837	10,228
49,900	49,950	11,191	9,325	11,852	10,242
49,950	50,000	11,205	9,339	11,868	10,256

* This column must also be used by a qualifying widow(er).

Continued on next page

1992 Tax Rate Schedules

Caution: *Use **only** if your taxable income (Form 1040, line 37) is $100,000 or more. If less, use the **Tax Table.** Even though you cannot use the tax rate schedules below if your taxable income is less than $100,000, all levels of taxable income are shown so taxpayers can see the tax rate that applies to each level.*

Schedule X—Use if your filing status is **Single**

If the amount on Form 1040, line 37, is: Over—	But not over—	Enter on Form 1040, line 38	of the amount over—
$0	$21,450	.... 15%	$0
21,450	51,900	$3,217.50 + 28%	21,450
51,900	....	11,743.50 + 31%	51,900

Schedule Y-1—Use if your filing status is **Married filing jointly** or **Qualifying widow(er)**

If the amount on Form 1040, line 37, is: Over—	But not over—	Enter on Form 1040, line 38	of the amount over—
$0	$35,800	.... 15%	$0
35,800	86,500	$5,370.00 + 28%	35,800
86,500	....	19,566.00 + 31%	86,500

Schedule Y-2—Use if your filing status is **Married filing separately**

If the amount on Form 1040, line 37, is: Over—	But not over—	Enter on Form 1040, line 38	of the amount over—
$0	$17,900	.... 15%	$0
17,900	43,250	$2,685.00 + 28%	17,900
43,250	....	9,783.00 + 31%	43,250

Schedule Z—Use if your filing status is **Head of household**

If the amount on Form 1040, line 37, is: Over—	But not over—	Enter on Form 1040, line 38	of the amount over—
$0	$28,750	.... 15%	$0
28,750	74,150	$4,312.50 + 28%	28,750
74,150	....	17,024.50 + 31%	74,150

Highlights for 1992

Several of the tax incentives the authors discuss in the book expired in 1992. However, among tax professionals a difference of opinion exists whether the next Congress will renew them. Some professionals assume a retroactive renewal. Others believe renewal is out of the question. To glean an outcome clue, the authors look at Congressional actions via the Revenue Bill of 1992. While the President did not sign this bill, Congress did pass the following legislation:

Extended permanently:
- Low-income housing credit
- Mortgage revenue bond authority
- Targeted jobs tax credit
- Alternative minimum tax exemption for charitable gifts of appreciated property
    Include all appreciated property, including real estate, stocks, and bonds in 1993

Extended for 15 month, through September 30, 1993:
- Small issue industrial development bond authority

Extended for 12 month, through June 30, 1993:
- Exclusion of employer-provided educational assistance
- Deduction of health insurance costs of self-employed persons
- Research and experimentation credit
- Orphan drug credit

Not extended:
- Employer-provided group legal services

Chapter 1

In this chapter, the authors discuss individual tax returns and why we pay taxes. They explain why a taxpayer's filing status is important and discuss the filing choices. The authors present two tax base formulas and define formula terms. They also tie the formula for individual taxpayers to the Internal Revenue Code. With the formula discussion, the authors look at the trade off between itemized deductions and the standard deduction (including the additional standard deduction).

At the end of the formula discussion, the authors provide a clarifying tax base illustration. Next, they discuss exemptions (personal and dependency) and provide clarifying examples. They present the filing requirements for self-employed and employed persons. For employed persons, the authors provide clarifying computation charts. Near the end of the chapter, they discuss tax filer responsibilities. Next, they provide an overview of property transactions. They also define property terms and provide a clarifying example. Finally, the authors discuss tax planning principles and how to use them to reduce the tax bite.

Chapter 2

In this chapter, the authors present the tax rates and computation process for individuals. Before illustrating Form 1040EZ and Form 1040A, they present a filled-in Form W-2, Wage and Tax Statement. They discuss the kiddie tax, and the wage bases and rates for social security (OASDI) and Medicare (HIP) taxes. OASDI stands for old age, survivors, and disability insurance. HIP stands for health insurance program. They also discuss three Form 1040A credits: child and dependent care credit, elderly or disabled credit, and refundable earned income credit. The earned income credit consists of three integrated credits: basic earned income credit, health insurance credit, and supplemental young child credit. At the end of the chapter, the authors present a comprehensive Form 1040A illustration.

Chapter 3

At the start of this chapter the authors present a road map for understanding the taxation of individuals. They also present an overview of the remaining materials on individual taxation. The road map is Form 1040. Throughout the chapter, the authors discuss several gross income items and present clarifying examples and illustrations. They include a table at the end of the chapter that lists several gross income items. Taxpayers can use the table to determine the proper gross income reporting Form(s).

Chapter 4

In this chapter, the authors examine exclusions from gross income and adjustments to income. Adjustments to income are deductions from gross income to arrive at adjusted gross income (above the line deductions). At the chapter's end there is a filled-in Form 1040A and page 1 of Form 1040 with supporting schedules. Upon completion of Chapter 4, a reader will have covered most of the common gross income items and adjustments to income. It also means they will have covered most items taxpayers report on Form 1040EZ, Form 1040A, and page 1 of Form 1040.

Chapter 5 and 6

Chapter 5 covers medical expenses, taxes, interest expenses, charitable contributions, and losses from casualties and thefts. In Chapter 6 the authors cover moving expenses and miscellaneous itemized deductions. To reduce the tax bite, taxpayers should itemize deductions when they exceed their standard deduction. Self-employed taxpayers who pay their own health insurance can deduct 25% of the cost as an adjustment to income.

For 1992, the standard automobile mileage rate for business travel is 28 cents per mile. For medical and moving expense travel, it is 9 cents per mile. Taxpayers above a certain income level must phase down some of their itemized deductions. The reduction is 3% of their adjusted gross income that is more than $105,250 (more than $52,625 if married filing separately). However, medical expenses, losses from casualties and thefts, and investment interest expense are not part of this phase down. Also, the phase down never can be more than 80% of the phase down items. For 1992 a taxpayer must limit the de-

duction for investment interest expense to his or her net investment income.

Chapter 7

This chapter focuses on page 2 of Form 1040. Here, the authors discuss Form 1040 information needs. They also show the calculations for the amount due to or from the government. This chapter contains an extensive coverage of the self-employment tax. The OASDI tax on self-employed taxpayers is 12.4% of taxable self-employment income up to $55,500. The HIP tax rate on these taxpayers is 2.9% of taxable self-employment income up to $130,200. The combined rate is 15.3% on taxable self-employment income up to $55,500. Other topics discussed in this chapter are penalties and related interest, filing extension requests, amended tax returns, and the dreaded tax audit.

Chapter 8

This chapter covers the reporting requirements of self-employed taxpayers. These taxpayers can deduct one-half of their self-employment tax as an adjustment to income. Starting in 1992, some sole proprietors can use a simplified reporting schedule to report their business income. It is Schedule C-EZ (Form 1040), Net Profit From Business. Taxpayers cannot use this schedule if the business has a loss. To use it, the business must use the cash method of accounting and have no employees. Also, the business must not have inventories or depreciable property. The business' gross receipts must be less than $25,000 and its expenses cannot exceed $2,000. Finally, to use the simplified reporting schedule the proprietor cannot take a home office deduction. In this chapter, the authors discuss Form 8829, Expenses for Business Use of Your Home.

Chapter 9

This chapter covers depreciation, cost recovery deductions, depletion, and amortization. The 1992 cost recovery deduction limits on automobiles are: first year—$2,760, second year—$4,400, third year—$2,650, and each later year—$1,575. Taxpayers who elect first year expensing must limit the total of their immediate expensing amount and cost recovery deduction to $2,760.

Chapter 10

In this chapter the authors scrutinize a taxpayer's supplemental income activities and illustrate Schedule E (Form 1040), Supplemental Income and Loss. The focus of the discussion is rental properties, including vacation homes. The authors also cover the passive activity and at-risk rules. Here, they discuss passive activity limits, suspended losses, and tax credits for passive activities.

Chapters 11 and 12

The authors use these chapters to discuss gains and losses from property transactions. They present a three step tax determination process for property transactions. Here, they explain how to calculate a realized and recognized gain or loss. They also comment on the tax treatment.

In Chapter 11 the authors examine the gain or loss calculation and recognition steps. They also discuss the basis of property, involuntary conversions, nontaxable exchanges, and the sale of a principal residence. In Chapter 12 they discuss the tax treatment of gains and losses from property disposals and the reporting process. They also discuss disposals of business property (Section 1231) and depreciation considerations. Finally, the authors discuss the maximum rate of tax on an individual's net capital gain.

Chapter 13

In this chapter the authors discuss several topics that affect entrepreneurs and investors. These topics include tax credits, alternative minimum tax, net operating losses, installment sales, long-term contracts, and information returns.

Chapter 14

In Chapter 14, the authors provide background information about income tax withholding, payroll taxes, and estimated income taxes. They discuss several aspects of the Treasury's new employment tax deposit regulations. Then, they illustrate new Form 941, Employer's Quarterly Federal Tax Report. The new deposit regulations and the new Form 941 go into effect in 1993. The authors also discuss new Form 8109, Federal Tax Deposit Coupon booklet. In addition to Social Security and Medicare taxes, the authors present a short discussion on the FUTA tax (Federal Unemployment Tax Act) with clarifying examples. In addition to the filled-in Forms 941 and 8109 illustrations, the authors illustrate other tax forms. They are Forms W-2, W-3, W-4, W-4P, 1040-ES worksheet, and 1040-ES Payment Voucher.

Chapter 15

In this chapter, the authors provide a comprehensive coverage of partnership tax reporting. They discuss the basis of partner interests and basis for gain or loss on contributed and distributed property. The authors include a section on structuring family partnerships for tax savings.

Chapter 16

In this edition, the authors cover the basis of S corporation stock, reporting separately stated items for a zero basis shareholder, and distributions of appreciated property. They also cover tax elections, terminations, and tax planning concepts. Then, they provide a filled-in Form 1120S.

Chapter 17

The authors use this chapter to identify an organization's tax nature. They present criteria for separating different business organizations. They also provide background on professional corporations and personal holding companies. However, the main focus of this chapter is the tax and reporting principles for C corporations. Throughout the chapter the authors provide examples of the reporting process. At the end of the chapter, the authors provide a filled-in Form 1120.

Chapter 18

This chapter addresses a variety of tax issues facing corporations. They include estimated and accumulated earnings taxes, personal holding company tax, and controlled groups. The authors also discuss pay outs to shareholders, as well as corporate reorganizations. As part of the pay out discussion, the authors focus on liquidating and nonliquidating distributions. Near the end of the chapter, the authors discuss the tax rules applicable to tax-exempt organizations.

INTRODUCTION TO FEDERAL INCOME TAXATION

➡ Classification of individual taxpayers

➡ Tax formulas

➡ How to determine the standard deduction

➡ How to determine the number of dependency exemptions

➡ How to determine filing status

➡ How to calculate the tax

➡ How to complete the Form 1040EZ

➡ Form 1040A and the tax credits

➡ Filing Requirements

Overview of the
Tax Structure

The Sixteenth Amendment to the Constitution gave Congress the power to collect income taxes. After its ratification, the Revenue Act of 1913 was enacted. It stated that all income earned after February 28, 1913 was taxable.

Unlike our current tax rates, the early ones were small (1 percent normal tax, and 1 to 6 percent surtax on high income taxpayers). Today, our tax rates range from 15 to 31 percent. Like the first tax system, our current one is self-reporting. Here, each taxpayer must determine his or her tax liability, file a proper return on time, and pay the tax when due. Taxpayers who do not meet these responsibilities face possible fines, penalties, and imprisonment. In addition, the IRS charges them interest on unpaid taxes. To meet these responsibilities, many taxpayers seek professional help. Last year, approximately half of all filed returns were prepared by tax professionals.

While many taxpayers use paid professionals, every taxpayer should have a basic understanding of the tax laws. This understanding will help them prepare their own return or identify data needed by their preparer. It will also help them review their professionally prepared return for errors before they file it. In addition, understanding the tax laws can help in recognizing potential problems before events take place. Through proper tax planning, taxpayers can minimize some of the tax bite. The first part of this chapter provides an overview of our current tax system. The latter part discusses tax planning principles.

Why Do We Pay Taxes?

Some people say we pay taxes to cover the cost of government operations. Others say we pay them to maintain price stability, redistribute the country's wealth, and encourage growth and full employment. In reality, our tax payments are used for all of these purposes. Theoretically, our federal government could operate without collecting taxes since it controls the money system. It could create money with its printing presses. It could also spend more than it takes in by borrowing funds. However, long-run use of these money-creating methods may not be in the best interest of most Americans.

What Individual Income Tax Returns Must Be Filed?

The returns which most taxpayers file and the related book discussion appear below:

1. Form 1040EZ, Income Tax Return for Single Filers With No Dependents (Chapter 2)
2. Form 1040A, U.S. Individual Income Tax Return (Chapters 2 and 4)
3. Form 1040, U.S. Individual Income Tax Return (Chapters 3 through 7)

Taxpayers file income tax returns to report income and claim deductions, exemptions, and credits (including advance tax payments to the government). In addition, the government collects data about taxpayers from other sources (employers, banks, etc.) which it uses to test the accuracy of tax return data.

Filing Status—Why Is It Important?

Every taxpayer who files a return must select his or her filing status. In some cases, filing status determines if a taxpayer can use a specific tax return. When a taxpayer takes a standard deduction, instead of itemizing, he or she selects the proper amount using filing status. A taxpayer also uses his or her filing status to determine which tax rate schedule or table to use to calculate the tax. Finally, filing status is important since it is a part of our tax system's filing requirements (discussed later). The five filing status choices are:

1. Single
2. Head of household (HOH)
3. Married filing a joint return
4. Married filing a separate return
5. Surviving spouse (a qualifying widow or widower with a dependent child)

Single Taxpayer

An unmarried person is a single taxpayer. A person separated by a final divorce decree or separate maintenance agreement is single. Status as a single taxpayer may include certain widow(er)s and abandoned spouses.

Widow(er)s. On a 1992 return a widow(er) without a dependent child, whose spouse dies before 1992, is a single person. If the widow(er) remarries before the end of 1992, a married status applies. If a widow(er) qualifies as a head of household (HOH) or a surviving spouse, this status applies. Status as a surviving spouse takes precedence over head of household status.

Abandoned Spouses (Married Persons Who Live Apart). Married persons may file separate returns. However, a married person who does not live with his or her spouse for the last half of the year may qualify as an abandoned spouse. The tax laws treat such a person as being single. With this treatment, the person may qualify as a head of household (HOH). To qualify as an abandoned spouse, the taxpayer and spouse must meet certain tests for a "married person who lives apart". The tests for an abandoned spouse are:

1. The taxpayer files a separate return.
2. For more than six months of the year, a taxpayer's natural, adopted, or stepchild lives with him or her. If it's a foster child, the child has to pass the **live-with test** (live with the taxpayer for the entire year).
3. The taxpayer pays more than half the home's upkeep cost for the tax year.
4. One of the children qualifies the taxpayer for a dependency exemption. This requirement does not apply if the taxpayer is eligible to claim the exemption but, by written agreement, gives it to the noncustodial parent.
5. The taxpayer's spouse did not live in the home at any time during the last six months of the tax year.

Head of Household (HOH)

A *head of household* is usually an unmarried person. However, an abandoned spouse can be a HOH. Also, a U.S. citizen married to a nonresident alien is a single person for HOH purposes. Neither a nonresident alien nor a surviving spouse can be a HOH. The rates for HOH status are higher than those for married persons filing jointly, but lower than those for single persons. In addition, to be a HOH the taxpayer must meet one of the following two tests:

1. The taxpayer maintains a home for more than half the year and lives in it with one of the following:

    a. An *unmarried* natural, step, adopted, or grandchild of the taxpayer. The child may or may not qualify the taxpayer for a dependency exemption. When a taxpayer gets HOH status by an unmarried child, the taxpayer enters the child's name on his or her tax return. For HOH purposes a grandchild is the same as the taxpayer's natural, step, or adopted child.

    b. A *married* natural, step, adopted, or grandchild must qualify the taxpayer for a dependency exemption. The taxpayer enters the name of every person qualifying him or her for a dependency exemption on the return. HOH status is available even if the taxpayer waives the right to claim the exemption. For a divorce or separation after 1984, the custodial parent makes the waiver by completing Form 8332, Release of Claim to Exemption for Child of Divorced or Separated Parents. Illustration 1-4 shows this form. The custodial parent can write a similar substitute release statement. The taxpayer gives the form or substitute statement to the noncustodial parent for inclusion with his or her return. HOH status is still available when the noncustodial parent gets the exemption by a pre-1985 divorce or separation document.

    c. For HOH purposes, a foster child is the same as the taxpayer's natural child.

To receive this treatment the foster child must pass the live-with test (live with the taxpayer for the entire year). A foster child does not have to come to the taxpayer's household by a placement agency. However, a foster parent must care for the child as his or her own child.

    d. Other relatives who qualify the taxpayer for a dependency exemption include a grandparent, brother, sister, brother-in-law, stepsister, mother-in-law, aunt, nephew, and the like.

2. The taxpayer maintains a household for more than half the year which is the principal home of the taxpayer's parent. Note, the parent does not have to live with the taxpayer. However, if the parent lives elsewhere, the taxpayer must maintain the household for the entire year. Regardless of where the parent lives, he or she must qualify the taxpayer for a dependency exemption.

Maintaining a household means the taxpayer is paying more than half the **household upkeep or maintenance cost**. Upkeep costs usually include those costs which are for the mutual benefit of household's occupants, such as food, telephone, water, fuel, electricity, and repairs. Household upkeep cost does not include the value of services supplied by the taxpayer or household members.

While taxpayers may claim dependency exemptions through multiple support agreements, such agreements will *not* help them get HOH status. For HOH purposes, a taxpayer may not claim a dependency exemption through a multiple support agreement.

Married Filing a Joint Return

A husband and wife may file a joint return even if only one has income. If both have income, they must have the same tax year to file jointly. A husband and wife both sign the return or have their authorized agents sign it. Usually, both spouses are individually liable for the tax.

A taxpayer who is not married for the entire year may file a joint return. It's the taxpayer's *marital status at the close of the year, or at the death of his or her spouse, that governs.* Thus, a taxpayer who marries on the last day of the year may file a joint return. A taxpayer who re-ceives a legal divorce or separation at the end of a year may not file a joint return. However, if the divorce or separation is not final by the year end, the couple may file a joint return.

Surviving Spouse in Year of Death. When a spouse dies during the year, the survivor may file a joint return with the decedent and claim two full personal exemptions. Special reporting rules apply if the spouse dies in 1992, or in 1993 before filing a 1992 return. The survivor should enter the word *deceased* and the date of the spouse's death in the name and address space on the return. In the signature space, the survivor should enter *filing as a surviving spouse*. If the survivor remarries before the end of the year, he or she may file a joint return with his or her new spouse.

Married Filing a Separate Return

When a husband and wife have separate incomes, savings may result by filing separate returns. Taxpayers should test both situations to see which one yields the smallest tax. The one producing the smallest tax usually determines filing status.

On a separate return, a taxpayer may list a spouse as an exemption. To do so, the spouse cannot have any gross income. The spouse cannot qualify another taxpayer for a dependency exemption. Also, the spouse cannot file a separate return. The taxpayer reports the full name and social security number of the spouse on the return.

Several factors may work against filing separate returns. When a married couple files separately, neither may claim the child and de-

---

Top Five Errors by Paid Tax Professionals on Form 1040A

1. Incorrect income when figuring earned income credit
2. Did not claim earned income credit when entitled
3. Used incorrect standard deduction amount
4. Omitted primary taxpayer's social security number
5. Omitted primary taxpayer's zip code

SOURCE: IRS Publication 1514 (Rev 4-92)

pendent care or earned income credit. However, an abandoned spouse may claim both credits. If a married couple lives together at any time during the tax year and files separately, neither may claim an elderly or disabled person credit.

When a couple who files separately provides more than half of a dependent's support, they may not split the dependency exemption. The person providing the larger support claims the exemption.

When a couple receives monthly social security or railroad retirement benefits, up to one-half may be part of gross income (discussed in Chapter 3). Why? When a married couple files separately, they may loose the special deduction (base amount) used to compute the taxable portion of these benefits. The loss of the special deduction takes place if the couple lives together at any time during the year.

Filing Separate Returns in Community Property States. The state laws of residence determine what is community property and what is separate property. Usually, expenses are community or separate according to the type of income from which they arise. If a taxpayer and spouse live in the same community property state and itemize deductions, they usually divide expenses paid from joint funds equally.

Election to File Joint or Separate Return. The election to file a joint or separate return is not binding on future years. After a couple files a joint return, they cannot change to separate returns after the return's due date. However, a married couple who file separately may change to a joint return even after the due date passes. However, they must make the change within three years of the return's due date.

Surviving Spouse [A Qualifying Widow(er) With Dependent Child]

For two years after a spouse's death, status as a surviving spouse is possible. The technical name of a **surviving spouse** is a qualifying widow(er) with dependent child. Note, the spouse that survives the death of his or her spouse may or may not qualify for surviving spouse status. To qualify for surviving spouse status, the widow(er) must:

1. Be eligible to file a joint return with the deceased spouse in the year of death.

2. Pay over half the upkeep cost of a home for a child who qualifies the taxpayer for a dependency exemption. A taxpayer's child includes a natural, step, adopted, and foster child.
3. Live with the qualifying child for the entire year.
4. Not remarry before the end of the year.

A surviving spouse gets the benefit of the married filing jointly rates in calculating the tax. This taxpayer also gets a basic standard deduction which equals the one for a married person filing jointly. However, a surviving spouse *cannot* file a joint return or claim an exemption for the deceased spouse. Also, this person *cannot* take an additional standard deduction because the decedent was blind or elderly at death. Surviving spouse status ends with remarriage.

A taxpayer cannot use Form 1040EZ to file as a surviving spouse. To claim this status, the taxpayer uses Form 1040A or Form 1040. Temporary absences from the household do not affect the status of a surviving spouse. Thus, a child attending school and returning home for vacation periods is a member of the surviving spouse's household.

What Is the Tax Calculation Formula?

Our federal income tax is directly applicable to individuals, regular corporations, estates, and trusts. Indirectly, it applies to **flow through en-**

Top Five Errors by Paid Tax Professionals on Form 1040

1. Omitted one-half of self-employment tax (adjustments to income)
2. Did not claim earned credit when entitled
3. Used incorrect income when figuring earned income credit
4. Used incorrect standard deduction amount
5. Omitted spouse's social security number

SOURCE: IRS Publication 1514 (Rev 4-92)

tities (partnerships and S corporations). Usually, the owners of a flow through entity pay taxes on the entity's taxable income. While different tax rates and reporting requirements apply to different taxpayers, all taxpayers use the same basic computation formula (reporting structure). After a brief discussion of gross income and introductory deduction comments, the book presents an expanded formula for individual taxpayers.

Tax Calculation Formula for All Taxpayers

```
  Total income
− Exempt income
= Gross income
− Deductions
= Taxable income
```

Gross Income

The Internal Revenue Code defines gross income as all wealth that flows to a taxpayer from whatever source derived. Then, it indicates other parts of the Code may exempt some income. It lists 15 different income sources and indicates the list is not all inclusive. The list includes

1. Compensation for services, including fees, commissions, fringe benefits, and similar items
2. Gross income from business
3. Gains from dealing in property
4. Interest
5. Rents
6. Royalties
7. Dividends
8. Alimony & separate maintenance payments
9. Annuities
10. Income from life insurance and endowment contracts
11. Pensions
12. Income from discharge of indebtedness
13. Distributive share of partnership income
14. Income in respect of a decedent
15. Income from an interest in an estate or trust

First, taxpayers determine their total income. Then, they reduce it by exclusions (income exempt from tax) to arrive at gross income. Taxpayers must have appropriate authority to exclude an item from gross income.

Authority for some exclusions exists in the tax statutes, the U.S. Constitution, and IRS de minimis rules. An IRS **de minimis rule** is an administrative rule that usually applies to small amounts. Regardless of an item's form or name, when no exclusion authority exists it is gross income. From gross income, authorized deductions are subtracted to calculate taxable income. Chapter 3 covers gross income inclusions. Chapter 4 discusses gross income exclusions.

Deductions

Individuals have two broad groups of deductions. Some are subtracted from gross income to arrive at an amount called adjusted gross income (AGI). The remaining deductions are subtracted from AGI to arrive at taxable income. Some people call them *for* or *from* deductions. Others call them above or below the line deductions. **Above the line deductions (*for* deductions)** are deductions from gross income to arrive at AGI. **Below the line deductions (*from* deductions)** are deductions from AGI to arrive at taxable income. All above the line deductions are not separately listed on page 1 of Form 1040. For those that are listed on page 1, the IRS refers to them as **adjustments to income.**

Below the line deductions fall into two broad groups. These groups include a taxpayer's itemized deductions or standard deduction, and exemptions (personal and dependency). Sometimes, AGI forms a limiting base for certain below the line deductions. At other times, it forms a base for phasing down specific benefits. Corporations, partnerships, estates, and trusts do not calculate AGI.

Deductions for AGI. The Internal Revenue Code states that an individual's AGI includes his or her gross income less certain deductions. Some of the deductions are specific; others are broad in scope. The deductions include:

1. Trade and business deductions
2. Certain expenses of performing artists
3. Losses from sale or exchange of certain property
4. Deductions attributable to rents and royalties
5. Certain deductions of life tenants and income beneficiaries of property
6. Pension, profit-sharing, and annuity plans of self-employed individuals
7. Retirement savings

Tax Calculation Formula for Individual Taxpayers

    Total income
  − <u>Exempt income</u>
  = Gross income
  − <u>Deductions for AGI</u>
  = AGI (adjusted gross income)
  − Deductions from AGI:
     Itemized or standard deduction, and
     <u>exemptions (personal & dependency)</u>
  = Taxable income

---

8. Certain lump-sum distributions from pension plans
9. Penalties forfeited because of premature withdrawal of funds from time savings accounts or deposits
10. Alimony
11. Reforestation expenses
12. Certain required repayments of supplemental unemployment compensation benefits
13. Jury duty pay remitted by employer

Itemized Deductions. After a taxpayer determines his or her AGI, he or she itemizes deductions or uses the standard deduction. Itemized deductions fall into the following eight groups (discussed in Chapters 5 and 6):

1. Medical expenses
2. Taxes
3. Interest
4. Charitable contributions
5. Casualty and theft losses
6. Moving expenses
7. Job expenses and most other miscellaneous deductions
8. Certain miscellaneous itemized deductions

Standard Deduction. A taxpayer uses the standard deduction when itemized deductions are small or when he or she doesn't want to keep supporting records. Note, a taxpayer who files Form 1040EZ or Form 1040A has no choice. Such a filer *must* use the standard deduction.

The schedule below contains amounts for the 1992 *basic standard deduction*. They do not apply to a person who qualifies another taxpayer for a dependency exemption deduction. Also, they do not include additional amounts for blind and elderly taxpayers. Blind and elderly taxpayers claim the basic standard deduction plus the proper additional standard deduction.

Taxpayer Status	Amount
Married filing jointly and qualifying widow(er)	$6,000
Head of Household	5,250
Single	3,600
Married filing separately	3,000

When a person (child) qualifies another taxpayer (parent) for a dependency exemption, he or she usually completes a standard deduction worksheet (Illustration 1-1). This worksheet shows that a dependent's standard deduction is usually the greater of $600 or his or her earned income (up to the basic standard deduction). Any additional standard deductions to which the dependent taxpayer is entitled increase the $600 and the basic standard deduction. However, a married person who qualifies another taxpayer for a dependency exemption may fall under a special rule. If the married person's spouse itemizes deductions, the special rule applies. Here, the taxpayer's standard deduction is zero.

A married person filing separately places a check in the proper box near the top of page 2 of Form 1040A or Form 1040. A check in one of these boxes says the taxpayer is a married person who is filing separately. It also says that the taxpayer's spouse is itemizing deductions on Form 1040. Form 1040EZ does not have a separate line for identifying a married taxpayer. Only single taxpayers with no dependents can use Form 1040EZ.

Illustration 1-1

This illustration presents a filled-in Standard Deduction Worksheet for Gloria Markus. Gloria is 16 years old. Her parents are eligible to claim her as a dependency exemption on their joint return. Gloria is not blind. For the current year, she has $1,400 of earned income from a weekend office job. Her standard deduction is $1,400, the larger of $600 or her earned income. This amount does not exceed the basic standard deduction for a single individual ($3,600).

Illustration 1-1
Filled-In Standard Deduction Worksheet for Dependents

Standard deduction worksheet for dependents (keep for your records)
Use this worksheet ONLY if someone can claim you as a dependent.

1.	Enter the amount from Form 1040A, line 7. If none, enter -0-.	1. 1,400.00
2.	Minimum amount.	2. 600.00
3.	Look at lines 1 and 2. Enter the larger of the two amounts here.	3. 1,400.00
4.	Enter on line 4 the amount shown below for your filing status. • Single, enter $3,600 • Married filing a separate return, enter $3,000 • Married filing a joint return or Qualifying widow(er) with dependent child, enter $6,000 • Head of household, enter $5,250	4. 3,600.00
5.	Standard deduction.	
a.	Look at lines 3 and 4. Enter the **smaller** of the two amounts here. If under 65 and not blind, stop here and enter this amount on Form 1040A, line 19. Otherwise, go to line 5b.	5a. 1,400.00
b.	If 65 or older or blind, multiply $900 ($700 if married filing a joint or separate return, or qualifying widow(er) with dependent child) by the number on Form 1040A, line 18a.	5b.
c.	Add lines 5a and 5b. Enter the total here and on Form 1040A, line 19.	5c.

Additional Standard Deduction. Taxpayers who are elderly or blind can claim an amount in addition to the basic standard deduction. A taxpayer is elderly when he or she reaches 65 years of age. The additional amount for each taxpayer is:

	Elderly or Blind	Both Elderly and Blind
Married	$700	$1,400
Single	900	1,800

Status as elderly or blind must exist at the end of the tax year (or at death). A taxpayer becomes 65 for income tax purposes the day before his or her 65th birthday. Thus, a taxpayer whose 65th birthday is on January 1, 1993, can claim the basic and one additional standard deduction for 1992. A taxpayer whose spouse dies during the year can claim the additional standard deductions for age and blindness. The additional amounts are claimable if the deceased spouse was legally age 65 and blind at death.

For total blindness, a taxpayer should attach a statement to his or her return to this effect. For partial blindness, a taxpayer claims the additional standard deduction when he or she meets one of two visual eye tests. The taxpayer must meet either of the tests on the last day of the tax year (or at death). For one test, the taxpayer's visual ability cannot exceed 20/200 in the better eye with correcting lenses. For the other test, the taxpayer's visual field cannot be more than 20 degrees. Taxpayers must support a partial blindness claim for the additional standard deduction with a certified statement from an eye doctor (ophthalmologist or optometrist). The statement must say that the taxpayer's vision does not exceed the described visual ability or field at the end time of the tax year. If the taxpayer's eye condition will never improve, he or she attaches such a statement to his or her return. For each following year, the taxpayer refers to this statement.

Exemptions. The *personal exemption* amount for 1992 for most taxpayers is $2,300. Usually, each taxpayer can claim the following:

1. One personal exemption
2. One personal exemption for the taxpayer's spouse. On a married-filing-separately return, a taxpayer can claim an exemption for his or her spouse when the spouse meets three conditions. Here, the spouse must:

   • Have no gross income
   • Not qualify another taxpayer for a dependency exemption
   • Not file a separate return

   If divorced or legally separated under a final decree, the taxpayer cannot claim a spouse exemption. If separated by a divorce that is not final (interlocutory decree), the taxpayer can claim a spouse exemption. Note, it is a personal exemption; not a dependency exemption. A spouse is never the dependent of his or her spouse.

3. One exemption for each qualifying dependent of the taxpayer

A person who qualifies another taxpayer for a dependency exemption cannot claim his or her own personal exemption. This statement is true even if the other taxpayer on his or her tax return does not claim the dependent. When a taxpayer changes his or her accounting period, he or she files a fractional year (short year) return. Here, the taxpayer prorates the exemptions.

In 1992, taxpayers with high AGI must reduce their personal and dependency exemptions. The reduction is 2 percentage points for each $2,500 of AGI, *or fraction thereof*, over a specified amount. When the number of $2,500 amounts, *or fraction thereof*, exceeds 49 the phase out is complete. Married taxpayers filing separately use $1,250 instead of $2,500. By filing status, the starting and upper limit amounts of AGI appear below:

Filing Status	Start When AGI Over	Stop When AGI Over
Married filing jointly	$157,900	$280,400
Qualifying widow(er)	157,900	280,400
Head of Household	131,550	254,050
Single	105,250	227,750
Married filing separately	78,950	140,200

For a single person with no dependents, the number of $2,500 amounts, *or fraction thereof*, exceeds 49 when AGI is over $227,750 [($227,751 − $105,250) / $2,500 = 49+)].

Illustration 1-2

This illustration shows the worksheet Jack and Lora Johnson use to calculate the phase down of their four personal and dependency exemptions. At the start of the worksheet, they enter their $9,200 exemption amount (4 x $2,300). They also enter their AGI of $163,000 and the phase down starting point of $157,900 for joint return filers. Next, they compute the difference of $5,100 ($163,000 − $157,900) and divide it by $2,500. The result is 2.04 which they round to 3. The Johnsons multiply the 3 by 2% to get 0.06 (6%), and enter the 3 and 0.06 on the worksheet. Then, they multiply the $9,200 by the 0.06 and enter the product of $552 on the worksheet. From the $9,200 exemption amount they subtract the $552 to get their exemption deduction of $8,648. The Johnsons could have calculated their $8,648 exemption deduction by multiplying the $9,200 by 94% (the complement of 6%).

Tax Base Illustration

A good review of Table 1-1 will help clarify the meaning of the tax formula definitions.

Table 1-1. This table shows how to compute the 1992 tax base for an unmarried taxpayer with single filing status. While the table

Illustration 1-2
Filled-In Personal Exemption Worksheet

Deduction for Exemptions Worksheet—Line 36 (keep for your records)

Use this worksheet **only** if the amount on Form 1040, line 32, is more than the dollar amount shown on line 3 below for your filing status. If the amount on Form 1040, line 32, is equal to or less than the dollar amount shown on line 3, multiply $2,300 by the total number of exemptions claimed on Form 1040, line 6e, and enter the result on line 36.

1. Multiply $2,300 by the total number of exemptions claimed on Form 1040, line 6e **1.** 9,200
2. Enter the amount from Form 1040, line 32 . . **2.** 163,000
3. Enter on line 3 the amount shown below for your filing status:
   - Married filing separately, enter $78,950
   - Single, enter $105,250
   - Head of household, enter $131,550
   - Married filing jointly or Qualifying widow(er), enter $157,900 . . . . **3.** 157,900
4. Subtract line 3 from line 2. If zero or less, **stop here**; enter the amount from line 1 above on Form 1040, line 36 . . . . **4.** 5,100

   Note: *If line 4 is more than $122,500 (more than $61,250 if married filing separately),* **stop here;** *you* **cannot** *take a deduction for exemptions. Enter -0- on Form 1040, line 36.*
5. Divide line 4 by $2,500 ($1,250 if married filing separately). If the result is not a whole number, round it up to the next higher whole number . **5.** 3
6. Multiply line 5 by 2% (.02) and enter the result as a decimal amount . . . . **6.** .06
7. Multiply line 1 by line 6 . . . . **7.** 552
8. **Deduction for exemptions.** Subtract line 7 from line 1. Enter the result here and on Form 1040, line 36 . . . . **8.** 8,648

presents all computation classes, it leaves some items within classes for later discussion.

Table 1-1
Computation of 1992 Taxable Income

INCOME:
Rent from apartment, $2,400; Salary, $16,200;
  Dividends on common stock, $720;
  Interest on savings, $80; Municipal bond
  interest, $30 . . . . $19,430
GROSS INCOME EXCLUSIONS:
Municipal bond interest $30   30
GROSS INCOME INCLUSIONS:
Rent from apartment, $2,400; Salary, $16,200;
  Dividends on common stock, $720;
  Interest on savings, $80 . . . . $19,400
DEDUCTIONS FOR AGI:
Expenses of apartment   1,400
AGI:
Net rent from apartment, $1,000; Salary,
  $16,200; Dividends on common stock,
  $720; Interest on savings, $80 . . . . . $18,000
DEDUCTIONS FROM AGI:
  STANDARD DEDUCTION OR
  ITEMIZED DEDUCTION
    Single Person $3,600
  EXEMPTIONS:
    One personal exemption   2,300   5,900
TAXABLE INCOME:
AGI, $18,000; less standard deduction,
  $3,600 and 1 exemption, $2,300 . . . . $12,100

Who Can Be Claimed as a Dependent?

Before a taxpayer may claim a dependency exemption for another person, the person must be a qualifying dependent of the taxpayer. A *qualifying dependent* must meet *five* tests:

1. Gross income less than exemption amount
2. Member of household or closely related
3. Resident or U.S. citizen
4. Support of more than 50%
5. Absence of joint return

Most of a taxpayer's young children will meet these tests, or one of the exceptions. When a child is born alive on the last day of the year before midnight, the parents get a full dependency exemption. However, a taxpayer may not claim an exemption for a stillbirth.

Gross Income Less Than Exemption Amount

Usually, a dependent's gross income must be less than the exemption amount. For 1992, this amount is $2,300. For the gross income test when a taxpayer reports on a fiscal-year basis, a dependent's tax year is the calendar year in which the taxpayer's fiscal year begins.

Gross income includes gross receipts from rental property, not the net amount after deducting expenses. Gross income of a business usually is sales minus the cost of goods sold, plus miscellaneous income. A dependent's social security benefits and tax-exempt municipal bond interest usually are not part of gross income.

Exceptions. The gross income test *does not* apply to a taxpayer's children under age 19 at the end of the tax year. If the taxpayer's children are under age 24 at year end and full-time students, it also does not apply.

To qualify as a full-time student, a child usually must attend an educational institution for five months of the year. The institution must maintain a regular faculty and curriculum. It must also have a regular body of students in attendance. The child need not be attending school at the end of the tax year. While a child may have graduated during the year, a parent may still be eligible to claim an exemption. However, the parent must meet the other dependency exemption tests. A child employed full-time during the day and attending school at night does not qualify as a full-time student. Enrollment in correspondence or employment training courses will not qualify a person as a full-time student.

Child Defined. The definition of a child for tax purposes includes natural and adopted children as well as stepchildren. It also includes a child placed by an authorized adoption agency when the child is a member of the taxpayer's household. The definition includes a foster child who lives with the taxpayer for the entire year. Temporary absences from the home do not affect a foster child's classification. Also, the birth or death of a foster child during the year does not affect this classification. Full-time students under age 24 who are foster children have no gross income test. The exemption for a dependent child is claimable on only one tax return.

Member of Household or Closely Related

A person unrelated to the taxpayer must pass the live-with test to qualify the taxpayer for a dependency exemption. Here, the unrelated person must be a member of the taxpayer's household for the entire year. In addition to truly unrelated individuals, the live-with test also applies to a cousin and a foster individual, child or adult. An exception exists for *temporary absences*. Here, a taxpayer may claim an exemption for the unrelated person when he or she is temporarily away from the taxpayer's household. Temporary absences include school attendance, vacations, and an indefinite nursing home confinement.

EXAMPLE 1 ————————————————

Cathy is Mary's elderly cousin who has been living with her for the past two years. For medical reasons, Cathy went to live in a nursing home in January of this year. Cathy's doctor says she will be in the nursing home for an indefinite period. However, Mary can still claim a dependency exemption for Cathy if she meets the other four tests.

Closely related relatives of the taxpayer need not be members of the taxpayer's household. A closely related relative is one of the following:

- A descendant of the taxpayer, including a legally adopted child
- A stepchild of the taxpayer, but not the stepchild's descendants
- A brother, sister, stepbrother, or stepsister
- A parent, grandparent, or other direct ancestor (but not a foster parent, foster grandparent, foster grandchild, etc.)
- A stepparent
- A nephew or niece (but not if related only by marriage instead of by blood)
- An uncle or aunt (but not if related only by marriage instead of by blood)
- A father-in-law, mother-in-law, son-in-law, daughter-in-law, brother-in-law, or sister-in-law

At the time of a couple's marriage, the tax laws set up permanent relationships between the couple and their in-laws. These relationships continue after a couple gets a divorce or a spouse dies. Thus, after a spouse's death, a mother-in-law may qualify a daughter-in-law for an exemption on her married filing separately return. In the years after the husband's death, the mother-in-law may also qualify the daughter-in-law for an exemption on the daughter-in-law's return as a single person. In both situations, the mother-in-law does not have to pass the live-with test (be a member of the daughter-in-law's household for the entire year). However, for "button-hole" relatives the tax laws do not set up permanent relationships at the time of marriage. A **"button-hole" relative** is an aunt, uncle, nephew, or niece of a taxpayer's spouse. For a spouse who survives the death of his or her spouse, and who also has a "button-hole" relative, the live-with test applies to a surviving spouse's married filing separately return. It also applies to this person's returns as a single person in the years after the spouse's death. In both situations, the "button-hole" relative must be a member of the surviving spouse's household for the entire year.

For dependency exemption purposes, the taxpayer is never the dependent of his or her spouse. On a joint or married filing separately return, a spouse may claim an exemption for his or her spouse. However, it is not a dependency exemption. It is either a **spousal exemption** or the spouse's own exemption.

Resident or U. S. Citizen

Dependents must be citizens of the United States. Persons who are not U.S. citizens must be residents of the United States, Canada, or Mexico for part of the tax year. This requirement usually means that foreign-born relatives who live in another country will not qualify. However, an alien child adopted by a U.S. citizen living abroad will qualify when the child lives with the taxpayer for the entire year.

Support of More Than 50%

The taxpayer claiming the dependency exemption must provide more than half of a dependent's *total support* during the calendar year. Support includes payments for food, clothing, lodging, education, medical and dental care, entertainment, transportation, and other needs. When a taxpayer furnishes lodging, its amount equals the lodging's fair rental value. **Fair rental value** is the amount that the taxpayer could expect to receive from a stranger for the same lodging. Lodging expense includes taxes, interest, depreciation, insurance, heat, and utilities. The amount included may be for one room or a proportionate share of a house, depending on the dependent's use. Capital items such as automobiles and furniture qualify as support items if given to (or purchased for) a dependent.

Scholarships children receive at educational institutions are not part of child support. Thus, a child may receive a $4,500 college scholarship in a year when the taxpayer provides only $3,800 of support. If no other sources of support exist, the taxpayer may claim a dependency exemption because he or she provides 100 percent of the child's support.

An amount paid by a state for training and educating a handicapped or mentally retarded child is a scholarship. Such amounts are not taken into account when applying the support test. Also, funeral expenses and life insurance premiums are not part of support.

The status and source of the money used for support is usually immaterial. Tax-exempt income such as social security benefits, veterans' schooling receipts, and welfare benefits may be support items. If a taxpayer uses such income to buy support items, it is part of the person's support. On a joint return, support from either spouse counts.

To determine if a taxpayer provides over half of a dependent's support, the taxpayer first determines a dependent's total support. Total support consists of three amounts:

1. Fair rental value of lodging
2. All appropriate expenses incurred or paid directly to or for the dependent
3. Share of proper expenses (excluding lodging) that are unrelated to specific household members such as food

EXAMPLE 2 ——————————————

Robert is a 21-year-old college student whose total support for the year is $11,000. It consists of $2,500 for lodging, $7,000 for college tuition and expenses, and $1,500 for miscellaneous items. Robert's parents pay $7,000 of his support. This amount is more than one-half of his total support (one-half of $11,000 equals $5,500). Thus, Robert's parents meet the support test to claim him as a dependency exemption on their tax return.

EXAMPLE 3 ——————————————

Martha's parents live with her for the entire year. They share the home with Martha, her husband, and dependent child without paying rent. The market value of the lodging used by the parents is $3,800 ($1,900 for each parent). Martha's father receives nontaxable social security of $3,250. He uses it to buy equal amounts of support items for himself and his wife. Dental expenses for Martha's mother are $2,200. Martha pays $700 of these expenses and her brother pays the remaining expenses. Martha's parents eat their meals with Martha and her family. Cost of all meals consumed in the home is $4,670. Each parent's share is $934 (⅕ of $4,670). The separate and combined support for Martha's parents for the year is:

	Mother	Father	Total
Lodging (fair rental value provided by Martha)	$1,900	$1,900	$ 3,800
Direct expenses:			
Social security spent by parents	1,625	1,625	3,250
Dental expense paid by Martha	700	—	700
Dental expense paid by Martha's brother	1,500	—	1,500
Share of food provided by Martha	934	934	1,868
	$6,659	$4,459	$11,118

Martha provides more than half the support of her parents. The support amount for her mother is $3,534 ($1,900 + $700 + $934). For her father, it is $2,834 ($1,900 + $934). Martha passes the support test to claim each parent as a dependency exemption. She paid over one-half of the total support for each parent.

Multiple Support Declaration. A special rule allows a qualifying group member to claim a dependency exemption when no one provides more than half of a person's support. Group members, and the claiming member, may vary from year to year. Everyone who passes the following tests is a group member for the year:

1. Provides more than 10% of the person's support
2. Meets the four non-support tests to claim the person as a dependency exemption
3. Provides, with the other group members, more than 50% of the person's support

For the multiple support rule to apply, the:

1. Group members who do not claim the exemption must complete and deliver a *Multiple Support Declaration* to the claiming member.
2. Claiming member must file the Multiple Support Declarations with his or her tax return.

EXAMPLE 4 ───────────────────────

Elinore lives with Logan the entire year. Logan, Marty, Nancy, Otey, and Lynette provide 100% of Elinore's support. Relationship to Elinore, support amounts, and percentages are:

	Amounts	%
Logan (Elinore's son)	$ 1,000	10
Marty (Elinore's son-in-law)	2,500	25
Nancy (Elinore's step-daughter)	2,500	25
Otey (Elinore's brother)	2,500	25
Lynette (Elinore's friend)	1,500	15
Total	$10,000	100

Qualifying group members are Marty, Nancy, and Otey. Logan and Lynette are not qualifying members. Why? Logan does not provide more than 10% of Elinore's support. Lynette is not a relative. For Lynette to qualify, Elinore must pass the live-with test (live with Lynette the entire year). Since Marty, Nancy, and Otey are relatives, Elinore does not have to live with them.

Illustration 1-3

This illustration presents a filled-in Form 2120, Multiple Support Declaration, for Joseph R. Calder for 1992. The preparer is Robert A. Calder, Joe's son. Bob lives at 321 Valley Road, Cincinnati, Ohio 45209-2402. His social security number is 132-48-9866. The declaration states that Helen B. Justin may claim Joe as a dependency exemption on her tax return. Helen is Joe's daughter. She lives at 1621 Appletree Lane, Cincinnati, Ohio 45226-1661. After dating and signing the declaration, Bob gives it to his sister. Helen will include the Multiple Support Declaration with her tax return. Helen's social security number is 134-62-8736.

Note that the declaration requests the name of the supported person and the claiming member's name and address. The person signing the form agrees to three preprinted statements. These statements say that the form's signer:

1. Provided more than 10% of the person's support
2. Could have claimed the exemption if she or he provided more than 50% of the support.
3. Will not claim the exemption for the years

Dependency Exemption for Child of Divorced or Separated Parents. For divorced or legally separated parents to claim an exemption for their child, the parents must pass the *divorced parent rules*. These rules say that the parents acting together:

1. Must provide more than 50% of the child's support
2. Must have custody of the child more than 50% of the year

The divorced parent rules apply to legally separated parents if they live apart during the last half of the year. The law treats the parent with the longest custody as the provider of more than half the child's support. This person is the **custodial parent**. The parent with the shortest custody is the **noncustodial parent**. When the spouse of a remarried parent provides the support, the law treats it as coming from the parent. Divorced parent rules do not apply in multiple support cases.

After passing the divorced parent rules and other dependency exemption tests, the custodial parent may claim the exemption. The custodial parent may release the claiming right to the other parent by completing Form 8332 (Illustration 1-4) and delivering it to him or her. If a Form 8332 release is not available, the custodial parent may deliver a signed and dated release statement to the other parent. This document should state that the custodial parent (signing parent) will not claim the exemption. The release may be for one or several years. The other parent files it with his or her tax return.

Divorce decrees or separation agreements before January 1, 1985 are under different rules. Here, the parent with the shortest custody may claim the exemption when:

1. This parent provides at least $600 for the child's support.
2. The decree or separation agreement specifies this parent may claim the exemption.

Illustration 1-3
Filled-In Form 2120

Form **2120**
(Rev. May 1991)

Department of the Treasury
Internal Revenue Service

Multiple Support Declaration

▶ **Attach to Form 1040 or Form 1040A.**

OMB No. 1545-0071
Expires 5-31-94

Attachment
Sequence No. **50**

Name of taxpayer claiming person as a dependent

Helen B. Justin

Social security number

134 62 8736

During the calendar year 19 **92** , I paid over 10% of the support of

Joseph R. Calder
(Name of person)

I could have claimed this person as a dependent except that I did not pay over 50% of his or her support. I understand that this person is being claimed as a dependent on the income tax return of

Helen B. Justin
(Name)

1621 Appletree Lane, Cincinnati, OH 45226-1661
(Address)

I agree not to claim this person as a dependent on my Federal income tax return for any tax year that began in this calendar year.

Robert J Calder
(Your signature)

132 48 9866
(Your social security number)

January 18, 1993   321 Valley Rd., Cincinnati, OH 45209-2402
(Date)   (Address)

Also, under these earlier rules, the noncustodial parent can claim the exemption when:

1. This parent provides at least $1,200 for the child's support.
2. The custodial parent cannot prove that he or she provides more support for the child than the noncustodial parent.

Illustration 1-4

This illustration shows a completed Form 8332, Release of Claim to Exemption for Child of Divorced or Separated Parents. The release is for Martha A. Krueger, the daughter of Anthony B. Krueger and Joyce C. Kappa. Joyce's social security number is 693-24-6802. If Tony delivers completed Form 8332 to Joyce Kappa, his former spouse, he cannot claim Martha as a dependent for 1992. Joyce can claim her as a dependent on her 1992 tax return. Tony places the current date on the form, signs it, and gives it to his former wife. Joyce files it with her tax return for 1992.

The instructions to Form 8332 say that the parent who has custody of the child prepares the form. The form asks for the names and social security numbers of the preparer and the person claiming the dependency exemption. It also asks for the name of the dependent child. Form 8332 is a two part form. The top part is for the current year, and the bottom part is for future years.

Absence of Joint Return

One of the dependency exemption tests is the absence of a joint return by the person the tax-

Illustration 1-4
Filled-In Form 8332

Form **8332**
(Rev. September 1990)

Department of the Treasury
Internal Revenue Service

Release of Claim to Exemption
for Child of Divorced or Separated Parents
▶ Attach to Tax Return of Parent Claiming Exemption.

OMB No. 1545-0915
Expires 6-30-93

Attachment
Sequence No. **51**

Name(s) of parent claiming exemption

Joyce C. Kappa

Social security number

693 : 24 : 6802

Part I   Release of Claim to Exemption for Current Year

I agree not to claim an exemption for   Martha A. Krueger

Name(s) of child (or children)

for the tax year 19 **92** .

Anthony B. Krueger   280-64-2396   8-5-92

Signature of parent releasing claim to exemption   Social security number   Date

If you choose not to claim an exemption for this child (or children) for future tax years, complete Part II, as explained in the instructions below.

Part II   Release of Claim to Exemption for Future Years

I agree not to claim an exemption for ______________________________

Name(s) of child (or children)

for tax year(s) ______________________________

(Specify. See instructions.)

____

Signature of parent releasing claim to exemption   Social security number   Date

---

payer is trying to claim as an exemption. It sometimes causes problems for dependency exemption claims when a married couple files jointly. If the joint return is only a refund claim, a dependency exemption for one spouse may be possible. The IRS says a joint return is a refund claim if it meets the following conditions:

1. Neither spouse must file a return.
2. Neither spouse files a separate return.
3. No tax would be due for either spouse on a married filing separate return.
4. No other taxpayer is entitled to claim a dependency exemption for the spouse of the person claimed as a dependency exemption.

EXAMPLE 5

In the current year, Karen separately furnishes 75% of the support of Sam (her son) and Diane (her daughter-in-law). All parties live in Ohio, a common law state. Sam is a part-time student at an Ohio college. Diane is a full-time student at the same col-

lege. At the end of the year, Sam will be 22 and Diane will be 21. During the year, Sam earns $2,500 as a part-time clerk. Diane receives a $2,500 tax-exempt scholarship. To obtain a refund of income taxes withheld from Sam's pay, Sam and Diane file a joint return.

Karen cannot claim a dependency exemption for Sam because his gross income is too high (over $2,299.99). The gross income exception applies to a taxpayer's children who are full-time, not part-time, students.

Since Diane's scholarship is tax-exempt, she has no gross income. If Sam files separately, no tax is due. Does Sam fall under the joint return filing requirements or the married filing separately filing requirements? If Sam files a separate return, or if a taxpayer other than Karen can claim an exemption for him, Sam falls under the married filing separately filing requirements. Sam did not file a separate return. Since

Karen furnishes 75% of Sam's support, no other taxpayer can claim a dependency exemption for him. Finally, by filing jointly with Diane, Sam does not save taxes. Thus, Karen can claim a dependency exemption for Diane.

Who Must File Income Tax Returns?

Under our self-reporting tax system, a taxpayer who meets certain conditions must file a return. While some low income persons do not have to file a return, most of us must file under our current tax system. The basis of the current filing requirements is either:

1. A person's net earnings from self-employment, or
2. A person's gross income and filing status

The filing requirements apply to all minor and adult, single and married, U.S. citizens and resident aliens. The requirements also apply to nonresident aliens married to U.S. citizens and resident aliens electing to be taxed on their world income by filing joint returns. Nonresident aliens who earn income in the U.S. must also file income tax returns. The latter part of this chapter discusses filing status types.

Self-Employment Income Test

A *self-employed* person must file a tax return when his or her net income from self-employment is at least $400. Note, it is net, not gross, income that determines when a self-employed person must file a return.

Gross Income Test

Since *gross income* is the filing requirement threshold amount for persons not self-employed, understanding its composition is important. A taxpayer's return of capital and income exempt from tax are not part of gross income. Also, it excludes **de minimis** income (usually small amounts exempt from tax for administrative reasons). Taxpayers using Chart A of Table 1-2 must file a return when their gross income is *equal to or greater than* the applicable amount. Taxpayers using Chart B must file a return when their gross income is *more than* the applicable amount.

Chart A of Table 1-2 shows threshold filing requirement amounts for persons who do not qualify another taxpayer for a dependency exemption. The basis for them is usually a taxpayer's personal exemptions and standard deduction. Dependency exemptions are not part of these amounts. For elderly taxpayers (age 65 or over), the filing threshold increases by one additional standard deduction amount. Note, blindness has no effect on these threshold amounts. A married taxpayer filing jointly with gross income of $2,300 or more, who does not live with his or her spouse at year end or at the spouse's death, must file a return. A married taxpayer filing separately, who does not qualify another taxpayer for a dependency exemption, must file a return when his or her gross income is $2,300 or more. A special rule applies when a married taxpayer qualifies another taxpayer for a dependency exemption, and this taxpayer's spouse itemizes deductions on a separate return. Here, the taxpayer must file a return when his or her gross income is more than $4.99. This special filing requirement is found in Chart B of Table 1-2.

Chart B of Table 1-2 shows threshold filing requirement amounts for individuals who qualify someone else for a dependency exemption. Their basis is usually the taxpayer's standard deduction and earned income. Here, age as well as blindness cause the standard deduction and earned income to increase. Earned income is personal service income. Unearned income includes interest and dividends from portfolio investments.

Even if no tax is due, a return must be filed when the law requires it. If a taxpayer's gross income is less than the applicable threshold amount, a return must still be filed if a tax is due to the government.

EXAMPLE 6 ————————————

John Jones is a part-time waiter at a local restaurant. John receives tips from customers that he does not report to his employer for income tax withholding purposes. Since John owes social security taxes on these tips, he must file a return and pay the tax.

Table 1-2: Who Must File in 1992

CHART A: Persons Who Do Not Qualify Another Taxpayer for a Dependency Exemption

NOT ELDERLY, & GROSS INCOME OF AT LEAST

	Single	HOH	* Married Filing Jointly	Surviving Spouse
Exemption–self	$2,300	$2,300	$ 2,300	$2,300
–spouse			2,300	
Standard deduction	3,600	5,250	6,000	6,000
Totals	$5,900	$7,550	$10,600	$8,300

ELDERLY, & GROSS INCOME OF AT LEAST

	Single	HOH	* Married Filing Jointly	Surviving Spouse
Exemption–self	$2,300	$2,300	$ 2,300	$2,300
–spouse			2,300	
Standard deduction	3,600	5,250	6,000	6,000
Additional Standard deduction–self	900	900	700	700
			11,300	
–spouse			700	
Totals	$6,800	$8,450	$12,000	$9,000

* Married persons not qualifying another taxpayer for a dependency exemption
  Filing jointly
  — Not living with spouse at year end or at spouse's death, and GROSS INCOME OF AT LEAST $2,300
  Filing separately
  — Living or not living with spouse at year end or at spouse's death, and GROSS INCOME OF AT LEAST $2,300
  Married persons who qualify another taxpayer for a dependency exemption, and whose spouse itemizes deductions, see Chart B

CHART B: Persons Who Qualify Another Taxpayer for a Dependency Exemption

SINGLE TAXPAYERS

Unearned Income	Earned Income	GROSS INCOME OF MORE THAN		
		Not Blind Not Elderly	Blind or Elderly	Blind and Elderly
No	Yes	$3,600	$4,500	$5,400
Yes	No	$ 600	$1,500	$2,400

Unearned Income	Earned Income	GROSS INCOME OF MORE THAN THE HIGHER OF		
Yes	Yes	$600 or EI with maximum of $3,600	$1,500 or EI plus $900 with maximum of $4,500	$2,400 or EI plus $1,800 with maximum of $5,400

MARRIED TAXPAYERS

Unearned Income	Earned Income	GROSS INCOME OF MORE THAN		
		Not Blind Not Elderly	Blind or Elderly	Blind and Elderly
No	Yes	$3,000	$3,700	$4,400
Yes	No	$ 600	$1,300	$2,000

Unearned Income	Earned Income	GROSS INCOME OF MORE THAN THE HIGHER OF		
Yes	Yes	$600 or EI with maximum of $3,000	$1,300 or EI plus $700 with maximum of $3,700	$2,000 or EI plus $1,400 with maximum of $4,400

NOTE: Married persons filing separately who qualify another taxpayer for a dependency exemption, and whose spouse itemizes deductions, must file when GROSS INCOME IS MORE THAN $4.99.

What Is a Tax Year?

While most individuals use the calendar year for tax reporting, a few use the fiscal year. Corporate taxpayers and partnerships are probably the largest fiscal year users. A **fiscal year** is any twelve-month period ending on the last day of a calendar month other than December. Unless otherwise stated, this book assumes all taxpayers use the calendar year.

How Is the Tax Due To or From the Government Calculated?

Many tax provisions control the tax base calculation process, making it difficult to determine gross income, deductions, and taxable income. Once taxpayers determine their base, they calculate their tax by applying the rates for their filing status. From the tax, they subtract prepayments and credits to determine a balance due to or from the government. Chapter 2 discusses the tax calculation process and some of the tax credits.

What Are a Tax Filer's Responsibilities?

Under our self-reporting tax system, each taxpayer must determine his or her tax liability, file a proper return on time, and pay the tax when due. Taxpayers who do not meet these responsibilities face possible fines, penalties, and imprisonment. In addition, the IRS charges them interest on unpaid taxes. The IRS requires taxpayers to file their returns directly with its regional service centers. Taxpayers should use the self-addressed envelope in their return package to mail their return. In addition to these responsibilities, taxpayers should maintain supporting records and make every attempt to minimize filing errors.

Maintain Records

Taxpayers must keep adequate records to support all return items. The retention period (return's closing date) usually ends three years after a return's due date, or filing date if later. However, taxpayers should retain the records which prove the basis of property (principal home) longer. Taxpayers should also keep a photocopy of their return and tax calculations. Last year's return and calculations can serve as a checklist for next year's return. It can also be useful at an IRS audit.

Minimize Errors

Honesty and care in preparing a return will help reduce the chances of controversies. Here, taxpayers should follow the suggestions below:

1. *Get appropriate forms, schedules and instructions.* Forms, schedules and instructions are normally mailed to taxpayers by the IRS. If a taxpayer does not receive them, get them from the local IRS office or appropriate IRS regional service center. The instructions contain toll-free telephone numbers for ordering forms.
2. Study the instructions and assemble data before preparing the return.
3. Be certain the IRS identification label is correct. Supply all data. Recheck all calculations. Minor omissions due to carelessness or haste delay processing.

General Responsibilities of Tax Filers

1. Prepare proper tax return
2. Determine proper tax liability
3. Pay tax due on-time
4. File return on-time with proper IRS Regional Service Center
5. Use envelope enclosed with tax form instructions to mail return
6. Keep evidence of on-time mailing to proper IRS Regional Service Center
7. Maintain records and documents to support tax return data
8. Try to minimize tax return errors

How are Property Disposals Treated?

Earlier, this chapter indicated that gains from dealings in property are part of gross income. It also stated that losses from the sale or exchange of certain property can qualify as a deduction for AGI. The following overview shows how these transactions mesh with earlier concepts and the tax calculation process. For more discussion, see Chapters 10 through 12.

Rate of Tax on Capital Gains

Before 1988, certain gains from dealing in property (capital assets) were taxed at a lower rate than other income. From 1988 through 1990, they were taxed like other income. Now, some of these gains again qualify for a lower rate (28%) when two conditions are met. First, the taxpayer must have a net capital gain. Second, he or she must be in the 31% marginal rate bracket.

Capital Asset

The Internal Revenue Code defines a **capital asset** by *what it is not*. It lists items that are not capital assets. Some people call it the *not list*. The capital asset not list includes accounts and notes receivable from the sale of goods or services in a taxpayer's trade or business. Inventory and stock in trade held for sale to customers are on the list. It also includes depreciable and real property used in a taxpayer's trade or business. For individuals, most property items are capital assets.

> ### Closing Dates of Tax Years
> ### Statutory Limit for Assessing
> ### Additional Taxes
>
> NORMAL CLOSING—3 years after later of return's due date or filing date.
>
> INCOME OMISSION—6 years after later of return's due date or filing date for taxpayer's inadvertent omission of more than 25% of gross income reported on return.
>
> FRAUDULENT RETURN—A tax year never closes.

Uses of Property

Taxpayers can hold property for personal-use purposes. They can also hold it for investment (income-producing) or trade or business purposes. Most gains from property disposals are taxable. However, some fall under the non-taxable sale or exchange rules. Chapter 11 discusses these rules.

Usually, taxpayers who dispose of personal-use property at a loss cannot deduct it. An exception exists for property that is destroyed by a casualty or is stolen. Chapter 5 covers these losses. When a taxpayer sells investment property at a loss, it is usually deductible. However, in a related party transaction it is not! Chapter 11 discusses them.

Holding Period

To understand the term *net capital gain*, one must first understand some of the holding period rules. Usually, the holding period of property starts the day after a taxpayer gets it. Thus, the purchase date belongs to the seller. The same numeric date in the next month as the buyer's *start date* marks the start date of the second holding month. Taxpayers who hold property more than 12 months and dispose of it usually get long-term treatment. When the property is a capital asset, the tax laws call it a long-term capital gain or loss.

Net Capital Gain

To understand the meaning of a net capital gain, the discussion below focuses on capital assets held for investment. In this context, a **net capital gain** is the excess of a taxpayer's net long-term capital gain over net short-term capital loss. To determine it, taxpayers net their short-term capital gains and losses. Then, they net their long-term capital gains and losses. Next, they net the results to produce a net gain or loss from all capital assets held for investment. If the final netting is a gain, it can be a *net capital gain*. If the final netting is a loss, individual taxpayers can deduct up to $3,000 from other income.

Under the offset rules for individuals, short-term capital losses offset other income before long-term capital losses. Losses not offset against other income in the current year go forward for an indefinite period. In the next year, the carry forward short-term and long-term losses offset respective gains. Remaining losses offset other income up to $3,000. Here, short-term losses are offset first. Note, it is the remaining loss after the offset against other income that has an indefinite carry forward period. For corporate taxpayers, capital losses can only offset capital gains. They carry these losses back three years and forward five. Like individuals, they use them to offset capital gains. Regardless of the holding period, the tax laws treat a corporate capital loss carry back or carry forward as short-term.

EXAMPLE 7 ——————————————

During the year, Abby Marcus sold several shares of stock held for investment. She had a short-term capital gain of $700 and a short-term capital loss of $200. She also had a long-term capital gain of $1,200 and a long-term capital loss of $300. From these transactions, Abby has a net gain of $1,400.

Short-term capital gain		$ 700
Short-term capital loss		(200)
Net short-term capital gain		$ 500
Long-term capital gain	$ 1,200	
Long-term capital loss	(300)	900
Net gain		$ 1,400

Since Abby does not have a net short-term capital loss, her net capital gain equals her net long-term capital gain of $900.

Net long-term capital gain	$900
Net short-term capital loss	–0–
Net capital gain	$900

If Abby's taxable income is inside the 31% marginal rate bracket by $900, all of her net capital gain ($900) gets taxed at the 28% rate. However, her net short-term capital gain gets taxed like other income.

Income Relationships

While a taxpayer's net capital gain is part of AGI and taxable income, only the gain part is included in gross income. Related losses are deductions from gross income to arrive at AGI. In Example 7, Abby includes her $900 net capital gain in AGI and taxable income. However, her gross income from these transactions is $1,900 ($700 + $1,200).

Common Tax Return Errors

1. Not attaching all Forms W-2 to front of return
2. Not including all forms and schedules with return
3. Use of wrong standard deduction
4. Failure to enclose payment
5. Incorrect or incomplete address
6. Incorrect or incomplete social security number
7. Omission of required data
8. Unallowed exclusions, deductions, or credits
9. Misstated entries
10. Failure to check filing status blank
11. Failure to list dependents properly
12. Incorrect use of tax tables or schedules
13. Incomplete data for tax deduction
14. Math errors
15. Items on wrong line
16. Failure to sign and date return

Importance of Proper Determination

A proper determination of gross income is important to taxpayers and the IRS since it is part of the basis of our tax system's filing requirements. Failure to file a proper return on time can result in tax penalties. A proper determination of gross income is also important because the IRS can extend a tax year's closing date when a taxpayer omits too much gross income from his or her return. When a closing date is extended, the IRS has more time to audit that year's return.

How Can I Minimize the Tax Bite?

Taxpayers have the right to use all legal means to avoid or postpone a tax. Through proper tax planning, taxpayer's can usually minimize the tax bite. The first goal should be to pay the smallest tax at the latest possible time. While a taxpayer's personal objectives can alter this goal, it should be the starting point of any tax plan. In setting up a plan, taxpayers should follow known tax planning principles.

> ## Tax Planning Principles
>
> 1. Acquire working knowledge of tax laws
> 2. Plan transactions in advance to reduce taxes
> 3. Keep good records

Acquire Working Knowledge of Tax Laws

The tax laws contain many elections which taxpayers must understand if they want to pay the smallest tax at the latest possible time. They involve transaction timing, tax years, gain postponement, methods of depreciation, and execution methods. For execution methods, taxpayers should know that an outright property sale produces one result while an installment sale or exchange produces another.

To increase expense deductions, taxpayers should know a deduction amount before completing a transaction. For charitable contributions, taxpayers should understand the tax impact of cash and property gifts, carry forward provisions, a market value election, and bargain sales (sales below market value).

For property disposals, holding period, nature of the property, and disposal date all influence the tax results. Taxpayers who want their property gains taxed at the 28% rate must meet specific conditions. This rate is available for gains from business, investment, and personal-use property when taxpayers meet the conditions.

Taxpayers who sell property at a loss should know when it is and is not deductible. If a loss is not fully deductible in the year of disposal, taxpayers should know if and when it can be deducted in the future.

Individuals who cannot keep up with the impact of tax law changes should seek professional advice. In addition to return preparation, this advice should include a tax analysis of planned transactions.

Plan Transactions in Advance to Reduce Taxes

Taxpayers who receive good tax advice can reduce their taxes by careful planning. The plan can be short-term or long-term. A short-term plan tries to reduce taxes over the next few years. A long-term plan tries to reduce taxes over a longer time span. Long-term plans usu-ally involve complex techniques beyond the scope of this book. They include selecting a retirement plan, and developing estate, gift, and trust strategies.

For taxpayers whose income, deductions, exemptions, and credits are stable, a one- to three-year tax plan is probably long enough. When uncertainty exists, they should use liberal, conservative, and middle of the road assumptions. In all cases, they should update the plan annually.

Taxpayers in a service business who use the cash method of accounting can control their end of the year income. They can increase income by speeding up service billings, or postpone it by delaying them. Other taxpayers who use the cash method of accounting (most persons) can control end of the year gains and losses by speeding up or slowing down the closing dates of property transactions. Taxpayers who control transaction timing can adjust their income and deductions to take full advantage of the tax laws.

Taxpayers whose itemized deduction dollars are close to their standard deduction amount can use a bunching technique. **Bunching** is the process of slowing down or speeding up cash payments for itemized deductions so that the maximum amount falls in a given year. Taxpayers who use this technique itemize their deductions in one year and take the standard deduction in the next. The easiest deductions to bunch are charitable contributions, medical expenses, property taxes, and state income taxes.

Personal exemptions are usually not controllable. However, couples can arrange their marriage date and the date they have a child (December or January) to minimize the tax bite. Through the amount taxpayers pay to support another taxpayer, they can control their dependency exemption claim. To some degree, taxpayers can control their tax credits. Here, they should try to take them as early as possible.

Keep Good Records

A good record-keeping system is an essential part of all tax planning models. It allows taxpayers easy access to the nature, purpose, and amount of old transactions. The underlying files should contain invoices, canceled notes or checks, payment receipts, property titles, and copies of old tax returns. An orderly indexing system will help taxpayers find stored documents. Finally, a good record-keeping system can keep a taxpayer from overlooking deductions at tax return time.

Summary

The more an individual knows about the tax laws, the easier it is to spot tax planning opportunities. Remember the tax planner's first goal: pay the smallest tax at the latest possible time. As you study the book, keep this goal in mind and be aware of ways to reduce the tax bite.

Deductions and Credits—What's the Difference?

Each deduction dollar reduces a taxpayer's liability by a fractional amount (amount equal to taxpayer's marginal tax rate). When a taxpayer's liability equals or exceeds his or her credit dollars, each credit dollar reduces the liability by a dollar. Also, some credit dollars are refundable.

C H A P T E R 1

Questions and Problems

1. **a.** For 1992 John Summers, age 16, is claimed as a dependency exemption on his parents' tax return. He earned $905 from his paper route and other after school jobs. John deposited most of his earnings in a savings account at the local bank. The bank notified him that for 1992 his interest income was $800. Must John file an income tax return for 1992? Provide a full explanation for your answer, including how his threshold filing requirement is calculated.

   b. For 1992 Frank Daniels, age 25, is claimed as a dependency exemption on his parents' tax return. He is one of several full-time students at Carroll College who receive a $5,000 tax-free academic scholarship. Also, his bank informed him that for 1992 he has interest income of $100. Frank also earned $425 in 1992 from his work as an independent art consultant to a local outdoor advertising agency. His expenses in connection with this work were $15. Must Frank file an income tax return for 1992? Provide a full explanation for your answer, including how his threshold filing requirement is calculated.

2. Each taxpayer must designate a filing status on his or her Form 1040A or Form 1040 for 1992. To use Form 1040EZ, a taxpayer must be single at the end of his or her tax year or at death. If the taxpayer is deceased, the executor or executrix of his or her estate will file the final income tax return. Using the data below, indicate each taxpayer's proper filing status for 1992.

   a. Married; separated from spouse by a separate maintenance decree; has no dependents . . . . __________________

   b. Widower; spouse died January 16, 1991; has not remarried; has a dependent parent who did not live with the taxpayer during 1992; maintained parent's home for the entire year . . . . __________________

   c. Unmarried; maintains a principal residence for entire year for self and an 8-year-old grandchild who is not a dependent . . . . __________________

   d. Married; has $15,000 of gross income; spouse has filed a separate return . . __________________

   e. Married; maintains a household for more than half the year for self and an adopted 4-year-old child who is a dependent; spouse left home on February 15 of current year and has not been seen since . . . . __________________

   f. Married; spouse has been properly claimed as a dependent on another taxpayer's return . . . . __________________

   g. Unmarried; divorced last year; no dependents . . . . __________________

   h. Married on December 31, 1992; no dependents . . . . __________________

   i. Widower; spouse died on December 3, 1991; has a dependent 6-year-old child who lived with the taxpayer for 1992; has not remarried . . . . . . __________________

3. Henry and Margaret were married on December 28, 1992. Henry had no gross income during the year and was supported by his parents prior to his marriage. Such support represented 50% of his total support cost for the entire year. The other 50% of his support came from tax-free interest he earned on his State of Florida general obligations bonds. Margaret was paid a gross salary of $35,000 in 1992.
   a. Under what circumstances is Margaret entitled to claim an exemption for Henry?

   b. Under what circumstances are Henry's parents entitled to claim an exemption for him?

4. How many exemptions can be claimed on an income tax return by an employed taxpayer who is married and has two children? One child is 17 and has no income, and the other is a 23-year-old, full-time college student, who earned $2,500 during the year. Both children are dependents of the taxpayer. The taxpayer has one employer and the spouse is not employed.

5. Orlin Ayers, age 67 and blind, is married to Susan Ayers, age 56 with good vision. They have a daughter, age 37, who is living with them along with her 18-year-old son. Mr. and Mrs. Orlin Ayers have provided more than one-half of the support of the daughter and her son. The daughter has earned wages of $1,600 during 1992, and her son, who is a full-time college student, has earned wages of $3,200. How many exemptions can Mr. and Mrs. Orlin Ayers claim on their 1992 tax return? Explain.

6. Indicate by inserting an "X" in the proper column which of the following persons may qualify as dependents for the purpose of claiming a dependency exemption. Assume the listed person is not a member of the taxpayer's household.

Dependents	Yes	No
a. Taxpayer's cousin	______	______
b. Taxpayer's father	______	______
c. Taxpayer's foster mother	______	______
d. Taxpayer's dependent friend	______	______
e. Taxpayer's spouse's brother	______	______
f. Taxpayer's foster grandparent	______	______
g. Taxpayer's half brother	______	______
h. Taxpayer's nephew by blood	______	______
i. Taxpayer's spouse	______	______
j. Taxpayer's uncle (on deceased spouse's side)	______	______
k. Taxpayer's daughter's husband	______	______
l. Taxpayer's grandfather	______	______
m. Taxpayer's mother-in-law (taxpayer's spouse deceased)	______	______

7. The date a tax year closes is an important date from a taxpayer's view since it stops a Revenue Agent from assessing a tax deficiency on a closed tax year. It is an important date from the government's view, since it stops a taxpayer from making a refund claim on a closed tax year.

 a. If a taxpayer files his or her tax return for 1992 on April 1, 1993, when does this taxpayer's 1992 tax year close under the normal closing rule? In your answer, provide a specific closing date and time.

 b. If a taxpayer inadvertently omits too much gross income from his or her income tax return, the normal closing of a tax year is extended by three years. What percentage of the taxpayer's gross income has to be omitted from his or her income tax return to have the closing year extended? As part of your answer, indicate exactly how this percentage is applied.

c. Joe Blystone, age 23 and single, had gross income of $5,000 from a part-time job in 1992. He had no other income sources. While he used some of his earned income for support items, the majority of his support came from his parents. Joe is not required to file a return for 1992. Should Joe file a return and why?

8. Vera and Billy Cohen were divorced during 1992. Vera was awarded custody of the children, George, age 6, and Jean, age 9. There was no agreement about who would receive the dependency exemptions for the children. All support for the children is provided by Billy.
   a. Who is to receive the dependency exemptions?

   b. Might the other parent receive the exemptions under certain conditions? Explain.

9. a. If Shirley Brown has a child born at 10 p.m. on December 31 of the taxable year, can she claim an exemption for this child for the year without proration?

   b. If a qualifying dependent of a taxpayer dies on January 4 of the taxable year, may the taxpayer claim an exemption for the dependent for the year without proration?

   c. If Mark Freeze's divorce decree is finalized before the end of the taxable year, can he claim an exemption for his spouse for the part of the year in which he was married? Explain.

10. During the current tax year, Graciela Autry, an unmarried taxpayer, received the following cash items: wages of $18,090, dividends of $490, interest of $240 from a bank savings account, and interest of $200 from general obligation municipal bonds. All of the bank interest was credited to her account in 1992. Graciela also received 50 shares of common stock from Top Brand Industries for a stock split. The number of shares received was related to the 100 shares of stock in Top Brand she owned before the split. The market value of each share of stock after the split was $25.
    a. What is the amount of her AGI?

   b. If Graciela maintains a home for her widowed mother for eight months of the year and claims her as a dependency exemption, can she file a return as a HOH if her mother lives alone? Explain the reason behind your answer.

11. **a.** What is the amount of each personal exemption in 1992?

     b. How does income affect the amount allowed for each exemption?

12. **a.** Clarence Archer is eligible to claim itemized deductions. Explain how itemized deductions relate to the determination of taxable income in 1992.

     b. The additional standard deduction and special standard deduction rules apply to what groups of taxpayers?

13. **a.** The statutes which govern our current income tax system are found in the 1986 Internal Revenue Code. What is the starting date of our current income tax system? What specific piece of legislation made the income tax a viable part of today's legal tax system?

     b. Name several objectives of our income tax system.

   c. Most individual taxpayers use the calendar year for reporting their taxable income. However, a few use the fiscal year. What is a fiscal year?

   d. Is the basic tax calculation formula for most taxpayers the same? What is the difference between the basic formula and the expanded calculation formula for individuals?

   e. The definition of gross income in the Internal Revenue Code lists 15 different sources. When a taxpayer receives something that is not one of the listed items, is it exempt from tax? Explain your answer.

   f. When a taxpayer doesn't want to include an item in gross income, what are the possible authoritative sources that permit an exclusion?

14. Itemized deductions fall into one of eight groups. Two of the groupings are (1) job expenses and most other miscellaneous itemized deductions, and (2) other itemized deductions. What are the other six groups?

15. a. In the tax laws, a capital asset is defined in terms of what it is not. What broad groups of items appear on the "not" list (are not capital assets)?

b. For investment assets, what is the definition of a net capital gain?

c. Explain the general holding period rules for capital assets, and indicate the period of time an asset has to be held under these rules to be long-term.

16. a. Jerry Long sold several stock certificates held for investment during the year. From the following sales, calculate Jerry's net long-term gain or loss, net short-term gain or loss, gross income, and net capital gain.

Purchase Date	Sale Date	Cost	Selling Price
1-5-91	1-5-92	$10,000	$13,000
4-4-91	5-7-92	8,000	7,500
8-9-91	9-8-92	6,000	10,500
2-3-92	8-1-92	4,200	1,100

b. If the selling price of the stock Jerry sold on 8-1-92 was $4,600 (instead of $1,100), what would be his net long-term gain or loss, net short-term gain or loss, gross income, and net capital gain?

17. a. Define the concept of tax planning and distinguish between short-term and long-term tax planning.

b. What is the primary reason for doing tax planning?

c. Identify three tax-planning principles that will help a taxpayer achieve a tax-planning objective.

d. Under what circumstances should a taxpayer plan to control the timing of payments that are deductible as itemized deductions?

e. Identify several treatments of income and expenses that are subject to the taxpayer's control in the process of tax planning to minimize income taxes.

18. Susan Klammer uses a local tax professional to prepare her tax return each year. She sees no reason for her to learn more about the tax laws. At tax return time every year, all she wants to know is "what is the fastest route to my tax preparer's office." After she files her return each year, she just wants to forget the whole thing. Indicate why it would be to Susan's advantage to know about the tax law.

Tax Determination

Chapter 1 discussed the tax structure and process for determining taxable income. This chapter expands the discussion and shows how individuals compute their tax liability. It reviews estimated tax payments, tax withholdings, and illustrates Form W-2 (form for reporting annual earnings and withholdings to employees). The chapter also discusses the tax computation process, simplified income tax Form 1040EZ, and "kiddie tax." After this discussion, it examines overpayments and tax credits. Taxpayers use overpayments and credits to determine the final amount due to or from the government. Finally, it looks at Form 1040A and illustrates its use for reporting one of the personal tax credits.

Individual Income Tax Rates

The Internal Revenue Code specifies the tax rates persons must use to figure their tax. The IRS presents them in the form of *Tax Rate Schedules* or *Tax Tables*. Understanding their structure helps in understanding the tax calculation process.

Tax Rate Schedules

The four Tax Rate Schedules that apply in 1992 are on page xiii. Note that each uses the same three rates (15%, 28%, and 31%). Taxpayers using Form 1040EZ or Form 1040A, who have less than $50,000 of taxable income, cannot use the rate schedules. Also, taxpayers using Form 1040 with less than $100,000 of taxable income cannot use the rate schedules. These taxpayers *must* determine their tax from the Tax Table.

Tax Table Cannot Be Used By

1. A person whose return is for a short period (less than 12 months) because of a change in accounting period.
2. A person claiming the foreign earned income exclusion.
3. A person filing Form 1040 with taxable income of $100,000 or more.
4. An estate or trust.

EXAMPLE 1 ——————————

Four taxpayers each have $100,000 of taxable income. Two of them are married. The filing status of these taxpayers and their tax for 1992 appear below:

Filing Status	Tax
Married, filing jointly	$23,751.00
Head of Household	25,038.00
Single	26,654.50
Married, filing separately	27,375.50

Tax calculations for the married filing jointly taxpayer are:

	Computations	Tax
Taxable income (TI)	$100,000	
Less:	86,500*	$19,566
TI taxed at 31% rate	$ 13,500	
Multiply by rate	x 31%	4,185
Tax on TI of $100,000		$23,751

* Note that the tax on the first $35,800 of TI is at 15% ($35,800 x 15% = $5,370). Also note that the tax on the next $50,700 of TI is at 28% ($50,700 x 28% = $14,196). Thus, the tax on the first $86,500 of TI ($35,800 + $50,700) is $19,566 ($5,370 + $14,196).

Tax Tables

The 1992 Tax Table for Form 1040 filers is on pages x. Like the rate schedules, it is subdivided by filing status. Taxpayers who use it need to know their taxable income and filing status. The Tax Tables for Form 1040EZ and Form 1040A filers are not part of this book. However, except for the upper income limit on taxable income (less than $50,000) and tax form line numbers, their construction and use are the same as the Form 1040 table. Thus, use of the Form 1040 table by a Form 1040EZ or Form 1040A filer will produce the same tax result.

The calculation base for Tax Table amounts is the midpoint of each income bracket. Each amount is calculated from the rate schedules, with nearest dollar rounding. For a single per-

---

Taxpayer Ranking by Filing Status for Given Amount of Taxable Income

Lowest to Highest Tax:

1. Married filing jointly
2. Head of household
3. Single
4. Married filing separately

son with $20,000 of taxable income, the table amount is $3,004. In the portion of the Tax Table reproduced below, a user determines the tax by first finding the line where taxable income of $20,000 falls. Then, the user finds the right column for his or her filing status. At the intersection of the line and column is the proper tax. Confirming calculations using the single taxpayer rate schedule appear below:

Midpoint of income bracket($20,000-$20,050)	$20,025.00
Tax Rate Schedule X:	
Tax of $20,025 @ 15%	$ 3,003.75
Tax Table amount rounded to nearest dollar	$ 3,004.00

If line 37 (taxable income) is—		And you are—			
At least	But less than	Single	Married filing jointly *	Married filing separately	Head of a household
			Your tax is—		
20,000					
20,000	20,050	3,004	3,004	3,280	3,004

Indexing

Congress legislated inflation adjustments for the standard deduction, additional standard deduction, and personal exemptions. It also legislated inflation adjustments for the rate schedules, rate tables, and starting points for phasing down personal exemptions and certain itemized deductions. Annually, the IRS adjusts these items using change numbers for the Consumer Price Index. The indexing base for each year ends on August 31 of the prior year.

Estimated Tax Payments and Withholding

Many taxpayers make estimated income tax payments or pay their taxes through the tax withholding system. Persons making estimated payments are self-employed. Persons making payments through the withholding system are employees. Chapter 14 discusses estimated tax payments and portions of the payroll tax withholding system. Below is an overview of these items.

Estimated Tax Payments

Under our pay-as-you-go tax system, self-employed persons and wage earners pay income and social security taxes throughout the year. Since a tax withholding system does not exist for self-employed persons, they estimate their taxes for the year. Then, they make quarterly payments to the IRS against these estimates. At filing time, self-employed persons show the estimated payments as credits against the tax on their returns.

Federal Income Taxes Withheld

Wages of most employees are subject to income, social security, and Medicare tax withholding. However, a few wage classes are exempt from income tax withholding, and some are exempt from all tax withholding. When a wage class is exempt from income tax withholding, voluntary withholding is possible by employer/employee agreement.

To help employers determine correct tax withholdings, the IRS publishes tax withholding tables. Employers deposit withheld taxes with a Federal Reserve bank or designated financial depository. Deposit frequency is usually a function of the amount withheld during a base pay period. Employers file withholding and deposit reports with the government throughout the year, and after the year ends.

Before February 1 of each year, employers must inform employees of their earnings for the past year and taxes withheld. Employers use Form W-2, Wage and Tax Statement, to give this information to their employees. At tax filing time, employees show their income tax withholdings as credits against the tax on their returns.

Filled-In Form W-2, Copy A

Illustration 2-1

This illustration shows filled-in Copy A of Form W-2, Wage and Tax Statement, for

Amelia Z. Sanchez. Ms. Sanchez is an unmarried 20-year-old department store employee with social security number 295-24-1408. She lives alone at 104 Bayside Drive, Green Bay, WI 54307 and works for Goodby's Department Store, 2722 Grandview Blvd., Green Bay, WI 54305. Goodby's identification number is 88-6045185.

On Form W-2, Goodby's payroll clerk, Bob Peters, enters Goodby's name and address (box 2) and identification number (box 3). He also enters Amelia's social security number (box 5), name (box 19a), and address (box 19b). Bob enters Amelia's 1992 wages of $12,920 on the form (boxes 10, 12, 14, and 25). He also enters withheld federal income taxes of $1,375 (box 9), Social Security taxes of $801.04 (box 11),

Medicare taxes of $187.34 (box 15), and Wisconsin income taxes of $332 (box 24). To identify Wisconsin, Peters enters "WI" (box 26).

Before February 1, 1993, Peters must send Copies 2, B, and C of Form W-2 to Ms. Sanchez. She should file Copy 2 with her 1992 Wisconsin income tax return, and Copy B with her 1992 Form 1040EZ. She stores Copy C with copies of her tax returns. Before March 1, 1993, Peters must file Copy A with the Social Security Administration and Copy 1 with the Wisconsin Department of Revenue. Peters files Copy D with Goodby's payroll records.

Illustration 2-2 provides more data about Ms. Sanchez and shows her Form 1040EZ.

Illustration 2-1
Filled-In Form W-2, Copy A

a Control number	22222	Void ☐	For Official Use Only ▶		
b Employer's identification number 88-6045185				1 Wages, tips, other compensation 12,920.00	2 Federal income tax withheld 1,375.00
c Employer's name, address, and ZIP code Goodby's Department Store 2722 Grandview Blvd. Green Bay, WI 54305				3 Social security wages 12,920.00	4 Social security tax withheld 801.04
				5 Medicare wages and tips 12,920.00	6 Medicare tax withheld 187.34
				7 Social security tips	8 Allocated tips
d Employee's social security number 295-24-1408				9 Advance EIC payment	10 Dependent care benefits
e Employee's name (first, middle initial, last) Amelia Z. Sanchez 104 Bayside Drive Green Bay, WI 54307				11 Nonqualified plans	12 Benefits included in Box 1
				13 See Instrs. for Box 13	14 Other
f Employee's address and ZIP code				15 Statutory employee ☐ Deceased ☐ Pension plan ☐ Legal rep. ☐ 942 emp. ☐ Subtotal ☐ Deferred compensation ☐	

16 State WI	Employer's state I.D. No.	17 State wages, tips, etc. 12,920.00	18 State income tax 332.00	19 Locality name	20 Local wages, tips, etc.	21 Local income tax

Cat. No. 10134D   Department of the Treasury—Internal Revenue Service

Form **W-2** Wage and Tax Statement **1993**

Copy A For Social Security Administration

For Paperwork Reduction Act Notice, see separate instructions.

OMB No. 1545-0008

Form 1040EZ

Form 1040EZ, Income Tax Return for Single Filers with No Dependents, is a return that reduces filing complexities. Only single taxpayers with no dependents can use it. For 1988, the latest years for which filing statistics are complete, about 19.2 million taxpayers (18%) used Form 1040EZ. This form has six sections that are easy to complete. The following discussion focuses on these sections.

Form 1040EZ Tests—Users Must

1. Be single, under age 65, and not blind.
2. Claim the standard deduction.
3. Make no claim for a dependency exemption.
4. Have gross income only from wages, salaries, tips, taxable scholarship or fellowship grants, and interest.
5. Have taxable income of less than $50,000.
6. Have total wages of $55,500 or less if employed by more than one employer.
7. Have taxable interest income of $400 or less.
8. Have no dividend income.
9. Not earn $20 or more in monthly tips which are omitted from Form W-2.

Taxpayer Identification

For a fair administration of the tax laws, clear identification of each taxpayer is necessary. Form 1040EZ filers insert their name, address, and social security number in the identification spaces at the top of the form. However, for taxpayers who filed Form 1040EZ last year the IRS sends them a Form 1040EZ instruction booklet with blank forms. The booklet has a preaddressed, peel-off, taxpayer identification label. Taxpayers should examine the label carefully, correct errors in ink, and paste it over the identification spaces on their completed Form 1040EZ. When the data on the identification label is not clear, taxpayers should insert their own in the proper spaces at the top of their return.

Presidential Election Campaign Fund

Taxpayers can instruct the IRS to give $1 of their tax payments to the presidential election campaign fund. It is an optional instruction that does not affect the amount of tax. Taxpayers give the instruction by placing an "X" in the proper YES or NO box (above line 1).

Reporting Taxable Income

Taxpayers using Form 1040EZ report their total income from wages, salaries, taxable scholarships or fellowships, and tips in the proper boxes at the right of the form (line 1). They also report their total taxable interest income in the proper boxes (line 2). This interest cannot be more than $400. Taxpayers who have tax-exempt interest income enter the letters "TEI" in the blank space immediately after the words "Form 1040EZ" (line 2). After the letters "TEI" they enter their tax-exempt interest income. They do *not* enter this interest in the boxes at the right of the form. Next, Form 1040EZ filers add the amounts in the two sets of boxes (lines 1 and 2) and enter the total on the form (line 3). This amount is their AGI.

Taxpayers place an "X" in the second set of YES or NO boxes (line 4) to show if another taxpayer is eligible to claim them as an exemption. Taxpayers who place an "X" in the YES box complete the worksheet on the back of the form. The worksheet helps them calculate their standard deduction. It is the greater of $600 or their earned income. However, it cannot exceed the basic standard deduction of $3,600 for a single person. They enter the amount from the last line of this worksheet in the proper end of the line boxes (line 4). Taxpayers placing an "X" in the YES box cannot claim their own exemption. Taxpayers placing an "X" in the NO box enter $5,900 in the proper end of the line boxes (line 4). This amount is their standard deduction ($3,600) and personal exemption ($2,300). All Form 1040EZ filers subtract the determined amount (line 4) from their AGI (line 3) and enter the difference (line 5). It is their taxable income.

Figuring the Income Tax

After figuring the amount of taxable income, taxpayers enter the taxes withheld by their employers (line 6 boxes) from Copy B of Forms W-2 (box 9). If they receive a Form 1099-INT from a payer of interest showing withheld income taxes, they add them to those on Forms W-2 (box 9). Then, they enter the total on Form 1040EZ (line 6 boxes). To the left of this line, they print the words *Form 1099*. After these entries, they use their taxable income (line 5) to determine their tax liability from the Tax Table (page x). They enter this liability on Form 1040EZ (line 7).

Don't Make a Payment to "IRS"

Due to some taxpayers' remittances (checks or money orders) being altered and stolen, make all payments to the "Internal Revenue Service." Never leave the payee line blank or use the initials IRS. Also, include the following taxpayer data and form identification on each remittance:

1. Name
2. Address
3. Social Security number
4. Daytime phone number
5. Year and form name (1992 Form 1040EZ, 1992 Form 1040A, or 1992 Form 1040)

SOURCES: IR-92-78 and Forms 1040EZ, 1040A, and 1040

Refund or Amount Owed

Once Form 1040EZ filers enter their tax withheld and tax liability (lines 6 and 7), they're ready to calculate the amount due to or from the government. If the total income tax withheld (line 6) is larger than their tax liability (line 7), they enter the difference due from the government (line 8). If the income tax withheld (line 6) is smaller than their tax liability (line 7), they enter the difference due to the government (line 9). To their Form 1040EZ, taxpayers attach a check for the amount due the government (line 9). They also attach Copy B, Form W-2. Attachment instructions are at the left of Form 1040EZ (next to lines 2 and 3).

Signature and Certification

Taxpayers *must* sign Form 1040EZ under the printed certification statement and enter their occupation and current date. They should sign and file their return before Friday, April 16, 1993. The tax return due date for calendar year filers is April 15, 1993.

Privacy Act and Paperwork Reduction Act Notice

Each 1992 income tax return contains a reference to the Privacy Act and Paper Reduction Act Notice in the instruction booklet. Form 1040EZ filers can find more information on this topic there.

Filled-In Form 1040EZ

Illustration 2-2

Earlier, Illustration 2-1 presented a filled-in Form W-2, Wage and Tax Statement, for Amelia Z. Sanchez. Illustration 2-2 shows how Amelia reports the W-2 data on her tax return. In addition to her sales clerk's wages, she received a credit of $395 in her bank savings account in December. The credit was for interest earned during the year and was her only other income. Amelia is not eligible to claim another person as a dependency exemption. Since her taxable income is less than $50,000, and her interest income is $400 or less, she decides to file Form 1040EZ.

After entering her taxpayer identification data at the top of the form, Amelia instructs the IRS to send $1 of her taxes to the Presidential Election Campaign Fund. She does this by placing an "X" in the YES box immediately after her name and address data. She enters her department store earnings of $12,920 (line 1) and her interest of $395 (line 2). Then, she adds the amounts on these lines and enters the total $13,315 (line 3). This is Amelia's AGI. Near the start of the line with the second set of YES or NO boxes (line 4), Amelia places an "X" in the NO box. It tells the IRS that no one else may claim an exemption for her. At the end of this line she enters $5,900. It is her personal exemption ($2,300) and standard deduction ($3,600).

Amelia determines her taxable income by subtracting the $5,900 (line 4) from her AGI of $13,315 (line 3). She enters the difference of $7,415 (line 5).

From her Form W-2 (box 9), Amelia enters her withheld federal income taxes of $1,375 (line 6). She uses the Tax Table to determine her tax. In working with the Tax Table, Amelia finds that her taxable income of $7,415 (line 5) falls in the $7,400 to $7,450 tax bracket. Using the Tax Table column for single filers, Amelia finds her tax is $1,114. She enters it on her return (line 7). When Amelia compares her withheld income taxes of $1,375 (line 6) with her tax of $1,114 (line 7), she finds that the withheld taxes are more than her tax. She enters the difference of $261 on her return (line 8). This is the refund the government owes her. At the bottom of the page, near the "X" line, she signs the return, lists her occupation, and enters April 5, 1993.

After attaching Copy B of Form W-2 to her return, Ms. Sanchez places it in the filing envelope and takes it to a U.S. Post Office. At the post office, she completes a certified or registered mail sticker and return receipt post card. She gives the envelope, sticker, and card to the postal clerk who enters the proper information. The clerk attaches the sticker, return receipt card, and postage to the envelope. Then, the clerk removes the stub from the bottom portion of the sticker, stamps the date on it, and gives it to Ms. Sanchez after collecting the postal fees. Ms. Sanchez stores the sticker stub with copies of her 1992 Federal and State income tax returns. This is her mailing receipt.

parents' highest rate when this rate exceeds the child's.

Note the distinction between types of income. The higher tax rates apply to net unearned investment income. It is usually the residual income that is more than $1,200 from such items as interest, dividends, capital gains, rents, royalties, annuities, and beneficiary trusts. Earned income of a child under 14 is not taxed at the parent's higher rates. Earned income includes a child's wages, tips, and other payments for personal services. Thus, a child's paper route and baby sitting income are taxed at the child's rates.

Filing Form 8615

If a child under age 14 has investment income of more than $1,200, he or she may (with parental help) have to file Form 8615. If the investment income is $1,200 or less, the child will not have to file Form 8615. However, the child may still have to file a tax return. Children can file Form 8615 with Form 1040A, Form 1040, or Form 1040NR, U.S. Nonresident Alien Income Tax Return. Certain tax situations require additional or alternate forms that are beyond the scope of this book.

When a child under age 14 has more than $1,200 of unearned investment income, and the child's parents file Form 1040A, the child usually must file Form 8615. If neither parent is alive on December 31, 1992, the child does not file Form 8615. Here, the child calculates the tax using his or her own rate. If the child's parents are married and filing separately, the child uses the rate of the parent with the highest taxable income. A different rate applies if the parents are not married, treated as single, or separated by a decree of divorce or a maintenance agreement. Here, the child uses the **custodial parent's** rate (parent with longest custody).

Form 8615, The Kiddie Tax Form

Before enactment of the provisions behind Form 8615, parents could avoid taxes by transferring investment property to their children. Here, the children paid the taxes on the investment income. Since most children were in a lower tax bracket, there was considerable tax savings. Now, the Code taxes the net unearned investment income of a child under 14 at the

Investment Income Worksheet

The instructions to Form 8615 contain a worksheet for computing a child's investment income. Children filing Form 1040A enter the total income from their return (line 14) on the first line of the worksheet. Children filing Form 1040 or Form 1040NR also enter this amount from their return (line 23). Illustration 2-3 contains an example of the worksheet. The work-

Illustration 2-2
Filled-In Form 1040EZ

Department of the Treasury—Internal Revenue Service

Form 1040EZ

Income Tax Return for Single Filers With No Dependents

1992

OMB No. 1545-0675

Name & address

Use the IRS label (see page 10). If you don't have one, please print.

LABEL HERE

Print your name (first, initial, last)
Amelia Z. Sanchez

Home address (number and street). If you have a P.O. box, see page 10.   Apt. no.
104 Bayside Drive

City, town or post office, state, and ZIP code. If you have a foreign address, see page 10.
Green Bay, WI 54307

Please print your numbers like this:

9 8 7 6 5 4 3 2 1 0

Your social security number

295 24 1408

Please see instructions on the back. Also, see the Form 1040EZ booklet.

Presidential Election Campaign (See page 10.)
Do you want $1 to go to this fund?

Note: Checking "Yes" will not change your tax or reduce your refund. ▶

Yes No
[X]

Dollars   Cents

Report your income

Attach Copy B of Form(s) W-2 here. Attach tax payment on top of Form(s) W-2.

Note: *You must check Yes or No.*

1   Total wages, salaries, and tips. This should be shown in box 10 of your W-2 form(s). Attach your W-2 form(s).   1

12,920.00

2   Taxable interest income of $400 or less. If the total is more than $400, you cannot use Form 1040EZ.   2

395.00

3   Add lines 1 and 2. This is your **adjusted gross income.**   3

13,315.00

4   Can your parents (or someone else) claim you on their return?
   [ ] Yes. Do worksheet on back; enter amount from line E here.
   [X] No. Enter 5,900.00. This is the total of your standard deduction and personal exemption.   4

5,900.00

5   Subtract line 4 from line 3. If line 4 is larger than line 3, enter 0. This is your **taxable income.**   5

7,415.00

Figure your tax

6   Enter your Federal income tax withheld from box 9 of your W-2 form(s).   6

1,375.00

7   Tax. Look at line 5 above. Use the amount on line 5 to find your tax in the tax table on pages 22-24 of the booklet. Then, enter the tax from the table on this line.   7

1,114.00

Refund or amount you owe

8   If line 6 is larger than line 7, subtract line 7 from line 6. This is your **refund.**   8

261.00

9   If line 7 is larger than line 6, subtract line 6 from line 7. This is the amount you owe. Attach your payment for full amount payable to the "Internal Revenue Service." Write your name, address, social security number, daytime phone number, and "1992 Form 1040EZ" on it.   9

Sign your return

Keep a copy of this form for your records.

I have read this return. Under penalties of perjury, I declare that to the best of my knowledge and belief, the return is true, correct, and complete.

Your signature
X *Amelia Z. Sanchez*

Date
4-5-93

Your occupation
Sales Clerk

For IRS Use Only — Please do not write in boxes below.

For Privacy Act and Paperwork Reduction Act Notice, see page 4 in the booklet. Cat. No. 11329W Form 1040EZ (1992)

sheet asks taxpayers (line 2) to enter their earned income plus any financial institution penalty for early savings withdrawals. It refers them to Form 1040 (line 28) and Form 1040NR (line 27) for the penalty. Note, the worksheet does not contain a reference to the penalty line on Form 1040A. This form does not have such a line. Taxpayers who want to reduce their investment income by an early withdrawal penalty should not use Form 1040A.

Illustration 2-3

Harold A. Lunde will be 14 on October 20, 1993. His social security number is 612-81-9206. Illustration 2-3 shows Harold's Form 8615 worksheet. His 1992 income consists of the following items:

Interest income, City of X tax-exempt bond	$ 500
Interest income, ABC Corporation bond	2,500
U.S. Series HH savings bond interest	2,000
Earnings from paper route, Daily Journal	1,100
Dividends, DDD Manufacturing Corporation	600
Total cash received	$6,700

On the first line of the worksheet, Harold enters $6,200 ($2,500 + $2,000 + $1,100 + $600). Interest on the tax-exempt bond is not part of Harold's gross income. He enters his earned income of $1,100 (line 2), and the $5,100 ($6,200 less $1,100) difference (line 3). He places the $5,100 difference on the first line of Step 1 of Form 8615.

Filled-In Form 8615

Illustration 2-4

The entries on Form 8615 follow the facts in Illustration 2-3 and the data below. On his own return, Harold Lunde does not claim an exemption for himself since his parents claim him as a dependent. George H. and Shirley O. Lunde, Harold's parents, file a joint tax return on Form 1040A. On this return, they show taxable income of $45,202 and a tax of $8,009. George's social

Illustration 2-3
Investment Income Worksheet

Worksheet (keep for your records)

1. Enter the amount from the child's Form 1040, line 23; Form 1040A, line 14; or Form 1040NR, line 23, whichever applies . . . **6,200**

2. Enter the child's **earned income** (defined below) plus any deduction the child claims on Form 1040, line 28, or Form 1040NR, line 27, whichever applies **1,100**

3. Subtract line 2 from line 1. Enter the result here and on Form 8615, line 1 . . **5,100**

security number is 360-29-4126 and Shirley's is 831-32-6101.

When completing Form 8615, taxpayers place the identification numbers of one parent and the child at the top of the form. On the first unnumbered line of Form 8615, they enter the child's name and social security number as shown on his or her Form 1040A or Form 1040. On the next two unnumbered lines, they enter the name, filing status, and social security number of the parent entered first on the parents' return. Since George's name appears first on the parents' return, Harold (with parental help) enters George's name and ID number. On the fourth unnumbered line, Harold enters the number 3 in the box. This shows that his parents took three exemptions on their joint return.

Step 1 of Form 8615 is to calculate the child's net unearned investment income. Harold starts the calculation process by entering $5,100 on Form 8615 (line 1) from his investment income worksheet (line 3). Children with no earned income can enter their AGI directly on Form 8615 (line 1). Since Harold did not itemize deductions, he enters $1,200 on Form 8615 (line 2). This is his $600 minimum standard deduction and another $600. Harold enters the difference of $3,900 ($5,100 less $1,200) on Form 8615 (line 3). This is his net unearned investment income. Then, Harold enters his taxable income of $5,100 (line 4). He determines his taxable income as follows:

Wages	$1,100
Taxable interest	4,500
Dividends	600
AGI	$6,200
Less: allowable standard deduction	1,100*
Taxable income	$5,100

* Since Harold's parents can claim him as a dependent on their return, his standard deduction is the greater of his earned income ($1,100) or $600.

Harold enters the smaller of $3,900 (line 3) or $5,100 (line 4) on the form (line 5).

Step 2 in figuring the tentative tax at the parents' rate involves using the Tax Table and following the Form 8615 instructions. Harold (with parental help) enters his parents' taxable income of $45,202 on Form 8615 (line 6). Since he has no brothers or sisters, he leaves the next line blank.

To figure his tentative tax, Harold adds his net unearned investment income of $3,900 (line 5) to his parents' taxable income of $45,202 (line 6). He enters the total of $49,102 ($3,900 + $45,202) on the form (line 8). Then, he determines that the tax on the $49,102 from the Tax Table is $9,101 and enters it (line 9). From his parents' tax return, he enters their tax of $8,009 on Form 8615 (line 10). Now, the difference between the taxes is calculated, $1,092 ($9,101 − $8,009), and entered (line 11). Since Harold has no brothers or sisters, he skips the tax allocation lines (12a and 12b) and enters the $1,092 again (line 13).

In Step 3, Harold calculates his actual tax liability. First, the difference between $5,100 (line 4) and $3,900 (line 5) is entered, $1,200 (line 14). Then, he determines that the tax on the $1,200 from the Tax Table is $182 and enters it (line 15). Now, Harold adds the $182 (line 15) to his tentative tax of $1,092 (line 13) and enters the total, $1,274 (line 16). Next, Harold determines that the tax on $5,100 (line 4) at his rate from the Tax Table is $769 and enters it

(line 17). Finally, Harold compares the $1,274 (line 16) with the $769 (line 17) and enters the larger amount on Form 8615 (line 18). He also enters the $1,274 on Form 1040A (line 23).

Income of Minor Child

Parents who file Form 1040 or Form 1040NR may avoid filing Form 8615 for a minor child. They do this by choosing to include the child's unearned income of more than $1,000 on their return. With such an election, the child will not have to file a return. Note, by making this election, an additional $200 of the child's unearned income may be taxed at the parents' higher rate. Why? First, the $1,200 on Form 8615 (line 2) is based on $1,000 which is indexed for inflation. Second, on Form 8814, Parent's Election to Report Child's Interest and Dividends, the $1,000 (line 4) is not indexed for inflation.

Form 8814 can be used when the child's income is (1) only from interest and dividends, (2) between $500 and $5,000, and (3) not subject to income tax withholding. Also, the child must not pay any estimated taxes in his or her name or TIN. Chapter 3 contains additional Form 8814 discussion. Parents who file Form 1040A may not choose to report a child's unearned income on their return. Thus, these filers cannot use Form 8814.

Tax Payments

The income tax reporting system lets taxpayers reduce their tax liability by advance and excess payments. Taxpayers group these items together and deduct them from their tax liability to determine the net amount due to or from the government. Excess withholding of income taxes, FICA taxes, Tier I railroad retirement taxes, and hospital insurance taxes on some U.S. government employees can result in refunds. Since the rates and bases for FICA and Tier I railroad retirement taxes are the same, the remainder of this discussion focuses on FICA taxes.

FICA taxes consist of two elements: (1) social security or OASDI taxes (old age, survivors, and

Illustration 2-4
Filled-In Form 8615

Form **8615**

Department of the Treasury
Internal Revenue Service

**Tax for Children Under Age 14
Who Have Investment Income of More Than $1,200**
▶ See instructions below and on back.
▶ Attach ONLY to the child's Form 1040, Form 1040A, or Form 1040NR.

OMB No. 1545-0998

1992

Attachment
Sequence No. **33**

General Instructions

Purpose of Form. For children under age 14, investment income (such as taxable interest and dividends) over $1,200 is taxed at the parent's rate if the parent's rate is higher than the child's rate. If the child's investment income is more than $1,200, use this form to figure the child's tax.

Investment Income. As used on this form, "investment income" includes all taxable income other than earned income as defined on page 2. It includes income such as taxable interest, dividends, capital gains, rents, royalties, etc. It also includes pension and annuity income and income (other than earned income) received as the beneficiary of a trust.

Who Must File. Generally, Form 8615 must be filed for any child who was under age 14 on January 1, 1993, and who had more than $1,200 of investment income. If neither parent was alive on December 31, 1992, do not use Form 8615. Instead, figure the child's tax in the normal manner.

Note: *The parent may be able to elect to report the child's interest and dividends on his or her return. If the parent makes this election, the child will not have to file a return or Form 8615. For more details, see the instructions for Form 1040 or Form 1040A, or get Form 8814,* Parents' Election To Report Child's Interest and Dividends.

Additional Information. For more details, get **Pub. 929,** Tax Rules for Children and Dependents.

Incomplete Information for Parent. If a child's parent or guardian cannot obtain the information needed to complete Form 8615 before the due date of the child's return, reasonable estimates of the parent's taxable income or filing status and the net investment income of the parent's other children may be made. The appropriate line(s) of Form 8615 must be marked "Estimated." For more details, see Pub. 929.

(Instructions continue on back.)

Child's name shown on return	Child's social security number	
Harold A. Lunde	612 : 81 : 9206	

A Parent's name (first, initial, and last). **Caution:** *See instructions on back before completing.*

George H. Lunde

B Parent's social security number
360 : 29 : 4126

C Parent's filing status (check one):
☐ Single   ☒ Married filing jointly   ☐ Married filing separately   ☐ Head of household   ☐ Qualifying widow(er)

Step 1   Figure child's net investment income

1	Enter child's investment income, such as taxable interest and dividend income. See instructions. If this amount is $1,200 or less, **stop here;** do not file this form	1	5,100 00
2	If the child DID NOT itemize deductions on Schedule A (Form 1040 or Form 1040NR), enter $1,200. If the child ITEMIZED deductions, see instructions	2	1,200 00
3	Subtract line 2 from line 1. If the result is zero or less, **stop here;** do not complete the rest of this form but ATTACH it to the child's return	3	3,900 00
4	Enter child's **taxable** income from Form 1040, line 37; Form 1040A, line 22; or Form 1040NR, line 35	4	5,100 00
5	Enter the **smaller** of line 3 or line 4 here ▶	5	3,900 00

Step 2   Figure tentative tax based on the tax rate of the parent listed on line A

6	Enter parent's **taxable** income from Form 1040, line 37; Form 1040A, line 22; Form 1040EZ, line 5; or Form 1040NR, line 35. If the parent transferred property to a trust, see instructions	6	45,202 00
7	Enter the total, if any, of the net investment income from Forms 8615, line 5, of ALL OTHER children of the parent. **Do not** include the amount from line 5 above	7	
8	Add lines 5, 6, and 7	8	49,102 00
9	Tax on line 8 based on the **parent's** filing status. See instructions. If from Schedule D, enter amount from line 22 of that Schedule D here ▶ _______	9	9,101 00
10	Enter parent's tax from Form 1040, line 38; Form 1040A, line 23; Form 1040EZ, line 7; or Form 1040NR, line 36. If from Schedule D, enter amount from line 22 of that Schedule D here ▶ _______	10	8,009 00
11	Subtract line 10 from line 9. If line 7 is blank, enter on line 13 the amount from line 11; skip lines 12a and 12b	11	1,092 00
12a	Add lines 5 and 7 ... **12a**		
b	Divide line 5 by line 12a. Enter the result as a decimal (rounded to two places)	12b	× .
13	Multiply line 11 by line 12b ▶	13	1,092 00

Step 3   Figure child's tax

14	**Note:** *If lines 4 and 5 above are the same, go to line 16.* Subtract line 5 from line 4 ... **14** 1,200 00		
15	Tax on line 14 based on the **child's** filing status. See instructions. If from Schedule D, enter amount from line 22 of that Schedule D here ▶ _______	15	182 00
16	Add lines 13 and 15	16	1,274 00
17	Tax on line 4 based on the **child's** filing status. See instructions. If from Schedule D, check here ▶ ☐	17	769 00
18	Enter the **larger** of line 16 or line 17 here and on Form 1040, line 38; Form 1040A, line 23; or Form 1040NR, line 36. Be sure to check the box for "Form 8615" even if line 17 is more than line 16 ▶	18	1,274 00

For Paperwork Reduction Act Notice, see back of form.   Cat. No. 64113U   Form **8615** (1992)

disability insurance), and (2) Medicare or HIP taxes (hospital insurance program). For OASDI, the maximum tax per person for 1992 is $3,441.00 (6.20% x $55,500). For HIP, the maximum tax for 1992 is $1,887.90 (1.45% x $130,200).

Excess Social Security, Medicare, or Railroad Retirement Tax

Sometimes employees have too much FICA tax withheld from wages. Over-withholding can occur when a person works for two or more employers. Here, each employer withholds OASDI taxes on the first $55,500 of wages, and HIP taxes on the first $130,200 of wages. When a taxpayer's Forms W-2, Wage and Tax Statements, show excess FICA withholdings via multiple employers, the excess is recoverable through the tax reporting system.

Form 1040EZ and Form 1040A filers add the excess FICA withholdings to their withheld federal income taxes and report the total on their return (line 6 or 28a). Then, to the left of the reporting line they write "excess OASDI or HIP" and the proper amount. Form 1040 filers also show the excess FICA withholding on their return, but as a separate item (line 58). When one employer deducts too much FICA tax, the taxpayer should ask the employer for a refund. Recovery of the withheld excess through the tax reporting system is *not* possible.

On a joint return, a taxpayer and spouse separately determine their withheld OASDI and HIP taxes. Then, each subtracts the proper tax from his or her maximum to determine if any excess withholding exists.

EXAMPLE 2 ──────────────────────

Forms W-2 for Elaine and Morton Levy contain OASDI information. No part of the withheld OASDI tax for Mrs. Levy is recoverable since it is not more than $3,441. Mr. Levy claims a credit for excess OASDI taxes of $502.20 ($3,943.20 − 3,441.00).

Employer	Total Social Security Wages Paid in 1992	OASDI Tax Withheld
Elaine Levy:		
Melville Dye Co.	$14,000	$ 868.00
Morton Levy:		
Step Mfg. Co.	$40,000	$2,480.00
United Corp.	23,600	1,463.20
	$63,600	$3,943.20

Excess Hospital Insurance Program Tax

U.S. government employees with two jobs may have paid too much HIP tax. To get a refund, the employee's wages must exceed $130,200. Here, the employee completes the Excess Social Security and Medicare Tax Worksheet in the Form 1040 instructions. The amount on the last line of the worksheet is the amount the employee enters on his or her tax return (line 58). If one employer withheld more than $1,887.90 in HIP taxes, the employee should ask the employer for a refund. The excess is *not* recoverable through the income tax reporting system.

Credits Against the Tax

In addition to reducing the tax liability by advance and excess payments, the tax system lets taxpayers reduce it by certain credits. Taxpayers who file Form 1040A can claim two non-refundable credits, plus a refundable one.

Credit for Child and Dependent Care Payments

Taxpayers who maintain a home that includes one or more qualifying persons may claim the child and dependent care credit. The credit is usually a percentage of paid employment-related care expenses that let the taxpayer work or look for work. To receive the credit, a taxpayer must usually have earned income.

Qualifying Person. A taxpayer who claims the child and dependent care credit must maintain and live in a household with one of the following:

1. A dependent under age 13 who the taxpayer claims on his or her return (or the noncustodial parent claims under the divorced or separated parent rules)
2. A spouse who is physically or mentally incapable of self-care
3. Any person who is physically or mentally incapable of self-care whom the taxpayer claims as a dependent (or could claim if the person's gross income was less than $2,300)

Employment-Related Care Expenses. *Employment-related expenses* for the child and dependent care credit must be for the care of a qualifying person. Such care can include the household services of a cook, housekeeper, or maid. However, the main function of these persons must be the protection and care of a qualifying person.

Payments for food, clothing, entertainment, and education are not care expenses. When care payments cover small unseparable non-care items, the full amount qualifies as care expense. Thus, payments to send a child to a day care center or nursery school qualify even if they include the child's lunches. However, payments to send a child to the first or higher grade, or an overnight camp, are not employment-related care expenses.

Employment-related care expenses can include payments for out-of-home care. Here, the qualifying person must spend at least eight hours a day in the taxpayer's home. Payments to a dependent care center qualify if the center follows state and local regulations.

Payments to a relative who does not qualify the taxpayer for a dependency exemption can qualify as employment-related care expenses. However, payments to a relative who qualifies the taxpayer for a dependency, the taxpayer's spouse, or taxpayer's child under 19 do not qualify. Employer payments to a relative of an employee, or an employee's dependent child under 19, are not care expenses. They are gross income to the employee.

Amount of Child and Dependent Care Credit. The child and dependent care credit for a taxpayer with $10,000 or less AGI usually is 30% of the employment-related care expenses. For a taxpayer with more than $10,000 of AGI, the 30% goes down by one percentage point for each $2,000 of AGI more than $10,000. For a taxpayer with AGI more than $28,000, the credit is 20% of qualifying expenses. The upper limit on care expenses is $2,400 for one qualifying person. For two or more qualifying persons, it is $4,800. Table 2-1 shows maximum credit amounts.

Reimbursements from an employer's dependent care help plan (Chapter 4) which the employee excludes from gross income reduce employment-related care expenses. It is a dollar for dollar reduction when determining the child and dependent care credit.

Table 2-1
Child and Dependent Care Credit

Amount of AGI	Applicable Percent of Employment-Related Expenses	Maximum Credit	
		One Qualifying Person	Two or More Qalifying Persons
Up to $10,000	30%	$720	$1,440
$10,001-12,000	29%	696	1,392
12,001-14,000	28%	672	1,344
14,001-16,000	27%	648	1,296
16,001-18,000	26%	624	1,248
18,001-20,000	25%	600	1,200
20,001-22,000	24%	576	1,152
22,001-24,000	23%	552	1,104
24,001-26,000	22%	528	1,056
26,001-28,000	21%	504	1,008
$28,001 and over	20%	480	960

EXAMPLE 3 ———————————————

Marvin Jones is a taxpayer with a child, age 7. His AGI is $15,000. Marvin spent $2,100 for employment-related care expenses in 1992 and qualifies for the dependent care credit. His employer has a non-discriminating employee benefit plan. In 1992, Marvin receives $500 under the plan as dependent care payments. If Marvin does not have to include the $500 in gross income, it reduces his allowable employment-related care expenses.

First, assume Marvin does not have to include the $500 in gross income. Here, he determines his credit percentage from Table 2-1. It is 27%. Then, he applies it to his net care payments. While Marvin paid $2,100 for qualifying services, the $500 from his employer reduces the $2,100. Thus, Marvin's net employment-related care expenses are $1,600 ($2,100 – $500). Now, he applies the 27% to the net amount and arrives at his nonrefundable care credit of $432 ($1,600 x 27%). If Marvin's qualified employment-related care expenses were more than $2,400, he would reduce the $2,400 by the $500. Now, assume Marvin includes the $500 reimbursement in gross income and his care expenses remain at $2,100. Here, his care credit is $567 ($2,100 x 27%).

Earned Income Limitation. Unmarried taxpayers use employment-related expenses up to their earned income. Married taxpayers use employment-related expense up to the earned income of the spouse with the smallest earnings.

The upper limit for these expenses is $2,400 or $4,800. It depends on whether there is one or more qualifying persons.

Usually, the credit is not available for a spouse with no earned income. However, if a nonworking spouse is physically or mentally disabled, or is a full-time student at an educational institution for five months of the year, a special rule applies. Here, the law assumes an earned income of $200 per month if there is one qualifying person. If there is more than one qualifying person, the law assumes an earned income of $400 per month. The earnings assumption is for each month the spouse is disabled or is a full-time student. For any month this spouse is not disabled or a full-time student, actual earnings count.

EXAMPLE 4 ————————————————

A taxpayer with two children, ages 3 and 5, works full-time while his spouse is a full-time business school student. The student spouse attends school 10 months of the year. Earlier, each spouse had a full-time job. During this period, they saved $20,000 to cover child care and educational expenses. In the current year the taxpayer earns $12,500 and pays $4,600 for child care employment-related expenses. The student spouse is treated as employed with earnings of $4,000 ($400 per month for 10 months). The student spouse did not work outside the home during the other two months of the year. The taxpayer and spouse use the $4,000 to figure the child care credit. The credit percentage of 28 is based on AGI of $12,500. The credit is $1,120 (28% x $4,000).

Claiming the Credit. Married taxpayers claiming a child and dependent care credit must file a joint return. An exception exists for an abandoned spouse. Here, the abandoned spouse must be separated from his or her spouse for the last six months of the year and file a separate return. Also, he or she must live with a qualifying person for over half the year and furnish over half the household maintenance cost.

A divorced or separated parent who has custody of his or her child under age 13 can claim a care credit. Regardless of age, the parent can claim the credit when the child is mentally or physically incapable of self-care. Here, the child does not have to qualify the parent for a dependency exemption. However, the claiming parent must have custody of the child for a longer period during the year than the other parent.

Taxpayers claiming a child and dependent care credit must provide information about care providers (name, address, and SSN or EIN). Failure to provide it can cause a credit disallowance. **SSN** refers to the payee's social security number (sometimes called a **TIN** or taxpayer identification number). **EIN** refers to the payee's employer identification number. This information is needed when care is provided under an employer's dependent care assistance plan. Taxpayers claim the credit on Schedule 2 (Form 1040A), Credit for Child and Dependent Care Expenses for Form 1040A Filers.

Filled-In Schedule 2 (Form 1040A)

Illustration 2-5

This illustration shows a filled-in Schedule 2 for Clyde R. and Patricia E. Smith. Their SSNs are 317-09-6291 and 376-78-7371, respectively. The Smiths are civil service workers in Chicago. Mr. Smith works full-time as an administrative clerk and receives a salary of $15,340. Mrs. Smith works part-time as a teacher and receives a salary of $5,950. They have no other source of income.

The Smith's son Michael, age 10, lives with them. He qualifies them for a dependency exemption. The Smiths have no deductions for AGI. Thus, their AGI equals their earned income. During the year, the Smiths paid Lucy Burke $1,621.50 to care for their son during working hours. Mrs. Burke's TIN is 677-33-6605. She lives at 1606 North Elm Street in the house next to the Smiths. The zip code for the neighborhood is 60631-1314.

On the unnumbered line at the top of Schedule 2, the Smiths enter their names. At the end of this line they enter Mr. Smith's SSN since they entered it first on Form 1040A. For Part I, they enter Lucy's name, address, TIN (line 1), and the $1,621.50 of child care cost (lines 1 and 2).

From Part II, the Smiths enter the number 1 (line 3). This informs the IRS that they have one qualifying dependent. They also enter their child care cost of $1,621.50 (line 4). Since the Smiths have only one qualifying person, they enter $2,400 (lines 5 and 7). While it is the maximum amount on which they can calculate the credit, it is greater than their actual cost (line 8). Next, they enter Mr. Smith's earnings of $15,340 (line 9) and Mrs. Smith's of $5,950 (line 10). Then, they enter $1,621.50 again (line 11). It is the smaller of their child care cost ($1,621.50), Mr. Smith's earnings ($15,340), and Mrs. Smith's earnings ($5,950). The Smiths enter their AGI (line 12) of $21,290 ($15,340 + $5,950) and use it and the table (line 13) to determine their credit decimal. They enter this decimal (0.24) to the right of the table (line 13). The Smiths multiply the $21,290 (line 12) by the decimal (line 13) and enter the product of $389.16 (line 14). This is their child care credit.

Taxpayers who file Form 1040 should use Form 2441, Child and Dependent Care Expenses, to calculate the child and dependent care credit. Since Form 2441 is similar to Schedule 2 (Form 1040A), the book does not illustrate it. However, note that Form 2441 provides for an addition to the care credit for the current year. The addition is for child and dependent care expenses that were incurred in 1991 and paid in 1992. This credit can be claimed in 1992 when it doesn't exceed the 1991 care credit limitation.

Elderly or Disabled Credit

Persons under age 65, who retire with a *permanent and total disability* and have *taxable disability income*, may receive a nonrefundable credit. To qualify for the credit, these persons, at the start of the tax year, must be younger than their employer's mandatory retirement age. Also, if these persons retire in 1992 they must be permanently and totally disabled at their retirement date. If they retired before January 1, 1977, they had to be permanently and totally disabled on January 1, 1976, or on January 1, 1977. The credit is also available to persons at least 65 years of age with or without a permanent and total disability. For both groups, the credit is 15% of a calculated amount. Usually, nonresident aliens cannot claim the credit. However, an exception exists when a nonresident alien is married to a U.S. citizen or resident alien. To claim the credit, this couple must agree to be taxed on their worldwide income.

A person with a permanent and total disability is one who is unable to engage in any large gainful activity. To qualify, the disability must be due to a physical or mental impairment. A physician must confirm it and state he or she expects it to last for at least 12 continual months or never improve. *Disability income* includes the taxable payments from an employer's pension or accident and health plan.

Persons filing Form 1040A use Schedule 3 to claim their elderly or disabled credit. Persons filing Form 1040 use Schedule R to claim this credit. Since Schedule 3 (Form 1040A) and Schedule R (Form 1040) are similar, the book does not illustrate the latter. However, it does present Schedule 3 (Form 1040A) in Illustration 2-6. Both schedules have three parts:

1. Filing status and age
2. Statement of permanent and total disability
3. Figure your credit

Filing Status and Age. Part I of Schedule 3 (Form 1040A) and Schedule R (Form 1040) contains nine numbered boxes. Taxpayers place an "X" in the proper box to show their filing status, age group, and whether they are retired with a permanent and total disability. They use this information to determine their statutory start amount for calculating the credit. They also use it during the calculation process to determine the reduction amount for their AGI.

Statement of Permanent and Total Disability. Part II of Schedule 3 (Form 1040A) and Schedule R (Form 1040) covers a disability statement on file with the IRS. It remains blank if the taxpayer (and spouse if applicable) is at least 65 years of age. The first statement of Part II focuses on a *physician's* disability statement filed before 1984. It continues with a focus on the *taxpayer's* disability statement filed after 1983 which contains a physician's confirming signature. Finally, this sentence focuses on the taxpayer's inability to engage in any large gainful activity. When a taxpayer agrees with the sentence, he or she places an "X" in the box after the sentence (right side of form). A taxpayer who places an "X" in the box does not have to

Illustration 2-5
Filled-In Schedule 2 (Form 1040A)

Schedule 2
(Form 1040A)

Department of the Treasury—Internal Revenue Service

Child and Dependent Care Expenses for Form 1040A Filers **1992**

OMB No. 1545-0085

Name(s) shown on Form 1040A

Clyde R. and Patricia E. Smith

Your social security number

317 :09 :6291

Caution: • If you have a child who was born in 1992 and the amount on Form 1040A, line 17, is less than $22,370, see **A change to note** on page 56 before completing this schedule.

• If you paid cash wages of $50 or more in a calendar quarter to an individual for services performed in your home, you must file an employment tax return. Get **Form 942** for details.

Part I

Persons or organizations who provided the care

You MUST complete this part. (See page 57.)

	(a) Care provider's name	(b) Address (number, street, apt. no., city, state, and ZIP code)	(c) Identifying number (SSN or EIN)	(d) Amount paid (see page 57)	
1	Lucy Burke	1606 North Elm Street Chicago, IL 60631-1314	677-33-6605	1,621	50

(If you need more space, use the bottom of page 2.)

2 Add the amounts in column (d) of line 1.   **2** 1,621 | 50

Next: Did you receive employer-provided dependent care benefits?
• **YES.** Complete Part III on the back now.
• **NO.** Complete Part II below.

Part II

Credit for child and dependent care expenses

3 Enter the number of qualifying persons cared for in 1992. You must have shared the same home with the qualifying person(s). See page 57 to find out who is a qualifying person.   **3** 1

4 Enter the amount of **qualified** expenses you incurred and actually paid in 1992. See page 58 to find out which expenses qualify.
Caution: If you completed Part III on page 2, DO NOT include on this line any excluded benefits shown on line 23.   **4** 1,621 | 50

5 Enter $2,400 ($4,800 if you paid for the care of two or more qualifying persons).   **5** 2,400 | 00

6 If you completed Part III on page 2, enter the **excluded benefits**, if any, from line 23.   **6**

7 Subtract line 6 from line 5. If line 6 is equal to or more than line 5, STOP HERE; you cannot claim the credit.   **7** 2,400 | 00

8 Look at lines 4 and 7. Enter the **smaller** of the two amounts here.   **8** 1,621 | 50

9 You **must** enter your **earned income.** See page 58 for the definition of earned income.   **9** 15,340 | 00

Note: If you are not filing a joint return, go to "All other filers" on line 11 now.

10 If you are filing a joint return, you **must** enter your spouse's earned income. If your spouse was a student or disabled, see page 59 for the amount to enter.   **10** 5,950 | 00

11 • If you are filing a joint return, look at lines 8, 9, and 10. Enter the **smallest** of the three amounts here.
• All other filers, look at lines 8 and 9. Enter the **smaller** of the two amounts here.   **11** 1,621 | 50

12 Enter the amount from Form 1040A, line 17.   **12** 21,290 | 00

13 Enter the decimal amount shown below that applies to the amount on line 12.

If line 12 is—		Decimal amount is—	If line 12 is—		Decimal amount is—
Over	But not over		Over	But not over	
$0	10,000	.30	$20,000	22,000	.24
10,000	12,000	.29	22,000	24,000	.23
12,000	14,000	.28	24,000	26,000	.22
14,000	16,000	.27	26,000	28,000	.21
16,000	18,000	.26	28,000	No limit	.20
18,000	20,000	.25			

13 × .24

14 Multiply line 11 above by the decimal amount on line 13. Enter the result here and on Form 1040A, line 24a.   **14** = 389 | 16

For Paperwork Reduction Act Notice, see Form 1040A instructions.   Cat. No. 10749I   1992 Schedule 2 (Form 1040A) page 1

file another disability statement. If the taxpayer disagrees with the sentence, his or her physician must complete the physician's disability statement at the bottom of Part II.

Before giving Schedule 3 (Form 1040A) or Schedule R (Form 1040) to a physician, the taxpayer enters his or her name on the physician's statement (first blank line). The physician's statement refers to two conditions and three dates. It is an "either/or" statement. The first part states that the taxpayer had a permanent and total disability on January 1, 1976, or on January 1, 1977. The second part of the "either/or" statement indicates that the taxpayer retired with a permanent and total disability after December 31, 1976. The taxpayer enters his or her retirement date on the blank line after the physician's statement. After completing the proper blanks, the taxpayer gives the schedule to his or her physician for impairment confirmation. If the physician agrees with one of the following statements on the form, he or she signs and dates the proper one (blank line to right of statement):

1. The disability has lasted, or can be expected to last, continuously for at least a year.
2. There is no reasonable probability that the disabling condition will ever improve.

At the bottom of Part II, the physician enters his or her name and address and returns the schedule to the taxpayer for filing.

Instead of filing a physician's statement, a person may file a Department of Veterans Affairs (VA) form. It is VA Form 21-0172, Certification of Permanent and Total Disability. If the taxpayer uses the VA form, the signing physician must be one who is authorized by the VA to sign it.

Figure Your Credit. Part III of Schedule 3 (Form 1040A) and of Schedule R (Form 1040) is used to compute the elderly or disabled credit. The credit calculations for a qualified elderly or disabled person depend on two amounts. One of them is determined by the taxpayer's (and spouse's if applicable) statutory start amount (line 10). The other is the taxpayer's (and spouse's if applicable) *taxable* disability income (line 11). The taxpayer enters the smaller amount (line 12) and uses it as the calculation amount to determine the credit.

Sometimes, a special addition of $5,000 is made to taxable disability income. The addition is made when a married taxpayer age 65 or older files a joint return, and his or her spouse is under age 65 and retired with a permanent and total disability. Here, the $5,000 is added to the taxable disability income of the spouse under age 65. Also, taxable disability income does not include amounts a taxpayer receives from an employer's pension plan after reaching the employer's mandatory retirement age.

Two items reduce the calculation amount (line 12). One item is the taxpayer's (and spouse's if applicable) *tax-free* income from pensions, annuities, social security, railroad retirement, and other disability plans (line 13). The other is one-half the taxpayer's AGI (line 14) in excess of an AGI reduction amount (line 15). The reduction amounts are printed on the schedule (line 15). After reducing AGI by the proper reduction amount, the taxpayer enters the difference on the schedule (line 16). Then, he or she divides it by 2 and enters the result (line 17). Since the statutory start amount is reduced by the sum of these two items, the taxpayer adds them (lines 13c and 17) and enters the total (line 18). Then, the taxpayer subtracts the total (line 18) from the calculation amount (line 12) and enters the difference (line 19).

If the difference (line 19) is positive, the taxpayer multiplies it by 15% and enters the product on the schedule (line 21), and on Form 1040A (line 24b) or Form 1040 (line 42). If the difference is zero or less, the taxpayer cannot claim an elderly or disabled credit.

Filled-In Schedule 3 (Form 1040A)

Illustration 2-6

This illustration shows Schedule 3 (Form 1040A) for Ruth E. Wiseman. Ms. Wiseman, age 59, is an unmarried school teacher who retired on June 30, 1991 with a permanent and total disability. Her SSN is 187-90-6731. When she filed her 1991 tax return she included her physician's disability statement. This statement indicated she would never work again in any large gainful employment. It also indicated there is no reasonable chance that her disabling condition will improve. For the current year, Ms. Wiseman's AGI is $8,520. It consists of $6,000 from taxable disability income and $2,520 from interest and dividend income. During the year Ms. Wiseman received $3,100 in social security benefits.

At the top of Schedule 3 (Form 1040A), Ms. Wiseman enters her name and SSN. In Part I, she places an "X" (box 2) to show she is under age 65 and retired with a permanent and total disability. In Part II, she places an "X" after the disability statement to indicate such a statement is already on file with the IRS.

Since Ms. Wiseman is single, under age 65, and retired with a permanent and total disability, she enters $5,000 in Part III (line 10). This is her statutory start amount. Then, she enters her taxable disability income of $6,000 (line 11), compares the two amounts (lines 10 and 11), and enters the smaller (line 12).

Ms. Wiseman enters her tax-free social security income of $3,100 (line 13a). Since she did not receive a tax-free pension, annuity, or other disability benefit, she enters a zero (line 13b). She adds the two amounts (lines 13a and 13b) and enters the total $3,100 (line 13c).

After entering her AGI of $8,520 (line 14), she enters her AGI reduction amount of $7,500 (line 15). Then, she subtracts her AGI reduction amount (line 15) from her AGI (line 14) and enters the $1,020 difference (line 16). After dividing the difference (line 16) amount by 2, she enters the $510 result (line 17).

Ms. Wiseman enters $3,610 (line 18). It is the sum of $3,100 (line 13c) and $510 (line 17). Then, she subtracts this sum from her calculation amount (line 12) and enters the $1,390 difference (line 19). She multiplies the $1,390 difference by 15% and enters the product $208.50 (line 21). It is her disabled tax credit. She also enters the $208.50 (line 21) on Form 1040A (line 24b).

Earned Income Credit (EIC)

The refundable earned income is a form of negative income tax. Taxpayers can get a refund even if they have no tax liability. This credit has three parts: (1) basic EIC, (2) health insurance credit, and (3) supplemental young child credit. Illustration 2-8 in the next section shows their presentation on Schedule EIC (Form 1040 and 1040A), EIC.

Qualifying Children. To claim the EIC, a taxpayer must have a qualifying child who is:

1. A son or daughter, or grandchild
2. A stepson or stepdaughter
3. An eligible foster or adopted child

The qualifying child must live with the taxpayer in the United States for more than half the year. If the child is a foster child, it's a one year live with the taxpayer test. In addition, the child must meet one of the following conditions:

1. Be under 19 at the end of the year
2. Be a full-time student who is under age 24 at the end of the year
3. Be permanently or totally disabled at any time during the year, regardless of age

Elderly or Disabled Credit—Statutory Start Point and AGI Reduction Amount

Filing Status	Number of Qualifying Taxpayers	Statutory Start Amounts	AGI Reduction Amounts
Single, HOH, Surviving Spouse	1	$5,000	$ 7,500
Married, filing jointly			
One person qualifies	1	5,000	10,000
Two persons qualify	2	7,500	10,000
Married, filing separately and have not lived with spouse for			
entire year*	1	3,750	5,000

* For a couple who lives together part of the year and files separately, no statutory start point exists. Thus, they cannot claim the elderly or disabled credit.

Illustration 2-6
Filled-In Schedule 3 (Form 1040A)—Page 1

Schedule 3
(Form 1040A)

Department of the Treasury—Internal Revenue Service

**Credit for the Elderly or the Disabled
for Form 1040A Filers**

1992

OMB No. 1545-0085

Name(s) shown on Form 1040A

Ruth E. Wiseman

Your social security number

187 : 90: 6731

You may be able to use Schedule 3 to reduce your tax if by the end of 1992:

- You were age 65 or older, **OR** • You were under age 65, you retired on **permanent and total** disability, and you received taxable disability income.

But you must also meet other tests. See the separate instructions for Schedule 3.

Note: *In most cases, the IRS can figure the credit for you. See page 37 of the Form 1040A instructions.*

Part I	If your filing status is:	And by the end of 1992:	Check only one box:
Check the box for your filing status and age	Single, Head of household, or Qualifying widow(er) with dependent child	1 You were 65 or older.	1 ☐
		2 You were under 65 and you retired on permanent and total disability	2 ☒
	Married filing a joint return	3 Both spouses were 65 or older	3 ☐
		4 Both spouses were under 65, but only one spouse retired on permanent and total disability	4 ☐
		5 Both spouses were under 65, and both retired on permanent and total disability	5 ☐
		6 One spouse was 65 or older, and the other spouse was under 65 and retired on permanent and total disability	6 ☐
		7 One spouse was 65 or older, and the other spouse was under 65 and **NOT** retired on permanent and total disability	7 ☐
	Married filing a separate return	8 You were 65 or older and you did not live with your spouse at any time in 1992	8 ☐
		9 You were under 65, you retired on permanent and total disability, and you did not live with your spouse at any time in 1992	9 ☐

If you checked box 1, 3, 7, or 8, skip Part II and complete Part III on the back. All others, complete Parts II and III.

Part II

Statement of permanent and total disability

Complete this part **only** if you checked box 2, 4, 5, 6, or 9 above.

IF: 1 You filed a physician's statement for this disability for 1983 or an earlier year, or you filed a statement for tax years after 1983 and your physician signed line B on the statement, **AND**

2 Due to your continued disabled condition, you were unable to engage in any substantial gainful activity in 1992, check this box . . . . ▶   ☒

- If you checked this box, you do not have to file another statement for 1992.
- If you **did not** check this box, have your physician complete the following statement:

Physician's statement (See instructions at bottom of page 2.)

I certify that ____

Name of disabled person

was permanently and totally disabled on January 1, 1976, or January 1, 1977, **OR** was permanently and totally disabled on the date he or she retired. If retired after December 31, 1976, enter the date retired ▶ _______________

Physician: Sign your name on **either** line A or B below.

A The disability has lasted or can be expected to last continuously for at least a year . . . . . ___________________________________

Physician's signature   Date

B There is no reasonable probability that the disabled condition will ever improve . . . . . ___________________________________

Physician's signature   Date

Physician's name | Physician's address

Illustration 2-6
Filled-In Schedule 3 (Form 1040A)—Page 2

1992 Schedule 3 (Form 1040A) page 2

Name(s) shown on page 1	Your social security number
Ruth E. Wiseman	187 : 90 : 6731

Part III

Figure your credit

10 If you checked (in Part I): **Enter:**
Box 1, 2, 4, or 7 . . . . $5,000
Box 3, 5, or 6 . . . . $7,500
Box 8 or 9 . . . . $3,750   **10** 5,000 00

Caution: *If you checked box 2, 4, 5, 6, or 9 in Part I, you* **MUST** *complete line 11 below. All others, skip line 11 and enter the amount from line 10 on line 12.*

11
- If you checked box 6 in Part I, add $5,000 to the taxable disability income of the spouse who was under age 65. Enter the total here.
- If you checked box 2, 4, or 9 in Part I, enter your taxable disability income here.
- If you checked box 5 in Part I, add your taxable disability income to your spouse's taxable disability income. Enter the total here.

TIP: For more details on what to include on line 11, see the instructions.   **11** 6,000 00

12
- If you completed line 11 above, look at lines 10 and 11. Enter the **smaller** of the two amounts here.
- All others, enter the amount from line 10 here.   **12** 5,000 00

13 Enter the following pensions, annuities, or disability income that you (and your spouse if filing a joint return) received in 1992 (see instructions):

a Nontaxable part of social security benefits, and

Nontaxable part of railroad retirement benefits treated as social security.   **13a** 3,100 | 00

b Nontaxable veterans' pensions and any other pension, annuity, or disability benefit that is excluded from income under any other provision of law.   **13b** –0–

c Add lines 13a and 13b. (Even though these income items are not taxable, they **must** be included here to figure your credit.) If you did not receive any of the types of nontaxable income listed on line 13a or 13b, enter -0- on line 13c.   **13c** 3,100 | 00

14 Enter the amount from Form 1040A, line 17.   **14** 8,520 | 00

15 If you checked (in Part I): **Enter:**
Box 1 or 2 . . . . $7,500
Box 3, 4, 5, 6, or 7 . . . . $10,000
Box 8 or 9 . . . . $5,000   **15** 7,500 | 00

16 Subtract line 15 from line 14. If line 15 is more than line 14, enter -0-.   **16** 1,020 | 00

17 Divide line 16 above by 2.   **17** 510 | 00

18 Add lines 13c and 17.   **18** 3,610 00

19 Subtract line 18 from line 12. If line 18 is more than line 12, stop here; you **cannot** take the credit. Otherwise, go to line 21.   **19** 1,390 00

20 Decimal amount used to figure the credit.   **20** × .15

21 Multiply line 19 above by the decimal amount (.15) on line 20. Enter the result here and on Form 1040A, line 24b.   **21** 208 50

Instructions for physician's statement

Taxpayer.—If you retired after December 31, 1976, enter the date you retired in the space provided in Part II.

Physician.—A person is permanently and totally disabled if **both** of the following apply:

1. He or she cannot engage in any substantial gainful activity because of a physical or mental condition, and
2. A physician determines that the disability has lasted or can be expected to last continuously for at least a year or can lead to death.

1992 Schedule 3 (Form 1040A) page 2

Elderly or Disabled Credit Calculation Format

Smaller of statutory start amount ($5,000) or taxable disability income ($6,000)			$5,000.00
Less:			
Nontaxable pensions, annuities, or, disability income		$3,100.00	
AGI	$8,520.00		
Less: AGI reduction amount	(7,500.00)		
Net amount	1,020.00		
Times	x 1/2	510.00	(3,610.00)
Base for applying statutory percent			1,390.00
Statutory percent			x 15%
Elderly or disabled credit			$ 208.50

Credit Rates and Dollars. According to the IRS credit tables, each credit starts with earned income of $1.00 and builds until earned income reaches $7,500. Then, each credit starts to decrease when the larger of the taxpayer's earned income or AGI reaches $11,850. The phase-down of each credit is complete when the larger of the taxpayer's earned income or AGI reaches $22,370.

For the basic EIC, there is a higher rate and faster phase-down for more than one qualifying child. For the health insurance and supplemental young child credits, the increases and decreases are the same regardless of the number of qualifying children. In addition, the health insurance credit cannot exceed the amount paid for health care insurance for at least one qualifying child. Finally, to claim the supplemental young child credit, the qualifying child must be under age one at year end. Table 2-2 shows the increasing and decreasing credit rates and dollar amounts for each credit.

The IRS provides credit tables, and taxpayers must use them to determine their credits. Tables 2-3, 2-4, and 2-5 in this text contain excerpts from IRS Credit Tables A (Basic Credit), B (Health Insurance Credit), and C (Extra Credit for Child Born in 1992). Like the income tax rate table, the IRS calculates the credits at the midpoint of each bracket. Then, they round them to the nearest whole number. Table 2-3 shows that the basic credit for a tax-

Table 2-2
Rates and Dollars for Earned Income Credit (EIC)

	One Qualifying Child		More Than One Qualifying Child	
	Credit Rate	Phase Down Rate	Credit Rate	Phase Down Rate
Basic EIC	17.6%	12.570%	18.4%	13.140%
Health insurance credit	6.0	4.285	6.0	4.285
Supplemental young child credit	5.0	3.570	5.0	3.570
Total	28.6%	20.425%	29.4%	20.995%
Maximum dollars (rounded)*				
Basic EIC				
17.600% x $7,520	$1,324			
18.400% x $7,520			$1,384	
Health Insurance Credit				
6.000% x $7,520	451		451	
Supplemental Young Child Credit				
5.000% x $7,520	376		376	
Phase down starts when the larger of earned income or AGI reaches	$11,840		$11,840	
Phase down ends when the larger of earned income or AGI reaches	22,370		22,370	

* Maximum earned income indexed for inflation.

Table 2-3
Excerpts from Basic EIC Table

TABLE A—Basic Credit

1992 Earned Income Credit

Caution: This is **not** a tax table.

To find your basic credit: First, read down the "At least — But less than" columns and find the line that includes the amount you entered on line 7 or line 9 of Schedule EIC. Next, read across to the column that includes the number of qualifying children you listed on Schedule EIC. Then, enter the credit from that column on Schedule EIC, line 8 or line 10, whichever applies.

| If the amount on Schedule EIC, line 7 or line 9, is— | | And you listed— | | If the amount on Schedule EIC, line 7 or line 9, is— | | And you listed— | | If the amount on Schedule EIC, line 7 or line 9, is— | | And you listed— | | If the amount on Schedule EIC, line 7 or line 9, is— | | And you listed— | |
| At least | But less than | One child | Two children | At least | But less than | One child | Two children | At least | But less than | One child | Two children | At least | But less than | One child | Two children |
		Your basic credit is—				Your basic credit is—				Your basic credit is—				Your basic credit is—	
$1	$50	$4	$5	$2,800	$2,850	$497	$520	$5,600	$5,650	$990	$1,035	$12,700	$12,750	$1,212	$1,267
50	100	13	14	2,850	2,900	506	529	5,650	5,700	999	1,044	12,750	12,800	1,206	1,261
100	150	22	23	2,900	2,950	515	538	5,700	5,750	1,008	1,053	12,800	12,850	1,200	1,254
150	200	31	32	2,950	3,000	524	547	5,750	5,800	1,016	1,063	12,850	12,900	1,193	1,248
1,000	1,050	180	189	3,800	3,850	673	704	6,600	6,650	1,166	1,219	13,700	13,750	1,087	1,136
1,050	1,100	189	198	3,850	3,900	682	713	6,650	6,700	1,175	1,228	13,750	13,800	1,080	1,129
1,100	1,150	198	207	3,900	3,950	691	722	6,700	6,750	1,184	1,237	13,800	13,850	1,074	1,123
1,150	1,200	207	216	3,950	4,000	700	731	6,750	6,800	1,192	1,247	13,850	13,900	1,068	1,116
1,200	1,250	216	225	4,000	4,050	708	741	6,800	6,850	1,201	1,256	13,900	13,950	1,061	1,110
1,250	1,300	224	235	4,050	4,100	717	750	6,850	6,900	1,210	1,265	13,950	14,000	1,055	1,103
1,300	1,350	233	244	4,100	4,150	726	759	6,900	6,950	1,219	1,274	14,000	14,050	1,049	1,097
1,350	1,400	242	253	4,150	4,200	735	768	6,950	7,000	1,228	1,283	14,050	14,100	1,043	1,090
1,400	1,450	251	262	4,200	4,250	744	777	7,000	7,050	1,236	1,293	14,100	14,150	1,036	1,083
1,450	1,500	260	271	4,250	4,300	752	787	7,050	7,100	1,245	1,302	14,150	14,200	1,030	1,077
1,500	1,550	268	281	4,300	4,350	761	796	7,100	7,150	1,254	1,311	14,200	14,250	1,024	1,070
1,550	1,600	277	290	4,350	4,400	770	805	7,150	7,200	1,263	1,320	14,250	14,300	1,017	1,064
1,600	1,650	286	299	4,400	4,450	779	814	7,200	7,250	1,272	1,329	14,300	14,350	1,011	1,057
1,650	1,700	295	308	4,450	4,500	788	823	7,250	7,300	1,280	1,339	14,350	14,400	1,005	1,051
1,700	1,750	304	317	4,500	4,550	796	833	7,300	7,350	1,289	1,348	14,400	14,450	999	1,044
1,750	1,800	312	327	4,550	4,600	805	842	7,350	7,400	1,298	1,357	14,450	14,500	992	1,037
1,800	1,850	321	336	4,600	4,650	814	851	7,400	7,450	1,307	1,366	14,500	14,550	986	1,031
1,850	1,900	330	345	4,650	4,700	823	860	7,450	7,500	1,316	1,375	14,550	14,600	980	1,024
1,900	1,950	339	354	4,700	4,750	832	869	7,500	11,850	1,324	1,384	14,600	14,650	973	1,018
1,950	2,000	348	363	4,750	4,800	840	879	11,850	11,900	1,319	1,379	14,650	14,700	967	1,011

1992 Earned Income Credit TABLE A—Basic Credit *Continued*

| If the amount on Schedule EIC, line 7 or line 9, is— | | And you listed— | | If the amount on Schedule EIC, line 7 or line 9, is— | | And you listed— | | If the amount on Schedule EIC, line 7 or line 9, is— | | And you listed— | |
| At least | But less than | One child | Two children | At least | But less than | One child | Two children | At least | But less than | One child | Two children |
		Your basic credit is—				Your basic credit is—				Your basic credit is—	
15,700	15,750	835	873	18,900	18,950	433	453	22,100	22,150	31	32
15,750	15,800	829	867	18,950	19,000	427	446	22,150	22,200	24	26
15,800	15,850	823	860	19,000	19,050	420	440	22,200	22,250	18	19
15,850	15,900	816	853	19,050	19,100	414	433	22,250	22,300	12	13
15,900	15,950	810	847	19,100	19,150	408	426	22,300	22,350	6	6
15,950	16,000	804	840	19,150	19,200	402	420	22,350	22,370	1	1
16,000	16,050	797	834	19,200	19,250	395	413				
16,050	16,100	791	827	19,250	19,300	389	407				
16,100	16,150	785	821	19,300	19,350	383	400				
16,150	16,200	779	814	19,350	19,400	376	394	**$22,370 or more**—you may not take the credit			
16,200	16,250	772	807	19,400	19,450	370	387				
16,250	16,300	766	801	19,450	19,500	364	380				

Table 2-4
Excerpts from Health Insurance Credit Table

TABLE B—Health Insurance Credit

1992 Earned Income Credit

Caution: This is **not** a tax table.

To find your health insurance credit: First, read down the "At least—But less than" columns and find the line that includes the amount you entered on line 7 or line 9 of Schedule EIC. Next, read across and find the credit. Then, enter the credit on Schedule EIC, line 12 or line 13, whichever applies.

If the amount on Schedule EIC, line 7 or line 9, is—		Your health insurance credit is—	If the amount on Schedule EIC, line 7 or line 9, is—		Your health insurance credit is—	If the amount on Schedule EIC, line 7 or line 9, is—		Your health insurance credit is—	If the amount on Schedule EIC, line 7 or line 9, is—		Your health insurance credit is—	If the amount on Schedule EIC, line 7 or line 9, is—		Your health insurance credit is—
At least	But less than		At least	But less than		At least	But less than		At least	But less than		At least	But less than	
$1	$50	$2	$3,800	$3,850	$230	$11,900	$11,950	$448	$15,700	$15,750	$285	$19,500	$19,550	$122
50	100	5	3,850	3,900	233	11,950	12,000	445	15,750	15,800	283	19,550	19,600	120
100	150	8	3,900	3,950	236	12,000	12,050	443	15,800	15,850	280	19,600	19,650	118
150	200	11	3,950	4,000	239	12,050	12,100	441	15,850	15,900	278	19,650	19,700	115
200	250	14	4,000	4,050	242	12,100	12,150	439	15,900	15,950	276	19,700	19,750	113
250	300	17	4,050	4,100	245	12,150	12,200	437	15,950	16,000	274	19,750	19,800	111
300	350	20	4,100	4,150	248	12,200	12,250	435	16,000	16,050	272	19,800	19,850	109
350	400	23	4,150	4,200	251	12,250	12,300	433	16,050	16,100	270	19,850	19,900	107
3,200	3,250	194	7,000	7,050	422	15,100	15,150	310	18,900	18,950	148			
3,250	3,300	197	7,050	7,100	425	15,150	15,200	308	18,950	19,000	145			
3,300	3,350	200	7,100	7,150	428	15,200	15,250	306	19,000	19,050	143			
3,350	3,400	203	7,150	7,200	431	15,250	15,300	304	19,050	19,100	141		TABLE B	
3,400	3,450	206	7,200	7,250	434	15,300	15,350	302	19,100	19,150	139			
3,450	3,500	209	7,250	7,300	437	15,350	15,400	300	19,150	19,200	137			
3,500	3,550	212	7,300	7,350	440	15,400	15,450	298	19,200	19,250	135			
3,550	3,600	215	7,350	7,400	443	15,450	15,500	295	19,250	19,300	133			
3,600	3,650	218	7,400	7,450	446	15,500	15,550	293	19,300	19,350	130			
3,650	3,700	221	7,450	7,500	449	15,550	15,600	291	19,350	19,400	128			
3,700	3,750	224	7,500	11,850	451	15,600	15,650	289	19,400	19,450	126			
3,750	3,800	227	11,850	11,900	450	15,650	15,700	287	19,450	19,500	124			

Table 2-5
Excerpts from Extra Credit for Child Born in 1992 Credit Table

TABLE C—Extra Credit for Child Born in 1992

1992 Earned Income Credit

Caution: This is **not** a tax table.

To find your extra credit for a child born in 1992: First, read down the "At least—But less than" columns and find the line that includes the amount you entered on line 7 or line 9 of Schedule EIC. Next, read across and find the credit. Then, enter the credit on Schedule EIC, line 17 or line 18, whichever applies.

If the amount on Schedule EIC, line 7 or line 9, is—		Your credit for a child born in 1992 is—	If the amount on Schedule EIC, line 7 or line 9, is—		Your credit for a child born in 1992 is—	If the amount on Schedule EIC, line 7 or line 9, is—		Your credit for a child born in 1992 is—	If the amount on Schedule EIC, line 7 or line 9, is—		Your credit for a child born in 1992 is—	If the amount on Schedule EIC, line 7 or line 9, is—		Your credit for a child born in 1992 is—
At least	But less than		At least	But less than		At least	But less than		At least	But less than		At least	But less than	
$1	$50	$1	$3,800	$3,850	$191	$11,900	$11,950	$373	$15,700	$15,750	$237	$19,500	$19,550	$102
50	100	4	3,850	3,900	194	11,950	12,000	371	15,750	15,800	236	19,550	19,600	100
100	150	6	3,900	3,950	196	12,000	12,050	369	15,800	15,850	234	19,600	19,650	98
150	200	9	3,950	4,000	199	12,050	12,100	368	15,850	15,900	232	19,650	19,700	96
200	250	11	4,000	4,050	201	12,100	12,150	366	15,900	15,950	230	19,700	19,750	95
250	300	14	4,050	4,100	204	12,150	12,200	364	15,950	16,000	228	19,750	19,800	93
300	350	16	4,100	4,150	206	12,200	12,250	362	16,000	16,050	227	19,800	19,850	91
350	400	19	4,150	4,200	209	12,250	12,300	360	16,050	16,100	225	19,850	19,900	89
3,200	3,250	161	7,000	7,050	351	15,100	15,150	259	18,900	18,950	123			
3,250	3,300	164	7,050	7,100	354	15,150	15,200	257	18,950	19,000	121			
3,300	3,350	166	7,100	7,150	356	15,200	15,250	255	19,000	19,050	119		TABLE C	
3,350	3,400	169	7,150	7,200	359	15,250	15,300	253	19,050	19,100	118			
3,400	3,450	171	7,200	7,250	361	15,300	15,350	252	19,100	19,150	116			
3,450	3,500	174	7,250	7,300	364	15,350	15,400	250	19,150	19,200	114			
3,500	3,550	176	7,300	7,350	366	15,400	15,450	248	19,200	19,250	112			
3,550	3,600	179	7,350	7,400	369	15,450	15,500	246	19,250	19,300	111			
3,600	3,650	181	7,400	7,450	371	15,500	15,550	244	19,300	19,350	109			
3,650	3,700	184	7,450	7,500	374	15,550	15,600	243	19,350	19,400	107			
3,700	3,750	186	7,500	11,850	376	15,600	15,650	241	19,400	19,450	105			
3,750	3,800	189	11,850	11,900	375	15,650	15,700	239	19,450	19,500	103			

payer with $6,700 of earned income and one qualifying individual is $1,184. The basis for this amount is the midpoint of the $6,700 – $6,750 bracket ($6,725.00 x 17.6% = $1,183.60 or $1,184 rounded).

Advance Payment of Basic Earned Income Credit (Form W-5)

Employers must inform employees whose wages are not subject to income tax withholding of their advance payment right. Eligible employees can get advance payments for the basic EIC. Since the advance payments are not wages, they do not change an employer's withholding of social security and Medicare taxes. Employers report the advance EIC payments to employees and the IRS through Form W-2, Wage and Tax Statement (box 8).

Taxpayers who receive advance payment of the basic EIC must file an income tax return, even if they do not meet the general tax return filing requirements. Also, taxpayers who want to claim the supplemental young child and health insurance credits must file a tax return. Employers cannot pay these credits to employees. When a taxpayer's advance credit payments are more than their allowable EIC, the taxpayer is liable to the government for the excess.

Filled-In Form W-5

Illustration 2-7

A filled-in Form W-5, Earned Income Credit Advance Payment Certificate, for Robert F. Grazier, an unmarried eligible employee, is shown in Illustration 2-7. Mr. Grazier lives at 1629 Applewood Hill Road, Belleville, IL 62221-1480. His SSN is 321-09-8674. He expects to work all year for the Happy Valley Bottling Company.

Eligible employees who do not want to receive advance EIC payments can claim the credit when they file their tax return. These employees should not file a Form W-5 with their employer. Eligible employees who want to receive advance EIC payments for the basic credit *must* file a Form W-5 with their employer.

A filled-in Form W-5 filed with an employer usually remains in effect until the end of the calendar year. However, employees who want to stop these payments, or are no longer eligible to receive them, *must* file a new Form W-5. When an eligible employee's spouse files a Form W-5 with an employer, the employee *must* file a new Form W-5 with his or her employer. On the new Form W-5, this employee places an "X" in the YES box (line 3) to show his or her spouse has filed a Form W-5. At the start of each year, eligible employees *must* file a new Form W-5 to have their employer continue (or start) advance EIC payments.

Form 1040A with EIC

Form 1040A, U.S. Individual Income Tax Return, is a two-page tax return for wage earners and persons with limited income sources. It has four supporting schedules. Taxpayers use Schedule 1 to report their interest and dividend income. They use Schedule 2 to calculate their child and dependent care credit, and Schedule 3 to calculate their elderly or disabled credit. The next paragraph contains a brief discussion of Form 1040A. It precedes Illustration 2-8 which shows taxpayers how to use it and Schedule EIC (Form 1040A and 1040) to get the EIC. Chapter 4 contains the main discussion of Form 1040A.

Who May Use Form 1040A

Only taxpayers with taxable incomes of less than $50,000 can use Form 1040A. The income of Form 1040A filers must be from wages, salaries, interest, dividends, tips, annuities, pensions, social security benefits (including Tier I railroad retirement benefits), distributions from individual retirement arrangements (IRAs), unemployment compensation, and taxable scholarships and fellowships. Chapters 3 and 4 discuss these items. Form 1040A permits only one deduction for AGI: a qualifying IRA contribution. Also, only the standard deduction and allowable exemptions are deductible from AGI.

Illustration 2-7
Filled-In Form W-5

Form **W-5**

Earned Income Credit
Advance Payment Certificate

1992

Department of the Treasury
Internal Revenue Service

▶ **This certificate expires on December 31, 1992.**

Type or print your full name

Robert F. Grazier

Your social security number

321 09 8674

Home address (number, street or rural route, apt. no.)

1629 Applewood Hill Road

City, town or post office, state, and ZIP code

Belleville, IL 62221-1480

Note: *If you file Form W-5 with an employer to receive advance payments of the earned income credit for 1992, you must file Form 1040 or Form 1040A for 1992. If married, you must file a joint return, but see the instructions for an exception.*

		Yes	No
1	I expect to be eligible for the earned income credit for 1992, I have no other certificate in effect with any other current employer, and I choose to receive advance payment of the earned income credit	X	
2	Are you married?		X
3	If you are married, does your spouse have a certificate in effect for 1992 with any employer?		

Under penalties of perjury, I declare that the information I have furnished above is, to the best of my knowledge, true, correct, and complete.

Signature ▶ *Robert F. Grazier*   Date ▶ 1-2-92

Cat. No. 10227P

Filled-In Form 1040A and Schedule EIC (Form 1040A and 1040)

Illustration 2-8

This illustration shows a filled-in Form 1040A and Schedule EIC (Form 1040A and 1040), Earned Income Credit, for Sarah R. and James E. Wilson. The Wilsons live at 1648 West Third Street in Muskegon, Michigan 49441. Sarah's SSN is 282-56-9320, and James' is 271-04-7926. They are both age 32 and neither is blind.

During the year, Mr. Wilson earned $9,665 in wages as a maintenance specialist. His employer did not withhold income taxes since he claimed 5 exemptions on his Form W-4, Employee's Withholding Allowance Certificate. Mrs. Wilson earned $6,100 in wages as a short order cook. Her employer withheld $384 for federal income taxes since she did not claim any Form W-4 exemptions. She also earned $150 of interest on her bank savings account. Since the Wilsons will have no tax liability, they cannot give tax money to the presidential election campaign fund.

The Wilsons file a joint tax return on February 26, 1993 and claim three dependency exemptions for their children. The children's names, SSN, and ages are Martha A. (826-45-3710) 10, Karl B. (850-21-5263) 7, and Susan K. (860-40-5721) less than one. Susan was born on March 1, 1992. As a protection against rising health costs, they bought medical insurance from the Midwest Health Cooperative for $710. It covers the medical expenses of their children.

From Schedule EIC (Forms 1040 and 1040A) and Tables 2-2, 2-3, and 2-4, the Wilsons determine that they have an EIC of $1,353. It consists of a $847 basic credit (line 11), a $276 health insurance credit (line 16), and a $230 supplemental young child credit (line 19). To confirm it, they made the following calculations:

Credit before phase down (Table 2-2)
   [29.400% x $7,520] $2,210.88
Less: credit phase down (Table 2-2)
   [20.995% x ($15,915 AGI - $11,840)]   855.55
Estimate of EIC $1,355.33

    Two reasons account for the difference in the amount of the Schedule EIC (Form 1040A and 1040) credit of $1,353 and the Wilsons' figure of $1,355.33. The reasons are rounding and the use of bracket midpoints in the tables to calculate the credit.

EIC on Form 1040

Taxpayers filing Form 1040 also should use an EIC schedule to calculate their EIC. For these filers, Schedule EIC (Form 1040A and Form 1040), Earned Income Credit, provides a place for inserting self-employment income (line 6) and adding it to other earned income.

Illustration 2-8
Filled-In Form 1040A—Page 1

Form **1040A**

Department of the Treasury—Internal Revenue Service

U.S. Individual Income Tax Return   **1992**   IRS Use Only—Do not write or staple in this space.

OMB No. 1545-0085

Label (See page 14.)

Use the IRS label. Otherwise, please print or type.

Your first name and initial	Last name		Your social security number
Sarah R. Wilson			282 : 56 : 9320
If a joint return, spouse's first name and initial	Last name		Spouse's social security number
James E. Wilson			271 : 04 : 7926
Home address (number and street). If you have a P.O. box, see page 15.		Apt. no.	
1648 West Third Street			For Privacy Act and Paperwork Reduction Act Notice, see page 4.
City, town or post office, state, and ZIP code. If you have a foreign address, see page 15.			
Muskegon, MI 49441			

Presidential Election Campaign Fund (See page 15.)   Yes   No

Do you want $1 to go to this fund? . . . .

If a joint return, does your spouse want $1 to go to this fund?

Note: *Checking "Yes" will not change your tax or reduce your refund.*

Check the box for your filing status (See page 15.)

Check only one box.

1   ☐ Single
2   ☒ Married filing joint return (even if only one had income)
3   ☐ Married filing separate return. Enter spouse's social security number above and full name here. ▶ _______________
4   ☐ Head of household (with qualifying person). (See page 16.) If the qualifying person is a child but not your dependent, enter this child's name here. ▶ _______________
5   ☐ Qualifying widow(er) with dependent child (year spouse died ▶ 19 ____). (See page 17.)

Figure your exemptions (See page 18.)

If more than seven dependents, see page 21.

6a ☒ **Yourself.** If your parent (or someone else) can claim you as a dependent on his or her tax return, do not check box 6a. But be sure to check the box on line 18b on page 2.

b   ☒ **Spouse**

c Dependents: (1) Name (first, initial, and last name)	(2) Check if under age 1	(3) If age 1 or older, dependent's social security number	(4) Dependent's relationship to you	(5) No. of months lived in your home in 1992
Martha A. Wilson	10	826 : 45 : 3710	daughter	12
Karl B. Wilson	7	850 : 21 : 5263	son	12
Susan K. Wilson	X	860 : 40 : 5721	daughter	10
		: :		
		: :		
		: :		

No. of boxes checked on 6a and 6b   **2**

No. of your children on 6c who:
• lived with you   **3**
• didn't live with you due to divorce or separation (see page 21)   ____

No. of other dependents on 6c   ____

d   If your child didn't live with you but is claimed as your dependent under a pre-1985 agreement, check here . . . . ▶ ☐

e   Total number of exemptions claimed.

Add numbers entered on lines above   **5**

Figure your total income

Attach Copy B of your Forms W-2 and 1099-R here.

If you didn't get a W-2, see page 22.

Attach check or money order on top of any Forms W-2 or 1099-R.

7	Wages, salaries, tips, etc. This should be shown in box 10 of your W-2 form(s). Attach Form(s) W-2.	7	15,765 | 00
8a	Taxable interest income (see page 24). If over $400, also complete and attach Schedule 1, Part I.	8a	150 | 00
b	Tax-exempt interest. DO NOT include on line 8a. 8b		
9	Dividends. If over $400, also complete and attach Schedule 1, Part II.	9	
10a	Total IRA distributions. 10a **10b** Taxable amount (see page 25).	10b	
11a	Total pensions and annuities. 11a **11b** Taxable amount (see page 25).	11b	
12	Unemployment compensation (see page 29).	12	
13a	Social security benefits. 13a **13b** Taxable amount (see page 29).	13b	
14	Add lines 7 through 13b (far right column). This is your **total income**. ▶	14	15,915 | 00

Figure your adjusted gross income

15a	Your IRA deduction from applicable worksheet. 15a		
b	Spouse's IRA deduction from applicable worksheet. Note: *Rules for IRAs begin on page 31.* 15b		
c	Add lines 15a and 15b. These are your **total adjustments**.	15c	
16	Subtract line 15c from line 14. This is your **adjusted gross income**. If less than $22,370, see "Earned income credit" on page 39. ▶	16	15,915 | 00

Cat. No. 11327A   1992 Form 1040A page 1

Illustration 2-8
Filled-In Form 1040A—Page 2

1992 Form 1040A page 2

Name(s) shown on page 1

Sara R. and James E. Wilson

Your social security number: 282 : 56 : 9320

Figure your standard deduction, exemption amount, and taxable income

17 Enter the amount from line 16. — **17** 15,915 00

18a Check if: ☐ You were 65 or older ☐ Blind / ☐ Spouse was 65 or older ☐ Blind } **Enter number of boxes checked ▶ 18a** ☐

b If your parent (or someone else) can claim you as a dependent, check here . . . . ▶ **18b** ☐

c If you are married filing separately and your spouse files Form 1040 and itemizes deductions, see page 35 and check here ▶ **18c** ☐

19 Enter the **standard deduction** shown below for your filing status. **But if you checked any box on line 18a or b,** go to page 35 to find your standard deduction. **If you checked box 18c,** enter -0-.
- Single—$3,600   • Head of household—$5,250
- Married filing jointly or Qualifying widow(er)—$6,000
- Married filing separately—$3,000 — **19** 6,000 00

20 Subtract line 19 from line 17. (If line 19 is more than line 17, enter -0-.) **20** 9,915 00

21 Multiply $2,300 by the total number of exemptions claimed on line 6e. **21** 11,500 00

22 Subtract line 21 from line 20. (If line 21 is more than line 20, enter -0-.) This is your **taxable income.** ▶ **22** –0–

Figure your tax, credits, and payments

If you want the IRS to figure your tax, see the instructions for line 22 on page 36.

23 Find the tax on the amount on line 22. Check if from: ☐ Tax Table (pages 48–53) or ☐ Form 8615 (see page 37). **23** –0–

24a Credit for child and dependent care expenses. Complete and attach Schedule 2. **24a**

b Credit for the elderly or the disabled. Complete and attach Schedule 3. **24b**

c Add lines 24a and 24b. These are your **total credits.** **24c** –0–

25 Subtract line 24c from line 23. (If line 24c is more than line 23, enter -0-.) **25** –0–

26 Advance earned income credit payments from Form W-2. **26**

27 Add lines 25 and 26. This is your **total tax.** ▶ **27** –0–

28a Total Federal income tax withheld. If any tax is from Form(s) 1099, check here. ▶ ☐ **28a** 384 00

b 1992 estimated tax payments and amount applied from 1991 return. **28b**

c **Earned income credit.** Complete and attach Schedule EIC. **28c** 1,353 00

d Add lines 28a, 28b, and 28c. These are your **total payments.** ▶ **28d** 1,737 00

Figure your refund or amount you owe

Attach check or money order on top of Form(s) W-2, etc., on page 1.

29 If line 28d is more than line 27, subtract line 27 from line 28d. This is the amount you **overpaid.** **29** 1,737 00

30 Amount of line 29 you want **refunded to you.** **30** 1,737 00

31 Amount of line 29 you want **applied to your 1993 estimated tax.** **31**

32 If line 27 is more than line 28d, subtract line 28d from line 27. This is the **amount you owe.** Attach check or money order for full amount payable to the "Internal Revenue Service". Write your name, address, social security number, daytime phone number, and "1992 Form 1040A" on it. **32**

33 Estimated tax penalty (see page 41). **33**

Sign your return

Keep a copy of this return for your records.

Under penalties of perjury, I declare that I have examined this return and accompanying schedules and statements, and to the best of my knowledge and belief, they are true, correct, and complete. Declaration of preparer (other than the taxpayer) is based on all information of which the preparer has any knowledge.

Your signature: *Sara R. Wilson* Date: 2-26-93 Your occupation: Short order cook

Spouse's signature. If joint return, BOTH must sign. *James E. Wilson* Date: 2-26-93 Spouse's occupation: Maintenance specialist

Paid preparer's use only

Preparer's signature ▶ Date Check if self-employed ☐ Preparer's social security no.

Firm's name (or yours if self-employed) and address ▶ E.I. No. ZIP code

Illustration 2-8
Filled-In Schedule EIC (Form 1040A)—Page 1

| SCHEDULE EIC
(Form 1040A or 1040)

Department of the Treasury
Internal Revenue Service | **Earned Income Credit**
▶ Attach to Form 1040A or 1040. ▶ See Instructions for Schedule EIC.
TIP: Why not let the IRS figure the credit for you? Give us only the information asked for on this page and we'll do the rest. | OMB No. 1545-0074
19**92**
Attachment Sequence No. **43** |

Name(s) shown on return   Sarah R. and James E. Wilson   Your social security number   282 : 56 : 9320

Part I   General Information

To take this credit ▶
- You MUST have worked and earned **LESS** than $22,370, **AND**
- Your adjusted gross income (Form 1040A, line 16, or Form 1040, line 31) MUST be **LESS** than $22,370, **AND**
- Your filing status can be any status **except** married filing a separate return, **AND**
- You MUST have at least one qualifying child (see boxes below), **AND**
- You cannot be a qualifying child yourself.

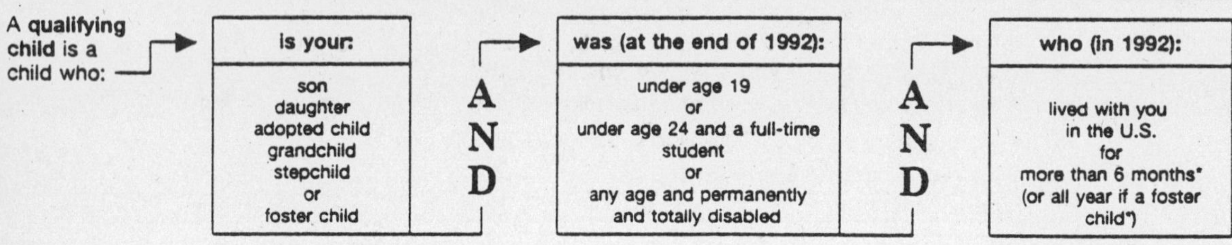

*If the child didn't live with you for the required time (for example, was born in 1992), see the **Exception** on page 61 of 1040A booklet (or page EIC-2 of 1040 booklet).

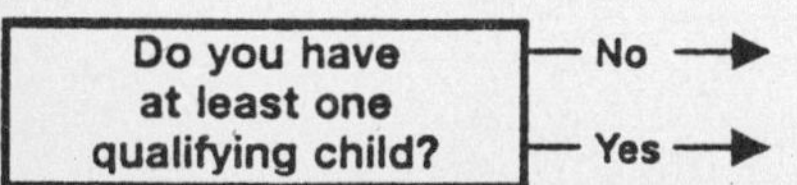

No ▶ You **cannot** take the credit. Enter "NO" next to line 28c of Form 1040A (or line 56 of Form 1040).

Yes ▶ Go to Part II. But if the child was married or is also a qualifying child of another person, first see page 61 of 1040A booklet (or page EIC-2 of 1040 booklet).

Part II   Information About Your Two Youngest Qualifying Children

If more than two qualifying children, see page 62 of 1040A booklet (or page EIC-2 of 1040 booklet). 1(a) Child's name (first, initial, and last name)	(b) Child's year of birth	For a child born BEFORE 1974, check if child was—		(e) If child was born BEFORE 1992, enter the child's social security number	(f) Child's relationship to you (for example, son, grandchild, etc.)	(g) Number of months child lived with you in the U.S. in 1992
		(c) a student under age 24 at end of 1992	(d) disabled (see booklet)			
Susan K. Wilson	19 92			: :	daughter	10
Karl B. Wilson	19 85			850 : 21 : 5263	son	12

Caution: If a child you listed above was born in 1992 **AND** you chose to claim the credit or exclusion for child care expenses for this child on **Schedule 2 (Form 1040A)** or **Form 2441 (Form 1040)**, check here . . . . ▶ ☐

Do you want the IRS to figure the credit for you?

Yes ▶ Fill in Part III below.   **AND** ▶ Enter the amount from Form 1040A, line 16, or Form 1040, line 31, here. ▶ . . . .

No ▶ Go to Part IV on the back now.

Part III   Other Information

2   If you had any **nontaxable earned income** (see page 62 of 1040A booklet or page EIC-2 of 1040 booklet) such as military housing and subsistence or contributions to a 401(k) plan, enter the total of that income on line 2. Also, list type and amount here. ▶ **2**

3   Enter the total amount you paid in 1992 for health insurance that covered at least one qualifying child. (See page 63 of 1040A booklet or page EIC-2 of 1040 booklet.) **3**

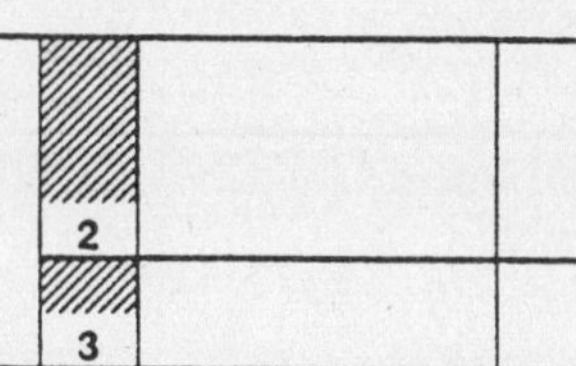

If you want the IRS to figure the credit for you,   **STOP** !

Attach this schedule to your return. If filing Form 1040A, print "EIC" on the line next to line 28c.
If filing Form 1040, print "EIC" on the dotted line next to line 56.

For Paperwork Reduction Act Notice, see Form 1040A or 1040 instructions.   Cat. No. 13339M   Schedule EIC (Form 1040A or 1040) 1992

Illustration 2-8
Filled-In Schedule EIC (Form 1040A)—Page 2

Schedule EIC (Form 1040A or 1040) 1992   Page **2**

Part IV **Figure Your Earned Income Credit**—You can take **ALL THREE** parts of the credit if you qualify

BASIC CREDIT

4 Enter the amount from line 7 of Form 1040A or Form 1040 (wages, salaries, tips, etc.). If you received a taxable scholarship or fellowship grant, see page 64 of 1040A booklet (or page EIC-3 of 1040 booklet) for the amount to enter **4** 15,765 00

5 If you had any **nontaxable earned income** (see page 62 of 1040A booklet or page EIC-2 of 1040 booklet) such as military housing and subsistence or contributions to a 401(k) plan, enter the total of that income on line 5. Also, list type and amount here. ▶ .... **5** –0–

6 **Form 1040 Filers Only:** If you were self-employed or reported income and expenses on Sch. C or C-EZ as a statutory employee, enter the amount from the worksheet on page EIC-3 of 1040 booklet **6**

7 Add lines 4, 5, and 6. This is your **earned income.** If $22,370 or more, you **cannot** take the earned income credit. Enter "NO" next to line 28c of Form 1040A (or line 56 of Form 1040) ▶ **7** 15,765 00

8 Use the amount on **line 7** above to look up your credit in **TABLE A** on pages **65 and 66** of 1040A booklet (or pages **EIC-4 and 5** of 1040 booklet). Then, enter the credit here **8** 867 00

9 Enter your **adjusted gross income** (from Form 1040A, line 16, or Form 1040, line 31). If $22,370 or more, you **cannot** take the credit . . . . ▶ **9** 15,915 00

10 **Is line 9 $11,850 or more?**

  • **YES.** Use the amount on **line 9** to look up your credit in **TABLE A** on pages **65 and 66** of 1040A booklet (or pages **EIC-4 and 5** of 1040 booklet). Then, enter the credit here **10** 847 00

  • **NO.** Enter the amount from line 8 on line 11.

11 If you answered "YES" to line 10, enter the **smaller** of line 8 or line 10 here. This is your **basic credit** . . **11** 847 00

NEXT: *To take the health insurance credit, fill in lines 12–16. To take the extra credit for a child born in 1992, fill in lines 17–19. Otherwise, go to line 20 now.*

HEALTH INSURANCE CREDIT —Take this credit **ONLY** if you paid for health insurance that covered at least one qualifying child.

12 Look at the amount on **line 7** above. Use that amount to look up your credit in **TABLE B** on page **67** of 1040A booklet (or page **EIC-6** of 1040 booklet). Then, enter the credit here **12** 283 00

13 Look at the amount on **line 9** above. **Is line 9 $11,850 or more?**

  • **YES.** Use the amount on **line 9** to look up your credit in **TABLE B** on page **67** of 1040A booklet (or page **EIC-6** of 1040 booklet). Then, enter the credit here **13** 276 00

  • **NO.** Enter the amount from line 12 on line 14.

14 If you answered "YES" to line 13, enter the **smaller** of line 12 or line 13 here. **14** 276 00

15 Enter the total amount you paid in 1992 for health insurance that covered at least one qualifying child. (See page 64 of 1040A booklet or page EIC-3 of 1040 booklet.) **15** 710 00

16 Enter the **smaller** of line 14 or line 15 here. This is your **health insurance credit** **16** 276 00

EXTRA CREDIT FOR CHILD BORN IN 1992 —Take this credit **ONLY** if:

  • You listed in Part II a child born in 1992, **AND**
  • You did not take the credit or exclusion for child care expenses on **Schedule 2** or **Form 2441** for the same child.

TIP: You can take **both** the basic credit and the **extra credit** for your child born in 1992.

17 Look at the amount on **line 7** above. Use that amount to look up your credit in **TABLE C** on page **68** of 1040A booklet (or page **EIC-7** of 1040 booklet). Then, enter the credit here **17** 236 00

18 Look at the amount on **line 9** above. **Is line 9 $11,850 or more?**

  • **YES.** Use the amount on **line 9** to look up your credit in **TABLE C** on page 68 of 1040A booklet (or page EIC-7 of 1040 booklet). Then, enter the credit here **18** 230 00

  • **NO.** Enter the amount from line 17 on line 19.

19 If you answered "YES" to line 18, enter the **smaller** of line 17 or line 18 here. This is your **extra credit for a child born in 1992** **19** 230 00

TOTAL EARNED INCOME CREDIT

20 Add lines 11, 16, and 19. Enter the total here and on Form 1040A, line 28c (or on Form 1040, line 56). This is your **total earned income credit** . . . . ▶ **20** 1,353 00

C H A P T E R   2

Questions and Problems

1. The IRS publishes Tax Rate Schedules and Tax Tables. In the space below, indicate which taxpayers cannot use the Tax Tables to figure their tax?

2. For 1992, the Tax Tables have been expanded. Now, some Form 1040 filers may have to use them to figure their tax. Form 1040EZ and Form 1040A filers must use the Tax Tables. In the space below, describe the exact steps a taxpayer follows to find his or her tax in the Tax Tables.

3. Mark Long, a single person, files his tax return as a HOH. He has taxable income of $40,125.
   a. Enter Mark's tax liability in the space below.

   b. Using the proper Tax Rate Schedule, prove that your answer to part *a.* is correct. Show all calculations in the space below.

4. When must taxpayers use the Tax Rate Schedules to calculate their income tax liability?

5. Barbara Landerson, age 25 and single, is employed at a monthly salary of $1,050. She claims one exemption on her tax return. Her employer withheld $1,428 from her wages for income taxes for 12 months of work. Calculate the amount of Barbara's 1992 income tax due to or from the government.

6. Determine the 1992 taxable income and income tax liability for each of the following taxpayers who claim a standard deduction:

Item	A	B	C	D	E
AGI*	$39,600	$14,642	$11,700	$17,736	$39,980
Exemptions	2	1	2	3	4
Filing status	Qualifying Widow	Single	Married Filing Separately	HOH	Married Filing Jointly
Other	—	Over 65	—	—	1 spouse blind
Taxable income	$________	$________	$________	$________	$________
Income tax	$________	$________	$________	$________	$________

* Salaries

7. For 1992, the taxpayers described below want to file Form 1040EZ. For each taxpayer, state whether he or she can file Form 1040EZ. If a taxpayer cannot file Form 1040EZ, state the reason(s) for your answer.

a. A single taxpayer has tax-exempt interest income of $401 and taxable income of $49,900. The taxable income is from wages.

b. A married taxpayer filing a separate return has taxable income of $47,290, including interest income of $100.

c. A single taxpayer has taxable income of $15,683, including $500 of interest income. The taxpayer also has $200 of tax-exempt interest.

d. A HOH taxpayer has taxable income of $30,400, including interest income of $250. The taxpayer has 2 dependents.

e. A single taxpayer has taxable income of $17,800, including dividend income of $300.

f. A single taxpayer has taxable income of $31,654, including tip income of $4,500 shown on his Form W-2 and interest income of $75.

8. Jeanne Searson is a 27-year-old unmarried accountant. She lives at 4502 Lakeside Drive, Eagle River, California 92040-1234. Her SSN is 369-48-5783. Her Forms W-2, Wage and Tax Statements, for 1992 contain the following information:

	Gross Wages	Income Tax Withheld	FICA Wages	FICA Tax Withheld
Arnold Corporation, Eagle River	$15,400	$2,042	$15,400	$1,178.10
Ace Company, Eagle River (present employer)	6,280	790	6,280	480.42
Totals	$21,680	$2,832	$21,680	$1,658.52

In addition to her wages, Ms. Searson received $250 in interest on her passbook account at the Eagle River Savings and Loan Association. She wants $1 of her tax money to go to the presidential election campaign fund. Using the Form 1040EZ provided on the next page, prepare her tax return for 1992. She will sign the return on February 6, 1993.

9. a. What is an individual's TIN and what is its purpose?

b. When must a taxpayer report a dependent's TIN?

10. a. For 1992, Patricia Crowley has AGI of $40,200. She fully supported Mike Crowley, her disabled husband who has tax-exempt interest income of $1,000. This interest is from State of Ohio general obligation bonds. Can Pat file a separate Form 1040A return and claim an exemption for Mike? Why or why not?

b. Is the exemption for Mike in *a.* a dependency exemption? Explain.

Department of the Treasury—Internal Revenue Service

Form
1040EZ

Income Tax Return for
Single Filers With No Dependents   **1992**

OMB No. 1545-0675

Name & address

Use the IRS label (see page 10). If you don't have one, please print.

LABEL HERE

Print your name (first, initial, last)

Home address (number and street). If you have a P.O. box, see page 10.   Apt. no.

City, town or post office, state, and ZIP code. If you have a foreign address, see page 10.

Please print your numbers like this:

9 8 7 6 5 4 3 2 1 0

Your social security number

Please see instructions on the back. Also, see the Form 1040EZ booklet.

Presidential Election Campaign (See page 10.)
Do you want $1 to go to this fund?

Note: Checking "Yes" will not change your tax or reduce your refund. ▶

Yes No

Dollars   Cents

Report your income

1 Total wages, salaries, and tips. This should be shown in box 10 of your W-2 form(s). Attach your W-2 form(s).   1

Attach Copy B of Form(s) W-2 here. Attach tax payment on top of Form(s) W-2.

2 Taxable interest income of $400 or less. If the total is more than $400, you cannot use Form 1040EZ.   2

3 Add lines 1 and 2. This is your **adjusted gross income.**   3

4 Can your parents (or someone else) claim you on their return?
☐ Yes. Do worksheet on back; enter amount from line E here.
☐ No. Enter 5,900.00. This is the total of your standard deduction and personal exemption.   4

Note: *You must check Yes or No.*

5 Subtract line 4 from line 3. If line 4 is larger than line 3, enter 0. This is your **taxable income.**   5

Figure your tax

6 Enter your Federal income tax withheld from box 9 of your W-2 form(s).   6

7 **Tax.** Look at line 5 above. Use the amount on **line 5** to find your tax in the tax table on pages 22-24 of the booklet. Then, enter the tax from the table on this line.   7

Refund or amount you owe

8 If line 6 is larger than line 7, subtract line 7 from line 6. This is your **refund.**   8

9 If line 7 is larger than line 6, subtract line 6 from line 7. This is the amount you owe. Attach your payment for full amount payable to the "Internal Revenue Service." Write your name, address, social security number, daytime phone number, and "1992 Form 1040EZ" on it.   9

Sign your return

Keep a copy of this form for your records.

I have read this return. Under penalties of perjury, I declare that to the best of my knowledge and belief, the return is true, correct, and complete.

Your signature

Date

Your occupation

X

For IRS Use Only — Please do not write in boxes below.

For Privacy Act and Paperwork Reduction Act Notice, see page 4 in the booklet. Cat. No. 11329W Form 1040EZ (1992)

c. If the Crowleys want to minimize the income tax bite, what filing status should they use? Why? In your answer, indicate why you think Pat may not want to use this filing status.

d. Would your answer to *a.* change if Mike's interest income was from taxable corporate bonds? Why or why not?

11. Marilyn Dorning and Charles Smith, unmarried individuals, are each age 29. Each has only one income source, and it is wages. For 1992, each will earn gross wages of $11,000. They are thinking about getting married in late December. Before they get married, they want to know how much they will save in federal income taxes if they file a joint return. They ask you to compare their combined federal income taxes as single individuals with their taxes as a married couple filing jointly. No other taxpayer qualifies them for a dependency exemption. Regardless of their marital status, they will claim the standard deduction(s). What advice do you have for Marilyn and Charles? Illustrate your answer with calculations.

12. Cele Goldman, age 46, received interest income of $940 on her bank savings account in 1992. She had no other income. Marvin, her 48-year-old husband, received wages of $24,600. He is thinking about filing a separate return. Neither Cele nor Marvin is blind. No one qualifies them for a dependency exemption. Should Cele and Marvin file a joint return or separate returns? Explain and illustrate.

13. Both John J. Jackson, age 66, and Mary C. Johnson, age 65, have good vision. For 1992, no one qualifies them for a dependency exemption. Two years ago they were divorced from each other. For 1990, they filed their income tax returns as single individuals. In 1992, Mr. Jackson's gross wage income will be $21,900 and Miss Johnson's will be $21,800. They have no other income. Their only deductions from AGI will consist of standard deductions and personal exemptions. They are considering a remarriage to each other before the end of 1992. What are the income tax consequences of a remarriage? From a 1992 income tax savings viewpoint, should they remarry during 1992 and file a joint return, remarry and file separate returns, or defer the wedding until 1993 and file as single individuals in 1992? Show calculations to support your answer.

14. Bill B. and Nancy A. Carlson are married and have no dependents. Neither qualifies another taxpayer for a dependency exemption. Bill is 48 years old and Nancy is 45. Both have good vision. During 1992, Bill earned $49,200 in gross wages. His wife received $980 in tax-exempt interest on State of Oregon general obligations bonds. Bill doesn't want Nancy to know his income. For 1992, Bill files Form 1040A as a married filing separately taxpayer. What is his tax cost for not informing Nancy of his income so he could file a joint return with her?

15. a. Is a parent required to report his or her child's investment income of $3,000 on the parent's 1992 income tax return? Assume the child is 12 years old. Explain.

    b. Is the parent responsible for paying the income tax of this child? Explain.

    c. Under what conditions can parents include their 12-year-old child's income on their 1992 tax return?

16. Mark C. and Melinda K. Johnson have SSNs of 841-38-1020 and 655-36-3216, respectively. The Johnsons file a joint return and claim 4 personal exemptions. Mark is 43 years of age and Melinda is 41. Their taxable income for 1992 is $36,000, and their tax is $5,433. They fully support their two children (Colleen C. and Anita R.). The children live with them at 610 Glenway Drive, Milwaukee, Wisconsin 53201-4532. Colleen is 8 years old. Her SSN is 961-14-8611. Anita is 13 and her SSN is 961-14-8610. The children had no itemized deductions for 1992. They had the following income for 1992:

	Colleen	Anita
Interest income from Second Bank	$ 500	$1,200
U.S. Series EE savings bonds (tax-deferred interest)	200	200
Interest income from general obligation municipal bonds	450	400
Dividends on Electric Utility Co. common stock	400	400
Wages earned	-0-	200
Mad money (allowance) from parents	300	300
Totals	$1,850	$2,700

a. Are Colleen and Anita required to file Form 8615? Why or why not?

b. Calculate Anita's standard deduction using the provided Standard Deduction Worksheet for Dependents. Then, compute her tax using the provided Form 8615. Finally, prepare Anita's tax return through line 23 using the provided Form 1040A. Assume that Anita has already prepared Schedule 1 (Form 1040A) and that she elects to contribute $1 to the presidential election campaign fund.

Standard deduction worksheet for dependents (keep for your records)
Use this worksheet ONLY if someone can claim you as a dependent.

1. Enter the amount from Form 1040A, line 7. If none, enter -0-.   **1.** [   ]

2. Minimum amount.   **2.** [600.00]

3. Look at lines 1 and 2. Enter the **larger** of the two amounts here.   **3.** [   ]

4. Enter on line 4 the amount shown below for your filing status.
- Single, enter $3,600
- Married filing a separate return, enter $3,000
- Married filing a joint return or Qualifying widow(er) with dependent child, enter $6,000
- Head of household, enter $5,250   **4.** [   ]

5. Standard deduction.
- **a.** Look at lines 3 and 4. Enter the **smaller** of the two amounts here. If under 65 and not blind, stop here and enter this amount on Form 1040A, line 19. Otherwise, go to line 5b.   **5a.** [   ]
- **b.** If 65 or older or blind, multiply $900 ($700 if married filing a joint or separate return, or qualifying widow(er) with dependent child) by the number on Form 1040A, line 18a.   **5b.** [   ]
- **c.** Add lines 5a and 5b. Enter the total here and on Form 1040A, line 19.   **5c.** [   ]

Form **8615**

Department of the Treasury
Internal Revenue Service

Tax for Children Under Age 14
Who Have Investment Income of More Than $1,200

▶ See instructions below and on back.
▶ Attach ONLY to the child's Form 1040, Form 1040A, or Form 1040NR.

OMB No. 1545-0998

19**92**

Attachment
Sequence No. **33**

General Instructions

Purpose of Form. For children under age 14, investment income (such as taxable interest and dividends) over $1,200 is taxed at the parent's rate if the parent's rate is higher than the child's rate. If the child's investment income is more than $1,200, use this form to figure the child's tax.

Investment Income. As used on this form, "investment income" includes all taxable income other than earned income as defined on page 2. It includes income such as taxable interest, dividends, capital gains, rents, royalties, etc. It also includes pension and annuity income and income (other than earned income) received as the beneficiary of a trust.

Who Must File. Generally, Form 8615 must be filed for any child who was under age 14 on January 1, 1993, and who had more than $1,200 of investment income. If neither parent was alive on December 31, 1992, do not use Form 8615. Instead, figure the child's tax in the normal manner.

Note: *The parent may be able to elect to report the child's interest and dividends on his or her return. If the parent makes this election, the child will not have to file a return or Form 8615. For more details, see the instructions for Form 1040 or Form 1040A, or get Form 8814,* Parents' Election To Report Child's Interest and Dividends.

Additional Information. For more details, get **Pub. 929,** Tax Rules for Children and Dependents.

Incomplete Information for Parent. If a child's parent or guardian cannot obtain the information needed to complete Form 8615 before the due date of the child's return, reasonable estimates of the parent's taxable income or filing status and the net investment income of the parent's other children may be made. The appropriate line(s) of Form 8615 must be marked "Estimated." For more details, see Pub. 929.

(Instructions continue on back.)

Child's name shown on return	Child's social security number

A Parent's name (first, initial, and last). **Caution:** *See instructions on back before completing.*		**B** Parent's social security number

C Parent's filing status (check one):

☐ Single ☐ Married filing jointly ☐ Married filing separately ☐ Head of household ☐ Qualifying widow(er)

Step 1 Figure child's net investment income

1	Enter child's investment income, such as taxable interest and dividend income. See instructions. If this amount is $1,200 or less, **stop here;** do not file this form	1
2	If the child DID NOT itemize deductions on Schedule A (Form 1040 or Form 1040NR), enter $1,200. If the child ITEMIZED deductions, see instructions	2
3	Subtract line 2 from line 1. If the result is zero or less, **stop here;** do not complete the rest of this form but ATTACH it to the child's return	3
4	Enter child's **taxable** income from Form 1040, line 37; Form 1040A, line 22; or Form 1040NR, line 35	4
5	Enter the **smaller** of line 3 or line 4 here ▶	5

Step 2 Figure tentative tax based on the tax rate of the parent listed on line A

6	Enter parent's **taxable** income from Form 1040, line 37; Form 1040A, line 22; Form 1040EZ, line 5; or Form 1040NR, line 35. If the parent transferred property to a trust, see instructions	6
7	Enter the total, if any, of the net investment income from Forms 8615, line 5, of ALL OTHER children of the parent. **Do not** include the amount from line 5 above	7
8	Add lines 5, 6, and 7	8
9	Tax on line 8 based on the **parent's** filing status. See instructions. If from Schedule D, enter amount from line 22 of that Schedule D here ▶ _______	9
10	Enter parent's tax from Form 1040, line 38; Form 1040A, line 23; Form 1040EZ, line 7; or Form 1040NR, line 36. If from Schedule D, enter amount from line 22 of that Schedule D here ▶ _______	10
11	Subtract line 10 from line 9. If line 7 is blank, enter on line 13 the amount from line 11; skip lines 12a and 12b	11
12a	Add lines 5 and 7 . . . 12a	
b	Divide line 5 by line 12a. Enter the result as a decimal (rounded to two places) ▶	12b ✕
13	Multiply line 11 by line 12b ▶	13

Step 3 Figure child's tax

	Note: *If lines 4 and 5 above are the same, go to line 16.*	
14	Subtract line 5 from line 4 . . . 14	
15	Tax on line 14 based on the **child's** filing status. See instructions. If from Schedule D, enter amount from line 22 of that Schedule D here ▶ _______	15
16	Add lines 13 and 15	16
17	Tax on line 4 based on the **child's** filing status. See instructions. If from Schedule D, check here ▶ ☐	17
18	Enter the **larger** of line 16 or line 17 here and on Form 1040, line 38; Form 1040A, line 23; or Form 1040NR, line 36. Be sure to check the box for "Form 8615" even if line 17 is more than line 16 . ▶	18

For Paperwork Reduction Act Notice, see back of form. Cat. No. 64113U Form **8615** (1992)

Form
1040A

Department of the Treasury—Internal Revenue Service

U.S. Individual Income Tax Return   1992

IRS Use Only—Do not write or staple in this space.

Label
(See page 14.)

Use the IRS label. Otherwise, please print or type.

LABEL HERE

Your first name and initial   Last name

If a joint return, spouse's first name and initial   Last name

Home address (number and street). If you have a P.O. box, see page 15.   Apt. no.

City, town or post office, state, and ZIP code. If you have a foreign address, see page 15.

OMB No. 1545-0085

Your social security number

Spouse's social security number

For Privacy Act and Paperwork Reduction Act Notice, see page 4.

Presidential Election Campaign Fund (See page 15.)

Do you want $1 to go to this fund? . . . .

If a joint return, does your spouse want $1 to go to this fund?

Yes	No

Note: *Checking "Yes" will not change your tax or reduce your refund.*

Check the box for your filing status
(See page 15.)

Check only one box.

1   ☐ Single

2   ☐ Married filing joint return (even if only one had income)

3   ☐ Married filing separate return. Enter spouse's social security number above and full name here. ▶ ______________

4   ☐ Head of household (with qualifying person). (See page 16.) If the qualifying person is a child but not your dependent, enter this child's name here. ▶ ______________

5   ☐ Qualifying widow(er) with dependent child (year spouse died ▶ 19 ____). (See page 17.)

Figure your exemptions
(See page 18.)

If more than seven dependents, see page 21.

6a   ☐ Yourself. If your parent (or someone else) can claim you as a dependent on his or her tax return, do not check box 6a. But be sure to check the box on line 18b on page 2.

b   ☐ Spouse

c   Dependents:

(1) Name (first, initial, and last name)	(2) Check if under age 1	(3) If age 1 or older, dependent's social security number	(4) Dependent's relationship to you	(5) No. of months lived in your home in 1992
____________________				
____________________				
____________________				
____________________				
____________________				
____________________				
____________________				

d   If your child didn't live with you but is claimed as your dependent under a pre-1985 agreement, check here . . . . ▶ ☐

e   Total number of exemptions claimed.

No. of boxes checked on 6a and 6b ____

No. of your children on 6c who:
- lived with you ____
- didn't live with you due to divorce or separation (see page 21) ____

No. of other dependents on 6c ____

Add numbers entered on lines above ☐

Figure your total income

Attach Copy B of your Forms W-2 and 1099-R here.

If you didn't get a W-2, see page 22.

Attach check or money order on top of any Forms W-2 or 1099-R.

7   Wages, salaries, tips, etc. This should be shown in box 10 of your W-2 form(s). Attach Form(s) W-2.   7

8a   **Taxable** interest income (see page 24). If over $400, also complete and attach Schedule 1, Part I.   8a

b   **Tax-exempt** interest. DO NOT include on line 8a.   8b

9   Dividends. If over $400, also complete and attach Schedule 1, Part II.   9

10a   Total IRA distributions.   10a   10b   Taxable amount (see page 25).   10b

11a   Total pensions and annuities.   11a   11b   Taxable amount (see page 25).   11b

12   Unemployment compensation (see page 29).   12

13a   Social security benefits.   13a   13b   Taxable amount (see page 29).   13b

14   Add lines 7 through 13b (far right column). This is your **total income.** ▶ 14

Figure your adjusted gross income

15a   Your IRA deduction from applicable worksheet.   15a

b   Spouse's IRA deduction from applicable worksheet. **Note:** *Rules for IRAs begin on page 31.*   15b

c   Add lines 15a and 15b. These are your **total adjustments.**   15c

16   Subtract line 15c from line 14. This is your **adjusted gross income.** If less than $22,370, see "Earned income credit" on page 39. ▶ 16

Cat. No. 11327A   **1992 Form 1040A page 1**

■ 1992 Form 1040A page 2

Name(s) shown on page 1	Your social security number

Figure your standard deduction, exemption amount, and taxable income

17 Enter the amount from line 16. **17**

18a Check if: ☐ You were 65 or older ☐ Blind   ☐ Spouse was 65 or older ☐ Blind   Enter number of boxes checked ▶ **18a**

b If your parent (or someone else) can claim you as a dependent, check here . . . . ▶ **18b** ☐

c If you are married filing separately and your spouse files Form 1040 and itemizes deductions, see page 35 and check here ▶ **18c** ☐

19 Enter the **standard deduction** shown below for your filing status. **But if you checked any box on line 18a or b,** go to page 35 to find your standard deduction. **If you checked box 18c,** enter -0-.

* Single—$3,600   • Head of household—$5,250
* Married filing jointly or Qualifying widow(er)—$6,000
* Married filing separately—$3,000 **19**

20 Subtract line 19 from line 17. (If line 19 is more than line 17, enter -0-.) **20**

21 Multiply $2,300 by the total number of exemptions claimed on line 6e. **21**

22 Subtract line 21 from line 20. (If line 21 is more than line 20, enter -0-.) This is your **taxable income.** ▶ **22**

Figure your tax, credits, and payments

If you want the IRS to figure your tax, see the instructions for line 22 on page 36.

23 Find the tax on the amount on line 22. Check if from: ☐ Tax Table (pages 48–53) or ☐ Form 8615 (see page 37). **23**

24a Credit for child and dependent care expenses. Complete and attach Schedule 2. **24a**

b Credit for the elderly or the disabled. Complete and attach Schedule 3. **24b**

c Add lines 24a and 24b. These are your **total credits.** **24c**

25 Subtract line 24c from line 23. (If line 24c is more than line 23, enter -0-.) **25**

26 Advance earned income credit payments from Form W-2. **26**

27 Add lines 25 and 26. This is your **total tax.** ▶ **27**

28a Total Federal income tax withheld. If any tax is from Form(s) 1099, check here. ▶ ☐ **28a**

b 1992 estimated tax payments and amount applied from 1991 return. **28b**

c **Earned income credit.** Complete and attach Schedule EIC. **28c**

d Add lines 28a, 28b, and 28c. These are your **total payments.** ▶ **28d**

Figure your refund or amount you owe

Attach check or money order on top of Form(s) W-2, etc., on page 1.

29 If line 28d is more than line 27, subtract line 27 from line 28d. This is the amount you **overpaid.** **29**

30 Amount of line 29 you want **refunded to you.** **30**

31 Amount of line 29 you want **applied to your** 1993 estimated tax. **31**

32 If line 27 is more than line 28d, subtract line 28d from line 27. This is the **amount you owe.** Attach check or money order for full amount payable to the "Internal Revenue Service". Write your name, address, social security number, daytime phone number, and "1992 Form 1040A" on it. **32**

33 Estimated tax penalty (see page 41). **33**

Sign your return

Keep a copy of this return for your records.

Under penalties of perjury, I declare that I have examined this return and accompanying schedules and statements, and to the best of my knowledge and belief, they are true, correct, and complete. Declaration of preparer (other than the taxpayer) is based on all information of which the preparer has any knowledge.

Your signature	Date	Your occupation
Spouse's signature. If joint return, BOTH must sign.	Date	Spouse's occupation

Paid preparer's use only

Preparer's signature	Date	Check if self-employed ☐	Preparer's social security no.
Firm's name (or yours if self-employed) and address		E.I. No.	
		ZIP code	

17. Howard and Jane Preston, married taxpayers filing a joint return, are both employed. Howard's SSN is 977-45-9711 and Jane's is 986-27-3145. They are eligible to file Form 1040A. For 1992 Howard had earned wages of $8,600, and Jane had an earned salary of $12,600. They have a dependent daughter, Nancy, who is 3 years of age. The Prestons paid the following expenses for their daughter's care so that they could work:

Housekeeper	$2,800
Clothing for daughter	150
Food for daughter while parents worked	200
To dependent grandmother for care of daughter	750
To Jane's sister for care of daughter	600
Total	$4,500

The Prestons' housekeeper is Lynn Klug. Lynn's SSN is 821-37-9101. She resides at 1648 West 4th. St., Ashtabula, Ohio 44004-3711. The grandmother's name is Ethel Rybak. She resides at 876 Walnut Blvd., Ashtabula, Ohio 44004-3711. Mrs. Rybak's SSN is 290-75-2132. Jane's sister, Sarah Buchanan, resides at 481 Haven Rd., Ashtabula, Ohio 44004-3711. Her SSN is 463-85-1980.

  a. What employment-related expenses can be claimed by Mr. and Mrs. Preston when determining their child and dependent care credit?

  b. Using the Schedule 2 (Form 1040A) reproduced on the next page, calculate the child and dependent care credit claimed by Mr. and Mrs. Preston.

  c. Would your solution to *b.* be different if the care was for the dependent father of Mr. Preston rather than for the child? Explain.

18.   **a.** In general, which groups of taxpayers might be eligible to claim the elderly and disabled credit?

Schedule 2
(Form 1040A)

Department of the Treasury—Internal Revenue Service

Child and Dependent Care Expenses for Form 1040A Filers

1992

OMB No. 1545-0085

Name(s) shown on Form 1040A	Your social security number

Caution: • If you have a child who was born in 1992 and the amount on Form 1040A, line 17, is less than $22,370, see **A change to note** on page 56 before completing this schedule.

• If you paid cash wages of $50 or more in a calendar quarter to an individual for services performed in your home, you must file an employment tax return. Get **Form 942** for details.

Part I

Persons or organizations who provided the care

You MUST complete this part. (See page 57.)

1

(a) Care provider's name	(b) Address (number, street, apt. no., city, state, and ZIP code)	(c) Identifying number (SSN or EIN)	(d) Amount paid (see page 57)

(If you need more space, use the bottom of page 2.)

2 Add the amounts in column (d) of line 1. ... 2

Next: Did you receive employer-provided dependent care benefits?
• **YES.** Complete Part III on the back now.
• **NO.** Complete Part II below.

Part II

Credit for child and dependent care expenses

3 Enter the number of qualifying persons cared for in 1992. You must have shared the same home with the qualifying person(s). See page 57 to find out who is a qualifying person. ... 3

4 Enter the amount of **qualified** expenses you incurred and actually paid in 1992. See page 58 to find out which expenses qualify.
Caution: If you completed Part III on page 2, DO NOT include on this line any excluded benefits shown on line 23. ... 4

5 Enter $2,400 ($4,800 if you paid for the care of two or more qualifying persons). ... 5

6 If you completed Part III on page 2, enter the **excluded benefits,** if any, from line 23. ... 6

7 Subtract line 6 from line 5. If line 6 is equal to or more than line 5, STOP HERE; you cannot claim the credit. ... 7

8 Look at lines 4 and 7. Enter the **smaller** of the two amounts here. ... 8

9 You **must** enter your **earned income.** See page 58 for the definition of earned income. ... 9

Note: If you are not filing a joint return, go to "All other filers" on line 11 now.

10 If you are filing a joint return, you **must** enter your spouse's earned income. If your spouse was a student or disabled, see page 59 for the amount to enter. ... 10

11 • If you are filing a joint return, look at lines 8, 9, and 10. Enter the **smallest** of the three amounts here.
• All other filers, look at lines 8 and 9. Enter the **smaller** of the two amounts here. ... 11

12 Enter the amount from Form 1040A, line 17. ... 12

13 Enter the decimal amount shown below that applies to the amount on line 12.

If line 12 is—		Decimal amount is—	If line 12 is—		Decimal amount is—
Over	But not over		Over	But not over	
$0	10,000	.30	$20,000	22,000	.24
10,000	12,000	.29	22,000	24,000	.23
12,000	14,000	.28	24,000	26,000	.22
14,000	16,000	.27	26,000	28,000	.21
16,000	18,000	.26	28,000	No limit	.20
18,000	20,000	.25			

13 ×

14 Multiply line 11 above by the decimal amount on line 13. Enter the result here and on Form 1040A, line 24a. ... 14 =

For Paperwork Reduction Act Notice, see Form 1040A instructions.   Cat. No. 10749I   1992 Schedule 2 (Form 1040A) page 1

b. Complete the following schedule pertaining to the elderly and disabled credit by placing your answers in the provided blanks to indicate (1) the filing status of all applicable taxpayers, (2) the statutory start base amounts for these taxpayers, and (3) the AGI reduction amounts for these taxpayers.

Filing Status	Number of Qualifying Taxpayers	Statutory Start Amounts	AGI Reduction Amounts
_______________________	1	_________	$7,500
Married, filing jointly			
One person qualifies	1	_________	_________
Two persons qualify	2	_________	_________
Married, filing separately and have lived with spouse entire year	______	3,750	5,000

c. In the blank space below, show the computation setup (format) for calculating the elderly or disabled credit. Use XXX for dollar amounts.

GROSS INCOME

- ➡ Overview of Form 1040 (road map to tax knowledge)
- ➡ Gross income inclusions
- ➡ Gross income exclusions
- ➡ How to complete the alimony recapture worksheet
- ➡ How to complete Schedules 1 and 2 of Form 1040A
- ➡ How to complete Schedules A and B of Form 1040
- ➡ How to report a "kiddie's" income on Form 8814
- ➡ How to complete the social security worksheet
- ➡ How to complete Form 8815 for the U.S. Savings Bonds exclusion
- ➡ How to complete the worksheets for an IRA deduction
- ➡ How to report nondeductible IRA contributions on Form 8606
- ➡ How to complete Form 1040A and Form 1040

Gross Income Inclusions

Your Rights as a Taxpayer

Courtesy and Consideration. You are always entitled to courteous and considerate treatment from IRS employees. If you ever feel that you are not being treated with fairness, courtesy, and consideration by an IRS employee, you should tell the employee's supervisor.

Source: Internal Revenue Service, Publication 1

Chapters 1 and 2 discussed the tax base and reporting structure for federal income taxes. They illustrated several tax forms, schedules, and tables, including two simplified returns, Form 1040EZ and Form 1040A. Chapters 3 through 13 focus on more complex items that are part of the tax base. The road map for understanding them is tax return Form 1040, U.S. Individual Income Tax Return. It is a two-page return supported by many schedules.

This chapter and the next cover items taxpayers should consider when determining AGI on Form 1040 (page 1). Understanding these items requires a knowledge of three reporting groups: gross income exclusions, gross income inclusions, and adjustments to income. Chapters 5 through 13 cover page 2 items. These items take taxpayers from AGI to taxable income, and to the amount due to or from the government.

Overview of Form 1040

Form 1040 is the tax system's most complex return for individuals. Understanding its structure gives insights into the full tax reporting process. Illustration 3-1 shows this form.

Blank Form 1040

Illustration 3-1

On Form 1040 (page 1), taxpayers report their filing status and exemptions (lines 1-6). Next, they report their income (lines 7-22) and **total income** (line 23). The bold heading to the left of this reporting section is **income**, not gross income. The term is broad enough to include income items before gross income exclusions, gross income items, and **net income items** (gross income less adjustments to income not reported on page 1).

In the next section, taxpayers report specific **adjustments to income** (lines 24-29). These adjustments are the **IRA** (individual retirement account) deduction, one-half any self-employment tax, self-employed health insurance deduction, self-employment retirement plan deductions, penalty on the early withdrawal of savings, and paid alimony. Taxpayers add these items and enter the **total adjustments** (line 30). See *Highlights* (page xiv) for discussion of extension of self-employed health insurance deduction.

Total adjustments to income (line 30) are subtracted from total income (line 23) to arrive at **adjusted gross income (AGI)**. AGI (line 31) serves as a limiting base for certain deductions and credits, and a phase-down base for other benefits.

On page 2, in the tax computation section, taxpayers enter their AGI (line 32) from page 1 (line 31). The IRS uses check-boxes (line 33) to collect data it needs to verify a standard deduction claim. Here, the IRS determines the age range and blind condition of the taxpayer and spouse. It also determines if a taxpayer qualifies another taxpayer for a dependency exemption claim. Finally, it determines if the spouse of a married-filing-separately taxpayer is itemizing deductions. The IRS also uses the last box (line 33) to determine if a taxpayer is a dual-status alien. However, dual-status aliens who file a joint return with a U.S. citizen or U.S. resident do not check this box.

Next, taxpayers enter their standard deduction or itemized deduction amount (line 34), subtract it from AGI, and enter the remainder (line 35). The dollar amount of their personal and dependency exemptions (line 36) is subtracted to arrive at **taxable income** (line 37).

The regular income tax (line 38) is calculated on the taxable income amount (line 37). The tax on lump-sum distributions and accumulation distributions from trusts (line 39) is added to the regular tax and the total entered (line 40). Through check-boxes (lines 38 and 39), taxpayers identify their tax calculation route and IRS computation form (if any).

Several credits (lines 41-44) may be subtracted from the tax (line 40). These credits include the child and dependent care credit, elderly or disabled credit, foreign tax credit, general business credit, and prior year minimum tax credit. Taxpayers add these credits and enter the total (line 45). Total credits are subtracted from the tax (line 40) and the difference entered (line 46).

Taxpayers enter other tax liabilities (lines 47-52) in the next section. They consist of self-employment taxes, alternative minimum tax, special recapture taxes, social security and medicare taxes for tips not on Form W-2, taxes for an IRA or qualified retirement plan, and advance EIC payments. Taxpayers add these items and enter a total (line 53). It is the **total tax.**

Taxpayers enter various payments and credits (lines 54-59) that reduce their tax liability. These items include withheld federal income taxes, estimated tax payments, overpayment on last year's taxes that apply to the current year, EIC, payments made with a due date extension request, excess withholdings for social security, medicare, and railroad retirement taxes, federal fuel tax credit, and regulated investment company credit. Taxpayers add them and enter the total (line 60). It is the **total payments.**

If total payments (line 60) are greater than the total tax (line 53), the overpayment is entered (line 61). If the taxpayer wants a total refund, the total overpayment is entered (line 62). If they want to apply some of the overpayment to next year's taxes, they indicate that amount (line 63).

When the total tax (line 53) is more than the total payments (line 60), taxpayers enter the amount due to the government (line 64). Then, they attach their check or money order made payable to the "Internal Revenue Service" for the amount due (line 64).

Taxpayers who have an estimated tax penalty include it with the amount they owe (line 64). They also enter it separately (line 65). The remaining portion of page 2 is for signatures and certification. It contains the same information as the signature and certification section on Form 1040A.

Gross Income Inclusions

Gross income is income from any source except capital recoveries and specific exclusions. It is the filing requirements' base for individuals who are not self-employed. Elements of gross income can appear as net or summary items on page 1 of Form 1040. Form 1040 does not include a gross income summary line.

This chapter discusses several of the more common gross income items. At the end of the chapter, Table 3-2 shows the returns taxpayers can use to report selected gross income items.

Alimony Received

A spouse or former spouse who gets alimony or separate maintenance payments includes them in income on Form 1040 (line 11). The payer deducts them for AGI on Form 1040 (line 29). Taxpayers cannot use Form 1040EZ or Form 1040A to report alimony payments.

The receiver of alimony must give the payer his or her **SSN** (social security number). The payer enters this number in the SSN spaces (line 29). The receiver or payer who does not provide this number can get a $50 penalty.

Child support payments are not alimony. A recipient of child support payments excludes them from gross income. The payer can't deduct them.

Application of the tax rules to alimony payments depends on the date of the divorce decree, separate maintenance agreement, or written divorce instrument. In some cases, a change date applies. The tax rules are divisible by periods: pre-1985 and post-1984. A knowledge of the property transfer rules helps in understanding the alimony rules.

Alimony: Property Transfers Between Spouses. Except transfers to a nonresident alien spouse, property transfers to a spouse in settlement of marital debts are nontaxable. While the transferring spouse doesn't get a tax deduction, he or she avoids having to pay taxes on the property's unrealized appreciation. The receiving spouse gets a carryover basis (the same basis as the transferor). Before July 19, 1984, such transfers were usually taxable.

Alimony: Post-1984 Agreements. The post-1984 alimony rules apply to a pre-1985 divorce or

Illustration 3-1
Blank Form 1040—Page 1

Form 1040

Department of the Treasury—Internal Revenue Service

U.S. Individual Income Tax Return **1992**

IRS Use Only—Do not write or staple in this space.

For the year Jan. 1–Dec. 31, 1992, or other tax year beginning _______ , 1992, ending _______ , 19 ___

OMB No. 1545-0074

Label

(See instructions on page 10.)

Use the IRS label. Otherwise, please print or type.

LABEL HERE

Your first name and initial — Last name — Your social security number

If a joint return, spouse's first name and initial — Last name — Spouse's social security number

Home address (number and street). If you have a P.O. box, see page 10. — Apt. no.

City, town or post office, state, and ZIP code. If you have a foreign address, see page 10.

For Privacy Act and Paperwork Reduction Act Notice, see page 4.

Presidential Election Campaign
(See page 10.)

Do you want $1 to go to this fund? . . . . Yes / No

If a joint return, does your spouse want $1 to go to this fund? . Yes / No

Note: Checking "Yes" will not change your tax or reduce your refund.

Filing Status

(See page 10.)

Check only one box.

1 ☐ Single

2 ☐ Married filing joint return (even if only one had income)

3 ☐ Married filing separate return. Enter spouse's social security no. above and full name here. ▶ _____________

4 ☐ Head of household (with qualifying person). (See page 11.) If the qualifying person is a child but not your dependent, enter this child's name here. ▶ _____________

5 ☐ Qualifying widow(er) with dependent child (year spouse died ▶ 19 ___). (See page 11.)

Exemptions

(See page 11.)

6a ☐ Yourself. If your parent (or someone else) can claim you as a dependent on his or her tax return, do not check box 6a. But be sure to check the box on line 33b on page 2

b ☐ Spouse . . . .

c Dependents:

(1) Name (first, initial, and last name)	(2) Check if under age 1	(3) If age 1 or older, dependent's social security number	(4) Dependent's relationship to you	(5) No. of months lived in your home in 1992

If more than six dependents, see page 12.

d If your child didn't live with you but is claimed as your dependent under a pre-1985 agreement, check here ▶ ☐

e Total number of exemptions claimed

No. of boxes checked on 6a and 6b ___

No. of your children on 6c who:
- lived with you ___
- didn't live with you due to divorce or separation (see page 13) ___

No. of other dependents on 6c ___

Add numbers entered on lines above ▶ ___

Income

Attach Copy B of your Forms W-2, W-2G, and 1099-R here.

If you did not get a W-2, see page 9.

Attach check or money order on top of any Forms W-2, W-2G, or 1099-R.

7 Wages, salaries, tips, etc. Attach Form(s) W-2 . . . . **7**

8a Taxable interest income. Attach Schedule B if over $400 . . . **8a**

b Tax-exempt interest income (see page 15). DON'T include on line 8a **8b**

9 Dividend income. Attach Schedule B if over $400 . . . . . **9**

10 Taxable refunds, credits, or offsets of state and local income taxes from worksheet on page 16 **10**

11 Alimony received **11**

12 Business income or (loss). Attach Schedule C or C-EZ **12**

13 Capital gain or (loss). Attach Schedule D **13**

14 Capital gain distributions not reported on line 13 (see page 15) . . **14**

15 Other gains or (losses). Attach Form 4797 . . . . **15**

16a Total IRA distributions . **16a** _____ b Taxable amount (see page 16) **16b**

17a Total pensions and annuities **17a** _____ b Taxable amount (see page 16) **17b**

18 Rents, royalties, partnerships, estates, trusts, etc. Attach Schedule E . . . **18**

19 Farm income or (loss). Attach Schedule F **19**

20 Unemployment compensation (see page 17) **20**

21a Social security benefits **21a** _____ b Taxable amount (see page 17) **21b**

22 Other income. List type and amount—see page 18 .... **22**

23 Add the amounts in the far right column for lines 7 through 22. This is your total income . . . ▶ **23**

Adjustments to Income

(See page 18.)

24a Your IRA deduction from applicable worksheet on page 19 or 20 **24a**

b Spouse's IRA deduction from applicable worksheet on page 19 or 20 **24b**

25 One-half of self-employment tax (see page 20) . . . **25**

26 Self-employed health insurance deduction (see page 20) **26**

27 Keogh retirement plan and self-employed SEP deduction **27**

28 Penalty on early withdrawal of savings **28**

29 Alimony paid. Recipient's SSN ▶ _____ **29**

30 Add lines 24a through 29. These are your total adjustments . . . . ▶ **30**

Adjusted Gross Income

31 Subtract line 30 from line 23. This is your **adjusted gross income.** If this amount is less than $22,370 and a child lived with you, see page EIC-1 to find out if you can claim the "Earned Income Credit" on line 56 . . . . ▶ **31**

Cat. No. 11320B

Form **1040** (1992)

Illustration 3-1
Blank Form 1040—Page 2

Form 1040 (1992)   Page **2**

Tax Computation

(See page 22.)

32   Amount from line 31 (adjusted gross income)   **32**

33a   Check if: ☐ **You** were 65 or older, ☐ Blind; ☐ **Spouse** was 65 or older, ☐ Blind.
Add the number of boxes checked above and enter the total here ▶ **33a**

b   If your parent (or someone else) can claim you as a dependent, check here ▶ **33b** ☐

c   If you are married filing separately and your spouse itemizes deductions or you are a dual-status alien, see page 22 and check here ▶ **33c** ☐

34   Enter the larger of your:
> Itemized deductions from Schedule A, line 26, OR
> Standard deduction shown below for your filing status. **But if you checked any box on line 33a or b, go to page 22 to find your standard deduction. If you checked box 33c, your standard deduction is zero.**
> - Single—$3,600
> - Head of household—$5,250
> - Married filing jointly or Qualifying widow(er)—$6,000
> - Married filing separately—$3,000

34

35   Subtract line 34 from line 32   **35**

36   If line 32 is $78,950 or less, multiply $2,300 by the total number of exemptions claimed on line 6e. If line 32 is over $78,950, see the worksheet on page 23 for the amount to enter   **36**

If you want the IRS to figure your tax, see page 23.

37   **Taxable income.** Subtract line 36 from line 35. If line 36 is more than line 35, enter -0-   **37**

38   Enter tax. Check if from a ☐ Tax Table, b ☐ Tax Rate Schedules, c ☐ Schedule D, or d ☐ Form 8615 (see page 23). Amount, if any, from Form(s) 8814 ▶ e ______   **38**

39   Additional taxes (see page 23). Check if from a ☐ Form 4970 b ☐ Form 4972   **39**

40   Add lines 38 and 39   ▶ **40**

Credits

(See page 23.)

41   Credit for child and dependent care expenses. Attach Form 2441   **41**

42   Credit for the elderly or the disabled. Attach Schedule R   **42**

43   Foreign tax credit. Attach Form 1116   **43**

44   Other credits (see page 24). Check if from a ☐ Form 3800 b ☐ Form 8396 c ☐ Form 8801 d ☐ Form (specify) ______   **44**

45   Add lines 41 through 44   **45**

46   Subtract line 45 from line 40. If line 45 is more than line 40, enter -0-   ▶ **46**

Other Taxes

47   Self-employment tax. Attach Schedule SE. Also, see line 25   **47**

48   Alternative minimum tax. Attach Form 6251   **48**

49   Recapture taxes (see page 25). Check if from a ☐ Form 4255 b ☐ Form 8611 c ☐ Form 8828   **49**

50   Social security and Medicare tax on tip income not reported to employer. Attach Form 4137   **50**

51   Tax on qualified retirement plans, including IRAs. Attach Form 5329   **51**

52   Advance earned income credit payments from Form W-2   **52**

53   Add lines 46 through 52. This is your **total tax**   ▶ **53**

Payments

Attach Forms W-2, W-2G, and 1099-R on the front.

54   Federal income tax withheld. If any is from Form(s) 1099, check ▶ ☐   **54**

55   1992 estimated tax payments and amount applied from 1991 return   **55**

56   **Earned income credit.** Attach Schedule EIC   **56**

57   Amount paid with Form 4868 (extension request)   **57**

58   Excess social security, Medicare, and RRTA tax withheld (see page 26)   **58**

59   Other payments (see page 26). Check if from a ☐ Form 2439 b ☐ Form 4136   **59**

60   Add lines 54 through 59. These are your **total payments**   ▶ **60**

Refund or Amount You Owe

Attach check or money order on top of Form(s) W-2, etc., on the front.

61   If line 60 is more than line 53, subtract line 53 from line 60. This is the amount you **OVERPAID**   ▶ **61**

62   Amount of line 61 you want **REFUNDED TO YOU**   ▶ **62**

63   Amount of line 61 you want **APPLIED TO YOUR 1993 ESTIMATED TAX** ▶ **63**

64   If line 53 is more than line 60, subtract line 60 from line 53. This is the **AMOUNT YOU OWE.** Attach check or money order for full amount payable to "Internal Revenue Service." Write your name, address, social security number, daytime phone number, and "1992 Form 1040" on it   **64**

65   Estimated tax penalty (see page 27). Also include on line 64   **65**

Sign Here

Keep a copy of this return for your records.

Under penalties of perjury, I declare that I have examined this return and accompanying schedules and statements, and to the best of my knowledge and belief, they are true, correct, and complete. Declaration of preparer (other than taxpayer) is based on all information of which preparer has any knowledge.

Your signature	Date	Your occupation
Spouse's signature. If a joint return, BOTH must sign.	Date	Spouse's occupation

Paid Preparer's Use Only

Preparer's signature	Date	Check if self-employed ☐	Preparer's social security no.
Firm's name (or yours if self-employed) and address		E.I. No.	
		ZIP code	

separation when a proper change document makes such a specification. Under the post-1984 rules, alimony payments must meet certain conditions to be taxable to the recipient and deductible by the payer.

Alimony Payment Requirements

1. Payments must be in cash.
2. Payments cannot be for child support.
3. Payments are made under a decree of divorce or separate maintenance, or written divorce instrument.
4. Governing decree or written instrument doesn't specify that the payments are something other than alimony.
5. Payer is not required to make payments after the recipient's death.
6. Parties to the divorce or separation are not members of the same household at the time of payments and are legally separated under a decree of divorce or separate maintenance.

When the parties are legally separated and remain in the same home, but physically separate themselves, payments between them are not alimony. An exception applies to individuals who are not legally separated under a decree of divorce or separate maintenance. Here, the payments may qualify as alimony. Another exception applies to a party under a decree of divorce or separate maintenance who is preparing to leave the household. The exception applies when this party leaves within one month after the payment date. Here, the law treats this party as not occupying the same household for this payment.

Alimony: Recapture Worksheet. Persons making property payments for the release of marital rights want to treat them as alimony. Usually, such property payments take place in the early years of a divorce or separation. A front-loading recapture provision discourages early payment. This provision says alimony payers must include in income a portion of alimony deducted earlier when there is a large drop in the payments. To fall under the provision, the drop must take place during the first three years of a divorce or separation. In the third post-separa-

tion year, the payer picks up recapture income and the receiver gets a like amount deduction for AGI. For years after 1986, there is a payment exemption drop of $15,000. Illustration 3-2 shows an alimony recapture worksheet.

Illustration 3-2
Alimony Recapture Worksheet

Daisy and Mike's divorce became final in early 1990. The divorce decree indicates Daisy is to pay Mike the following alimony: $42,000 in 1990, $31,000 in 1991, $14,000 in 1992, and $4,000 a year for the next three years. The decree also indicates that the alimony payments stop if Mike dies before Daisy makes the last one. Daisy and Mike are not living together.

While Daisy gets a $14,000 alimony deduction for AGI in 1992, she also has gross income of $7,500. On the other hand, while Mike's gross income increases by the $14,000 alimony payment in 1992, he gets a $7,500 deduction for AGI. Daisy enters $7,500 on Form 1040 (alimony received line 11). She crosses out the word "received" and enters the word "recapture." Mike enters $7,500 on Form 1040 (alimony paid line 29). He crosses out the word "paid" and enters the word "recapture." Recapture calculations start with the second post-separation year and proceed to the first post-separation year. All recapture takes place in the third post-separation year.

For a divorce or separation in 1985 and 1986, the recapture rules are more complex. Persons under these rules, and persons with a divorce or separation before 1985, should consult a tax adviser for the proper handling of alimony payments.

Alimony: Child Support Payments. After 1984, payments designated as child support in the decree of divorce or separate maintenance, or in the divorce instrument, are not alimony. Also, payments that are contingent upon a child's status are child support payments (the payments decline when the child reaches age 18). For a divorce or separation before 1985, the

Illustration 3-2
Alimony Recapture Worksheet

EXCESS PAYMENT FOR SECOND POST-SEPARATION YEAR

1. Second post-separation year payment		$31,000	
2. Third post-separation year payment	$14,000		
3. Add: statutory exemption from recapture	15,000	29,000	
4. Recapture from second post-separation year			$2,000

EXCESS PAYMENT FOR FIRST POST-SEPARATION YEAR

5. First post-separation year payment		$42,000	
6. Less:			
a. Paid in second post-separation year	$31,000		
b. Less: recapture from second post-separation year	2,000		
c. Net amount	29,000		
d. Plus: third post-separation year payment	14,000		
7. Total amount	$43,000		
8. Simple yearly average ($43,000/2)	$21,500		
9. Add: statutory exemption from recapture	15,000	36,500	
10. Recapture from first post-separation year			5,500

RECAPTURE IN THIRD POST-SEPARATION YEAR

11. Total recapture in third post-separation year			$7,500

governing decree or instrument had to specify that a declining portion of the alimony payments was child support. Without the specification, all payments were alimony.

Business or Professional Income or Loss

The profit from a business or profession is taxable. A loss is usually deductible. Taxpayers report business profit or loss on Form 1040 (line 12) with supporting details on a separate schedule. Chapter 8 discusses this schedule.

Divorce and Property Settlements

Both parties to a divorce or legal separation should know that the alimony recapture rules do not apply to declining payments after the third post-separation year. Thus, alimony payers could arrange for declining payments of more than $15,000 to start after the third post-separation year and avoid the recapture rules. Also excluded from the recapture rules are level payments and increasing payments during the three year period.

Compensation, Wages, Salaries, Tips, Bonuses, and Commissions

All compensation taxpayers receive for services is taxable, whether its form is cash or property. Also, its name makes no difference. Thus, honorariums for speeches and "so-called" gifts for furnishing names of potential customers are taxable compensation. When a person receives compensation in the form of property, its FMV is taxable.

Gross income includes fees for baby sitting, grass cutting, snow shoveling, and commissions or salaries for delivering newspapers. Employee fringe benefits are also part of gross income unless exempt by statute, U.S. Constitution, or an IRS **de minimis** rule (small item rule). Social security taxes, income taxes, union dues, insurance premiums, and health and accident insurance premiums withheld from wages do not reduce gross income. A person who receives a service fee as an independent contractor has gross income. While some exceptions exist, gross income includes military service pay. Chapter 4 discusses the exceptions.

Employees who receive less than $20.00 in any one month in tips while working for any one employer, do not have to report their tips to their employers. However, employees must report these tips as part of gross income. Em-

Fair Market Value (FMV)

FMV is the price that a buyer is willing to pay, and a seller is willing to accept. FMV assumes that neither buyer nor seller is required to buy or sell. FMV also assumes that both buyer and seller have reasonable knowledge of all necessary facts. Finally, in the absence of an actual sale or exchange, FMV can be determined by expert appraisal and supporting other evidence.

ployees do not have to pay social security, Medicare, or railroad retirement taxes on these tips.

Employees who receive $20.00 or more in any one month in tips while working for any one employer, must report them to their employer. Employees can use Form 4070, Employee's Report of Tips to Employer. Employees who do not use Form 4070 must supply the same data in their tip report that this form requests. The due date of each tip report is the 10th of the month following the month in which an employee receives the tips. If the 10th of the month falls on a Saturday, Sunday, or holiday, the report is due on the next business day. Note, an employer may require more frequent reporting.

Employees who do not report tips when required may receive a penalty. Also, these employees will have to fill-in Form 4137, Social Security and Medicare Tax on Unreported Tip Income, include it with their Form 1040, and pay the taxes. The penalty for not reporting these tips is 50% of the social security or railroad retirement tax and Medicare tax. This penalty is an additional amount these employees must pay the government. The IRS will not assess the penalty if the reporting failure is due to a reasonable cause. Willful neglect is not a reasonable cause.

To help employees with their record keeping, the IRS makes available Form 4070-A, Employee's Daily Record of Tips. While employees do not have to use this form, they must keep some form of daily tip record or other reliable evidence of their tip income. This other evidence can be copies of restaurant bills, credit card charge slips, or some other tip add on arrangement. Employees also should keep a copy of the tip reports given to their employer.

Sometimes, a business asks customers who use their dining or banquet rooms to pay a service fee instead of tipping. Later, the business apportions and pays this fee to employees. Employees receiving a share of this fee do not include it on their Form 4070 tip reports. When they receive their annual Form W-2, Wage and Tax Statement, they will find it is part of their total wage income.

For income tax reporting purposes, the IRS says that tips reported to an employer are part of gross income on the day an employee turns in a tip report. Thus, tips an employee receives in December 1992 and reports to an employer in January 1993, are part of the employee's 1993 gross income. After the 1992 calendar year ends, employers include the tips on reports received in 1992 on each receiving employee's Form W-2 as wages. When an employee fails to turn in a tip report, or does not turn in one because his or her tips are less than $20.00 in one month, the IRS says such tips are part of gross income when the employee receives them.

To be sure employees properly report tips, employers must keep verifiable sales and tip records. Restaurants and cocktail lounges employing more than ten persons on a typical business day must file annual information returns with the IRS on their gross sales and employee tip income. When total tip income reported by all tipped employees is less than 8% of total sales (or an approved lower level), employers must assign tips to some employees. Employees receiving this assignment are those who report tips of less than 8% (or the approved lower level). When determining total sales, employers exclude carry out sales, state and local taxes, and sales with a service fee of 10% or more. When customers of a business tip less than 8%, an employer should petition the IRS District Director to approve a lower base assignment. However, in no event may the District Director approve an assignment base that is below 2%. Also, no income, social security, or Medicare taxes have been withheld from employees receiving an assignment of tip income. Thus, these employees must fill-in a Form 4137, attach it their Form 1040, and pay related taxes.

Taxpayers report all compensation (including wages, salaries, tips, bonuses, and commissions) on page 1 of Form 1040EZ, Form 1040A, and Form 1040. However, taxpayers using Form 1040EZ or Form 1040A must be certain taxable income is less than $50,000.

Dividend Income

Corporations distribute cash, property, stock, rights to acquire stock, services, and other accommodations to shareholders. Annually, they report them to shareholders on information return Form 1099-DIV, Dividends and Distributions. Chapter 13 discusses information returns.

Ordinary Dividends. Distributions from a corporation's earnings and profits are ordinary dividends. Receiving shareholders include them in gross income. When a corporation makes an ordinary non-cash property distribution, receiving shareholders increase gross income by the property's distribution date market value. Unless a corporation identifies a distribution for special tax treatment, it is an ordinary dividend.

Nominee Dividends. Sometimes taxpayers receive ordinary dividends as nominees for other taxpayers. Thus, parents can receive dividends for their children. If the paying corporation shows the nominee's taxpayer identification number **(TIN)** on information return Form 1099-DIV, the nominee must usually prepare a Form 1099-DIV. He or she sends the original to the IRS, retains a copy, and sends one to the shareholder.

Dividend Reinvestment Plans (DRIPs). Some corporations offer shareholders dividend reinvestment plans. A trustee usually purchases additional stock in the paying corporation for participating shareholders. Thus, they never receive the dividends. However, they must include them in gross income as ordinary dividends.

Return of Capital Distributions. Sometimes, corporations with no earnings and profits distribute cash or property to shareholders. These distributions are a return-of-capital. Shareholders reduce the stock's basis until it reaches zero. Then, the law taxes the excess distributions as capital gains. The gains get long-term or short-term treatment depending on the shareholder's stock holding period.

Distributions of Mutual Funds. Mutual funds make five types of distributions: (1) ordinary dividends, (2) return of capital distributions, (3) capital gain distributions, (4) exempt interest dividends, and (5) foreign investment dividends. The above discussion covered ordinary dividends and return of capital distributions.

A **capital gain distribution** is a distribution of net long-term capital gains from an investment company. The distributing company reports them to shareholders on information return Form 1099-DIV. Receivers treat them as long-term capital gains. Some mutual funds keep long-term capital gains and pay an undistributed capital gains tax. Then, they pass the tax on to shareholders who claim it as a credit on Form 1040 (line 59). The shareholders increase their basis in the mutual fund shares. Mutual funds report them to shareholders on Form 2439, Notice to Shareholder of Undistributed Long-Term Capital Gains. Shareholders attach this form to their tax return.

EXAMPLE 1 ─────────────────────────────

Assume a mutual fund has undistributed capital gains in 1992 of $2 per share. Also assume it pays a capital gains tax of $0.56 per share. A taxpayer owning 100 shares of the fund reports a capital gain distribution of $200 (100 x $2). Then, the taxpayer claims a $56 capital gains tax (100 x $0.56) credit on Form 1040 (line 59). The basis of the shareholder's stock goes up by $144 ($200 − $56). This is the difference between the taxpayer's share of the undistributed capital gain and the tax credit.

An **exempt interest dividend** from a mutual fund is a tax-free distribution. To be tax-free, the fund must hold 50% or more of its investments in tax-exempt municipal bonds at the close of each quarter of its year. Also, it must pay out 90% or more of this interest to shareholders annually.

Some mutual funds pay **foreign investment dividends**. Annually, these funds tell shareholders their share of the foreign taxes. The shareholders deduct the taxes as itemized deductions or claim a foreign tax credit on Form 1116, Foreign Tax Credit (Individual Fiduciary, or Nonresident Alien Individual). Chapter 13 discusses the foreign tax credit.

Reporting Dividend Income. Taxpayers cannot use Form 1040EZ to report corporate dividends. However, they can report exempt bond interest from a mutual fund on Form 1040EZ with identifying letters **TEI** (tax-exempt interest). Taxpayers enter TEI and the exempt interest amount after the words "Form 1040EZ" (line 2).

Taxpayers can use Form 1040A to report ordinary dividends, nominee dividends, and tax-exempt mutual fund bond interest. They cannot use it to report capital gain and return of capital distributions. Taxpayers who receive these distributions must use Form 1040.

Form 1040A, Filled-In Schedule 1, Part II

Illustration 3-3

This illustration shows how Jackie Anderson uses Schedule 1 (Form 1040A), Part II to report the ordinary dividends she receives. Jackie receives the dividends from the Kabetogama Publishing Company and Namakan Corporation as a nominee for her 10-year-old son. Jackie owns the stock of the Alexandria Bay Weaving Company and Eva Lake Moving Company. Thus, these dividends belong to her.

Form 1040, Filled-In Schedule B, Part II

Illustration 3-4

This illustration shows how Clyde Dowling uses Schedule B, Part II, of Form 1040 to report ordinary dividends, a capital gain distribution, and a return of capital distribution. Clyde receives ordinary dividends from Kabetogama and Namakan as a nominee for his 8-year-old daughter. He owns the stock in the other corporations. The dividends from Alexandria Bay and Eva Lake are ordinary dividends. Of the $200 from the Mainville Distributing Company, $50 is a return of capital. The remainder is an ordinary dividend. The distribution from the Melema Mutual Fund is a capital gain distribution.

Illustration 3-3
Filled-In Schedule 1, Part II, Form 1040A

Part II

Dividend income

(See pages 24 and 55.)

Complete this part and attach Schedule 1 to Form 1040A if you had over $400 in dividends.

If you received, as a nominee, dividends that actually belong to another person, see page 55.

Note: *If you received a Form 1099–DIV, or substitute statement, from a brokerage firm, enter the firm's name and the total dividends shown on that form.*

5	List name of payer	Amount	
5			
	Kabetogama Publishing Company	210	00
	Namakan Corporation	75	00
	Nominee Distribution	285	00
	Alexandria Bay Weaving Company	30	00
	Eva Lake Moving Company	40	00
	Total	355	00
	Less: Nominee Distribution	285	00

6 Add the amounts on line 5. Enter the total here and on Form 1040A, line 9.   6 | 70 | 00

Illustration 3-4
Filled-In Schedule B, Part II, Form 1040

Part II
Dividend
Income

(See pages 15 and B-1.)

Note: If you received a Form 1099-DIV or substitute statement from a brokerage firm, list the firm's name as the payer and enter the total dividends shown on that form.

If you had over $400 in gross dividends and/or other distributions on stock, you must complete this part and Part III. If you received, as a nominee, dividends that actually belong to another person, see page B-1.

Dividend Income		Amount
5 List name of payer—include on this line capital gain distributions, nontaxable distributions, etc. ▶	5	
Kabetogama Publishing Company		420 00
Namakan Corporation		150 00
Nominee Distribution		570 00
Alexandria Bay Weaving Company		60 00
Eva Lake Moving Corporation		80 00
Mainville Distributing Company		200 00
Melema Mutual Fund		90 00
Total		1,000 00
Less: Nominee Distribution		570 00
6 Add the amounts on line 5	6	430 00
7 Capital gain distributions. Enter here and on Schedule D*. [7 90 00]		
8 Nontaxable distributions. (See the inst. for Form 1040, line 9.) [8 50 00]		
9 Add lines 7 and 8	9	140 00
10 Subtract line 9 from line 6. Enter the result here and on Form 1040, line 9 . ▶	10	290 00

If you received capital gain distributions but do not need Schedule D to report any other gains or losses, see the instructions for Form 1040, lines 13 and 14.

Farm Income or Loss

Net income (or loss) from farming is reported on Form 1040 (line 19). Special rules govern farming businesses since income and expense recognition is unique to growing crops, raising animals, and maintaining land and other resources. Chapter 8 discusses farm income (or loss).

Foreign Accounts and Foreign Trusts

Most taxpayers who file Schedule B (Form 1040) must answer both questions in Part III. Answers to the questions provide the IRS with information about foreign financial accounts and trusts. A foreign financial account includes a bank account, securities account, and any other foreign financial account. Taxpayers who earn $400 or less in interest or dividends, have no interest in a foreign financial account, and are not the grantor of or transferor to a foreign trust are exempt from answering.

The first question determines if a taxpayer had an interest in, or signature or other authority over, a financial account in a foreign country at any time during 1992. In addition to a direct interest, the question applies to taxpayers who own more than 50 percent of a corporation's stock that owns one or more foreign bank accounts. The Form 1040 instruction booklet contains a few situations where an interest exists, but the taxpayer can answer "No."

A taxpayer answering "Yes" to the first question must enter the name of the proper foreign country. This taxpayer must also file Form TD F 90-22.1, Report of Foreign Bank and Financial Accounts, directly with the Treasury Department before July 1, 1992. This form should not be filed with the IRS. A taxpayer can get a copy of Form TD F 90-22.1 from the IRS Forms Distribution Center that serves his or her state.

The second question determines if a taxpayer was the grantor of, or transferor to, a foreign trust that was in existence during 1992. Taxpayers must answer this question whether or not they have a beneficial interest in the trust. A taxpayer answering "Yes" to this question may have to file Form 926, Form 3520, or Form 3520-A. **Form 926** is for U.S. taxpayers transferring property to a foreign corporation, estate, trust, or partnership. **Form 3520** is an information return for the creation of or transfers to a foreign trust. **Form 3520-A** is the annual information return of a foreign trust with U.S. beneficiaries. Taxpayers answering "Yes" may wish to contact the IRS to determine if one of the mentioned forms must be filed.

Gains and Losses: Capital Asset Transactions

Taxpayers report the sale or exchange of property on their tax return. The amount and type of gain or loss depends on the property's basis, type, period held, and amount realized. Gains from the sale or exchange of personal-use property usually are part of gross income in the transaction year. However, losses from such transactions are not deductible.

When a taxpayer sells or exchanges property, sometimes the resulting gain or loss is **ordinary** instead of **capital**. If the property is a capital asset that is held one year or less, the resulting gain or loss is **short-term**. If the property is held more than one year, the resulting gain or loss is usually **long-term**. Taxpayers include all recognized gains in gross income. Recognized losses from the sale or exchange of business use or investment property are deductible from gross income to arrive at AGI. Losses from the sale or exchange of personal use property are not deductible. Brokers report the sale of stocks, bonds, and other securities to taxpayers on information return Form 1099-B, Proceeds From Broker and Barter Exchange Transactions. Brokers can also report them on a substitute statement. Receiving taxpayers should reconcile the Form 1099-B amounts with tax return amounts.

Special rules apply to the sale or exchange of a principal residence (a personal-use capital asset). In general, gain on the sale or exchange of a principal residence is taxable. Loss from such a transaction is not deductible. Under some circumstances, taxpayers can postpone the gain recognition. Under other circumstances, gain on the sale or exchange of a principal residence is completely tax-free. Chapter 10 discusses the tax rules which govern the sale or exchange of a principal residence.

Taxpayers report a capital gain or loss on Form 1040 (line 13). For more than one capital asset transaction, taxpayers support the gain or loss amount with a schedule. Chapter 11 discusses the reporting process for capital gains and losses.

Gains and Losses: Other Transactions

Taxpayers report gains and losses from the sale, exchange, and involuntary conversion of business use assets on Form 4797, Sale of Business Property. They report a summary amount from these transactions on Form 1040 (line 15). Chapter 11 discusses the reporting details for Form 4797.

Interest Income

Gross income includes interest on bank deposits, notes, mortgages (including seller-financed mortgages), corporate bonds, and debts of the United States. Interest on an income tax refund is part of gross income. Unless an exception applies, taxpayers include all interest in gross income in the year they receive it or have a right to receive it (constructive receipt).

Some organizations pay interest and call it something else. Its name makes no difference. It is still payment for the use of money (interest), and is part of gross income. For some credit instruments, interest income is imputed.

Dividends That Are Actually Interest. Taxpayers include some dividend distributions in gross income as interest. These distributions include deposit and share account dividends in cooperative banks, credit unions, domestic building and loan associations, savings and loan associations, and mutual savings banks. Taxpayers report, but do not include in gross income, distributions of exempt interest (tax-free) from a mutual fund. However, taxpayers report dividends they receive on money market funds as dividends.

Savings Accounts and Certificates. Gross income includes interest from banks, savings bonds, and seller-financed mortgages. Interest on a passbook savings account is part of gross income in the year the financial institution credits it to a depositor's account (constructive receipt). This statement is true even if time passes before a depositor presents his or her passbook to the institution for the income entry. An exception exists for frozen financial institution deposits. Here, interest which cannot be withdrawn because of a financial institution's bankruptcy or insolvency is omitted from gross income. The exception also applies when a state limits withdrawals because other banks in the state are bankrupt or insolvent.

Gross income includes interest on deposit certificates. If the interest is deferred for more than one year, it is treated as original issue discount (OID). Taxpayers usually include a ratable portion of the discount in gross income each month.

Merchandise Premiums. Some banks, savings and loan associations, and credit unions offer customers merchandise to make a deposit. Such merchandise is prepaid interest and is taxable at the property's FMV when the taxpayer receives it.

Interest on Insurance Dividends. Interest on insurance dividends left as a demand deposit with an insurance carrier is part of gross income when the company adds it to the taxpayer's account. If the interest can only be withdrawn on the policy's anniversary date, it is part of gross income in the year this date falls. However, interest on National Service Life Insurance dividends left on deposit with the Veterans Administration is not part of gross income. Also, dividends on unmatured mutual life insurance are a return of a policy's premiums (rebate) and are not part of gross income.

U.S. Savings Bonds. Usually, taxpayers report interest on discounted United States Savings Bonds at the time of redemption. These bonds are Series E and EE. An exemption for educational purposes exists for the interest on certain Series EE bonds. Chapter 4 discusses the exemption and its phase-down. For Series E and EE bonds that don't qualify for the exemption, taxpayers can elect to report the increase in redemption value each year. When a taxpayer elects this reporting, he or she reports the redemption value increase to date in the election year. Then, the taxpayer reports annual redemption value increases each year. The election applies to all Series E or EE bonds the taxpayer owns at the time of election, and all he or she acquires later. An automatic reversal procedure exists.

Taxpayers who want to reverse a U.S. Savings Bond election can file Form 3115, Application for Change in Accounting Method, with

their tax return. At the top of the form they enter: Filed Under Rev. Proc. 89-46. For automatic approval, taxpayers attach a reporting statement. The statement says the taxpayer will report at the time of disposal, redemption, or final maturity (whichever occurs first) all interest on Series E or EE bonds he or she acquires in the change year. It also says the taxpayer will report all interest on such bonds he or she already owns or acquires in later years. Of course, the government only taxes the interest once.

Series E bonds issued before December 1965 mature 40 years after the issue date. Series E bonds issued after November 1965, and Series EE bonds, mature 30 years after the issue date. Once a bond reaches final maturity, it no longer pays interest. Under certain conditions, taxpayers can exchange Series E and EE bonds for Series HH bonds for up to one year after a final maturity date. Then, the interest on the Series E and EE bonds is deferred until the taxpayer cashes the Series HH bonds. Series HH bonds are current income bonds which the Treasury issues at par. Semiannually, the Treasury mails interest checks to Series HH bondholders which they include in gross income in the year of receipt.

Series HH bonds cannot be purchased. They can only be acquired by exchanging Series E and EE bonds, and U.S. Savings notes, with a combined redemption value of $500 or more. The exchange can be made through a Federal Reserve Bank or the Bureau of Public Debt. Taxpayers should make the exchange near the final maturity date to avoid lost interest. Most banks will help by providing exchange Form PD F 3253 and sending it with the bonds to the district Federal Reserve Bank for redemption.

There are two ways to acquire Series EE U.S. Savings Bonds: payroll deduction plan and an order placed through a participating financial institution. Taxpayers acquiring Series EE bonds through a payroll savings plan complete card Form SBD-2003, Authorization for Purchase and Request for Change, United States Series EE Savings Bonds. Those placing an order through a financial institution complete Form PD F 5263, Order for Series EE U.S. Savings Bonds.

U.S. Treasury Bills, Notes, and Bonds. Treasury bills are issued at a discount. The difference between issue price and face value at maturity is interest. Taxpayers include this interest in gross income when they receive it at maturity. Treasury notes and bonds are bought in coupon or registered form and usually pay interest every six months. The interest is taxable when a taxpayer receives it or has the right to receive it. However, the interest on U.S. Treasury bills, notes, and bonds is exempt from all state and local income taxes.

Accrued Interest Purchased. When a taxpayer acquires a bond between interest dates, the interest up to the purchase date belongs to the seller. The buyer adds it to the bond's purchase price. Then, the buyer deducts it from the first interest payment he or she receives. The buyer includes the remaining interest in gross income.

Appreciation of Growth-Type Certificates. Interest on appreciation of growth-type savings certificates is taxable. It is taxable in the year the owner has the right to receive the added value. Taxpayers include this interest in gross income though they don't receive it until the certificate's redemption date.

Original Issue Discount for Publicly-Traded Debt Instruments. Usually, interest on debt instruments is part of gross income. When a corporation issues debt instruments at a discount (issues them for less than the stated maturity value), taxpayers must determine the original issue discount (OID). **Original issue discount** is the difference between a debt instrument's **face value** (maturity or principal value) and issue price.

EXAMPLE 2 ——————————————

Assume that a corporation issues a 20-year, zero-coupon bond with a face value of $100,000 for $12,861. Here, the OID is $87,139 ($100,000 – $12,861).

For some situations, OID amount is treated as a zero amount. The zero treatment applies when the discount is **de minimis** (a small amount). It is de minimis when the discount is less than ¼ of 1% of the maturity redemption price times the number of complete years to maturity.

EXAMPLE 3 ——————————————

Assume that a corporation issues a 10-year, zero-coupon bond with a $100,000 face value for $98,000. While the real OID is $2,000, it is treated as being zero. Here, there is no discount to amortize. Use of the de minimis discount formula shows the discount is less than $2,500 [(.0025 x $100,000 face value of bond) x 10 full years to maturity].

Taxpayers usually amortize OID over a debt obligation's life by including a portion in gross income each year. For publicly-traded OID debt issued after July 1, 1982, taxpayers determine their interest income by applying a constant interest rate over the debt's life. The rate is the yield to maturity.

First, taxpayers amortizing OID determine a yield-to-maturity amount for the interest period using the compound interest method. To make this computation, they apply the yield-to-maturity rate to the instrument's amortized debt basis. At issue date, the instrument's amortized debt basis equals its cost. This calculation produces the interest income amount that taxpayers add to the amortized debt basis. At maturity the amortized debt basis equals its maturity value. While the coupon portion of the yield amount is part of interest income, it is not added to the amortized debt basis. For long-term zero-coupon debt, Treasury Regulations say that the proper compounding period is six months.

EXAMPLE 4 ——————————————

A 30-year, zero-coupon bond with a face value of $1,000,000 and a yield-to-maturity of 15.25% is issued to a calendar-year taxpayer on October 1, 1992, for $12,170. The original issue discount is $987,830 ($1,000,000 – $12,170). The interest for the first six-month period is $927.96 ([15.25% x $12,170] ÷ 2). The interest for the second six-month period is $998.72 ([15.25% x ($12,170 + $927.96)] ÷ 2). The interest for the third six-month period is $1,074.87 ([15.25% x ($12,170 + $927.96 + $998.72)] ÷ 2).

The interest for 1992 is $463.98. It is half of the $927.96 interest for the period October 1, 1992 through March 31, 1993. The interest for 1993 is $2,000.14. It consists of $463.98 for January 1 through March 31, 1993 (50% x $927.96), $998.72 for April 1 through September 31, 1993, and $537.44 for October 1 through December 31, 1993

(50% x $1,074.87). At the bond's maturity, the taxpayer's total interest for the 30 years is $987,830. The taxpayer amortizes the OID at a compound annual yield of 15.25%.

For original discount debts issued before July 1, 1982, different rules apply in determining the discount amount. Debt instruments that are not subject to the OID rules include short-term government debts, tax-exempt debts, bonds issued by individuals before March 2, 1984, loans of less than $10,000 between individuals, U.S. savings bonds, and several uncommon debts.

Issuers of debt instruments send the IRS and debt owner a copy of information return Form 1099-OID, Statement for Recipients of Original Issue Discount. This information reporting requirement applies when the calendar year OID is $10 or more and the debt instrument's term is more than one year. For original purchasers of OID debt instruments, Form 1099-OID shows the interest amount they include in gross income.

Stripping Interest Coupons from Bonds. Coupon-stripping is the process of separating bond interest coupons from the bonds. Special stripping rules apply to bond purchases after July 1, 1982. These rules prevent artificial losses from the sale of rights to receive future income.

When a stripped bond or detached interest coupon is sold or redeemed, the owner assigns the bond's basis between the sold or redeemed and retained parts. The owner uses the relative FMV of each to make the assignment. This process applies to taxable, as well as tax-exempt, corporate, noncorporate, and government obligations. For the taxable obligations, the seller and purchaser include a portion of any discount in income each year using the OID rules above.

Bond Premium on Taxable Bonds. Taxpayers can elect to offset interest income by a ratable portion of a taxable bond's premium. The amortization election applies to all bonds a taxpayer owns, not a specific issue. For bond purchases before October 23, 1986, taxpayers deduct the monthly premium amortization as a **miscellaneous itemized deduction**. Chapter 6 discusses miscellaneous itemized deductions. For bond purchases after October 22, 1986, and before January 1, 1988, taxpayers deduct the amortization as **investment interest**. Chapter 5 discusses

---

Imputed Interest Situations

1. Deferred payment sales where payments are due more than one year after the sale date and there is unstated interest
2. Excess payments to corporate executives when corporate control changes (golden parachute payments)
3. Rent agreements for tangible property where at least one use payment for a calendar year is paid after the close of the next calendar year (deferred payments). Imputed interest also applies to increasing rent agreements for tangible property (stepped rents).
4. Private placement of debt instruments
5. Loans with below-market interest rates:
   a. Gift loans (parents to children)
   b. Loans between a corporation and a shareholder
   c. Compensation-related loans between an employer and employee
   d. Tax-avoidance loans

---

investment interest expense. For bond purchases after December 31, 1987, the amortization is an **offset to bond interest income**. Taxpayers decrease the basis of the bonds by the amount of premium amortization.

Imputed Interest. When a loan is made without an interest rate, or the stated rate is low, interest may be imputed. The rates for imputing interest are called **AFRs** (applicable federal rates). AFRs are based on the interest rates the federal government pays on new borrowings. These rates apply to a variety of debt instruments.

Each month the IRS publishes AFR rates for short-term, mid-term, and long-term securities. They include monthly, quarterly, semiannual, and annual compounding rates. Taxpayers use the short-term rates for demand loans and loans maturing in 3 years or less. They use the mid-term rates for debt with a 3- to 9-year maturity, and long-term rates for debt maturing in more than 9 years. In addition, the IRS publishes Adjusted AFRs for determining the amount of exempt interest on tax-exempt original issue discount obligations. It also publishes Adjusted Federal Long-Term Rates and Applicable Credit Percentages for Low-Income Housing.

Loans to family members (gift loans) fall under the imputed interest rules. If an exception does not apply, interest on a gift loan must be imputed. In addition, the person making the loan is treated as gifting funds to the borrower each year equal to the imputed interest amount. Here, the lender may have to file a gift tax return. Then, the lender includes the interest income from the loan in his or her gross income.

EXAMPLE 5 ————————————————

John and Rita O'Neil-Grady are a young couple with two children. They have been saving money for some time for a down payment on a house. However, it seems every time they get enough money, a financial emergency occurs. Usually, it's a medical problem with one of the children. Rita's parents remember how hard it was for them to scrape together funds for a down payment. They offer to lend John and Rita $10,000 without interest, provided John and Rita sign a note due in 10 years for the funds. John and Rita agree to these terms and sign the note. If John and Rita use the loan proceeds for a house down payment, and not to buy income producing property, no interest will be imputed.

EXAMPLE 6 ————————————————

Marilyn and Bob Lawler are a young couple who have been saving money for a down payment on a house. Bob's parents offer to lend them $10,000 on an interest-free loan so they can invest the funds and earn more money for a down payment. If Marilyn and Bob buy income producing property with the loan proceeds, interest might be imputed. It will depend on their total net investment income. If their net investment income for the year is $1,000 or less, no interest will be imputed. If it exceeds $1,000, interest will be imputed. However, the imputed interest cannot exceed their net investment income.

For compensated related loans and corporation-shareholder loans, a $10,000 imputed interest exception applies. If one of these loans is for tax avoidance purposes, the exception does not apply to that loan, and interest is imputed.

Reporting Interest Income. Taxpayers can use Form 1040EZ, Form 1040A, and Form 1040 to report taxable and tax-exempt interest income. Chapter 4 discusses tax-exempt interest income. A maximum taxable interest income limitation exists for Form 1040EZ filers.

Form 1040EZ filers report taxable interest income of $400 or less on page 1 in the boxes at the right of the taxable interest income line. For tax-exempt interest income, they enter it in the descriptive part of this line with the letters "TEI." However, taxpayers who exclude Educational Savings Bond interest from gross income cannot use Form 1040EZ. Chapter 4 discusses the Educational Savings Bond Program. Sometimes, taxpayers withdraw funds early on a fixed maturity instrument (certificate of deposit) and receive a penalty. Taxpayers who wish to deduct the penalty use Form 1040 (line 28). They cannot use Form 1040EZ or Form 1040A to deduct the penalty. Finally, taxpayers with $50,000 or more of taxable income cannot use Form 1040EZ.

With a few exceptions, taxpayers can use Form 1040A to report all taxable interest income. One exception concerns taxable income. Here, taxpayers with $50,000 or more of taxable income cannot use Form 1040A. Form 1040A users with taxable interest income of less than $400 report tax-exempt interest on page 1 on the interest income line. However, they do not add it to the other interest income.

Taxpayers cannot use Form 1040A to report OID when it is over or under the amount shown on a Form 1099-OID. Also, they cannot use Form 1040A to report accrued interest on security transfers between interest dates. Finally, taxpayers who purchase taxable bonds after 1987 and choose to offset interest income by amortizing a bond premium cannot use Form 1040A.

Form 1040A filers with taxable interest income of more than $400 complete Schedule 1, Part I. Illustration 3-5 shows a filled-in Schedule 1, Part I, for a Form 1040A filer. These filers separately list the interest amounts from each payer on Schedule 1. The listing should include all tax-exempt interest listed on Form 1099-INT, U.S. Information Return for Recipients of Interest Income, interest received as a nominee, and Educational Savings Bond interest excluded from gross income.

After listing all interest, Form 1040A filers add the amounts together and enter it near the bottom of the interest income section. They enter separate subtotals for tax-exempt and nominee interest above the total line for all interest. Note, Form 1040A does not have special lines for the total and subtotals. Next to the subtotal for tax-exempt interest, receiving taxpayers write "Tax-Exempt Interest." Next to the subtotal for nominee interest, they write "Nominee Distribution."

After entering the subtotals and subtracting them from total interest income, taxpayers enter the difference (line 2). They enter excludable Educational Savings Bond interest from Form 8815, Exclusion of Interest From Series EE U.S. Savings Bonds Issued After 1989 (line 3). After subtracting the excludable interest (line 3), they enter the difference (line 4) and transfer the amount to the taxable interest income line on Form 1040A (line 8a).

Taxpayers use Form 1040 to report all kinds of interest income. When taxable interest income is $400 or less, there is no need to prepare a separate listing. Unless a specific exemption applies, all interest income is part of gross income. Taxpayers with more than $400 of taxable interest income list each item separately on Schedule B, Part I. Illustration 3-6 shows a filled-in Schedule B (Form 1040), Part I. While the listing includes all interest income, some of it may not be taxable. This income includes: (1) interest a taxpayer receives as a nominee, (2) accrued interest a taxpayer receives or pays on the transfer of securities between interest dates, (3) tax-exempt interest, and (4) OID when it is less than the amount shown on Form 1099-OID. After the last interest income listing, taxpayers enter a total for all items. Above this total, they enter and label subtotals for the nontaxable items as follows:

Amount	Identification
1 Paid to those for whom nominee distributions were made	1 Nominee distributions
2 Paid for accrued interest purchased	2 Accrued interest
3 Paid as tax-exempt interest	3 Tax-exempt
4 Received for OID that was less than the amount shown on Form 1099-OID	4 OID adjustment

After entering and labeling the subtotals, taxpayers subtract them from the total of all interest income and enter the difference (line 2). Like Form 1040A, Form 1040 does not have special lines for the total and subtotals.

On Schedule B (line 3), taxpayers enter excludable Educational Savings Bond interest

Imputed Interest Gift Loan Exceptions and Limitations

1. No interest imputed on loans of $10,000 or less between individuals, unless loan proceeds used to purchase income-producing property
2. No imputed interest on loans of $100,000 or less between individuals if the borrower's net investment income for the year does not exceed $1,000
3. Imputed interest cannot exceed borrower's net investment income for the year on loans of $100,000 or less between individuals
4. Limitations on imputed interest for gift loans do not apply if the loan's principal purpose is tax avoidance

from Form 8815, Exclusion of Interest From Series EE U.S. Savings Bonds Issued After 1989. They subtract it from the total interest income (line 2) and enter the remainder (line 4) and transfer the amount to Form 1040 (line 8a).

Taxpayers enter their tax-exempt interest income on Form 1040, page 1 (line 8b). A married person who files a separate return, and properly claims an exemption for his or her spouse, does not have to report the spouse's tax-exempt interest income. If the spouse feels uneasy about not reporting this income, he or she can report it with the label "spouse's tax-exempt interest income." However, a married couple filing a joint return must report all tax-exempt interest income they receive.

Form 1040A, Filled-In Schedule 1, Part I

Illustration 3-5

This illustration shows how Rachel Q. Baker uses Schedule 1, Part I, of Form 1040A to report the interest income she receives. Rachel receives the interest from the Agnes Lake Distributing Company and Buckeye Lake Brewing Company as a nominee for her 7-year-old daughter. The remaining interest that Rachel lists on Schedule 1 belongs to her. Rachel's SSN is 727-69-3205.

Illustration 3-5
Filled-In Schedule 1, Form 1040A, Part I

Schedule 1 Department of the Treasury—Internal Revenue Service
(Form 1040A) **Interest and Dividend Income**
for Form 1040A Filers   **1992**

OMB No. 1545-0085

Name(s) shown on Form 1040A

Rachael Q. Baker

Your social security number
727 : 69 : 3205

Part I

Interest income

(See pages 24 and 54.)

Complete this part and attach Schedule 1 to Form 1040A if:

● You had over $400 in taxable interest, or

● You are claiming the exclusion of interest from series EE U.S. savings bonds issued after 1989.

If you received, as a nominee, interest that actually belongs to another person, see page 54.

Note: *If you received a Form 1099–INT, Form 1099–OID, or substitute statement, from a brokerage firm, enter the firm's name and the total interest shown on that form.*

1 List name of payer—if any interest is from seller-financed mortgages, see page 54	Amount	
1		
Agnes Lake Distributing Company	700	00
Buckeye Lake Brewing Company	250	00
Nominee Distribution	950	00
Franklin Lake Winery, Inc.	175	00
Nym Lake Distilled Water Company	80	00
Second Federal National Bank	200	00
Total interest	1,405	00
Less: Nominee Distribution	950	00
2 Add the amounts on line 1. **2**	455	00
3 Excludable interest on series EE U.S. savings bonds issued after 1989 from Form 8815, line 14. You MUST attach Form 8815 to Form 1040A. **3**	–0–	
4 Subtract line 3 from line 2. Enter the result here and on Form 1040A, line 8a. **4**	455	00

Form 1040, Filled-In Schedule B, Parts I and III

Illustration 3-6

John R. and Jean K. Williams file Schedule B, Part I, to support the interest income item on Form 1040 (line 8a). Illustration 3-6 shows filled-in Schedule B. The total amount of interest income Mr. and Mrs. Williams receive in 1992 is:

Buckeye Savings and Loan	$ 351.81
First City Bank Certificate of Deposit	706.10
City of Milwaukee bond interest . .	60.00
Interest received on U.S. Treasury Bills	201.90
City Credit Union dividend	558.10
Gross interest	$1,877.91

Although the $60 of interest from the Milwaukee bond is tax-exempt, the City reports it as interest income on information return Form 1099-INT. On Schedule B, the Williams include the exempt interest with their other interest. Then, they subtract it from the total of all interest. The Williams list the tax-exempt interest on Form 1040 (line 8b). It is not part of total income (line 23). The taxable interest income they report in Schedule B, Part I (line 4) is $1,817.91 ($1,877.91 – $60). They carry it ($1,817.91) to Form 1040 (line 8a).

The total dividend income Mr. and Mrs. Williams receive in 1992 is:

Dividends received on common stock of Armco Corp. and reinvested through the company's dividend reinvestment plan		$ 49.75
Dividends received on common stock of United Corp.		35.00
Dividends received from BCA Mutual Fund:		
Capital gains	$152.00	
Ordinary dividend . . .	10.00	162.00
Gross dividends		$246.75

Since $246.75 is less than $400, the Williams do not complete Part II of Schedule B. The Williams report $94.75 ($246.75 – $152 capital gain distribution) as dividend income on Form 1040 (line 9). They report the $152 of capital gains on Schedule D (line 12).

The Williams have no foreign accounts or foreign trusts, and enter an "X" in the "No" boxes to answer the questions in Schedule B, Part III (lines 11a and 12). Chapter 12 discusses Schedule D.

for 1992, and the taxpayer has the higher taxable income.

3. Taxpayer is unmarried, treated as unmarried for tax purposes, or separated from child's other parent by a divorce or separate maintenance decree. Taxpayer must be the **custodial parent** (the parent with longest custody).

If the taxpayer (custodial parent) remarries and files a joint return, the election to report the child's income may be taken with the new spouse. However, if the taxpayer and new spouse (child's stepparent) file separate returns there is an election restriction. Here, the election may be taken only if the taxpayer's taxable income is higher than the new spouse's.

Making the Election. To make the election, a parent fills in Form 8814, Parent's Election To Report Child's Interest and Dividends, and attaches it to his or her Form 1040. For each child whose income he or she chooses to report, the parent completes a separate Form 8814.

Completing Form 8814 is a two-step process. In step 1, the parent determines the amount of the child's income that he or she will report. In step 2, the parent calculates the additional tax that is due to the government. Illustration 3-7 shows a filled-in Form 8814.

On Form 8814 (line 1a), the parent enters the child's taxable interest. If the child receives interest as a nominee, the parent enters this interest on the dotted line portion (line 1a). Next

Interest and Dividends of Children Under Age 14

Parents may choose to report their child's interest and dividend income on Form 1040 or Form 1040NR, but not on Form 1040EZ or Form 1040A. If parents choose this reporting, the child will not have to file a return.

Parent Qualifications. To qualify for this election, the taxpayer (parent) must file Form 1040 or 1040NR and meet one of the following requirements:

1. Taxpayer and child's other parent are married to each other and file a joint return for 1992.
2. Taxpayer and child's other parent are married to each other and file separate returns

To Report Kiddie's Interest and Dividends on Parent's Form 1040, Kiddie Must

1. Be under age 14
2. Have income only from interest and dividends
3. Have gross income for 1992 that is more than $500, but less than $5,000
4. Not have made estimated tax payments for 1992
5. Not have a 1991 tax return overpayment that is applied to his or her 1992 tax
6. Not have federal income tax withheld from income (including backup withholding)

Illustration 3-6
Filled-In Schedule B, Form 1040, Parts I and III

Schedules A&B (Form 1040) 1992   OMB No. 1545-0074   Page **2**

Name(s) shown on Form 1040. Do not enter name and social security number if shown on other side.   Your social security number

John R. and Jean K. Williams   272 : 11 : 8245

Schedule B—Interest and Dividend Income

Attachment Sequence No. **08**

Part I Interest Income

(See pages 14 and B-1.)

Note: If you received a Form 1099-INT, Form 1099-OID, or substitute statement from a brokerage firm, list the firm's name as the payer and enter the total interest shown on that form.

If you had over $400 in taxable interest income OR are claiming the exclusion of interest from series EE U.S. savings bonds issued after 1989, you must complete this part. List ALL interest you received. If you had over $400 in taxable interest income, you must also complete Part III. If you received, as a nominee, interest that actually belongs to another person, or you received or paid accrued interest on securities transferred between interest payment dates, see page B-1.

Interest Income	Amount	
1 List name of payer—if any interest income is from seller-financed mortgages, see page B-1 and list this interest first ▶		
Buckeye Savings and Loan	351	81
First City Bank	706	10
City of Milwaukee	60	00
U.S. Treasury	201	90
City Credit Union	558	10
Subtotal	1,877	91
Less: Tax-exempt interest	60	00
2 Add the amounts on line 1	**2** 1,817	91
3 Excludable interest on series EE U.S. savings bonds issued after 1989 from Form 8815, line 14. You MUST attach Form 8815 to Form 1040	**3**	
4 Subtract line 3 from line 2. Enter the result here and on Form 1040, line 8a. ▶	**4** 1,817	91

Part III Foreign Accounts and Foreign Trusts

(See page B-2.)

If you had over $400 of interest or dividends OR had a foreign account or were a grantor of, or a transferor to, a foreign trust, you must complete this part.

	Yes	No
11a At any time during 1992, did you have an interest in or a signature or other authority over a financial account in a foreign country, such as a bank account, securities account, or other financial account? See page B-2 for exceptions and filing requirements for Form TD F 90-22.1		X
b If "Yes," enter the name of the foreign country ▶		
12 Were you the grantor of, or transferor to, a foreign trust that existed during 1992, whether or not you have any beneficial interest in it? If "Yes," you may have to file Form 3520, 3520-A, or 926 .		X

For Paperwork Reduction Act Notice, see Form 1040 instructions.   Schedule B (Form 1040) 1992

to this amount the parent writes the letters "ND" for nominee distribution. If the child has tax-exempt interest, the parent enters it (line 1b).

The parent enters the child's dividends (line 2a). These dividends include capital gain and nontaxable distributions. However, if the parent has capital gains and losses, he or she reports the capital gain and nontaxable distributions with them. If the child receives dividends as a nominee, the taxpayer enters them on the dotted line portion (line 2a). Then, the parent enters the letters "ND" next to this amount.

Filled-In Form 8814

Illustration 3-7

Kenneth A. and Violet M. Wong file a joint return and decide to include their daughter's income on their tax return. During the year, Helen, age 12, receives $975 in interest income from a savings account and $200 in interest from municipal bonds. These items are Helen's only income. Kenneth's SSN is 324-51-9234, and Helen's is 344-72-0156. Illustration 3-7 shows the Wong's filled-in Form 8814. The amount the Wongs enter on Form 1040 (line 38e) and include in their tax liability (line 38) is $71.25. Note, the $200 municipal bond interest is tax-exempt.

IRA Distributions

Taxpayers can use Form 1040A or Form 1040 to report distributions (payments) from **IRAs** (Individual Retirements Arrangements). This reporting includes regular distributions, early distributions, rollovers, and any other money or property from an IRA. However, they cannot use Form 1040EZ for this reporting. Taxpayers who owe an additional tax for an early IRA distribution must use Form 1040. They can use Form 1040A when they don't owe additional taxes. When taxpayers roll over all the proceeds of one IRA to another IRA within a certain period, there are no additional taxes.

IRA rules provide a recovery formula for determining the nontaxable portion of an IRA

distribution. Taxpayers reporting nontaxable IRA distributions on Form 1040A enter the total distribution (line 10a). They also enter the taxable portion (line 10b).

When all IRA distributions are taxable, taxpayers enter the total (line 10b). Taxpayers also report rollovers from one IRA to another IRA (lines 10a and 10b), and rollovers from a qualified employer's pension plan to an IRA (lines 11a and 11b). The taxable income of taxpayers using Form 1040A to report IRA distributions must be less than $50,000.

On Form 1040, taxpayers report regular IRA distributions and IRA rollovers (lines 16a and 16b). If the IRA distributions are fully taxable, taxpayers enter them (line 16b). If only part of them are taxable, they enter the full distribution (line 16a) and the taxable part (line 16b). Taxpayers also report rollovers from a qualified employer's pension plan to an IRA (lines 17a and 17b).

Partnership, S Corporation, Estate, and Trust Income or Loss

Taxpayers with income or loss from a partnership, S corporation (Subchapter S), estate, or trust must file Form 1040. They report their share of the net profit or loss from these units on Form 1040 (line 18). A discussion of trust and estate returns is beyond the scope of this book.

Pensions and Annuities

Payments from pension and annuity plans usually consist of two elements: return of capital and income. Recipients of pension and annuity payments report them on Form 1040A (lines 11a and 11b) or on Form 1040 (lines 17a and 17b). Use of these forms also applies to payments from profit-sharing plans, employee retirement plans, employee savings plans, and salary reduction plans. Payment recipients cannot use Form 1040EZ.

Receivers of pensions and annuities usually get a series of regular cash payments for a definite time or their remaining life. The law does not tax the recovery of their after-tax annuity or pension investments. For pensions and annuities starting before 1987, recipients determine a recovery exclusion for their after-tax investments and use it for as long as they receive payments. For those starting after 1986, recipients

Illustration 3-7
Filled-In Form 8814

Form **8814** Department of the Treasury Internal Revenue Service	**Parent's Election To Report Child's Interest and Dividends** ▶ **See instructions below and on back.** ▶ **Attach to Parent's Form 1040 or Form 1040NR.**	OMB No. 1545-1128 **1991** Attachment Sequence No. **40**

General Instructions

Purpose of Form. Use this form if you are a parent and choose to report the income of your child on your return. If you do, the child will not have to file a return. You can file this form if your child meets **all** of the following conditions:

● Was under age 14 on January 1, 1992.

● Had income only from interest and dividends (including Alaska Permanent Fund dividends).

● Had gross income for 1991 that was more than $500 but less than $5,000.

● Had no estimated tax payments for 1991.

● Did not have any overpayment of tax shown on his or her 1990 return applied to the 1991 return.

● Had no Federal income tax withheld from his or her income (backup withholding).

The parent(s) must also qualify as explained on page 2 of these instructions.

Step 1 is used to figure the amount of the child's income to report on the parent's return. **Step 2** is used to figure an additional tax that must be added to the parent's tax.

How To Make the Election. To make the election, complete and attach Form 8814 to your tax return and file your return by the due date (including extensions). A separate Form 8814 must be filed for each child whose income you choose to report.

Caution: *The Federal income tax on your child's income may be less if you file a tax return for the child instead of making this election. This is because you cannot take certain deductions that your child would be entitled to on his or her own return. For details, see **Deductions You May Not Take** on page 2.*

(Instructions continue on back.)

Name(s) shown on parent's return Kenneth A. and Violet M. Wong	Your social security number 324 51 9234
Child's name (first, initial, and last) Helen I. Wong	Child's social security number 344 72 0156

Caution: If more than one Form 8814 is attached, check here . . . . ▶ ☐

Step 1	**Figure amount of child's interest and dividend income to report on your return**		
1a	Enter your child's **taxable** interest income. If this amount is different from the amounts shown on the child's Forms 1099-INT and 1099-OID, see the instructions	1a	975 00
b	Enter your child's **tax-exempt** interest income. **DO NOT** include this amount on line 1a. 1b 200 00		
2a	Enter your child's gross dividends (including any Alaska Permanent Fund dividends). If none, enter -0- on line 2c and go to line 3. If your child received any capital gain distributions or dividends as a nominee, see the instructions . . . 2a		
b	Enter your child's nontaxable distributions (from Form 1099-DIV, Box 1d) included on line 2a 2b		
c	Subtract line 2b from line 2a	2c	-0-
3	Add lines 1a and 2c. If the total is $1,000 or less, skip lines 4 and 5 and go to line 6. If the total is $5,000 or more, **do not** file this form. Your child **must** file his or her own return to report the income	3	975 00
4	Base amount	4	1,000 00
5	Subtract line 4 from line 3. (If filing more than one Form 8814 or if line 2a includes any capital gain distributions, see the instructions.) Also include this amount in the total on Form 1040, line 22, or Form 1040NR, line 22. In the space next to line 22, enter "Form 8814" and show the amount. Go on to line 6 below . . . . ▶	5	

Step 2	**Figure your tax on the first $1,000 of child's interest and dividend income**		
6	Amount not taxed	6	500 00
7	Subtract line 6 from line 3. If the result is zero or less, enter -0-	7	475 00
8	**Tax.** ● If the amount on line 7 is $500 or more, enter $75 here. (Also, see the **Note** below.) ● If the amount on line 7 is less than $500, multiply the amount on line 7 by 15% (.15) and enter the result here. (Also, see the **Note** below.)	8	71 25

Note: *Include the amount from line 8 in the tax you enter on Form 1040, line 38, or Form 1040NR, line 36. On Form 1040, also enter the amount from line 8 in the space provided next to line 38. On Form 1040NR, enter the amount from line 8 in the space provided next to line 36. (If filing more than one Form 8814, see the instructions.)*

For Paperwork Reduction Act Notice, see back of form.   Cat. No. 10750J   Form **8814** (1991)

use their recovery exclusion until they get their investment back. Then, all remaining payments are taxable. Annuitants consider several items when determining their recovery exclusion.

Nontaxable IRA Distribution Formula

     Total Nondeductible Contributions
÷ Total Value of IRA
     (including contributions & earnings)
x Distribution
     Nontaxable Distributions

EXAMPLE 7 ─────────────────────

Assume Sally Smith purchases a life annuity for $72,000, which is payable in annual installments of $8,000 beginning January 1, 1992. Sally's life expectancy at the annuity start date is 12 years. The calculations below show how Sally determines her recovery exclusion and taxable portion of each payment.

Investment in contract	$72,000
Expected return ($8,000 x 12 years)	$96,000
Percentage of income to be excluded ($72,000 ÷ $96,000)	75%
Amount received during year	$ 8,000
Recovery exclusion ($8,000 x 75%)	6,000
Taxable portion	$ 2,000

Sally's annuity income for 12 years is $2,000 a year. If she outlives her life expectancy, the $8,000 she receives each year after the 12th payment is gross income. If her regular annuity payments started before 1987, she could exclude $2,000 a year for her remaining life.

For pensions and annuities starting after 1986, a miscellaneous itemized deduction is available when a recipient dies before recovering his or her capital (investment). The estate's executor or executrix takes the deduction on the decedent's final income tax return. While it is a miscellaneous itemized deduction, it is not subject to the 2% of AGI limitation. Chapter 6 discusses miscellaneous itemized deductions.

Lump-sum payments under annuity, endowment, or life insurance contracts are not annuity payments. Recipients include them in gross income when they exceed their investment. A beneficiary of a life insurance policy treats the policy's face value as his or her investment. When a life insurance beneficiary chooses to receive the proceeds in installments, he or she treats each payment like an annuity.

Payments taxpayers receive under annuity contracts before the annuity start date are not annuity payments. The start date of an annuity is the later of two dates. One date is the day the annuity contract becomes fixed. The other is the first day of the first annuity period. The date an annuity contract becomes fixed is usually the day a recipient tells the contract payer how to pay the annuity. The first day of the first annuity period is usually one annuity period before the day an annuitant receives the first payment. For an annual annuity, it is usually the same numeric date in the prior year.

EXAMPLE 8 ─────────────────────

Arlene Wyler purchased an annuity five years ago. At that time she told her insurance company she wanted to receive a fixed amount for the remainder of her life. She also told the company to send her the first payment on July 17 of the year she becomes 65. On July 17 of the current year, Arlene became 65. On this date she received her first annuity check. The start

---

Pensions and Annuities Recovery Exclusion Items

1. **Exclusion ratio**. Numerator of exclusion ratio is after-tax investment in the contract. Denominator is expected return.
2. **Expected return**. For an annual annuity, multiply annual payment by expected return multiple.
3. **Expected return multiple**. For an annual annuity, expected return multiple is number of years annuity is expected to continue or recipient's expected life (whichever applies). Recipient determines expected life from IRS life tables using nearest age at annuity start date.
4. **Recovery exclusion**. Recipient multiplies annuity payment by exclusion ratio to determine recovery exclusion (tax-free capital recovery amount).

date of Arlene's annuity is July 17 of last year. Technically, the last day of the first period ends at midnight on July 16 of the current year. The instant after midnight on July 16 is the start date of the second annual annuity period.

Various tax rules apply to payments from annuity contracts before the start date. A discussion of these rules is beyond the scope of this book.

Rents and Royalties

Taxpayers who receive rent or royalty income usually report it on Form 1040 (line 18). However, when the rents or royalties are business income, taxpayers report it as business income or loss (line 12). Forms 1040EZ and 1040A cannot be used to report rent or royalty income. The gross income equals the gross rent or royalty taxpayers receive. Deductions for ordinary, necessary, and reasonable business expenses are allowable in calculating AGI. If allowable deductions exceed income, the loss within certain limits may be deductible from other income in calculating the taxpayer's AGI.

Social Security (and Tier 1 Railroad Retirement) Benefits

For some retirees, a portion of monthly social security and Tier 1 Railroad Retirement benefits is taxable. Tier 1 monthly benefits usually equal the amount a railroad retiree would receive if under social security. Here, pension personnel apply the benefit formula to a retiree's wage history after 1936 under both retirement systems. The law limits the amount subject to tax. Taxpayers using Form 1040A report gross and taxable social security (and Tier 1 Railroad Retirement) benefits on their return (lines 13a and 13b). Taxpayers using Form 1040 also report them on their return (lines 21a and 21b). Instructions to these forms contain similar worksheets for calculating taxable benefits.

Filled-In Social Security Benefits Worksheet

Taxable Social Security

Taxable social security (and Tier 1 Railroad Retirement) benefits equal lesser of (a) one-half benefits or (b) following formula results:

1. Increase AGI by the following:
   a. One-half social security (and Tier 1 Railroad Retirement) benefits for year
   b. Tax-exempt interest for year
   c. Educational exclusion for U.S. Savings Bonds, Series EE
   d. Exclusion for income of U.S. citizens or residents living abroad
   e. Exclusion for income from Guam, American Somoa, and Northern Mariana Islands
   f. Exclusion for income from Puerto Rico
2. Determine base exemption:
   a. $25,000—Single taxpayers, or married taxpayers filing separately who do not live with their spouse at any time during the year
   b. $32,000—Married taxpayers filing jointly
   c. $ -0- —Married taxpayers filing separately who live with their spouse at some time during the year
3. Decrease amount in Step 1 by base exemption from Step 2
4. Multiply remainder by 50 percent

Illustration 3-8

Nancy O. Calkins, a 66-year-old married taxpayer, files a joint return with her husband, Robert B. Calkins. Bob has no income. The Calkins have taxable income before social security benefits of $28,600, total of Form 1040 (lines 7 through 20, plus line 22). Nancy also reports $1,500 as tax-exempt interest on her Spring City bonds (line 8b). For the current year, Nancy receives $9,250 in social security benefits.

In calculating Nancy's taxable social security benefits, she enters her $9,250 of social security on the benefits worksheet (line 1). Then, she enters half this amount or $4,625 (line 2). She enters the Calkins' total income before social security benefits (line 3). It is $30,100 ($28,600 of taxable income + $1,500 of tax-exempt income). She then adds half of the social security benefits (line 2) and total income (line 3), and enters the $34,725 total (line 4). Since the Calkins have no deduction for AGI, Form 1040 (line 30), she enters the $34,725 on the worksheet (line 6). Then, she enters the $32,000 joint return social security base exemption (line 7). Nancy deducts the base exemption (line 7) from the $34,725 (line 6) and enters the difference of $2,725 (line 8). She divides this amount ($2,725) by 2 and enters the results, $1,362.50 (line 9).

Nancy enters the $9,250 (line 1) of the Form 1040 worksheet (line 21a). By this entry she shows her total social security benefits on page 1 of Form 1040. Then, she enters on Form 1040 (line 21b) the smaller of the worksheet amounts [$4,625 (line 2) or $1,362.50 (line 9)]. Her taxable social security is $1,362.50.

Illustration 3-8
Filled-In Social Security Benefits Worksheet

Social Security Benefits Worksheet—Lines 21a and 21b (keep for your records)

If you are married filing separately and you did not live with your spouse at any time in 1992, enter "0" to the left of line 21a.

1. Enter the total amount from box 5 of all your Forms SSA-1099 and Forms RRB-1099 (if applicable) **1.** 9,250

Note: If line 1 is zero or less, stop here; none of your benefits are taxable. Otherwise, go to line 2.

2. Divide line 1 above by 2 . . . . **2.** 4,625

3. Add the amounts on Form 1040, lines 7, 8a, 9 through 15, 16b, 17b, 18 through 20, and line 22. Do not include here any amounts from box 5 of Forms SSA-1099 or RRB-1099 . . **3.** 30,100

4. Enter the amount from Form 1040, line 8b . . . . . . **4.** -0-

5. Add lines 2, 3, and 4 . . . . **5.** 34,725

6. Enter the total adjustments from Form 1040, line 30 . . . **6.** -0-

7. Subtract line 6 from line 5 . . . . **7.** 34,725

8. Enter on line 8 the amount shown below for your filing status:
   - Single, Head of household, or Qualifying widow(er), enter $25,000
   - Married filing jointly, enter $32,000
   - Married filing separately, enter -0- ($25,000 if you did not live with your spouse at any time in 1992) **8.** 32,000

9. Subtract line 8 from line 7. If zero or less, enter -0-. **9.** 2,725
   - If line 9 is zero, stop here. None of your benefits are taxable. Do not enter any amounts on lines 21a or 21b. But if you are married filing separately and you did not live with your spouse at any time in 1992, enter -0- on line 21b. Be sure you entered "0" to the left of line 21a.
   - If line 9 is more than zero, go to line 10.

10. Divide line 9 above by 2 . . . . **10.** 1,362.50

11. **Taxable social security benefits.**
    - First, enter on Form 1040, line 21a, the amount from line 1.
    - Then, enter the smaller of line 2 or line 10 here and on Form 1040, line 21b **11.** 1,362.50

Note: If part of your benefits are taxable for 1992 and they include benefits paid in 1992 that were for an earlier year, you may be able to reduce the taxable amount shown on the worksheet. Get Pub. 915 for details.

Unemployment Compensation (Insurance)

Unemployment compensation is the amount workers receive under a federal or state law for short periods of unemployment. Recipients of unemployment compensation must report it on Form 1040A (line 12) or Form 1040 (line 20). Payers of $10 or more of unemployment compensation report the payments annually to the IRS on Form 1099-G, Statement for Recipients of Certain Government Payments. These payers also send recipients a copy of Form 1099-G before February of the year following the payment year.

State and Local Income Tax Refunds

Taxpayers receiving a refund of state and local income taxes deducted in a prior year may have gross income from the refund. For the portion that is taxable, they enter it on Form 1040 (line 10). Taxpayers cannot use Form 1040EZ or Form 1040A to report the refund.

Taxpayers who deducted state and local taxes in a prior tax year usually received a **tax benefit** (saved tax by the deduction). To eliminate this benefit, taxpayers include the refund in gross income in the year they get it to the extent the prior year's deduction saved taxes. The next section discusses the tax benefit rule and the amount included in gross income.

A refund of state and local income taxes that were not deducted in a prior year is not part of gross income. Also, a refund of federal income taxes is not part of gross income. In both cases, there were no prior tax benefits. Taxable income in these years was not reduced by a tax deduction.

Tax Benefit Rule

Under the tax benefit rule, taxpayers who recover amounts deducted in a prior tax year may have to include the recovery in gross income in the refund year. The includable part of the recovery is usually the portion of the prior year's deduction that reduced that year's tax liability. Thus, a refund of deducted state and local income taxes or deducted medical expenses in a prior year falls under this rule.

Special rules apply for amounts deducted as itemized deductions after 1986 when taxable income for the deduction year was equal to or greater than zero. Here, all recoveries (recovery year) are included in gross income if their total amount (aggregate recovery amount) is equal to or less than the taxpayer's **excess itemized deductions** for the deduction year. Excess itemized deductions for the deduction year equal the deduction year's itemized deductions less the standard deduction for the taxpayer's filing status for that year. When aggregate recoveries (recovery year) exceed excess itemized deductions (deduction year), an amount equal to the excess itemized deduction (deduction year) is included in gross income (recovery year).

Other Income

Taxpayers must report income from other sources. This income includes awards and prizes, bad debt recoveries for which a deduction was taken in a prior year, and reimbursements for health and accident expenses deducted in an earlier year.

Gambling winnings are part of gross income. Taxpayers deduct gambling losses up to the amount of winnings. Persons in the trade or business of gambling deduct them for AGI. Everyone else deducts them from AGI. However, these losses are not subject to the 2% of AGI limitation on miscellaneous itemized deductions. Chapter 6 discusses miscellaneous itemized deductions.

Amounts taxpayers receive from sales contests, raffles, and radio and television contestant programs are taxable. Also, the value of door prizes, and prizes and awards from employers are taxable. There is a limited exclusion for specific employee service and safety awards. All other awards or prizes from employers are part of gross income unless de minimis rules apply (hams and turkeys for special holidays). Taxpayers include prizes and awards they receive in the form of goods or services in gross income at fair market value. Awards in recognition of past religious, charitable, scientific, educational, artistic, literary, or civic accomplishments, such as the Pulitzer and Nobel prizes, are part of gross income. An exception applies if the recipient of such an award immediately assigns it to a qualified governmental unit or tax-exempt charity.

Reporting Gross Income

Table 3-1 summarizes some of the reporting requirements in the previous paragraphs. Chapter 4 examines gross income exclusions and **adjustments to income** (deductions from gross income to arrive at AGI). Then, the chapter illustrates Form 1040A and Form 1040.

Table 3-1
Reporting Gross Income Items

	Form 1040EZ	Form 1040A	Form 1040
Alimony paid, received, and recaptured			X
Annuities, endowments, life insurance, & pensions		X	X
Business income or loss (self-employed)			X
Capital gain distributions			X
Compensation:			
As employee:			
Awards included in wages	X	X	X
Awards not included in wages, taxable			X
Baby sitting wages	X	X	X
Bonuses included in wages	X	X	X
Commissions included in wages	X	X	X
Fringe benefits included in wages	X	X	X
Fringe benefits not included in wages, taxable			X
Grass cutting wages	X	X	X

Table 3-1   (Continued)
Reporting Gross Income Items

	Form 1040EZ	Form 1040A	Form 1040
Military wages or armed services pay	X	X	X
Moving expense reimbursement included in wages	X	X	X
Moving expense reimbursement not included in wages			X
Newspaper delivery wages	X	X	X
Salaries	X	X	X
Sick pay included in wages	X	X	X
Sick pay not included in wages			X
Snow shoveling wages	X	X	X
Supplemental unemployment benefits			X
Tips:			
Allocated to employee by employer			X
Less than $20, not reported to employer	X	X	X
$20 or more, not reported to employer			X
$20 or more, reported to employer	X	X	X
Wages	X	X	X
As self-employed person			X
Dividend income:			
Dividend reinvestment plan		X	X
Money market accounts	X	X	X
Mutual fund dividend		X	X
Ordinary dividends		X	X
Estate income or loss			X
Farm income or loss			X
Fellowships, taxable portion	X	X	X
Gain or loss: capital asset transactions			X
Gain or loss: other transactions			X
Interest income	X	X	X
IRA distributions		X	X
Other income:			
Awards			X
Bad debt recoveries, non-business			X
Gambling winnings (not in trade or business of gambling)			X
Prizes			X
Real estate tax refunds, taxable portion			X
Reimbursements for accident and health benefits, taxable portion			X
Reimbursements for medical expenses, taxable portion			X
Partnership income or loss			X
Railroad retirement benefits		X	X
Rents			X
Royalties			X
S corporation income or loss			X
Scholarships, taxable portion	X	X	X
Social security benefits		X	X
State and local income tax refunds, taxable portion			X
Trust income or loss			X
Unemployment compensation		X	X

Name ______________________________

Section ____________ Date ______________

C H A P T E R 3

Questions and Problems

1. For a divorce or legal separation after 1984, alimony payments are deductible by the payer and includable in the payee's gross income. However, to be alimony the payments must meet six conditions. What are these conditions?

2. Richard and Janet Dixon, a childless couple, were divorced in early 1990. Since that time they have not lived together. The divorce decree says that Richard is to pay Janet the following amounts annually: 1990—$56,400, 1991—$45,600, 1992—$20,000, and for every year thereafter—$20,000. The decree also says that all payments stop if Janet dies or remarries. Using the alimony recapture worksheet below, calculate the amount Richard must include in his 1992 gross income from the alimony payments.

EXCESS PAYMENT FOR SECOND POST-SEPARATION YEAR

    1. Second post-separation year payment $ __________

    2. Third post-separation year payment $ __________

    3. Add: statutory exemption from recapture   __________   __________

    4. Recapture from second post-separation year $ __________

EXCESS PAYMENT FOR FIRST POST-SEPARATION YEAR

    5. First post-separation year payment $ __________

    6. Less:

        a. Paid in second post-separation year $ __________

        b. Less: recapture from second post-separation year   __________

        c. Net amount   __________

        d. Add: third post-separation year payment   __________

    7. Total amount $ __________

    8. Simple yearly average ($ __________ / 2) $ __________

    9. Add: statutory exemption from recapture   __________   __________

   10. Recapture from first post-separation year   __________

RECAPTURE IN THIRD POST-SEPARATION YEAR

   11. Total recapture in third post-separation year $ __________

3. On September 30, 1992, Shelma Glick purchased a $20,000 par value bond of the QPD Corporation. She paid the seller $20,400 ($20,000 par value + $400 accrued interest). The bond pays 8% interest semiannually on December 31 and June 30. Shelma received the first semiannual interest payment of $800 on December 31, 1992. From the QPD Corporation bonds, how much interest income does Mrs. Glick have in 1992? Explain.

4. **a.** Listed below are the issue price, original maturity value, and selected redemption values of Series E bonds owned by Richard Grady.

| | | Redemption Value | |
Issue Price	Original Maturity Value	End of Current Year	End of Subsequent Year
$375	$ 500	$ 648.00	$ 673.20
150	200	232.56	240.72
750	1,000	1,015.60	1,051.60
75	100	79.60	82.64
150	200	156.08	162.24

In 1992, Grady elects to report the increase in redemption value each year on Series E bonds. At the election date he owned no other United States bonds. What is Grady's gross income from these bonds in 1992? In 1993 (assuming no redemptions or additional purchases)?

   b. Norma Demar, age 30 and single, who has never owned U.S. Savings bonds, wants to invest $2,000 in either Series EE or Series HH bonds. When she cashes her bonds at maturity, she does not plan to use the proceeds for educational purposes. Does Norma have the option of purchasing Series EE or Series HH bonds? Explain your answer. Also, explain how Norma reports the interest on the bonds. Assume Norma does not make any elections.

5. Explain the tax benefit rule as it applies to refunds of a) state and local income taxes and b) federal income taxes.

6. For self-employed persons who work full-time in their business or profession, to what extent are the profits (or losses) from these activities added to (or deducted from) their other income when calculating taxable income?

7. Ten years ago, Ted Brock purchased an annuity contract for $96,000. The contract says he will receive $500 a month for life, starting on January 1, 1989. On this date, Ted's remaining life expectancy is 20 years. For 1992, how much of the annuity payments can Ted exclude from his gross income?

8. On August 10, 1992, Don Wilson became 65 years of age and received his first annuity check. Earlier, he had purchased the annuity at a total cost of $68,985. The annuity contract says Don is to receive monthly annuity payments of $425 on the same day every month for the remainder of his life. On his 65th birthday, he has a life expectancy of 15 years.
   a. From the annuity payments Don receives in 1992, what amount is part of his gross income?

   b. If Don receives 12 annuity payments in 1993, what is his gross income from these payments?

   c. If Don lives longer than his expected 15 years, how much of his annual annuity receipts are part of his gross income?

9. Taxpayers A through D have reported the following social security information for 1992. Fill in blank lines *e.* through *h.* on the table for each taxpayer and, in the space below, show how to calculate the amount of the taxable social security benefits included in income for each taxpayer on line *h*.

Item		A	B	C	D
a.	Taxpayer status	Single	Married filing jointly	Married filing separately	Married filing jointly
b.	AGI before social security benefits	$45,000	$32,300	$41,200	$24,000
c.	Social security received in 1992	7,800	9,400	6,200	11,000
d.	Tax-exempt interest	500	–0–	–0–	400
e.	Revised AGI	$________	$________	$________	$________
f.	Less base exemption	$________	$________	$________	$________
g.	Difference (combined income)	$________	$________	$________	$________
h.	Taxable social security benefits included in income	$________	$________	$________	$________

10. **a.** During 1992, Ann Miller, age 67 and single, received social security benefits of $7,482. Her AGI before the social security benefits was $22,200. During the year, Ann received tax-exempt interest of $2,800. Use the worksheet at the right to determine the portion of the social security benefits that are part of her gross income.

Social Security Benefits Worksheet—Lines 21a and 21b (keep for your records)

If you are married filing separately and you did not live with your spouse at any time in 1992, enter "D" to the left of line 21a.

1. Enter the total amount from box 5 of all your **Forms SSA-1099** and **Forms RRB-1099** (if applicable) . . . .   **1.** ________

   Note: *If line 1 is zero or less, stop here; none of your benefits are taxable. Otherwise, go to line 2.*

2. Divide line 1 above by 2 . . . .   **2.** ________
3. Add the amounts on Form 1040, lines 7, 8a, 9 through 15, 16b, 17b, 18 through 20, and line 22. Do not include here any amounts from box 5 of Forms SSA-1099 or RRB-1099 . . .   **3.** ________
4. Enter the amount from Form 1040, line 8b . . . .   **4.** ________
5. Add lines 2, 3, and 4 . . . .   **5.** ________
6. Enter the total adjustments from Form 1040, line 30 . . . .   **6.** ________
7. Subtract line 6 from line 5 . . . .   **7.** ________
8. Enter on line 8 the amount shown below for your filing status:
   - Single, Head of household, or Qualifying widow(er), enter $25,000
   - Married filing jointly, enter $32,000   **8.** ________
   - Married filing separately, enter -0- ($25,000 if you did not live with your spouse at any time in 1992)
9. Subtract line 8 from line 7. If zero or less, enter -0-. . . .   **9.** ________
   - If line 9 is zero, stop here. None of your benefits are taxable. Do not enter any amounts on lines 21a or 21b. But if you are married filing separately and you did not live with your spouse at any time in 1992, enter -0- on line 21b. Be sure you entered "D" to the left of line 21a.
   - If line 9 is more than zero, go to line 10.
10. Divide line 9 above by 2 . . . .   **10.** ________
11. **Taxable social security benefits.**
   - First, enter on Form 1040, line 21a, the amount from line 1.
   - Then, enter the **smaller** of line 2 or line 10 here and on Form 1040, line 21b . . . .   **11.** ________

Note: *If part of your benefits are taxable for 1992 and they include benefits paid in 1992 that were for an earlier year, you may be able to reduce the taxable amount shown on the worksheet. Get Pub. 915 for details.*

b. Assume that in 1992, Ann Miller received $3,850 in social security benefits and $6,000 in tax-exempt bond interest. Also assume her AGI before the social security benefits remains at $22,200. Use the worksheet at the right to determine the portion of the social security benefits that are part of her gross income.

Social Security Benefits Worksheet—Lines 21a and 21b (keep for your records)

If you are married filing separately and you did not live with your spouse at any time in 1992, enter "D" to the left of line 21a.

1. Enter the total amount from box 5 of all your **Forms SSA-1099** and **Forms RRB-1099** (if applicable) . . . .   **1.** ________

   Note: *If line 1 is zero or less, stop here; none of your benefits are taxable. Otherwise, go to line 2.*

2. Divide line 1 above by 2 . . . .   **2.** ________
3. Add the amounts on Form 1040, lines 7, 8a, 9 through 15, 16b, 17b, 18 through 20, and line 22. Do not include here any amounts from box 5 of Forms SSA-1099 or RRB-1099 . . .   **3.** ________
4. Enter the amount from Form 1040, line 8b . . . .   **4.** ________
5. Add lines 2, 3, and 4 . . . .   **5.** ________
6. Enter the total adjustments from Form 1040, line 30 . . . .   **6.** ________
7. Subtract line 6 from line 5 . . . .   **7.** ________
8. Enter on line 8 the amount shown below for your filing status:
   - Single, Head of household, or Qualifying widow(er), enter $25,000
   - Married filing jointly, enter $32,000   **8.** ________
   - Married filing separately, enter -0- ($25,000 if you did not live with your spouse at any time in 1992)
9. Subtract line 8 from line 7. If zero or less, enter -0-. . . .   **9.** ________
   - If line 9 is zero, stop here. None of your benefits are taxable. Do not enter any amounts on lines 21a or 21b. But if you are married filing separately and you did not live with your spouse at any time in 1992, enter -0- on line 21b. Be sure you entered "D" to the left of line 21a.
   - If line 9 is more than zero, go to line 10.
10. Divide line 9 above by 2 . . . .   **10.** ________
11. **Taxable social security benefits.**
   - First, enter on Form 1040, line 21a, the amount from line 1.
   - Then, enter the **smaller** of line 2 or line 10 here and on Form 1040, line 21b . . . .   **11.** ________

Note: *If part of your benefits are taxable for 1992 and they include benefits paid in 1992 that were for an earlier year, you may be able to reduce the taxable amount shown on the worksheet. Get Pub. 915 for details.*

11. List four types of interest income taxpayers report on Form 1040, Schedule B (line 1) that are not part of this schedule's line 2 total. Explain the mechanics of reporting these items on Schedule B.

12. a. What are AFRs? What are their bases?

    b. Janet Bowman's parents lend Janet and her husband $125,000 to purchase a new home. The loan is for 10 years with zero interest. Must interest be imputed on the loan? Explain your answer and indicate the limitations (if any).

    c. If the loan to Janet and her husband in question *b.* was $100,000, must interest be imputed? Explain your answer and indicate the limitations (if any).

13. On July 1, 1992, Gerald Johnson purchased a 25-year, zero-coupon bond with a maturity value of $1,000,000 for $52,911.96. The yield-to-maturity is 15.25%.

    a. What is the OID on the bond?

    b. What portion of the OID would be included in taxable interest income for 1992?

    c. What portion of the OID would be included in taxable interest income for 1993?

d. When is a Form 1099-OID prepared? Who prepares it? To whom are copies sent? What information does it contain?

14. List two types of interest items that taxpayers report on Form 1040A, Schedule 1, Part I, line 1, that they do not include in the line 2 total. Where on Schedule 1 do taxpayers enter their excludable Educational Savings Bond interest? Explain the mechanics of reporting these items on Schedule 1.

15. **a.** Name five types of distributions that a taxpayer might receive from a mutual fund.

   b. For Form 1040A filers with more than $400 of gross dividends, what kinds of dividend distributions can they report on Schedule 1?

16. Susan Rhiner owns shares of stock in a mutual investment fund. In January 1993, the fund sent her a distribution notice which shows that she received the following distributions from the fund in 1992:

Regular cash dividend	$526
Capital gains distributed	150
Capital gains undistributed	370

Ms. Rhiner verifies the above data from her records. The mutual fund also sent her a Form 2439 showing that her share of the income tax paid by the fund in 1992 on its undistributed capital gains is $132.86. Ms. Rhiner has no other investments. She paid $10,100 for her mutual fund shares on January 16, 1992.

   a. What amount of the distribution of the mutual fund is reported on Ms. Rhiner's Form 1040, and where is it reported?

   b. If the mutual fund shares are sold by Ms. Rhiner in January 1993 for $10,200, what is the amount of gain or loss on the sale? (Show calculation.)

17. Form 1040, Schedule B, Part III contains questions about foreign financial accounts and trusts.

    a. Do all taxpayers who file Schedule B of Form 1040 have to answer the questions in Part III? If your answer is "No," indicate which taxpayers are exempt from answering the questions.

    b. For the foreign financial accounts question (line 11a), what kinds of financial accounts does the question apply to?

    c. If a taxpayer's answer to the foreign accounts question is "Yes," what additional information must he or she enter on Schedule B (line 11b)?

    d. If a taxpayer's answer to the foreign accounts question is "Yes," does the taxpayer have to file any additional forms? If you answer yes, indicate the name of the government agency or department where the taxpayer files the form(s).

18. Neale D. and Judith L. Hamilton file a Form 1040 joint return for 1992. Neale's SSN is 394-57-7584. Judith's is 746-38-4457. The Hamiltons have no foreign accounts or trusts. During 1992, they received the interest and dividends shown below.

    a. Prepare the Form 1040, Schedule B, Interest and Dividend Income, for the Hamiltons using the Schedule B reproduced on the following page. Assume they received an information return from all payers.

Schedules A&B (Form 1040) 1992 OMB No. 1545-0074 **Page 2**

Name(s) shown on Form 1040. Do not enter name and social security number if shown on other side. | **Your social security number**

Schedule B—Interest and Dividend Income

Attachment Sequence No. **08**

Part I Interest Income

(See pages 14 and B-1.)

If you had over $400 in taxable interest income OR are claiming the exclusion of interest from series EE U.S. savings bonds issued after 1989, you must complete this part. List ALL interest you received. If you had over $400 in taxable interest income, you must also complete Part III. If you received, as a nominee, interest that actually belongs to another person, or you received or paid accrued interest on securities transferred between interest payment dates, see page B-1.

Note: If you received a Form 1099-INT, Form 1099-OID, or substitute statement from a brokerage firm, list the firm's name as the payer and enter the total interest shown on that form.

Interest Income	Amount
1 List name of payer—if any interest income is from seller-financed mortgages, see page B-1 and list this interest first ▶	**1**
2 Add the amounts on line 1	**2**
3 Excludable interest on series EE U.S. savings bonds issued after 1989 from Form 8815, line 14. You MUST attach Form 8815 to Form 1040	**3**
4 Subtract line 3 from line 2. Enter the result here and on Form 1040, line 8a. ▶	**4**

Part II Dividend Income

(See pages 15 and B-1.)

If you had over $400 in gross dividends and/or other distributions on stock, you must complete this part and Part III. If you received, as a nominee, dividends that actually belong to another person, see page B-1.

Note: If you received a Form 1099-DIV or substitute statement from a brokerage firm, list the firm's name as the payer and enter the total dividends shown on that form.

Dividend Income	Amount
5 List name of payer—include on this line capital gain distributions, nontaxable distributions, etc. ▶	**5**
6 Add the amounts on line 5	**6**
7 Capital gain distributions. Enter here and on Schedule D* . **7**	
8 Nontaxable distributions. (See the inst. for Form 1040, line 9.) **8**	
9 Add lines 7 and 8	**9**
10 Subtract line 9 from line 6. Enter the result here and on Form 1040, line 9 . ▶	**10**

If you received capital gain distributions but do not need Schedule D to report any other gains or losses, see the instructions for Form 1040, lines 13 and 14.

Part III Foreign Accounts and Foreign Trusts

(See page B-2.)

If you had over $400 of interest or dividends OR had a foreign account or were a grantor of, or a transferor to, a foreign trust, you must complete this part.

	Yes	No
11a At any time during 1992, did you have an interest in or a signature or other authority over a financial account in a foreign country, such as a bank account, securities account, or other financial account? See page B-2 for exceptions and filing requirements for Form TD F 90-22.1		
b If "Yes," enter the name of the foreign country ▶		
12 Were you the grantor of, or transferor to, a foreign trust that existed during 1992, whether or not you have any beneficial interest in it? If "Yes," you may have to file Form 3520, 3520-A, or 926 .		

For Paperwork Reduction Act Notice, see Form 1040 instructions. **Schedule B (Form 1040) 1992**

b. From the items below, identify those that the Hamiltons do not report on Schedule B. For each item not reported on Schedule B that they must report, identify where they should report it.

Interest Received in Cash	Amount
U.S. Treasury bond	$600.00
State of Michigan general obligation bond	75.00
City of Meadowood utility bond	160.00
Mortgage of Mr. and Mrs. K. J. Roe (purchased from E. Johnson)	732.50
Ace Manufacturing Company note	50.00
K. R. Smith, personal note	115.00
American Telephone and Telegraph debenture note	60.00

Dividends Received in Cash	Amount
BXL Mutual Fund return-of-capital dividend	$450.00
Mutual Life Insurance Company policy dividend	81.25
Red Corporation preferred stock dividend	280.00
Credit union dividend	90.00
L.M.O. Mutual Fund capital gains distribution	15.00
USX Corporation common stock dividend	341.20
Dow Chemical Company common stock dividend reinvested in common stock through company dividend reinvestment plan ($185 dividend less service charge $3.27)	181.73

Other Income	Amount
Prize won at Red Corporation annual stockholders' meeting: color TV set FMV to Mrs. Hamilton	$325.00
Blue Corporation, 2-for-1 stock split market value of each share of stock owned jointly by Mr. and Mrs. Hamilton after split, $22	200 shares
ART Corporation dividend in ART Corporation stock total market value of stock, $720. No election for cash to taxpayer, Mrs. Hamilton	100 shares

Gross Income Exclusions and Adjustments to Income

Chapter 3 examined gross income inclusions. This chapter examines gross income exclusions and adjustments to income. **Adjustments to income** are deductions from gross income to arrive at AGI. Illustrations 4-5 and 4-9 show how taxpayers report income and adjustments to income on Form 1040A and Form 1040.

Gross Income Exclusions

Gross income is all wealth that flows to a taxpayer after considering capital recoveries and certain statutory, Constitutional, and IRS-approved exclusions. This section discusses several income items that are fully or partially excluded from gross income (exempt from tax).

Armed Forces Pay

The pay of military personnel is usually part of gross income. If the pay covers combat zone activities, it can be fully or partially exempt from tax.

Combat Zone Benefits. For each month of service in a combat zone, the pay of enlisted personnel and warrant officers is tax-exempt. For commissioned officers, up to $500 a month is tax-exempt. When enlisted personnel and warrant officers serve as commissioned officers in a combat zone, the $500-a-month exemption applies. The exemption usually covers all months in a hospital with combat-zone injuries. Also, military personnel serving part of a month in a combat zone get a full month's exemption. If the service person's Form W-2, Wage and Tax Statement, includes such pay, he or she should ask for a new one.

Currently, income taxes are not withheld from combat pay. Thus, officers may discover that additional taxes are due when they file their tax return.

Military personnel who die from combat-zone wounds, disease, or injuries are exempt from income taxes in the year of death. The exemption covers income taxes for any prior year that *ends on or after* the decedent's first day of combat-zone service. The exemption also covers taxes for the last year that ends before the wound or injury year. In addition, military personnel who die from wounds or injuries in certain terroristic or military actions outside the United States get the exemption.

A **combat zone** is an area identified by the President where U.S. armed forces engage in combat. Service outside these zones can qualify as combat-zone service when a person receives Hostile Fire Pay. The exemption does not cover the pay of military personnel in a combat zone on personal business. Also, it does not cover the pay of military personnel in a combat zone on leave from places outside the zone. Finally, the exemption does not cover military pay for trips which take the traveler over or through the zone.

Other Tax Exempt Military Benefits. In addition to combat pay, other military benefits can be exempt from tax. Specific definitions and limitations govern each exemption.

Tax-exempt Military Benefits

1. Disability pay
2. Educational aid pay
3. Family allowance pay for counseling, dependent education, emergency aid, evacuations, and separation
4. Group-term life insurance
5. Living allowances for basic quarters, basic subsistence, and living expenses abroad
6. Medical and dental care pay for dependents
7. Moving allowances for household goods and personal items, moving trailers and mobile homes, storage, and some temporary lodging
8. Mustering-out pay (discharge pay)
9. Professional education pay
10. ROTC subsistence allowance pay
11. Survivor and retirement protection insurance pay
12. Travel allowances for an annual round trip for dependent students who are away from home, and travel allowances for dependents and self for leaves between consecutive overseas duty tours
13. Living expenses during a ship's overhaul or inactivation
14. Uniform pay to officers
15. Uniforms furnished to enlisted personnel

Veteran Benefits. The bonus a veteran receives from a state government is not part of gross income. Also exempt from tax are the proceeds from veteran insurance and endowment policies paid before death. In addition, several benefits from the Department of Veterans Affairs (VA) are tax-exempt.

Tax-exempt Veteran Benefits

1. Education, training, and living allowance pay
2. Disability compensation and pensions
3. Grants for homes designed for wheelchair living
4. Grants for motor vehicles for veterans who lost their sight or limb use
5. Veterans' pensions paid either to the veterans or veterans' families

---

Bequests and Inheritances

The value of property a taxpayer gets by bequest, devise, or inheritance is exempt from income tax. However, any income from the property is part of gross income.

Dividends, Tax-Exempt

Some corporate distributions are exempt from tax. For a distribution to be a dividend, the distributing corporation must have earnings and profits (E&P). To the extent corporate E&P cover a distribution, it's a dividend. To the extent earnings and profits don't cover a distribution, it's a nontaxable distribution.

Nontaxable Distributions. Distributions which return a shareholder's capital are **nontaxable distributions**. When a **return-of-capital** exceeds a shareholder's stock basis, the excess is a capital gain. Nontaxable distributions can include stock and stock rights.

Liquidating distributions are similar to return-of-capital distributions. However, sometimes they can result in a gain or loss. Taxpayers who receive a liquidating distribution should consult a tax adviser.

Common stock dividends and **stock rights** are usually nontaxable distributions. A shareholder assigns a portion of the existing stock basis to the new shares. Sometimes, a shareholder's stock holdings are so small that he or she is not entitled to get a full share of stock. Here, the corporation usually gives the shareholder cash. The cash is an ordinary dividend up to the corporation's E&P. However, sometimes it gives the shareholder a fractional share. If the fractional share is saleable, the shareholders recognize capital gain or loss at the time of sale. In some situations, stock dividends and stock rights are taxable. The rules governing stock dividends also govern stock rights.

A common stock dividend is taxable when a shareholder has an option to receive cash or property instead of the stock. Without this taxing rule, a shareholder could get cash and avoid a taxable dividend. Several rules govern the taxability of stock dividends.

Stock splits are nontaxable distributions. Here, a corporation issues additional stock to existing shareholders. The number of shares going to any shareholder depends on the number of shares he or she already owns.

Other Nontaxable Dividends. Some dividends are not true dividends for tax purposes. Dividends to policyholders of mutual insurance companies are a partial return of premiums. Until these dividends exceed the policyholder's paid premiums, he or she excludes them from gross income.

Stock Dividend Rules

1. A stock dividend is taxable when an election exists to take cash or property.
2. A stock dividend is taxable when the distribution is disproportionate. This rule applies when some shareholders get cash or property, and the proportionate interests of other shareholders increase. For this rule, the Code treats convertible debentures like stock.
3. A distribution of preferred stock to some common shareholders and common stock to other common shareholders is taxable.
4. Unless there is a change in conversion ratio to reflect a stock dividend or stock split, a distribution on preferred stock is taxable.
5. A disproportionate distribution of convertible preferred stock is taxable.

Fringe Benefits

Employers often provide employees with **fringe benefits**, some of which are taxable. Others are partially or fully tax-exempt. Table 4-1 lists several fringe benefits. The discussion below covers some of the more common ones.

Cafeteria Plans. A **cafeteria plan** allows employees to customize their fringe benefit package. According to the IRS, a qualifying cafeteria plan must be in writing and be available to all employees. Also, there must be two or more benefits that include cash and a qualifying tax-free benefit. Qualifying tax-free benefits include dependent care help, educational aid, and group legal services. These benefits also include group-term life insurance, health and accident insurance, and life insurance for a spouse or child. Qualifying scholarships, fellowships, and tuition reductions can be tax-free benefits. Also, tax-free benefits can include no-additional-cost services, employee discounts, working condition fringes, deferred compensation options, and several de minimis (small value) items. See *Highlights* (page xiv) for discussion of group legal services.

Dependent Care Help. An employee can exclude up to $5,000 from gross income for dependent care help from an employer that lets them go to work. The help must be for an employee's children and dependents (qualifying persons). The plan cannot favor high-pay employees. Instead of outside payments, the employer can provide the care at the work site. Frequency of use and value of the work site service is a factor in determining the exclusion amount.

There is an annual earnings limit on the dependent care exclusion. The limitation is $5,000, or the earned income of the spouse with the smallest earnings. For married persons filing separately, the dollar limit is $2,500. For the care of one person, the law assigns $200 a month of earnings to the spouse who is a full-time student or is incapacitated. When two persons receive care, the $200 a month of earnings assignment goes to $400.

Persons who use the exclusion cannot claim the child and dependent care credit. Taxpayers who claim the exclusion must report the name, address, and **TIN** (taxpayer identification number) of the care provider on their tax return.

Educational Help. See *Highlights* (page xiv) for discussion of employer-provided educational assistance. Under a qualifying educational help plan, employees can exclude annually up to $5,250 of educational benefits an employer provides. The exclusion covers tuition, fees, books, and supplies for undergraduate and graduate students. This exclusion is in addition to any

---

Table 4-1
Employer-Provided Fringe Benefits

Airfares	Gifts	Profit-sharing plans
Airplanes	Golden parachute payments	Property and noncash payments
Athletic facilities	Holidays	Residence
Awards	Home office	Retirement plans
Bonuses	Incentive stock plans	Scholarships and fellowships
Cafeteria plans	Insurance (life, health,	Sick pay
Cars and commuting vehicles	and accident)	Simplified pension plans
Computers	IRAs (employer-sponsored)	Stock bonus plans
Conventions	Jury duty pay	Supplemental unemployment
Death benefits	Loans to employees	benefits
Deferred compensation plans	Maternity and paternity leaves	Taxes of employee paid by
De minimis benefits	Meals and lodging	employer
Disability pay	Membership fees	Travel
Discounts	Military pay	Tuition reductions
Eating facilities	Moving expenses	Uniforms and special clothing
Employee stock ownership plans	No-additional-cost services	Vacations
Entertainment	Out-placement	Van pooling
Equipment and tools	Parking facilities	Wage continuation plans
Financial planning assistance	Pension plans	Workers' compensation
401(k) plans	Prizes	Working condition benefits

job-related educational help. However, the exclusion is not available when more than 5% of the employer's help goes to 5% owners and their families.

Group Legal Services. See *Highlights* (page xiv) for discussion of group legal services. Under a qualifying group legal services plan, employers can provide tax-free insurance to pay for employee legal services. The plan can include the legal services of an employee's spouse and dependents. The maximum annual exclusion per employee is $70 of insurance premium value. The exclusion is not available for the next plan year when the consecutive three year benefits for 5% owners, spouses, and dependents exceed 25% of all benefits paid under the plan.

Group-Term Life Insurance. Sometimes employers buy group-term life insurance for employees. Employees who get the insurance can exclude up to $50,000 of insurance coverage cost. To qualify, employers must provide the insurance under a plan that doesn't favor officers, shareholders, or high-pay personnel. When coverage exceeds $50,000, the employee may pay taxes on the excess cost. Employers use a uniform premium table to determine the excess cost (Table 4-2). Employees subtract amounts they pay for the insurance from the excess cost to determine their taxable amount.

Table 4-2
Uniform 1-Year Premiums for $1,000 of Group-Term Life Insurance Protection

Age*	Cost Per $1,000
Under 30	$ .96
30-34	1.08
35-39	1.32
40-44	2.04
45-49	3.48
50-54	5.76
55-59	9.00
60-64	14.04
65-69	25.20
70 and over	45.12

*The age of the taxpayer on the last day of the tax year is used to determine the appropriate bracket.

EXAMPLE 1 ————————————————

The Bow Manufacturing Company pays the premium on a $90,000 nondiscrimina-tory group-term life insurance policy for Harry R. Lewis. Mr. Lewis is the company's Vice-President of Sales. He is 56 years of age and names his wife as beneficiary. The annual policy cost from the uniform premium table (Table 4-2) is $9 per $1,000 of insurance coverage. Of this amount, Mr. Lewis pays $3 per $1,000 through payroll deductions. He must include $90 in gross income for his insurance coverage.

Group-term life insurance coverage	$90,000
Exempt coverage	50,000
Coverage subject to gross income inclusion	$40,000
Cost subject to gross income inclusion [$40,000/$1,000=40;40x$9 (Table 4-2)]	$ 360
Payments by Lewis (90 x $3)	270
Includable in gross income	$ 90

For key employees to qualify for the group-term life insurance exclusion, the plan must not favor them. When a plan favors key employees, or the type and amount of their benefits, it is discriminatory. A **key employee** is an officer of the company, one of the company's ten largest owners, or a 5% owner. Also, a key employee is a 1% owner with annual earnings of more than $150,000. In addition to the current plan year, these tests apply to the prior four plan years.

Employers must withhold FICA taxes on the taxable portion of group-term life insurance. Employers include the taxable portion on the employee's Form W-2, Wage and Tax Statement. The employee reports the taxable portion of the insurance coverage on his or her tax return as wages. Premiums employers pay for *nongroup life insurance* for an employee, where the employee names the beneficiary, are gross income to the employee.

Health and Accident Plans. Premiums that employers pay for health and accident insurance for employees are usually tax-exempt. However, a self-insured health and accident plan that favors key employees can increase their gross income.

Noncash Compensation. Certain noncash employee benefits are also tax-exempt. Most must not favor key employees. However, fringe benefits for special receiver groups can be tax-exempt. Thus, tax-free benefits can go to full-time em-

> ## Group-term Life Insurance Must Meet 1 of Following Conditions:
>
> 1. The plan must benefit at least 70% of all employees.
> 2. At least 85% of employees participating in the plan are not key employees.
> 3. The plan does not favor key employees.
> 4. The plan is part of a qualifying cafeteria plan

ployees with seniority and employees in certain job groups. When an employer fails the discrimination tests, only employees outside the special receiver group get the tax-free benefits. Fringe benefits that are taxable are part of an employee's wages. Six groups of tax-free fringe benefits appear below:

1. **Subsidized eating facility** operated by an employer is tax-free if the facility meets certain conditions. First, the facility must be on or near the employer's business premises. Second, the revenue from the facility must equal or exceed the facility's direct operating costs. Finally, the facility's operations must not favor key personnel. When an employer provides free employee meals on the business premises for the employer's convenience, the meals are not part of gross income.
2. **De minimis (small-value) fringe benefits** such as the use of copy machines, stationery, and office supplies. These benefits also include low-value holiday gifts such as turkeys and hams. The IRS excludes them from gross income because accounting for them is impractical. When property or service frequency is large, the benefits can be taxable. Discrimination rules do not apply to these benefits.
3. **Qualifying employee discounts** can be tax-free. Such discounts include clothing discounts, brokerage fee discounts, and lodging or meal discounts. Employees exclude the discounts from gross income when they are usual for the employer's trade or business. The receiving employee must work in the employer's business line. The employer must meet any discrimination tests. For a qualifying service to be tax-free, the discount cannot exceed 20% of the retail value of the service. For property, the discount cannot exceed the employer's gross profit percentage. This percentage is the average markup for the type of property. The exclusion is not available for an employee's purchase of gold coins, securities, or interests in mineral-producing property. Also, it is not available for residential or commercial real estate.
4. **Working condition fringe benefits** include goods and services for use in the employer's business. Discrimination rules do not apply to them. Employee parking, business periodicals, and company automobiles or airplanes for business use can be working condition fringe benefits. These benefits are tax-free when they help an employee's job performance. Under certain conditions, demonstrator automobiles for full-time car salespersons qualify for the exclusion. Also tax-free are ordinary and necessary expenses for the protection and safety of executives, or for on-the-job training or travel. Good usage records are helpful in proving a fringe benefit should be tax-free.

   To be tax-free, working condition fringe benefits must be deductible to employees if they paid for them. However, three kinds of benefits do not require an employee deduction. They are parking, limited use of demonstrator automobiles by car salespersons, and expenses that don't exceed the percentage limitation on miscellaneous itemized deductions.
5. **No-additional-cost service** includes airline, railroad, and subway travel, hotel rooms, and telephone service. Services are tax-exempt when they do not cause large additional costs or lost revenues. These services must also be in the business line where the employee works. When the employer's plan favors key employees, these services are taxable to the key employees.
6. **Athletic facilities** include the use value of any on-premise athletic facility such as tennis courts and swimming pools. To be tax-free, most of the use must be by employees, spouses, and dependent children.

Retirement Plans. Employers often provide retirement plans for employees. The employees pay taxes on the benefits when they receive retirement income.

Gifts

The value of property of all kinds that a taxpayer receives as a gift is exempt from income tax. However, the value of so-called gifts a taxpayer receives as pay for personal services is part of gross income.

Income of Minors

The parents of a minor child (individuals having parental rights and duties) are responsible for the child. Under some local laws, a parent can contract for a minor's services, claim the earnings, and receive them. However, for income tax purposes, minors are separate taxpayers who pay taxes on their earnings. Parents do not include a minor's earned income on their tax return.

The tax on the earned income of a minor that he or she does not pay is a debt of the parent. **Earned income** includes wages for services. **Unearned income** includes income from investments and trusts.

If a minor cannot file an income tax return, the parent must file it. The parent should sign the return as follows: *By (signature), parent for minor child.*

Parents can deduct reasonable wage payments to their children for business and farm work. The children report the wages on their tax return. If a child uses his or her wages to purchase clothes and other needs, the availability of the deduction does not change. However, parents cannot deduct the cost of meals and lodging for their children. Meal and lodging payments received from a working child are taxable to the parents when they exceed the child's share of household expenses.

Insurance, Proceeds From Life Policy

The face value of a life insurance policy for a beneficiary is usually tax-exempt. Thus, payment of the policy's face amount in a lump sum or in installments does not affect taxability. When an insurance company holds the proceeds under an agreement to pay interest, the interest is usually taxable. Proceeds of matured National Service Life Insurance contracts, and dividends on unmatured contracts, are not includable in gross income.

Interest on dividends left with an insurance company is taxable when the company adds the interest to the taxpayer's account. If the interest can only be withdrawn on the policy's anniversary date, it is income on this date. Interest on dividend deposits with the Veterans Administration for National Service Life Insurance is no longer taxable.

Interest, Tax-Exempt

Interest on the debt of a state, territory, or District of Columbia is usually tax-exempt. The exemption applies to any political subdivision of these units, including cities, counties, and school districts. Investors frequently refer to this interest as **muni-bond interest** (municipal-bond interest). Interest on student loan bonds and qualifying scholarship funding bonds is also tax-exempt. Interest on U.S. Savings Bonds used to finance the higher education of taxpayers, spouses, and dependents can be tax-exempt.

Interest on bonds issued after 1980 by a volunteer fire department can qualify for exempt treatment. The fire department must use the funds to improve, purchase, or construct a firehouse or fire truck. When a state or municipal subdivision invests the proceeds of issued bonds in short-term Treasury bills, it usually has no effect on the exempt status.

While tax-exempt interest is not part of gross income, taxpayers must report this interest separately on their return. Sometimes, government units issue bonds and use some of the proceeds for nongovernment activities. These are **industrial development** or **private activity** bonds. Learning how to determine the taxability of specific bond issues is a difficult undertaking. However, below is a brief discussion for persons who own them, or are thinking about getting them. See *Highlights* (page xiv) for discussion of extension of authority to issue these bonds.

Industrial Development Bonds. Interest is tax-exempt on certain bonds of cities and other government units for industrial development. The exemption encourages public improvements and local industrial development. Exemption is also available for certain bonds these units issue to provide an exempt facility, such as air terminals. The exemption also applies to some *small issues*. Restrictions on industrial development bond interest appear below.

Interest on all industrial development bonds issued *before* May 1, 1968, is tax-exempt.

The exemption also applies to bonds where there was a commitment before this date to issue them. After April 30, 1968, only certain issues qualify for the exemption. Then, after 1982, only under certain conditions is the interest on these industrial development bond issues tax-exempt. To be tax-exempt, an elected legislative body or public official must approve the issue after a public notice and hearing. Industrial development bond issues that the voters approve in a referendum do not require a hearing or public official approval. Other restrictions on industrial development bonds slow their growth, availability, and use.

Private Activity Bonds. Private activity bonds are an alternative to financing real property with conventional bonds. In general, a governmental unit issues private activity bonds. Then, a private business uses more than 10 percent of the proceeds to construct permanent facilities. The issuing unit usually secures more than 10 percent of the debt service through an interest in the facility. **Debt service** includes principal and interest payments. The issuing unit can also secure this service through payments from the using business. In addition, **loan financing bonds** can be private activity bonds.

Bonds issued by a governmental unit are private activity bonds when the issuer uses the smaller of two amounts to finance loans to persons other than governmental units. The amounts are $5 million, and more than 5 percent of the bond proceeds. The Code definition of private activity bonds is long and complex. A short definition causes confusion. To avoid these issues, the book does not present a clarifying definition of private activity bonds. Private activity bonds are tax-exempt when they meet several conditions.

U.S. Savings Bonds, Series EE. Under certain conditions, interest on Series EE U.S. Savings Bonds a taxpayer redeems is tax-exempt. Taxpayers use Form 8815, Exclusion of Interest from Series EE U.S. Savings Bonds Issued After 1989, to qualify for the exemption. The exemption applies when a taxpayer uses bond redemption proceeds to pay for certain educational expenses at eligible institutions.

Redemption proceeds include the bond principal and interest. Qualifying educational expenses include tuition and fees paid to eligible institutions. However, these expenses do not include payments for room and board, and courses involving sports, games, or hobbies unless they are part of a degree or certificate-granting program. Eligible institutions include most public and non-profit higher education and post-secondary institutions eligible for federal help. The help must be under the Higher Education Act of 1965 or the Carl D. Perkins Vocational Educational Act. The definition of eligible institutions does not include proprietary schools.

The government must issue the bonds in the name of the taxpayer, or the taxpayer and spouse. To prevent bond owners from avoiding AGI phase down limitations, the owners must be 24 or older at issue date. The beneficiary in case of death can be anyone. The exclusion is available to persons who pay qualifying education expenses during the year with certain Series EE bond redemption proceeds. Persons who report Series EE bond interest on a year-by-year basis will not get much of an exclusion in the redemption year.

Qualifying expenses can be for the taxpayer, spouse, and dependents. When the expenses are for a dependent, he or she must qualify the taxpayer for a dependency exemp-

---

Private Activity Bonds Tax-exempt Under Following Conditions

1. The bonds are Code Section 501(c)(3) bonds which a qualifying charitable organization issues.
2. The bond proceeds finance certain exempt facilities. These facilities include airports, docks, wharves, and those for mass commuting. They also include certain water, sewage, and solid waste disposal plants. Bonds for local district heating and cooling facilities, certain residential rental projects, and electric and gas facilities can be private activity bonds.
3. The bonds are qualifying mortgage bonds.
4. The bonds are qualifying veterans' mortgage bonds.
5. The bonds are qualifying redevelopment bonds, small-issue bonds, student loan bonds, and supplemental student loan bonds.

tion. Taxpayers reduce these expenses by certain nontaxable items a qualifying student receives during the year.

In addition, a qualifying taxpayer must meet the following conditions during 1992 to exclude educational savings bond interest:

1. Cash Series EE U.S. Savings Bonds
2. Pay qualifying education expenses
3. Don't file a separate return if married
4. Have modified AGI of less than $59,150 (less than $96,200 if married filing a joint return)

To exclude all 1992 interest, a qualifying taxpayer's modified AGI must be less than $44,150 (less than $66,200 for a joint return filer). In addition, the taxpayer must use all redemption proceeds for qualifying expenses. When redemption proceeds exceed qualifying expenses, a taxpayer can only exclude part of the interest. Here, the taxpayer determines the excludable amount by a formula.

Single filers and HOH for 1992 reduce excludable bond interest when their modified AGI is between $44,150 and $59,150. Joint return filers reduce excludable bond interest when their modified AGI is between $66,200 and $96,200. Thus, a taxpayer's excludable bond interest is reduced by a fraction when modified AGI exceeds a threshold amount.

To determine a taxpayer's modified AGI for Form 1040A or Form 1040, add all income items on page 1 except taxable interest income. The figure for interest income comes from Form 1040A, Schedule 1 (line 2) or Form 1040, Schedule B (line 2). It includes the interest on the cashed Series EE bonds before any educational savings bond exclusion. The total of any foreign earned income or housing exclusions or deductions, and any exclusions for income from U.S. possessions and Puerto Rico, are also added. Total **adjustments to income** from Form 1040A (line 15c) or Form 1040 (line 30) are subtracted

from the total income calculation to arrive at modified AGI for Form 8815 purposes.

Tax-exempt Items that Reduce Educational Savings Bonds Expenses

1. Tax-exempt scholarships and fellowships
2. Veterans' educational help benefits
3. Employer-provided educational help benefits, see *Highlights* (page xiv)
4. Other educational payments exempt from tax which are not gifts, bequests, and inheritances

---

Filled-In Form 8815, Exclusion of Interest From Series EE U.S. Savings Bonds Issued After 1989

Illustration 4-1

For the current year, Frederick B. and Ida A. Smith file a joint return. Fred is 44, and his SSN is 382-60-1057. Ida is 42, and her SSN is 491-02-8729. Fred and Ida's daughter, Inez I. Smith, is a full-time student at Kent State University. She qualifies her parents for a dependency exemption.

During the current year the Smiths pay $2,000 of Inez's qualifying educational expenses. Also during this year, Inez receives a $1,000 nontaxable scholarship in two installments. She receives the first installment on January 20, and the second on September 15. For the year, the Smiths' salary income is $74,000. The Smiths have no deductions for AGI. On December 31 of the current year Fred redeems a $10,000 Series EE bond ($1,000 interest and $9,000 principal).

Fred and Ida decide to file Form 1040 and claim the bond interest exclusion on Form 8815, Exclusion of Interest From Series EE U.S. Savings Bonds Issued After 1989. At the top of the form Fred enters his name and SSN. He uses his name because it comes first on the Smiths' Form 1040. Fred enters Inez's name (column 1a).

Excludable Educational Savings Bonds Interest Before Phase Down

Interest part of redemption proceeds x [qualifying expenses after reduction for nontaxable items ÷ total redemption proceeds]

Phase Down of Excludable Educational Savings Bonds Interest

Excludable bond interest x [modified AGI − $44,150 ($66,200 for a joint return) ÷ $15,000 ($30,000 for a joint return)]

Then, he enters the name and address of Kent State University (column 1b).

Fred enters the $2,000 of qualifying expenses for Inez (line 2), and Inez's $1,000 nontaxable scholarship (line 3). Then, Fred subtracts the nontaxable scholarship (line 3) from the qualifying expenses (line 2), and enters the difference of $1,000 (line 4). Fred enters the bond redemption proceeds of $10,000 (line 5), and the $1,000 of bond interest (line 6). He divides the difference between expenses and benefits (line 4) by the total Series EE bonds (principal and interest) cashed in 1992 (line 5), and enters the decimal of 0.10 (line 7).

Next, Fred multiplies the interest amount (line 6) by the 0.10 and enters the product of $100 (line 8). To determine the phase down of the interest income exclusion, Fred must determine the Smiths' modified AGI. He uses the worksheet on the back of Form 8815 for this calculation. Fred enters the Series EE bond interest of $1,000 (line A) and the Smiths' salary income of $74,000 (line B). He adds the two amounts and enters the $75,000 total (lines C and E). This is the Smiths' modified AGI. Fred also enters it on Form 8815 (line 9).

Since the Smiths are filing jointly, Fred reduces the $75,000 (modified AGI) by $66,200 (line 10) and enters the $8,800 remainder (line 11). Following the instructions, Fred divides the $8,800 (line 11) by $30,000, and enters the 0.29 decimal results (line 12). Fred multiplies the $100 (line 8) by this decimal, and enters the $29 product (line 13). He subtracts this amount from the $100 (line 8) and enters the $71 difference (line 14). Finally, Fred enters the $71 of excludable interest on Form 1040 Schedule B (line 3).

Illustration 4-1
Filled-in Worksheet Modified AGI

Worksheet—Line 9 (keep for your records)

1. • If you are filing Form 1040, enter the amount from Schedule B, line 2.
   • If you are filing Form 1040A, enter the amount from Schedule 1, line 2. .... **1,000**

2. • If you are filing Form 1040, add the amounts on lines 7, 9 through 15, 16b, 17b, 18 through 20, 21b, and 22. Enter the total.
   • If you are filing Form 1040A, add the amounts on lines 7, 9, 10b, 11b, 12, and 13b. Enter the total. **74,000**

3. Add lines 1 and 2 . . . . **75,000**

4. • If you are filing Form 1040, enter the amount from line 30.
   • If you are filing Form 1040A, enter the amount from line 15c. .... **–0–**

5. Subtract line 4 from line 3. Enter the result here and on Form 8815, line 9 . . . . **75,000**

Scholarship and Fellowship Grants

A taxpayer's gross income does not include some scholarship and fellowship grants. Only degree candidates get the exclusion. The award exclusion applies to tuition and course-required fees, as well as required books, supplies, and equipment. A degree candidate is an undergraduate or graduate student who is pursuing studies to meet the requirements for an academic or professional degree. Post-doctoral fellows are not degree candidates. The award exclusion is not available for room, board, or other expenses. Nondegree candidates cannot claim an exclusion. Also, the exclusion is not available for certain federal grants when the recipient performs services as a federal employee to get the grant. Graduate students who do teaching or research at a degree institution can exclude educational tuition reductions from gross income.

Social Security Benefits

Social security includes payments for a disability and railroad retirement, and for old-age

Illustration 4-1 (continued)
Filled-In Form 8815

Form **8815**	**Exclusion of Interest From Series EE U.S. Savings Bonds Issued After 1989** (For Filers With Qualified Higher Education Expenses) ▶ Attach to Form 1040 or Form 1040A. ▶ See instructions on back.	OMB No. 1545-1173 **1992** Attachment Sequence No. **57**
Department of the Treasury Internal Revenue Service		

Caution: *If your filing status is married filing a separate return, **do not** file this form. You **cannot** take the exclusion even if you paid qualified higher education expenses in 1992.*

Name(s) shown on return   **Frederick B. Smith**

Your social security number   382 : 60 : 1057

1	(a) Name of person (you, your spouse, or your dependent) who was enrolled at or attended an eligible educational institution	(b) Name and address of eligible educational institution
	Inez I. Smith	Kent State University West Lake Road, Ashtabula, OH 44004

If you need more space, attach a statement.

2	Enter the total qualified higher education expenses you paid in 1992 for the persons listed in column (a) of line 1. See the instructions to find out which expenses qualify	**2**	2,000 | 00
3	Enter the total of any nontaxable educational benefits (such as nontaxable scholarship or fellowship grants) received for 1992 for the persons listed in column (a) of line 1. See instructions	**3**	1,000 | 00
4	Subtract line 3 from line 2. If the result is less than zero, enter -0- **Note:** *If line 4 is zero, stop here; you **cannot** take the exclusion.*	**4**	1,000 | 00
5	Enter the total proceeds (principal and interest) from all series EE U.S. savings bonds **issued after 1989** that you **cashed during 1992**	**5**	10,000 | 00
6	Enter the interest included on line 5. See instructions	**6**	1,000 | 00
7	Look at lines 4 and 5 above. Is line 4 **less than** line 5? • **Yes.** Divide line 4 by line 5. Enter the result as a decimal (to at least two places). • **No.** Enter "1.00."	**7**	× 0.10
8	Multiply line 6 by line 7	**8**	100 | 00
9	Enter your modified adjusted gross income. See instructions **9** 75,000 00 **Note:** *If line 9 is $59,150 or more ($96,200 or more if married filing a joint return), stop here; you **cannot** take the exclusion.*		
10	Enter $44,150 ($66,200 if married filing a joint return) **10** 66,200 00		
11	Subtract line 10 from line 9. If the result is zero or less, skip line 12, enter -0- on line 13, and go to line 14 **11** 8,800 00		
12	Divide line 11 by $15,000 (by $30,000 if married filing a joint return). Enter the result as a decimal (to at least two places)	**12**	× .29
13	Multiply line 8 by line 12	**13**	29 | 00
14	**Excludable savings bond interest.** Subtract line 13 from line 8. Enter the result here and on Schedule B (Form 1040), line 3, or Schedule 1 (Form 1040A), line 3, whichever applies ▶	**14**	71 | 00

Paperwork Reduction Act Notice

We ask for the information on this form to carry out the Internal Revenue laws of the United States. You are required to give us the information. We need it to ensure that you are complying with these laws and to allow us to figure and collect the right amount of tax.

The time needed to complete and file this form will vary depending on individual circumstances. The estimated average time is: **Recordkeeping, 53 min.; Learning about the law or the form, 11 min.; Preparing the form, 35 min.; and Copying, assembling, and sending the form to the IRS, 34 min.**

If you have comments concerning the accuracy of these time estimates or suggestions for making this form more simple, we would be happy to hear from you. You can write to both the IRS and the Office of Management and Budget at the addresses listed in the instructions of the tax return with which this form is filed.

help. For high income taxpayers, a portion of these benefits is taxable. For taxpayers with low income, the benefits are usually tax-free.

Workers' Compensation and Health Insurance Benefits

Taxpayers who receive workers' compensation payments for a physical injury or illness exclude them from gross income. Some awards for damages are tax-exempt. Also, payments from accident and health insurance are not part of gross income.

Adjustments to Income

Adjustments to income are deductions *from* gross income to arrive at AGI. Taxpayers using Form 1040EZ have no adjustments to income. For 1040A filers, there is one adjustment to income. This adjustment is the deduction for contributions to an individual retirement arrangement (line 10). Form 1040 filers can enter the six types (seven items) of adjustments to income listed in Table 4-3 (lines 24-29). They can also write in five more on the dotted line portion (line 30) before they enter the total adjustments (line 30).

Table 4-3
Adjustments to Income

Form 1040 Line	Description
24a	Taxpayer IRA deduction (from applicable worksheet)
24b	Spouse's IRA deduction (from applicable worksheet)
25	Deduction for self-employment tax (from applicable worksheet)
26	Self-employed health insurance deduction*
27	Keogh retirement plan and self-employed SEP deduction
28	Penalty on early withdrawal of savings
29	Alimony paid

* See *Highlights* (page xiv) for discussion of extension of self-employed health insurance deduction.

In addition, Form 1040 filers enter some adjustments to income on supporting forms and schedules. When they enter these income items on Form 1040 (page 1), it is after deducting the proper adjustments to income. The discussion below covers several adjustments to income for Form 1040. It also includes the IRA deduction for Form 1040A filers.

Alimony

Payers of alimony deduct it for AGI. Receivers include alimony payments in gross income. When an alimony payer has recapture income, the receiver gets an adjustment to income for a like amount.

Individual Retirement Arrangement (IRA)

Taxpayers have been taking IRA deductions since 1974. Married taxpayers do not have to file a joint return to take one. In the year a taxpayer reaches age 70½, deduction availability usually stops. However, a 70½-year-old person can still take a deduction for a spousal IRA contribution. This availability stops in the year his or her spouse reaches age 70½. The government taxes deductible IRA contributions and related earnings when the taxpayer receives them.

Eligible IRA Programs. Eligible taxpayers can make IRA contributions to either of the following retirement programs:

1. A domestic trust or custodial account. Here, the trustee can be an employer or employee's labor union. The trustee can also be a bank, savings and loan, credit union, insurance company, or regulated investment company. Under certain conditions, other organizations can qualify as the trustee.
2. Individual annuity contracts issued by an insurance company

While the retirement funds are under the control of a trustee or custodian, the taxpayer can still direct investments.

Deductible IRA Payments. When both spouses receive compensation and qualify for an IRA deduction, they calculate the deduction separately. The maximum deduction for each is the smaller of $2,000 or 100% of his or her annual

Write-In Adjustments to Income on Form 1040 (line 30)

1. Some expenses of qualifying performing artist
2. Jury duty pay an employee gives to his or her employer for regular pay
3. Foreign housing deduction
4. Write off of forestations or reforestations cost
5. Certain repayments of supplemental unemployment benefits

compensation. A spousal IRA provides the largest deduction when a taxpayer's spouse receives compensation of less than $250, and the taxpayer receives $2,250 or more. The maximum deduction is $2,250. Here, if each spouse has a separate IRA, the maximum deduction is less than $2,250. For the spousal IRA, not more than $2,000 of a contribution can be in the name of one spouse. Also, taxpayers can make IRA contributions in 1993 between January 1 and April 15 and deduct them on their 1992 return.

The maximum IRA deduction is available in two situations. First, persons who do not participate in an employer's retirement plan can get the full deduction without phase down. For married persons, neither can be an active participant in such a retirement plan. An exception exists for a non-participating married taxpayer filing separately who does not live with his or her spouse for the entire year. Here, the spouse can participate in an employer's retirement plan and not disqualify the taxpayer for the full deduction. The participation test is for the employer's plan year that ends with or within the taxpayer's year. Second, a taxpayer who participates in an employer's retirement plan and has net AGI of not more than his or her phase down starting point can get the full deduction. Net AGI is the taxpayer's AGI before the IRA deduction and exclusion for educational Series EE bonds interest. Net AGI is also before the foreign earned income exclusion and foreign housing exclusion or deduction.

For single participants in an employer's retirement plan, the IRA deduction phase down starts at $25,000 of net AGI. The phase down also starts at this point for a participating head of household. For participating married per-

sons filing jointly, the phase down starts at $40,000. For participating married persons living apart the entire year and filing separately, the starting point is $25,000. The law treats them as single persons. However, if a participating married person lives with his or her spouse at any time during the year and files a separate return, the starting point is zero. Each taxpayer reduces his or her maximum IRA deduction until net AGI is $10,000 higher than the phase down start point. The reduction is 20 percent of net AGI over the start point. Thus, no deduction is available for a participating single person when his or her net AGI reaches $35,000.

$$\text{Maximum deduction} = \$2,000 - (20\% \times [\$35,000 - \$25,000])$$
$$= \$2,000 - \$2,000$$
$$= \$ \text{-0-}$$

An employer's retirement plan includes a qualifying pension, profit-sharing, stock bonus plan, qualifying annuity plan, and a simplified employee pension plan (SEP). Retirement plans of the United States, a state, political subdivision, or agency are employer's retirement plans. A retirement plan includes a tax-sheltered annuity and pension plan under Section 501(c)(18).

Individuals with enough compensation, who do not qualify for an IRA deduction, can still make nondeductible contributions. Here, the maximum contribution for an individual is $2,000. For contributions to a spousal IRA, the maximum contribution is $2,250. The government taxes the earnings on nondeductible contributions at the time of withdrawal.

Adjustments to Income Not Listed Separately on Form 1040 (page 1)

1. Employee business expenses, Form 2106 (Chapter 6)
2. Trade or business deductions, Schedule C (Chapter 8)
3. Losses from property sales, Schedule D (Chapter 11)
4. Rent and royalty expenses, Schedule E (Chapter 10)
5. Expenses of life tenants and income beneficiaries, Schedule E (Chapter 10)

Individual Retirement Arrangement Worksheets. The IRS provides two IRA worksheets with the instructions to Forms 1040A and 1040. Except for line numbers, the worksheets are similar. The worksheets help taxpayers arrive at the proper amount of deductible and nondeductible IRA contributions. Taxpayers who complete a worksheet should file it with their tax records. IRA Worksheet 2 is for married taxpayers who file separately and live together. IRA Worksheet 1 is for use when:

1. Taxpayers (and spouse if filing jointly) are not covered by an employer's retirement plan.
2. Taxpayers (or spouse if filing jointly) are covered by an employer's retirement plan and have a limited amount of net AGI. Here, their net AGI must be:
   a. $25,000 or less if the taxpayers are single, a HOH, or married filing separately and living apart
   b. $40,000 or less for married taxpayers filing jointly

The net AGI of Form 1040A filers with no Series EE educational savings bond interest is total income (line 14). The calculation of net AGI for Form 1040 filers with no educational savings bond interest is total income (line 23) less adjustments (lines 25-29, plus line 30 write-ins). Form 1040A and Form 1040 filers who have this interest and file Form 8815 should get a copy of IRS Publication 590, Tax Information on Individual Retirement Arrangements. This publication contains special instructions on figuring the IRA deduction. Previous Illustration 4-1 contains a filled-in

Form 8815, Exclusion of Interest From Series EE U.S. Savings Bonds Issued After 1989.

Filled-In Form 1040A IRA Worksheet 1

Illustration 4-2

This illustration shows a filled-in IRA Worksheet 1 for Joseph C. and Karen R. Phillips. The Phillips file a joint return on Form 1040A. Mr. Phillips has $23,500 of income from wages and $800 of interest income. Mrs. Phillips has $300 of dividend income. The Phillips total income is $24,600. Mr. Phillips contributes $2,250 to a spousal IRA ($2,000 for himself and $250 for Mrs. Phillips).

He completes IRA Worksheet 1 (lines 1-8) using the information above. Then, he transfers his IRA deduction of $2,000 (line 3) from IRA Worksheet 1 to Form 1040A (line 15a). He also transfers Mrs. Phillips' IRA deduction of $250 from Worksheet 1 (line 8) to Form 1040A (line 15b).

Illustration 4-2
Filled-In Form 1040A IRA Worksheet 1

IRA Worksheet 1—Lines 24a and 24b (keep for your records)

	(a) Your IRA	(b) Your working spouse's IRA
1. Enter IRA contributions you made, or will make by April 15, 1993, for 1992. But do not enter more than $2,000 in either column — **1.**	2,000.00	
2. For each person, enter wages and other earned income from Form 1040, minus any deductions on Form 1040, lines 25 and 27. Do not reduce wages by any loss from self-employment — **2.**	23,500.00	
3. Enter the **smaller** of line 1 or line 2. Enter on Form 1040, line 24a, the amount from line 3, column (a), you choose to deduct. Enter on Form 1040, line 24b, the amount, if any, from line 3, column (b), you choose to deduct. If filing a joint return and contributions were made to your nonworking spouse's IRA, go to line 4 — **3.**	2,000.00	

	Nonworking spouse's IRA
4. Enter the **smaller** of line 2, column (a), or $2,250 — **4.**	2,250.00
5. Enter the amount from line 3, column (a) — **5.**	2,000.00
6. Subtract line 5 from line 4 — **6.**	250.00
7. Enter IRA contributions made, or that will be made by April 15, 1993, for 1992 for your nonworking spouse. But do not enter more than $2,000 — **7.**	250.00
8. Enter the **smaller** of line 6 or line 7. Enter on Form 1040, line 24b, the amount from line 8 you choose to deduct — **8.**	250.00

IRA Deduction— Net AGI Phase Down Start Points for Participates in Employer's Retirement Plan

Single	$25,000
HOH	25,000
Married, filing jointly	40,000
Married, filing separately and does not live with spouse part of the year	25,000
Married, filing separately and lives with spouse part of year	–0–

Filled-In Form 1040 IRA Worksheet 2

Illustration 4-3

This illustration shows a filled-in IRA Worksheet 2 for Neal R. and Betty Jo Richards. The Richards file a joint return using Form 1040. Both participate in an employer's retirement plan. Mr. Richards receives wages of $17,600 and dividend income of $600. His total income is $18,200. Mrs. Richards' only income source is her wages of $27,400. Neal contributes $2,000 to his IRA for 1992. Betty Jo contributes $500 to her IRA.

Since the Richards file jointly, they enter $50,000 on IRA Worksheet 2 (line 1) and total income of $45,600 (line 2). Since they have no adjustments to income (Form 1040, lines 25-30, plus write-in line 30), they enter a zero (line 3). The Richards calculate the difference of $4,400 (line 5) between the $50,000 phase down stop point (line 1) and their $45,600 income amount (line 4). Then, they figure the deductible IRA contribution available to each (line 6). Here, the Richards multiply $4,400 (line 5) by 20% and enter the $880 product (line 6).

The Richards list their wages (line 7): $17,600 for Neal and $27,400 for Betty Jo. Then, they enter their individual IRA contributions of $2,000 for Neal and $500 for Betty Jo (line 8). The Richards enter the smaller of their available contribution (line 6), wage amount (line 7), or actual contribution (line 8). For Neal this amount is $880 (line 9). For Betty Jo it is $500 (line 9). These amounts are the Richards' deductible IRA contributions. Finally, the Richards determine their nondeductible IRA contributions (line 10). Neal's nondeductible contribution is $1,120, the $2,000 amount (line 8) less the $880 deductible amount (line 9). All of Betty Jo's $500 contribution is deductible. The last part of IRA Worksheet 2 (lines 11-20) deals with nonworking spouses and is not part of this illustration.

The Richards transfer their deductible contributions (line 9) from the worksheets to Form 1040 (lines 24a and 24b). Illustration 4-9 at the end of this chapter shows how the Richards enter their IRA contributions on Form 1040 (page 1). Neal supports his nondeductible contribution with Form 8606, Nondeductible IRA Contributions, IRA Basis, and Nontaxable IRA Distributions. The next section illustrates this form.

IRA Records. Tax year 1992 is the fifth year for nondeductible IRA contributions. Taxpayers who make deductible and nondeductible contributions to the same IRA account must keep good records. To help them with this record-keeping task, the IRS provides Form 8606. Taxpayers who make a nondeductible IRA contribution, but don't file a tax return, must still file Form 8606.

Taxpayers should keep their IRA records until all IRA funds are received and all distribution tax years are closed. They are responsible for maintaining adequate records for the nontaxable portion of an IRA distribution. Taxpayers with an IRA should retain the following records:

1. The tax return (including Form 8606) for each year that nondeductible contributions were made.
2. Form 5498, Individual Retirement Arrangement Information, which shows the taxpayer's contributions.
3. Form 5498 or other statement which shows the IRA value for each distribution year.
4. Form 1099-R, Distributions From Pensions, Annuities, Retirement or Profit-Sharing Plans, IRAs, Insurance Contracts, etc., which reports annual IRA distributions.

Filled-In Form 8606, Nondeductible IRA Contributions, IRA Basis, and Nontaxable IRA Distributions

Illustration 4-4

In Illustration 4-3, Neal Richards made a nondeductible IRA contribution. Thus, he files Form 8606 with the Richards' Form 1040. Illustration 4-4 shows Neal's filled-in

Illustration 4-3
Filled-In Form 1040 IRA Worksheet 2

IRA Worksheet 2—Lines 24a and 24b (keep for your records)

1. If you checked Filing Status box:
   - 1 or 4, enter $35,000
   - 2 or 5, enter $50,000
   - 3, enter $10,000 ($35,000 if you **did not** live with your spouse at any time in 1992)

   1. 50,000

2. Enter the amount from Form 1040, line 23 . . . . **2.** 45,600

3. Add amounts on Form 1040, lines 25 through 29, and any write-in amount included on line 30 . . . . **3.** –0–

4. Subtract line 3 from line 2. If the result is equal to or more than the amount on line 1, none of your IRA contributions are deductible. Stop here. If you want to make a nondeductible IRA contribution, see Form 8606 . . . . **4.** 45,600

5. Subtract line 4 from line 1. **If the result is $10,000 or more, stop here and use Worksheet 1** **5.** 4,400

6. Multiply line 5 above by 20% (.20). If the result is not a multiple of $10, round it up to the next multiple of $10 (for example, round $490.30 to $500). If the result is $200 or more, enter the result. But if it is less than $200, enter $200. Go to line 7. . . **6.** 880

Deductible IRA contributions	(a) Your IRA	(b) Your working spouse's IRA
7. For each person, enter wages and other earned income from Form 1040, minus any deductions on Form 1040, lines 25 and 27. Do not reduce wages by any loss from self-employment . . **7.**	17,600	27,400
8. Enter IRA contributions you made, or will make by April 15, 1993, for 1992. But **do not** enter more than $2,000 in either column . . . . **8.**	2,000	500
9. Enter the **smallest** of line 6, 7, or 8. This is the most you can deduct. Enter on Form 1040, line 24a, the amount from line 9, column (a), you choose to deduct. Enter on Form 1040, line 24b, the amount, if any, from line 9, column (b), you choose to deduct. If line 8 is more than line 9, go to line 10 . . . . **9.**	880	500

Nondeductible IRA contributions

	(a)	(b)
10. Subtract line 9 from the **smaller** of line 7 or line 8. Enter on line 2 of your Form 8606 the amount from line 10 you choose to make nondeductible **10.**	1,120	–0–

If filing a joint return and contributions were made to your nonworking spouse's IRA, go to line 11.

Deductible IRA contributions for nonworking spouse

11. Enter the **smaller** of line 7, column (a), or $2,250 . . . . . **11.** _______

12. Add the amount on line 9, column (a), to the part of line 10, column (a), that you choose to make nondeductible . . . **12.** _______

13. Subtract line 12 from line 11. If the result is zero or less, stop here. You cannot make deductible or nondeductible IRA contributions for your nonworking spouse . . . . . . **13.** _______

14. Enter the **smallest** of **(a)** IRA contributions made, or that will be made by April 15, 1993, for 1992 for your nonworking spouse; **(b)** $2,000; or **(c)** the amount on line 13 . . . . **14.** _______

15. Multiply line 5 above by 22.5% (.225). If the result is not a multiple of $10, round it up to the next multiple of $10. If the result is $200 or more, enter the result. But if it is less than $200, enter $200 . . . . **15.** _______

16. Enter the amount from line 9, column (a) . . . . **16.** _______

17. Subtract line 16 from line 15 . . . . **17.** _______

18. Enter the **smaller** of line 14 or line 17 . . . . **18.** _______

19. Enter the **smallest** of line 6, 7, or 18. This is the most you can deduct. Enter on Form 1040, line 24b, the amount from line 19 you choose to deduct. If line 14 is more than line 19, go to line 20 . . . . **19.** _______

Nondeductible IRA contributions for nonworking spouse

20. Subtract line 19 from line 14. Enter on line 2 of your spouse's Form 8606 the amount from line 20 that you choose to make nondeductible . . . . **20.** _______

Form 8606. Illustration 4-9 shows page 1 of the Richards' Form 1040. In preparing Form 8606, Mr. Richards enters his name and SSN at the top of the form (678-42-1720). He enters the December 31, 1992, value of $9,617.42 for his only IRA (line 1). He got this figure from the First National Bank of Dallas trustee report.

Mr. Richards reports his nondeductible 1992 IRA contributions of $1,120 (line 2). He got this amount from his IRA Worksheet 2 (Illustration 4-3, line 10). He made two deposits to his IRA for 1992. On February 15, 1992, he deposited $1,800. On February 15, 1993, he deposited $200. Of the $2,000 total, $880 is deductible and $1,120 is nondeductible.

Mr. Richards reports his IRA basis for 1991 and prior years of $920 (line 3). This basis is the total of all his nondeductible IRA contributions after 1986. If Mr. Richards filed a Form 8606 in 1991, the $920 would be on that form (line 14).

The total of the 1992 nondeductible (line 2) and prior years' (line 3) contributions is entered (line 4). Since Mr. Richards did not receive an IRA distribution in 1992, he leaves the next section blank (lines 5-13). Thus, the amount of $2,040 (line 4) is the total IRA basis for 1992 and prior years (line 14).

If Mr. Richards had received any IRA distributions in 1992, he would have used that section (lines 5-13) to determine the amount of 1992 nontaxable distributions. Any nontaxable distributions received in 1992 would have reduced Mr. Richards' total IRA basis for 1992 and prior years.

IRA Investment in Collectibles. When taxpayers invest their IRA contributions in collectibles, the amount is treated as a taxable distribution. Collectibles include art works, rugs, gems, coins, stamps, metals, and antiques. However, when taxpayers invest IRA funds in certain United States gold or silver coins, the investment is not treated as a taxable distribution.

Excess Contributions to an IRA. No tax deduction is allowed for *excess contributions* to an IRA. If contributions exceed the allowable limit, the IRS assesses an additional nondeductible 6% excise tax. There is no additional tax when taxpayers get the excess contribution back. Here, taxpayers must receive the refund by their return's due date, including extensions, to avoid the excise tax. However, these taxpayers must include the amount they receive in gross income. Taxpayers report excess contributions on Form 5329, Return For Additional Taxes Attributable to Qualifying Retirement Plans (including IRAs), Annuities, and Modified Endowment Contracts.

Distributions from an IRA. When taxpayers retire and receive IRA distributions, they divide them according to deductible and nondeductible contributions. The portion that comes from the deductible contributions is taxed as ordinary income. Taxpayers cannot use a special 10-year averaging rule that is available for other pension distributions.

If a taxpayer receives an IRA distribution before reaching age 59½, the IRS usually assesses an early 10 percent distribution tax. However, the IRS does not assess this tax on distributions to disabled taxpayers. If the distribution is to fund beneficiaries because of the taxpayer's death, the IRS does not assess the tax. When a taxpayer rolls over an IRA within a short time (moves one IRA to another IRA), the IRS does not assess the tax. The IRS does not assess the tax for timely withdrawals of contributions. Here, the taxpayer must complete the withdrawal before the due date of his or her return, including extensions. Finally, a special rule covers installment annuity distributions.

Taxpayers report the distribution tax on Form 5329. A discussion of each early distribution is beyond the scope of this book. However, taxpayers who receive them should get a copy of IRS Publication 590, Tax Information on Individual Retirement Arrangements.

Taxpayers do not have to start withdrawing IRA funds until April 1 of the calendar year after the year they reach age 70½. Thus, taxpayers who reach age 70½ in 1992 do not have to start withdrawing IRA funds until April 1, 1993.

Penalty on Early Withdrawal of Savings

Deposits in special time certificates or savings accounts usually get a higher return rate than a

Illustration 4-4
Filled-In Form 8606

Form **8606**

Department of the Treasury
Internal Revenue Service

Nondeductible IRA Contributions, IRA Basis, and Nontaxable IRA Distributions

▶ Please see Recordkeeping Requirements on page 2.
▶ Attach to Form 1040, Form 1040A, or Form 1040NR.

OMB No. 1545-1007

1991

Attachment
Sequence No. **47**

Name. (If married, file a separate Form 8606 for each spouse. See instructions.)

Neal R. Richards

Your social security number

678 : 42 : 1720

Fill in Your Address Only If You Are Filing This Form by Itself and Not With Your Tax Return

Home address (number and street, or P.O. box if mail is not delivered to your home)

Apt. no.

City, town or post office, state, and ZIP code

1	Enter the total value of **ALL** your IRAs as of 12/31/91. (See instructions.)	1	9,617 42
2	Enter your IRA contributions for 1991 that you choose to be nondeductible. Include those made during 1/1/92–4/15/92 that were for 1991. (See instructions.)	2	1,120 00
3	Enter your total IRA basis for 1990 and prior years. (See instructions.)	3	920 00
4	Add lines 2 and 3. If you did not receive any IRA distributions (withdrawals) in 1991, skip lines 5 through 13 and enter this amount on line 14	4	2,040 00
5	Enter only those contributions included on line 2 that were made during 1/1/92–4/15/92. (This amount will be the same as line 2 if all of your nondeductible contributions for 1991 were made in 1992 by 4/15/92.) (See instructions.)	5	
6	Subtract line 5 from line 4	6	
7	Enter the amount from line 1 plus any outstanding rollovers. (See instructions.)	7	
8	Enter the total IRA distributions received during 1991. Do not include amounts rolled over before 1/1/92. (See instructions.)	8	
9	Add lines 7 and 8	9	
10	Divide line 6 by line 9 and enter the result as a decimal (to at least two places). Do not enter more than "1.00"	10	.
11	Multiply line 8 by line 10. This is the amount of your **nontaxable distributions for 1991.** (See instructions.) ▶	11	
12	Subtract line 11 from line 6. This is the **basis in your IRA(s) as of 12/31/91**	12	
13	Enter the amount, if any, from line 5	13	
14	Add lines 12 and 13. This is your **total IRA basis for 1991 and prior years** ▶	14	2,040 00

Sign Here Only If You Are Filing This Form by Itself and Not With Your Tax Return

Under penalties of perjury, I declare that I have examined this form, including accompanying attachments, and to the best of my knowledge and belief, it is true, correct, and complete.

Your signature

Date

Paperwork Reduction Act Notice.—We ask for the information on this form to carry out the Internal Revenue laws of the United States. You are required to give us the information. We need it to ensure that you are complying with these laws and to allow us to figure and collect the right amount of tax.

The time needed to complete and file this form will vary depending on individual circumstances. The estimated average time is: **Recordkeeping,** 26 minutes; **Learning about the law or the form,** 7 minutes; **Preparing the form,** 22 minutes; and **Copying, assembling, and sending the form to the IRS,** 20 minutes.

If you have comments concerning the accuracy of these time estimates or suggestions for making this form more simple, we would be happy to hear from you. You can write to both the **Internal Revenue Service,** Washington, DC 20224, Attention: IRS Reports Clearance Officer, T:FP; and the **Office of Management and Budget,** Paperwork Reduction Project (1545-1007), Washington, DC 20503. **DO**

NOT send this form to either of these offices. Instead, see **When and Where To File** on this page.

General Instructions

Purpose of Form.—You must use Form 8606 to report your IRA contributions that you choose to be nondeductible. You may wish to make nondeductible contributions, for example, if all or part of your contributions are not deductible because of the income limitations for IRAs. First, figure your deductible contributions using the instructions for Form 1040 or Form 1040A, whichever apply to you. Report the deductible contributions on Form 1040, Form 1040A, or Form 1040NR. Then, enter on line 2 of Form 8606 the amount you choose to be nondeductible.

The part of any distributions you receive attributable to nondeductible contributions will not be taxable. If you have at any time made nondeductible contributions, also use Form 8606 to figure the nontaxable part of any IRA distributions you received in 1991. Line 11 will show the amount that is not taxable.

Who Must File.—You must file Form 8606 for 1991 if **either** of the following applies:

● You made nondeductible contributions to your IRA for 1991, or

● You received IRA distributions in 1991 **and** you have at any time made nondeductible contributions to any of your IRAs.

When and Where To File.—Attach Form 8606 to your 1991 Form 1040, Form 1040A, or Form 1040NR.

If you are required to file Form 8606, but do not have to file an income tax return because you do not meet the requirements for filing a return, you still have to file a Form 8606 with the Internal Revenue Service at the time and place you would be required to file Form 1040, Form 1040A, or Form 1040NR.

Penalty for Not Filing Form 8606.—The law provides for a penalty if you make nondeductible IRA contributions and do not file Form 8606. You will have to pay a $50 penalty for each failure to file Form 8606, unless you can show that the failure to file was due to reasonable cause.

Cat. No. 63966F

Form **8606** (1991)

passbook account. The financial institution guarantees the higher rate for funds that remain on deposit until maturity. Often, the governing instrument contains interest forfeiture and penalty provisions for early withdrawals. Taxpayers who withdraw funds early include the full interest income in gross income on Form 1040 (line 8a), and deduct the forfeited interest (line 28). Usually, the interest payer reports the forfeited interest on Form 1099-INT, U.S. Information Return For Recipients of Interest Income.

Self-Employed Health Insurance Deduction

See *Highlights* (page xiv) for discussion of self-employed health insurance deduction. A self-employed taxpayer with net profit can get a business expense deduction for medical insurance payments. When eligible, taxpayers take the deduction for AGI (above the line). The deduction equals the smaller of two amounts. One of the two amounts is 25 percent of the taxpayer's health insurance premiums. These premiums can cover the taxpayer, spouse, and dependents. The other amount is the taxpayer's net self-employment profit. To this amount the taxpayer adds other earned income, and subtracts any Form 1040 deduction for a Keogh or SEP retirement plan.

Taxpayers who are eligible to participate in a spouse's health plan maintained by his or her employer cannot take the deduction. A self-employed taxpayer with employees can take the deduction only if the health insurance plan is available to employees. When the plan discriminates in favor of the taxpayer, the deduction is not available. For the portion of the insurance premiums not deductible above the line, taxpayers deduct it as a medical expense.

Self-Employed Keogh Retirement Plan

Certain limited payments made by self-employed individuals to *Keogh* retirement plans can be deducted *for* AGI. Taxpayers take the deduction on Form 1040 (line 27).

The maximum deduction for a contribution to a Keogh *defined contribution* plan is the lesser of $30,000 or 25% of the participant's compensation. For self-employed taxpayers, *compensation* is net earnings from self-employment. However, taxpayers must reduce this amount

by contributions to qualifying retirement plans for their benefit. Two major types of defined contribution plans are available to an owner-employee. These are the *profit-sharing plan* and the *money-purchase plan*. An owner-employee can contribute to both plans, as long as his or her contributions to both do not exceed the allowable maximum.

The maximum contribution for self-employed taxpayers in a *money-purchase plan* is 20% of net earnings. Net earnings are after deducting qualifying contributions for employees. Taxpayers figure the 20% limit by dividing the 25% maximum Keogh contribution by 125% (100% for net earnings + 25% for maximum contribution rate).

For self-employed taxpayers in a *profit-sharing plan*, the maximum deduction is 13.0435% of net earnings. Taxpayers can determine the 13.0435% by dividing the 15% maximum contribution by 115% (100% for net earnings + 15% for maximum contribution rate).

In addition to defined contribution plans, there are defined benefit plans. These plans are set up at the time taxpayers set up the retirement fund. Tax advisers usually recommend a profit-sharing and money-purchase plan to get the maximum tax deduction.

Self-Employed SEP

A simplified employees pension plan (SEP) allows self-employed persons to make deductible contribution to a retirement plan for themselves and employees. As a minimum, the employer must set up an IRA (SEP-IRA) for each qualifying employee. Under a SEP, there is no requirement that an employer contribute to the plan. However, if the employer contributes to the plan there can be no discrimination in favor of officers, shareholders, or high-pay employees.

Review of Gross Income Inclusions and Exclusions, Adjustments to Income, and Form 1040 Reporting Structure

Chapter 3 covered gross income inclusions. The focus of this chapter was on gross income exclusions and adjustments to income. Table 4-4 is a checklist of gross income inclusions and exclusions. It brings together many items found in Chapters 3 and 4. Review this table and Table 4-5 before studying the reporting illustrations. Table 4-5 contains gross income inclusions and adjustments to income, as well as the remaining portions of the tax reporting structure presented in Chapter 1. This table is laid out in a Form 1040 format and contains references to many supporting schedules and forms. The book discusses the items after the AGI line in later chapters.

Reporting Illustrations

Illustrations 4-5 through 4-8 show how taxpayers report gross income, adjustments to income, and other items on Forms 1040A. These illustrations contain the 1992 tax return and related schedules for William E. and Lori R. Fisher. Illustration 4-5 contains general filing data for the Fishers. Illustration 4-6 contains the dividend income data. Illustration 4-7 contains the data for the Fishers' IRA deduction. Finally, Illustration 4-8 contains the Fishers' child and dependent care credit data. Then, Illustration 4-9 shows how taxpayers report these items on Form 1040, page 1 and on Schedule B.

Filled-In Form 1040A

Illustration 4-5

William E. Fisher, a 36-year-old clerk, is married to Lori R. Fisher. Lori is 34 years of age and a part-time teller. For 1992 the Fishers file a joint Form 1040A tax return. They fully support their 6-year-old only child, Marian C. Fisher. Marian's SSN is 624-18-1111. Marian's only income is $200 of interest from a savings account at the Friendly Credit Union. The Fishers live at 400 South Elm Street, Chicago, IL 60631-1314. Mr. and Mrs. Fishers' SSN are 269-09-9092 and 390-16-2222, respectively. Since they filed a Form 1040A return last year, the IRS mailed them a 1992 Form

1040A booklet with instructions.

The Fishers enter their taxpayer identification label on Form 1040A, page 1 and place an "X" in the proper boxes to designate $1 each for the presidential election campaign fund. They also place an "X" in the proper box to indicate their married filing jointly filing status. The Fishers claim three exemptions and supply the necessary information about Marian.

Employers of the Fishers withheld payroll taxes from their gross wages. For 1992, the Fishers had combined gross wages of $22,150 ($16,200 for William and $5,950 for Lori). Table 4-6 presents needed payroll data to support their wages and withholdings. Their employers entered the Fishers' gross wages and withheld federal income and FICA taxes on Forms W-2. Then, their employers sent them a copy of their Form W-2. Mr. Fisher's employer carries a shared-cost, $10,000, group-term insurance policy on his life. During 1992, Mr. Fisher's employer withheld 50 cents a month for each $1,000 of group-term for his share of the premium. The total premium withheld from Fisher for 1992 is $60. The balance of the insurance premium is paid by Mr. Fisher's employer. While the net wages received by the Fishers were $17,119.52, their gross wages are reported on Form 1040A (line 7). The Fishers report $22,150 here.

The Fishers' did not withdraw their 1992 interest income of $230 from a bank savings account. They enter this interest directly on Form 1040A (line 8a) since it is not more than $400.

Filled-In Schedule 1, Form 1040A

Illustration 4-6

Cash dividends of $410 were received by the Fishers on RPM Manufacturing Company stock in 1992. Since these dividends exceeded $400, the Fishers enter related information on Schedule 1, Part II (Form

Table 4-4
Gross Income Checklist for 1992

Item	Gross Income Incl.	Gross Income Excl.
Accident insurance proceeds		X
Alimony payments (periodic)	X	
Back-pay awards	X	
Bad debt recovered, up to prior tax benefit	X	
Bequests		X
Board (meals) unless furnished for employer's convenience on premises	X	
Bonuses received as compensation	X	
Capital gains	X	
Car pool receipts		X
Clergy:		
Rental value of parsonage as part of compensation		X
Salaries, fees, etc., for personal services	X	
Commissions received as compensation for services	X	
Compensatory damages received:		
For patent infringement	X	
For personal injuries		X
For slander or libel		X
Disability payments from health or accident insurance		X
Dismissal pay received	X	
Dividends:		
From corporate earnings accumulated after February 28, 1913	X	
In stock if proportionate interest of stockholders is unaffected		X
On mutual life insurance policy		X
Education assistance (job-related) paid by employer		X**
Embezzlement proceeds	X	
Executor's fees	X	
Federal income tax refund		X
Gambling winnings (gross)	X	
Gifts		X
Health resort expenses paid by employer	X	
Inheritances		X
Interest on:		
Bank savings accounts	X	
Bonds (general obligation) of a state, city, or other political subdivision		X
Building and loan savings	X	
Educational savings bonds		X**
Federal obligations issued	X	
Federal tax refund	X	
Industrial bonds	X	
Notes receivable	X	

Item	Gross Income Incl.	Gross Income Excl.
Jury fees	X	
Kickbacks	X	
Legacies		X
Life insurance:		
Group-term premiums paid by employer (up to $50,000 of insurance)		X**
Proceeds paid on death		X
Lodging, unless furnished for employer's convenience on premises and is a condition of employment	X	
Marriage settlement, lump-sum payment		X
Moving expenses paid by employer (permanent move)	X	
Notary public fees	X	
Old-age benefits:		
Railroad retirement		X*
Social security		X*
Partnership income, share of partnership profits	X	
Peace Corps basic living and travel allowances		X
Prizes won in contests, fairs, raffles, etc.	X	
Professional fees	X	
Refunds of state and local taxes, to extent of prior tax benefit	X	
Rents	X	
Retirement pay after cost recovery (except veteran's disability)	X	
Rewards	X	
Royalties	X	
Salaries and wages	X	
State and federal employees' salaries	X	
Strike benefits from union (established fund)	X	
Tips	X	
Unemployment benefits:		
Area Redevelopment Act	X	
Manpower Development and Training Act	X	
Railroad Unemployment Insurance Act	X	
State unemployment compensation laws	X	
Veterans:		
Bonuses		X
Disability		X
Retirement pension	X	
Workers' compensation		X

* A portion of social security and railroad benefits may be included in the gross income.
** May be taxable if certain requirements are not met.

Table 4-5
Income Tax Return Structure (Form 1040)

INCOME:

Wages, salaries, tips, and other employee compensation (Form(s) W-2)	$XX
Taxable interest income (Schedule B) .	XX
Tax-exempt interest income . . . . $XX	
Dividend income	XX
Taxable refunds of state and local income taxes	XX
Alimony received	XX
Business income or (loss) (Schedule C)	XX
Capital gain or (loss) (Schedule D) . .	XX
Other gains or (losses) (Form 4797) . .	XX
Pensions, IRA distributions, and annuities (including rollovers) received . . . . $XX	
Taxable amount of pensions, IRA distributions, and annuities	XX
Rents, royalties, partnerships, estates, trusts, etc. (Schedule E)	XX
Farm income or (loss) (Schedule F) . .	XX
Unemployment compensation (insurance)	XX
Social security benefits . . . . $XX	
Taxable amount of social security benefits	XX
Other income	XX
TOTAL INCOME	$XX

LESS ADJUSTMENTS TO INCOME:

Taxpayer IRA deductions . . . . $XX	
Spouse's IRA deductions XX	
Deduction for self-employment tax . . XX	
Self-employed health insurance deduction . . . . XX*	
Keogh retirement plan and self-employed SEP deduction XX	
Penalty on early withdrawal of savings XX	
Alimony paid (recipient's name and social security number) XX	
TOTAL ADJUSTMENTS TO INCOME	XX
ADJUSTED GROSS INCOME	$XX
Less (1) itemized deductions (Schedule A) or (2) standard deduction	XX
Difference	$XX
Less number of exemptions multiplied by $2,300	XX
TAXABLE INCOME (tax base amount used to determine tax)	$XX

TAX COMPUTATION:

Amount of income tax (from Tax Table, Tax Rate Schedules X, Y, or Z, or Form 8615)		$XX
Plus additional taxes (Form 4970 or Form 4972)		XX
TOTAL TAX		$XX

LESS CREDITS:

Credit for child care and dependent care expenses (Form 2441)	$XX	
Credit for the elderly or for the permanently and totally disabled (Schedule R)	XX	XX
Net, but not less than zero		$XX
Foreign tax credit (Form 1116)	$XX	
General business credit (Form 3800, Form 3468, Form 5884, Form 6478, Form 6765, or Form 8586)	XX	XX
Net, but not less than zero		$XX

PLUS OTHER TAXES:

Self-employment tax (Schedule SE) . .	$XX	
Alternative minimum tax (Form 6251)	XX	
Tax from recapture of investment credit (Form 4255)	XX	
Social security tax on tip income not reported to employer (Form 4137) .	XX	
Tax on an IRA or qualified retirement plans (Form 5329)	XX	
Advance earned income credit payments received (Form W-2)	XX	XX
TOTAL TAX		$XX

LESS PAYMENTS:

Federal income tax withheld (Forms W-2 and W-2P)	$XX	
1992 estimated tax payments and amount applied from 1991 return	XX	
Earned income credit	XX	
Amount paid with Form 4868	XX	
Excess social security tax and RRTA tax withheld	XX	
Credit for federal tax on gasoline and special fuels (Form 4136)	XX	
Regulated investment company credit (Form 2439)	XX	XX

REFUND OR AMOUNT OWED:

Refund or amount owed		$XX

* See Highlights (page xiv)

Table 4-6
Payroll Information for William E. and Lori R. Fisher

Employer	Wages	Federal Income Tax Withheld	FICA Taxes Withheld	Other Deductions	Net
Aeron Corporation:				$ 60 Ins.	
William E. Fisher	$16,200	$1,392	$1,239.30	1,500 IRA	$12,008.70
First Bank:					
Lori R. Fisher	5,950	384	455.18	—	5,110.82
Totals	$22,150	$1,776	$1,694.48	$1,560	$17,119.52

1040A). The Fishers enter the total dividend of $410 on Form 1040A (line 9). The Fishers then enter their total income of $22,790 on Form 1040A (line 14).

Filled-In Worksheet for IRA Deduction

Illustration 4-7

William Fisher set up an IRA account with the Aeron Corporation Credit Union on January 4, 1991. During 1991 and 1992, he made contributions of $125 per month by payroll deductions. Earnings on the account are compounded monthly. The credit union reports them to Fisher and the IRS. The interest income is $92.85 for 1991, and $228.16 for 1992. This interest, as well as Fisher's monthly contributions for the two years, is tax deferred. The total deferment on December 31, 1992, is $3,321.01 [($125 x 12 x 2) + ($92.85 + $228.16)]. The Fishers do not report the 1992 interest of $228.16 on their tax return.

The Fishers use an IRA worksheet, but do not file it with their tax return. Note, the Fishers were eligible to contribute and deduct $4,000 ($2,000 each). If they increased their IRA contribution to $4,000, their tax refund would almost double.

The Fishers enter the $1,500 IRA payment for 1992 on Form 1040A (line 15a and 15c). If they had made a qualifying IRA payment in 1993 for 1992, they would include this payment (line 15a). The Fishers enter their AGI of $21,290 (line 16) and carry it to page 2 (line 17).

Illustration 4-7
Filled-In Worksheet for IRA Deduction

IRA Worksheet 1—Lines 24a and 24b (keep for your records)

	(a) Your IRA	(b) Your working spouse's IRA
1. Enter IRA contributions you made, or will make by April 15, 1993, for 1992. But do not enter more than $2,000 in either column	1. 1,500	
2. For each person, enter wages and other earned income from Form 1040, minus any deductions on Form 1040, lines 25 and 27. Do not reduce wages by any loss from self-employment	2. 16,200	
3. Enter the **smaller** of line 1 or line 2. Enter on Form 1040, line 24a, the amount from line 3, column (a), you choose to deduct. Enter on Form 1040, line 24b, the amount, if any, from line 3, column (b), you choose to deduct. If filing a joint return and contributions were made to your nonworking spouse's IRA, go to line 4	3. 1,500	

	Nonworking spouse's IRA
4. Enter the **smaller** of line 2, column (a), or $2,250	4.
5. Enter the amount from line 3, column (a)	5.
6. Subtract line 5 from line 4	6.
7. Enter IRA contributions made, or that will be made by April 15, 1993, for 1992 for your nonworking spouse. But do not enter more than $2,000	7.
8. Enter the **smaller** of line 6 or line 7. Enter on Form 1040, line 24b, the amount from line 8 you choose to deduct	8.

Filled-In Schedule 2, Form 1040A

Illustration 4-8

In 1992, the Fishers paid Helen Johnson to care for their daughter, Marian, while they were at work. Mrs. Johnson is a neighbor who lives at 406 South Elm St. The Fishers paid her $1,621.50 in 1992. Helen's TIN is 492-23-5605. The Fishers enter her name, address, TIN, and the $1,621.50 on Schedule 2, Part I (lines 1 and 2). They enter the

Illustration 4-5
Filled-In Form 1040A, Page 1

Form **1040A**

Department of the Treasury—Internal Revenue Service

U.S. Individual Income Tax Return   **1992**

IRS Use Only—Do not write or staple in this space.

OMB No. 1545-0085

Label (See page 14.)

Use the IRS label. Otherwise, please print or type.

Your first name and initial / Last name

William E. Fisher

If a joint return, spouse's first name and initial / Last name

Lori R. Fisher

Home address (number and street). If you have a P.O. box, see page 15. / Apt. no.

400 South Elm Street

City, town or post office, state, and ZIP code. If you have a foreign address, see page 15.

Chicago, IL 60631-1314

Your social security number

269 09 9092

Spouse's social security number

390 16 2222

For Privacy Act and Paperwork Reduction Act Notice, see page 4.

Presidential Election Campaign Fund (See page 15.)

	Yes	No
Do you want $1 to go to this fund?	X	
If a joint return, does your spouse want $1 to go to this fund?	X	

Note: *Checking "Yes" will not change your tax or reduce your refund.*

Check the box for your filing status (See page 15.)

Check only one box.

1 ☐ Single
2 ☒ Married filing joint return (even if only one had income)
3 ☐ Married filing separate return. Enter spouse's social security number above and full name here. ▶ _______________
4 ☐ Head of household (with qualifying person). (See page 16.) If the qualifying person is a child but not your dependent, enter this child's name here. ▶ _______________
5 ☐ Qualifying widow(er) with dependent child (year spouse died ▶ 19 ____). (See page 17.)

Figure your exemptions (See page 18.)

If more than seven dependents, see page 21.

6a ☒ Yourself. If your parent (or someone else) can claim you as a dependent on his or her tax return, do not check box 6a. But be sure to check the box on line 18b on page 2.

b ☒ Spouse

c Dependents:

(1) Name (first, initial, and last name)	(2) Check if under age 1	(3) If age 1 or older, dependent's social security number	(4) Dependent's relationship to you	(5) No. of months lived in your home in 1992
Marian C. Fisher		624 18 1111	daughter	12

d If your child didn't live with you but is claimed as your dependent under a pre-1985 agreement, check here . . . . ▶ ☐

e Total number of exemptions claimed.

No. of boxes checked on 6a and 6b **2**

No. of your children on 6c who:
• lived with you **1**
• didn't live with you due to divorce or separation (see page 21) ____

No. of other dependents on 6c ____

Add numbers entered on lines above **3**

Figure your total income

Attach Copy B of your Forms W-2 and 1099-R here.

If you didn't get a W-2, see page 22.

Attach check or money order on top of any Forms W-2 or 1099-R.

7	Wages, salaries, tips, etc. This should be shown in box 10 of your W-2 form(s). Attach Form(s) W-2.	7	22,150 00
8a	**Taxable** interest income (see page 24). If over $400, also complete and attach Schedule 1, Part I.	8a	230 00
b	Tax-exempt interest. DO NOT include on line 8a. 8b		
9	Dividends. If over $400, also complete and attach Schedule 1, Part II.	9	410 00
10a	Total IRA distributions. 10a	10b Taxable amount (see page 25). 10b	
11a	Total pensions and annuities. 11a	11b Taxable amount (see page 25). 11b	
12	Unemployment compensation (see page 29).	12	
13a	Social security benefits. 13a	13b Taxable amount (see page 29). 13b	
14	Add lines 7 through 13b (far right column). This is your total income. ▶	14	22,790 00

Figure your adjusted gross income

15a	Your IRA deduction from applicable worksheet. 15a 1,500 00		
b	Spouse's IRA deduction from applicable worksheet. Note: *Rules for IRAs begin on page 31.* 15b		
c	Add lines 15a and 15b. These are your **total adjustments**.	15c	1,500 00
16	Subtract line 15c from line 14. This is your **adjusted gross income**. If less than $22,370, see "Earned income credit" on page 39. ▶	16	21,290 00

Cat. No. 11327A

1992 Form 1040A page 1

Illustration 4-5
Filled-In Form 1040A, Page 2

1992 Form 1040A page 2

Name(s) shown on page 1	Your social security number
William E. & Lori R. Fisher	269 09 9092

Figure your standard deduction, exemption amount, and taxable income

17	Enter the amount from line 16.	17	21,290 00

18a Check if: ☐ You were 65 or older ☐ Blind / ☐ Spouse was 65 or older ☐ Blind } Enter number of boxes checked ▶ 18a ☐

b If your parent (or someone else) can claim you as a dependent, check here . . . . ▶ 18b ☐

c If you are married filing separately and your spouse files Form 1040 and itemizes deductions, see page 35 and check here ▶ 18c ☐

19 Enter the **standard deduction** shown below for your filing status. **But if you checked any box on line 18a or b,** go to page 35 to find your standard deduction. **If you checked box 18c,** enter -0-.

- Single—$3,600
- Head of household—$5,250
- Married filing jointly or Qualifying widow(er)—$6,000
- Married filing separately—$3,000

		19	6,000 00
20	Subtract line 19 from line 17. (If line 19 is more than line 17, enter -0-.)	20	15,290 00
21	Multiply $2,300 by the total number of exemptions claimed on line 6e.	21	6,900 00
22	Subtract line 21 from line 20. (If line 21 is more than line 20, enter -0-.) This is your **taxable income.** ▶	22	8,390 00

Figure your tax, credits, and payments

If you want the IRS to figure your tax, see the instructions for line 22 on page 36.

23	Find the tax on the amount on line 22. Check if from: ☒ Tax Table (pages 48–53) or ☐ Form 8615 (see page 37).	23	1,256 00
24a	Credit for child and dependent care expenses. Complete and attach Schedule 2. 24a 389 16		
b	Credit for the elderly or the disabled. Complete and attach Schedule 3. 24b		
c	Add lines 24a and 24b. These are your **total credits.**	24c	389 16
25	Subtract line 24c from line 23. (If line 24c is more than line 23, enter -0-.)	25	866 84
26	Advance earned income credit payments from Form W-2.	26	
27	Add lines 25 and 26. This is your **total tax.** ▶	27	866 84
28a	Total Federal income tax withheld. If any tax is from Form(s) 1099, check here. ▶ ☐ 28a 1,776 00		
b	1992 estimated tax payments and amount applied from 1991 return. 28b		
c	**Earned income credit.** Complete and attach Schedule EIC. 28c		
d	Add lines 28a, 28b, and 28c. These are your **total payments.** ▶	28d	1,776 00

Figure your refund or amount you owe

Attach check or money order on top of Form(s) W-2, etc., on page 1.

29	If line 28d is more than line 27, subtract line 27 from line 28d. This is the amount you **overpaid.**	29	909 16
30	Amount of line 29 you want **refunded to you.**	30	909 16
31	Amount of line 29 you want **applied to your** 1993 estimated tax. 31		
32	If line 27 is more than line 28d, subtract line 28d from line 27. This is the **amount you owe.** Attach check or money order for full amount payable to the "Internal Revenue Service". Write your name, address, social security number, daytime phone number, and "1992 Form 1040A" on it.	32	
33	Estimated tax penalty (see page 41). 33		

Sign your return

Under penalties of perjury, I declare that I have examined this return and accompanying schedules and statements, and to the best of my knowledge and belief, they are true, correct, and complete. Declaration of preparer (other than the taxpayer) is based on all information of which the preparer has any knowledge.

Keep a copy of this return for your records.

Your signature	Date	Your occupation
William E. Fisher	2/16/93	Clerk

Spouse's signature. If joint return, BOTH must sign.	Date	Spouse's occupation
Lori R. Fisher	2/16/93	Teller

Paid preparer's use only

Preparer's signature ▶	Date	Check if self-employed ☐	Preparer's social security no.
Firm's name (or yours if self-employed) and address ▶		E.I. No.	
		ZIP code	

Illustration 4-6
Filled-In Schedule 1, Form 1040A

Schedule 1
(Form 1040A)

Department of the Treasury—Internal Revenue Service

Interest and Dividend Income
for Form 1040A Filers   **1992**

OMB No. 1545-0085

Name(s) shown on Form 1040A

William E. & Lori R. Fisher

Your social security number

269 : 09 : 9092

Part I

Interest income

(See pages 24 and 54.)

Complete this part and attach Schedule 1 to Form 1040A if:

- You had over $400 in taxable interest, or
- You are claiming the exclusion of interest from series EE U.S. savings bonds issued after 1989.

If you received, as a nominee, interest that actually belongs to another person, see page 54.

Note: *If you received a Form 1099–INT, Form 1099–OID, or substitute statement, from a brokerage firm, enter the firm's name and the total interest shown on that form.*

1 List name of payer—if any interest is from seller-financed mortgages, see page 54		Amount
	1	
2 Add the amounts on line 1.	2	
3 Excludable interest on series EE U.S. savings bonds issued after 1989 from Form 8815, line 14. You MUST attach Form 8815 to Form 1040A.	3	
4 Subtract line 3 from line 2. Enter the result here and on Form 1040A, line 8a.	4	

Part II

Dividend income

(See pages 24 and 55.)

Complete this part and attach Schedule 1 to Form 1040A if you had over $400 in dividends.

If you received, as a nominee, dividends that actually belong to another person, see page 55.

Note: *If you received a Form 1099–DIV, or substitute statement, from a brokerage firm, enter the firm's name and the total dividends shown on that form.*

5 List name of payer		Amount
RPM Manufacturing Company	5	410 00
6 Add the amounts on line 5. Enter the total here and on Form 1040A, line 9.	6	410 00

number "1" in Part II (line 3). This tells the IRS that the Fishers have only one qualifying dependent. They also enter the $1,621.50 of qualifying expenses (line 4).

The Fishers enter their maximum credit amount of $2,400 (lines 5 and 7). Next, they enter the smaller of the qualified expenses of $1,621.50 (line 4) or the maximum credit amount of $2,400 (line 7). Then, they enter Mr. Fisher's earned income of $16,200 (line 9) and Mrs. Fisher's earned income of $5,950 (line 10). They enter (line 11) the smallest of actual expenses of $1,621.50 (line 8), Mr. Fisher's income of $16,200 (line 9), or Mrs. Fisher's income of $5,950 (line 10).

The Fishers multiply the entered $1,621.50 (line 11) by the decimal entered earlier (line 13). To arrive at the decimal, the Fishers entered their AGI from Form 1040A (line 17) of $21,290 on Schedule 2 (line 12) and used the printed table (line 13) to find the proper decimal. They entered 0.24 (line 13), calculated their child care credit of $389.16 (line 14), and entered it on Form 1040A (lines 24a and 24c).

Deductions. On Form 1040A, page 2, the Fishers enter their $6,000 standard deduction (line 19). They deduct $6,900 (3 x $2,300) for three exemptions (line 21). Then, the Fishers enter their taxable income of $8,390 (line 22).

Tax, Credits, and Payments. The Fishers use the tax table to figure their tax. They find that their taxable income of $8,390 falls in the bracket "At least $8,350, but less than $8,400." Since the Fishers are filing a joint return, they follow the line across to the "Married filing jointly" column. Here, they find $1,256. The Fishers enter this amount (line 23) and place an "X" in the first box on this line. This "X" tells the IRS that the Fishers used the tax table to figure their tax.

The Fishers enter their $389.16 credit for child and dependent care expense (lines 24a and 24c) and deduct it from their $1,256 tax. The difference is the total tax of $866.84 (lines 25 and 27). They report their withheld income tax of $1,776 (lines 28a and 28d). Since the amount of income tax withheld of $1,776 is larger than the total tax of $866.84, they are entitled to a refund. They enter the refund of $909.16 (line 29). Since the Fishers want the IRS to send them the refund, they enter the refund amount again (line 30). Both William and Lori Fisher sign and date the return and enter their occupations.

When and Where Filed. The Fishers file their tax return with the Internal Revenue Service Center in Kansas City. Since they mailed the return on February 16, 1993, they don't have to worry about a late filing penalty.

Filled-In Form 1040, Page 1

Illustration 4-9

This illustration shows how Neal R. and Betty Jo Richards in Illustration 4-3 enter their tax data on Form 1040, page 1. Illustration 4-4 contains Neal's SSN. Betty Jo's SSN is 701-62-3714. They live at 1002 Lakeview Lane, Dallas, Texas 75211-3674.

Both Neal and Betty Jo want $1.00 of their tax money to go to the Presidential Election Fund. The Richards have no dependency exemptions. They combine their salaries ($17,600 for Neal and $27,400 for Betty Jo) and enter the $45,000 total (line 7). Since the Richards have over $400 in dividend income, they prepare Schedule B, Form 1040, Parts II and III. In Part II they enter the $600 dividend (lines 5, 6, and 10). They also enter the Bula Hoe and Fork Company name (line 5). They place an "X" in the Part III "NO" boxes (lines 11a and 12), and enter the $600 dividend on Form 1040 (line 9).

The Richards add the Form 1040 income items (lines 7 and 9) and enter $45,600 (line 23). They enter Neal's deductible IRA contribution of $880 (line 24a), and Betty Jo's of $500 (line 24b). They add these amounts and enter the $1,380 total (line 30). Then, they subtract the total adjustments (line 30) from total income (line 23) and enter the $44,220 difference (line 31). It is the Richards' AGI.

Illustration 4-8
Filled-In Schedule 2, Form 1040A

Schedule 2
(Form 1040A)

Department of the Treasury—Internal Revenue Service
Child and Dependent Care
Expenses for Form 1040A Filers   **1992**

OMB No. 1545-0085

Name(s) shown on Form 1040A

William E. & Lori R. Fisher

Your social security number
269 : 09 : 9092

Caution: • *If you have a child who was born in 1992 and the amount on Form 1040A, line 17, is less than $22,370, see A change to note on page 56 before completing this schedule.*

• *If you paid cash wages of $50 or more in a calendar quarter to an individual for services performed in your home, you must file an employment tax return. Get Form 942 for details.*

Part I

Persons or organizations who provided the care

You MUST complete this part. (See page 57.)

	(a) Care provider's name	(b) Address (number, street, apt. no., city, state, and ZIP code)	(c) Identifying number (SSN or EIN)	(d) Amount paid (see page 57)
1	Helen Johnson	406 South Elm Street Chicago, IL 60631–1314	492–23–5605	1,621 50

(If you need more space, use the bottom of page 2.)
2 Add the amounts in column (d) of line 1.   **2**   1,621 50

Next: Did you receive employer-provided dependent care benefits?
• **YES.** Complete Part III on the back now.
• **NO.** Complete Part II below.

Part II

Credit for child and dependent care expenses

3 Enter the number of qualifying persons cared for in 1992. You must have shared the same home with the qualifying person(s). See page 57 to find out who is a qualifying person.   **3**   1

4 Enter the amount of **qualified** expenses you incurred and actually paid in 1992. See page 58 to find out which expenses qualify.
Caution: *If you completed Part III on page 2, DO NOT include on this line any excluded benefits shown on line 23.*   **4**   1,621 50

5 Enter $2,400 ($4,800 if you paid for the care of two or more qualifying persons).   **5**   2,400 00

6 If you completed Part III on page 2, enter the **excluded benefits,** if any, from line 23.   **6**

7 Subtract line 6 from line 5. If line 6 is equal to or more than line 5, STOP HERE; you cannot claim the credit.   **7**   2,400 00

8 Look at lines 4 and 7. Enter the **smaller** of the two amounts here.   **8**   1,621 50

9 You **must** enter your **earned income.** See page 58 for the definition of earned income.   **9**   16,200 00

Note: *If you are not filing a joint return, go to "All other filers" on line 11 now.*

10 If you are filing a joint return, you **must** enter your spouse's earned income. If your spouse was a student or disabled, see page 59 for the amount to enter.   **10**   5,950 00

11 • If you are filing a joint return, look at lines 8, 9, and 10. Enter the **smallest** of the three amounts here.
• All other filers, look at lines 8 and 9. Enter the **smaller** of the two amounts here.   **11**   1,621 50

12 Enter the amount from Form 1040A, line 17.   **12**   21,290 00

13 Enter the decimal amount shown below that applies to the amount on line 12.

If line 12 is—		Decimal amount is—	If line 12 is—		Decimal amount is—
Over	But not over		Over	But not over	
$0	10,000	.30	$20,000	22,000	.24
10,000	12,000	.29	22,000	24,000	.23
12,000	14,000	.28	24,000	26,000	.22
14,000	16,000	.27	26,000	28,000	.21
16,000	18,000	.26	28,000	No limit	.20
18,000	20,000	.25			

13   ×.24

14 Multiply line 11 above by the decimal amount on line 13. Enter the result here and on Form 1040A, line 24a.   **14** = 389 16

For Paperwork Reduction Act Notice, see Form 1040A instructions.   Cat. No. 10749I   1992 Schedule 2 (Form 1040A) page 1

Illustration 4-9
Filled-In Form 1040, Page 1

Form **1040** Department of the Treasury—Internal Revenue Service
U.S. Individual Income Tax Return 19**92**   IRS Use Only—Do not write or staple in this space.

For the year Jan. 1–Dec. 31, 1992, or other tax year beginning _______, 1992, ending _______, 19___   OMB No. 1545-0074

Label (See instructions on page 10.) Use the IRS label. Otherwise, please print or type.

Your first name and initial — Last name: **Neal R. Richards**
Your social security number: **678 : 42 : 1720**

If a joint return, spouse's first name and initial — Last name: **Betty Jo Richards**
Spouse's social security number: **701 : 62 : 3714**

Home address (number and street). If you have a P.O. box, see page 10. Apt. no.: **1002 Lakeview Lane**

For Privacy Act and Paperwork Reduction Act Notice, see page 4.

City, town or post office, state, and ZIP code. If you have a foreign address, see page 10.: **Dallas, TX 75211-3674**

Presidential Election Campaign (See page 10.)
Do you want $1 to go to this fund? . . . . [X] Yes [ ] No
If a joint return, does your spouse want $1 to go to this fund? . [X] Yes [ ] No
Note: Checking "Yes" will not change your tax or reduce your refund.

Filing Status (See page 10.) Check only one box.

1 [ ] Single
2 [X] Married filing joint return (even if only one had income)
3 [ ] Married filing separate return. Enter spouse's social security no. above and full name here. ▶ ___________
4 [ ] Head of household (with qualifying person). (See page 11.) If the qualifying person is a child but not your dependent, enter this child's name here. ▶ ___________
5 [ ] Qualifying widow(er) with dependent child (year spouse died ▶ 19___). (See page 11.)

Exemptions (See page 11.)

6a [X] Yourself. If your parent (or someone else) can claim you as a dependent on his or her tax return, do not check box 6a. But be sure to check the box on line 33b on page 2

b [X] Spouse

No. of boxes checked on 6a and 6b: **2**

c Dependents:

(1) Name (first, initial, and last name)	(2) Check if under age 1	(3) If age 1 or older, dependent's social security number	(4) Dependent's relationship to you	(5) No. of months lived in your home in 1992

No. of your children on 6c who:
• lived with you
• didn't live with you due to divorce or separation (see page 13)
No. of other dependents on 6c

If more than six dependents, see page 12.

d If your child didn't live with you but is claimed as your dependent under a pre-1985 agreement, check here ▶ [ ]
e Total number of exemptions claimed . . . .

Add numbers entered on lines above ▶ **2**

Income

Attach Copy B of your Forms W-2, W-2G, and 1099-R here.

If you did not get a W-2, see page 9.

Attach check or money order on top of any Forms W-2, W-2G, or 1099-R.

7	Wages, salaries, tips, etc. Attach Form(s) W-2	7	45,000 00
8a	Taxable interest income. Attach Schedule B if over $400	8a	
b	Tax-exempt interest income (see page 15). DON'T include on line 8a [8b]		
9	Dividend income. Attach Schedule B if over $400	9	600 00
10	Taxable refunds, credits, or offsets of state and local income taxes from worksheet on page 16	10	
11	Alimony received	11	
12	Business income or (loss). Attach Schedule C or C-EZ	12	
13	Capital gain or (loss). Attach Schedule D	13	
14	Capital gain distributions not reported on line 13 (see page 15)	14	
15	Other gains or (losses). Attach Form 4797	15	
16a	Total IRA distributions [16a]	b Taxable amount (see page 16)	16b	
17a	Total pensions and annuities [17a]	b Taxable amount (see page 16)	17b	
18	Rents, royalties, partnerships, estates, trusts, etc. Attach Schedule E	18	
19	Farm income or (loss). Attach Schedule F	19	
20	Unemployment compensation (see page 17)	20	
21a	Social security benefits [21a]	b Taxable amount (see page 17)	21b	
22	Other income. List type and amount—see page 18	22	
23	Add the amounts in the far right column for lines 7 through 22. This is your total income ▶	23	45,600 00

Adjustments to Income (See page 18.)

24a	Your IRA deduction from applicable worksheet on page 19 or 20	24a	880 00
b	Spouse's IRA deduction from applicable worksheet on page 19 or 20	24b	500 00
25	One-half of self-employment tax (see page 20)	25	
26	Self-employed health insurance deduction (see page 20)	26	
27	Keogh retirement plan and self-employed SEP deduction	27	
28	Penalty on early withdrawal of savings	28	
29	Alimony paid. Recipient's SSN ▶ ___________	29	
30	Add lines 24a through 29. These are your total adjustments . . . . ▶	30	1,380 00

Adjusted Gross Income

31 Subtract line 30 from line 23. This is your **adjusted gross income**. If this amount is less than $22,370 and a child lived with you, see page EIC-1 to find out if you can claim the "Earned Income Credit" on line 56 . . . . ▶ | 31 | 44,220 00 |

Cat. No. 11320B

Illustration 4-9
Filled-In Parts II and III, Schedule B, Form 1040, Page 2

Schedules A&B (Form 1040) 1992   OMB No. 1545-0074   Page **2**

Name(s) shown on Form 1040. Do not enter name and social security number if shown on other side. | Your social security number

Neal R. & Betty Jo Richards   678 42 1720

Schedule B—Interest and Dividend Income
Attachment Sequence No. **08**

Part I
Interest Income

(See pages 14 and B-1.)

If you had over $400 in taxable interest income OR are claiming the exclusion of interest from series EE U.S. savings bonds issued after 1989, you must complete this part. List ALL interest you received. If you had over $400 in taxable interest income, you must also complete Part III. If you received, as a nominee, interest that actually belongs to another person, or you received or paid accrued interest on securities transferred between interest payment dates, see page B-1.

Interest Income	Amount
1 List name of payer—if any interest income is from seller-financed mortgages, see page B-1 and list this interest first ▶	1

Note: If you received a Form 1099-INT, Form 1099-OID, or substitute statement from a brokerage firm, list the firm's name as the payer and enter the total interest shown on that form.

2 Add the amounts on line 1	2
3 Excludable interest on series EE U.S. savings bonds issued after 1989 from Form 8815, line 14. You MUST attach Form 8815 to Form 1040	3
4 Subtract line 3 from line 2. Enter the result here and on Form 1040, line 8a. ▶	4

Part II
Dividend Income

(See pages 15 and B-1.)

If you had over $400 in gross dividends and/or other distributions on stock, you must complete this part and Part III. If you received, as a nominee, dividends that actually belong to another person, see page B-1.

Dividend Income	Amount	
5 List name of payer—include on this line capital gain distributions, nontaxable distributions, etc. ▶		
Bula Hoe and Fork Company	600	00
	5	

Note: If you received a Form 1099-DIV or substitute statement from a brokerage firm, list the firm's name as the payer and enter the total dividends shown on that form.

6 Add the amounts on line 5	6	600	00
7 Capital gain distributions. Enter here and on Schedule D*.	7	
8 Nontaxable distributions. (See the inst. for Form 1040, line 9.)	8	
9 Add lines 7 and 8	9	
10 Subtract line 9 from line 6. Enter the result here and on Form 1040, line 9 ▶	10	600	00

*If you received capital gain distributions but do not need Schedule D to report any other gains or losses, see the instructions for Form 1040, lines 13 and 14.

Part III
Foreign Accounts and Foreign Trusts

(See page B-2.)

If you had over $400 of interest or dividends OR had a foreign account or were a grantor of, or a transferor to, a foreign trust, you must complete this part.

	Yes	No
11a At any time during 1992, did you have an interest in or a signature or other authority over a financial account in a foreign country, such as a bank account, securities account, or other financial account? See page B-2 for exceptions and filing requirements for Form TD F 90-22.1		X
b If "Yes," enter the name of the foreign country ▶		
12 Were you the grantor of, or transferor to, a foreign trust that existed during 1992, whether or not you have any beneficial interest in it? If "Yes," you may have to file Form 3520, 3520-A, or 926		X

For Paperwork Reduction Act Notice, see Form 1040 instructions.   Schedule B (Form 1040) 1992

C H A P T E R   4

Questions and Problems

1. **a.** Name six types of tax-exempt benefits for members of the Armed Forces of the United States that are not related to combat-zone activities.

   b. Members of the Armed Forces of the United States who serve in a combat zone can exclude certain pay and benefits from gross income. By Executive Order, the President of the United States identifies a combat zone. Some military personnel in a combat zone are not eligible for the exclusion. Who are they?

   c. From time to time, former members of the Armed Forces of the United States receive benefits from the Veterans Administration (VA). Name five VA benefits that are exempt from federal income taxation.

2. During 1992, Jacob C. Steiner receives $10,000 ($8,000 principal and $2,000 of interest) from the redemption of U.S. Savings Bond, Series EE. The bonds qualify for the educational exclusion. He uses the proceeds to pay university tuition and fees of $5,500 for his two dependent children, Sharon A. and Joseph P. Steiner. Sharon is 21 years of age, and Joseph is 20. With the exception of temporary absences away from home to attend the University of Michigan in Ann Arbor (48104) as full-time students, they live with their parents. During the year, Sharon and Joseph each receive a tax-exempt university scholarship of $1,500.

   The Steiner's home address is 2790 Lakeview Road, Muskegon, MI 49441. Mr. Steiner's SSN is 372-90-6729. He receives an annual salary of $72,900 and files a joint return with his wife Rachael on Form 1040. Rachael has no gross income. Prepare Form 8815 on the following page for the Steiners.

Form **8815** Department of the Treasury Internal Revenue Service	**Exclusion of Interest From Series EE U.S. Savings Bonds Issued After 1989** (For Filers With Qualified Higher Education Expenses) ▶ Attach to Form 1040 or Form 1040A. ▶ See instructions on back.	OMB No. 1545-1173 **1992** Attachment Sequence No. **57**

Caution: *If your filing status is married filing a separate return, **do not** file this form. You **cannot** take the exclusion even if you paid qualified higher education expenses in 1992.*

Name(s) shown on return | Your social security number

1	**(a)** Name of person (you, your spouse, or your dependent) who was enrolled at or attended an eligible educational institution	**(b)** Name and address of eligible educational institution

If you need more space, attach a statement.

2	Enter the total qualified higher education expenses you paid in 1992 for the persons listed in column (a) of line 1. See the instructions to find out which expenses qualify	2	
3	Enter the total of any nontaxable educational benefits (such as nontaxable scholarship or fellowship grants) received for 1992 for the persons listed in column (a) of line 1. See instructions	3	
4	Subtract line 3 from line 2. If the result is less than zero, enter -0- . . . . **Note:** *If line 4 is zero, stop here; you **cannot** take the exclusion.*	4	
5	Enter the total proceeds (principal and interest) from all series EE U.S. savings bonds **issued after 1989** that you **cashed during 1992**.	5	
6	Enter the interest included on line 5. See instructions	6	
7	Look at lines 4 and 5 above. Is line 4 **less than** line 5? • **Yes.** Divide line 4 by line 5. Enter the result as a decimal (to at least two places). • **No.** Enter "1.00."	7	× .
8	Multiply line 6 by line 7	8	
9	Enter your modified adjusted gross income. See instructions . . . **9**	
	Note: *If line 9 is $59,150 or more ($96,200 or more if married filing a joint return), stop here; you **cannot** take the exclusion.*		
10	Enter $44,150 ($66,200 if married filing a joint return). **10**	
11	Subtract line 10 from line 9. If the result is zero or less, skip line 12, enter -0- on line 13, and go to line 14 . . . . **11**	
12	Divide line 11 by $15,000 (by $30,000 if married filing a joint return). Enter the result as a decimal (to at least two places)	12	× .
13	Multiply line 8 by line 12	13	
14	**Excludable savings bond interest.** Subtract line 13 from line 8. Enter the result here and on Schedule B (Form 1040), line 3, or Schedule 1 (Form 1040A), line 3, whichever applies . . ▶	14	

Paperwork Reduction Act Notice

We ask for the information on this form to carry out the Internal Revenue laws of the United States. You are required to give us the information. We need it to ensure that you are complying with these laws and to allow us to figure and collect the right amount of tax.

The time needed to complete and file this form will vary depending on individual circumstances. The estimated average time is: **Recordkeeping, 53 min.; Learning about the law or the form, 11 min.; Preparing the form, 35 min.; and Copying, assembling, and sending the form to the IRS, 34 min.**

If you have comments concerning the accuracy of these time estimates or suggestions for making this form more simple, we would be happy to hear from you. You can write to both the IRS and the Office of Management and Budget at the addresses listed in the instructions of the tax return with which this form is filed.

Cat. No. 10822S Form **8815** (1992)

3. On August 1, 1992, Marion DeNoble was granted a $6,000 scholarship for each of 4 academic years (9 months each year) to earn a degree from Birdhaven University. The scholarship grant includes $4,000 for tuition, fees, and books and $2,000 for room and board. Payment is 1/9 each month, starting September 10, 1992, and is made on the 10th of each month thereafter.

   a. How much of the scholarship payments can Ms. DeNoble exclude from gross income in 1992? Why?

   b. If Ms. DeNoble is not a degree candidate, is there any limitation to the amount of her exclusion? Explain.

4. Certain fringe benefits must comply with the nondiscrimination rules, while other fringe benefits are not required to meet these rules.

   a. What are nondiscrimination rules? What are the consequences for failing to meet the nondiscrimination rules?

   b. For each category of fringe benefits given below, state whether the nondiscrimination rules apply and give two examples of specific fringe benefits in that category.

Fringe Benefit Category	Nondiscrimination Rules Apply (Yes or No)	Examples of Specific Fringe Benefits in Each Category
De minimis fringe benefits	_____________	_________________________
Qualified employee discounts	_____________	_________________________
Working condition fringe benefits	_____________	_________________________
No-additional-cost services	_____________	_________________________
On-premise athletic facilities	_____________	_________________________

5. Marilyn A. Sippola, a single taxpayer who is not eligible to file Form 1040EZ, owns bonds from each of the issues listed below. She does not own any stock certificates. During the current year she purchased a number of bonds and received the interest amounts shown. In the space provided, state the amount of interest to be included in or excluded from gross income in 1992 and, if excluded, state why.

Bond	Issue	Date Purchased Bonds Owned	Interest Received
A	City of Jefferson	7- 1-82	$400
B	Pymatuming School District	7-10-81	250
C	U.S. Treasury	2- 1-87	300
D	Bow & Socket Company	12-10-79	184
E	Series HH U.S. Savings	11- 1-83	800

Bond	Interest Includable	Interest Excludable and Why
A	$	$
B	$	$
C	$	$
D	$	$
E	$	$

6. Doris Koffman owns a Series E bond with an original maturity of $1,000 which she purchased for $750 several years ago. The redemption value during 1992 is $1,012, and the extended maturity value ten years from the current year is $1,467.20. Assume Ms. Koffman has not elected to report the bond interest on a year-by-year basis. In the space below, indicate the amount of her 1992 gross income from bond interest if

   a. The bond is redeemed during 1992.

   b. The bond is not redeemed during 1992.

7. Using the 1992 information that follows for an unmarried taxpayer with no dependents, prepare an analysis listing in appropriate sequence the tax base. Show each item and amount under the appropriate headings of (a) income, (b) gross income exclusions, (c) gross income inclusions, (d) deductions for AGI, (e) AGI, (f) deductions from AGI, including both the standard deduction and exemptions, and (g) taxable income. In addition, show the total amount for each heading.

Cash Received

Interest on savings account	$ 3,350.00
Subsistence allowance for student's advanced ROTC training	1,296.00
Gift of money from parent	500.00
Rent from farmland owned	20,000.00
Proceeds of life insurance policy of parent	40,000.00
Nondegree candidate fellowship, granted 8/20/91, of $450 per month for 4 months	1,800.00
Gross salary of $32,000 less $8,100 state and federal income taxes, $1,984 social security taxes, and $464 health insurance program. Net pay received	21,452.00
De minimis employee fringe benefits valued at $20	-0-
Company automobile, working condition, fringe benefit, costing employer $200 per month for 12 months. Not in compliance with IRS nondiscrimination rules	-0-
Total cash received	$88,398.00

Cash Payments

Expenses of farmland rental	$ 2,000.00
Cost of living expenditures	6,600.00
Total cash payments	$ 8,600.00

8. The Speedy-Tanner Company pays an annual premium for $87,000 of nondiscriminatory group-term life insurance coverage on its president, William R. Logan. Bill is 44 years of age. His wife, Rachael, is the policy's beneficiary. For this group-term life insurance, Bill pays Speedy-Tanner $0.80 per year for each $1,000 of coverage. His share of the insurance premium is deducted from his gross salary under Speedy-Tanner's payroll deduction plan. What portion of the group-term life insurance cost must Mr. Logan include in his gross income for 1992?

9. Joyce and Barry Bright are both employed. Each is 56 years of age. In 1992 Barry has earned wages of $1,500 and Joyce has earned wages of $17,530. Joyce is an active participant in her employer-maintained qualified annuity pension plan. For 1992, the Brights plan to file a joint tax return and claim the maximum deduction for payments made to an IRA.

   a. What is the latest date by which an IRA payment must be made in order for it to be claimed on the Brights' 1992 return?

   b. Can the payments be claimed on Form 1040EZ? On Form 1040A?

   c. What is the maximum amount Joyce and Barry can each pay into an IRA and deduct for 1992?

   d. Are the earnings on the IRA payments made in 1992 subject to federal income taxes in 1992? Explain.

10. Fred and Diane Workingman file a joint return. Neither taxpayer is covered by a retirement plan at work. For 1992, Fred's gross income from wages is $17,900. Diane's gross income from wages in 1992 is $21,500. Diane also received taxable interest income of $600 in 1992. Since establishing their IRAs, Diane and Fred have contributed the following amounts to them:

Diane:	April 6, 1992	$500
	July 1, 1992	500
	October 3, 1992	500
	January 4, 1993	500
Fred:	June 16, 1992	$1,000
	February 3, 1993	1,000

Earnings from their IRAs during 1992 were $890 for Diane and $340 for Fred. Calculate the Workingmans' allowable 1992 IRA deductions and their AGI.

11. Susan and Andrew Lee file a joint return for 1992. Susan has taxable interest income of $400. Andrew has income of $29,000 which consists of $8,000 in wages, $13,000 in tips, $5,500 in taxable dividends, and $2,500 in tax-exempt interest. The Lees plan to make the maximum allowable IRA contribution for 1992. Neither is covered by a retirement plan at work. Determine the Lees' maximum IRA contribution by preparing IRA Worksheet 1 provided below.

IRA Worksheet 1—Lines 24a and 24b (keep for your records)

	(a) Your IRA	(b) Your working spouse's IRA
1. Enter IRA contributions you made, or will make by April 15, 1993, for 1992. But **do not** enter more than $2,000 in either column . . . . . . 1.	_________	_________
2. For each person, enter wages and other earned income from Form 1040, minus any deductions on Form 1040, lines 25 and 27. Do not reduce wages by any loss from self-employment . . 2.	_________	_________
3. Enter the **smaller** of line 1 or line 2. Enter on Form 1040, line 24a, the amount from line 3, column (a), you choose to deduct. Enter on Form 1040, line 24b, the amount, if any, from line 3, column (b), you choose to deduct. If filing a joint return and contributions were made to your nonworking spouse's IRA, go to line 4 . . . . 3.	_________	_________.

		Nonworking spouse's IRA
4. Enter the **smaller** of line 2, column (a), or $2,250	4.	_________
5. Enter the amount from line 3, column (a)	5.	_________
6. Subtract line 5 from line 4	6.	_________
7. Enter IRA contributions made, or that will be made by April 15, 1993, for 1992 for your nonworking spouse. But **do not** enter more than $2,000	7.	_________
8. Enter the **smaller** of line 6 or line 7. Enter on Form 1040, line 24b, the amount from line 8 you choose to deduct	8.	_________

12. For 1992, Ken Daniel has gross income of $14,995. Fran Daniel, his wife, has gross income of $3,898. Ken and Fran are each 42 years of age. Each contributed $1,000 to an IRA and is entitled to claim an IRA deduction of $1,000. The Daniels will use the standard deduction to determine their tax liability. They are entitled to claim three exemptions.

a. What will be the amount of their income tax if they file a joint return using Form 1040A?

b. If the Daniels file separate returns and Ken claims 2 exemptions and Fran claims 1, what will be the amount of income tax on each return and the total combined tax?

13. Relative to gross income, indicate by placing an "X" in the proper column the includable or excludable status of the following 1992 income items received.

Item	Includable	Excludable
a. Worker's compensation	_________	_________
b. Rental value of parsonage for clergy	_________	_________
c. Embezzlement proceeds	_________	_________
d. Health resort fee paid for taxpayer by employer	_________	_________
e. Dividends from employees credit union	_________	_________
f. Free parking in employer's lot	_________	_________
g. FMV of an automobile won at a television giveaway program	_________	_________

	Item	Includable	Excludable
h.	Veteran's disability compensation	__________	__________
i.	Gambling winnings (no losses)	__________	__________
j.	Proceeds of a life insurance policy paid because of the death of the insured	__________	__________
k.	Dismissal pay received by employee	__________	__________
l.	Combat pay of enlisted personnel	__________	__________
m.	Gold necklace found in ocean	__________	__________

14. Distinguish between items that are deductions for AGI and adjustments to income. Give several examples of each.

15. Check whether the following statements are true or false.

		True	False
a.	The maximum deductible amount for contributions to an IRA in 1992 is $2,250 by a married couple who both work and each earns $10,000	______	______
b.	Contributions to an IRA are deductible in the determination of AGI for a single employee with earned income of $15,000	______	______
c.	The earnings of an IRA are taxed to the employee in the year earned	______	______
d.	Contributions to a nonworking spouse's IRA must be equally divided between the two spouses, up to the maximum limit of the combined deduction of $2,250	______	______
e.	Distributions from an IRA must begin no later than April 1 of the calendar year after an IRA depositor reaches age 70½	______	______
f.	The income earned on nondeductible IRA contributions is not taxable until it is withdrawn	______	______

16. Donald O. and Paula C. Light, married taxpayers filing jointly, reside at 1642 East Terrace Ave., Rochester, New York 14692-8854. They each have an IRA maintained by the Trust Department, Second National Bank, Rochester, New York 14692-3736. Donald's SSN is 672-01-8611 and Paula's is 362-84-9931. Donald's IRA has a value of $8,216.10 on December 31, 1992. All of the contributions for the 1992 IRA were made in 1992. Even though they are both covered by an employer-maintained retirement plan, they are eligible for partially deductible IRA contributions in 1992. Both Mr. and Mrs. Light have decided to contribute the maximum amount to their IRAs for 1992, consisting of partially deductible and partially nondeductible contributions. Nondeductible contributions of $1,100 had been made in prior years and had been recorded as the IRA basis as of December 31, 1991, on the 1991 Form 8606.

Mr. Light has determined that his deductible IRA contribution for 1992 is limited to $1,200 with the remainder nondeductible. He makes the total deposit in the account on December 15, 1992.

a. Prepare Form 8606 on the following page for Mr. Light to attach to the income tax return.

b. Explain how any distribution from Mr. Light's IRA in 1993 would be split between the deductible and nondeductible portions.

Form 8606

Department of the Treasury
Internal Revenue Service

Nondeductible IRA Contributions, IRA Basis, and Nontaxable IRA Distributions

▶ Please see Recordkeeping Requirements on page 2.
▶ Attach to Form 1040, Form 1040A, or Form 1040NR.

OMB No. 1545-1007

1991

Attachment
Sequence No. 47

Name. (If married, file a separate Form 8606 for each spouse. See instructions.)

Your social security number

Fill in Your Address Only If You Are Filing This Form by Itself and Not With Your Tax Return ▷

Home address (number and street, or P.O. box if mail is not delivered to your home)

Apt. no.

City, town or post office, state, and ZIP code

1	Enter the total value of **ALL** your IRAs as of 12/31/91. (See instructions.)	**1**
2	Enter your IRA contributions for 1991 that you choose to be nondeductible. Include those made during 1/1/92–4/15/92 that were for 1991. (See instructions.)	**2**
3	Enter your total IRA basis for 1990 and prior years. (See instructions.)	**3**
4	Add lines 2 and 3. If you did not receive any IRA distributions (withdrawals) in 1991, skip lines 5 through 13 and enter this amount on line 14	**4**
5	Enter only those contributions included on line 2 that were made during 1/1/92–4/15/92. (This amount will be the same as line 2 if all of your nondeductible contributions for 1991 were made in 1992 by 4/15/92.) (See instructions.)	**5**
6	Subtract line 5 from line 4	**6**
7	Enter the amount from line 1 plus any outstanding rollovers. (See instructions.)	**7**
8	Enter the total IRA distributions received during 1991. Do not include amounts rolled over before 1/1/92. (See instructions.)	**8**
9	Add lines 7 and 8	**9**
10	Divide line 6 by line 9 and enter the result as a decimal (to at least two places). Do not enter more than "1.00"	**10**
11	Multiply line 8 by line 10. This is the amount of your **nontaxable distributions for 1991.** (See instructions.) ▶	**11**
12	Subtract line 11 from line 6. This is the **basis in your IRA(s) as of 12/31/91**	**12**
13	Enter the amount, if any, from line 5	**13**
14	Add lines 12 and 13. This is your **total IRA basis for 1991 and prior years** ▶	**14**

Sign Here Only If You Are Filing This Form by Itself and Not With Your Tax Return

Under penalties of perjury, I declare that I have examined this form, including accompanying attachments, and to the best of my knowledge and belief, it is true, correct, and complete.

▶ Your signature   ▶ Date

Paperwork Reduction Act Notice.—We ask for the information on this form to carry out the Internal Revenue laws of the United States. You are required to give us the information. We need it to ensure that you are complying with these laws and to allow us to figure and collect the right amount of tax.

The time needed to complete and file this form will vary depending on individual circumstances. The estimated average time is: **Recordkeeping,** 26 minutes; **Learning about the law or the form,** 7 minutes; **Preparing the form,** 22 minutes; and **Copying, assembling, and sending the form to the IRS,** 20 minutes.

If you have comments concerning the accuracy of these time estimates or suggestions for making this form more simple, we would be happy to hear from you. You can write to both the **Internal Revenue Service,** Washington, DC 20224, Attention: IRS Reports Clearance Officer, T:FP; and the **Office of Management and Budget,** Paperwork Reduction Project (1545-1007), Washington, DC 20503. **DO**

NOT send this form to either of these offices. Instead, see **When and Where To File** on this page.

General Instructions

Purpose of Form.—You must use Form 8606 to report your IRA contributions that you choose to be nondeductible. You may wish to make nondeductible contributions, for example, if all or part of your contributions are not deductible because of the income limitations for IRAs. First, figure your deductible contributions using the instructions for Form 1040 or Form 1040A, whichever apply to you. Report the deductible contributions on Form 1040, Form 1040A, or Form 1040NR. Then, enter on line 2 of Form 8606 the amount you choose to be nondeductible.

The part of any distributions you receive attributable to nondeductible contributions will not be taxable. If you have at any time made nondeductible contributions, also use Form 8606 to figure the nontaxable part of any IRA distributions you received in 1991. Line 11 will show the amount that is not taxable.

Who Must File.—You must file Form 8606 for 1991 if **either** of the following applies:

• You made nondeductible contributions to your IRA for 1991, or

• You received IRA distributions in 1991 **and** you have at any time made nondeductible contributions to any of your IRAs.

When and Where To File.—Attach Form 8606 to your 1991 Form 1040, Form 1040A, or Form 1040NR.

If you are required to file Form 8606, but do not have to file an income tax return because you do not meet the requirements for filing a return, you still have to file a Form 8606 with the Internal Revenue Service at the time and place you would be required to file Form 1040, Form 1040A, or Form 1040NR.

Penalty for Not Filing Form 8606.—The law provides for a penalty if you make nondeductible IRA contributions and do not file Form 8606. You will have to pay a $50 penalty for each failure to file Form 8606, unless you can show that the failure to file was due to reasonable cause.

---

17. **a.** What is the maximum self-employed health insurance deduction that can be claimed as an adjustment to income?

    b. Under what conditions would a taxpayer not be eligible for the self-employed health insurance deduction?

18. **a.** What is the maximum deduction that can be claimed by a self-employed taxpayer for a money-purchase plan and for a profit-sharing plan under the defined contribution provisions of Keogh retirement plans?

    b. Explain the deduction for the penalty on the early withdrawal of savings.

    c. What is the income tax consequence of the transfer of property from one spouse to the other incidental to a divorce on February 6, 1992, when the FMV of the property is greater than the cost or tax basis?

PERSONAL DEDUCTIONS AND OTHER TAX CONSIDERATIONS

➡ The itemized deductions

➡ How to complete Schedule A

➡ How to report self-employment tax

➡ How to report alternative minimum tax (AMT)

➡ How to complete the earned income credit worksheet

➡ How to determine interest on underpayment or overpayment of taxes

➡ The penalties for taxpayers

➡ How to file an amended individual income return

Personal Itemized Deductions

Your Rights as a Taxpayer

Representation and Recordings. You can represent yourself, or generally with proper written authorization, have someone represent you in your absence. During an interview, you can have someone accompany you.

Source: Internal Revenue Service, Publication 1

Introduction to Itemized Deductions

This chapter covers the basic tax principles relating to those *itemized deductions* which constitute deductible personal expenses. These expenses include medical and dental expenses, taxes, interest expense, charitable contributions, and casualty and theft losses. The five types of itemized deductions presented in this chapter are the typical personal expenses incurred by taxpayers. These expenses may provide an opportunity for a larger deduction in computing taxable income than is provided through the standard deduction. Other itemized deductions related to employment and investment activities, which include moving expenses and miscellaneous deductions, are covered in Chapter 6. Taxpayers whose total itemized deductions are greater than their standard deduction can and should use their itemized deductions in calculating taxable income. Taking itemized deductions that are higher than the standard deduction will minimize their tax liability. Readers are referred to Chapter 1 for a detailed discussion of the standard deduction.

The calculation of itemized deductions has been relatively unchanged in recent years. However, certain changes occurred in the deductibility of personal interest and investment interest. These transition rules limited the deductibility of personal interest and investment interest. In tax years starting in 1991, personal interest expense is no longer deductible and investment interest expense is deductible only to the extent of investment income. The Tax Reconciliation Act of 1990 further restricted itemized deductions by excluding unnecessary cosmetic surgery as a medical expense deduction and by reducing total allowable itemized deductions (other than medical expenses, casualty and theft losses, and investment interest) by 3% of a taxpayer's AGI in excess of $100,000, ($105,250 in 1992) subject to some exceptions. The limitations on medical expenses and interest expense, which are applicable to tax years 1991, 1992, and later years, are discussed in Chapter 5. The limitations on total itemized deductions are discussed in Chapter 5.

Taxpayers should carefully plan their payments for itemized deductions so that they can be claimed in a year in which the total will exceed the standard deduction. This planning may result in a substantial reduction in tax liability.

Reporting Itemized Deductions (Schedule A)

Any taxpayer is eligible to deduct the total amount of itemized deductions when that total exceeds the standard deduction amount. Total itemized deductions are calculated by adding the dollar amounts allowed for each of these categories on Schedule A. The first five of these categories are described and illustrated in Chapter 5. The final three categories are discussed and illustrated in Chapter 6. Before discussing individual types of itemized deductions, readers should be aware of the maximum dollar amounts of the standard deduction for different taxpayer categories that must be exceeded in order for the taxpayer to benefit from taking itemized deductions.

Itemized Deductions Reported on Schedule A of Form 1040

1. Medical and Dental Expenses
2. Taxes You Paid
3. Interest You Paid
4. Gifts to Charity
5. Casualty and Theft Losses
6. Moving Expenses
7. Job Expenses
8. Other Miscellaneous Deductions

Guidelines

In general, a taxpayer should itemize deductions in 1992 if the following qualifications are applicable:

1. Married filing jointly or a qualifying widow(er) with dependent child, if the total itemized deductions are more than the allowed standard deduction of $6,000. Add $650 to the standard deduction for each married individual who is 65 or older, and add another $650 for each spouse who is blind.
2. Married filing separately, if the total itemized deductions are more than $3,000. Add $650 if the taxpayer is age 65 or older and another $650 if the taxpayer is blind.
3. Single, if the total itemized deductions are more than $3,600. Add $850 if the taxpayer

is age 65 or older and another $850 if the taxpayer is blind.

4. HOH, if total itemized deductions are more than $5,250. Add $850 if the taxpayer is age 65 or older and another $850 if the taxpayer is blind.

Medical and Dental Expenses

Medical and dental expenses paid during 1992 for the taxpayer, spouse, or a dependent are eligible for consideration as itemized deductions. Also included are medical expenses paid for a person who otherwise would be a dependent except that they do not meet the gross income test or the joint return test. For example, a taxpayer can deduct the medical expenses of a child who cannot be claimed as a dependent only because (1) the child's gross income exceeds $2,150 or (2) the child filed a joint return with his or her spouse on which there was a tax liability.

Expenses related to health care that are eligible for inclusion as itemized deductions include the following types:

1. Qualified medicines and drugs: only medicines and drugs prescribed by a physician, and insulin
2. All medical and dental insurance premiums
3. Other medical and dental expenses

The total of these includable medical expenses is treated as an itemized deduction to the extent such expenses *exceed 7½% of AGI*. Special considerations and limitations related to the deductibility of each of the above types of expenses are discussed below.

Prescription Medicines and Drugs; Insulin

The deductibility of medicines and drugs is very restrictive under the current tax rules. Only medicines and drugs prescribed by a physician and expenditures for insulin can be included under the medicines and drugs category of medical expenses. In other words, if it is not a prescription medicine or drug, or insulin, it is not deductible as a medicine or drug. Thus, taxpayers cannot treat vitamins and iron supplements purchased without a prescription as deductible medicines and drugs. Likewise, no

deduction is allowed for special foods that take the place of foods normally consumed. But the cost of special foods prescribed by a physician that supplement a normal diet and are not part of the nutritional needs would be includable as a medicine or drug. For example, if a restaurant charges extra to prepare food to meet a salt-free diet prescribed by a physician, the extra charge would be includable as a medical expense. Also includable as a medicine or drug would be birth control pills if prescribed by a physician.

Illustration 5-1

All deductible medical expenses are listed in the Medical and Dental Expenses section on Schedule A (line 1) including prescription medicines and drugs, and insulin; payments to doctors, dentists, nurses, and hospitals; premiums paid for medical and dental insurance; and other types of medical expenses, such as transportation and lodging related to medical care, hearing aids, dentures, and eyeglasses. In Illustration 5-1, the total of the medical expenses is $3,565.69 (line 1) after deducting any reimbursements from insurance and other sources as described later. The taxpayer's AGI, Form 1040 (line 32), in this case $33,900.44, is entered in the Medical and Dental section of Schedule A (line 2). The AGI is then multiplied by 7½ percent to arrive at the amount of $2,542.53 ($33,900.44 x 7½%, line 3). The amount (line 3) is the portion of medical expenses not allowed as an itemized deduction. The amount, $1,023.16 (line 4), is the deductible portion of medical expenses.

The following paragraphs elaborate on the types of medical expense payments, less reimbursements, that can be included in the Medical and Dental Expenses section of Schedule A (Form 1040).

Other Common Medical Expenses

Generally, deductible medical expenses would include *payments made directly to doctors, dentists, nurses, and hospitals*. Such expenses would

Illustration 5-1
Medical and Dental Expenses section of Form 1040

Medical and Dental Expenses				
	Caution: *Do not include expenses reimbursed or paid by others.*			
1	Medical and dental expenses (see page A-1)	**1**	3,565	69
2	Enter amount from Form 1040, line 32. **2** 33,900 44			
3	Multiply line 2 above by 7.5% (.075)	**3**	2,542	53
4	Subtract line 3 from line 1. If zero or less, enter -0- ▶	**4**	1,023	16

include payments for the fees of physicians, surgeons, dentists, authorized Christian Science practitioners, chiropractors, osteopaths, podiatrists, physiotherapists, psychologists, psychoanalysts (medical care only), obstetricians, and nurses. Also included are hospital costs, costs of outpatient clinics, diagnostic fees, laboratory fees, X-ray examinations or treatments, therapy treatments, and insulin treatments. Surgical vasectomies and abortions are also included if the procedures are legal when performed. Expenses of a kidney donor and other operations that affect a structure of the body, such as a face-lift (if allowable), are includable (line 1) as deductible medical expenses.

Nursing Home Care. The entire cost of maintenance, including meals and lodging, may be included as a medical expense (line 1) for an individual in a *nursing home* or a *home for the aged*. These expenses are allowable if the principal reason for being there is an adverse physical condition and the availability of medical care. The cost of meals and lodging of an individual who is in such an institution for personal or family reasons cannot be included. In such instances, only the portion of the cost attributable to medical or nursing care is includable as medical expense. An additional tax saving can often substantially benefit a taxpayer if the individual being maintained in a nursing home or a home for the aged is a parent, because HOH status may possibly be claimed by the person paying the bills.

Medical Insurance. The full amount of an *insurance premium* covering medical and dental care is eligible to be included (line 1). Self-employed taxpayers who pay their own and their family's health insurance may deduct 25% of the cost of this insurance as an adjustment to income on Form 1040 (line 26) even if they do not itemize deductions. The other 75% is included with other medical expenses subject to the 7½% of AGI floor. A premium paid for the replacement cost of lost or damaged contact lenses is also considered as an amount paid for medical care. The portion of the social security tax paid by the employee or a self-employed individual for hospitalization is not deductible, but voluntary additional monthly payments for supplementary medical insurance under Medicare can be deducted. If the monthly supplementary medical insurance is paid by the employer, it cannot be deducted by the taxpayer and is not included in the taxpayer's gross income.

Only actual medical and dental insurance coverage is deductible. Accident and health insurance premiums cannot be deducted unless the health or medical coverage is specifically identified. When identified, the health or medical portion of the premium is deductible. Premiums cannot be deducted on life insurance policies or on policies providing reimbursement for loss of earnings or for accidental loss of life, limb, sight, etc. Also excluded are policies that guarantee a specific amount each week for a specific period, regardless of the hospital or medical costs.

Transportation Expenses. *Transportation* primarily for and essential to medical care is deductible (line 1). The IRS has authorized the use of a standard mileage rate of 9 cents per mile for out-of-pocket expenses incurred in operating an automobile in connection with medical care. (Note that the standard mileage rate for operating an automobile for charitable purposes is 12 cents per mile.) The expense to and from a doctor's office is clearly deductible.

The use of the standard mileage rate is optional rather than mandatory; allowable expenses actually incurred can still be claimed. It should be noted that depreciation or the rental value of a taxpayer's automobile used for medical purposes do not qualify as an "amount paid," and, therefore, only out-of-pocket expenses qualify as a deduction. Parking fees and tolls are deductible in addition to the amount allowed for standard mileage. Certain long-distance travel can also qualify as transportation essential to medical care. For instance, the cost of a parent's transportation to accompany a sick child (or the cost of transportation for a nurse to attend the child) is deductible.

Travel Expenses. The deductibility of travel expenses for medical care (line 1) has been extended to specifically allow a limited deductibility of *meals and lodging expenses* incurred to enable an individual to obtain medical care away from home. The deductibility of these expenses for meals and lodging en route is different than that for meals and lodging after arrival. The deductibility of meals and lodging after arrival at the out-of-town medical facility is dependent upon whether the patient is treated as an inpatient or as an outpatient. These differences are as follows:

1. If a taxpayer incurs meals and lodging expenses en route to a medical facility, these expenses are considered travel costs for medical purposes. Only 80% of the cost of meals en route is deductible.
2. After a patient arrives at an out-of-town medical facility, the deductibility of medical expenses depends on whether the patient is treated as an inpatient or as an outpatient.
   a. If the patient is hospitalized in a medical care facility as an inpatient, the entire cost of meals and lodging is deductible as part of the cost of medical treatment.
   b. If the patient is treated on an outpatient basis, the cost of meals is not deductible. The cost of lodging is limited to $50 per night per individual, including lodging costs for a spouse, parent, or nurse.

The lodging for the outpatient is deductible as long as the expenses incurred are primarily for and essential to receiving medical care. These outpatient expenses must be provided by a physician in a licensed hospital or in a medical care facility that is the equivalent of a hospital or related to a hospital. To prevent possible abuses of this deduction, the law specifies that the lodging may not be lavish or extravagant.

Also, there can be no significant element of personal pleasure, recreation, or vacation during the time of the medical care away from home.

If a taxpayer or family member is away from home for medical treatment that does not require the patient to be housed in a medical facility, the cost of meals and lodging while away from home are not deductible as medical expenses even if the trip was made on the advice of a doctor. In such a case only the patient's share of transportation expenses would be deductible along with the cost of visits to the doctor's office, as reflected in Example 1.

EXAMPLE 1 ————————————————

A husband has a lung problem. On the advice of his doctor, he and his wife spend the winter in a rented condo in the warm climate of Arizona. Since they will need the use of an automobile, they decide to drive to Arizona from their home in Chicago. The husband incurs expenses in Arizona for visits to a local doctor for checkups. The only medical expenses allowed as a deduction in this situation are the husband's share of transportation expenses to Arizona and the expenses for the visits to the doctor's office. The wife's transportation to and from Arizona and the meals and lodging for both the husband and the wife on the trip to and from Arizona and while in Arizona are not deductible.

School for the Handicapped. Amounts paid for sending a *mentally or physically handicapped* dependent to a special school are deductible (line 1) if the principal reason for the attendance is the institution's resources for alleviating the handicap. The amounts paid for sending a problem child to a special school for the benefits obtainable from its curriculum and disciplinary methods are not includable.

Capital Expenditures. When there is a capital expenditure directly related to medical care, such as special equipment installed in a home or similar improvements for medical purposes, the expenditure will be allowed as a medical expense (line 1). The capital expenditure is includible only for the amount by which the expense exceeds the increase in value of the property improved. In addition, the annual amount for the operation and maintenance of capital assets used for medical care can be included as a medical expense. The full costs of certain home improvements made for physically handicapped persons may be included in medical expenses. The full cost is included as a medical expense regardless of its effect on the value of the property. These improvements include ramps, railings, widened hallways and doors, and other adjustments that make cabinets and other facilities more accessible.

Other Medical Expenses. Other deductible medical expenses include amounts paid for hearing aids, dentures, eyeglasses, and other equipment needed for medical purposes. Amounts can be deducted for artificial teeth and limbs, braces, sacroiliac belts, orthopedic shoes, crutches, wheelchairs, ambulance hire, and the cost and care of guide dogs. Also includible is that part of tuition paid to a school or college that is identified for health or medical care. (Even the cost of regular school attendance *may* be deductible if it is incidental to a primary medical care function of treating the patient.) In general, amounts paid for the prevention, cure, correction, or treatment of a mental or physical defect or illness can be deducted.

Expenses Not Allowed as Deductible Medical Expenses

Amounts paid for the preservation of general health, such as nonprescription drugs, dues for health clubs, steam baths, and vacations are not deductible. Also excluded are funeral expenses and cemetery plots, illegal operations or drugs, premiums on life insurance, and travel ordered or suggested by a doctor for rest or change. In addition, the Revenue Reconciliation Act of 1990 disallows unnecessary cosmetic surgery as a medical expense. Unnecessary cosmetic surgery is defined as surgery designed to correct a deformity that is not a congenital abnormality or one caused by a personal injury or disease.

Reimbursement

The total medical and dental expenses claimed for the year must be reduced by the total *reimbursement* received from insurance or other sources for those expenses paid during the year. Medical and dental expenses must be reduced by the amount of the reimbursement before application of the 7½% total medical and dental expense limitation.

If a taxpayer pays the entire premium on a medical insurance policy or similar plan, and the reimbursement received from that policy or plan equals or exceeds the medical expenses for the year, the taxpayer may deduct the cost of the policy but not the medical expenses. Any excess reimbursement is *not* included in gross income. If a taxpayer and the employer both contribute to the medical insurance plan, the part of the excess reimbursement attributable to the employer's contributions must be included in gross income. If the employer paid the total cost of the medical insurance plan and the premiums paid by the employer were not included in gross income of the taxpayer, the excess reimbursement would be included in gross income.

If a deduction for medical expenses is allowed in one year and the taxpayer is reimbursed for all or a part of the expense in a later year, as a general rule the taxpayer must include the reimbursement in gross income in the year it is received. However, taxpayers are required to include in gross income no more than the amount previously deducted as medical expenses. If medical expenses had not been deducted in prior years because the taxpayer had no itemized deductions or for other reasons, the reimbursement is not taxable when received in a later year.

Employee Physicals

If an employer requires an employee to have a periodic medical checkup, and the employee must pay for it personally, it is an employee business expense that is deductible as an itemized deduction (enter as a miscellaneous deduction on Schedule A, line 20). The 7½%-of-AGI limitation for medical expenses *does not* apply. However the 2%-of-AGI limit for miscellaneous deductions does apply as described later in Chapter 6.

Calculation of Allowable Deduction for Medical and Dental Expenses

Two calculations of the allowable deduction for medical and dental expenses are illustrated below. In studying these calculations, it should be kept in mind that medical expenses are excluded from the new provision in the Revenue Reconciliation Act of 1990 that requires total itemized deductions to be reduced by 3 percent of AGI in excess of $100,000 ($105,250 in 1992).

EXAMPLE 2 ————————————————

A taxpayer, age 51, has AGI for the taxable year of $22,000. During the year the medical and dental expenses (not reimbursed by insurance) were as follows:

Medical and Dental Expenses

Prescription medicines and drugs	$ 150
Medical insurance premiums	750
Doctors and dentists	600
Hospital	800
Total, Schedule A (line 1)	$2,300

Calculation of Deduction

Schedule A (line 2), AGI from Form 1040 (line 32)	$22,000
Schedule A (line 3), Amount not deductible (7½% of $22,000)	1,650
Schedule A (line 1)	$ 2,300
Schedule A (line 3)	1,650
Schedule A (line 4), Total deductible medical and dental expenses	$ 650

EXAMPLE 3 ————————————————

A taxpayer, age 66, and spouse, age 64, provide 80% support for a daughter, age 41. The daughter earned $2,400 during the year and is not a full-time student. A joint return is filed on which adjusted gross income for the taxable year is $35,000. Payments for medical and dental expenses during the year (not reimbursed by insurance) are as follows:

	Daughter	Tax-payer	Spouse	Total
Prescription medicines and drugs	$ 15	$ 35	$ 35	$ 85
Medical insurance premiums	240	405	190	835
Doctors and dentists	225	800	380	1,405
Hospital	—	490	—	490
Total	$480	$1,730	$605	$2,815

Computation of Deduction

Prescription medicines and drugs	$ 85
Total medical insurance premiums	835
Doctors, dentists, and hospital	1,895
Total, Schedule A (line 1)	$ 2,815
Schedule A (line 2): AGI from Form 1040, (line 32)	$35,000
Schedule A (line 3): Amount not deductible (7½% of $35,000)	$ 2,625
Schedule A (line 1)	$ 2,815
Schedule A (line 3)	2,625
Schedule A (line 4): Total deductible medical and dental expenses	$ 190

The daughter's medical expenses are deductible even though she does not qualify as a dependent. Medical expenses are allowed in such a case since dependency has been denied only because her gross income exceeds $2,150.

Taxes You Paid

This section covers the deductibility of state and local taxes that are allowed as itemized deductions for the 1992 tax year. Only specified state and local taxes can be deducted from AGI in 1992.

To be deductible, state and local taxes must be imposed on the taxpayer during the taxable year. In general, taxpayers on the cash method can deduct only taxes actually paid, while taxpayers on the accrual method deduct taxes as they accrue. The two taxes that account for the majority of the deductible taxes for most taxpayers are (1) state and local income taxes and (2) real estate taxes.

Illustration 5-2

This illustration shows how deductible taxes are reported. State and local income tax payments are entered (line 5); real estate taxes (line 6); and other taxes, such as personal property taxes, (line 7). In Illustration 5-2, the $2,083.85 total of these three amounts is entered on Schedule A (line 8). The types of taxes that can be deducted (lines 5, 6, and 7) are described in the following paragraphs.

State and Local Income Taxes

State and local income taxes are deductible on Schedule A (line 5) by cash-method taxpayers in the year paid. The amount deductible is the sum of amounts withheld from payments to employees, paid on declarations of estimated state or local taxes, paid when returns are filed, or paid as additional assessments by the state or local government. Refunds of prior-year taxes cannot be offset against current-year tax deductions on Schedule A. Taxable refunds of prior-year taxes are included as income on Form 1040 (line 10.)

EXAMPLE 4 —————————————————

The following information is presented regarding state and local tax payments to illustrate the calculation of the 1992 itemized deduction for such taxes:

State income tax withheld during 1992	$ 650
Estimated state income tax paid during 1992	400
1991 state income tax paid with 1991 return when filed in 1992	175
Additional assessment on 1990 state income tax paid in 1992	55
Total deduction for state income taxes on 1992 return	$1,280

Real Estate Taxes

These taxes are deductible on Schedule A (line 6) by cash-method taxpayers in the year paid. Under this rule, payments can be timed to enable the taxpayer to "double up" by paying two years of tax in one year (when an itemized deduction would be applicable). Then, the taxpayer would not pay any real estate taxes in the next year (when itemized deductions may not be applicable).

When real estate is bought or sold during the year, the deduction for real estate taxes must be allocated between the buyer and seller. The allocation is in proportion to the number of days in the year each owned the property—even though the tax was imposed on only one of the parties and there had been a different agreement as to the apportionment. This apportionment rule assumes that the purchaser owns the property on the date of sale. The property

---

State and Local Taxes Allowed as Itemized Deductions

1. State and local income taxes
2. State and local unincorporated business taxes (do not include on Schedule C)
3. Real estate taxes
4. Other taxes such as (1) personal property tax, and (2) foreign income tax if not taken as a tax credit

---

taxes actually paid by the buyer and seller may be different than the amount based on the number of days in the year each owned the property. If there is a difference between the amount paid and the amount apportioned to each party, the difference is treated as an adjustment of the selling price by the seller and an adjustment of the cost basis by the purchaser.

EXAMPLE 5 —————————————————

Robert Smith sells a house to Mr. and Mrs. Gordon Bell on May 27, 1992 for $165,000. Taxes of $2,500 are levied on this property for the 1992 calendar year with payment due on March 31 of the following year. There is no provision in the sales agreement regarding the apportionment of taxes. Accordingly, Mr. and Mrs. Bell are obligated to pay the 1992 property taxes when they become due since they are the legal owners of the property on the date that the taxes are due. Assuming that Mr. and Mrs. Bell pay the full amount of the 1992 property taxes in December, 1992, the tax law assumes that 40% of the taxes ($1,000) are

---

Illustration 5-2
Taxes You Paid section of Form 1040

Taxes You Paid (See page A-1.)	5	State and local income taxes	5	1,130	00			
	6	Real estate taxes (see page A-2)	6	857	67			
	7	Other taxes. List—include personal property taxes . ▶ Personal Property Tax	7	96	18			
	8	Add lines 5 through 7 . . . . ▶	8				2,083	85

the obligation of Robert Smith (146 days from January 1 through May 26 = 146/366 = 40% x $2,500 = $1,000) and $1,500 of taxes (60%) are the obligation of Mr. and Mrs. Bell (219/366 = 60% x $2,500 = $1,500). Therefore, Smith will be allowed to deduct $1,000 as an itemized property tax deduction on his 1992 return, and the Bells will be allowed a property tax deduction of $1,500. The deductions are allowed in the year the taxes are paid, in this case 1992. In addition, since the Bells paid $1,000 of Smith's tax obligation, this $1,000 is treated as an additional part of the selling price of the property. Therefore, the purchase price to the Bells is $166,000, and the selling price to Smith for the purpose of calculating the gain on the sale of the house is also $166,000.

Condominium owners may deduct real estate taxes assessed and paid on their interests in the property. However, homeowners' association assessments for promoting recreation, health, safety, and welfare of residents or for maintaining common areas are not deductible. Tax surcharges for increased real estate taxes imposed on tenants as rent are not deductible by tenants.

Personal Property Taxes. To qualify for deduction, state or local personal property taxes must (1) be based on the value of the personal property, (2) be imposed on an annual basis even if collected more or less frequently, and (3) be imposed on personal property. In states in which the automobile registration fee meets these three requirements, the fee can be deducted as a personal property tax.

Interest Expense

Illustration 5-3

Interest expenses are deductible either for AGI as a business expense or from AGI as an itemized deduction. Interest expenses incurred in an active trade or business are deductible for AGI (see Chapter 8). Interest expenses that are deductible as itemized deductions in full or in part can be classified as being either of two types: interest on qualified personal residences or investment interest. Allowable interest in each of these categories is deductible on Schedule A Interest You Paid section (lines 9a-12). The total amount of interest expense deducted in Illustration 5-3 is $1,268.46, with $1,068.46 representing home mortgage interest and $200.00 representing investment interest. Personal interest deduction was not allowed beginning in 1991.

Nondeductible Taxes

- State and local sales taxes
- State inheritance, estate, and gift taxes
- Assessments for local benefits, such as street improvements, sewers, etc. (except in a few special instances)
- Regulatory fees, such as a dog or cat license, hunting or fishing license, automobile inspection fee, or fee for certificate of automobile registration (unless based on the value of the automobile)
- Federal income, estate, and gift taxes
- Federal excise taxes on personal goods or for such items as transportation, telephone, and gasoline (except as an ordinary and necessary business expense)
- Federal social security and railroad retirement taxes
- State and local taxes on such items as cigarettes, gasoline, alcoholic beverages, water, admission fees, marriage licenses, and drivers' licenses
- Qualified taxes paid for another person
- Taxes incurred in a trade or business or for the production of rents and royalties (should be deducted *for* AGI)

Illustration 5-3
Interest You Paid section of Form 1040

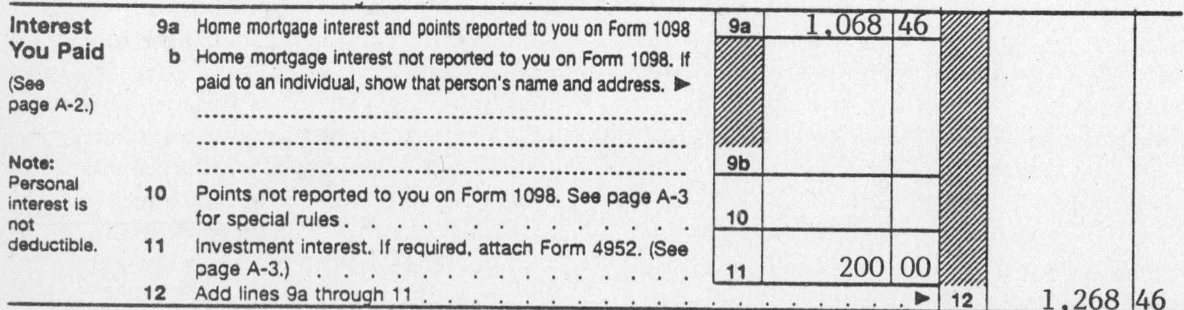

Interest on Qualified Personal Residences

The Revenue Act of 1987, which modified the Tax Reform Act of 1986, allows the deduction of interest expense attributable to qualified residences. Qualified residences include the taxpayer's principal residence (including condominiums and cooperative units) and one second residence, such as a vacation home. To be a qualified residence, a taxpayer must establish that the unit is used for personal purposes. A residential unit is considered to be a qualified residence if the taxpayer (or family or relatives) used the unit for personal purposes for more than a specified number of days. If the unit is used for the greater of 14 days or 10% of the number of days during the year for which the unit was rented at fair market value (FMV), the unit is considered to be a qualified residence. Any day during which a unit is rented to relatives at less than FMV is considered to be a personal use day of the taxpayer. A unit cannot be treated as rented at FMV for any day for which it is used for personal purposes. If the unit is not rented during the year and is not used personally by the taxpayer during the year, it may still be treated as a personal residence.

The Revenue Act of 1987 specifies that two types of interest are deductible on qualified residences, interest on acquisition indebtedness and home equity interest. Qualified residence interest is any interest which is paid or accrued during the taxable year on (1) acquisition indebtedness with respect to any qualified residence of the taxpayer or on (2) home equity indebtedness.

Acquisition Indebtedness. Acquisition indebtedness is indebtedness which is (1) incurred in acquiring, constructing, or substantially improving any qualified residence of the taxpayer, and (2) is secured by such residence. The indebtedness only qualifies as acquisition indebtedness if it is incurred during the period beginning 24 months prior to the date the residence was completed and ending on the date the debt was incurred, i.e. usually the date of closing. Refinancing of indebtedness with new indebtedness that does not exceed the amount of the original indebtedness will be considered to be acquisition debt, subject to a maximum acquisition indebtedness, original or refinanced, of not more than $1,000,000 for any tax year ($500,000 for a married couple filing separate returns). Acquisition indebtedness is reduced as payments are made and cannot be increased by refinancing unless the additional refinancing proceeds are used to make substantial improvements to the residence.

EXAMPLE 6

Assume a taxpayer acquires a principal residence for $180,000, using $140,000 of mortgage financing. The entire $140,000 is acquisition financing. If the taxpayer subsequently pays down $40,000 of the mortgage balance and obtains a second mortgage of $40,000 to be used to finance the purchase of an automobile plus some investments, only the remaining $100,000 balance of the original indebtedness is acquisition indebtedness. In this case, the interest on the $40,000 second mortgage would be treated as interest on a home equity loan. The deductibility of interest on home equity loans is discussed below. If the taxpayer used the $40,000 second mortgage to make substantial improvements to the principal residence, then the additional $40,000 borrowed would be acquisition indebtedness for which the interest would be eligible for deduction as mortgage interest. Acquisition indebtedness incurred on or before October 13, 1987, will not be subject to the $1,000,000 limitation, but such indebtedness does apply toward the limit when considering further debt.

Home Equity Indebtedness. Home equity indebtedness refers to any debt, other than acquisition indebtedness, which is secured by a qualified residence. However, the total amount of such indebtedness cannot exceed the FMV of the qualified residence reduced by the amount of acquisition indebtedness on such residence. The maximum amount of home equity indebtedness is also limited to $100,000 ($50,000 for a married couple filing separate returns). The $100,000 limitation applies to the total amount of home equity indebtedness for any year on both a principal and second residence. Home equity indebtedness rules allow a homeowner to borrow up to $100,000 on the equity in the home with no limit on how such funds are used and yet deduct the interest as qualified residence interest.

EXAMPLE 7 ───────────────────────

To illustrate the limits on home equity indebtedness, assume that a taxpayer owns a home with a FMV of $240,000 on which there is a first mortgage of $175,000. If the taxpayer wanted to borrow money on a home equity loan to invest in the stock market, the maximum loan that the taxpayer can make and still treat the interest as residence interest is $65,000 ($240,000 – $175,000). A $65,000 limit applies in this example since any loan exceeding the FMV of the residence would be treated as investment interest.

If a taxpayer *refinances* a home or takes out what is commonly called a home equity loan in order to make substantial improvements on the home, that indebtedness qualifies as *acquisition* indebtedness. It is subject to the $1,000,000 maximum, but it is not subject to the $100,000 limit on home equity loans. In other words, to the extent that the borrowed funds are used to substantially improve the home and are not used for other personal or investment purposes, the loan is classified as acquisition indebtedness. The new rules related to acquisition indebtedness and home equity loans also apply to boats and motor homes that are used as second homes.

Mortgage interest paid to financial institutions is deducted on Schedule A (line 9a), while mortgage interest paid to individuals is deducted on Schedule A (line 9b). Interest paid to individuals is reported separately in order to provide the IRS with information to check on whether the recipients are reporting interest received as income. The name and address of the individual to whom the home mortgage interest was paid must be shown (line 9b).

Loan Processing Fees (Points). A loan processing fee, sometimes referred to as a loan-origination fee or "points," is deductible as interest when paid as compensation to the home mortgage lender solely for the use of money. Points as defined by the IRS are similar to a prepayment of interest; thus they are to be treated as paid over the term of the loan for purposes of the prepaid interest rule. There are, however, special provisions for points paid for home mortgages. Points paid for home mortgages can be deducted in the year of payment by a cash-method taxpayer on any indebtedness incurred in connection with the purchase or improvement of, and secured by, the taxpayer's *principal residence* if four conditions are met.

1. Points are an established business practice in the area where the loan is incurred.
2. The amount of the payment does not exceed the amount generally charged in the area.
3. If the loan is used to **improve** your main home, the points must be paid with funds other than funds obtained from the lender.
4. If the loan is used to **buy** your main home, the taxpayer must provide funds at the time of closing at least equal to the points charged. Funds the taxpayer provides include down payments, escrow deposits, earnest money applied at closing, and funds actually paid at closing.

So-called "points" charged by a lender for services provided by the lender are not considered interest. Such charges include appraisal fees, loan preparation fees, and notary fees. These and other expenses a taxpayer pays in connection with a mortgage, such as recording fees and commissions, are treated as capital expenditures and are added to the tax basis (cost) of the property.

EXAMPLE 8 ————————————————

Roy Apple acquired a loan in 1992 from the local savings and loan association to buy a new home. The purchase price of the home was $135,000. Apple paid the S&L a loan origination fee of 1% and an additional 1% to cover appraisal fees, trust preparation, and settlement fees. In addition, Apple paid a commission to the realtor of $2,500 and recording fees of $50. Based on these costs, Apple would need to determine how to treat each one of these costs for tax purposes. If the loan origination fee of 1% is an established practice in that area, Apple could deduct $1,350 ($135,000 x 1%) as interest on home acquisition indebtedness in 1992. The other 1% ($1,350) plus $2,500 commission and $50 recording fee, a total of $3,900, would be added to the cost of the home to arrive at the tax basis of the home of $138,900 ($135,000 + $1,350 + $2,500 + $50).

Points may be deducted in the year the home is purchased even if included with other costs and fees in the closing statement and therefore not paid by a separate check. Points withheld by a lender from loan proceeds are not deductible by the borrower in the year of withholding. Points paid in refinancing a mortgage are not deductible in full in the year paid (except to the extent the loan is used to make improvements), but must be deducted ratably over the term of the new loan regardless of when the points are paid.

Points paid by the *seller* of a residence as a condition of FHA financing are *not* deductible as interest. Such a charge is a selling expense that reduces the amount realized. The amount of deductible points is entered on Schedule A (line 10).

Investment Interest Expense

Some taxpayers incur large investment interest expenses in purchasing or holding investment property that produces little or no current income. In 1991 and later years, the investment interest income deduction is limited to an amount not exceeding net investment income. For this purpose, net investment income includes dividends, interest, certain rents, royalties, and any gains from the sale of investment property. The limitation on investment expense deductions applies to all taxpayers except corporations. Form 4952, Investment Interest Expense Deduction, is available to calculate the allowable investment interest deduction.

Disallowed investment interest arising because of limitations can be carried over to the following year or years and is subject to the same limitations.

Qualified investment interest that is deductible as an itemized deduction is listed on Schedule A, Form 1040 (line 11). Illustration 5-3 includes a deduction of $200 for investment interest.

Personal Interest

Personal interest is not deductible and includes interest paid or incurred to purchase assets for personal use, including interest expense on consumer credit card charges for personal purchases. Personal interest also includes interest on tax underpayments, on revolving charge accounts, on bank credit cards, and on insurance policy loans. Personal interest does not include (1) interest paid or incurred in carrying on a trade or business or a passive business activity, (2) interest expense incurred in income-producing activities, or (3) interest expense on a personal residence that meets the requirements as interest on acquisition indebtedness or interest on home equity loans subject to the limitations discussed earlier.

Other Interest Expense Considerations

Prepaid Interest. Cash-method taxpayers must use the accrual method for purposes of deducting prepaid interest. Generally, this means that interest can be deducted only in the year in which the interest would be a charge for the use of money. Since prepaid interest is interest paid in advance of the year in which it is an actual charge, cash-method taxpayers cannot take a deduction until the later period or periods to which the prepaid interest actually applies. To achieve the deduction of prepaid interest only in the year to which it applies, the prepaid interest amounts are accumulated in an appropriate capital (asset) account and deducted in the period and to the extent that interest represents the cost of using the borrowed money in that year. The prepaid interest deduction rule covers interest paid for personal, business, or investment purposes. The prepaid interest deduction rule does not change the rules on whether a payment is in fact interest (such as situations where a payment represents an additional purchase price or where the interest is treated as a dividend on a capital contribution). Interest paid as part of a level constant payment, such as principal and interest on most home mortgages, is not subject to the rule.

In some cases, the IRS may require that interest payments under a variable interest rate be treated partly as interest paid under an average effective rate of interest and partly as an interest prepayment that is allocable to later years of a loan. Interest at a stated rate tied to the "prime rate" will usually not be considered to be prepaid interest.

Finance Charges

The *Consumer Credit Protection Act (Truth-in-Lending)* generally requires the lender to show interest charges as an annual percentage rate (APR) on the customer's billing statement. Thus, even though the interest rate is not stated on the original agreement, the taxpayer can determine the actual interest charges from billing statements. If a finance charge is levied on the unpaid balance of a loan and if it is levied only in the event that payment is not made within a specified period of time, it may be a deductible interest expense for the taxpayer. In what category the interest expense is deductible depends on the limitations described above for the various categories of interest expense.

Finance charges on *revolving charge accounts* are deductible as interest as long as the charge is based on the customer's unpaid balance at the beginning of the month and is expressed as an APR on the customer's billing statement in accordance with the Truth-in-Lending Act. Under this type of agreement, if the customer pays for a purchase within 30 days from the billing date on the statement, no charge is made on the account. If full payment is not made within 30 days, a charge is made based on the unpaid balance, stated as a finance charge and expressed as an APR. This finance charge is considered deductible interest for the taxpayer in 1992 only if it qualifies as home mortgage interest, home equity interest, or investment interest.

Bank Credit Cards. For 1992 tax returns, holders of bank credit cards may deduct interest expense charged on those cards only to the extent that it qualifies as deductible investment interest. Therefore, if a bank charges an amount to a cardholder's account at a rate of 1½% per month on the unpaid balance of an account after a period of 25 days, this charge would be deductible interest only to the extent allowed under the investment interest rules.

Insurance Policy Loans. To the extent that interest on insurance policy loans qualifies as a deductible category of interest, a taxpayer on the cash method may deduct interest on an insurance policy loan paid when due. However, if the interest is not paid but added to the amount of the loan, the interest is not deductible. If this interest is paid later, the amount will be treated as interest expense in the year paid.

Tax Delinquency Payments. Interest paid on delinquent federal income or estate taxes is deductible only in the rare case that it is not classified as personal interest. Interest is payable on any underpayment of tax from the original due date (regardless of extensions) to the date on which payment is received. The rates are set quarterly and are based on the three-month Treasury bill rate plus three percentage points. New rates become effective two months after the date of each adjustment. The rate applicable for the first three quarters of 1992 was 8%. An exception to the normal stated rate applies to interest accrued on substantial underpayments of more than $1,000 arising from tax-motivated transactions, which are transactions entered into primarily to avoid taxes. Interest on these underpayments is calculated at 120% of the annual interest rate (i.e., 8% x 120% = 9.6%).

The interest rates in effect for delinquent taxes also are applied to amounts of estimated income taxes unpaid by specified quarterly dates. However, the calculated amount is not considered to be interest, but rather is a penalty for failure to pay estimated taxes on time and therefore is not deductible.

Discount Payable in Installments. When interest is paid in advance through a discount from the principal or face amount of the loan, a proportionate part of the discount is deductible as interest expense for the taxable year within the limits of the appropriate interest expense category. This proportionate part is based on the number of months paid in the taxable year compared to the total number of months to be paid. Examples are home-improvement loans or bank loans on a discount basis.

Other Nondeductible Interest. Interest on money borrowed to buy or carry tax-exempt securities or single premium life insurance is not deductible.

Gifts to Charity

Payments made to approved charitable institutions are deductible as charitable contributions if the institutions are operated exclusively for religious, charitable, scientific, humanitarian, cultural, or literary purposes; for the prevention of cruelty to animals or children; or for educational purposes. Examples of such institutions are churches, temples, synagogues, United Way, American Red Cross, Salvation Army, YMCA, YWCA, Boy Scouts, Girl Scouts, American Library Association, CARE, Boys Club of America, Goodwill Industries, and American School Citizenship League.

The recipient of a deductible contribution must be a nonprofit, domestic organization. Gifts to the United States or any state or political subdivision of a state are deductible if made exclusively for public purposes. For example, contributions to the "Bureau of Public Debt" to reduce the public debt are deductible. Gifts to veterans' organizations and their auxiliaries and trusts or foundations for such organizations are deductible if no part of their net earnings is for the benefit of an individual.

Tax-exempt status has been granted for certain joint hospital service organizations if organized and operated specifically for data processing, purchasing, warehousing, billing and collecting, food service, industrial engineering, laboratories, printing, communication, record center, or personnel services.

Contributions to nonprofit organizations primarily engaged in research or education for the alleviation and treatment of various diseases are deductible. These diseases include cerebral palsy, cystic fibrosis, arthritis, birth defects, asthma, diseases of the heart, cancer, diabetes, hemophilia, mental illness and mental retardation, multiple sclerosis, muscular dystrophy, poliomyelitis, tuberculosis, and AIDS.

Reporting Contributions

Illustration 5-4

Contributions eligible for deduction are reported on the Gifts to Charity section of Schedule A (lines 13-16), shown in Illustration 5-4. As Illustration 5-4 shows, contributions by cash (line 13) amounted to $787, contributions other than cash (line 14) amounted to $18, and carryover contributions from prior years (line 15) amounted to $200, for total deductible contributions of $1,005 (line 16). The types of contributions deductible in each of these categories are described in the paragraphs that follow.

Cash Contributions

Only contributions actually paid by cash or credit card during the year can be deducted, regardless of whether the cash or accrual method is used by the taxpayer. Unpaid subscriptions are not deductible. Out-of-pocket expenses not reimbursed, such as gas, oil, etc., for volunteer work with a charitable organization, may be deducted. Instead of listing actual expenses of operating an automobile, the standard rate of 12 cents per mile can be used when driving for charitable purposes.

All cash contributions are entered on Schedule A (line 13). For cash contributions that total $3,000 or more to any one organization, the taxpayer must show to whom the gift was given and the amount.

Illustration 5-4
Gifts to Charity section of Form 1040

Gifts to Charity		Caution: *If you made a charitable contribution and received a benefit in return, see page A-3.*			
(See page A-3.)	**13**	Contributions by cash or check	**13**	787	00
	14	Other than by cash or check. If over $500, you **MUST** attach Form 8283	**14**	18	00
	15	Carryover from prior year	**15**	200	00
	16	Add lines 13 through 15 . . . . ▶	**16**	1,005	00

Noncash Contributions

Common noncash charitable contributions include household goods, used clothing, objects of art, books, stocks, bonds, and land. Unusual items would be rights to air space, wild animals, and antiques. Such noncash contributions generally would be reported on Schedule A (line 14) at their FMV. However, if the property has increased in value, in certain cases the taxpayer may be only allowed to deduct an amount that is less than the property's FMV. The amount of the deduction is dependent on (1) whether the property is ordinary income property or capital gains property and (2) how the property is used by the charity. The deductibility of gifts based on the type of property and how it is used by the charity is discussed below.

Fair Market Value (FMV). In determining the amount of the deduction for contributions of property, it is often necessary to determine the FMV of the property on the date of the donation. FMV is the price at which the property would change hands between a buyer and a seller, neither being required to buy or sell, and both having reasonable knowledge of all necessary facts. Certain property contributions to charity are often likely to have a value much less than their original cost. This situation would normally apply to used clothing, used household goods, and used cars, trucks, and boats. The taxpayer must rely on appraisals or quotations from thrift shops, commerical firms, and/or trade associations for guidance in determining the donated property's FMV. If a taxpayer wants to donate an automobile to his church, for example, he or she could obtain a "blue book" value on the automobile from a bank or autombile dealership. The "blue book" would identify several values depending on the condition of the car when it is donated. Except for official appraisals, other sources of FMV are only guides which the taxpayer must justify as representing the true FMV for taking a deduction on his or her tax return.

Gift of Ordinary Income Property. Ordinary income property is property whose income from sale would be reported either as ordinary income or as a short-term capital gain. Examples of ordinary income property would include inventory, manuscripts or art work created by the donor, and stocks and bonds held for not more than one year. The charitable contribution deduction for ordinary income property is determined by subtracting the ordinary income or short-term capital gain from the FMV at the date of the contribution. In effect, this rule limits the deduction to the lesser of the property's tax basis or its FMV.

EXAMPLE 9 ———————

A sole proprietor who operates a grocery store donates selected fruits and vegetables to a charitable nursing home after closing on Saturday evenings, since some of these perishable products will not be saleable when the store reopens on Monday morning. Over the course of a tax year, the FMV of the fruits and vegetables donated totaled $2,750. The proprietor's tax basis in these inventoriable items was $2,000. Since the $750 gain would be considered ordinary income because inventory is ordinary income property, the charitable deduction that the sole proprietor would take on his own tax return would be $2,000. This amount is the donated inventory's FMV less the appreciation above the tax basis of the inventory deduction ($2,750 − $750 = $2,000). The $2,000 would be reported on Schedule A (line 14).

Gift of Long-Term Capital Gain Property. Property is long-term capital gain property if a gain resulting from the sale of the property at FMV is recognizable as a long-term capital gain. Capital gains property includes stocks and bonds and other capital assets **held for more than one year** as well as certain real property and depreciable property used in a trade or business that has been held more than one year. As a general rule, a taxpayer who contributes long-term capital gains property to a charity can deduct its FMV, with limitations on the amount of the deduction for **tangible personal property** depending on how the charity uses that type of property. Example 10 illustrates the general rule.

EXAMPLE 10 ───────────────────────

A taxpayer contributes stock with a FMV of $3,500 to his church to be used in support of an elementary school operated by the church. The stock, which had originally cost $2,100, had been held for three years when it was transferred to the church. The taxpayer would take a charitable contribution deduction of $3,500 and would not need to report the $1,400 appreciation as a gain. Since the stock is classified as intangi-

---

Gifts of Property to Charities

Types of Property:
   Amount Deductible

Ordinary Income Property:
   Basis = FMV − Ordinary Income
Short-term Capital Gains Property:
   Basis = FMV − Short-Term Gain
Long-Term Intangible Personal Property:
   FMV
Long-Term Tangible Personal Property
   Related to Charitable Function:
   FMV
Long-Term Tangible Personal Property
   Not Related to Charitable Function:
   Basis = FMV − Long-Term Gain

---

ble capital gains property and has been held for more than one year, the property qualifies for a charitable contribution deduction in the amount of its FMV on the date of the donation.

If the appreciated property that was contributed is **tangible personal property**, such as a painting or a statue, and the charitable organization does not use the property for its intended purpose, the charitable deduction is limited to the FMV less 100% of the appreciation in value. In effect, the deduction is limited to the tax basis of the property. This rule would apply if the charitable organization decides to sell the painting or the statue instead of displaying it for the benefit of its members, such as for the benefit of art students in a university or for an art museum open to the public.

EXAMPLE 11 ───────────────────────

A taxpayer contributes a painting to the art museum of a university for use by art students in painting classes. The painting has a FMV of $15,000 and originally cost the donor $2,500. If the university displays the painting in its museum for use by the art students, the donor taxpayer would be allowed a charitable deduction of $15,000, subject to the percentage of AGI limitations discussed later. On the other hand, if the university chose to sell the painting for $15,000 and use the cash for other purposes, the donor taxpayer would be allowed to deduct only $2,500, its adjusted basis for tax purposes. (**Adjusted basis** is the original cost or other initially determined basis plus capital additions and less capital recoveries, such as depreciation.) This situation suggests that the taxpayer should have strong assurances from the donee charity as to what its plans are for the use of tangible personal property in order to satisfy the taxpayer that a deduction of the FMV will be allowed. A statement from the charity to the donor that can be kept in the donor's file would provide evidence for deducting the FMV of the donated capital gains property.

Unlike the limited tax treatment of gifts of tangible personal property to charities where the gift is not used in the charity's exempt function, gifts of appreciated *long-term capital gain intangible property,* such as stocks and bonds, to charities are eligible for a deduction of the full FMV of the property, whether the charity sells the securities or keeps them for the use of the income.

Other rules related to gifts of property cover gifts of depreciable business property and gifts of government publications, as follows: (1) The gift of depreciable property used in business will be reduced by any potential recapture income (such as the additional depreciation on a building through use of an accelerated depreciation method over the amount that would have been taken by the straight-line method); and (2) Government publications received by a taxpayer at a reduced price or without charge, such as copies of the Congressional Record received by members of Congress, are not to be treated as a capital asset for contribution purposes. Thus, the full FMV deduction cannot be claimed for government publications contributed to a charity, such as a university or library, even if the use is related to the charity's exempt purpose.

Tax Preferences. The appreciated value of capital gains property (real, personal, or intangible) given to charity constitutes a tax preference item. Under the alternative minimum tax (AMT), a taxpayer's tax preferences, including the appreciated portion of the value of capital gains property given to charities, generally are subject to the AMT. The AMT rate increased from 21% in 1990 to 24% in 1991 under the Revenue Reconciliation Act of 1990. However, along with the increase in the AMT rate, the appreciated portion of the value of **tangible personal property** given to charities is not considered to be a tax preference item subject to the AMT if contributed in 1991 or before July 1, 1992. Thus, the tax year 1991 and half of the 1992 tax year provided a window of opportunity for taxpayers who have donated to charity appreciated tangible personal assets, such as paintings and antiques. If securities were given to public charities in 1991 or before July 1, 1992, the taxpayer can take a charitable contribution deduction of the FMV of such assets without the **appreciated gain** being subject to either the regular income tax or the AMT. The appreciated portion of property given to charity will be considered to be a tax preference item for purposes of the AMT if the property is donated to a char-

ity after June 30, 1992. The 1991-1992 waiver of an asset's appreciation as a tax preference item was designed to provide benefits to public charities since taxpayers giving appreciated property to charities often fall into the trap of being subject to the AMT because the appreciation in the asset is counted as a tax preference. Without this exception for tangible personal property, if the tax computed under the minimum tax rules is higher than the tax computed on the regular tax return, then the taxpayer would pay the higher minimum tax amount.

Bargain Sales to Charities. Another method of taking a tax deduction when transfering property to a charity is by making a sale to a charity at a bargain price. Tax benefits apply when property that has appreciated in value is sold to a charity at a *bargain price,* i.e. at less than FMV. The basis of the property contributed must be allocated between the part of the property that is sold and the part that is contributed. The taxpayer must pay tax on the gain on the part sold and gets a charitable contribution deduction for the part donated based on the rules cited above for appreciated property.

EXAMPLE 12 ———————————————

Assume a taxpayer sold securities (original cost $9,000), with a FMV of $20,000, to a charity for cash of $16,000. The *cost basis* of $9,000 is allocated between the portion sold and the portion donated on the basis of selling price in relation to its FMV.

$$\frac{\text{Cost}}{\text{Basis}} \times \frac{\text{Selling Price}}{\text{FMV}} = \frac{\text{Basis Assigned}}{\text{to Portion Sold}}$$

$$\$9,000 \times \frac{\$16,000}{\$20,000} = \$7,200$$

$$\frac{\text{Cost}}{\text{Basis}} - \frac{\text{Basis Assigned}}{\text{to Portion Sold}} = \frac{\text{Basis Assigned}}{\text{to Portion Donated}}$$

$$\$9,000 - \$7,200 = \$1,800$$

The gain to be reported is:

Selling price	$16,000
Basis of portion sold	7,200
Gain	$ 8,800*

*Long-term capital gain if asset is a capital asset held for more than 12 months.

The *contribution deduction* for the donated portion of a bargain sale depends upon the type of property involved and the type of charity to which the property is being donated. The deduction is based on the appreciated property rules set forth above.

EXAMPLE 13

If the property in the illustration above had been tangible personal property and the use of the property was related to the charity's exempt function, the charitable deduction for the portion donated would be equal to the FMV of the portion donated, i.e., $4,000 ($20,000 – $16,000). If the use of the property was **not related** to the charitable organization's intended functions, then the charitable deduction would have been the FMV of the portion donated, $4,000 ($20,000 – $16,000), less 100% of the appreciation.

FMV of the portion donated ($20,000 – $16,000)	$4,000
Less: All of the appreciation ($4,000 – $1,800)	2,200
Contribution deduction	$1,800

Gifts of a Partial Interest in Property. If a taxpayer donates a partial interest in property to a qualified charity, the transfer of the undivided interest in the property will qualify for a charitable deduction if the recipient has the right to take possession within one year or less from the date of the gift.

Thus, a taxpayer is allowed to take a charitable deduction for donating a 10% interest in a group of paintings to a museum. The museum is allowed to take possession of the paintings for 10% of the time, but need not actually take possession. The charitable deduction hinges on the right to take possession, not the exercising of the right of possession.

Gift of Future Interest in Property. Contributions of future interests in *tangible personal property* generally are not deductible until the gift is complete. The deduction can be claimed when all intervening rights held by the donor or the relatives have expired. Future interests in *real property* are deductible, subject to reduction for straight-line depreciation and depletion. The amount of the deduction is the value of the future interest when the taxpayer no longer has an interest in the property.

EXAMPLE 14

A taxpayer contributes a $40,000 home and paintings worth $20,000 to an alma mater, reserving for lifetime the right to live in the home and to retain possession of the paintings. No deduction is allowed for the contribution of the paintings in the current year, since they are tangible personal property and the gift is not complete. The calculated value of the future interest in the home qualifies in the current year because the home is real property. The IRS provides guidelines as to how to calculate the present value of a future interest in real property.

Admissions to Charitable Affairs. When *something of value is received* for making a contribution, only the excess of the contribution over the FMV of the item received can be deducted. To be deductible there must be a gift, meaning a payment of money or transfer of property without adequate consideration. The taxpayer must establish that any amount paid is not the purchase price of privileges or benefits, and that the payment is in fact a gift. Evidence is required that the payment exceeds the FMV of the privileges or other benefits received by the amount claimed to have been paid as a gift.

EXAMPLE 15

If $20 is paid for a ticket to a church fund-raising dinner and a meal with a FMV of $5.50 is received, only $14.50 ($20 – $5.50) can be deducted.

Fund-raising events for charities, such as charity balls, banquets, shows, and athletic events, are covered by the rule. When an event is reasonably comparable to events for which there are established charges for admission, such charge would fix the FMV of the admission or privilege. How the proceeds are used has no bearing on the amount deductible as a contribution.

The test of deductibility does not hinge on exercising the right to admission, but is determined by whether the right is available. Therefore, if a taxpayer pays $30 for a ticket to a charity concert and the FMV of the ticket is $10, the charitable deduction is limited to $20, whether or not the taxpayer actually attends the concert.

Charitable Contributions of Art.   Taxpayers who contribute works of art with an aggregate value of at least $20,000 must attach to their returns a complete copy of a qualified appraisal of the work of art plus an 8x10-inch color photograph or a color transparency no smaller than 4x5 inches. The appraisal and the photograph will be reviewed by an IRS art advisory panel to determine the appropriateness of the deduction. Included as art are sculptures, watercolors, prints, drawings, ceramics, antique furniture, decorative arts, textiles, carpets, silver, rare manuscripts, and historical memorabilia. Gems, jewelry, and books are excluded.

Reporting Requirements for Noncash Contributions. When contributions of property are made, the taxpayer is required to keep receipts and written records showing the date of the contribution, the kind of property given, the method of valuation at the date of the gift, the name of the organization to which it was given, and whether it was capital gain or ordinary income property.

If a taxpayer donates used items to charity, such as clothing or furniture, the deduction is figured at the FMV of the property at the time it was given.

Additional Information Required for All Gifts Valued Above $500

1. Address of the organization to which the property was given
2. Description of the property
3. Any conditions attached to the gift
4. How the donor acquired the property
5. Cost or other basis of the property *if*:
   a. the donor owned it less than 12 months, *or*
   b. the donor reduced the value by any ordinary income or capital gain that would have resulted if the property had been sold at its FMV.
6. How the taxpayer figured the deduction if the choice was made to reduce the taxpayer's deduction for contributions of capital gain property

---

If a taxpayer's total deduction for gifts of property exceeds $500 in value, it may be necessary to obtain appraisals of the property values. Form 8283, Noncash Charitable Contributions, must be completed and attached to the tax return. Section A provides for the reporting of noncash gifts from $500 to $5,000 and all publicly-traded stock. No appraisals need to be filed, but the taxpayer should keep records of them. Section B provides for the reporting of noncash gifts, other than publicly-traded stock, totaling over $5,000. The property must be appraised, and both the organization receiving the gift and the appraiser must complete portions of this section of Form 8283. An appraisal summary, signed by the appraiser and an authorized officer of the charitable organization, must accompany Form 8283. The taxpayer should keep a copy of Form 8283, the appraisal summary, and the appraisal.

Nondeductible Contributions. A deduction for a contribution to a private foundation is denied unless the foundation either has exempt status or has applied to the IRS for recognition of exempt status. Other nondeductible contributions include:

1. Gifts to individuals, including friends and relatives, even though made as an act of charity.
2. Dues to social clubs, country clubs, lodges, or fraternal groups
3. Tuition to a private school
4. Gifts to foreign organizations, labor unions, chambers of commerce, civic leagues, and groups whose purpose is to lobby for changes in the law

Buying a raffle ticket from a charitable organization does not provide a deduction. The purchaser has not made a gift, but has bought a chance to obtain valuable merchandise at a low price. The value of time or services contributed to a qualified organization cannot be deducted, nor can the value of blood given to a blood bank or the value of property used by a qualified organization. Thus, the value of real estate used by a church for a church picnic cannot be deducted.

Maximum Deduction Limitation

The *maximum deduction* for charitable contributions is limited each year to 50%, 30%, or 20% of a taxpayer's AGI, depending on the type of contribution.

50% Limitation. The deduction of charitable contributions for individuals is limited to 50% of AGI (before net operating loss carryback deduction) for contributions of cash and property, other than appreciated capital gains property. This 50% limitation applies to certain educational organizations, churches or a convention or association of churches, hospitals, medical organizations, state university endowment foundations, governmental units, and to charities receiving a substantial part of their support from the government or from the general public. Included are contributions to certain qualified private foundations, exempt charitable organizations, and contributions made exclusively for public purposes to the United States, a state, a possession of the United States, a political subdivision of a state or possession of the United States, or the District of Columbia. Also eligible are contributions to certain corporations, trusts, United Way, etc., organized and operated exclusively for religious, charitable, scientific, literary, or educational purposes or for the prevention of cruelty to children or animals. Also included are publicly or governmentally supported museums of history, art, or science; libraries; organizations providing facilities for the support of an opera, symphony orchestra, ballet, or repertory drama; and organizations such as the American Red Cross, Cancer Society, and Boy Scouts of America.

EXAMPLE 16 ────────────────

To illustrate the 50% maximum contribution allowable, assume that an individual's AGI for the taxable year is $12,000. The taxpayer may deduct charitable contributions amounting to $6,000 (50% of $12,000) provided the contributions have been made directly to approved organizations. If husband and wife file a joint return, they are treated as one person in applying the limitation. Carryovers for five years of excess deductions of the 50% type are permitted, with the nature of the deduction carryover remaining the same.

30% Limitation. A maximum deduction limitation of 30% of AGI applies to contributions to public charities of *appreciated capital gain property* that are not reduced by any amount of appreciation. The 30% limit also applies to contributions of cash and ordinary income property made to private nonoperating foundations. Appreciated capital gain property is any

capital asset that would have a long-term capital gain if sold at its FMV. *Such a contribution is considered to be the last deduction taken,* and if disallowed, can be carried over for five years subject to a 30% limit in carryover years.

EXAMPLE 17 ────────────────

During 1992, a taxpayer with AGI of $20,000 contributed cash of $4,000 to the First Church and gave appreciated securities held more than 12 months and valued at $10,000 (costing $1,000) to the City Hospital. The stock contribution is first limited in the year to $6,000 (30% of $20,000). The stock and cash contributions total $14,000, but the maximum deduction is $10,000 (50% of $20,000). Since the stock is the last deduction taken, the cash of $4,000 and stock of $6,000 make up the $10,000 contribution deductible for the current year. The $4,000 balance of the stock contributed can be carried to the next five years.

The 30% of AGI maximum deduction limitation applies also to contributions made "for the use of" rather than "directly to" a public charity. The amount of the deduction is the lesser of (1) 30% of AGI or (2) 50% of AGI over the amount of contribution to public charities without regard to the 30% limitation.

20% Limitation. A maximum deduction limitation of 20% of AGI applies to all gifts of capital-gain property by individuals to private nonoperating foundations (that is, not operating for the public benefit). The excess of the total of the 20% limitation type contribution may be carried forward to future years.

Carryover of Charitable Contributions

Individual taxpayers may carry forward to the next five years the amount of any contributions that exceeds the percentage limitations. In the years to which excess contributions are carried over, the total deduction, including carryovers, is again limited to the 50%, 30%, and 20% of AGI limitation. The carryover maintains its status and is treated as though the contributions had been paid in the year to which they were carried, taking the years in sequence. Prior-year contribution carryovers are claimed on Schedule A (line 15).

All contributions recorded on Schedule A (lines 13-15) are totaled, and the total is recorded on line 16 to be included in calculating total itemized deductions.

Casualty and Theft Loss(es)

Losses of a taxpayer's property resulting from accidents, fires, storms, shipwrecks, or other casualties, or from theft, not covered by insurance or other reimbursement, are deductible if the event is due to some sudden, unexpected, or unusual cause.

A list of deductible and nondeductible casualty losses that an individual may sustain from the operation of an automobile for personal purposes is shown in Table 5-1. It should be noted from the first item in the list that the loss is deductible regardless of whether the taxpayer is at fault. However, if the damage is due to the taxpayer's willful negligence, the deduction will not be allowed. Casualty losses are deductible regardless of whether the taxpayer's property is used in trade or business and regardless of whether the losses were incurred in transactions entered into for profit. Thus, casualty losses to personal-use property, such as the taxpayer's personal residence, personal automobile used for personal purposes, or any other personal property not used in business, are deductible. With respect to theft losses, the taxpayer must prove that the property was really stolen, not simply lost. If the theft loss can be proven, the cost of recovering the property is deductible as part of the theft loss.

Losses that cannot be deducted include breakage of china, glassware, furniture, and similar items under normal conditions; money or property that has been misplaced or lost; and damage to property such as buildings, clothes, and trees caused by termites, moths, other insects, or diseases.

Amount of Deductible Loss

To calculate the amount of casualty loss that is deductible, it is necessary to know certain specific information.

For personal-use property, the deductible casualty or theft loss is the lesser of the actual loss (FMV before the loss minus FMV after the loss) or the adjusted basis of each item of property reduced by the following three items:

1. Any insurance or other reimbursement received
2. A $100 floor
3. 10% of AGI

The $100 reduction applies to each casualty or theft loss as a separate occurrence. When two or more items are lost in a single casualty or theft occurrence, however, a single $100 reduction applies. A taxpayer and a spouse filing a

Table 5-1
Deductiblity of Automobile Losses

Item	Deductible	Not Deductible
Loss resulting from damage to taxpayer's automobile caused by collision, taxpayer at fault	X	
Loss resulting from damage to taxpayer's automobile caused by collision, taxpayer not at fault	X	
Loss resulting from damage to taxpayer's automobile from skidding on icy street	X	
Loss resulting from damage to taxpayer's automobile caused by freezing motor (unexpected freeze)	X	
Loss resulting from theft of taxpayer's automobile	X	
Loss resulting from damage to taxpayer's automobile caused by fire	X	
Loss resulting from damage to other taxpayer's property caused by taxpayer's automobile		X
Loss from sale of taxpayer's automobile		X
Loss on trade-in of taxpayer's automobile		X

joint return are considered as one taxpayer, with the $100 reduction applying to each casualty or theft occurrence, even though both the husband and wife suffered the loss. Married taxpayers filing separate returns who have a loss of property owned jointly must each exclude $100 of their loss. The $100 reduction does not apply to losses on property used in a trade or business or held for the production of income.

EXAMPLE 18 ——————————————————

To illustrate the calculation of the casualty loss for personal-use property, assume that James R. Brown wrecked a personal automobile that had originally cost $8,500. Its FMV just before the accident was $6,000, and its FMV after the accident was $1,200. The amount of insurance collected was $2,700. Assuming that the AGI is $16,000, and that this is Brown's only casualty loss for the year 1992, the casualty loss deduction is $400, calculated as follows:

FMV of the casualty loss, $6,000–$1,200	$4,800
Cost basis of the auto	$8,500
Lesser of FMV of casualty loss or cost basis of auto	$4,800
Less insurance proceeds	(2,700)
Less $100 reduction	(100)
Remaining casualty loss	$2,000
Less 10% x $16,000	1,600
Casualty loss deduction	$ 400

Be aware that a casualty loss deduction for insured personal-use property will be disallowed to the extent of potential reimbursement, if the taxpayer has not filed with the insurance company an appropriate insurance claim.

Excess Living Expenses

A taxpayer is entitled to exclude from gross income the insurance payments received as reimbursements for extra living expenses incurred as a result of the principal residence being damaged or destroyed by fire or other casualty when there is a temporary necessity to find another residence while the home is being repaired. This exclusion also applies when a person is denied access to the principal residence by governmental authorities because of the casualty.

The exclusion is limited to the excess of the actual living expenses incurred by the taxpayer and members of the household over the normal living expenses they would have incurred during the period. Such additional living expenses would include such costs as rent for suitable housing and extraordinary expenses for transportation, food, utilities, and miscellaneous services. A taxpayer should be prepared to support a claim for a casualty loss deduction if requested by the IRS.

Reporting Casualty and Theft Losses

Illustration 5-5

Casualty and theft losses are reported in total on Schedule A (line 17), shown in Illustration 5-5 as $400. Form 4684, Casualties and Thefts, should be used by the taxpayer to explain the amount reported on Schedule A (line 17) in any of the following situations:

1. There was a net casualty or theft loss of $1,000 or more, after subtracting any insurance payments and the $100 reduction.
2. There was more than one casualty or theft loss during the taxable year.

Supporting Evidence to Justify a Casualty Loss Deduction

1. The nature of the incident, when the casualty occurred, and that the loss actually did occur
2. That the property is owned by the taxpayer
3. A description of the damaged property and its location
4. The cost or other adjusted basis of the property
5. If depreciable property, the depreciation allowed or allowable
6. The FMV of the property immediately before and after the casualty
7. The salvage value of the property
8. The amount of any insurance compensation received by the taxpayer

**Illustration 5-5
Casualty and Theft Losses section
Form 1040**

Casualty and Theft Losses	17	Casualty or theft loss(es). Attach Form 4684. (See page A-4.) . . . . ▶	17	400	00

3. There was more than one item lost or damaged by one or more casualties or thefts.
4. There was a gain from a casualty or theft.
5. The casualty or theft involved trade, business, or income-producing property.

Filled-In Form 4684

Illustration 5-6

A filled-in Form 4684 is presented in Illustration 5-6 to show the calculation of the deductible casualty loss for the wrecking of James R. Brown's personal automobile, discussed on the preceding page. The net deduction of $400 shown on Form 4684 would be the amount reported on Schedule A (line 17), provided that was Brown's only casualty loss for the year.

Summary of Common Itemized Deductions

If the only itemized deductions the taxpayer has are medical and dental expenses, taxes, interest expense, charitable contributions, and casualty and theft losses, these amounts are totaled on Schedule A (line 26). The total amount of itemized deductions on Schedule A (line 26) is compared with the amount that the taxpayer is allowed as a standard deduc-

tion. The larger of the total itemized deductions or the standard deduction is entered on Form 1040, page 2 (line 34). The amount entered (line 34) is subtracted from the AGI (line 32) with the difference entered (line 35). Personal exemptions (line 36) are subtracted to arrive at taxable income (line 37). By subtracting itemized deductions from AGI when itemized deductions are greater than the standard deduction, taxable income will be lower and the taxpayer will pay a lower amount of tax. However, an additional limitation on the total of itemized deductions is applied if the taxpayer's AGI is over $100,000. This further limitation is discussed later in this chapter.

Filled-In Schedule A

Illustration 5-7

Dewey R. (SSN 354-69-4351) and Janell S. Davis presented the following itemized deduction amounts to their accountant for the year 1992. The accountant prepared the filled-in Schedule A, Itemized Deductions, as shown in Illustration 5-7 based on an AGI of $30,000.

Amounts paid by check during the year which were used in determining itemized deductions on Schedule A were as follows (rounded to even dollars):

Medical and dental expenses paid
  (not compensated by insurance):

Dr. A. A. Forest	$ 640
Dr. S. B. Davis	300
Eyeglasses, Optical Clinic	145

Illustration 5-6
Filled-In Form 4684

Form **4684**

Department of the Treasury
Internal Revenue Service

Casualties and Thefts

▶ See separate instructions.
▶ Attach to your tax return.
▶ Use a separate Form 4684 for each different casualty or theft.

OMB No. 1545-0177

1992

Attachment
Sequence No. **26**

Name(s) shown on tax return

James R. Brown

Identifying number

264-19-1906

SECTION A.—Personal Use Property (Use this section to report casualties and thefts of property **not** used in a trade or business or for income-producing purposes.)

1 Description of properties (show kind, location, and date acquired for each):

Property **A** Personal automobile purchased September 1, 1985

Property **B**

Property **C**

Property **D**

		Properties (Use a separate column for each property lost or damaged from one casualty or theft.)			
		A	**B**	**C**	**D**
2 Cost or other basis of each property	2	8,500 00			
3 Insurance or other reimbursement (whether or not you submitted a claim). See instructions. **Note:** If line 2 is **more than** line 3, skip line 4.	3	2,700 00			
4 Gain from casualty or theft. If line 3 is **more than** line 2, enter the difference here and skip lines 5 through 9 for that column. If line 3 includes an amount that you did not receive, see instructions.	4				
5 Fair market value **before** casualty or theft	5	6,000 00			
6 Fair market value **after** casualty or theft	6	1,200 00			
7 Subtract line 6 from line 5	7	4,800 00			
8 Enter the **smaller** of line 2 or line 7	8	4,800 00			
9 Subtract line 3 from line 8. If zero or less, enter -0-	9	2,100 00			

10 Casualty or theft loss. Add the amounts on line 9. Enter the total	10	2,100 00
11 Enter the amount from line 10 or $100, whichever is **smaller**	11	100 00
12 Subtract line 11 from line 10	12	2,000 00
13 **Caution:** Use only one Form 4684 for lines 13 through 18. Add the amounts on line 12 of all Forms 4684	13	2,000 00
14 Combine the amounts from line 4 of all Forms 4684	14	–0–
15 • If line 14 is **more than** line 13, enter the difference here and on Schedule D. Do not complete the rest of this section (see instructions). • If line 14 is **less than** line 13, enter -0- here and continue with the form. • If line 14 is **equal to** line 13, enter -0- here. Do not complete the rest of this section.	15	–0–
16 If line 14 is **less than** line 13, enter the difference	16	2,000 00
17 Enter 10% of your adjusted gross income (Form 1040, line 32). Estates and trusts, see instructions	17	1,600 00
18 Subtract line 17 from line 16. If zero or less, enter -0-. Also enter result on Schedule A (Form 1040), line 17. Estates and trusts, enter on the "Other deductions" line of your tax return	18	400 00

For Paperwork Reduction Act Notice, see page 1 of separate instructions.   Cat. No. 12997O   Form **4684** (1992)

County Hospital	1,230	
Premium on medical insurance	690	
Prescription drugs	270	$3,275
State income taxes		1,150
Real estate taxes paid on residence		1,337
Personal property taxes		126
Interest on home mortgage		1,227
Interest on credit card charges		53
Contributions:		
March of Dimes	$ 25	
Salvation Army	15	
American Red Cross	20	
United Way	17	
Used clothing to thrift shop, FMV	25	
Trinity Church	550	652
Property damage sustained as a result of auto collision:		
FMV of loss (less than cost basis)	$5,820	
Less insurance proceeds	2,000	
	$3,820	
Less $100 reduction	100	
	$3,720	
Less 10% of $30,000.00	3,000	
Deductible casualty loss		720

Mr. Davis drove his personal automobile 200 miles on special church business. Instead of calculating the actual cost of driving on church business, he claimed a $24 deduction using the standard 12 cents per mile figure. The deduction was entered on Schedule A (line 14).

As Schedule A illustrates, the total itemized deductions calculated for Dewey and Janell Davis amounted to $6,261 for 1992. Since the amount of itemized deductions is larger than the $6,000 of standard deduction, the total of itemized deductions, $6,261, would be reported on Form 1040, page 2 (line 34) and subtracted from AGI in computing their taxable income and tax liability. Itemized deductions totaling $6,261 is the correct amount for Mr. and Mrs. Davis as long as their AGI does not exceed $100,000. If AGI does exceed $100,000 in 1992 or later years, there is an overall limitation on the total amount of itemized deductions.

Limitation on Itemized Deductions

For tax years beginning after 1990 and before January 1, 1995, the Revenue Reconciliation Act of 1990 provides that total otherwise allowable itemized deductions (other than medical expenses, casualty and theft losses, and investment interest) are reduced by 3% of the taxpayer's AGI in excess of $105,250 for all taxpayers except married filing separately, in which case the adjustment applies for AGI in excess of $52,625 for 1992. However, the phase out is limited in that total otherwise allowable itemized deductions may not be reduced by more than 80%. This limitation on itemized deductions effectively increases the marginal tax rate by slightly less than 1%.

EXAMPLE 19

To illustrate the limitation on itemized deductions for 1992 provided by the Revenue Reconciliation Act of 1990, assume that a taxpayer who files a joint return with his wife had an AGI in 1992 of $140,000. Also assume that the couple's expenses of the type listed on Schedule A for itemized deductions consisted of the following amounts before applying the limitations for medical expenses, casualty losses, and the overall limitation required by the Revenue Reconciliation Act of 1990:

Medical Expenses, $12,000; Taxes, $3,300; Mortgage Interest, $2,500; Investment Interest, $1,800; Charitable Contributions, $4,200; Casualty Losses (not covered by insurance), $8,500.

Based on this information, the itemized deductions for this married couple in 1992 would be $12,100, calculated as follows:

Medical Expenses	
[$12,000 − (7.5% x $140,450)]	$ 1,466*
Taxes	3,300
Interest Expense	
($2,500 + $1,800)	4,300
Charitable Contributions	4,200
Casualty Losses	
[$8,500 − (10% x $140,450) − $100]	0
Deductible Expenses Before Overall	
Limitation	$13,266

Illustration 5-7
Filled-In Schedule A, Itemized Deductions

SCHEDULES A&B (Form 1040) Department of the Treasury Internal Revenue Service	**Schedule A—Itemized Deductions** (Schedule B is on back) ▶ Attach to Form 1040. ▶ See Instructions for Schedules A and B (Form 1040).	OMB No. 1545-0074 19**92** Attachment Sequence No. **07**

Name(s) shown on Form 1040

Dewey R. and Janell S. Davis

Your social security number: 354 : 69 : 4351

Medical and Dental Expenses

Caution: *Do not include expenses reimbursed or paid by others.*

1	Medical and dental expenses (see page A-1)	1	3,275 00
2	Enter amount from Form 1040, line 32. **2** 30,000 00		
3	Multiply line 2 above by 7.5% (.075)	3	2,250 00
4	Subtract line 3 from line 1. If zero or less, enter -0- ▶	4	1,025 00

Taxes You Paid
(See page A-1.)

5	State and local income taxes	5	1,150 00
6	Real estate taxes (see page A-2)	6	1,337 00
7	Other taxes. List—include personal property taxes ▶ Personal property tax	7	126 00
8	Add lines 5 through 7 ▶	8	2,613 00

Interest You Paid
(See page A-2.)

Note: Personal interest is not deductible.

9a	Home mortgage interest and points reported to you on Form 1098	9a	1,227 00
b	Home mortgage interest not reported to you on Form 1098. If paid to an individual, show that person's name and address. ▶		
		9b	
10	Points not reported to you on Form 1098. See page A-3 for special rules	10	
11	Investment interest. If required, attach Form 4952. (See page A-3.)	11	
12	Add lines 9a through 11 ▶	12	1,227 00

Gifts to Charity
(See page A-3.)

Caution: *If you made a charitable contribution and received a benefit in return, see page A-3.*

13	Contributions by cash or check	13	627 00
14	Other than by cash or check. If over $500, you **MUST** attach Form 8283	14	49 00
15	Carryover from prior year	15	
16	Add lines 13 through 15 ▶	16	676 00

Casualty and Theft Losses

17	Casualty or theft loss(es). Attach Form 4684. (See page A-4.) ▶	17	720 00

Moving Expenses

18	Moving expenses. Attach Form 3903 or 3903F. (See page A-4.) ▶	18	

Job Expenses and Most Other Miscellaneous Deductions
(See page A-5 for expenses to deduct here.)

19	Unreimbursed employee expenses—job travel, union dues, job education, etc. If required, you **MUST** attach Form 2106. (See page A-4.) ▶	19	
20	Other expenses—investment, tax preparation, safe deposit box, etc. List type and amount ▶	20	
21	Add lines 19 and 20	21	
22	Enter amount from Form 1040, line 32. **22**		
23	Multiply line 22 above by 2% (.02)	23	
24	Subtract line 23 from line 21. If zero or less, enter -0- ▶	24	

Other Miscellaneous Deductions

25	Other—from list on page A-5. List type and amount ▶	25	

Total Itemized Deductions

26	Is the amount on Form 1040, line 32, more than $105,250 (more than $52,625 if married filing separately)? • **NO.** Your deduction is not limited. Add lines 4, 8, 12, 16, 17, 18, 24, and 25. • **YES.** Your deduction may be limited. See page A-5 for the amount to enter. ▶	26	6,261 00

Caution: *Be sure to enter on Form 1040, line 34, the **LARGER** of the amount on line 26 above or your standard deduction.*

For Paperwork Reduction Act Notice, see Form 1040 instructions.   Cat. No. 11330X   Schedule A (Form 1040) 1992

Itemized Deductions Subject to Limitation:

Taxes	$ 3,300
Mortgage Interest	2,500
Charitable Contributions	4,200
Total	$10,000

Reduce Otherwise Allowable Itemized Deductions by the Lesser of $10,613 (80% x $13,266) or 3% ($140,450 – $105,250) = ... (1,056)

Total Itemized Deductions Allowed in 1992 .... $12,210

Chapter Summary

This chapter covered the types of itemized deductions related to personal expenses that are common to most taxpayers. These itemized deductions include medical expenses, taxes, interest expense, charitable contributions, and casualty and theft losses. In addition to demonstrating the extent of deductibility of these five common types of itemized deductions, also discussed in this chapter is the overall limitation on the amount of allowable itemized deductions provided for in the Revenue Reconciliation Act of 1990 when AGI exceeds $100,000.

Itemized deductions related to employment and investment activities, such as moving expenses and miscellaneous itemized deductions are covered in Chapter 6 along with disclosures of tax information, regulation of preparers, and tax planning principles. A more comprehensive Schedule A covering all itemized deductions is presented in Chapter 6 after moving expenses and miscellaneous itemized deductions are covered.

C H A P T E R   5

Questions and Problems

1. Roger Brown and his wife, Jenny, maintain a home in which they live with their invalid daughter, Brenda, age 24. AGI on Mr. and Mrs. Brown's joint return is $24,000, and payments for medical and dental expenses during the year are as follows:

	Brenda	Mr. & Mrs. Brown
R. J. Stone, M.D. (not paid by insurance)	$260	$ 250
G. O. Wright, M.D. (not paid by insurance)	220	200
Hearing Aid		525
Premium on Hospital Insurance		240
Eyeglasses		130
Toothpaste	20	35
Prescription Drugs (not paid by insurance)	275	125
Total	$775	$1,505

Calculate the itemized deduction from AGI that could be claimed by Mr. and Mrs. Brown for medical and dental expenses on Schedule A (line 4).

2. Edna Rogerson, a single taxpayer, has paid the following expenses during the year. Her AGI is $17,900.
   a. In the spaces below, enter the letter indicating whether each item listed is subject to deduction as (A) medicines, doctors, dentists, nurses, hospitals, and premiums on medical insurance; (B) transportation and lodging; (C) other medical and dental expenses; or (D) not deductible. If deductible, also enter the amount (without regard to the 7½% of AGI limitation). Assume that these amounts have already been reduced by the insurance reimbursement, when applicable.

Item	Subject To Deduction as	Deductible Amount
a. Premium on health insurance, $386	___________	___________
b. Premium on life insurance policy, $275	___________	___________
c. Premium on automobile accident insurance policy, $610 .	___________	___________
d. Toothpaste, $9.48	___________	___________
e. Drugs prescribed by doctor, $300	___________	___________
f. Vitamins, $60	___________	___________

	Item	Subject To Deduction as	Deductible Amount
g.	Cosmetics, $150		
h.	Dr. Beth K. Wall, dentist, $120		
i.	Dues to health spa, $325		
j.	X-ray examination, $60		
k.	City Hospital for room and other services, $375		
l.	Ace Optical Center for glasses, $125		
m.	Cemetery plot, $600		
n.	Transportation from residence to doctor's office and return, standard mileage rate for 180 miles		
o.	Illegal drugs, $135		
p.	Vacation for rest to improve general health, $875 to Mountain Retreat Resort		
q.	Dr. C. B. Root, surgeon, $350		
r.	Purchase of wheelchair, $275		
s.	Dr. A. Spencer for false teeth, $480, and services, $100 . . .		

b. Complete for Ms. Rogerson the Medical and Dental Expenses section of Schedule A that is reproduced below.

Medical and Dental Expenses			
	Caution: *Do not include expenses reimbursed or paid by others.*		
1	Medical and dental expenses (see page A-1)	1	
2	Enter amount from Form 1040, line 32 . $\boxed{2}$ |_____________|		
3	Multiply line 2 above by 7.5% (.075)	3	
4	Subtract line 3 from line 1. If zero or less, enter -0-. . . . . ▶	4	

3. A taxpayer receives reimbursement for a medical expense of $455 in the current year. What is the proper tax treatment of the $455 if:
   a. The expense being reimbursed had also been paid in the current year?

   b. The expense being reimbursed had been paid in a prior year when itemized deductions had not been claimed?

   c. The expense being reimbursed had been paid in a prior year when itemized deductions had been claimed, including medical expenses of $840?

d. The expense being reimbursed had been paid in a prior year when itemized deductions had been claimed, including medical expenses of $350?

e. The total includes $75 that is in excess of the taxpayer's current year's medical expense? The premium on the policy being reimbursed had been paid by the taxpayer.

f. The total includes $75 that is in excess of the taxpayer's current year's medical expense? The employer had paid the total cost of the medical insurance plan, and the cost of the medical premium had not been included in gross income of the taxpayer.

4. If an employee pays for a periodic medical checkup required by an employer, can the amount paid be deducted, and if so, is there any limitation? Explain.

5. Maurice and June Prior, Milwaukee, Wisconsin, cash-method taxpayers, file a joint income tax return. One dependent child, Jeff, is claimed on the return for 1992. AGI is $24,650. The Priors elect to itemize deductions. From the information given, prepare the Taxes You Paid section of Schedule A for Mr. and Mrs. Prior, using the form provided on the next page.

a. State income tax withheld by employer in 1992 was $1,697.15.

b. Quarterly payments on declaration of state income tax for 1991 and 1992 were as follows:

1991		1992	
April 15, 1991	$100	April 13, 1992	$120
July 15, 1991	100	July 10, 1992	120
October 14, 1991	100	October 15, 1992	120
January 10, 1992	100	January 12, 1993	120

c. Payments on real estate tax levies on personal residence were as follows:

July 31, 1991	$450	
January 30, 1992	450	$900 for 1991
July 30, 1992	$450	
January 29, 1993	500	$950 for 1992

d. Personal property tax on boat, paid on January 23, 1992, was $96. The tax bill had been received on December 28, 1991.

e. Other taxes paid in 1992 include $1,511.05 for social security tax, $800 for special assessment against real estate for a new sidewalk, and $32 federal excise tax on telephone bills.

Taxes You Paid						
Taxes You Paid	5	State and local income taxes	5			
Paid	6	Real estate taxes (see page A-2)	6			
(See page A-1.)	7	Other taxes. List—include personal property taxes . ▶	7			
	8	Add lines 5 through 7 . . . . ▶	8			

6. On March 14, 1991, Rudy Valquez sold a 10-acre piece of property to Eric Volkan for $40,000. In closing the transaction, nothing was stipulated about the payment of the property taxes for the year 1991. Eric paid the entire 1991 property tax bill on January 31, 1992, in the amount of $800. Based on these facts, answer the following:

a. How much of the paid property tax can Eric deduct on his tax return? Show calculations if needed.

b. In which year is Eric allowed to take the property tax deduction on Schedule A for the amount of taxes calculated in *a.* above? Explain.

c. Calculate the amount of paid property taxes, if any, that Eric is not allowed to take as an itemized deduction, and explain how, if at all, Eric and Rudy should account for this portion of the taxes.

d. What could Rudy and Eric have done to avoid the above complications in handling the deductibility of property taxes?

7. During 1992, Barbara Newton borrowed money on two different occasions from the local Savings and Loan Association. The first loan was entered into on March 1, 1992, to purchase land as a place for keeping horses and livestock as an investment activity. Newton paid $33,000 for the land, making a down payment of $6,000 and borrowing $27,000 for 10 years at 9% interest. She was required to pay two points to initiate the loan, amounting to $540 (2% x $27,000). In August, 1992, Newton bought a new house to be used as her residence. The loan was for $48,000 at 8% for 20 years. The lender required Newton to pay one point at the closing to initiate the loan (1% x $48,000 = $480).

a. How much interest expense is Newton allowed to deduct in 1992 in connection with the points paid on the two loans? Show calculations.

b. What is the tax treatment of any amounts paid as points to the extent not deductible in 1992?

8. On May 10, 1992, Roy and Jane Wilde's home was damaged by a severe storm. The home had been purchased in 1980 for $73,000, excluding the cost of the land. Its FMV just before the storm was estimated to be $97,000, and its FMV after the storm was estimated at $79,000. They collected $15,000 of insurance. Their AGI was $22,000 for 1992.

    a. Complete Form 4684 on the next page to determine the amount that Mr. and Mrs. Wilde can report as a casualty loss on Schedule A, Itemized Deductions, if they itemize their deductions on their 1992 tax return. The SSN to be entered on the form is 182-78-2641.

    b. Mr. and Mrs. Wilde's normal living expenses are $900 per month. They were reimbursed at the rate of $1,200 per month for actual living expenses during the three months they lived in a motel while their house was being repaired. What are the tax consequences of the $1,200 per month reimbursement for living costs?

9. Can each of the following payments be deducted from AGI (as an itemized deduction on Schedule A), assuming the amount is within any limitation applicable? Check "Yes" or "No" in the appropriate column. If the answer is "Yes," indicate the line no. on Schedule A where the amount paid would be entered.

Item	Yes	No	Line No. on Schedule A
a. Payment to home for the aged for person physically incapable of self-care:			
(1) Meals	_____	_____	__________
(2) Lodging	_____	_____	__________
(3) Nursing care	_____	_____	__________
b. Interest paid to purchase municipal bonds	_____	_____	__________
c. Supplementary medical insurance premium under Medicare	_____	_____	__________
d. Interest on credit card	_____	_____	__________
e. Interest on gambling debt	_____	_____	__________
f. Addition to rent for tenant because of increases in real estate taxes paid by the landlord	_____	_____	__________
g. Interest paid on delinquent federal income tax	_____	_____	__________
h. Interest paid on loan to purchase bonds of the City of Wilmington	_____	_____	__________
i. Finance charge on revolving credit on amount of unpaid balance	_____	_____	__________
j. Interest paid on life insurance policy loan	_____	_____	__________

Form **4684**

Department of the Treasury
Internal Revenue Service

Casualties and Thefts

▶ See separate instructions.
▶ Attach to your tax return.
▶ **Use a separate Form 4684 for each different casualty or theft.**

OMB No. 1545-0177

19**92**

Attachment
Sequence No. **26**

Name(s) shown on tax return

Identifying number

SECTION A.—Personal Use Property (Use this section to report casualties and thefts of property **not** used in a trade or business or for income-producing purposes.)

1 Description of properties (show kind, location, and date acquired for each):

Property **A** ....

Property **B** ....

Property **C** ....

Property **D** ....

Properties (Use a separate column for each property lost or damaged from one casualty or theft.)

	A	B	C	D
2 Cost or other basis of each property				
3 Insurance or other reimbursement (whether or not you submitted a claim). See instructions. **Note:** *If line 2 is **more than** line 3, skip line 4.*				
4 Gain from casualty or theft. If line 3 is **more than** line 2, enter the difference here and skip lines 5 through 9 for that column. If line 3 includes an amount that you did not receive, see instructions				
5 Fair market value **before** casualty or theft				
6 Fair market value **after** casualty or theft				
7 Subtract line 6 from line 5				
8 Enter the **smaller** of line 2 or line 7				
9 Subtract line 3 from line 8. If zero or less, enter -0-				

10 Casualty or theft loss. Add the amounts on line 9. Enter the total **10**

11 Enter the amount from line 10 or $100, whichever is **smaller** **11**

12 Subtract line 11 from line 10 .... **12**

Caution: *Use only one Form 4684 for lines 13 through 18.*

13 Add the amounts on line 12 of all Forms 4684 .... **13**

14 Combine the amounts from line 4 of all Forms 4684 .... **14**

15 • If line 14 is **more than** line 13, enter the difference here and on Schedule D. Do not complete the rest of this section (see instructions).

   • If line 14 is **less than** line 13, enter -0- here and continue with the form.

   • If line 14 is **equal to** line 13, enter -0- here. Do not complete the rest of this section. **15**

16 If line 14 is **less than** line 13, enter the difference **16**

17 Enter 10% of your adjusted gross income (Form 1040, line 32). Estates and trusts, see instructions **17**

18 Subtract line 17 from line 16. If zero or less, enter -0-. Also enter result on Schedule A (Form 1040), line 17. Estates and trusts, enter on the "Other deductions" line of your tax return **18**

For Paperwork Reduction Act Notice, see page 1 of separate instructions.   Cat. No. 12997O   Form **4684** (1992)

10. Gloria S. and John A. Peters obtained a loan from the County Savings and Loan Association to purchase a new residence. The loan was negotiated for $56,550, and the security for the loan was the new residence purchased on July 2, 1992. The following statement from the County Savings and Loan Association, listing the disbursements made from the loan and other information about the purchase of the new residence, was received by Mr. and Mrs. Peters on July 25, 1992. All transactions had been completed and the loan properly accounted for.

For each item **(a)** through **(j)** in the statement from the County Savings and Loan Association, insert in the space provided in the "Letter" column one of the letters shown below, indicating the appropriate 1992 income tax treatment of each payment made. State in the "Amount" column the amount applicable for each item identified.

A   Add to the cost of the residence
B   Deduct from gross income to arrive at AGI
C   Deduct from AGI (itemized deduction, Schedule A)
D   Personal, not deductible
E   Other

COUNTY SAVINGS AND LOAN ASSOCIATION
Loan Statement for Gloria S. and John A. Peters
July 25, 1992

	Amount	Item No.	Letter	Amount
Purchase price of residence	$ 62,500			
Deposit with purchase offer, 5-28-92	(2,500)	(a)	_______	_______
Balance due at closing	$ 60,000			
Down payment in cash	(10,000)	(b)	_______	_______
Purchase price to be financed	$ 50,000	(c)	_______	_______
Premium on homeowner's insurance policy (fire, casualty liability, etc.) assumed from prior owner, 7-2-92 through 12-31-94	480	(d)	_______	_______
Estimated real estate taxes for 1992 from prior owner (to be levied at end of year by city) of $1,950 for 1-1-92 through 6-30-92	(975)	(e)	_______	_______
Full tank of fuel oil for heating on hand, 7-2-92	245	(f)	_______	_______
Attorney fee for title examination, recordings, and legal representation at closing (selling expenses)	375	(g)	_______	_______
Appraisal fee to obtain loan (selling expenses)	215	(h)	_______	_______
Points for making loan—2% of loan (2% point payment is the business practice in the area	1,000	(i)	_______	_______
Paid to Mr. and Mrs. Peters jointly with City Improvement Company for remodeling of kitchen in new residence	3,360	(j)	_______	_______
Total	$ 54,700			

11. George (SSN 286-53-6215) and Mary Greenfield (SSN 473-51-7632), who had an AGI of $98,500 in 1992, incurred the following interest expenses during the year:

Credit card interest	$ 79.32
Automobile loan (older car)	337.15
Mortgage interest—personal residence	13,500.00
Investment interest on broker's margin account to carry a portfolio of corporate stocks	543.20
Investment interest on broker's margin account to carry tax-exempt bonds	381.75
Mortgage interest on vacation home	3,080.00
Points paid on vacation home mortgage ($48,000 x 2 points)	960.00

The original cost of their personal residence was $160,000, which has a FMV of $166,000. There have been no capitalized improvements. The balance of the mortgage was $140,000 on January 1, 1992, and $139,000 on December 31, 1992 (average 1992 balance $139,500). The vacation home was originally acquired in 1983 at a cost of $56,400, including subsequent improvements, and was without a mortgage until May 1, 1992, when the Greenfields decided to take out a 10-year mortgage secured by the vacation home in the amount of $48,000 in order to purchase a new car and consolidate several other loans. The balance of the mortgage at December 31, 1992, was $47,400 (average 1992 balance $47,700).

a. Based on the information regarding interest costs incurred by the Greenfields in 1992, determine how much mortgage interest can be deducted in each category of interest expense.

b. Complete the Interest You Paid section of Schedule A below to show how the deductible interest allowed to George and Mary Greenfield for 1992 is to be reported.

Interest You Paid (See page A-2.)	9a	Home mortgage interest and points reported to you on Form 1098	9a			
	b	Home mortgage interest not reported to you on Form 1098. If paid to an individual, show that person's name and address. ▶				
		....				
		....	9b			
Note: Personal interest is not deductible.		....				
	10	Points not reported to you on Form 1098. See page A-3 for special rules.	10			
	11	Investment interest. If required, attach Form 4952. (See page A-3.)	11			
	12	Add lines 9a through 11 ▶	12			

12. a. A taxpayer incurs a debt of $40,000 to purchase a residential lot on August 1, 1990. The debt is secured by the lot. On March 1, 1992, the taxpayer begins construction on a residence and spends his own funds for construction to the extent of $210,000. The residence is completed on October 1, 1992, and immediately becomes the taxpayer's principal residence. On December 1, 1992, the taxpayer incurs a debt of $200,000 secured by the residence. Of the proceeds, $40,000 is sent by the lender directly to the holder of the debt on the lot to pay off the existing debt, and $160,000 is disbursed directly to the taxpayer.

1) Is the initial debt of $40,000 on the lot treated as acquisition indebtedness on the principal residence? Explain.

2) Is the $200,000 debt, used to refinance the initial debt and reimburse the taxpayer for construction funds supplied to build the residence, treated as acquisition indebtedness on the residence? Explain.

b. Assume the same facts as in *a.* above except that the taxpayer used his own cash, rather than incurring debt, to purchase the lot. How much of the $200,000 debt on the residence can be treated as acquisition indebtedness? Explain.

13. a. Can a contribution of a book, an antique, a wild animal, used furniture, or a future right to a work of art be deducted? If so, how are such contributions reported?

b. If deductible contributions exceed the amount that can be deducted in the current year, is the excess deduction lost? Explain.

14. a. An individual transfers common stock with a market value of $15,000 to an educational institution to be used for scholarships. The stock originally cost $3,575 six years ago. What amount may be claimed as an itemized deduction because of this contribution? It may be assumed that the amount claimed is not in excess of 50% of AGI.

b. What must a taxpayer consider before contributing appreciated securities to a charity?

15. An appreciated security with a FMV of $9,500 was contributed to the City General Hospital in 1992. The security had been held for five months and had cost $4,200. The taxpayer had AGI for 1992 of $32,000. What amount of contribution deduction could be claimed by a taxpayer?

16. In 1992, a taxpayer who itemizes deductions sells to the First Church for $12,000 tangible personal property that cost $6,000 in 1985. The FMV of the property is $20,000. What contribution amount can be claimed if:

    a. The contribution was related to the charity's exempt function?

    b. The contribution was not related to the charity's exempt function?

    c. Does the taxpayer need to report the bargain sale in any other place on Form 1040? If so, where and how?

17. A professional football team plays a game for the benefit of the local hospital each year. The admission charge is $32 per ticket, the usual admission price for a professional football game, with one-half of the purchase price going directly to the hospital. Denise Clarke purchases four tickets at a total cost of $128. Ms. Clarke itemizes deductions on Schedule A.

    a. How much can Ms. Clarke deduct per ticket as a charitable contribution on her income tax return? Explain.

    b. How would your answer to *a.* differ if Ms. Clarke had no intention of going to the football game, and in fact stayed home, with the tickets not being used? Explain.

    c. Would your answer be different if $32 had been paid for each ticket when the usual admission charge is $20 per ticket? Explain.

18. Indicate by placing an "X" in the proper column whether each of the following gifts or other expenditures is deductible as a contribution, deductible but not as a contribution, or not deductible.

Gift or Expenditure	Deductible as a Contribution	Deductible But Not as a Contribution	Not Deductible
a. Cash to American Red Cross			
b. Pledge to church			
c. Auto expense of church employee			
d. Cash to Girl Scouts of America			
e. Building to American Legion			
f. Cash to political party			
g. Cash to American Library Association			
h. Clothing to Salvation Army			
i. Common stock to church			
j. Cash to local university			
k. U.S. bond to local hospital			
l. Service to church (10 hours @ $3.50 per hour)			
m. Auto expense for volunteer church work			

19. Kevin and Jane Steele file a joint return each year. During 1992 their house was broken into and the following items were taken. Their AGI for 1992 is $20,000.

	Cost	FMV of Loss
Television Set	$ 595	$ 375
Microwave Oven	575	400
VCR	850	700
Jewelry	2,200	2,500

The Steeles collected $500 from their insurance company. What amount may they deduct as an itemized deduction in 1992 for this theft?

20. John Saad files a joint return with his wife Mary for the year 1992. Their AGI for the year amounted to $132,000. They assembled for their accountant's use the following list of potential itemized deductions for which they had excellent backup records: medical expenses, $10,400; property taxes, $3,400; state and local income taxes, $4,600; mortgage interest, $4,800; investment interest, $3,700; and charitable contributions, $6,400. Assume that the investment interest is fully deductible. John Saad's SSN is 432-61-7809.

   a. Assume that you are serving as Mr. and Mrs. Saad's tax accountant for the year 1992. Calculate the total amount of itemized deductions they would be entitled to on their 1992 income tax return.

   b. Prepare Schedule A on the following page for Mr. and Mrs. Saad for 1992.

SCHEDULES A&B
(Form 1040)

Department of the Treasury
Internal Revenue Service

Schedule A—Itemized Deductions

(Schedule B is on back)

▶ Attach to Form 1040. ▶ See Instructions for Schedules A and B (Form 1040).

OMB No. 1545-0074

1992

Attachment
Sequence No. **07**

Name(s) shown on Form 1040

Your social security number

Medical and Dental Expenses

Caution: *Do not include expenses reimbursed or paid by others.*

1 Medical and dental expenses (see page A-1) . . . . | 1
2 Enter amount from Form 1040, line 32. | 2 |
3 Multiply line 2 above by 7.5% (.075) . . . . . . | 3
4 Subtract line 3 from line 1. If zero or less, enter -0- . . . . . . ▶ | 4

Taxes You Paid

(See page A-1.)

5 State and local income taxes . . . . | 5
6 Real estate taxes (see page A-2) . . . . | 6
7 Other taxes. List—include personal property taxes · ▶
.... | 7
8 Add lines 5 through 7 . . . . ▶ | 8

Interest You Paid

(See page A-2.)

Note: Personal interest is not deductible.

9a Home mortgage interest and points reported to you on Form 1098 | 9a
 b Home mortgage interest not reported to you on Form 1098. If paid to an individual, show that person's name and address. ▶
....
....
.... | 9b
10 Points not reported to you on Form 1098. See page A-3 for special rules . . . . | 10
11 Investment interest. If required, attach Form 4952. (See page A-3.) . . . . | 11
12 Add lines 9a through 11 . . . . ▶ | 12

Gifts to Charity

(See page A-3.)

Caution: *If you made a charitable contribution and received a benefit in return, see page A-3.*

13 Contributions by cash or check . . . . | 13
14 Other than by cash or check. If over $500, you **MUST** attach Form 8283 . . . . | 14
15 Carryover from prior year . . . . | 15
16 Add lines 13 through 15 . . . . ▶ | 16

Casualty and Theft Losses

17 Casualty or theft loss(es). Attach Form 4684. (See page A-4.) . . . . ▶ | 17

Moving Expenses

18 Moving expenses. Attach Form 3903 or 3903F. (See page A-4.). . . . . . . ▶ | 18

Job Expenses and Most Other Miscellaneous Deductions

(See page A-5 for expenses to deduct here.)

19 Unreimbursed employee expenses—job travel, union dues, job education, etc. If required, you **MUST** attach Form 2106. (See page A-4.) ▶ ....
.... | 19
20 Other expenses—investment, tax preparation, safe deposit box, etc. List type and amount ▶ ....
....
.... | 20
21 Add lines 19 and 20 . . . . | 21
22 Enter amount from Form 1040, line 32. | 22 |
23 Multiply line 22 above by 2% (.02) . . . . | 23
24 Subtract line 23 from line 21. If zero or less, enter -0- . . . . ▶ | 24

Other Miscellaneous Deductions

25 Other—from list on page A-5. List type and amount ▶ ....
.... ▶ | 25

Total Itemized Deductions

26 Is the amount on Form 1040, line 32, more than $105,250 (more than $52,625 if married filing separately)?

• **NO.** Your deduction is not limited. Add lines 4, 8, 12, 16, 17, 18, 24, and 25. } ▶ | 26
• **YES.** Your deduction may be limited. See page A-5 for the amount to enter. }

Caution: *Be sure to enter on Form 1040, line 34, the **LARGER** of the amount on line 26 above or your standard deduction.*

For Paperwork Reduction Act Notice, see Form 1040 instructions.   Cat. No. 11330X   Schedule A (Form 1040) 1992

Other Itemized Deductions: Moving Expenses and Miscellaneous Deductions

---

Your Rights as a Taxpayer

Incorrect Lien. You have the right to appeal an IRS filing of a Notice of Federal Tax Lien if you believe the IRS filed the lien in error.

Source: Internal Revenue Service, Publication 1

The more common types of itemized deductions were covered in Chapter 5, including medical expenses, taxes, interest expense, charitable contributions, and casualty and theft losses. Itemized deductions related to employment and investment activities (moving expenses and miscellaneous itemized deductions) are discussed in this chapter along with a discussion of tax information disclosures, and certain tax planning principles.

Moving Expenses

Expenses incurred to move a taxpayer, the taxpayer's family, and their personal property to a new employment location are classified as moving expenses. All employees, old or new, and self-employed individuals are eligible to deduct moving expenses as itemized deductions if they meet certain mileage and employment tests. Items include (1) personal property, (2) people, (3) house hunting, (4) temporary quarters, and (5) buying/selling a house. Some items are totally deductible, others are deductible subject to certain limitations. Beginning on January 1, 1987, the Tax Reform Act of 1986 required that all moving expenses be allowed only as itemized deductions. For 1992, deductible moving expenses are reported on Schedule A (line 18).

Illustration 6-1
Schedule A—Moving Expenses

The calculation of the moving expense deduction is explained in detail in the following paragraphs. Qualified moving expenses are deductible in full, since they are not classified as miscellaneous deductions subject to the 2% of AGI floor. If moving expenses are reimbursed in whole or in part by the employer, the reimbursed amount must be included in income.

To qualify as eligible moving expenses, the expenses must meet a number of tests involving (1) the time of the move, (2) the definition of a principal residence, (3) whether fully deductible or deductible with limits, (4) the distance of the move, and (5) the length of time in the new job. Each of these tests is discussed in the following pages.

The Timing of the Move

A usual assumption is that the taxpayer will move to the location of the new employment at the time the new employment starts. However, a physical move by the family may be delayed because of children in school at the old job location or not wanting to move until the current residence at the old job location has been sold. In order to deduct moving expenses, they must be related in time to the start of work at the new location. Moving expenses are considered to be closely related in time to the start of work at the new location if the expenses are incurred within one year from the date the taxpayer first reported to work. If the moving expenses are incurred later than one year after the start of work, they are not deductible unless the taxpayer can prove to the satisfaction of the IRS that there were circumstances which prevented an earlier move, such as waiting for a child to finish his or her senior year in high school. Inability to sell the residence at the old location is not an acceptable reason for delaying the incurrence of the expenses for the move to the new home.

Illustration 6-1
Schedule A—Moving Expenses

Moving Expenses			
18 Moving expenses. Attach Form 3903 or 3903F. (See page A-4.) . . . . ▶	18	4,380	00

The Definition of the Principal Residence

In order to deduct moving expenses, the taxpayer must be moving from a former principal residence to a new principal residence. The old and the new principal residences must be the taxpayer's primary home, including a house, a condominium, or an apartment. A secondary residence, such as a beach house or some other seasonal or temporary residence will not qualify as a principal residence from which a move is being made or to which a move is being made. The need for a principal residence may be a problem in some cases for a college graduate who is seeking a first job. A person seeking a job for the first time is eligible to deduct moving expenses as long as the job-seeker is moving from a former principal residence to a new principal residence. A student residence at college generally will not qualify as a principal residence from which a job hunter is moving.

Fully Deductible Moving Expenses

Fully deductible moving expenses (except for meals) include the costs incurred by the taxpayer in moving the family and the family's personal property to a new residence at the general location of a new principal place of employment.

Fully deductible moving expenses include the reasonable expenses of transportation, meals (limited to 80%), and lodging for the taxpayer and members of the household while en route (including the day of arrival) and the cost of moving household goods and personal effects. Only one trip is deductible, although it is not necessary for the taxpayer and all members of the household to travel together or at the same time. Deductible moving expenses generally do not include the cost of moving such individuals as a nurse or a personal attendant. Included in moving expenses are such items as packing, crating, special handling of the family pets, and in-transit storage of goods. In one recent case, the taxpayer was allowed to include in moving expenses the cost of transporting a sailboat to the new residence since the boat was used regularly by the taxpayer for recreation. Expenses must be for moving from a former residence to a new residence in connection with a new principal place of employment.

EXAMPLE 1 ——————————————————

A taxpayer incurred the following expenses in moving his family to a distant city in connection with the acceptance of a new job. The expenses incurred in moving the family and the household goods were: moving van, $3,500; transportation, $550; and meals $150; a total of $4,200. All of these expenses are deductible as moving expenses except for $30 (20% x $150) of the meal cost. Thus, the deductible moving expenses in this category are $4,170.

A taxpayer using a personal automobile for transportation in connection with moving can deduct only the actual out-of-pocket expenses, such as gasoline, oil, repairs, etc., or 9 cents per mile. Parking fees and tolls paid can be added to the expenses with either method. If out-of-pocket expenses are claimed, an adequate record must be maintained, while only the mileage needs to be verified when the optional 9 cents-per-mile method is used.

Moving Expenses with Deduction Limits

The following three categories of moving expenses are deductible subject to certain limitations:

1. The cost of transportation, meals (80%), and lodging for the taxpayer and members of the household incurred for the principal purpose of *househunting* near the place of new employment can be deducted. Employment must have been obtained before the househunting trip begins.
2. *Temporary living expenses* at the new location can be deducted if incurred within any 30 consecutive days after obtaining employment. Such items include the cost of meals and lodging for the taxpayer and members of the household while waiting to move into permanent quarters.
3. Qualified expenses relating to the sale, purchase, or lease of a residence can be deducted. *Sales-related* expenses include such items as brokers' commissions and escrow fees. Fixing-up costs cannot be deducted. *Purchase-related* expenses include such items as attorney fees, escrow fees, appraisal fees, title and closing costs, and "points" or loan placement charges not deductible as interest. Prorated expenses, such as property taxes between a buyer

and seller, cannot be deducted as moving expenses. Deductible *lease-related* expenses include both the expenses related to the settling of an old lease and those related to the acquisition of a new lease. Security and rent deposits are not deductible.

Other Limitations. Deduction of moving expenses under these three categories (but not the other categories of moving expenses listed earlier) is limited to an overall amount of $3,000. Househunting trips and temporary living expenses at the new job location cannot exceed $1,500 of the $3,000.

EXAMPLE 2 ————————————————

Assume that Roger C. and Nancy J. Clarke incur pre-moving expenses for househunting of $870, including $120 for meals; incur temporary living expenses of $1,000, including $250 for meals; pay sales commissions of $1,800 on the sale of the old residence; and incur purchased-related expenses on the new residence of $700.

Qualified moving expenses in these three categories would amount to a maximum of $3,000, calculated as follows:

Pre-move expenses excluding meals ($870 – $120)	$ 750	
Meals ($120 x 80%)	96	$ 846
Temporary living expenses excluding meals ($1,000 – $250)	$ 750	
Meals ($250 x 80%)	200	950
Total pre-move & temporary living expenses		$1,796
Limitation on deductibility of pre-move and temporary expenses		$1,500
Expenses incurred for sale and purchase of residences		$2,500
Limitation on deductibility of sale and purchase expenses (total, $2,500) limit		1,500
Total deductible qualified moving expenses		$3,000

The $1,000 ($2,500 – $1,500) of expenses incurred in connection with the sale and purchase of residences that are not deductible as moving expenses can be used to reduce the sale price of the old residence and increase the cost of the new residence. The $1,000 of nondeductible moving expenses would be prorated between sales and purchase expenses based on the relative amounts paid in the form of sales commissions, $1,800, and the $700 paid in connection with the purchase of the new residence, as follows:

Total commissions paid	$1,800
Deducted as moving expenses (($1,800/$2,500) x $1,500)	1,080
Commission expense applied to reduce selling price of old residence	$ 720
Total purchase-related expenses on new residence	$ 700
Deducted as moving expenses (($700/$2,500) x $1,500)	420
Purchase-related expenses applied to the cost of the new residence	$ 280

Limits for Certain Married Persons. The limit for a married person filing a separate return is $1,500, and househunting and temporary living expenses are limited to $750 of the $1,500. This limit for a married person filing a separate return also applies where *both* spouses begin work at a new principal place of work and share the same residence.

However, where a taxpayer and spouse who file separate returns both begin work at a new principal place of work, but *do not* share the same new residence, the deduction is limited to an overall amount of $3,000 for each return, with househunting trips and temporary living expenses not exceeding $1,500. If a joint return is filed in this case, the overall limitation is $6,000, with househunting trips and temporary living expenses not exceeding $3,000.

Expenses deducted as moving expenses may not be used to reduce the selling price of the old residence or to increase the basis of the new residence.

Moving Expense Deductions for Foreign Job-Related Moves. The deduction for foreign pre-move house searching, temporary living expenses, and qualified sale or lease expenses incurred by an employee in a foreign move is limited to $6,000. The expenses relating to such househunting trips and temporary living expenses at the new job location are deductible to a maximum of $4,500 of the overall $6,000 limit. In addition, the period during which the cost of living in temporary facilities would be deductible as moving expenses is 90 days.

The moving expense deduction is extended to apply to bona fide retirees who have worked in a foreign country and are returning to the

United States. The deduction is also extended to apply to survivors of taxpayers who worked abroad, if these survivors returned to the United States within six months of the taxpayer's death.

Form 3903F, Foreign Moving Expenses, is available for U.S. citizens or residents who move to a new principal place of work outside the United States or its possessions.

Nondeductible Expenses. Nondeductible moving expenses include such items as the costs of mortgage prepayment penalties, refitting rugs and draperies, expenses of connecting and disconnecting utilities, losses arising from the disposal of property, or similar items.

Meeting the Mileage and Employment Tests

Mileage Test. Moving expenses can be deducted only if the distance between the employee's *new* job location and the *former* residence is at least 35 miles greater than the distance between the *old* job location and the *former* residence.

EXAMPLE 3 ———————————————

If the distance between a taxpayer's old residence and the taxpayer's former place of employment was 12 miles, the location of the new place of employment must be at least 47 miles (35 miles plus 12 miles) from the old residence. If there is no old job location, the new place of work must be at least 35 miles from the former residence. The distance is measured by the shortest of the more commonly traveled routes between the two points.

Employment Test. An employee deducting moving expenses must be employed *full time* in the new job location for 39 weeks during the 12 months immediately following the move. This requirement is waived if failure to comply with the rule is due to disability, death, discharge not due to willful misconduct, or transfer for the employer's benefit.

The moving expense deduction can be claimed even though the 39-week employment test of deductibility is not met by the time the income tax return is due.

EXAMPLE 4 ———————————————

Assume that a taxpayer moved to a new job on September 1, 1992 and expected to work at the new location indefinitely. Deductible moving expenses amounted to $3,450. The taxpayer can deduct these moving expenses on his or her 1992 tax return even though the 39-week employment test will not be met until June 1, 1993.

A taxpayer may take the moving expense deduction for the tax year the moving expenses are incurred. However, if the taxpayer fails to meet the employment test, previously deducted amounts must be reported as income by the taxpayer for the year in which the taxpayer fails to qualify for the moving expense deduction. As an alternate method, the taxpayer can take the deduction in the year in which the employment test is satisfied.

Reimbursement of Moving Expenses

A reimbursement of moving expenses received from either a new or old employer must be included in gross income as compensation for services. Qualified moving expenses are then deducted as an itemized deduction. For moving expense reimbursements that include meals during the move, the employee's deduction for meals is reduced by 20%. Moving expense reimbursements or payments are considered compensation for personal services and are thus subject to withholding and social security taxes. Withholding of income taxes would not be applicable unless there is reason to expect that the moving expenses will not be allowed as a deduction.

No deduction will be allowed for expenses incurred in a prior year if the reimbursement is not included in gross income.

The reimbursement rule does not apply to moving and storage expenses furnished in kind by the government as a part of a permanent change of station for a member of the armed forces on active duty.

Self-Employed Individuals

A self-employed individual is eligible to deduct most of the types of moving expenses that employees are allowed to deduct if the mileage test (discussed above) and the employment test are met. However, a self-employed individual is not allowed to deduct pre-move househunting trips and temporary living expenses unless substantial arrangements have been made to begin work at the new location. Substantial arrangements would include the acquisition of a store or office, the acquisition of inventory and supplies, and specific arrangements with employees and customers at the new location. If no other actions have been taken other than to rent an office, a store, or an apartment, then the IRS is likely to deny the pre-move trip costs because insufficient arrangements have been made to assure a move to the new location.

To meet the employment test, the self-employed individual must, during the 24-month period immediately following the arrival at a new principal place of work, perform services on a full-time basis (either self-employed or as an employee) for at least 78 weeks, of which 39 weeks are within the 12-month period immediately following the arrival at the new place of employment.

The moving expense deduction can be claimed even though the 78-week employment test of deductibility is not met by the time the income tax return is due. The taxpayer may take the moving expense deduction in the year the expenses were incurred. However, if the taxpayer fails to meet the employment test, previously deducted amounts must be reported as income by the taxpayer for the year in which the taxpayer fails to qualify for the moving expense deduction. As an alternate method, the taxpayer can wait until the test is met and then file an amended return for the prior year.

Filled-In Form 4782

Illustration 6-2

Employers must furnish employees with a detailed breakdown of payments for, or reimbursement of, moving expenses. Form 4782, Employee Moving Expense Information, is provided for this purpose. A filled-in Form 4782 provided by Newendorf Company to Roger C. Clarke, Social Security No. 296-26-6254, is shown in Illustration 6-2. Employers are also required to include the total payments on the employee's Form W-2, Wage and Tax

Statement. Nondeductible expenses are subject to withholding and are included in the "Wages" block of Form W-2. Payments for deductible expenses are not subject to withholding and are also included in the "Wages" block. A Form 4782 is to be completed for each move made by an employee for which reimbursement or payment is made. Form 4782 is an information form only, and is not filed with the individual income tax return.

Filled-In Form 3903

Illustration 6-3

Form 3903, Moving Expenses, is available for use in reporting the deduction for moving expenses. The moving expense information on filled-in Form 3903 shown in Illustration 6-3 is reported for Roger C. and Nancy J. Clarke.

Roger C. (SSN 296-26-6254) and Nancy J. Clarke file a joint return and have moved from Chicago, IL to Rockford, IL. The distance between Roger Clarke's new job location and his former residence is 85 miles greater than the distance between his old job location and his former residence. He spent $4,380 for moving expenses in the following amounts: transporting household goods, $2,105; travel and lodging not including meals, $125; total meals during the move, $62.50; pre-move travel expenses excluding meals, $90; pre-move meal expenses, $75; expenses of selling their old residence, $145; and expenses of buying a new home, $1,805. The moving expense deduction of $4,380 is carried to Form 1040, Schedule A (line 18) as shown in Illustration 6-1. The Clarkes were reimbursed by his employer to the extent of $3,485. The $3,485 paid by Newendorf Company to Roger Clarke, as reported on Form 4782 (See Illustration 6-2), is included on his Form W-2 and must be reported by Clarke on Form 1040 (line 7).

Illustration 6-2
Filled-In Form 4782

Form 4782
(Rev. October 1992)

Department of the Treasury
Internal Revenue Service

Employee Moving Expense Information

Payments made during the calendar year 19 91...

▶ See instructions on back.

OMB No. 1545-0182
Expires 9-30-95

**Do not file.
Keep for your records.**

Name of employee

Roger C. Clarke

Social security number

296 : 26 : 6254

Moving Expense Payments		(a) Amount paid to employee		(b) Amount paid to a third party for employee's benefit and value of services furnished in kind		(c) Total (Add columns (a) and (b).)	
Section A—Transportation of Household Goods							
1 Transportation and storage of household goods and personal effects	1	1,405	00			1,405	00
Section B—Expenses of Moving From Old To New Home							
2 Travel and lodging payments **not** including meals	2	75	00			75	00
3 Meal payments for travel	3	50	00			50	00
Section C—Pre-move Househunting Expenses and Temporary Quarters for any 30 Days in a Row After Obtaining Employment (90 Days for a Foreign Move)							
4 Pre-move travel and lodging payments **not** including meals	4	90	00			90	00
5 Temporary quarters payments **not** including meals	5	–0–				–0–	
6 Total meal payments for both pre-move househunting and temporary quarters	6	60	00			60	00
Section D—Qualified Real Estate Expenses							
7 Qualified expenses of selling, buying, or renting a home	7	1,805	00			1,805	00
Section E—Miscellaneous Payments							
8 List all other payments (specify) ▶	8						
9 Total moving expense payments. Add the amounts in column (c) of lines 1 through 8 ▶	9					3,485	00

Note: *The amount on line 9 must be included in the employee's income.*

For Paperwork Reduction Act Notice, see back of form.   Cat. No. 13079T   Form **4782** (Rev. 10-92)

Illustration 6-3
Filled-In Form 3903

Form **3903**	**Moving Expenses**	OMB No. 1545-0062

Department of the Treasury
Internal Revenue Service

▶ **Attach to Form 1040.**

▶ **See separate instructions.**

19**92**

Attachment Sequence No. **62**

Name(s) shown on Form 1040: Roger C. and Nancy J. Clarke

Your social security number: 296 : 26 : 6254

1	Enter the number of miles from your **old home** to your **new workplace**	**1**	100
2	Enter the number of miles from your **old home** to your **old workplace**	**2**	15
3	Subtract line 2 from line 1. Enter the result but not less than zero. ▶	**3**	85

If line 3 is 35 or more miles, complete the rest of this form. If line 3 is less than 35 miles, you may not deduct your moving expenses. This rule does not apply to members of the armed forces.

Caution: *If you are a member of the armed forces, see the instructions before continuing.*

Part I   Moving Expenses

Note: *Any payments your employer made for any part of your move (including the value of any services furnished in kind) should be included on your W-2 form. Report that amount on* **Form 1040, line 7.** *See* **Reimbursements** *in the instructions.*

Section A—Transportation of Household Goods

4	Transportation and storage for household goods and personal effects	**4**	2,105 00

Section B—Expenses of Moving From Old To New Home

5	Travel and lodging **not** including meals	**5**	125 00
6	Total meals	**6**	62 50
7	Multiply line 6 by 80% (.80)	**7**	50 00
8	Add lines 5 and 7	**8**	175 00

Section C—Pre-move Househunting Expenses and Temporary Quarters (for any 30 days in a row after getting your job)

9	Pre-move travel and lodging **not** including meals	**9**	90 00
10	Temporary quarters expenses **not** including meals	**10**	
11	Total meal expenses for both pre-move househunting and temporary quarters	**11**	75 00
12	Multiply line 11 by 80% (.80)	**12**	60 00
13	Add lines 9, 10, and 12	**13**	150 00

Section D—Qualified Real Estate Expenses

14	Expenses of (check one): a ☐ selling or exchanging your old home, or / b ☐ if renting, settling an unexpired lease. }	**14**	145 00
15	Expenses of (check one): a ☐ buying your new home, or / b ☐ if renting, getting a new lease. }	**15**	1,805 00

Part II   Dollar Limits and Moving Expense Deduction

16	Enter the **smaller** of: • The amount on line 13, or • $1,500 ($750 if married filing a separate return and at the end of 1992 you lived with your spouse who also started work in 1992). }	**16**	150 00
17	Add lines 14, 15, and 16	**17**	2,100 00
18	Enter the **smaller** of: • The amount on line 17, or • $3,000 ($1,500 if married filing a separate return and at the end of 1992 you lived with your spouse who also started work in 1992). }	**18**	2,100 00
19	Add lines 4, 8, and 18. Enter the total here and on Schedule A, line 18. This is your **moving expense deduction** ▶	**19**	4,380 00

For Paperwork Reduction Act Notice, see separate instructions.   Cat. No. 12490K   Form **3903** (1992)

Note that to the extent expenses in Sections B and C of Form 3903 include meals, only 80% of those meals can be counted as moving expenses. It also should be noted that qualified real estate expenses (Section D, Form 3903) are limited to $3,000. If these expenses exceed $3,000, the excess expenses for the sale of the old residence can be used to reduce the gain on the sale of the residence and the excess expenses involved in buying the new residence can be added to the basis of the new residence. Expenses for the sale of a residence include commissions, points paid on the loan, attorney's fees, state transfer taxes, title fees, and escrow fees. Expenses of buying a new home include appraisal fees, title search, attorney's fees and escrow fees. To the extent possible, expenses incurred in buying and selling a home should be deducted as moving expenses since moving expenses can be deducted in the current year as itemized deductions. If these expenses exceed the maximums allowed for the moving expense deduction, then the taxpayer will be benefited in the current year by expenses that can reduce the selling price of the old residence and in future years by expenses that are included in the basis of the new residence.

Job Expenses and Most Other Miscellaneous Deductions

This section of Schedule A, which follows the Moving Expense section, allows certain deductions that are not listed individually in earlier, separate sections of Schedule A. Beginning after 1986, the Tax Reform Act of 1986 places limitations on certain miscellaneous itemized deductions, which are deductible only in excess of 2% of AGI. This section of Schedule A should not be confused with Schedule A, Other Miscellaneous Deductions, which allows certain, relatively uncommon, deductions without limitation (to be briefly discussed later in this chapter).

Job expenses and certain other miscellaneous expenses subject to deduction limits include unreimbursed employee business expenses attributable to job and other expenses which are quasi-business in nature, such as investment expenses. Current tax provisions allow these types of expenses to be deducted

only to the extent that the total of these expenses exceeds 2% of AGI. Also, to the extent that unreimbursed employee business expenses constitute expenses for meals and entertainment, only 80% of these costs can be included in miscellaneous expenses subject to the 2% of AGI limitation.

Miscellaneous Itemized Deductions Subject to 2% of AGI Limitation Include

1. Unreimbursed employee business expense (fill out Form 2106):
   a. Travel and transportation expenses
   b. 80% of business meals and entertainment expenses
   c. Business lodgings
   d. Outside salespersons' expenses

2. Investment expenses:
   a. Safety deposit box rent
   b. Investment publications
   c. Subscriptions to investment periodicals
   d. Legal and accounting fees
   e. Custodial fees
   f. Tax preparation fees

3. Other unreimbursed business expenses

Reimbursed Employee Business Expenses

An employee's reimbursed business expenses are generally not deductible on the tax return in calculating AGI. Likewise, the reimbursement is not reported in gross income. To avoid both the reporting and deducting of reimbursements on the tax return, the business expenses must be paid or incurred by the employee under a qualified "reimbursement or other allowance arrangement" with the employer. Qualified plans must meet *both* of the following conditions:

1. The employee must substantiate the expenses to the employer.
2. The employee must return any amount in excess of the substantiated expenses covered under the arrangement.

Amounts paid by the employer under a qualified arrangement are not reported as wages on the employee's Form W-2. If the employee seeks to deduct expenses in excess of the amounts paid under a qualified arrangement, the total expenses and the amount of the reimbursement by the employer are reported on Form 2106, Employee Business Expenses. The excess expenses over the reimbursement also are calculated on Form 2106 and are included as part of the employee's miscellaneous itemized deductions on Schedule A, subject to the 2% AGI limitation.

If the arrangement does not require the employee to substantiate the expenses or allows the employee to keep any excess amount, the reimbursement plan is not a qualified arrangement and the amount paid by the employer must be reported by the employer as wages in Boxes 10 and 12 of the employee's Form W-2. In addition, *all* employee expenses, both reimbursed and unreimbursed, must be deducted as part of the employee's miscellaneous itemized deductions on Schedule A, subject to the 2% AGI limitation.

If an employee does not account to an employer for expenses, a statement must be filed with the return showing the appropriate detail. In any instance, accurate records should be kept of all expenses paid or incurred.

The Internal Revenue Code provides special rules for certain *qualified performing artists*. These people are permitted to deduct their employee expenses from gross income to arrive at AGI, regardless of the above rules. The expenses are to be reported on Form 2106 with the total expenses entered as a "write-in amount" on Form 1040 (line 30), the "total adjustments" line. The taxpayer should keep records that show proof of the expenses paid and that provide the information to calculate the total home office expenses reported on Schedule A.

Unreimbursed Employee Business Expenses

All unreimbursed **employee** business expenses are classified as miscellaneous itemized deductions. For the purpose of the miscellaneous deductions section of Schedule A, an unreimbursed employee business expense is an expense which was incurred for the benefit of the employer and was not reimbursed. It may also be an expense incurred by the employee who is reimbursed under a "nonqualified" reimbursement program (defined above). Reimbursements under a nonqualified program are included in income, and the expenses are

treated as miscellaneous itemized deductions. If the employee is reimbursed in the form of allowances (such as a per diem allowance) and does not account to the employer for his expenses and/or does not return any excess reimbursement, the total amount reimbursed is included in income and the incurred expenses are reported on Schedule A subject to the 2% AGI limitation. Also note that most employee business meals and entertainment expenses are only included in itemized deductions to the extent of 80% of their cost. As noted in Chapter 4, the 80% limit does not apply to *de minimis* expenses.

Form 2106, Employee Business Expenses, shown in Illustration 6-4, is provided to report the details of employee business expenses incurred for employers' benefit. Moving expenses, which are classified separately from employee business expenses, are reported on Schedule A separately.

Vehicle Expenses. Vehicle expenses claimed by employees are reported on Form 2106, Section A, Part II. The taxpayer can elect the larger of actual expenses or the expense as determined by use of the standard mileage rates. Space is provided for data related to two vehicles. If more vehicles are involved, the additional information can be provided by the use of a supplementary schedule. General information about the date each vehicle was placed in service, total mileage for 1992, total mileage for business use, and the percentage of mileage for business use must be reported for each vehicle.

Not deductible as a business expense are (1) the costs of commuting to and from work and (2) other personal use mileage. Four spe-

---

Unreimbursed Employee Business Expenses Reported on Form 2106

1. Vehicle for business use
2. Parking fees, tolls, and local transportation
3. Travel while away from home, including lodging, airplane, car rental, etc.
4. Other business expenses (excluding meals and entertainment): business gifts, education (tuition and books), and home office
5. Meals and entertainment

cific questions must be answered about (1) the availability of another vehicle for personal use, (2) whether an employer-provided vehicle is available for personal use during off-duty hours, (3) the availability of evidence to support the deductions, and (4) whether the evidence is written.

Standard Mileage Rate. A simplified method of calculating the deductible cost of operating a car for business purposes is available on Form 2106, Section B, Part II. As an alternative to claiming actual expenses, taxpayers may elect to use a *standard mileage rate* of 28 cents per mile for all business miles driven during the year. The standard mileage rate may be claimed whether actual expenses were greater than or less than the standard mileage rate. The standard mileage rate is optional and is used in place of claiming all operating and fixed costs of the automobile, such as gasoline, oil, repairs, licenses, insurance, and depreciation. However, if the taxpayer does not choose the standard mileage rate in the first year the car is placed in service, the standard rate cannot be used on that car in any year. To claim the standard mileage rate, the time, place, business purpose, and actual number of miles traveled must be established.

EXAMPLE 5 ————————————————

Assume that Roger Palmer, an employee, is expected to use his own car for transportation on company business. During 1992 the employee had total transportation of 7,200 miles with his own personal car, of which 1,800 miles was on company business. The taxpayer would be entitled to treat $504 (1,800 miles @ $.28) as vehicle expense in connection with his employment. The $504 would be first reported on Form 2106, page 2 (line 22) and then would be carried to Form 2106, page 1 (line 1).

Even though the standard mileage rate is used, taxpayers may still claim the business portion of interest on car loans and personal property taxes as allowable business expenses. Parking fees and tolls incurred while the vehicle is being used for business can be deducted as separate items. Use of the standard mileage rate is considered to be an election not to use the MACRS (Modified Accelerated Cost Recovery System) depreciation deduction on the car in the

future. The nonbusiness portion of interest does not qualify as an itemized deduction in 1992.

Taxpayers who use the standard mileage rate are required to reduce the adjusted basis of their automobiles according to the following schedule:

Year	Rate Per Mile
1991	11 cents
1990	11 cents
1989	11 cents
1988	10.5 cents
1987	10 cents
1986	9 cents

For tax years before 1990, the rate applied to the first 15,000 miles. For tax years after 1989, the depreciation rate of 11 cents applies to all business miles.

If an individual replaces one automobile with another during the year, or if more than one automobile is owned and used for business purposes, the standard mileage rate is applied to the combined business mileage of all vehicles owned in the period.

The standard mileage rate is available for use by employees who are not reimbursed by their employers. It can also be used by an employee who is reimbursed by the employer for such expense, provided such reimbursement or allowance is reflected in the return. Generally, the reimbursement is deducted from expenses other than meals and entertainment on Form 2106.

An employee can be reimbursed by an employer at a rate of up to 28 cents per mile and not be required to report the reimbursement on the income tax return nor deduct the expenses on the return, provided the employer is given a statement showing the business purpose of the travel, the number of miles traveled, the date, and the place. Reimbursement up to 28 cents per mile can be paid by the employer regardless of the age of the vehicle or the number of miles driven during the year.

Actual Vehicle Expenses. Rather than using the standard mileage rate, taxpayers can claim actual expenses incurred for the business use of a vehicle providing proper records documenting the expenses are maintained. Actual expenses include vehicle rentals, gasoline, oil, repairs, insurance on vehicle, etc. In addition, the value of employer-provided vehicles may be claimed if included on Form W-2 at 100% of the fair rental value. In calculating deductible vehicle expenses, the employee must first report total actual vehicle expenses for the year. Then total expenses are multiplied by the percentage of business use to determine the applicable business expense.

Added to the actual expenses is an amount for depreciation which is determined on Form 2106, Part II, Section D. Vehicles used 50% or less for business must use straight-line depreciation. Vehicles used more than 50% for business may use various accelerated depreciation or cost recovery methods depending on when the vehicle was placed in service. These methods generally allow for a larger depreciation deduction in the early years of the vehicle's service.

Parking Fees, Tolls, and Local Transportation. Parking fees, tolls, and local transportation, including train, bus, and taxi fares are entered on Form 2106, Part I. Also included are air fares which do not include overnight travel. Expenses of commuting to and from work are not deductible. However, an individual who is employed by two different employers on the same day may deduct the cost of traveling from the first job to the second job. An employee who works on the same day for the same employer at two different locations and is not paid for the cost of traveling between the two locations may deduct the cost of this local transportation.

EXAMPLE 6 ————————————————

Assume that Roger Palmer incurred $35 of parking fees, tolls, and local transportation in 1992 in connection with his work as an employee. This amount would be reported on Form 2106, Part I (line 2).

Travel Expenses. *Travel expenses* are expenses paid or incurred for travel and lodging while temporarily away from home in connection with employment. The IRS has consistently held that travel expenses must be away from home "overnight." *Home,* for determining deductibility of travel expenses, is an individual's place of business, employment, station, or post of duty, regardless of where the family lives. Travel expenses include such items as air, bus, train and taxi fares, hotel expenses, baggage charges, tips, and telephone expenses.

EXAMPLE 7 ————————————————

Roger Palmer incurred the following expenses, other than meals and entertain-

ment, while away from home overnight in connection with his employment: Air fare $120, hotel $75, and car rental $35, a total of $230. These employee expenses are reported on Form 2106, Part I (line 3).

A state legislator is considered to be away from home on any day that the legislature is in session or on any day that the legislator's presence is recorded at a committee meeting. However, legislators whose place of residence is 50 miles or less from the state capital may not elect to have these away-from-home rules apply to them.

If a taxpayer's spouse accompanies the taxpayer on a business trip, the spouse's traveling expenses are not deductible unless the main purpose of the spouse's presence is business.

Meals and Entertainment Expenses. Employee's business meals and entertainment expenses must be reported separately on Form 2106. Only 80% of these expenses are eligible to be considered for deduction. Generally, the cost of meals cannot be deducted unless the taxpayer is "away from home overnight." To be deductible, meals must be for a business purpose and must include a business discussion directly before, during, or following the meal, or the meal must be directly related to the active conduct of the taxpayer's employment. Similarly the entertainment must be directly related to or associated with the active conduct of the taxpayer's employment. The taxpayer must generally be present at the meeting. Included in meals and entertainment expenses are taxes and tips.

EXAMPLE 8 ————————————————

Roger Palmer incurred $150 of meals and entertainment while away from home overnight in connection with his employment.

This amount is reported on Form 2106, Part I, Column B (lines 5, 6, and 8). This $150 of expense is reduced by 20% in Column B (line 9), resulting in a deductible amount for meals and entertainment of $120 (line 10). Then the amounts $710, Column A (line 10), and $120, Column B, are added to arrive at Roger Palmer's deductible employee business expenses of $880, calculated as follows: transportation, $495 + parking fees and tolls, $35 + travel expenses away from home overnight, $230 + deductible meals and entertainment, $120.

Money provided to an employee to buy dinner while occasionally working overtime is excluded from gross income as a *de minimis* fringe benefit. However, if the payment is actually disguised compensation, it is considered to be taxable wages.

Only 80% of meals provided as an integral part of a banquet meeting are eligible for a deduction. A qualified banquet meeting is a seminar, convention, annual meeting, or similar business program at which:

1. The price of the meal is not separately stated in the price of the meeting.
2. More than half of the participants are away from home.
3. At least 40 individuals are in attendance.
4. The meal is a part of a program that includes a speaker.

If an employee incurs entertainment or meal expenses related to a business purpose and these expenses are fully reimbursed by the employer, it is the employer who is limited to a deduction of 80% of the meal and entertainment expenses.

Combined Business and Pleasure Trips. An employee traveling away from home on a combined business and pleasure trip may deduct the entire travel expenses to and from the business destination provided the trip is primarily (over 50%) for business. If the trip is primarily for personal purposes, such expenses are not deductible. Business expenses at the destination of the trip are deductible, whether the trip is business or personal.

EXAMPLE 9 ───────────────────

Mary Davis took a combined business-pleasure trip to New York City and spent $650 for travel expenses. The trip included two days spent in travel, eight days on business, and four days visiting friends in New York. The full $650 travel expenses and the expenses incurred in the eight days of business are deductible. However, the costs incurred in the four days of visiting friends would be personal expenses and not deductible.

Travel expenses of employees on a combined business/pleasure trip outside of the United States usually are allocated, with only the business portion being deductible. Allocation may not be required even in this instance if an employee has no substantial control over arranging the trip (i.e., is not a managing executive or a 10% or greater owner); if the taxpayer is away from home for seven days or less; or if less than 25% of the time was for personal purposes.

No deduction is allowed for traveling expenses to a convention outside the North American area unless the taxpayer can prove that the meeting is directly related to the taxpayer's employment, and that it is "as reasonable" for the meeting to be held outside the North American area as within it. The definition of North American area includes the United States and its possessions, the Trust Territory of the Pacific Islands, Canada, and Mexico.

Home Office Deduction. Under certain circumstances employees are allowed to deduct home office expenses. Eligible employees will report home office expenses on Schedule A, Job Expenses and Most Other Miscellaneous Deductions (line 19). The opportunity for employees to deduct home office expenses is very limited. A primary requirement for deducting such expenses is that the office maintained in the home must be for the convenience of the employer. Based on the requirement that the office must be for the convenience of the employer, most teachers and college professors would not qualify for a home office deduction on Schedule A. In a case where the standard was applied strictly, a college professor was denied a deduction for home office expenses even though the college did not provide the professor with an office at the college. In a more recent court case, a college professor was allowed to deduct home office expenses because the principal place of his work was in his home office where he actively engaged in the research and writing required by the college in order to retain his position.

EXAMPLE 10 ───────────────────────

A professor does research and writing using his own home library of rare books. The university was not in a position to provide proper library facilities to maintain the rare classical books in an acceptable condition so a request was made that the professor maintain the books in his own home. This agreement to do research in his own home using rare books not available at the university is for the convenience of the employer and meets the requirements for a deduction of home office expenses by the professor. It is an example of a rare opportunity for a college professor to deduct home office expenses. The college professor would solidify his position for the home office deduction by asking the university to supply him with a letter stating that the maintenance of the home office to house the rare books that support the professor's research and writing responsibilities is for the university's convenience.

"Exclusive use" of a portion of the residence means that the employee must use a specific part of the residence *only* for carrying on his or her duties strictly for the convenience of the employer. The test is not met if the specified portion of the residence is used for both business and personal purposes. The "regular basis" rule implies that occasional or incidental trade or business use of an exclusive portion of the home will not justify expense deductions. The term "place of business" includes a separate structure on the property which is used in connection with the employee's business activity for the convenience of the employer. Home office deductions are normally not allowed when an employee rents a portion of his or her home to an employer.

Calculating the Home Office Deduction. The amount of the home office deduction is for the specific expenses related to operating the home office space. The deductible expenses include the specific expenses of operating the office, such as supplies, long distance business phone calls, repairs and painting within the office and depreciation of office furniture and equipment. In addition, as a general rule, home office expenses will include a proportionate amount of the expenses incurred in maintaining the entire home based on the percentage of business use. A business use portion of such expenses as depreciation of the house, real estate taxes, insurance, interest expense, repair of the roof, utilities, trash removal, cleaning services, and painting the exterior of the home would be considered appropriate home office expenses. Excluded from classification as home office expenses would be repairs to other personal-use rooms, expenses of lawn care and landscaping,

and the value of the taxpayer's own labor in performing repairs and other general services around the house.

EXAMPLE 11 ─────────────────

Assume that an employee maintains a home office for the convenience of her employer. The office portion is 20% of the total residence space. Real estate taxes and mortgage interest on the entire residence amount to $9,000. Assume further that the office expenses are $750 and that other total expenses of operating the house include depreciation, utilities, repairs, and insurance in the amount of $7,000. Based on this information, the employee would be entitled to include on Schedule A (line 19) a total home office expense of $3,950, which includes $1,800 ($9,000 x 20%) for real estate taxes and interest, $1,400 ($7,000 x 20%) for depreciation, insurance, repairs, and utilities, and $750 for specific home office expenses. The $3,950 would be reduced by 2% of AGI to calculate what portion of the total would be deductible.

Education Expenses. Unreimbursed education expenses incurred by employees for the benefit of their employers or required by law or regulation are *deductible.*The education (1) must maintain or improve skills required by the employee's present employment, or (2) meet the requirements of the employer or law or regulations that are a condition of keeping the employee's salary, status, or employment. This is true even if the education leads to a degree. However, educational expenses are *nondeductible* if they are personal expenditures which are necessary (1) to meet the minimum education requirements for the employee's present job, (2) to obtain a new position or substantial advancement in position, or (3) to qualify an individual for a new trade or business. Education expenses of an employee may fall into one of four categories as to deductibility: (1) deductible for AGI, (2) deductible from AGI (as miscellaneous itemized deduction), (3) reimbursed by the employer and excluded from income, or (4) not deductible because they are considered to be personal expenses.

Employees deduct the *unreimbursed* cost of tuition, books, supplies, laboratory fees, travel expenses, and the like as an itemized miscellaneous deduction subject to the 2% of AGI floor.

Reimbursed job-related, benefit-of-the-employer educational expenses do not have to be reported as income if (1) the taxpayer accounts to the employer for the expenses, (2) the expense equals or exceeds the reimbursement, and (3) the taxpayer does not claim a deduction for these business-related, deductible expenses. Travel expenses incurred as a form of education are not allowed as an education expense deduction.

EXAMPLE 12 ─────────────────────

A business executive who pursues an education to maintain or improve business skills would be allowed a miscellaneous itemized deduction subject to the 2% rule. A CPA who seeks a law degree would not be allowed an education expense deduction because the CPA would be qualifying for a new trade or profession. A teacher who is required to take additional education courses to maintain his or her teaching certificate would be allowed to deduct such education expenses as a miscellaneous itemized deduction. Expenses incurred to take the bar exam or the CPA exam would be considered to be personal expenses and therefore not deductible.

A veteran of the armed forces cannot deduct educational expenses for courses to maintain and improve job skills if these expenses are reimbursed by a tax-exempt Veterans Administration educational payment.

Outside Salespersons. *Outside salespersons* are full-time employees engaged principally in soliciting business at places other than the employer's place of business. Outside salespersons are treated the same as other business employees for income tax purposes.

Substantiation of Employee Business Expenses

A taxpayer must substantiate any expenses claimed for entertainment, business, gifts, and travel away from home by keeping adequate records or sufficient evidence that will corroborate the taxpayer's statements. An employee must have documentary evidence for all expenditures of $25 or more.

The extent of documentation that taxpayers are required to maintain on expenditures and that the recordkeeping must substantiate include:

1. Amount of expenditure
2. Time and place of travel or entertainment (or use of entertainment facility)
3. Date and description of gift or expenditure
4. Business purpose of expenditure
5. Business relationship to the taxpayer of each person being entertained, using an entertainment facility, or receiving a gift

Written evidence for substantiation purposes would include:

1. Account books, diaries, and logs
2. Documentary evidence, such as receipts and paid bills
3. Trip sheets
4. Expense reports
5. Written statements of witnesses

Taxpayers should take appropriate action to obtain and preserve related documentation to substantiate expenses.

If a *per diem* allowance does not exceed $66 per day (or a higher per diem rate authorized by the federal government in the locality in which travel is performed) and the mileage allowance does not exceed 28 cents per mile, and if the other elements (other than the amount of expenditure) of the business expense are substantiated, the employee will be considered as having met the substantiation requirement.

If an employee is reimbursed on a per diem basis that is within the IRS-specified rate and the per diem allowance exceeds the actual expense incurred by the employee, the excess does not have to be returned to the employer. Accordingly, there is deemed to be no excess retained by the employee.

Filled-In Form 2106

Illustration 6-4

The filled-in Form 2106, Employee Business Expenses, for Roy E. Mack, SSN 369-18-4201, a district representative for the Drake Corporation, is shown in Illustration 6-4. Mack took a 5-day business trip for his employer in November. The Drake Corporation does not have a qualified reimbursement plan; however, the company reimbursed the direct expense incurred to meet with a client ($95) and air travel ($210). Mack was expected to pay his own meals ($125) and lodging ($250) and other transportation (taxi fares) expenses ($12), totaling $387. In addition to the New York trip, Mack had driven his personal automobile on business a total of 23,842 miles of the 34,060 miles driven. Employer reimbursement of $5,364.45 (at 22.5 cents per mile) had been received for mileage. Reimbursements from his employer of $5,669.45 ($5,364.45 + $95 + $210) was included on Mack's Form W-2 for 1992.

Parking fees and tolls paid for business totaled $445.

Mack completed Form 2106, Parts I and II. He elected to claim the standard mileage amount of $6,676* (23,842 miles x $0.28) over the actual vehicle expenses on Form 2106, Part I (line 1). The vehicle expenses were added to the other expenses in Part I to obtain the total expense of $7,688 in Column A and $125 in Column B. The reimbursement of $5,669.45 was reported to Mack on Form W-2 in Box 10 and Box 13 and was included in income on Form 1040 (line 7). Since the reimbursement was paid under a nonqualified arrangement, all of Mack's expenses (meals and entertainment less 20%), $7,788, are deductible as a miscellaneous itemized deduction subject to the 2%-of-AGI floor.

* Amount is rounded.

Other Unreimbursed Quasi-Business Expenses

Investment Expenses. Investment expenses are reported as other miscellaneous deductions subject to the 2% of AGI rule on Schedule A (line 20). Expenses identified as investment expenses are includable because they are considered to be ordinary and necessary expenses of producing or collecting income. Included in this category are mutual fund administrative fees and other investment expenses, both subject to the 2% of AGI limitation.

Special Clothing. The cost of clothing worn by an employee at work is generally a nondeductible personal expense. When special uniforms are required as a condition of employment and are not adaptable for general or continued use in place of ordinary clothing, the cost of the uniforms and their maintenance is deductible. For example, uniforms of police officers, fire fighters, letter carriers, nurses, bus drivers, railway workers, jockeys, and professional baseball players are deductible. In certain instances, special work clothes used solely in the course of employment do not have to be specifically required as a condition of employment in order to be deductible.

Armed Services. The *cost of equipment of a member of the armed services* is deductible only to the extent that it exceeds the nontaxable allowances received for such equipment and to the extent that the equipment is especially required by the profession and does not merely take the place of articles required in civilian life. For example, the cost of insignia is an allowable deduction in

---

Other Unreimbursed Business Expenses

- Business use of part of home that is used exclusively and regularly for business for the convenience of the employer
- Educational expenses required by employer, law, or regulations to maintain present salary or job
- Fees to employment agencies and other costs to look for a new job in the taxpayer's present occupation
- Physical exams required by employer
- Protective clothing required in job, such as hard hats, safety shoes, and glasses
- Safety equipment, small tools, and supplies needed in job
- Subscriptions to professional and trade publicaitons
- Uniforms required by employer that are not suitable for street wear
- Union and professional dues

Illustration 6-4
Filled-In Form 2106, Page 1

Form 2106

Department of the Treasury
Internal Revenue Service

Employee Business Expenses

▶ See separate instructions.

▶ Attach to Form 1040.

OMB No. 1545-0139

1992

Attachment
Sequence No. **54**

Your name	Social security number	Occupation in which expenses were incurred
Roy Mack	369 18 4201	District Representative

Part I Employee Business Expenses and Reimbursements

STEP 1 Enter Your Expenses

		Column A Other Than Meals and Entertainment	Column B Meals and Entertainment
1	Vehicle expense from line 22 or line 29	6,676 00	
2	Parking fees, tolls, and local transportation, including train, bus, etc.	445 00	
3	Travel expense while away from home overnight, including lodging, airplane, car rental, etc. **Do not** include meals and entertainment	472 00	
4	Business expenses not included on lines 1 through 3. **Do not** include meals and entertainment	95 00	
5	Meals and entertainment expenses (see instructions)		125 00
6	**Total expenses.** In Column A, add lines 1 through 4 and enter the result. In Column B, enter the amount from line 5	7,688 00	125 00

Note: *If you were not reimbursed for any expenses in Step 1, skip line 7 and enter the amount from line 6 on line 8.*

STEP 2 Enter Amounts Your Employer Gave You for Expenses Listed in STEP 1

7	Enter amounts your employer gave you that were **not** reported to you in box 10 of Form W-2. Include any amount reported under code "L" in box 17 of your Form W-2 (see instructions)		

STEP 3 Figure Expenses To Deduct on Schedule A (Form 1040)

		Column A	Column B
8	Subtract line 7 from line 6	7,688 00	125 00
	Note: *If **both columns** of line 8 are zero, **stop here**. If Column A is less than zero, report the amount as income and enter -0- on line 10, Column A. See the instructions for how to report.*		
9	Enter 20% (.20) of line 8, Column B		25 00
10	Subtract line 9 from line 8	7,688 00	100 00
11	Add the amounts on line 10 of both columns and enter the total here. **Also, enter the total on Schedule A (Form 1040), line 19.** (Qualified performing artists and individuals with disabilities, see the instructions for special rules on where to enter the total.) ▶		7,788 00

For Paperwork Reduction Act Notice, see instructions.   Cat. No. 11700N   Form **2106** (1992)

Illustration 6-4
Filled-In Form 2106, Page 2

Form 2106 (1992)   Page **2**

Part II   **Vehicle Expenses** (See instructions to find out which sections to complete.)

Section A.—General Information

			(a) Vehicle 1	(b) Vehicle 2
12	Enter the date vehicle was placed in service	12	1 / 2 / 91	/ /
13	Total miles vehicle was driven during 1992	13	34060 miles	miles
14	Business miles included on line 13	14	23842 miles	miles
15	Percent of business use. Divide line 14 by line 13	15	70 %	%
16	Average daily round trip commuting distance	16	10 miles	miles
17	Commuting miles included on line 13	17	2500 miles	miles
18	Other personal miles. Add lines 14 and 17 and subtract the total from line 13.	18	7718 miles	miles

19   Do you (or your spouse) have another vehicle available for personal purposes?   ☐ Yes   ☐ No

20   If your employer provided you with a vehicle, is personal use during off duty hours permitted? ☐ Yes   ☐ No   ☐ Not applicable

21a   Do you have evidence to support your deduction?   ☐ Yes   ☐ No

21b   If "Yes," is the evidence written?   ☐ Yes   ☐ No

Section B.—Standard Mileage Rate (Use this section only if you own the vehicle.)

22	Multiply line 14 by 28¢ (.28). Enter the result here and on line 1. (Rural mail carriers, see instructions.)	22	6,676 00

Section C.—Actual Expenses

			(a) Vehicle 1	(b) Vehicle 2
23	Gasoline, oil, repairs, vehicle insurance, etc.	23		
24a	Vehicle rentals	24a		
b	Inclusion amount (see instructions)	24b		
c	Subtract line 24b from line 24a	24c		
25	Value of employer-provided vehicle (applies only if 100% of annual lease value was included on Form W-2—see instructions)	25		
26	Add lines 23, 24c, and 25	26		
27	Multiply line 26 by the percentage on line 15	27		
28	Depreciation. Enter amount from line 38 below	28		
29	Add lines 27 and 28. Enter total here and on line 1.	29		

Section D.—Depreciation of Vehicles (Use this section only if you own the vehicle.)

			(a) Vehicle 1	(b) Vehicle 2
30	Enter cost or other basis (see instructions)	30		
31	Enter amount of section 179 deduction (see instructions)	31		
32	Multiply line 30 by line 15 (see instructions if you elected the section 179 deduction)	32		
33	Enter depreciation method and percentage (see instructions)	33		
34	Multiply line 32 by the percentage on line 33 (see instructions)	34		
35	Add lines 31 and 34	35		
36	Enter the limitation amount from the table in the line 36 instructions	36		
37	Multiply line 36 by the percentage on line 15	37		
38	Enter the smaller of line 35 or line 37. Also, enter this amount on line 28 above	38		

calculating taxable income, but the cost of a uniform is not. However, amounts expended by a reservist for the purchase and maintenance of uniforms which may be worn only when on active duty, for training for temporary periods when attending service school courses, or when attending training assemblies are deductible except to the extent that nontaxable allowances are received for such amounts. Amounts expended by members of the armed services of the United States on active duty for the purchase and maintenance of required military fatigue uniforms, where local military regulations prohibit their off-duty wear, are, to the extent the expenses exceed allowances received, deductible as a miscellaneous expense.

Other Expenses Reported on Schedule A (line 20). The cost of a license or examination to *qualify* for a trade or profession is not deductible. Thus, the expense of taking a state examination leading to a certificate as a certified public accountant and expenses for law courses and bar review courses are all nondeductible. However, the *annual* fee for a license to engage in a trade or profession is deductible as an expense of an employee in connection with employment.

Schedule A Reporting of Job Expenses and Most Other Miscellaneous Deductions

Illustration 6-5

Qualified expenses that are classified as unreimbursed employee business expenses are reported on Schedule A (line 19), with the detail shown on Form 2106, Employee Business Expenses, when necessary. Investment expenses and tax preparation fees must be listed by type and amount (line 20). The total (lines 19 and 20) is reported (line 21). The amount of AGI on Form 1040 (line 32) is included on Schedule A (line 22) from which 2% of AGI is calculated (line 23). The amount (line 23) is subtracted from the total (line 21) to calculate the amount allowable for Job Expenses and Most Other Miscellaneous Deductions (line 24). Qualified miscellaneous expenses that are deductible in full must be listed by type on Schedule A (line 25).

Other Miscellaneous Expenses Fully Deductible

The last category of itemized deductions on Schedule A are Other Miscellaneous Deductions. These expenses are not subject to the 2% of AGI floor or the 80% limit on meals and entertainment. Other Miscellaneous Deductions are deductible in full when allowable expenses are itemized.

EXAMPLE 13

To illustrate the tax treatment of gambling gains and losses, assume that a taxpayer had $5,000 of gambling gains and $8,000 of gambling losses in 1992. The gambling gains of $5,000 would be reported in gross income on Form 1040 (line 22). If the taxpayer itemizes deductions, gambling losses in this example would be deducted on Schedule A (line 25), as shown in Illustration 6-5, to the extent of $5,000, which is an amount no larger than the amount of gambling gains. In other words, net gambling gains are included in income, but net gambling losses are not deductible.

Gambling gains include winnings from ticket raffles and lotteries. If the winnings are in the form of property, such as cars, houses, securities, or other noncash items, they are reported at their FMV. Taxpayers who participate in gambling activities are required to keep an accurate written record of winnings and losses and be able to prove the amounts by means of receipts, ticket stubs, or other evidence.

Summary of Itemized Deductions

Once all categories of itemized deductions are identified and their dollar amounts are listed under the appropriate categories on Schedule A, the total amount of itemized deductions is listed on Schedule A (line 26). This total amount of itemized deductions on Schedule A (line 26) is compared with the amount that the taxpayer is allowed as a standard deduction. The larger of total itemized deductions or the standard deduction is entered on Form 1040, page 2 (line 34). The amount (line 34) is subtracted from the AGI (line 32) to calculate the balance (line 35).

Illustration 6-5
Schedule A, Miscellaneous Deductions

Job Expenses and Most Other Miscellaneous Deductions (See page A-5 for expenses to deduct here.)		
19 Unreimbursed employee expenses—job travel, union dues, job education, etc. If required, you **MUST** attach Form 2106. (See page A-4.) ▶	**19** 880	00
20 Other expenses—investment, tax preparation, safe deposit box, etc. List type and amount ▶ Tax preparation 220 Safety deposit box 30	**20** 250	00
21 Add lines 19 and 20	**21** 1,130	00
22 Enter amount from Form 1040, line 32. **22** 33,900 00		
23 Multiply line 22 above by 2% (.02)	**23** 678	01
24 Subtract line 23 from line 21. If zero or less, enter -0- ▶	**24** 451	99
Other Miscellaneous Deductions		
25 Other—from list on page A-5. List type and amount ▶		
▶	**25** —0—	

Personal exemptions are subtracted from the amount (line 35) to arrive at taxable income (line 37). By subtracting itemized deductions from AGI when itemized deductions are greater than the standard deduction, taxable income will be lower and the taxpayer will pay a lower amount of tax.

Remember that there is an overall limitation on the amount of allowable itemized deductions (Chapter 5). If AGI exceeds $105,250, itemized deductions otherwise allowable are reduced by 3% of the taxpayer's AGI in excess of $105,250. The total itemized deductions need not be reduced by more than 80%. The reduction does not apply to medical expenses, casualty and theft losses, and investment interest.

Filled-In Schedule A

Illustration 6-6

A comprehensive illustration of itemized deductions discussed in Chapters 5 and 6 is shown here for John R. and Jean K. Williams of Verona, Wisconsin, whose Form 1040 is shown in Illustration 7-3 of Chapter 7, including an itemization of their deductions from AGI. The filled-in Schedule A, Itemized Deductions, is shown in Illustration 6-6.

Amounts paid by check during the year which were used to determine itemized deductions on Schedule A as follows:

Medical and dental expenses paid (not compensated by insurance)
    Dr. W. A. Davis, $660.00
    Dr. K. U. Able, $980.00
    Dr. M. R. Rambler, $250.00
    Eyeglasses, Optical Center, $155.69
    City Hospital, $2,560.00
    Premium on medical insurance, $720.00
    Prescription drugs, $240.00
       Total medical expenses, $5,565.69
Income and property taxes:
    State of Wisconsin income taxes, $1,130.00
    Real estate taxes paid on residence, $2,857.67
    Personal property taxes, $96.18
Interest expenses:
    Interest on home mortgage, $1,426.50
    Interest on credit card charges, $112.60
Charitable Contributions:
    Cancer Society, $25.00
    Salvation Army, $15.00
    United Way, $20.00
    University of Wisconsin, $100.00
    United Church, $827.00
    Non-Cash Clothing & Furniture to Thrift Shop, $460.00
Casualty and theft losses:
    Property damage sustained as the result of an automobile collision:

FMV of loss (less than cost basis)	$5,733.59
Less: Insurance proceeds	2,000.00
Balance	$3,733.59
Less:	100.00
Balance	$3,633.59
Less: 10% of $66,721.92	6,672.19
Deductible casualty loss	0

Miscellaneous Itemized Deductions:

Income tax preparation fee	$400.00
Safety deposit box rent	50.00
Subscriptions to investment periodicals	273.00
Unreimbursed business expenses (reported on Form 2106):	
Professional dues	$289.00
Subscriptions to trade publications	104.01
Meals and entertainment (Gross $450 x 80%)	360.00

Mr. Williams drove his personal automobile 150 miles on special church business. Instead of calculating the actual cost of driving on church business, he claimed an $18 deduction using the standard 12 cents per mile figure. The deduction was entered on Schedule A (line 14).

During 1991, the Williams contributed a large amount of appreciated capital stock, acquired 15 years ago and owned jointly, to the United Church building expansion fund. Since the amount deductible (FMV) was substantial, their total charitable contributions for 1991 were $200 in excess of the 50% maximum contribution allowance for that year.

The $200 can be carried forward to the next 5 years, if needed. Since the entire $200 carryforward can be claimed in 1992, the $200 was entered on Schedule A (line 15).

Average Itemized Deductions

Taxpayers can determine whether the individual amounts claimed for itemized deductions agree with the average amounts deducted by other taxpayers by a comparison with the averages. The average itemized deductions claimed by taxpayers in 1989, based on IRS income tax statistics, are shown in Table 6-1. Comparison with the averages could signal an area in which allowable deductions are being overlooked. Above-average itemized deductions could also identify an area in which the taxpayer could expect the IRS to require documentation to be produced. Keep in mind, however, that comparison of certain itemized deductions for 1992 with the averages for some previous years will not be valid because the Tax Reform Act of 1986 has altered the rules for deduction of taxes, interest, and miscellaneous itemized deductions.

Regardless of size, itemized deductions are subject to verification. Taxpayers should claim the amount of documentable itemized deductions to which they are entitled whether the total is higher or lower than the average amount shown in this table.

A checklist of common items that can and cannot be itemized as deductions from AGI is shown in Table 6-2.

Tax Planning for Itemized Deductions

For taxpayers whose itemized deductions are relatively close in amount to the taxpayer's standard deduction amount, the tax liability can be minimized by bunching itemized deductions in one year and using the standard deduction amount in the other year. The itemized deductions that are easiest to control are charitable contributions, medical expenses, and estimated state income taxes. For cash-method taxpayers, the expense is deductible when the payment is made. Thus, charitable contributions can be made in December or January, depending upon which year the taxpayer chooses to use the standard deduction and which year itemized deductions are to be taken. Likewise, medical expenses payable near year-end can be

Other Miscellaneous Deductions Not Subject to 2% of AGI Floor

1. Impairment-related work expenses for handicapped employees
2. Estate tax related to income in respect of a decedent
3. Certain amortizable bond premiums
4. Gambling losses to the extent of gambling gains (see Example 14)
5. Certain expenses of short sales
6. Certain costs of cooperative housing corporations
7. Balance of an employee's investment in an annuity contract where the employee dies before recovering the entire investment

paid in December or January as determined by the tax plan. Taxpayers who pay estimated state income taxes quarterly can make the fourth quarterly payment in December of the current year or in January of the following year. It is important to remember that the deduction is taken in the year the check is mailed or in the year the credit charge is made (and not when the credit card bill is paid).

Table 6-1
Average Amounts of Itemized Deductions—1989

AGI	Medical Expenses	Taxes	Contributions	Interest
$25,000-$30,000	$ 3,128	$ 1,975	$ 1,109	$ 4,314
$30,000-$40,000	2,849	2,342	1,184	4,887
$40,000-$50,000	3,546	2,947	1,318	5,400
$50,000-$75,000	4,713	3,943	1,607	6,271
$75,000-$100,000	6,448	5,713	2,108	8,531
$100,000-$200,000	10,090	9,020	3,532	12,150
$200,000-$500,000	24,134	19,645	7,213	19,853
$500,000-$1,000,000	40,556	43,499	18,374	29,788
$1,000,000+	66,478	148,529	83,929	68,303

Source: Research Institute of America based on preliminary IRS data

Illustration 6-6
Schedule A, Itemized Deductions

SCHEDULES A&B (Form 1040)

Department of the Treasury
Internal Revenue Service

Schedule A—Itemized Deductions
(Schedule B is on back)

▶ Attach to Form 1040. ▶ See Instructions for Schedules A and B (Form 1040).

OMB No. 1545-0074

1992

Attachment Sequence No. **07**

Name(s) shown on Form 1040: **John R. and Jean K. Williams**

Your social security number: **272 : 11 : 8425**

Medical and Dental Expenses

Caution: *Do not include expenses reimbursed or paid by others.*

1	Medical and dental expenses (see page A-1)	1 5,565 69
2	Enter amount from Form 1040, line 32.	2 66,721 92
3	Multiply line 2 above by 7.5% (.075)	3 5,004 14
4	Subtract line 3 from line 1. If zero or less, enter -0- ▶	4 561 55

Taxes You Paid (See page A-1.)

5	State and local income taxes	5 1,130 00
6	Real estate taxes (see page A-2)	6 2,857 67
7	Other taxes. List—include personal property taxes ▶ Personal Property Tax	7 96 18
8	Add lines 5 through 7 ▶	8 4,083 85

Interest You Paid (See page A-2.)

Note: Personal interest is not deductible.

9a	Home mortgage interest and points reported to you on Form 1098	9a 1,426 50
b	Home mortgage interest not reported to you on Form 1098. If paid to an individual, show that person's name and address. ▶	9b
10	Points not reported to you on Form 1098. See page A-3 for special rules	10
11	Investment interest. If required, attach Form 4952. (See page A-3.)	11
12	Add lines 9a through 11 ▶	12 1,426 50

Gifts to Charity (See page A-3.)

Caution: *If you made a charitable contribution and received a benefit in return, see page A-3.*

13	Contributions by cash or check	13 987 00
14	Other than by cash or check. If over $500, you **MUST** attach Form 8283	14 478 00
15	Carryover from prior year	15 200 00
16	Add lines 13 through 15 ▶	16 1,665 00

Casualty and Theft Losses

17	Casualty or theft loss(es). Attach Form 4684. (See page A-4.) ▶	17 –0–

Moving Expenses

18	Moving expenses. Attach Form 3903 or 3903F. (See page A-4.) ▶	18

Job Expenses and Most Other Miscellaneous Deductions (See page A-5 for expenses to deduct here.)

19	Unreimbursed employee expenses—job travel, union dues, job education, etc. If required, you **MUST** attach Form 2106. (See page A-4.) ▶	19 753 01
20	Other expenses—investment, tax preparation, safe deposit box, etc. List type and amount ▶ Tax prep 400: Safe dep box 50 Invest. sub 273	20 723 00
21	Add lines 19 and 20	21 1,476 01
22	Enter amount from Form 1040, line 32.	22 66,721 92
23	Multiply line 22 above by 2% (.02)	23 1,334 44
24	Subtract line 23 from line 21. If zero or less, enter -0- ▶	24 141 57

Other Miscellaneous Deductions

25	Other—from list on page A-5. List type and amount ▶	25

Total Itemized Deductions

26	Is the amount on Form 1040, line 32, more than $105,250 (more than $52,625 if married filing separately)? • **NO.** Your deduction is not limited. Add lines 4, 8, 12, 16, 17, 18, 24, and 25. • **YES.** Your deduction may be limited. See page A-5 for the amount to enter. ▶	26 7,878 47

Caution: *Be sure to enter on Form 1040, line 34, the **LARGER** of the amount on line 26 above or your standard deduction.*

For Paperwork Reduction Act Notice, see Form 1040 instructions.

Cat. No. 11330X

Schedule A (Form 1040) 1992

Table 6-2
Checklist of Itemized Deductions

Item	Deductible	Nondeductible
Administrative fees of mutual funds (subject to limitations)	X	
Automobile expenses (car used exclusively for personal purposes):		
Gasoline taxes (state portion) imposed on consumer		X
Interest on finance loans (subject to limitations)	X	
Ordinary upkeep, operating expenses, and license fees		X
Business entertainment for employer (subject to limitations)	X	
Casualty and theft losses not covered by insurance (fire, flood, earthquakes, etc.), in excess of $100 and exceeding 10% of AGI	X	
Charitable contributions to approved institutions	X	
Domestic servants, wages paid		X
Dues, social and sports clubs for personal use		X
Employment fees paid to agencies for job in the same trade (subject to limitations)	X	
Entertainemnt of friends		X
Federal income taxes, gift taxes, and inheritance taxes		X
Fines for violation of laws and regulations		X
Funeral expenses		X
Gambling losses (to extent of gains only)	X	
Gifts to relatives and other individuals		X
Interest paid on personal loans		X
License to engage in trade or profession	X*	
Life insurance premiums		X
Medical expenses in excess of 7½% of AGI (including the cost of prescription drugs, artifical limbs, dentures, eyeglasses, hearing aids, doctor and dental fees, hospital expenses) to extent not covered by insurance	X	
Professional organization dues (subject to limitations)	X*	
Property taxes, real and personal	X	
Residence for personal use:		
Insurance		X
Interest on mortgage loan and property taxes	X	
Loss from sale of		X
Rent paid		X
Repairs or improvements		X
Safe-deposit box rent (used for the safekeeping of income-producing assets) (subject to limitations)	X	
Safety equipment, tools and supplies used on job (subject to limitations)	X	
Social security taxes withheld by employer		X
State and local income taxes	X	
State and local sales taxes		X
Traveling expenses attending professional meetings (subject to limitations)	X*	
Traveling expenses to and from place of buisness or employment		X
Uniforms, including cost and upkeep, if not adaptable for general use (nurses, police, baseball players, etc.) (subject to limitations)	X	

* Deductible as an itemized deduction if incurred as a business expense by an employee.

C H A P T E R   6

Questions and Problems

1. **a.** What categories of moving expenses are deductible by an employee who moves to a new job that meets the mileage and employment tests?

   b. To what extent are deductible moving expenses subject to dollar limitations?

   c. If a taxpayer's moving expenses are wholly or partially reimbursed by the employer, how are the reimbursed expenses reported?

2. Paul Wescott, an employee of the Nordic Manufacturing Company, was transferred to a new place of permanent employment in one of the company branch plants located in a city 450 miles away. Mr. Wescott paid the expenses listed below connected with his move during the current year.
   a. Insert the amount deductible for moving expenses in the space provided.

Item	Amount Paid	Amount Deductible
1. Actual out-of-pocket expenses paid (auto depreciation excluded) for 475 miles for use of personal automobile in moving self and family	$ 138	__________
2. Cutting draperies to proper size for new home	60	__________
3. Penalty for breaking lease on old home	100	__________
4. Meals en route for Mr. Wescott ($36.00) Mrs. Wescott ($40.50) and children ($50.50)	127	__________
5. Actual out-of-pocket expenses paid (auto depreciation excluded) for use of personal automobile on a preliminary trip of 1,000 miles to arrange for housing in the new community	283	__________
6. Motel expense en route, one room for Mr. and Mrs. Wescott and one room for the children at $46.00 per room	92	__________
7. Toll road fees en route	21	__________
8. Expense of moving model train maintained as a hobby	150	__________
9. Meals at restaurant on day of arrival in city of new residence	48	__________
10. Expense of packing and transporting furniture	2,400	__________
Total	$3,419	__________

b. Would the moving expense deduction be allowed if itemized deductions are not claimed?

c. If the move had been from one part of the city to another, a distance of 30 miles, would the moving expense deduction be allowed? Explain.

d. If the move had been temporary instead of permanent, would moving expenses be deductible? Explain.

3. Place an "X" in the space provided to indicate whether each of the following unreimbursed expenses of a taxpayer in moving to a new residence at the general location of a new principal place of employment is deductible as an itemized deduction on Schedule A, Form 1040.

Expense	Yes	No
a. Expense of using own personal automobile		
b. Expense of trip to arrange for the move		
c. Expense of trip to actually move after (b) above		
d. Expense of waiting at location of new residence for household goods to arrive		
e. Expense of moving pets		
f. Expense of self-employed individual who expects to be at a new principal place of work for 62 weeks		
g. Expenses at the former location in connection with the move:		
(1) Mortgage prepayment penalty		
(2) Expense of disconnecting utilities		
(3) Loss on sale of residence		
h. Expense of moving to a job if in the following year, after 24 weeks, the employee moves again to accept a new position with a new company		

4. Carolyn and Pete Gipple are married, file jointly, and currently reside in California. Pete was transferred by his company from Richmond, Virginia, to a new plant in California during 1992. The distance from his former residence to his former business location was 15 miles. The company reimbursed $14,599 for moving expenses, all of which was reported on Pete's Form W-2. Actual moving expenses were incurred and reimbursed as follows:

	Actual Expense	Amount Reimbursed
Moving household goods	$8,500.00	$6,500.00
Travel expenses in driving family from Richmond to Los Angeles, excluding meals (3,510 miles)	975.00	975.00
Meals	160.00	100.00
Travel expenses for a preliminary trip to California to buy a home, excluding meals	1,014.00	1,014.00
Meals while on a preliminary trip	230.00	200.00
Expenses incident to selling residence in Richmond	4,550.00	4,550.00
Expenses incident to purchasing a residence in L.A.	1,860.00	1,260.00

a. Prepare the employer statement detailing actual reimbursement on the Form 4782 below. Pete's SSN is 342-67-5610.

Form 4782
(Rev. October 1992)
Department of the Treasury
Internal Revenue Service

Employee Moving Expense Information

Payments made during the calendar year 19 ....

▶ See instructions on back.

OMB No. 1545-0182
Expires 9-30-95

Do not file.
Keep for your records.

Name of employee

Social security number

Moving Expense Payments	(a) Amount paid to employee	(b) Amount paid to a third party for employee's benefit and value of services furnished in kind	(c) Total (Add columns (a) and (b))
Section A—Transportation of Household Goods			
1 Transportation and storage of household goods and personal effects			
Section B—Expenses of Moving From Old To New Home			
2 Travel and lodging payments not including meals			
3 Meal payments for travel			
Section C—Pre-move Househunting Expenses and Temporary Quarters for any 30 Days in a Row After Obtaining Employment (90 Days for a Foreign Move)			
4 Pre-move travel and lodging payments not including meals			
5 Temporary quarters payments not including meals			
6 Total meal payments for both pre-move househunting and temporary quarters			
Section D—Qualified Real Estate Expenses			
7 Qualified expenses of selling, buying, or renting a home			
Section E—Miscellaneous Payments			
8 List all other payments (specify) ▶			
9 Total moving expense payments. Add the amounts in column (c) of lines 1 through 8 ▶			

Note: *The amount on line 9 must be included in the employee's income.*

For Paperwork Reduction Act Notice, see back of form.   Cat. No. 13079T   Form **4782** (Rev. 10-92)

b. Use Form 3903, shown on the following page, to calculate the amount of moving expense deduction, if any, that Carolyn and Pete will be able to deduct on their 1992 income tax return.

5. How do the rules for the deduction of moving expenses differ for self-employed taxpayers from those for employees?

6. Wendy Rogers, a single taxpayer, is a certified public accountant (CPA) employed by a CPA firm in the city where she lives. She attends the monthly dinner meetings of the local CPA chapter of the state society. During 1992, she incurred and paid $125 for attending these meetings and drove a total of 170 miles for this purpose. Her AICPA dues are $110 per year; her state society CPA dues are $85 per year; and her CPA license fee is $35 per year.

    a. What amount may Ms. Rogers include as an itemized deduction for 1992 in connection with her work?

    b. Explain the rules for the deductibility of employee business expenses in 1992.

7. Identify the following as (A) deductible for AGI, (B) deductible from AGI, or (C) not deductible. Ignore the AGI limitations that are used to determine the deductibility of certain types of deductions.

Item	Answer
a. State inheritance taxes	_______
b. Cost of transportation between home and place of business	_______
c. Rental of safe-deposit box used for safekeeping of securities	_______
d. Fee paid to state for CPA examination	_______
e. Federal income tax penalty assessed for delinquency in filing a tax return	_______
f. Fee paid to accountant to prepare personal property tax return on rental property	_______
g. Loss incurred in operating a book store (filed Schedule C)	_______
h. License fee for business automobile	_______
i. Cost of uniforms suitable for street wear	_______
j. Insurance on house used by owner as residence	_______
k. Union dues paid by employee of steel company	_______
l. Expense of travel for job-related activities, paid by employee for which no specific reimbursement was made	_______
m. Interest on mortgage on apartment house owned by taxpayer	_______
n. Loss of trees on property owned and used as a home, caused by windstorm (balance after deducting insurance, $100 floor, and 10% of AGI)	_______
o. Loss on sale of automobile used as pleasure car	_______
p. Damage paid by taxpayer to X for damage to X's car as a result of a collision, taxpayer at fault	_______

Form **3903** Department of the Treasury Internal Revenue Service	**Moving Expenses** ▶ Attach to Form 1040. ▶ See separate instructions.	OMB No. 1545-0062 19**92** Attachment Sequence No. **62**

Name(s) shown on Form 1040	Your social security number

1 Enter the number of miles from your **old home** to your **new workplace** **1**
2 Enter the number of miles from your **old home** to your **old workplace** **2**
3 Subtract line 2 from line 1. Enter the result but not less than zero . . . . ▶ **3**

If line 3 is 35 or more miles, complete the rest of this form. If line 3 is less than 35 miles, you may not deduct your moving expenses. This rule does not apply to members of the armed forces.

Caution: *If you are a member of the armed forces, see the instructions before continuing.*

Part I Moving Expenses

Note: *Any payments your employer made for any part of your move (including the value of any services furnished in kind) should be included on your W-2 form. Report that amount on* **Form 1040, line 7.** *See* **Reimbursements** *in the instructions.*

Section A—Transportation of Household Goods

4 Transportation and storage for household goods and personal effects **4**

Section B—Expenses of Moving From Old To New Home

5 Travel and lodging **not** including meals **5**

6 Total meals **6**

7 Multiply line 6 by 80% (.80) **7**

8 Add lines 5 and 7 . . . . **8**

Section C—Pre-move Househunting Expenses and Temporary Quarters
    (for any 30 days in a row after getting your job)

9 Pre-move travel and lodging **not** including meals **9**

10 Temporary quarters expenses **not** including meals **10**

11 Total meal expenses for both pre-move househunting and temporary quarters **11**

12 Multiply line 11 by 80% (.80) **12**

13 Add lines 9, 10, and 12 . . . . **13**

Section D—Qualified Real Estate Expenses

14 Expenses of (check one): **a** ☐ selling or exchanging your old home, or
    b ☐ if renting, settling an unexpired lease. } **14**

15 Expenses of (check one): **a** ☐ buying your new home, or
    b ☐ if renting, getting a new lease. } **15**

Part II Dollar Limits and Moving Expense Deduction

16 Enter the **smaller** of:
- The amount on line 13, or
- $1,500 ($750 if married filing a separate return and at the end of } **16**
1992 you lived with your spouse who also started work in 1992). }

17 Add lines 14, 15, and 16 . . . . **17**

18 Enter the **smaller** of:
- The amount on line 17, or
- $3,000 ($1,500 if married filing a separate return and at the end } **18**
of 1992 you lived with your spouse who also started work in 1992). }

19 Add lines 4, 8, and 18. Enter the total here and on Schedule A, line 18. This is your **moving expense deduction** . . . . ▶ **19**

For Paperwork Reduction Act Notice, see separate instructions.   Cat. No. 12490K   Form **3903** (1992)

Item	Answer

q. Loss on sale of securities (filed Schedule D) . . . .   _________

r. Interest paid on loan, money borrowed in order to pay vacation expenses . . . . .   _________

s. Unreimbursed traveling expense incurred by a salesperson in connection with
     employment . . . .   _________

t. Depreciation on apartment building owned and rented by taxpayer who is a doctor .   _________

u. Charitable contribution to a university . . . .   _________

v. Interest on money borrowed to purchase an apartment building . . . .   _________

w. Windstorm damage to house held for rental purposes by a farmer (not covered by
     insurance) . . . .   _________

8. During 1992, Mark Downing won $1,400 from football bets. He also lost $750 from basket-
ball bets and lost $1,150 at the horse races.
  a. To what extent, if at all, are the above gains and losses to be reported on the taxpayer's
     income tax return? Explain.

  b. Where would the appropriate amounts be entered on Form 1040 and supporting schedules?

9. Mr. and Mrs. Virgil Creque had AGI for 1992 of $47,400. They incurred the following miscel-
laneous expenses during 1992:

Mr. Creque
Employee travel expenses:

Transportation expenses (1,964 miles @ $.28)	$550
Meals away from home overnight (all reimbursed)	85
Hotels	185
Miscellaneous travel expenses	18
Total Travel Expenses	$838
Travel Expenses Reimbursed by Employer (including all meals)	(462)
Travel expenses paid out of pocket	$376

Other Business Expenses

Subscriptions to professional journals	$115
Business meals and entertainment (not reimbursed)	160
Tax return preparation fee	175

Other miscellaneous itemized deductions:

Total gambling losses (gambling gains included in AGI, $85)	$120

Mrs. Creque

Safe-deposit box rent for storage of securities	$ 40
Investment periodicals	120
Nurse's uniforms: cost and upkeep	340
Professional dues	85

Using appropriate amounts from above, complete the Miscellaneous Deductions section of
Schedule A, on the next page.

Job Expenses and Most Other Miscellaneous Deductions (See page A-5 for expenses to deduct here.)	19	Unreimbursed employee expenses—job travel, union dues, job education, etc. If required, you **MUST** attach Form 2106. (See page A-4.) ▶		19				
	20	Other expenses—investment, tax preparation, safe deposit box, etc. List type and amount ▶		20				
	21	Add lines 19 and 20		21				
	22	Enter amount from Form 1040, line 32 . ⌊ 22 ⌋						
	23	Multiply line 22 above by 2% (.02)		23				
	24	Subtract line 23 from line 21. If zero or less, enter -0- . . . . ▶	24					
Other Miscellaneous Deductions	25	Other—from list on page A-5. List type and amount ▶ .... ▶	25					

10. Charlie P. and Maggie S. Church are married and file a joint return. They reside in Evanston, Illinois. Mr. Church's SSN is 367-83-9403, and Mrs. Church's is 361-73-4098. Mr. Church was employed as a chemist by Drake Corporation for the first six months of the year and by Potter Company for the remaining six months of the year. Mrs. Church worked part time as a nurse at City Hospital. Their AGI on their 1992 income tax return was $74,105.20.

The following payments were made during the year. Canceled checks or receipts exist for each payment unless noted.

Interest on residence mortgage	$4,200
Church	900
Hunting license	90
Automobile license (pleasure car)	16
John and Ellen Newton (poor family)	50
Red Cross	20
March of Dimes (no canceled check or receipt)	10
Property tax on residence	2,450
Sales tax actually paid	625
R. K. Snell, M.D. (not reimbursed by insurance)	980
E. I. Newman, M.D. (not reimbursed by insurance)	290
Hospital Insurance Premiums Paid	556
Rental of safe-deposit box (contains stock certificates)	22
Evanston Drug Co. for non-prescription medicines and drugs (not reimbursed by insurance)	160
State Income Taxes Withheld	890

Prepare a Schedule A (shown on the next page) for Mr. and Mrs. Church for the year 1992.

SCHEDULES A&B
(Form 1040)

Department of the Treasury
Internal Revenue Service

Schedule A—Itemized Deductions

(Schedule B is on back)

▶ Attach to Form 1040. ▶ See Instructions for Schedules A and B (Form 1040).

OMB No. 1545-0074

1992

Attachment
Sequence No. **07**

Name(s) shown on Form 1040

Your social security number

Medical and Dental Expenses

Caution: *Do not include expenses reimbursed or paid by others.*

1 Medical and dental expenses (see page A-1) . . . . . | 1
2 Enter amount from Form 1040, line 32. | 2 |
3 Multiply line 2 above by 7.5% (.075) . . . . | 3
4 Subtract line 3 from line 1. If zero or less, enter -0- . . . . ▶ | 4

Taxes You Paid

(See page A-1.)

5 State and local income taxes . . . . | 5
6 Real estate taxes (see page A-2) . . . . | 6
7 Other taxes. List—include personal property taxes . ▶ | 7
8 Add lines 5 through 7 . . . . ▶ | 8

Interest You Paid

(See page A-2.)

Note:
Personal interest is not deductible.

9a Home mortgage interest and points reported to you on Form 1098 | 9a
b Home mortgage interest not reported to you on Form 1098. If paid to an individual, show that person's name and address. ▶
  | 9b
10 Points not reported to you on Form 1098. See page A-3 for special rules . . . . | 10
11 Investment interest. If required, attach Form 4952. (See page A-3.) . . . . | 11
12 Add lines 9a through 11 . . . . ▶ | 12

Gifts to Charity

(See page A-3.)

Caution: *If you made a charitable contribution and received a benefit in return, see page A-3.*

13 Contributions by cash or check . . . . | 13
14 Other than by cash or check. If over $500, you **MUST** attach Form 8283 . . . . | 14
15 Carryover from prior year . . . . | 15
16 Add lines 13 through 15 . . . . ▶ | 16

Casualty and Theft Losses

17 Casualty or theft loss(es). Attach Form 4684. (See page A-4.) . . . . ▶ | 17

Moving Expenses

18 Moving expenses. Attach Form 3903 or 3903F. (See page A-4.) . . . . . . ▶ | 18

Job Expenses and Most Other Miscellaneous Deductions

(See page A-5 for expenses to deduct here.)

19 Unreimbursed employee expenses—job travel, union dues, job education, etc. If required, you **MUST** attach Form 2106. (See page A-4.) ▶ | 19
20 Other expenses—investment, tax preparation, safe deposit box, etc. List type and amount ▶ | 20
21 Add lines 19 and 20 . . . . | 21
22 Enter amount from Form 1040, line 32. | 22 |
23 Multiply line 22 above by 2% (.02) . . . . | 23
24 Subtract line 23 from line 21. If zero or less, enter -0- . . . . ▶ | 24

Other Miscellaneous Deductions

25 Other—from list on page A-5. List type and amount ▶
  . . . . ▶ | 25

Total Itemized Deductions

26 Is the amount on Form 1040, line 32, more than $105,250 (more than $52,625 if married filing separately)?

● **NO.** Your deduction is not limited. Add lines 4, 8, 12, 16, 17, 18, 24, and 25. ▶ | 26
● **YES.** Your deduction may be limited. See page A-5 for the amount to enter.

Caution: *Be sure to enter on Form 1040, line 34, the **LARGER** of the amount on line 26 above or your standard deduction.*

For Paperwork Reduction Act Notice, see Form 1040 instructions.   Cat. No. 11330X   Schedule A (Form 1040) 1992

11. For each situation described below, state whether the expenses paid qualify as education expenses. If the expenses do qualify as education expenses, indicate whether the expenses are deductible for AGI or from AGI.

   a. Accounting courses taken by a self-employed CPA to meet the state's continuing professional education requirement. Total CPE expenses in 1992 were $525.

   b. Tuition and books in the amount of $3,500 for a CPA enrolled in law school.

   c. Tuition and books in the amount of $2,700 for a high school teacher enrolled in graduate school to meet state law requirements in order to renew her teaching certificate.

   d. A company executive paid tuition, transportation, and book expenses of $8,000 during 1992 to attend an executive MBA program to improve his business skills on the job.

12. Betty McGregor is a single person whose primary job is to teach the third grade class at the local public school. In the past few years the school budget has been very tight, making funds for classroom supplies relatively scarce. Betty, being a conscientious teacher, often buys paper, pencils, drawing materials, and other supplies for use by her children. With a tight budget she cannot get reimbursed for these materials, so she pays for them out of her own funds.

   a. To what extent do these expenses paid by Betty for these materials meet the qualifications for being treated as employee expenses under miscellaneous itemized deductions?

   b. To what extent do these expenses meet the qualifications for being reported as charitable contributions to a tax-exempt public institution?

   c. Based on your answers to *a.* and *b.* above, how should Betty report the expenses for school materials on her tax return?

13. Roberto Gomez and his wife are both working in professional jobs. They filed a joint tax return for 1992 which reported an AGI of $125,000. The return included a Schedule A for itemized deductions which showed the following gross expenses: Medical expenses, $12,000; Taxes, $4,500; Mortgage interest, $3,000; Investment interest, $2,000; Charitable contributions, $4,000; and Moving expenses, $3,300.

   a. What is the total amount of itemized deductions allowed on Form 1040, page 2 as a deduction against AGI in calculating taxable income? Show calculations.

   b. Assuming Mr. and Mrs. Gomez are entitled to three personal exemptions, by how much in dollars and in tax rate did their income taxes increase as a result of the limitation on the deductibility of certain itemized deductions?

      (1) Increase in amount of tax liability:

      (2) Effect on their marginal tax rate:

14. **a.** Under what circumstances should a taxpayer plan to control the timing of payments that are deductible as itemized deductions?

   b. Identify some specific ways in which the current tax law affects tax planning for expenses that could be treated as itemized deductions in 1993.

Tax Ethics Case*

15. Assume that you are Nick Steven's CPA tax preparer. Nick informs you that he does not want his wife to know that he has been gambling and therefore wants you to leave his gambling losses and gains off of his tax return. He is aware that no tax liability is due on his gambling gains, since they are less than his gambling losses. Since his individual winnings were all under the limit, the IRS will have no record of his winnings and probably will not discover his failure to report his gambling transactions. Nick says that you will be doing him a big favor by leaving his gambling transactions off of his return, since his wife studies the return carefully before she signs it.

   a. What are the ethical issues in this case?

   b. What alternative courses of action do you, as Nick's tax preparer, have?

   c. What course of action would you take if you were the tax preparer?

---

* Case adapted from ethics cases prepared for publication by the American Accounting Association.

Other Tax Considerations

The information presented in this chapter will enable the taxpayer to complete Form 1040 and to calculate the amount of any additional taxes that might be owed to the government or applied to next year's tax.

Chapters 3 and 4 focused on the financial information needed to calculate AGI and complete page 1 of Form 1040. Included in this chapter is a discussion of the information needed on page 2 of Form 1040.

Occasionally, taxpayers will be subject to interest and penalties for improprieties in filing their tax return or paying their taxes. Some taxpayers need an extension of time to file their returns, or they may need to amend a previously filed return. Still others are troubled by the possibility of a tax audit or the procedure to be followed in appealing the findings of an unfavorable tax audit. These taxpayer concerns will also be addressed in this chapter. Taxpayers with a basic knowledge of the laws affecting these areas of concern will be better prepared to minimize their tax payments and avoid unnecessary hassles with the government.

Finalizing the Tax

The information presented in chapters 5 and 6 will enable the taxpayer to determine whether to itemize deductions or use the standard deduction. Once determined, the appropriate amount is deducted from AGI. AGI (described in Chapter 4) is listed on Form 1040 (lines 31 and 32).

Next, the taxpayer deducts the amount available for personal and dependency exemptions ($2,300 x number of exemptions). The result is taxable income, Form 1040 (line 37). Exemptions are discussed in Chapter 1.

Taxable Income Summary:
```
    Total Income
  – Adjustments to Income
  = AGI
  – Larger of:  1) Standard Deduction, or
                2) Itemized Deductions
  – Exemptions @ $2,300
  = TAXABLE INCOME
```

Taxable income is an important figure for the taxpayer. It is the income on which the basic amount of income tax is determined. This basic tax will either be found on the Tax Table or calculated using the Tax Rate Schedules. Certain children under the age of 14 who have more than $1,200 of investment income may figure their tax on Form 8615. For information on the calculation of the tax see Chapter 2.

Once the basic tax calculation has been completed on Form 1040, (line 38), several other factors must be considered before the total tax owed to the government can be calculated on Form 1040, (line 53). These factors include the possible addition of several extra taxes and the possible application of a number of tax credits.

To determine the amount of tax owed or the refund due, the amount paid or credited towards the tax liability must be considered. All payments must be listed and subtracted from the total tax (line 53) to arrive at the additional taxes owed or the amount overpaid.

Summary—Form 1040, page 2:
```
    Tax Computation
  – Credits
  + Other Taxes
  – Payments
  = Refund or Amount Owed
```

The extra taxes and tax payments are examined in this chapter. Personal tax credits are discussed in Chapter 2, and business tax credits are covered in Chapter 13.

Extra Taxes

In this segment of Chapter 7, two extra categories of taxes are considered: "additional taxes" and "other taxes." These taxes are included in the "total tax" shown on Form 1040 (line 53).

Additional Taxes Reported

Two of the extra taxes that are collected through the income tax system are labeled as "additional taxes." One of the taxes is the Tax on Accumulation Distribution of Trusts, Form 4970. The other tax is the Tax on Lump-Sum Distributions, Form 4972. While these two taxes are calculated on separate forms, they are reported in the "Tax Computation" section of Form 1040. They are listed (line 39) and are included in the total tax shown (line 40). The appropriate box (line 39) is checked to identify the source of these taxes.

Other Taxes

Form 1040 also enables the IRS to obtain reports and to collect certain other taxes, to adjust for prior-year tax calculations, and to adjust for other payments received. The amount of the other tax items must be entered on Form 1040 (lines 47-51), and a separate schedule or form attached to Form 1040 with the needed details. "Other taxes" are discussed as follows:

1. Self-employment tax (Schedule SE)
2. Alternative minimum tax (Form 6251)
3. Recapture taxes (Form 4255, Form 8611, or Form 8828)
4. Social security tax on tip income not reported to employer (Form 4137)
5. Tax on an IRA or a qualified retirement plan (Form 5329)
6. Advance EIC payments received (Form W-2)

Self-Employment Tax

Self-employed taxpayers must file a tax return if they had taxable net earnings from self-employment of $400 or more. In addition, they are liable for self-employment tax. This tax is comparable to the social security tax withheld from an employee's wages. It is used to provide funds for Social Security and Medicare benefits. Self-employment tax is calculated on Schedule SE which must be attached to the taxpayer's Form 1040. Approximately 10% of all taxpayers pay self-employment tax.

Taxpayers are required to pay self-employment tax on taxable self-employment income regardless of their age. Taxpayers who receive Social Security benefits are also liable for the tax if they receive taxable self-employment income of $400 or more. Generally, no self-employment tax is payable when net self-employment income is less than $400. However, all net self-employment income must be reported in gross income.

Self-Employment Tax Rates

Self-employment tax is composed of two elements:

1 OASDI (Old-Age, Survivors, and Disablility Insurance)
   1992: 12.4% of taxable net earnings from self-employment up to $55,500
2. HIP (Health Insurance Plan)
   1992: 2.9% of taxable net earnings from self-employment up to $130,200

The combined rate is 15.3% up to $55,500. Only 2.9% applies above $55,500. The base is adjusted yearly and must be published on or before November 1 and is effective the following January.

Self-employment tax rates are applied against the *taxable* net earnings from self-employment. *Taxable* net earnings from self-employment are determined by multiplying net self-employment income by .9235. The taxpayer must have $400 or more of net earnings from self-employment after applying the .9235 factor to be subject to the tax. One half of self-employment tax will be allowed as an adjustment to income (Form 1040, line 25) in calculating AGI.

When a self-employed individual also has earned wages subject to social security taxes, the wages are deducted from the maximum earnings base that is subject to self-employment tax.

EXAMPLE 1 ——————————————

Ramona receives wages of $50,000 during the tax year. She also has $12,000 of *taxable* net earnings from self-employment. Only $5,500 ($55,500 – $50,000) of Ramona's self-employment income is subject to the OASDI tax rate of 12.4%. However, the entire $12,000 is subject to the HIP tax rate of 2.9%.

Self-Employment Income

Taxpayers generate self-employment income when they engage in a business or profession as a sole proprietor, an independent contractor, a member of a partnership, or are otherwise in business for themselves. One does not have to carry on regular full-time business activities to be self-employed. Part-time work may also be self-employment. Generally, the self-employment income of a sole proprietor is the amount shown on Schedule C. A partner's self-employment income is the amount reported on Schedule K-1, Form 1065.

Special Rules

Some types of income may not be treated as self-employment income. The following paragraphs list self-employment tax rules for special situations.

Aliens. Nonresident aliens do not have to pay self-employment tax. Residents of the Virgin Islands, Puerto Rico, Guam, or American Samoa, however, are subject to the tax.

Gains and Losses. Generally, capital gains and losses, such as gain or loss on the sale of investment property, are excluded from self-employment income. Gains and losses from the sale, exchange, or involuntary conversion of fixed assets used in a trade or business are also excluded in the calculation of self-employment income.

Corporate Director. Fees received for performing services as a director of a corporation are self-employment income. Such fees may be received for going to director's meetings or for serving on committees. The income is recognized in the year in which the fee is received.

Corporate Employee. Any income received by an employee or officer of the corporation is not self-employment income, even if the person owns all of the stock of the corporation.

S Corporations. Shareholders in an S corporation do not treat their share of the corporation's taxable income as self-employment income.

Dividends. Dividends on securities are not self-employment income unless the taxpayer is a dealer in securities.

Newspaper Carriers. Generally, the income newspaper carriers receive for delivering newspapers or shopping news to customers is not

> ## Avoiding Underpayment Penalties
>
> Self-employment tax is collected through the income tax system. Taxpayers must include self-employment tax when they figure their estimated tax for the year. Underpayment of a required installment of estimated taxes may invoke a penalty.

self-employment income. However, if the carrier is age 18 or over, the income is subject to social security tax (FICA).

Interest. Interest is not self-employment income unless it is received in a trade or business, such as interest on accounts receivable or interest received from bonds or notes by a dealer in securities.

Clergy. Members of the clergy and Christian Science practitioners are generally subject to self-employment tax unless they qualify and apply for an exemption (Form 4361). If the church has elected exemption from social security taxes, a special rule applies to church employees who are not ministers. These people have to pay self-employment tax if they are paid $108.28 or more during the year. However, employees of certain religious sects that are opposed to insurance generally qualify for an exemption from the self-employment tax. Also, members who have taken a vow of poverty are automatically exempt from self-employment tax on amounts received for work performed for the church.

Real Estate Rentals. Rent from real estate and from personal property leased with real estate is not self-employment income. However, if the rent is received in the normal course of business by a real estate dealer, it is self-employment income. Also, rents received for the use or occupancy of hotels, boarding houses, or apartment houses are not treated as real estate rentals if substantial services are provided to the occupants. These rentals are included in figuring net earnings from self-employment.

Babysitters. Babysitters who provide child care in their own home generate self-employment income. However, babysitters who provide child care in the parent's home are considered employees of the parents and do not have self-employment income.

Nurses. Registered nurses or licensed practical nurses who are employed directly by the patient to provide private nursing services are treated as self-employed individuals. If these nurses receive their compensation from an agency that assigns them to different jobs, the nurses are generally considered to be employees of the agency and not self-employed. Nurses employed directly by a doctor, a hospital, or other health care facility are employees.

Unlicensed persons who classify themselves as practical nurses are treated as employees. It makes no difference who employs such a person—a doctor, a patient, or a hospital.

Authors. Royalties paid to authors are self-employment income.

Lecturers. Taxpayers who give an occasional lecture do not generate self-employment income from their lectures. Professional lecturers who seek out lecture engagements and give lectures on a regular basis are treated as receiving self-employment income.

Real Estate Agents. Licensed real estate agents working out of a real estate agency are generally treated as self-employed. To receive this treatment two conditions must be met: 1) they must have a contract with the agency specifying that they are not employees of the agency, and 2) substantially all of their compensation is based on sales rather than on the number of hours worked.

Direct Marketing Distributors. People who receive a commission for selling or brokering products and services from their homes or other non-retail establishments are treated as self-employed individuals.

Consultants. Consultants are generally treated as self-employed individuals.

Executors. A professional executor is considered to be self-employed. Nonprofessional executors, however, are not treated as self-employed unless all of the following criteria are met: 1) the estate includes a business, 2) the executor actively participates in the operation of the business, and 3) all or part of the executor's fee is related to the operation of the business.

Employees of Foreign Governments. If a U.S. citizen is working in the United States as an employee of a foreign government, any compensation received is treated as self-employment income.

Partnership Income

General partners must include their distributive share of partnership income or loss in net earnings from self-employment. Any guaranteed payments should also be included.

Limited partners include in self-employment income only those payments that are guaranteed, such as salary and professional fees that are received for services performed during the year. Self-employment income does not include a distributive share of partnership income or loss.

Retired partners pay no self-employment tax on retirement income received from the partnership under a written plan if:

1. The retired partner receives life-long periodic payments.
2. The retired partner's share of the partnership capital was fully repaid to the retired partner.
3. The retired partner performs no services for the partnership during the year.
4. The partnership owes the retired partner nothing but the retirement payments.

Different Tax Years. If the partner's tax year is not the same as the partnership's tax year, the partner's distributive share of the partnership gain or loss is reported in the partner's tax year that includes the end of the partnership tax year.

EXAMPLE 2 ————————————

Jose files his return on a calendar year basis, but the partnership uses the fiscal year ending January 31. Jose must include his distributive share of partnership earnings and his guaranteed payments for the fiscal year ending January 31, 1992, on his return for the calendar year 1992.

Calculating Net Self-Employment Income

There are three ways to figure self-employment net earnings: 1) the regular method, 2) the farm optional method, and 3) the nonfarm optional method. The following will explain the regular method. The optional methods are discussed later.

Regular Method of Calculating Net Self-Employment Income

Net self-employment income generally includes all business income less all business deductions allowed for income tax purposes. Net earnings from self-employment must be determined by using the same accounting method used for income tax purposes. All allowable deductions must be subtracted when figuring net earnings from self-employment. False statements made to receive or to increase social security benefits could subject the taxpayer to penalties.

If a taxpayer has more than one trade or business, the net earnings from each business must be combined to determine the net self-employment income. A loss incurred in one business will reduce the gain in another business. These gains and losses are netted only for purposes of the self-employment tax. Separate records must be kept for each business and the appropriate form or schedule must be filed for each separate business.

EXAMPLE 3 ————————————————

Ryan is the sole proprietor of two separate businesses. He operates a yard maintenance business which made a net profit of $30,000 last year. He also has a clothing store which had a net loss of $4,000 last year. Ryan files one Schedule SE showing net self-employment income of $26,000. He must also file a Schedule C for each business—a Schedule C for the yard business showing a net profit of $30,000, and another Schedule C for the clothing store showing a net loss of $4,000.

Deductions and Exemptions. Certain deductions and exemptions used to compute taxable income are not deductible in calculating self-employment income. Specifically, the following are not used:

1. Deductions for personal exemptions for the taxpayer, spouse, or dependents
2. The standard deduction
3. The net operating loss deduction
4. The foreign expropriation loss deduction
5. Nonbusiness deductions
6. The self-employed health insurance deduction

EXAMPLE 4 ————————————————

Mildred owns a grocery store which had the following items for the year:

Gross profit on sales	$94,700
Salaries	48,000
Rent	12,000
Heat, light, and air conditioning . . .	6,000
Other expenses	3,800
Gain on sale of equipment	200
Fire loss on store building	2,800
Net operating loss carryover	3,000

In determining taxable income, all the above items are considered. However, in calculating **net earnings from self employment**, only the following are used:

Gross profit on sales		$94,700
Expenses:		
Salaries	$48,000	
Rent	12,000	
Heat, light, and air		
conditioning	6,000	
Other expenses	3,800	
Total expenses		69,800
Net operating profit		$24,900

The $24,900 is Mildred's net earnings from self-employment. The equipment sale, the fire loss, and the net operating loss carried over from a previous year are specifically excluded in the calculation of self-employment income.

Married Couples

If both the taxpayer and spouse have self-employment earnings, both are required to pay the self-employment tax, and both are required to file a separate Schedule SE with their income tax return. When spouses participate in a joint business operation, the net earnings (loss) from the business are generally shared between them.

Community Income. If any income from a trade or business is community income under state law, it is subject to self-employment tax as the income of the spouse carrying on the trade or business. Such income is not treated as community property for self-employment tax purposes. The identity of the person carrying on the trade or business is determined based on the facts in each situation.

Short Schedule SE

Schedule SE, Self-Employment Tax, shown in Illustration 7-1, is a two-page form designed to provide two reporting structures in which to calculate self-employment tax. Self-employment tax is calculated in Section A, Short Schedule SE, or in Section B, Long Schedule SE. The Short Schedule SE calculation of self-employment earnings requires the entry of the amount of net profit as determined from Schedule C for business proprietorships, Schedule F for farm proprietorships, or Schedule K-1, Form 1065, for partnerships.

Long Schedule SE

The Long Schedule SE, Section B, is used by taxpayers for whom the Short Schedule SE is not appropriate. Included among these taxpayers are those who elect to use an optional method to calculate self-employment income. Taxpayers who receive wages must use the Long Schedule SE when the total of their wages and their net earnings from self-employment exceed $55,500. The longer schedule is also required by certain ministers and church employees. In addition, those who have not reported taxable tips to their employer must use the Long Schedule SE.

Optional Method of Calculating Net Self-Employment Income

Taxpayers may choose to use an optional method to calculate their net self-employment income if their *taxable* net self-employment income is less than $1,600 (or even a loss), and:

1. They want to increase their social security benefit base.
2. They incurred child or dependent care expenses to be self-employed (this method will increase earned income which could increase the child and dependent care tax credit).
3. They are entitled to the EIC (this method will increase earned income which could increase the earned income tax credit).

Taxpayers using this method must pay self-employment tax, even if they are not otherwise required to do so.

Nonfarm Optional Method. The nonfarm optional method is used only for self-employment income that does not come from farming. Taxpayers may use this method if they meet all the following tests which are based on nonfarm self-employment income:

1. Actual net earnings, figured by the regular method, are less than $1,733 (.9235 x $1,733 = $1,600.43).
2. Actual *net* earnings are less than 72.189% of *gross* income.
3. Taxable net earnings are $400 or more in at least two of the preceding three tax years.

The nonfarm option may only be used five times during the taxpayer's lifetime.

Gross income $2,400 or less. If gross income from all nonfarm trades or businesses is $2,400 or less, the taxpayer may report two-thirds of the gross income as net earnings from self-employment if this amount is greater than the actual net earnings.

EXAMPLE 5 ────────────────────────

Angela Lopez, who qualifies to use the optional method, reports earnings from her craft business as follows:

Gross income $2,100
Net earnings $1,000

Because her actual net earnings from self-employment are less than $1,733 and less than 72.189% of her total gross nonfarm income, Angela may either report her actual net earnings of $1,000 or she may use the optional method to report $1,400 (two-thirds of $2,100).

EXAMPLE 6 ────────────────────────

Assume that in Example 5 Angela Lopez has gross income of $1,200 and net earnings of $900. Angela must report her actual net earnings of $900. She may not use the optional method because her actual net earnings are not less than 72.189% of her gross income.

EXAMPLE 7 ————————————————

Assume that in Example 5 Angela has a net loss of $800. Angela may choose to report $1,400 (two thirds of $2,100) as her net earnings under the optional method.

Gross income more than $2,400. If gross income from all nonfarm trades or businesses is more than $2,400, the taxpayer may report $1,600 as net earnings from self-employment if this amount is greater than the actual net earnings.

EXAMPLE 8 ————————————————

Goro Wakui operates a hot dog concession. Goro, who qualifies to use the optional method, reports earnings as follows:

Gross income	$14,000
Net earnings	$1,400

Since Goro's net earnings from self-employment ($1,400) are less than $1,733 and less than 72.189% of gross income, he may choose to report $1,600 as his net earnings from self-employment, or he may report $1,400 under the regular method.

Farm Optional Method. Farmers may report two-thirds of their gross income from farming as net earnings from farming, if their gross income is not more than $2,400. If their gross income from farming is more than $2,400 and net earnings are less than $1,733, they may use $1,600 as net earnings from self-employment.

This option may be used whether the farmer is on a cash or accrual method. Also the farm optional method is not limited to just five uses during the farmer's lifetime. It is available on an unlimited basis.

Filled-in Schedule SE

Illustration 7-1

Schedule SE (Form 1040), Self-Employment Tax, is used to calculate the amount of self-employment tax and to provide the means by which self-employed individuals receive social security credit for the payments they make through their income tax returns. Self-employment tax is based on net earnings from self-employment.

The filled-in Schedule SE in Illustration 7-1, showing John Williams' net earnings from self-employment, includes both the income from his hardware store ($57,959) and his share of the income from the partnership of Willard and Williams ($5,002) for total self-employment income of $62,961.00. Since Mr. Williams qualified for the Short Schedule SE, only Section A of Schedule SE was completed.

Self-employment tax of $8,568.19, calculated on Schedule SE, is entered on Form 1040 (line 47). This tax is added to the amount of income tax in determining the balance of tax due or overpayment.

The information on Schedule SE will be processed by the IRS and the data forwarded to the social security offices.

If both husband and wife have net earnings from self-employment, both are subject to the tax. Each must file a Schedule SE.

Alternative Minimum Tax (AMT)

Through the effective use of tax incentives, some taxpayers pay little or no tax on their sizable economic incomes. The alternative minimum tax (AMT) is designed to exact at least some minimum amount of tax from these people.

The AMT for individuals is calculated on Schedule 6251, Alternative Minimum Tax—Individuals. The AMT is computed at the flat rate of 24%. The amount of the AMT is compared with the amount of the regular income tax liability. The taxpayer must pay the regular tax liability plus the amount by which the AMT exceeds the regular income tax on Form 1040 (line 48).

The calculation of the AMT starts with the conversion of the taxpayer's taxable income into an **alternative minimum taxable income** (AMTI) figure. This conversion is accomplished by modifying taxable income with specified increases and decreases that are aimed at minimizing certain excessive tax benefits enjoyed by the taxpayer. The AMTI is then reduced by a special exemption to arrive at the **net alternative minimum taxable income**. The exemption

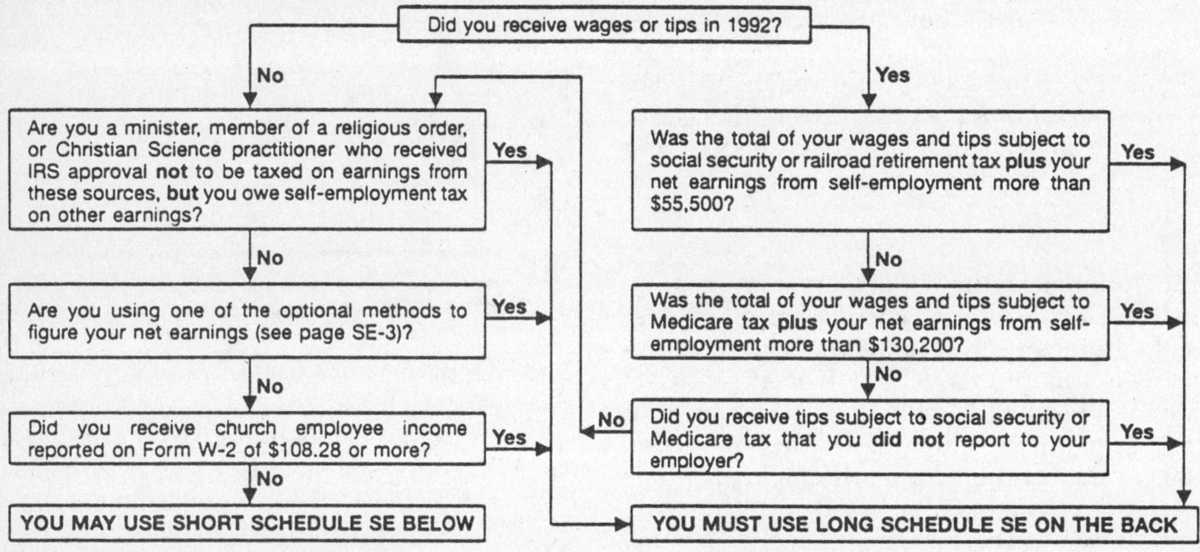

Illustration 7-1
Filled-In Schedule SE (Form 1040)

SCHEDULE SE **(Form 1040)** Department of the Treasury Internal Revenue Service	**Self-Employment Tax** ▶ See Instructions for Schedule SE (Form 1040). ▶ Attach to Form 1040.	OMB No. 1545-0074 **1992** Attachment Sequence No. **17**

Name of person with **self-employment** income (as shown on Form 1040) John R. Williams	Social security number of person with **self-employment** income ▶ 272 : 11 : 8245

Who Must File Schedule SE

You must file Schedule SE if:

- Your wages (and tips) subject to social security AND Medicare tax (or railroad retirement tax) were less than $130,200; **AND**
- Your *net earnings from self-employment from other than church employee income* (line 4 of Short Schedule SE or line 4c of Long Schedule SE) were $400 or more;
  OR
- You had church employee income (as defined on page SE-1) of $108.28 or more.

Exception. If your only self-employment income was from earnings as a minister, member of a religious order, or Christian Science practitioner, AND you filed **Form 4361** and received IRS approval not to be taxed on those earnings, DO NOT file Schedule SE. Instead, write "Exempt–Form 4361" on Form 1040, line 47.

May I Use Short Schedule SE or MUST I Use Long Schedule SE?

Section A—Short Schedule SE. Caution: *Read above to see if you must use Long Schedule SE on the back (Section B).*

1	Net farm profit or (loss) from Schedule F, line 36, and farm partnerships, Schedule K-1 (Form 1065), line 15a	**1**	
2	Net profit or (loss) from Schedule C, line 31; Schedule C-EZ, line 3; and Schedule K-1 (Form 1065), line 15a (other than farming). See page SE-2 for other income to report	**2**	62,961 00
3	Combine lines 1 and 2	**3**	62,961 00
4	**Net earnings from self-employment.** Multiply line 3 by 92.35% (.9235). If less than $400, **do not** file this schedule; you do not owe self-employment tax . . . . ▶	**4**	58,144 48
5	**Self-employment tax.** If the amount on line 4 is: • $55,500 or less, multiply line 4 by 15.3% (.153) and enter the result. • More than $55,500 but less than $130,200, multiply the amount in excess of $55,500 by 2.9% (.029). Then, add $8,491.50 to the result and enter the total. • $130,200 or more, enter $10,657.80. Also, enter this amount on Form 1040, line 47	**5**	8,568 19

Note: *Also, enter **one-half** of the amount from line 5 on **Form 1040, line 25.***

For Paperwork Reduction Act Notice, see Form 1040 instructions.   Cat. No. 11358Z   Schedule SE (Form 1040) 1992

is $40,000 for married taxpayers filing jointly and surviving spouses, $30,000 for single or head of household (HOH) taxpayers, and $20,000 for a married taxpayer filing separately.

These exemptions are phased out for taxpayers with a high AMTI by a reduction of $0.25 for each dollar that the AMTI exceeds $150,000 for married taxpayers filing jointly and surviving spouses, $112,500 for single taxpayers and HOHs, and $75,000 for married taxpayers filing separately.

The amount of the AMT is calculated at the 24% rate on the net AMTI. For some taxpayers, the AMT has become a separate tax system which significantly complicates filing the tax return. The AMT is described more fully in Chapter 13.

Recapture Taxes

The IRS has established recapture provisions for tax benefits allowed to the taxpayer that are based on conditions that were anticipated but did not occur. Two such situations are the investment credit and the low-income housing credit. Recapture taxes are added to the tax liability on Form 1040 (line 49).

Investment Credit Recapture

Prior to 1986, taxpayers were eligible to claim an investment tax credit for certain business assets in the taxable year that an asset was acquired. If an asset on which the credit has been claimed is disposed of before the end of the asset's cost recovery period, the investment credit must be recalculated. The difference between the amount of the credit previously claimed and the amount to which the taxpayer is actually entitled, based on the actual date the property ceased to be investment credit property, is determined on Form 4255, Recapture of Investment Credit. This amount is recaptured in the year of the asset's disposal by placing an "X" in the box for Form 4255 on Form 1040 (line 49) and treating it as a tax and adding it to the taxpayer's income tax liability.

Low-Income Housing Credit Recapture

After 1986, owners of qualified low-income residential rental housing have available a special tax credit. The credit may be taken in each of 10 years starting with the year the building is placed in service. Each year the credit is equal to a specified percentage (4 to 9%) of the building's qualified cost.

The project must continue to meet certain requirements over a period of 15 years or recapture of a portion of the credit can occur. Recapture occurs because of a "recapture event" in which requirements are not met, such as early disposition of a building. Form 8611, Recapture of Low-Income Housing Credit, is available to calculate and support the amount of the credit recaptured and to determine the amount of increase in the liability of the taxpayer. The box for Form 8611 is marked with an "X" on Form 1040 (line 49), and the recapture amount is added to the tax liability of the taxpayer.

Social Security Tax on Tip Income Not Reported to Employer

If tips of $20 or more have been received by a taxpayer in any month, they must be reported to the employer. If a taxpayer has any tip income that has not been reported to the employer, Form 4137, Social Security and Medicare Tax on Unreported Tip Income, *must* be filed by the employee with the income tax return. Tips of less than $20 per month are not subject to Social Security taxes, however, they must be reported as income on Form 1040 (line 7). The Social Security tax on unreported tip income in excess of $20 per month must be reported on the employee's Form 1040 (line 50). Form 4137 is used to calculate this tax. Schedule U (Form 1040), attached to Form 4137, provides information for the employee's social security account which is important for determining possible future benefits. If all tip income has been reported to the employer, Form 4137 does not have to be filed.

Filled-In Form 4137 and Schedule U

Illustration 7-2

A filled-in Form 4137, Social Security and Medicare Tax on Unreported Tip Income, and Schedule U, U.S. Schedule of Unreported Tip Income, for Robert L. Long, a part-time waiter, are both presented in Illustration 7-2. Robert Long has unreported tip income of $63.25 for the taxable year 1992. He must report the $63.25 as income on Form 1040 (line 7). He must also pay social security tax of $4.84 (7.65% x $63.25) on this income. The tax is entered on Form 4137 (line 16) and also on Form 1040 (line 50).

Tax on IRAs and Qualified Retirement Plans

IRAs and qualified retirement plans are subject to a penalty tax on premature distributions and on excess accumulation in IRA and annuities. The tax is reported on Form 5329, Return for Additional Taxes Attributable to Qualified Retirement Plans (including IRAs), Annuities, and Modified Endowment Contracts, and then entered on Form 1040 (line 51).

Advance Earned Income Credit (EIC)

Advance EIC payments are amounts advanced by employers to employees as part of their regular wage payments. The advance is based on the EIC to which the employee is entitled. This additional payment enables the employee to enjoy the benefits of the EIC before the annual tax return is filed. The amount of the advance is entered (line 52).

Special Taxes

Three other taxes are reported on Form 1040 (line 53). The amount of these taxes is added to the total tax reported on that line. The tax and the amount should be identified on the dotted line next to the total tax. These three taxes are discussed below.

The *Section 72 penalty tax* is assessed if the taxpayer is a 5% owner of a business and receives income from an early or excessive distribution from a Keogh (HR 10) plan or trust. The penalty tax is 10% of the distribution. "Section 72 penalty" and the amount are written on the dotted line (line 53).

When an employee has *uncollected social security or railroad retirement tax due on tips reported to the employer*, the amount of tax is shown on the employee's Form W-2. "Uncollected tax on tips" and the amount are written on the dotted line (line 53).

Golden parachute payments are those made by a corporation to key employees to compensate them when control of the corporation changes. A 20% tax is levied on any excess parachute payments received. The letters "EPP" and the amount are written on the dotted line (line 53).

Payment and Filing Concerns

This portion of the chapter deals with payments and credits that may be used to offset the total tax. It also examines filing deadlines and penalties. In addition, a filled-in Form 1040 is illustrated.

Payments Claimed on Form 1040

A taxpayer may claim on Form 1040 payments already made on the various tax liabilities, and certain refunds to which the taxpayer is entitled. Payments serve to reduce the amount of tax due or to increase the amount of the refund claimed on the taxpayer's return. The following payments and credits can be claimed on Form 1040:

1. Federal income tax withheld (Forms W-2 and W-2P)
2. Estimated tax payments for 1992 and overpayment on 1991 tax return applied on 1992 estimated tax payments
3. EIC
4. Payments made with Form 4868, Application for Automatic Extension of Time to File U.S. Individual Income Tax Return
5. Excess social security, Medicare, and railroad retirement tax withheld

Illustration 7-2
Filled-In Form 4137 and Schedule U

Form 4137

Department of the Treasury
Internal Revenue Service

Social Security and Medicare Tax on Unreported Tip Income
▶ See instructions on back.
▶ Attach to Form 1040.

OMB No. 1545-0059

1992

Attachment Sequence No. **24**

Name of person who received tip income (as shown on Form 1040)

Robert L. Long

Social security number

123 : 45 : 4321

Name(s) of employer(s) to whom you were required to, but did not, report your tip income:

Town & Country Inn

1 Total cash and charge tips you **received** in 1992. See instructions	1	4,206 | 00
2 Total cash and charge tips you **reported** to your employer in 1992	2	4,142 | 75
3 Subtract line 2 from line 1. This amount is income you **must** include in the total on Form 1040, line 7	3	63 | 25
4 Cash and charge tips you received but did not report to your employer because the total was less than $20 in a calendar month. See instructions	4	–0–
5 Subtract line 4 from line 3	5	63 | 25
6 Maximum amount of wages (including tips) subject to social security tax **6** 55,500 |00		
7 Total social security wages and social security tips (shown on Form(s) W-2) or railroad retirement (tier 1) compensation **7** 15,210 |50		
8 Subtract line 7 from line 6. If line 7 is more than line 6, enter -0- here and on line 9 and go to line 11	8	40,289 | 50
9 Unreported tips subject to social security tax. Compare the amounts on lines 5 and 8 above. Enter the **smaller** of the two amounts here and on line 1 of Schedule U below. If you received tips as a Federal, state, or local government employee, see the instructions	9	63 |25
10 Multiply line 9 by .062	10	3 |92
11 Maximum amount of wages (including tips) subject to Medicare tax **11** 130,200 |00		
12 Total Medicare wages and tips (shown on Form(s) W-2) or railroad retirement (tier 1) compensation **12** 15,210 |50		
13 Subtract line 12 from line 11. If line 12 is more than line 11, enter -0- here and on line 14 and go to line 16	13	114,989 | 50
14 Unreported tips subject to Medicare tax. Compare the amounts on lines 5 and 13 above. Enter the **smaller** of the two amounts here and on line 2 of Schedule U below	14	63 | 25
15 Multiply line 14 by .0145	15	92
16 Add lines 10 and 15. Enter the result here and on Form 1040, line 50 ▶	16	4 | 84

For Paperwork Reduction Act Notice, see instructions on back.

Form **4137** (1992)

- Do Not Detach -

SCHEDULE U (Form 1040)

Department of the Treasury
Internal Revenue Service

U.S. Schedule of Unreported Tip Income
For crediting to your social security record

1992

Note: *The amounts you report below are for your social security record. This record is used to figure any benefits, based on your earnings, payable to you and your dependents, or your survivors. Fill in each item accurately and completely.*

Print or type name of person who received tip income (as shown on Form 1040)

Robert L. Long

Social security number

123 : 45 : 4321

Address (number, street, and apt. no., or P.O. box if mail is not delivered to your home)

264 West Vernon Place

Occupation

Waiter

City, town or post office, state, and ZIP code

Maderia, OH 45243–1030

1 Unreported tips subject to social security tax. Enter the amount from line 9 (Form 4137) above ▶	1	63 | 25
2 Unreported tips subject to Medicare tax. Enter the amount from line 14 (Form 4137) above ▶	2	63 | 25

Please do not write in this space

DLN—

Cat. No. 12626C

6. Credit for federal tax on gasoline and special fuels, Form 4136
7. Regulated investment company credit, Form 2439

Federal Income Tax Withheld

Amounts withheld by an employer from an employee's wages or amounts withheld by a payer from other income are claimed on Form 1040 (line 54). The employer or payer has deposited these withheld amounts in an authorized bank depository, and the total amount withheld from each employee or payee is reported on Form W-2, Form W-2P, Form W-2G, or Form 1099-R. Copy B of these forms should be attached to Form 1040.

Estimated Tax Payments and Prior-Year Overpayments

Self-employed individuals are required to pay income taxes on a current basis by *estimating the amount of tax* for the year in advance and making periodic payments. In addition, a taxpayer can elect to apply any *prior-year overpayment* to reduce estimated tax payments for the coming year instead of receiving a refund. Both the amount paid in advance on a taxpayer's estimated tax and any overpayment from prior years is claimed for the current year on Form 1040 (line 55).

Earned Income Credit (EIC)

The EIC was discussed in Chapter 2 in connection with taxpayers who file Form 1040A. Taxpayers who file Form 1040 may make a more complex calculation of the EIC, because self-employment income (or loss) can be added to the calculation of earned income.

The EIC is not like the other credits listed on Form 1040 (lines 41-44). Those credits can only be deducted up to the amount of the tax liability. Depending on the credit, the excess is either lost or carried over. The EIC, however, is treated as if it were a tax payment that is refundable when all of the tax liability has been offset. This refundable credit is claimed on Form 1040 (line 45). Taxpayers claiming the EIC on Form 1040 must attach Schedule EIC to their Form 1040.

Excess Social Security, Medicare, and Railroad Retirement Tax

The excess social security, medicare, and railroad retirement tax withheld from a taxpayer can be claimed on Form 1040 (line 58). The recovery of these excess taxes through the income tax return was discussed in Chapter 2 in connection with Form 1040A.

Credit for Federal Tax on Fuels

A credit may be claimed by a taxpayer for the federal excise tax paid on gasoline and gasohol, diesel fuel, and other special fuels used for certain types of business purposes. The credit is claimed on Form 1040 (line 59). Form 4136, Computation of Credit for Federal Tax on Fuels, is filed to provide the details of the amount claimed. In addition, a credit is allowed on the purchase of a qualified diesel-powered highway vehicle. Included is any diesel-powered highway vehicle with at least four wheels, a gross vehicle weight of 10,000 pounds or less, and a registration for highway use in the U.S. under the laws of any state.

Credit from a Regulated Investment Company

The amount of tax paid by a regulated investment company (mutual fund) on its undistributed long-term capital gains is constructively distributed to shareholders. Shareholders must be notified on Form 2439, Notice to Shareholder of Undistributed Long-Term Capital Gains, of the amount of tax paid by the company on their share of the undistributed long-term capital gains within 30 days after the close of the tax year. The credit is claimed on Form 1040 (line 59).

Filled-In Form 1040

Illustration 7-3

A filled-in joint return for John R. Williams, 43 years of age, SSN 272-11-8245, and his wife, Jean K. Williams, 41 years of age,

SSN 369-41-3822, is reproduced in Illustration 7-3. Mr. Williams is a retail hardware dealer who keeps his accounts on the calendar-year basis. Mrs. Williams is a part-time legal secretary and homemaker.

Mr. and Mrs. Williams reside at 1438 East Second Street, Verona, Wisconsin 53593-9088. They both elected to designate $1 of their 1992 tax for the presidential election campaign fund. Their filing status as a married couple filing a joint return is indicated by placing a check mark (line 2). Mr. and Mrs. Williams claimed five exemptions. One exemption was claimed for Mr. Williams, one for Mrs. Williams, one for each of their two dependent children, Mary R. Williams, age 12, SSN 453-26-8190, and Douglas J. Williams, age 15, SSN 453-26-8189, and one for Mr. Williams' 63-year-old dependent mother, Mildred A. Williams, SSN 168-29-4501. Mr. Williams' mother and children had no income in 1992 and lived with the Williams family for the entire year. The separate schedule for dependents, line 6c, was filled in to claim all dependents.

Mrs. Jean K. Williams had received $8,400 ($700 per month) as a part-time secretary for Roe and Quinby, attorneys, 1615 East Second Street, Verona, Wisconsin. Her Form W-2 indicated the following:

Total wages	$8,400.00
Social security tax withheld	642.60
Federal income tax withheld	1,260.00

Supporting Schedules and Forms

Following the building-block concept of supporting the amounts entered on Form 1040, the basic individual income tax return, Mr. and Mrs. Williams assembled their supporting schedules and forms shown in Table 7-1.

Wages, Dividends, and Interest

The amount for wages of $8,400 from Mrs. Williams' Form W-2 was entered on Form 1040 (line 7).

Mr. and Mrs. Williams reported their gross interest income for the year on Part I—Interest Income, Schedule B. The amount of total interest income of $1,817.91 was carried to Form 1040 (line 8a). Tax-exempt interest income from City of Madison bonds of $60 was entered on Form 1040 (line 8b). Mr. and Mrs. Williams reported their gross dividends for the year of $94.75 on Form 1040 (line 9).

Income Other Than Wages, Dividends, and Interest

In May of 1992 the Williams received refunds of 1991 income tax from the state of Wisconsin of $342.16 and from the federal government of $866.17. The $342.16 is taxable since the Williams had deducted this amount on their 1991 return. The refund was entered on Form 1040 (line 10). Mr. Williams owns and operates the Williams Hardware Store, and he reported the business's net income of $57,959 (line 12). Mr. Williams prepared Schedule C, Profit or Loss From Business, to be filed in support of the tax return.

Table 7-1
Supporting Schedules and Forms for 199 Form 1040

Form or Schedule	Description	Amount
Form W-2	Wage and Tax Statement	$ 8,400.00
Schedule A	Itemized Deductions	7,878.47
Schedule B	Part I—Interest Income	1,817.91
Schedule C	Profit or Loss From Business or Profession (Sole Proprietorship)	57,959.00
Schedule D	Capital Gains and Losses and Reconciliation of Forms 1099-B	250.00
Schedule E	Supplemental Income and Loss	5,212.00
Schedule SE	Self-Employment Tax	8,568.19

Illustration 7-3
Filled-In Form 1040, Page 1

Form **1040** Department of the Treasury—Internal Revenue Service
U.S. Individual Income Tax Return **1992** | IRS Use Only—Do not write or staple in this space.

For the year Jan. 1–Dec. 31, 1992, or other tax year beginning ______ , 1992, ending ______ , 19 ___ | OMB No. 1545-0074

Label
(See instructions on page 10.)
Use the IRS label. Otherwise, please print or type.

LABEL HERE

Your first name and initial: John R. | Last name: Williams | Your social security number: 272 : 11 : 8245

If a joint return, spouse's first name and initial: Jean K. | Last name: Williams | Spouse's social security number: 369 : 41 : 3822

Home address (number and street). If you have a P.O. box, see page 10.: 1438 East Second Street | Apt. no.

City, town or post office, state, and ZIP code. If you have a foreign address, see page 10.: Verona, WI 53593-9088

For Privacy Act and Paperwork Reduction Act Notice, see page 4.

Presidential Election Campaign (See page 10.)
Do you want $1 to go to this fund? . . . . | X Yes | No
If a joint return, does your spouse want $1 to go to this fund? . | X Yes | No
Note: Checking "Yes" will not change your tax or reduce your refund.

Filing Status
(See page 10.)
Check only one box.

1 [ ] Single
2 [X] Married filing joint return (even if only one had income)
3 [ ] Married filing separate return. Enter spouse's social security no. above and full name here. ▶ ______
4 [ ] Head of household (with qualifying person). (See page 11.) If the qualifying person is a child but not your dependent, enter this child's name here. ▶ ______
5 [ ] Qualifying widow(er) with dependent child (year spouse died ▶ 19 ___). (See page 11.)

Exemptions
(See page 11.)

6a [X] Yourself. If your parent (or someone else) can claim you as a dependent on his or her tax return, do not check box 6a. But be sure to check the box on line 33b on page 2 .
b [X] Spouse . . . .

No. of boxes checked on 6a and 6b: 2

c Dependents:

(1) Name (first, initial, and last name)	(2) Check if under age 1	(3) If age 1 or older, dependent's social security number	(4) Dependent's relationship to you	(5) No. of months lived in your home in 1992
Mary R. Williams		453 :26 : 8190	daughter	12
Douglas J. Williams		453 :26 : 8189	son	12
Mildred A. Williams		168 :29 : 4501	mother	12

If more than six dependents, see page 12.

No. of your children on 6c who:
• lived with you: 2
• didn't live with you due to divorce or separation (see page 13): ___
No. of other dependents on 6c: 1

d If your child didn't live with you but is claimed as your dependent under a pre-1985 agreement, check here ▶ [ ]
e Total number of exemptions claimed . . . .

Add numbers entered on lines above ▶ 5

Income

Attach Copy B of your Forms W-2, W-2G, and 1099-R here.

If you did not get a W-2, see page 9.

Attach check or money order on top of any Forms W-2, W-2G, or 1099-R.

7	Wages, salaries, tips, etc. Attach Form(s) W-2	7	8,400 00
8a	Taxable interest income. Attach Schedule B if over $400 .	8a	1,817 91
b	Tax-exempt interest income (see page 15). DON'T include on line 8a	8b 60 00	
9	Dividend income. Attach Schedule B if over $400 .	9	94 75
10	Taxable refunds, credits, or offsets of state and local income taxes from worksheet on page 16	10	342 16
11	Alimony received	11	
12	Business income or (loss). Attach Schedule C or C-EZ	12	57,959 00
13	Capital gain or (loss). Attach Schedule D .	13	250 00
14	Capital gain distributions not reported on line 13 (see page 15)	14	
15	Other gains or (losses). Attach Form 4797 . . .	15	
16a	Total IRA distributions . 16a ___ b Taxable amount (see page 16)	16b	
17a	Total pensions and annuities 17a ___ b Taxable amount (see page 16)	17b	
18	Rents, royalties, partnerships, estates, trusts, etc. Attach Schedule E	18	5,212 00
19	Farm income or (loss). Attach Schedule F .	19	
20	Unemployment compensation (see page 17) . .	20	
21a	Social security benefits 21a ___ b Taxable amount (see page 17)	21b	
22	Other income. List type and amount—see page 18	22	800 00
23	Add the amounts in the far right column for lines 7 through 22. This is your total income . . ▶	23	74,875 82

Adjustments to Income
(See page 18.)

24a	Your IRA deduction from applicable worksheet on page 19 or 20	24a 2,000 00	
b	Spouse's IRA deduction from applicable worksheet on page 19 or 20	24b 2,000 00	
25	One-half of self-employment tax (see page 20) . . .	25 4,284 10	
26	Self-employed health insurance deduction (see page 20)	26	
27	Keogh retirement plan and self-employed SEP deduction	27	
28	Penalty on early withdrawal of savings . .	28	
29	Alimony paid. Recipient's SSN ▶ . . .	29	
30	Add lines 24a through 29. These are your total adjustments . . . . . ▶	30	8,284 10

Adjusted Gross Income

31 Subtract line 30 from line 23. This is your **adjusted gross income**. If this amount is less than $22,370 and a child lived with you, see page EIC-1 to find out if you can claim the "Earned Income Credit" on line 56 . . . . . ▶ | 31 | 66,591 72

Cat. No. 11320B | Form **1040** (1992)

Illustration 7-3
Filled-In Form 1040, Page 2

Form 1040 (1992) Page **2**

Tax Computation (See page 22.)	32 Amount from line 31 (adjusted gross income)	32	66,591 72

33a Check if: ☐ You were 65 or older, ☐ Blind; ☐ Spouse was 65 or older, ☐ Blind.
Add the number of boxes checked above and enter the total here ▶ 33a

b If your parent (or someone else) can claim you as a dependent, check here ▶ 33b ☐

c If you are married filing separately and your spouse itemizes deductions or you are a dual-status alien, see page 22 and check here ▶ 33c ☐

34 Enter the larger of your:
> Itemized deductions from Schedule A, line 26, OR
> Standard deduction shown below for your filing status. But if you checked any box on line 33a or b, go to page 22 to find your standard deduction. If you checked box 33c, your standard deduction is zero.
> - Single—$3,600
> - Head of household—$5,250
> - Married filing jointly or Qualifying widow(er)—$6,000
> - Married filing separately—$3,000

34 7,878 47

35 Subtract line 34 from line 32 — 35 58,713 25

36 If line 32 is $78,950 or less, multiply $2,300 by the total number of exemptions claimed on line 6e. If line 32 is over $78,950, see the worksheet on page 23 for the amount to enter — 36 11,500 00

If you want the IRS to figure your tax, see page 23.

37 **Taxable income.** Subtract line 36 from line 35. If line 36 is more than line 35, enter -0- — 37 47,213 25

38 Enter tax. Check if from a ☒ Tax Table, b ☐ Tax Rate Schedules, c ☐ Schedule D, or d ☐ Form 8615 (see page 23). Amount, if any, from Form(s) 8814 ▶ e _______ — 38 8,569 00

39 Additional taxes (see page 23). Check if from a ☐ Form 4970 b ☐ Form 4972 — 39

40 Add lines 38 and 39 ▶ 40 8,569 00

Credits (See page 23.)

41 Credit for child and dependent care expenses. Attach Form 2441 | 41

42 Credit for the elderly or the disabled. Attach Schedule R | 42

43 Foreign tax credit. Attach Form 1116 | 43

44 Other credits (see page 24). Check if from a ☐ Form 3800 b ☐ Form 8396 c ☐ Form 8801 d ☐ Form (specify)_______ | 44

45 Add lines 41 through 44 — 45

46 Subtract line 45 from line 40. If line 45 is more than line 40, enter -0- ▶ 46 8,569 00

Other Taxes

47 Self-employment tax. Attach Schedule SE. Also, see line 25 — 47 8,568 19

48 Alternative minimum tax. Attach Form 6251 — 48

49 Recapture taxes (see page 25). Check if from a ☐ Form 4255 b ☐ Form 8611 c ☐ Form 8828 — 49

50 Social security and Medicare tax on tip income not reported to employer. Attach Form 4137 — 50

51 Tax on qualified retirement plans, including IRAs. Attach Form 5329 — 51

52 Advance earned income credit payments from Form W-2 — 52

53 Add lines 46 through 52. This is your **total tax** ▶ 53 17,137 19

Payments

Attach Forms W-2, W-2G, and 1099-R on the front.

54 Federal income tax withheld. If any is from Form(s) 1099, check ▶ ☐ | 54 | 1,260 00

55 1992 estimated tax payments and amount applied from 1991 return | 55 | 16,000 00

56 **Earned income credit.** Attach Schedule EIC | 56

57 Amount paid with Form 4868 (extension request) | 57

58 Excess social security, Medicare, and RRTA tax withheld (see page 26) | 58

59 Other payments (see page 26). Check if from a ☐ Form 2439 b ☐ Form 4136 | 59

60 Add lines 54 through 59. These are your **total payments** ▶ 60 17,260 00

Refund or Amount You Owe

61 If line 60 is more than line 53, subtract line 53 from line 60. This is the amount you **OVERPAID.** ▶ 61 122 81

62 Amount of line 61 you want **REFUNDED TO YOU.** ▶ 62 122 81

63 Amount of line 61 you want **APPLIED TO YOUR 1993 ESTIMATED TAX** ▶ 63

Attach check or money order on top of Form(s) W-2, etc., on the front.

64 If line 53 is more than line 60, subtract line 60 from line 53. This is the **AMOUNT YOU OWE.** Attach check or money order for full amount payable to "Internal Revenue Service." Write your name, address, social security number, daytime phone number, and "1992 Form 1040" on it | 64

65 Estimated tax penalty (see page 27). Also include on line 64 | 65

Sign Here

Keep a copy of this return for your records.

Under penalties of perjury, I declare that I have examined this return and accompanying schedules and statements, and to the best of my knowledge and belief, they are true, correct, and complete. Declaration of preparer (other than taxpayer) is based on all information of which preparer has any knowledge.

Your signature *John R. Williams* Date 4-12-93 Your occupation Retailer

Spouse's signature. If a joint return, BOTH must sign. *Jean K. Williams* Date 4-12-93 Spouse's occupation Legal Secretary

Paid Preparer's Use Only

Preparer's signature ▶ Date Check if self-employed ☐ Preparer's social security no.

Firm's name (or yours if self-employed) and address ▶ E.I. No. ZIP code

The net gain from capital assets of $250 was entered on Form 1040 (line 13) from Schedule D, Capital Gains and Losses.

Net rental income of $210 from an 8-unit apartment building, owned jointly by Mr. and Mrs. Williams, plus partnership income of $5,002 were reported on Schedule E, Supplemental Income and Loss, and the total of $5,212 was entered on Form 1040 (line 18). Mrs. Williams had won a door prize of $800 in cash at the City of Verona 4th of July celebration. The $800 was entered on Form 1040 (line 22). The total of $74,875.82 (lines 7-22) was entered on Form 1040 (line 23).

Adjustments to Income

Mr. and Mrs. Williams had three adjustments to income to report on Form 1040 (lines 24 and 25). For 1992, Mr. and Mrs. Williams had each paid the maximum of $2,000 for IRAs. Thus, the maximum deduction of $2,000 available to each qualified person filing jointly was entered (lines 24a and 24b). Mr. Williams' self-employment earnings is qualified compensation for an IRA. Mr. Williams had made his payment of $2,000 on April 2, 1992. Mrs. Williams had made her payment in two parts, the first part of $1,500 on July 2, 1992, and the balance of $500 on April 6, 1993, after the end of the 1992 tax year but before the return was filed on April 12, 1993. Although Mrs. Williams made her last payment to her 1992 IRA in 1993 (prior to the due date of Form 1040), the total amount of the IRA payments made by Mrs. Williams was shown on Form 1040 (line 24b).

The third adjustment to income is for the self-employment tax. Mr. Williams' self-employment income was $62,961 ($57,959 + $5,002). Of this amount, only $58,144.48 (.9235 x $62,961) is subject to self-employment tax. His total self-employment tax is $8,568.19. This amount was calculated on Schedule SE, Self-Employment Tax. One-half of Mr. Williams' self-employment tax, $4,284.10 ($8,568.19/2), is deductible on Form 1040 (line 25).

The total of the adjustments to income, $8,284.10, was subtracted from the total income, $74,875.82, and the difference of $66,591.72 was entered as the *AGI* (lines 31 and 32).

Tax Calculation

Mr. and Mrs. Williams decided that they would determine their own tax and that they would claim itemized deductions. They did not check the boxes (lines 33a, 33b or 33c) as they were not applicable. The amount of their itemized deductions, $7,878.47, was entered (line 34). The itemized deductions were deducted from AGI and the difference of $58,713.25 was entered (line 35). If the Williams had *not* claimed itemized deductions, they could have deducted the standard deduction of $6,000. Because their itemized deductions are greater than the standard deduction, the Williams will pay less tax by claiming their itemized deductions.

The Williams then entered $11,500 (line 36), $2,300 for each of the five exemptions claimed (line 6e). The difference of $47,213.25, the amount of taxable income, was entered (line 37). The Williams used the Tax Tables to determine their tax. Their taxable income was located in the "At least $47,200, but less than $47,250" bracket of the Tax Tables and, following the line for this bracket across to the "married filing jointly" column, the amount of tax, $8,569, was found. This amount was entered (line 38), and a check mark was placed in the box to show that the tax came from the Tax Tables. Since there were no additional taxes to enter (line 39), the $8,569 (line 38) was also entered (line 40).

Credits

The Williams are not entitled to claim any credits, thus the total of $8,569 (line 40) was entered again (line 46).

Other Taxes

The only other tax owed by Mr. and Mrs. Williams was a self-employment tax of $8,568.19 from Schedule SE, Self-Employment Tax. This amount was entered (line 47) and then added to the total regular tax of $8,569 (line 46). The total tax sum of $17,137.19 was entered (line 53).

Other Payments

From the total tax, taxpayers deduct the payments they have previously made in order to determine the balance still due or the amount of the overpayment. Seven types of payments can be entered on Form 1040.

Mr. and Mrs. Williams reported their advance payments on their 1992 tax liability on

Form 1040 (lines 54 and 55). The amount of $1,260 withheld from Mrs. Williams' wage and reported by her employer on Copy B of Form W-2 was entered (line 54). Copy B of Form W-2 would be attached to the front of Form 1040 to support the payment claimed, and Copy C would be retained by Mr. and Mrs. Williams as their record copy. In addition, Mr. and Mrs. Williams had paid $4,000 each quarter on their 1992 estimated tax. The total paid of $16,000 was claimed (line 55). The Williams were not eligible for the EIC (line 56). Since there were no other payments to enter, the total amount of payments of $17,260 ($1,260 + $16,000) was entered (line 60).

Amount Owed or Refund

The Williams' overpayment amounted to $122.81 (line 61), and they elected to receive this amount as a refund (line 62). If elected, the amount of the overpayment could be credited on the 1993 estimated tax (line 63). The total (lines 62 and 63) should be equal to the overpayment (line 61).

When there is an underpayment of estimated taxes, the difference between the total tax (line 53) and the total payments (line 60) is the amount of tax still owed (line 64).

If the amount (line 64) is more than $500 and more than 10% of the total tax, the taxpayer may be subject to a penalty. Form 2210, Underpayment of Estimated Tax by Individuals, or Form 2210F, Underpayment of Estimated Tax by Farmers and Fishermen, should be attached to explain the nature and amount of the penalty due, or to explain the exception to the penalty, if applicable. In addition, the IRS requests that the amount of the penalty be reported in the space provided (line 65) and paid by adding to (line 64) or subtracting from (line 61) as appropriate.

Signatures and Certifications

Both Mr. and Mrs. Williams must sign Form 1040, and both are liable for the payment of the tax and any penalties or interest. Both certify under the penalties of perjury that the return has been examined, including all of the accompanying schedules and statements, and that they are to the best of their knowledge true, correct, and complete. The date of the signature and their occupations are entered. If a person other than Mr. or Mrs. Williams was paid to prepare the return, the signature and identifying number of the preparer would be entered on Form 1040 (bottom of page 2), along with either the preparer's address or the employer's name, address, EIN, and the date.

Special care should be taken to assure that supporting forms and schedules are securely fastened to Form 1040 in the proper number sequence so that they cannot become separated and lost during processing. The signed Form 1040 for the Williams, with all supporting forms and schedules, would be mailed to the Internal Revenue Service Center at Kansas City, MO 64999.

Interest on Under- or Overpayment of Taxes

The rate of interest that the IRS charges for underpayment of taxes, or pays for refunds made more than 45 days after the due date of the return, is adjusted quarterly. The rates are determined by adding three percentage points for underpayments and two percentage points for overpayments to the federal short-term rate. The rates for 1991 and 1992 are:

Quarter Beginning	Overpayment Interest Rate	Underpayment Interest Rate
1-1-91	10	11
4-1-91	9	10
7-1-91	9	10
10-1-91	9	10
1-1-92	8	9
4-1-92	7	8
7-1-92	7	8
10-1-92	6	7

Penalties for Taxpayers

The penalties discussed in the paragraphs below may be charged to individual taxpayers by the IRS unless it is shown that these failures are due to reasonable causes.

Penalty for Filing and Paying Late

The *penalty for late filing* is 5% of the tax due for each month or fraction of a month that the return is late, unless the taxpayer can show a reasonable cause for the delay. The maximum penalty for late filing is 25% of the tax due. The *penalty for late payment* is generally ½ of 1% of the unpaid amount for each month or fraction of a month that the tax is unpaid. The maximum late payment penalty is 25% of the unpaid tax. Taxpayers may reduce the filing penalty by the late payment penalty when both penalties apply.

Fraud Penalty

If there is a deficiency of taxes because of fraud, the penalty is 75% of the underpayment due to fraud. When the fraud penalty applies, neither the negligence penalty nor the delinquency penalty applies.

Penalty for Filing Frivolous Return

A penalty of $500, in addition to any other penalties, can be imposed upon any individual who files a frivolous return. The penalty applies to those who take a frivolous position or try to delay or impede administration of the tax law by filing a return that fails to contain information from which the tax liability can be correctly calculated or on which the tax liability shown is substantially incorrect.

Reasonable Cause

The IRS has guidelines listing the circumstances in which a taxpayer can be excused from certain civil penalties for failure to comply with tax laws. Such circumstances are:

1. Death or serious illness
2. Unavoidable absence
3. Destruction of certain facilities or records
4. Timely mailing
5. Wrong filing place
6. Reliance on competent tax adviser
7. Unobtainable records
8. IRS office visit in which an IRS employee was unable to be seen for reasons beyond taxpayer control
9. Erroneous IRS information

Other reasonable causes may exist, and each case is judged by the IRS on its merits.

Avoiding the Late Filing Penalty

Taxpayers who do not have the money to pay the tax should file on time even though payment cannot be made. Although interest will be charged for late payment, the penalty charge for late filing can be avoided.

Extension of Time to File

Illustration 7-4

Form 4868, Application for Automatic Extension of Time to File U.S. Individual Income Tax Return, can be used by a taxpayer to request an automatic four-month extension of time to file the basic income tax return, Form 1040. An extension will be granted by proper filing of Form 4868 with payment of the balance due as reported on Form 4868 (line 6). This payment is an important aspect of the automatic extension. A filled-in Form 4868 is shown in Illustration 7-4.

When Form 1040 is finally filed, the amount of the payment made with Form 4868 is claimed on Form 1040 (line 57). If a taxpayer and spouse file a joint Form 4868, but do not file a joint Form 1040, the total of the automatic extension tax payment may be claimed on the separate return of either spouse, or divided in any agreed amounts. Likewise, if separate Forms 4868 were filed, the sum of the amounts paid on the separate Forms 4868 can be claimed on a joint return. Form 4868 should be filed with the IRS Center where the taxpayer is required to file Form 1040.

If a taxpayer needs an extension of time to file beyond the four months automatically granted with Form 4868, then Form 2688, Application for Extension of Time to File, should be filed later with the IRS. An extension beyond a total of six months (two months additional) is seldom allowed.

Illustration 7-4
Filled-In Form 4868

Form **4868** Department of the Treasury Internal Revenue Service	**Application for Automatic Extension of Time To File U.S. Individual Income Tax Return**	OMB No. 1545-0188 19**92**

Please Type or Print	Your first name and initial	Last name	Your social security number
	Carla A. Kramer		652 19 9990
	If a joint return, spouse's first name and initial	Last name	Spouse's social security number
	Home address (number, street, and apt. no. or rural route). If you have a P.O. box, see the instructions.		
	6820 W. 59th Street		
	City, town or post office, state, and ZIP code		
	Memphis, TN 38105–1960		

Note: *File this form with the Internal Revenue Service Center where you file your income tax return and pay any amount(s) you owe. This is not an extension of time to pay your tax.*

I request an automatic 4-month extension of time to August 16, 1993, to file Form 1040A or Form 1040 for the calendar year 1992 or to ___________ , 19 ______ , for the fiscal tax year ending ___________ , 19 ______ .

1	Total tax liability for 1992. This is the amount you expect to enter on Form 1040A, line 27, or Form 1040, line 53. If you do not expect to owe tax, enter -0-	**1**	4,580	00

Caution: *You **MUST** enter an amount on line 1 or your extension will be denied. You can estimate this amount, but be as exact as you can with the information you have. If we later find that your estimate was not reasonable, the extension will be null and void.*

2	Federal income tax withheld	**2**	2,400	00
3	1992 estimated tax payments. Include 1991 overpayment allowed as a credit	**3**	2,000	00
4	Other payments and credits you expect to show on Form 1040A or Form 1040 .	**4**	–0–	
5	Add lines 2, 3, and 4	**5**	4,400	00
6	**BALANCE DUE.** Subtract line 5 from line 1. If zero or less, enter -0-. **To get this extension, you MUST pay in full the balance due with this form. Attach check or money order for full amount payable to "Internal Revenue Service." Write your name, address, social security number, daytime phone number, and "1992 Form 4868" on it** . . . . ▶	**6**	180	00

If you expect to owe gift or generation-skipping transfer (GST) tax, complete line 7 (and 8a or 8b if applicable). Do not include income tax on these lines. See the instructions.

7	If you or your spouse plan to file a gift tax return (Form 709 or 709-A) for 1992, generally due by April 15, 1993, see the instructions and check here . . . . { Yourself ▶ ☐ Spouse ▶ ☐	
8a	Enter the amount of gift or GST tax **you** are paying with this form	**8a**
b	Enter the amount of gift or GST tax **your spouse** is paying with this form	**8b**

Signature and Verification

Under penalties of perjury, I declare that I have examined this form, including accompanying schedules and statements, and to the best of my knowledge and belief, it is true, correct, and complete; and, if prepared by someone other than the taxpayer, that I am authorized to prepare this form.

▶ *Carla A. Kramer* | 4/14/93   ▶ ___________________________________
Your signature   Date   Spouse's signature, if filing jointly   Date

▶ ___________________________________
Preparer's signature (other than taxpayer)   Date

If correspondence regarding this extension is to be sent to you at an address other than that shown above or to an agent acting for you, please enter the name of the agent and/or the address where it should be sent.

Please Type or Print	Name
	Number and street (include suite, room, or apt. no.) or P.O. box number if mail is not delivered to street address
	City, town or post office, state, and ZIP code

General Instructions

Purpose of Form

Use Form 4868 to ask for 4 more months to file **Form 1040A** or **Form 1040.** You do not have to explain why you are asking for the extension. We will contact you only if your request is denied.

To get the extra time you **MUST:**

• Fill in Form 4868 correctly, **AND**

• File it by the due date of your return, **AND**
• Pay ALL of the amount shown on line 6.

If you already had 2 extra months to file because you were "out of the country" (explained on page 2) when your return was due, then use this form to ask for an additional 2 months to file.

Do not file Form 4868 if you want the IRS to figure your tax or are under a court order to file your return by the regular due date.

Note: *An extension of time to file your 1992 calendar year income tax return also extends the time to file a gift tax return (**Form 709** or **709-A**) for 1992.*

If the automatic extension does not give you enough time, you can later ask for additional time. But you'll have to give a good reason, and it must be approved by the IRS. To ask for the additional time, you must do **either** of the following:

For Paperwork Reduction Act Notice, see back of form.   Cat. No. 13141W   Form **4868** (1992)

Individual Income Tax Return in Year of Death

A final income tax return must be filed on Form 1040 for a taxpayer in the year of death if, from the beginning of the taxable year up to the date of death, one of the following situations applies:

1. The decedent was subject to one of the gross income requirements for filing a return
2. Social security tax on tips was owed (which would be paid with the final return)
3. The decedent's income was under the gross income requirement for filing a return, but tax was withheld or estimated tax was paid. In this situation Form 1310, Statement of Person Claiming Refund Due a Deceased Taxpayer, should be attached to the return.

The final return of a taxpayer is due on the date it would have been due had the taxpayer lived. Thus the income tax return for a calendar-year taxpayer who died during 1992, regardless of the date of death, would be due on or before April 15, 1993.

The final return and any other return or returns still due would be filed by the executor, administrator, legal representative, or survivor. A joint return can be filed by a surviving spouse, and would usually be filed together by the surviving spouse and the executor or administrator. If no executor or administrator has been appointed before the due date, the surviving spouse can file a joint return anyway. A joint return cannot be filed with a deceased spouse if the surviving spouse is remarried before the end of the year in which the spouse died.

Avoiding the Late Payment Penalty

Form 4868 is an extension of time to file the return, but not an extension of time to pay the tax. Therefore, when filing Form 4868, the taxpayer should pay any taxes due. There could be a penalty for late payment of tax if payment does not accompany this form.

An executor or administrator appointed after a surviving spouse has filed a joint return with a decedent may, within one year from the due date of the return, disaffirm the joint return by filing a separate return for the decedent. The joint return filed by the surviving spouse will then be considered the survivor's separate return and the tax will be recalculated.

If an executor or administrator has been appointed, that person must sign the decedent's final return. If a joint return is filed, the surviving spouse also must sign. If no executor or administrator has been appointed and a joint return is filed, the surviving spouse should sign the return and write in the signature area "Filing as surviving spouse."

In general, *no allocations* of tax deductions are required on a final tax return. If qualified, the full $2,300 for the 1992 personal exemption is allowed for the deceased taxpayer. Medical expenses paid for a decedent may be treated as paid at the time incurred, even when they are paid after the date of death.

Technical assistance should be obtained when the affairs of a decedent are complex, especially when the problems relate to the determination of income and expenses properly reported on the taxpayer's final return and those properly recognized after the date of death and not included on the final return.

Filing an Amended Individual Income Tax Return

Form 1040X, Amended U.S. Individual Income Tax Return, is available to amend an individual income tax return within three years after the date the original return was due or three years after the date it was filed, whichever was later. Use of Form 1040X to correct either a Form 1040 or Form 1040A and to possibly claim a refund could be advantageous to a taxpayer, since Form 1040X is designed to expedite processing by the IRS.

The use of Form 1040X is not mandatory, but is preferred by the IRS over the use of a regular Form 1040 marked "Revised" or a Form 1040A marked "Revised." Form 1040X can be filed only after a taxpayer has filed an original return.

Filled-In Form 1040X

Illustration 7-5

Mr. and Mrs. Steven M. Martin discovered that they had failed to claim a $100 contribution made during 1991 to the General Hospital, Peoria, Illinois, a qualifying hospital. Mr. and Mrs. Martin amended their Form 1040 for 1991 and claimed a refund for 1991 by filing a Form 1040X, shown in Illustration 7-5 on June 15, 1992. Steven's SSN is 471-91-0417, and his spouse's (Sarah J. Martin) is 916-38-2142. The Martins reside at 2886 Linwood Court, Peoria, Illinois 61604-5417.

Mr. and Mrs. Martin entered on Form 1040X, Columns A and C (line 1), their total income of $49,733.66 from their 1991 Form 1040 (line 23). They entered their adjustment to income, $640 (line 2) of original Form 1040 (line 30), and their AGI, $49,093.66 (line 3) of original Form 1040 (line 31). The $100 itemized deduction they had failed to claim was entered on Form 1040X, Column B (line 4). This deduction changed their taxable income on Form 1040X (line 7) from $36,580.68 to $36,480.68.

The tax of $5,821 from the 1991 Tax Tables claimed by the Martins on their original Form 1040 was entered on Form 1040X, Column A (line 8). The Martins determined that their corrected tax (from the Tax Tables) based on taxable income of $36,480.68 was $5,793, and this was entered on Form 1040X, Column C (line 8). The 1991 self-employment tax of $4,177.20 was entered on Columns A and C (line 11).

The original total tax liability of $9,998.20 was then entered on Column A (line 12), and the corrected total tax liability of $9,970.20 was entered on Column C (line 12).

The Martin's total 1991 tax payments of $10,356 ($856 + $9,500) are summarized (line 19). Originally, the Martins received a $357.80 refund (line 20). The balance of their original payments, $9,998.20 (line 21) exceeds their amended tax liability of $9,970.20, Column C (line 12) by $28.00 (line 23). This is the additional refund to which the Martins are entitled.

On Form 1040X, page 2 the Martins made no entry in Part I since the exemptions they had claimed on their Form 1040 had not changed. In Part II, they stated the reason for the change in their deductions.

Certain Procedural Concerns

In this final section of the chapter certain procedural concerns are examined. These include regulations affecting preparers and accounting period requirements. The tax audit procedure and the taxpayer appeal procedure are also reviewed.

Disclosures and Regulation of Preparers

Subject to several exceptions, the Internal Revenue Code provides confidentiality protection to the taxpayer for information provided to tax return preparers. A criminal penalty applies to persons who disclose or use information obtained from a taxpayer for any purpose other than to prepare or assist in the preparation of a return or declaration. Preparers are subject to a fine of $1,000 and/or a 1-year imprisonment for each violation.

The criminal penalty applies to those persons engaged in the business of preparing or providing services in connection with the preparation of income tax returns and individual estimated tax returns, or any person who receives compensation for preparing such a return.

An exception to the penalty is made when disclosure of information is required by the Internal Revenue Code or by a court. Information can also be used for preparation of state and local tax returns and declarations. The Secretary of the Treasury is also authorized to issue regulations stating other uses and disclosures that will be exempted from penalty.

The IRS has estimated that more than 50% of the taxpayers filing income tax returns seek some type of professional or commercial tax advice. An extensive series of provisions related to persons who prepare, for compensation, all

Illustration 7-5
Filled-In Form 1040X, Page 1

Form 1040X
(Rev. November 1991)

Department of the Treasury—Internal Revenue Service

Amended U.S. Individual Income Tax Return
▶ See separate instructions.

OMB No. 1545-0091
Expires 10-31-94

This return is for calendar year ▶ 1991 , OR fiscal year ended ▶ , 19 .

Your first name and initial / Last name	Your social security number
Steven M. Martin	471 : 91 : 0417
If a joint return, spouse's first name and initial / Last name	Spouse's social security number
Sarah J. Martin	916 : 38 : 2142
Home address (number and street). (If you have a P.O. box, see instructions.) Apt. no.	Telephone number (optional)
2886 Linwood Court	(309) 721-0846
City, town or post office, state, and ZIP code. (If you have a foreign address, see instructions.)	For Paperwork Reduction Act Notice, see page 1 of separate instructions.
Peoria, IL 61604-5417	

Please print or type

Enter name and address as shown on original return (if same as above, write "Same"). If changing from separate to joint return, enter names and addresses from original returns.

same

A Service center where original return was filed

Kansas City, MO 64999

B Has original return been changed or audited by the IRS? ☐ Yes ☒ No
If "No," have you been notified that it will be? . . . . ☐ Yes ☒ No
If "Yes," identify the IRS office ▶

C Are you amending your return to include any item (loss, credit, deduction, other tax benefit, or income) relating to a tax shelter required to be registered? . . . . ☐ Yes ☒ No
If "Yes," you **MUST** attach **Form 8271**, Investor Reporting of Tax Shelter Registration Number.

D Filing status claimed. (Note: *You cannot change from joint to separate returns after the due date has passed.*)

On original return ▶ ☐ Single ☒ Married filing joint return ☐ Married filing separate return ☐ Head of household ☐ Qualifying widow(er)
On this return ▶ ☐ Single ☒ Married filing joint return ☐ Married filing separate return ☐ Head of household ☐ Qualifying widow(er)

Income and Deductions (see instructions) (Note: *Be sure to complete page 2.*)		A. As originally reported or as adjusted (see instructions)	B. Net change— Increase or (Decrease)—explain on page 2	C. Correct amount
1	Total income	49,733.66		49,733.66
2	Adjustments to income	640.00		640.00
3	Adjusted gross income (subtract line 2 from line 1)	49,093.66		49,093.66
4	Itemized deductions or standard deduction	6,062.98	100.00	6,162.98
5	Subtract line 4 from line 3	43,030.68		42,930.68
6	Exemptions (if changing, fill in Parts I and II on page 2)	6,450.00		6,450.00
7	Taxable income (subtract line 6 from line 5)	36,580.68		36,480.68
8	Tax (see instructions). (Method used in col. C ________)	5,821.00		5,793.00
9	Credits (see instructions)	–0–		–0–
10	Subtract line 9 from line 8. Enter the result but not less than zero	5,821.00		5,793.00
11	Other taxes (such as self-employment tax, alternative minimum tax)	4,177.20		4,177.20
12	Total tax (add lines 10 and 11)	9,998.20		9,970.20
13	Federal income tax withheld and excess social security, Medicare, and RRTA taxes withheld	856.00		856.00
14	Estimated tax payments	9,500.00		9,500.00
15	Earned income credit			
16	Credits for Federal tax on fuels, regulated investment company, etc.			
17	Amount paid with Form 4868, Form 2688, or Form 2350 (application for extension of time to file)			
18	Amount paid with original return plus additional tax paid after it was filed			
19	Add lines 13 through 18 in column C			10,356.00

Refund or Amount You Owe

20	Overpayment, if any, as shown on original return (or as previously adjusted by the IRS)	357.80
21	Subtract line 20 from line 19 (see instructions)	9,998.20
22	**AMOUNT YOU OWE.** If line 12, col. C, is more than line 21, enter the difference and see instructions	
23	**REFUND** to be received. If line 12, column C, is less than line 21, enter the difference	28.00

Please Sign Here

Under penalties of perjury, I declare that I have filed an original return and that I have examined this amended return, including accompanying schedules and statements, and to the best of my knowledge and belief, this amended return is true, correct, and complete. Declaration of preparer (other than taxpayer) is based on all information of which the preparer has any knowledge.

▶ *Steven M Martin* | 6/15/93   ▶ *Sarah J. Martin* | 6/15/93
Your signature   Date   Spouse's signature (if joint return, BOTH must sign)   Date

Paid Preparer's Use Only

Preparer's signature ▶	Date	Check if self-employed ☐	Preparer's social security no.
Firm's name (or yours if self-employed) and address ▶		E.I. No.	
		ZIP code	

Cat. No. 11360L

Illustration 7-5
Filled-In Form 1040X, Page 2

Form 1040X (Rev. 11-91)   Page **2**

Part I Exemptions (see Form 1040 or Form 1040A instructions)	A. Number originally reported	B. Net change	C. Correct number

If you are not changing your exemptions, do not complete this part.
If claiming more exemptions, complete lines 24–30 and, if applicable, line 31.
If claiming fewer exemptions, complete lines 24–29.

	A. Number originally reported	B. Net change	C. Correct number
24 Yourself and spouse			
Caution: *If your parents (or someone else) can claim you as a dependent (even if they chose not to), you cannot claim an exemption for yourself.*			
25 Your dependent children who lived with you			
26 Your dependent children who did not live with you due to divorce or separation			
27 Other dependents			
28 Total number of exemptions (add lines 24 through 27)			
29 **For tax year 1991,** if the amount on page 1, line 3, is more than $75,000, see the instructions. If line 3 is $75,000 or less, multiply $2,150 by the number of exemptions claimed on line 28. **For tax year 1990,** use $2,050: **for tax year 1989,** use $2,000: **for tax year 1988,** use $1,950. Enter the result here and on page 1. line 6.			

30 Dependents (children and other) not claimed on original return:

No. of your children on line 30 who lived with you ▶ ☐

(a) Dependent's name (first, initial, and last name)	(b) Check if under age 1 (under age 2 if a 1989 or 1990 return: under age 5 if a 1988 return)	(c) If age 1 or older (age 2 or older if a 1989 or 1990 return: age 5 or older if a 1988 return), enter dependent's social security number	(d) Dependent's relationship to you	(e) No. of months lived in your home

No. of your children on line 30 who didn't live with you due to divorce or separation (see instructions) ▶ ☐

No. of other dependents listed on line 30 ▶ ☐

31 If your child listed on line 30 didn't live with you but is claimed as your dependent under a pre-1985 agreement, check here . . . ▶ ☐

Part II Explanation of Changes to Income, Deductions, and Credits

Enter the line number from page 1 for each item you are changing and give the reason for each change. Attach all supporting forms and schedules for items changed. Be sure to include your name and social security number on any attachments.

If the change pertains to a net operating loss carryback or a general business credit carryback, attach the schedule or form that shows the year in which the loss or credit occurred. See instructions. Also, check here . . . ▶ ☐

Line 4:   Contribution of $100 paid to General Hospital. Peoria. Illinois. on July 15.

1991. was omitted in error on Line 13. Schedule A. Form 1040.

Part III Presidential Election Campaign Fund

Checking below will not increase your tax or reduce your refund.

If you did not previously want to have $1 go to the fund but now want to, check here . . . ▶ ☐
If a joint return and your spouse did not previously want to have $1 go to the fund but now wants to, check here . . . ▶ ☐

or a substantial part of any return or claim for refund of tax are included under the income tax provisions of the Internal Revenue Code. These provisions cover the employers of return preparers in addition to the actual preparers. The provisions are to regulate preparers, to provide the IRS with power to enforce proper practices, and to provide procedures to make it easier to identify and deter dishonest or negligent preparers who consistently make errors on large numbers of returns. Substantial civil penalties for understatement of taxpayers' income tax liabilities on returns or claims for refund due to negligent or willful attempts to understate liability are provided.

A tax return preparer must furnish a completed copy of the return or claim for refund to the taxpayer at the time the return is presented for the taxpayer's signature. Preparers are also required to retain for three years, and make available for inspection, a completed copy of each return or claim prepared or a list of the names and TINs of taxpayers for whom returns or claims were prepared. A $25 penalty will be assessed a tax return preparer who fails to sign a return, fails to furnish a copy of the return to the taxpayer, or fails to furnish an TIN. There is a $1,000 penalty for preparers who aid and abet a taxpayer in understating the amount of the tax liability.

Public Disclosure of Written Determinations

Any written determination issued by the IRS, such as a private letter ruling, as well as any background file documents relating to it, is open to public inspection after identifying details and various commercial and financial information have been deleted.

A *written determination* is a statement issued by the National Office of the IRS for the interpretation and application of tax laws for a specific situation. A taxpayer may request from the District Director a determination letter for the application of policies that have already been interpreted by the National Office.

On the basis that full public disclosure of its written determinations would hinder the IRS ruling program, Congress has provided for a system of review for private rulings and other determinations of confidential information before they are made public. In addition, certain categories of confidential information have been specified to be deleted before disclosures are made.

Disclosure of Returns and Return Information

The Internal Revenue Code has been amended to control what had been largely executive and administrative practices regarding confidentiality and disclosure of tax returns and tax return information.

The provisions provide assurance for the taxpayer that tax returns and return information are confidential and not subject to disclosure to federal or state agencies or employees except as provided by the Internal Revenue Code.

In relationship to confidentiality rules, the terms "return" and "return information" have specific, limited meanings. A *return* means any tax return, information return, declaration of estimated tax, or claim for refund filed under the Internal Revenue Code on behalf of or with respect to any persons. Included with these items are any amendment, supplement, supporting schedule, or attachment filed with the return. Written determinations, as discussed in the preceding section of this text, that are included with or attached to a filed return by a taxpayer are not returns. *Return information* must be in a form that is associated or identified with a particular person. Included are the following:

1. The taxpayer's identity
2. The nature, source, or amount of income, payments, receipts, deductions, net worth, tax liability, deficiencies, etc.
3. Data received or prepared by the IRS regarding a return, deficiency, penalty, interest, offense, etc.
4. Information regarding actual or possible investigations of a return
5. Any part of an IRS written determination or background file document not open to public inspection

The provisions specify to whom returns and return information may be disclosed and the purposes for which disclosed returns and information may be used. Persons to whom returns and return information may be disclosed are the designee of the taxpayer, state tax officials, persons having a material interest, Congressional committees, the White House and other federal agencies, the Treasury Department and Justice Department in civil and criminal tax cases, federal agencies in nontax criminal cases, and the General Accounting Office. Restrictions as to exceptions, use, and conditions of disclosure are specified.

Accounting Periods

The income tax returns of individuals are prepared on the basis of a taxable year. The Tax Reform Act of 1986 requires that most individual taxpayers file their tax returns for a calendar year, but in some circumstances a fiscal year can be used. The *calendar year* is a period of 12 months ending on December 31. A *fiscal year* is a period of 12 months ending on the last day of any month other than December. A taxable year may be either the calendar year or a fiscal year depending upon the basis on which the net income of the taxpayer is calculated. Most individuals file their returns on the calendar-year basis. However, individuals who are allowed to keep their regular books of account on a fiscal-year basis must file their returns on the same basis.

Under no circumstances may an income tax return be made for an accounting period of more than 12 months. When there is a change in the basis of calculating net income from one taxable year to another taxable year, it is necessary to file a return for a fractional part of a year. Thus, if an individual changes the taxable year from a fiscal year ending on March 31 to a calendar year, a return must be filed for a period of 9 months extending from April 1 to December 31 inclusive. When a return is filed for a period of less than a year because of a change in the accounting period, the income must be calculated on an annual basis. This is done by multiplying the amount of the taxable income for the period (exemptions must be prorated and itemized deductions must be claimed in the determination of taxable income) by 12 and dividing by the number of months in the short period for which the return is made.

EXAMPLE 9 ——————————————

If a taxpayer files a return for a period of 9 months, during which the actual taxable income amounted to $6,000, it would be necessary to calculate the income on an annual basis as follows:

$ 6,000 x (12 months/9 months) = $8,000

The tax should then be calculated on the basis of the annual taxable income of $8,000. After calculating the tax on the basis of the annual income, the amount of the tax to be paid is ascertained by multiplying the result by the number of months in the short period for which the return is made and dividing by 12. Thus, if the tax on an annual income of $8,000 amounted to $1,204, the actual tax to be paid would be calculated as follows:

$1,204 x (9 months/12 months) = $903

If no books are kept, returns must be made on the basis of the calendar year. Keeping books means the maintenance of a systematic record that will adequately and clearly provide information to the taxpayer about income and expenses. It does not mean the keeping of a few casual notes that only enable the taxpayer to estimate income in lieu of calculating actual income.

Except in the case of a first return, taxpayers must make a return for the current taxable year on the same basis as the return for the previous taxable year, unless the accounting period has been changed with the approval of the Commissioner of the IRS. When a change in the accounting period is made, a short-period return is required to effect the change. Official consent is required before the change of an accounting period. Application for change in accounting period must be filed on Form 1128, Application for Change in Accounting Period, with the IRS on or before the fifteenth day of the second month following the close of the short period for which a return is required.

A change in accounting period must serve a business purpose. The only cases where individual taxpayers may change their accounting periods without obtaining prior permission from the Commissioner are:

1. In the case of a partnership where individual partners need to change to the same taxable year as the partnership.
2. In the case of a newly married husband or wife who want the same accounting period so that they may file a joint return.

When a taxpayer who has been filing calendar-year returns begins a new business as a sole proprietor, the calendar-year basis must be used for filing the business return. This is because income and deductions of the business must be included in the taxpayer's individual return.

A fiscal-year taxpayer will ordinarily file a final return and pay the balance of any tax due on or before the fifteenth day of the fourth month following the close of the fiscal year. Thus, if the fiscal year ends on June 30, the final return must be filed on or before October 15.

However, a final return may be filed on or before the last day of the month following the close of the fiscal year. This would avoid the necessity of paying the fourth installment of the estimated tax or of filing an amended declaration of the tax for the preceding year to avoid a penalty for underestimation of the tax.

Audit

Illustration 7-6

The IRS uses computers to identify income tax returns that might need an audit. A diagram of the income tax audit procedure of the IRS is shown in Illustration 7-6.

Mathematical or Clerical Errors

When returns are filed with the IRS Centers, they are initially checked for mathematical or clerical errors. These errors are defined as:

1. An error in arithmetic shown on the return
2. Incorrect use of any IRS table, if the incorrect use is apparent from the existence of other information on the return
3. Inconsistent entries on the return
4. Omission of information necessary to substantiate a return entry
5. Entry of a deduction or credit item amount that exceeds a statutory limit of a specified monetary amount, percentage, ratio, or fraction, if the items entering into the application of that limit appear on the return

The mathematical errors are corrected and a notice of the correction is sent to the taxpayer, asking for payment of any additional tax or enclosing a refund for any overpayment.

Selection of Returns to be Audited

Returns that are most in need of an examination are identified by the computer through means of mathematical formulas developed by the IRS under what it calls the *Discriminant*

Function System. A high mathematical score indicates a probability of significant tax changes on a return. Some examples of high-level audit items include claims for refunds of $200,000 or more, claims involving mathematical errors that cannot be resolved without looking over the taxpayer's records, claims involving income from pension or profit-sharing plans, or estate tax claims. Examples of average-level audit items include an increase of three or more exemptions, a decrease of $2,000 or more in interest or dividend income, moving expenses exceeding $5,000, a decrease in net rental income of $2,000 or more, or decreases in capital gains or increases in capital losses exceeding $10,000. Returns may also be selected for examination under the *Taxpayer Compliance Measurement Program,* a random selection system designed to measure and evaluate taxpayer compliance characteristics.

Returns containing items that might not be considered allowable (such as certain charitable contributions or medical expenses) are delivered to the audit division at the Regional Service Center for correction by *correspondence.* Returns having the greatest audit possibility are sent to the District audit division to be examined. Within the District audit division, there are two types of audits. One is the *office audit* made either by correspondence or office interviews. In the latter case, a short talk may be all that is needed to clear up any questions. The other is the *field audit* conducted by IRS agents either in the IRS office or by calling on the taxpayer.

Disclosure of IRS Audit Standards. To eliminate attempts by taxpayers to obtain disclosure of the IRS audit-selection standards, the Economic Recovery Tax Act of 1981 makes it clear that, after July 19, 1981, the Federal statutory disclosure requirements do not apply to standards used or to be used for the selection of returns for examination whenever the Treasury Department determines that such disclosures will seriously impair the assessment, collection, or enforcement of the federal tax laws.

Length of Time of Audit

At the present time, the National Office of the IRS requires examination of income tax returns to be completed within 26 months after the due date of the return or the date filed, whichever is later. In the course of an audit,

Illustration 7-6
Income Tax Audit Procedure

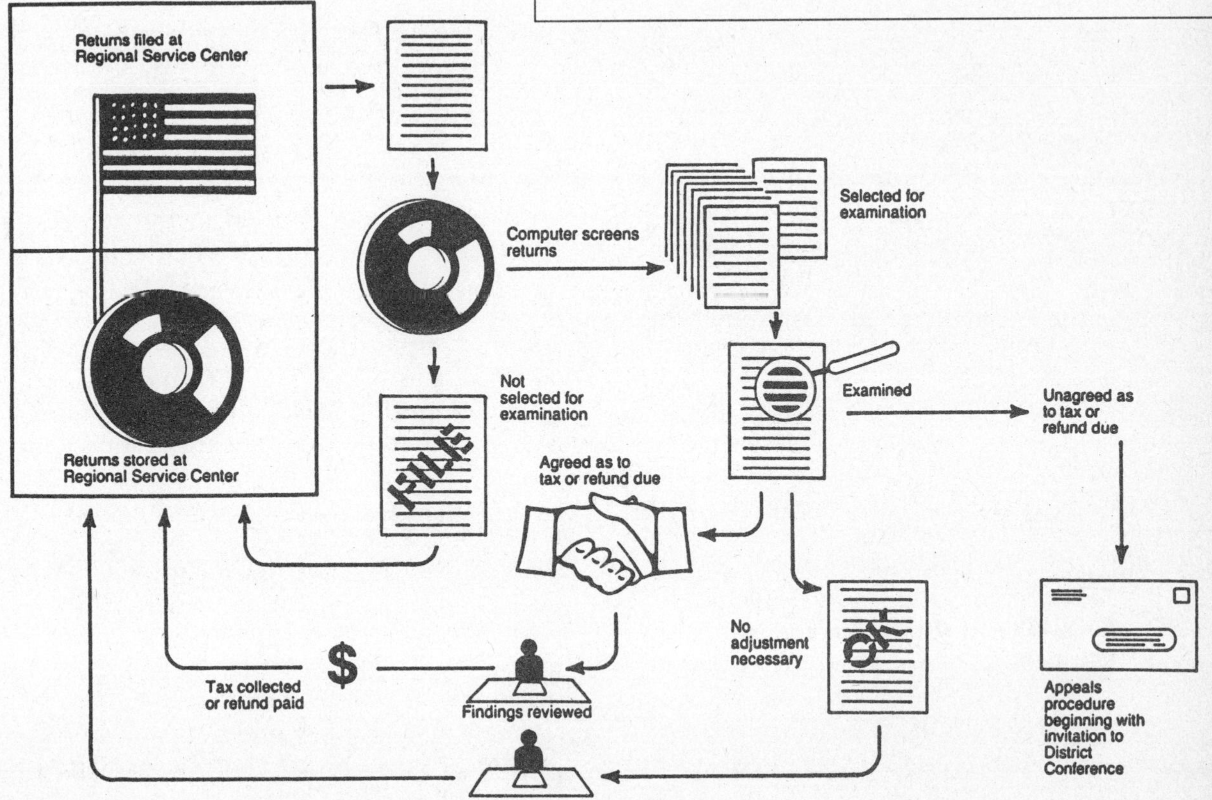

an agent may need to audit the returns for the other years that are within the statute of limitations. As a general rule, the law gives the government three years after a return is filed in which to assess any additional tax. There are exceptions to this rule. For example, if anyone who is required to file a return fails to do so, or if anyone files a fraudulent return with the intention of evading the tax, the tax may be assessed or court proceedings may be begun at any time. If a taxpayer omits from a return an amount in excess of 25% of reported gross income, the government has six years in which to assess more tax.

Appeal

If a taxpayer does not agree with the findings of an audit, appeal procedures are available. In a correspondence audit, the taxpayer will receive a report of the findings along with a *30-day letter* describing the taxpayer's appeal rights. In a field audit, the taxpayer will receive a copy of the examination report along with the 30-day letter. The taxpayer has a right to request a conference with the examining officer within 15 days from the date of the letter. If a conference is not desired, the taxpayer must advise the District within 30 days what the choice of action will be.

An *Appeals Office* headed by a Regional Director of Appeals is established in each of the seven IRS Regions, and each office has the authority to settle cases fully. If the total amount of the proposed additional tax or claimed refund does not exceed $2,500 for the year, the taxpayer will be granted an Appeals Office conference merely by requesting it. If the proposed additional tax or claimed refund exceeds $2,500 for the year, an Appeals Office conference will be granted when the taxpayer files a written protest stating the facts upon which the appeal is based.

If the taxpayer and the Appeals Office cannot agree on the issues in dispute, the taxpayer would receive a *90-day deficiency notice*. This must be mailed to the taxpayer within three years of the date that the income tax return was filed. The taxpayer may petition for a review in Tax Court within 90 days after the deficiency notice is mailed.

A taxpayer can petition for a review of the Tax Court decision by the Court of Appeals. Final disposition of the case may be taken to the United States Supreme Court. It may take years for all these steps, but final assessment of tax due from a taxpayer may not be made until the case is closed. The Commissioner then has 60 days from the final decision to make an assessment of tax from the taxpayer.

Taxpayer Rights

Taxpayers have the right to plan their business and personal affairs so that they will pay the least amount of tax that is due under the law. They also have the right to be treated fairly, professionally, promptly, and courteously by the IRS.

Taxpayers are entitled to information and IRS assistance in complying with the tax laws. The IRS provides a wide variety of informational material, educational programs, and tax assistance programs to aid people in understanding and complying with the tax laws. IRS Publication 910, *Guide to Free Tax Services*, is a catalog of free IRS services and publications.

Taxpayers needing a copy of a prior year tax return may receive such by completing Form 4506, Request for Copy of Tax Form, and sending it to the IRS along with a small fee. If only certain information is needed, such as reported income from a prior year, the taxpayer may get this information free by writing, visiting, or calling an IRS office.

Special assistance programs are available to people who cannot resolve their tax problems through normal channels or whose tax problems cause significant hardship—inability to provide necessities.

People having a complaint about the IRS may write to the District Director or the Service Center Director for their area. Additional information on taxpayer rights may be found in IRS Publication 1, *Your Rights as a Taxpayer.*

Illustration 7-7

Illustration 7-7 shows a diagram of the income tax appeal procedure.

Illustration 7-7
Income Tax Appeal Procedure

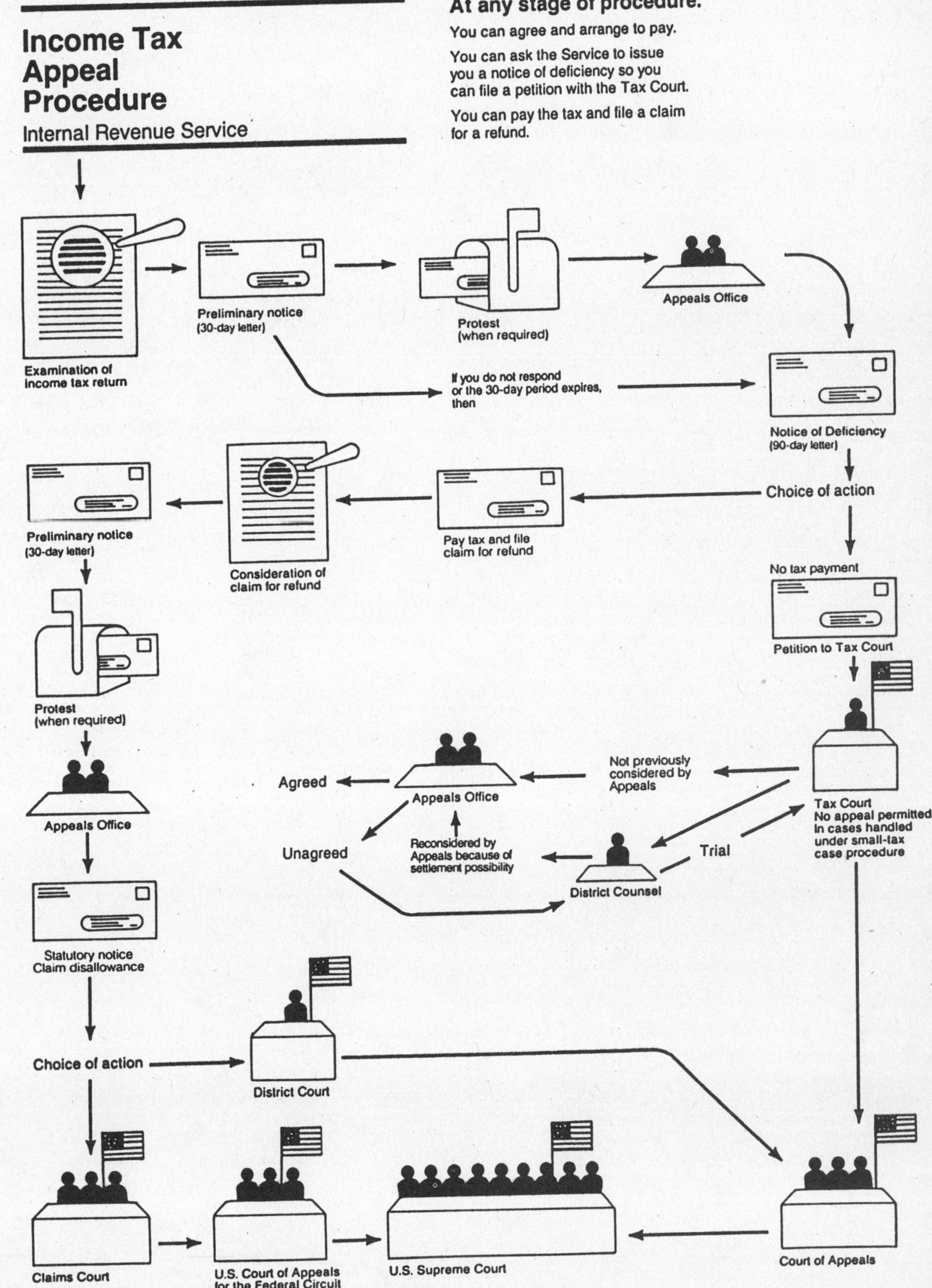

C H A P T E R   7

Questions and Problems

1. **a.** Rosemary R. James is employed as an attorney and also operates a consulting business on the side. If net earnings from self-employment (consulting business) in 1992 were $350, how much self-employment tax would be paid?

   b. If net earnings from self-employment were $10,000, how much self-employment tax would be paid if her salary as an attorney was $40,000?

   c. If net earnings from self-employment were $130,000, how much self-employment tax would be paid if her salary as an attorney was $40,000?

   d. If net earnings from self-employment were $130,000, how much self-employment tax would be paid if her salary as an attorney was $80,000?

2. Indicate T (true) or F (false) for each statement regarding self-employment tax:

   _____ **a.** Resident aliens do not have to pay self-employment tax.

   _____ **b.** Shareholders in an S corporation must treat their share of the corporation's taxable income as self-employment income.

   _____ **c.** Interest on accounts receivable received in a trade or business is treated as self-employment income.

   _____ **d.** Babysitters who provide child care in the parent's home must treat their earnings as self-employment income.

   _____ **e.** Registered nurses who are hired directly by the patient to provide private nursing services are treated as self-employed individuals.

_____ **f.** Licensed real estate agents working out of a real estate agency are generally treated as employees of the real estate agency.

_____ **g.** Amway, Avon, Shaklee, and Tupperware distributors are treated as self-employed individuals.

_____ **h.** All executors of estates are treated as self-employed.

3. Charles A. Roderick, a professor at Carlock Central College, is a part-time computer consultant. Charles received a salary of $45,000 from the college. Income taxes and social security taxes have been properly withheld by the employer. Charles' net profit from consulting was $30,000. Using Schedule SE on the following pages, calculate Charles' self-employment tax. His SSN is 346-69-3674.

4. Indicate T (true) and F (false) for each statement regarding the AMT:

_____ **a.** The AMT for individuals is calculated at the rate of 21%.

_____ **b.** Within limitations, married taxpayers, filing jointly, may reduce their taxable income by a $30,000 exemption.

_____ **c.** Within limitations, HOH filers may reduce their taxable income by a $20,000 exemption.

_____ **d.** Exemptions are phased out at the rate of $.25 for each dollar in excess of a specified income figure.

_____ **e.** For single taxpayers, the exemption phase out begins when AMTI exceeds $75,000.

5. Indicate T (true) and F (false) for each statement regarding an extension of time to file.

_____ **a.** Taxpayers may receive an automatic extension of six months to file their tax return.

_____ **b.** To receive an automatic extension, taxpayers should file Form 2608, Application for Extension of Time to File.

_____ **c.** An automatic extension to file also extends the payment of the tax.

_____ **d.** If a taxpayer requests an automatic extension of time to file, no penalty will be assessed for late payment of the tax.

_____ **e.** An extension of time to file beyond six months is seldom allowed.

6. Mildred K. Hayworth, a single taxpayer 55 years of age and with good vision, SSN 484-58-4637, resides at 916 Wellington Street, Fresno, California 93730-3236. She is a sales representative and was in a serious automobile accident on April 2, 1993. As a result of the accident she was hospitalized and unable to complete her income tax return for 1992 by the due date of April 15, 1993. The following information was available:

Federal income tax withheld	$ 4,952
Social security employee tax	$ 2,295
Wages paid subject to withholding	$30,000
Social security wages paid	$30,000

In addition to the above, Miss Hayworth estimated that her other income for 1992 would be approximately $6,500. She is entitled to claim one exemption and paid $700 estimated tax. She is unsure of her total itemized deductions, so she used the standard deduction in figuring her tentative tax.

a. Using the above data, calculate the tentative 1992 income tax liability for Miss Hayworth.

<table>
<tr>
<td>SCHEDULE SE
(Form 1040)

Department of the Treasury
Internal Revenue Service</td>
<td align="center">Self-Employment Tax

▶ See Instructions for Schedule SE (Form 1040).

▶ Attach to Form 1040.</td>
<td>OMB No. 1545-0074
1992
Attachment
Sequence No. 17</td>
</tr>
<tr>
<td colspan="2">Name of person with self-employment income (as shown on Form 1040)</td>
<td>Social security number of person
with self-employment income ▶</td>
</tr>
</table>

Who Must File Schedule SE

You must file Schedule SE if:

- Your wages (and tips) subject to social security AND Medicare tax (or railroad retirement tax) were less than $130,200; **AND**
- Your *net earnings from self-employment from other than church employee income* (line 4 of Short Schedule SE or line 4c of Long Schedule SE) were $400 or more;
  OR
- You had church employee income (as defined on page SE-1) of $108.28 or more.

Exception. If your only self-employment income was from earnings as a minister, member of a religious order, or Christian Science practitioner, AND you filed **Form 4361** and received IRS approval not to be taxed on those earnings, DO NOT file Schedule SE. Instead, write "Exempt–Form 4361" on Form 1040, line 47.

May I Use Short Schedule SE or MUST I Use Long Schedule SE?

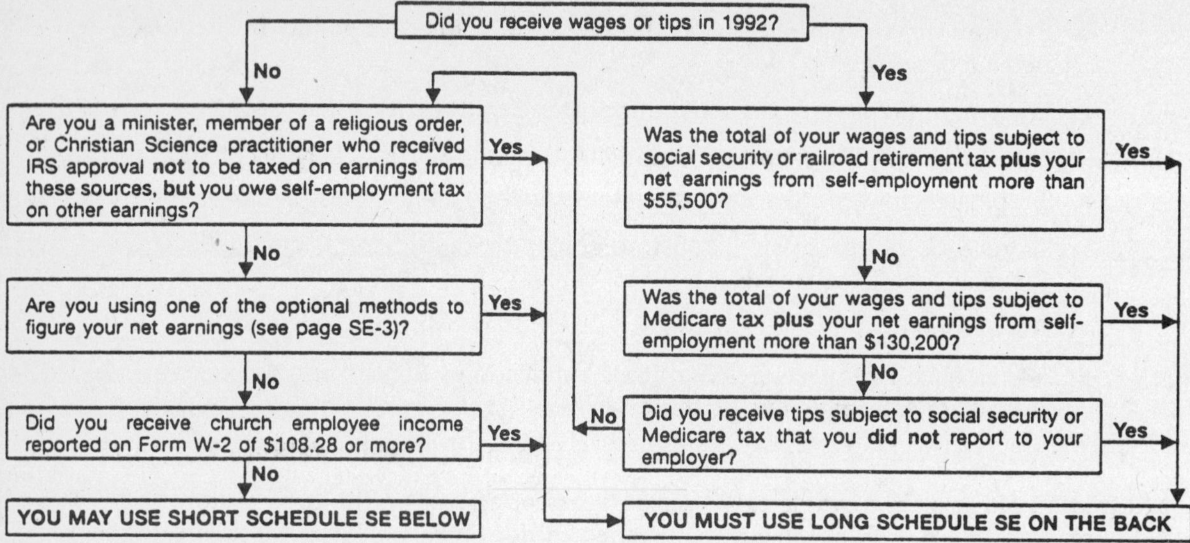

Section A—Short Schedule SE. Caution: *Read above to see if you must use Long Schedule SE on the back (Section B).*

1	Net farm profit or (loss) from Schedule F, line 36, and farm partnerships, Schedule K-1 (Form 1065), line 15a	**1**
2	Net profit or (loss) from Schedule C, line 31; Schedule C-EZ, line 3; and Schedule K-1 (Form 1065), line 15a (other than farming). See page SE-2 for other income to report	**2**
3	Combine lines 1 and 2	**3**
4	**Net earnings from self-employment.** Multiply line 3 by 92.35% (.9235). If less than $400, **do not** file this schedule; you do not owe self-employment tax . . . . ▶	**4**
5	**Self-employment tax.** If the amount on line 4 is: • $55,500 or less, multiply line 4 by 15.3% (.153) and enter the result. • More than $55,500 but less than $130,200, multiply the amount in excess of $55,500 by 2.9% (.029). Then, add $8,491.50 to the result and enter the total. • $130,200 or more, enter $10,657.80. Also, enter this amount on Form 1040, line 47	**5**

Note: *Also, enter one-half of the amount from line 5 on Form 1040, line 25.*

Schedule SE (Form 1040) 1992   Attachment Sequence No. **17**   Page **2**

Name of person with **self-employment** income (as shown on Form 1040)	Social security number of person with **self-employment** income ▶

Section B—Long Schedule SE

A   If you are a minister, member of a religious order, or Christian Science practitioner AND you filed **Form 4361,** but you had $400 or more of **other** net earnings from self-employment, check here and continue with Part I . . . . ▶ ☐

B   If your only income subject to self-employment tax is church employee income and you are **not** a minister or a member of a religious order, skip lines 1 through 4b. Enter -0- on line 4c and go to line 5a.

Part I   **Self-Employment Tax**

1	Net farm profit or (loss) from Schedule F, line 36, and farm partnerships, Schedule K-1 (Form 1065), line 15a. **Note:** *Skip this line if you use the farm optional method. See requirements in Part II below and on page SE-3* .	**1**	
2	Net profit or (loss) from Schedule C, line 31; Schedule C-EZ, line 3; and Schedule K-1 (Form 1065), line 15a (other than farming). See page SE-2 for other income to report. **Note:** *Skip this line if you use the nonfarm optional method. See requirements in Part II below and on page SE-3*	**2**	
3	Combine lines 1 and 2	**3**	
4a	If line 3 is more than zero, multiply line 3 by 92.35% (.9235). Otherwise, enter amount from line 3	**4a**	
b	If you elected one or both of the optional methods, enter the total of lines 17 and 19 here . .	**4b**	
c	Combine lines 4a and 4b. If less than $400, **do not** file this schedule; you do not owe self-employment tax. **Exception.** If less than $400 and you had church employee income, enter -0- and continue . ▶	**4c**	
5a	Enter your church employee income from Form W-2. **Caution:** *See page SE-1 for definition of church employee income* **5a**		
b	Multiply line 5a by 92.35% (.9235). If less than $100, enter -0- . . .	**5b**	
6	**Net earnings from self-employment.** Add lines 4c and 5b	**6**	
7	Maximum amount of combined wages and self-employment earnings subject to social security tax or the 6.2% portion of the 7.65% railroad retirement (tier 1) tax for 1992	**7**	55,500 00
8a	Total social security wages and tips (from Form(s) W-2) and railroad retirement (tier 1) compensation **8a**		
b	Unreported tips subject to social security tax (from Form 4137, line 9) **8b**		
c	Add lines 8a and 8b	**8c**	
9	Subtract line 8c from line 7. If zero or less, enter -0- here and on line 10 and go to line 12a ▶	**9**	
10	Multiply the **smaller** of line 6 or line 9 by 12.4% (.124)	**10**	
11	Maximum amount of combined wages and self-employment earnings subject to Medicare tax or the 1.45% portion of the 7.65% railroad retirement (tier 1) tax for 1992	**11**	130,200 00
12a	Total Medicare wages and tips (from Form(s) W-2) and railroad retirement (tier 1) compensation **12a**		
b	Unreported tips subject to Medicare tax (from Form 4137, line 14) **12b**		
c	Add lines 12a and 12b	**12c**	
13	Subtract line 12c from line 11. If zero or less, enter -0- here and on line 14 and go to line 15 .	**13**	
14	Multiply the **smaller** of line 6 or line 13 by 2.9% (.029)	**14**	
15	**Self-employment tax.** Add lines 10 and 14. Enter the result here and on Form 1040, line 47 . **Note:** *Also, enter one-half of the amount from line 15 on Form 1040, line 25.*	**15**	

Part II   **Optional Methods To Figure Net Earnings** (See **Who Can File Schedule SE** on page SE-1 and **Optional Methods** on page SE-3.)

Farm Optional Method. You may use this method **only** if **(a)** Your gross farm income[1] was not more than $2,400 **or (b)** Your gross farm income[1] was more than $2,400 and your net farm profits[2] were less than $1,733.

16	Maximum income for optional methods	**16**	1,600 00
17	Enter the **smaller** of: two-thirds (⅔) of gross farm income[1] or $1,600. Also, include this amount on line 4b above	**17**	

Nonfarm Optional Method. You may use this method **only** if **(a)** Your net nonfarm profits[3] were less than $1,733 and also less than 72.189% of your gross nonfarm income,[4] **and (b)** You had net earnings from self-employment of at least $400 in 2 of the prior 3 years. **Caution:** *You may use this method no more than five times.*

18	Subtract line 17 from line 16	**18**	
19	Enter the **smaller** of: two-thirds (⅔) of gross nonfarm income **or** the amount on line 18. Also, include this amount on line 4b above	**19**	

[1] From Schedule F, line 11, and Schedule K-1 (Form 1065), line 15b.   [3] From Schedule C, line 31; Schedule C-EZ, line 3; and Schedule K-1 (Form 1065), line 15a.
[2] From Schedule F, line 36, and Schedule K-1 (Form 1065), line 15a.   [4] From Schedule C, line 7; Schedule C-EZ, line 1; and Schedule K-1 (Form 1065), line 15c.

b. Prepare Form 4868, Application for Automatic Extension of Time to File U.S. Individual Income Tax Return, using the blank form reproduced below, for Mildred K. Hayworth. The form was signed April 12, 1993.

Form **4868** Department of the Treasury Internal Revenue Service	**Application for Automatic Extension of Time To File U.S. Individual Income Tax Return**	OMB No. 1545-0188 19**92**

Please Type or Print	Your first name and initial	Last name	Your social security number
	If a joint return, spouse's first name and initial	Last name	Spouse's social security number
	Home address (number, street, and apt. no. or rural route). If you have a P.O. box, see the instructions.		
	City, town or post office, state, and ZIP code		

Note: *File this form with the Internal Revenue Service Center where you file your income tax return and pay any amount(s) you owe. **This is not an extension of time to pay your tax.***

I request an automatic 4-month extension of time to August 16, 1993, to file Form 1040A or Form 1040 for the calendar year 1992 or to _____________ , 19 _______ , for the fiscal tax year ending _______________________ , 19 _____

1 Total tax liability for 1992. This is the amount you expect to enter on Form 1040A, line 27, or Form 1040, line 53. If you do not expect to owe tax, enter -0- **1**

   Caution: *You **MUST** enter an amount on line 1 or your extension will be denied. You can estimate this amount, but be as exact as you can with the information you have. If we later find that your estimate was not reasonable, the extension will be null and void.*

2 Federal income tax withheld **2**
3 1992 estimated tax payments. Include 1991 overpayment allowed as a credit **3**
4 Other payments and credits you expect to show on Form 1040A or Form 1040 . **4**
5 Add lines 2, 3, and 4 **5**
6 **BALANCE DUE.** Subtract line 5 from line 1. If zero or less, enter -0-. **To get this extension, you MUST pay in full the balance due with this form. Attach check or money order for full amount payable to "Internal Revenue Service." Write your name, address, social security number, daytime phone number, and "1992 Form 4868" on it** . . . . ▶ **6**

If you expect to owe gift or generation-skipping transfer (GST) tax, complete line 7 (and 8a or 8b if applicable). Do not include income tax on these lines. See the instructions.

7 If you or your spouse plan to file a gift tax return (Form 709 or 709-A) for 1992, generally due by April 15, 1993, see the instructions and check here . . . Yourself ▶ ☐   Spouse ▶ ☐

8a Enter the amount of gift or GST tax **you** are paying with this form **8a**
  b Enter the amount of gift or GST tax **your spouse** is paying with this form **8b**

Signature and Verification

Under penalties of perjury, I declare that I have examined this form, including accompanying schedules and statements, and to the best of my knowledge and belief, it is true, correct, and complete; and, if prepared by someone other than the taxpayer, that I am authorized to prepare this form.

▶ Your signature ______________________ Date ________   ▶ Spouse's signature, if filing jointly ______________ Date ________

▶ Preparer's signature (other than taxpayer) __________________________ Date ________

If correspondence regarding this extension is to be sent to you at an address other than that shown above or to an agent acting for you, please enter the name of the agent and/or the address where it should be sent.

Please Type or Print	Name
	Number and street (include suite, room, or apt. no.) or P.O. box number if mail is not delivered to street address
	City, town or post office, state, and ZIP code

General Instructions

Purpose of Form

Use Form 4868 to ask for 4 more months to file **Form 1040A** or **Form 1040.** You do not have to explain why you are asking for the extension. We will contact you only if your request is denied.

To get the extra time you **MUST:**
- Fill in Form 4868 correctly, **AND**
- File it by the due date of your return, **AND**
- Pay ALL of the amount shown on line 6.

   If you already had 2 extra months to file because you were "out of the country" (explained on page 2) when your return was due, then use this form to ask for an additional 2 months to file.

   Do not file Form 4868 if you want the IRS to figure your tax or are under a court order to file your return by the regular due date.

Note: *An extension of time to file your 1992 calendar year income tax return also extends the time to file a gift tax return (**Form 709** or **709-A**) for 1992.*

   If the automatic extension does not give you enough time, you can later ask for additional time. But you'll have to give a good reason, and it must be approved by the IRS. To ask for the additional time, you must do **either** of the following:

For Paperwork Reduction Act Notice, see back of form.   Cat. No. 13141W   Form **4868** (1992)

7. On May 8, 1993, Mildred K. Hayworth (see Problem 6) was recovered from the accident sufficiently to complete her records and obtain the additional data needed to file her Form 1040 for 1992. Mildred paid the balance due when Form 4868 was filed with the IRS on April 12, 1993. The information from Problem 6 about her income as a sales representative is correct as stated. The specifics of the other income estimated at $6,500 in Problem 6 were actually as follows:

a. Interest received on bank account . . . . $ 300.00
b. Prize received as contestant on TV quiz show 3,800.00
c. Self-employment income of $100 per month for special weekend consulting on sales
    management (no business expenses were incurred) 1,200.00
d. State income tax refund for 1991 (itemized deductions were claimed in 1991) 350.00
e. A 1992 Form W-2 for wages received for 1 week of employment with another employer
    during her vacation from her regular employer, reported the following:

Wages paid subject to withholding	$205.00
Federal income taxes withheld	(41.00)
Social security employee tax	(15.68)
Net take-home pay received from above	148.32
Total	$5,798.32

Miss Hayworth actually paid $3,800 for itemized deductions. Miss Hayworth elected to have $1 of her tax go to the presidential election campaign fund.

Prepare Form 1040, reproduced on the following pages, for Mildred K. Hayworth. Assume that the needed schedules have already been completed.

8. Ms. Arlene K. Kildow, SSN 366-57-4672, 42 years of age, is a widow and provides for the full support of a daughter, 17 years of age. The daughter, Marie T. Kildow, SSN 642-08-9131, resides with Arlene at 1421 Blue Acre Dr., Shorewood Hills, Wisconsin 53711-2014. Arlene claims Marie as a dependent. George K. Kildow, Arlene's deceased husband, had died on November 4, 1991.

Arlene Kildow, employed as an accountant, received a Form W-2 from her employer for 1992 reporting the following:

Wages	$36,000
Federal income tax withheld	4,260
Wisconsin income tax withheld	2,160
Social security tax withheld	2,754

All itemized deductions that can be claimed by Arlene in 1992, *excluding* Wisconsin income tax mentioned above, totaled $2,800, including $800 of charitable contributions. Dividends and interest received in 1992 were as follows:

	Dividends
Delhi Manufacturing Co. common stock dividend (cash)	$220
Ace Corporation preferred stock dividend (cash)	160

	Interest
U.S. Treasury bonds	$160
Shorewood Savings and Loan Company	80
First National Bank savings account	30
Certificate of Deposit, First Bank	134
City of Eagle, Wisconsin, bonds	720

Marie T. Kildow earned $1,820 working at a summer camp as a counselor. Social security tax of $139.23, federal income tax of $208, and Wisconsin income tax of $69.60 had been withheld from her earnings. In addition, she received $1,400 of interest income from Ace Corporation bonds. A worksheet is provided on page 266 to assist in calculating Marie's standard deduction.

Form **1040**

Department of the Treasury—Internal Revenue Service

U.S. Individual Income Tax Return   **1992**

IRS Use Only—Do not write or staple in this space.

For the year Jan. 1–Dec. 31, 1992, or other tax year beginning _______ , 1992, ending _______ , 19 ___   OMB No. 1545-0074

Label

(See instructions on page 10.)

Use the IRS label. Otherwise, please print or type.

LABEL HERE

Your first name and initial   Last name

Your social security number

If a joint return, spouse's first name and initial   Last name

Spouse's social security number

Home address (number and street). If you have a P.O. box, see page 10.   Apt. no.

City, town or post office, state, and ZIP code. If you have a foreign address, see page 10.

For Privacy Act and Paperwork Reduction Act Notice, see page 4.

Presidential Election Campaign
(See page 10.)

Do you want $1 to go to this fund? · · · · · · · Yes ☐ No ☐

If a joint return, does your spouse want $1 to go to this fund?   Yes ☐ No ☐

Note: *Checking "Yes" will not change your tax or reduce your refund.*

Filing Status

(See page 10.)

Check only one box.

1 ☐ Single

2 ☐ Married filing joint return (even if only one had income)

3 ☐ Married filing separate return. Enter spouse's social security no. above and full name here. ▶ _______

4 ☐ Head of household (with qualifying person). (See page 11.) If the qualifying person is a child but not your dependent, enter this child's name here. ▶ _______

5 ☐ Qualifying widow(er) with dependent child (year spouse died ▶ 19 ___). (See page 11.)

Exemptions

(See page 11.)

6a ☐ **Yourself.** If your parent (or someone else) can claim you as a dependent on his or her tax return, do not check box 6a. But be sure to check the box on line 33b on page 2

b ☐ **Spouse**

c **Dependents:**

(1) Name (first, initial, and last name)	(2) Check if under age 1	(3) If age 1 or older, dependent's social security number	(4) Dependent's relationship to you	(5) No. of months lived in your home in 1992

If more than six dependents, see page 12.

d If your child didn't live with you but is claimed as your dependent under a pre-1985 agreement, check here ▶ ☐

e Total number of exemptions claimed

No. of boxes checked on 6a and 6b _______

No. of your children on 6c who:
- lived with you _______
- didn't live with you due to divorce or separation (see page 13) _______

No. of other dependents on 6c _______

Add numbers entered on lines above ▶ ☐

Income

Attach Copy B of your Forms W-2, W-2G, and 1099-R here.

If you did not get a W-2, see page 9.

Attach check or money order on top of any Forms W-2, W-2G, or 1099-R.

7 Wages, salaries, tips, etc. Attach Form(s) W-2 · · · · · ·   **7**

8a Taxable interest income. Attach Schedule B if over $400 · · ·   **8a**

b Tax-exempt interest income (see page 15). DON'T include on line 8a   **8b**

9 Dividend income. Attach Schedule B if over $400 · · · ·   **9**

10 Taxable refunds, credits, or offsets of state and local income taxes from worksheet on page 16   **10**

11 Alimony received   **11**

12 Business income or (loss). Attach Schedule C or C-EZ   **12**

13 Capital gain or (loss). Attach Schedule D · · · · ·   **13**

14 Capital gain distributions not reported on line 13 (see page 15)   **14**

15 Other gains or (losses). Attach Form 4797 · · · ·   **15**

16a Total IRA distributions · **16a** _______ b Taxable amount (see page 16)   **16b**

17a Total pensions and annuities   **17a** _______ b Taxable amount (see page 16)   **17b**

18 Rents, royalties, partnerships, estates, trusts, etc. Attach Schedule E · · ·   **18**

19 Farm income or (loss). Attach Schedule F · · · ·   **19**

20 Unemployment compensation (see page 17) · · ·   **20**

21a Social security benefits   **21a** _______ b Taxable amount (see page 17)   **21b**

22 Other income. List type and amount—see page 18 ....   **22**

23 Add the amounts in the far right column for lines 7 through 22. This is your total income · ▶   **23**

Adjustments to Income

(See page 18.)

24a Your IRA deduction from applicable worksheet on page 19 or 20   **24a**

b Spouse's IRA deduction from applicable worksheet on page 19 or 20   **24b**

25 One-half of self-employment tax (see page 20) · · ·   **25**

26 Self-employed health insurance deduction (see page 20)   **26**

27 Keogh retirement plan and self-employed SEP deduction   **27**

28 Penalty on early withdrawal of savings · · · ·   **28**

29 Alimony paid. Recipient's SSN ▶ _______   **29**

30 Add lines 24a through 29. These are your total adjustments · · · ▶   **30**

Adjusted Gross Income

31 Subtract line 30 from line 23. This is your **adjusted gross income.** *If this amount is less than $22,370 and a child lived with you, see page EIC-1 to find out if you can claim the "Earned Income Credit" on line 56*   ▶   **31**

Form 1040 (1992)   Page **2**

Tax Computation (See page 22.)	**32** Amount from line 31 (adjusted gross income)	**32**
	33a Check if: ☐ **You** were 65 or older, ☐ Blind; ☐ **Spouse** was 65 or older, ☐ Blind. Add the number of boxes checked above and enter the total here . . . . ▶ **33a**	
	b If your parent (or someone else) can claim you as a dependent, check here . ▶ **33b** ☐	
	c If you are married filing separately and your spouse itemizes deductions or you are a dual-status alien, see page 22 and check here . . . . ▶ **33c** ☐	
	34 Enter the larger of your: { Itemized deductions from Schedule A, line 26, **OR** **Standard deduction** shown below for your filing status. But if you checked any box on line **33a** or **b**, go to page 22 to find your standard deduction. If you checked box **33c**, your standard deduction is zero. ● Single—$3,600 ● Head of household—$5,250 ● Married filing jointly or Qualifying widow(er)—$6,000 ● Married filing separately—$3,000 }	**34**

	35 Subtract line 34 from line 32	**35**
	36 If line 32 is $78,950 or less, multiply $2,300 by the total number of exemptions claimed on line 6e. If line 32 is over $78,950, see the worksheet on page 23 for the amount to enter .	**36**
If you want the IRS to figure your tax, see page 23.	**37** **Taxable income.** Subtract line 36 from line 35. If line 36 is more than line 35, enter -0- .	**37**
	38 Enter tax. Check if from a ☐ Tax Table, b ☐ Tax Rate Schedules, c ☐ Schedule D, or d ☐ Form 8615 (see page 23). Amount, if any, from Form(s) 8814 ▶ e ________	**38**
	39 Additional taxes (see page 23). Check if from a ☐ Form 4970 b ☐ Form 4972 . .	**39**
	40 Add lines 38 and 39 . . . . ▶	**40**

Credits (See page 23.)	**41** Credit for child and dependent care expenses. Attach Form 2441 | **41**	
	42 Credit for the elderly or the disabled. Attach Schedule R . . | **42**	
	43 Foreign tax credit. Attach Form 1116 . . . . | **43**	
	44 Other credits (see page 24). Check if from a ☐ Form 3800 b ☐ Form 8396 c ☐ Form 8801 d ☐ Form (specify)______ | **44**	
	45 Add lines 41 through 44	**45**
	46 Subtract line 45 from line 40. If line 45 is more than line 40, enter -0- . . . . . ▶	**46**

Other Taxes	**47** Self-employment tax. Attach Schedule SE. Also, see line 25	**47**
	48 Alternative minimum tax. Attach Form 6251	**48**
	49 Recapture taxes (see page 25). Check if from a ☐ Form 4255 b ☐ Form 8611 c ☐ Form 8828	**49**
	50 Social security and Medicare tax on tip income not reported to employer. Attach Form 4137 .	**50**
	51 Tax on qualified retirement plans, including IRAs. Attach Form 5329	**51**
	52 Advance earned income credit payments from Form W-2	**52**
	53 Add lines 46 through 52. This is your **total tax** . . . . ▶	**53**

Payments Attach Forms W-2, W-2G, and 1099-R on the front.	**54** Federal income tax withheld. If any is from Form(s) 1099, check ▶ ☐ | **54**	
	55 1992 estimated tax payments and amount applied from 1991 return . | **55**	
	56 **Earned income credit.** Attach Schedule EIC . . . . . | **56**	
	57 Amount paid with Form 4868 (extension request) . . . . | **57**	
	58 Excess social security, Medicare, and RRTA tax withheld (see page 26) . | **58**	
	59 Other payments (see page 26). Check if from a ☐ Form 2439 b ☐ Form 4136 . . | **59**	
	60 Add lines 54 through 59. These are your **total payments** . . . . ▶	**60**

Refund or Amount You Owe Attach check or money order on top of Form(s) W-2, etc., on the front.	**61** If line 60 is more than line 53, subtract line 53 from line 60. This is the amount you **OVERPAID**. ▶	**61**
	62 Amount of line 61 you want **REFUNDED TO YOU** . . . . ▶	**62**
	63 Amount of line 61 you want **APPLIED TO YOUR 1993 ESTIMATED TAX** ▶ | **63** |	
	64 If line 53 is more than line 60, subtract line 60 from line 53. This is the **AMOUNT YOU OWE.** Attach check or money order for full amount payable to "Internal Revenue Service." Write your name, address, social security number, daytime phone number, and "1992 Form 1040" on it	**64**
	65 Estimated tax penalty (see page 27). Also include on line 64 | **65** |	

Sign Here Keep a copy of this return for your records.	Under penalties of perjury, I declare that I have examined this return and accompanying schedules and statements, and to the best of my knowledge and belief, they are true, correct, and complete. Declaration of preparer (other than taxpayer) is based on all information of which preparer has any knowledge. ▶ Your signature | Date | Your occupation ▶ Spouse's signature. If a joint return, BOTH must sign. | Date | Spouse's occupation
Paid Preparer's Use Only	Preparer's signature ▶ | Date | Check if self-employed ☐ | Preparer's social security no. Firm's name (or yours if self-employed) and address ▶ _______ | E.I. No. | ZIP code

Standard Deduction Worksheet for Dependents—Line 34 (keep for your records)

Use this worksheet **only** if someone can claim you as a dependent.

1. Enter your **earned income** (defined below). If none, enter -0-   **1.** _______________

2. Minimum amount **2.** 600.00

3. Enter the **larger** of line 1 or line 2 . . . .   **3.** _______________

4. Enter on line 4 the amount shown below for your filing status:
   - Single, enter $3,600
   - Married filing separately, enter $3,000
   - Married filing jointly or Qualifying widow(er), enter $6,000   **4.** _______________
   - Head of household, enter $5,250

5. **Standard deduction.**

   a. Enter the **smaller** of line 3 or line 4. If under 65 and not blind, stop here and enter this amount on Form 1040, line 34. Otherwise, go to line 5b . . . .   **5a.** _______________

   b. If 65 or older or blind, multiply $900 ($700 if married filing jointly or separately, or qualifying widow(er)) by the number on Form 1040, line 33a . . . .   **5b.** _______________

   c. Add lines 5a and 5b. Enter the total here and on Form 1040, line 34 . . . .   **5c.** _______________

Earned income includes wages, salaries, tips, professional fees, and other compensation received for personal services you performed. It also includes any amount received as a scholarship that you must include in your income. Generally, your earned income is the total of the amount(s) you reported on Form 1040, lines 7, 12, and 19, minus the amount, if any, on line 25.

a. Using Form 1040 on pages 267 and 268, prepare the 1992 income tax return for Ms. Arlene K. Kildow, who signed her return 4-2-93. She elects to have $1 go to the presidential election campaign fund.

b. Using Form 1040 on pages 269 and 270, prepare the income tax return for Marie T. Kildow, who signed her return 3-18-93. The total of the interest income should be entered on Form 1040 (line 8). (Although interest income over $400 must be reported on Schedule B, the solution of this problem does *not* require the preparation of this schedule.) She elects to have $1 go to the presidential election campaign fund.

Form **1040**

Department of the Treasury—Internal Revenue Service

U.S. Individual Income Tax Return **1992**

IRS Use Only—Do not write or staple in this space.

For the year Jan. 1–Dec. 31, 1992, or other tax year beginning _______, 1992, ending _______, 19___

OMB No. 1545-0074

Label

(See instructions on page 10.)

Use the IRS label. Otherwise, please print or type.

L A B E L H E R E	Your first name and initial	Last name	Your social security number
	If a joint return, spouse's first name and initial	Last name	Spouse's social security number
	Home address (number and street). If you have a P.O. box, see page 10.	Apt. no.	**For Privacy Act and Paperwork Reduction Act Notice, see page 4.**
	City, town or post office, state, and ZIP code. If you have a foreign address, see page 10.		

Presidential Election Campaign

(See page 10.)

Do you want $1 to go to this fund? . . . . Yes No

If a joint return, does your spouse want $1 to go to this fund? . Yes No

Note: *Checking "Yes" will not change your tax or reduce your refund.*

Filing Status

(See page 10.)

Check only one box.

1 ☐ Single

2 ☐ Married filing joint return (even if only one had income)

3 ☐ Married filing separate return. Enter spouse's social security no. above and full name here. ▶ _______

4 ☐ Head of household (with qualifying person). (See page 11.) If the qualifying person is a child but not your dependent, enter this child's name here. ▶ _______

5 ☐ Qualifying widow(er) with dependent child (year spouse died ▶ 19___). (See page 11.)

Exemptions

(See page 11.)

6a ☐ **Yourself.** If your parent (or someone else) can claim you as a dependent on his or her tax return, do not check box 6a. But be sure to check the box on line 33b on page 2 .

b ☐ **Spouse** . . . .

c **Dependents:**

(1) Name (first, initial, and last name)	(2) Check if under age 1	(3) If age 1 or older, dependent's social security number	(4) Dependent's relationship to you	(5) No. of months lived in your home in 1992

If more than six dependents, see page 12.

No. of boxes checked on 6a and 6b _______

No. of your children on 6c who:
- lived with you
- didn't live with you due to divorce or separation (see page 13)

No. of other dependents on 6c _______

d If your child didn't live with you but is claimed as your dependent under a pre-1985 agreement, check here ▶ ☐

e Total number of exemptions claimed

Add numbers entered on lines above ▶ _______

Income

Attach Copy B of your Forms W-2, W-2G, and 1099-R here.

If you did not get a W-2, see page 9.

Attach check or money order on top of any Forms W-2, W-2G, or 1099-R.

7	Wages, salaries, tips, etc. Attach Form(s) W-2	7
8a	Taxable interest income. Attach Schedule B if over $400 . . .	8a
b	Tax-exempt interest income (see page 15). DON'T include on line 8a 8b	
9	Dividend income. Attach Schedule B if over $400	9
10	Taxable refunds, credits, or offsets of state and local income taxes from worksheet on page 16	10
11	Alimony received	11
12	Business income or (loss). Attach Schedule C or C-EZ	12
13	Capital gain or (loss). Attach Schedule D	13
14	Capital gain distributions not reported on line 13 (see page 15) .	14
15	Other gains or (losses). Attach Form 4797	15
16a	Total IRA distributions . 16a _______ b Taxable amount (see page 16)	16b
17a	Total pensions and annuities 17a _______ b Taxable amount (see page 16)	17b
18	Rents, royalties, partnerships, estates, trusts, etc. Attach Schedule E . . .	18
19	Farm income or (loss). Attach Schedule F	19
20	Unemployment compensation (see page 17)	20
21a	Social security benefits 21a _______ b Taxable amount (see page 17)	21b
22	Other income. List type and amount—see page 18	22
23	Add the amounts in the far right column for lines 7 through 22. This is your total income . ▶	23

Adjustments to Income

(See page 18.)

24a	Your IRA deduction from applicable worksheet on page 19 or 20	24a	
b	Spouse's IRA deduction from applicable worksheet on page 19 or 20	24b	
25	One-half of self-employment tax (see page 20) . . .	25	
26	Self-employed health insurance deduction (see page 20)	26	
27	Keogh retirement plan and self-employed SEP deduction	27	
28	Penalty on early withdrawal of savings	28	
29	Alimony paid. Recipient's SSN ▶ _______	29	
30	Add lines 24a through 29. These are your total adjustments . . . . ▶		30

Adjusted Gross Income

31 Subtract line 30 from line 23. This is your **adjusted gross income**. *If this amount is less than $22,370 and a child lived with you, see page EIC-1 to find out if you can claim the "Earned Income Credit" on line 56* . . . . ▶ | 31

Cat. No. 11320B

Form **1040** (1992)

Form 1040 (1992)   Page **2**

				32	

Tax Computation

(See page 22.)

32 Amount from line 31 (adjusted gross income) **32**

33a Check if: ☐ You were 65 or older, ☐ Blind; ☐ Spouse was 65 or older, ☐ Blind.
Add the number of boxes checked above and enter the total here . . . . ▶ **33a**

b If your parent (or someone else) can claim you as a dependent, check here ▶ **33b** ☐

c If you are married filing separately and your spouse itemizes deductions or you are a dual-status alien, see page 22 and check here . . . . ▶ **33c** ☐

34 Enter the larger of your:
{ Itemized deductions from Schedule A, line 26, **OR**
Standard deduction shown below for your filing status. **But if you checked any box on line 33a or b, go to page 22 to find your standard deduction. If you checked box 33c, your standard deduction is zero.**
• Single—$3,600   • Head of household—$5,250
• Married filing jointly or Qualifying widow(er)—$6,000
• Married filing separately—$3,000 }   **34**

35 Subtract line 34 from line 32 . . . .   **35**

36 If line 32 is $78,950 or less, multiply $2,300 by the total number of exemptions claimed on line 6e. If line 32 is over $78,950, see the worksheet on page 23 for the amount to enter .   **36**

If you want the IRS to figure your tax, see page 23.

37 **Taxable income.** Subtract line 36 from line 35. If line 36 is more than line 35, enter -0-   **37**

38 Enter tax. Check if from a ☐ Tax Table, b ☐ Tax Rate Schedules, c ☐ Schedule D, or d ☐ Form 8615 (see page 23). Amount, if any, from Form(s) 8814 ▶ e _______   **38**

39 Additional taxes (see page 23). Check if from a ☐ Form 4970 b ☐ Form 4972 . . .   **39**

40 Add lines 38 and 39 . . . . ▶   **40**

Credits

(See page 23.)

41 Credit for child and dependent care expenses. Attach Form 2441   **41**

42 Credit for the elderly or the disabled. Attach Schedule R . .   **42**

43 Foreign tax credit. Attach Form 1116 . . . .   **43**

44 Other credits (see page 24). Check if from a ☐ Form 3800 b ☐ Form 8396 c ☐ Form 8801 d ☐ Form (specify)_______   **44**

45 Add lines 41 through 44 . . . .   **45**

46 Subtract line 45 from line 40. If line 45 is more than line 40, enter -0- . . . . ▶   **46**

Other Taxes

47 Self-employment tax. Attach Schedule SE. Also, see line 25 .   **47**

48 Alternative minimum tax. Attach Form 6251 . . . .   **48**

49 Recapture taxes (see page 25). Check if from a ☐ Form 4255 b ☐ Form 8611 c ☐ Form 8828   **49**

50 Social security and Medicare tax on tip income not reported to employer. Attach Form 4137 .   **50**

51 Tax on qualified retirement plans, including IRAs. Attach Form 5329 . . . .   **51**

52 Advance earned income credit payments from Form W-2 . . . .   **52**

53 Add lines 46 through 52. This is your **total tax** . . . . ▶   **53**

Payments

Attach Forms W-2, W-2G, and 1099-R on the front.

54 Federal income tax withheld. If any is from Form(s) 1099, check ▶ ☐   **54**

55 1992 estimated tax payments and amount applied from 1991 return .   **55**

56 **Earned income credit.** Attach Schedule EIC **56**

57 Amount paid with Form 4868 (extension request) **57**

58 Excess social security, Medicare, and RRTA tax withheld (see page 26) .   **58**

59 Other payments (see page 26). Check if from a ☐ Form 2439 b ☐ Form 4136 . . . . . .   **59**

60 Add lines 54 through 59. These are your **total payments** . . . . ▶   **60**

Refund or Amount You Owe

Attach check or money order on top of Form(s) W-2, etc., on the front.

61 If line 60 is more than line 53, subtract line 53 from line 60. This is the amount you OVERPAID. ▶   **61**

62 Amount of line 61 you want REFUNDED TO YOU . . . . ▶   **62**

63 Amount of line 61 you want APPLIED TO YOUR 1993 ESTIMATED TAX ▶ **63**

64 If line 53 is more than line 60, subtract line 60 from line 53. This is the **AMOUNT YOU OWE.** Attach check or money order for full amount payable to "Internal Revenue Service." Write your name, address, social security number, daytime phone number, and "1992 Form 1040" on it   **64**

65 Estimated tax penalty (see page 27). Also include on line 64   **65**

Sign Here

Keep a copy of this return for your records.

Under penalties of perjury, I declare that I have examined this return and accompanying schedules and statements, and to the best of my knowledge and belief, they are true, correct, and complete. Declaration of preparer (other than taxpayer) is based on all information of which preparer has any knowledge.

▶ Your signature	Date	Your occupation
▶ Spouse's signature. If a joint return, BOTH must sign.	Date	Spouse's occupation

Paid Preparer's Use Only

Preparer's signature ▶	Date	Check if self-employed ☐	Preparer's social security no.
Firm's name (or yours if self-employed) and address ▶		E.I. No.	
		ZIP code	

Form **1040** Department of the Treasury—Internal Revenue Service
U.S. Individual Income Tax Return 19**92** IRS Use Only—Do not write or staple in this space.

For the year Jan. 1–Dec. 31, 1992, or other tax year beginning   , 1992, ending   , 19 | OMB No. 1545-0074

Label

(See instructions on page 10.)

Use the IRS label. Otherwise, please print or type.

L A B E L   H E R E

Your first name and initial | Last name | Your social security number

If a joint return, spouse's first name and initial | Last name | Spouse's social security number

Home address (number and street). If you have a P.O. box, see page 10. | Apt. no.

City, town or post office, state, and ZIP code. If you have a foreign address, see page 10.

For Privacy Act and Paperwork Reduction Act Notice, see page 4.

Presidential Election Campaign
(See page 10.)

Do you want $1 to go to this fund? . . . . | Yes | No
If a joint return, does your spouse want $1 to go to this fund? . | Yes | No

Note: *Checking "Yes" will not change your tax or reduce your refund.*

Filing Status

(See page 10.)

Check only one box.

1 Single
2 Married filing joint return (even if only one had income)
3 Married filing separate return. Enter spouse's social security no. above and full name here. ▶ _______
4 Head of household (with qualifying person). (See page 11.) If the qualifying person is a child but not your dependent, enter this child's name here. ▶ _______
5 Qualifying widow(er) with dependent child (year spouse died ▶ 19   ). (See page 11.)

Exemptions

(See page 11.)

6a ☐ **Yourself.** If your parent (or someone else) can claim you as a dependent on his or her tax return, do not check box 6a. But be sure to check the box on line 33b on page 2
b ☐ **Spouse** . . . .
c Dependents:

(1) Name (first, initial, and last name)	(2) Check if under age 1	(3) If age 1 or older, dependent's social security number	(4) Dependent's relationship to you	(5) No. of months lived in your home in 1992

If more than six dependents, see page 12.

d If your child didn't live with you but is claimed as your dependent under a pre-1985 agreement, check here ▶ ☐
e Total number of exemptions claimed

No. of boxes checked on 6a and 6b _______
No. of your children on 6c who:
• lived with you _______
• didn't live with you due to divorce or separation (see page 13) _______
No. of other dependents on 6c _______
Add numbers entered on lines above ▶ _______

Income

Attach Copy B of your Forms W-2, W-2G, and 1099-R here.

If you did not get a W-2, see page 9.

Attach check or money order on top of any Forms W-2, W-2G, or 1099-R.

7 Wages, salaries, tips, etc. Attach Form(s) W-2 . . . . | 7
8a Taxable interest income. Attach Schedule B if over $400 . . . | 8a
b Tax-exempt interest income (see page 15). DON'T include on line 8a | 8b |
9 Dividend income. Attach Schedule B if over $400 . . . . . . | 9
10 Taxable refunds, credits, or offsets of state and local income taxes from worksheet on page 16 | 10
11 Alimony received . . . . | 11
12 Business income or (loss). Attach Schedule C or C-EZ . . . . | 12
13 Capital gain or (loss). Attach Schedule D . . . . | 13
14 Capital gain distributions not reported on line 13 (see page 15) . | 14
15 Other gains or (losses). Attach Form 4797 . . . . | 15
16a Total IRA distributions . | 16a | b Taxable amount (see page 16) | 16b
17a Total pensions and annuities | 17a | b Taxable amount (see page 16) | 17b
18 Rents, royalties, partnerships, estates, trusts, etc. Attach Schedule E | 18
19 Farm income or (loss). Attach Schedule F . . . . | 19
20 Unemployment compensation (see page 17) . . . . | 20
21a Social security benefits | 21a | b Taxable amount (see page 17) | 21b
22 Other income. List type and amount—see page 18 . . . . | 22
23 Add the amounts in the far right column for lines 7 through 22. This is your total income ▶ | 23

Adjustments to Income

(See page 18.)

24a Your IRA deduction from applicable worksheet on page 19 or 20 | 24a
b Spouse's IRA deduction from applicable worksheet on page 19 or 20 | 24b
25 One-half of self-employment tax (see page 20) . . . | 25
26 Self-employed health insurance deduction (see page 20) | 26
27 Keogh retirement plan and self-employed SEP deduction | 27
28 Penalty on early withdrawal of savings . . . . . | 28
29 Alimony paid. Recipient's SSN ▶ | 29
30 Add lines 24a through 29. These are your total adjustments . . . . ▶ | 30

Adjusted Gross Income

31 Subtract line 30 from line 23. This is your **adjusted gross income.** *If this amount is less than $22,370 and a child lived with you, see page EIC-1 to find out if you can claim the "Earned Income Credit" on line 56* . . . . ▶ | 31

Cat. No. 11320B   Form **1040** (1992)

Form 1040 (1992)   Page **2**

Tax Compu-tation

(See page 22.)

32 Amount from line 31 (adjusted gross income) **32**

33a Check if: ☐ You were 65 or older, ☐ Blind; ☐ Spouse was 65 or older, ☐ Blind.
Add the number of boxes checked above and enter the total here . . . . ▶ **33a**

b If your parent (or someone else) can claim you as a dependent, check here . ▶ **33b** ☐

c If you are married filing separately and your spouse itemizes deductions or you are a dual-status alien, see page 22 and check here . . . . ▶ **33c** ☐

34 Enter the larger of your:
Itemized deductions from Schedule A, line 26, **OR**
Standard deduction shown below for your filing status. **But if you checked any box on line 33a or b, go to page 22 to find your standard deduction. If you checked box 33c, your standard deduction is zero.**
• Single—$3,600   • Head of household—$5,250
• Married filing jointly or Qualifying widow(er)—$6,000
• Married filing separately—$3,000
   34

35 Subtract line 34 from line 32 . . . .   **35**

36 If line 32 is $78,950 or less, multiply $2,300 by the total number of exemptions claimed on line 6e. If line 32 is over $78,950, see the worksheet on page 23 for the amount to enter .   **36**

If you want the IRS to figure your tax, see page 23.

37 **Taxable income.** Subtract line 36 from line 35. If line 36 is more than line 35, enter -0- .   **37**

38 Enter tax. Check if from **a** ☐ Tax Table, **b** ☐ Tax Rate Schedules, **c** ☐ Schedule D, or **d** ☐ Form 8615 (see page 23). Amount, if any, from Form(s) 8814 ▶ **e** _______   **38**

39 Additional taxes (see page 23). Check if from **a** ☐ Form 4970 **b** ☐ Form 4972 . . .   **39**

40 Add lines 38 and 39 . . . . ▶ **40**

Credits

(See page 23.)

41 Credit for child and dependent care expenses. Attach Form 2441   **41**

42 Credit for the elderly or the disabled. Attach Schedule R . .   **42**

43 Foreign tax credit. Attach Form 1116 . . . .   **43**

44 Other credits (see page 24). Check if from **a** ☐ Form 3800 **b** ☐ Form 8396 **c** ☐ Form 8801 **d** ☐ Form (specify)______   **44**

45 Add lines 41 through 44 . . . .   **45**

46 Subtract line 45 from line 40. If line 45 is more than line 40, enter -0- . . . . . . ▶ **46**

Other Taxes

47 Self-employment tax. Attach Schedule SE. Also, see line 25. . .   **47**

48 Alternative minimum tax. Attach Form 6251 . . . .   **48**

49 Recapture taxes (see page 25). Check if from **a** ☐ Form 4255 **b** ☐ Form 8611 **c** ☐ Form 8828 .   **49**

50 Social security and Medicare tax on tip income not reported to employer. Attach Form 4137 .   **50**

51 Tax on qualified retirement plans, including IRAs. Attach Form 5329 . . . . . .   **51**

52 Advance earned income credit payments from Form W-2 . . . .   **52**

53 Add lines 46 through 52. This is your **total tax** . . . . ▶ **53**

Payments

Attach Forms W-2, W-2G, and 1099-R on the front.

54 Federal income tax withheld. If any is from Form(s) 1099, check ▶ ☐   **54**

55 1992 estimated tax payments and amount applied from 1991 return .   **55**

56 **Earned income credit.** Attach Schedule EIC **56**

57 Amount paid with Form 4868 (extension request) **57**

58 Excess social security, Medicare, and RRTA tax withheld (see page 26) .   **58**

59 Other payments (see page 26). Check if from **a** ☐ Form 2439 **b** ☐ Form 4136 . . . .   **59**

60 Add lines 54 through 59. These are your **total payments** . . . . ▶ **60**

Refund or Amount You Owe

Attach check or money order on top of Form(s) W-2, etc., on the front.

61 If line 60 is more than line 53, subtract line 53 from line 60. This is the amount you **OVERPAID** . . ▶ **61**

62 Amount of line 61 you want **REFUNDED TO YOU** . . . . ▶ **62**

63 Amount of line 61 you want **APPLIED TO YOUR 1993 ESTIMATED TAX** ▶ **63**

64 If line 53 is more than line 60, subtract line 60 from line 53. This is the **AMOUNT YOU OWE.** Attach check or money order for full amount payable to "Internal Revenue Service." Write your name, address, social security number, daytime phone number, and "1992 Form 1040" on it   **64**

65 Estimated tax penalty (see page 27). Also include on line 64   **65**

Sign Here

Keep a copy of this return for your records.

Under penalties of perjury, I declare that I have examined this return and accompanying schedules and statements, and to the best of my knowledge and belief, they are true, correct, and complete. Declaration of preparer (other than taxpayer) is based on all information of which preparer has any knowledge.

Your signature   Date   Your occupation

Spouse's signature. If a joint return, BOTH must sign.   Date   Spouse's occupation

Paid Preparer's Use Only

Preparer's signature   Date   Check if self-employed ☐   Preparer's social security no.

Firm's name (or yours if self-employed) and address   E.I. No.   ZIP code

9. David R. Johnson, age 66 and with good vision, and his wife Betty L. Johnson, age 62 and also with good vision, have filed cash-method joint income tax returns for many years. On November 8, 1992, Mr. Johnson died, leaving his complete estate to his wife. No administrator or executor has been appointed as yet. Mr. Johnson had retired, but prior to his death in 1992 he had received interest income on corporate bonds of $2,220 and had realized a gain of $2,500 on the sale of HYT Corporation common stock that had been owned since May 6, 1978. He had received dividends on various domestic corporations of an additional $6,560, including a dividend of $800 payable November 1, 1992, but received November 12, 1992 (after his death).

   a. Would an income tax return be filed for Mr. Johnson for 1992? Explain.

   b. Could Mrs. Johnson file a 1992 joint return with her deceased husband? Explain.

   c. When would the final income tax return be due for Mr. Johnson, and what form would be used?

10. Indicate T (true) or F (false) for each statement regarding a decedent's income tax return:

   _____ a. If a tax return is required, Form 1040 should be used.

   _____ b. The final return of a taxpayer is due 3½ months after the date of death.

   _____ c. A joint return cannot be filed with a deceased spouse if the executor of the estate officially objects to such a filing.

   _____ d. A "full" personal exemption is allowed for the deceased taxpayer.

   _____ e. Medical expenses paid after the date of death may not be included on the decedent's final return.

11. a. What is the penalty for fraud in 1992?

    b. Explain the penalty for filing a frivolous return.

12. In what circumstances can a taxpayer be excused from civil penalties for failure to comply with tax laws?

13. How are interest rates determined by the IRS for underpayments and overpayments of taxes?

14. Shortly after filing their Form 1040 for 1992 with the IRS Center in Memphis, Tennessee, Jack L. and Judith K. Keith, 1618 Redford Lane, Kingsport, Tennessee 37664-3322, discovered several items that had been omitted from their original return. These items are:

  a. A contribution of 20 shares of stock in the ABC Corporation to the Building Fund of the Second Church on January 7, 1992, had not been claimed. The stock had been owned by Mrs. Keith and had cost $600 when purchased on August 6, 1980. FMV on January 7, 1992, was $950.

  b. Dividends from domestic corporations received during 1992 that had not been reported:

Wye Corporation (owned by Mr. Keith)	$46.25
ABC Corporation (owned by Mrs. Keith). Dividend had been declared on December 22, 1991, to shareholders of record January 2, 1992. Paid February 1, 1992.	$51.75

Information available from the 1992 Form 1040 that had been filed by Mr. and Mrs. Keith is as follows:

Married filing jointly, claiming 2 personal exemptions and 1 dependent exemption

Total income, Form 1040 (line 23), and AGI, Form 1040 (line 31)	$21,000
Itemized deductions, Form 1040 (line 34)	6,370
Taxable income, Form 1040 (line 37)	7,730
Total tax liability, Form 1040 (line 53)	1,159
Federal income tax withheld, Form 1040 (line 54)	1,484
Amount to be refunded on original return	325

The SSN for Jack L. Keith is 347-47-5784 and for Judith K. Keith is 457-58-4758. They have not been advised that their 1992 income tax return is under audit. Total dividend income that had been reported was $280.16; total interest income that had been reported was $150. Prepare an Amended U.S. Individual Income Tax Return, Form 1040X, for Mr. and Mrs. Keith, using the form on the following pages. The return was filed July 9, 1993.

15. Rixie Jefferson files his tax return on April 28. He also encloses a check for $2,000 to cover the balance of his tax liability. What penalties must Rixie pay (disregard interest)?

16. Nancy Fess changed her tax year. As a consequence, she had to file a return for a period of four months. During this four-month period her actual taxable income was $8,000.

  a. Calculate the annualized taxable income on which Nancy's tax will be based.

  b. If the tax on this annualized income is $4,200, what is Nancy's tax liability for this short-period return?

Form 1040X (Rev. November 1991)

Department of the Treasury—Internal Revenue Service

Amended U.S. Individual Income Tax Return

▶ See separate instructions.

OMB No. 1545-0091
Expires 10-31-94

This return is for calendar year ▶ 19______ , OR fiscal year ended ▶ ____________ , 19______ .

Please print or type	

Your first name and initial | Last name | Your social security number

If a joint return, spouse's first name and initial | Last name | Spouse's social security number

Home address (number and street). (If you have a P.O. box, see instructions.) | Apt. no. | Telephone number (optional) (   )

City, town or post office, state, and ZIP code. (If you have a foreign address, see instructions.) | For Paperwork Reduction Act Notice, see page 1 of separate instructions.

Enter name and address as shown on original return (if same as above, write "Same"). If changing from separate to joint return, enter names and addresses from original returns.

A Service center where original return was filed

B Has original return been changed or audited by the IRS? ☐ Yes ☐ No
If "No," have you been notified that it will be? . . . . . ☐ Yes ☐ No
If "Yes," identify the IRS office ▶

C Are you amending your return to include any item (loss, credit, deduction, other tax benefit, or income) relating to a tax shelter required to be registered? . . . . ☐ Yes ☐ No
If "Yes," you **MUST** attach **Form 8271**, Investor Reporting of Tax Shelter Registration Number.

D Filing status claimed. (**Note:** *You cannot change from joint to separate returns after the due date has passed.*)

On original return ▶ ☐ Single ☐ Married filing joint return ☐ Married filing separate return ☐ Head of household ☐ Qualifying widow(er)
On this return ▶ ☐ Single ☐ Married filing joint return ☐ Married filing separate return ☐ Head of household ☐ Qualifying widow(er)

Income and Deductions (see instructions)

(**Note:** *Be sure to complete page 2.*)

		A. As originally reported or as adjusted (see instructions)	B. Net change—Increase or (Decrease)—explain on page 2	C. Correct amount
1	Total income			
2	Adjustments to income			
3	Adjusted gross income (subtract line 2 from line 1) . . .			
4	Itemized deductions or standard deduction			
5	Subtract line 4 from line 3			
6	Exemptions (if changing, fill in Parts I and II on page 2) . .			
7	Taxable income (subtract line 6 from line 5)			
8	Tax (see instructions). (Method used in col. C________________)			
9	Credits (see instructions)			
10	Subtract line 9 from line 8. Enter the result but not less than zero .			
11	Other taxes (such as self-employment tax, alternative minimum tax) .			
12	Total tax (add lines 10 and 11)			
13	Federal income tax withheld and excess social security, Medicare, and RRTA taxes withheld .			
14	Estimated tax payments			
15	Earned income credit			
16	Credits for Federal tax on fuels, regulated investment company, etc.			
17	Amount paid with Form 4868, Form 2688, or Form 2350 (application for extension of time to file) . . .			
18	Amount paid with original return plus additional tax paid after it was filed			
19	Add lines 13 through 18 in column C			

Tax Liability (lines 8–12) · **Payments** (lines 13–16)

Refund or Amount You Owe

20	Overpayment, if any, as shown on original return (or as previously adjusted by the IRS) . .	
21	Subtract line 20 from line 19 (see instructions)	
22	**AMOUNT YOU OWE.** If line 12, col. C, is more than line 21, enter the difference and see instructions . .	
23	**REFUND** to be received. If line 12, column C, is less than line 21, enter the difference . . .	

Please Sign Here

Under penalties of perjury, I declare that I have filed an original return and that I have examined this amended return, including accompanying schedules and statements, and to the best of my knowledge and belief, this amended return is true, correct, and complete. Declaration of preparer (other than taxpayer) is based on all information of which the preparer has any knowledge.

▶ Your signature | Date | ▶ Spouse's signature (if joint return, BOTH must sign) | Date

Paid Preparer's Use Only

Preparer's signature ▶ | Date | Check if self-employed ☐ | Preparer's social security no.

Firm's name (or yours if self-employed) and address ▶ | E.I. No. | ZIP code

Cat. No. 11360L

Form 1040X (Rev. 11-91)   Page **2**

Part I	**Exemptions** (see Form 1040 or Form 1040A instructions)	A. Number originally reported	B. Net change	C. Correct number

If you are not changing your exemptions, do not complete this part.
If claiming more exemptions, complete lines 24–30 and, if applicable, line 31.
If claiming fewer exemptions, complete lines 24–29.

		A. Number originally reported	B. Net change	C. Correct number
24	Yourself and spouse			
	Caution: *If your parents (or someone else) can claim you as a dependent (even if they chose not to), you cannot claim an exemption for yourself.*			
25	Your dependent children who lived with you			
26	Your dependent children who did not live with you due to divorce or separation			
27	Other dependents.			
28	Total number of exemptions (add lines 24 through 27)			
29	**For tax year 1991,** if the amount on page 1, line 3, is more than $75,000, see the instructions. If line 3 is $75,000 or less, multiply $2,150 by the number of exemptions claimed on line 28. **For tax year 1990,** use $2,050; **for tax year 1989,** use $2,000; **for tax year 1988,** use $1,950. Enter the result here and on page 1, line 6.			

30 Dependents (children and other) not claimed on original return:

No. of your children on line 30 who lived with you ▶ ☐

No. of your children on line 30 who didn't live with you due to divorce or separation (see instructions) ▶ ☐

No. of other dependents listed on line 30 ▶ ☐

(a) Dependent's name (first, initial, and last name)	(b) Check if under age 1 (under age 2 if a 1989 or 1990 return; under age 5 if a 1988 return)	(c) If age 1 or older (age 2 or older if a 1989 or 1990 return; age 5 or older if a 1988 return), enter dependent's social security number	(d) Dependent's relationship to you	(e) No. of months lived in your home

31 If your child listed on line 30 didn't live with you but is claimed as your dependent under a pre-1985 agreement, check here . . . ▶ ☐

Part II	**Explanation of Changes to Income, Deductions, and Credits**

Enter the line number from page 1 for each item you are changing and give the reason for each change. Attach all supporting forms and schedules for items changed. Be sure to include your name and social security number on any attachments.

If the change pertains to a net operating loss carryback or a general business credit carryback, attach the schedule or form that shows the year in which the loss or credit occurred. See instructions. Also, check here . . . . ▶ ☐

Part III	**Presidential Election Campaign Fund**

Checking below will not increase your tax or reduce your refund.

If you did not previously want to have $1 go to the fund but now want to, check here . . . . ▶ ☐
If a joint return and your spouse did not previously want to have $1 go to the fund but now wants to, check here . . . . . ▶ ☐

17. Indicate T (true) and F (false) for each statement:

_____ **a.** At the Regional Service Center there are two types of audits: the office audit and the field audit.

_____ **b.** The Economic Recovery Act of 1981 protects the Treasury Department from disclosing its standards used to select returns for examination.

_____ **c.** Presently, examination of income tax returns must be completed within 24 months after the later of the due date or the filing date of the return.

_____ **d.** In a correspondence audit, the taxpayer will receive a report of the findings along with a 90-day deficiency notice.

_____ **e.** At any stage of the appeal procedure, the taxpayer may pay the tax requested and file a claim for a refund.

BUSINESS AND PROFESSIONAL RETURNS

- ➡ The different accounting methods
- ➡ How to complete Schedule C
- ➡ How to complete Schedule SE
- ➡ How to calculate depreciation
- ➡ How to complete Form 4562
- ➡ How to complete Form 8829

Reporting Requirements for Self-Employed Taxpayers

Your Rights as a Taxpayer

Payment of Only the Required Tax. You have the right to plan your business and personal finances so that you will pay the least tax that is due under the law.

Source: Internal Revenue Service, Publication 1

Chapters 1 through 7 presented the basic structure for reporting income and deductions. Excluded were the special reporting requirements for a taxpayer who earns income as an independent contractor, a sole proprietor, a professional, or a farmer. This chapter focuses on self-employed individual taxpayers and their tax reporting.

Self-employed taxpayers must determine their self-employment income, self-employment tax (Chapter 7), and net income from operations. Schedule C (Form 1040), Profit or Loss From Business, is the reporting form for all sole proprietors except farmers, who report on Schedule F (Form 1040), Profit or Loss From Farming.

The net income calculated in the process of preparing Schedule C for a self-employed taxpayer may not be equal to the net income reflected by the books of the business or profession. Different rules govern items that are to be included in, or excluded from, the tax return. Certain transactions not reported in tax schedules are reported elsewhere. The gain or loss on sale or exchange of business property is reported on Schedule D (Form 1040), Capital Gains and Losses, or on Form 4797, Sales of Business Property.

Accounting Methods

All taxpayers are required to keep records that will enable them to calculate the amount of their net income or (loss). In preparing the annual tax return, income must be calculated in accordance with the method of accounting regularly employed in keeping the records, except to the extent that the Internal Revenue Code allows deviations. Accounting records are generally kept on either the (1) cash method or (2) accrual method.

Cash Method

The cash method of accounting generally recognizes income in the period in which it is actually or constructively received and recognizes expenses only as they are paid. Business and professional enterprises that sell services rather than merchandise and materials frequently use this method of accounting. For example, a lawyer using the cash method maintains a memorandum record of fees charged to clients, recording the fees as income only when cash is collected. Since the income from services is recognized only when received, taxpayers cannot deduct worthless receivables. Bills for rent, electricity, and other expenses are recorded only when the cash is paid.

If income is received in a form other than cash, the amount of the income is the FMV of the property or services received.

EXAMPLE 1 ───────────────────

If a taxpayer receives ten shares of stock as a bonus when the market value of a share is $28, the taxpayer realizes income of $280. If the taxpayer sells the stock at a later date, the difference between the sale proceeds and basis of $280 constitutes a capital gain or loss.

Income is constructively received when it is available to the taxpayer without any limitations.

EXAMPLE 2 ───────────────────

On December 31, the last day of the tax year, a taxpayer receives a check in payment of fees. This income should be reported in the current tax year even though the check may not be cashed until the following year.

If a taxpayer has interest income credited to a savings account on the last day of the year, it is income in that year regardless of when it is withdrawn. Bond interest coupons should be reported as income in the year in which they mature even though they are cashed in a later year, because the taxpayer is considered to have constructively received the cash on the coupon's maturity date since the taxpayer has the right to payment on that date.

Accounting for business assets that will be used for more than one year is the same under both methods, cash and accrual. The amount paid in a particular year for plant and equipment is not an expense of the period. Only cost recovery (depreciation) is deductible each year. Payments for services to be received in a future taxable year or years are also not deductible in the year of payment.

Rent paid in advance can be deducted only in the year for which the rent is incurred. Similarly, when property or casualty insurance premiums are paid in advance for more than a year, only the pro rata amount is deductible in that year.

EXAMPLE 3 ——————————————————

Assume that rent paid in advance on a building covered a two-year period from October 1, 1992 to September 30, 1994. If the taxpayer on the cash method paid the entire amount, $36,000, on October 1, 1992, the amount deductible in 1992 would be $4,500 ($36,000 ÷ 24 x 3).

However, for a taxpayer who makes a **mandatory** payment for an expense item that expires before the end of the year following payment, a full deduction is allowed in the year of the payment. This special rule does not apply to prepaid interest which is deductible only in the year to which it is properly allocable.

Amounts received as principal on a loan are not income and amounts paid as principal repayments are not an expense.

Most individuals not engaged in a business of their own use the cash method. When a taxpayer's income is composed exclusively of salary, dividends, interest, and royalties, this method is simple and yields satisfactory results. Taxpayers who do not maintain books of account are required to calculate income on the cash method. In service businesses, where inventories usually are not a material factor in measuring income, the taxpayer is given a choice in keeping the accounts on either the cash method or the accrual method. However, unincorporated businesses with $5 million or more in annual gross receipts from any of the prior three years will no longer be eligible to use the cash method and must use the accrual method in determining income.

Accrual Method

With the accrual method, the calculation of net income includes amounts earned or accrued but not received and liabilities incurred but not paid. The controlling factor is the right to receive income rather than the time of actual receipt in cash, or the obligation to pay for expenses incurred rather than the time of actual payment in cash.

EXAMPLE 4 ——————————————————

Assume that salaries accrued for the week ended December 31 are paid by the employer on January 4. If the accrual method is used, the salaries should be reported as an expense of December; if the cash method is used, the salaries should be reported as an expense of January.

The accounting for prepaid expenses is the same as under the cash method. Only the amount properly allocable to the year is deductible, the remainder being carried forward as an asset to the following period. On the other hand, with the exception of prepaid subscription income and certain advance payments for goods and services, income of future years collected in advance generally may not be deferred; it must be reported as income in the year received. However, an accrual-method taxpayer in a *service business* is not required to accrue service revenue that is probably uncollectible based on experience.

In determining the income from a business in which the production, purchase, or sale of merchandise is a material factor, the taxpayer is required to make appropriate adjustments for inventories and account for purchases and sales on the accrual method. As indicated above, the accrual method can be modified for income from personal services which, based on experience, will not be collected. Such income need not be accrued unless interest or late fees are charged.

Taxpayers who want to change their method of accounting in preparing their returns from the cash method to the accrual method, or vice versa, must first obtain the consent of the IRS by filing Form 3115, Application for Change in Accounting Method, within the first 180 days of the tax year of the change.

Reporting Profit or Loss by Individuals, Partnerships, and Corporations

Individuals who, as sole proprietors, own a business or practice a trade or profession, must report the net profit or (loss) from their business, trade, or profession on Form 1040, U.S. Individual Income Tax Return. Schedule C (Form 1040), Profit or Loss From Business, provides for the detailed reporting of revenue and expenses by sole proprietors, except for farmers, whose revenues and expenses from farming are reported on Schedule F (Form 1040), Profit or Loss From Farming.

Businesses organized and operated as partnerships and corporations are entities separate from the individual owners. Accordingly, partnerships and corporations (including S corporations and C corporations) generally must file separate returns.

Generally, the rules for recognition of revenues and expenses for a business, trade, profession, or farm are comparable regardless of the form of organization. These similarities include the election of such items as method of accounting (cash or accrual), method of calculating depreciation or cost recovery, method of recording the disposal of long-lived assets, guidelines for the expensing or capitalization of expenditures, and the jobs credit and/or energy credit. Certain differences are specifically legislated. For example, special provisions are made for situations unique to certain entities, such as partnerships and/or corporations. Special provisions are also made for situations unique to certain taxpayers, such as the loss of a growing crop, sale of a breeding animal, earning of self-employment income, or provision for a special method for reporting sales.

To be deductible, expenses paid or incurred in a business, trade, or profession during the period must be ordinary and necessary for its operation. With a few exceptions, there is no limit on the amounts that can be deducted by a business, trade, or profession for a specific ordinary and necessary expense as long as the amount deducted is reasonable. It is not necessary to have more revenue than expense in any given year. An exception regarding the deduction of a net operating loss involves hobby losses which are discussed later.

The remainder of this chapter will be devoted to businesses operated as sole proprietorships, but the reader should keep in mind that the tax treatment of revenues and expenses for sole proprietorships generally will apply to entities operating as partnerships and corporations as well.

Deductible Business Expenses

The following expenses, to the extent that they are ordinary, necessary, and reasonable in amount, are deductible:

- Accounting and legal fees
- Advertising
- Bank service charges
- Bookkeeping, reference books, & subscriptions to professional publications
- Car and truck costs
- Commissions
- Computer and printing services
- Depletion
- Depreciation
- Dues
- Education
- Employee benefit programs
- Employment agency fees
- Entertainment, gifts, and gratuities
- Insurance, license fees, and taxes
- Interest on business loans
- Lobbying
- Maintenance and repairs
- Office equipment rental
- Office supplies
- Pension plan for employees
- Professional assistance
- Profit-sharing plan for employees
- Public transportation
- Rent
- Salaries
- Tax advisory and preparation fees
- Telephone and utilities
- Travel away from home
- Work clothes

Profit or (Loss) Reporting by Sole Proprietorships

Any profit or (loss) derived from a business or a profession operated as a sole proprietorship is taxable (or deductible). In calculating the amount of profit, deduction may be made for the cost of goods sold and for all ordinary and necessary business expenses to the extent reasonable in amount. If a business or profession is operated at a loss, the loss may be deducted from other income in calculating the individual taxpayer's taxable income.

The following tests may be applied in determining what expenses may be deducted when calculating the net profit or (loss) of a business or profession operated as a sole proprietorship:

1. Only ordinary, necessary, and reasonable expenses paid or incurred during the taxable year in carrying on a trade or business are deductible.
2. Any necessary expense that is not a capital investment incurred in good faith in a particular business is to be considered an ordinary expense.
3. Capital expenditures which are not deductible should be treated as long-term investments and be added to the cost of the property to which they apply. Capital expenditures can usually be recovered by cost recovery deductions such as depreciation.

Sole proprietorships report their income on either Schedule C-EZ, Net Profit From Business or on Schedule C, Profit or Loss From Business. Schedule C-EZ is a new form for 1992. Since Schedule C-EZ can only be used by a limited number of sole proprietors, the following discussion regarding the reporting of income by sole proprietors is focused on Schedule C, Profit or Loss From Business.

Structure of Schedule C

Schedule C, Profit or Loss from Business (Sole Proprietorship), is a two-page schedule for reporting the profit or (loss) from a business operating as a proprietorship. Schedule C, shown in Illustration 8-1, is a "building block" schedule filed in support of Form 1040, page 1 (line 12). The following five types of information are reported in Schedule C, page 1:

1. Identification of proprietor
2. Identification of business and other business data
3. Income
4. Expenses
5. Net profit or (loss)

The name of the proprietor as it appears on Form 1040 and the proprietor's SSN are entered on the first line of Schedule C. If a joint return is filed, only the name of the proprietor appears on Schedule C. If both taxpayers on a joint re-

---

A Sole Proprietor's Requirements for Using Schedule C-EZ

- Had gross receipts from business of $25,000 or less
- Had business expenses of $2,000 or less
- Used the cash method of accounting
- Did not have an inventory at any time during the year
- Did not have a net loss
- Had only one business as a sole proprietor
- Had no employees during the year
- Was not required to file Form 4562, Depreciation and Amortization
- Did not deduct expenses for business use of home
- Did not have prior year unallowed passive activity losses from this business

---

turn each own a business, a separate Schedule C is filed for each proprietor. If more than one business is owned by a proprietor, a separate Schedule C must be filed for each business.

The identification of the business and other data about the business are entered as Items A–J. This information identifies the business and informs the IRS of the business practices being used.

The third type of data on Schedule C is income (which is usually referred to as revenue for financial reporting purposes). Net receipts or sales is calculated by subtracting returns and allowances from gross receipts or sales. Cost of goods sold, calculated in Part III of Schedule C, is subtracted from net receipts or sales to obtain gross profit. Other income is added to obtain the amount of gross income.

In Part II of Schedule C, deductions for ordinary, necessary, and reasonable expenses are listed. Total expenses before expenses for the business use of the home are listed. This amount is subtracted from gross income to arrive at the tentative profit (loss). Expenses related to the business use of the taxpayer's home (reported in detail on Form 8829) would be deducted to arrive at the net profit or (loss). The amount of profit or (loss) is carried to Form 1040 (line 12), and the amount of profit, but not a loss, is carried to Schedule SE, Self-Employment Tax.

If there is a net loss, the proprietor must describe his or her investment in the business as being "all investment is at risk" (line 32a) or "some investment is not at risk" (line 32b) by checking the appropriate box. The limitation on losses of "at risk" amounts is discussed in Chapter 10.

Schedule C, Page 2 includes Part III and Part IV. Part III is used to calculate the cost of goods sold. Total cost of goods sold is carried to page 1 and subtracted to calculate gross profit. Part IV furnishes the codes for the principal business or professional activity of the business. The code that most closely describes the business is entered on page 1 (line B).

Filled-In Schedule C

Illustration 8-1

A filled-in Schedule C filed in support of the Form 1040 for George L. Monroe is shown. Mr. Monroe owns a management consulting business, George L. Monroe, Consulting. His EIN is 39-6420797. The cash method of accounting is used. As there is no merchandise inventory in the business, Mr. Monroe answered "Does Not Apply" to Question G regarding the method used to value closing inventory and did not complete Part III of Schedule C, Cost of Goods Sold. Since he materially participated in the operation of his consulting business, he answered "Yes" to Question I. He included total gross receipts under the cash method in Part I (Income), and he has included all expenses pertaining to the business in Part II. Since Mr. Monroe is self-employed, he also would have completed Schedule SE. Schedule SE was discussed in Chapter 7 so will be mentioned only briefly later.

Item-by-Item Reporting on Schedule C

To provide a further understanding of the components of Schedule C reporting of Income in Part I and Expenses in Part II, comments follow regarding each item of Schedule C. The amounts described relate to the filled-in Schedule C for George L. Monroe shown in Illustration 8-1.

Schedule C, Part I: Income

Gross receipts or sales (line 1) totaled $156,921.40.

Returns and allowances (lines 2 & 3) would be subtracted from gross receipts or sales to arrive at net receipts or net sales (line 3). Since Monroe did not have any returns or allowances, the amount shown is $156,921.40.

Cost of goods sold (line 4) is deducted from net receipts or sales to calculate gross profit (line 5). Cost of goods sold is calculated on Schedule C, Part III. George Monroe did not complete Part III since he does not sell a product and, therefore, has no cost of goods sold.

Gross profit (line 5) is calculated by subtracting cost of goods sold from net receipts or sales. If cost of goods sold is not calculated because inventories are not a major source of business, then gross profit (line 5) will be the same amount as net receipts or sales (line 3) as is the case for George Monroe, or $156,921.40.

Other income (line 6) includes a refund or tax credit for Federal and state gasoline tax. Other income is an infrequent category in a sole proprietorship.

Gross income (line 7) is calculated by adding other income (line 6), if any, to the gross profit (line 5). Since George Monroe did not have any income to report (line 6), the gross income (line 7) of $156,921.40 is the same as the gross profit (line 5).

Schedule C, Part II: Expenses

Advertising (line 8) expenses are deductible if they are ordinary, necessary, and reasonable in amount and are business related. Advertising expenses cannot be deducted if the purpose is to influence legislation. Expenses for public service advertising which is designed to keep the public regularly aware of the company's name are generally deductible if the amount of the expense is reasonably related to the amount of business expected to be gained in the future. Examples of such advertising would be that which encourages people to contribute to charities, buy savings bonds, or participate in similar public activities. George Monroe shows $492 spent for advertising during 1992.

Illustration 8-1
Filled-In Schedule C, Form 1040

SCHEDULE C
(Form 1040)

Department of the Treasury
Internal Revenue Service

Profit or Loss From Business
(Sole Proprietorship)

▶ Partnerships, joint ventures, etc., must file Form 1065.

▶ Attach to Form 1040 or Form 1041.   ▶ See Instructions for Schedule C (Form 1040).

OMB No. 1545-0074

1992

Attachment Sequence No. **09**

Name of proprietor: **George L. Monroe**

Social security number (SSN)

A Principal business or profession, including product or service (see page C-1)
Management Consultant

B Enter principal business code (from page 2) ▶ 7 2 8 6

C Business name **George L. Monroe, Consulting**

D Employer ID number (Not SSN) 3 9 6 4 2 0 7 9 7

E Business address (including suite or room no.) ▶ ....
City, town or post office, state, and ZIP code

F Accounting method: (1) ☒ Cash (2) ☐ Accrual (3) ☐ Other (specify) ▶ ....

G Method(s) used to value closing inventory: (1) ☐ Cost (2) ☐ Lower of cost or market (3) ☐ Other (attach explanation) (4) ☒ Does not apply (if checked, skip line H)

		Yes	No
H	Was there any change in determining quantities, costs, or valuations between opening and closing inventory? If "Yes," attach explanation		X
I	Did you "materially participate" in the operation of this business during 1992? If "No," see page C-2 for limitations on losses	X	
J	Was this business in operation at the end of 1992?	12	
K	How many months was this business in operation during 1992? ▶		
L	If this is the first Schedule C filed for this business, check here ▶ ☐		

Part I Income

1	Gross receipts or sales. **Caution:** *If this income was reported to you on Form W-2 and the "Statutory employee" box on that form was checked, see page C-2 and check here* ▶ ☐	1	156,921 40
2	Returns and allowances	2	
3	Subtract line 2 from line 1	3	156,921 40
4	Cost of goods sold (from line 40 on page 2)	4	
5	**Gross profit.** Subtract line 4 from line 3	5	156,921 40
6	Other income, including Federal and state gasoline or fuel tax credit or refund (see page C-2)	6	
7	**Gross income.** Add lines 5 and 6 ▶	7	156,921 40

Part II Expenses (Caution: *Do not enter expenses for business use of your home on lines 8–27. Instead, see line 30.*)

8	Advertising	8	492 00	21	Repairs and maintenance	21	1,389 00
9	Bad debts from sales or services (see page C-3)	9		22	Supplies (not included in Part III)	22	1,641 86
10	Car and truck expenses (see page C-3—also attach **Form 4562**)	10	2,842 00	23	Taxes and licenses	23	7,210 15
11	Commissions and fees	11		24	Travel, meals, and entertainment:		
12	Depletion	12		a Travel		24a	842 10
13	Depreciation and section 179 expense deduction (not included in Part III) (see page C-3)	13	1,619 40	b Meals and entertainment	430 18		
14	Employee benefit programs (other than on line 19)	14		c Enter 20% of line 24b subject to limitations (see page C-4)	86 04		
15	Insurance (other than health)	15	742 00	d Subtract line 24c from line 24b		24d	344 14
16	Interest:			25 Utilities		25	3,600 15
a	Mortgage (paid to banks, etc.)	16a		26 Wages (less jobs credit)		26	40,615 82
b	Other	16b		27a Other expenses (list type and amount):			
17	Legal and professional services	17	310 00	Bank service charges 205.15			
18	Office expense	18	1,640 00	Prof. Sub. 575.00			
19	Pension and profit-sharing plans	19					
20	Rent or lease (see page C-4):						
a	Vehicles, machinery, and equipment	20a	1,200 00				
b	Other business property	20b	7,200 00	27b Total other expenses		27b	780 15

28	**Total expenses** before expenses for business use of home. Add lines 8 through 27b in columns ▶	28	72,468 87
29	Tentative profit (loss). Subtract line 28 from line 7	29	84,452 53
30	Expenses for business use of your home. Attach **Form 8829**	30	
31	**Net profit or (loss).** Subtract line 30 from line 29. If a profit, enter here and on Form 1040, line 12. Also, enter the net profit on Schedule SE, line 2 (statutory employees, see page C-5). If a loss, you MUST go on to line 32 (fiduciaries, see page C-5)	31	84,452 53
32	If you have a loss, you MUST check the box that describes your investment in this activity (see page C-5)	32a ☐ All investment is at risk. 32b ☐ Some investment is not at risk.	

If you checked 32a, enter the loss on Form 1040, line 12, and Schedule SE, line 2 (statutory employees, see page C-5). If you checked 32b, you MUST attach **Form 6198**.

For Paperwork Reduction Act Notice, see Form 1040 instructions.   Cat. No. 11334P   Schedule C (Form 1040) 1992

Bad debts from sales or services (line 9). Business bad debts that arise out of the operations of a business, such as credit sales to customers or loans to suppliers, clients, employees, or distributors are deductible. There must be a true creditor-debtor relationship between the taxpayer (creditor) and the debtor. There must be a legal obligation to pay a fixed sum of money. The taxpayer must realize a loss because of inability to collect the money owed. The taxpayer must show that the debt is worthless and will remain worthless, and must have taken reasonable steps to collect the debt, including going to court unless it can be shown that a judgment from the court would be uncollectible, such as in a bankruptcy situation. The taxpayer must have an actual loss of money or have reported the amount owed in gross income (accrual method) of the current or an earlier tax year.

To be deductible, a business bad debt must be closely related to the activity of the business and the taxpayer must have had a dominant business reason to enter into the transaction. If any part of accounts or notes receivable are uncollectible, the uncollectible part is a business bad debt. Under current tax law, business taxpayers (with the exception of certain financial institutions) must use the specific charge-off method in which the bad debt is deductible in the year it is actually determined to be worthless. A business bad debt may be deducted even if it became worthless after the taxpayer went out of business. Since George Monroe reports on the cash method, there are no bad debts to be reported.

Car and truck expenses (line 10). Transportation includes the ordinary and necessary expenses of getting from one work place to another in the course of the taxpayer's business or profession when not traveling away from home. Transportation expenses when traveling away from home are deductible as travel expenses. Costs of operating a vehicle for business use are deductible. If a vehicle is used for both business and personal purposes, special rules apply and only the percent of expenses allocated to business use is deductible. Special rules apply if the car is used less than 50% for business. Commuting expenses in going between the taxpayer's home and the regular place of work or fees paid for parking at the taxpayer's place of business are not deductible.

A taxpayer must keep records to show when he or she started using the car (or truck) for business and the cost or other basis of the vehicle. Also, a taxpayer must show the total miles and the business miles the car was driven during the year. If a taxpayer uses the actual expenses, he or she must keep records of the cost of operating the car. If actual expenses are not deducted for the use of a car or truck for business, the standard mileage rate of 28 cents per mile may be deducted for an unlimited number of business miles. If the taxpayer chooses to use the standard mileage rate, it must be used in the first year the car is placed in service in the business and can then be used in each successive year for use of the car in business. If the taxpayer chooses not to use the standard mileage rate in the first year, that rate cannot be used in any future year for that car. When the standard mileage rate is elected in the first year of business use for the car, the taxpayer is considered to have made an election not to use the MACRS (Chapter 9). To use the standard mileage rate, the taxpayer must (1) own the car, (2) not use the car for hire, and (3) not operate a fleet of cars using two or more at the same time. Parking fees and tolls can be deducted in addition to the standard mileage rate. Interest expense on car loans is considered to be personal interest which is not deductible. The parenthetical instruction on this line specifies that the taxpayer must attach Form 4562, Depreciation and Amortization. For 1992 George Monroe reported $2,842.10.

Commissions and fees (line 11) paid in the course of business are deductible. For 1992 George Monroe did not incur any expenses for commissions or fees.

Deductible Car & Truck Expenses

- Garage rent, parking, and tolls
- Gasoline, oil, and lubrication
- Insurance, licenses, and auto club
- Lease payments
- Maintenance and repairs
- Property taxes
- Tires and batteries
- Washing and polishing

Depletion (line 12). Two methods of depletion are available for calculating the depletion allowance for a proprietor to recover an economic investment in mineral deposits or oil and gas wells. The two methods are cost depletion and percentage depletion. Readers are referred to advanced texts for explanations of the use of these two methods in recovering an economic interest in natural resources. Monroe's business had no investment in natural resources.

Depreciation and Section 179 expense deduction (line 13). Cost recovery in the form of a depreciation deduction for the use of business property is discussed in Chapter 9. The amount of $1,619.40 deducted by George Monroe would have been supported by completing and attaching Form 4562, Depreciation and Amortization.

Employee benefit programs (line 14). Employee benefit programs other than pension and profit sharing plans are deductible. George Monroe had no benefit plans for employees.

Insurance (line 15). Premiums on business property, such as real estate, furniture and equipment, and transportation equipment are deductible. The year of deduction depends upon whether the taxpayer is on the cash method or the accrual method. If the taxpayer uses the cash method of reporting, the premiums generally are deductible in the year paid. However, if a taxpayer makes an advance payment of a premium on a policy that covers more than one tax year, the taxpayer cannot deduct the entire premium in the year paid even if the taxpayer is using the cash method of accounting. Only that portion of the premium that applies to the tax reporting year is deductible. The portion of the premium related to future years is deductible in the applicable years.

EXAMPLE 5 ————————————————

Assume a fire insurance premium on an office building is $2,400 for a two-year period from November 1, 1991 to October 31, 1993. If the taxpayer on the cash method paid the entire $2,400 premium on November 1, 1991, only $1,200 of the premium is deductible on the taxpayer's 1992 return ($2,400/2). $1,000 would be deductible in 1993. On the accrual method, the applicable portion of the premium would be deductible for the year that the insurance protec-

tion is provided. In this example, the premiums would be deductible each year on the accrual method in the same amount as on the cash method. If the taxpayer on the cash method paid the entire $2,400 premium on January 15, 1992, the amount deductible in 1992 would be $1,400, which covers $200 for 1991 and $1,200 for 1992. On the accrual method, $200 would be deductible in 1991. George Monroe deducted $742 of insurance premiums paid in 1992 applicable to 1992 coverage on business property.

Interest (line 16). Included are business interest on mortgages and on other borrowings for business use. If money was borrowed to provide working capital for the business, for instance, the interest expense paid during the year on such a loan would be deductible (line 16b). If loan proceeds are used partly for nonbusiness purposes, then an allocation must be made so that only the interest on the business use of borrowed money is deductible. George Monroe incurred no interest expense in 1992.

EXAMPLE 6 ————————————————

If a taxpayer borrows funds that are secured by business property, but uses the funds to buy an automobile for personal use, none of the interest expense is allocable for business purposes and would not be deductible on Schedule C.

Legal and professional services (line 17). Legal and professional services are deductible. George Monroe deducted $310 that was paid for accounting advice related to his business.

Office expense (line 18). Included are postage, stationery, and other general expenses of operating a business office. George Monroe paid $1,640 in 1992 for office expense.

Pension and profit-sharing plans (line 19). Pension and profit-sharing plans for employees are deductible and are discussed later in this chapter. George Monroe had no pension or profit-sharing plan for employees.

Rent or lease (line 20). Rent or lease expense is the amount paid for the use of property not owned by the taxpayer. In general, rent is deductible as an expense when the property is used in the taxpayer's trade or business. If the taxpayer will receive equity in, or title to, the property, the rent is a capital expenditure and not rent expense. If rent is paid in advance, the taxpayer can only deduct the amount that applies to the use of the property during the tax year in which the rent payment was made with the remainder deductible in the years to which the rent applies. During 1992 George Monroe paid $1,200 for the lease of equipment and $7,200 for the rent of office space. These amounts are reported on Schedule C (lines 20a and 20b). If a car is leased, the costs related to business use portion of the lease payment is deductible. Any advance lease payments must be spread over the entire lease period. Payments made to buy the car are not deductible even if these payments are described as lease payments.

Repairs and maintenance (line 21). The costs of maintaining business property are deductible. Repair expenses must be distinguished from capital expenditures. Expenses for keeping business property in a normal and efficient operating condition which (1) do not add to the value or usefulness of the property and (2) do not significantly increase the property's life can be deducted as repairs and maintenance. These expenses are incurred to maintain the property in a normal operating condition. The costs deductible under these guidelines include labor, supplies, and other related types of expenses. If the repairs and maintenance are allocable to cost of goods sold, they should be deducted on Schedule C under Part III in calculating cost of goods sold rather than under Part II. George Monroe deducted $1,389 as repairs and maintenance related to his furniture, office equipment, and vehicles.

Supplies (line 22). Included are wrapping paper, cost of books, professional instruments, and like items provided that the normal use of these types of materials is less than one year. If unusually large purchases of supplies are made, the taxpayer may only be allowed to deduct that portion which represents the amount of supplies normally used within one operating year. George Monroe deducted $1,641.86 of supplies for the year 1992.

Taxes and licenses (line 23). Taxes and licenses, such as business licenses required by state and local governments for operating a trade or business and vehicle licenses for operating business vehicles, are deductible in the year paid. Deductible taxes include property taxes on business buildings and equipment, the employer's share of social security taxes paid for employees, and state and federal unemployment taxes paid on employees. The total of all of these types of taxes amounted to $7,210.15.

Travel, meals, and entertainment (lines 24, 24a, 24b). Travel expenses incurred and paid while traveling away from home for business or professional purposes are deductible. Travel expenses for personal or vacation purposes or that are lavish or extravagant are not deductible. A taxpayer is traveling away from home if the business activities require the taxpayer to be away from the general area of the tax home substantially longer than an ordinary day's work and, during the time off while away, the taxpayer needs to get sleep or rest to meet the demands of the business. Generally, the tax home is the general area or entire city in which the taxpayer's business is located. The location of the family home is not a factor since the taxpayer, in some cases, may be considered to be traveling away from home even while working in the city in which the taxpayer and family are living. If the taxpayer has two or more offices in separate areas, the tax home is the general area where the main place of business or main office is located. The following factors should be used in determining what location is the main place of business: (1) the total time ordinarily spent working in each area, (2) the degree of business activity in each area, and (3) the relative amount of income from each area. The taxpayer need not be away from the tax home for a whole day or from dusk to dawn as long as the relief from duty is long enough to get necessary sleep or rest. Travel expenses do not include transportation expenses while not traveling away from home.

Schedule C requires travel expenses to be reported separately from meals and entertainment since qualified meal and entertainment expenses are only deductible to the extent of 80% of the total. George Monroe incurred and paid $842.10 for travel expenses (line 24a).

Business entertainment expenses are deductible only if incurred and paid while carrying on the taxpayer's trade or business. The taxpayer must be able to show that the ex-

Deductible Travel Expenses

- Air, rail, and bus transportation
- Baggage charges
- Cleaning and laundry
- Lodgings
- Meals and entertainment (subject to limitation)
- Operating and maintaining a car
- Other expenses related to travel
- Public stenographer's fee
- Taxi fares from the airport to the hotel, from one customer to another, or from one place of business to another
- Telephone and telegraph
- Tips that are related to travel

penses are (1) directly related to the active conduct of the business or (2) associated with the active conduct of the business, in which case entertainment must directly precede or follow a substantial business discussion. Entertainment includes any activity generally considered to provide entertainment, amusement, or recreation. It also includes satisfying the personal, living, or family needs of individuals, such as providing food, hotel, and/or a car for business customers or their families. Entertainment includes the cost of a meal provided to a customer or client. Generally the taxpayer must be present when the food or beverages are provided for the entertainment-related meal to be deductible. When figuring the deduction for the cost of tickets for entertainment or recreation, no more than the face value of the ticket is allowed. This rule excludes deducting extra costs for scalping, ticket agencies, and brokers.

In general, only 80% of business-related entertainment is deductible. This rule applies to self-employed persons, their clients, and their employees to the extent reimbursed. The 80% limit applies to entertainment expenses incurred while traveling away from home on business, entertaining customers at your place of business or other locations such as a restaurant, or attending a business meeting, convention, or a business meal at a club. Taxes and tips related to a meal or entertainment are included in the amount subject to the 80% limit. Also included are cover charges for admission to a club, rent paid for a room for meals and entertainment, and the amount paid for parking at a sports arena. Not included in the 80% limit is the cost of transportation to and from a business meal or entertainment activity. If the taxpayer makes payments that include other expenses in addition to meals and entertainment, an allocation must be made, on a reasonable basis, between the expenses for meals and entertainment and the expenses for other services, such as separating out meal costs from hotel charges for both room and meals. The 80% limit is applied after determining the amount of entertainment expenses that would be otherwise deductible.

George Monroe incurred and paid $430.18 for meals and entertainment (line 24b). However, 20% of these expenses or $86.04 (20% x $430.18) is not deductible (line 24c). Only $344.14 are deductible meal and entertainment expenses (line 24d).

EXAMPLE 7 ————————————————————

A taxpayer incurs $450 of expenses for clients for rooms, meals, and entertainment. The room charge is $190, and $50 of the meals and entertainment is considered to be lavish and extravagant. The deduction for meals and entertainment would be $168, calculated as follows:

$450 - $190 = $260 - $50 = $210 x 80% = $168

Utilities (line 25). Utilities include heat, light, power, and telephones and are not deductible to the extent that they are incurred for personal use. If the taxpayer has an office in the home, the cost of basic telephone service for the first telephone line is not deductible as a business expense. The operating cost of cellular telephone equipment may be a business expense, but such equipment is classified as "listed property" after December 31, 1989. The concept of listed property is discussed in Chapter 9 and relates to limitations on the allowable depreciation deduction. George Monroe incurred and paid $3,600.15 of utility expenses in 1992.

Wages (line 26). Wages paid to employees totaled $40,615.82 during 1992. Nothing is included for payments directly to George Monroe or for any withdrawals by Monroe from the business. A business must *excluded* any wages which are *included* in cost of goods sold.

Salaries of employees who are also stockholders must meet the same tests of deductibility as those of any other employee, such as being ordinary and necessary, reasonable in amount, and paid for services actually performed for the business.

Other expenses (line 27). Included are expenses that are not deductible elsewhere on Schedule C. Each of these expenses that are applicable to a sole proprietor should be listed by type and dollar amount. Other expenses totaled $780.15.

Total expenses (line 28). Total expenses (lines 8 through 27) equaled $72,468.87. This amount is subtracted from gross income (line 7) to arrive at tentative profit or (loss) amount (line 29). The tentative profit or (loss) for Monroe's consulting business is $84,452.53 for 1992. This amount is brought forward (line 31) if no expenses for business use of the home are deducted as calculated on Form 8829. The net profit or (loss) amount (line 31) is carried to Form 1040, page 1 (line 12) and to Schedule SE, Self-Employment Tax (line 2), for the purpose of calculating self-employment tax (Chapter 7).

Schedule C, Part III: Cost of Goods Sold

To complete the discussion of the preparation of Schedule C, readers need to understand the calculation of cost of goods sold for proprietors in a manufacturing, wholesale, or retail business. The amount of cost of goods sold is calculated by completing Schedule C, Part III. The calculation of cost of goods sold consists of adding to beginning inventory (line 33), the cost of net purchases, labor, materials and supplies, and other costs for the year (line 38). Ending inventory (line 39) is subtracted to arrive at cost of goods sold (line 40). Cost of goods sold (line 40) is reported on Schedule C, Part I (line 4). The amount of cost of goods sold should not include selling expenses or any other expenses that are not directly related to obtaining or producing the goods sold.

EXAMPLE 8 —————————————————

The following schedule illustrates the calculation of cost of goods sold:

Inventory at beginning of year	$ 74,500
Less: Cost of merchandise contributed to charity	2,500
	$ 72,000
Add: Merchandise purchased during year	$ 98,500
Labor	32,000
Materials and supplies	6,300
Other costs	9,700
	$146,500
Merchandise available for sale	$218,500
Less: Inventory at end of year	79,200
Cost of goods sold	$139,300

For a manufacturer, the total value of the beginning inventory includes the sum of raw materials, work in process, finished goods, and materials and supplies used in manufacturing the products. For merchants, the beginning inventory consists of merchandise held for sale. The beginning inventory of one year usually should be identical to the ending inventory of the previous year.

For merchants, merchandise purchased includes all goods bought for sale during the year. For manufacturers or producers, raw materials purchased includes all of the raw materials acquired during the year to be used in manufacturing the finished product. In recording purchases of merchandise or raw materials, trade discounts should be deducted to arrive at the actual price paid. Cash discounts can be credited to a separate discount account or they may be deducted from total purchases for the year. Whichever method is used, it must be consistently followed from year to year. To arrive at net purchases, all returns and allowances must be deducted from total purchases during the year.

Freight In is included in the cost of purchases to arrive at the merchandise available for sale. Readers are referred to advanced accounting texts for more information about the calculation of cost of goods sold for a manufacturing firm.

The assigned value of ending inventory is subtracted from the merchandise available for sale to arrive at cost of goods sold. After the cost of goods sold is calculated on Schedule C, Part III, the amount is carried to Schedule C (line 4) to be subtracted from net receipts from sales in arriving at gross profit from manufacturing or merchandising activities. Finally the operating expenses for the year are subtracted from gross profit or (loss) to arrive at the net profit or (loss) for the year. Illustration 8-2 shows the presentation of a Schedule C when a determination of cost of goods sold is a factor in calculating net business income in a case where the taxpayer is a retail merchant.

Filled-In Schedule C

Illustration 8-2

John R. Williams, whose Form 1040, U.S. Individual Income Tax Return, was shown in Illustration 7-3 in Chapter 7, is the sole proprietor of the Williams Hardware Store. His business revenues, cost of goods sold, and expenses for the year ended December 31, 1992, are shown on the income statement in Table 8-1. A filled-in Schedule C for Mr. Williams is shown in Illustration 8-2. Schedule C was prepared in support of the amount of net income subject to the income tax reported by Mr. Williams on Form 1040, page 1 (line 12).

Schedule C provides for taxpayer identification data and information on accounting methods. The same accounting methods must be followed consistently in preparing Schedule C, unless the necessary permission to change is obtained from the IRS. The taxpayer must answer questions relating to deductions for the method of valuing inventories, and any substantial change in the manner of determining quantities, costs, or valuations between the opening and closing inventories. Inventories are important factors in the determination of net income or (loss), and any change could be a change in an accounting method, which is subject to special rules.

An additional question asks if the taxpayer materially participated in the operation of the business in 1992. The degree of participation in operations will determine whether the net profit or (loss) from the business is to be treated as active income (loss) or passive income (loss).

Part I of Schedule C is used to report income from the sale of goods, land, services, and other sources. The calculation of cost of goods sold is determined in Part III. Under the regula-

tions, a taxpayer is given the option of reporting cash discounts as income or of deducting cash discounts from purchases in calculating the cost of goods sold, as long as a consistent procedure is followed. Schedule C, Part III (line 34) reflects gross purchases for Williams Hardware Store of $180,716 less purchase discounts of $3,614 and the cost of merchandise withdrawals of $400 to give a balance of $176,702. The cost of the merchandise withdrawals is deducted from purchases so that the correct cost of goods sold can be calculated to support the entry on Schedule C, Part I (line 4).

The net profit shown on Schedule C, Part II, amounts to $57,959, whereas the net income shown in the income statement amounted to only $57,102. Part of the difference is accounted for by the fact that the charitable contributions paid by the business, amounting to $787, are entered on Mr. Williams' individual return as a deduction from AGI instead of as a business deduction on Schedule C. The remaining difference, $70, is the result of having to reduce meal and entertainment expenses by 20% on Schedule C.

Schedule C also requires a summary of the items used in determining gross profit and total income as well as a listing of business expenses. The net profit reported on Schedule C (line 31) is carried to Form 1040 (line 12) and is also entered on Schedule SE, Self-Employment Tax (line 2). A loss on Schedule C (line 31) also would be reported on Form 1040 (line 12) as negative income. However, if the business does have a loss, the question on Schedule C (line 32) must be answered regarding whether some or all amounts are at risk for the taxpayer. If only some are at risk, the taxpayer must attach Form 6198, At-Risk Limitations, which will determine how much, if any, of the loss is deductible on Form 1040 (line 12).

Business expenses are listed in Schedule C, Part II, including the deduction for cost recovery (depreciation). Mr. Williams used Form 4562, Depreciation and Amortization, to calculate the depreciation deduction of $4,200 on Form 4562 (line 20), based on the assets he had in service during 1992. The $4,200 is then carried to Schedule C, Part II (line 13) to be used along with other business expenses in calculating net profit for the year. The detailed calculation of the $4,200 of depreciation for Mr. Williams' Schedule C is presented in Chapter 9, Table 9-9, in connection with a detailed discussion of cost recovery and depreciation.

Other Business Expenses

This section covers some ordinary and necessary business expenses a sole proprietor may incur in operating a business that have not been explained earlier.

Business Use of the Home

If a sole proprietor uses part of his or her home as a place of business, the taxpayer is allowed to deduct the expenses of that part of the home used for business. These expenses may be deducted only if that part of the home is used regularly and exclusively as (1) the principal place of business or (2) a place to meet or deal with patients, clients, or customers in the nor-

---

Table 8-1
Income Statement for Williams Hardware Store

WILLIAMS HARDWARE STORE
Income Statement
For Year Ended December 31, 1992

Operating revenue:			
Sales		$284,280	
Less sales returns and allowances		2,751	
Net sales			$281,529
Cost of merchandise sold:			
Merchandise inventory, beginning of period		$131,216	
Purchases	$180,716		
Less purchases discount	3,614		
Net purchases	$177,102		
Less merchandise withdrawn for personal use	400	176,702	
Merchandise available for sale		$307,918	
Less merchandise inventory, end of period		167,546	
Cost of merchandise sold			140,372
Gross profit on sales			$141,157
Operating expenses:			
Advertising expense		$ 3,906	
Bad debts from sales or services		1,531	
Charitable contributions		787	
Cost recovery (depreciation expense)		4,200	
Entertainment expense		350	
Insurance expense		2,250	
Legal and professional services		6,693	
Miscellaneous expense		15	
Payroll taxes		8,845	
Personal property taxes		960	
Rent expense		10,200	
Repairs to store equipment		2,125	
Supplies expense		3,400	
Telephone expense		1,258	
Travel		184	
Truck expense		2,498	
Utilities expense		3,908	
Wages expense		31,297	
Total operating expenses			84,407
Operating income			$ 56,750
Other income:			
Interest income			584
			$ 57,334
Other expenses:			
Interest expense			232
Net income			$ 57,102

Illustration 8-2
Filled-In Schedule C, Form 1040, Page 1

SCHEDULE C
(Form 1040)

Department of the Treasury
Internal Revenue Service

Profit or Loss From Business
(Sole Proprietorship)

▶ Partnerships, joint ventures, etc., must file Form 1065.

▶ Attach to Form 1040 or Form 1041.   ▶ See Instructions for Schedule C (Form 1040).

OMB No. 1545-0074

1992

Attachment
Sequence No. **09**

Name of proprietor: **John R. Williams**

Social security number (SSN): 272 : 11 : 8245

A Principal business or profession, including product or service (see page C-1): **Retail Hardware**

B Enter principal business code (from page 2) ▶ | 4 | 4 | 5 | 7 |

C Business name: **Williams Hardware Store**

D Employer ID number (Not SSN): 9 | 1 : 0 | 6 | 2 | 4 | 4 | 3 | 1 |

E Business address (including suite or room no.) ▶ **Verona, WI 53593-3644**
   City, town or post office, state, and ZIP code

F Accounting method: (1) ☐ Cash (2) ☒ Accrual (3) ☐ Other (specify) ▶ ....

G Method(s) used to value closing inventory: (1) ☒ Cost (2) ☐ Lower of cost or market (3) ☐ Other (attach explanation) (4) ☐ Does not apply (if checked, skip line H)

		Yes	No
H	Was there any change in determining quantities, costs, or valuations between opening and closing inventory? If "Yes," attach explanation		X
I	Did you "materially participate" in the operation of this business during 1992? If "No," see page C-2 for limitations on losses	X	
J	Was this business in operation at the end of 1992?	X	

K How many months was this business in operation during 1992? ▶ 12

L If this is the first Schedule C filed for this business, check here ▶ ☐

Part I Income

1	Gross receipts or sales. **Caution:** *If this income was reported to you on Form W-2 and the "Statutory employee" box on that form was checked, see page C-2 and check here* ▶ ☐	1	284,280 00
2	Returns and allowances	2	2,751 00
3	Subtract line 2 from line 1	3	281,529 00
4	Cost of goods sold (from line 40 on page 2)	4	140,372 00
5	**Gross profit.** Subtract line 4 from line 3	5	141,157 00
6	Other income, including Federal and state gasoline or fuel tax credit or refund (see page C-2)	6	584 00
7	**Gross income.** Add lines 5 and 6 ▶	7	141,741 00

Part II Expenses (Caution: *Do not enter expenses for business use of your home on lines 8–27. Instead, see line 30.*)

8	Advertising	8	3,906 00	21	Repairs and maintenance	21	2,125 00
9	Bad debts from sales or services (see page C-3)	9	1,531 00	22	Supplies (not included in Part III)	22	3,400 00
10	Car and truck expenses (see page C-3—also attach Form 4562)	10	2,498 00	23	Taxes and licenses	23	9,805 00
11	Commissions and fees	11		24	Travel, meals, and entertainment:		
12	Depletion	12			a Travel	24a	184 00
13	Depreciation and section 179 expense deduction (not included in Part III) (see page C-3)	13	4,200 00		b Meals and entertainment . 350 00		
14	Employee benefit programs (other than on line 19)	14			c Enter 20% of line 24b subject to limitations (see page C-4) . 70 00		
15	Insurance (other than health)	15	2,250 00		d Subtract line 24c from line 24b	24d	280 00
16	Interest:			25	Utilities	25	5,166 00
a	Mortgage (paid to banks, etc.)	16a		26	Wages (less jobs credit)	26	31,297 00
b	Other	16b	232 00	27a	Other expenses (list type and amount):		
17	Legal and professional services	17	6,693 00		....		
18	Office expense	18			....		
19	Pension and profit-sharing plans	19			....		
20	Rent or lease (see page C-4):				....		
a	Vehicles, machinery, and equipment	20a			....		
b	Other business property	20b	10,200 00	27b	Total other expenses	27b	15 00

28	**Total expenses** before expenses for business use of home. Add lines 8 through 27b in columns ▶	28	83,782 00
29	Tentative profit (loss). Subtract line 28 from line 7	29	57,959 00
30	Expenses for business use of your home. Attach **Form 8829**	30	
31	**Net profit or (loss).** Subtract line 30 from line 29. If a profit, enter here and on Form 1040, line 12. Also, enter the net profit on Schedule SE, line 2 (statutory employees, see page C-5). If a loss, you MUST go on to line 32 (fiduciaries, see page C-5)	31	57,959 00

32 If you have a loss, you MUST check the box that describes your investment in this activity (see page C-5)

   32a ☐ All investment is at risk.
   32b ☐ Some investment is not at risk.

   If you checked 32a, enter the loss on Form 1040, line 12, and Schedule SE, line 2 (statutory employees, see page C-5). If you checked 32b, you MUST attach **Form 6198.**

For Paperwork Reduction Act Notice, see Form 1040 instructions.   Cat. No. 11334P   Schedule C (Form 1040) 1992

Illustration 8-2
Filled-In Schedule C, Form 1040, Page 2

Schedule C (Form 1040) 1992   Page **2**

Part III   Cost of Goods Sold (see page C-5)

33	Inventory at beginning of year. If different from last year's closing inventory, attach explanation . .	33	131,216	00
34	Purchases less cost of items withdrawn for personal use.	34	176,702	00
35	Cost of labor. Do not include salary paid to yourself	35		
36	Materials and supplies	36		
37	Other costs	37		
38	Add lines 33 through 37.	38	307,918	00
39	Inventory at end of year.	39	167,546	00
40	Cost of goods sold. Subtract line 39 from line 38. Enter the result here and on page 1, line 4 . .	40	140,372	00

Part IV   Principal Business or Professional Activity Codes

Locate the major category that best describes your activity. Within the major category, select the activity code that most closely identifies the business or profession that is the principal source of your sales or receipts. Enter this 4-digit code on page 1, line B. For example, real estate agent is under the major category of "**Real Estate**," and the code is "**5520**." Note: *If your principal source of income is from farming activities, you should file **Schedule F (Form 1040)**, Profit or Loss From Farming.*

Agricultural Services, Forestry, Fishing
Code
- 1990 Animal services, other than breeding
- 1933 Crop services
- 2113 Farm labor & management services
- 2246 Fishing, commercial
- 2238 Forestry, except logging
- 2212 Horticulture & landscaping
- 2469 Hunting & trapping
- 1974 Livestock breeding
- 0836 Logging
- 1958 Veterinary services, including pets

Construction
- 0018 Operative builders (for own account)

Building Trade Contractors, Including Repairs
- 0414 Carpentering & flooring
- 0455 Concrete work
- 0273 Electrical work
- 0299 Masonry, dry wall, stone, & tile
- 0257 Painting & paper hanging
- 0232 Plumbing, heating, & air conditioning
- 0430 Roofing, siding & sheet metal
- 0885 Other building trade contractors (excavation, glazing, etc.)

General Contractors
- 0075 Highway & street construction
- 0059 Nonresidential building
- 0034 Residential building
- 3889 Other heavy construction (pipe laying, bridge construction, etc.)

Finance, Insurance, & Related Services
- 6064 Brokers & dealers of securities
- 6080 Commodity contracts brokers & dealers; security & commodity exchanges
- 6148 Credit institutions & mortgage bankers
- 5702 Insurance agents or brokers
- 5744 Insurance services (appraisal, consulting, inspection, etc.)
- 6130 Investment advisors & services
- 5777 Other financial services

Manufacturing, Including Printing & Publishing
- 0679 Apparel & other textile products
- 1115 Electric & electronic equipment
- 1073 Fabricated metal products
- 0638 Food products & beverages
- 0810 Furniture & fixtures
- 0695 Leather footwear, handbags, etc.
- 0836 Lumber & other wood products
- 1099 Machinery & machine shops
- 0877 Paper & allied products
- 1057 Primary metal industries
- 0851 Printing & publishing
- 1032 Stone, clay, & glass products
- 0653 Textile mill products
- 1883 Other manufacturing industries

Mining & Mineral Extraction
- 1537 Coal mining
- 1511 Metal mining

- 1552 Oil & gas
- 1719 Quarrying & nonmetallic mining

Real Estate
- 5538 Operators & lessors of buildings, including residential
- 5553 Operators & lessors of other real property
- 5520 Real estate agents & brokers
- 5579 Real estate property managers
- 5710 Subdividers & developers, except cemeteries
- 6155 Title abstract offices

Services: Personal, Professional, & Business Services
Amusement & Recreational Services
- 9670 Bowling centers
- 9688 Motion picture & tape distribution & allied services
- 9597 Motion picture & video production
- 9639 Motion picture theaters
- 8557 Physical fitness facilities
- 9696 Professional sports & racing, including promoters & managers
- 9811 Theatrical performers, musicians, agents, producers & related services
- 9613 Video tape rental
- 9837 Other amusement & recreational services

Automotive Services
- 8813 Automotive rental or leasing, without driver
- 8953 Automotive repairs, general & specialized
- 8839 Parking, except valet
- 8896 Other automotive services (wash, towing, etc.)

Business & Personal Services
- 7658 Accounting & bookkeeping
- 7716 Advertising, except direct mail
- 7682 Architectural services
- 8318 Barber shop (or barber)
- 8110 Beauty shop (or beautician)
- 8714 Child day care
- 7872 Computer programming, processing, data preparation & related services
- 7922 Computer repair, maintenance, & leasing
- 7286 Consulting services
- 7799 Consumer credit reporting & collection services
- 8755 Counseling (except health practitioners)
- 7732 Employment agencies & personnel supply
- 7518 Engineering services
- 7773 Equipment rental & leasing (except computer or automotive)
- 8532 Funeral services & crematories
- 7633 Income tax preparation
- 7914 Investigative & protective services
- 7617 Legal services (or lawyer)
- 7856 Mailing, reproduction, commercial art, photography, & stenographic services
- 7245 Management services
- 8771 Ministers & chaplains
- 8334 Photographic studios
- 7260 Public relations
- 8733 Research services

- 7708 Surveying services
- 8730 Teaching or tutoring
- 7880 Other business services
- 6882 Other personal services

Hotels & Other Lodging Places
- 7237 Camps & camping parks
- 7096 Hotels, motels, & tourist homes
- 7211 Rooming & boarding houses

Laundry & Cleaning Services
- 7450 Carpet & upholstery cleaning
- 7419 Coin-operated laundries & dry cleaning
- 7435 Full-service laundry, dry cleaning, & garment service
- 7476 Janitorial & related services (building, house, & window cleaning)

Medical & Health Services
- 9274 Chiropractors
- 9233 Dentist's office or clinic
- 9217 Doctor's (M.D.) office or clinic
- 9456 Medical & dental laboratories
- 9472 Nursing & personal care facilities
- 9290 Optometrists
- 9258 Osteopathic physicians & surgeons
- 9241 Podiatrists
- 9415 Registered & practical nurses
- 9431 Offices & clinics of other health practitioners (dieticians, midwives, speech pathologists, etc.)
- 9886 Other health services

Miscellaneous Repair, Except Computers
- 9019 Audio equipment & TV repair
- 9035 Electrical & electronic equipment repair, except audio & TV
- 9050 Furniture repair & reupholstery
- 2881 Other equipment repair

Trade, Retail—Selling Goods to Individuals & Households
- 3038 Catalog or mail order
- 3012 Selling door to door, by telephone or party plan, or from mobile unit
- 3053 Vending machine selling

Selling From Showroom, Store, or Other Fixed Location

Apparel & Accessories
- 3921 Accessory & specialty stores & furriers for women
- 3939 Clothing, family
- 3772 Clothing, men's & boys'
- 3913 Clothing, women's
- 3756 Shoe stores
- 3954 Other apparel & accessory stores

Automotive & Service Stations
- 3558 Gasoline service stations
- 3319 New car dealers (franchised)
- 3533 Tires, accessories, & parts
- 3335 Used car dealers
- 3517 Other automotive dealers (motorcycles, recreational vehicles, etc.)

Building, Hardware, & Garden Supply
- 4416 Building materials dealers
- 4457 Hardware stores
- 4473 Nurseries & garden supply stores
- 4432 Paint, glass, & wallpaper stores

Food & Beverages
- 0612 Bakeries selling at retail
- 3086 Catering services
- 3095 Drinking places (bars, taverns, pubs, saloons, etc.)
- 3079 Eating places, meals & snacks
- 3210 Grocery stores (general line)
- 3251 Liquor stores
- 3236 Specialized food stores (meat, produce, candy, health food, etc.)

Furniture & General Merchandise
- 3988 Computer & software stores
- 3970 Furniture stores
- 4317 Home furnishings stores (china, floor coverings, drapes)
- 4119 Household appliance stores
- 4333 Music & record stores
- 3996 TV, audio & electronic stores
- 3715 Variety stores
- 3731 Other general merchandise stores

Miscellaneous Retail Stores
- 4812 Boat dealers
- 5017 Book stores, excluding newsstands
- 4853 Camera & photo supply stores
- 3277 Drug stores
- 5058 Fabric & needlework stores
- 4655 Florists
- 5090 Fuel dealers (except gasoline)
- 4630 Gift, novelty & souvenir shops
- 4838 Hobby, toy, & game shops
- 4671 Jewelry stores
- 4895 Luggage & leather goods stores
- 5074 Mobile home dealers
- 4879 Optical goods stores
- 4697 Sporting goods & bicycle shops
- 5033 Stationery stores
- 4614 Used merchandise & antique stores (except motor vehicle parts)
- 5884 Other retail stores

Trade, Wholesale—Selling Goods to Other Businesses, etc.
Durable Goods, Including Machinery Equipment, Wood, Metals, etc.
- 2634 Agent or broker for other firms— more than 50% of gross sales on commission
- 2618 Selling for your own account

Nondurable Goods, Including Food, Fiber, Chemicals, etc.
- 2675 Agent or broker for other firms— more than 50% of gross sales on commission
- 2659 Selling for your own account

Transportation, Communications, Public Utilities, & Related Services
- 6619 Air transportation
- 6312 Bus & limousine transportation
- 6676 Communication services
- 6395 Courier or package delivery
- 6361 Highway passenger transportation (except chartered service)
- 6536 Public warehousing
- 6114 Taxicabs
- 6510 Trash collection without own dump
- 6635 Travel agents & tour operators
- 6338 Trucking (except trash collection)
- 6692 Utilities (dumps, snow plowing, road cleaning, etc.)
- 6551 Water transportation
- 6650 Other transportation services

- 8888 Unable to classify

mal course of the taxpayer's trade or business. The taxpayer also may be allowed to deduct expenses for the use of part of the home as a day-care facility or as a place to store inventory that is sold in the business, even if that part of the home is sometimes used for personal purposes. If a home office deduction is claimed for meeting with patients, clients, or customers, the taxpayer must meet with them on the premises of the home and the meetings must be integral to the conduct of the business, rather than being simply occasional meetings or telephone calls. The home may be the principal place of business for the owner yet need not be the principal place of business for the owner's employees. The following example illustrates how to calculate the deductible portion of home office expenses to be reported on Schedule C (line 30).

situation where the income from the business activity carried on in the home is greater that the total of the business expenses, including the home office expenses. In addition to meeting the "exclusive use" and "regular basis" rules, there is a further limit on the amount of the deduction a taxpayer may take for the business use of a portion of a residence. The deductible expenses are limited to the amount of gross income derived from such business. Gross income for purposes of this discussion is defined as gross income less deductions having no connection with the business (such as mortgage interest and real estate taxes) and expenses of the business that are not related to the place of business (such as salaries and office supplies). To determine the proper amount of home office expense deduction, the business deductions for the business use of the home must be deducted in the following order:

1. The business percentage of home office expenses that would be allowable as deductions if no business was operated in the home, such as mortgage interest, real estate taxes, and deductible casualty losses
2. Direct business expenses incurred in operating the business in the taxpayer's home, such as repairs and maintenance, insurance, and utilities
3. Depreciation on home office portion of house

The last deduction taken would be the depreciation on the home office portion of the home since that depreciation reduces the tax basis of the home. Example 9 illustrates the application of the sequencing rules for calculating the home office expense deduction.

Illustration 8-3

A taxpayer conducts a consulting practice in his home, with the office constituting 10% of the total square footage (3,400 sq. ft.). The adjusted basis of the home is $75,000, including the land value of $12,000. The home's FMV is $128,000. The tentative profit reported by the taxpayer on Schedule C (line 29) is $12,200. This tentative profit and the expenses listed below are reported on Form 8829, Illustration 8-3.

Mortgage interest (line 10)	$2,300
Real estate taxes (line 11)	3,500
Repairs & maintenance (indirect) (line 13)	750
Insurance (line 17)	480
Utilities (line 19)	1,810
Home office depreciation (line 28)	200

Expenses not attributed to business use of the home, such as supplies, depreciation on home office furniture and equipment (see Chapter 9), computer services, postage, photocopying, etc., would be included on Schedule C in calculating the sole proprietor's tentative profit from his consulting business.

EXAMPLE 9 ————————————

A taxpayer conducts a tax practice from an office in his home. The office constitutes 20% of the total square footage of the home. Expenses in operating the home generally include utilities, $3,500; real estate taxes, $4,000; mortgage interest, $6,000; insurance, $800; general purpose home repairs, $2,000; and depreciation of the office portion of the home's tax basis, $900. Gross income from the tax practice amounted to $3,300. Based on this information, the taxpayer would calculate his home office expense deduction to be reported on Schedule C, line 30, as follows:

Illustration 8-3 reflects the calculation of the deduction for home office expenses in a

Illustration 8-3
Filled-In Form 8829

Form **8829**	**Expenses for Business Use of Your Home**	OMB No. 1545-1266
Department of the Treasury Internal Revenue Service	▶ File with Schedule C (Form 1040). Use a separate Form 8829 for each home you used for business during the year. ▶ See Instructions on back.	**19 92** Attachment Sequence No. **66**

Name(s) of proprietor(s)   Your social security number

Part I Part of Your Home Used for Business

1	Area used exclusively for business (see instructions). Include area that does not meet exclusive use test and either used for inventory storage or regularly used as part of a day-care facility	1	340
2	Total area of home	2	3,400
3	Divide line 1 by line 2. Enter the result as a percentage	3	10 %

- For day-care facilities not used exclusively for business, also complete lines 4–6.
- All others, skip lines 4–6 and enter the amount from line 3 on line 7.

4	Multiply days used for day care during year by hours used per day	4	hr.
5	Total hours available for use during the year (366 days × 24 hours). See instructions	5	8,784 hr.
6	Divide line 4 by line 5. Enter the result as a decimal amount	6	
7	Business percentage. For day-care facilities not used exclusively for business, multiply line 6 by line 3 (enter the result as a percentage). All others, enter the amount from line 3 ▶	7	10 %

Part II Figure Your Allowable Deduction

			(a) Direct expenses	(b) Indirect expenses		
8	Enter the amount from Schedule C, line 29, **plus** any net gain or (loss) derived from the business use of your home and shown on Schedule D or Form 4797. If more than one place of business, see instructions				8	12,200 00
	See instructions for columns (a) and (b) before completing lines 9–20.					
9	Casualty losses. See instructions	9				
10	Deductible mortgage interest. See instructions	10		2,300 00		
11	Real estate taxes. See instructions	11		3,500 00		
12	Add lines 9, 10, and 11	12		5,800 00		
13	Multiply line 12, column (b) by line 7	13		580 00		
14	Add line 12, column (a) and line 13				14	580 00
15	Subtract line 14 from line 8. If zero or less, enter -0-				15	11,640 00
16	Excess mortgage interest. See instructions	16				
17	Insurance	17		480 00		
18	Repairs and maintenance	18		750 00		
19	Utilities	19		1,810 00		
20	Other expenses. See instructions	20				
21	Add lines 16 through 20	21		3,040 00		
22	Multiply line 21, column (b) by line 7	22		304 00		
23	Carryover of operating expenses from 1991 Form 8829, line 41	23				
24	Add line 21 in column (a), line 22, and line 23				24	304 00
25	Allowable operating expenses. Enter the **smaller** of line 15 or line 24				25	304 00
26	Limit on excess casualty losses and depreciation. Subtract line 25 from line 15				26	11,336 00
27	Excess casualty losses. See instructions	27				
28	Depreciation of your home from Part III below	28	200 00			
29	Carryover of excess casualty losses and depreciation from 1991 Form 8829, line 42	29				
30	Add lines 27 through 29				30	200 00
31	Allowable excess casualty losses and depreciation. Enter the **smaller** of line 26 or line 30				31	200 00
32	Add lines 14, 25, and 31				32	1,084 00
33	Casualty loss portion, if any, from lines 14 and 31. Carry amount to **Form 4684**, Section B				33	
34	Allowable expenses for business use of your home. Subtract line 33 from line 32. Enter here and on Schedule C, line 30. If your home was used for more than one business, see instructions ▶				34	1,084 00

Part III Depreciation of Your Home

35	Enter the **smaller** of your home's adjusted basis or its fair market value. See instructions	35	75,000 00
36	Value of land included on line 35	36	12,000 00
37	Basis of building. Subtract line 36 from line 35	37	63,000 00
38	Business basis of building. Multiply line 37 by line 7	38	6,300 00
39	Depreciation percentage. See instructions	39	3.175 %
40	Depreciation allowable. Multiply line 38 by line 39. Enter here and on line 28 above. See instructions	40	200 00

Part IV Carryover of Unallowed Expenses to 1993

41	Operating expenses. Subtract line 25 from line 24. If less than zero, enter -0-	41	
42	Excess casualty losses and depreciation. Subtract line 31 from line 30. If less than zero, enter -0-	42	

For Paperwork Reduction Act Notice, see back of form.   Cat. No. 13232M   Form **8829** (1992)

Gross income from business use of home .	$3,300
Less: Business portion of mortgage interest and real estate taxes 20% x ($6,000 + $5,000)	2,200
Modified net income (limit on deductibility of business portion of other home office expenses)	$1,100
Business use of other home office expenses	
Utilities, insurance, repairs	$1,260
Depreciation on home office	900
Total other home office expenses	$2,160
Deductible expenses limited to modified net income	1,100
Home office expenses not deductible in 1992 to be carried forward to 1993 subject to the 1993 limits	$1,060

The $1,100 of deductible home office expenses are considered to consist of the home office portion of expenses for utilities, insurance, and repairs. This means that the carryover losses of $1,060 consist of $160 ($1,260 – $1,100) of utilities, insurance, and repairs and $900 of depreciation expense. Recognizing these components of the carryover expenses is important because the $900 of depreciation on the home office part of the home will not be used to reduce the tax basis of the home until the $900 is actually deducted in a future year.

The general principle of this calculation of the deductibility of home office expenses is that the deductions for the business use of a home cannot cause a business loss or increase a business loss. Instead, excess home office expenses can be carried forward to next year and/or future years when income is sufficient to absorb the carryover expenses.

Education Expenses

The two types of deductible business education expenses are (1) education expenses for employees and (2) education expenses for the owner (sole proprietor). The education expenses paid for employees are deductible as long as they are ordinary and necessary to the operation of the business. The education expenses for the owner-employee include amounts spent on the owner's own education related to the trade or business, including tuition, books, transportation, meals (subject to 80% rule), and lodging. To qualify for the education deduction, the taxpayer must show that the education maintains and improves skills that are required in the taxpayer's trade, business, or profession, or that it is required by law or regulation for keeping a job. The sole proprietor cannot deduct the cost of education expenses that are incurred to meet the minimum requirements of his or her present trade, business, or profession, or those that qualify the taxpayer for a new trade, business, or profession, even if such education maintains or improves skills that are presently required.

Business Gifts

The self-employed taxpayer can deduct the cost of business gifts to customers and clients. However, the maximum deduction cannot exceed $25 for business gifts given, directly or indirectly, to any one individual during the tax year. A gift to a company that is not intended for the personal use or benefit of a particular person or class of people, or a gift to a spouse of a person the taxpayer is doing business with, is treated as an indirect gift to the person the taxpayer is doing business with. The following are not considered gifts subject to the $25 limit:

1. At item that costs $4 or less on which the donor's company name is clearly and permanently imprinted, and is one of a number of items that is widely distributed, such as pens, desk sets, etc.
2. Signs, display racks, and other promotional material to be used on the business premises of the recipient
3. Incidental costs, such as engraving, packaging, insuring, and mailing

Any item that might be considered either a gift or entertainment generally will be considered to be entertainment, unless it is intended for use at a later date. If you provide tickets to events to a business customer and do not go with the customer to the event, the taxpayer can treat the tickets as either a gift or as entertainment, whichever is to the taxpayer's advantage. If you go with the customer to the event, it must be treated as entertainment. Employee achievement awards are not treated as gifts.

Hobby Losses

Losses from a hobby are not deductible from other income. A hobby is an activity from which a taxpayer does not expect to make a profit. The question of whether a profit motive exists in a business usually arises in cases where an activity has elements of both personal pleasure and profit. If the activity is deemed to be a profit activity, any net loss for the year may be offset against other income reported by the taxpayer. If the activity is deemed to be a hobby, expenses of the activity are only deductible to the extent of the activity's gross income. Some of the factors considered by the IRS in determining whether an activity is a business or a hobby include the following:

1. Was it the taxpayer's intention to make a profit?
2. Were books and records kept for the activity?
3. Have there been profits in some years and losses in other years?
4. What was the relative amount of pleasure derived from the activity?
5. To what extent does the taxpayer depend on this activity for financial support?
6. How much time and effort is devoted to the activity?

The burden of proof for determining whether the activity is a business for profit generally rests with the taxpayer. The taxpayer must show that the activity is being pursued for profit, but does not need to justify that the expectation of profit is necessarily reasonable. Furthermore, the taxpayer does not need to show a profit each year.

If the activity shows a profit in any three of five consecutive years (two years out of seven for activities involving horses), the burden of proof that the activity is a hobby shifts to the IRS. An election is also available to the taxpayer to postpone any IRS challenge until five years of business activity has been completed. The five-year period gives the taxpayer the opportunity to have three taxable years to justify that it is an activity for profit. However, having three years of profitable activity does not automatically cancel any challenges by the IRS. The election must be filed within three years of the due date of the tax return for the taxable year in which the taxpayer first initiates the activity.

If the activity is considered to be a hobby, expenses incurred in carrying out the hobby are only deductible to the extent of the activity's gross income reduced by expenses that would be deductible whether or not the activity was a hobby.

EXAMPLE 10

Assume that a taxpayer paints pictures as a hobby. The painting is done on the taxpayer's premises in a separate studio. The taxpayer sold some paintings during the year for $2,300. $3,025 was paid for expenses as follows: $400 for real estate taxes on the studio; $125 for interest on a loan to buy painting supplies; and $2,500 for painting supplies and utilities. The amount of expenses deductible against the gross income of the hobby would be $1,900, calculated as follows:

Gross income		$2,300
Expenses deductible whether or not activity is a hobby:		
Property taxes		400
Maximum deductible hobby losses		$1,900
Expenses related to the hobby:		
Interest on loan for supplies	$ 125	
Painting supplies	2,500	
Total hobby expenses	$2,625	

Deductible hobby expenses (limited to remaining gross income, but deductible only as miscellaneous itemized deductions)	1,900
Net reportable hobby gain or loss	0

The net effect of this situation is that the taxpayer must report the income from the hobby as gross income, is allowed to deduct the real estate taxes as an itemized deduction under taxes, and can include $1,900 of the remaining expenses as a miscellaneous itemized deduction subject to the 2% of AGI (which includes the hobby income). If a portion of the $1,900 was interest expense on the supplies, that portion would be a nondeductible personal interest expense and the amount includable as a miscellaneous itemized deduction would be less than $1,900. In this example, no deduction is allowed for the $600 of painting supplies over and above the $1,900 and no deduction is allowed for the $125 of personal interest on the loan for supplies.

The significant impact on the taxpayer of having an activity treated as a hobby should help explain why taxpayers make considerable effort to treat their activities as a business by making profits in three out of every five years and taking other steps to justify that the activity is engaged in for profit. As a profit activity, all expenses are deductible and net losses can be used to offset income from other sources.

Deducting the Cost of Retirement Plans

When employers decide to provide retirement benefits for employees, they usually prefer that the plan achieve the following tax benefits:

1. The contributions by the employer must be deductible in the current year.
2. The income earned by the fund is not currently taxable to the employees.
3. The pension benefits are not taxable to employees until the employees retire and start collecting the benefits.

In order to achieve these tax benefits, the retirement plan must be constituted as a qualified plan for income tax purposes, which means that it must meet major requirements involving participation, vesting, contributions, benefits, and distributions. The same general rules with respect to these requirements apply whether the employer is a corporation, partnership, or proprietorship.

Qualified Retirement Plans

In order to understand the deductibility of contributions and the characteristics of benefits, it is necessary to recognize the different forms of qualified retirement plans. Most qualified retirement plans are *pension, profit-sharing, or stock bonus plans.* Pension and profit-sharing plans are discussed in the sections that follow. Refer to advanced tax texts to learn more about stock bonus plans (including ESOPs—employee stock ownership plans).

Pension Plans. Pension plans are basically of two types. One type, called a **defined benefit plan**, provides specified benefits based on levels of compensation and years of service. The contributions to the plan are actually calculated to ensure that the promised benefits will be available at retirement. In this type of pension plan, the contributions are usually not allocated to individual employee accounts. The other type of pension plan is called a **defined contribution plan**. In this type of plan, the employer promises to make a specific contribution for the benefit of each employee participating in the plan, usually a percentage of compensation or a percentage of profits. The contributions are assigned to specific employees. When the contributions assigned to individual employee accounts are based on a specific compensation formula, the plan is referred to as a **money-purchase plan**. No specific benefits are promised, but the employee will receive whatever benefits can be provided by the accumulated contributions.

Profit-Sharing Plans. A **profit-sharing plan** is a retirement plan in which employer contributions are based on profits. Some profit-sharing plans require that a fixed percentage of profits be contributed each year, whereas other plans permit considerable flexibility by the employer as to how much is contributed to the pension fund each year. Whenever contributions are made, the employer must allocate the contributions among the employees based on a specific written formula. Since individual accounts are maintained for the employee participants, a profit-sharing plan is also classified as a defined contribution plan. Money-purchase and profit-sharing plans are discussed further in the section on *Retirement Plans for Self-Employed Individuals.*

Deductibility of Contributions to Pension and Profit-Sharing Plans

For taxable years after 1983, there is little or no distinction between the deductibility rules for pension plans established by corporations and those established by partnerships and sole proprietorships. The only stipulation since 1983 for partners and sole proprietors is that contributions on their behalf must be based on their own compensation, which is defined to mean the person's earned income from the business. Thus, withdrawals from the proprietorship or partnership cannot be treated as "earned income."

Earned income is income derived from personal services. If total income is from investments, the individual is not eligible for a retirement pension plan because there is no earned income. When both capital and personal services are material income-producing factors, net profit is considered earned income for purposes of calculating the amount of contribution to a retirement plan. Professional fees or commissions, less business deductions, are treated as earned income even though an individual may employ assistants to perform part of the services, provided the individual is responsible for the services.

In a corporation, all participants in the retirement plan are employees. Therefore, the maximum contribution for any employee would be based on the employee's compensation, subject to the maximum deduction allowed for the corporation as a whole, and on the type of plan in effect. Self-employed individuals are subject to these same maximums, and their contributions to a retirement plan for self-employed individuals are deductible on Form 1040 (line 27).

Self-employed individuals are divided into two groups—those who are "owner-employees" and those who are not. This distinction is important because plans covering "owner-employees" are subject to a number of special requirements.

Retirement Plans for Self-Employed Individuals (Owner-Employees)

The term owner-employee means a self-employed individual who owns the entire interest in an unincorporated business (sole proprietorship) or a partner in a partnership who owns more than a 10% interest in the partnership profits or capital. Owner-employees who establish retirement plans may have to provide benefits for certain other employees (part-time and seasonal employees may be excluded). There are two main types of retirement plans that a self-employed individual may open. These are defined contribution plans and defined benefit plans.

Defined Contribution Plan. Under a defined contribution plan, an individual account is established for each person in the plan (the owner-employee and any covered employees). The major types of defined contribution plans are profit-sharing plans and money-purchase plans.

The maximum amount that a self-employed individual (owner-employee) is allowed to contribute to a defined contribution plan depends on whether the plan is a profit-sharing plan or money-purchase plan. In a money-purchase plan, the maximum is limited to 25% of the participant's compensation, while in a profit-sharing plan the maximum is limited to 15%. The maximum amount is limited to $30,000 whether the contribution is to a money-purchase plan, profit-sharing plan, or some combination of the two. Compensation is defined as net earnings from self-employment after deducting the owner-employee's plan contribution.

To illustrate the maximum deductible for a money purchase plan, assume that a self-employed taxpayer had Schedule C earned income of $72,000 and has in existence a money-purchase plan requiring a 25% contribution each year. Since the 25% is determined after deducting the contribution, this taxpayer can contribute and deduct a maximum of $14,400, calculated by using either of the following two equations:

25% (Net Income − Deduction) = Deduction

For this example, the equation would read:

25% ($72,000 − Deduction) = Deduction

Thus:

Deduction = $18,000 − 25% Deduction

Therefore:

1.25 Deduction = $18,000

This results in a net deduction of $14,400. The calculation can also be expressed as:

($72,000 x 20%) = $14,400; or
($72,000 −$14,400) x 25% = $14,400

In other words, 20% of the Schedule C income (before deducting the pension contribution) is equal to 25% of the Schedule C income reduced by the pension contribution. Note, however, the money-purchase plan deduction can only be made in the amount of 25% if the plan specifies that percentage, which also means that the owner-employee must make a required contribution of that percentage each year.

Unlike the money-purchase plan, the maximum contribution to a profit-sharing plan is 15% of Schedule C income after deducting the contribution.

If the taxpayer has Schedule C income of $72,000, the maximum deductible contribution to a profit-sharing plan would be $9,391, calculated by using either of the following two equations:

15% (Net Income − Deduction) = Deduction

or:

15% x $72,000 − 15% Deduction = Deduction

Solving for the deduction: 1.15 Deduction = 10,800, resulting in a net deduction of $9,391. A second equation would be as follows:

($72,000 x .130435) = $9,391 = ($72,000 – $9,391) x 15% = $9,391

In other words, 13.0435% ($9,391/$72,000) of the Schedule C income of $72,000 (before deducting the pension contribution) is equal to 15% of the Schedule C income reduced by the pension contribution.

Profit-Sharing Plan. An owner-employee may establish a profit-sharing plan which requires a fixed percentage of profits (up to 15%) to be contributed to the plan each year and/or have a profit-sharing plan that allows for flexibility in the amount of contributions. If the owner-employee elects a plan which allows for flexibility, a decision must be made each year as to how much, if any, will be contributed that year to the plan. The maximum amount that can be contributed is the lesser of 15% of compensation (after deducting the contribution) or $30,000. It is important to note that owner-employees are allowed to stipulate contributions to the profit-sharing plan for their benefit in any amount up to 15%, as long as the same percent is contributed for other eligible employees. Also note that, if the sole proprietor has both a money-purchase and a profit-sharing plan, the maximum combined amount that can be contributed to both plans is 20% of Schedule C income up to a maximum deductible amount of $30,000.

Money-Purchase Plan. If an owner-employee elects a money-purchase plan, the contributions of both the owner-employee and the employees are a fixed percentage of their compensation (defined in the same way as described earlier). The plan requires regular contributions for the designated percentage of compensation each year. The maximum contribution is 25% of each participant's compensation (after deducting the contribution) but not more than $30,000.

Combined Money-Purchase Plan and Profit-Sharing Plan. An owner-employee can take advantage of the maximum deductible contribution percentage limit of 25% of compensation (up to $30,000) by combining a money-purchase plan with a profit-sharing plan. The contribution for the money-purchase plan must be a fixed percentage of compensation each year, while the contribution to a flexible profit-sharing plan, up to a maximum of 15%, is optional each year. In any case, the total contributions for both plans in any one year cannot exceed 25% of each participant's compensation as defined earlier.

The $30,000 defined contribution limit will remain unchanged until the defined benefit limit reaches $120,000 (for 1992 the defined benefit limit is $112,221). The $30,000 defined contribution limit will be increased as the defined benefit limit is adjusted above $120,000 by reference to the consumer price index.

Defined Benefit Plan. A defined benefit plan is any plan that is not a defined contribution plan. The retirement benefits an individual will receive at retirement under this plan are specified at the time the plan is established. There are special rules concerning the maximum amounts that may be received under a defined benefit plan, as well as rules limiting the yearly contribution.

Under a defined benefit plan, the maximum allowable contribution in 1992 is the amount that would purchase an annual retirement benefit equal to the lesser of $112,221 or 100% of compensation (based on an average of the participant's three highest-paid consecutive years). There are some restrictions on defined benefit plans for individual participants. Those restrictions include the stipulation that the defined benefit limit must generally be reduced for each year the participant is short of 10 years of participation. Thus, an employer who shifts from a defined contribution plan to a defined benefit plan cannot provide benefits to employees based on years of service prior to the year of establishing the new defined benefit plan. Furthermore, benefits from a defined benefit plan may be reduced substantially for a participant who retires before age 65. An overall cap is provided for the amount of deductible contributions to a defined benefit plan in order to allow a tax deduction for only the actual liability incurred. Deductions are not allowed for contributions to a defined benefit plan to an extent that contributions cause plan assets to exceed 150% of termination liabilities, or any alternative limitations that may be developed by the Secretary of the Treasury.

Historically, self-employed individuals were more likely to contribute to one or more defined contribution plans rather than to a defined benefit plan. The choice of defined contribution plans has been motivated by more flexibility in the compliance provisions and in the amount of contributions made each year in the face of uncertainty about future financial viability of the business. However, defined benefit plans have become more popular in recent years.

Timing of Contributions

The time for making the deductible qualified retirement plan contributions extends to the due date of the tax return (including extensions), provided the plan was in existence by December 31 of the tax year during which the deduction is taken. The effect of extending the time for making the contribution is that a cash-method taxpayer can take a deduction on his or her 1992 tax return for plan contributions paid by April 15, 1993 (or later if there is an extension of time to file). If the self-employed person elects to take the extension, the election is irrevocable. It should be noted, however, that the sooner the contributions to the plan are actually made, the sooner the income earned by the plan becomes nontaxable until withdrawn at retirement.

Funding of Retirement Plans

A variety of arrangements may be made for investing the funds of qualified retirement plans. Contributions may be used to purchase annuity contracts, various types of insurance contracts, shares in regulated investment companies, certain other types of investment contracts, or a United States obligation designed for this purpose.

Minimum funding requirements are specified by the IRS for each type of retirement plan. If employer contributions to a plan are not sufficient to meet the minimum funding requirements, the employer will be subject to an excise tax. This tax is 5% of the accumulated funding deficiency and is imposed each year in which the accumulated funding deficiency is not corrected.

Annual Reporting of Retirement Plans

The following is a list of specific rules relating to the reporting of retirement plans which are either profit-sharing plans or money-purchase plans:

1. Annual reporting for retirement plans is required, even if the only participant is the owner-employee.
2. Administrators or sponsors of employee benefit plans with 100 or more participants must file Form 5500, Annual Return/Report of Employee Benefit Plan.
3. Form 5500EZ may be filed by a "One-Participant Plan" which is a pension benefit plan that covers only an individual or an individual and his or her spouse who wholly own a trade or business which is either incorporated or unincorporated.
4. Plans with less than 100 participants may qualify in certain cases to file Form 5500EZ also. If the plan does not qualify to file Form 5500EZ, then Form 5500-C/R must be filed.
5. If the pension plan is a one-participant plan that has no more than $100,000 of assets at the end of the year or if there are two or more one-participant plans with no more than $100,000 of total assets for the combined plans, the trustee of the plan(s) is not required to file a Form 5500EZ. However, if there are two or more one-participant plans and the total assets of those plans exceed $100,000 at the end of the year a Form 5500EZ must be filed for each plan.

The applicable reporting form for pension plans for sole proprietors must be filed by the end of the seventh month following the end of the plan year, with the opportunity for an extension of up to an additional 2½ months.

Simplified Employer Pension Plans (SEP)

Another option in owner-employee retirement plans is the SEP. A SEP is an IRA established for the benefit of employees. Employers are permitted to make contributions to such retirement plans on behalf of employees, including the owner-employee, whether or not there are other employees. Employer contributions must not discriminate in favor of officers, shareholders, or other highly-compensated employees. Thus, the employer must make contributions for each employee who has reached age 21, has performed service for the employer during the calendar year and for at least three of five preceding calendar years, and has received at least $300 (to be indexed in the future) in compensation from the employer for the year. Two classes of employees may be excluded: (1) employees covered by a collective bargaining agreement made in good faith, and (2) employees who are nonresident aliens and who have received no earned income from the employer constituting income from sources within the U. S.

Under a SEP, an employee for whom the employer makes contributions is considered to be an active participant in a qualified employer plan and, therefore, may make contributions to a separate IRA, subject to the IRA phase-out rules. Employer SEP contributions are excluded from the employee's gross income. The maximum elective contribution by an employee for all salary reduction plans (other than tax-sheltered annuities) is $7,627. Thus, up to $30,000 of employer SEP contributions, including up to $7,627 of elective contributions, are excluded from the employee's gross income. SEPs may contain a salary-reduction provision allowing employees to reduce their salaries and to have the reduction amount (i.e. an elective contribution) deposited in the plan and treated as an employer contribution.

The elective provision for employee contributions to a SEP is generally limited to employers with 25 or fewer employees, at least half of whom contribute to the SEP. Special discrimination tests comparing deferrals by highly-compensated employees to rank-and-file employees may apply.

The employer contributions to a SEP-IRA must be immediately vested. Contributions by the employee to a SEP-IRA or to a separate IRA must be made no later than the due date for filing the tax return, with no exception for extensions. Therefore, for most taxpayers, the contribution deadline is April 15.

Section 401(k) Plans

An alternative to a SEP is a Section 401(k) plan. This type of plan permits employee participants to receive up to $7,000 in cash from their employer and choose a reduced salary, with the amount being contributed to a retirement plan in the employee's name. The amount contributed to the 401(k) plan is not taxed to the employee until withdrawn at or after retirement. If the 401(k) plan is in the form of a salary reduction agreement with the employer, the employee may elect to reduce current compensation or elect to forego a pay raise. The amount elected up to $7,000 is not only tax-deferred, including interest earnings, but is

100% vested when the contribution is made to the plan. The $7,000 maximum is reduced on a per-dollar basis for contributions to tax-sheltered annuities or SEPs. Section 401(k) plans are subject to precise nondiscrimination rules.

Tax Planning for Retirement Plans by Self-Employed Individuals

A self-employed individual who establishes a qualified retirement plan has several options, including money-purchase and/or profit-sharing plans (Keogh plans), a SEP plan, a Section 401(k) plan, and/or a regular IRA subject to the phase out rules. Taxpayers who are not sole proprietors or partners cannot set up Keogh, SEP, or 401(k) types of plans on their own initiative. The choice or choices of plans will depend on the extent of compliance requirements, maximum contributions, and flexibility. Contributions to retirement plans should be made as early in the year as possible in order to exclude as much of the earnings from such funds as possible from the current year's taxable income.

EXAMPLE 13 ———————————————

If a contribution of $30,000 was made on January 2, 1992, to a qualified plan and the earnings on the contribution amounted to $3,000 for the year, all $3,000 would be deferred until retirement. If the taxpayer held the $30,000 as a taxable investment until late December, 1992, all $3,000 of the earnings would be taxable in 1992.

Qualified retirement plan contributions other than SEP and IRA contributions can be made up to the date of filing the tax return, including extensions, if the plan was in effect by the last day of the tax year (December 31 for calendar-year taxpayers) for which the deduction is to be taken. Contributions to SEP and IRA plans must be made by the original due date of the return, exclusive of extensions (by April 15 for calendar-year taxpayers), but a regular IRA need not have been established prior to the date of the contributions to the plan. Owner-employees considering the establishment of a retirement plan should carefully review the requirements and limitations of each type of plan before determining which type or types of plans are most suited to their situation.

Self-Employment Tax for Self-Employed Individuals

The sole proprietor of a business, trade, profession, or farm is a self-employed individual unless specifically exempted by the law. A self-employment tax must be paid by a self-employed individual regardless of age or whether social security benefits are being received. As indicated in Chapter 7, net earnings from self-employment include:

1. Net profit derived by an individual from any trade or business as shown on Schedule C (Form 1040)
2. Net profit derived by an individual from farming as shown on Schedule F (Form 1040)
3. Individuals's distributive share (whether or not distributed) of the ordinary net income (or loss) from a partnership or joint venture

Net earnings of less than $400 from self-employment are not subject to tax. In 1992:

1. The maximum amount of self-employment income subject to social security tax is limited to $55,500. Therefore, the maximum social security tax for 1992 is $8,491.50 ($55,500 x 15.3%).
2. The maximum amount of self-employment earnings subject to Medicare tax is $130,200. If the self-employment income is more than $55,500, but less than $130,200, the excess above $55,500 is subject to a Medicare tax of 2.9% which is added to the $8,491.50 social security tax. The maximum Medicare tax is $2,166.30 ($130,200 − $55,500 = $74,700 x 2.9%).
3. The maximum social security and Medicare tax on self-employment income would be $10,657.80 ($8,491.50 + $2,166.30).

Other Aspects of the Self-Employment Tax

The *self-employment tax* (discussed in Chapter 7) is paid by self-employed individuals on their *self-employment taxable earnings*. The self-employment tax normally is paid with the individual taxpayer's estimated tax, and/or with the individual's final income tax payment when Form 1040 is filed. Self-employment tax payments permit self-employed individuals to become eligible for social security benefits. As described below, the tax burden of the self-employment tax is at least partially offset by allowing self-employed individuals to deduct one-half of the self-employment taxes paid as an adjustment to income. See Chapter 7 for a detailed discussion of the self-employment tax, including an illustration of a filled-in Schedule SE.

Deduction of Self-Employment Tax

Those taxpayers who pay the self-employment tax of 15.3% are really paying the equivalent of both the employer's share and the employee's share of the FICA tax. Because the employer's share is a business expense, starting with the 1990 tax return self-employed taxpayers are allowed to deduct one-half of the total self-employment tax as a deduction for AGI on Form 1040, page 1 (line 25).

The IRS has included a worksheet in the instructions that accompany Form 1040 to help self-employed taxpayers calculate the amount of the deduction for self-employment tax.

EXAMPLE 14 ————————————————

If a self-employed taxpayer was subject to the maximum self-employment tax for social security and Medicare in the amount of $8,491.50 on the maximum self-employment income of $55,500 in 1992, the taxpayer is allowed to deduct $4,245.75 ($8,491.50 x 50%) as an adjustment to income on Form 1040 (line 25).

Farm Income and Expenses

A taxpayer engaged in the business of farming reports net farm income or (loss) on Form 1040 (line 19). The detail of farm income and expense is reported separately on Schedule F, Profit or Loss from Farming. Schedule F specifically states that if the taxpayer's principal source of income is from providing agricultural services such as soil preparation, veterinary, farm labor, horticultural, or management for a fee or on a contract basis, such taxpayers should file Schedule C instead of Schedule F. Farmers eligible to use Schedule F normally report on the cash method, the accrual method, or the crop method, whichever reflects income and expenses most accurately. The records of the farmer must follow the same method as used for income tax reporting purposes. Under the **cash method** all taxable income, whether received in cash or property, is included in income in the year it is actually or constructively received. Inventories are not used to determine income, and expenses can be deducted only in the year paid.

Under the **accrual method** all taxable income is included in income in the year earned, regardless of when payment is received, and expenses are deducted in the year incurred, regardless of when paid. Farmers using this method must use inventories taken at the end of the year.

Under the **crop method** the cost of growing the crop, including expenses for seeds or young plants, must be deducted in the year the income from the crop is realized. The crop method can be used by farmers whose crops take more than one year from the time of planting to the time of harvesting. Consent of the IRS is necessary to use this method. It has the advantage of expenses not being offset during years in which there might be no income.

Schedule F is provided to report the detail of farm revenue or expenses. Farm revenue may be reported either by the cash method, Parts I and II, or the accrual method, Parts II and III. If a farmer disposed of commodities and received payment in the form of commodity credit loan proceeds, this information must be disclosed by checking the applicable box or boxes just below the owner's name on Schedule F, page 1. Depreciation for either the cash or the accrual method is figured on Form 4562, Depreciation and Amortization, and the total is entered on Schedule F (line 16). The net profit shown on Schedule F is carried to Form 1040 (line 19).

Net earnings from farm self-employment and the calculation of social security self-employment tax are reported in Section A of short-form Schedule SE.

A cash method farmer's deduction for feed, seed, fertilizer, and other items generally will be limited if they exceed 50% of the farmer's other deductible farming expenses for the taxable year. In certain limited situations, farmers may be required to capitalize the cost of producing inventoriable items. Soil and water conservation expenses will only be deductible if consistent with a conservation plan approved by the U.S. Department of Agriculture or a comparable state agency. The election to deduct land clearing expenses has been repealed. Such expenses must be capitalized as part of the cost of land, except for brush clearing and other ordinary maintenance expenses.

Farm Losses

Losses incurred in the operation of a farm as a business are deductible in the same manner as any other net loss from a business, including carryover and carryback of net operating losses (Chapter 13). A farm loss appears as a "minus" item in arriving at farm net profit on Schedule F, and is also entered as a "minus" item on Form 1040 (line 19). Passive farm losses must be considered in calculating the AMT (Chapter 13).

Credit for Federal Tax on Gasoline and Certain Other Fuels

A credit may be claimed by a taxpayer for the federal excise tax on gasoline and gasohol, diesel fuel, and other special fuels used for certain types of business purposes. Although the emphasis here is on the use of the credit for gasoline used in farm vehicles, it also applies to qualified diesel-powered highway vehicles, various buses, commercial fishing vessels, and other off-highway business vehicles. The credit can be claimed on Form 1040 (line 59), if supported by Form 4136, Computation of Credit for Federal Tax on Gasoline and Special Fuels. The credit is figured by multiplying the number of gallons used by the rate of the federal excise tax paid or the allowable rate, if less. The rate varies for each type of eligible fuel. The amount claimed is allowed only if the taxpayer's income tax return is filed on time (including extensions).

For any of the first three quarters of the tax year, a taxpayer may file for a refund of the tax, instead of claiming the credit on Form 4136, if the taxpayer has paid an excise tax of $1,000 or more ($50 or more for a qualified taxicab and $200 or more for gasoline/alcohol mixtures). The refund is claimed on Form 843, Claim for Refund and Request for Abatement, before the end of the quarter following the one in which the refund is sought.

Form 4136 also applies to a qualified diesel-powered highway vehicle which is any diesel-powered highway vehicle with at least four wheels and a gross vehicle weight of 10,000 pounds or less, and which is registered for highway use in the U.S. under the laws of any state. For such a vehicle purchased after January 1, 1986, for use other than resale and whose owner, the taxpayer, is the original purchaser, a credit may be claimed of $102 for an automobile or $198 for a light truck or van. Note that the credit is for the purchase of the vehicle in addition to subsequent credits for fuel use if the business use meets requirements of Form 4136.

In addition, there are further restrictions on deductions by farming syndicates (partnerships) and corporations. There is also a special tax treatment for certain crop disaster payments and a special elective tax treatment for income from the forced sale of livestock resulting from drought conditions in an area designated as eligible by the federal government.

There are many special rules relating to the reporting of farm income and expenses. A pamphlet entitled "Farmer's Tax Guide" (Publication 225) can be obtained free from the IRS to explain the detailed procedures.

Filled-In Schedule F

Illustration 8-4

A filled-in Schedule F for Milton R. Watson is shown in Illustration 8-4. Since Mr. Watson grows field crops, such as cotton, peanuts, corn, wheat, tobacco, or potatoes, he must record the three-digit code number for that category (#120) on page 1 (line B). Other code numbers are also listed on of Schedule F, page 2, under Part IV.

Mr. Watson reports on the cash method and has, therefore, completed Parts I and II. Had he been reporting on the accrual method, he would have been expected to complete Parts II and III. Schedule F, Part III, page 2 is not illustrated here. The net farm profit of $35,895 was determined on Schedule F (line 36), and also entered on short-form Schedule SE (line 1) for the calculation of Mr. Watson's net earnings from farm self-employment. The total net earnings of $35,895 from short-form Schedule SE (line 1) is multiplied by .9235 and the result, $33,149.03, is entered (line 3 and line 8) for the calculation of his social security self-employment tax of $5,071.80 (15.3% x $33,149.03). This amount of $5,071.80 is entered on Form 1040, page 2 (line 47). In addition, one-half of the $5,071.80 of self-employment tax, $2,535.90 ($5071.80 x 50%), is also entered on Form 1040 (line 25) as an adjustment to income.

Illustration 8-4
Filled-In Schedule F, Form 1040

SCHEDULE F
(Form 1040)

Department of the Treasury
Internal Revenue Service

Profit or Loss From Farming

▶ Attach to Form 1040, Form 1041, or Form 1065.

▶ See Instructions for Schedule F (Form 1040).

OMB No. 1545-0074

1992

Attachment
Sequence No. **14**

Name of proprietor

Milton R. Watson

Social security number (SSN)

268 29 4316

A Principal product. Describe in one or two words your principal crop or activity for the current tax year.

General Livestock

B Enter principal agricultural activity code (from page 2) ▶ 1 2 0

D Employer ID number (Not SSN)

4 9 9 6 8 5 2 8 1

C Accounting method: (1) ☒ Cash (2) ☐ Accrual

E Did you "materially participate" in the operation of this business during 1992? If "No," see page F-1 for limitations on losses. ☒ Yes ☐ No

Part I Farm Income—Cash Method—Complete Parts I and II (Accrual method taxpayers complete Parts II and III, and line 11 of Part I.)
Do not include sales of livestock held for draft, breeding, sport, or dairy purposes; report these sales on Form 4797.

1	Sales of livestock and other items you bought for resale	1	37,000 00	
2	Cost or other basis of livestock and other items reported on line 1	2	10,000 00	
3	Subtract line 2 from line 1			3 27,000 00
4	Sales of livestock, produce, grains, and other products you raised			4 43,398 00
5a	Total cooperative distributions (Form(s) 1099-PATR)	5a 140 00	5b Taxable amount	5b 140 00
6a	Agricultural program payments (see page F-2)	6a 3,400 00	6b Taxable amount	6b 3,400 00
7	Commodity Credit Corporation (CCC) loans (see page F-2):			
a	CCC loans reported under election			7a
b	CCC loans forfeited or repaid with certificates	7b –0–	7c Taxable amount	7c
8	Crop insurance proceeds and certain disaster payments (see page F-2):			
a	Amount received in 1992	8a –0–	8b Taxable amount	8b
c	If election to defer to 1993 is attached, check here ▶ ☐		8d Amount deferred from 1991	8d
9	Custom hire (machine work) income			9 1,216 00
10	Other income, including Federal and state gasoline or fuel tax credit or refund (see page F-3)			10 160 00
11	**Gross income.** Add amounts in the right column for lines 3 through 10. If accrual method taxpayer, enter the amount from page 2, line 51 ▶			11 75,314 00

Part II Farm Expenses—Cash and Accrual Method (Do not include personal or living expenses such as taxes, insurance, repairs, etc., on your home.)

12	Car and truck expenses (see page F-3—also attach Form 4562)	12	25	Pension and profit-sharing plans	25 2,000 00
13	Chemicals	13	26	Rent or lease (see page F-4):	
14	Conservation expenses. Attach Form 8645	14 190 00	a	Vehicles, machinery, and equipment	26a
15	Custom hire (machine work)	15	b	Other (land, animals, etc.)	26b
16	Depreciation and section 179 expense deduction not claimed elsewhere (see page F-3)	16 6,910 00	27	Repairs and maintenance	27 1,000 00
			28	Seeds and plants purchased	28 826 00
			29	Storage and warehousing	29
17	Employee benefit programs other than on line 25	17	30	Supplies purchased	30 680 00
			31	Taxes	31 1,032 00
18	Feed purchased	18 6,205 00	32	Utilities	32 1,884 00
19	Fertilizers and lime	19 1,925 00	33	Veterinary, breeding, and medicine	33 1,275 00
20	Freight and trucking	20 250 00	34	Other expenses (specify):	
21	Gasoline, fuel, and oil	21 2,080 00	a **Farm Org. Pufs.**	34a 25 00
22	Insurance (other than health)	22 920 00	b **Farm Publication**	34b 35 00
23	Interest:		c		34c
a	Mortgage (paid to banks, etc.)	23a 4,002 00	d		34d
b	Other	23b	e		34e
24	Labor hired (less jobs credit)	24 8,180 00	f		34f

35	**Total expenses.** Add lines 12 through 34f ▶	35	39,419 00
36	**Net farm profit or (loss).** Subtract line 35 from line 11. If a profit, enter on Form 1040, line 19, and on Schedule SE, line 1. If a loss, you MUST go on to line 37 (fiduciaries and partnerships, see page F-5)	36	35,895 00
37	If you have a loss, you MUST check the box that describes your investment in this activity (see page F-5). If you checked 37a, enter the loss on Form 1040, line 19, and Schedule SE, line 1. If you checked 37b, you MUST attach Form 6198.	37a ☐ All investment is at risk. 37b ☐ Some investment is not at risk.	

For Paperwork Reduction Act Notice, see Form 1040 instructions. Cat. No. 11346H Schedule F (Form 1040) 1992

Name _______________________________

Section _______________ Date _______________

C H A P T E R   8

Questions and Problems

1. Ramon S. Torres, an attorney reporting professional revenues and expenses on the cash method, wants to determine how each of the following items would be reported in his Schedule C and how the reporting would differ if he were to use the accrual method. In the space provided below, enter the correct amount to be included on Schedule C assuming the cash method is used. Then enter the correct amount assuming the use of the accrual method. If there is no amount to be reported, enter a zero.

			Included in Schedule C	
			Cash Method	Accrual Method
a.	Cash received from last year's fees	$ 7,200	$__________	$__________
b.	Cash received from current year's fees	49,000	__________	__________
c.	Fees billed for current year for which cash has not been received	10,200	__________	__________
d.	Cash received for typewriter with a book value of $75	75	__________	__________
e.	Cash received from bank loan	2,500	__________	__________
f.	Cash received from client to repay loan made last year	500	__________	__________
g.	Cash received for retainer from client for whom work is to be done next year	3,800	__________	__________
h.	Repaid loan at bank:			
	Principal	1,000	__________	__________
	Interest	60	__________	__________
i.	Paid contribution pledged to church	1,000	__________	__________
j.	Paid for supplies used last year	150	__________	__________
k.	Paid for supplies used during the current year	850	__________	__________
l.	Paid for legal books	200	__________	__________
m.	Supplies not used during the current year and not paid for	40	__________	__________
n.	Paid for a new typewriter	564	__________	__________

			Included in Schedule C	
			Cash Method	Accrual Method
o.	Paid to son for yard work at the office on Saturday and after school	$ 175	__________	__________
p.	Salary paid to secretary	12,500	__________	__________
q.	Advance paid for client to title company for their work performed during the current year. To be reimbursed by client next year	120	__________	__________
r.	Wrote off advance made to client for toll call charges paid last year	4	__________	__________
s.	Wrote off client billing for fees. Work performed current year.	150	__________	__________
t.	Wrote off client billing for fees. Work performed last year.	135	__________	__________
u.	Paid annual subscription to magazines for office . .	50	__________	__________
v.	Paid life insurance premium on owner	516	__________	__________
w.	Paid Chamber of Commerce dues	125	__________	__________

2. Marie Lopez, 190 Glenn Drive, Grand Rapids, Michigan 49527-2005, SSN 318-01-6921, is a single taxpayer entitled to one exemption only. Ms. Lopez owns and operates the Reliable Drug Company at 1816 First Street in Grand Rapids, Michigan 49503-1902, in which she actively participates the entire year. Her principal business code is 3277. Her EIN is 38-9654321. Employer quarterly payroll tax returns were filed as required, and she values inventory at cost. The income statement for 1992 is reproduced on the following page. Ms. Lopez reports on the accrual method. She does not deduct expenses for an office in her home.

An examination of the business records reveals that the depreciable assets include furniture and fixtures, a heavy-duty delivery truck, and store equipment. The depreciation expense shown on the 1992 income statement meets the income tax requirements for depreciation for using the above assets during 1992. Ms. Lopez rounds calculations to the nearest dollar. Miscellaneous expenses include:

Reimbursement to Ms. Lopez for actual expenses of a purchasing trip ($256 for airfare and lodging, $70 for meals)	$326
Contributions to Red Cross and United Way	350
Chamber of Commerce dues	125
Personal electrical bill for August	80
Total miscellaneous expenses	$881

The only other income for Ms. Lopez was a salary of $100 each month for her services as a member of a working committee of the Drug Association. Her Form W-2 from the association showed gross wages of $1,200; income tax withheld of $96; and social security tax of $91.80.

Prepare Schedules C and SE for Ms. Lopez, using the forms provided on pages 309-312. Also show the calculation for how much self-employment tax Ms. Lopez will be allowed to deduct in 1992 as an adjustment to income on Form 1040 (line 25).

RELIABLE DRUG COMPANY
Income Statement for Year Ended December 31, 1992

Operating revenue:

Sales		$324,200
Less sales returns and allowances		3,390
Net sales		$320,810

Cost of merchandise sold:

Merchandise inventory, beginning (FIFO)	$ 68,920	
Purchases	$198,240	
Less purchases returns and allowances	8,100	
Net purchases	$190,140	
Merchandise available for sale	$259,060	
Merchandise inventory, ending (FIFO)	69,185	
Cost of merchandise sold		189,875
Gross profit on sales		$130,935

Operating expenses:

Advertising expense	$ 6,541	
Car and truck expense	7,967	
Depreciation expense	3,396	
Insurance expense (other than health)	644	
Miscellaneous expense	881	
Payroll taxes	3,471	
Rent expense (business property)	12,000	
Telephone and utilities expense	2,395	
Uncollectible accounts expense	850	
Wages expense	62,500	
Total operating expenses		100,645
Net income		$ 30,290

3. Roger Harkins operates a novelty shop as a sole proprietor. You have been asked to calculate the Cost of Goods Sold section of Schedule C for his 1992 income tax return since he is unfamiliar with detailed accounting concepts. You have been given the following information from his records to help meet his request:

Sales revenue	$200,000
Purchases	80,000
Cash operating expenses	40,000
Depreciation expense	15,000
Beginning inventory	60,000
Ending inventory	54,000
Bad debts written off	3,200

Using the appropriate information from Roger Harkins' books, prepare the Cost of Goods Sold section of Schedule C for 1992.

Schedule C (Form 1040) 1992   Page **2**

Part III   **Cost of Goods Sold** (see page C-5)

#			
33	Inventory at beginning of year. If different from last year's closing inventory, attach explanation	33	
34	Purchases less cost of items withdrawn for personal use.	34	
35	Cost of labor. Do not include salary paid to yourself	35	
36	Materials and supplies	36	
37	Other costs	37	
38	Add lines 33 through 37.	38	
39	Inventory at end of year.	39	
40	**Cost of goods sold.** Subtract line 39 from line 38. Enter the result here and on page 1, line 4	40	

SCHEDULE C
(Form 1040)

Department of the Treasury
Internal Revenue Service

Profit or Loss From Business

(Sole Proprietorship)

▶ Partnerships, joint ventures, etc., must file Form 1065.

▶ Attach to Form 1040 or Form 1041.   ▶ See Instructions for Schedule C (Form 1040).

OMB No. 1545-0074

1992

Attachment
Sequence No. **09**

Name of proprietor

Social security number (SSN)

A Principal business or profession, including product or service (see page C-1)

B Enter principal business code (from page 2) ▶

C Business name

D Employer ID number (Not SSN)

E Business address (including suite or room no.) ▶ ....
City, town or post office, state, and ZIP code

F Accounting method: (1) ☐ Cash   (2) ☐ Accrual   (3) ☐ Other (specify) ▶ ....

G Method(s) used to value closing inventory: (1) ☐ Cost   (2) ☐ Lower of cost or market   (3) ☐ Other (attach explanation)   (4) ☐ Does not apply (if checked, skip line H)

	Yes	No
H Was there any change in determining quantities, costs, or valuations between opening and closing inventory? If "Yes," attach explanation		
I Did you "materially participate" in the operation of this business during 1992? If "No," see page C-2 for limitations on losses		
J Was this business in operation at the end of 1992?		
K How many months was this business in operation during 1992? ▶		
L If this is the first Schedule C filed for this business, check here ▶ ☐		

Part I Income

1 Gross receipts or sales. **Caution:** *If this income was reported to you on Form W-2 and the "Statutory employee" box on that form was checked, see page C-2 and check here* ▶ ☐	**1**	
2 Returns and allowances	**2**	
3 Subtract line 2 from line 1	**3**	
4 Cost of goods sold (from line 40 on page 2)	**4**	
5 **Gross profit.** Subtract line 4 from line 3	**5**	
6 Other income, including Federal and state gasoline or fuel tax credit or refund (see page C-2)	**6**	
7 **Gross income.** Add lines 5 and 6 ▶	**7**	

Part II Expenses (Caution: *Do not enter expenses for business use of your home on lines 8–27. Instead, see line 30.*)

8 Advertising	**8**		**21** Repairs and maintenance	**21**	
9 Bad debts from sales or services (see page C-3)	**9**		**22** Supplies (not included in Part III)	**22**	
10 Car and truck expenses (see page C-3—also attach Form 4562)	**10**		**23** Taxes and licenses	**23**	
11 Commissions and fees	**11**		**24** Travel, meals, and entertainment:		
12 Depletion	**12**		a Travel	**24a**	
13 Depreciation and section 179 expense deduction (not included in Part III) (see page C-3)	**13**		b Meals and entertainment		
14 Employee benefit programs (other than on line 19)	**14**		c Enter 20% of line 24b subject to limitations (see page C-4)		
15 Insurance (other than health)	**15**		d Subtract line 24c from line 24b	**24d**	
16 Interest:			**25** Utilities	**25**	
a Mortgage (paid to banks, etc.)	**16a**		**26** Wages (less jobs credit)	**26**	
b Other	**16b**		**27a** Other expenses (**list type and amount**):		
17 Legal and professional services	**17**		....		
18 Office expense	**18**		....		
19 Pension and profit-sharing plans	**19**		....		
20 Rent or lease (see page C-4):			....		
a Vehicles, machinery, and equipment	**20a**				
b Other business property	**20b**		**27b** Total other expenses	**27b**	

28 **Total expenses** before expenses for business use of home. Add lines 8 through 27b in columns ▶	**28**	
29 Tentative profit (loss). Subtract line 28 from line 7	**29**	
30 Expenses for business use of your home. Attach **Form 8829**	**30**	
31 **Net profit or (loss).** Subtract line 30 from line 29. If a profit, enter here and on Form 1040, line 12. Also, enter the net profit on Schedule SE, line 2 (statutory employees, see page C-5). If a loss, you MUST go on to line 32 (fiduciaries, see page C-5)	**31**	
32 If you have a loss, you MUST check the box that describes your investment in this activity (see page C-5). If you checked 32a, enter the loss on Form 1040, line 12, and Schedule SE, line 2 (statutory employees, see page C-5). If you checked 32b, you MUST attach **Form 6198**.	**32a** ☐ All investment is at risk. **32b** ☐ Some investment is not at risk.	

For Paperwork Reduction Act Notice, see Form 1040 instructions.   Cat. No. 11334P   Schedule C (Form 1040) 1992

Schedule C (Form 1040) 1992

Page **2**

Part III   Cost of Goods Sold (see page C-5)

33	Inventory at beginning of year. If different from last year's closing inventory, attach explanation	33	
34	Purchases less cost of items withdrawn for personal use	34	
35	Cost of labor. Do not include salary paid to yourself	35	
36	Materials and supplies	36	
37	Other costs	37	
38	Add lines 33 through 37	38	
39	Inventory at end of year	39	
40	**Cost of goods sold.** Subtract line 39 from line 38. Enter the result here and on page 1, line 4	40	

Part IV   Principal Business or Professional Activity Codes

Locate the major category that best describes your activity. Within the major category, select the activity code that most closely identifies the business or profession that is the principal source of your sales or receipts. Enter this 4-digit code on page 1, line B. For example, real estate agent is under the major category of "**Real Estate**," and the code is "5520." **Note:** *If your principal source of income is from farming activities, you should file **Schedule F (Form 1040)**, Profit or Loss From Farming.*

Agricultural Services, Forestry, Fishing
Code
1990 Animal services, other than breeding
1933 Crop services
2113 Farm labor & management services
2246 Fishing, commercial
2238 Forestry, except logging
2212 Horticulture & landscaping
2469 Hunting & trapping
1974 Livestock breeding
0836 Logging
1958 Veterinary services, including pets

Construction
0018 Operative builders (for own account)

Building Trade Contractors, Including Repairs
0414 Carpentering & flooring
0455 Concrete work
0273 Electrical work
0299 Masonry, dry wall, stone, & tile
0257 Painting & paper hanging
0232 Plumbing, heating, & air conditioning
0430 Roofing, siding & sheet metal
0885 Other building trade contractors (excavation, glazing, etc.)

General Contractors
0075 Highway & street construction
0059 Nonresidential building
0034 Residential building
3889 Other heavy construction (pipe laying, bridge construction, etc.)

Finance, Insurance, & Related Services
6064 Brokers & dealers of securities
6080 Commodity contracts brokers & dealers; security & commodity exchanges
6148 Credit institutions & mortgage bankers
5702 Insurance agents or brokers
5744 Insurance services (appraisal, consulting, inspection, etc.)
6130 Investment advisors & services
5777 Other financial services

Manufacturing, Including Printing & Publishing
0679 Apparel & other textile products
1115 Electric & electronic equipment
1073 Fabricated metal products
0638 Food products & beverages
0810 Furniture & fixtures
0695 Leather footwear, handbags, etc.
0836 Lumber & other wood products
1099 Machinery & machine shops
0877 Paper & allied products
1057 Primary metal industries
0851 Printing & publishing
1032 Stone, clay, & glass products
0653 Textile mill products
1883 Other manufacturing industries

Mining & Mineral Extraction
1537 Coal mining
1511 Metal mining

1552 Oil & gas
1719 Quarrying & nonmetallic mining

Real Estate
5538 Operators & lessors of buildings, including residential
5553 Operators & lessors of other real property
5520 Real estate agents & brokers
5579 Real estate property managers
5710 Subdividers & developers, except cemeteries
6155 Title abstract offices

Services: Personal, Professional, & Business Services
Amusement & Recreational Services
9670 Bowling centers
9688 Motion picture & tape distribution & allied services
9597 Motion picture & video production
9639 Motion picture theaters
8557 Physical fitness facilities
9696 Professional sports & racing, including promoters & managers
9811 Theatrical performers, musicians, agents, producers & related services
9613 Video tape rental
9837 Other amusement & recreational services

Automotive Services
8813 Automotive rental or leasing, without driver
8953 Automotive repairs, general & specialized
8839 Parking, except valet
8896 Other automotive services (wash, towing, etc.)

Business & Personal Services
7658 Accounting & bookkeeping
7716 Advertising, except direct mail
7682 Architectural services
8318 Barber shop (or barber)
8110 Beauty shop (or beautician)
8714 Child day care
7872 Computer programming, processing, data preparation & related services
7922 Computer repair, maintenance, & leasing
7286 Consulting services
7799 Consumer credit reporting & collection services
8755 Counseling (except health practitioners)
7732 Employment agencies & personnel supply
7518 Engineering services
7773 Equipment rental & leasing (except computer or automotive)
8532 Funeral services & crematories
7633 Income tax preparation
7914 Investigative & protective services
7617 Legal services (or lawyer)
7856 Mailing, reproduction, commercial art, photography, & stenographic services
7245 Management services
8771 Ministers & chaplains
8334 Photographic studios
7260 Public relations
8733 Research services

7708 Surveying services
8730 Teaching or tutoring
7880 Other business services
6882 Other personal services

Hotels & Other Lodging Places
7237 Camps & camping parks
7096 Hotels, motels, & tourist homes
7211 Rooming & boarding houses

Laundry & Cleaning Services
7450 Carpet & upholstery cleaning
7419 Coin-operated laundries & dry cleaning
7435 Full-service laundry, dry cleaning, & garment service
7476 Janitorial & related services (building, house, & window cleaning)

Medical & Health Services
9274 Chiropractors
9233 Dentist's office or clinic
9217 Doctor's (M.D.) office or clinic
9456 Medical & dental laboratories
9472 Nursing & personal care facilities
9290 Optometrists
9258 Osteopathic physicians & surgeons
9241 Podiatrists
9415 Registered & practical nurses
9431 Offices & clinics of other health practitioners (dieticians, midwives, speech pathologists, etc.)
9886 Other health services

Miscellaneous Repair, Except Computers
9019 Audio equipment & TV repair
9035 Electrical & electronic equipment repair, except audio & TV
9050 Furniture repair & reupholstery
2881 Other equipment repair

Trade, Retail—Selling Goods to Individuals & Households
3038 Catalog or mail order
3012 Selling door to door, by telephone or party plan, or from mobile unit
3053 Vending machine selling

Selling From Showroom, Store, or Other Fixed Location
Apparel & Accessories
3921 Accessory & specialty stores & furriers for women
3939 Clothing, family
3772 Clothing, men's & boys'
3913 Clothing, women's
3756 Shoe stores
3954 Other apparel & accessory stores

Automotive & Service Stations
3558 Gasoline service stations
3319 New car dealers (franchised)
3533 Tires, accessories, & parts
3335 Used car dealers
3517 Other automotive dealers (motorcycles, recreational vehicles, etc.)

Building, Hardware, & Garden Supply
4416 Building materials dealers
4457 Hardware stores
4473 Nurseries & garden supply stores
4432 Paint, glass, & wallpaper stores

Food & Beverages
0612 Bakeries selling at retail
3086 Catering services
3095 Drinking places (bars, taverns, pubs, saloons, etc.)
3079 Eating places, meals & snacks
3210 Grocery stores (general line)
3251 Liquor stores
3236 Specialized food stores (meat, produce, candy, health food, etc.)

Furniture & General Merchandise
3988 Computer & software stores
3970 Furniture stores
4317 Home furnishings stores (china, floor coverings, drapes)
4119 Household appliance stores
4333 Music & record stores
3996 TV, audio & electronic stores
3715 Variety stores
3731 Other general merchandise stores

Miscellaneous Retail Stores
4812 Boat dealers
5017 Book stores, excluding newsstands
4853 Camera & photo supply stores
3277 Drug stores
5058 Fabric & needlework stores
4655 Florists
5090 Fuel dealers (except gasoline)
4630 Gift, novelty & souvenir shops
4838 Hobby, toy, & game shops
4671 Jewelry stores
4895 Luggage & leather goods stores
5074 Mobile home dealers
4879 Optical goods stores
4697 Sporting goods & bicycle shops
5033 Stationery stores
4614 Used merchandise & antique stores (except motor vehicle parts)
5884 Other retail stores

Trade, Wholesale—Selling Goods to Other Businesses, etc.
Durable Goods, Including Machinery Equipment, Wood, Metals, etc.
2634 Agent or broker for other firms— more than 50% of gross sales on commission
2618 Selling for your own account

Nondurable Goods, Including Food, Fiber, Chemicals, etc.
2675 Agent or broker for other firms— more than 50% of gross sales on commission
2659 Selling for your own account

Transportation, Communications, Public Utilities, & Related Services
6619 Air transportation
6312 Bus & limousine transportation
6676 Communication services
6395 Courier or package delivery
6361 Highway passenger transportation (except chartered service)
6536 Public warehousing
6114 Taxicabs
6510 Trash collection without own dump
6635 Travel agents & tour operators
6338 Trucking (except trash collection)
6692 Utilities (dumps, snow plowing, road cleaning, etc.)
6551 Water transportation
6650 Other transportation services

8888 Unable to classify

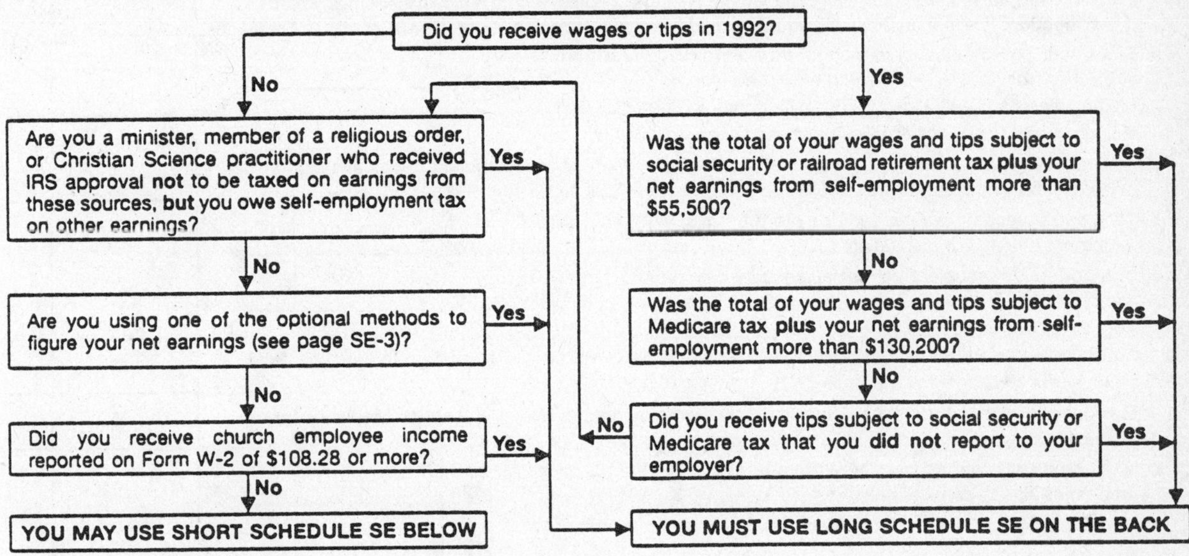

| **SCHEDULE SE**
(Form 1040)

Department of the Treasury
Internal Revenue Service | **Self-Employment Tax**

► See Instructions for Schedule SE (Form 1040).

► Attach to Form 1040. | OMB No. 1545-0074
1992
Attachment
Sequence No. **17** |

Name of person with **self-employment** income (as shown on Form 1040) | Social security number of person with **self-employment income** ►

Who Must File Schedule SE

You must file Schedule SE if:

- Your wages (and tips) subject to social security AND Medicare tax (or railroad retirement tax) were less than $130,200; **AND**
- Your *net earnings from self-employment from other than church employee income* (line 4 of Short Schedule SE or line 4c of Long Schedule SE) were $400 or more;
  OR
- You had church employee income (as defined on page SE-1) of $108.28 or more.

Exception. If your only self-employment income was from earnings as a minister, member of a religious order, or Christian Science practitioner, AND you filed **Form 4361** and received IRS approval not to be taxed on those earnings, DO NOT file Schedule SE. Instead, write "Exempt–Form 4361" on Form 1040, line 47.

May I Use Short Schedule SE or MUST I Use Long Schedule SE?

Section A—Short Schedule SE. Caution: *Read above to see if you must use Long Schedule SE on the back (Section B).*

1 Net farm profit or (loss) from Schedule F, line 36, and farm partnerships, Schedule K-1 (Form 1065), line 15a	1	
2 Net profit or (loss) from Schedule C, line 31; Schedule C-EZ, line 3; and Schedule K-1 (Form 1065), line 15a (other than farming). See page SE-2 for other income to report	2	
3 Combine lines 1 and 2	3	
4 **Net earnings from self-employment.** Multiply line 3 by 92.35% (.9235). If less than $400, do not file this schedule; you do not owe self-employment tax ►	4	
5 **Self-employment tax.** If the amount on line 4 is: • $55,500 or less, multiply line 4 by 15.3% (.153) and enter the result. • More than $55,500 but less than $130,200, multiply the amount in excess of $55,500 by 2.9% (.029). Then, add $8,491.50 to the result and enter the total. • $130,200 or more, enter $10,657.80. Also, enter this amount on Form 1040, line 47 **Note:** *Also, enter **one-half** of the amount from line 5 on **Form 1040, line 25.***	5	

For Paperwork Reduction Act Notice, see Form 1040 instructions.   Cat. No. 11358Z   Schedule SE (Form 1040) 1992

Schedule SE (Form 1040) 1992   Attachment Sequence No. **17**   Page **2**

Name of person with **self-employment** income (as shown on Form 1040)	Social security number of person with **self-employment** income ▶	

Section B—Long Schedule SE

A   If you are a minister, member of a religious order, or Christian Science practitioner AND you filed **Form 4361,** but you had $400 or more of **other** net earnings from self-employment, check here and continue with Part I . . . . . . ▶ ☐

B   If your only income subject to self-employment tax is church employee income and you are **not** a minister or a member of a religious order, skip lines 1 through 4b. Enter -0- on line 4c and go to line 5a.

Part I   Self-Employment Tax

1	Net farm profit or (loss) from Schedule F, line 36, and farm partnerships, Schedule K-1 (Form 1065), line 15a. **Note:** *Skip this line if you use the farm optional method. See requirements in Part II below and on page SE-3*	**1**		
2	Net profit or (loss) from Schedule C, line 31; Schedule C-EZ, line 3; and Schedule K-1 (Form 1065), line 15a (other than farming). See page SE-2 for other income to report. **Note:** *Skip this line if you use the nonfarm optional method. See requirements in Part II below and on page SE-3*	**2**		
3	Combine lines 1 and 2	**3**		
4a	If line 3 is more than zero, multiply line 3 by 92.35% (.9235). Otherwise, enter amount from line 3	**4a**		
b	If you elected one or both of the optional methods, enter the total of lines 17 and 19 here . .	**4b**		
c	Combine lines 4a and 4b. If less than $400, do **not** file this schedule; you do not owe self-employment tax. **Exception.** If less than $400 and you had church employee income, enter -0- and continue . ▶	**4c**		
5a	Enter your church employee income from Form W-2. **Caution:** *See page SE-1 for definition of church employee income* **5a**			
b	Multiply line 5a by 92.35% (.9235). If less than $100, enter -0-	**5b**		
6	**Net earnings from self-employment.** Add lines 4c and 5b	**6**		
7	Maximum amount of combined wages and self-employment earnings subject to social security tax or the 6.2% portion of the 7.65% railroad retirement (tier 1) tax for 1992	**7**	55,500	00
8a	Total social security wages and tips (from Form(s) W-2) and railroad retirement (tier 1) compensation **8a**			
b	Unreported tips subject to social security tax (from Form 4137, line 9) **8b**			
c	Add lines 8a and 8b	**8c**		
9	Subtract line 8c from line 7. If zero or less, enter -0- here and on line 10 and go to line 12a ▶	**9**		
10	Multiply the **smaller** of line 6 or line 9 by 12.4% (.124)	**10**		
11	Maximum amount of combined wages and self-employment earnings subject to Medicare tax or the 1.45% portion of the 7.65% railroad retirement (tier 1) tax for 1992	**11**	130,200	00
12a	Total Medicare wages and tips (from Form(s) W-2) and railroad retirement (tier 1) compensation **12a**			
b	Unreported tips subject to Medicare tax (from Form 4137, line 14) **12b**			
c	Add lines 12a and 12b	**12c**		
13	Subtract line 12c from line 11. If zero or less, enter -0- here and on line 14 and go to line 15 .	**13**		
14	Multiply the **smaller** of line 6 or line 13 by 2.9% (.029)	**14**		
15	**Self-employment tax.** Add lines 10 and 14. Enter the result here and on Form 1040, line 47 .	**15**		
	Note: *Also, enter one-half of the amount from line 15 on* ***Form 1040, line 25.***			

Part II   Optional Methods To Figure Net Earnings (See **Who Can File Schedule SE** on page SE-1 and **Optional Methods** on page SE-3.)

Farm Optional Method. You may use this method **only** if **(a)** Your gross farm income[1] was not more than $2,400 **or (b)** Your gross farm income[1] was more than $2,400 and your net farm profits[2] were less than $1,733.

16	Maximum income for optional methods	**16**	1,600	00
17	Enter the **smaller** of: two-thirds (⅔) of gross farm income[1] or $1,600. Also, include this amount on line 4b above	**17**		

Nonfarm Optional Method. You may use this method **only** if **(a)** Your net nonfarm profits[3] were less than $1,733 and also less than 72.189% of your gross nonfarm income,[4] **and (b)** You had net earnings from self-employment of at least $400 in 2 of the prior 3 years. **Caution:** *You may use this method no more than five times.*

18	Subtract line 17 from line 16	**18**		
19	Enter the **smaller** of: two-thirds (⅔) of gross nonfarm income[4] or the amount on line 18. Also, include this amount on line 4b above	**19**		

[1]From Schedule F, line 11, and Schedule K-1 (Form 1065), line 15b.   [3]From Schedule C, line 31; Schedule C-EZ, line 3; and Schedule K-1 (Form 1065), line 15a.
[2]From Schedule F, line 36, and Schedule K-1 (Form 1065), line 15a.   [4]From Schedule C, line 7; Schedule C-EZ, line 1; and Schedule K-1 (Form 1065), line 15c.

4. Davidson Company makes and sells clothing to stores throughout the country.

On December 31, 1992, before year-end adjustments were made to the accounting records, the company had the following account balances on its books:

Sales revenue, 1992 (60% were credit sales)	$1,300,000
Accounts receivable	73,100
Allowance for uncollectible accounts (credit)	450

Based on past experience, the company expects 3% of ending accounts receivable to be uncollectible. Accordingly, it was determined that the *Allowance for uncollectible accounts* should be increased to $2,193 ($73,100 x 3%).

During the year the company wrote off accounts that were uncollectible in the amount of $3,500.

a. What method of writing off uncollectible accounts must the company use in preparing its 1992 tax return?

b. What is the amount of the company's income tax deduction for uncollectible accounts for 1992?

5. A sole proprietor who operates a warehouse purchases insurance for his building and equipment in three-year increments in order to get a good insurance premium rate. The insurance policy in force was acquired on October 1, 1991, for $4,800 and will be in effect until September 30, 1994. The premium on this policy was paid in three installments of $1,600 each on the following dates: October 1, 1991; July 1, 1992; and January 2, 1993.

a. What amount of insurance premium can the taxpayer include as an expense on Schedule C for 1992 assuming use of the cash method of accounting? Show calculations.

b. What amount of insurance premium is deductible in 1992 if the taxpayer is on the accrual method?

6. Robert Applewood works as an accountant for the Craft Manufacturing Company. He also moonlights at night and on weekends preparing tax returns for a regular set of clients. He does not have a regular office in his home, so he does not take a deduction for a home office. However, he does prepare a Schedule C to reflect the income from his tax practice. He has asked you to review his Schedule C to determine whether he is properly reporting the operating expenses of his business in relation to other aspects of his tax return. He has included the following expenses on Schedule C:

Supplies and postage	$ 72.00
Professional dues paid to AICPA tax division	120.00
Professional dues to the Institute of Management Accountants (IMA)	175.00
Meals ($80) and entertainment ($120) for tax clients	200.00
Transportation Expenses for tax clients (236 miles @ $.28)	67.00
Contribution to State Accounting Society's Political Action Committee	100.00
CPE course fees to meet the annual requirements to be a member of AICPA and the state society	600.00
Cost of new printer for use with tax clients (shown under repairs and maintenance)	650.00
Long distance telephone charges related to his tax clients	44.00
Interest expense on bank loan used to buy a computer for tax and personal use (Used for tax clients 60% of the time during the tax year)	400.00

Of these expenses, indicate what amounts, if any, are not eligible for inclusion on Schedule C and explain why in each case.

7. **a.** Briefly explain the differences in the following retirement plans and the maximum contribution that can be made in 1992 to each plan: money-purchase plan, profit-sharing plan, and SEP.

b. Under what conditions may a taxpayer with a money-purchase or profit-sharing plan be exempt from filing a Form 5500EZ?

8. **a.** If Louise Bell earned $14,000 from self-employment in 1992 and paid $2,800 for a money-purchase defined contribution retirement plan for a self-employed person, how much of the payment can be deducted from gross income on her 1992 income tax return? How is the deduction claimed?

b. If Bell earned $3,000 from self-employment in 1992, what is the maximum deductible amount she can pay into a qualified profit-sharing plan for a self-employed person?

9. Indicate T (true) or F (false) for each statements regarding pension plans for self-employed individuals for 1992:

    a. The maximum allowable contribution to a defined contribution plan in 1992 is 25% of the owner-employee's gross compensation,, up to $30,000

    b. An employee who is less than a 5% owner is subject to a nondeductible 10% penalty tax for distributions of retirement plan benefits that start before age 59½

    c. A lump-sum distribution from a qualified retirement plan may be rolled over into an IRA

    d. Employers may make contributions to an IRA through a SEP plan

10. Denise Smith, a self-employed individual, operates a consulting service by herself, with no employees. For the tax year 1992, her gross consulting revenue was $140,000, and her operating expenses, not including retirement plan contributions, amounted to $30,000. In addition to her consulting income, she also received $5,000 of earned income in 1992 for writing a chapter in a book about management consulting. During 1992, she established both a money-purchase pension plan and a profit-sharing plan. The money-purchase plan stipulated a fixed percentage of 10% of compensation as the amount of the required annual contribution. The profit-sharing plan allowed for varying amounts of contributions up to 15%.

a. What is the required dollar contribution that Smith must make to her money-purchase plan for 1992?

b. Considering the required contribution to the money-purchase plan for 1992, how much additional deductible contribution can Smith make to her profit-sharing plan for 1992?

c. By what date must the money-purchase and profit-sharing plans be established in order for Smith to take a deductible contribution on her 1992 tax return?

d. By what date must the contributions be paid into the money-purchase and profit-sharing plans in order for Smith to take a deduction on her 1992 tax return?

11. Rita Porter operates a child-care service out of her home. The rooms used for this purpose constitute 30% of the total living space of the house. Expenses of operating the home generally during 1992 included electricity, $480; water, $340; heating, $3,600; property taxes, $4,000; and home repairs, $800. The depreciation on the rooms and related equipment used for child care amounted to $1,800.

What is the total amount of Schedule C expenses that Porter can deduct for using her own home to provide the child-care services?

12. Robin Clark incurs travel and entertainment expenses as a traveling salesperson for her company, which is a sole proprietorship. She has the company reimburse her for transportation and hotel expenses based on her submitted expense reports. However, she reimbursed herself at the rate of $500 per month for meals and entertainment ($6,000 per year) without any specific accounting. Assuming that Clark incurred meal expenses of $2,400 and entertainment expenses of $5,500 during 1992, answer the following questions about how her expenses and the reimbursements are reported on her Form 1040 for 1992. Assume that $400 of the meal expenses and $600 of the entertainment expenses are considered to be lavish and were not reimbursed by her employer.

a. To what extent must Clark report reimbursements from her company as income? Explain how reimbursements must be reported.

b. How much expense may Clark deduct for meals and entertainment? Show calculations and explain where these expenses are reported on Form 1040.

13. a. What are the criteria for determining whether an activity is a legitimate business or a hobby?

b. If a doctor operates a farm on the side that is used to graze cattle, will the showing of a Schedule C profit automatically exempt the doctor from the possibility that the activity will be considered by the IRS to be a hobby? Explain.

14. Russell Long is retired from his regular work and now is spending his time painting landscapes in a studio set up in his home. The studio occupies 12% of the living space in his home. During 1992 he sold some of his paintings for the first time. Now he is not certain whether he is required to file a tax return, and if so, whether he will be required to pay any taxes as a business. The revenue from selling paintings in 1992 was $2,300. His expenses were as follows: property taxes on his home, $3,600; interest on loan for painting supplies, $140; painting supplies, $1,750; electricity for the home, $2,400; and heat for the home, $2,900.

    a. How much can Long deduct of the above expenses if his painting activity is treated as a business? Show calculations.

    b. How much can Long deduct of the above expenses if his painting activity is treated as a hobby? Show calculations.

    c. Explain what Long might do in the way of tax planning to further support a claim that this is a business activity.

15. Indicate Y (yes) or N (no) if the following items are net earnings from self-employment:

Item

_____ a. Net earnings from apartment building

_____ b. Net income from accounting practice

_____ c. Interest income on loan

_____ d. Share of net income from manufacturing partnership

_____ e. Net income for service as a minister

_____ f. Dividends from domestic corporations

_____ g. Gross rent received on office building

_____ h. Gross profit from doctor's practice

_____ i. Prize for winning essay contest

_____ j. Salary for secretary

_____ k. Net gain on the sale of property

_____ l. Director's fees

16. Determine the self-employment tax that would be paid for 1992 by each of the following taxpayers. If there is no self-employment tax, explain why.

Taxpayer A: Age, 42; net business income, $39,000; dividend income, $300; salary subject to social security, $5,000; gross rental income, $6,000; and net rental income, $1,500.

Taxpayer B: Age, 71; net business income, $9,000; dividend income, $500; salary subject to social security, $42,900.

Taxpayer C: Age, 35; net business income, $60,000; dividend income, $200.

Taxpayer D: Age, 27; net business income, $15,000; dividend income, $100; salary subject to social security, $20,000.

Taxpayer E: Age, 56; net business income, $3,000; dividend income, $450; gross rental income, $4,000; and net rental income, ($500).

Taxpayer F: Age, 64; net business income, $300; dividend income, $50; salary subject to social security, $400.

17. Elaine Gerber conducts a business in her home. Tentative profit from Schedule C (line 29) was $9,600. Complete Form 8829 on the next page.

Form **8829**	**Expenses for Business Use of Your Home**	OMB No. 1545-1266
Department of the Treasury Internal Revenue Service	▶ File with Schedule C (Form 1040). Use a separate Form 8829 for each home you used for business during the year. ▶ See instructions on back.	**19**92 Attachment Sequence No. **66**.

Name(s) of proprietor(s)   Your social security number

Elaine Gerber

Part I Part of Your Home Used for Business

1	Area used exclusively for business (see instructions). Include area that does not meet exclusive use test and either used for inventory storage or regularly used as part of a day-care facility	1	240
2	Total area of home	2	3,000
3	Divide line 1 by line 2. Enter the result as a percentage	3	%

- **For day-care facilities not used exclusively for business, also complete lines 4–6.**
- **All others, skip lines 4–6 and enter the amount from line 3 on line 7.**

4	Multiply days used for day care during year by hours used per day .	4	hr.
5	Total hours available for use during the year (366 days × 24 hours). See instructions	5	8,784 hr.
6	Divide line 4 by line 5. Enter the result as a decimal amount	6	
7	Business percentage. For day-care facilities not used exclusively for business, multiply line 6 by line 3 (enter the result as a percentage). All others, enter the amount from line 3 . . . . . ▶	7	%

Part II Figure Your Allowable Deduction

			(a) Direct expenses	(b) Indirect expenses		
8	Enter the amount from Schedule C, line 29, **plus** any net gain or (loss) derived from the business use of your home and shown on Schedule D or Form 4797. If more than one place of business, see instructions	8				
	See instructions for columns (a) and (b) before completing lines 9–20.					
9	Casualty losses. See instructions	9				
10	Deductible mortgage interest. See instructions .	10		1,800 00		
11	Real estate taxes. See instructions	11		1,500 00		
12	Add lines 9, 10, and 11	12				
13	Multiply line 12, column (b) by line 7	13			13	
14	Add line 12, column (a) and line 13				14	
15	Subtract line 14 from line 8. If zero or less, enter -0- .				15	
16	Excess mortgage interest. See instructions . .	16				
17	Insurance	17		500 00		
18	Repairs and maintenance	18				
19	Utilities	19		750 00		
20	Other expenses. See instructions	20				
21	Add lines 16 through 20	21				
22	Multiply line 21, column (b) by line 7		22			
23	Carryover of operating expenses from 1991 Form 8829, line 41 . .		23			
24	Add line 21 in column (a), line 22, and line 23	24				
25	Allowable operating expenses. Enter the **smaller** of line 15 or line 24	25				
26	Limit on excess casualty losses and depreciation. Subtract line 25 from line 15	26				
27	Excess casualty losses. See instructions	27				
28	Depreciation of your home from Part III below	28				
29	Carryover of excess casualty losses and depreciation from 1991 Form 8829, line 42	29				
30	Add lines 27 through 29	30				
31	Allowable excess casualty losses and depreciation. Enter the **smaller** of line 26 or line 30 . .	31				
32	Add lines 14, 25, and 31	32				
33	Casualty loss portion, if any, from lines 14 and 31. Carry amount to **Form 4684**, Section B .	33				
34	Allowable expenses for business use of your home. Subtract line 33 from line 32. Enter here and on Schedule C, line 30. If your home was used for more than one business, see instructions ▶	34				

Part III Depreciation of Your Home

35	Enter the **smaller** of your home's adjusted basis or its fair market value. See instructions . .	35	60,000 00
36	Value of land included on line 35	36	10,000 00
37	Basis of building. Subtract line 36 from line 35	37	
38	Business basis of building. Multiply line 37 by line 7	38	
39	Depreciation percentage. See instructions	39	3.175 %
40	Depreciation allowable. Multiply line 38 by line 39. Enter here and on line 28 above. See instructions	40	

Part IV Carryover of Unallowed Expenses to 1993

41	Operating expenses. Subtract line 25 from line 24. If less than zero, enter -0-	41	
42	Excess casualty losses and depreciation. Subtract line 31 from line 30. If less than zero, enter -0-	42	

For Paperwork Reduction Act Notice, see back of form.   Cat. No. 13232M   Form **8829** (1992)

18. Harold R. and Helen K. Westgate, RFD #1, Box 231, Newville, Iowa 52315-4221, file a joint income tax return. They claim as dependents their two sons, James R., age 16, SSN 941-23-5814, and Orville K., age 15, SSN 948-42-8153. Mr. Westgage, age 53, SSN 311-58-5849, and Mrs. Westgate, age 55, SSN 233-58-4765, own and operate a dairy farm. Over half of the support is provided for both of the sons who are going to school and live at home. The Westgate's farm EIN is 32-5748365. They uses the cash method and has cash receipts and disbursements for the year as follows:

Cash Receipts

Salary as school board member (gross $1,200 less social security $91.80)	$ 1,108.20
Dairy product sales	48,650.00
Hay sales	1,530.10
Corn sales	462.00
Machine work which Mr. Westgate had done	1,100.00
Taxable agricultural program receipts (cash)	3,200.00
Steers raised, sold 7-3-92	2,300.00
Steers sold, 9-14-92. Acquired 11-4-91, cost $3,200	6,800.00
Interest from savings and loan deposit	400.00
Dividends from Minnesota Mfg. Corporation (joint)	160.00
State gasoline tax refund	110.00

Cash Disbursements

Medical insurance premiums for the family	1,500.00
Labor hired	2,200.00
Labor hired	
—son James	1,200.00
—son Orville	850.00
Repairs and maintenance	820.00
Feed purchased	4,000.00
Seeds and plants purchased	2,100.00
Supplies purchased	180.00
Veterinary fees	135.00
Taxes—farm	2,113.40
Insurance—farm	630.00
Life insurance—Mr. Westgate	915.00
Farm publications	18.50
Preparation of 1991 income tax return	250.00
Other miscellaneous deductions	120.00
Contribution to First Newville Church	960.00
Other qualified contributions	360.00
Purchased 4 dairy cows, 12-30-92	1,511.50
Purchased new combine, 1-30-92	43,600.00
Interest expense	
—farm mortgage paid to financial institution	800.00
—note covering purchase of personal auto in 1991	400.00
State income tax	3,640.00
Property taxes on residence	1,625.00
Estimated federal income tax payments made in 1992	8,200.00

Depreciation (from Form 4562) on farm animals, buildings, and equipment for 1992 is $9,280, which can be accepted as the complete and correct amount for filing the income tax return for the Westgates.

From the above information, prepare the U.S. Individual Income Tax return for Mr. and Mrs. Westgate for 1992 using Form 1040 and Schedules A, F, and SE provided the following pages.

The Westgates sign and date the return on March 28, 1993. They must use Part I, Regular Method, of Schedule SE to calculate net earnings from farm self-employment.

Form **1040** Department of the Treasury—Internal Revenue Service
U.S. Individual Income Tax Return **1992** | IRS Use Only—Do not write or staple in this space.

For the year Jan. 1–Dec. 31, 1992, or other tax year beginning , 1992, ending , 19 OMB No. 1545-0074

Label
(See instructions on page 10.)
Use the IRS label. Otherwise, please print or type.

L A B E L   H E R E

Your first name and initial | Last name | Your social security number

If a joint return, spouse's first name and initial | Last name | Spouse's social security number

Home address (number and street). If you have a P.O. box, see page 10. | Apt. no.

City, town or post office, state, and ZIP code. If you have a foreign address, see page 10.

For Privacy Act and Paperwork Reduction Act Notice, see page 4.

Presidential Election Campaign (See page 10.)

Do you want $1 to go to this fund? . . . . · Yes ▨ No
If a joint return, does your spouse want $1 to go to this fund? . Yes ▨ No

Note: *Checking "Yes" will not change your tax or reduce your refund.*

Filing Status
(See page 10.)
Check only one box.

1 ☐ Single
2 ☐ Married filing joint return (even if only one had income)
3 ☐ Married filing separate return. Enter spouse's social security no. above and full name here. ▶ _______
4 ☐ Head of household (with qualifying person). (See page 11.) If the qualifying person is a child but not your dependent, enter this child's name here. ▶ _______
5 ☐ Qualifying widow(er) with dependent child (year spouse died ▶ 19). (See page 11.)

Exemptions
(See page 11.)

6a ☐ **Yourself.** If your parent (or someone else) can claim you as a dependent on his or her tax return, do not check box 6a. But be sure to check the box on line 33b on page 2
b ☐ **Spouse** . . . .
c **Dependents:**

If more than six dependents, see page 12.

(1) Name (first, initial, and last name)	(2) Check if under age 1	(3) If age 1 or older, dependent's social security number	(4) Dependent's relationship to you	(5) No. of months lived in your home in 1992

No. of boxes checked on 6a and 6b _____
No. of your children on 6c who:
• lived with you _____
• didn't live with you due to divorce or separation (see page 13) _____
No. of other dependents on 6c _____

d If your child didn't live with you but is claimed as your dependent under a pre-1985 agreement, check here ▶ ☐
e Total number of exemptions claimed . . . .

Add numbers entered on lines above ▶ ☐

Income

Attach Copy B of your Forms W-2, W-2G, and 1099-R here.

If you did not get a W-2, see page 9.

Attach check or money order on top of any Forms W-2, W-2G, or 1099-R.

7 Wages, salaries, tips, etc. Attach Form(s) W-2 . . . . | 7 |
8a Taxable interest income. Attach Schedule B if over $400 . . . . | 8a |
b Tax-exempt interest income (see page 15). DON'T include on line 8a | 8b | |
9 Dividend income. Attach Schedule B if over $400 . . . . . . | 9 |
10 Taxable refunds, credits, or offsets of state and local income taxes from worksheet on page 16 | 10 |
11 Alimony received . . . . | 11 |
12 Business income or (loss). Attach Schedule C or C-EZ . . . . . | 12 |
13 Capital gain or (loss). Attach Schedule D . . . . | 13 |
14 Capital gain distributions not reported on line 13 (see page 15) . . | 14 |
15 Other gains or (losses). Attach Form 4797 . . . . | 15 |
16a Total IRA distributions . | 16a | b Taxable amount (see page 16) | 16b |
17a Total pensions and annuities | 17a | b Taxable amount (see page 16) | 17b |
18 Rents, royalties, partnerships, estates, trusts, etc. Attach Schedule E . . . . . | 18 |
19 Farm income or (loss). Attach Schedule F . . . . | 19 |
20 Unemployment compensation (see page 17) . . . . | 20 |
21a Social security benefits | 21a | b Taxable amount (see page 17) | 21b |
22 Other income. List type and amount—see page 18 . . . . . . | 22 |
23 Add the amounts in the far right column for lines 7 through 22. This is your total income . . ▶ | 23 |

Adjustments to Income
(See page 18.)

24a Your IRA deduction from applicable worksheet on page 19 or 20 | 24a |
b Spouse's IRA deduction from applicable worksheet on page 19 or 20 | 24b |
25 One-half of self-employment tax (see page 20) . . . | 25 |
26 Self-employed health insurance deduction (see page 20) | 26 |
27 Keogh retirement plan and self-employed SEP deduction | 27 |
28 Penalty on early withdrawal of savings . . . . . | 28 |
29 Alimony paid. Recipient's SSN ▶ | 29 |
30 Add lines 24a through 29. These are your total adjustments . . . . ▶ | 30 |

Adjusted Gross Income

31 Subtract line 30 from line 23. This is your **adjusted gross income.** *If this amount is less than $22,370 and a child lived with you, see page EIC-1 to find out if you can claim the "Earned Income Credit" on line 56* . . . . ▶ | 31 |

Cat. No. 11320B   Form **1040** (1992)

Form 1040 (1992)   Page **2**

Tax Computation

(See page 22.)

32 Amount from line 31 (adjusted gross income)   **32**

33a Check if: ☐ You were 65 or older, ☐ Blind; ☐ Spouse was 65 or older, ☐ Blind.
Add the number of boxes checked above and enter the total here ▶ **33a** ☐

b If your parent (or someone else) can claim you as a dependent, check here ▶ **33b** ☐

c If you are married filing separately and your spouse itemizes deductions or you are a dual-status alien, see page 22 and check here ▶ **33c** ☐

34 Enter the larger of your:
- Itemized deductions from Schedule A, line 26, OR
- Standard deduction shown below for your filing status. But if you checked any box on line 33a or b, go to page 22 to find your standard deduction. If you checked box 33c, your standard deduction is zero.
  - Single—$3,600
  - Head of household—$5,250
  - Married filing jointly or Qualifying widow(er)—$6,000
  - Married filing separately—$3,000

34

35 Subtract line 34 from line 32   **35**

36 If line 32 is $78,950 or less, multiply $2,300 by the total number of exemptions claimed on line 6e. If line 32 is over $78,950, see the worksheet on page 23 for the amount to enter   **36**

(If you want the IRS to figure your tax, see page 23.)

37 Taxable income. Subtract line 36 from line 35. If line 36 is more than line 35, enter -0-   **37**

38 Enter tax. Check if from a ☐ Tax Table, b ☐ Tax Rate Schedules, c ☐ Schedule D, or d ☐ Form 8615 (see page 23). Amount, if any, from Form(s) 8814 ▶ e _______   **38**

39 Additional taxes (see page 23). Check if from a ☐ Form 4970 b ☐ Form 4972   **39**

40 Add lines 38 and 39   ▶ **40**

Credits

(See page 23.)

41 Credit for child and dependent care expenses. Attach Form 2441   **41**

42 Credit for the elderly or the disabled. Attach Schedule R   **42**

43 Foreign tax credit. Attach Form 1116   **43**

44 Other credits (see page 24). Check if from a ☐ Form 3800 b ☐ Form 8396 c ☐ Form 8801 d ☐ Form (specify)_______   **44**

45 Add lines 41 through 44   **45**

46 Subtract line 45 from line 40. If line 45 is more than line 40, enter -0-   ▶ **46**

Other Taxes

47 Self-employment tax. Attach Schedule SE. Also, see line 25   **47**

48 Alternative minimum tax. Attach Form 6251   **48**

49 Recapture taxes (see page 25). Check if from a ☐ Form 4255 b ☐ Form 8611 c ☐ Form 8828   **49**

50 Social security and Medicare tax on tip income not reported to employer. Attach Form 4137   **50**

51 Tax on qualified retirement plans, including IRAs. Attach Form 5329   **51**

52 Advance earned income credit payments from Form W-2   **52**

53 Add lines 46 through 52. This is your **total tax**   ▶ **53**

Payments

Attach Forms W-2, W-2G, and 1099-R on the front.

54 Federal income tax withheld. If any is from Form(s) 1099, check ▶ ☐   **54**

55 1992 estimated tax payments and amount applied from 1991 return   **55**

56 Earned income credit. Attach Schedule EIC   **56**

57 Amount paid with Form 4868 (extension request)   **57**

58 Excess social security, Medicare, and RRTA tax withheld (see page 26)   **58**

59 Other payments (see page 26). Check if from a ☐ Form 2439 b ☐ Form 4136   **59**

60 Add lines 54 through 59. These are your **total payments**   ▶ **60**

Refund or Amount You Owe

Attach check or money order on top of Form(s) W-2, etc., on the front.

61 If line 60 is more than line 53, subtract line 53 from line 60. This is the amount you **OVERPAID**   ▶ **61**

62 Amount of line 61 you want **REFUNDED TO YOU**   ▶ **62**

63 Amount of line 61 you want **APPLIED TO YOUR 1993 ESTIMATED TAX** ▶ **63**

64 If line 53 is more than line 60, subtract line 60 from line 53. This is the **AMOUNT YOU OWE.** Attach check or money order for full amount payable to "Internal Revenue Service." Write your name, address, social security number, daytime phone number, and "1992 Form 1040" on it   **64**

65 Estimated tax penalty (see page 27). Also include on line 64   **65**

Sign Here

Keep a copy of this return for your records.

Under penalties of perjury, I declare that I have examined this return and accompanying schedules and statements, and to the best of my knowledge and belief, they are true, correct, and complete. Declaration of preparer (other than taxpayer) is based on all information of which preparer has any knowledge.

▶ Your signature   Date   Your occupation

▶ Spouse's signature. If a joint return, BOTH must sign.   Date   Spouse's occupation

Paid Preparer's Use Only

Preparer's signature ▶   Date   Check if self-employed ☐   Preparer's social security no.

Firm's name (or yours if self-employed) and address ▶   E.I. No.

ZIP code

SCHEDULES A&B
(Form 1040)

Department of the Treasury
Internal Revenue Service

Schedule A—Itemized Deductions

(Schedule B is on back)

▶ Attach to Form 1040. ▶ See Instructions for Schedules A and B (Form 1040).

OMB No. 1545-0074

1992

Attachment
Sequence No. **07**

Name(s) shown on Form 1040

Your social security number

Medical and Dental Expenses		Caution: *Do not include expenses reimbursed or paid by others.*		
	1	Medical and dental expenses (see page A-1)	1	
	2	Enter amount from Form 1040, line 32 .	2		
	3	Multiply line 2 above by 7.5% (.075)	3	
	4	Subtract line 3 from line 1. If zero or less, enter -0- . . . . . . ▶	4	

Taxes You Paid (See page A-1.)				
	5	State and local income taxes	5	
	6	Real estate taxes (see page A-2)	6	
	7	Other taxes. List—include personal property taxes . ▶	7	
	8	Add lines 5 through 7 . . . . ▶	8	

Interest You Paid (See page A-2.) **Note: Personal interest is not deductible.**				
	9a	Home mortgage interest and points reported to you on Form 1098	9a	
	b	Home mortgage interest not reported to you on Form 1098. If paid to an individual, show that person's name and address. ▶	9b	
	10	Points not reported to you on Form 1098. See page A-3 for special rules .	10	
	11	Investment interest. If required, attach Form 4952. (See page A-3.)	11	
	12	Add lines 9a through 11 . . . . ▶	12	

Gifts to Charity (See page A-3.)		Caution: *If you made a charitable contribution and received a benefit in return, see page A-3.*		
	13	Contributions by cash or check	13	
	14	Other than by cash or check. If over $500, you **MUST** attach Form 8283	14	
	15	Carryover from prior year	15	
	16	Add lines 13 through 15 . . . . ▶	16	

Casualty and Theft Losses	17	Casualty or theft loss(es). Attach Form 4684. (See page A-4.) . . . . . . ▶	17	

Moving Expenses	18	Moving expenses. Attach Form 3903 or 3903F. (See page A-4.) . . . . . . ▶	18	

Job Expenses and Most Other Miscellaneous Deductions (See page A-5 for expenses to deduct here.)				
	19	Unreimbursed employee expenses—job travel, union dues, job education, etc. If required, you **MUST** attach Form 2106. (See page A-4.) ▶	19	
	20	Other expenses—investment, tax preparation, safe deposit box, etc. List type and amount ▶	20	
	21	Add lines 19 and 20	21	
	22	Enter amount from Form 1040, line 32 .	22		
	23	Multiply line 22 above by 2% (.02)	23	
	24	Subtract line 23 from line 21. If zero or less, enter -0- . . . . ▶	24	

Other Miscellaneous Deductions	25	Other—from list on page A-5. List type and amount ▶	25	

Total Itemized Deductions	26	Is the amount on Form 1040, line 32, more than $105,250 (more than $52,625 if married filing separately)? • **NO.** Your deduction is not limited. Add lines 4, 8, 12, 16, 17, 18, 24, and 25. } ▶ • **YES.** Your deduction may be limited. See page A-5 for the amount to enter. }	26	

Caution: *Be sure to enter on Form 1040, line 34, the **LARGER** of the amount on line 26 above or your standard deduction.*

For Paperwork Reduction Act Notice, see Form 1040 instructions.   Cat. No. 11330X   Schedule A (Form 1040) 1992

SCHEDULE F
(Form 1040)

Department of the Treasury
Internal Revenue Service

Profit or Loss From Farming

▶ Attach to Form 1040, Form 1041, or Form 1065.

▶ See Instructions for Schedule F (Form 1040).

OMB No. 1545-0074

1992

Attachment
Sequence No. **14**

Name of proprietor

Social security number (SSN)

A Principal product. Describe in one or two words your principal crop or activity for the current tax year.

B Enter principal agricultural activity code (from page 2) ▶

D Employer ID number (Not SSN)

C Accounting method: (1) ☐ Cash   (2) ☐ Accrual

E Did you "materially participate" in the operation of this business during 1992? If "No," see page F-1 for limitations on losses. ☐ Yes ☐ No

Part I   **Farm Income—Cash Method—Complete Parts I and II** (Accrual method taxpayers complete Parts II and III, and line 11 of Part I.)
Do not include sales of livestock held for draft, breeding, sport, or dairy purposes; report these sales on Form 4797.

1	Sales of livestock and other items you bought for resale	**1**	
2	Cost or other basis of livestock and other items reported on line 1	**2**	
3	Subtract line 2 from line 1		**3**
4	Sales of livestock, produce, grains, and other products you raised		**4**
5a	Total cooperative distributions (Form(s) 1099-PATR) **5a**	5b Taxable amount	**5b**
6a	Agricultural program payments (see page F-2) **6a**	6b Taxable amount	**6b**
7	Commodity Credit Corporation (CCC) loans (see page F-2):		
a	CCC loans reported under election		**7a**
b	CCC loans forfeited or repaid with certificates **7b**	7c Taxable amount	**7c**
8	Crop insurance proceeds and certain disaster payments (see page F-2):		
a	Amount received in 1992 **8a**	8b Taxable amount	**8b**
c	If election to defer to 1993 is attached, check here ▶ ☐	8d Amount deferred from 1991	**8d**
9	Custom hire (machine work) income		**9**
10	Other income, including Federal and state gasoline or fuel tax credit or refund (see page F-3)		**10**
11	**Gross income.** Add amounts in the right column for lines 3 through 10. If accrual method taxpayer, enter the amount from page 2, line 51 ▶		**11**

Part II   **Farm Expenses—Cash and Accrual Method** (Do not include personal or living expenses such as taxes, insurance, repairs, etc., on your home.)

12	Car and truck expenses (see page F-3—also attach Form 4562)	**12**		25	Pension and profit-sharing plans	**25**	
13	Chemicals	**13**		26	Rent or lease (see page F-4):		
14	Conservation expenses. Attach Form 8645	**14**		a	Vehicles, machinery, and equipment	**26a**	
15	Custom hire (machine work)	**15**		b	Other (land, animals, etc.)	**26b**	
16	Depreciation and section 179 expense deduction not claimed elsewhere (see page F-3)	**16**		27	Repairs and maintenance	**27**	
				28	Seeds and plants purchased	**28**	
				29	Storage and warehousing	**29**	
17	Employee benefit programs other than on line 25	**17**		30	Supplies purchased	**30**	
				31	Taxes	**31**	
18	Feed purchased	**18**		32	Utilities	**32**	
19	Fertilizers and lime	**19**		33	Veterinary, breeding, and medicine	**33**	
20	Freight and trucking	**20**		34	Other expenses (specify):		
21	Gasoline, fuel, and oil	**21**		a	....	**34a**	
22	Insurance (other than health)	**22**		b	....	**34b**	
23	Interest:			c	....	**34c**	
a	Mortgage (paid to banks, etc.)	**23a**		d	....	**34d**	
b	Other	**23b**		e	....	**34e**	
24	Labor hired (less jobs credit)	**24**		f		**34f**	

35	**Total expenses.** Add lines 12 through 34f ▶		**35**
36	**Net farm profit or (loss).** Subtract line 35 from line 11. If a profit, enter on Form 1040, line 19, and on Schedule SE, line 1. If a loss, you MUST go on to line 37 (fiduciaries and partnerships, see page F-5)		**36**
37	If you have a loss, you MUST check the box that describes your investment in this activity (see page F-5). If you checked 37a, enter the loss on Form 1040, line 19, and Schedule SE, line 1. If you checked 37b, you MUST attach Form 6198.	**37a** ☐ All investment is at risk. **37b** ☐ Some investment is not at risk.	

For Paperwork Reduction Act Notice, see Form 1040 instructions.   Cat. No. 11346H   **Schedule F (Form 1040) 1992**

Schedule F (Form 1040) 1992   Page **2**

Part III Farm Income—Accrual Method (see page F-5)

Do not include sales of livestock held for draft, breeding, sport, or dairy purposes; report these sales on Form 4797 and do not include this livestock on line 46 below.

38	Sales of livestock, produce, grains, and other products during the year.		**38**
39a	Total cooperative distributions (Form(s) 1099-PATR) **39a** ______ **39b** Taxable amount		**39b**
40a	Agricultural program payments **40a** ______ **40b** Taxable amount		**40b**
41	Commodity Credit Corporation (CCC) loans:		
a	CCC loans reported under election		**41a**
b	CCC loans forfeited or repaid with certificates **41b** ______ **41c** Taxable amount		**41c**
42	Crop insurance proceeds		**42**
43	Custom hire (machine work) income		**43**
44	Other income, including Federal and state gasoline or fuel tax credit or refund		**44**
45	Add amounts in the right column for lines 38 through 44		**45**
46	Inventory of livestock, produce, grains, and other products at beginning of the year.	**46**	
47	Cost of livestock, produce, grains, and other products purchased during the year.	**47**	
48	Add lines 46 and 47	**48**	
49	Inventory of livestock, produce, grains, and other products at end of year	**49**	
50	Cost of livestock, produce, grains, and other products sold. Subtract line 49 from line 48*		**50**
51	**Gross income.** Subtract line 50 from line 45. Enter the result here and on page 1, line 11 ▶		**51**

*If you use the unit-livestock-price method or the farm-price method of valuing inventory and the amount on line 49 is larger than the amount on line 48, subtract line 48 from line 49. Enter the result on line 50. Add lines 45 and 50. Enter the total on line 51.

Part IV Principal Agricultural Activity Codes

Caution: *File **Schedule C** (Form 1040), Profit or Loss From Business, or **Schedule C-EZ** (Form 1040), Net Profit From Business, instead of Schedule F if:*

● Your principal source of income is from providing agricultural services such as soil preparation, veterinary, farm labor, horticultural, or management for a fee or on a contract basis, or

● You are engaged in the business of breeding, raising, and caring for dogs, cats, or other pet animals.

Select one of the following codes and write the 3-digit number on page 1, line B:

120 **Field crop,** including grains and nongrains such as cotton, peanuts, feed corn, wheat, tobacco, Irish potatoes, etc.

160 **Vegetables and melons,** garden-type vegetables and melons, such as sweet corn, tomatoes, squash, etc.

170 **Fruit and tree nuts,** including grapes, berries, olives, etc.

180 **Ornamental floriculture and nursery products**

185 **Food crops grown under cover,** including hydroponic crops

211 **Beefcattle feedlots**

212 **Beefcattle,** except feedlots

215 **Hogs, sheep, and goats**

240 **Dairy**

250 **Poultry and eggs,** including chickens, ducks, pigeons, quail, etc.

260 **General livestock,** not specializing in any one livestock category

270 **Animal specialty,** including bees, fur-bearing animals, horses, snakes, etc.

280 **Animal aquaculture,** including fish, shellfish, mollusks, frogs, etc., produced within confined space

290 **Forest products,** including forest nurseries and seed gathering, extraction of pine gum, and gathering of forest products

300 **Agricultural production,** not specified

<table>
<tr><td>SCHEDULE SE
(Form 1040)

Department of the Treasury
Internal Revenue Service</td><td align="center">Self-Employment Tax

▶ See Instructions for Schedule SE (Form 1040).

▶ Attach to Form 1040.</td><td>OMB No. 1545-0074
1992
Attachment
Sequence No. 17</td></tr>
<tr><td colspan="2">Name of person with self-employment income (as shown on Form 1040)</td><td>Social security number of person
with self-employment income ▶</td></tr>
</table>

Who Must File Schedule SE

You must file Schedule SE if:

- Your wages (and tips) subject to social security AND Medicare tax (or railroad retirement tax) were less than $130,200; **AND**
- Your *net earnings from self-employment from other than church employee income* (line 4 of Short Schedule SE or line 4c of Long Schedule SE) were $400 or more;
  OR
- You had church employee income (as defined on page SE-1) of $108.28 or more.

Exception. If your only self-employment income was from earnings as a minister, member of a religious order, or Christian Science practitioner, AND you filed **Form 4361** and received IRS approval not to be taxed on those earnings, DO NOT file Schedule SE. Instead, write "Exempt–Form 4361" on Form 1040, line 47.

May I Use Short Schedule SE or MUST I Use Long Schedule SE?

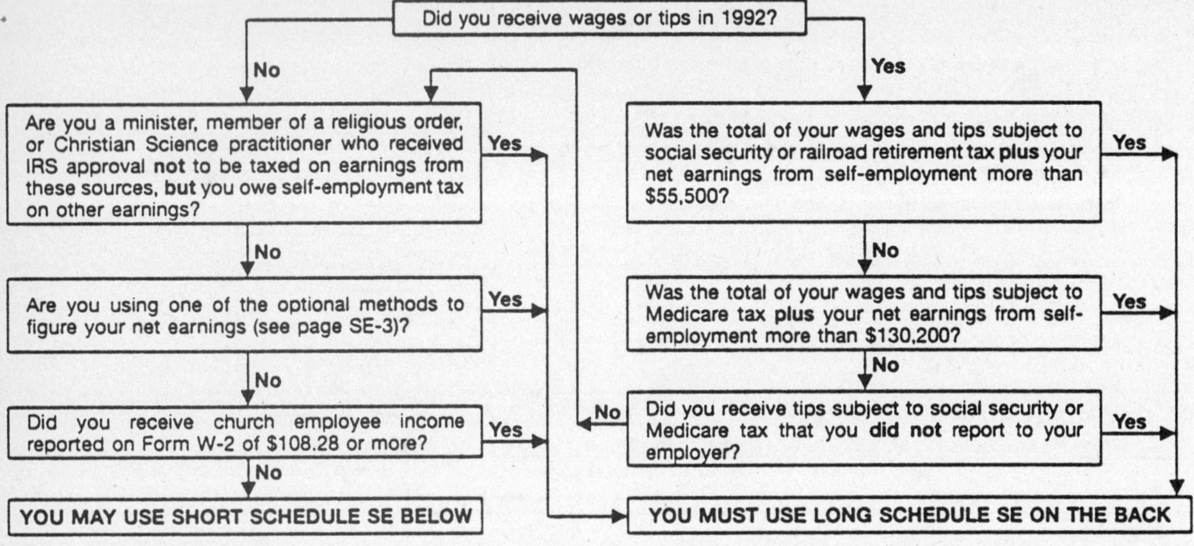

Section A—Short Schedule SE. Caution: *Read above to see if you must use Long Schedule SE on the back (Section B).*

1	Net farm profit or (loss) from Schedule F, line 36, and farm partnerships, Schedule K-1 (Form 1065), line 15a	1
2	Net profit or (loss) from Schedule C, line 31; Schedule C-EZ, line 3; and Schedule K-1 (Form 1065), line 15a (other than farming). See page SE-2 for other income to report	2
3	Combine lines 1 and 2	3
4	**Net earnings from self-employment.** Multiply line 3 by 92.35% (.9235). If less than $400, **do not** file this schedule; you do not owe self-employment tax . . . . ▶	4
5	**Self-employment tax.** If the amount on line 4 is: • $55,500 or less, multiply line 4 by 15.3% (.153) and enter the result. • More than $55,500 but less than $130,200, multiply the amount in excess of $55,500 by 2.9% (.029). Then, add $8,491.50 to the result and enter the total. • $130,200 or more, enter $10,657.80. Also, enter this amount on Form 1040, line 47 . . . . **Note:** *Also, enter one-half of the amount from line 5 on Form 1040, line 25.*	5

For Paperwork Reduction Act Notice, see Form 1040 instructions.   Cat. No. 11358Z   **Schedule SE (Form 1040) 1992**

Schedule SE (Form 1040) 1992   Attachment Sequence No. **17**   Page **2**

Name of person with **self-employment** income (as shown on Form 1040)	Social security number of person with **self-employment** income ▶	

Section B—Long Schedule SE

A   If you are a minister, member of a religious order, or Christian Science practitioner AND you filed **Form 4361**, but you had $400 or more of **other** net earnings from self-employment, check here and continue with Part I . . . . . ▶ ☐

B   If your only income subject to self-employment tax is church employee income and you are **not** a minister or a member of a religious order, skip lines 1 through 4b. Enter -0- on line 4c and go to line 5a.

Part I   Self-Employment Tax

1	Net farm profit or (loss) from Schedule F, line 36, and farm partnerships, Schedule K-1 (Form 1065), line 15a. **Note:** *Skip this line if you use the farm optional method. See requirements in Part II below and on page SE-3*	**1**	
2	Net profit or (loss) from Schedule C, line 31; Schedule C-EZ, line 3; and Schedule K-1 (Form 1065), line 15a (other than farming). See page SE-2 for other income to report. **Note:** *Skip this line if you use the nonfarm optional method. See requirements in Part II below and on page SE-3*	**2**	
3	Combine lines 1 and 2	**3**	
4a	If line 3 is more than zero, multiply line 3 by 92.35% (.9235). Otherwise, enter amount from line 3	**4a**	
b	If you elected one or both of the optional methods, enter the total of lines 17 and 19 here . .	**4b**	
c	Combine lines 4a and 4b. If less than $400, **do not file this schedule; you do not owe self-employment tax. Exception.** If less than $400 and you had church employee income, enter -0- and continue . ▶	**4c**	
5a	Enter your church employee income from Form W-2. **Caution:** *See page SE-1 for definition of church employee income* **5a**	**5b**	
b	Multiply line 5a by 92.35% (.9235). If less than $100, enter -0-		
6	**Net earnings from self-employment.** Add lines 4c and 5b	**6**	
7	Maximum amount of combined wages and self-employment earnings subject to social security tax or the 6.2% portion of the 7.65% railroad retirement (tier 1) tax for 1992	**7**	55,500 00
8a	Total social security wages and tips (from Form(s) W-2) and railroad retirement (tier 1) compensation **8a**		
b	Unreported tips subject to social security tax (from Form 4137, line 9) **8b**		
c	Add lines 8a and 8b	**8c**	
9	Subtract line 8c from line 7. If zero or less, enter -0- here and on line 10 and go to line 12a ▶	**9**	
10	Multiply the **smaller** of line 6 or line 9 by 12.4% (.124)	**10**	
11	Maximum amount of combined wages and self-employment earnings subject to Medicare tax or the 1.45% portion of the 7.65% railroad retirement (tier 1) tax for 1992	**11**	130,200 00
12a	Total Medicare wages and tips (from Form(s) W-2) and railroad retirement (tier 1) compensation **12a**		
b	Unreported tips subject to Medicare tax (from Form 4137, line 14) **12b**		
c	Add lines 12a and 12b	**12c**	
13	Subtract line 12c from line 11. If zero or less, enter -0- here and on line 14 and go to line 15 .	**13**	
14	Multiply the **smaller** of line 6 or line 13 by 2.9% (.029)	**14**	
15	**Self-employment tax.** Add lines 10 and 14. Enter the result here and on Form 1040, line 47 . . **Note:** *Also, enter one-half of the amount from line 15 on Form 1040, line 25.*	**15**	

Part II   Optional Methods To Figure Net Earnings (See Who Can File Schedule SE on page SE-1 and Optional Methods on page SE-3.)

Farm Optional Method. You may use this method **only** if **(a)** Your gross farm income[1] was not more than $2,400 **or (b)** Your gross farm income[1] was more than $2,400 and your net farm profits[2] were less than $1,733.

16	Maximum income for optional methods	**16**	1,600 00
17	Enter the **smaller** of: two-thirds (⅔) of gross farm income[1] or $1,600. Also, include this amount on line 4b above	**17**	

Nonfarm Optional Method. You may use this method **only** if **(a)** Your net nonfarm profits[3] were less than $1,733 and also less than 72.189% of your gross nonfarm income,[4] **and (b)** You had net earnings from self-employment of at least $400 in 2 of the prior 3 years. **Caution:** *You may use this method no more than five times.*

18	Subtract line 17 from line 16	**18**	
19	Enter the **smaller** of: two-thirds (⅔) of gross nonfarm income[4] or the amount on line 18. Also, include this amount on line 4b above	**19**	

[1] From Schedule F, line 11, and Schedule K-1 (Form 1065), line 15b.   [3] From Schedule C, line 31; Schedule C-EZ, line 3; and Schedule K-1 (Form 1065), line 15a.
[2] From Schedule F, line 36, and Schedule K-1 (Form 1065), line 15a.   [4] From Schedule C, line 7; Schedule C-EZ, line 1; and Schedule K-1 (Form 1065), line 15c.

Tax Ethics Case*

19. The date is April 14. Helen Baldwin, CPA tax practitioner, sits at her desk pondering over the tax return she has before her. She has spent plenty of time pondering during the past year since moving from her home in a large eastern city to set up her new tax practice in a small western town. Clients in this small town have not exactly beaten a path to her door to take advantage of her services. Building a client base has proven much more difficult than Helen had anticipated.

The return in front of her was completed on behalf of her newest client, Billy Joe Carter, who owns Honest Bill's Used Car Lot. He is a cousin of half of the members of the town council and is very influential in the local business community. Establishing a client relationship with Billy is the break that Helen has been looking for. In fact, Billy has made it clear that if Helen can complete and file his return before the April 15th deadline, Helen will receive his tax return business, as well as that of his family, for years to come.

Of concern to Helen, however, are several items on Billy's return. Billy insists that he is entitled to a business deduction for his new 4-wheel-drive truck, since he uses the truck 100% of the time for business errands (such as traveling to car auctions, picking up parts, etc.). Helen thinks she has seen Billy driving the truck a number of times on what appeared to be personal trips. Also, Billy insists that the expenses associated with several trips to Las Vegas are deductible since the trips were "primarily of a business nature." Billy also claims several other large deductions without offering what Helen would consider to be "substantial documentation." As if anticipating Helen's skepticism, Billy said, "I don't know how things were in the big city where you came from, but around here people believe that a person's word is worth something. You'll just have to trust good old 'Honest Bill' this year, and next year I'll try to keep some better records."

a. What are the ethical issues in this case?

b. Who and what are the "stakeholders" who will be affected directly or indirectly by an inappropriate decision on Helen's part?

c. What are Helen's options in this situation?

d. What do you recommend that Helen should do?*

---

* Case adapted from ethics cases prepared for publication by the American Accounting Association.

Depreciation, Cost Recovery, Depletion, and Amortization

> ### Your Rights as a Taxpayer
>
> **Complaints.** You may write to the District Director or Service Center Director for your area if for any reason you have a complaint about the IRS.
>
> *Source: Internal Revenue Service, Publication 1*

In Chapter 8, the reporting requirements for sole proprietors operating as a trade, business, or profession were discussed. The primary reporting forms for reporting business activities of a sole proprietor are Schedule C, and Form 4562, Depreciation and Amortization. For the two Schedule C's illustrated in Chapter 8, one for George Monroe (Illustration 8-1) and one for John Williams (Illustration 8-2), an amount was recorded for depreciation on Schedule C, Part II (line 13), without explaining how the depreciation amounts were determined. The primary purpose of this chapter is to present a comprehensive discussion of the concepts and calculations related to the recovery of the cost of business assets used for more than one year. As a part of these explanations, the depreciation deduction of $4,200 shown on the 1992 Schedule C (line 13) for Mr. John Williams will be calculated and reported on Form 4562.

Cost Recovery and Depreciation for a Business, Trade, or Profession

When a business buys assets that will have a useful life of more than one year, the cost is recovered over a specified number of years by taking deductions from gross income. The methods and timing of the recovery depend upon whether the asset is real property or tangible personal property. For tangible personal property, such as furniture and fixtures, machinery and equipment, and vehicles, a limited amount of cost may be deducted as an expense in the year of acquisition before any regular depreciation is calculated, referred to as a Section 179 deduction. After taking a Section 179 deduction, if applicable, the taxpayer must spread the remainder of the cost of Section 179 property and other business property over more than one year and claim depreciation deductions over the recovery period of the property. Following the depreciation rules carefully is important because, if any allowable depreciation is not claimed in an earlier year, the taxpayer must still reduce the basis of the property in determining subsequent amounts of cost recovery. If the overlooked allowable depreciation is discovered later, an amended return may be filed to deduct the unclaimed depreciation provided the amended return is filed within three years of the due date of the original return on which the allowable depreciation was not taken.

The calculation of the annual depreciation deduction for business property is complicated because, over a period of time from the 1970s to the present, three regular depreciation systems and one alternate system have been used to determine the allowable depreciation deduction for tax purposes.

Since taxpayers may own assets that were acquired when each of these systems was in effect, it is important to understand the depreciation requirements that were applicable when the depreciable asset was acquired.

Keep in mind that the cost recovery rules for certain assets were changed within each of these periods, such as the placing of limitations on the use of accelerated depreciation in 1969, the change in the useful life for buildings during the ACRS period, and changes in the cost recovery rules for luxury automobiles during the MACRS period.

Historical Perspective on Depreciation and Cost Recovery

Assets Acquired Before 1981. For assets acquired before 1981, the deductions from gross income are taken over the useful life of the asset and are referred to as depreciation expense. *Depreciation expense* is each year's portion of the asset's cost that is written off because of wear and tear, deterioration and decay, and normal obsolescence resulting from technological changes. Therefore, the asset's cost is recovered over the economic or useful life of the asset. The IRS provided guides to determine the economic life if such life was not otherwise determinable by the business.

Assets Acquired During the Years 1981-86. For assets acquired during the period 1981 through 1986, the Economic Recovery Tax Act of 1981 allowed businesses and taxpayers owning income-producing property to take accelerated cost recovery deductions instead of "depreciation" deductions. The *Accelerated Cost Recovery System (ACRS)* provided for a more rapid capital cost recovery than had been previously possible under the depreciation rules in effect for assets acquired before 1981. The purpose of this accelerated cost recovery was to encourage more reinvestment of capital in depreciable assets and to help revitalize the economy by reducing the federal income tax burden on businesses and on income-producing property. During the tax years 1981 through 1986, certain taxpayers also could elect to expense, in the year an asset was acquired, up to $5,000 of the cost of tangible personal property.

Assets Acquired After 1986. The Tax Reform Act of 1986 modified the ACRS rules by revising the recovery periods and/or rates of recovery, and by prescribing depreciation methods rather than statutory rates. Tangible personal property acquired after the end of 1986 is depreciable in one of six classes and real property is generally depreciable in two classes. The depreciation rules for assets **placed in service** before 1981, the original ACRS for assets placed in service during 1981-1986, and MACRS for assets placed in service after 1986 continue to apply. In effect, each of these depreciation or cost recovery systems is applicable for assets placed in service during the period each system was being used.

In the following pages there will be a brief discussion of depreciation prior to 1981 and the original ACRS system applicable to the period 1981 through 1986, before beginning a detailed discussion of the MACRS system.

Depreciation Prior to 1981

The cost of buildings, equipment, and other assets of a capital nature placed in service by the taxpayer before 1981 and used in the business or held for the production of income could be deducted from gross income as **depreciation expense**.

Land *cannot* be depreciated because of its permanent nature. When land and buildings were purchased for a lump sum, the cost had to be apportioned between the two on the basis of their relative FMV in order to establish a basis for determining the annual charge for depreciation of the buildings. Four factors had to be considered in calculating the annual depreciation deduction: (1) the basis of the property, which ordinarily is cost, (2) the estimated life, which is usually stated in years, but may be stated in terms of machine hours or units of production, (3) the estimated residual or salvage value, and (4) the method of allocating basis (usually cost) over the useful life (referred to as the depreciation method to be used).

In general, the annual depreciation expense deduction could be determined by any reasonable method. However, three methods were specifically authorized in the Internal Revenue Code: *straight-line, declining-balance, and sum-of-the-years-digits*. The straight-line method was allowed for any depreciable asset. The declining-balance and the sum-of-the-years-digits methods, known as *accelerated methods*, were applicable to tangible property having a useful life of three years or more. There were certain restrictions on the use of accelerated methods.

Straight-Line Method. The most commonly used depreciation method for financial reporting prior to 1981 was the straight-line method in which *cost minus estimated salvage value* is spread ratably over the estimated life of the asset. The annual depreciation deduction for tax purposes could be determined without using the salvage value, even though salvage value had to be considered for financial reporting purposes.

EXAMPLE 1 ————————————————

Assume the straight-line rate is applied to a $10,000 asset with an estimated life of 10 years and an estimated salvage value of $1,000. For property acquired at the beginning of a year, the depreciation expense for each year would be $900 (($10,000 − $1,000)/10 years) if salvage value was considered. If salvage value was not considered, the depreciation would be $1,000 ($10,000/10 years).

Declining-Balance Method. The declining-balance method, which yields greater deductions during the earlier years of life and lower deductions during later laters, applied a uniform rate at not more than twice the straight-line rate (for example, 125%, 150%, 175%, or 200%) to the unrecovered basis of the property. Estimated salvage value did not need to be considered in calculating the rate or the base. However, an asset could not be depreciated below its estimated salvage value. Taxpayers who wished to elect the declining-balance method at twice the straight-line rate had to do so in the year the asset could first be depreciated. A change could be made to the straight-line rate at any time during the asset's life without obtaining permission from the IRS.

<hr>

EXAMPLE 2

If the declining-balance method at twice the straight-line rate were applied to a $10,000 asset with an estimated life of 10 years and an estimated salvage value of $1,000, the accelerated rate would be 20% (2 x 10%) and the initial tax basis against which the rate would be applied would be $10,000. Thus, the first year's depreciation for an asset used the entire year would be $2,000 ($10,000 x 20%). Note that the percentage is applied before deducting the salvage value. However, an asset cannot be depreciated below its estimated salvage value.

Sum-of-the-Years-Digits Method. Depreciation using the sum-of-the-years-digits method also was allowed prior to 1981. The rules for the time of election were the same as those applicable to the declining-balance method. Depreciation expense under the sum-of-the years-digits method was determined by applying a constantly reducing fraction to the cost less the salvage value. The numerator of the changing fraction was the number of remaining years of the estimated life and the denominator was the sum of the digits representing the total years of life. Assuming an estimated life of 10 years, the denominator of the fraction is 55 (10+9+8+7+6+5+4+3+2+1). The denominator can also be calculated by using the formula $n[(n+1)/2]$ as follows: $10 \times (10+1)/2 = 55$. Thus, for the first year's depreciation using the sum-of-the-years-digits method, the cost less salvage value would be multiplied by the fraction with

a numerator of 10 and a denominator of 55, i.e 10/55. For the second year, the fraction would be 9/55; for the fifth year, 6/55 and so on.

<hr>

EXAMPLE 3

If the sum-of-the-years-digits method is applied to an asset that cost $10,000, has a $1,000 salvage value, and a useful life of 10 years, the first year's depreciation would be $1,636, 10/55 x ($10,000 – $1,000), assuming the taxpayer elected to consider the salvage value in the calculation. The $1,636 for the first year of depreciation under the sum-of-the-years digits method is somewhat less than the $2,000 for the first year under the 200% declining-balance method.

Depreciation Methods for Property Placed in Service After July 24, 1969. Certain limitations existed on the use of accelerated depreciation for property placed in service after July 24, 1969. The limitations under the depreciation provisions prior to 1981 appear below.

1. Depreciation on new commercial real estate could be calculated by the declining-balance method at 150% of the straight-line rate. However, used commercial real estate was limited to straight-line depreciation.

2. Depreciation on new residential rental property where at least 80% of the gross rental income comes from dwelling units could be calculated by the sum-of-the-years-digits method or the declining-balance method at 200% of the straight-line rate. However, used residential rental property having a useful life of 20 years or more was limited to the declining-balance method at 125% of the straight-line rate. For used residential rental property having less than a 20-year life, straight-line depreciation had to be used. The declining balance method at 200% of the straight-line rate applied to residential rental property only in years that the 80%-of-gross-rental-income test was met.

3. Depreciation on new tangible personal business property (such as equipment) having a useful life of 3 years or more could be calculated by either the sum-of-the-years-digits method or the declining-balance method at 200% of the straight-line rate. However, used tangible personal business property with a useful life of 3 years or more was limited to

the declining-balance method at not more than 150% of the straight-line rate.

In any year that the 80% test was not met for residential rental property, the taxpayer was required to change to a method equivalent to 150% of the straight-line rate. The rental value of a unit occupied by an owner is not income. Therefore, if an owner occupied one unit of a four-unit apartment, depreciation could be taken on only three-fourths of the rental property. This rule still applies if the taxpayer is using such property in 1992.

Table 9-1 summarizes the rules for the maximum depreciation allowed on depreciable assets in any one year if acquired before 1981.

Table 9-1
Maximum Depreciation for Assets Placed In Service After July 24, 1969, Not Under ACRS, MACRS, or ADS (Straight-Line Rate = 100%)

	New	Used
Commercial and industrial assets		
Real estate (buildings)	150%	100%
Equipment (3-yr. life or more)	200	150
Residential rental property		
New buildings	200%	
Used buildings (20-yr. life or more)		125%
Used buildings (less than 20-yr. life)		100
Furniture & equipment (3-yr. life or more)	200	150

Additional First-Year Depreciation. For new or used tangible personal property acquired before 1981 with a useful life of six years or more, an initial depreciation deduction of 20% of the cost could be claimed anytime during the year in which the property was acquired. This deduction was in addition to the ordinary first-year depreciation. The total cost of property to which the extra 20% deduction could be applied was $10,000 per taxpayer. This additional first-year depreciation deduction was repealed by the Economic Recovery Act of 1981 for property placed in service after 1980. If an initial 20% deduction had been taken in the year the asset could first be depreciated, it reduced the amount of the depreciation deduction in subsequent years.

Useful Life. In calculating the depreciation deduction, the taxpayer had two choices in terms of selecting the useful life of an asset. The taxpayer could choose an asset life that represented the useful life for that asset based on the taxpayer's personal experience. As long as the useful life selected could be justified, the taxpayer could use that life in calculating the depreciation deduction.

Instead of selecting a life based on personal experience, the taxpayer could elect to use the class life system adopted by Congress. Under the class life system, the taxpayer could choose an asset life that varied as much as 20% shorter or longer than the guideline class life for that type of asset. All of the assets in a particular guideline class acquired during the taxable year were placed in vintage accounts and depreciated in groups.

Accelerated Cost Recovery System (ACRS)

In 1981, the traditional system of tax depreciation was abandoned and was replaced with a simplified cost recovery system that allowed depreciable assets to be written off at a much faster rate. ACRS provided for cost recovery of eligible assets, whether new or used, over a period of 3, 5, or 10 years for most tangible personal property and over 15, 18, or 19 years for most real property. A summary of the assets recovery classes and the methods and rates of recovery allowed after 1980 under ACRS is shown in Table 9-2.

Calculating the Cost Recovery Deduction (1981-1986). In calculating the annual cost recovery deduction for the various classes of assets listed in Table 9-2 that were acquired during the period 1981 through 1986, certain operating procedures must be applied:

1. The calculation of the cost recovery deduction involved applying the correct percentage from the statutory rate schedule for the property's recovery class to the unadjusted basis of the property. For property acquired by purchase, the unadjusted basis would include the cost incurred to get the property ready for use at its intended location. For property acquired in other ways, such as by exchange, by gift, or as a beneficiary in a death transfer, specific rules for determining the basis of property would apply. The

Table 9-2
Cost Recovery Data for Assets Under Original ACRS (1981-1986)

Recovery Class	Rates and Methods	Types of Assets by Class
3-year	150% Declining Balance: 25%, 38%, 37%	Tangible personal property with an ADR life of 4 years or less. Includes light trucks, autos, and R&D equipment
5-year	150% Declining Balance: 15%, 22%, 21%, 21%, 21%	All tangible personal property not included elsewhere. Includes machinery and equipment, furniture and fixtures, computers, and single purpose agricultural and horticultural structures
18-year with no mid-month convention	175% Declining Balance: Identified % for each year per IRS tables	Depreciable Section 1250 property. All buildings and their structural components with a guideline class life of 12½ years or more acquired after March 15, 1984, and before June 23, 1984
18-year with mid-month convention	175% Declining Balance: Identified % for each year per IRS tables	Real property placed in service after June 22, 1984, and before May 9, 1985
19-year	175% Declining Balance: Identified % for each year per Table 9-4	Real property placed in service May 8, 1985, and before January 1987. (Taxpayers may elect under the modified ACRS for assets)

ACRS rules apply to both new and used property; salvage value is ignored.

2. For tangible personal property a *half-year convention* is used (all assets are assumed to be placed in service on the first day of the second half of the tax year), with a conversion to the straight-line method at the appropriate point in the recovery period for that class. For tangible personal property, no cost recovery is allowed in the year of disposition if the asset is disposed of before the end of the normal recovery period.

3. Recovery percentages for real property were determined according to the month in the taxable year in which the property was placed in service. If real property was sold before the end of the recovery period, the ACRS deduction for the year of disposition had to reflect only the months of that year during which the property was in service. Property placed in service after June 22, 1984, was considered to have been placed in service or disposed of in the middle of the month, regardless of the actual date of placement in service or of disposal. This rule is called the *mid-month convention*. Thus, a one-half month's cost recovery is allowed for the month the property is placed in service and for the month in which the property is disposed of prior to the end of the recovery period. This approach differs from the original ACRS rules under which a full-month convention was applied, but only in the year of acquisition. In essence, the original ACRS rules allowed a full month's recovery for the month of acquisition and none for the month of disposition.

4. Certain property does not qualify as ACRS property. Excluded from ACRS is property depreciated under the production-units method of depreciation and property used outside of the United States. Such property had to be depreciated under the rules relative to properties placed in service before 1981.

Election to Expense Certain Depreciable Assets. An expense deduction was provided for taxpayers who acquired qualifying Section 179 property. Section 179 of the Internal Revenue Code allowed an expense deduction, rather than capitalization as an asset, up to a dollar limitation on the total cost for 1986 and earlier years amounting to $5,000. Under the Tax Reform Act of 1984, the dollar amount that could be expensed was $5,000 through 1986. The Tax Reform Act of 1986 increased this amount to $10,000 for taxable years beginning in 1987. *Section 179 property* is *personal property* that is cost recovery property and has been acquired by *purchase for use in a trade or business*. Property held for the production of income but not used in a trade or business (such as rental property) is not eligible for the expense deduction.

Generally, for passenger automobiles placed in service in a trade or business after June 18, 1984, and before April 3, 1985, the maximum amount that could be expensed was limited to $4,000. For automobiles placed in service after April 2, 1985, this maximum amount was reduced to $3,200. For 1992 the maximum amount is $2,760.

When electing to expense up to the annual dollar limitation, the taxpayer must specify the items of property to which the election applies and the portion of each property's cost to be expensed currently. The election must be made on the original tax return for the year in which the property is placed in service.

A Section 179 expense deduction is treated as a depreciation deduction and therefore is subject to depreciation recapture as ordinary income if the asset is disposed of at a gain.

Optional Recovery Periods. Instead of using ACRS, a taxpayer could elect to use a straight-line recovery over the applicable class-life recovery periods shown in Table 9-3.

Table 9-3
Optional Recovery Periods

Recovery Class	Straight-line Recovery Periods Available
3-Year Class	3, 5, or 12 years
5-Year Class	5, 12, or 25 years
10-Year Class	10, 25, or 35 years
15-Year Class	15, 35, or 45 years
18-Year Class	18, 35, or 45 years
19-Year Class	19, 35, or 45 years

If the optional straight-line recovery period was elected, the election applied to all *personal property* in that class placed in service during the tax year in which the election was made, and the half-year convention had to be used.

For *real property*, the optional straight-line recovery election was made on a property-by-property basis. The half-year convention did not apply. Instead, the straight-line ACRS recovery percentages were prorated over the months the property was in service for the first year and year of disposition.

Listed Property Eligible for ACRS. The ACRS rules for depreciation were designed to limit the opportunity for accelerated depreciation and the Section 179 expense deduction for specified assets that are popularly used for both business and personal purposes. These specified assets are referred to as listed assets. Under ACRS, listed assets are designated types of tangible personal property that must be used more than 50% in a qualified business in order to be eligible for ACRS deductions and for a Section 179 expense deduction. The types of property to which these limitations apply are passenger automobiles, other means of transportation subject to personal use (trucks, buses, boats, airplanes and motorcycles), property generally used for entertainment, recreation, or amusement (cameras, VCRs, stereo equipment, and communication equipment), and computers (with their related equipment). If the business use of these types of equipment is 50% or less for the tax year, the following limitations apply:

1. The ACRS deduction is limited to straight-line depreciation using 5 years for 3-year class property and 12 years for 5-year class property.
2. The $10,000 expense deduction is not allowed.

For passenger automobiles and other transportation equipment, the 50% test should be based on *miles used for business* in relation to total miles used. For other types of equipment that are listed property, appropriate *units of time* should be the basis of the allocation between business use and other use. Qualified business use for meeting the more-than-50% test *does not include* the use of the listed property for *generating investment income*. However, if the more-than-50%-business-use test is not met, the ACRS deductions (using lives allowed for E & P calculations) are determined using both the trade and business use and the use for investment activities.

Modified ACRS (MACRS) for 1987 and Later Years

ACRS was significantly modified by the Tax Reform Act of 1986. MACRS is generally less advantageous to taxpayers. MACRS is designed to match class lives more closely with the economic or useful lives of depreciable assets. For tangible personal property, the changes are partly mitigated by the fact that the 200% declining-balance method is allowed, whereas, under the original ACRS, only the 150% declining-balance method was allowed. The principal differences between the original ACRS and MACRS are in the class life designations for assets and the allowable recovery methods.

Cost Recovery for Tangible Personal Property. In the modified system, tangible personal property is assigned to one of six classes for determining the depreciation method and the period of write off, while real property is assigned to one of two classes. The class that a tangible personal asset is assigned to is determined primarily by the pre-1981 *Asset Depreciation Range (ADR)* guidelines. In some cases new ADR lives are specified for certain assets. For short-lived assets (3, 5, 7, or 10 years), costs are recovered using 200% declining-balance depreciation, with a switch to straight-line permitted to maximize the annual depreciation deduction. Costs of depreciable tangible personal assets (assets not classified as real property) are recovered using 150% declining-balance depreciation, also with a switch to straight-line. The component method of depreciation is prohibited for all recovery property. A summary of the method applicable to each class of tangible personal property is shown in Table 9-5. A MACRS table for 3-, 5-, 7-, and 10-year classes using the half-year convention (see discussion on averaging conventions later) is provided in Table 9-4.

Excluded Property. As with the original ACRS, property depreciated under the units-of-completion method or under other recovery methods not expressed in years is excluded.

Table 9-4
MACRS Table for 3-, 5-, 7-, and 10-Year Classes Using a Half-Year Convention

Year	3 Year	5 Year	7 Year	10 Year
		Recovery Period		
1	33.33%	20.00%	14.29%	10.00%
2	44.45	32.00	24.49	18.00
3	14.81*	19.20	17.49	14.40
4	7.41	11.52*	12.49	11.52
5		11.52	8.93*	9.22
6		5.76	8.92	7.37
7			8.93	6.55*
8			4.46	6.55
9				6.56
10				6.55
11				3.28

* Year to switch to the straight-line method to achieve the maximum depreciation deduction.

Averaging Conventions. For depreciable tangible personal property, a half-year convention applies to both first-year and last-year allowances. Under MACRS with a half-year convention applicable to the year of purchase and the last year of use, the total cost recovery deduction is spread over one year longer than the class life to which the asset is assigned.

EXAMPLE 4 ────────────────

Assume a 3-year class asset costing $2,000 under MACRS.

Yr.		MACRS
1	$ 667	($2,000 x 33.33%)
2	889	($2,000 x 44.45%)
3	296	($2,000 x 14.81%)*
4	148	($2,000 x 7.41%)
	$2,000	

* Switched to straight-line method.

Under MACRS, the cost of a 3-year asset is recovered in 4 years. Likewise, the cost of a 5-year asset would be recovered in 6 years. The half-year convention applies to tangible personal property both in the year acquired and in the ending year of the asset whether using the declining-balance method or the straight-line method.

Another change in the averaging conventions for MACRS is that when more than 40% of asset additions in any one year are placed in service in the last quarter of the taxable year, a mid-quarter convention is used to calculate the cost recovery allowances for all additions in that year. Table 9-6 shows the MACRS table for 3-, 5-, and 7-year classes for each of the four mid-quarter conventions.

Elections Choices

Alternate MACRS Method. Taxpayers have the option to elect out of the regular **accelerated** deductions that have been described above for MACRS. This election is referred to as the Alternate MACRS Method. Under this method, the MACRS system allows taxpayers to elect the straight-line method instead of the accelerated method. If the taxpayer elects the straight-line method, all of the other rules that normally apply under MACRS continue to apply, including the applicable recovery period and the account-

Table 9-5
Cost Recovery Data for Assets Under the Tax Reform Act of 1986
(Modified Accelerated Cost Recovery System)

Recovery Class	Rate & Method	ADR Midpoint	Special Rules for Each Asset Class
3-year	200% D.B.	4 years or less	Excludes automobiles and light trucks. Includes tractors, race horses, and special tools
5-year	200% D.B.	Over 4 years to less than 10 years	Includes automobiles, light trucks, and computers
7-year	200% D.B.	10 years to less than 16 years	Includes machinery and equipment, office furniture and fixtures, single purpose agricultural and horticultural structures, railroad tracks, and assets with no ADR midpoint
10-year	200% D.B.	16 years to less than 20 years	No special rules
15-year	150% D.B.	20 years to less than 25 years	Includes sewage treatment plants and telephone distribution plants
20-year	150% D.B.	25 years or more	Includes municipal sewers; excludes real property with an ADR midpoint of 27½ years or more
27½-year	St. Line	N.A.	Residential rental property
31½-year	St. Line	N.A.	Commercial and industrial real property other than residential rental property

ing conventions. The election to use the straight-line method is made annually by class of property. For example, if the taxpayer elected the straight-line method for 5-year class property, then all 5-year class assets acquired in that year would need to be depreciated using the straight-line method. The election to use the straight-line method for one class does not require the taxpayer to use the straight-line method for other classes in the same year or in the same class in a subsequent year.

As another alternative to electing the straight-line method as described above, Congress also established the Alternative Depreciation System.

Alternative Depreciation System (ADS). T h e alternative system to the accelerated system described above for the MACRS is similar to MACRS in that salvage value is ignored and the same averaging conventions apply. The major differences are that under the ADS system the recovery periods are longer for most assets, and the taxpayer has a choice between the straight-line method and the 150% declining-balance method for most personal property. Only the straight-line method applies to real property.

The following recovery periods under MACRS and ADS illustrate the similarities and differences between the two systems:

	MACRS	ADS
Furniture, fixtures & equipment	7 yrs.	10 yrs.
Automobiles	5 yrs.	5 yrs.
Data handling equipment (except computers)	5 yrs.	6 yrs.
Heavy general purpose trucks	5 yrs.	6 yrs.

If there is no designated class life for personal property, the recovery period under ADS is 12 years. Nonresidential and residential rental property with no designated class life must be depreciated on a 40-year recovery basis.

Except for real property, the election to use ADS is the same as for the MACRS system. Except for real property, the taxpayer may elect to use ADS on a class-by-class, year-by-year basis. For real property, the election must be made on a property-by-property basis. Once an election is made it is irrevocable for assets acquired in that year.

For certain property the use of ADS is mandatory. ADS must be used for recovering the cost of the following types of assets: (1) property used outside the United States, (2) tax-exempt use property, (3) property financed with tax-exempt bonds, and (4) designated imported property. Furthermore, ADS using straight-line depreciation must be used in calculating E & P and in calculating depreciation under the AMT.

Table 9-6
MACRS Table for 3-, 5-, and 7-year Classes Using Mid-Quarter Conventions

Property Placed In Service In:	Years							
	1	2	3	4	5	6	7	8
1st quarter								
3-yr.	58.33%	27.78%	12.35%	1.54%				
5-yr.	35.00	26.00	15.60	11.01	11.01%	1.38%		
7-yr.	25.00	21.43	15.31	10.93	8.75	8.74	8.75%	1.09%
2nd quarter								
3-yr.	41.67	38.89	14.14	5.30				
5-yr.	25.00	30.00	18.00	11.37	11.37	4.26		
7-yr.	17.85	23.47	16.76	11.97	8.87	8.87	8.87	3.33
3rd quarter								
3-yr.	25.00	50.00	16.67	8.33				
5-yr.	15.00	34.00	20.40	12.24	11.30	7.06		
7-yr.	10.71	25.51	18.22	13.02	9.30	8.85	8.86	5.33
4th quarter								
3-yr.	8.33	61.11	20.37	10.19				
5-yr.	5.00	38.00	22.80	13.68	10.94	9.58		
7-yr.	3.57	27.55	19.68	14.06	10.04	8.73	8.73	7.64

The availability of the alternate MACRS election and the ADS election suggests that a taxpayer has up to four choices available for 3-, 5-, 7-, and 10-year personal business property that is not covered by any mandatory requirements:

EXAMPLE 5 ——————————————

A taxpayer acquires a desk for $10,000. In choosing the amount of depreciation for the desk in the year of acquisition, the taxpayer has the following choices:

1. Under MACRS:
   a. 200% declining-balance over 7 years
   b. Straight-line over 7 years
2. Under ADS:
   a. Straight-line over 10 years
   b. 150% declining-balance over 10 years

The choice that the taxpayer should make in applying the tax planning principle of paying the least tax at the latest possible time would be to select the depreciation method that provides the greatest tax savings at the earliest point in time.

The election to expense tangible personal property is retained with the amount eligible for expensing increased to $10,000 with a reduc-

tion dollar-for-dollar as the cost of qualified property placed in service exceeds $200,000. The amount expensed is further limited to the taxable income derived from any trade or business. Disallowed costs may be carried forward.

Filled-in Form 4562

Illustration 9-1

To illustrate the calculation of cost recovery for tangible personal property, this example uses the assets that John Williams had in service during 1992 as shown in Table 9-7. Table 9-7 also shows the cost recovery calculation for each asset used in the Williams Hardware Store.

The cost recovery of $643 for the shop equipment is shown in Illustration 9-1, Form 4562, Part I (line 14c) for 7-year class property under MACRS. The amount of cost recovery of $643 from Table 9-9 is based on 200% declining-balance using a half-year convention ($4,500 x 14.29% = $643).

The computer acquired in 1991 and used 80% for business is in its second year of use, meaning the statutory recovery percentage is 40% of the remaining business basis of $1,440 ($2,250 x 80% = $1,800 – $360) with a 1992 cost recovery of $576 ($1,440 x 40%). Since computers are listed property, the depreciation deduction is first recorded in Form 4562, Part V, and the $576 depreciation deduction is entered on Form 4562, Part IV (line 19). The storage building was acquired in 1981 and is located on a lot owned by Mr. Williams. Since it was a used building and was placed in service in 1981, Mr. Williams could elect a depreciation period of 20 years using the straight-line method. The building is in its 12th year of service, resulting in a 1992 cost recovery of $180 ($3,600/20 yrs.). The machinery was acquired in 1991 and is being depreciated over its recovery period of 7 years on an elected 150% declining-balance method, with a cost recovery in 1992 of $2,801, ($14,640 – $1,569 x .21429). The cost recovery for the machinery and the storage shed in 1992, $2,981 ($2,801 + $180), is reported on Form 4562 (line 18). The total cost recovery of $4,200 for 1992 is reported on Form 4562 (line 20) and is then transferred to the Williams' Schedule C, Part II (line 13).

Cost Recovery for Real Property. Under MACRS real property must be depreciated on a straight-line basis over a period of 27½ years for residential rental property and over 31½ years for commercial and industrial property other than residential rental property. Like tangible personal property, the component method of depreciation is prohibited for real property. Under an alternative cost recovery system, real property is depreciable over a life of 40 years (27½ years for low-income property). The alternative cost recovery system is mandatory for recovery of the cost of (1) property used outside of the United States, (2) property used for tax-exempt purposes, and (3) certain imported property. The alternative system is also used for calculating E&P and for the AMT calculation. Taxpayers can elect to use the alternative cost recovery system for real property in lieu of the regular straight-line deductions. The election of the alternative system for real property is on a property-by-property basis.

EXAMPLE 6 ──────────────────

For the calculation of cost recovery for real property (Section 1250 property), assume that a taxpayer owned the following buildings:

Apt. building #1:   Acquired 5-20-86 at a cost of $140,000
Apt. building #2:   Acquired 3-25-91 at a cost of $160,000
Office building: Acquired 7-01-92 at a cost of $75,000

Apartment building #1, acquired in 1986, has a class life of 19 years under ACRS and would be allowed a statutory cost recovery rate in the seventh year of use of 5.3%. The cost recovery amount for 1992 would be $7,420 ($140,000 x 5.3%). Apartment building #2, acquired in March, 1991, has a class life of 27½ years under MACRS and must be depreciated on a straight-line basis over 27½ years. For this building, the cost recovery for 1992 would be $5,818 ($160,000/27.5 years). The office building

Table 9-7
Calculation of Cost Recovery for Williams Hardware Store

Asset	Year Acquired	Basis for Depreciation	Recovery Period	% or Method	Recovery in 1992
Shop Equipment	1992	$ 4,500	7 years	200% D.B.	$ 643
Computer (80% Business)	1991	$ 1,800	5 years	200% D.B.	576
Storage Shed (used)	1981	$ 3,600	20 years	St. Line	180
Machinery	1991	$14,640	7 years	150% D.B.	2,801
Total Cost Recovery					$4,200

Illustration 9-1
Filled-In Form 4562, Page 1

Form **4562**

Department of the Treasury
Internal Revenue Service

Depreciation and Amortization
(Including Information on Listed Property)

▶ See separate instructions.   ▶ Attach this form to your return.

OMB No. 1545-0172

1992

Attachment
Sequence No. **67**

Name(s) shown on return:
John R. Williams

Identifying number
272-11-8245

Business or activity to which this form relates:
Williams Hardware Store

Part I   Election To Expense Certain Tangible Property (Section 179) (Note: *If you have any "Listed Property," complete Part V before you complete Part I.*)

1	Maximum dollar limitation (see instructions)	**1** $10,000
2	Total cost of section 179 property placed in service during the tax year (see instructions)	**2**
3	Threshold cost of section 179 property before reduction in limitation	**3** $200,000
4	Reduction in limitation. Subtract line 3 from line 2, but do not enter less than -0-	**4**
5	Dollar limitation for tax year. Subtract line 4 from line 1, but do not enter less than -0-	**5**

(a) Description of property	(b) Cost	(c) Elected cost
6		

7	Listed property. Enter amount from line 26.	**7**
8	Total elected cost of section 179 property. Add amounts in column (c), lines 6 and 7	**8**
9	Tentative deduction. Enter the smaller of line 5 or line 8	**9**
10	Carryover of disallowed deduction from 1991 (see instructions)	**10**
11	Taxable income limitation. Enter the smaller of taxable income or line 5 (see instructions)	**11**
12	Section 179 expense deduction. Add lines 9 and 10, but do not enter more than line 11	**12**
13	Carryover of disallowed deduction to 1993. Add lines 9 and 10, less line 12 ▶	**13**

Note: *Do not use Part II or Part III below for automobiles, certain other vehicles, cellular telephones, computers, or property used for entertainment, recreation, or amusement (listed property). Instead, use Part V for listed property.*

Part II   MACRS Depreciation For Assets Placed in Service ONLY During Your 1992 Tax Year (Do Not Include Listed Property)

(a) Classification of property	(b) Month and year placed in service	(c) Basis for depreciation (business/investment use only—see instructions)	(d) Recovery period	(e) Convention	(f) Method	(g) Depreciation deduction
14 General Depreciation System (GDS) (see instructions):						
a 3-year property						
b 5-year property						
c 7-year property		4,500	7 yr.	$\frac{1}{2}$ yr.	DDB	643
d 10-year property						
e 15-year property						
f 20-year property						
g Residential rental property			27.5 yrs.	MM	S/L	
			27.5 yrs.	MM	S/L	
h Nonresidential real property			31.5 yrs.	MM	S/L	
			31.5 yrs.	MM	S/L	
15 Alternative Depreciation System (ADS) (see instructions):						
a Class life					S/L	
b 12-year			12 yrs.		S/L	
c 40-year			40 yrs.	MM	S/L	

Part III   Other Depreciation (Do Not Include Listed Property)

16	GDS and ADS deductions for assets placed in service in tax years beginning before 1992 (see instructions)	**16**
17	Property subject to section 168(f)(1) election (see instructions)	**17**
18	ACRS and other depreciation (see instructions)	**18** 2,981

Part IV   Summary

19	Listed property. Enter amount from line 25.	**19** 576
20	**Total.** Add deductions on line 12, lines 14 and 15 in column (g), and lines 16 through 19. Enter here and on the appropriate lines of your return. (Partnerships and S corporations—see instructions)	**20** 4,200
21	For assets shown above and placed in service during the current year, enter the portion of the basis attributable to section 263A costs (see instructions)	**21**

For Paperwork Reduction Act Notice, see page 1 of the separate instructions.   Cat. No. 12906N   Form **4562** (1992)

Illustration 9-1
Filled-In Form 4562, Page 2

Form 4562 (1992)   Page **2**

Part V Listed Property—Automobiles, Certain Other Vehicles, Cellular Telephones, Computers, and Property Used for Entertainment, Recreation, or Amusement

*For any vehicle for which you are using the standard mileage rate or deducting lease expense, complete **only** 22a, 22b, columns (a) through (c) of Section A, all of Section B, and Section C if applicable.*

Section A—Depreciation (Caution: See instructions for limitations for automobiles.)

22a Do you have evidence to support the business/investment use claimed? ☐ Yes ☐ No 22b If "Yes," is the evidence written? ☐ Yes ☐ No

(a) Type of property (list vehicles first)	(b) Date placed in service	(c) Business/ investment use percentage	(d) Cost or other basis	(e) Basis for depreciation (business/investment use only)	(f) Recovery period	(g) Method/ Convention	(h) Depreciation deduction	(i) Elected section 179 cost
23 Property used more than 50% in a qualified business use (see instructions):								
Computer	2/1/90	80 %	2,250	1,800	5 yr.	DDB ½	576	
		%						
		%						
24 Property used 50% or less in a qualified business use (see instructions):								
		%				S/L –		
		%				S/L –		
		%				S/L –		

25 Add amounts in column (h). Enter the total here and on line 19, page 1 . . . . . . **25** 576

26 Add amounts in column (i). Enter the total here and on line 7, page 1 . . . . **26**

Section B—Information Regarding Use of Vehicles—If you deduct expenses for vehicles:
- *Always complete this section for vehicles used by a sole proprietor, partner, or other "more than 5% owner," or related person.*
- *If you provided vehicles to your employees, first answer the questions in Section C to see if you meet an exception to completing this section for those vehicles.*

	(a) Vehicle 1	(b) Vehicle 2	(c) Vehicle 3	(d) Vehicle 4	(e) Vehicle 5	(f) Vehicle 6
27 Total business/investment miles driven during the year (DO NOT include commuting miles)						
28 Total commuting miles driven during the year						
29 Total other personal (noncommuting) miles driven						
30 Total miles driven during the year. Add lines 27 through 29.						

	Yes	No	Yes	No	Yes	No	Yes	No	Yes	No	Yes	No
31 Was the vehicle available for personal use during off-duty hours?												
32 Was the vehicle used primarily by a more than 5% owner or related person?												
33 Is another vehicle available for personal use?												

Section C—Questions for Employers Who Provide Vehicles for Use by Their Employees
Answer these questions to determine if you meet an exception to completing Section B. Note: Section B must always be completed for vehicles used by sole proprietors, partners, or other more than 5% owners or related persons.

	Yes	No
34 Do you maintain a written policy statement that prohibits all personal use of vehicles, including commuting, by your employees?		
35 Do you maintain a written policy statement that prohibits personal use of vehicles, except commuting, by your employees? (See instructions for vehicles used by corporate officers, directors, or 1% or more owners.)		
36 Do you treat all use of vehicles by employees as personal use?		
37 Do you provide more than five vehicles to your employees and retain the information received from your employees concerning the use of the vehicles?		
38 Do you meet the requirements concerning qualified automobile demonstration use (see instructions)? . .		

Note: If your answer to 34, 35, 36, 37, or 38 is "Yes," you need not complete Section B for the covered vehicles.

Part VI Amortization

(a) Description of costs	(b) Date amortization begins	(c) Amortizable amount	(d) Code section	(e) Amortization period or percentage	(f) Amortization for this year
39 Amortization of costs that begins during your 1992 tax year:					

40 Amortization of costs that began before 1992	**40**	
41 Total. Enter here and on "Other Deductions" or "Other Expenses" line of your return . . .	**41**	

acquired in July, 1992, has a class life of 31½ years under MACRS and must be depreciated on a straight-line basis over 31½ years using the mid-month convention. The 1992 cost recovery amount for the office building would be $1,091 ($75,000/31.5 years) x (5.5/12 months).

Depreciation of Office in the Home. If a taxpayer uses his or her home in a trade or business, the taxpayer can take a depreciation deduction for that part of the home used regularly and exclusively as the principal place of business. Part of the home used for both personal and business purposes would not meet the exclusive-use test and therefore depreciation and other business expenses related to using that part of the home would not be deductible as business expenses. To calculate the deduction for depreciation and other expenses related to that part of the home used for business, the taxpayer must calculate that percentage of the square footage of the space in the home that is used for business in relation to the total square footage in the home. An alternative approach would be to relate the number of rooms used in the business to the total rooms in the home, provided the rooms are all of approximately equal size. The percentage of the home calculated for business use is applied to the total of each home expense (such as depreciation, real estate taxes, mortgage interest, insurance, and utilities) to calculate the allowable expenses on Form 8829, Expenses for Business Use of Your Home, for a sole proprietor. Example 7 illustrates how the depreciation deduction would be calculated.

EXAMPLE 7 —————————————————

Assume a taxpayer owns a home with an adjusted basis of $240,000 (excluding land cost) on December 31, 1991, for which one room is used as an office starting in January, 1992, for consulting services. The square footage of the office used exclusively for consulting purposes is 200 out of a total of 4,000 square feet. Thus, the part of the home used for the consulting services would constitute 5% (200 sq.ft./ 4,000 sq.ft.). Therefore, the portion of the adjusted basis of the home that is eligible to be depreciated is $12,000 ($240,000 x 5%). Since the business portion of the home is classified as commercial use property, the

depreciation calculation must be based on the straight-line method using a life of 31.5 years. For this taxpayer, the depreciation deduction for the use of the home for consulting in 1992 would be $381 ($12,000/31.5 years). This amount can be reported directly on Form 8829, Expenses for Business Use of Your Home, Part III, while depreciation of business equipment used in the office would be reported on Form 4562, Depreciation and Amortization. However, Form 4562 is necessary, in addition to Form 8829, if 1992 is the first year a taxpayer uses the home for business or if depreciation is being taken for improvements or additions made in 1992.

The depreciation deduction for a use of the home for a trade or business activity cannot result in the creation of a business loss or increase a loss from your business. Business deductions for the business use of the taxpayer's home must be deducted in the following order:

1. The business portion of expenses that would be allowable as deductions if no business activity were carried on in the home, such as real estate taxes, interest on the home mortgage, and casualty losses
2. The business expenses related to the business use of the home, such as the business portion of repairs and maintenance, utilities, and insurance
3. Depreciation on the home and any other deductions that adjust the taxable basis of the home

The part of these expenses that results in a business loss for the year is not deductible on Schedule C in the current year. The loss can be carried forward to subsequent years.

EXAMPLE 8 —————————————————

Assume that Cliff Adams has a tentative profit on Schedule C (line 29) from the business use of a part of his home of $1,600 in 1992. He uses a room exclusively as an office in providing consulting advice on computers. The office represents 10% of the square footage of the entire house. Cliff has the following expenses for the year for the entire house: interest and real estate taxes, $4,200; expenses related to the business use of the home (10% of repairs, insurance, utilities), $1,000; and depreciation on the office part of the home, $650. The calculation of Cliff's deduction on Form 8829 for the business use of his home is as follows:

Tentative profit (line 8)	$1,600
Less: interest & taxes (lines 10,11,13,14)	
10% x $4,200	420
Modified net income (line 15)	$1,180
Less: Expenses related to business use of	
home: insur., repairs, util.	1,000
Limit on depreciation (line 26)	$ 180
Depreciation (line 28)	650
Current expenses not deductible in 1992	
(carried forward to 1993) (line 42)	($ 470)

The carryover expenses would be $470. The $470 of carryover expenses would come from the total of $650 of depreciation expenses. Thus, all of the business expenses except $470 of depreciation expenses would have been offset against 1992 income. Since the $470 of depreciation expenses is not deductible in 1992, the basis of the home office portion of the home would only be reduced by the $180 of depreciation expenses that are deductible in 1992. The basis in the home will not be reduced for the other $470 of depreciation expenses until that amount is actually deducted in a future year.

Listed Property. Form 4562, page 2, asks for specific information concerning **listed property**, such as computers and automobiles or other vehicles used in business. Depreciation and the Section 179 expense deduction must be recorded on Form 4562, Part V, Section A. If the listed property is used 50% or less in a trade or business, depreciation must be calculated under ADS using the straight-line method. Part V, Section B must be completed by all taxpayers who use vehicles in their business. These questions must be completed to support the business mileage and the actual business use of the vehicles. Section C must be completed by employers who provide vehicles for use by their employees. If the employer has a written policy statement regarding the use of vehicles provided by the employer, the employee will not be required to keep separate records.

EXAMPLE 9 ————————————————————

To illustrate the rules related to partial personal use of listed property, assume that a computer costing $4,000 is placed in service in 1992 to the extent of 40% for business, 25% for investment purposes, and 35% for personal use. Since the computer was used less than 50% for business purposes, the taxpayer is not eligible for the $10,000 expense deduction (or any fraction of the expense deduction) and is not allowed to use the MACRS. The ADS deduction would be $260 [($4,000 x (20% x 50%) x 65%)] for the business activity and the investment activity combined. The deduction is based on the straight-line method using a 5-year recovery period and a half-year convention. Applicable recovery rates for listed property are in tables provided by the IRS.

EXAMPLE 10 ————————————————————

If the computer had been used 60% for business, 15% for investment purposes, and 25% for personal use, the MACRS deduction would have been based on a 5-year recovery period for 75% of the computer's use (60% business plus 15% investment), using either the 200% declining-balance or the straight-line method. Thus, the cost recovery deduction in 1992 would be either $600 [($4,000 x (40% x 50%) x 75%)] using the 200% declining-balance method with a half-year convention, or $300 [($4,000 x (20% x 50%) x 75%)] using the straight-line method with a half-year convention.

EXAMPLE 11————————————————————

When the business use is greater than 50% (i.e 60% in Example 10), the taxpayer may elect to expense up to $2,400 ($4,000 x 60%) of the cost in the first year. If the payer made such an election and also elected to use the 200% declining-balance method with a half-year convention for the remainder of the cost, the depreciation for 1992 would have been $2,640: $2,400 + ($1,600 x (40% x 50%) x 75%).

Luxury Automobiles and Cost Recovery

In addition to the cost recovery limitations on over 50% of personal use of listed business property (such as computers and automobiles), there are additional limits on cost recovery for luxury automobiles. The ACRS limits were enacted by Congress in 1984 to cover luxury automobiles used for business that were put into service after June 18, 1984. The original ACRS deductions for 100% business use of a luxury automobile (which was 3-year class property until 1987) was limited to $4,000 for the first year of use and $6,000 for each succeeding year. These rules were changed in 1985 (for business automobiles acquired and placed into service after April 2, 1985) to limit the first-year cost recovery deduction to $3,200 and to $4,800 in subsequent years. Under MACRS specified by the Tax Reform Act of 1986, automobiles were shifted from the 3-year class to the 5-year class, for which the first year cost recovery deduction in 1992 is limited to $2,760. A $4,400 deduction is allowed in the second year, $2,650 in the third year, and $1,575 in each succeeding year until the entire cost is recovered. These limits are applied before any reductions for personal use are taken into consideration. The $2,760 limitation in the first year of use also applies to the $10,000 expense election.

Based on the limits indicated above for cost recovery deductions of business automobiles, it can be concluded that Congress considers a luxury automobile to be one that costs more than $14,535. This amount can be assumed by comparing the limits with the amount allowed using MACRS (Table 9-4).

Year	Limits	MACRS, $13,800 cost
1	$ 2,760	$ 2,907 (20% x $13,800)
2	4,400	4,651 (32% x $13,800)
3	2,650	2,791 (19.2% x $13,800)
4	1,575	1,674 (11.52% x $13,800)*
5	1,575	1,674 (11.52% x $13,800)
6	1,575	838 (5.76% x $13,800)
Totals	$14,535	$14,535

* Switched to straight-line method.

EXAMPLE 12 ——————————

To illustrate the combined application of the rules for listed property used only partly for business and the rules for luxury automobiles, assume a taxpayer buys a luxury automobile for $25,000 on April 2, 1992, that will be used 80% for business. The automobile is 5-year class property under the modified ACRS rules. The cost recovery deductions under the limits for luxury automobiles are shown in Table 9-8.

Without the limitation for luxury automobiles, the taxpayer could have deducted the entire $20,000 (80% x $25,000) of allowable depreciation in the first six years. With the luxury automobile limitation, the taxpayer can deduct only $11,628 in the first six years. If the auto is sold or traded at the end of six years, the business portion of the basis of the luxury car is $8,372 ($20,000 – $11,628). If the taxpayer continues to use the car for business, this $8,372 may be treated as MACRS allowances in subsequent years up to a maximum of $1,260 (for 80% business use: 80% x $1,575) in each year until the unrecovered basis is used up. If the taxpayer continued to use the luxury auto 80% of the time in business, $1,260 (80% x $1,575 per table limits) can be deducted for six and a fraction more years, i.e. 1998 through 2004, for a total of $20,000 of cost recovery over a 13-year period ($11,628 in the period 1992 through 1997 and $8,372 in the period 1998 through 2004). These recovery deductions are allowable in years beyond the 5-year class life only if the property continues to be eligible for a cost recovery deduction in each year due to business use, adjusted for the specific percentage of business use.

If the automobile is sold, traded, or junked at the end of six years, the basis for disposition of the business portion would be $8,372 and the basis for disposition of the personal portion would be $5,000 ($25,000 – $20,000).

Depletion

Depletion is the process of deducting the cost (economic interest) of natural resources as the recoverable units of the resource are sold (under the accrual method) or sold and payment received (under the cash method). The typical types of natural resources that are subject to depletion rules are minerals, oil and gas, geothermal wells, and standing timber. The depletion deduction is available to the taxpayer as the owner and operator if the taxpayer has an economic interest in the natural resource. The depletion deduction is calculated separately for each property. A "property" is defined as each separate interest owned by the taxpayer in each mineral deposit in each separate tract or parcel of land. There are two methods for calculating the depletion deduction: the cost method and the percentage depletion method.

Cost Depletion

The cost depletion method provides for the deduction of the cost of the natural resource as the resource units are recovered. The deduction is calculated by dividing the adjusted basis of the investment in the natural resource by the total number of recoverable units in the deposit, and then multiplying the resulting rate per unit by the appropriate number of units produced or sold, dependent on whether the cash method or the accrual method of accounting is used. Thus, when the cash method is used, the rate per recoverable unit is multiplied by the number of units sold for which the taxpayer has received payment during the tax year; and when the accrual method is used, the rate per unit is multiplied by the number of units sold (whether or not payment has been received by the taxpayer).

EXAMPLE 13 ───────────

Assume that a taxpayer purchased the rights to a coal deposit for $800,000 in 1992 that is estimated to contain 200,000 tons of coal. During 1992 the taxpayer recovered 25,000 tons of coal from the deposit and sold 20,000 tons by year-end. Cash was collected on 18,000 tons, with the selling price of 2,000 tons shown as an accounts receivable. The recoverable cost per ton is $4.00 ($800,000/200,000 tons). If the taxpayer is on the accrual method, the

cost depletion for 1992 is $80,000 (20,000 tons x $4). If the taxpayer is on the cash method, the cost depletion for 1992 is $72,000 (18,000 tons x $4). The accrual-method taxpayer will recover the investment cost on the 5,000 tons not sold in 1992 when that tonnage is sold the next year. The cash-method taxpayer will recover the investment cost on the 2,000 tons in the year the accounts receivable are collected and will recover the investment cost in the 5,000 tons in inventory when those tons are sold **and** payment is received.

If it is discovered at a later time that the estimated number of units of the natural resource is different than originally estimated, the recoverable cost per unit must be revised based on the newly estimated number of available units.

EXAMPLE 14 ───────────

Assume the same facts as in Example 13, except that, beginning in 1993, the estimate of the remaining number of tons of coal in the deposit is 280,000. For the cash-method taxpayer, the remaining cost to be recovered is $728,000 ($800,000 – $72,000) and the remaining units on which to recover depletion is 287,000 tons (280,000 tons in the coal deposit + 5,000 tons in inventory + 2,000 tons sold but for which collection has not been received). The new recoverable cost per unit for the cash method taxpayer would be $2.537 ($728,000/ 287,000 tons). If payment was received on 20,000 tons in 1993, the taxpayer would have a cost depletion deduction of $50,740 (20,000 tons x $2.537).

Table 9-8
1992 Cost Recovery Limitations for a $25,000 Luxury Automobile (80% Business Use)

Year	Potential MACRS Deduction		Luxury Car Limitation	
'92	$ 4,000	($25,000 x 80% x 20%)	$ 2,208	(80% x $2,760)
'93	6,400	($25,000 x 80% x 32%)	3,520	(80% x $4,400)
'94	3,840	($25,000 x 80% x 19.2%)	2,120	(80% x $2,650)
'95	2,304	($25,000 x 80% x 11.52%)*	1,260	(80% x $1,575)
'96	2,304	($25,000 x 80% x 11.52%)	1,260	(80% x $1,575)
'97	1,152	($25,000 x 80% x 5.76%)	1,260	(80% x $1,575)
	$20,000		$11,628	

* Switched to straight-line method.

EXAMPLE 15 ——————————

Assume the same facts as in Examples 13 and 14, except that the taxpayer is on the accrual method. The taxpayer's remaining cost to be recovered at the end of 1992 would be $720,000 ($800,000 − $80,000), and the remaining units on which to recover depletion is 285,000 tons (280,000 tons in the coal deposit + 5,000 tons in inventory). The new recoverable cost per unit for the accrual-method taxpayer would be $2.526 ($720,000/285,000 ton). If 20,000 tons were sold in 1993, the accrual-method taxpayer would have cost depletion deduction of $50,520 (20,000 tons x $2.526).

Percentage Depletion

Percentage depletion gets its name because a percentage is applied to gross income from the property to be depleted to determine the depletion deduction, subject to a limitation. The percentage applied to gross income is specified for each natural resource, with a higher percentage usually prescribed for those natural resources that are more important to the public interest of the country. Percentage depletion rates vary from a low of 5% of gross income for sand and gravel, to 10% for coal, 14% for granite, slate, and limestone, 15% for copper, gold, silver, iron, oil, and gas, and 22% for lead, zinc, tin, and sulfur. This is not an exhaustive list. Percentage depletion does not apply to timber. Furthermore, the percentage depletion deduction for any tax year cannot exceed 50% of taxable income from the property, figured without the depletion deduction. If the taxpayer is an independent producer or royalty owner, the percentage depletion deduction is limited to the *lesser of* 65% of *total taxable income* (calculated without regard to any net operating loss) or 50% of the *taxable income from the property* (calculated before the deduction for depletion is claimed).

A significant advantage of the percentage depletion provision is that the taxpayer can continue to take the percentage depletion deduction even if the cost invested in the natural resources has already been recovered. Thus, unlike the depreciation deduction, the percentage depletion deduction is applicable after the adjusted basis of the investment is zero. Furthermore, if percentage depletion for a given year is less than cost depletion, the taxpayer is required to use cost depletion for that year. This means that the taxpayer can use the higher of cost or percentage depletion each year and continue to use percentage depletion when all of the cost has been recovered.

EXAMPLE 16 ——————————

Assume a taxpayer has gross income in 1992 from a depletable coal deposit of $200,000. Assume further that cost depletion for the year 1992 would be $15,000. Since coal has a 10% depletion percentage, the taxpayer can choose the higher percentage depletion of $20,000 ($200,000 x 10%) over the lower cost depletion of $15,000, as long as the percentage depletion does not exceed 50% of $200,000 of gross income. Since the 50% limitation rule does not apply in this example, the taxpayer's percentage depletion deduction for 1992 is $20,000. Thus, the percentage depletion deduction for 1992 is determined by first comparing the percentage depletion of $20,000 ($200,000 x 10%) with the gross income limitation of $100,000 ($200,000 x 50%). The lower of these two amounts is compared with the cost depletion, in this case $15,000, to determine whether the percentage depletion (as limited) is higher or lower than the cost depletion for the year. Since the percentage depletion of $20,000 does not exceed the maximum limit of 50% of gross income and is higher than the cost depletion of $15,000, the actual depletion deduction for 1992 would be $20,000.

Special Rules for Depletion of Timber

Only the cost method of depletion applies to timber. The depletion is based on the cost or other basis for the standing timber. The depletion deduction is allowed only after the timber is cut and the quantity cut is accurately measured. The depletion allowed for a given year is calculated by multiplying the number of timber units cut (such as board feet or number of cords of wood) by the depletion cost per unit. A taxpayer may elect, under certain circumstances, to treat the cutting of timber as a sale or exchange. If readers are interested in a more detailed discussion of depletion rules for timber, they are referred to advanced tax texts.

Amortization of Intangible Property

The term "depreciation" generally applies to the cost recovery of real and tangible personal business property and the term "amortization" applies to the cost recovery of intangible personal property, such as patents, copyrights, and leasehold improvements, provided such property has a definite and limited legal life. The tax law does not make a clear distinction between depreciation and amortization but allows cost recovery of intangible property that has a limited life, such as patents and franchises. The tax law disallows a write off for goodwill because it does not have an identifiable limited life. Costs for trademarks and trade names are treated in the same way as goodwill. They must be capitalized and cannot be depreciated or amortized for tax purposes.

In amortizing (or depreciating) intangible assets for tax purposes, the cost recovery must be calculated using the straight-line method. If the asset has a specific legal life, like a patent or a copyright, the cost is recoverable over that legal life. However, if the patent or copyright becomes valueless in any year before it expires, the remaining unrecovered cost (adjusted basis) may be deducted in the year it becomes valueless.

Leasehold Improvements

If a lessee makes a leasehold improvement, the lease period for calculating the straight-line depreciation (amortization) includes all of the renewal periods, except that a renewal period or periods need not be considered if including a renewal period would extend the period taken into account to a period which exceeds the remaining useful life of the improvement. This same rule applies to the cost of acquiring a lease.

EXAMPLE 17

Assume that a lessee enters into the lease of an office building at the beginning of 1992 for five years with the lease renewable for two additional three-year periods. The lessee makes improvements to the lease that are completed early in the first year of the lease at a cost of $32,000. The improvements are estimated to have a useful life of 8 years. Since the lease life after the first year, including the renewal periods, is 10 years and the useful life of the leasehold improvement is 8 years, the taxpayer may depreciate (amortize) the cost of the improvement over 8 years on a straight-line basis. Thus, the depreciation for the year 1992, the first year the leasehold improvement was put in service, would be $4,000 ($32,000/8 years).

Tax Planning for the Depreciation Deduction

In determining the depreciation and/or amortization deduction for a given tax year, it is often assumed that the taxpayer should take the maximum deduction allowed at the earliest possible time. If this policy was followed literally, taxpayers would always take any first-year expense deduction that was allowed and use the most rapid accelerated depreciation method that was allowed. In many cases this is a good strategy to meet the test of paying the least legal tax at the latest possible date. Recognize, however, that taking the largest deduction at the earliest point in the life of a depreciable or amortizable asset may not be the best policy. If the taxpayer is in a low tax bracket now, but expects to be in a higher tax bracket in future years, the taxpayer will benefit most by delaying the large depreciation deductions until he or she is in the higher tax bracket. This can be accomplished by using alternative methods that allow for a longer life to be selected and/or by using a straight-line method instead of an accelerated method. Careful planning for the depreciation deduction is an important element in the overall tax policy of paying the least legal tax at the latest possible date.

Name ________________________________

Section ______________ Date ________________

C H A P T E R   9

Questions and Problems

1. For each of the following types of assets, briefly summarize a specified or typical life expectancy and depreciation method(s) for each of the following periods: Before 1981, 1981-1986, and 1987-present.

Before 1981	**Useful Life**	**Method or Methods**
Automobiles	__________	__________
Light trucks	__________	__________
Computers	__________	__________
Furniture and fixtures	__________	__________
Machinery and equipment	__________	__________
Commercial buildings	__________	__________
Residential buildings	__________	__________

1981-1986		
Automobiles	__________	__________
Light trucks	__________	__________
Computers	__________	__________
Furniture and fixtures	__________	__________
Machinery and equipment	__________	__________
Commercial buildings	__________	__________
Residential buildings	__________	__________

1987-Present		
Automobiles	__________	__________
Light trucks	__________	__________
Computers	__________	__________
Furniture and fixtures	__________	__________
Machinery and equipment	__________	__________
Commercial buildings	__________	__________
Residential buildings	__________	__________

2. Peter Baker used the following assets in his business for the year 1992:

Machinery: Acquired in 1987 at a cost of $72,000
Furniture: Acquired in 1989 at a cost of $30,000
Computer: Acquired in 1990 at a cost of $50,000

a. Calculate the depreciation deduction Baker would be entitled to based on the information regarding the date of purchase and cost of each asset. Assume that each asset was acquired in early January of the year indicated. Baker elected the optional straight-line method with a 12-year life for the machinery when it was acquired in 1987. The maximum allowable depreciation was used for the furniture and the computer without taking the first year expense allowance.

b. Now assume that Peter Baker purchased each of these assets in early January 1992. Calculate the cost recovery for each of these assets for the year 1992 using the maximum depreciation allowed for each asset without taking the first year expense allowance.

3. Refer to Problem 2 and calculate the following requirements:

    a. Assume that each of the assets was purchased in 1992. Calculate the depreciation for 1992 using the optional straight-line method with a recovery period equal to the period used in Problem 2b.

    b. Assume that each of the assets was purchased in 1992. Calculate the cost recovery for 1992 using an ADR midpoint life of 8 years for the computer and 12 years for the furniture and the machinery.

4. Quentin Miller, a calendar year taxpayer, acquired four machines in 1992 on the dates indicated at the costs stated:

February 1	$25,000
April 1	35,000
October 1	30,000
December 1	20,000

    a. Calculate Miller's cost recovery deduction for 1992 that would be reported on Schedule C using MACRS with the appropriate averaging convention.

b. Calculate the MACRS cost recovery for 1992 if half-year convention had been applicable for all of 1992 purchases, and comment on the significance of the difference from the answer to *a.* above.

5. In early January, 1992, a taxpayer purchased two buildings—one was an office building for $320,000 and the other was an apartment building for $400,000.

   a. Calculate the regular cost recovery for each building in 1992.

   b. Calculate the depreciation for each building for 1992 if the taxpayer had elected the alternative cost recovery system for each building in 1992.

6. The H.B. Fields Company acquired the following business assets in 1992:

Date of Acquisition	Item	Cost
July 2	Automobile (new)	$18,000
March 10	Garage for auto (new)	31,500
February 1	Electric typewriter (used)	1,246
February 1	Office desk (new)	910

   a. Calculate the H.B. Fields Company's cost recovery deduction for 1992 that would be reported on Schedule C, using MACRS. The cost recovery period must be determined for each asset.

   b. Complete Form 4562, Depreciation and Amortization, on the following pages to report the depreciation deduction reported on Schedule C as calculated in Part *a.*

Form **4562**

Department of the Treasury
Internal Revenue Service

Depreciation and Amortization
(Including Information on Listed Property)

▶ See separate instructions. ▶ Attach this form to your return.

OMB No. 1545-0172

1992

Attachment
Sequence No. **67**

Name(s) shown on return

Identifying number

Business or activity to which this form relates

Part I Election To Expense Certain Tangible Property (Section 179) (Note: *If you have any "Listed Property," complete Part V before you complete Part I.*)

1	Maximum dollar limitation (see instructions)	1	$10,000
2	Total cost of section 179 property placed in service during the tax year (see instructions) . .	2	
3	Threshold cost of section 179 property before reduction in limitation	3	$200,000
4	Reduction in limitation. Subtract line 3 from line 2, but do not enter less than -0-	4	
5	Dollar limitation for tax year. Subtract line 4 from line 1, but do not enter less than -0- . .	5	

(a) Description of property	(b) Cost	(c) Elected cost	
6			

7	Listed property. Enter amount from line 26	7	
8	Total elected cost of section 179 property. Add amounts in column (c), lines 6 and 7 . . .	8	
9	Tentative deduction. Enter the smaller of line 5 or line 8	9	
10	Carryover of disallowed deduction from 1991 (see instructions).	10	
11	Taxable income limitation. Enter the smaller of taxable income or line 5 (see instructions) . .	11	
12	Section 179 expense deduction. Add lines 9 and 10, but do not enter more than line 11 . .	12	
13	Carryover of disallowed deduction to 1993. Add lines 9 and 10, less line 12 ▶	13	

Note: *Do not use Part II or Part III below for automobiles, certain other vehicles, cellular telephones, computers, or property used for entertainment, recreation, or amusement (listed property). Instead, use Part V for listed property.*

Part II MACRS Depreciation For Assets Placed in Service ONLY During Your 1992 Tax Year (Do Not Include Listed Property)

(a) Classification of property	(b) Month and year placed in service	(c) Basis for depreciation (business/investment use only—see instructions)	(d) Recovery period	(e) Convention	(f) Method	(g) Depreciation deduction
14 General Depreciation System (GDS) (see instructions):						
a 3-year property						
b 5-year property						
c 7-year property						
d 10-year property						
e 15-year property						
f 20-year property						
g Residential rental property			27.5 yrs.	MM	S/L	
			27.5 yrs.	MM	S/L	
h Nonresidential real property			31.5 yrs.	MM	S/L	
			31.5 yrs.	MM	S/L	
15 Alternative Depreciation System (ADS) (see instructions):						
a Class life					S/L	
b 12-year			12 yrs.		S/L	
c 40-year			40 yrs.	MM	S/L	

Part III Other Depreciation (Do Not Include Listed Property)

16	GDS and ADS deductions for assets placed in service in tax years beginning before 1992 (see instructions)	16	
17	Property subject to section 168(f)(1) election (see instructions)	17	
18	ACRS and other depreciation (see instructions)	18	

Part IV Summary

19	Listed property. Enter amount from line 25	19	
20	**Total.** Add deductions on line 12, lines 14 and 15 in column (g), and lines 16 through 19. Enter here and on the appropriate lines of your return. (Partnerships and S corporations—see instructions)	20	
21	For assets shown above and placed in service during the current year, enter the portion of the basis attributable to section 263A costs (see instructions)	21	

For Paperwork Reduction Act Notice, see page 1 of the separate instructions. Cat. No. 12906N Form **4562** (1992)

Form 4562 (1992)

Page **2**

Part V Listed Property—Automobiles, Certain Other Vehicles, Cellular Telephones, Computers, and Property Used for Entertainment, Recreation, or Amusement

*For any vehicle for which you are using the standard mileage rate or deducting lease expense, complete **only** 22a, 22b, columns (a) through (c) of Section A, all of Section B, and Section C if applicable.*

Section A—Depreciation (Caution: See instructions for limitations for automobiles.)

22a Do you have evidence to support the business/investment use claimed? ☐ Yes ☐ No   22b If "Yes," is the evidence written? ☐ Yes ☐ No

(a) Type of property (list vehicles first)	(b) Date placed in service	(c) Business/investment use percentage	(d) Cost or other basis	(e) Basis for depreciation (business/investment use only)	(f) Recovery period	(g) Method/Convention	(h) Depreciation deduction	(i) Elected section 179 cost
23 Property used more than 50% in a qualified business use (see instructions):								
		%						
		%						
		%						
24 Property used 50% or less in a qualified business use (see instructions):								
		%				S/L –		
		%				S/L –		
		%				S/L –		

25 Add amounts in column (h). Enter the total here and on line 19, page 1 . . . . **25**

26 Add amounts in column (i). Enter the total here and on line 7, page 1 . . . . **26**

Section B—Information Regarding Use of Vehicles—If you deduct expenses for vehicles:

- Always complete this section for vehicles used by a sole proprietor, partner, or other "more than 5% owner," or related person.
- If you provided vehicles to your employees, first answer the questions in Section C to see if you meet an exception to completing this section for those vehicles.

	(a) Vehicle 1		(b) Vehicle 2		(c) Vehicle 3		(d) Vehicle 4		(e) Vehicle 5		(f) Vehicle 6	
27 Total business/investment miles driven during the year (DO NOT include commuting miles)												
28 Total commuting miles driven during the year												
29 Total other personal (noncommuting) miles driven												
30 Total miles driven during the year. Add lines 27 through 29												
	Yes	No	Yes	No	Yes	No	Yes	No	Yes	No	Yes	No
31 Was the vehicle available for personal use during off-duty hours?												
32 Was the vehicle used primarily by a more than 5% owner or related person?												
33 Is another vehicle available for personal use?												

Section C—Questions for Employers Who Provide Vehicles for Use by Their Employees

Answer these questions to determine if you meet an exception to completing Section B. **Note:** *Section B must always be completed for vehicles used by sole proprietors, partners, or other more than 5% owners or related persons.*

	Yes	No
34 Do you maintain a written policy statement that prohibits all personal use of vehicles, including commuting, by your employees?		
35 Do you maintain a written policy statement that prohibits personal use of vehicles, except commuting, by your employees? (See instructions for vehicles used by corporate officers, directors, or 1% or more owners.)		
36 Do you treat all use of vehicles by employees as personal use?		
37 Do you provide more than five vehicles to your employees and retain the information received from your employees concerning the use of the vehicles?		
38 Do you meet the requirements concerning qualified automobile demonstration use (see instructions)? . . .		

Note: *If your answer to 34, 35, 36, 37, or 38 is "Yes," you need not complete Section B for the covered vehicles.*

Part VI Amortization

(a) Description of costs	(b) Date amortization begins	(c) Amortizable amount	(d) Code section	(e) Amortization period or percentage	(f) Amortization for this year
39 Amortization of costs that begins during your 1992 tax year:					

40 Amortization of costs that began before 1992 . . . . **40**

41 Total. Enter here and on "Other Deductions" or "Other Expenses" line of your return . . . **41**

7. The Redwood Company, which is on a calendar-year basis for income tax purposes, acquired the following tangible depreciable properties during 1992:

Item	Cost	Date Acquired	Class Life-Years	ADR Life Years
Automobile (new)	$ 18,500	February 2, 1992	5	6
Light truck (new)	14,200	March 1, 1992	5	8
Machinery (used)	42,000	June 1, 1992	7	10
Equipment (new)	77,000	June 30, 1992	7	12
Warehouse (new)	110,250	January 9, 1992	31.5	40

Assuming all of these assets were placed in service when acquired, what are the alternative amounts of MACRS deduction that the taxpayer can elect on each of these properties?

8. Dewey Terrell is a personal financial adviser who operates out of an office in his rented personal residence. In March 1991, he purchased a computer with related equipment for $4,800 and an automobile for $12,600. During 1992, he used the computer 60% of the time in providing financial advice to clients, 15% of the time for his own investments, and 25% of the time for personal use. He used the automobile 70% of the time for business, 10% of the time for his investments, and 20% of the time for personal use. Assume that the car is not subject to the luxury car limitations.

   a. Indicate what Terrell's options are with respect to the way he calculates depreciation for 1992 with respect to the computer and the automobile.

   b. How much of MACRS deduction is Terrell entitled to take in 1992 for the computer and the automobile, assuming he elected to take the maximum MACRS deduction?

9. Charlotte Milone is a computer consultant. She advises on and helps install computer systems for a wide variety of clients. Since she often drives considerable distances to work in client offices, she decides to buy a luxury automobile to use in her work. She purchased the car on March 1, 1992 for $30,000 and has used it 80% of the time during 1992 for business purposes. As her tax consultant, she asks you to prepare a schedule for her which shows the maximum cost recovery she will be entitled to take in each of the years 1992 through 1997, assuming that she uses the automobile 80% of the time for business each year.

10. On January 1, 1992, Bradford Company had the following assets on its books. You are asked to calculate the allowable depreciation deduction for 1992 for each of these assets, all of which were sold on the dates indicated.

Asset	Date Acquired	Original Cost	Depreciation Method	Accumulated Depreciation	Date of Sale
Computer	7-1-89	$ 4,200	DDB	$ 2,990	3-5-92
Automobile	4-1-90	12,000	DDB	6,240	9-1-92
Furniture	8-1-88	24,000	SL*	8,400	8-1-92

* Used the straight-line depreciation method with an ADS life of 10 years

11. An independent crude oil producer purchased a newly developed oil well for $1,200,000. An independent geologist estimated that the well would generate 900,000 barrels of oil. During 1992, 40,000 barrels of oil were pumped from the well and 35,000 barrels were sold at $25 per barrel.

The company's records indicate that the cost of producing the oil was $12 per barrel. Assume that the percentage depletion rate for this oil producer is 15% in 1992 and that the company uses the accrual method of accounting.

a. Determine the cost depletion that this producer would be allowed on his 1992 tax return.

b. Determine the percentage depletion that this producer would be allowed on his 1992 tax return.

c. Based on your calculations in a. and b. above, indicate what amount you would recommend that this oil producer use as the depletion deduction on his 1992 tax return.

12. A taxpayer purchased the rights to a coal mine for $660,000 in 1992 that is estimated to contain 300,000 tons of coal. During 1992 18,000 tons were mined and 15,000 tons were sold. Cash was collected on 12,000 of the tons sold with the selling price of 3,000 tons shown as accounts receivable.

   a. What is the cost depletion for 1992 if the taxpayer uses the cash method of accounting?

   b. What is the cost depletion for 1992 if the taxpayer uses the accrual method of accounting?

   c. When will the taxpayer be allowed to take the depletion deduction for the tons not sold in 1992 if (1) the taxpayer uses the cash method, and (2) if the taxpayer uses the accrual method?

13. A taxpayer acquired the rights to certain mineral deposits at an initial price of $1,200,000. The taxpayer then incurred an additional $100,000 in further exploration costs plus $150,000 of development costs prior to starting the extraction of the ore. Geologists estimated that the deposit contained 40,000 tons of minerals. Mining experts estimated that the property would be worth $10,000 after all of the usable ore had been removed from the mine. If the 1992 production amounted to 12,000 tons, how much would the cost depletion be for the year, assuming that 10,000 tons were sold in 1992, leaving 2,000 tons in inventory? The taxpayer uses the accrual method of accounting.

14. Assume the same fact as in Problem 13 above. At the end of 1992, geologists made a new estimate of the remaining ore in the deposit, determining that the remaining usable ore not yet extracted would amount to 36,000 tons. If 15,000 tons were extracted in 1993 and 14,000 tons were sold (including the 2,000 tons in inventory at the end of 1992), how much would the taxpayer's cost depletion be for the year 1993?

15. An independent crude oil producer provided the following financial and production information regarding his business activities for 1992:

Gross income from an oil well	$300,000
Taxable income from oil well (before the depletion deduction) . . .	60,000
Cost depletion on the oil well	25,000
Percentage depletion rate on oil well	20%
Taxable income from other activities	4,000

    a. What is the maximum depletion deduction allowed to the taxpayer for 1992? Show calculations.

    b. What is the taxpayer's total taxable income for 1992 after taking the appropriate deduction for depletion?

16. The taxpayer, a lessee, enters into an 8-year lease of a warehouse for storing spare parts for one of the lessee's products. In order to use the building efficiently, the lessee incurred costs for improvements in the amount of $32,000. It is estimated that the improvements will have a useful life of 5 years after which further improvements will be necessary to maintain an efficient operation of the warehouse. Assume that the lease contract was entered into on July 1, 1992.

    a. Assuming that the lease is not renewable at the end of the lease term and that the warehouse improvements were completed on October 1, 1992, what deduction is the taxpayer entitled to for the calendar year 1992 in connection with the lease, if any?

    b. Assume the same facts as for *a.* above, except that the improvements to the warehouse will have a useful life of 10 years. What deduction, if any, can the lessee take in 1992 in connection with the lease of the warehouse?

17. Explain what flexibility a taxpayer has in doing tax planning with respect to the depreciation deduction in order to be consistent with the tax planning principle of "paying the least legal tax at the latest possible time."

PROPERTY TRANSACTIONS

➥ How to calculate rental income and expenses

➥ How to complete Schedule E

➥ How to determine passive activity losses

➥ How to determine gain or loss on property transactions

➥ How to determine holding period for capital assets

➥ How to complete Schedule D

➥ How to complete Form 4797

➥ How to account for transactions involving Section 1231, Section 1245, and Section 1250 assets

Supplemental Income Activities

Income diversification is a fact of life. Successful individuals generally have more than one source of income. Many employees operate their own trade or business on the side to generate additional income. Some people invest in real estate, stocks, bonds, mutual funds, and other standard investment items. Some individuals are involved with royalty producing properties. People have many different sources of supplemental income. The tax ramifications of operating a trade or business were explained in previous chapters. Dividends and interest were also covered in previous chapters. Investments in capital assets held for appreciation will be covered in Chapters 11 and 12. This chapter will examine rental and other passive activities, royalties, and other items reported on Schedule E.

Rental Income and Expense

One of the more popular areas of income diversification is rental properties. This segment of the chapter will examine rental activities and explain how rental income and expenses are to be reported on the tax return.

Rental Income

Rental income is any payment received for the use or occupation of property. Generally, all amounts received as rent must be included in gross income. In addition to amounts received as normal rent payments, there are other amounts that may be rental income.

Advance Rent. Rent received in advance of the rental period should be included in rental income in the year of receipt regardless of the period covered or the method of accounting used.

EXAMPLE 1 ──────────────

Mary Haas signed a 5-year lease to rent her property. In the first year, she received $6,000 as rent for the first year and $6,000 in advance as rent for the last year of the lease. Mary must include $12,000 in her income in the first year.

Security Deposits. A security deposit is not included in income when received if it is to be returned to the tenant at the end of the lease. But, if during any year, part or all of the security deposit is not returned because the tenant does not live up to the terms of the lease, the amount not returned is included in income for that year. If a security deposit is to be used as a final payment of rent, it is advance rent and included in income when received.

Payment for Cancelling a Lease. Any payment received from a tenant to cancel a lease is rent. The payment is included in income in the year it is received.

Expense Paid by a Tenant. Any expenses (e.g., real estate taxes) paid by a tenant for the landlord are rental income and must be included in the income of the landlord. However, any rental expenses paid by a tenant may be deducted by the landlord.

Rental of Taxpayer's Home. If the taxpayer rents out his/her home for less than 15 days during the tax year, the rent received is not included in gross income. However, expenses other than allowable interest, taxes, and casualty and theft losses cannot be deducted.

Part Interest. If a taxpayer owns a partial interest in rental property, the taxpayer's portion of the rental income must be reported as income by the taxpayer.

Rental Expenses

The ordinary expenses of renting property can be deducted from gross rental income. This section discusses expenses that can be deducted if part of the property is rented, or if the property is changed to rental use.

If a part interest in rental property is owned, the part of the expenses the taxpayer actually paid can be deducted. Rental expenses are generally deducted in the year the expenses are paid or incurred.

Repairs and Improvements

The cost of repairs made to a rental property may be deducted. However, the cost of improvements cannot be deducted. The costs of improvements are recovered by taking depreciation.

Accurate records should be kept separating the cost of repairs and improvements. The cost of improvements is needed when the property is sold or depreciation is determined.

Repairs. A repair keeps a property in good operating condition. It does not materially add to the value of the property or substantially prolong its life. Repainting property inside or out, fixing gutters or floors, fixing leaks, plastering, and replacing broken windows are examples of repairs. If repairs are made as part of an extensive remodeling or restoration of the property, the entire job is an improvement.

Improvements. An improvement adds to the value of the property, prolongs its useful life, or adapts it to new uses. Building a recreation room in an unfinished basement; paneling a den; adding a bathroom or bedroom; installing a fence, new plumbing or wiring, new cabinets, a new roof, or decorative grillwork on a balcony; and paving a driveway are examples of improvements. Improvements must be capitalized and depreciated.

Depreciation

Depreciation is the annual deduction taken to recover the cost of rental property that is used for more than one year. Several factors determine how much depreciation can be deducted. The main factors are: (1) the basis in the property, and (2) the recovery period for the property.

Depreciation can be deducted only on the part of the property used for rental purposes. Depreciation reduces the basis for figuring gain or loss on a later sale or exchange. Form 4562, Depreciation and Amortization, is used to report depreciation (Chapter 9).

Other Expenses

Expenses for advertising, janitor and maid service, utilities, fire and liability insurance, taxes, interest commissions for the collection of rent, ordinary and necessary travel and transportation, and other expenses discussed below may be deducted from gross rental income.

Salaries and Wages. Reasonable salaries and wages paid to employees can be deducted. Bonuses paid to employees can also be deducted if, when added to the regular salaries or wages, the total is not more than reasonable pay.

Reasonable wages paid to a dependent child can be deducted if the child is a bona fide employee. However, the cost of meals and lodging for the child cannot be deducted.

Rental Payments for Property. Rent paid for property that is used for rental purposes can be deducted. If a leasehold is purchased for rental purposes, an equal part of the cost can be deducted each year over the term of the lease.

Rental of Equipment. Rent paid for equipment that is used for rental purposes is deductible. However, if the lease contract is actually a purchase contract, these payments cannot be deducted. The payments for such equipment must be capitalized and recovered through depreciation.

Insurance Premiums. Insurance premiums can be deducted. If the premiums are paid in advance for more than one year, only that part of the premium payment applicable to the current year can be deducted.

Local Benefits. Generally, special assessments for local benefits that increase the value of the property, such as for putting in streets, sidewalks, or water and sewer systems, cannot be deducted. The assessment must be added to the basis of the property. Local benefit taxes can be deducted if they are for maintaining, repairing, or paying interest charges for the benefits.

Charges for Services. Charges paid to obtain services for rental property, such as water, sewer, and trash collection are deductible.

Renting Part of a Property

If only part of a property is rented, certain expenses must be divided between the part of the property used for rental purposes and the part of the property used for personal purposes. The property is treated as two separate pieces of property.

Part of some expenses (mortgage interest and real estate taxes) can be deducted as a rental expense. The remaining part, subject to certain limitations, can be claimed as an itemized deduction. A portion of the expenses that are normally nondeductible personal expenses (electricity or painting the outside of a house) are deductible as rental expenses.

Expenses that relate only to the rental part of the property do not have to be divided. If a room that is rented is painted, or if premiums are paid for liability insurance in connection with renting a room, the entire cost is a rental expense. Depreciation can also be deducted on that part of any qualified property used for rental purposes.

Allocation of Expenses. If an expense is for both rental use and personal use (mortgage interest or heat for the entire house), the expense must be divided between the rental use and the personal use. Any reasonable method for dividing the expenses can be used. The two most common methods are one based on the number of rooms in the home and one based on area.

The number of participants may be the best method to use in dividing certain expenses. For example, if both room and board are provided to tenants, the most accurate method of dividing food costs between rental and personal expenses may be one based on the total number of people eating the food. If tenants have unrestricted use of the telephone, the number of people using it may be the proper method for allocating the monthly telephone charge.

Limits on Deductions for Rental Expenses. When a property is held for both personal and rental use, the amount of the rental expenses that are deductible on the tax return may be limited. People that rent out their vacation home, for example, may not be able to deduct all of the rental expenses. (See *Vacation Homes and Other Dwelling Units*)

Property Changed to Rental Use

If a personal residence, apartment, or other property is changed to rental use at any time

Choosing a Method

Since there are a number of "reasonable" methods that are acceptable in allocating expenses, the taxpayer should choose that method which produces the most favorable tax result.

other than at the beginning of the tax year, yearly expenses such as depreciation, taxes, and insurance must be divided between rental use and personal use. Only that portion of the expense that relates to the period the property was used or held for rental purposes is deductible as a rental expense.

Depreciation and insurance cannot be deducted for any property held for personal use. However, the allowable part of the interest and tax expenses for personal use can be used as an itemized deduction on Schedule A (Form 1040).

Avoiding Taxation of Gains

Taxpayers who sell their residence and reinvest the sales proceeds in another residence avoid taxation of any realized gain. However, if part of the residence has been rented out, the gain attributable to the rental portion will generally be taxed. This tax can be avoided if the rental portion of the dwelling is converted back and used as a personal residence before the sale takes place.

EXAMPLE 2 ——————————————

Sylvia moved from her home in June and started renting it out on July 1. She can deduct as rental expenses 6/12 of her yearly expenses such as taxes and insurance. Sylvia can also deduct as rental expenses, starting with July, the amounts paid for items generally billed monthly, such as utilities.

Vacation Homes and Other Dwelling Units

If part or all of a vacation home or other dwelling unit is rented out and any part of the dwelling unit is also used as a home during the year, the tax treatment of the rental income and deductions depends on how many days the property was used for personal use and rental use.

Basically, if a rented dwelling qualifies as a "home," deductible expenses are limited to the amount of rental income. Whereas, a rented dwelling that does not qualify as a "home" does not carry this limitation. In this situation, rental expenses can exceed rental income and actually create a deductible loss.

Rented Less Than 15 Days

If a dwelling unit is used as a home and is rented for less than 15 days during the year, none of the rental income needs to be reported. However, none of the expenses can be deducted as rental expenses. Allowable interest, taxes, and casualty and theft losses are deductible on Schedule A (Form 1040) if deductions are itemized.

Rented 15 Days or More

If a dwelling unit is used as a home and it is rented for 15 days or more during the year, all of the rental income must be reported. Expenses must be divided between the personal use and the rental use based on the number of days used for each purpose.

Dwelling Unit

The above paragraphs outline the basic treatment of revenues and expenses for dwellings that serve as a home and also generate rental income. To better understand this treatment, the following paragraphs will describe the meaning of: a dwelling unit, a home, personal use, and rental use.

For purposes of the rules that apply to vacation homes and other dwelling units, a dwelling unit includes a house, apartment, condominium, mobile home, boat, or similar property. It does not include property used exclusively as a hotel, motel, inn, or similar establishment. Property is used exclusively as a hotel, motel, inn, or similar establishment if it is regularly available for occupancy by paying customers and is not used by an owner as a home during the year.

Home

A dwelling unit is used as a home during the tax year if it is used for personal purposes for more than 14 days and more than 10% of the number of days during the year that it is rented at a fair rental price. In determining whether a dwelling unit qualifies as a home, any day of personal use cannot be counted as a day on which it is rented at a fair rental price. See *Personal Use* later for information on how to determine days of personal use.

Fair Rental Price. A fair rental price for a property generally is an amount that a person who is not related would be willing to pay. The rent charged is **not** a fair rental price if it is substantially less than the rents charged for other properties that are similar to the property.

To determine whether another property is similar to the property being rented, the following questions should be asked:

1. Is it used for the same purposes?
2. Is it approximately the same size?
3. Is it in approximately the same condition?
4. Does it have similar furnishings?
5. Is it in a similar location?

If any of the answers are no, the properties probably are not similar.

Examples. The following examples illustrate the classification of rental properties as dwelling units; homes; or as hotels, motels or similar properties.

EXAMPLE 3 ────────────────────

Deborah converted the basement of her residence into an apartment with a bedroom, a bathroom, and a small kitchen. She rents the apartment to college students during the regular school year. She rents to them on a 9-month (273 days) lease.

During the summer, Deborah's nephews stay with her for a month (30 days) and live in the apartment.

Deborah's basement apartment is a dwelling unit (and not a hotel, motel, inn, or similar establishment) because she used it as a home (that is, for personal purposes for more than 14 days and more than 10% of the number of days for which it is rented).

EXAMPLE 4 ────────────────────

Stewart rents out the guest bedroom in his residence during the local college's homecoming, commencement, and football weekends (a total of 27 days). His sister-in-law stays in the room, rent-free, for the last three weeks (21 days) in July.

The room itself is not a dwelling unit, but it is part of a dwelling unit. The room is not used exclusively as a hotel, motel, inn, or similar establishment because Stewart uses it as a home (that is, for personal purposes for more than 14 days and more than 10% of the number of days for which it is rented).

EXAMPLE 5 ————————————————

Harry rents out a room in his residence that is always available for occupancy by paying customers. He does not use the room himself and does not allow anyone other than paying customers to use the room. The room is used exclusively as a hotel, motel, inn, or similar establishment and is therefore not a dwelling unit.

EXAMPLE 6 ————————————————

Maren owns a cottage at the shore. She rents it out from June 1 through August 31, a total of 92 days. The tenant who rented the cottage for the month of July was unable to use it from July 4 through July 8. The tenant allowed Maren to use the cottage for those 5 days. The tenant did not ask for a refund of or a reduction in the rent. Maren's family used the cottage for 3 of those days.

For purposes of determining whether Maren used the cottage as a home, the 3 days are not counted as days on which the cottage was rented at a fair rental price. The cottage was rented at a fair rental price for 89 days (92 − 3 = 89).

She would have used the cottage as a home if she had used it for personal purposes for more than 14 days.

Personal Use

A dwelling unit is used for personal purposes on any day that it is used by:

1. The owner or by any other person who has an interest in it, unless it is rented as a main home under a shared equity financing agreement (defined later)
2. A member of the owner's family or by a member of the family of any other person who has an interest in it, unless the family member uses the dwelling unit as their main home and pays a fair rental price (Family includes only brothers and sisters, half-brothers and half-sisters, spouses, ancestors (parents, grandparents, etc.) and lineal descendants (children, grandchildren, etc.))
3. Anyone under an arrangement that lets the owner use some other dwelling unit
4. Anyone at less than a fair rental price

Rental to Person with Interest in Unit.   A dwelling unit is used for personal purposes if it is rented to someone who has an interest in it unless the rental is under a shared equity financing agreement.

Shared equity financing agreement. This is an agreement under which two or more persons acquire undivided interests for more than 50 years in an entire dwelling unit, including the land, and one or more of the co-owners is entitled to occupy the unit as their main home upon payment of rent to the other co-owner or owners.

Rental to Family Member. A dwelling unit is not used for personal purposes if it is rented at a fair rental price to a member of the owner's family who uses it as their principal residence (unless they have an interest in the unit).

Charitable Contributions. A dwelling unit is used for personal purposes if:

1. The use of the unit is donated to a charitable organization
2. The organization sells the use of the unit at a fund-raising event
3. The purchaser uses the unit

Examples. The following examples show how to determine days of personal use.

EXAMPLE 7 ————————————————

Loren and his neighbor, Bill, are co-owners of a condominium at the beach. Loren rents the unit out to vacationers whenever possible. The unit is not used as a main home by anyone. Bill uses the unit for two weeks every year.

Because Bill has an interest in the unit, both Loren and Bill are considered to have used the unit for personal purposes during those two weeks.

EXAMPLE 8

Marie and her neighbors are co-owners of a house under a shared equity financing agreement. Her neighbors live in the house and pay her a fair rental price.

Even though Marie's neighbors have an interest in the house, the days her neighbors live there are not counted as days of personal use by Marie. This is because her neighbors rent the house as their main home under a shared equity financing agreement.

EXAMPLE 9

Jane owns a rental property that she rents to her son. Her son has no interest in this dwelling unit. He uses it as his main home. He pays her a fair rental price for the property.

Her son's use of the property is not personal use by Jane because her son is using it as his main home, he has no interest in the property, and he is paying her a fair rental price.

EXAMPLE 10

Byron rents his beach house to Mary Smith. Mary rents her house in the mountains to Byron. Both pay a fair rental price.

Byron is using his house for personal purposes on the days that Mary uses it because his house is used by Mary under an arrangement that allows him to use her house.

EXAMPLE 11

Bruce rents an apartment to his mother at less than a fair rental price. He is using the apartment for personal purposes during the period that his mother rents it.

Days Not Counted as Personal Use

Some days spent at the dwelling unit are not counted as days of personal use. Two types of days that do not count as personal use days are discussed below.

Repairs and Maintenance. Any day that is spent repairing and maintaining a property on a full-time basis is not counted as a day of personal use. Such a day is not counted as a day of personal use even if relatives use the property for recreational purposes on the same day.

Use as a Residence Before or After Renting. Days on which a property is used as a residence are not counted as days of personal use if the property is used as a residence before or after renting it or offering it for rent, **and either:**

1. The property is rented or offered for rent for 12 or more consecutive months
2. The property is rented or offered for rent for a period of less than 12 consecutive months and the period ended because the property was sold or exchanged

EXAMPLE 12

Harlan Fuller accepted a position in another city and moved out of his residence on March 15, 1992. He had lived in the house for 5 years. Harlan rented the house at a fair rental price from May 1, 1992, to June 30, 1993. On September 1, 1993, Harlan returned to the community and moved back into his former residence.

Since the house was rented for at least 12 consecutive months, Harlan's use of the house as his main residence from January 1, 1992, to March 15, 1992, and from September 1, 1993, to December 31, 1993, is not counted as personal use.

Division of Expenses

If a dwelling unit is used for both rental and personal purposes, expenses must be divided between the rental use and the personal use. This division is required even if the dwelling unit does not qualify as a "home." For purposes of dividing expenses:

1. Any day that the unit is rented at a fair rental price is a day of rental use even if it is personally used for that day.
2. A unit is **not** considered used for rental during the time that it is held out for rent but not actually rented.

Please note that the rules for determining "personal use" for purposes of dividing expenses is different from the "personal use" rules used for determining whether a dwelling unit qualifies as a home.

EXAMPLE 13 —————————————————

Nikolette offers her beach cottage for rent from June 1 through August 31 (92 days). Her family uses the cottage during the last 2 weeks in May (14 days). During the year, she was unable to find a renter for the first week in August (7 days). The person who rented the cottage for July allowed her to use it over a weekend (2 days) without any reduction in or refund of rent. The cottage was not used at all before May 14 or after August 31.

The cottage was used for rental a total of 85 days (92 – 7 = 85). The days it was held out for rent but not rented (7 days) are not days of rental use. For purposes of dividing expenses, the July weekend on which Nikolette used it (2 days) is rental use because she received a fair rental price for the weekend.

Nikolette used the cottage for personal purposes for 14 days (the last 2 weeks in May). Thus, the expenses are divided as follows: 14.1% (14/99) for personal use and 85.9% (85/99) for rental use.

Expense Limitations on Rental Property

If a dwelling unit is not used as a home, deductible rental expenses can be more than gross rental income, thus creating a loss. However, the passive activity rules may limit the amount of the loss that is deductible. Rental activities are usually classified as passive activities. Losses from passive activities are generally deductible only to the extent of income from passive activities.

Exception

If losses from rental real estate activities are $25,000 or less ($12,500 if married filing separately), the passive activity limits probably do not apply. (See *Rental Real Estate Activities* later in the chapter for more information.) Also the passive activity rules do not apply to any income, deductions, gain, or loss related to the rental of property, if the property is used as a home. A home is a dwelling unit used for personal purposes for more than 14 days and more than 10% of the number of days for which it was rented at a fair rental price. The passive activity rules are explained in more detail later in the chapter.

Property Used as a Home

If a qualified home is rented for less than 15 days, none of the expenses can be deducted as *rental expense*. However, none of the rental income is reported as income.

If a qualified home is rented for more than 15 days, rental expenses are deductible as follows:

1. If there is a net profit from the rental property for the year (that is, if rental income is more than the total of rental expenses, including depreciation), all of the rental expenses are deductible.
2. If there is not a net profit from the rental property for the year, the deductible rental expenses will be limited to the amount of gross rental income. In addition, the rental expenses for the year will be deductible in the following order:

    a. The rental use portion of interest and taxes
    b. Rental expenses that are not directly related to the dwelling unit itself. This includes expenses such as rental agent fees, office supplies, depreciation on office equipment used exclusively in the business of renting property, and advertising fees.
    c. The rental use portion of any expenses not described in **a.** or **b.** (other than depreciation and other basis adjustments). This includes expenses such as repairs, insurance, and utilities.
    d. The rental use portion of depreciation and other basis adjustments to that rental property

The expenses in each of the above categories can only be deducted as a rental expense to the extent there is sufficient unabsorbed gross rent to offset the expense. Excess expenses may be carried forward. See *Carryover of Expenses*, later.

Where to Report. Reportable rental income and all of the deductible rental expenses are reported on Schedule E (Form 1040), Supplemental Income and Loss. Allowable interest, taxes, and casualty losses for the personal use of the property can be deducted on Schedule A (Form 1040) if deductions are itemized.

Other Reporting Considerations

Rental income is reported on the tax return for the year it is actually or constructively received. Income is considered to be constructively received when it is made available, for example, by being credited to the taxpayer's bank account.

Carryover of Expenses

If some of a prior year's rental expenses could not be deducted because the property was used as a home, the part not deductible in the prior year is treated as a current rental expense. The expenses carried over to a year can be deducted only up to the amount of gross rental income for that year, even if the property was not used as a home for that year.

Reporting Income and Expenses

Where rental income and expenses, including depreciation, is reported depends on whether certain services are provided to the tenant. If buildings, rooms, or apartments, are rented out and only heat, light, trash collection, etc., are provided, rental income and expenses are normally reported on Schedule E (Form 1040), Supplemental Income and Loss, Part I.

If additional services are provided that are primarily for the tenant's convenience, such as regular cleaning, changing linen, or maid service, rental income and expenses are reported on Schedule C (Form 1040), Profit or Loss from Business. Self-employment tax may also have to be paid on the rental income.

Royalty Income

Royalty income is the amount received for use of property covered by copyrights or patents, or for extraction from oil, gas, and mineral properties. Like rental income, royalty income must be included by the taxpayer in gross income.

Royalties from copyrights on literary, musical, artistic work, and similar property are generally paid to the taxpayer on the basis of units sold, such as for the sale of tickets, books, and records. Taxpayers are permitted to recover their cost or other basis through depreciation over the life of the copyright or patent. If the copyright or patent becomes valueless in any year before its expiration, the unrecovered cost or basis can be deducted in the next year.

Royalty income from oil, gas, and mineral properties is the amount per unit, such as ton or barrel, paid to the taxpayer by a lessee when the material resource is extracted from the property. The taxpayer with an economic interest in mineral deposits, oil and gas wells, or standing timber is entitled to a deduction for depletion on the tax return.

Schedule E provides the reporting structure for royalty income as well as rent income. However, persons who own and operate a business involving oil, gas, or mineral properties should report their gross income and expenses on Schedule C (Form 1040). Schedule C should also be used by self-employed writers, inventors, and artists.

Sale of Property Rights

When taxpayers sell their complete interest in oil, gas, or mineral rights, the amount received is considered to be payment for the sale of property, not royalty income. Such a sale may be reported on the installment basis if at least one payment is received after the tax year in which the sale took place.

The sale of a royalty producing property is generally treated as a capital asset transaction subject to capital gain or loss treatment on Schedule D (Form 1040), Capital Gains and Losses (see Chapter 12). However, copyrights and artistic works created by the taxpayer's personal efforts do not qualify for capital gain or loss treatment. These gains and losses are reported as ordinary items on Form 1040.

Sale of Future Production

Taxpayers who own a mineral property may sell a part of their future production. Generally, the money received from the buyer at the time of sale is treated as a loan from the buyer. This money is not included in income nor is it used as a basis for depletion.

When production begins, all proceeds received should be included in income. All production expenses, and depletion, should be deducted from this income to arrive at taxable income from the property.

Payments made by the taxpayer to the buyer representing the buyer's share of the proceeds are treated as a loan repayment. The buyer will treat these proceeds as a return of capital. Thus, the loan repayment will not be included in income nor will it be subject to a depletion allowance. Also, any interest factor received by the buyer will be treated as ordinary income not subject to the allowance for depletion.

Retaining a Royalty

Taxpayers who retain a royalty, an overriding royalty, or a net profit interest in a mineral property for the life of the property, are treated as having made a lease or a sublease. Any cash received for the assignment is ordinary income subject to a depletion allowance.

Supplemental Income Schedule

Schedule E (Form 1040), Supplemental Income Schedule, is used to report income or (loss) from rents and royalties. Schedule E is also used to report the taxpayer's share of income or (loss) from partnerships, S corporations, estates, trusts, and real estate mortgage investment conduits (REMICs). Any deductible losses reported on Schedule E must be sustained from activities in which the taxpayer has an investment that is at risk. These losses must also be allowable under the passive activity rules, if ap-

plicable. The at-risk rules and the passive activity rules are explained later in the chapter. Schedule E is shown in Illustration 10-1.

Schedule E, Part I

Schedule E, Part I is used for the reporting of rent and royalty income or (loss). A description of the kind and location of rental properties is required (Part I, line 1). Information regarding the taxpayer's personal usage of the rental property is also requested (line 2). This question is asked because of limitations that apply to taxpayers who use the rental property for personal purposes as well as collecting rent from the property.

Entered in the income section is the amount received for rents (line 3) and royalties (line 4). Expenses relating to rent and royalty activities, such as advertising, auto and travel, cleaning and maintenance, utilities, and taxes, are listed in the appropriate column for each property (lines 5 through 18). Depreciation is shown separately (line 20). The income and expenses from each property are netted to produce a net income or (loss) for each property (line 22), and these figures are combined to form a total income or (loss) amount for all rent and royalty properties (line 26). Approximately 10% of all taxpayers report net income or (loss) from rents and royalties.

Schedule E, Parts II and III

Schedule E, Parts II and III, provide the structure in which individual taxpayers report their share of income or (loss) from partnerships, S corporations (small business corporations), estates, and trusts. These entities are required to file tax returns and report the allocation of income and expenses between the individual taxpayers. Roughly 5% of the taxpayers report net income or (loss) from partnerships and S corporations. Only about .5% report income or (loss) from estates and trusts.

Generally, partnerships, S corporations, estates, and trusts do not pay taxes. Instead these entities serve as a channel to the individual for the taxing of income or deducting of expenses. Partnership and S corporation ordinary income (loss) that channels to the individual taxpayer is reported on Schedule E, Part II. For example, the taxpayer's share of ordinary partnership in-

---

> ### Overview of Schedule E
>
> Schedule E is a two-page schedule with five parts:
>
> | Part | Description |
> | --- | --- |
> | I | Rent and royalty income or loss |
> | II | Income or loss from partnerships and S corporations |
> | III | Income or loss from estates and trusts |
> | IV | Income or loss from REMICs— residual holder |
> | V | Summary of Parts I through IV |

come is reported as either passive (columns g and h) or nonpassive (columns i, j, and k) on Schedule E, Part II. Ordinary income (loss) from estates and trusts is reported in a similar manner on Schedule E, Part III.

Certain special items that channel through to the individual are not reported on Schedule E. Instead, these special items are reported on other, more appropriate schedules. For example, capital gains and losses channel through to the individual's Schedule D, Capital Gains and Losses. Charitable contributions are reported on the individual's Schedule A, Itemized Deductions.

Reporting on Schedule E, Parts II and III. In reporting the amount of income or expense from partnerships, S corporations, estates, and trusts, the name and EIN of the entity is reported by the individual taxpayer. When appropriate, the code symbols "P" for partnership or "S" for S corporation are entered in Part II, Column b, to aid in identification. With this information the individual return can be traced and verified through the computer system to the entity making the original report. Foreign partnerships are identified by a check mark in Column c. Similar reporting for estates and trusts is entered on Schedule E, Part III.

Schedule E, Parts IV and V

Schedule E, Part IV is for reporting income or (loss) from REMICs—residual holders.

Schedule E, Part V (line 39) is used to report the amount of farm rental income and expenses from Form 4835, Farm Rental Income and Expenses. Farm income is reported on Schedule E by a taxpayer if two tests are met:

1. The rental income received by the taxpayer from the farm was based on crops or livestock produced by a tenant.
2. The taxpayer did not manage or operate the farm to any great extent.

Total income or (loss) from all of the parts of Schedule E must be summarized (line 40) and entered on Form 1040 (line 18).

Farmers and fisherman are requested to reconcile (line 41) their total gross income from farming and fishing reported in Parts II and III and on Schedule E (line 39).

Filled-In Schedule E

Illustration 10-1

A filled-in Schedule E, Supplemental Income Schedule, for John and Jean Williams is shown in Illustration 10-1.

The Williams received gross rents of $38,168 from an 8-unit apartment during 1992. Expenses for advertising, maintenance, insurance, interest, legal fees, repairs, taxes, depreciation, and utilities totaled $37,958. Total rental income of $210 was determined on Schedule E, Part I (line 26).

John R. Williams received notification that his 1992 share of the ordinary income reported by the partnership of Willard & Williams (a partnership in which Mr. Williams has a 20% ownership interest) on Form 1065 was $5,002. John Williams actively participates in managing the partnership and, therefore, the income is considered to be nonpassive. This amount was entered with the appropriate partnership identification on Schedule E, Part II.

Income from the Willard & Williams partnership had also been considered by Mr. Williams in other ways in his tax planning and on his tax return. At the beginning of the year, Mr. Williams had estimated his share of income from the partnership (not subject to withholding) and included the amount in determining the estimated income tax on which he would make required quarterly payments. In addition, Mr. Williams' share of partnership income is self-employment income and must be considered in the calculation of the social security self-employment tax. The total income on Schedule E (line 40), $5,212, is reported by Mr. and Mrs. Williams on their Form 1040 (line 18).

At-Risk Limits

Generally, the at-risk rules limit a taxpayer's loss to the amount the taxpayer has at risk and could actually lose from an activity.

Illustration 10-1
Filled-In Schedule E, Form 1040, Page 1

SCHEDULE E
(Form 1040)

Department of the Treasury
Internal Revenue Service

Supplemental Income and Loss

(From rental real estate, royalties, partnerships, estates, trusts, REMICs, etc.)
▶ Attach to Form 1040 or Form 1041.
▶ See Instructions for Schedule E (Form 1040).

OMB No. 1545-0074

19 92

Attachment
Sequence No. **13**

Name(s) shown on return

John R. and Jean K. Williams

Your social security number

272 : 11 : 8245

Part I   **Income or Loss From Rental Real Estate and Royalties**   Note: *Report income and expenses from the rental of personal property on Schedule C or C-EZ. Report farm rental income or loss from Form 4835 on page 2, line 39.*

1 Show the kind and location of each rental real estate property:

A   8-unit apt. bldg.
     505 West Street, Verona, WI

B

C

2 For each rental real estate property listed on line 1, did you or your family use it for personal purposes for more than the greater of 14 days or 10% of the total days rented at fair rental value during the tax year? (See page E-1.)

	Yes	No
A		X
B		
C		

Income:

		Properties			Totals
		A	B	C	(Add columns A, B, and C.)
3 Rents received	3	38,168 00			3 38,168 00
4 Royalties received	4				4

Expenses:

		A	B	C	
5 Advertising	5	250 00			
6 Auto and travel (see page E-2)	6				
7 Cleaning and maintenance	7	2,500 00			
8 Commissions	8				
9 Insurance	9	1,227 00			
10 Legal and other professional fees	10	300 00			
11 Management fees	11				
12 Mortgage interest paid to banks, etc. (see page E-2)	12	14,329 00			12 14,329 00
13 Other interest	13				
14 Repairs	14				
15 Supplies	15	3,262 00			
16 Taxes	16	4,290 00			
17 Utilities	17	1,800 00			
18 Other (list) ▶	18				
19 Add lines 5 through 18	19	27,958 00			19 27,958 00
20 Depreciation expense or depletion (see page E-2)	20	10,000 00			20 10,000 00
21 Total expenses. Add lines 19 and 20	21	37,958 00			
22 Income or (loss) from rental real estate or royalty properties. Subtract line 21 from line 3 (rents) or line 4 (royalties). If the result is a (loss), see page E-2 to find out if you must file **Form 6198**	22	210 00			
23 Deductible rental real estate loss. **Caution:** *Your rental real estate loss on line 22 may be limited. See page E-3 to find out if you must file Form 8582*	23	(	)(	)(	)

24 Income. Add positive amounts shown on line 22. **Do not** include any losses | 24 | 210 00 |

25 Losses. Add royalty losses from line 22 and rental real estate losses from line 23. Enter the total losses here | 25 | (   ) |

26 Total rental real estate and royalty income or (loss). Combine lines 24 and 25. Enter the result here. If Parts II, III, IV, and line 39 on page 2 do not apply to you, also enter this amount on Form 1040, line 18. Otherwise, include this amount in the total on line 40 on page 2 | 26 | 210 00 |

For Paperwork Reduction Act Notice, see Form 1040 instructions.   Cat. No. 11344L   **Schedule E (Form 1040) 1992**

Rental Activity

Rental activities are deemed to be passive activities regardless of the form of ownership and the amount of time the taxpayer spends on the rental activity.

A rental activity is an activity in which the taxpayer provides tangible real or personal property to customers or holds the property for use by customers. It does not matter whether the use is under a lease, a service contract, or some other arrangement. Gross income from the activity must be mainly for the use of the property.

A rental activity is considered a passive activity even if the taxpayer materially participated (defined earlier).

Exceptions. An activity is **not a rental activity** if any of the following apply:

1. The average period of customer use is 7 days or less. The average period of use is figured by dividing the total number of days for all rental periods by the number of rentals.
2. The average period of customer use is 30 days or less, as figured in 1, and the taxpayer provided significant personal services in connection with the rentals. Significant personal services are services performed by an individual other than:
   a. Services needed to permit the lawful use of the rental property
   b. Services to repair or improve property that would extend its useful life
   c. Services that are similar to those commonly provided with rentals. For example, cleaning and maintenance of common areas or routine repairs
3. The taxpayer provides extraordinary personal services in connection with customer use. Extraordinary personal services are services performed by individuals and are incidental to the use of the rental property.
4. The rental activity is incidental to the taxpayer's business activity. The rental of property is incidental to the trade or business if all of the following apply:
   a. The taxpayer owns an interest in the trade or business at all times during the year,.
   b. The rental property was used mainly in the trade or business during the current year, or during at least 2 of the 5 preceding tax years.

   c. The gross rental income from the property is less than 2% of the unadjusted basis of the property, or 2% of the FMV of the property if this amount is smaller. (The unadjusted basis of the property is its cost without reducing it by depreciation or any other basis adjustment.)

5. The taxpayer usually makes the property available during business hours for use by various customers.
6. The taxpayer provides the property to his or her partnership, S corporation, or joint venture.

If any of the six exceptions listed above are met, the rental of the property **is not a rental activity.**

Rental Real Estate Activities

Generally, taxpayers who have losses from rental real estate activities can deduct up to $25,000 of such losses from active and portfolio income. This exception to the passive loss rules allows taxpayers to use up to $25,000 of otherwise unallowable losses from rental real estate activities as a deduction against salary, interest, dividends, and other nonpassive income. The deduction is limited to $12,500 for married taxpayers filing separately and living apart at all times during the year. If they have not lived apart for the entire year, this special deduction is not available.

To qualify for this $25,000 deduction, the following requirements must be met:

1. Taxpayer must *actively participate* in the rental real estate activity.
2. Taxpayer must own at least 10% of the value of all interests in the activity throughout the entire year.

Active participation is not the same as material participation (defined earlier). Active participation is a less stringent requirement than material participation. Active participation does not require regular, continuous, and substantial involvement in operations. However, the taxpayer must participate in management decisions in a significant and bona fide sense, such as approving new tenants, deciding on rental terms, approving improvements or repairs, or arranging for others to provide services such as repairs. Only individuals and qualifying estates can actively participate in a rental estate activity. Generally, limited partners cannot actively participate.

EXAMPLE 15

Tom, a bachelor, had the following income and losses during the tax year:

Salary	$52,300
Dividends	500
Interest	1,600
Rental loss	(6,000)

The rental loss came from the rental of a house Tom owned. Tom advertised and rented the house to the current tenant himself. He also collected the rents, and either did the repairs or hired someone to do them. Even though the rental loss is a loss from a passive activity, Tom can use the entire $6,000 loss to offset his other income because he actively participated.

Phase-Out Rule

The annual deduction available for qualifying rental real estate activities is reduced by 50% of the taxpayer's modified AGI in excess of $100,000 ($50,000 for married individuals filing separately). Consequently, the entire deduction is phased out when modified AGI reaches $150,000 ($75,000 for married individuals filing separately).

Modified AGI is AGI modified so as *not* to include the following items:

1. Social security and railroad retirement payments
2. Deductible contributions to IRA and SEP
3. Any passive activity loss

EXAMPLE 16

During 1992, John was unmarried. For 1992, he had $120,000 in salary, $5,000 of partnership income from a limited partnership in which he invested on December 31, 1986, and a $31,000 loss from his rental real estate activities in which he actively participated and that he acquired on November 30, 1986. He had no social security or railroad retirement benefits, nor did he make contributions to an IRA or a SEP. When John files his 1992 return,

he may deduct only $15,000 of his passive activity loss. He must carry over the remaining $11,000 passive activity loss to 1993. John's deduction and carryover are calculated as follows:

AGI, modified as required (The passive activity loss of $26,000 ($31,000-$5,000) is not considered.)	$120,000
Less amount not subject to phase-out	100,000
Amount subject to phase-out rule	$ 20,000
Multiply by applicable percentage	x 50%
Required reduction to APRRE* offset amount	$ 10,000
Maximum offset	$ 25,000
Less required reduction (see above)	10,000
Adjusted offset amount for APRRE* activities	$ 15,000
Passive loss from rental real estate	$31,000
Less passive income	5,000
Passive activity loss	$26,000
Deduction allowable/ Adjusted offset amount	15,000
Amount that must be carried forward (suspended loss)	$ 11,000

*Active Participation Rental Real Estate

Suspended Losses

Any passive activity losses that cannot be deducted in the current tax year are carried forward to the next year. However, the taxpayer's basis in the passive activity is reduced by all allowable deductions even though the deductions are not usable on the current tax return because of the passive loss rule.

EXAMPLE 17

Sara Lee invested $15,000 in a passive activity on January 5, 1992. During the year she had a loss from this activity of $5,000. Sara doesn't have an interest in any other passive activities. As Sara has no passive income, she cannot deduct the $5,000 loss. Consequently, Sara's amount at risk and adjusted basis in the activity is $10,000 ($15,000 – $5,000). She also has a $5,000 suspended loss.

EXAMPLE 18

In 1993, Sara, in Example 17, realized a loss of $14,000 in her passive activity. This loss exceeds Sara's amount at risk ($10,000) by $4,000. Thus, under the at-risk rules, $4,000 of her loss is disallowed. The remaining $10,000 loss is also not deductible because she has no passive income that she may offset it against. As a result, Sara has a $4,000 suspended loss under the at-risk rules, $15,000 ($5,000 for 1992 + $10,000 for 1993) of suspended passive losses, and an adjusted basis of zero in her passive activity.

EXAMPLE 19

In 1994, Sara's passive activity, in Example 17, produced $3,000 of income. This income increased her amount at risk to $3,000. Thus, $3,000 of the $4,000 suspended loss can be reclassified as passive loss. The passive income of $3,000 can then be used to absorb $3,000 of the $18,000 ($15,000 + $3,000 of reclassified losses) of suspended passive losses on the 1994 tax return. At the end of 1994, Sara's situation is as follows: She has $1,000 of suspended losses under the at-risk rules, $15,000 of suspended passive losses, and an adjusted basis of zero in her passive activity.

Multiple Activities

When taxpayers have multiple activities of a passive nature, the suspended loss for each separate activity must be determined through an allocation process. The loss allocation to each activity is calculated as follows:

$$\textbf{Total disallowed loss} \times \frac{\text{Loss from separate activity}}{\text{Sum of all losses}}$$

EXAMPLE 20

Dick White reports the following income and losses from his four passive activities for the year:

Activity A	($40,000)
Activity B	30,000
Activity C	(32,000)
Activity D	(8,000)
Net Passive Loss	($50,000)

The net passive loss of $50,000 is allocated to activities A, C, and D as follows:

A: ($50,000 x $40,000/$80,000)	$25,000
C: ($50,000 x $32,000/$80,000)	20,000
D: ($50,000 x $8,000/$80,000)	5,000
Total Suspended Losses	$50,000

These suspended losses are carried forward indefinitely and treated as a deduction associated with the activity to which each relates.

Tax Credits on Passive Activities

Tax credits arising from passive activities can only be used against the regular tax attributable to passive income. This tax is calculated as follows:

Tax on **all** income (passive and nonpassive)
– Tax on **nonpassive** income
= Tax attributable to passive income

Examples of passive activity credits include: rehabilitation credit, low-income housing credit, jobs credit, and research activities credit.

If passive activities result in a net loss for the year, the taxpayer cannot utilize any passive activity credits in that year. Also, if the AMT must be paid for the year, no passive credits can be applied against the tax. Unused credits resulting from passive activities may be carried forward indefinitely. However, when an activity is disposed of in a taxable transaction, any suspended passive credits related to that activity will be lost forever if these credits exceed the tax attributable to passive income for the year.

Credits on Rental Real Estate Activities

Tax credits generated by rental real estate activities may be applied against the tax on nonpassive income to a limited extent. If income does not exceed specified limits, active, 10% rental real estate owners have available a special $25,000 passive loss deduction (described earlier). When net passive losses from real estate rental activities are less than $25,000, the balance of this allowance is available for tax credit deduction equivalents.

To determine the maximum amount of passive credits that may be applied to the tax liability, the remaining balance of the special

$25,000 allowance is multiplied by the tax-payer's marginal tax rate.

EXAMPLE 21 ─────────────

Walter Weed is an active participant in a 30% owned rental real estate activity. This activity produces a net passive loss for the year and also generates some tax credits. Walter's share of the loss and credits is $20,000 and $1,600, respectively. After Walter deducts the $20,000 loss, he has available a deduction equivalent of $5,000 (25,000 – $20,000). Walter, who is in the 28% tax bracket, may claim up to $1,400 ($5,000 x .28) of tax credits on his tax return. The remaining credits of $200 ($1,600 – $1,400) carry forward.

Dispositions of Passive Interest

Generally, any passive activity losses (**but not credits**) from an activity that have not been allowed as a deduction on a tax return are allowed in full in the tax year in which taxpayers dispose of their entire interest in the activity. However, in order for the losses to be allowed, taxpayers must dispose of their entire interest in the activity in a transaction in which all realized gain or loss is recognized. Furthermore, the person acquiring the property must not be related to the taxpayer.

Capital Losses

Taxpayers realizing a capital loss on the disposition of an interest in a passive activity will be subject to the rules governing capital gains and losses. Generally, capital losses are used to offset capital gains. If a net loss results, individuals may deduct up to $3,000 of the loss on their tax return. Any remaining loss carries forward as a capital loss.

This loss is no longer considered as a loss from a passive activity. Capital gains and losses are explained more fully in Chapter 12.

EXAMPLE 22 ─────────────

Ray, whose only other income during the year was his $60,000 salary, had a 5% interest in the B Limited Partnership, which had an adjusted basis of $42,000 at the date of sale. He had carried over $2,000 of passive activity losses from prior years and then sold his entire interest in the current tax year to an unrelated person for $50,000. Ray realized an $8,000 gain from the sale, but may offset $2,000 of that gain with his $2,000 carryover loss. Ray's $6,000 net gain is calculated as follows:

Sales price	$50,000
Minus: adjusted basis	42,000
Gain	$ 8,000
Minus: carryover losses allowable .	2,000
Net gain	$ 6,000

Ray will treat the $6,000 net gain as income from a passive activity. However, on the tax return, Ray will report an $8,000 capital gain on Schedule D. His carryover loss of $2,000 will be shown as an allowable deduction on Schedule E.

If Ray sold his interest for $30,000, instead of $50,000, his deductible loss would be $5,000, calculated as follows:

Sales price	$30,000
Minus: adjusted basis	42,000
Capital loss	$12,000
Minus: capital loss limit	3,000
Capital loss carryover	$ 9,000
Allowable capital loss on sale	$ 3,000
Carryover losses allowable	2,000
Total current deductible loss	$ 5,000

The $5,000 total current deductible loss calculated above is deductible in the current tax year. The $3,000 capital loss will be reported on Schedule D, and the carryover loss of $2,000 will be shown on Schedule E. The $9,000 capital loss carryover is not subject to the passive activity loss limit. Ray will treat it in the same manner as any other capital loss carryover.

Installment Sales

When an installment sale of an entire interest in a passive activity takes place, the general rules explained above apply. However, not all of the accumulated unused passive activity losses are allowed in the year of sale. The accumulated losses are allowed as deductions in installments over the term of the installment sale. The losses are allowed in the same ratio as the recognized gain. For example, if 30% of the total gain is recognized in the year of sale, 30% of the accumulated losses are also allowed. Thus, the full amount of accumulated losses will not be recovered until the year that the last amount of the installment gain is recognized.

Dispositions by Gift

When an interest in a passive activity is given away, the accumulated unused passive activity losses on that activity cannot be deducted in any tax year. Instead, these accumulated losses are added to the basis of the passive interest being transferred.

Dispositions by Death

When a passive activity interest is transferred by reason of the owner's death, the accumulated unused losses may be available as a deduction on the deceased taxpayer's final return. However, the suspended losses are deductible only to the extent that they exceed the step-up in basis for the property transferred. (The basis of inherited property is normally the FMV at the date of death—see Chapter 11.)

EXAMPLE 23 ────────────────────

Information relating to a decedent's passive activity at the date of her death follows:

Basis (investment) in passive interest	$20,000
FMV of passive interest	26,000
Suspended losses in passive interest	8,000

The beneficiary's basis in the inherited property is $26,000 (FMV at date of death).

The loss allowed on the decedent's final tax return is limited to $2,000 ($8,000 − $6,000 step up in basis).

Reporting Passive Activity Losses

Reporting the results of passive activities requires the use of more than one form or schedule. The actual number of forms required depends on the number and types of activities in which the taxpayer is engaged. Some of the forms that may be required are:

Schedule A (Form 1040), Itemized Deductions
Schedule C (Form 1040), Profit or Loss From Business
Schedule D (Form 1040), Capital Gains and Losses
Schedule E (Form 1040), Supplemental Income Schedule
Schedule F (Form 1040), Profit or Loss From Farming
Form 8582, Passive Activity Loss Limitations
Form 8582-CR, Passive Activity Credit Limitations

Other activities, such as those involving low-income housing, may require the use of forms not mentioned above.

Form 8582. Regardless of the number or complexity of passive activities, only one Form 8582, Passive Activity Loss Limitations, should be used by the taxpayer.

Each individual activity should be reported on the form normally required for that activity. For example, Schedule E is used to report rental activities, and Form 4797 is used to report gains and losses from the sale of business assets. Form 8582 is then prepared to determine if the passive loss rules disallow any of the losses.

Name ________________________________

Section ______________ Date ______________

C H A P T E R   1 0

Questions and Problems

1. **a.** State the amount of rent income that must be reported on Schedule E for 1992 by each of the following taxpayers:

Taxpayer	Description	Amount
A	On November 30, 1992, a tenant pays her landlord $1,000 as a security deposit, $1,000 for the December rent, and an advance payment of $5,000 for an additional five months of rent	$________
B	Rent of $350 per month was received the first of each month in 1992. In addition, $900 was paid by the tenant for property taxes: $450 in February, $450 in July	$________
C	Rent of $1,200 is received when taxpayer rents personal residence to friends for twelve days during the Mardi Gras festivities	$________

    b. State the maximum amount of depreciation and other expenses attributable to the property that can be claimed by each of the following taxpayers:

D	Based on property rented to a friend for $100 per month for the entire year, with a fair rental value of $275 per month	$________
E	Based on personal dwelling unit rented for 12 days during 1992 for a total of $300	$________

2. Derek Quinn owns a two-family home. He rents out the first floor and resides on the second floor. The following expenses attributable to the building were incurred by Quinn for the year ended December 31, 1992:

	Expenses For		
	Entire Building	**First Floor**	**Second Floor**
Depreciation	$4,000		
Real estate taxes	2,000		
Mortgage interest	1,600		
Utilities	1,200		
Repairs		$500	
Painting			$400

    a. What portion of the expenses can Quinn deduct on Schedule E of Form 1040?

    b. What portion of the expenses can Quinn take as itemized deductions on Schedule A of Form 1040?

3. Sandee Scott, a cash-method taxpayer, is the owner of a house with two identical apartments. She resides in one apartment and rents the other apartment to a tenant. The tenant made timely monthly rental payments of $500 for the months of January through November 1992. Rents for December 1992 and January 1993 were paid by the tenant on January 5, 1993. The following additional information for 1992 was available:

Fuel and utilities	$3,600
Depreciation of building	3,000
Maintenance and repairs (rental apartment)	400
Insurance on building	600

What amount should Scott report as net rental income for 1992?

4. Henry Schuller owns a fishing cabin in Wisconsin. He offers the cottage for rent from June 1 through September 30. However, his family uses the cabin for 14 days in the month of August. Henry was unable to rent the cabin for 2 weeks (14 days) during the remaining rental period. At all other times, the cabin was rented.

The family that rented the cabin the last week in June was unable to use it over a weekend. There was no refund or reduction in the rent, and Henry used the cabin for these two days.

   a. Will Henry's cabin be treated as a home? Explain.

   b. What tax advantage is available if the cabin is not treated as a home?

   c. What disadvantage does Henry face if the cabin is considered a home?

   d. For division of expense purposes, how many days of rental use and personal use does Henry have?

5. During the year, Barry Barone rents his vacation home for three months and spends two months there. Gross rental income from the property was $6,000. Barry incurred the following expenses for the year:

Mortgage interest	$3,000
Real estate taxes	1,500
Utilities	800
Maintenance	400
Depreciation	4,000

Calculate Barry's net rent for the vacation home.

6. On which tax form or schedule would each of the following be reported:

   a. Royalty paid to author based on units sold, ________________________________.

   b. Payment made to author who is self-employed, ________________________________.

   c. Gain on sale of copyright by the author, ________________________________.

   d. Payment received by person holding an operating interest in an oil property, ________.

   e. Gain on the sale of a complete interest in an oil property, ________________________.

7. Janis R. Jetson, a cash-method taxpayer, SSN 344-46-5768, purchased a two-unit apartment building at 1626 Flat Street, Detroit, Michigan 48270-8224, on January 2, 1983. The land cost was $15,000, and the building cost was $52,500. The building has an estimated life of 35 years with normal maintenance, after which it is estimated that the cost to raze the building would be about equal to the salvage value. Both apartments are the same size, with one on the ground floor and the other upstairs. Ms. Jetson has lived in the upstairs apartment since she acquired the building. The tenant in the ground floor apartment at the time the building was purchased has continued to rent from Ms. Jetson. The tenant was paying $350 per month in rent on January 1, 1992. In March, Ms. Jetson served notice that effective July 1 the rent would be increased to $375 per month. On June 30 the tenant moved. The apartment was vacant until September 1, although Ms. Jetson advertised and attempted to rent it. On September 1, a new tenant moved in, paying rent of $365 per month, with one month's rent in advance. Rent is due on the 1st day of the month. Ms. Jetson is not subject to passive activity loss limitations. Information on the apartment is as follows:

Revenue:

Rent from the first tenant (6 months @ $350)	$2,100
Rent from the second tenant (5 months, including 1 month advance @ $365)	1,825
Total revenue	$3,925

Expenses:

Total house:

Real estate taxes	$1,700
Janitor and yard work	160
Lights and water	440
Repairs	1,000
Heat	800
Interest on 1st Federal Savings & Loan mortgage	1,100
Insurance	376
Depreciation*	1,500
	$7,076

Ground apartment:

Advertising	$ 100
Painting and papering	420
Repairs	70
Ms. Jetson's personal labor @ $5.00 per hour	660
	$1,250

Upstairs apartment:

Repairs	$ 90
Cleaning assistance	480
	$ 570

* Depreciation is reported on a straight-line basis over 35 years.

Ms. Jetson also received taxable income of $600 from nonpassive activities reported to her from her father's trust, the Jack J. Jetson Trust, EIN 25-1020862. Ms. Jetson's share of the partnership income reported on Schedule K-1 from the Marsh-Jetson Company, EIN 39-6043961, was $8,200. Ms. Jetson was an active participant in the Marsh-Jetson Company, and her entire investment is considered "at risk."

Prepare the Schedule E, Supplemental Income and Loss, reproduced on the following pages to support the income tax return, Form 1040, that would be filed by Ms. Jetson.

SCHEDULE E
(Form 1040)

Department of the Treasury
Internal Revenue Service

Supplemental Income and Loss

(From rental real estate, royalties, partnerships, estates, trusts, REMICs, etc.)

▶ Attach to Form 1040 or Form 1041.
▶ See Instructions for Schedule E (Form 1040).

OMB No. 1545-0074

1992

Attachment
Sequence No. **13**

Name(s) shown on return

Your social security number

Part I **Income or Loss From Rental Real Estate and Royalties** Note: *Report income and expenses from the rental of personal property on **Schedule C** or **C-EZ**. Report farm rental income or loss from **Form 4835** on page 2, line 39.*

1 Show the kind and location of each **rental real estate property**:

A ....

B ....

C ....

2 For each rental real estate property listed on line 1, did you or your family use it for personal purposes for more than the greater of 14 days or 10% of the total days rented at fair rental value during the tax year? (See page E-1.)

	Yes	No
A		
B		
C		

Income:

		Properties A	B	C	Totals (Add columns A, B, and C.)
3	Rents received	3			3
4	Royalties received	4			4

Expenses:

			A	B	C	
5	Advertising	5				
6	Auto and travel (see page E-2)	6				
7	Cleaning and maintenance	7				
8	Commissions	8				
9	Insurance	9				
10	Legal and other professional fees	10				
11	Management fees	11				
12	Mortgage interest paid to banks, etc. (see page E-2)	12				12
13	Other interest	13				
14	Repairs	14				
15	Supplies	15				
16	Taxes	16				
17	Utilities	17				
18	Other (list) ▶	18				
19	Add lines 5 through 18	19				19
20	Depreciation expense or depletion (see page E-2)	20				20
21	Total expenses. Add lines 19 and 20	21				
22	Income or (loss) from rental real estate or royalty properties. Subtract line 21 from line 3 (rents) or line 4 (royalties). If the result is a (loss), see page E-2 to find out if you must file **Form 6198**	22				
23	Deductible rental real estate loss. **Caution:** *Your rental real estate loss on line 22 may be limited. See page E-3 to find out if you must file **Form 8582***	23 (	)(	)(	)	

24 **Income.** Add positive amounts shown on line 22. **Do not** include any losses . . . . | 24 |

25 **Losses.** Add royalty losses from line 22 and rental real estate losses from line 23. Enter the total losses here . . . . | 25 (|) |

26 Total rental real estate and royalty income or (loss). Combine lines 24 and 25. Enter the result here. If Parts II, III, IV, and line 39 on page 2 do not apply to you, also enter this amount on Form 1040, line 18. Otherwise, include this amount in the total on line 40 on page 2 . . . . | 26 |

For Paperwork Reduction Act Notice, see Form 1040 instructions.   Cat. No. 11344L   **Schedule E (Form 1040) 1992**

Schedule E (Form 1040) 1992   Attachment Sequence No **13**   Page **2**

Name(s) shown on return. Do not enter name and social security number if shown on other side.

Your social security number

Note: *If you report amounts from farming or fishing on Schedule E, you must enter your gross income from those activities on line 41 below.*

Part II   Income or Loss From Partnerships and S Corporations

If you report a loss from an at-risk activity, you MUST check either column **(e)** or **(f)** of line 27 to describe your investment in the activity. See page E-3. If you check column **(f)**, you must attach **Form 6198.**

27	(a) Name	(b) Enter P for partnership; S for S corporation	(c) Check if foreign partnership	(d) Employer identification number	Investment At Risk? (e) All is at risk	(f) Some is not at risk
A						
B						
C						
D						
E						

	Passive Income and Loss		Nonpassive Income and Loss		
	(g) Passive loss allowed (attach **Form 8582** if required)	(h) Passive income from **Schedule K-1**	(i) Nonpassive loss from **Schedule K-1**	(j) Section 179 expense deduction from **Form 4562**	(k) Nonpassive income from **Schedule K-1**
A					
B					
C					
D					
E					
28a Totals					
b Totals					

29	Add columns (h) and (k) of line 28a	29	
30	Add columns (g), (i), and (j) of line 28b	30 (	)
31	Total partnership and S corporation income or (loss). Combine lines 29 and 30. Enter the result here and include in the total on line 40 below	31	

Part III   Income or Loss From Estates and Trusts

32	(a) Name	(b) Employer identification number
A		
B		
C		

	Passive Income and Loss		Nonpassive Income and Loss	
	(c) Passive deduction or loss allowed (attach **Form 8582** if required)	(d) Passive income from **Schedule K-1**	(e) Deduction or loss from **Schedule K-1**	(f) Other income from **Schedule K-1**
A				
B				
C				
33a Totals				
b Totals				

34	Add columns (d) and (f) of line 33a	34	
35	Add columns (c) and (e) of line 33b	35 (	)
36	Total estate and trust income or (loss). Combine lines 34 and 35. Enter the result here and include in the total on line 40 below	36	

Part IV   Income or Loss From Real Estate Mortgage Investment Conduits (REMICs)—Residual Holder

37	(a) Name	(b) Employer identification number	(c) Excess inclusion from Schedules Q, line 2c (see page E-4)	(d) Taxable income (net loss) from Schedules Q, line 1b	(e) Income from Schedules Q, line 3b

38	Combine columns (d) and (e) only. Enter the result here and include in the total on line 40 below	38	

Part V   Summary

39	Net farm rental income or (loss) from **Form 4835.** Also, complete line 41 below	39	
40	TOTAL income or (loss). Combine lines 26, 31, 36, 38, and 39. Enter the result here and on Form 1040, line 18 . . . . ▶	40	
41	**Reconciliation of Farming and Fishing Income:** Enter your gross farming and fishing income reported in Parts II and III and on line 39 (see page E-4) 41		

8. **a.** What is the significance of "at risk" rules?

   b. What activities are subject to "at risk" loss limitations?

9. **a.** What types of trade or business activity are considered to be passive activities?

   b. Distinguish between material participation and active participation in rental activities and explain why the difference is significant.

   c. Historically, dividends and interest income have been treated as passive income. How are these categories of income treated in relation to the passive loss limitations of the 1986 Tax Reform Act?

10. Assume that a taxpayer owned the following passive activities during 1992 with operating results as indicated below:

Passive Activity	Gross Income	Deductions	Net Income or (Loss)
A	$12,000	$ 8,000	$ 4,000
B	20,000	30,000	(10,000)
C	3,000	5,000	(2,000)
D	14,000	12,000	2,000

Calculate (a) the amount of passive loss that can offset passive income in 1992 and (b) the amount of passive loss that can be carried forward for each activity.

11. Mark and Martha Matthews have $130,000 of AGI before considering a $22,000 loss from their rental real estate activities in which they actively participate. What amount of loss can Mark and Martha deduct on their joint return?

12. Bobby Southworth is active in three different rental real estate activities. Bobby's income and losses from these activities are as follows:

Activity	Income or (loss)
X	$(10,000)
Y	(20,000)
Z	9,000

Bobby also had a $2,400 tax credit for property X. Bobby is in the 28% tax bracket and has AGI of $80,000 before consideration of the rental real estate activities. Calculate his deductions and credits allowed and any suspended losses and credits.

a. Deduction allowed _________________________

b. Credit allowed ___________________________

c. Suspended loss __________________________

d. Suspended credit ________________________

13. Bob Jefferson has investments in three passive activities. As of January 1, 1992, the suspended losses on these activities are:

Partnership	Suspended Losses
X	$(20,000)
Y	(30,000)
Z	0

In 1992 Bob sold his interest in Y at a loss of $8,000. In addition, his passive activities generated the following income and losses during the year:

Partnership	Income or (loss)
X	$ 10,000
Y	(10,000)
Z	20,000

How will Bob report the results of his activities for 1992?

14. Sue Brew sold a passive activity in 1992 for $200,000. Her adjusted basis was $100,000. Sue chose to report her gain on the sale under the installment method. Suspended losses on this activity totaled $20,000. Sue received $80,000 in 1992.

a. How much gain is recognized in 1992?

b. How much of the suspended losses are deductible in 1992?

15. Fred Elias gave his sister, Elvira, a passive activity property having an adjusted basis of $50,000. At the date of the gift, the property has a FMV of $80,000. There is also $5,000 of suspended losses on the property.

   a. What loss can Fred deduct when he transfers the property to his sister?

   b. What is Elvira's basis (investment) in the property she received from Fred?

16. Terry Taxpayer died during the current year while owning an interest in a passive activity. Information relating to Terry's interest in this activity at the date of his death follows:

Basis (investment) in passive activity	$50,000
FMV of passive activity	60,000
Suspended losses in passive activity	8,000

   a. How much passive activity loss can be deducted on Terry's final tax return?

   b. What is the beneficiary's basis (investment) in the inherited passive activity?

Property Transactions: Recognizing Gains and Losses

When property is sold, exchanged, or otherwise disposed of, a gain or loss usually results. This property may be a personal asset such as a personal residence. It may be stocks, bonds, or other investment property; or it may be an asset used in a trade or business. The gain may or may not be taxable, and the loss may or may not be deductible.

Chapter 11 will examine the calculation of gains and losses from property dispositions. Gain or loss is measured as the difference between the value of the property received and the *basis* of the property given up. Establishing the basis of property is also explained in the chapter.

Once the gain or loss has been calculated, the amount of gain or loss to be recognized on the tax return must be determined. This chapter will identify those gains and losses that are to be recognized. The treatment of the unrecognized gains and losses will also be described. Chapter 12 will address the tax treatment of the recognized gains and losses.

The time and manner in which a person chooses to dispose of an asset may determine the amount that must be paid in taxes. Chapters 11 and 12 will examine various property transactions and describe the tax consequences of each. These chapters warrant special attention since the gains and losses generated by sales and exchanges of property are frequently quite large compared to the other items that enter into the calculation of taxable income. The information in these two chapters will help the taxpayer to minimize or defer any tax burden that may be imposed.

Determination of Gain or Loss

The first step in determining the tax treatment of a property disposition is to calculate the gain or loss on the transaction. This will involve measuring the value of the property received and establishing a value for the property given up.

Realized Gain or Loss

Gain or loss from the sale, exchange, or other disposition of property is measured by comparing the amount realized from the transaction with the adjusted basis of the property given up. A *realized gain* results when the amount realized exceeds the adjusted basis of the property. When the adjusted basis of the property is greater than the amount realized, the difference is a *realized loss*.

Amount Realized

The amount realized from the disposition of property includes the total of all money received plus the FMV of all property and services received. Selling expenses are subtracted from this total to arrive at the amount realized.

Fair Market Value (FMV). The FMV of property and services received is the price at which the property would change hands between a buyer and a seller, neither being required to buy or sell, and both have reasonable knowledge of all necessary facts.

Indebtedness. If the seller has any indebtedness that is paid off or assumed by the buyer, the amount of such indebtedness must be included in the amount realized.

EXAMPLE 1 ————————————

Martha sells stock which she had pledged for a bank loan of $6,000. Her basis in the stock is $4,000. The buyer pays off Martha's bank loan and pays her $18,000 in cash. The amount realized is $24,000 ($18,000 + $6,000). Martha's realized gain is $20,000 ($24,000 − $4,000).

EXAMPLE 2 ————————————

Robert trades ABC Company stock with an adjusted basis of $8,000 for XYZ Company stock with a FMV of $12,000. Robert also receives a note for $5,000 that has a discount value of $4,000. Robert has a realized gain of $8,000 ($12,000 + $4,000 − $8,000).

Adjusted Basis

The adjusted basis of property is the original cost, or other original basis of the property, increased by capital additions and decreased by capital recoveries.

Capital additions include the cost of improvements that add to the value of the property, lengthen its life, or convert the property to a different use. These costs must be added to the basis of the property. Expenditures incurred to effect the transfer of title, such as purchase commissions, legal fees, and delinquent property taxes, are also added to the basis of the property.

Capital recoveries represent a return of capital. Capital is recovered through events such as depreciation, casualties and thefts, and the granting of an easement. Capital recoveries must be subtracted from the adjusted basis of the property.

Basis summary:

> Cost (or other basis) at acquisition
> + Capital additions
> – Capital recoveries
> = Adjusted basis

A more detailed description of basis is presented later in *Basis of Property*.

Recognized Gain or Loss

Once the realized gain or loss has been calculated, the next step is to determine whether the gain or loss will be recognized on the tax return. As a general rule, most gains will be recognized and included in the taxpayer's gross income. Losses, on the other hand, are only deductible in certain situations.

Losses on the *sale, exchange,* or *condemnation* of personal assets are not recognized for tax purposes. A loss on the sale of a personal residence or an automobile is not deductible on the tax return. However, a *casualty* or *theft* loss on a personal asset is deductible as an itemized deduction within specified limits (see Chapter 5).

Losses on the disposition of business or income producing property are generally recognized on the tax return. Exceptions include nontaxable exchanges, involuntary conversions, and loss transactions between related parties.

Recognized gains and losses are covered in more detail later in *Recognition of Gains and Losses*.

Tax Treatment of Recognized Gains and Losses

If a gain or loss is to be recognized on the tax return, it may be treated as either a capital gain or loss or an ordinary gain or loss, depending on the circumstances. In some situations, part of the gain or loss may be capital gain or loss and part may be ordinary gain or loss. The tax treatment of recognized gains and losses is examined in Chapter 12.

Basis of Property

Basis is a way of measuring the taxpayer's investment in property for tax purposes. The basis of property is used to figure the deductions for depreciation, amortization, depletion, and casualty losses. Basis is also used to figure gain or loss on the sale or other disposition of property. Taxpayers should keep accurate records of all items that affect the basis of their property.

This segment of the chapter is divided into three sections: *Cost Basis, Adjusted Basis,* and *Other Basis.*

The basis of property is usually its cost. This cost may include items, such as sales tax, certain real estate taxes, and settlement fees.

The original basis in property (whether cost or other) must be increased or decreased for certain events. Improvements to the property will increase its basis. Deductions for depreciation or casualty losses will reduce basis.

Basis in some assets cannot be determined by cost. This includes property received as a gift or inheritance. It also applies to property received in an involuntary conversion and certain other circumstances.

Cost Basis

The basis of property acquired by purchase is usually its cost. Cost is the amount of cash paid and the FMV of other property or services given up in the transaction. Cost also includes amounts paid for:

1. The sales tax charged on the purchase
2. Freight charges to obtain the property
3. Installation and testing charges

In addition, the cost basis of real estate and business assets will include other items.

Unstated Interest. When property is purchased on any time-payment plan that charges little or no interest, the basis of the property is the stated purchase price, less the amount considered to be unstated interest.

Real Property

Certain fees and expenses paid to acquire real property are part of the basis in the property.

Assumption of a Mortgage. If the taxpayer becomes liable for an existing mortgage on the property being purchased, basis is the amount paid for the property in cash plus the unpaid mortgage assumed.

Real Estate Taxes. If the buyer of real property agrees to pay taxes that were owed by the seller, the taxes paid by the buyer are treated as part of the cost of the property. Such taxes may not be deducted on the tax return as taxes paid. On the other hand, if the seller pays taxes on behalf of the buyer, any reimbursement provided by the buyer to the seller, is usually deductible as a tax paid. This type of reimbursement should not be included as a cost of the property.

Settlement Fees or Closing Costs Included in the Basis of Property

- Abstract fees
- Charges for installing utility services
- Legal and recording fees
- Surveys
- Transfer taxes
- Title insurance
- Any amounts owed by the seller that the buyer agrees to pay, such as back taxes or interest, recording or mortgage fees, charges for improvements or repairs, and sales commissions

The taxpayer must reasonably allocate these fees or costs between land and improvements to figure the basis for depreciation of the improvements. Settlement fees do not include amounts placed in escrow for the future payment of items such as taxes and insurance.

Adjusted Basis

Certain adjustments (increases and decreases) must be made to the basis of the property. The result of these adjustments to the basis is the adjusted basis.

Increases to Basis

The basis of any property is increased by all items that are properly added to a capital account. This includes the cost of any improvements having a useful life of more than one year and amounts spent after a casualty to restore the damaged property. Other items added to the basis of property include the cost of extending utility service lines to the property, and legal fees, such as the cost of defending and perfecting title.

Improvements. The cost of improvements that add to the value of property, lengthen its life, or adapt it to a different use is added to the basis in the property. For example, building a recreation room in an unfinished basement, adding another bathroom or bedroom, erecting a fence, putting in new plumbing or wiring, installing a new roof, or paving the driveway are improvements and their costs are added to the basis in the home.

Special Assessments. Special assessments for local improvements, which tend to increase the value of the property, must be added to the basis of the property and not deducted as taxes. For example, if the city puts in a paved sidewalk along the street in front of the home and assesses the affected landowners for the cost of the sidewalk, the assessment must be added to the basis of the property. However, assessments for maintenance or repair or meeting interest charges on the improvements are deductible as taxes.

Decreases to Basis

A property's basis must be decreased by any items that represent a return of capital.

Casualties and Thefts. Taxpayers suffering casualty or theft losses must decrease the basis of their property by the amount of any insurance or other reimbursement received to cover the loss. Any loss deducted on the taxpayer's return must also be subtracted from the basis of the property. Amounts expended to restore damaged property are added to the property's basis.

Easements. The amount received for granting an easement is usually considered to be from the sale of an interest in real property. It reduces the basis of the affected part of the property. If the amount received is more than the basis of the part of the property affected by the easement, basis is reduced to zero, and the excess is a recognized gain.

Section 179 Election. Taxpayer's electing to take the Section 179 deduction for any part of the cost of property, must decrease the basis of the property by the amount of the Section 179 deduction (Chapter 9).

Depreciation. At a minimum, the basis of a taxpayer's property must be reduced by the amount of depreciation *allowable*. Allowable depreciation is the amount of depreciation that the taxpayer is entitled to take under the method of depreciation selected. Thus, if a taxpayer fails to take depreciation on a business asset, the basis of the asset must nevertheless be reduced by the depreciation allowable.

If the taxpayer deducts more depreciation than was allowable, the excess depreciation deduction also reduces the property's basis to the extent that the excess deduction resulted in a decrease in the tax liability for any year.

Adjusted Basis Example

EXAMPLE 3 ───────────────────────

Liz Cameron owned a duplex used as rental property that cost her $42,000. The $42,000 cost was allocated as $36,000 for the building and $6,000 for the land. Liz added an improvement to the duplex that cost $10,000. On September 1, 1991, the duplex was damaged by fire. Up to that time, Liz had been allowed depreciation of $22,000. She sold the salvage for $1,500 and collected $19,500 from her insurance company. She deducted a casualty loss of $3,000 on her 1991 income tax return. Liz spent $29,000 for restoration of the duplex, which was completed in 1992. The adjusted basis of the duplex, after the restoration, is figured as follows:

Original cost of duplex		$36,000
Addition to duplex		10,000
Total cost of duplex		$46,000
Minus: Depreciation		22,000
Adjusted basis before casualty . . .		$24,000
Minus: Casualty loss . . .	$ 3,000	
Insurance proceeds	19,500	
Salvage proceeds .	1,500	24,000

Adjusted basis after casualty	$	–0–
Add: Cost of restoring duplex		29,000
Adjusted basis after restoration . . .		$29,000

Her basis in the land is its original cost of $6,000.

Other Basis

While the basis of purchased property is usually its cost, there are many situations when cost cannot be used as a basis. In these cases, the FMV or the adjusted basis of certain property may be important. The following paragraphs will examine the basis of properties obtained through various methods of acquisition.

Property Received for Services

When property is received for services rendered the property's FMV is income. The amount included in income becomes the basis of the property.

If the property is subject to certain restrictions, basis in the property is its FMV when it can be transferred or when it is not subject to a substantial risk of forfeiture.

Bargain Purchases

A bargain purchase takes place when employees or shareholders purchase goods or other property at less than FMV from the company. They must include the difference between the FMV and the purchase price of the property in their income. However, if this difference represents a qualified employee discount, the taxpayer does not include the difference in income. The basis in the property is its FMV, that is, the purchase price plus the amount (if any) included in income.

Inherited Property

The basis of inherited property is usually its FMV at the date of the decedent's death. FMV six months after death is an alternative if this produces a lower value for the gross estate *and* a lower estate tax liability. If the alternative value is chosen and property is disposed of before the six-month period has expired, that property shall be valued at the FMV at the date of disposition. The basis of inherited property may also be figured under the special farm or closely held business real property valuation method, if chosen for estate tax purposes.

Property Received as a Gift

To determine the basis of property received as a gift, the taxpayer (donee) must have available the following information:

1. The donor's adjusted basis in the property
2. The FMV of the property at the time it was given
3. The amount of gift tax paid on the property by the donor

Property received by gift carries a dual basis. Consequently, the basis used to calculate a gain may not be the same basis used to calculate a loss.

Gain Basis. If the taxpayer disposes of gift property in a transaction that produces a gain, the gain is measured from the *gain basis*. The gain basis is the donor's adjusted basis, plus a possible adjustment for gift tax. This basis figure is also used for depreciation, depletion, and amortization.

On gifts received before 1977, the total gift tax paid by the donor is added to the donor's adjusted basis, but this tax adjustment cannot raise the basis of the property above its FMV at the date of the gift. Thus, if FMV is less than the donor's adjusted basis, no gift tax can be added.

EXAMPLE 4

Frank was given a house in 1976. At that time, it had a FMV of $21,000, and the donor's adjusted basis was $20,000. The donor paid a gift tax of $500. His basis for gain or loss and for depreciation is $20,500, the donor's adjusted basis plus the gift tax paid.

EXAMPLE 5

If, in Example 4, the gift tax paid had been $1,500, Frank's basis would be $21,000. This is the donor's adjusted basis plus the gift tax paid, but it is limited to the FMV of the house at the time he received the gift.

On gifts received after 1976, the basis of the property is increased only by the gift tax attributable to the net appreciation in the value of the gift property. However, the donor's basis cannot be raised above the FMV of the property at the date of the gift.

The tax attributable to the net appreciation is calculated by multiplying the gift tax paid on the gift by a fraction. The numerator of the fraction is the net appreciation in the value of the gift, and the denominator is the FMV of the gift. The net appreciation in the value of the gift is the FMV of the gift minus the donor's adjusted basis.

Summary of the formula:

Donor's adjusted basis
+ (Appreciation/FMV of gift x gift tax)
= Donee's Gain Basis

EXAMPLE 6

In 1991 Susan received a gift of property from her father. At that time the property had a FMV of $50,000, and his adjusted basis was $20,000. He paid a gift tax of $9,000 on the property. For figuring depreciation, depletion, amortization, and gain or loss, Susan's basis is $25,400, figured as follows:

FMV	$50,000
Minus: Adjusted basis	20,000
Net appreciation in value	$30,000
Gift tax paid	$ 9,000
Multiplied by ($30,000/$50,000)	.60
Gift tax due to net appreciation in value	$ 5,400
Adjusted basis of property to father	20,000
Susan's basis in the property	$25,400

Loss Basis. If the taxpayer disposes of gift property in a transaction that produces a loss, the loss is measured from the *loss basis*. The loss basis is the lower of:

1. The donor's adjusted basis plus a possible adjustment for gift tax (see *Gain Basis*), or
2. The FMV of the property at the date of the gift.

EXAMPLE 7

In 1985, Mike received a gift of property from his mother. At that time the property had a FMV of $50,000, and her adjusted basis was $60,000. She paid a gift tax of $9,000 on the property. The basis that would be used to calculate a loss is $50,000. The basis that would be used for gain, depreciation, depletion, and amortization is $60,000. No gift tax can be added.

In certain situations neither a gain nor a loss can be calculated on the sale of property received by gift. In such a situation, the selling price is less than the gain basis and more than the loss basis.

EXAMPLE 8

Carlos received 100 shares of XYZ stock in 1988 as a gift from his father. The stock cost his father $12,000. At the date of the gift, the market value of the stock was $8,000, and no gift tax was paid.

If Carlos sells the stock for $14,000, his gain is $2,000 ($14,000 – $12,000). If Carlos sells the stock for $5,000, the loss is $3,000 ($8,000 – $5,000). Finally, if Carlos sells the stock for $10,000, there is no gain or loss on the transaction since the selling price is less than the gain basis ($12,000) and more than the loss basis ($8,000).

Property Transferred From a Spouse

The basis of property transferred to a taxpayer by a spouse, or by a former spouse if the transfer is incident to divorce, is the same as the transferor's adjusted basis of the property. This also applies to property transferred in trust for the taxpayer's benefit. Generally, no gain or loss is recognized by the spouse (transferor) when a transfer is made. However, the basis is adjusted for any gain recognized by the transferor on a transfer of property in trust in which the sum of the liabilities assumed, plus the liabilities to which the property is subject, is more than the adjusted basis of the property transferred.

If the property transferred is a Series E or EE United States savings bond, the transferor must include in income the interest accrued to the date of transfer. The transferee's basis in the bond immediately after the transfer is equal to the transferor's adjusted basis in the bond increased by the interest income includable in the transferor's income.

The transferor must supply the transferee with records necessary to determine the adjusted basis of the property as of the date of the transfer.

Property Changed to Business or Rental Use

If property held for personal use is changed to business use or rental use, such as the renting out of a former personal residence, the basis for depreciation must be determined.

The *basis for depreciation* equals the lesser of:

1. The FMV of the property on the date of the change
2. Its adjusted basis on the date of the change

EXAMPLE 9

Several years ago Sam built his home for $40,000 on a lot that cost him $4,000. Before changing the property to rental use last year, he added $8,000 of permanent improvements to the house and claimed a $1,000 deduction for a casualty loss to the house. Because land is not depreciable, he can only include the cost of the house when figuring the basis for depreciation.

Sam's adjusted basis in the house at the time of the change in use is $47,000 ($40,000 + $8,000 – $1,000). On the date of the change in use, his property has a FMV of $48,000, of which $6,000 is for the land and $42,000 is for the house. The basis for depreciation on the house is the FMV at the date of the change ($42,000) because it is less than his adjusted basis ($47,000).

Subsequent Disposition. If the converted property is later sold or disposed of, the basis of the property will depend on whether it is sold at a gain or a loss.

The *gain basis* is the adjusted basis when the property is sold—that is the original cost or other basis, plus capital improvements or additions, less depreciation deduction.

The *loss basis* is figured using the smaller of the adjusted basis at the time of sale or the FMV of the property at the date of conversion after certain adjustments. The FMV at conversion is increased by the cost of improvements and additions made after the conversion, and reduced by depreciation and casualty loss deductions claimed after the change in use.

EXAMPLE 10 ————————————————————

Emily sold her house, which she had changed to rental property after using it as her home. She originally bought the house for $35,000. When she changed it to rental use, it had a FMV of $33,000. During the rental period, Emily claimed $3,000 depreciation, figured under the straight-line method. Her adjusted basis at the time of the sale for figuring gain, is $32,000 ($35,000 – $3,000). Her loss basis is $30,000 ($33,000 – $3,000). If the sales price is between $30,000 and $32,000, there is neither a gain nor a loss on the sale.

Stocks and Bonds

The cost basis of stocks or bonds is the purchase price plus the costs of purchase such as commissions and recording or transfer fees. If stocks or bonds are acquired other than by purchase, the basis is usually determined by the FMV or the donor's adjusted basis, as previously discussed.

The basis of the stocks or bonds must be adjusted for certain events that occur after purchase. For example, if additional stock is received from nontaxable stock dividends or stock splits, the basis of the original stock must be allocated to all of the shares held. Basis also must be reduced if nontaxable distributions are received since these are a return of capital. In certain situations, stock dividends are taxable. If such is the case, the basis of the stock received is its FMV, and the basis of the original shares remains the same.

EXAMPLE 11 ————————————————————

In 1987, Sarah bought 100 shares of XYZ stock for $1,000, or $10 a share. In 1988, she bought 50 shares of XYZ stock for $800, or $16 a share. In 1991, XYZ declared a 2-for-1 stock split. Sarah now has 200 shares of stock with a basis of $5 ($1,000 / 200) a share and 100 shares with a basis of $8 ($800 / 100) a share.

Identifying shares. If securities are bought and sold at different times in varying quantities and are not adequately identified, the basis of the securities sold is determined under the first-in first-out method. If the shares can be properly identified, the basis of the securities sold will be the actual basis of the securities given up. An adequate identification can be made if certificates for securities that were purchased on a certain date or for a specific price are delivered to the broker or agent.

If the broker or agent holds the security certificates, an adequate identification is made if the seller:

1. Notifies the broker of the particular security to be sold or transferred at the time of the sale or transfer
2. Receives a written confirmation of the identification from the broker or agent within a reasonable time

Other Acquisitions

The basis of property acquired in certain transactions is more appropriatedly described in the following section of the chapter—*Recognition of Gains and Losses*. These acquisitions include properties obtained as a result of:

- Involuntary conversions
- Nontaxable exchanges
- Taxable exchanges
- Sale and purchase of a residence
- Wash sales

Recognition of Gains and Losses

When taxpayers dispose of property items, they are required to determine if they have a gain or loss that should be reported on their tax return. In a preceding section, *Determination of Gain or Loss*, emphasis was placed on the calculation of a taxpayer's actual gain or loss experienced as a result of a property disposition. Once this realized gain or loss has been calculated, the amount of the gain or loss to be included on the tax return must be determined. Not all gains and losses will be included on the return. This section of the chapter will focus on the identification of those gains and losses that are to be recognized for tax purposes. It will also describe the treatment of those gains and losses that are not recognized. Chapter 12 will deal with the tax treatment of recognized gains and losses.

Gains

Generally, if a taxpayer disposes of an asset and realizes a gain, the gain is taxed. In certain transactions the gain is not currently recognized, but it is postponed and recognized in some manner in a future tax year. In some situations the gain is never recognized. These transactions are described below.

Losses

Losses on the sale, exchange, or condemnation of personal assets are not recognized. Neither are they postponed. The only losses associated with personal assets that are deductible on the tax return are those resulting from casualty or theft (see Chapter 5).

Losses on the sale or condemnation of business or income-producing property are generally deductible. However, if such property is sold to a related party, the loss is not recognized. A loss resulting from an exchange of business property is frequently postponed. These and other exceptions are described below.

Postponements

In certain transactions, some or all of the gain or loss may be postponed. Postponement is accomplished by modifying the basis of the replacement property. Thus, postponement is possible only if replacement property is acquired.

When postponement is appropriate, the basis of the replacement property is determined by using the following guidelines:

Postponed gains. *Decrease* the basis (FMV) of the replacement property by the amount of the unrecognized gain.

Postponed losses. *Increase* the basis (FMV) of the replacement property by the amount of the unrecognized loss.

The remainder of the chapter examines those transactions which carry special problems regarding the recognition of gains and losses.

Involuntary Conversions

An involuntary conversion results from occurrences such as casualty or condemnation. These events cause destruction of property (partial or complete), loss of property, or the sale or exchange of property under the threat or imminence of condemnation. While the taxpayer may suffer a loss on an involuntary conversion, gain is also a possibility. As a result of receiving insurance and other reimbursement proceeds or sales proceeds from the property or salvage, the taxpayer frequently experiences a realized gain.

Losses

The tax treatment of casualty and theft losses depends on whether the property converted is a personal asset or is an asset used in a business or income-producing activity.

Personal Assets. Condemnation losses on personal assets are not deductible, nor are they postponable. Casualty and theft losses, however, are deductible within limits. These losses are recognized only to the extent that they exceed $100 for each casualty or theft event. In addition, the deduction on the tax return for casualty and theft losses is further limited to the excess of all such losses for the year over 10% of AGI. Casualty and theft losses are deductible on Schedule A (line 17). See Chapter 5 for a more complete description of casualty and theft losses.

Business or Income-Producing Assets. Casualty, theft and condemnation losses on business or income-producing property are generally deductible on the tax return. If the property is completely destroyed, the deductible loss is the adjusted basis of the property, minus any salvage value and any insurance or other reimbursement received or expected to be received. If the property is only partially destroyed, the deductible loss is the decrease in FMV of the property or the adjusted basis of the property, whichever is less. This amount must be reduced by any insurance or other reimbursement received or expected to be received.

The loss on each individual, identifiable property that is damaged or destroyed must be figured separately.

Gains

A gain realized on an involuntary conversion may be totally recognized, partially recognized, or totally postponed. Postponement of the realized gain is allowed to the extent the taxpayer reinvests the amount realized in appropriate replacement property. However, the taxpayer may elect to have the entire gain taxed. A realized gain will be recognized to the extent the amount reinvested in replacement property is *less than* the amount realized. The unrecognized gain is postponed. If the amount reinvested in replacement property equals or exceeds the amount realized, no gain is recognized. The entire gain is postponed. If the taxpayer does not acquire replacement property, the entire gain is taxed.

Replacement Period

Taxpayers electing to postpone the gain on an involuntary conversion must replace the converted property within a specified period.

Casualty or Theft. The replacement period for a casualty or theft begins on the date the property was damaged, destroyed, or stolen. The replacement period ends two years after the *close* of the first tax year in which any part of the gain on the casualty or theft is realized.

Condemnation. The replacement period for a condemnation begins on the earlier of:

1. The date on which the condemned property was disposed of
2. The date on which the threat of condemnation began

The replacement period ends two years after the close of the first tax year in which any part of the gain on the condemnation is realized. The replacement period is extended to three years if the property is real property held for use in a trade or business or for investment (not including property held primarily for sale).

EXAMPLE 12 ————————————

Alexis, a calendar-year taxpayer, was notified by the city council on December 1, 1991, of its intention to acquire by negotiation or by condemnation real property used in her business. On June 1, 1992, when Alexis' adjusted basis in the property was $40,000, the city condemned the property and paid her $50,000. The replacement period began on December 1, 1991, the date Alexis was notified of the intention to condemn the property. Because the condemned property was real estate used in her business, the re-

placement period ends on December 31, 1995, three years after the last day of the year in which the gain was realized.

An extension of the replacement period may be obtained by applying to the District Director of the IRS. The request should be made before the end of the replacement period.

Basis of Replacement Property

To qualify as replacement property, the new property must be similar or related in service or use to the involuntarily converted property.

Similar or Related Property. If qualified replacement property is acquired, the basis of the new property is its cost minus any unrecognized gain. The basis of the replacement property may also be found by reducing the basis of the old property by any proceeds not spent on similar property and adding the recognized gain or subtracting the recognized loss.

Not Similar or Related Property. If the replacement property is not similar or related in service or use to the involuntarily converted property, the basis of the new property is the cost of the new property. Any gain would be taxed.

EXAMPLE 13 ————————————

Robert's property was condemned by the state. The property had an adjusted basis of $26,000, and the state paid him $31,000 for it. Robert realized a gain of $5,000 ($31,000 − $26,000). He bought new property that is similar in use to the old property for $29,000. He must recognize a gain of at least $2,000 ($31,000 − $29,000), the unspent part of the payment from the state. The basis of the new property is figured as follows:

Cost of new property	$29,000
Minus: Gain not recognized	3,000
Basis of the new property	$26,000

Allocating the Basis. The basis must be allocated among the parts of the property acquired as a result of an involuntary exchange. This allocation is usually based on the ratios of the FMV of each part of the new property to the total FMV of the whole new property.

If more than one piece of replacement property is acquired, the basis is allocated among the properties based on their respective costs. If in Example 13, the state had condemned unimproved real property, and the new property acquired was improved real property with both land and buildings, the basis of the new property, $26,000, would be allocated between land and buildings based on their FMV.

EXAMPLES 14

Antonio Perez operates a furniture store. In April, his warehouse was totally destroyed by a fire. The insurance company paid him $200,000 for the building which had a basis of $80,000. Antonio decided to buy another warehouse rather than rebuild the old one. He expended $250,000 to acquire the new facility—$175,000 for the building and $75,000 for the land. Since Antonio did not spend all of his insurance proceeds on qualified replacement property (a warehouse), his gain is recognized to the extent of the proceeds left over ($25,000).

Insurance settlement	$200,000
Basis of warehouse	80,000
Realized gain	$120,000
Insurance settlement	$200,000
Cost of new warehouse	175,000
Gain recognized	$ 25,000
Realized gain	$120,000
Recognized gain	25,000
Postponed gain	$ 95,000

The basis of the land acquired is $75,000 and the basis of the replacement property (warehouse) is:

Cost of new warehouse	$175,000
Minus: Gain not recognized	95,000
Basis of new warehouse	$ 80,000

EXAMPLE 15

Yoko Yukimura operated a restaurant. The city condemned the property and paid her $300,000 for it. Yoko's basis in the property is $100,000. Yoko decided to buy two restaurants (A and B) with the proceeds. She paid $240,000 for A and $160,000 for B, a total of $400,000.

As Yoko paid out all of the condemnation proceeds to acquire qualified replacement property, no gain is recognized. The basis of the two facilities is determined as follows:

Condemnation proceeds	$300,000
Basis of condemned restaurant . . .	100,000
Realized gain (postponed)	$200,000
Cost of A	$240,000
Minus: Postponed gain	
($200,000 x $240,000/$400,000)	120,000
Basis of A	$120,000
Cost of B	$160,000
Minus: Postponed gain	
($200,000 x $160,000/$400,000)	80,000
Basis of B	$ 80,000

Nontaxable Exchanges

Certain trades or exchanges are nontaxable. This means that some or all of the realized gain or loss on an exchange will not be recognized for tax purposes. Such gain or loss is postponed. As a result, the basis of the property given up will carry over to the newly acquired property.

Under a sale and purchase arrangement, any realized gain on the sale of the old asset is recognized, and the basis of the new equipment is its cost. Conversely, the taxpayer may be in a position to trade the old equipment for new equipment. This exchange of equipment may qualify for nontaxable exchange treatment.

Like-Kind Exchanges

The exchange of property for the same kind of property is the most common type of nontaxable exchange. To be nontaxable, a like-kind exchange must meet all six of the following conditions:

1. The property must be business or investment property. Both the property traded

Making Use of Nontaxable Exchanges

Taxpayers contemplating the replacement of equipment used in a trade or business may find it advantageous to structure the transaction as a nontaxable exchange rather than a sale of the old equipment and the purchase of new equipment.

and the property received must be held for business or investment purposes. Neither property may be used for personal purposes, such as a personal residence or a family car.

2. Neither the property traded nor the property received may be property held for sale to customers, such as merchandise.

3. There must be an exchange of like property. The exchange of real estate for real estate and the exchange of personal property for similar personal property are exchanges of like property. The trade of improved real estate for unimproved real estate or a panel truck for a pickup truck are like-kind exchanges. The exchange of a piece of machinery for a store building is not a like-kind exchange.

4. The property must be *tangible* property. These rules and benefits do not apply to exchanges of stocks, bonds, notes, choses in action, certificates of trust or beneficial interest, or other securities or evidence of indebtedness or interest, including the exchange of partnership interests. However, one may have a nontaxable exchange of corporate stocks, as discussed later.

5. The property to be received must be identified within 45 days after the old property is given up.

6. The property must be received on or before the earlier of:
   a. The 180th day after the old property is given up
   b. The due date, including extensions, for the tax return for the year in which the old property is given up

Gains

If a gain is realized on a nontaxable exchange of property, the gain is recognized to the extent of the FMV of any *boot received*. **Boot** is money or unlike property that is given or received in a like-kind exchange. Any unrecognized gain in a nontaxable exchange is postponed (deducted from the basis of the replacement property).

Losses

A loss incurred on a nontaxable exchange of property is not deductible. It is postponed (added to the basis of the replacement property).

Boot Given Up

A gain or loss may also be recognized on any unlike property that is given up on the exchange. The gain or loss to be recognized on this property is equal to the difference between the FMV of the unlike property and the property's adjusted basis.

Corporate Stocks

The following trades of corporate stocks generally do not result in a taxable gain or a deductible loss.

Stock for Stock of the Same Corporation. Common stock may be exchanged for common stock or preferred stock for preferred stock in the same corporation without having a recognized gain or loss. This is true for a trade between two persons as well as a trade between a stockholder and a corporation.

Convertible Stocks and Bonds. A gain or loss is not recognized if bonds are converted into stock or preferred stock is converted into common stock of the same corporation. Such conversions, however, must take place according to a conversion privilege in the terms of the bond or the preferred stock certificate.

Property for Stock. If a taxpayer transfers property to a corporation in exchange for stock or securities in that corporation, and immediately after the trade the taxpayer is in control of the corporation, a gain or loss will ordinarily not be recognized. This rule applies both to individuals and to groups who transfer property to a corporation. It does not apply if the corporation is an investment company. However, if there is a gain from the disposition of depreciable property from this transaction, part of the gain may be taxable.

For this purpose, to be in control of a corporation, the taxpayer (group) must own, immediately after the exchange, at least 80% of the total combined voting power of all classes of stock entitled to vote and at least 80% of the outstanding shares of each class of nonvoting stock of the corporation.

Insurance Policies and Annuities

A gain or loss will not be recognized if the following are traded:

1. A life insurance contract for another life insurance contract or for an endowment or an annuity contract
2. An endowment contract for an annuity contract or for another endowment contract providing for regular payments beginning at a date not later than the beginning date under the old contract
3. An annuity contract for another annuity contract

The insured or annuitant must stay the same as under the original contract. Exchanges that are not included in this list, such as an annuity contract for an endowment contract, are taxable.

U.S. Treasury Notes or Bonds

Certain issues of U.S. Treasury obligations may be traded for certain other issues with no gain or loss recognized on the trade. These obligations must be specifically designated by the Secretary of the Treasury as qualifying for this special treatment.

Basis of Property Acquired in a Nontaxable Exchange

The basis of like-kind property received in a nontaxable exchange can be determined by using the postponement procedures described previously in this section. The Internal Revenue Code provides an alternative procedure that may be used to determine the basis of the like-kind property received:

> Adjusted basis of all property given up
> + Gain recognized
> − FMV of boot received
> − Loss recognized
> = Basis of like-kind property received

The basis, as figured under this method, must be allocated among the properties, other than money, that are received in the exchange. In making this allocation, the basis of the unlike property is its FMV on the date of exchange. The remainder is the basis of the like property.

EXAMPLE 16 —————————————

Phil trades in an old truck, that has an adjusted basis of $4,700, for a new one costing $16,800. The dealer allows him $5,000 on the old truck, and he pays $11,800. This is a nontaxable exchange, and the basis of the new truck is $16,500, that is, the adjusted basis of the old one, $4,700, increased by the additional cost, $11,800. If Phil sells his old truck to a third party for $5,000 and then buys the new one from the dealer, he has a taxable gain on the sale, and the basis of the new truck is the price he pays the dealer.

Trade-in or Sale and Purchase. The basis of property for depreciation may not be increased by selling the old property outright to a dealer and then buying the new property from the same dealer if the sale and purchase are actually a single transaction. If the sale to the dealer of the old property and the purchase from that dealer of the new property are dependent on each other, the old property is considered to be traded in. The transaction is treated as an exchange no matter how it is carried out.

EXAMPLE 17 —————————————

Barney is a salesperson who uses one of his cars 100% for business. He has used this car in his sales activities for two years and has depreciated it. His adjusted basis in the car is $2,600, and its FMV is $3,100.

Barney is interested in a new car with a listed retail price of $8,695, which usually sells for $8,000. If he trades his old car for the new one and pays the dealer $4,900, his basis for depreciation for the new car would be $7,500 ($4,900 cash plus $2,600 basis of his old car). However, Barney wants a higher basis for depreciating the new car, so he agrees to pay the dealer $8,000 cash for the new car if the dealer will pay him $3,100 for his old car.

Since the sale and purchase are dependent on each other, Barney is treated as if he had exchanged his old car for the new one. His basis for depreciating the new car is $7,500, which is the same as it would be if he had traded the old car.

Taxable Exchanges

A taxable exchange exists when an exchange does not meet the criteria previously set forth under *Nontaxable Exchanges*. The trade-in of a personal automobile is an example of a taxable exchange.

Gains

Any realized gain on a taxable exchange will be recognized. Such a gain must be included on the taxpayer's return.

Losses

Losses on taxable exchanges are deductible or not deductible depending on how the property was used. Nondeductible losses are not postponed. They are simply lost.

Personal Assets. A loss incurred in a taxable exchange of a personal asset is not deductible. Neither is it postponed. The taxpayer receives no tax benefit from such a loss.

Business or Income-Producing Assets. A loss suffered in a taxable exchange of a business or income-producing asset is recognized. There is no loss to postpone.

Basis of Property Acquired in a Taxable Exchange

The basis of property acquired in a taxable exchange is usually its FMV at the time of the exchange. There is no postponed gain or loss to affect the basis.

Related Party Transactions

Special rules apply to the sale or trade of property between related parties. A loss on the sale or trade of property is not deductible if the transaction is directly or indirectly between the taxpayer and the following related parties:

1. Members of the taxpayers family—brothers, sisters, half-brothers, half-sisters, spouse, ancestors (parents, grandparents, etc.), and lineal descendants (children, grandchildren, etc.)
2. A corporation in which the taxpayer owns directly or indirectly more than 50% in value of the outstanding stock
3. An exempt charitable or educational organization that is controlled in any manner or by any method, directly or indirectly, by

the taxpayer or a family member, whether or not this control is legally enforceable

---

Making the Loss Deductible

Taxpayers who contemplate making a gift of investment or income producing property that has declined in value (FMV is less than basis), may find it advantageous to sell the property and make a gift of the cash. A sale of the property would give the taxpayer a recognized loss and a tax saving, whereas, a gift of such property would produce no tax benefit for the taxpayer.

Related parties transactions also include sales between commonly owned corporations, S corporations, and partnerships.

If a number of blocks of stock or pieces of property are sold or traded to a related party for a lump sum, the gain or loss must be determined separately for each block of stock or piece of property. The gain on each item may be taxable. However, the loss on any item may not be deducted. Also, the losses from the sales of any of these items may not be used to reduce the gains on the sales of any of the other items.

Indirect Transactions

Indirect transactions include sales through a stock exchange. A loss on the sale of stock through a broker may not be deducted if, for example, under a prearranged plan a related person or entity buys the same stock.

Constructive Ownership

In determining whether a taxpayer directly or indirectly owns any of the outstanding stock of a corporation, constructive ownership rules apply. Under constructive ownership rules, stock owned in a corporation by a taxpayer's spouse, children, grandchildren, and parents is attributed to the taxpayer in determining the ownership percentage. A taxpayer also constructively owns stock in a corporation held by any trust, estate, or partnership in which the taxpayer is a beneficiary or partner.

Sale or Trade of Property Received from a Related Party

If property received from a related party is sold or traded, any gain is recognized only to the extent that it is more than the loss previously disallowed to the transferor. This rule applies only to the original transferee. In addition, losses disallowed to the related party (transferor) cannot be deducted by the transferee in a future disposition of the property.

EXAMPLE 18

Steve, Lori's brother, sells Lori stock with a cost basis of $10,000 for $7,600. Steve cannot deduct the loss of $2,400. Later Lori sells the same stock to an unrelated party for $10,500, thus realizing a gain of $2,900. Her reportable gain is $500, the $2,900 gain minus the $2,400 loss not allowed to Steve.

EXAMPLE 19

Assume the same facts as before, except that Lori sold the stock for $6,900 instead of $10,500. Her recognized loss is only $700 ($7,600 basis minus $6,900). She cannot deduct the loss that was not allowed to Steve.

Gain on Sale or Trade of Depreciable Property

Capital gain treatment is denied when there is a recognized gain on the sale or trade of property between related parties and the property is depreciable property in the hands of the party who receives it. Such a gain is ordinary income and not capital gain.

Sale of Principal Residence

Property owned and used by a taxpayer solely as a residence is a capital asset. When a principal residence is sold (or exchanged), the sale must be reported in the year of sale on Form 2119, Sale or Exchange of Principal Residence, regardless of whether there is a gain or loss. When a principal residence is sold, any gain realized is a capital gain. Any taxable gain from such a sale is reportable on Schedule D (line 2 or 9). If sold at a loss, the loss is not deductible because it is a personal loss and not a loss sustained in a trade or business or in a transaction entered into for profit.

In calculating a gain or loss from the sale of a taxpayer's principal residence, the *basis* includes the original cost of the property, commissions, and other expenses incurred in its purchase, plus the cost of improvements, minus any energy credit taken, any casualty loss taken on the residence, any depreciation allowed or allowable (if there was ever any rental or business use of the residence), and the postponed gain on the sale or exchange of a previous principal residence.

EXAMPLE 20

If a taxpayer purchased a residence for $35,000, paid sales commission of $2,450, made capital improvements from time to time totaling $3,000, and sold the property 10 years after acquisition, the basis of the property for determining loss or gain would be $40,450 ($35,000 + $2,450 + $3,000).

Reinvestment in Another Principal Residence

Although the gain on the sale or exchange of a principal residence may be taxable, a special rule applies when the sale proceeds are reinvested in another principal residence. If a taxpayer buys a new principal residence within 24 months before or after the sale, or starts construction of a new residence within 24 months after sale and occupies it within 24 months after the sale, the gain on the sale is not recognized if the cost of the new residence exceeds the adjusted sales price of the old residence. The *adjusted sales price* is the selling price of the old residence less sales commission, other selling expenses, and fixing-up expenses (painting, papering, etc.). *Fixing-up expenses* must be for work performed during the 90 days preceding the sale of the old residence, be paid for not later than 30 days after the sale, be otherwise nondeductible in calculating taxable income, and not be capital expenditures or improvements. Fixing-up expenses are considered only in determining the amount of gain on which tax is postponed and cannot be deducted in determining the actual profit.

Sale of Residence Under Age 55

When a new principal residence is acquired within the specified replacement period, the special rule of deferring the gain on the sale of a principal residence by a taxpayer in the United States is mandatory for the taxpayer *under age 55*. The taxpayer, therefore, may not choose between reporting a gain or postponing it. However, if the adjusted sales price of the old residence is greater than the cost of the new residence, any gain on the transaction will be recognized to the extent of the difference between the two figures.

Taxpayers selling their home at a loss receive no tax benefit. The basis of the new, replacement home is its cost. Basis is not increased by the unrecognized loss.

EXAMPLE 21 ————————————————

To illustrate the postponement of gain on the sale of a principal residence for taxpayers under age 55 who reinvest in another principal residence, assume that Barbara S. and John F. Goddard, who are both under age 55, bought a residence 5 years ago for $40,000 and sold it on October 6, 1992, for $56,000. Within 90 days prior to the sale, they incurred fixing-up expenses of $600, paying for them upon completion of the work. They also paid selling expenses of $3,000. A month before the sale, on September 10, 1992, they purchased a new residence for $52,000. The recognized gain is calculated as follows:

Selling price of old residence	$56,000
Less selling expenses	3,000
Amount realized	$53,000
Basis of old residence	40,000
Realized gain	$13,000
Amount realized (from above)	$53,000
Less fixing-up expenses	600
Adjusted sales price	$52,400
Cost of new residence	52,000
Recognized gain	$ 400

Of the realized gain of $13,000, only $400 is recognized for income tax purposes. The $400 is a long-term capital gain. The postponed gain of $12,600 ($13,000 realized gain minus $400 recognized gain) is treated as a reduction of the cost basis of the new residence. In the event the taxpayer should sell the new residence at some later date, the basis of the residence for determining the gain would be $39,400 ($52,000 cost minus $12,600 postponed gain). If the cost of the new residence had been $52,400 or more, none of the gain would be recognized, and the basis of the new residence would be the cost reduced by the $13,000 of postponed gain.

The rule for postponement of gain on the sale of a principal residence generally applies only to the first residence sold and the last residence purchased within the 24-month period. However, if more than one residence is purchased within this 24-month period, a taxpayer is still allowed a tax-free rollover of a gain on the sale of any residence otherwise qualified if the taxpayer relocates for employment purposes. This rollover provision applies if the taxpayer commences work as an employee or as a self-employed person at a new principal place of work and the taxpayer meets the geographic rule (35 miles) and the length-of-employment rule (39 and 78 weeks) required for the deductibility of moving expenses.

Sometimes, a taxpayer and spouse may own an old residence jointly but may own the new residence separately (or vice versa). In such a case, the postponed gain and the resulting adjusted basis of the new residence may be divided between the taxpayer and spouse. This division may be made only if the old and new residences are each used as a principal residence and if a consent is signed by both the taxpayer and spouse. This may be done in the bottom margin of Form 2119 or on a separate attached statement by writing "We consent to reduce the basis of the new residence by the gain from selling the old residence."

Illustration 11-1

A filled-in Form 2119, Sale of Your Home, for John F. and Barbara S. Goddard, is shown in Illustration 11-1. Form 2119 is used to report any gain on the sale of a principal residence whether or not it is replaced with another principal residence. The $400 of taxable gain reported by the Goddards on Form 2119 (line 14c) must be entered on Schedule D, Form 1040 (line 9).

Illustration 11-1
Filled-In Form 2119, Sale of Your Home

Form **2119**

Department of the Treasury
Internal Revenue Service

Sale of Your Home

▶ Attach to Form 1040 for year of sale.

▶ See separate instructions. ▶ Please print or type.

OMB No. 1545-0072

19**92**

Attachment
Sequence No. **20**

Your first name and initial. If a joint return, also give spouse's name and initial.	Last name	Your social security number
John F. and Barbara S.	Goddard	642 : 34 : 5921

Fill in Your Address Only If You Are Filing This Form by Itself and Not With Your Tax Return

Present address (no., street, and apt. no., rural route, or P.O. box no. if mail is not delivered to street address)

7116 Felix Street

Spouse's social security number

372 : 87 : 8924

City, town or post office, state, and ZIP code

Oxford, Ohio 39674

Part I General Information

1 Date your former main home was sold (month, day, year) . . . . ▶ | **1** | 10 / 06 / 92

2 Face amount of any mortgage, note (e.g., second trust), or other financial instrument on which you will get periodic payments of principal or interest from this sale (see instructions) . . . | **2** |

3 Have you bought or built a new main home? . . . . [X] Yes [ ] No

4 Is or was any part of either main home rented out or used for business? If "Yes," see instructions . . . [ ] Yes [X] No

Part II Gain on Sale (Do not include amounts you deduct as moving expenses.)

5 Selling price of home. Do not include personal property items that you sold with your home .	**5**	56,000	00
6 Expense of sale. Include sales commissions, advertising, legal, etc.	**6**	3,000	00
7 Amount realized. Subtract line 6 from line 5	**7**	53,000	00
8 Basis of home sold (see instructions)	**8**	40,000	00
9 **Gain on sale.** Subtract line 8 from line 7	**9**	13,000	00

- If line 9 is zero or less, **stop here** and attach this form to your return.
- If line 3 is "Yes," you **must** go to Part III or Part IV, whichever applies. Otherwise, go to line 10.

10 If you haven't replaced your home, do you plan to do so within the replacement period (see instructions)? [ ] Yes [ ] No
- If line 10 is "Yes," stop here, attach this form to your return, and see **Additional Filing Requirements** in the instructions.
- If line 10 is "No," you **must** go to Part III or Part IV, whichever applies.

Part III One-Time Exclusion of Gain for People Age 55 or Older (If you are not taking the exclusion, go to Part IV now.)

11 Who was age 55 or older on date of sale? . . . . [ ] You [ ] Your spouse [ ] Both of you

12 Did the person who was age 55 or older own and use the property as his or her main home for a total of at least 3 years (except for short absences) of the 5-year period before the sale? If "No," go to Part IV now . . [ ] Yes [ ] No

13 **If line 12 is "Yes," do you elect to take the one-time exclusion?** If "No," go to Part IV now . . . . . [ ] Yes [ ] No

14 At time of sale, who owned the home? . . . . [ ] You [ ] Your spouse [ ] Both of you

15 Social security number of spouse at time of sale if you had a different spouse from the one above at time of sale. If you were not married at time of sale, enter "None" . . . . . ▶ | **15** |

16 **Exclusion.** Enter the **smaller** of line 9 or $125,000 ($62,500, if married filing separate return). Then, go to line 17 | **16** |

Part IV Adjusted Sales Price, Taxable Gain, and Adjusted Basis of New Home

17 Subtract line 16 from line 9	**17**	13,000	00

- If line 17 is zero, stop here and attach this form to your return.
- If line 3 is "Yes," go to line 18 now.
- If you are reporting this sale on the installment method, stop here and see the line 2 instructions.
- All others, stop here and **enter the amount from line 17 on Schedule D, line 2 or line 10.**

18 Fixing-up expenses (see instructions for time limits)	**18**	600	00
19 Add lines 16 and 18	**19**	52,400	00
20 **Adjusted sales price.** Subtract line 19 from line 7	**20**	52,000	00
21a Date you moved into new home (month, day, year) ▶ 11 / 01 / 92 **b** Cost of new home	**21b**	52,000	00
22 Subtract line 21b from line 20. If the result is zero or less, enter -0-	**22**	400	00
23 **Taxable gain.** Enter the **smaller** of line 17 or line 22	**23**	400	00

- If line 23 is zero, go to line 24 and attach this form to your return.
- If you are reporting this sale on the installment method, see the line 2 instructions and go to line 24.
- All others, **enter the amount from line 23 on Schedule D, line 2 or line 10,** and go to line 24.

24 Postponed gain. Subtract line 23 from line 17	**24**	12,600	00
25 Adjusted basis of new home. Subtract line 24 from line 21b	**25**	39,400	00

Sign Here Only If You Are Filing This Form by Itself and Not With Your Tax Return

Under penalties of perjury, I declare that I have examined this form, including attachments, and to the best of my knowledge and belief, it is true, correct, and complete.

Your signature	Date	Spouse's signature	Date
▶ *John F. Goddard*	4/10/93	▶ *Barbara S. Goddard*	4/10/93

If a joint return, both must sign.

For Paperwork Reduction Act Notice, see separate instructions.   Cat. No. 11710J   Form **2119** (1992)

Sale of Residence at Age 55 or Over

Taxpayers who have reached the *age of 55* before the date of sale of a residence may elect to exclude up to $125,000 of the gain realized on the sale of a principal residence, provided neither the taxpayer nor spouse had previously elected this exclusion. The taxpayer must have owned and used the residence for periods totaling at least 3 years within the 5-year period ending on the date of sale.

EXAMPLE 22 ————————————

To illustrate this application, assume that a taxpayer, age 60, sells a personal residence for $220,000 on June 1. The cost basis in the residence is $38,000. Selling expenses of $12,000 were incurred. The taxpayer purchased another residence for $80,000 and elected to take the $125,000 exclusion on the sale of the old residence. The taxpayer will be required to recognize $3,000 on the sale, as determined in Table 11-1.

Table 11-1
Recognized Gain on Sale

Selling price of old residence		$220,000
Less selling expenses		12,000
Amount realized		$208,000
Basis of old residence		38,000
Realized gain		$170,000
Gain excluded		125,000
Remaining gain		$ 45,000
Adjusted sales price		$208,000
Cost of new residence		80,000
Gain normally recognized		$128,000
Gain excluded		125,000
Recognized gain		$ 3,000
Cost of new residence		$ 80,000
Total gain on old residence .	$170,000	
Gain excluded	125,000	
Remaining gain	$ 45,000	
Gain recognized	3,000	
Gain postponed		42,000
Basis of new residence		$ 38,000

Only one lifetime election is available to a taxpayer, including married taxpayers. For married taxpayers filing separate returns, the maximum exclusion is $62,500 on each separate return. For residences owned jointly, if one spouse meets the age requirement, holding period, and use requirement for the exclusion, both spouses are considered to have met the requirements.

Reinvestment in Another Principal Residence by a Taxpayer Living Outside the U.S.

A taxpayer on active duty in the armed forces of the United States for more than 90 days who is stationed outside of the United States, or who, after returning to the United States, is required to reside in on-base government quarters because adequate off-base housing is not available at the remote base site, is allowed additional time for reinvesting in another principal residence after the date of selling the old residence. The taxpayer has a suspension of the 24-month period between the sale of the old home and the purchase of a new home to postpone recognition of the gain. A period for reinvestment is extended to four years after the sale of the old residence *or* one year after the member of the armed forces is no longer required to reside in government quarters, whichever is later. In addition, the total period cannot exceed eight years.

Wash Sales

There is an important limitation on the recognition of losses from the sale of certain securities. If a taxpayer sells stocks or other securities at a loss and, within 30 days before or after the sale, purchases substantially identical securities, the loss on the sale is not recognized in determining taxable income. Such a sale is termed a *wash sale.* The unrecognized loss on a wash sale is added to the cost of the securities purchased within 30 days before or after the sale. The loss becomes part of the basis of the newly acquired securities in determining the gain or loss from their disposition at any future date.

EXAMPLE 23 ————————————

To illustrate the effect of these rules, assume the following purchases and sales of ABC Corporation stock by a taxpayer:

June 5, 1982, purchased 100 shares	$3,000
Dec. 17, 1992, sold 100 shares	2,400
Jan. 10, 1993, purchased 100 shares	2,300

The $600 loss ($3,000 − $2,400) on the sale of 100 shares of ABC Corporation stock on December 17, 1992, is not recognized because within 30 days of that date the taxpayer acquired 100 shares of the same type of stock. The basis of the stock acquired on January 10, 1993, is the cost, $2,300, plus the unrecognized loss of $600, or a total of $2,900.

The wash sale provision applies *only* to losses; gains are taxable regardless of whether similar stock is acquired within the 30-day period. A dealer in securities is not affected by the provision inasmuch as securities constitute stock in trade. For shares of stock or other securities acquired in connection with a *wash sale,* the holding period of the acquired property includes the holding period of the original property.

Name _______________________________

Section _____________ Date _______________

C H A P T E R 1 1

Questions and Problems

1. Taxpayer sells land which is mortgaged for $60,000. In return for the land, the taxpayer receives cash of $40,000 and stock with a FMV of $30,000 ($20,000 par value). The buyer also assumes the mortgage. The taxpayer's adjusted basis in the land is $80,000.

   a. What is the amount realized?

   b. What is the realized gain?

   c. How would these amounts change if the buyer had not assumed the mortgage, but instead had paid the taxpayer an additional $60,000 to pay off the mortgage before the transfer of the land took place?

2. Leo Small purchased an apartment building. He paid $300,000 in cash and assumed a mortgage of $200,000. He also paid the following:

Brokerage commission	$35,000
Attorney's fee to acquire title	2,000
Back real estate taxes	40,000
Remodeling costs	20,000
Surveying expenses	2,500

   What is Small's basis for depreciation on this building if the FMV of the land and that of the building are $100,000 and $400,000, respectively?

3. George O'Brien, president of Sugarman Corporation, was given the opportunity to buy 1,000 shares of the corporation's stock for $120 per share. The par value of the stock was $100. George took advantage of this offer and purchased 100 shares of stock at a time when the stock was selling for $150 per share. The company also gave George an additional 100 shares of stock as a bonus when the stock was selling for $160 per share.

   a. What amount of income must George recognize as a result of these stock acquisitions?

   b. What is George's per share basis in the stock that he acquired?

4. Sharon inherited 10 shares of Alpha Corporation stock upon the death of her father. The stock cost her father $10,000 but was worth only $7,000 at the date of his death. Sharon sold the stock this year for $8,000. What gain or loss must be reported on the sale?

5. Terry Taylor purchased 5,000 shares of Ferrero Corporation stock in 1980 for $60,000. Mr. Taylor died on August 1, 1992, leaving the stock to his daughter, Tina. Tina received the stock on November 1, 1992. The alternate valuation date was elected for Terry's estate. The FMV of the stock for various dates is:

August 1, 1992	$80,000
November 1, 1992	78,000
February 1, 1993	77,000

What is Tina's basis for the stock?

6. Assume the same information as in Problem 5, except that Tina received the stock on March 1, 1993, when the FMV of the stock was $81,000. What is Tina's basis for the stock?

7. Max Fish purchased 100 shares of XQM stock in 1980 for $10,000. In 1985 Max gave the stock to his daughter, Linda, when the FMV of the stock was $8,000. No gift tax was paid.

   a. What is Linda's basis if she sells the stock in the current year for $11,000?

   b. What is Linda's basis if she sells the stock in the current year for $7,000?

   c. What is Linda's reportable gain or loss if she sells the stock in the current year for $9,000?

8. On February 10, 1992, Bruce gave Shirley a house worth $100,000 on a lot worth $25,000. Bruce's adjusted basis in the house and in the land were $80,000 and $20,000, respectively. Assume the gift tax paid was $10,000. If Shirley uses the house as rental property, what is her basis for depreciation?

9. H and W were divorced. Under the terms of the divorce agreement, H transferred 100 shares of Big Rig stock (cost $30,000, market value $45,000) to W in satisfaction of W's property rights. If W sells the stock for $50,000, what is W's gain?

10. Parker Lewis converted his personal residence to rental property on June 1. The house cost Lewis $90,000 ten years ago. On June 1, the FMV of the house was $70,000.

   a. What is Parker's basis for depreciation deduction on the house?

   b. If Parker sells the house for $100,000 after taking depreciation deductions of $10,000, what is his gain or loss?

   c. If Parker sells the house for $50,000 after taking depreciation deductions of $10,000, what is his gain or loss?

   d. If the house is sold for $70,000 after taking depreciation deductions of $10,000, what is the gain or loss?

11. Ima O. Witch had the following purchases of common stock of Halloween Tricks, Inc.:

   1980   400 shares at $10 per share
   1983   100 shares at $20 per share
   1986   300 shares at $30 per share
   1988   200 shares at $40 per share

   a. In 1992, Ima sold 500 shares at $35 per share. Assuming that incomplete records were kept by Ima and she could not identify which blocks of stock were sold, calculate her gain or loss on the sale.

b. If Ima's objective is to minimize taxes, and she can adequately identify which stock she is selling, which stock should she sell and what is the gain or loss that would result?

12. Diane owned 100 shares of common stock in the Delta Corporation when it had a two-for-one stock split. The original 100 shares cost $50 each, for a total cost of $5,000. After the split, Diane had 200 shares that were valued at $30 each, for a total value of $6,000. As a result of the stock split, what is Diane's basis in each share of stock and how much income must she recognize?

13. The Mini-Wini Dress Shop was destroyed by fire in January. The adjusted basis of the store was $150,000. In March the insurance company paid $140,000 to cover the loss. Shortly thereafter a new shop was purchased for $200,000.

   a. What, if any, is the gain or loss to be recognized?

   b. What is the basis of the new dress shop?

14. Duffy & Co.'s warehouse, which had an adjusted basis of $1,000,000, was destroyed by fire. Duffy received insurance in the amount of $2,000,000. Duffy invested $1,800,000 in a new warehouse and elected the nonrecognition provisions of the Internal Revenue Code.

   a. What is the amount of gain recognized for income tax purposes?

   b. What is the basis of the new warehouse?

   c. Assume that, instead of investing $1,800,000 in one new warehouse, Duffy invested in two new warehouses, as follows:

Warehouse A	$1,080,000
Warehouse B	720,000

   What is the basis of Warehouse A and Warehouse B?

15. On February 17, 1992, Alice Baker, a calendar-year taxpayer, was notified by the state that the land she owned as an investment was needed for a state park and that the land would be condemned. The state took possession of the land on May 15, 1992, and Alice received her condemnation award on that date. If she elects to postpone recognition of her gain, by what date must Alice purchase replacement property?

16. Dorsey Packard exchanges real estate held for investment for other real estate to be held for investment. The following facts relate to the exchange.

Adjusted basis of old property	$ 75,000
FMV of new property	100,000
Cash received by Packard	10,000
Mortgage on old property assumed by other party	30,000

    a. What is the amount of Packard's recognized gain?

    b. What is the adjusted basis of Packard's new property?

17. For each of the following nontaxable exchanges, calculate the actual (accounting) gain or loss, the recognized gain or loss, and the basis of the new property acquired.

Exchange a: The basis of the old asset is $8,000. The price of the new asset is $5,000. No cash is received or paid.

Exchange b: The basis of the old asset is $6,000. The price of the new asset is $10,000. Cash of $5,000 is paid.

Exchange c: The basis of the old asset is $6,000. The price of the new asset is $10,000. Cash of $2,000 is paid.

Exchange d: The basis of the old asset is $10,000. The price of the new asset is $7,000. Cash of $2,000 is received.

Exchange e: The basis of the old asset is $10,000. The price of the new asset is $7,000. Cash of $5,000 is received.

Exchange f: The basis of the old asset is $10,000. The price of the new asset is $11,000. Cash of $2,000 is received.

18. Ivan Petersen owned a Harley Davidson motorcycle. He traded it for a Honda motorcycle on September 5. The cycle he traded was purchased for $6,400 on April 10 of last year. The cycle received in the exchange had a FMV of $6,000. No boot was involved. Ivan sold his Honda on December 30 for $6,150. Determine Ivan's gain or loss on the sale.

19. Which of the following transactions qualify as a like-kind exchange?

   a. Grocery store for a rental house
   b. Apartment building for an apple orchard
   c. GM common stock for land to be held for investment
   d. 100 shares of Ford common stock for 100 shares of Chrysler common stock
   e. Duplex apartment (investment property) for a personal residence
   f. Old computer for a new computer (both used in business)
   g. Inventory traded for a computer (used in business)
   h. Old personal auto for new personal auto
   i. Convertible preferred stock of IBX for common stock of IBX under a conversion agreement
   j. A life insurance contract for an endowment contract

20. Patsy Oman trades one of her business machines, which has an adjusted basis of $50,000, and stock with an adjusted basis of $20,000 and a FMV of $25,000. She receives in return a new business machine with a FMV of $80,000. What gain or loss must Patsy recognize, and what is the basis of the new machine?

21. Bates wanted McKean's farm as a site for an amusement park and offered him $200,000 for the land. McKean did not want to sell his land, which had a basis of $50,000. Bates is presently considering the acquisition of another farm for $170,000 and the subsequent offering of this land and $20,000 in cash to McKean in exchange for his farm. If McKean accepts this offer, what tax consequences does he face?

22. Fred sold common stock, which cost him $12,000, to his sister, Sara, for $9,000. Three years later she sold the stock for $14,000 to an unrelated party.

   a. What was Fred's recognized loss when he sold the stock to Sara?

   b. What is Sara's basis in the stock she purchased from Fred?

   c. What is Sara's recognized gain or loss when she sells the stock?

d. If Sara had sold the stock for $11,000, what would her recognized gain or loss be?

e. If Sara had sold the stock for $7,000, what would her recognized gain or loss be?

23. During 1992 Cynthia Hodges, age 48, sold for $58,000 her residence which she had acquired several years ago for $44,000. Within 90 days prior to the sale, she incurred and paid fixing-up expenses of $400. She also paid a sales commission of $3,500. Fill in the blanks below under each of the following assumptions: **(a)** she purchased a new residence for $56,000 within 6 months; **(b)** she purchased a new residence for $64,000 within 6 months; **(c)** she sold the old residence for $59,500, instead of $58,000, and purchased a new residence for $43,000 within 6 months.

	(a)	(b)	(c)
Amount realized	__________	__________	__________
Realized gain	__________	__________	__________
Adjusted sales price	__________	__________	__________
Recognized gain	__________	__________	__________
Basis of new residence	__________	__________	__________

24. Brian A. Nimms, a single taxpayer 58 years of age, sold his personal residence during 1992 for $175,450. The cost of the residence to Mr. Nimms when acquired 20 years ago was $34,000. On April 14, 1992, the date of the sale, the remaining mortgage of $12,000 plus $800 interest was paid in full by Mr. Nimms.

One week before the sale, Mr. Nimms paid a painter $1,500 for painting and making other minor repairs to fix up the property for sale. A real estate agent was paid $7,200 as the commission from the proceeds of the sale. An additional $400 was paid for legal fees in connection with the sale. Mr. Nimms lived in the residence for the 20 years of his ownership and elects to exclude the maximum amount of the gain.

a. Calculate the realized gain on the sale, the gain excluded, and the remaining gain.

b. How often may a taxpayer age 55 or over claim the special exclusion from income of a portion of the gain from the sale of a personal residence, and how much can be excluded if the taxpayer is single? Married filing jointly? Married filing separately?

25. Scott Percy, single, is 57 years old and contemplating marriage. Scott is also considering the sale of his personal residence at a profit of $160,000. He plans to move into an apartment. His future bride is 60 years old and has previously elected to exclude $45,000 of the gain on the sale of her residence from taxation. What tax advice can you give Scott on the sale of his residence and the timing of his marriage?

26. Debra Cruise owns a personal residence. She resides in one-half of the building and rents the other half to a tenant. She purchased the building five years ago at a cost of $100,000. Depreciation deductions claimed on the property total $9,000. Debra plans to sell this property and acquire a new principal residence for $130,000. Her selling expenses are expected to be $9,000, and she anticipates a selling price of $120,000. She does not plan to rent any part of the new house to tenants. Describe in detail the tax treatment of these planned transactions.

27. Ed Ficek sold 100 shares of EPI stock for $10,000 on September 1, 1992. He had purchased the stock on July 1, 1980, for $18,000. On August 15, 1992, Ed purchased 50 shares of EPI stock for $5,500. What are the tax consequences of these transactions?

28. Fred A. and Ethyl B. Morris, both under 55, sold their home on June 23, 1992 for $120,000. The house was purchased in 1975 for $75,000. In selling the house, they incurred fixing-up expenses of $1,000 and selling expenses of $5,000. They subsequently purchased a new home on August 24, 1992 for $135,000. They moved in on September 3, 1992. Complete Form 2119, Sale of Your Home, on the following page. The Morrises present address is 427 W. Evans, Tucson, AZ, 92741. Their SSNs are 336-46-4101 and 367-41-9403, respectively.

Form **2119**	**Sale of Your Home**	OMB No. 1545-0072

▶ **Attach to Form 1040 for year of sale.**

Department of the Treasury
Internal Revenue Service

▶ **See separate instructions.** ▶ **Please print or type.**

19**92**

Attachment
Sequence No. **20**

Your first name and initial. If a joint return, also give spouse's name and initial. Last name **Your social security number**

Fill in Your Address Only If You Are Filing This Form by Itself and Not With Your Tax Return

Present address (no., street, and apt. no., rural route, or P.O. box no. if mail is not delivered to street address) **Spouse's social security number**

City, town or post office, state, and ZIP code

Part I General Information

1 Date your former main home was sold (month, day, year) . . . . ▶ **1** / /

2 Face amount of any mortgage, note (e.g., second trust), or other financial instrument on which you will get periodic payments of principal or interest from this sale (see instructions) . . . **2**

3 Have you bought or built a new main home? . . . . ☐ Yes ☐ No

4 Is or was any part of either main home rented out or used for business? If "Yes," see instructions . . . ☐ Yes ☐ No

Part II Gain on Sale (Do not include amounts you deduct as moving expenses.)

5 Selling price of home. Do not include personal property items that you sold with your home . **5**

6 Expense of sale. Include sales commissions, advertising, legal, etc. **6**

7 Amount realized. Subtract line 6 from line 5 . . . . **7**

8 Basis of home sold (see instructions) **8**

9 **Gain on sale.** Subtract line 8 from line 7 . . . . **9**

 • If line 9 is zero or less, **stop here** and attach this form to your return.

 • If line 3 is "Yes," you **must** go to Part III or Part IV, whichever applies. Otherwise, go to line 10.

10 If you haven't replaced your home, do you plan to do so within the replacement period (see instructions)? ☐ Yes ☐ No

 • If line 10 is "Yes," stop here, attach this form to your return, and see **Additional Filing Requirements** in the instructions.

 • If line 10 is "No," you **must** go to Part III or Part IV, whichever applies.

Part III One-Time Exclusion of Gain for People Age 55 or Older (If you are not taking the exclusion, go to Part IV now.)

11 Who was age 55 or older on date of sale? . . . . ☐ You ☐ Your spouse ☐ Both of you

12 Did the person who was age 55 or older own and use the property as his or her main home for a total of at least 3 years (except for short absences) of the 5-year period before the sale? If "No," go to Part IV now . . ☐ Yes ☐ No

13 **If line 12 is "Yes,"** do you elect to take the one-time exclusion? If "No," go to Part IV now . . . . . ☐ Yes ☐ No

14 At time of sale, who owned the home? . . . . ☐ You ☐ Your spouse ☐ Both of you

15 Social security number of spouse at time of sale if you had a different spouse from the one above at time of sale. If you were not married at time of sale, enter "None" . . . . . . ▶ **15**

16 **Exclusion.** Enter the **smaller** of line 9 or $125,000 ($62,500, if married filing separate return). Then, go to line 17 **16**

Part IV Adjusted Sales Price, Taxable Gain, and Adjusted Basis of New Home

17 Subtract line 16 from line 9 . . . . **17**

 • If line 17 is zero, stop here and attach this form to your return.

 • If line 3 is "Yes," go to line 18 now.

 • If you are reporting this sale on the installment method, stop here and see the line 2 instructions.

 • All others, stop here and **enter the amount from line 17 on Schedule D, line 2 or line 10.**

18 Fixing-up expenses (see instructions for time limits) **18**

19 Add lines 16 and 18 . . . . **19**

20 **Adjusted sales price.** Subtract line 19 from line 7 . . . . **20**

21a Date you moved into new home (month, day, year) ▶ / / **b** Cost of new home **21b**

22 Subtract line 21b from line 20. If the result is zero or less, enter -0- **22**

23 **Taxable gain.** Enter the **smaller** of line 17 or line 22 . . . . . **23**

 • If line 23 is zero, go to line 24 and attach this form to your return.

 • If you are reporting this sale on the installment method, see the line 2 instructions and go to line 24.

 • All others, **enter the amount from line 23 on Schedule D, line 2 or line 10,** and go to line 24.

24 Postponed gain. Subtract line 23 from line 17 . . . . **24**

25 **Adjusted basis of new home.** Subtract line 24 from line 21b **25**

Sign Here Only If You Are Filing This Form by Itself and Not With Your Tax Return

Under penalties of perjury, I declare that I have examined this form, including attachments, and to the best of my knowledge and belief, it is true, correct, and complete.

Your signature Date Spouse's signature Date

▶   ▶

If a joint return, both must sign.

For Paperwork Reduction Act Notice, see separate instructions. Cat. No. 11710J Form **2119** (1992)

Property Transactions: Tax Treatment of Gains and Losses

Normally, a gain or loss is realized when the taxpayer sells, exchanges, or otherwise disposes of property items. Chapter 11 examined various property dispositions focusing attention on the calculation of the gain or loss and the identification of those gains and losses that are to be recognized for tax purposes. When the taxpayer has determined that a gain or loss is to be recognized, the next step is to establish whether it is to be treated as a *capital* gain or loss or as an *ordinary* income or loss item.

Historically, capital gains were taxed at a much lower rate than ordinary income. Under current tax laws, capital gains are generally taxed at the same rate as ordinary income. However, the maximum tax rate applicable to a net capital gain is 28%.

While recognized ordinary losses are generally deducted in full, the deduction for net capital losses is limited. Such losses are deductible from gross income only to the extent of $3,000 each tax year. Any excess loss is carried forward indefinitely.

This chapter will address in more detail the tax treatment of recognized gains and losses from property transactions. The forms needed to report these gains and losses will also be illustrated.

Character of Gain or Loss

Taxpayers who have a taxable gain or a deductible loss from a property transaction, may have either a capital gain or loss or an ordinary gain or loss, depending on the circumstances. If the gain or loss is from the disposition of a capital asset, it is a capital gain or loss.

Taxpayers may also receive capital gain treatment from the disposition of a noncapital asset, if it is a Section 1231 property (business property, discussed later). However, a net loss resulting from the disposition of Section 1231 property is an ordinary loss. It is not treated as a capital loss. If a taxpayer disposes of depreciable 1231 property at a gain, all or part of the gain may be treated as ordinary income. This chapter sets forth the rules for calculating the amount of the gain on depreciable property that is ordinary income.

Not only is it important to properly classify gains and losses as either ordinary or capital in nature, but these gains and losses must also be identified as either short-term or long-term, depending on the holding period. The correct classification of gains and losses is important for determining the proper tax treatment for these gains and losses.

The information presented in this chapter should enable taxpayers to determine their capital gains and losses, ordinary income and losses, the holding period, and the tax treatment and reporting requirements for gains and losses recognized on property transactions.

Capital Assets

Taxpayers involved with property transactions should learn how to distinguish a capital asset from a noncapital asset. These taxpayers should also be familiar with those noncapital assets that may be treated like a capital asset under certain circumstances.

> ## Property Owned and Used for Personal Purposes, Pleasure, or Investment Is a Capital Asset
>
> - Gain from a sale or exchange is a capital gain.
> - Losses from sales and exchanges are not deductible (unless they result from personal casualties or thefts).
>
> Some examples are:
>
> - Car used for pleasure or commuting
> - Coin or stamp collections
> - Gems and jewelry
> - Gold, silver or any other metal
> - Household furnishings
> - Personal residence
> - Stocks or bonds held in a personal account

Definition: Capital Assets

The Internal Revenue Code defines **capital assets** as all property held by the taxpayer *except*:

1. **Property held mainly for sale to customers** or property that will physically become

a part of the merchandise that is for sale to customers

2. **Accounts or notes receivable** acquired in the ordinary course of a trade or business, or for services rendered as an employee, or from the sale of any of the properties described in Item *1*

3. **Depreciable property** used in a trade or business, even though fully depreciated

4. **Real property** used in a trade or business

5. **A copyright, a literary, musical, or artistic composition, a letter or memorandum,** or similar property that was created by the taxpayer's personal efforts; that was prepared or produced for the taxpayer as a letter, memorandum, or similar property; or that was acquired under circumstances (a gift) entitling the taxpayer to the basis of either the person who created the property or the person for whom it was prepared or produced

6. **U.S. Government publications** that were received free or for less than the normal sales price

Special Items

Some property items are given special tax treatment. A selected number of these items are discussed below.

Nonbusiness Bad Debts. Amounts owed to the taxpayer that prove to be uncollectible are bad debts. If the bad debt is *unrelated* to the taxpayer's trade or business, it is a nonbusiness bad debt. Nonbusiness bad debts are deducted only as short-term capital losses on Schedule D (Form 1040), Capital Gains and Losses. There are limits on how capital losses may be deducted. These limits are discussed later in the chapter.

Establishing a Bona Fide Loan

Taxpayers making loans to friends and family members should document the transaction in order to provide evidence that the amount loaned is not intended as a gift. Documentation may include a promissory note with provision for payment date(s) and interest.

For a bad debt to qualify for the deduction, there must be a true creditor-debtor relationship between the taxpayer and the person or organization that owes the money. There must be a legal obligation to pay a fixed sum of money. Taxpayers must realize a loss because of their inability to collect the money owed to them.

To be deductible, nonbusiness bad debts must be totally worthless. One cannot deduct a partially worthless nonbusiness bad debt.

Losses on Small Business Stock (Section 1244). Generally, losses on the sale of stock are capital losses. However, an individual (not including a trust or estate) may deduct as an ordinary loss, rather than as a capital loss, any loss on the sale, exchange, or worthlessness of small business stock. This ordinary loss is reported on Form 4797, Part II (line 10). Any gain on this stock, however, is a capital gain. Such gain is reported on Schedule D (Form 1040).

The ordinary loss deduction is available only to the original owner of this stock and is limited to $50,000. On a joint return, the limit is $100,000 even if only one spouse has this type of loss. Thus, if a married taxpayer's loss is $110,000, $100,000 may be deducted on a joint return. The excess of $10,000 is a capital loss.

Maximizing Ordinary Loss Deduction

If the loss on Section 1244 stock is expected to exceed the annual ordinary loss limit ($50,000/$100,000), the taxpayer should consider selling the stock in two different tax years.

In order to receive Section 1244 treatment, the corporation issuing the stock must meet certain qualifications. The basic qualification is that the total amount of contributed capital to the corporation does not exceed $1,000,000. Either common or preferred stock may qualify as Section 1244 stock.

Cancellation or Sale of a Lease. Payments received by a tenant (lessee) for the cancellation or sale of a lease may produce a capital gain or loss. A capital gain or loss will result if the property was used by the tenant for personal use. If the leased property was used in the tenant's trade or business, the gain or loss is a Section 1231 gain or loss as discussed later in the chapter. Payments received by a landlord (lessor) for the cancellation of a lease are ordinary income.

Options. Normally, the sale or exchange of an option to buy or sell property produces capital gain or loss if the property covered by the option is (or would be) a capital asset to the option holder.

Failure to Exercise Options. If an option is not exercised, the lapse of the option is treated as a sale or exchange of the option as of the option's expiration date. The lapse of options on stock, securities, commodities or commodity futures produces short-term capital gain to those grantors who do not hold options for sale to customers. Dealers must recognize such gain as ordinary income.

Exercise of Options by Grantee. When the grantee (buyer) exercises an option, the amount paid for the option is added to the cost (basis) of the property acquired. The amount paid for the option also adds to the proceeds from the sale of the property and increases the gain to the grantor. This gain is capital gain or ordinary income depending on the nature of the property transferred.

Patents. Generally, the *holder* of a patent may treat profits and royalties from the sale or exchange of the patent as long-term capital gains, regardless of how long the patent is held. In order to receive this special treatment, all *substantial rights* to the patent must be transferred.

The holder of a patent is usually the inventor. It may also be a person who acquires an interest in the patent from the inventor before the invention is reduced to practice. The holder, however, cannot be the inventor's employer or certain parties related to the inventor. If the employer has all the rights to an employee's invention, the patent would be an ordinary asset to the employer.

Inventors are eligible for long-term capital gain treatment on their patented inventions. It should be noted, however, that artists, authors, and composers do not receive such favorable treatment for their creative works.

Transfer of a Franchise, Trademark, or Trade Name. A franchise includes an agreement that gives one of the parties the right to distribute, sell, or provide goods, services, or facilities, within a specified area. Generally the transfer of a franchise, trademark, or trade name will not be treated as the transfer of a capital asset. However, capital gain or loss treatment is available if the transferor does not retain any *significant power*, *right*, or *continuing interest* in the franchise, trademark, or trade name. Amounts received for a franchise, trademark, or trade name that are contingent on the productivity, use or disposition of these assets are ordinary income to the transferor and ordinary expense to the transferee.

Subdivision of Real Estate. Generally, dealers who subdivide and sell real estate treat their income from such endeavors as ordinary income. However, Section 1237 enables certain taxpayers to receive capital gain treatment on limited subdivision activities. To receive capital treatment, the following requirements must be met:

1. The taxpayer cannot be a real estate dealer.
2. The taxpayer cannot be a corporation.
3. No substantial improvements may be made to the lots sold. Generally, filling, draining, clearing, and leveling operations are not considered as substantial improvements.
4. The taxpayer must hold the lots for at least five years before selling them. There is no minimum holding requirement for inherited property.

If the above requirements are met, all gains on the sale of lots are capital gains until the tax year in which the sixth lot is sold. In the tax year in which the sixth lot is sold, the gains on all lots sold during the year are subject to limited ordinary income treatment. The gain on each of these lot sales is taxed as ordinary income to the extent of five percent of the selling price. However, this ordinary income is offset by any selling expenses incurred to sell the lot. Any excess selling expenses are then used to reduce the capital gain on the sale.

EXAMPLE 1 ————————————————

Taxpayer bought a tract of land in 1980. He subdivides it during the current taxable year and sells three lots for $1,200 each. The adjusted basis for each lot is $900. Taxpayer has a long-term capital gain of $300 on the sale of each lot.

EXAMPLE 2 ———————————————

Assume the same facts as in Example 1. Except that in the current taxable year taxpayer sells three more lots, each having a $900 basis for gain or loss. The selling price of each lot is $1,200 and there are no selling expenses. Therefore, 5% of $1,200, or $60, of the gain on the sale of each lot is ordinary income. The balance of $1,140 ($1,200 – $60) is long-term capital gain. Total ordinary income is $360 ($60 x 6), and total long-term capital gain is $6,840 ($1,140 x 6).

If, after the taxpayer has sold some lots, no additional lots are sold for a period of five years, another five lots can be sold, and the gains can receive capital gain treatment. Sales commissions are frequently more than five percent of the sales price. Consequently, the ordinary income to be recognized on these sales is generally nonexistent.

Goodwill. Goodwill is a capital asset that may or may not exist within a business. It is the total of all those indefinable qualities that bring customers to a business. If it does exist at the time a business is sold, the seller can receive capital gain treatment on the part of the sales price that is for goodwill. The buyer cannot deduct any of the amount paid for goodwill because it is a capital asset with an unknown useful life and it cannot be depreciated or amortized. The amount paid by the buyer for goodwill becomes the basis of the goodwill to the business.

Holding Period of Capital Assets

Gains and losses from the sale or exchange of capital assets are classified as *short-term* or *long-term,* depending upon the period of time the capital asset was held. The separation between short-term and long-term capital gains was originally designed to reflect the distinction between speculative income and investment income.

If a capital asset is held for *one year or less,* the gain or loss is a *short-term capital gain or loss.* The aggregate of all short-term capital gains and losses for a taxable year is called "net short-term capital gain" or "net short-term capital loss."

If a capital asset is held for *more than one year,* the gain or loss is a *long-term capital gain or loss.* The sum of all long-term capital gains and losses for a taxable year is called "net long-term capital gain" or "net long-term capital loss."

The distinction between short-term and long-term capital gains and losses may be illustrated as follows. Assume that a taxpayer derived a gain of $2,000 on the sale of securities that qualified for short-term capital gain, and sustained a loss of $700 on the sale of another lot that qualified for short-term capital loss. The excess of the short-term capital gain of $2,000 over the short-term capital loss of $700 yields a net short-term capital gain of $1,300. Similarly, the grouping of gains and losses from the sale or exchange of capital assets that qualify for long-term capital gain or loss treatment results in a net long-term capital gain or a net long-term capital loss.

The gain or loss from the sale of a capital asset that has been held for exactly the one year is short-term. In counting the period held, the date of acquisition is excluded and the day of disposition is included.

EXAMPLE 3 ———————————————

If a capital asset acquired on January 18, 1991 is sold on January 18, 1992 the holding period is exactly twelve months and the gain or loss is short-term.

Holding Periods for Property

In general, the holding period for capital assets is the length of time between the date when the taxpayer acquires property and when the taxpayer disposes of it. In transactions in which some portion of the basis of an asset carries forward, the holding period begins at the time the carryover basis originated. Some unique situations are examined in the following paragraphs.

Stock. The holding period for *stock purchased* begins on the day following the purchase (rather than the later day when payment is made and delivery accepted) and ends with the day of sale (rather than the later day when payment is received and delivery made). The holding period for stock received as a *nontaxable stock dividend* starts from the date the original stock was acquired.

Gifts. If the donor's basis is used to establish the basis of the gift property, the holding period for the donee begins at the time the donor's basis originated. If the FMV is used as the basis of the gift property (a loss situation), the donee's holding period begins at the date of the gift.

Inherited Property. The holding period for property acquired by inheritance generally begins on the date of the decedent's death. However, any gain or loss on the later disposition of such property is treated as long-term capital gain or loss, regardless of the actual holding period.

Nontaxable Exchanges. The holding period for property received in a nontaxable exchange includes the holding period of the like-kind property given up in the exchange. However, the holding period for any boot received will start from the date of the exchange.

Other Carryover Situations. Other situations in which the holding period of the former asset (or owner) may carryover to the current asset (or owner) include:

1. Stock and securities acquired in a wash sale
2. Sale and replacement of a personal residence where a gain was realized and the residence was replaced within the specified time
3. Qualified replacement property acquired as a result of an involuntary conversion in which a gain was realized and the replacement took place within the specified time
4. Transfers of property between spouses or former spouses incident to divorce

Capital Gains and Losses

The special rules and limitations upon taxability of capital gains and deductibility of capital losses are not the same for corporations as for other taxpayers. The following discussion relates to all taxpayers other than corporations.

Capital gains and losses for the year are matched to determine the amount of net gain or loss to be included in AGI. Schedule D (Form 1040) is provided by the IRS for this determination. Approximately 11% of the taxpayers file Schedule D.

Capital Gain Taxation

Currently, the highest tax bracket applicable to an individual is 31%. However, the highest tax rate applied to a net capital gain is 28%. A net capital gain is defined as the excess of net long-term capital gain over net short-term capital loss for the year. Short-term capital gains may still be taxed at 31%.

At the outset, net capital gains are included in gross income and taxed as if they were ordinary income. To ensure that net capital gains are taxed at not more than 28%, the following procedure is used:

Step 1: The regular tax rates are applied to the greater of:
    a. Taxable income minus the net capital gain, or
    b. That segment of taxable income taxed at a rate below 28%

Step 2: Multiply the remaining taxable income from Step 1 by 28%.

Step 3: Total the results of Steps 1 and 2.

EXAMPLE 4 ——————————

In 1992, Maria Garcia, a single individual, had a salary of $80,000. She also had a net capital gain of $40,000. Her itemized deductions and exemptions totaled $10,000.

Based on this information, Maria's taxable income is $110,000 ($80,000 + $40,000 − $10,000). Her tax is $28,554.50.

Step 1: Tax the greater of:
    a. Taxable income less the net capital gain: $70,000 ($110,000 − $40,000), OR
    b. Taxable income below the 28% bracket: $21,450

Greater amount	$70,000	
Tax on	51,900	$11,743.50
Remainder	$18,100	
Marginal tax at	31%	5,611.00
TAX ON STEP 1		$17,354.50

Step 2: .28 ($110,000 − $70,000)		11,200.00
Step 3: TOTAL TAX		$28,554.50

If the maximum 28% tax rate were not in effect, Maria's tax liability for 1992 would have been $29,754.50: $11,743.50 + .31 ($110,000 − $51,900).

Net Gain

The following examples illustrate different combinations of net short-term and net long-term capital gains or losses. Any resulting *net capital gain* would be available for the maximum tax rate of 28%.

EXAMPLE 5

1. Net long-term capital gain	$5,000
2. Net short-term capital gain or loss	none
3. Net gain included in AGI	
(line 1 minus line 2)	$5,000
4. Net capital gain	$5,000

EXAMPLE 6

1. Net long-term capital gain	$5,000
2. Net short-term capital loss	(2,000)
3. Net gain included in AGI	
(line 1 minus line 2)	$3,000
4. Net capital gain	$3,000

EXAMPLE 7

1. Net long-term capital gain	$5,000
2. Net short-term capital gain	2,000
3. Net gain included in AGI	
(line 1 plus line 2)	$7,000
4. Net capital gain	$5,000

EXAMPLE 8

1. Net long-term capital loss	$(1,000)
2. Net short-term capital gain	3,000
3. Net gain included in AGI	
(line 2 minus line 1)	$2,000
4. Net capital gain	none

Net Loss

The netting of all capital asset transactions from current sales or exchanges may result in a net loss. The current deduction for net losses (both long-term and short-term) from sales or exchanges of capital assets is limited to the smallest of the following amounts:

1. $3,000 ($1,500 if married, filing separately)
2. The net loss

EXAMPLE 9

To illustrate a loss situation, a taxpayer filing jointly has a salary of $30,000 in 1992, and the following capital gains and losses:

	Long-term	Short-term
Gains	$ 3,000	$ 500
Losses	(15,000)	(1,400)
Net	$(12,000)	$(900)

The taxpayer can deduct $3,000 of the $12,900 net loss capital loss against ordinary income in 1992. The remaining loss of $9,900 ($12,900 − $3,000) is carried forward.

Capital Loss Carryovers

Any capital loss that is not deductible in the current year may be carried forward for an *unlimited period of time*. When capital losses are carried forward, they are first used to offset any capital gains originating in the carryover year. There is no limit on the amount of capital gain that may be offset. Up to $3,000 ($1,500, separate return) of any remaining capital loss will be used as a deduction from other income. Note that the $3,000 ($1,500) maximum deduction applies on an annual basis.

Losses carried forward are treated as long- or short-term in the carryover year, depending upon whether they were long- or short-term originally. Whenever capital losses exceed capital gains and there are both long-term and short-term capital losses, the short-term capital losses will be used to offset other income before the long-term losses are used.

EXAMPLE 10

To illustrate the provisions of capital loss carryover, assume that the taxpayer in the preceding example with the $900 net short-term capital loss and $12,000 net long-term capital loss had no additional capital gain or loss in 1993 or 1994. For the taxable year 1992, other income would be offset by the maximum amount of $3,000, consisting of $900 net short-term capital loss plus $2,100 of long-term capital loss. The balance of the net long-term capital loss of $9,900 ($12,000 − $2,100) would be carried forward to 1993.

In 1993, $3,000 of the loss would be deducted, leaving $6,900 ($9,900 − $3,000) as a carryover to 1994. Another $3,000 would be deducted in 1994, and $3,900 ($6,900 − $3,000) would carry over to 1995.

Reporting on Schedule D

Taxable gains and losses from the sale or exchange of property by an individual must be reported on separate Schedule D (Form 1040), Capital Gains and Losses. Form 4797, Sales of Business Property, is provided for reporting gains and losses from dispositions of trade or business property. It is filed in support of Schedule D. Schedule D is used to report information on capital gains and losses as shown in Table 12-1.

Table 12-1
Reporting on Schedule D

Part	Description
I	Short-term Capital Gains and Losses—Assets Held One Year or Less
II	Long-term Capital Gains and Losses—Assets Held More Than One Year
III	Summary of Parts I and II
IV	Tax Calculation Using Maximum Capital Gains Rate
V	Capital Loss Carryovers From 1991 to 1992
VI	Election Not To Use the Installment Method
VII	Reconciliation of Forms 1099-B for Bartering Transactions

Parts I and II, Short-Term and Long-Term Capital Gains and Losses

Parts I and II of Schedule D are of special importance to many individual taxpayers who sell or exchange property but who do not have a trade or business. The sale or exchange of capital assets, such as securities, personal residences, and jewelry, is reported in these two parts. The nature of capital assets, holding periods, and basis of property have already been discussed earlier in this chapter. For each transaction involving taxable gains or losses, the taxpayer must report the kind of property, the date acquired, the date sold, the gross sales price (less expense of sale), the cost or other basis, and the loss or gain.

All 1992 short-term capital gains or losses and any short-term capital losses carried over are listed in Part I (lines 1a through 6) and then summarized (line 7). These totals are combined to determine the net short-term gain or loss (line 8).

All 1992 long-term capital gains or losses and any long-term capital losses carried over are listed in Part II (lines 9a through 16) and then summarized (line 17). These total amounts are combined to form the net long-term gain or loss (line 18).

Part III, Summary of Parts I and II

Part III summarizes the net short-term and net long-term gains and losses from Parts I and II. The capital gain amount to be included in AGI or the capital loss amount to be deducted from other income is determined.

The net short-term gain or loss (line 8) and the net long-term gain or loss (line 18) are combined in Part III (line 19). If there is a *net gain* (line 19), this amount is entered on Form 1040 (line 13). If there is a *net loss* (line 19), the amount of loss to be deducted from AGI must be calculated (line 20). The loss that can be deducted is the smaller of the (a) net loss (line 19) or (b) $3,000 ($1,500 if married filing separately).

Part IV, Tax Calculation Using Maximum Capital Gains Rate

Part IV is used only by taxpayers that have a net capital gain and taxable income that is subject to the 31% tax rate. The tax calculation in Part IV (lines 21 through 29) applies the maximum capital gain tax rate of 28% to any long-term capital gain (line 19). The regular tax rates apply to taxable income other than the net capital gain.

The taxes on both the ordinary income and the net capital gain are included in the total tax (line 29). This tax is entered on Form 1040 (line 38), where the box for Schedule D is also checked.

Part V, Capital Loss Carryovers from 1992 to 1993

Part V is used only when there is an excess of deductible capital loss (line 19) over the amount of capital loss that can actually be claimed in 1992 (line 20). The short-term capital loss carryover and the long-term capital loss carryover retain their short-term or long-term status. Part V determines the portion of the short-term capital loss (line 38) and the portion of long-term capital loss (line 45) that can be carried over from 1992 to 1993.

Part VI, Election Not to Use the Installment Method

If property is sold at a gain and payment is received in the following tax year, the installment method of reporting must be used unless the taxpayer elects not to do so. If electing out of the installment method, the taxpayer checks the box (line 46).

Part VI must be completed if a taxpayer has a note or other obligation at less than full face value to report. The face amount of the note and the percentage of valuation must be reported.

Part VII, Reconciliation of Forms 1099-B for Bartering Transactions

Schedule D, Part VII is a schedule designed by the IRS to enable reconciliation and to verify taxpayer reporting compliance. The taxpayer summarizes the amounts of bartering income from Forms 1099-B which are included on the various appropriate income tax return forms and schedules. This part of Schedule D is used by the IRS to compare the data reported by taxpayers and the data reported on bartering transactions on Forms 1099-B. The taxpayer must attach to Schedule D any additional sheets used for an explanation of Part VII reporting.

Filled-In Schedule D

Illustration 12-1

A filled-in Schedule D, Capital Gains and Losses, for Mr. and Mrs. John R. Williams is shown in Illustration 12-1. Mr. and Mrs. Williams are in the 28% marginal tax bracket.

The Williams had two sales of stock during the year, and had received a Form 1099-B on each. Comco Corporation stock, purchased on June 27, 1992, at a cost of $750, was sold on November 20, 1992, at a gross sales price of $950. Since the stock had been held for less than one year, the gain of $200 was short-term and was reported on Schedule D (line 1a). Wilcox Industries stock, purchased on February 7, 1981, at a cost of $5,192, was sold on September 3, 1992, at a gross sales price of $6,090. Since a Form 1099-B had been received and the stock had been held for more than one year, the gain of $898 was long-term and was reported on Schedule D (line 9a).

In 1990, Mr. Williams had sold 900 shares of common stock in the CMA Corporation, recognizing a short-term loss of $7,000. There had been no other capital gain or loss transactions in either 1990 or 1991. Thus, it had been possible to deduct $3,000 (maximum for 1990) of the loss against other income in 1990. The remaining $4,000 had been carried forward to 1991, and another $3,000 (maximum for 1991) was deducted against other income in 1991. The remaining $1,000 was carried forward to 1992. Mr. and Mrs. Williams entered the $1,000 short-term capital loss carryover on Schedule D (line 6). The $1,000 short-term capital loss carryover was combined with the $200 short-term gain to give a net short-term loss of $800 (line 8).

A capital gain distribution from BCA Mutual Fund of $152 is entered on Schedule D (line 14). The total of the long-term transactions, $1,050, is entered on Schedule D (lines 17 and 18).

Part III of Schedule D combines the amounts of capital gains and losses. The result of the Williams' net short-term loss of $800 and net long-term gain of $1,050 is a net gain of $250. This gain is reported on Schedule D (line 19) and carried to Form 1040 (line 13).

Schedule D-1. If more space is needed to list transactions involving short-term and long-term capital gains and losses, Schedule D-1 provides additional lines for this listing. The total short-term capital gain (loss) from Schedule D-1 is reported on Schedule D (line 1b). Similarly, the total long-term capital gain (loss) is reported on Schedule D (line 9b). Taxpayers using Schedule D-1 must attach this form to Schedule D.

Illustration 12-1
Filled-In Schedule D, Form 1040, Page 1

SCHEDULE D
(Form 1040)

Department of the Treasury
Internal Revenue Service

Capital Gains and Losses
(And Reconciliation of Forms 1099-B for Bartering Transactions)

► Attach to Form 1040.   ► See Instructions for Schedule D (Form 1040).
► For more space to list transactions for lines 1a and 9a, get Schedule D-1 (Form 1040).

OMB No. 1545-0074

1992

Attachment
Sequence No. **12A**

Name(s) shown on Form 1040

John R. and Jean K. Williams

Your social security number
272 11 8245

Caution: *Add the following amounts reported to you for 1992 on Forms 1099-B and 1099-S (or on substitute statements): (a) proceeds from transactions involving stocks, bonds, and other securities, and (b) gross proceeds from real estate transactions not reported on another form or schedule. If this total does not equal the total of lines 1c and 9c, column (d), attach a statement explaining the difference.*

Part I — Short-Term Capital Gains and Losses—Assets Held One Year or Less

(a) Description of property (Example, 100 shares 7% preferred of "XYZ" Co.)	(b) Date acquired (Mo., day, yr.)	(c) Date sold (Mo., day, yr.)	(d) Sales price (see page D-2)	(e) Cost or other basis (see page D-3)	(f) LOSS If (e) is more than (d), subtract (d) from (e)	(g) GAIN If (d) is more than (e), subtract (e) from (d)
1a Stocks, Bonds, Other Securities, and Real Estate. Include Form 1099-B and 1099-S Transactions. See page D-3.						
100 shares Comco Corp.	6/27/92	11/20/92	950:00	750:00		200:00

1b Amounts from Schedule D-1, line 1b. Attach Schedule D-1		
1c Total of All Sales Price Amounts. Add column (d) of lines 1a and 1b . . ►	**1c**	950:00
1d Other Transactions.		

2 Short-term gain from sale or exchange of your home from Form 2119, line 17 or 23 .	**2**			
3 Short-term gain from installment sales from Form 6252, line 26 or 37	**3**			
4 Short-term gain or (loss) from like-kind exchanges from Form 8824	**4**			
5 Net short-term gain or (loss) from partnerships, S corporations, and fiduciaries .	**5**			
6 Short-term capital loss carryover from 1991 Schedule D, line 36	**6**	1,000:00		
7 Add lines 1a, 1b, 1d, and 2 through 6, in columns (f) and (g).	**7**	(1,000:00)		200:00
8 Net short-term capital gain or (loss). Combine columns (f) and (g) of line 7	**8**			(800:00)

Part II — Long-Term Capital Gains and Losses—Assets Held More Than One Year

9a Stocks, Bonds, Other Securities, and Real Estate. Include Form 1099-B and 1099-S Transactions. See page D-3.

(a) Description of property	(b) Date acquired	(c) Date sold	(d) Sales price	(e) Cost or other basis	(f) LOSS	(g) GAIN
100 shares Wilcox Industries	2/7/81	9/3/92	6,090:00	5,192:00		898:00

9b Amounts from Schedule D-1, line 9b. Attach Schedule D-1		
9c Total of All Sales Price Amounts. Add column (d) of lines 9a and 9b . . ►	**9c**	6,090:00
9d Other Transactions.		

10 Long-term gain from sale or exchange of your home from Form 2119, line 17 or 23 .	**10**			
11 Long-term gain from installment sales from Form 6252, line 26 or 37	**11**			
12 Long-term gain or (loss) from like-kind exchanges from Form 8824.	**12**			
13 Net long-term gain or (loss) from partnerships, S corporations, and fiduciaries .	**13**			
14 Capital gain distributions	**14**			152:00
15 Gain from Form 4797, line 8 or 10	**15**			
16 Long-term capital loss carryover from 1991 Schedule D, line 43	**16**			
17 Add lines 9a, 9b, 9d, and 10 through 16, in columns (f) and (g)	**17**	( )		1,050:00
18 Net long-term capital gain or (loss). Combine columns (f) and (g) of line 17	**18**			1,050:00

For Paperwork Reduction Act Notice, see Form 1040 instructions.   Cat. No. 11338H   Schedule D (Form 1040) 1992

Illustration 12-1
Filled-In Schedule D, Form 1040, Page 2

Schedule D (Form 1040) 1992   Attachment Sequence No. **12A**   Page **2**

Name(s) shown on Form 1040. Do not enter name and social security number if shown on other side.   Your social security number

Part III Summary of Parts I and II

19 Combine lines 8 and 18 and enter the net gain or (loss). If a gain, also enter the gain on Form 1040, line 13 . . . . **19** 250 | 00

  Note: *If both lines 18 and 19 are gains, see Part IV below.*

20 If line 19 is a (loss), enter here and as a (loss) on Form 1040, line 13, the **smaller** of:

  a The (loss) on line 19; **or**

  b ($3,000) or, if married filing a separate return, ($1,500) . . . . **20** (   )

  Note: *When figuring whether line 20a or 20b is smaller, treat both numbers as positive.*
  Complete Part V if the loss on line 19 is more than the loss on line 20 OR if Form 1040, line 37, is zero.

Part IV Tax Computation Using Maximum Capital Gains Rate

USE THIS PART TO FIGURE YOUR TAX ONLY IF BOTH LINES 18 AND 19 ARE GAINS, AND:

You checked filing status box:	AND	Form 1040, line 37, is over:	You checked filing status box:	AND	Form 1040, line 37, is over:
1		$51,900	3		$43,250
2 or 5		$86,500	4		$74,150

21 Enter the amount from Form 1040, line 37 . . . . **21**

22 Enter the **smaller** of line 18 or line 19 . . . . **22**

23 Subtract line 22 from line 21 . . . . **23**

24 Enter: $21,450 if you checked filing status box 1; $35,800 if you checked filing status box 2 or 5; $17,900 if you checked filing status box 3; or $28,750 if you checked filing status box 4 . . . . . **24**

25 Enter the **greater** of line 23 or line 24 . . . . **25**

26 Subtract line 25 from line 21 . . . . **26**

27 Figure the tax on the amount on line 25. Use the Tax Table or Tax Rate Schedules, whichever applies **27**

28 Multiply line 26 by 28% (.28) **28**

29 Add lines 27 and 28. Enter here and on Form 1040, line 38, and check the box for Schedule D . . **29**

Part V Capital Loss Carryovers from 1992 to 1993

30 Enter the amount from Form 1040, line 35. If a loss, enclose the amount in parentheses **30**

31 Enter the loss from line 20 as a positive amount **31**

32 Combine lines 30 and 31. If zero or less, enter -0- **32**

33 Enter the **smaller** of line 31 or line 32 . . . . **33**

  Note: *If both lines 8 and 20 are losses, go to line 34; otherwise, skip lines 34-38.*

34 Enter the loss from line 8 as a positive amount **34**

35 Enter the gain, if any, from line 18 . . . . **35**

36 Enter the amount from line 33 . . . . **36**

37 Add lines 35 and 36 . . . . **37**

38 **Short-term capital loss carryover to 1993.** Subtract line 37 from line 34. If zero or less, enter -0- . **38**

  Note: *If both lines 18 and 20 are losses, go to line 39; otherwise, skip lines 39-45.*

39 Enter the loss from line 18 as a positive amount **39**

40 Enter the gain, if any, from line 8 . . . . **40**

41 Enter the amount from line 33 . . . . **41**

42 Enter the amount, if any, from line 34 . . . **42**

43 Subtract line 42 from line 41. If zero or less, enter -0- **43**

44 Add lines 40 and 43 . . . . **44**

45 **Long-term capital loss carryover to 1993.** Subtract line 44 from line 39. If zero or less, enter -0- . **45**

Part VI Election Not To Use the Installment Method. Complete this part **only** if you elect out of the installment method and report a note or other obligation at less than full face value.

46 Check here if you elect out of the installment method . . . . ▶ ☐

47 Enter the face amount of the note or other obligation . . . . ▶ . . . .

48 Enter the percentage of valuation of the note or other obligation . . . . ▶ . . . . %

Part VII Reconciliation of Forms 1099-B for Bartering Transactions.
Complete this part **only** if you received one or more Forms 1099-B or substitute statements reporting **bartering income.**

Amount of bartering income from Form 1099-B or substitute statement reported on form or schedule

49 Form 1040, line 22 . . . . **49**

50 Schedule C, C-EZ, D, E, or F (specify) ▶ **50**

51 Other form or schedule (identify). If nontaxable, indicate reason—attach additional sheets if necessary:

. . . . **51**

52 **Total.** Add lines 49 through 51. This amount should be the same as the total bartering income on all Forms 1099-B and substitute statements received for bartering transactions **52**

Gains and Losses on Dispositions of Business Property

Real and depreciable personal property used in a trade or business are not capital assets, but, under certain conditions, they are entitled to capital gains treatment. If these assets are held for more than 12 months, they are referred to as *Section 1231 assets*. When such assets are sold, exchanged, or involuntarily converted, the gains and losses on their disposition receive special tax treatment. Net gains may be treated as long-term capital gain, and net losses may be treated as ordinary expenses. In many cases, however, previous deductions for depreciation may convert the potential capital gain into ordinary income. The specific tax treatment of gains and losses on real and depreciable personal property used in a trade or business is governed by Internal Revenue Code Sections 1231, 1245, and 1250, which are interrelated in their impact. Each of these sections is discussed briefly with an example following to show their interrelationship.

Section 1231 Gains and Losses

Section 1231 provides that *net* gains from the sale, exchange, or involuntary conversion of real and depreciable property used in a trade or business may be eligible for long-term capital gains treatment even though such assets are not defined as capital assets. To be eligible for Section 1231 treatment, the assets must have been held for more than 12 months, and the gains must exceed the losses from all Section 1231 transactions.

In addition to the sale or exchange of depreciable and real property, Section 1231 transactions include the following situations:

1. The *involuntary conversion* of *real and depreciable property* used in the trade or business, and held for more than 12 months (The term "involuntary conversion" is applied to property which has been destroyed accidentally, has been stolen, or has been seized through condemnation proceedings.)
2. The *involuntary conversion* of *capital assets* used for business or held for profit when the holding period is more than 12 months
3. The sale or exchange of certain livestock and unharvested crops
4. Cutting or disposal of timber under certain conditions
5. Disposal of coal or iron ore under certain conditions

Involuntary Conversions. To correctly apply Section 1231, transactions in the form of involuntary conversions due to casualty or theft of business property are separated from all other transactions involving Section 1231 assets. The gains and losses from involuntary conversions due to casualty or theft of business property and property held for profit are considered as a separate group and are first reported on Form 4684, Casualties and Thefts. If the gains exceed the losses when these transactions are combined, the net gain is transferred to Form 4797, Sales of Business Property, Part I (line 3), to be considered along with all other Section 1231 gains and losses described below.

If the losses from the casualty and theft transactions exceed the gains from such transactions when combined on Form 4684, the net loss is transferred to Form 4797, Part II (line 14). This net loss is deductible as an ordinary loss. Condemnations are not grouped with casualty and theft items. They are grouped with the other Section 1231 assets.

Note: Gains and losses from casualties or thefts of nonbusiness property are not combined with similar gains and losses on business property under Section 1231. If nonbusiness losses exceed the nonbusiness gains, the net loss is reported as a casualty and theft loss on Schedule A (Form 1040). However, if the total gains are more than the total losses, the difference will be treated as capital gain on Schedule D (Form 1040).

Net 1231 Gain. All other transactions involving Section 1231 assets (except for the limitations of Sections 1245 and 1250 described below) are reported on Form 4797, Part I (line 2). These transactions include sales and exchanges of real and depreciable property used in a trade or business and condemnations of such property. If the total of all transactions reported on Section 4797, Part I is a net gain (including the net gain transferred from Form 4684), this gain will be treated as ordinary income to the extent of any unrecaptured Section 1231 losses claimed by the taxpayer in the previous five years. Any remaining gain is a net long-term capital gain and is reported as such on Schedule D (Form 1040).

Net 1231 Loss. If the total of all transactions reported in Part I of Form 4797 is a net loss, the loss is an ordinary loss and is entered on Form 4797, Part II (line 12). As an ordinary loss, the loss can be deducted each year without limitation rather than being subject to the capital loss limitations. The proper classification and reporting of Section 1231 transactions is very important in assuring that the taxpayer gets the maximum tax benefit in the form of capital gains treatment for net gains and ordinary loss treatment for net losses.

EXAMPLE 11 —————————————————

Assume in a particular year that a business has two transactions in eligible Section 1231 assets, an $18,000 gain from the sale of land and a $10,000 casualty loss on a building from a fire. The $18,000 gain and the $10,000 loss are separately reported. Since the business has a net casualty loss of $10,000, the loss is deductible as an ordinary expense and is not netted with the 1231 gain. Thus, the net 1231 gain of $18,000 is treated as a long-term capital gain. However, if there are any unrecaptured 1231 losses from the previous five years, some or all of the $18,000 gain will be ordinary income.

EXAMPLE 12 —————————————————

Jose Mendella started a business in 1987 and experienced the following 1231 gains and losses over the period 1987-1992:

Year	Net Section 1231 Gain	Net Section 1231 Loss
1987		$4,000
1988	$1,000	
1989		$8,000
1990	$5,000	
1991		$10,000
1992	$30,000	

The net 1231 losses in 1987, 1989, and 1991 are deductible expenses for AGI on the tax return for each of those years.

The net 1231 gain in 1988 ($1,000) will all be recaptured as ordinary income. The 1990 gain of $5,000 will also be treated as ordinary income since the unrecaptured 1231 losses deducted in the previous years, $11,000 ($4,000 − $1,000 + $8,000), exceed the gain.

The $30,000 net 1231 gain in 1992 is treated as ordinary income to the extent of unrecaptured Section 1231 losses in the previous years, $16,000 ($11,000 − $5,000 + $10,000). The remaining $14,000 of gain ($30,000 − $16,000, ordinary income) is treated as long-term capital gain.

Depreciation Recapture

In the discussion of Section 1231 thus far, it has been assumed that all of the gain from a transaction in eligible property was a potential long-term capital gain. In the past, business taxpayers had the incentive to take deductions for depreciation as rapidly and in as accelerated a manner as possible. They would then sell the asset at a gain which was taxed as a long-term capital gain. This approach had the effect of converting ordinary income into long-term capital gain.

To limit the opportunity of converting ordinary income into a long-term capital gain, Congress introduced *depreciation recapture*: if a business asset is sold at a gain, some or all of that gain will be treated as ordinary income to the extent of a specified amount of depreciation taken on the asset over its lifetime. That portion of the gain not treated as ordinary income remains as a Section 1231 gain which may become a long-term capital gain.

Treating some or all of the gain as ordinary income under the depreciation recapture rules has been mitigated by the fact that capital gains have been taxed as ordinary income since 1987 with only a small tax advantage accruing to individuals after 1990. However, the concept is still important because capital gains and losses must still be calculated to determine the maximum deduction of capital losses against ordinary income. Therefore, it continues to be necessary, because of the capital loss limitations and the depreciation recapture rules, to distinguish between income classified as ordinary and income classified as Section 1231 gains which may be converted to long-term gains.

In addition to generally taxing capital gains as ordinary income, the Tax Reform Act of 1986 modified the ACRS rules to require that all real property be depreciated on a straight-line basis. Because of these changes, the 1986 Act eliminated any recapture requirements for real property acquired after 1986.

Recapture of Depreciation on Section 1245 Assets

Section 1245 provides for the recapture of depreciation on personal property used in a trade or business. The primary assets affected are machinery, equipment, furniture, fixtures, and motor vehicles. Section 1245 assets also include elevators and escalators, single purpose agricultural and horticultural structures, storage facilities used in connection with the distribution of petroleum and its primary products, and livestock held for breeding, dairy, or sport purposes.

Section 1245 also provides for the recapture of ACRS deductions on Section 1245 *recovery property*. Recovery property includes all *real* and *personal* ACRS property other than the following classes of real property: (1) real property that is residential rental property, (2) real property that is used predominantly outside of the United States, (3) low-income housing, and (4) real property for which a straight-line election is made.

Ordinary Income. If a Section 1245 asset is sold at a gain, the gain will be treated as ordinary income to the extent of *all* depreciation or ACRS deductions taken since 1961. If the gain is greater than the amount of depreciation or ACRS deductions recaptured as ordinary income, the excess gain is treated as a Section 1231 gain. Such a gain may be eligible for capital gains treatment when combined with other Section 1231 gains and losses on Form 4797.

EXAMPLE 13 ──────────────

Assume a taxpayer acquired a business machine on January 2, 1991, for $20,000. Depreciation was taken using accelerated depreciation based on a 5-year life in the following amounts: 1991, $4,000; 1992, $3,200; a total of $7,200. The machine was sold on January 25, 1992, for $21,000.

The calculation of the gain or loss and the amount of gain to be classified as (1) ordinary income and (2) capital gain is determined as follows:

1. Determine the realized gain:

Selling price	$21,000
Adjusted basis ($20,000 − $7,200)	12,800
Realized gain	$ 8,200

2. Determine the Section 1245 ordinary income equal to the amount of depreciation taken since 1961, but not exceeding the realized gain:

Depreciation taken since 1961	$7,200
Realized gain	$8,200
Ordinary income (lesser of $7,200 and $8,200)	$7,200

3. Determine the gain to be included as Section 1231 gain:

Total realized gain	$8,200
Less Section 1245 ordinary income (not exceeding realized gain)	7,200
Section 1231 gain	$1,000

The amount of depreciation taken since 1961 is a key figure in determining Section 1245 ordinary income. Any gain up to the amount of the depreciation taken since 1961 is Section 1245 ordinary income. If the sale or exchange results in a gain that is more than the amount of depreciation taken since 1961, the amount of gain in excess of Section 1245 income is treated as a Section 1231 gain. For a Section 1231 gain to occur, however, the selling price of the used 1245 asset would have to exceed its original cost.

It should also be noted that Section 1245 recapture applies only to gains. Losses on Section 1245 property are actually 1231 losses. Such losses are netted against 1231 gains.

Recapture of Depreciation on Section 1250 Assets

Section 1250 provides for the recapture of depreciation from the disposition of certain depreciable realty, including all intangible real property (leases) and all tangible real property except those defined in Section 1245. But unlike Section 1245 which provides for depreciation recapture on *all* depreciation taken, Section 1250 provides for the recapture of only *excess* depreciation taken since 1969. If a Section 1250 asset is sold at a gain, that gain is considered to be ordinary income to the extent that the actual depreciation taken exceeds straight-line depreciation. The recapture rules are somewhat different for commercial and industrial buildings than for residential rental property. For both types of buildings, however, the recapture is more lenient than for Section 1245 assets because only the excess depreciation is recaptured.

Note: The Tax Reform Act of 1986 eliminated the recapture requirements for real property acquired after 1986. However, the recapture rules still apply to real property acquired before 1987.

EXAMPLE 14

Chad Chevalier purchased a grocery store in April, 1985, for $400,000. He sold the store in July of 1992 for $390,000. Chad used accelerated depreciation on the building and claimed $186,833 during the period that he owned the facility. Straight-line depreciation during the same period would have been $138,888.

Chad's realized gain is $176,833. His Section 1250 ordinary income is $47,945, and his Section 1231 gain is $128,888.

Sales proceeds		$390,000
Basis ($400,000 – $186,833)		213,167
Realized gain		$176,833
Depreciation recapture:		
Depreciation claimed	$186,833	
Straight-line depreciation	138,888	
Excess depreciation (ordinary income)		47,945
Section 1231 gain		$128,888

Reporting Sales of Business Property

Form 4797, Sales of Business Property, pages 1 and 2, shown in Illustration 12-2, is used to report all transactions involving the sale or exchange of Section 1231, 1245, and 1250 assets. Part I, Sales or Exchanges of Property Used in a Trade or Business and Involuntary Conversions From Other Than Casualty and Theft —Property Held More Than 1 Year, is used for Section 1231 transactions except for certain livestock.

Part II, Ordinary Gains and Losses, is used for transactions in which the property involved is not a capital asset or is not entitled to capital gains treatment. This includes business assets held 12 months or less. Part III, Gain from Disposition of Property Under Section 1245, 1250, 1252, 1254, and 1255, is used for calculating the amount of gain that must be reported as ordinary income under the depreciation recapture provisions of Section 1245. It is important to note that Sections 1231, 1245, and 1250 (for real property placed in service before 1987) are applicable to all business property whether held by an individual, a partnership, or a corporation. Transactions in-

volving these sections are reported on Form 4797 regardless of the type of taxpayer. It is beyond the scope of this text to discuss the recapture rules related to Sections 1252, 1254, and 1255 which deal with such topics as the recapture of expenditures related to conservation, land clearing, and intangible drilling costs.

Section 1231 gains of Form 4797, Part I, are carried to the long-term capital gains section of Schedule D, Form 1040. Section 1231 net losses are carried to Form 4797, Part II, Ordinary Gains and Losses. If the net losses in Part II are identified as casualty losses, they are carried to Schedule A, Form 1040 (line 17). If there is a remaining gain (or loss) in Part II not identified as a casualty loss, it is carried to Form 1040 (line 15). The net gain from disposition of Section 1245 property reported in Part III is transferred to Form 4797, Part II (line 14) to the extent that the gain is ordinary income and to Part I (line 6) to the extent that the gain is to be treated as a capital gain under Section 1231.

Filled-In Form 4797

Illustration 12-2

To illustrate the application of the recapture rules, assume that Pauline Christopher completed the construction of a commercial building at a cost of $200,000 on July 3, 1980. She used accelerated depreciation and a 40-year useful life. The building was sold on January 3, 1992, for $166,000. If the accumulated depreciation taken from July 3, 1980 to January 3, 1992 amounted to $71,110, the basis of the property would be $128,890 ($200,000 – $71,110), and the realized gain would be $37,110 ($166,000 – $128,890). This gain is reported on Form 4797, Part III, since Pauline used an accelerated depreciation method which is subject to depreciation recapture. Straight-line depreciation for the same period would have amounted to $57,500. The difference of $13,610 ($71,110 – $57,500) is ordinary income, and the remaining gain, $23,500 ($37,110 – $13,610), is a Section 1231 gain. The $13,610 is reported on Form 4797 (line 33) and carried (line 14) where it is combined with other ordinary gains and losses on Form 4797, Part II. The $23,500 is calculated (line 34) and carried (line 6). The $23,500 is added to the long-term gain calculated on Form 4797, Part I.

Also assume that Pauline Christopher has the following gains and losses from designated transactions during the taxable year 1992 for properties used in a business and held for more than one year:

Gain from the sale of land ($22,800 – $15,000)	$7,800
Loss from the involuntary conversion of real estate condemned by city ($30,200 – $33,200)	(3,000)
Loss on the involuntary conversion of machinery—due to fire loss ($4,500 – $11,400)	(6,900)

Pauline has no unrecaptured 1231 losses from the preceding five years.

The gross proceeds from the sales or exchanges of real estate, $223,500 ($166,000 + $22,800 + $30,200 + $4,500), is reported on Form 4797 (line 1). The gain from the sale of land and the loss from the condemned real estate are reported (line 2). The gain of $28,300 ($7,800 + $23,500 – $3,000) will be entered as long-term capital gain on Ms. Christopher's Schedule D (Form 1040).

The $6,900 fire loss is first reported on Form 4864, and then the loss is transferred to Form 4797, Part II (line 15). Since this $6,900 is a business casualty loss and not a personal casualty loss, it will be combined with the other ordinary business gains and losses (line 20) for a net gain of $6,710. Thus, the long-term capital gain of $28,300 will be transferred from Form 4797 (line 10) to Schedule D (Form 1040). The ordinary gain of $6,710 will be transferred to Form 1040 directly from Form 4797 (line 20).

Gains from Sales Between Related Persons

Capital gains treatment for gains realized on a sale or exchange of depreciable property between related persons [spouse or between an individual and a corporation which the individual controls [over 50% ownership)] is not allowed. Also under constructive stock ownership rules, stock owned in a corporation by a taxpayer's spouse and minor children or grandchildren is attributed to the taxpayer in determination of control. These rules apply specifically to sales between commonly owned corporations, as well as to the situations given above. Constructive stock ownership rules are also expanded to include the taxpayer's parents, adult children, and any trust, estate, or partnership in which the taxpayer is a beneficiary or partner.

Corporate Comparison

Corporations net out capital gains and losses in the same manner as individuals. Any net capital gain is taxed as ordinary income.

In contrast to an individual, however, no part of a net capital loss is deductible from ordinary income by a corporation. Corporations can only use capital losses to offset capital gains. Consequently, the law provides that capital losses may be carried back three years and forward five years to offset capital gains in these other tax years. It should also be noted that all capital losses carry over as *short-term* capital losses.

Section 1231 Transactions

Corporations will handle 1231 property transactions much the same as individuals. Depreciation recapture provisions also apply to corporations.

Section 291 Recapture. Corporations (other than S corporations) also face an additional recapture provision. A corporation's ordinary income on the sale of Section 1250 real property will be increased by 20% of the additional amount which would have been ordinary income if the property had been "Section 1245 property." This additional ordinary income is calculated as follows:

Ordinary income under 1245 recapture rules
– Ordinary income under 1250 recapture rules
= Additional ordinary income under 1245 rules
x 20%
= Increase in corporation's ordinary income

Any gain on Section 1231 property that is not recaptured as ordinary income is 1231 gain.

Illustration 12-2
Filled-In Form 4797, Page 1

Form 4797

Department of the Treasury
Internal Revenue Service

Sales of Business Property
(Also Involuntary Conversions and Recapture Amounts Under Sections 179 and 280F)
▶ Attach to your tax return.   ▶ See separate instructions.

OMB No. 1545-0184

1992

Attachment Sequence No. 27

Name(s) shown on return: **Pauline Christopher**

Identifying number: **271-57-2696**

1 Enter here the gross proceeds from the sale or exchange of real estate reported to you for 1992 on Form(s) 1099-S (or a substitute statement) that you will be including on line 2, 11, or 22 . . . . **1**

Part I Sales or Exchanges of Property Used in a Trade or Business and Involuntary Conversions From Other Than Casualty or Theft—Property Held More Than 1 Year

(a) Description of property	(b) Date acquired (mo., day, yr.)	(c) Date sold (mo., day, yr.)	(d) Gross sales price	(e) Depreciation allowed or allowable since acquisition	(f) Cost or other basis, plus improvements and expense of sale	(g) LOSS ((f) minus the sum of (d) and (e))	(h) GAIN ((d) plus (e) minus (f))
2 Land	2/6/78	5/9/92	22,800		15,000		7,800
Real Estate (involuntary conversion)	3/5/83	6/2/92	30,200	47,100	80,300	(3,000)	

		(g)	(h)
3	Gain, if any, from Form 4684, line 39 . . . . **3**		
4	Section 1231 gain from installment sales from Form 6252, line 26 or 37 . . . . **4**		
5	Section 1231 gain or (loss) from like-kind exchanges from Form 8824 . . . . **5**		
6	Gain, if any, from line 34, from other than casualty or theft **6**		23,500
7	Add lines 2 through 6 in columns (g) and (h) **7**	(3,000)	31,300

8 Combine columns (g) and (h) of line 7. Enter gain or (loss) here, and on the appropriate line as follows: **8** 28,300

Partnerships—Enter the gain or (loss) on Form 1065, Schedule K, line 6. Skip lines 9, 10, 12, and 13 below.

S corporations—Report the gain or (loss) following the instructions for Form 1120S, Schedule K, lines 5 and 6. Skip lines 9, 10, 12, and 13 below, unless line 8 is a gain and the S corporation is subject to the capital gains tax.

All others—If line 8 is zero or a loss, enter the amount on line 12 below and skip lines 9 and 10. If line 8 is a gain and you did not have any prior year section 1231 losses, or they were recaptured in an earlier year, enter the gain as a long-term capital gain on Schedule D and skip lines 9, 10, and 13 below.

9 Nonrecaptured net section 1231 losses from prior years (see instructions) **9**

10 Subtract line 9 from line 8. If zero or less, enter -0-. Also enter on the appropriate line as follows (see instructions): **10** 28,300

S corporations—Enter this amount (if more than zero) on Schedule D (Form 1120S), line 13, and skip lines 12 and 13 below.

All others—If line 10 is zero, enter the amount from line 8 on line 13 below. If line 10 is more than zero, enter the amount from line 9 on line 13 below, and enter the amount from line 10 as a long-term capital gain on Schedule D.

Part II Ordinary Gains and Losses

11 Ordinary gains and losses not included on lines 12 through 18 (include property held 1 year or less):

(a)	(b)	(c)	(d)	(e)	(f)	(g)	(h)

		(g)	(h)
12	Loss, if any, from line 8 . . . . **12**	-0-	
13	Gain, if any, from line 8, or amount from line 9 if applicable **13**		
14	Gain, if any, from line 33 . . . . **14**		13,610
15	Net gain or (loss) from Form 4684, lines 31 and 38a **15**	6,900	
16	Ordinary gain from installment sales from Form 6252, line 25 or 36 . . . . **16**		
17	Ordinary gain or (loss) from like-kind exchanges from Form 8824 . . . . **17**		
18	Recapture of section 179 expense deduction for partners and S corporation shareholders from property dispositions by partnerships and S corporations (see instructions) **18**		
19	Add lines 11 through 18 in columns (g) and (h) **19**	(6,900)	13,610

20 Combine columns (g) and (h) of line 19. Enter gain or (loss) here, and on the appropriate line as follows: . . . **20** 6,710

a For all except individual returns: Enter the gain or (loss) from line 20 on the return being filed.

b For individual returns:

(1) If the loss on line 12 includes a loss from Form 4684, line 35, column (b)(ii), enter that part of the loss here and on line 20 of Schedule A (Form 1040). Identify as from "Form 4797, line 20b(1)." See instructions . . . . **20b(1)** -0-

(2) Redetermine the gain or (loss) on line 20, excluding the loss, if any, on line 20b(1). Enter here and on Form 1040, line 15 . **20b(2)** 6,710

For Paperwork Reduction Act Notice, see page 1 of separate instructions.   Cat. No. 13086I   Form **4797** (1992)

Form 4797 (1992)   Page **2**

Part III **Gain From Disposition of Property Under Sections 1245, 1250, 1252, 1254, and 1255**

21	(a) Description of section 1245, 1250, 1252, 1254, or 1255 property:			(b) Date acquired (mo., day, yr.)	(c) Date sold (mo., day, yr.)
A	Commercial building			7/3/80	1/3/92
B					
C					
D					

	Relate lines 21A through 21D to these columns ▶		Property A	Property B	Property C	Property D
22	Gross sales price (Note: *See line 1 before completing.*)	22	166,000			
23	Cost or other basis plus expense of sale	23	200,000			
24	Depreciation (or depletion) allowed or allowable	24	71,110			
25	Adjusted basis. Subtract line 24 from line 23	25	128,890			
26	Total gain. Subtract line 25 from line 22	26	37,110			
27	**If section 1245 property:**					
a	Depreciation allowed or allowable from line 24	27a				
b	Enter the **smaller** of line 26 or 27a	27b				
28	**If section 1250 property:** If straight line depreciation was used, enter -0- on line 28g, except for a corporation subject to section 291.					
a	Additional depreciation after 1975 (see instructions)	28a	13,610			
b	Applicable percentage multiplied by the **smaller** of line 26 or line 28a (see instructions)	28b	13,610			
c	Subtract line 28a from line 26. If line 26 is not more than line 28a, skip lines 28d and 28e	28c	23,500			
d	Additional depreciation after 1969 and before 1976	28d				
e	Applicable percentage multiplied by the **smaller** of line 28c or 28d (see instructions)	28e				
f	Section 291 amount (corporations only)	28f				
g	Add lines 28b, 28e, and 28f	28g	13,610			
29	**If section 1252 property:** Skip this section if you did not dispose of farmland or if this form is being completed for a partnership.					
a	Soil, water, and land clearing expenses	29a				
b	Line 29a multiplied by applicable percentage (see instructions)	29b				
c	Enter the **smaller** of line 26 or 29b	29c				
30	**If section 1254 property:**					
a	Intangible drilling and development costs, expenditures for development of mines and other natural deposits, and mining exploration costs (see instructions)	30a				
b	Enter the **smaller** of line 26 or 30a	30b				
31	**If section 1255 property:**					
a	Applicable percentage of payments excluded from income under section 126 (see instructions)	31a				
b	Enter the **smaller** of line 26 or 31a	31b				

Summary of Part III Gains. Complete property columns A through D, through line 31b before going to line 32.

32	Total gains for all properties. Add columns A through D, line 26	32	37,110
33	Add columns A through D, lines 27b, 28g, 29c, 30b, and 31b. Enter here and on line 14. See the instructions for Part IV if this is an installment sale	33	13,610
34	Subtract line 33 from line 32. Enter the portion from casualty or theft on Form 4684, line 33. Enter the portion from other than casualty or theft on Form 4797, line 6	34	23,500

Part IV **Election Not to Use the Installment Method.** Complete this part only if you elect out of the installment method and report a note or other obligation at less than full face value.

35	Check here if you elect out of the installment method	▶ ☐
36	Enter the face amount of the note or other obligation	▶ $
37	Enter the percentage of valuation of the note or other obligation	▶ %

Part V **Recapture Amounts Under Sections 179 and 280F When Business Use Drops to 50% or Less** See instructions for Part V.

			(a) Section 179	(b) Section 280F
38	Section 179 expense deduction or depreciation allowable in prior years	38		
39	Recomputed depreciation (see instructions)	39		
40	Recapture amount. Subtract line 39 from line 38. See instructions for where to report	40		

C H A P T E R   1 2

Questions and Problems

1. Are the following properties capital assets? (Indicate your answer by writing "yes" or "no" in the column at the right.)

Item	Answer
a. House occupied as a residence by the owner	__________
b. Delivery truck used in a contractor's business	__________
c. Corporate stocks owned by a doctor	__________
d. Valuable jewelry held for sale by Jones Jewelers	__________
e. Building lot held as speculation by an accountant	__________
f. Automobile used for personal purposes by owner	__________
g. Business suits worn only to work	__________
h. House used strictly as a summer residence	__________
i. Franchise	__________
j. Goodwill	__________
k. Patent	__________
l. Musical copyright owned by the composer	__________

2. **a.** Distinguish between long-term capital gain and short-term capital gain for capital assets acquired January 10, 1992.

   b. If an individual has gains and losses from the sale of stocks and other investments, in addition to other income and deductions, what schedule is used to supplement Form 1040 in reporting this gain or loss?

3. State the time when the holding period begins on capital assets acquired by the following methods:
   a. Capital asset acquired by gift, if sold at a gain

   b. Capital asset acquired by gift, if sold at a loss

   c. Property transmitted at death

4. Juan Alvarez, a farmer, subdivided an unimproved tract of land that he acquired 20 years ago. In the current year, he sold 4 lots for $10,000 each. The basis of each lot is $2,000, and the selling expenses are $400 per lot.
   a. What is the gain or loss on these transactions, and how will these transactions be taxed?

   b. Assuming that Alvarez sells 5 lots next year at the same price with selling expenses of $400 per lot, what will be the gain or loss, and how will these transactions be taxed?

5. Benji Baba, a real estate dealer, purchased two lots for $12,000 each last year in May. On August 30 of the current year, he sold the tracts of land for $20,000 each. Calculate the gain and describe how it will be treated on the tax return.

6. Roger Razaki sells 1000 shares of his Section 1244 stock ("small business corporation" stock) at a loss of $200,000. If Roger and his wife file a joint return, how will this loss be treated on the tax return?

7. a. An individual taxpayer, not a dealer or trader in securities, completed the following transactions in Micro Products Company common stock:

   September 15, current year, purchased 100 shares at a cost of $4,800
   December 10, current year, sold the above shares for $3,200
   January 4, succeeding year, purchased 100 shares at a cost of $3,000

      (1) What is the total taxable capital gain or deductible capital loss from the sale on December 10?

(2) What is the cost basis of the stock purchased on January 4?

b. Assume that the selling price of the 100 shares sold on December 10 was $5,300; all other facts stated in *7. a.*, above, remain the same.

    (1) What is the total capital gain or deductible capital loss from the sale on December 10?

    (2) What is the cost basis of the stock purchased on January 4?

c. Assume that the selling price of the shares sold on December 10 was $3,200 and that the original 100 shares of stock had been inherited by the taxpayer from the taxpayer's father on September 15, current year, at which time they were valued at $2,500. The stock had been purchased by the taxpayer's father five years earlier for $1,000.

    (1) What is the total capital gain or deductible loss from the sale on December 10?

    (2) What is the cost basis of the stock purchased on January 4?

8. What is the amount of capital loss deduction that can be claimed against other income for 1992 for each of the following taxpayers? Also, what is the capital loss carryover to 1993 by type of loss? If none, insert "None."

Gains and Losses	A	B	C	D	E
Short-term capital gains	$ 900	$ 800	$ 0	$ 400	$ 3,200
Short-term capital losses	(6,200)	(1,200)	(400)	(2,400)	(8,600)
Long-term capital gains	800	2,200	800	1,600	1,400
Long-term capital losses	(600)	(800)	(1,150)	(4,200)	(2,600)
Capital loss claimed against 1992 other income	$________	$________	$________	$________	$________
Short-term loss carryover to 1993	$________	$________	$________	$________	$________
Long-term loss carryover to 1993	$________	$________	$________	$________	$________

9. In each of the following cases, determine the amount of the capital gain or loss to be included with AGI in the 1992 tax return of an individual and the capital loss carryover, if any, with its type.

  a. Net short-term capital loss, $2,000; net long-term capital gain, $6,000.

  b. Net short-term capital gain, $2,000; net long-term capital loss, $6,000.

c. Net short-term capital gain or loss, none; net long-term capital gain, $6,000.

d. Net short-term capital gain, $4,000; net long-term capital loss, $8,000.

10. A taxpayer sold 100 shares of stock on April 13, 1992, for $7,500 cash. Before the sale, this taxpayer owned shares in the company as evidenced by the following certificates:

Certificate Number	Date Acquired	Number of Shares	Cost
CR642	4-11-77	300	$15,000
DO111	9-10-82	100	9,000
EA002	8-13-84	100	6,000

Which certificate should be delivered to the broker to cover the stock sold, and what is the tax consequence of the selection in 1992?

11. In March of 1992, Shirley Thompson sold stock of the Wingate Corporation for $15,000. She had acquired the stock several years earlier at a cost of $11,600. Exclusive of this gain she expects to have a taxable income of $34,000 (after deductions and exemptions) for the year. Ms. Thompson files a joint return with her husband, who has no income. She also is contemplating selling stock of the Roberts Printing Company in December 1992, which she acquired on January 15, 1991, at a cost of $18,000, and which has since declined in price to $13,000.

a. Calculate her total tax liability for 1992 assuming that she does not sell the Roberts stock in 1992.

b. Calculate her total tax liability for 1992 assuming that she does sell the Roberts stock for $13,000 in 1992. Also calculate the amount of tax savings that will result from the sale.

12. Michael L. and Joyce A. Sea, married taxpayers filing a joint return, SSNs 374-47-7774 and 642-81-9982, respectively, sold the following securities in 1992:

No. of Shares	Company	Date Acquired	Cost or Other Basis	Date Sold	Gross Sales Price
20	Red Corporation	7-1-91	$1,661	12-6-92	$2,311
50	Lee Corporation	9-15-91	5,820	11-14-92	4,320
60	Alf Corporation	6-10-92	850	10-15-92	715
100	RST Corporation	5-10-81	4,600	3-5-92	2,430
—	$1,000 par value bond, TF Company	5-5-92	800	10-15-92	900

A capital gain distribution from the Equity Capital Mutual Fund of $320 was received on July 16, 1992. A short-term capital loss of $260 and a long-term capital loss of $2,500 were carried over from 1991 to 1992.

Prepare Schedule D, Capital Gains and Losses and Reconciliation of Forms 1099-B, for Mr. and Mrs. Sea for 1992, using the Schedule D reproduced on the following pages. Assume that the income from Form 1040 (line 35), is $34,300 for Mr. and Mrs. Sea.

13. Rita loaned her brother, Richard, $7,500 on February 14, 1991. Richard filed for bankruptcy in 1992, and Rita learned that she could only expect to receive $.70 on the dollar on the personal loan that she had made to him. On April 10, 1993, Rita received a final settlement of $4,000.

   a. How much loss can Rita deduct in 1992?

   b. How much loss can Rita deduct in 1993?

   c. How will this loss be treated on Rita's tax return?

14. From the following information, please answer the questions listed below:

	Period Property Was Held	Amount 100%
Bad debt loss due to loan to friend	3 years	$(2,600)
Sale of equipment used in business	2 months	(1,500)
Sale of equipment used in business	2 years	(3,000)
Sale of corporate stock	5 years	2,500
Sale of land used in business	4 years	5,000
Net Gain (Loss)		$ 400

   a. What, if any, is the amount of short term capital loss?

   b. What, if any, is the amount of net "1231" gain or (loss)?

   c. What, if any, is the ordinary loss deduction?

SCHEDULE D
(Form 1040)

Department of the Treasury
Internal Revenue Service

Capital Gains and Losses

(And Reconciliation of Forms 1099-B for Bartering Transactions)

▶ Attach to Form 1040.   ▶ See Instructions for Schedule D (Form 1040).

▶ For more space to list transactions for lines 1a and 9a, get Schedule D-1 (Form 1040).

OMB No. 1545-0074

1992

Attachment
Sequence No. **12A**

Name(s) shown on Form 1040

Your social security number

Caution: Add the following amounts reported to you for 1992 on Forms 1099-B and 1099-S (or on substitute statements): (a) proceeds from transactions involving stocks, bonds, and other securities, and (b) gross proceeds from real estate transactions not reported on another form or schedule. If this total does not equal the total of lines 1c and 9c, column (d), attach a statement explaining the difference.

Part I   Short-Term Capital Gains and Losses—Assets Held One Year or Less

(a) Description of property (Example, 100 shares 7% preferred of "XYZ" Co.)	(b) Date acquired (Mo., day, yr.)	(c) Date sold (Mo., day, yr.)	(d) Sales price (see page D-2)	(e) Cost or other basis (see page D-3)	(f) LOSS If (e) is more than (d), subtract (d) from (e)	(g) GAIN If (d) is more than (e), subtract (e) from (d)
1a Stocks, Bonds, Other Securities, and Real Estate. Include Form 1099-B and 1099-S Transactions. See page D-3.						

1b Amounts from Schedule D-1, line 1b. Attach Schedule D-1					
1c Total of All Sales Price Amounts. Add column (d) of lines 1a and 1b ▶ **1c**					

1d Other Transactions.

2 Short-term gain from sale or exchange of your home from Form 2119, line 17 or 23 .	**2**	
3 Short-term gain from installment sales from Form 6252, line 26 or 37	**3**	
4 Short-term gain or (loss) from like-kind exchanges from Form 8824	**4**	
5 Net short-term gain or (loss) from partnerships, S corporations, and fiduciaries .	**5**	
6 Short-term capital loss carryover from 1991 Schedule D, line 36	**6**	
7 Add lines 1a, 1b, 1d, and 2 through 6, in columns (f) and (g).	**7** ( )	
8 Net short-term capital gain or (loss). Combine columns (f) and (g) of line 7	**8**	

Part II   Long-Term Capital Gains and Losses—Assets Held More Than One Year

9a Stocks, Bonds, Other Securities, and Real Estate. Include Form 1099-B and 1099-S Transactions. See page D-3.

9b Amounts from Schedule D-1, line 9b. Attach Schedule D-1					
9c Total of All Sales Price Amounts. Add column (d) of lines 9a and 9b ▶ **9c**					

9d Other Transactions.

10 Long-term gain from sale or exchange of your home from Form 2119, line 17 or 23 .	**10**	
11 Long-term gain from installment sales from Form 6252, line 26 or 37	**11**	
12 Long-term gain or (loss) from like-kind exchanges from Form 8824	**12**	
13 Net long-term gain or (loss) from partnerships, S corporations, and fiduciaries .	**13**	
14 Capital gain distributions	**14**	
15 Gain from Form 4797, line 8 or 10	**15**	
16 Long-term capital loss carryover from 1991 Schedule D, line 43	**16**	
17 Add lines 9a, 9b, 9d, and 10 through 16, in columns (f) and (g).	**17** ( )	
18 Net long-term capital gain or (loss). Combine columns (f) and (g) of line 17	**18**	

For Paperwork Reduction Act Notice, see Form 1040 instructions.   Cat. No. 11338H   Schedule D (Form 1040) 1992

Schedule D (Form 1040) 1992   Attachment Sequence No. **12A**   Page **2**

Name(s) shown on Form 1040. Do not enter name and social security number if shown on other side. | Your social security number

Part III Summary of Parts I and II

19 Combine lines 8 and 18 and enter the net gain or (loss). If a gain, also enter the gain on Form 1040, line 13 . . . . **19**

  Note: *If both lines 18 and 19 are gains, see Part IV below.*

20 If line 19 is a (loss), enter here and as a (loss) on Form 1040, line 13, the **smaller** of:

  a The (loss) on line 19; **or**

  b ($3,000) or, if married filing a separate return, ($1,500) . . . . **20** ( )

  Note: *When figuring whether line 20a or 20b is smaller, treat both numbers as positive.*
  Complete Part V if the loss on line 19 is more than the loss on line 20 OR if Form 1040, line 37, is zero.

Part IV Tax Computation Using Maximum Capital Gains Rate

USE THIS PART TO FIGURE YOUR TAX ONLY IF BOTH LINES 18 AND 19 ARE GAINS, AND:

You checked filing status box:	AND	Form 1040, line 37, is over:	You checked filing status box:	AND	Form 1040, line 37, is over:
1		$51,900	3		$43,250
2 or 5		$86,500	4		$74,150

21 Enter the amount from Form 1040, line 37 . . . . **21**

22 Enter the **smaller** of line 18 or line 19 . . . . **22**

23 Subtract line 22 from line 21 . . . . **23**

24 Enter: $21,450 if you checked filing status box 1; $35,800 if you checked filing status box 2 or 5; $17,900 if you checked filing status box 3; or $28,750 if you checked filing status box 4 . . . . . **24**

25 Enter the **greater** of line 23 or line 24 . . . . **25**

26 Subtract line 25 from line 21 . . . . **26**

27 Figure the tax on the amount on line 25. Use the Tax Table or Tax Rate Schedules, whichever applies **27**

28 Multiply line 26 by 28% (.28) **28**

29 Add lines 27 and 28. Enter here and on Form 1040, line 38, and check the box for Schedule D . . **29**

Part V Capital Loss Carryovers from 1992 to 1993

30 Enter the amount from Form 1040, line 35. If a loss, enclose the amount in parentheses **30**

31 Enter the loss from line 20 as a positive amount **31**

32 Combine lines 30 and 31. If zero or less, enter -0- **32**

33 Enter the **smaller** of line 31 or line 32 . . . . **33**

  Note: *If both lines 8 and 20 are losses, go to line 34; otherwise, skip lines 34-38.*

34 Enter the loss from line 8 as a positive amount **34**

35 Enter the gain, if any, from line 18 . . . . **35**

36 Enter the amount from line 33 . . . . **36**

37 Add lines 35 and 36 . . . . **37**

38 **Short-term capital loss carryover to 1993.** Subtract line 37 from line 34. If zero or less, enter -0- . **38**

  Note: *If both lines 18 and 20 are losses, go to line 39; otherwise, skip lines 39-45.*

39 Enter the loss from line 18 as a positive amount **39**

40 Enter the gain, if any, from line 8 . . . . **40**

41 Enter the amount from line 33 . . . . . . **41**

42 Enter the amount, if any, from line 34 . . . **42**

43 Subtract line 42 from line 41. If zero or less, enter -0- **43**

44 Add lines 40 and 43 . . . . **44**

45 **Long-term capital loss carryover to 1993.** Subtract line 44 from line 39. If zero or less, enter -0- . **45**

Part VI Election Not To Use the Installment Method. Complete this part **only** if you elect out of the installment method and report a note or other obligation at less than full face value.

46 Check here if you elect out of the installment method . . . . ▶ ☐

47 Enter the face amount of the note or other obligation . . . . ▶ . . . .

48 Enter the percentage of valuation of the note or other obligation . . . . ▶ . . . . %

Part VII Reconciliation of Forms 1099-B for Bartering Transactions.
  Complete this part **only** if you received one or more Forms 1099-B or substitute statements reporting **bartering income.**

Amount of bartering income from Form 1099-B or substitute statement reported on form or schedule

49 Form 1040, line 22 . . . . **49**

50 Schedule C, C-EZ, D, E, or F (specify) ▶ **50**

51 Other form or schedule (identify). If nontaxable, indicate reason—attach additional sheets if necessary:

. . . . **51**

52 **Total.** Add lines 49 through 51. This amount should be the same as the total bartering income on all Forms 1099-B and substitute statements received for bartering transactions **52**

15. Joji Kato experienced the following 1231 gains and losses in his business over the period 1987-1992.

Year	Net Section 1231 Gain	Net Section 1231 Loss
1987		$10,000
1988	$ 6,000	
1989		$15,000
1990		$ 8,000
1991	$20,000	
1992	$12,000	

How will the 1231 gains in 1991 and 1992 be treated?

16. Carlota Sanchez purchased a machine for her business on 1-20-91 for $50,000. On 11-05-92 she sold the machine for $55,000. Depreciation information is as follows:

MACRS deduction claimed	$18,000
Straight-line depreciation (5-year life) would have been	$10,000

What is Carlota's gain or loss on the sale of this machine and how will it be treated?

17. Victor Soto purchased a warehouse for his business in 1980 for $1,000,000. Soto sold the warehouse in December of 1992 for $1,200,000. Soto used an accelerated method of depreciation and claimed $400,000 of depreciation during the period when he owned the building. Straight-line depreciation during the same period would have been $275,000. How will this transaction be reported on the tax return?

18. In 1992, Virginia Banks, a calendar-year taxpayer, SSN 364-25-8153, had the following transactions involving assets used in her manufacturing business:

a. A warehouse was sold on April 6, 1992 for $39,300. The building had been purchased on July 3, 1986 for $28,000. Using accelerated depreciation, $11,893 was claimed for depreciation during the period July 3, 1986 through April 6, 1992. Straight-line depreciation for this same period would have been $8,475. Applicable percentage for Form 4797 (lines 26b and 26e) is 100%.

b. The land on which the warehouse was sitting was sold for $23,000. The land had a basis of $16,000.

c. A small tool shed was destroyed by fire during 1992. The loss was not covered by insurance. The shed had been used for several years and had an adjusted basis of $2,500 at the time of the fire. The loss was initially reported on Form 4684.

d. A building that the business had purchased for $60,000 on August 1, 1975, was condemned by the city in order to acquire the land upon which it stood for a new highway. Banks was paid $25,000 for the building on May 1, 1992. Depreciation totaled $30,000, with a loss of $5,000 on the sale.

e. Banks received $36,000 for the condemned land on which the building was sitting. The land had a basis of $30,000.

Prepare Form 4797, Sales of Business Property, using the blank forms provided.

Form **4797**	**Sales of Business Property** (Also Involuntary Conversions and Recapture Amounts Under Sections 179 and 280F)	OMB No. 1545-0184 **1992**
Department of the Treasury Internal Revenue Service	► Attach to your tax return. ► See separate instructions.	Attachment Sequence No. **27**

Name(s) shown on return	Identifying number

1 Enter here the gross proceeds from the sale or exchange of real estate reported to you for 1992 on Form(s) 1099-S (or a substitute statement) that you will be including on line 2, 11, or 22 . . . . **1**

Part I Sales or Exchanges of Property Used in a Trade or Business and Involuntary Conversions From Other Than Casualty or Theft—Property Held More Than 1 Year

(a) Description of property	(b) Date acquired (mo., day, yr.)	(c) Date sold (mo., day, yr.)	(d) Gross sales price	(e) Depreciation allowed or allowable since acquisition	(f) Cost or other basis, plus improvements and expense of sale	(g) LOSS ((f) minus the sum of (d) and (e))	(h) GAIN ((d) plus (e) minus (f))
2							

3 Gain, if any, from Form 4684, line 39 . . . . **3**

4 Section 1231 gain from installment sales from Form 6252, line 26 or 37 . . . . . . **4**

5 Section 1231 gain or (loss) from like-kind exchanges from Form 8824 . . . . . . **5**

6 Gain, if any, from line 34, from other than casualty or theft **6**

7 Add lines 2 through 6 in columns (g) and (h) . . . . **7** ( )

8 Combine columns (g) and (h) of line 7. Enter gain or (loss) here, and on the appropriate line as follows: **8**

    Partnerships—Enter the gain or (loss) on Form 1065, Schedule K, line 6. Skip lines 9, 10, 12, and 13 below.

    S corporations—Report the gain or (loss) following the instructions for Form 1120S, Schedule K, lines 5 and 6. Skip lines 9, 10, 12, and 13 below, unless line 8 is a gain and the S corporation is subject to the capital gains tax.

    All others—If line 8 is zero or a loss, enter the amount on line 12 below and skip lines 9 and 10. If line 8 is a gain and you did not have any prior year section 1231 losses, or they were recaptured in an earlier year, enter the gain as a long-term capital gain on Schedule D and skip lines 9, 10, and 13 below.

9 Nonrecaptured net section 1231 losses from prior years (see instructions) **9**

10 Subtract line 9 from line 8. If zero or less, enter -0-. Also enter on the appropriate line as follows (see instructions): **10**

    S corporations—Enter this amount (if more than zero) on Schedule D (Form 1120S), line 13, and skip lines 12 and 13 below.

    All others—If line 10 is zero, enter the amount from line 8 on line 13 below. If line 10 is more than zero, enter the amount from line 9 on line 13 below, and enter the amount from line 10 as a long-term capital gain on Schedule D.

Part II Ordinary Gains and Losses

11 Ordinary gains and losses not included on lines 12 through 18 (include property held 1 year or less):

12 Loss, if any, from line 8 . . . . **12**

13 Gain, if any, from line 8, or amount from line 9 if applicable **13**

14 Gain, if any, from line 33 . . . . **14**

15 Net gain or (loss) from Form 4684, lines 31 and 38a **15**

16 Ordinary gain from installment sales from Form 6252, line 25 or 36 . . . . . . **16**

17 Ordinary gain or (loss) from like-kind exchanges from Form 8824 . . . . . . **17**

18 Recapture of section 179 expense deduction for partners and S corporation shareholders from property dispositions by partnerships and S corporations (see instructions) **18**

19 Add lines 11 through 18 in columns (g) and (h) . . . . **19** ( )

20 Combine columns (g) and (h) of line 19. Enter gain or (loss) here, and on the appropriate line as follows: . . . **20**

  a For all except individual returns: Enter the gain or (loss) from line 20 on the return being filed.

  b For individual returns:

    (1) If the loss on line 12 includes a loss from Form 4684, line 35, column (b)(ii), enter that part of the loss here and on line 20 of Schedule A (Form 1040). Identify as from "Form 4797, line 20b(1)." See instructions . . . . **20b(1)**

    (2) Redetermine the gain or (loss) on line 20, excluding the loss, if any, on line 20b(1). Enter here and on Form 1040, line 15 . **20b(2)**

For Paperwork Reduction Act Notice, see page 1 of separate instructions.　　　　Cat. No. 13086I　　　　Form **4797** (1992)

Form 4797 (1992)   Page **2**

Part III Gain From Disposition of Property Under Sections 1245, 1250, 1252, 1254, and 1255

21 (a) Description of section 1245, 1250, 1252, 1254, or 1255 property: | (b) Date acquired (mo., day, yr.) | (c) Date sold (mo., day, yr.)

A

B

C

D

Relate lines 21A through 21D to these columns ▶		Property A	Property B	Property C	Property D
22 Gross sales price (Note: *See line 1 before completing.*)	22				
23 Cost or other basis plus expense of sale	23				
24 Depreciation (or depletion) allowed or allowable	24				
25 Adjusted basis. Subtract line 24 from line 23	25				
26 Total gain. Subtract line 25 from line 22	26				
27 If section 1245 property:					
a Depreciation allowed or allowable from line 24	27a				
b Enter the **smaller** of line 26 or 27a	27b				
28 If section 1250 property: If straight line depreciation was used, enter -0- on line 28g, except for a corporation subject to section 291.					
a Additional depreciation after 1975 (see instructions)	28a				
b Applicable percentage multiplied by the **smaller** of line 26 or line 28a (see instructions)	28b				
c Subtract line 28a from line 26. If line 26 is not more than line 28a, skip lines 28d and 28e	28c				
d Additional depreciation after 1969 and before 1976	28d				
e Applicable percentage multiplied by the **smaller** of line 28c or 28d (see instructions)	28e				
f Section 291 amount (corporations only)	28f				
g Add lines 28b, 28e, and 28f	28g				
29 If section 1252 property: Skip this section if you did not dispose of farmland or if this form is being completed for a partnership.					
a Soil, water, and land clearing expenses	29a				
b Line 29a multiplied by applicable percentage (see instructions)	29b				
c Enter the **smaller** of line 26 or 29b	29c				
30 If section 1254 property:					
a Intangible drilling and development costs, expenditures for development of mines and other natural deposits, and mining exploration costs (see instructions)	30a				
b Enter the **smaller** of line 26 or 30a	30b				
31 If section 1255 property:					
a Applicable percentage of payments excluded from income under section 126 (see instructions)	31a				
b Enter the **smaller** of line 26 or 31a	31b				

Summary of Part III Gains. Complete property columns A through D, through line 31b before going to line 32.

32 Total gains for all properties. Add columns A through D, line 26	32	
33 Add columns A through D, lines 27b, 28g, 29c, 30b, and 31b. Enter here and on line 14. See the instructions for Part IV if this is an installment sale	33	
34 Subtract line 33 from line 32. Enter the portion from casualty or theft on Form 4684, line 33. Enter the portion from other than casualty or theft on Form 4797, line 6	34	

Part IV Election Not to Use the Installment Method. Complete this part only if you elect out of the installment method and report a note or other obligation at less than full face value.

35 Check here if you elect out of the installment method . . . . ▶ ☐
36 Enter the face amount of the note or other obligation . . . . ▶ $ ______
37 Enter the percentage of valuation of the note or other obligation . . . . ▶ ______ %

Part V Recapture Amounts Under Sections 179 and 280F When Business Use Drops to 50% or Less
See instructions for Part V.

		(a) Section 179	(b) Section 280F
38 Section 179 expense deduction or depreciation allowable in prior years	38		
39 Recomputed depreciation (see instructions)	39		
40 Recapture amount. Subtract line 39 from line 38. See instructions for where to report	40		

TAX CREDITS AND OTHER TAX SITUATIONS

➡ The types of tax credits

➡ How to determine the alternative minimum tax

➡ How to complete Form 6251

➡ How to calculate a net operating loss (NOL)

➡ How to account for gains from installment sales

➡ How to account for income earned on long-term contracts

➡ Information returns

Tax Credits and Other Tax Situations

Your Rights as a Taxpayer

Cancellation of Penalties. You have the right to ask that certain penalties (but not interest) be cancelled (abated) if you can show reasonable cause for the failure that led to the penalty (or can show that you exercised due diligence, if that is the applicable standard for that penalty).

Source: Internal Revenue Service, Publication 1

$\mathbf{T}$his chapter will examine various tax situations that primarily affect entrepreneurs and investors. Some of the information presented in this chapter can be used by many taxpayers. Other information can be used by taxpayers only in limited situations.

These topics are discussed in this chapter:

1. Tax credits
2. Alternative Minimum Tax (AMT)
3. Net operating losses
4. Installment sales
5. Long-term contracts
6. Information returns

Tax Credits

Tax credits are specially calculated amounts that can be subtracted directly from the tax liability. Tax credits should be distinguished from income tax deductions. The tax reduction produced by a tax deduction is determined by the taxpayer's marginal tax rate. A tax deduction of $2,000 reduces the income tax by $560 if the taxpayer is in the 28% tax bracket. A tax credit of $2,000 reduces the tax liability by $2,000.

There are a number of credits that may be used to offset the income tax. Some of these are personal in nature and some relate to business activities.

Refundable and Nonrefundable Credits

Tax credits may also be grouped according to those which are refundable and those which are nonrefundable. Nonrefundable credits are allowed only as a reduction of the tax liability. If there is no tax liability, the credits cannot be used. Refundable credits, however, can be claimed even though there is no income tax liability against which they can be offset. They are entered on the tax return along with payments, and they can be refunded to the taxpayer. Refundable credits include:

1. Credit for withheld wages
2. Earned Income Credit (EIC)
3. Tax withheld from income of nonresident aliens and foreign corporations
4. Gasoline and special fuels credit
5. Regulated investment company credit

All other tax credits are nonrefundable.

Personal Credits

The following personal tax credits were examined in Chapter 2:

1. Child and dependent care credit
2. EIC
3. Credit for the elderly or for the permanently and totally disabled

Credit for Interest on Certain Home Mortgages

Interest paid or accrued on certain state and local government mortgage credit certificates entitles the home buyer to a credit of 10% to 50% (the certificate credit rate) times the mortgage interest paid or accrued by the taxpayer during any taxable year in which the certificate is in effect. The credit is limited to $2,000 if the taxpayer's credit rate is more than 20%. If the credit is taken, the mortgage interest deduction is reduced by the amount of the credit.

Foreign Tax Credit

The foreign tax credit applies to both individuals and to corporations. This credit is available as a reduction in the United States income tax for taxes paid to foreign countries. The credit results in greater equality in tax treatment since it prevents foreign income from being taxed twice, once by the foreign country and again by the United States. The taxpayer is not required to claim the foreign tax credit, although it is usually advantageous to do so. Instead, the foreign tax may be used as a deduction from the taxpayer's income.

There are "overall" limitations to the amount of the foreign tax credit that can be claimed. The amount that can be claimed is based on the total amount of taxes paid to all foreign countries and United States possessions. However, the amount of the foreign tax credit is limited:

$$\frac{\text{foreign income}}{\substack{\text{worldwide taxable income} \\ \text{(without any deductions} \\ \text{for personal exemptions)}}} \times \substack{\text{U.S. tax on} \\ \text{worldwide income}}$$

Form 1116, Computation of Foreign Tax Credit, is available from the IRS and should be used to compute the amount of foreign tax credit. The rules for the foreign tax credit are more complex than the average taxpayer discussions of this text.

Business Tax Credits

The remainder of this section on tax credits deals with business tax credits. These are credits that relate to various business activities.

Clinical Testing (Orphan Drug) Credit

The clinical testing (orphan drug) credit is 50% of the qualified clinical testing expense for the year. It is available for qualified clinical testing expenses in connection with the development of drugs for rare diseases and conditions.

The credit is elective, and in situations in which the election is not made, the qualified clinical testing expense may continue to qualify for the research expenditures credit.

Credit for Producing Fuel from a Nonconventional Source

A producer of alternative fuels may claim a credit for the domestic production of fuels, such as oil, gas, and synthetic fuels, from nonconventional sources. The credit generally is $3 multiplied by the fuel's barrel-of-oil equivalence, with a phase-out provision relating to oil prices.

The credit is available for fuels produced in facilities placed in service or wells drilled after 1979. In addition, the fuels must be sold before 2001. The credit is included on Form 1040 (line 45) by entering "FNS" on the dotted portion (line 45) and adding the amount of the credit to the credits entered (lines 41 through 44).

General Business Credit

After all other nonrefundable credits have been offset against the income tax liability, the taxpayer can claim the general business credit. The general business credit consists of the combined group of six credits as follows:

1. Investment tax credit (including the business energy credit and the credit for rehabilitation expenditures)—Form 3468
2. Targeted jobs credit—Form 5884
3. Credit for alcohol used as a fuel—Form 6478
4. Credit for increased research activities—Form 6765
5. Low-income housing credit—Form 8586
6. Disabled access credit—Form 8826

These individual credits are combined into one general business credit, including the current-year credits and the sum of the carrybacks and carryovers of the various component credits allowed for the taxable year. The carrybacks and carryovers lose their identity and become the allowable general business credit. The allowable general business credit is claimed first in the current tax year. The unused credit is carried back to the third tax year preceding the current tax year. If not used up, it is carried forward to the second preceding tax year and then the first preceding year. If there is still an unused credit it would be carried to the tax year after the current tax year and is combined with additional business credits if any in that year. The same procedure would be repeated in each succeeding year until the unused credit carried forward is used up or the 15-year carryover period is reached. In each carryover year, the oldest credit is used first, thus minimizing the possible expiration of any unused general business credit.

The amount of the general business credit that may be used to reduce the regular tax liability for the current tax year is limited to the taxpayer's *net income tax*, Form 1040 (line 46) reduced by the greater of:

1. The *tentative minimum tax*
2. 25% of the *net regular tax liability* in excess of $25,000

The *net regular tax liability* is the regular tax liability reduced by certain nonrefundable tax credits.

1. Child and dependent care expenses credit
2. Credit for the elderly and the permanently and totally disabled
3. Credit for mortgage interest paid
4. Foreign tax credit
5. Orphan drug testing credit
6. Credit for producing fuel from nonconventional sources

The *net income tax* is the *net regular tax liability* plus the alternative minimum tax. Form 3800 is used to calculate the general business credit.

Investment Tax Credit

There are two separate credits that continue to be considered as part of the investment tax credit. One of these credits is the business energy credit, and the other is the credit for rehabilitation expenditures.

Business Energy Investment Credit. A tax credit of 10% is available for qualified investment in *solar* and *geothermal* energy property. The basis of the energy property must be reduced by 50% of the energy credit taken. These business energy credits are calculated on Form 3468, Schedule B, Business Energy Investment Credit, and then they are entered on Form 3468, Investment Credit, to calculate the total amount of investment credit for the year.

Credit for Rehabilitation Expenditures. Expenditures incurred after 1981 for the rehabilitation of qualified buildings and certified historic structures are eligible for the investment tax credit, as follows:

Property	Credit
Certified historical structures (nonresidential and residential)	20%
Nonresidential buildings placed in service before 1936	10%

A basis adjustment to the property is also required for the full amount of the rehabilitation credit in the case of both the historic and nonhistoric buildings. Passive loss limitations are applicable in connection with the credit. This credit is reported on Form 3468, Investment Credit.

Targeted Jobs Credit

The targeted jobs credit, reported on Form 5884, Jobs Credit, is also called the *jobs credit*. It is available to employers who hire individuals who are certified as members of specified target groups. This credit is equal to 40% of the first $6,000 of qualified first-year wages. However, the total of all such qualified first-year wages may not exceed 30% of the total unemployment insurance (FUTA) wages paid by the employer during the current taxable year. The credit is not available if an employee works less than 90 days (14 days for qualified summer youth employees) or 120 hours. The targeted jobs credit is combined into the general business credit, and as such is subject to carryback and carryover rules. Employers who elect to claim this credit must reduce their wage expense deduction by the amount of the credit claimed.

Alcohol Fuels Credit

An alcohol fuels credit of 60 cents a gallon is allowed for sales or use of alcohol that is at least 190 proof, and 45 cents a gallon between 150 and 190 proof. It must be used as a fuel in a trade or business. The alcohol must be in a mixture with gasoline or special fuel, and either used as a fuel or sold at retail to another person who uses the fuel in a personal vehicle.

Credit for Increasing Research Activities

The research credit is designed to encourage businesses to increase the amounts they spend on research and experimental activities that is technological in nature. The total amount of the credit may consist of two components: an incremental research credit and a basic research credit.

The incremental research credit is 20% of the amount by which a company's research expenses for the year exceed its average base period amount. The average base period amount is a calculated amount that represents the company's expected average level of research activity in the last four years. The amount which is multiplied by 20% cannot exceed 50% of the current year's qualifying research expenditures.

A *corporation* may claim an additional tax credit for part of its payments to qualified basic research institutions. This portion of the research credit is equal to 20% of the amount by which current payments for basic research exceed a specially calculated base amount.

A business claiming a tax credit for any of its research expenses may also deduct these expenses on its tax return. As an alternative, the business may capitalize the research expenses and amortize them over a period of not less than 60 months. If the business elects to expense its research activities currently, it has two options:

1. Claim the full research credit and reduce its research expense deduction by 100% of the credit, OR
2. Deduct all of the research expense currently and reduce the research credit by half of the maximum corporate tax rate

The credit can be claimed on Form 6765, Credit for Increasing Research Activities. This credit is one of the components of the general business credit.

Low-Income Rental Housing Credit

The low-income rental housing act credit can be claimed by owners of residential rental property providing low-income housing. The credit replaced a number of tax incentives. Separate credits are provided for new construction and rehabilitation of low-income housing and certain costs of acquisition of existing housing to service low-income individuals.

The credit is claimed each year for a period of 10 years. The credit rate is set monthly by the IRS to reflect changes in the AFR. Once determined, however, the rate remains constant for that property.

The credit has a number of special requirements and interrelationships with other federal programs. The project must continue to meet requirements for 15 years or recapture of a portion of the credit may occur. The credit is part of the general business credit and can be claimed on Form 8586, Low-Income Housing Credit.

Disabled Access Credit

This nonrefundable credit is also part of the general business credit. It is an incentive to small businesses to make their business more accessible to disabled individuals.

The credit is equal to 50% of the eligible expenditures for the year that fall between $250 and $10,250. Thus, the maximum credit available is $5,000 (50% x $10,000). The depreciable basis of any property improvement must be reduced by the amount of the credit.

A business is eligible for the credit if one of the following criteria was satisfied in the previous tax year:

1. It had gross receipts of $1 million or less.
2. It had 30, or fewer, full-time employees.

Expenditures that qualify for the credit include those that lead to the removal of architectural, communication, physical, or transportation barriers that prevent a business from being accessible to, or usable by, disabled individuals. Amounts paid for qualified interpreters or readers to effect the communication of materials to hearing-impaired individuals and visually-impaired individuals also qualify.

Credit for Prior Year Minimum Tax

Form 1040 (line 44) is used to report and deduct the amount of the credit for prior year minimum tax. The credit for prior year minimum tax is available for taxpayers to claim the por-

tion of the prior year AMT paid that relates to deferral preferences and adjustments that do not result in a permanent exclusion of income for tax purposes. An understanding of the credit also requires an understanding of the AMT and the related calculation. The credit for prior year minimum tax can be claimed by filing Form 8801.

Alternative Minimum Tax (AMT)

Income tax rate schedules levy a graduated tax on a taxpayer's taxable income, taxing those with larger taxable incomes at a higher rate than those with lower taxable incomes. Because of certain gross income exclusions and other tax incentives or provisions, some individuals with high economic incomes pay little or no income tax.

In order to redistribute the tax burden, Congress enacted in 1978 an AMT. The AMT was designed to complement the regular income tax by assuring that taxpayers with high economic incomes, who pay relatively little or no regular income tax, will pay some amount of tax. The AMT operates as a completely separate tax system that parallels the regular income tax. The basic format for calculating the AMT is as follows:

> Regular taxable income
> Add: Tax preferences and other adjustments
>   Disallowed itemized deductions
> Less: Allowed net operating losses
> Equals: **Alternative Minimum Taxable Income**
> Less: Allowable exemption (subject to phase-out above certain incomes)
> Equals: Amount subject to tax
> Times: 24%
> Equals: **AMT**
> Tax liability equals: Regular income tax plus amount of AMT in excess of regular tax
> Less tax credit: Excess AMT paid is available as an offset to the regular income tax in later years.

Each of these components in the calculation of the AMT is discussed below.

Preferences and Adjustments

The calculation of Alternative Minimum Taxable Income (AMTI) is based on a set of adjustments that reconstructs regular taxable income. For example, if a business asset had been depreciated under the 200% declining-balance method of cost recovery in calculating regular taxable income, this amount would be added back to regular taxable income and depreciation on the business asset would be deducted using the 150% declining-balance method which is required in calculating AMTI.

Preferences and adjustments are tax incentives that permit a taxpayer to take a larger expense or an accelerated deduction in calculating regular taxable income. The AMT is designed to make certain that taxpayers pay some tax currently even if they took advantage of special provisions of the tax law in reducing or eliminating their regular income tax. The AMT calculation involves the cancellation of several preferences used in calculating the regular income tax and the making of a number of adjustments that are designed to reflect more realistic cost recovery periods for certain assets. Thus, the cost recovery periods are generally lengthened and certain items that were currently expensed for regular income tax purposes are amortized over a period of years for AMT purposes. The adjustments and preferences to be used in calculating the AMT are divided into four categories: (1) investment-related preferences and adjustments, (2) new timing adjustments, (3) tax shelter losses, and (4) tax-exempt or excluded items. The particular preferences and adjustments are discussed in the sections that follow.

It should be noted here that partnerships pass along tax preferences and adjustments in their entirety to the partners. Small business corporations (S corporations) also pass along tax preferences and adjustments with a few exceptions.

Investment-Related Preferences and Adjustments. These items include the following:

1. *Depreciation on real property.* Real property placed in service after 1986 and property placed in service in 1986 for which new depreciation rules are elected must be depreciated using straight-line depreciation over 40 years.
2. *Depreciation on personal property.* Personal property placed in service after 1986 and property placed in service in 1986 for which new depreciation rules are elected, must be depreciated using the 150% declining-balance method, switching to straight-line in the year that maximizes the deduction.

3. *Expensed intangible drilling costs.* Intangible drilling costs are a tax preference item to the extent that the current year's deduction exceeds the amount that would have been deducted if the intangible drilling costs had been capitalized and recovered through depletion. If the intangible drilling cost deducted during the current year had been $1,500 and the amortized portion of the tangible drilling costs, if capitalized and amortized over ten years, had been $150, the tax preference amount would have been $1,350.
4. *Percentage depletion.* Depletion is a preference item to the extent of the allowable depletion over the total adjusted basis of the property at year's end without adjustment for the year's depletion. The determination is made individually for each piece of property.
5. *Amortization of pollution control facilities.* Pollution control facilities are treated as personal property if acquired after 1986. If pollution control facilities were placed in service before 1987 and were amortized using the special 5-year rule, the excess amortization over the regular depreciation allowance (15, 18, or 19 years) is a preference item for AMT.
6. *Mining exploration and development costs.* These costs must be amortized ratably over ten years.
7. *Circulation expenditures.* Circulation expenditures must be amortized ratably over three years.
8. *R&D expenditures.* Research and experimentation expenditures must be amortized ratably over ten years.

The separate calculation of depreciation for AMT purposes not only indicates that the AMT calculation is clearly distinguished from the regular income tax calculation, but also indicates a unique feature of the adjustment approach to calculating AMTI. This unique feature is that the basis of an asset for regular income tax purposes will be different than the basis of the asset for AMT purposes.

EXAMPLE 1 ───────────────────

Assume the taxpayer has a business asset that cost $3,000 with a recovery period of five years for regular income tax purposes and an 8-year AMT life (its economic life).

The basis of this asset for regular income tax purposes and for AMT purposes is calculated as follows:

	Regular Income Tax	AMT
Cost	$3,000	$3,000
Less: Depreciation Yr. 1	(450)[1]	(281)[2]
Depreciation Yr. 2	(660)	(510)
Depreciation Yr. 3	(630)	(414)
Depreciation Yr. 4	(630)	(335)
Depreciation Yr. 5	(630)	(272)
Adjusted Basis (end of Yr. 5)	$ -0-	$1,178

1 150% DB, 5-year life
2 150% DB, 8-year life

If this asset were sold at the end of Year 5 for $1,500, the regular tax gain would be $1,500 ($1,500 − 0), and the AMT gain would be $322 ($1,500 − $1,178). The $322 gain would be reflected in the calculation of the AMT in the year of sale.

Timing Adjustments. The preferences and adjustments in this category are designed to reflect cost recovery that more clearly approximates the investment's useful life or the period over which benefits are to be realized. The items included in this category are income deferred under the completed-contract method and income deferred under the installment method.

A taxpayer who uses the completed-contract method for any long-term contract entered into after March 1, 1986, must make an adjustment in determining AMTI using the percentage-of-completion method. Thus, if the income deferred is $12,000 on a 2-year contract for the regular tax calculation, $6,000 must be included in AMTI for each of the two years.

For certain taxpayers who make installment sales after March 1, 1986, the installment sales method has to be disregarded in calculating AMTI. All of the gain attributable to the sale is included in AMTI in the year of disposition. This provision applies to dealers, sellers of real property used in a trade or business, and sellers of rental real property where the selling price exceeds $150,000.

Tax Shelter Losses. Losses arising from tax shelter activities are generally not deductibile in the year they occur for either the income tax or AMT calculations. Such losses are carried forward and used to offset passive income in future years or deducted in full when the taxpayer disposes of the entire interest in the activity. Tax shelter losses include both passive activity losses and passive farm losses.

While the loss recognition for both tax calculations is deferred, the amount of the loss to be deferred will generally differ. The difference occurs because the loss for AMT purposes is determined using all required AMT tax adjustments rather than the regular income tax deductions.

Tax shelter farm losses result from any farm activity (including a farming syndicate) that generates passive-activity losses. The rules for deducting passive farm losses are more restrictive than those applicable to nonfarm passive losses. Passive losses arising from one farming activity cannot be used to offset income from another farming activity or from nonfarming activities. However, passive losses from nonfarming activities can be used to offset income from farming activities.

In carryover years, a passive loss from a farming activity can only be used to offset income from the same activity. When the property is sold, however, any suspended losses are deductible in full.

Tax-Exempt Interest. Tax-exempt interest from private activity bonds must be included in AMTI. Any expenses incurred to carry these bonds is allowed as an offset to the interest income.

Incentive Stock Options. The exercise of an incentive stock option does not affect taxable income. In calculating AMTI, however, income is recognized for the excess of the FMV of the stock over the exercise price.

Disallowed Itemized Deductions, Exemptions, and Credits

In calculating AMTI, certain itemized deductions taken in calculating the regular income tax are disallowed. Actually, the taxpayer must add back to regular taxable income all itemized deductions except charitable contributions, allowable home-mortgage interest expense, casualty and theft losses, gambling losses, and income taxes in respect of a decedent. However, the 3% reduction in itemized deductions required for taxpayers with excessive AGI does not apply in calculating the itemized deductions for the AMT.

Charitable Contributons. Taxpayers who contribute qualified long-term capital gain property to a charity may deduct the FMV of the property as an itemized deduction without recognizing income on the appreciation. For AMTI purposes, the appreciation is recognized as income. This income may be offset by decreases in the value of other long-term capital assets that are contributed to charities.

State and Local Taxes. All state and local taxes that were deducted in calculating the regular income tax must be added back in calculating AMTI. State income tax refunds that are included in regular taxable income are not required to be included in AMTI.

Medical Expenses. Only medical expenses that exceed 10% of AGI may be deducted for AMTI purposes, even though medical expenses in excess of 7.5% of AGI may be deducted in calculating regular taxable income. Consequently, the taxpayer must add back to regular taxable income 2.5% of the lesser of AGI or the regular-tax medical deduction.

Personal Exemptions. No personal exemptions and no standard deduction are deductible for AMTI. Instead, after the AMTI base is calculated, a special exemption is allowed to assure that most middle income taxpayers will not be subject to the AMT. The special exemption varies by taxpayer category: married filing jointly, $40,000; single, $30,000; and married filing separately, $20,000. However, this special exemption is phased out after the AMTI reaches specified levels. The phase-out is 25% of the amount of AMTI above a specified level for each class of taxpayer. Table 13-1, AMT Exemptions, reflects the phase-out levels for the AMT exemption.

Making the Most of the Special Exemption

The annual special exemption can be used to offset a significant amount of tax preferences and positive adjustments. Thus, the taxpayer should attempt to spread out tax preferences and positive adjustments over two or more tax years when these items are expected to exceed the current exemption. To avoid the bunching of adjustments and tax preferences in one tax year, the taxpayer must control the timing of events generating these items.

Tax Credits. The only tax credit that can regularly reduce the AMT liability is the foreign tax credit, which is calculated using a special formula for AMT purposes. However, some portion of the amount by which the AMT exceeds the regular tax is carried forward indefinitely to be used to reduce the AMT tax in future years to avoid double taxing of certain deferred preferences. It is beyond the scope of this text to discuss the logic of the credit and the calculation of the amount of the carryover that is usable.

Calculation of AMT

EXAMPLE 2 ——————————————

To illustrate the calculation of the AMT, assume that Jeffry Lang's regular income tax calculation for 1992 was as follows:

Table 13-1
AMT Exemptions

	Special Exemption	Phase-Out Starts (AMTI)	Phase-Out Complete (AMTI)	Calculation
Married filing jointly	$40,000	$150,000	$310,000	25% ($310,000 − $150,000)
Single	30,000	112,500	232,500	25% ($232,500 − $112,500)
Married filing separately	20,000	75,000	155,000	25% ($155,000 − $ 75,000)

Salary		$95,000
Rental income	$ 6,000	
Rental expenses:		
Depreciation—real		
property	$2,400	
Depreciation—personal		
property	600	
Interest expense . . .	5,000	
Property taxes	800	
Other expenses	200	
Total rent expenses	9,000	
Net rental loss (active participation) . . .		(3,000)
Gain on installment sale of land recognized		
in 1992 (total gain $40,000)		5,000
Total income		$97,000
Less itemized deductions:		
Contributions (including		
$32,000 of appreciated gain		
on securities donated to the		
university)	$35,000	
State income taxes	7,500	
Local property taxes	4,400	
Total itemized deductions	46,900	
Income after itemized deductions,		
Form 1040 (line 35)		$50,100
Less personal exemption		2,300
Taxable income		$47,800
Regular tax liability (@ 1992 rates)		$10,603

Based on this information, Lang's AMT would be $15,924.00, calculated as follows:

Regular taxable income		$47,800.00
Add: (1) Excess depreciation		
Real property (assumed)	$ 2,200.00	
Personal prop. (assumed)	150.00	2,350.00
(2) Disallowed itemized deductions:		
Appreciated gain on		
donation	$32,000.00	
State income taxes .	7,500.00	
Local property taxes	4,400.00	
Total itemized deductions . . .		43,900.00
(3) Personal exemption		2,300.00
AMTI		$96,350.00
Less exemption		30,000.00
AMT base		$66,350.00
AMT ($66,350 x 24%)		$15,924.00

The gain from the installment sale did not require adjustment since Lang is not a dealer and the land was held for investment and not used as trade, business, or rental property.

Filled-In Form 6251

Illustration 13-1

A filled-in Form 6251, Alternative Minimum Tax—Individuals, for Jeffry Lang is shown in Illustration 13-1. The information for Form 6251 is taken from Example 2. Jeffry Lang's AMT is larger than his regular income tax by $5,321.00 ($15,924 – $10,603). This amount is included on Form 1040 (line 48) and thus is added to the regular income tax to arrive at Lang's total income tax for 1992 of $15,924.00.

Tax Planning for the AMT

The above discussion of the AMT and the calculation of the tax indicate that the AMT is a very complex concept. The AMT is more broadly based than the regular tax. Minimizing the effect of the AMT requires careful planning. Generally, taxpayers who invest in real and personal depreciable property will have AMT adjustments because of the differences in asset lives for the regular tax and the AMT. These differences can be reduced by electing the alternative depreciation system which provides for straight-line depreciation and economic lives that are the same as for the AMT. For personal property the straight-line life is the ADR midpoint life (or 12 years if there is no midpoint life), and for real property the straight-line life is 40 years.

Making elections as to how to report certain activities for regular tax purposes should be done with careful analysis of the effect of these elections on the AMT. In effect, taxpayers must carefully plan the mix of their investments and the methods and patterns of asset disposals if they want to mitigate the effect of the AMT. Planning is essential, and it must be done for extended periods of time and not just for one year at a time.

Illustration 13-1
Filled-In Form 6251

Form 6251

Alternative Minimum Tax—Individuals

▶ See separate instructions.

▶ Attach to Form 1040 or Form 1040NR.

Department of the Treasury
Internal Revenue Service

OMB No. 1545-0227

1992

Attachment Sequence No. **32**

Name(s) shown on Form 1040

Your social security number

#	Description		Amount	
1	Enter the amount from Form 1040, line 35. If less than zero, enter as a negative amount	1	50,100	00
2	Net operating loss deduction, if any, from Form 1040, line 22. Enter as a positive amount	2	0	00
3	Overall itemized deductions limitation amount (see instructions)	3	(0	00)
4	Combine lines 1, 2, and 3	4	50,100	00
5	**Adjustments:** (See instructions before completing.)			
a	Standard deduction, if any, from Form 1040, line 34	5a		
b	Medical and dental expenses. Enter the smaller of the amount from Schedule A (Form 1040), line 4, or 2½% (.025) of Form 1040, line 32	5b		
c	Miscellaneous itemized deductions from Schedule A (Form 1040), line 24	5c		
d	Taxes from Schedule A (Form 1040), line 8	5d	11,900	00
e	Refund of taxes	5e	(	)
f	Certain home mortgage interest	5f		
g	Investment interest expense	5g		
h	Depreciation of tangible property placed in service after 1986	5h	2,350	00
i	Circulation and research and experimental expenditures paid or incurred after 1986	5i		
j	Mining exploration and development costs paid or incurred after 1986	5j		
k	Long-term contracts entered into after 2/28/86	5k		
l	Pollution control facilities placed in service after 1986	5l		
m	Installment sales of certain property	5m		
n	Adjusted gain or loss	5n		
o	Incentive stock options	5o		
p	Certain loss limitations	5p		
q	Tax shelter farm activities	5q		
r	Passive activities	5r		
s	Beneficiaries of estates and trusts	5s		
t	Combine lines 5a through 5s	5t	14,250	00
6	**Tax preference items:** (See instructions before completing.)			
a	Appreciated property charitable deduction	6a	32,000	00
b	Tax-exempt interest from private activity bonds issued after 8/7/86	6b		
c	Depletion	6c		
d	Accelerated depreciation of real property placed in service before 1987	6d		
e	Accelerated depreciation of leased personal property placed in service before 1987	6e		
f	Intangible drilling costs	6f		
g	Add lines 6a through 6f	6g	32,000	00
7	Combine lines 4, 5t, and 6g	7	96,350	00
8	Energy preference adjustment for certain taxpayers. Do not enter more than 40% of line 7. See instructions	8	0	00
9	Subtract line 8 from line 7	9	96,350	00
10	Alternative tax net operating loss deduction. See instructions for limitations	10	0	00
11	**Alternative minimum taxable income.** Subtract line 10 from line 9. If married filing separately, see instructions	11	96,350	00
12	Enter: $40,000 ($20,000 if married filing separately; $30,000 if single or head of household)	12	30,000	00
13	Enter: $150,000 ($75,000 if married filing separately; $112,500 if single or head of household)	13	112,500	00
14	Subtract line 13 from line 11. If zero or less, enter -0- here and on line 15 and go to line 16	14	0	00
15	Multiply line 14 by 25% (.25)	15	0	00
16	**Exemption.** Subtract line 15 from line 12. If zero or less, enter -0-. If completing this form for a child under age 14, see instructions for amount to enter	16	30,000	00
17	Subtract line 16 from line 11. If zero or less, enter -0- here and on line 22 and skip lines 18 through 21	17	66,350	00
18	Multiply line 17 by 24% (.24)	18	15,924	00
19	Alternative minimum tax foreign tax credit. See instructions	19	0	00
20	Tentative minimum tax. Subtract line 19 from line 18	20	15,924	00
21	Enter your tax from Form 1040, line 38, minus any foreign tax credit on Form 1040, line 43. If an amount from Form 4970 is entered on line 39 of Form 1040, also include the amount from Form 4970 on this line	21	10,603	00
22	**Alternative minimum tax.** Subtract line 21 from line 20. If zero or less, enter -0-. Enter this amount on Form 1040, line 48. If completing this form for a child under age 14, see instructions for amount to enter	22	5,321	00

For Paperwork Reduction Act Notice, see separate instructions.   Cat. No. 13600G   Form **6251** (1992)

Fluctuating Income

Because of the graduated schedule of income tax rates, extreme fluctuations in the amount of taxable income from year to year should be avoided by taxpayers whenever possible. For example, an annual taxable income of (1) $30,000 for a 2-year period would be preferable to an annual taxable income of (2) $40,000 and $20,000, respectively, for the same two years. For a married taxpayer filing a joint return, the difference in the total amount of income tax (using the 1992 Tax Rate Schedule) would be $549 ($9,557 – $9,008) as calculated from the following table:

	(1)	(2)
Taxable income:		
First year	$30,000	$40,000
Second year	30,000	20,000
Total taxable income	$60,000	$60,000
Income tax:		
First year	$ 4,504	$ 6,553
Second year	4,504	3,004
Total income tax	$ 9,008	$ 9,557

This section of the chapter looks at several situations where certain types of income and loss may be spread out over a number of years in order to level out income and avoid major fluctuations in taxable income.

Net Operating Loss (NOL)

A type of income tax averaging applies in situations where an individual operating a business has a loss in one year and a profit in other years. It would be inequitable, for example, to tax an individual on a net income from business operations in one year if, in the following year, there was a net loss of the same amount which had no tax effect. In order to gain the benefit of a business loss, the Internal Revenue Code provides that an operating loss arising from a trade or profession (or from a casualty loss of personal property) may be carried back and offset against taxable income of certain previous years and may be carried forward against taxable income of certain succeeding years, in the order of the earliest year first. The current carryback is 3 years and the carryover is 15 years.

A taxpayer may elect to forego the carryback and carry the NOL forward only.

The NOL does not appear as such on the tax return. It appears only in the calculations and statements supporting a refund claim or a subsequent NOL deduction. If a NOL carryback entitles an individual taxpayer to a refund of prior-year taxes, a quick refund can be claimed on Form 1045, Application for Tentative Refund.

Calculation of NOL

The allowable NOL usually does not appear on Form 1040, page 2 (line 37), in place of what is typically taxable income. Instead, the *allowable* NOL is calculated on Form 1045, Schedule A, page 2 (not shown here). Form 1045, Schedule A, is used to calculate the allowable NOL in the process of applying for refund of prior year income taxes. The steps in the calculation of the NOL are illustrated in Table 13-2.

In general, the amount of the loss that may be carried back to preceding years and forward to subsequent years is restricted to the economic loss actually suffered. The economic loss is referred to as a *NOL* and is the excess of allowable business deductions over the sum of business gross income and nonbusiness net income in any taxable year, calculated with the following exceptions and limitations:

1. No deduction may be taken for personal and dependency exemptions.
2. A net capital loss is not deductible.
3. Nonbusiness capital losses may be offset only against nonbusiness capital gains. Nonbusiness capital gains and losses arise from transactions in nonbusiness assets.
4. The NOL of a preceding or a succeeding year cannot be included as a deduction in order to create a NOL for the current year.
5. For taxpayers other than corporations, nonbusiness deductions are allowed only to the extent of nonbusiness gross income plus net nonbusiness capital gains (the excess of nonbusiness capital gains over nonbusiness capital losses). Nonbusiness income is income from sources other than the taxpayer's trade, business, or profession. Salaries, capital gains and losses from business asset transactions, and rental income are treated as business income. Nonbusiness deductions include all itemized deductions except for casualty and theft

Table 13-2
Calculation of NOL

Summary of Net Loss on 1992 Tax Return

Ordinary business income	$200,600	
Ordinary nonbusiness income (dividends and interest)	1,500	
Long-term capital gain on business assets (treated as ordinary income)	6,000	
Total income		$208,100
Ordinary business deductions	$280,000	
Ordinary nonbusiness deductions (standard deductions or itemized deductions except casualty and theft losses)	6,680	
Personal and dependency exemptions	6,900	
Total deductions		293,580
Net loss shown on Form 1040		($ 85,480)

Calculation of Net Operating Loss

Net loss shown on 1992 tax return, above		($ 85,480)
a. Personal and dependency exemptions	$ 6,900	
b. Excess of nonbusiness deductions over nonbusiness income ($6,680 – $1,500)	5,180	
Total adjustments		12,080
NOL		($ 73,400)

losses and the deductible portion of employee business expenses, both types of which are treated as business losses and expenses.

6. Individual taxpayers who do not itemize deductions must treat an amount equal to their standard deduction as a nonbusiness deduction.

EXAMPLE 3 —————————————

Assume a taxpayer who is married and files a joint return has been operating a grocery store for the past year. The store generated $120,000 of gross revenues and $150,000 of operating expenses, resulting in an operating loss of $30,000 for 1992. He and his wife had other business and nonbusiness income and expenses for 1992 as follows:

Wife's salary	$15,000
Net business capital gains	3,000
Net nonbusiness long-term gains	4,000
Interest income on nonbusiness investments	1,500
Casualty loss from a house fire (the deductible portion)	(6,200)
Home mortgage interest	(9,500)

Based on this information, the taxpayer would show a loss on the tax return of $26,800 calculated as follows:

Business loss, (Schedule C)		($30,000)
Salary		15,000
Net business capital gains		3,000
Net nonbusiness capital gains		4,000
Investment interest income		1,500
AGI (loss)		($6,500)
Less: Itemized deductions		
Mortgage interest	$9,500	
Casualty loss	6,200	(15,700)
Less: Personal exemptions		(4,600)
Form 1040, (line 37)* Taxable income (loss)		($26,800)

* Assuming the actual loss is reported instead of reporting zero.

Using this information in preparing the taxpayer's tax return, the NOL for 1992 would be $18,200, calculated as follows:

Taxable loss			($26,800)
Add back:			
Personal exemptions		$4,600	
Net nonbusiness expenses			
Mortgage interest	$9,500		
Less nonbusiness income ($4,000 + $1,500)	5,500	4,000	8,600
NOL for 1992			($18,200)

NOL Deduction

The NOL calculated for a particular year, such as $18,200 for the year 1992 in the example above, can be carried back for three years, if elected, and/or carried forward for 15 years. The NOL calculated for 1992 can be carried back to 1989 to offset income taxed in that year. When a NOL is carried to another year, it is referred to as a *NOL deduction* which is treated as a *deduction for AGI in the year to which it is carried*. A NOL carried forward is shown on Form 1040, page 1 (line 22) as a *minus* item which reduces total income (line 23). Thus, since AGI will be reduced in that year, the NOL deduction may affect the extent to which certain itemized deductions are allowed. Other than charitable contributions, all itemized deductions based on AGI must be recalculated to determine the revised taxable income. If taxable income is completely eliminated by deducting the NOL, any tax credit previously claimed would not be allowed in that year.

The NOL deduction is the sum of the carrybacks and carryovers to the taxable year. If the NOL deduction exceeds the taxable income in the offset year, the taxpayer gets a refund of the entire tax paid. If the NOL deduction is less than the taxable income, the taxpayer will get a tax refund to the extent of the tax difference between the original taxable income and the taxable income after applying the NOL deduction.

When the NOL deduction exceeds the taxable income in the offset year, it usually is necessary to make certain adjustments to the unused loss to determine whether any of it can be carried forward to the next eligible year. It is beyond the scope of this text to discuss this recalculation in detail, but readers should recognize that the remaining NOL deduction must be reduced. At a minimum, the loss is reduced by the personal and dependency exemptions and any net capital losses in the offset year. Any loss that remains after making these adjustments is the amount that can be carried forward to the next eligible year.

Installment Sales

When assets are sold, a taxpayer generally has the option of collecting the sales price in full at the time of sale, or alternatively, to spread the collection period over a number of months or years. When collection is taken in full at the time of sale, the gain or loss on sale is reported on the tax return in the period in which the sale was made. When collections are received in a year (or years) after the year of sale, the sale is referred to as an installment sale. When certain conditions exist, the taxpayer is required to report the taxable gain (but not a deductible loss) over the period of collection *unless a specific election is made to report the gain on an accrual method in the year of sale*. A loss on an installment sale is deductible only in the year of sale. Thus, if a taxpayer's transactions meet the requirements for installment sale reporting, the recognition of income and the payment of income tax from the sale is deferred until the payments on the installment obligation are received.

The types of transactions eligible for installment reporting and the accounting treatment of installment sales reporting has changed frequently in recent years as Congress searched for an approach that would allow taxpayers to postpone income on certain transactions until collections of the receivables occurred, while at the same time requiring other taxpayers to report income on the accrual method in the year of the sale. Currently, the use of the installment method is prohibited for revolving credit sales and sales of stock, securities, and other properties traded in an established market. The installment sales method of accounting is also prohibited for dealers (i.e., those who sell property in a business setting) in personal property and real estate. In general, then, the installment sales method of reporting is still allowed in the following situations:

1. Casual sales of personal property and real property by nondealers

2. Sales of business and rental property by nondealers that exceed a selling price of $150,000 to the extent that the face amounts of real property obligations arising during any year do not exceed $5 million. For sales of business and rental property by nondealers that exceed $5 million for the year, the taxpayer may use the installment method, but is required to pay interest annually on the amount of deferred tax resulting from the use of the installment method.

3. Sales of residential lots and timeshares by dealers

For the purpose of these rules, a dealer is any person who regularly sells personal property on the installment plan or who holds real property for sale to customers in the ordinary course of a trade or business. A casual sale or occasional sale of real property held for rental purposes is not a "dealer disposition." For dealers who are no longer allowed to use the installment method, any deferred gains are generally taken into income over a period not to exceed four years.

The current tax law further eases the installment sales rules for nondealers by allowing the use of the installment method in determining AMT income and allows nondealers to elect the new rules for sales occurring after August 16, 1986. However, when installment obligations are pledged as security for a loan after December 17, 1987, the amount borrowed must be treated as a collection of the installment obligation. This rule applies to installment obligations arising from the sale of property for more than $150,000. The property must have been used in the taxpayer's trade or business or held for the production of rental income.

Installment Sales of Real Estate and Casual Sales of Personal Property

The installment method of reporting is automatic for sales of real estate (by taxpayers who are not dealers and by dealers for residential lots and timeshares) and for casual sales of personal property (non-inventory property) unless the taxpayer elects not to use it. The election for non-installment (accrual method) reporting must be made on or before the due date of the return for the tax year of sale. To elect non-installment reporting, the taxpayer reports the entire gain from the sale on the tax return for the tax year in which the sale was made *and* completes Schedule D (Form 1040), page 2, Part VI, by checking the box (line 46) and by entering information about the installment note payable (lines 47 and 48). The decision to report on the installment basis or to elect to report the entire gain in the year of sale will depend on many factors, such as current versus future tax rates, relative amounts of passive income and passive losses, and whether the property being sold is passive activity property.

A gain from the sale of real estate or a casual sale of personal property can be reported on the installment basis provided at least one payment is to be received after the close of the tax year in which the sale occurs. Therefore, installment reporting may be used where there is a lump-sum payment made in a tax year follow-ing the year of a sale. The installment method may not be used in reporting a loss.

Selling Price and Payments Received. The selling price of the property sold includes not only cash and other property received but also mortgage notes given by the purchaser or assumed by the purchaser. It is the total amount involved in the sale. Any interest received is excluded from the calculation of the selling price. The profit to be reported as income from an installment sale is that portion of the selling price considered to have been received in a given year. Payments received include cash and property other than notes or other obligations of the purchaser.

Gross Profit to be Realized. In determining the gain, or gross profit, to be realized from the sale, the cost or other basis of the property sold must be adjusted for any depreciation allowed or allowable and for the cost of any improvements. Commissions and other selling expenses should be added to the basis of the property in determining the gross profit, except for real estate dealers who report such expenses as business expenses.

EXAMPLE 4 ——————————————————

Assume that in 1992 a taxpayer engaged in business sells a piece of land for $18,000 that had been acquired at a cost of $11,700. A sales commission of $900 was paid. The amount of gross profit to be realized is shown as follows:

Selling price		$18,000
Cost	$11,700	
Plus commission	900	12,600
Gross profit to be realized		$ 5,400

Reporting the Gain. In order to determine the gain from an installment sale reportable in a current tax year, the gross profit ratio is calculated as follows: the gross profit to be realized is divided by the contract price. The *contract price* is the sum of the principal payments, excluding interest, to be received. The amount to be received may be the same amount as the selling price. If the purchaser assumes a mortgage on the property, however, the contract price will be less than the selling price, with a special adjustment necessary if the mortgage assumed exceeds the adjusted basis of the property. In the preceding illustration, the gross profit ratio would be calculated as follows:

$$\frac{\$5,400 \text{ (Gross Profit to be Realized)}}{\$18,000 \text{ (Contract Price)}} = 30\%$$

The gain to be included in the current year's income is calculated by multiplying the amount(s) received on the principal during the year by the gross profit ratio. Keep in mind, however, that the payments on the notes normally will include interest as well as principal. The interest received by the seller is ordinary income, whereas the profit element on the principal usually will be taxed as a capital gain, as discussed in the next section.

EXAMPLE 5

Assume that the purchaser, from the preceding example, makes a down payment of $4,000 in 1992 and gives a series of notes totaling $14,000 of principal, plus interest, of which $12,000 of principal falls due in 1992 and $2,000 falls due in 1993. Assuming the notes are paid when due, the seller's gain will be reported as follows:

Contract Price of $18,000		
1992	$ 4,000 x 30% =	$1,200
1992	12,000 x 30% =	3,600
1993	2,000 x 30% =	600
Total		$5,400

EXAMPLE 6

Now assume that the purchaser from the preceding illustration makes a $4,000 down payment in 1992, assumes a mortgage note of $2,000 owed on the property by the seller, and gives the seller a series of notes totaling $12,000, all of which fall due in 1993. The contract price will be $16,000 ($4,000 cash down payment plus $12,000 in notes). Assuming that the $12,000 of notes are paid at maturity, the gain will be reported as follows:

$$\frac{\$5,400 \text{ (Gross Profit to be Realized)}}{\$16,000 \text{ (Contract Price)}} = 33.75\%$$

Contract Price of $16,000		
1992	$ 4,000 x 33.75% =	$1,350
1993	12,000 x 33.75% =	4,050
Total		$5,400

It should be noted that the selling prices and the gross profits to be realized are the same in Examples 4, 5, and 6, but the amounts to be collected by the seller are different in Example 6. In Examples 4 and 5, the gross profit was allocated on the basis of $18,000 to be collected by the seller. In Example 6, it was allocated on the basis of $16,000 to be collected by the seller; the additional $2,000 of the selling price would be paid directly to the holder of the mortgage note that was assumed by the purchaser.

Capital Assets. When capital assets are sold on the installment basis, the taxpayer reports the gain as a capital gain. The taxpayer may elect to report the entire gain in the year of sale. Without an election the gain must be prorated in accordance with the collection of the installment payments. In either case, the sale is reported on a separate Schedule D.

EXAMPLE 7

Assume that an individual, who is less than age 55, sells a personal residence for $48,000, receiving a down payment of $4,000 and five notes of $8,800 each, plus interest, due at yearly intervals. The home was acquired a number of years ago at a cost of $28,800 and will not be replaced. Thus, because the home was held for more than one year, the gain of $19,200 (40% of the contract price: $19,200/$48,000) is a long-term capital gain. The taxpayer could elect to report the entire $19,200 in the year of the sale. If the individual reports on the installment basis, there would be a long-term capital gain of $1,600 in the year of sale (40% x $4,000) and a long-term capital gain of $3,520 (40% x $8,800) in each of the following five years.

In determining whether the gain on real estate or other group holdings should be reported as a short-term or long-term capital gain, the holding period includes only the period during which each property was held, regardless of when the installment obligations are finally liquidated. Thus, it is necessary to calculate the holding periods of land and improvements thereon separately, taking into consideration the length of the holding period applicable to each. Any interest collected on the notes is reported as ordinary income.

Depreciation Recapture. When real property or personal property is sold at a gain, the gain must be treated as ordinary income to the extent of the recapture of certain depreciation taken during the property's business life, as specified under Sections 1245 and 1250 of the Code. These recapture provisions also apply to installment sales as well as to regular sales. Historically, the first gains reported on the installment basis were treated as ordinary income until all appropriate depreciation charges were recaptured. If the gains on installments paid in the year of sale did not cover all of the depreciation to be recaptured, the gains on subsequent installments had to be treated as ordinary income for the remaining depreciation to be recaptured, after which the subsequent gains could be treated as capital gains or as Section 1231 gains.

Under current tax law, all of the depreciation to be recaptured must be included in ordinary income in the year of the property's disposition, even if the gain otherwise reportable in the year of sale is less than the depreciation to be recaptured. Thus, gain would be reported in the year of sale to reflect depreciation recapture, even though no payments were actually received in the year of sale. The gain reported in the first year as a recapture of depreciation is treated as an increase in the basis of the property disposed of (i.e., reduction in remaining gain) for the purpose of calculating the gross profit ratio and the amount of each installment to be included in income as a capital gain or Section 1231 gain. This treatment of depreciation recapture applies to depreciable property sold after June 6, 1984.

EXAMPLE 8 ─────────────────────

To illustrate, assume a taxpayer sells depreciated property for $180,000 (accepting five equal installments of $36,000) with the total gain calculated as follows:

Selling price		$180,000
Original cost	$90,000	
Accumulated depreciation	30,000	
Adjusted basis		60,000
Total gain		$120,000

Assume that all of the depreciation is to be recaptured as ordinary income and that the $36,000 is collected each year for five years, plus interest at current rates. The

$30,000 of depreciation would be recaptured as ordinary income in the year of sale plus additional income to be treated as a capital gain, based on a recalculation of the gross profit ratio, by adding the $30,000 of ordinary income to the basis of the property, as shown below:

Income Reportable in Year 1

Ordinary income (depreciation recapture)	$ 30,000

Capital gain or Section 1231 gain:

$$\text{Gross Profit Ratio} = \frac{\$120,000 - \$30,000}{\$180,000} = 50\%$$

Capital gain (Section 1231 gain) reportable in Year 1 (50% x $36,000)	$18,000
Total gain reportable in Year 1 ($30,000 + $18,000)	$48,000

Income Reportable in Years 2-5

Each year:	
50% x $36,000 = $18,000 x 4 years	$ 72,000
Total gain reportable in 5 years	$120,000

Disposition of Installment Obligations. If an installment obligation is sold or otherwise disposed of, the gain or loss must be reported at the time of disposal for the difference between the tax basis of the obligation and (1) the amount realized in a sale or exchange, or (2) the FMV of the obligation in case of disposal by other than a sale or exchange. Except for certain real estate transactions, the use of installment obligations as collateral for a loan is a way of receiving cash from installment obligations without recognizing income. Thus, using installment obligations as collateral for a loan is not considered to be a disposition of the obligation except for certain real estate transactions.

Tax Planning Issues. Taxpayers who sell rental property on the installment basis must keep in mind that any gain on the sale of rental property above $150,000 is considered to be passive income. If suspended passive losses (i.e., passive losses not deductible in the year incurred which can be carried forward to offset passive income of subsequent years) have been accumulated, the use of the installment method for reporting gains will extend the period over which suspended losses can be used up, since the installment method will postpone the reporting of the gain (which is passive income) from the sale of the property. Thus, the need to use up suspended passive losses may discourage the use of the installment method for reporting sales of rental property.

Long-Term Contracts

A *long-term contract* is defined as a contract for building, installing, constructing, or manufacturing that is entered into in one taxable year and completed in another taxable year. In addition, a manufacturing contract qualifies for a long-term contract method only if it involves the manufacture of unique items or items normally requiring more than 12 months to complete. Prior to the Tax Reform Act of 1986, long-term contracts could be reported under either of two methods: the *percentage-of-completion method* or the *completed-contract method*. The percentage-of-completion method has the effect of spreading income over two or more accounting periods as portions of the contract are completed. The completed-contract method results in reporting the entire profit on a contract in the year the contract is completed. The completed-contract method had to be used for contracts lasting one year or less even if the contract was not completed in one calendar year. There was no requirement that the company using either of these methods for tax purposes had to use the same method in reporting income on its financial statements. The two methods are described below since both methods continue to be applicable, although there now are significant restrictions on the use of the completed-contract method.

Percentage of Completion Method (PCM)

Prior to 1987, two approaches were available for estimating the percentage of the contract that had been completed. One approach was to use the percentage of cost incurred to date to total costs expected to be incurred on the contract. Another approach was for the architect or engineer to certify the percentage of work completed during the year. Whichever method was used, the percentage of the contract completed during the year was then applied to the total contract price to yield the amount of total contract income to be reported in that year. All expenditures attributed to the contract during the reporting year were deducted from the reported gross income to yield the net income that year from performing the contract, as illustrated in Example 9.

EXAMPLE 9 ————————————————

If the costs incurred in a particular year were \$120,000 and the total contract costs were expected to be \$200,000, then the contract would have been considered to be 60% completed (\$120,000 / \$200,000) in that year. If the total contract price was \$300,000, then the gross income to be reported in the measurement year would be \$180,000 (\$300,000 x 60%), and the profit to be reported would be \$60,000 (\$180,000 − \$120,000).

An engineer's estimate of the percentage of work completed is no longer acceptable for income tax purposes. Thus, the percentage of completion must be calculated by using the ratio of cost incurred this period to total expected costs for the entire contract.

The contractor is required to use the PCM for all *long-term* contracts unless the contractor qualifies to use the completed-contract method for home construction contracts and certain other contracts described later in the *Completed Contract* section. Two basic principles apply in using the PCM. First, the percentage of the contract considered to be completed can only be determined by comparing costs incurred to total estimated contract costs. Secondly, contract costs must include all direct costs and an allocable share of indirect costs, including an allocated portion of interest expense. Costs that the contractor cannot allocate to long-term contracts include independent R&D expenses; expenses of unsuccessful bids and proposals; and marketing, selling, and advertising expenses. In determining such expenditures, the inventories of materials and supplies at the beginning and end of the year should be considered. The amount of progress payments received by the contractor during the year has no effect on the determination of the expenditures.

EXAMPLE 10 ———————————————

To illustrate the application of the current PCM, assume that a taxpayer contracts to construct a building for $900,000 and that the work is spread over two taxable years. Other details include:

Taxable Year	Percentage of Completion at End of Year	Allocable Costs	Payment Received
Year 1	40%	$300,000	$350,000
Year 2	100%	500,000	550,000
		$800,000	$900,000

The net income from the contract to be reported in each of the two years would be:

Year 1	
Gross income, 40% of $900,000	$360,000
Expenditures	300,000
Net income	$ 60,000
Year 2	
Gross income, 60% of $900,000	$540,000
Expenditures	500,000
Net income	$ 40,000

Completed-Contract Method

Using the completed-contract method, the entire amount to be received under the contract is reported in the year in which the contract is completed. All expenditures attributable to the contract are then deducted in the year of completion regardless of the year in which the expenditures were made.

Applying the completed-contract method to the set of facts assumed in Example 10 would have the result that the entire profit of the contract would be reported in Year 2.

Year 2	
Gross income	$900,000
Expenditures	800,000
Net income	$100,000

The IRS has regulations that clarify when a contract is considered completed and whether contracts should be treated as one or several contracts. Under present rules, which are specified in the Revenue Reconciliation Act of 1989, the completed-contract method may be used only for (1) home construction contracts in which at least 80% of the estimated costs are for dwelling units in buildings with four units or less or (2) for construction projects built by smaller companies (those with average gross receipts of $10 million or less for the preceding three years) for contracts that are expected to take two years or less to complete.

When a contract is completed, the taxpayer is required to recalculate the annual income and tax liability for all years of the contract using actual contract costs rather than estimated contract costs. This is referred to as the "lookback" rule. Based on the recalculation of income and tax liability using actual data, the taxpayer calculates the overpayment or underpayment of tax for each year of the contract, and then determines an amount of interest due to or from the IRS.

Information Returns

Information returns are an important part of the IRS computerized taxpayer compliance program. Specific types of payments must be reported to the IRS and to the taxpayer by the organization or person who has made the payments. The taxpayer must then report these payments on his or her income tax return. The purpose of this reporting is to make it possible for the IRS to determine whether taxpayers have reported the appropriate amounts on their tax returns. The TIN (SSN), shown on both the information return and the income tax return, is the basis for comparing the data reported in these returns. Unlike Forms W-2 and W-2G, which are filed with the taxpayer's income tax return, information returns are not attached to the return. Taxpayers should, however, retain the copies of the information returns for their records.

Most organizations or persons required to file information returns use magnetic media to transmit the data. The IRS can then automatically collect and compare these data with the data in the taxpayer's computerized file. The IRS has implied that it would be possible to produce income tax returns automatically for large numbers of taxpayers from data reported on information returns. Payers filing information returns in paper form must use a separate transmittal Form 1096, Annual Summary and Transmittal of U.S. Information Returns, for each different type of information return.

If there is an error in the data reported on the information return, the preparer should be requested to correct it immediately and issue a corrected return. Care should be taken to report data from information returns clearly on the taxpayer's income tax return to minimize the need for an inquiry from the IRS about the reporting of this information.

IRS Comparisons. Because the IRS routinely compares the amounts reported on information returns filed by the payers of interest, dividends, and other types of payments to the amounts reported by the taxpayer on the income tax return, the taxpayer should report the same amounts on Schedule B. Therefore, if two Forms 1099-DIV are received from ABC Company, one for $300 for the dividend on stock held personally by the taxpayer, and another for $176.20 for the dividend on stock held by a trustee for a dividend reinvestment plan, then both amounts should be separately entered on Schedule B. If only one Form 1099-DIV is received for the $476.20 total, then only one amount is reported on Schedule B.

Avoiding Deficiency Notices

If the computer detects a difference between the amounts reported on the information returns and the amounts reported by the taxpayer, the computer may generate a deficiency notice that will require explanation by the taxpayer. Although the difference can be explained by the taxpayer and no penalty will be incurred, much time and effort will be saved if the taxpayer is careful to report the amounts as shown on the information returns.

Common Returns. Some of the common information returns include:

Form 1099-DIV, Dividends and Distributions
Form 1099-INT, Interest Income
Form 1099-G, Certain Government Payments
Form 1098, Mortgage Interest Statement
Form 1099-MISC, Miscellaneous Income
Form 1099-R, Distributions from Pensions, Annuities, Retirement or Profit-Sharing Plans, IRAs, Insurance Contracts, Etc.
Form 1099-B, Proceeds from Broker and Barter Exchange Transactions
Form 1099-S, Proceeds from Real Estate Transactions
Form 8027, Employer's Annual Information Return of Tip Income and Allocated Tips
Form 5498, Individual Retirement Arrangement Information

Penalty for Failure to File Information Returns

The penalty for failure to timely file an information return or a statement to a taxpayer is $50 for each return not filed up to a maximum of $100,000 for any calendar year.

If the failure to file is due to intentional disregard of filing requirements (except for brokers and direct sellers), the penalty will not be less than 10% of the total unreported amounts, and there will be no $100,000 maximum limit. For brokers and certain partnership interests or dispositions of donated property who intentionally fail to file information returns, the penalty is 5% of the gross proceeds with no maximum limit, and the penalty for intentionally failing to report a direct seller's name and address is $100 for each return with no limit.

The penalty for any failure to file an information return or a statement in connection with a deferred compensation plan or a trust, annuity, or bond purchase plan will be $25 for each day that a failure to file continues up to a maximum of $15,000 for any one person.

A penalty for filing information returns that contain incorrect information *or* omit correct information is $5 for each erroneous return up to a $20,000 maximum (except in cases of intentional disregard).

CHAPTER 13

Questions and Problems

1. **a.** Which nonrefundable credit is the last to be offset against the tax liability of an individual taxpayer in 1992?

   b. What are the credits that are combined into the general business credit?

   c. What is the option of a taxpayer who is unable to deduct all of the general business credit from the tax liability in a given year?

   d. When the general business credit is carried back or forward, in what order is it combined with the credits claimed in the past or future years to which it is carried?

   e. For purposes of calculating the general business credit, what is the maximum amount by which the general business credit may reduce the tax liability?

2. Gladys purchased an office building in the current year that had originally been placed in service in 1932. She paid $100,000 for the building and spent an additional $50,000 to rehabilitate it. The building was placed in service in May.

   a. What is Gladys' credit for rehabilitation expenditures?

   b. What is Gladys' basis in the building for depreciation purposes if she elects to take the rehabilitation credit?

3. During 1992, RST, Inc. hired three people (A, B, and C) all of whom qualified RST for the jobs credit. Wages were paid during the year as follows: A—$8,000, B—$9,000, and C—$5,000.

   a. What is RST's jobs credit for 1992?

   b. If RST paid a total of $180,000 to its employees during the year for wages, how much is deductible for wage expense in 1992 if the jobs credit is elected?

4. Harry Maxwell is a citizen and resident of the United States. Harry owns and operates a sporting goods business. During the year Harry has *taxable income* of $90,800. Included in this figure is $20,000 from foreign sources. Harry's foreign income tax on this foreign income is $13,000. His U.S. tax on worldwide income ($90,800) is $20,907. Harry files a joint return and claims his two children as dependents. If Harry elects to claim the foreign taxes as an income tax credit, what amount of credit may he claim?

5. What is meant by a NOL?

6. **a.** What types of adjustments must be made in order to convert an ordinary business loss into a NOL?

   b. If a taxpayer has ordinary gross income amounting to $70,000 and allowable business deductions of $98,000, what is the amount of the NOL assuming that no adjustments are necessary?

c. What would be the amount of the NOL if, in *b.* above, the taxpayer's gross income included an excess of net long-term capital gains over net short-term capital losses in the amount of $4,800?

d. Can an individual who is not in business have a NOL? Explain.

e. For what taxable years may a NOL in 1992 be used as a deduction from income?

7. Chris Rouse, a single lawyer, has opened his own law office. Following is a summary of the net loss related to his 1992 taxes. Calculate Mr. Rouse's NOL for 1992.

Business income	$54,500	
Nonbusiness income (dividends and interest)	2,300	
Long-term capital gain (nonbusiness income)	1,800	
Total income		$58,600
Business deductions	$58,800	
Ordinary nonbusiness deductions (other itemized deductions of $5,370 and a $400 theft loss)	5,770	
Personal and dependency exemptions	4,600	
Total deductions		69,170
Net loss as calculated by Chris		($10,570)

8. Yoko Saburo, a consulting engineer, decided to close her office and go back to study business. One of her most valuable assets was an automobile that she had purchased in 1991 for $12,000. She still owed $5,000 on the car when she sold it for $10,600 on January 10, 1992. The buyer agreed to assume the $5,000 note and further agreed to pay $1,600 as a down payment and pay $2,480 on January 10, 1993, and $2,240 on January 10, 1994 (the balance of $4,000 plus interest at 12%). Under the MACRS rules, Saburo had taken $2,400 of depreciation on the automobile on her 1991 tax return. Assume that Saburo has no other liabilities.

a. What is the realized gain to Saburo on the sale of the automobile?

b. If the realized gain is reported on the installment basis, how much and what type of gain will Yoko report as income in 1992, 1993, and 1994?

c. How much interest income will Yoko report in 1993 and 1994?

9. Refer to Problem *8* and assume that Yoko Saburo needs additional money in 1993. She sells to her bank for $2,050 the note for $2,240 due on January 10, 1994. The bank acquires the note on January 10, 1993.

   a. How much income, if any, would Yoko be required to report on her 1993 tax return as a result of selling the note to the bank?

   b. How would your answer to *a.* differ if Yoko pledged the note due on January 10, 1994, as collateral in the process of acquiring a loan from the bank on January 10, 1993?

10. Walter Spencer, a married taxpayer with no dependents, owns 200 acres of land which he acquired 10 years ago at a total cost of $30,000. There is no mortgage on the property. He has a chance to sell this land in November of 1992 as a site for a golf course on either of the following terms:

   a. For $100,000 cash

   b. For $100,000 with a down payment of $60,000 and the balance payable in two equal annual installments plus interest at 10%

Walter consults with you as to which of the above methods of selling the land would provide the greater tax savings. He and his spouse have income from wages amounting to $23,000 a year and allowable nonbusiness itemized deductions amounting to $7,400 in 1992. They expect to use the standard deduction in 1993 and 1994. (Assume that the standard deduction in 1993 and 1994 will be the same as the standard deduction for 1992.)

Their personal exemptions are $2,300 each in 1992. Assume that they will be the same in 1993 and 1994. Calculate their income taxes on a joint return for 1992, 1993, and 1994 under *a.* and *b.* before considering the AMT, and prepare a summary that will show the tax savings resulting from the best alternative method for selling the land. Assume that the income tax rates applicable to 1993 and 1994 are the same as for 1992.

11. **a.** The Soft-Tone Furniture Co. sells much of its merchandise on the installment basis. While their accounts receivable are collected on an installment basis, their profits must be reported on the accrual method. The installment sales and cost of goods sold figures reported for 1989, 1990, 1991, and 1992 are as follows:

	1989	1990	1991	1992
Installment sales	$160,000	$210,000	$230,000	$250,000
Cost of goods sold	96,000	115,500	103,500	125,000

During 1992 the company collected the following amounts of accounts receivable: 1989 accounts, $30,000; 1990 accounts, $70,000; 1991 accounts, $115,000; and 1992 accounts, $75,000. Determine the gross profit to be reported on the accrual method in 1992 from collections on 1989, 1990, and 1991 accounts and from sales in 1992.

b. Who is allowed to use the installment method of reporting income?

12. The Salem Construction Co. started a construction contract in 1992 that it expects to complete in 1994. Thus, the completion of this contract is to be spread over three years. The following is a list of the expenditures and receipts for each year:

	Expenditures	Receipts	Percentage of Completion at End of Year
First year	$2,250,000	$1,500,000	30%
Second year	3,250,000	3,250,000	75
Third year	1,750,000	3,000,000	100
Totals	$7,250,000	$7,750,000	

The taxpayer's average gross receipts for the three years preceding this contract did not exceed $10,000,000.

a. If the company elects to report the income from this long-term contract under PCM, what amount of net income should be reported each year?

b. How does the taxpayer determine the percentage to use in arriving at income to be reported under the PCM?

c. Would the taxpayer be allowed to report this contract during the period 1992-1994 using the completed-contract method? Explain.

13. Virginia Mann, a sole proprietor, sold depreciable real property for $70,000 on August 4, 1992. The buyer agreed to pay $10,000 at the time of sale and $20,000 on August 4 in each of the succeeding three years, excluding interest. The property cost $55,000 originally, and its book value at the date of sale was $25,000. Of the total depreciation taken, $18,000 is to be recaptured as ordinary income.

  a. Calculate the total gain from the sale.

  b. How much and what type of income must be reported in the year of sale?

  c. How much and what type of income must be reported in each of the succeeding three years?

14. Explain in general the calculation of AMT and how the calculation differs from the calculation of tax on the regular taxable income.

15. **a.** How must depreciation expense for real and personal property be determined in calculating the AMT?

  b. Explain the *types* of adjustments that must be made to regular taxable income in order to calculate the AMT income.

16. Gordon M. and Teresa S. Baker, SSNs 346-57-4657 and 465-46-3647 respectively, prepared a joint income tax return for 1992 and claimed four exemptions. The regular taxable income and tax liability were calculated as follows:

Salaries	$40,000
Schedule C income	52,000
Dividend income	4,700
Interest income	2,150
Total income	$98,850
Itemized deductions	18,000
Balance	$80,850
Personal exemptions	9,200
Taxable income	$71,650
Tax liability	$15,415

In calculating taxable income, the Bakers took depreciation on Schedule C in the amount of $7,000 using the 200%-declining-balance method on assets with a 7-year class life. The AMT life for these assets is 10 years, which would result in allowable 1992 AMT depreciation of $5,500. Itemized deductions include charitable contributions of $9,000 made after July 1 (which includes an appreciated gain on donated securities of $8,500), state and local property taxes of $4,712, casualty losses of $775, and state income taxes of $3,513. Calculate the Bakers' AMT and indicate what their federal tax liability is for 1992.

17. Indicate T (true) or F (false) for the following statements.

_____ a. To be eligible for the disabled access credit, a business must employ not more than 30 full-time employees.

_____ b. The maximum disabled access credit is $5,000.

_____ c. The penalty for failure to timely file an information return is $100 for each return.

_____ d. The penalty for filing information returns that contain incorrect information is $5 for each erroneous return.

_____ e. The penalty for failure to file an information return in connection with a deferred compensation plan is $25 for each day that the failure to file continues up to a maximum of $10,000 for any one person.

PART VII

WITHHOLDING, PAYROLL, AND ESTIMATED TAXES

➡ Pay-as-you-go withholding

➡ Income tax withholding rules for employers and employees

➡ Recording data on wage and tax statements

➡ FICA taxes

➡ Federal unemployment tax

➡ Federal tax deposit system

➡ Employer's quarterly federal tax return

➡ Transmitting tax statements to the government

➡ Estimated taxes for self-employed persons and others

Withholding, Payroll, and Estimated Taxes

On January 1, 1943, the income of most wage earners became subject to *pay-as-you-go withholding*. Under this system, the government collects a large portion of its revenue at the source. Unless exempt by law, employers must withhold income taxes from all wage earners. Before 1943, wage earners would earn their income in one year and pay related taxes in the following year.

By withholding taxes at the source, the government gets a steady cash flow throughout the year and reduces tax collection problems. Source withholding also lessens the cash needs of taxpayers at return time. This chapter provides background information about the tax withholding process. It also provides similar information about the payroll tax deposit system and the self-employment tax.

Withholding Taxes

Under the pay-as-you-go system, *employers* withhold taxes from *employees* that approximate their tax debts. Employers deposit them with a Federal Reserve bank, commercial depository, or financial agent of the United States. The depository or financial agent can be a bank, trust company, domestic building and loan association, or credit union. At tax return time, employees offset the withholdings against their tax debts.

To credit withheld amounts to the proper employee, and then to properly audit his or her tax return, the government needs each employee's correct identification number and related withholdings.

Identification Numbers

The IRS uses a computer examination program to process tax returns. A key factor in this process is the taxpayer's identification number. By law, taxpayers must request, receive, and enter a federal identification number on withholding forms and tax returns.

Taxpayer Identification Number (TIN)

Usually, a **TIN** is a taxpayer's SSN. A taxpayer who needs an SSN can apply for one with Form SS-5, Application for a Social Security Card. For a taxpayer not under the social security system, the law lets the IRS assign an identification number.

The law gives states and political subdivisions the right to request and use taxpayer identification numbers. Payers of dividends, interest, retirement benefits, and profit distributions may also request and use these numbers.

The IRS uses TINs to correlate taxpayer information. Taxpayers claiming a dependency exemption for a person age one or older record his or her SSN on their tax return. This number lets the IRS find the child's tax return (if any) and determine if the tax is correct.

Employer Identification Number (EIN)

Employers use a business identification number on payroll tax reporting forms, tax returns, and other government reports. Employers needing an EIN can apply for one with Form SS-4, Application for Employer Identification Number.

Penalty for Missing ID Number

When an identification number is missing from a return, statement, or document, the charge is $50 for each calendar year omission. The maximum penalty is $100,000.

Withholding Allowances

All compensation, regardless of its name or form, is part of gross income. Compensation includes wages, salaries, fees, tips, bonuses, commissions, and some retirement pay. From this compensation, an employer withholds income taxes which are about equal to the employee's tax debt. When a taxpayer receives property of any kind for services, the property's FMV is the pay measure. In some situations, payers of interest, dividends, and gambling winnings must withhold taxes.

Form W-4, Employee's Withholding Allowance Certificate, is the focal point of the income tax withholding system. Employees claim with-

> ### Fair Market Value (FMV)
>
> FMV is the price at which the property would change hands between a buyer and a seller, neither being required to buy or sell, and both having reasonable knowledge of all necessary facts. Finally, in the absence of an actual sale or exchange, FMV can be determined by expert appraisal and supporting other evidence.

holding allowances with this form. The definition of a **withholding allowance** includes expected personal and dependency exemptions. In 1992, each withholding allowance decreases an employee's withholding tax base by $2,300. Thus, each withholding allowance equals the amount a taxpayer claims for a personal or dependency exemption. Chapter 1 discussed personal and dependency exemptions. This chapter discusses three types of withholding allowances:

1. Personal and dependency allowances
2. Deduction and adjustment allowances
3. Additional allowances for two-earner/two-job employees

The chapter also discusses the process for claiming and changing withholding allowances, exemption from withholding, and penalties.

Withholding Allowance Certificate

Employees do not have to file a new Form W-4 with their employer each year. However, employees should be certain that the Form W-4 on file contains the proper number of allowances. While the IRS does not assess a penalty for over withholding, it does assess a penalty for under withholding. Form W-4 has five data groups and is shown in Illustration 14-1:

1. Background and key explanations
2. Personal allowances worksheet
3. Employee's withholding allowance certificate
4. Deductions and adjustments worksheet
5. Two-earner/two-job worksheet (including Tables 1 and 2)

Only the form portion of this set is given to an employer (page 1, bottom part). Employees should keep the remaining portion in their tax file.

Personal Withholding Allowances

On the personal allowance worksheet, page 1, employees enter whole numbers for their personal withholding allowances (lines A through F). Then, they add these numbers and enter the total (line G). Additional withholding allowances are available to reduce tax withholdings when an employee plans to itemize deductions or claim adjustments to income. Single employees with more than one job, who have total earnings of more than $29,000, may want to claim additional allowances. Married employees with more than one job, or with an employed spouse, who have combined total earnings of more than $50,000, may also want to claim additional allowances.

Deductions and Adjustments in Determining Withholding Allowances

Employees enter an estimate of their itemized deductions on the deduction and adjustments worksheet, page 2 (line 1). Then, they enter the standard deduction amount for their filing status (line 2), subtract this amount from their itemized deduction estimate, and enter the difference when it is more than zero (line 3). Otherwise, they enter zero (line 3). This difference is their estimated excess itemized deductions. Employees also enter an estimate of their alimony and IRA adjustments to income (line 4), add these adjustments to their excess itemized deductions (line 3), and enter a total (line 5). It is their estimated excess itemized deductions and adjustments.

Now, employees enter an estimate of their nonwage income (interest and dividends) on the worksheet (line 6). They subtract this estimate (line 6) from their excess itemized deductions and adjustments (line 5), and enter the difference when it is more than zero (line 7). Otherwise, they enter zero (line 7). This difference is their net excess itemized deductions and adjustments. They divide this difference (line 7) by $2,500, drop any fraction, and enter the remaining whole number (line 8). It represents additional withholding allowances employees can claim to reduce their income subject to withholding. Use of the additional allowances brings employer withholdings more in line with the tax debt for the withholding year. Next, employees enter their personal withholding allowances, page 1 (line G), on the deduc-

Withholding Allowances—Personal Allowance Worksheet (lines A-F)

A. One for employee, when he or she does not qualify another taxpayer for a dependency exemption

B. One for employee, when he or she:

1. Is single and has only one job
2. Receives wages from a second job of $1,000 or less
3. Has one job, and his or her spouse is not a wage earner
4. Has a spouse with wages of $1,000 or less
5. Has a spouse, and the couple's combined wages are $1,000 or less

C. One for employee's spouse. The IRS suggests that a married employee with more than one job or a wage earning spouse claim a zero spousal allowance. Using this suggestion may avoid an under withholding situation.

D. One for each person who qualifies the employee for a dependency exemption. Note, a taxpayer is never the dependent of his or her spouse.

E. One, if employee files as a HOH.

F. One, if employee plans to claim the child or dependent care credit for at least $1,500 of expenses.

tion and adjustments worksheet (line 9), add it to their additional withholding allowances (line 8), and enter a total (line 10). Employees who do not use the Two-Earner/Two-Job Worksheet enter the total (line 10) on Form W-4, page 1 (line 5). Employees who use the Two-Earner/Two-Job Worksheet enter the total (line 10) on the Two-Earner/Two-Job Worksheet (line 1).

Additional Withholding for Two-Earner/Two-Job Employees

The Two-Earner/Two-Job Worksheet is available for a married employee with more than one job or a wage-earning spouse, and combined earnings of at least $50,000. A single employee with more than one job uses this worksheet when his or her combined earnings are at least $29,000. The line instructions for

this worksheet are self-explanatory. Total income tax withholdings for an employee who follows the instructions should be close to this person's tax liability.

Filled-In Form W-4, Employee's Withholding Allowance Certificate

Illustration 14-1

This illustration shows a filled-in Form W-4 for Jerry J. Page. Mr. Page expects to file a joint tax return for 1992 with his wife Belle. The Pages decide that Jerry will claim all of their withholding allowances. Jerry determines his withholding allowances on one set of worksheets. In 1992, he expects to earn $22,000 a year as a preschool administrator. Belle expects to earn $17,900 as a school program adviser. Neither Jerry nor Belle qualify another taxpayer for a dependency exemption. The Pages provide all the support for their two minor children who have no income. Jerry and Belle estimate that they will pay or receive the following amounts during 1992:

Deductible IRA payment estimated for Belle	$1,000
Deductible IRA payment estimated for Jerry	1,000
Deductible interest expense payment on home mortgage	4,260
Property tax payment	1,400
Estimated child and dependent care expenses for credit	600
State income tax payment	1,000
Estimated charitable contribution payments	2,140
Interest income on corporate bonds	1,250
Dividend income on domestic public utility stock	1,000

From the deductions and adjustments worksheet, page 2 (line 10), Jerry determines that he can claim 4 withholding allowances. He enters this number on Form W-4 (line 5). Since Jerry does not want his employer to withhold additional amounts, he enters a "–0–" (line 6). Since he is not exempt from the withholding tax rules, he leaves the next line blank (line 7). He enters an "X" in the NO box (line 8). Then, he signs and dates the form and gives it to his employer.

Illustration 14-1
Filled-In Form W-4—Page 1

349   12-91   1037

19**92** Form W-4

Department of the Treasury
Internal Revenue Service

Purpose. Complete Form W-4 so that your employer can withhold the correct amount of Federal income tax from your pay.

Exemption From Withholding. Read line 7 of the certificate below to see if you can claim exempt status. *If exempt, complete line 7; but do not complete lines 5 and 6.* No Federal income tax will be withheld from your pay. Your exemption is good for one year only. It expires February 15, 1993.

Basic Instructions. Employees who are not exempt should complete the Personal Allowances Worksheet. Additional worksheets are provided on page 2 for employees to adjust their withholding allowances based on itemized deductions, adjustments to income, or two-earner/two-job situations. Complete all worksheets that apply to your situation. The worksheets will help you figure the number of withholding allowances you are entitled to claim. However, you may claim fewer allowances than this.

Head of Household. Generally, you may claim head of household filing status on your tax return only if you are unmarried and pay more than 50% of the costs of keeping up a home for yourself and your dependent(s) or other qualifying individuals.

Nonwage Income. If you have a large amount of nonwage income, such as interest or dividends, you should consider making estimated tax payments using Form 1040-ES. Otherwise, you may find that you owe additional tax at the end of the year.

Two-Earner/Two-Jobs. If you have a working spouse or more than one job, figure the total number of allowances you are entitled to claim on all jobs using worksheets from only one Form W-4. This total should be divided among all jobs. Your withholding will usually be most accurate when all allowances are claimed on the W-4 filed for the highest paying job and zero allowances are claimed for the others.

Advance Earned Income Credit. If you are eligible for this credit, you can receive it added to your paycheck throughout the year. For details, get Form W-5 from your employer.

Check Your Withholding. After your W-4 takes effect, you can use Pub. 919, Is My Withholding Correct for 1992?, to see how the dollar amount you are having withheld compares to your estimated total annual tax. Call 1-800-829-3676 to order this publication. Check your local telephone directory for the IRS assistance number if you need further help.

Personal Allowances Worksheet

For 1992, the value of your personal exemption(s) is reduced if your income is over $105,250 ($157,900 if married filing jointly, $131,550 if head of household, or $78,950 if married filing separately). Get Pub. 919 for details.

A	Enter "1" for **yourself** if no one else can claim you as a dependent	A __1__
B	Enter "1" if: • You are single and have only one job; or • You are married, have only one job, and your spouse does not work; or • Your wages from a second job or your spouse's wages (or the total of both) are $1,000 or less.	B ____
C	Enter "1" for your **spouse**. But, you may choose to enter -0- if you are married and have either a working spouse or more than one job (this may help you avoid having too little tax withheld)	C __0__
D	Enter number of **dependents** (other than your spouse or yourself) whom you will claim on your tax return	D __2__
E	Enter "1" if you will file as **head of household** on your tax return (see conditions under "Head of Household," above)	E ____
F	Enter "1" if you have at least $1,500 of **child or dependent care expenses** for which you plan to claim a credit	F ____
G	Add lines A through F and enter total here. Note: *This amount may be different from the number of exemptions you claim on your return* ▶	G __3__

For accuracy, do all worksheets that apply.

• If you plan to **itemize or claim adjustments to income** and want to reduce your withholding, see the Deductions and Adjustments Worksheet on page 2.

• If you are **single** and have **more than one job** and your combined earnings from all jobs exceed $29,000 OR if you are **married** and have a **working spouse or more than one job,** and the combined earnings from all jobs exceed $50,000, see the Two-Earner/Two-Job Worksheet on page 2 if you want to avoid having too little tax withheld.

• If **neither** of the above situations applies, **stop here** and enter the number from line G on line 5 of Form W-4 below.

·········· **Cut here and give the certificate to your employer. Keep the top portion for your records.** ··········

Form **W-4**
Department of the Treasury
Internal Revenue Service

Employee's Withholding Allowance Certificate

OMB No. 1545-0010

19**92**

▶ **For Privacy Act and Paperwork Reduction Act Notice, see reverse.**

1 Type or print your first name and middle initial	Last name	2 Your social security number
Jerry J.	Page	432–16–8410

Home address (number and street or rural route)
1222 West Main Street

3 ☐ Single ☒ Married ☐ Married, but withhold at higher Single rate.
Note: *If married, but legally separated, or spouse is a nonresident alien, check the Single box.*

City or town, state, and ZIP code
San Diego, CA 91344–8135

4 If your last name differs from that on your social security card, check here and call 1-800-772-1213 for more information ▶ ☐

5 Total number of allowances you are claiming (from line G above or from the Worksheets on back if they apply) — **5** | 4

6 Additional amount, if any, you want deducted from each paycheck — **6** $ –0–

7 I claim exemption from withholding and I certify that I meet **ALL** of the following conditions for exemption:

• Last year I had a right to a refund of **ALL** Federal income tax withheld because I had **NO** tax liability; **AND**
• This year I expect a refund of **ALL** Federal income tax withheld because I expect to have **NO** tax liability; **AND**
• This year if my income exceeds $600 and includes nonwage income, another person cannot claim me as a dependent.

If you meet all of the above conditions, enter the year effective and "EXEMPT" here ▶ **7** | 19

8 Are you a full-time student? (**Note:** *Full-time students are not automatically exempt.*) — **8** ☐ Yes ☒ No

Under penalties of perjury, I certify that I am entitled to the number of withholding allowances claimed on this certificate or entitled to claim exempt status.

Employee's signature ▶ *Jerry J. Page*   Date ▶ December 15   , 19 92

9 Employer's name and address (Employer: Complete 9 and 11 only if sending to the IRS) | **10** Office code (optional) | **11** Employer identification number

Cat. No. 10220Q

Illustration 14-1
Filled-In Form W-4—Page 2

1037-2

349 12-91

Form W-4 (1992) Page **2**

Deductions and Adjustments Worksheet

Note: *Use this worksheet only if you plan to itemize deductions or claim adjustments to income on your 1992 tax return.*

1 Enter an estimate of your 1992 itemized deductions. These include: qualifying home mortgage interest, charitable contributions, state and local taxes (but not sales taxes), medical expenses in excess of 7.5% of your income, and miscellaneous deductions. (For 1992, you may have to reduce your itemized deductions if your income is over \$105,250 (\$52,625 if married filing separately). Get Pub. 919 for details.) **1** \$8,800

2 Enter: { \$6,000 if married filing jointly or qualifying widow(er) / \$5,250 if head of household / \$3,600 if single / \$3,000 if married filing separately } **2** \$6,000

3 **Subtract** line 2 from line 1. If line 2 is greater than line 1, enter -0- **3** \$2,800

4 Enter an estimate of your 1992 adjustments to income. These include alimony paid and deductible IRA contributions **4** \$2,000

5 **Add** lines 3 and 4 and enter the total **5** \$4,800

6 Enter an estimate of your 1992 nonwage income (such as dividends or interest income) **6** \$2,250

7 **Subtract** line 6 from line 5. Enter the result, but not less than -0- **7** \$2,550

8 **Divide** the amount on line 7 by \$2,500 and enter the result here. Drop any fraction **8** 1

9 Enter the number from Personal Allowances Worksheet, line G, on page 1 **9** 3

10 **Add** lines 8 and 9 and enter the total here. If you plan to use the Two-Earner/Two-Job Worksheet, also enter the total on line 1, below. Otherwise, **stop here** and enter this total on Form W-4, line 5, on page 1 **10** 4

Two-Earner/Two-Job Worksheet

Note: *Use this worksheet only if the instructions for line G on page 1 direct you here.*

1 Enter the number from line G on page 1 (or from line 10 above if you used the Deductions and Adjustments Worksheet) **1**

2 Find the number in **Table 1** below that applies to the **LOWEST** paying job and enter it here **2**

3 If line 1 is **GREATER THAN OR EQUAL TO** line 2, subtract line 2 from line 1. Enter the result here (if zero, enter -0-) and on Form W-4, line 5, on page 1. **DO NOT** use the rest of this worksheet **3**

Note: *If line 1 is **LESS THAN** line 2, enter -0- on Form W-4, line 5, on page 1. Complete lines 4–9 to calculate the additional dollar withholding necessary to avoid a year-end tax bill.*

4 Enter the number from line 2 of this worksheet **4**

5 Enter the number from line 1 of this worksheet **5**

6 **Subtract** line 5 from line 4 **6**

7 Find the amount in **Table 2** below that applies to the **HIGHEST** paying job and enter it here **7** \$

8 **Multiply** line 7 by line 6 and enter the result here. This is the additional annual withholding amount needed **8** \$

9 Divide line 8 by the number of pay periods remaining in 1992. (For example, divide by 26 if you are paid every other week and you complete this form in December of 1991.) Enter the result here and on Form W-4, line 6, page 1. This is the additional amount to be withheld from each paycheck **9** \$

Table 1: Two-Earner/Two-Job Worksheet

Married Filing Jointly		All Others	
If wages from **LOWEST** paying job are—	Enter on line 2 above	If wages from **LOWEST** paying job are—	Enter on line 2 above
0 - \$4,000	0	0 - \$6,000	0
4,001 - 8,000	1	6,001 - 10,000	1
8,001 - 13,000	2	10,001 - 14,000	2
13,001 - 18,000	3	14,001 - 18,000	3
18,001 - 22,000	4	18,001 - 22,000	4
22,001 - 26,000	5	22,001 - 45,000	5
26,001 - 30,000	6	45,001 and over	6
30,001 - 35,000	7		
35,001 - 40,000	8		
40,001 - 60,000	9		
60,001 - 80,000	10		
80,001 and over	11		

Table 2: Two-Earner/Two-Job Worksheet

Married Filing Jointly		All Others	
If wages from **HIGHEST** paying job are—	Enter on line 7 above	If wages from **HIGHEST** paying job are—	Enter on line 7 above
0 - \$50,000	\$340	0 - \$27,000	\$340
50,001 - 100,000	640	27,001 - 58,000	640
100,001 and over	710	58,001 and over	710

Claiming Withholding Allowances

Employers must request a withholding allowance certificate from each employee. If an employee fails to furnish such a certificate, the employer treats the employee as claiming no withholding allowance. Married employees must show their status on Form W-4 to take advantage of a lower withholding rate.

If a person does not claim married status, an employer must withhold at the single status rate. If a married person wants an employer to withhold taxes at the single rate, he or she checks the proper box (line 3). This box states "Married, but withhold at higher Single rate." It also states "If married, but legally separated, or spouse is a nonresident alien, check the Single box."

An employer's basis for income tax withholding is the number of allowances an employee claims on Form W-4. By agreement, an employee can have his or her employer withhold additional taxes. Without proper authorization, an employer cannot withhold additional amounts. When an employee places an amount on Form W-4 (line 5), he or she authorizes additional withholding.

The basis for claiming withholding allowances is expectations. Taxpayers who are married at the start of the year usually assume the same status will exist at year end. If events take place during the year which alter the number of allowances, the employee can file an amended Form W-4. Note, sometimes an employee cannot claim all expected allowances. Though a single taxpayer expects to marry before year end, he or she cannot claim an allowance for a future spouse. The taxpayer must be eligible to claim an allowance when he or she gives Form W-4 to an employer.

A single taxpayer with no dependents, but more than one job, can claim only one withholding allowance at a time. He or she should claim this allowance with the employer paying the highest wage. At the other job(s), the taxpayer should claim zero withholding allowances. The income tax withholdings of a single taxpayer with only wage or salary income who follows this rule will be closer to his or her actual tax liability.

While a married taxpayer and spouse can choose how to divide their withholding allowances, the couple cannot claim the same allowance with more than one employer. Married taxpayers filing separately claim their allowances separately.

An employer must file copies of some Forms W-4 with the IRS. This filing includes the Forms W-4 for each employee claiming 11 or more allowances. This filing also includes the Forms W-4 for each employee with wages of more than $200 a week who claims exemption from withholding. Before sending copies to the IRS, employers complete the lines at the bottom of Form W-4 (lines 8, 9, and 10).

Changing Withholding Allowances

An employee usually does not have to file a new Form W-4 each year. However, when an employee's withholding allowances *decrease*, the employee must file a new Form W-4 within 10 days of the decreasing event (divorce or legal separation). If an event during the year *increases* an employee's withholding allowances, he or she can file a new Form W-4 or leave the old Form W-4 in effect.

When a new employee files a Form W-4, the employer starts withholding with the first wage payment. When a continuing employee files a replacement Form W-4, the employer places the replacement in effect by the later of two dates. One is the beginning of the next payroll period; the other is 30 days after the employer receives the employee's new Form W-4.

The death of a spouse or dependent during the year does not change an employee's withholding allowances. However, an employee should file a new Form W-4 by December 1 to assure that it will take effect at the start of the next year. For the two years after a spouse's death, a surviving spouse with a qualifying child can use the standard deduction for married persons filing jointly. A surviving spouse takes this fact into consideration on the Form W-4 deductions and adjustments worksheet, page 2 (line 2).

Exemption from Withholding

An employee can claim exemption from withholding on Form W-4 with more than one employer, page 1 (line 6). The exemption only applies to federal income taxes. Thus, an employer must still withhold social security taxes.

The provision to claim exemption from withholding is helpful to persons who work short periods or earn small amounts. Without this provision, employers would have to with-

Exemption from Withholding— To Claim Taxpayer Must

1. Have no federal income tax liability for last year
2. Have a right to a full refund of all income taxes withheld last year
3. Not expect to owe any federal income taxes for the current year
4. Expect to have a right to a full refund of all income taxes withheld this year
5. Not qualify another taxpayer for a dependency exemption claim when his or her income is more than $600 and includes nonwage income

hold taxes though no likelihood of a tax debt for the employee exists. If an employer withholds taxes when none are due, the employee must file an IRS refund claim to get them back.

The exemption from withholding for a given year expires on February 15 of the next year. When an employee wishes to continue a withholding exemption for the next year, he or she must file a new Form W-4 by February 15. The employee must also revoke the exemption within 10 days of an event that creates a tax expectation for the current year. When an employee expects a tax debt for the next tax year, he or she should revoke the exemption by filing a new Form W-4 before December 1.

Penalty for False Withholding Information

The *civil penalty* for entering false data on a Form W-4 is $500. This penalty applies when there is no reasonable basis for a Form W-4 statement. The IRS does not assess the penalty when the false statement results in correct or over withholding. Also, the IRS does not assess the penalty when a person's tax debt is less than his or her combined tax withholdings and estimated tax payments.

The *criminal penalty* for willfully supplying false withholding information is $1,000 or imprisonment for up to 1 year, or both. This penalty applies to all taxpayers who willfully furnish incorrect or false withholding information. The IRS can assess the criminal penalty when it assesses other penalties.

Penalty for Failure to Collect or Deposit Taxes

The IRS can assess a 100% penalty against employers who fail to collect or deposit Federal Insurance Contributions Act (FICA) taxes. The penalty does not apply to direct taxes, like the federal unemployment tax or employer's share of FICA taxes. The IRS can assess the 100% penalty against employers who willfully try to avoid withholding income and payroll taxes by classifying employees as independent contractors. The IRS can also assess the penalty against employees responsible for an employer's tax withholdings.

FICA Tax

The FICA Act provides for OASDI. This Act also provides for a HIP. On an employee's Form W-2, the IRS calls the OASDI portion, the *social security tax*. The HIP portion is the *Medicare tax*.

The government assesses an equal amount of FICA tax on employers and employees. Each employer withholds the employee's share from wages and deposits both shares (employer and employee) in a specific depository or Federal Reserve bank.

FICA wages include those of a child more than 17 years old who works in the parent's business (sole proprietorship or partnership). These wages also include those of the taxpayer's spouse who works in the business. Wages of any family member employed by a family member corporation are usually subject to FICA withholding. The wages of a child under age 21 who works for a parent are not subject to federal unemployment taxes. Also, the wages of a spouse working for a spouse are not subject to federal unemployment taxes. When an employer purchases group-term life insurance of more than $50,000 for an employee, the gross income amount for this coverage is part of the employee's FICA wages.

Social Security and Medicare Tax Rates

For 1992, the social security or OASDI tax rate is 6.20%. Employers apply the rate to each employee's wages up to $55,500, including employees who have already reached the maximum wage base with another employer. Thus, an employer's share of the OASDI tax per employee cannot be more than $3,441, (6.20% x $55,500). Since the OASDI tax is a matching tax, the employee's share cannot be more than $3,441.

The Medicare or HIP tax rate is 1.45%. This tax is also a matching tax on employers and employees. Employers apply the HIP rate to each employee's wages up to $130,200, including employees who have already reached the maximum wage base with another employer. Thus, both the employer and employee's share of the HIP tax cannot be more than $1,887.90, (1.45% x $130,200). The maximum FICA tax that an employer can withhold from an employee's wages is $5,328.90, ($3,441.00 + $1,887.90). The wage bases for the FICA rates are subject to cost-of-living adjustments.

Tax Rates and Bases

Calendar Year	OASDI (Social Security Rate)	HIP (Hospital Insurance Rate)	OASDI Base	HIP Base
1991	6.20	1.45	$53,400	$125,000
1992	6.20	1.45	55,500	130,200
1993	6.20	1.45	57,600	135,000

Special Social Security Tax Situations

Certain education organizations can purchase tax-sheltered annuities for employees. For income tax purposes, the purchase price is not part of an employee's gross income from wages. However, for FICA purposes the purchase price is part of wages. When an employer pays an employee's share of FICA taxes, the employee's gross, OASDI, and HIP wages increase.

Reporting to Employees and Government

Each January, employers give each employee a separate Form W-2, Wage and Tax Statement. Employers also give the Social Security Administration a copy of each Form W-2. Form W-2 shows an employee's wages (gross, OASDI, and HIP) and withheld taxes (income, OASDI, and HIP) for the past calendar year. While not a federal requirement, Form W-2 can show an employee's retirement contributions, withheld state income taxes, and other items. At tax return time, employees attach a completed Form W-2 copy to their tax return. The following discussion examines Form W-2.

Employers prepare six copies of Form W-2 for each eligible employee. Employers file Copy A with the Social Security Administration by the last day in February. If applicable, they file Copy 1 with the proper state or local government agency. Employers send Copies B, C, and 2 to each employee by January 31. When employment ends before the close of a calendar year, employers must send the leaving employee Copies B, C, and 2 no later than January 31 of the next year. A former employee can request a Form W-2 before this date. The former employer must give the former employee a Form W-2 within 30 days of his or her request or last wage payment, whichever is later.

Distribution of Form W-2

Copy	Distribution
Copy A	For Social Security Administration
Copy 1	For state, city, or local tax department
Copy B	To be filed with employee's federal tax return
Copy C	For employee's records
Copy 2	To be filed with employee's state, city, or local income tax return
Copy D	For employer

Reporting, Data Needs

The discussion below describes the data an employer needs to complete some of the 1993 Form W-2 boxes. It does not cover all boxes since the printed headings in most are descriptive of needed data. However, the *Instructions for Form W-2* describe the data needs of all boxes.

Control Number (box a). Employers can assign an identifying control number of up to seven digits to Form W-2. Employers who make such an assignment should include this number in all Form W-2 correspondence sent to the Social Security Administration.

Identifying Form Number (22222). The number 22222 appears at the top of Form W-2 (box to right of box a). The Social Security Administration uses electronic scanning equipment and this number to identify Form W-2.

Void. Employers mark this box when a form contains an erasure, white-out, strike over, or incorrect entry. Do not include amounts on voided forms in the subtotals on the 42nd form. (see *Subtotal* below.)

Statutory Employee, Deceased, Pension Plan Legal Rep., 942 Emp., Subtotal, Deferred Compensation (box 15). Employers place an "X" in the proper square (box 15) to identify the following employee or Form W-2 situation:

Statutory Employee. Employers withhold FICA taxes from the wages of statutory employees, but do not withhold federal income taxes from these employees. **Statutory employees** include four occupation groups who meet three Code tests. Group (1) includes agent-drivers or commission-drivers engaged in delivering laundry, dry-cleaning, and certain foods products (other than milk) to customers. Group (2) is full-time life insurance salespersons for a single life insurance company. Group (3) is home workers. Group (4) includes traveling or city salespersons soliciting orders for one business who are not agent-drivers or commission-drivers. For a group member to meet the three tests, he or she must:

1. Work under a service contract that states or implies that he or she will provide most of the services
2. Be working in a continuing (on-going) employment relationship
3. Have little or no investment in the equipment or property used to perform the contracted services (other than transportation facilities)

Home workers do not include household employees who perform domestic service. Any person who is a member of group (1) or (4) and meets the three Code tests is a statutory employee for the federal unemployment tax provisions.

Deceased. Employers mark this square for wages or other compensation paid to a deceased employee's estate.

Pension Plan. Employers place an "X" in this square to identify active participants in the employer's retirement plan. Employers do not mark this square for contributions to nonqualified pension plans or Section 457 plans. Section 457 covers the deferred compensation plans of state and local governments.

Legal Representative. Employers mark this square when the name in the *Employee's name and address* box is a trust (John Doe Trust). If the person or business name in the name box is acting as the employee's representative, employers mark this square. Words which describe an employee representative are custodian, parent, or attorney. Employers do not place an "X" in this square when the address is for someone other than the employee (John Doe, c/o Jane Smith).

942 Employee. Employers mark this square for household employees.

Subtotal. The government printing office prints two Forms W-2 on a single sheet of paper. To ease checking at the Social Security Administration, employers report subtotals on every 42nd form for the preceding 41 forms. Each set of 42 forms can include blank and void forms. The subtotals on the 42nd form do not contain amounts on the blank and void forms. Employers enter amounts on every 42nd form to the nearest cent without dollar signs, but with decimal points. The entry format is (000.00). Employers mark the subtotal box on the 42nd form to show that this form contains subtotals for the last 41 forms. When the last group of forms is less than 41, employers still mark this box. An employer with 86 employees shows subtotals on the 42nd, 84th, and 89th form. An employer filing less than 41 forms does not enter subtotals.

Deferred Compensation. Employers mark this square to show contributions to a Section 401(k), 403(b), 408(k)(6), 457, or 501(c)(18)(D) retirement plan for employees. Section 401(k) covers cash or deferred retirement arrangements. Section 403(b) covers salary reduction plans for the purchase of annuity contracts. Section 408(k)(6) covers salary reduction plans (SEP). Section 457 covers deferred compensation plans of state and local governments. Section 501(c)(18)(D) covers tax-exempt organization plans.

Other (box 14). Employers use this box to report the payment of union dues, moving expenses, and educational aid for employees.

Filled-In Form W-2, Wage and Tax Statement

Illustration 14-2

This illustration shows a 1993 filled-in Copy A of Form W-2 for Harriet R. Shawver. Her SSN is 364-74-6560. Her employer, Anderson, Berger, and Green, SC, has the following EIN: 92-0446587 (federal) and 104693 (state). Harriet lives at 2123 Fairmount Drive, Milwaukee, Wisconsin 53209-3685. Her employer's place of business is 2700 South Park Drive, Milwaukee, Wisconsin 53202-2645. Ms. Shawver's gross salary is $21,500. Her employer withheld federal income taxes of $3,264, social security taxes of $1,333, Medicare taxes of $311.75, and Wisconsin income taxes of $1,008.

Federal Unemployment Tax Act (FUTA)

In addition to income and FICA taxes, there is another payroll tax. This tax is the FUTA tax. Since the law levies the FUTA tax on employers, there is no FUTA withholding from wages.

FUTA Rate and Base

The FUTA rate is 6.2% of taxable wages that an employer pays during the year. However, employers are only liable for 6.2% of *each* employee's taxable wages up to $7,000. Employers can get a credit of up 5.4% which they can use to reduce the FUTA tax. Employers get this credit when they pay a proper state unemployment rate. For employers paying the proper state rate, 0.8% is the net FUTA rate. Employers reduce the state credit by 10% when they do not pay the state unemployment tax by the due date of the annual FUTA return. Without an extension, employers must file a FUTA return before February 1 of the next year. Depending on the situation, employers use either Form 940, Employer's Annual Federal Unemployment (FUTA) Tax Return, or Form 940EZ. Both forms have the same name.

Kimberly has two employees: Mike and Susan Thompson. Mike and Susan's gross wages for 1992 are $10,000 and $5,000, respectively. The Thompsons live and work in a state with a 5.4% unemployment tax. Kimberly's FUTA tax for 1992 is $96 ($56 for Mike's wages and $40 for Susan's).

	Mike	Susan
1. Gross wages	$10,000	$ 5,000
2. Maximum FUTA wages	$ 7,000	$ 7,000
3. Smaller of 1 or 2	$ 7,000	$ 5,000
4. Times net FUTA rate (6.2% – 5.4%)	x 0.8%	x 0.8%
5. FUTA tax	$ 56	$ 40

Depositing FUTA Taxes

Employers usually deposit FUTA taxes with a specific depository or Federal Reserve bank before a due date ends. The due date is the end of the month, following the end of a quarter, in which the employer's net FUTA liability is more than $100. If an employer's FUTA liability for any quarter is $100 or less, the deposit due date carries over to the next quarter. During the first three calendar quarters, employers make a deposit when their quarterly FUTA debt is more than $100. When the FUTA tax for the fourth quarter is $100 or less, employers can pay it directly to the IRS with their FUTA return. When the FUTA tax is more than $100, employers deposit the tax with a specific depository or Federal Reserve bank before February 1. Such a deposit extends the due date of the FUTA return by 10 days.

After reduction by the state credit, the Bucket Company's 1992 quarterly FUTA taxes are: 1st—$35, 2nd—$50, 3rd—$45, and 4th—$20. Bucket must deposit $130 ($35 + $50 + $45) before November 1, 1992. For the fourth quarter, Bucket can either deposit the tax before February 1, 1993 or attach the fourth quarter tax payment to its FUTA return. If Bucket does not deposit the fourth quarter's $20 FUTA tax on time, the FUTA return is due before February 1, 1993.

Illustration 14-2
Filled-In Form W-2, Copy A

a Control number	22222	Void ☐	For Official Use Only ►		

b Employer's identification number	1 Wages, tips, other compensation	2 Federal income tax withheld
92-0446587	21,500.00	3,264.00

c Employer's name, address, and ZIP code	3 Social security wages	4 Social security tax withheld
Anderson, Berger, and Green, SC 2700 South Park Drive Milwaukee, WI 53202-2645	21,500.00	1,333.00

	5 Medicare wages and tips	6 Medicare tax withheld
	21,500.00	311.75

	7 Social security tips	8 Allocated tips

d Employee's social security number	9 Advance EIC payment	10 Dependent care benefits
364-74-6560		

e Employee's name (first, middle initial, last)	11 Nonqualified plans	12 Benefits included in Box 1
Harriet R. Shawver		
2123 Fairmount Drive Milwaukee, WI 53209-3685	13 See Instrs. for Box 13	14 Other

15 Statutory employee ☐ Deceased ☐ Pension plan ☐ Legal rep. ☐ 942 emp. ☐ Subtotal ☐ Deferred compensation ☐

f Employee's address and ZIP code					

16 State	Employer's state I.D. No.	17 State wages, tips, etc.	18 State income tax	19 Locality name	20 Local wages, tips, etc.	21 Local income tax
WI	104693	21,500.00	1,008.00			

Cat. No. 10134D   Department of the Treasury—Internal Revenue Service

Form **W-2** Wage and Tax Statement **1993**

Copy A For Social Security Administration

For Paperwork Reduction Act Notice, see separate instructions.

OMB No. 1545-0008

Withholding on Pensions, Annuities, and Deferred Income

Withholding applies to *certain distributions.* These distributions include the taxable part of pensions, profit-sharing plans, stock bonuses, individual retirement accounts, and deferred compensation plans. Commercial annuity contracts, whether or not purchased under an employer's plan, come under the withholding rules. Withholding also applies to the partial surrender of annuity contracts and certain loans from employee pension plans and IRAs. Annuity payments and distributions by the Civil Service Retirement System come under the withholding rules.

Pension and annuity payments can be periodic or nonperiodic. Unless a recipient requests no tax withholding, payers must withhold taxes. Recipients can ask a payer not to withhold taxes for any reason. A taxpayer making this request fills out the top part of Form W-4P, Withholding Certificate for Pension or Annuity Payments. Then, he or she places an "X" in the proper box (end of line 1). After signing and dating the form, the taxpayer mails the form to the payer. Recipients who are U.S. citizens or resident aliens must provide the payer with a home address in the United States or a U.S. possession. Under some conditions, payers can send pension and annuity payments to addresses outside the United States or its possessions. A discussion of these conditions is beyond the scope of this book.

Pension and annuity payments at regular intervals over a period of more than one year are *periodic* payments. The one year begins with the start date of the pension or annuity. The payment interval can be annual, quarterly, monthly, etc. When a payer does not receive a withholding certificate from the payee, withholding must still take place. Here, the payer treats the payee as a married person claiming three withholding allowances.

For 1992, payers withhold taxes on a payee's pension or annuity when a payment is more than $883 per month [($2,300 exemption + $2,300 exemption + $6,000 standard deduction)/12 months]. As an alternative, a payee may request withholding on the basis of his or her marital status and withholding allowances. He or she makes this request by entering the proper number of withholding allowances on Form W-4P (line 2). If the payee wants the payer to withhold an additional amount, he or she enters this amount (line 3).

Usually, payers of *nonperiodic* pensions or annuities withhold taxes at a flat 10% rate. However, such payers do not withhold at this rate for a qualifying *total* pension or annuity distribution. Here, payers withhold taxes according to Treasury Department tables.

Some pension and annuity distributions are subject to a maximum withholding limit. A payer usually cannot withhold more than the market value of the property and money distributions.

Most payers of pensions and annuities are banks and insurance companies. These organizations deposit withheld taxes with a Federal Reserve bank or specific depository.

Filled-In Form W-4P, Withholding Certificate for Pension or Annuity Payments

Illustration 14-3

A filled-in Form W-4P is shown for Yang Li. Mr. Li's SSN is 836-48-1557. He lives at 5284 Elm Avenue, Louisville, Kentucky 40216-7550. His pension contract does not have an identification number. He uses Form W-4P to ask his pension payer not to withhold taxes on his pension payments. Mr. Li's Form W-4P remains in effect until he files another one with his pension payer.

Federal Tax Deposit System

Employers use the federal tax deposit system to transfer payroll taxes to the government. Employers usually deposit these taxes with a specific depository or the Federal Reserve Bank servicing the employer's geographic area. Under certain conditions, some tax payments go directly to the IRS.

Federal Tax Deposit Coupon Book

The IRS issues Form 8109, Federal Tax Deposit Coupon Book, to employers. Each coupon book issued after July 1, 1992 has a yellow cover and contains 24 deposit coupons. The sixth and seventh coupons contain a special identification number which automatically triggers a coupon reorder request. Depositors do not have to reorder a supply of deposit coupons. Old reorder coupon (Form 8109A) has been eliminated.

For each tax deposit transfer, employers prepare a deposit coupon by writing in the numerical data, omitting dollar signs, leading zeros, commas, and decimal points. Commas and decimal point already appear in the form's entry

Form 8109 Tax Deposit Types by Form Number

Form 941—Withheld Income and Social Security Tax
Form 990C—Exempt Cooperative Association Income Tax
Form 943—Agricultural Withheld Income and Social Security Tax
Form 720—Excise Tax
Form CT-1—Railroad Retirement Tax
Form 940—Federal Unemployment Tax
Schedule A—Backup Withholding (reported on Forms 941 and 941E)
Form 1120—Corporate Income Tax
Form 990T—Exempt Organization Income Tax
Form 990PF—Return of Private Foundation Exempt From Income Tax
Form 1042—Income Tax Withholding on Payments to Nonresident Aliens and Foreign Corporations

Illustration 14-3
Filled-In Form W-4P

.... Cut here and give the certificate to the payer of your pension or annuity. Keep the top portion for your records. ....

Form **W-4P**

Department of the Treasury
Internal Revenue Service

**Withholding Certificate for
Pension or Annuity Payments**

OMB No. 1545-0415

1992

Type or print your full name

Yang Li

Your social security number

836   48   1557

Home address (number and street or rural route)

5284 Elm Avenue

Claim or identification number
(if any) of your pension or
annuity contract

City or town, state, and ZIP code

Louisville, KY 40216–7550

Complete the following applicable lines:

1   I elect not to have income tax withheld from my pension or annuity. (Do not complete lines 2 or 3.) . . . . . ▶ X

2   I want my withholding from each **periodic** pension or annuity payment to be figured using the number of allowances
    and marital status shown. (You may also designate an amount on line 3.) . . . . ▶ _____

    Marital status: ☐ Single   ☐ Married   ☐ Married, but withhold at higher Single rate

    (Enter number of allowances.)

3   I want the following additional amount withheld from each pension or annuity payment. **Note:** For periodic payments,
    you cannot enter an amount here without entering the number (including zero) of allowances on line 2 . . . ▶ $ _____

Your signature ▶ Yang Li   Date ▶ 7-6-93

Cat. No. 10225T

area. When a deposit is for whole dollars only, employers write zeros in the boxes for cents.

At the top right of each deposit coupon is a list of tax period ovals. Employers darken one to show the quarter which a deposit covers. To the left of the period ovals is a list of payment ovals with related form numbers. Employers darken one to identify the deposit type.

Filled-In Form 8109, Federal Tax Deposit Coupon

Illustration 14-4

This illustration shows a filled-in Form 8109 deposit coupon for Martinez Enterprises, Inc., 64 Bay Road, Miami, FL 33139-5670. On the line below the preprinted EIN and address, Martinez enters its daytime telephone number of (305) 271-3544. In the center boxes at the top of the coupon, Martinez enters its deposit of $1,873.22. The deposit is for FICA and withheld income taxes. At the top right, Martinez darkens the first quarter

oval to show the deposit is for taxes on first quarter wages. Then, Martinez darkens the Form 941 oval.

Deposit Frequency for Employment Tax Accumulations

Starting on January 1, 1993, new rules for depositing employment taxes go into effect. However, a change rule lets employers choose to

Employment Taxes: What Are They?

1. Income and FICA taxes withheld from employees
2. Employer's share of FICA taxes
3. Taxes withheld from pensions, annuities, and some deferred income
4. Taxes withheld under the backup withholding rules

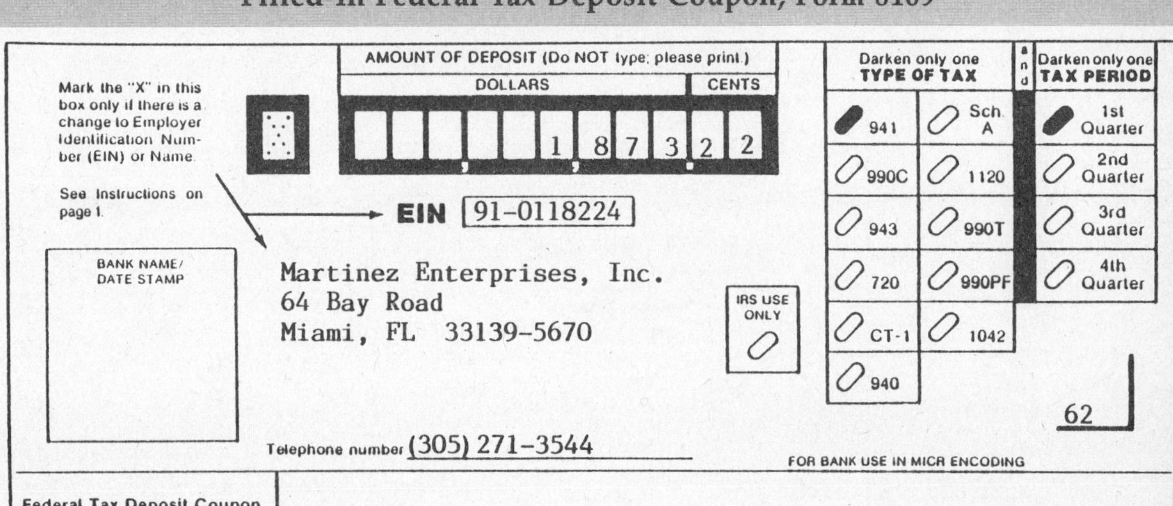

Illustration 14-4
Filled-In Federal Tax Deposit Coupon, Form 8109

continue with the old rules through December 31, 1993. After December 31, 1993, employers must deposit all employment tax accumulations under the new rules. Chart 14-1 provides an overview of these rules. Under them, employers are either monthly or semi-weekly depositors. Before the start of each calendar year, the IRS tells employers their status. To determine this status, the IRS usually uses the total employment tax accumulations for each employer's base (lookback) period.

What is the Base (Lookback) Period?

Each employer's base period is the 12 calendar months ending on the June 30 that precedes the next calendar year. For the calendar year 1993, the base period ends on June 30, 1992. The IRS adds the employment tax accumulations appearing on each Form 941, Employer's Quarterly Federal Tax Report, for the employer's base period. If an employer was not in existence during the base period, the IRS treats the employer as having zero tax accumulations.

Which Employers Are Semi-Weekly Depositors?

When total employment tax accumulations for an employer's base period are more than $50,000, the employer is a semiweekly depositor. A semi-weekly employer must deposit em-

ployment tax accumulations before the end of a Wednesday or Friday business day. Wednesday deposits include tax accumulations for Wednesday, Thursday, and Friday of the prior week. Friday deposits include tax accumulations for the prior Saturday, Sunday, Monday, and Tuesday. However, an overriding one-day rule (discussed below) applies when employment tax accumulations are $100,000 or more.

Semi-weekly depositors must make two deposits when the end of a calendar quarter is not a Wednesday or Friday. One deposit is for the last day(s) in the ended quarter. The other deposit is for the starting day(s) in the new quarter. Employers must prepare a separate Form 8109, Federal Tax Deposit Coupon, for each deposit. Both deposits are due on the next regular deposit date.

Which Employers Are Monthly Depositors?

When total employment tax accumulations for an employer's base period are $50,000 or less, the employer is a monthly employer. A monthly depositor must deposit employment taxes before the end of the 15th day of the next month. After a quarter ends, a monthly depositor makes one deposit for this quarter.

Under a special overriding condition, a monthly depositor becomes a semi-weekly depositor. This condition applies when an employer falls under the one-day rule.

Chart 14-1
Employment Tax Deposit Rules
An Overview

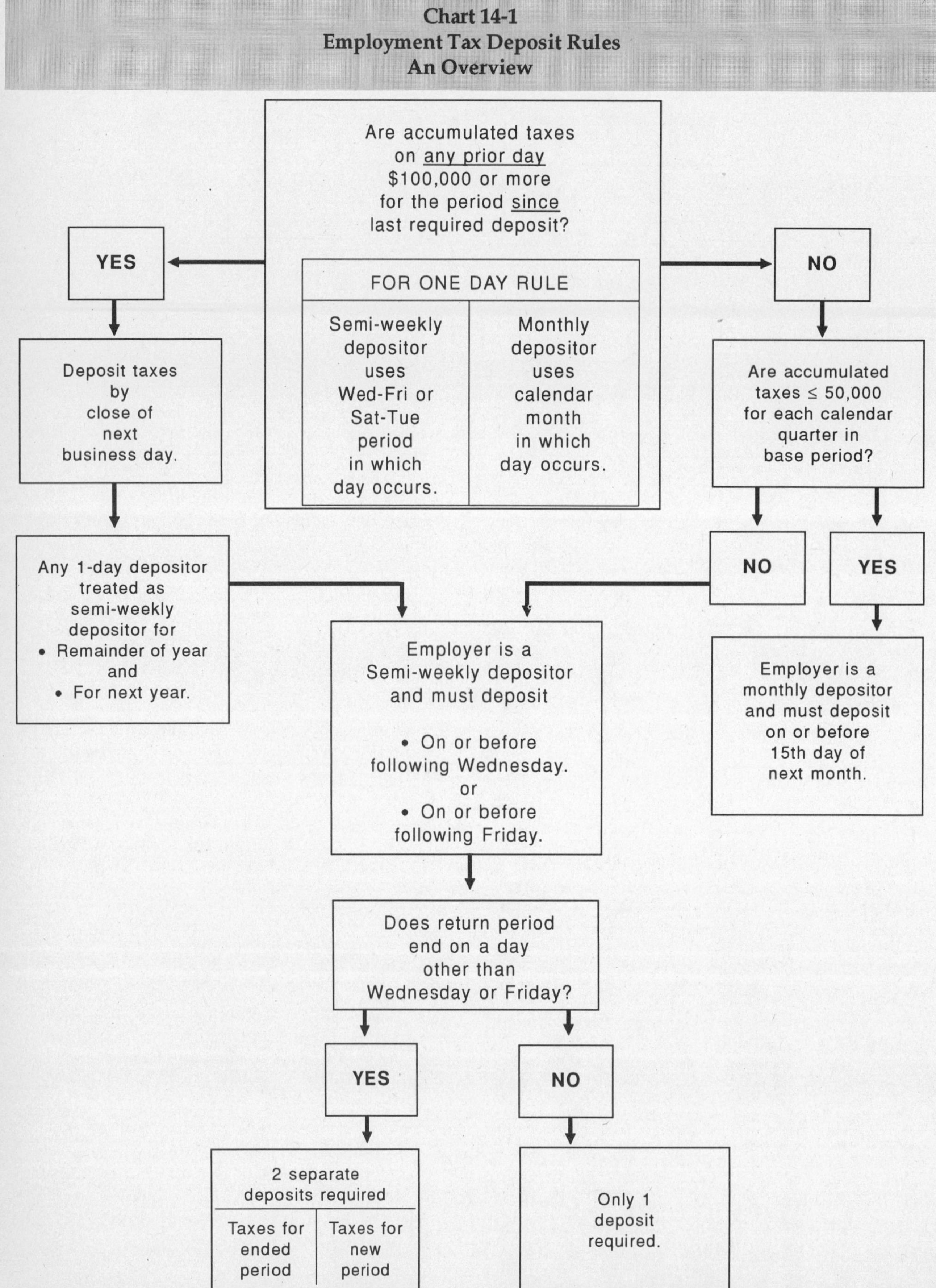

Which Employers Fall Under One-Day Rule?

Whenever an employer's employment tax accumulations are $100,000 or more, the one-day rule applies. Here, an employer must deposit employment taxes before the close of the depository's next business day. A monthly employer falling under the one-day rule is no longer a monthly employer. This employer is a semi-weekly employer for the remainder of the calendar year, and all of the next year.

Determining Accumulations

Semi-weekly depositors determine if they fall under the one-day rule by examining employment tax accumulations since the last deposit date. For them, the examination period is either Wednesday-Friday or Saturday-Tuesday. On the day their accumulations are $100,000 or more, they meet the test for the one-day rule. Monthly depositors determine if they fall under the one-day rule by examining their accumulations in the current month. They fall under the one-day rule on the day their accumulations are $100,000 or more.

When determining accumulations for the lookback period, the IRS only counts tax accumulations that appear on an employer's Forms 941. Sometimes, employers correct a prior quarter's tax accumulations on the Form 941 of a current quarter. Here, they attach a Form 941c, Statement to Correct Information. For the base period rule, these corrections are not part of the prior quarter's accumulations. They are part of the current quarter's accumulations.

Week-Ends and Holidays

What happens when a deposit date falls on a Saturday, Sunday, or other depository holiday? Here, a deposit will be timely if made on the next business banking day.

EXAMPLE 3 ─────────────────────

RST is a monthly depositor. During January 1993, RST has employment tax accumulations of $10,000. To be timely, RST must deposit these taxes before the end of the depository's February 15 business day. If February 15 is a depository holiday, RST must deposit the accumulations before the end of the next business depository day.

Semi-Weekly Depositors Get Three Extra Banking Days

Semi-weekly depositors have three banking days after the close of a payroll deposit period. This rule does not apply when a deposit falls under the one-day rule (a deposit of $100,000 or more).

EXAMPLE 4 ─────────────────────

On Wednesday of the current week, XYZ, a semi-weekly depositor, made an employment tax deposit. The deposit included the tax accumulations for its payrolls ending Wednesday, Thursday, and Friday of the prior week. Unless XYZ falls under the one-day rule, Friday of the current week is its next deposit date. This deposit would include XYZ's tax accumulations for payrolls ending on the prior Saturday, Sunday, Monday, and Tuesday. If Thursday of the current week is a depository holiday, XYZ can make a Monday deposit, and it will be timely.

Safe Harbor/De Minimis Rule

An employer satisfies its deposit requirement when a shortfall does not exceed the larger of $100 or 2% of a required deposit. **Shortfall** means the required deposit amount less the amount deposited before the end of a deposit date. To use this rule, employers must deposit unplanned shortfalls before the end of their make-up date. Unplanned shortfalls are unintentional.

The shortfall make-up date for monthly depositors is the Form 941 due date in which the shortfall occurs. Here, an employer must either send or deposit the shortfall before the end of the Form 941 due date. The shortfall make-up date for semi-weekly and one-day depositors is different. Here, an employer must deposit the accumluations by the first Wednesday or Friday after the 14th of the next month, whichever comes first. Also, the employer must make the deposit before the end of the depository's Wednesday or Friday business day.

A special deposit rule applies if the tax accumulations for a quarter are less than $500. To be timely, an employer must deposit them before the end of the quarterly Form 941 due date. If an employer sends a check for the accumulations with a timely filed Form 941, the IRS calls it a timely deposit.

Agricultural Employers

Special rules apply to agricultural employers. Such employers should get a copy of the deposit rules and study them carefully.

Employer's Quarterly Report

Usually, every employer who withholds income taxes, or who is liable for FICA taxes, must file a quarterly Form 941, Employer's Quarterly Federal Tax Return. Seasonal employers, who do not pay wages in a quarter, do not file a Form 941 for that quarter. On every Form 941 that seasonal employers file, they place an "X" in the seasonal employer's box (above line 1).

All depositors complete Form 941, page 1. Semi-weekly depositors, employers with $100,000 or more of employment tax accumulations, and employers who use the old deposit rules during 1993 also complete Schedule B (Form 941), Employer's Record of Federal Tax Liability. Employers completing Schedule B show their employment tax accumulations for each day of the reporting quarter.

Filing the Quarterly Report

Employers must file Form 941 before the end of the month after the close of a calendar quarter. For the quarter ending with December 31, employers must file a Form 941 before February 1 of the next year. When employers deposit all taxes before a due date ends, the law allows them an additional 10 days to file Form 941. Employers cannot use a Form 941 for more than one calendar quarter, or combine parts of quarters on one form.

Adjusting for Over Withholding or Under Withholding

Employers who find an error in withheld income tax for an earlier quarter of the same year, correct it on the current quarter's Form 941 (line 4). When the reporting error is for FICA taxes on an earlier return of the same year, employers also correct it on the current quarter's Form 941 (line 9). Employers also use this line (line 9) to correct a penalty or interest payment on taxes for earlier quarters. For every correction (adjustment), employers attach a statement which explains and identifies the earlier return with the error(s).

Employers who withhold *less than* the correct amount of tax from wages, deduct the under withholding from future wages. When employers withhold *more* than the correct amount, they can repay the excess to the proper employees in any quarter of the same year. Employers must keep the employee's dated and signed receipts for the repayment. These employers must also include excess withholdings that they do not repay during the withholding quarter on their quarterly Form 941.

Final Returns

When an employer goes out of business, or otherwise ceases to pay wages, a special procedure applies. Here, the employer inserts the word "Final" in the space at the top of the last Form 941. The employer also enters the final wage payment date. In addition, the employer attaches a statement which shows the location of employment records and the person responsible for them. Employers selling or transferring a business, enter the sale or transfer date and the new owner's name and address.

Employers who temporarily cease to pay wages continue to file Form 941 returns. On the front of a return for which no tax is due, employers show the last wage payment date. They also show the date they expect wage payments to start.

Filled-In Form 941, Employer's Quarterly Federal Tax Return

Illustration 14-5

This illustration shows the 1993 filled-in fourth quarter Form 941, Employer's Quarterly Federal Tax Return, for Martinez Enterprises, Inc. Martinez reports combined wage and other compensation payments of $22,396 for the quarter (line 2). During this quarter Martinez withheld $3,370 in income taxes from employees. It enters this amount (line 3).

Martinez enters total social security wages, $20,296 (line 6a, left hand column). Then Martinez multiplies this amount by 12.4% and enters the product, $2,516.71 (line 6a, right hand column). This product is the social security tax. Martinez enters Medicare wages, $20,296 (line 7, left hand column). Then, Martinez multiplies this amount by 2.9% and enters the product, $588.58 (line 7, right hand column). This product is the Medicare tax. Adding withheld income, social security, and Medicare taxes produces a total tax debt, $6,475.29 (line 14). Then, Martinez subtracts its advance EIC payments of $200 from $6,475.29 and enters the difference, $6,275.29 (line 16).

During the quarter, Martinez made cash deposits in a government depository for payroll taxes. It enters these deposits in the bottom portion of Form 941, page 1. Since the total debt for each month is less than $3,000, Martinez enters these totals on the "Total liability for month" line. The president, Edward L. Martinez, signs and dates the return. He also prints his name and title in the space between his signature and the date.

Upon receipt of Martinez' Form 941, the IRS transfers the data to magnetic tape. Then, the IRS uses its electronic data processing system to be sure Martinez deposited the amounts listed at the bottom of Form 941, page 1.

Sending Forms W-2 to the Government

Employers must send Copy A (Forms W-2) for all employees to the Social Security Administration before March 1, 1993. With these forms, they also include filled-in Form W-3, Transmittal of Income and Tax Statements 1992. Employers must type all data, omit dollar signs, and use decimal points and zeros to show cents (000.00).

Transmittal Form, Data Needs

The discussion below describes the data an employer needs to complete some of the Form W-3 boxes. However, the discussion does not cover every box since most box headings are descriptive. The instructions for Form W-3 describe the data needs of all boxes.

Control Number, box a. Like Form W-2, employers can assign and enter a *control* number of up to seven digits or leave the box blank.

Form Identifying Number, 33333. The government uses this number to identify all Forms W-3 with electronic scan equipment.

Kind of Payer, box b. Employers check one of the following six groups:

1. *941/941E.* Employers check this box when none of the other groups apply.
2. *Military.* Military employers check this box when sending Forms W-2 for members of the armed forces.
3. *943.* Employers check this box when filing a Form 943 for agricultural employees. When some employees are not agricultural workers, employers send a separate Form W-3 with each group of Forms W-2.
4. *CT-1.* Railroad employers check this box when sending Forms W-2 for employees under the Railroad Retirement Tax Act (RRTA).
5. *942.* Household employers check this box when sending Forms W-2 for household workers. When some employees are not household workers, employers use a separate Form W-3 to send these Forms W-2.
6. *Medicare Gov't. Emp.* For government and local agency employees who are only subject to the 1.45% HIP (Medicare) tax, employers check this box.

Total Number of Statements, box c. Employers enter the number of individual Forms W-2 they are sending with Form W-3. However, void and subtotal statements are not part of the count.

Establishment Number, Box d. Employers enter the number agreed upon with the Social Security Administration for an establishment reporting plan. For each establishment plan, employers file a separate Form W-3 with the Forms W-2. They must file a separate W-3 though each plan has the same EIN. For information about an optional reporting method, employers should contact a local Social Security Administration office.

Illustration 14-5
Filled-In Form 941

Form **941**
(Rev. January 1993)
Department of the Treasury
Internal Revenue Service

4141

Employer's Quarterly Federal Tax Return

► See Circular E for more information concerning employment tax returns.

Please type or print.

Exhibit A

OMB No. 1545-0029
Expires 5-31-93

Enter state code for state in which deposits made. ► ☐

Name (as distinguished from trade name)
Edward L. Martinez

Trade name, if any
Martinez Enterprises, Inc.

Address (number and street)
64 Bay Road, Miami, FL

Date quarter ended
12/31/93

Employer identification number
91–0118224

City, state, and ZIP code
33139–5670

T
FF
FD
FP
I
T

If address is different from prior return, check here ►

If you do not have to file returns in the future, check here . ► ☐   Date final wages paid ►

If you are a seasonal employer, see *Seasonal employers* on page 2 and check here . ► ☐

1	Number of employees (except household) employed in the pay period that includes March 12th . ►	
2	Total wages and tips subject to withholding, plus other compensation	**2** 22,396 00
3	Total income tax withheld from wages, tips, pensions, annuities, sick pay, gambling, etc.	**3** 3,370 00
4	Adjustment of withheld income tax for preceding quarters of calendar year (see instructions)	**4** –0–
5	Adjusted total of income tax withheld (line 3 as adjusted by line 4—see instructions)	**5** 3,370 00
6a	Taxable social security wages . . . $ 20,296 00 × 12.4% (.124) =	**6a** 2,516 71
b	Taxable social security tips . . . $ × 12.4% (.124) =	**6b**
7	Taxable Medicare wages and tips . $ 20,296 00 × 2.9% (.029) =	**7** 588 58
8	Total social security and Medicare taxes (add lines 6a, 6b, and 7)	**8** 3,105 29
9	Adjustment of social security and Medicare taxes (see instructions for required explanation) .	**9** –0–
10	Adjusted total of social security and Medicare taxes (line 8 as adjusted by line 9—see instructions)	**10** 3,105 29
11	Backup withholding (see instructions)	**11**
12	Adjustment of backup withholding tax for preceding quarters of calendar year	**12**
13	Adjusted total of backup withholding (line 11 as adjusted by line 12)	**13**
14	Total taxes (add lines 5, 10, and 13)	**14** 6,475 29
15	Advance earned income credit (EIC) payments made to employees, if any	**15** 200 00
16	Net taxes (subtract line 15 from line 14). This should equal line 20d below or line D on Schedule B (plus line D of Schedule A if you treated backup withholding as a separate liability)	**16** 6,275 29
17	Total deposits for quarter, including overpayment applied from a prior quarter, from your records	**17** 6,275 29
18	Balance due (subtract line 17 from line 16). This should be less than $500. Pay to the Internal Revenue Service	**18** –0–
19	Overpayment, if line 17 is more than line 16, enter excess here ► $ _______ and check if to be: ☐ Applied to next return OR ☐ Refunded.	

20   **Monthly Summary of Federal Tax Liability.** If you are a monthly depositor, summarize your monthly tax liability below. If you are a semiweekly depositor or have accumulated a liability of $100,000 or more on any day, attach Schedule B (Form 941) and check here (see instructions) . . . . ☐

	(a) First month	(b) Second month	(c) Third month	(d) Total for quarter
Liability for month	2,267.03	2,037.79	1,970.47	6,275.29

Sign Here

Under penalties of perjury, I declare that I have examined this return, including accompanying schedules and statements, and to the best of my knowledge and belief, it is true, correct, and complete.

Signature ► *Edward L. Martinez*   Print Your Name and Title ► President   Date ► 1/29/94

For Paperwork Reduction Act Notice, see page 2.   Cat. No. 17001Z   Form **941** (Rev. 1-93)

Employer's State I.D. Number, box i. Employers do not have to complete these boxes. However, a state in which an employer does business may assign an I.D. number. Employers that are reporting for two states, enter one state's I.D. number in each box.

Transmittal Form, Signature and Certification

The person completing Form W-3, Transmittal of Income and Tax Statements, signs and dates it at the bottom. This person also indicates his or her title in the space between the signature and date. By signing the form, the preparer certifies to the correctness and completeness of the accompanying Forms W-2 and the Form W-3. The certification is a statement under penalty of perjury that says the forms are true, correct, and complete to the signer's knowledge and belief.

Transmittal Form, Where to File

Employers file Form W-3 and the proper Forms W-2 with a regional Social Security Administration, Data Operations Center. The filing center is the one for the geographical area where the employer maintains a legal residence, principal place of business, office, or agency.

Filled-In Form W-3, Transmittal of Income and Tax Statements

Illustration 14-6

This illustration shows a filled-in 1993 Form W-3 with control number 01 for Martinez Enterprises, Inc. With this form, Martinez sends eight Forms W-2 to the Social Security Administration. The amounts entered in boxes 1, 2, 3, 4, 5, 6, and 9 are the totals of the separate amounts on the Forms W-2. Edward L. Martinez, the president, reviews and signs the form on January 29, 1994.

Estimated Taxes

Individuals usually pay income and self-employment taxes on a pay-as-you-go basis. Wage earners pay most taxes through the payroll withholding system. Others estimate taxes and make quarterly payments directly to the IRS. When a taxpayer's annual net self-employment earnings are less than $400, the self-employment tax does not apply. For 1992, quarterly tax payments are due on April 15, 1992, June 15, 1992, September 15, 1992, and January 15, 1993.

To help taxpayers prepare a tax estimate, the IRS provides Form 1040-ES, Estimated Tax for Individuals. The Form 1040-ES package includes four taxpayer identifying payment-vouchers, a tax worksheet, and a schedule of payments.

Who Must Pay an Estimated Tax?

Citizens and residents of the United States, residents of Puerto Rico, Virgin Islands, Guam, Northern Mariana Islands, and American Samoa, and nonresident aliens may need to make estimated tax payments. Usually, when their *estimated unpaid tax* is $500 or more for 1992, an estimated tax payment must be made when their tax withholdings and credits for 1992 are less than (1) 90% of the tax shown on their 1992 tax return or (2) 100% of the tax shown on their 1991 tax return (assuming the return covered all 12 months). Most taxpayers will not have to file an estimated tax return if they expect a tax refund *or* if their estimated unpaid tax for 1992 is less than $500. Four types of taxpayers usually make quarterly tax payments.

Taxpayers Usually Making Quarterly Tax Payments

1. Self-employed persons with business or professional income
2. Persons with large dividend, interest, rent, royalty, and property gain income
3. Wage earners whose income is not subject to withholding (some household servants)
4. Wage earners whose tax credits and withholdings fall short of their liability

Illustration 14-6
Filled-In Form W-3

a Control number	33333	For Official Use Only ▶ OMB No. 1545-0008		

b Kind of Payer ▶	941/941E [X] Military ☐ 943 ☐ CT-1 ☐ 942 ☐ Medicare govt. emp. ☐	1 Wages, tips, other compensation 89,560.00	2 Federal income tax withheld 13,518.40
		3 Social security wages 87,560.00	4 Social security tax withheld 5,428.72
c Total number of statements	d Establishment number	5 Medicare wages and tips 1,269.62	6 Medicare tax withheld 87,560.00
	e Employer's identification number 91–0118224	7 Social security tips	8 Allocated tips
f Employer's name Martinez Enterprises, Inc. 64 Bay Road Miami, FL 33139–5670		9 Advance EIC payments 600.00	10 Dependent care benefits
		11 Nonqualified plans	12 Deferred compensation
		13 Adjusted total social security wages and tips	
		14 Adjusted total Medicare wages and tips	
g Employer's address and ZIP code			
h Other EIN used this year		15 Income tax withheld by third-party payer	
i Employer's state I.D. No.			

Under penalties of perjury, I declare that I have examined this return and accompanying documents, and, to the best of my knowledge and belief, they are true, correct, and complete.

Signature ▶ *Edward L. Martinez*   Title ▶ President   Date ▶ 1/29/93
Telephone number 305–271–3544

Form **W-3** **Transmittal of Wage and Tax Statements 1993**   Department of the Treasury Internal Revenue Service

For 1992, some taxpayers cannot use the 100% rule. These taxpayers include those who meet all three of the following conditions:

1. They made estimated tax payments in any of the three prior years.
2. Their AGI for the current year is more than $75,000 (more than $37,500 for a married individual filing separately).
3. Their AGI for the current year is more than $40,000 above their AGI for last year (more than $20,000 for a married individual filing separately).

For the April 15, 1992 payment, taxpayers could still use the 100% rule. Also, taxpayers could use the 100% rule for any quarter in 1992 that their estimate of annualized AGI falls within the threshold. When determining if their AGI has increased over last year by more than $40,000 ($20,000 for a married-filing-separately taxpayer), two gains are omitted. Omitted gains come from involuntary conversions and sale of a principal residence. These gains are also omitted when calculating a taxpayer's estimated tax liability for the current year.

Nonresident aliens do not have to make estimated tax payments, unless they have income connected with the conduct of a U.S. trade or business. Then, the nonresident alien files Form 1040-ES (NR), U.S. Estimated Tax for Nonresident Alien Individuals.

Estimated tax payments do not remove the need for filing a final return. Any taxpayer who makes estimated tax payments must file a final Form 1040 return after the close of the tax year. On the final Form 1040 return, withheld taxes and estimated tax payments are shown as credits against the total tax. The filing taxpayer must pay any balance due in full.

When estimating gross income, a taxpayer must consider expected income from wages not subject to withholding. Such income could come from domestic service in a private home, local college group, or local chapter of a college fraternity or sorority. A partner must consider his or her share of any expected partnership net income.

The IRS provides a worksheet to help a taxpayer calculate the estimated tax. The difference between a taxpayer's total estimated tax and estimated credits and employer withholdings represents the *estimated unpaid tax*. Usually, this balance is the amount a taxpayer must pay now or in four equal installments.

Filled-In Estimated Tax Worksheet

Illustration 14-7

This illustration shows a filled-in 1992 Estimated Tax Worksheet for Audrey C. McGrath. Ms. McGrath is single, age 35, with good vision, and no dependents. She estimates her 1992 AGI and enters it on the worksheet (line 1). Her calculations show her estimated AGI to be $22,872.83.

Salary ($1,300 x 12)	$15,600.00
Net rentals from apartment building	5,600.00
Net income from business	1,800.00
Total income	$23,000.00
Less: 50% of self-employment tax	127.17
AGI	$22,872.83

Ms. McGrath does not expect to itemize deductions in 1992. Thus, she enters $3,600 for her standard deduction (line 2). Since she is single with no dependents, she enters $2,300 (line 4). She subtracts the standard deduction (line 2) and personal exemption (line 4) from her AGI and enters the difference (line 5). This amount is her taxable income estimate of $16,972.83 ($22,872.83 − $3,600 − $2,300). Then, she determines her tax from the 1992 Tax Rate Schedule (below worksheet) and enters this amount (line 6). It is $2,545.93 ($16,972.83 x 15%). Since she does not

expect additional taxes (line 7) or credits (line 9) in 1992, she places a zero on these lines and enters $2,545.93 (lines 8 and 10).

To arrive at the worksheet entry for her self-employment tax (line 11, end blank), Ms. McGrath calculates her remaining earnings subject to FICA taxes ($39,900 for social security tax, or $55,500 − $15,600) and ($114,600 for Medicare, or $130,200 − $15,600). Next, she determines and compares her net self-employment earnings of $1,662.30 (line 11, center blank) with these amounts. To get the $1,662.30 estimate, Ms. McGrath multiplies her gross self-employment earnings of $1,800 by 0.9235 [1.00 − (50% x {0.124 social security rate + 0.029 Medicare rate})]. The 0.9235 appears in Publication 505 mentioned in the worksheet (line 11). Since the $1,662.30 is less than her remaining FICA amounts ($39,900 and $114,600), all FICA taxes apply. To get the $254.33 self-employment tax (line 11, end blank), she multiplies her net self-employment earning ($1,662.30) by the 0.153 FICA self-employment rate (0.124 + 0.029).

Ms. McGrath enters the $1,662.30 and $254.33 in the proper worksheet blanks (line 11). She adds the $254.33 to her income tax estimate (line 10) and enters the total of $2,800.26 (lines 13a and 13c). This amount is her *total 1992 estimated tax*. When she prepares her income tax return, she deducts one-half of her self-employment tax or $127.17, Form 1040 (line 25) as an income adjustment ($127.17 = $254.33 x 50%).

To determine the minimum amount Ms. McGrath must pay to avoid an underpayment penalty, she multiples her total 1992 estimated tax by 90% and enters the product (line 14a). This product is $2,520.23 ($2,800.26 x 90%). She enters 100% of her 1991 tax debt of $2,831.00 (line 14b). The smaller of these figures ($2,520.23 or $2,831.00) is the total amount she must pay to avoid a penalty. She can pay a larger amount if she chooses.

Ms. McGrath chooses to pay $2,850 and enters this amount (line 14c). She estimates her employer's 1992 income tax withholding at $1,632 and enters it (line 15). Then, she subtracts $1,632 from the $2,850 and enters the difference of $1,218 (line 16). The $1,218 is her remaining estimated tax liability. Ms. McGrath chooses to pay the remaining liability in 4 equal installments of $304.50 ($1,218/4). If she has an overpayment carryover from 1991 that she wants to apply against her first quarter's payment, she reduces the $304.50 by this amount and enters the difference (line 17). Otherwise, she enters $304.50 (line 17).

Joint Estimated Tax Payments

A husband and wife can file a joint estimated tax return when both are citizens or residents of the United States. Making a joint or separate estimate does not commit the couple to the same final Form 1040. Thus, the couple can make a joint estimate and file separate tax returns. When a husband and wife make a joint estimate and file separate returns, they can divide the estimated tax payments as they choose. One of them could use all the payments as a credit. A joint estimate is not available for a couple separated under a decree of divorce or separate maintenance. Also, the joint estimate is not available when a husband and wife have different tax years or one is a nonresident alien.

Payment of Estimated Tax

Taxpayers who make estimated tax payments mail their payment-vouchers to the IRS Service Center for their district. The annual preprinted Form 1040-ES package contains four unnumbered and dated payment-vouchers (see Illustration 14-8) and mailing envelopes. A taxpayer who files an estimated tax return for the first time will receive a preprinted Form 1040-ES package. This package will arrive about two weeks before the second estimated payment is due.

For 1992, a taxpayer should file the first of the four payment-vouchers before April 16 (due date for payment ends with April 15). Later, the taxpayer should file the payment-vouchers due on June 15 and September 15 of 1992, and January 15, 1993. However, if the taxpayer meets the requirement for the first payment after March 31, 1992, the payment-vouchers are due as follows:

If the requirement is met after:	Payment due date is:
March 31 and before June 1	June 15, 1992
May 31 and before Sept. 1	Sept. 15, 1992
August 31	Jan. 15, 1993

When a taxpayer meets the requirement to file the first payment voucher after August 31, 1992, he or she can avoid the need for making an estimated payment. This taxpayer files his or her final tax return before February 1, 1993 and pays any tax due to the government.

Prior-Year Overpayments. If a final tax return shows an overpayment, the taxpayer can choose to get a refund. The taxpayer can also choose to apply the overpayment to any estimated tax due in the next year. This taxpayer can use the overpayment to reduce each installment in order until used up, *or* equally reduce each installment.

EXAMPLE 5

Below are the tax payments and 1992 estimated tax data for Betty Nystrum:

Estimated tax for the year	$1,500
Estimated income tax withholding during the year	900
Estimated unpaid tax	$ 600
Amount of quarterly installment	$ 150
Less amount of overpayment from previous year	200
Amount of payment with voucher	None

Betty's quarterly installment is $150 ($600 ÷ 4). She does not have to pay the first installment because the amount is less than her last year's overpayment of $200. When Betty's second installment is due, she pays $100 (second quarterly installment of $150 less the remaining $50 from her last year's overpayment). Betty's estimated tax payment due dates and installment payment amounts are:

April 15	$ 0
June 15	100
September 15	150
January 15, 1993	150

Betty could make an election to apply the overpayment evenly against each installment rather than in full against the first and succeeding installments. If Betty makes this election, she divides last year's overpayment by the number of installments ($200 ÷ 4) and applies the result to each installment. Here, she subtracts $50 from each installment and pays $100 each quarter.

Illustration 14-7
Filled-In Estimated Tax Worksheet—Audrey C. McGrath

1992 Estimated Tax Worksheet (keep for your records)

#	Description	Amount
1	Enter amount of adjusted gross income you expect in 1992	22,872 83
2	• If you plan to itemize deductions, enter the estimated total of your itemized deductions. **Caution:** If line 1 above is over $105,250 ($52,625 if married filing separately), your deduction may be reduced. See Pub. 505 for details. • If you do not plan to itemize deductions, see **Standard Deduction for 1992** on page 2, and enter your standard deduction here.	3,600 00
3	Subtract line 2 from line 1	19,272 83
4	Exemptions. Multiply $2,300 by the number of personal exemptions. If you can be claimed as a dependent on another person's 1992 return, your personal exemption is not allowed. **Caution:** If line 1 above is over $157,900 ($131,550 if head of household; $105,250 if single; $78,950 if married filing separately), get Pub. 505 to figure the amount to enter	2,300 00
5	Subtract line 4 from line 3	16,972 83
6	Tax. Figure your tax on the amount on line 5 by using the 1992 Tax Rate Schedules below. DO NOT use the Tax Table or the Tax Rate Schedules in the 1991 Form 1040 or Form 1040A instructions. **Caution:** If you have a net capital gain and line 5 is over $86,500 ($74,150 if head of household; $51,900 if single; $43,250 if married filing separately), get Pub. 505 to figure the tax	2,545 93
7	Additional taxes (see line 7 instructions)	–0–
8	Add lines 6 and 7	2,545 93
9	Credits (see line 9 instructions). Do not include any income tax withholding on this line	–0–
10	Subtract line 9 from line 8. Enter the result, but not less than zero	2,545 93
11	Self-employment tax. Estimate of 1992 net earnings from self-employment $ 1,662.30 if $55,500 or **less,** multiply the amount by .153; if **more than $55,500,** see line 11 instructions for the amount to enter. **Caution:** you also have wages subject to social security or Medicare tax, get Pub. 505 to figure the amount to enter	254 33
12	Other taxes (see line 12 instructions)	–0–
13a	Add lines 10 through 12	2,800 26
b	Earned income credit and credit from **Form 4136**	–0–
c	Subtract line 13b from line 13a. Enter the result, but not less than zero. THIS IS YOUR TOTAL 1992 ESTIMATED TAX ▶	2,800 26
14a	Multiply line 13c by 90% (66⅔% for farmers and fishermen) ... 14a 2,520 23	
b	Enter 100% of the tax shown on your 1991 tax return ... 14b 2,831 00 **Caution:** If 14b is **smaller** than 14a and line 1 above is over $75,000 ($37,500 if married filing separately), stop here and see **Limit on Use of Prior Year's Tax** on page 1 before continuing.	
c	Enter the **smaller** of line 14a or 14b. THIS IS YOUR REQUIRED ANNUAL PAYMENT ▶ **Caution:** Generally, if you do not prepay at least the amount on line 14c, you may owe a penalty for not paying enough estimated tax. To avoid a penalty, make sure your estimate on line 13c is as accurate as possible. If you prefer, you may pay 100% of your 1992 estimated tax (line 13c). For more details, get Pub. 505.	2,850 00
15	Income tax withheld and estimated to be withheld during 1992 (including income tax withholding on pensions, annuities, certain deferred income, etc.)	1,632 00
16	Subtract line 15 from line 14c. (**Note:** If line 13c minus line 15 is less than $500, you do not have to make estimated tax payments.) If you are applying an overpayment from 1991 to 1992 estimated tax, see **How To Complete and Use the Payment-Voucher** on page 4	1,218 00
17	If the first payment you are required to make is due April 15, 1992, enter ½ of line 16 (minus any 1991 overpayment that you are applying to this installment) here and on your payment-voucher(s)	304 50

1992 Tax Rate Schedules

Caution: Do not use these Tax Rate Schedules to figure your 1991 taxes. Use only to figure your 1992 estimated taxes.

Single—Schedule X

If line 5 is: Over—	But not over—	The tax is:	of the amount over—
$0	$21,450	...........15%	$0
21,450	51,900	$3,217.50 + 28%	21,450
51,900	....	11,743.50 + 31%	51,900

Head of household—Schedule Z

If line 5 is: Over—	But not over—	The tax is:	of the amount over—
$0	$28,750	.... 15%	$0
28,750	74,150	$4,312.50 + 28%	28,750
74,150	....	17,024.50 + 31%	74,150

Married filing jointly or Qualifying widow(er)—Schedule Y-1

If line 5 is: Over—	But not over—	The tax is:	of the amount over—
$0	$35,800	...........15%	$0
35,800	86,500	$5,370.00 + 28%	35,800
86,500	....	19,566.00 + 31%	86,500

Married filing separately—Schedule Y-2

If line 5 is: Over—	But not over—	The tax is:	of the amount over—
$0	$17,900	.... 15%	$0
17,900	43,250	$2,685.00 + 28%	17,900
43,250	....	9,783.00 + 31%	43,250

Filled-In Payment-Voucher

Illustration 14-8

This illustration shows the filled-in April 15, 1992 payment-voucher for the data in Illustration 14-7. Audrey C. McGrath's worksheet (line 17) shows her quarterly payments to be $304.50. However, assume her 1991 income tax return shows a tax overpayment of $25. If Audrey does not want a refund, she replaces the $304.50 (line 17) with $279.50 ($304.50 – $25.00). She also enters the $279.50 on her payment voucher (line 1). After entering her name, address, and SSN on the voucher, she attaches her check for $279.50. Then, she mails the payment-voucher to her district's IRS Service Center. As each remaining installment comes due, Audrey completes the proper voucher and mails it with her check to the IRS. For the remaining three installments, the IRS will not tell her that a payment is due.

Underpayment of Estimated Tax

Payments for estimated tax installments must be made on time to avoid a *mandatory additional underpayment charge.* A taxpayer will incur this penalty when withholdings, credits, and estimated tax payments are less than 90% (66⅔% for farmers and fishermen) of the amount due for any installment period. Under some conditions, a taxpayer who underpays his or her 1992 income tax debt by more than 10% will not owe any penalty. Here, the taxpayer must be a U.S. resident for all of 1991, have no 1991 tax debt, and have filed a 12-month 1991 tax return. The basis of any underpayment penalty is the underpayment amount for each quarter. However, the IRS treats employer withholdings as taking place evenly throughout the year.

The IRS may waive the underpayment penalty if the taxpayer's underpayment is due to one of the following situations:

1. A casualty, disaster, or other unusual circumstance such as a serious illness or death, or the imposition of the penalty is inequitable and against good conscience.
2. The taxpayer retires at 62 or later, or becomes disabled in the tax year when he or she must make estimated tax payments.

Illustration 14-8
Filled-In Form 1040-ES, Payment Voucher (Due April 15, 1992)

361   7-92   **2109-7**

Form 1040-ES (OCR) | **1992 Payment-Voucher 1**
Department of the Treasury
Internal Revenue Service

OMB No. 1545-0087

File only if you are **making a payment** of estimated tax. Cross out the **name** and **social security number** of a deceased or divorced spouse. If your address has changed, please complete **Form 8822**, Change of Address (see instructions).

Calendar year—
Due April 15, 1992

Audrey C. McGrath   270–09–3509
3312 Miami Road
Milford, OH   45150–1204

Amount of payment $ 279.50

If name or social security number is incorrect, please change.

For Paperwork Reduction Act Notice, see instructions.

Determining the Penalty Amount. A taxpayer determines his or her penalty amount with Form 2210, Underpayment of Estimated Tax by Individuals. Farmers and fishermen use Form 2210F. Taxpayers enter their penalty on Form 1040 (line 67). Then, they add it to any other amount due the government or subtract it from any refund. Taxpayers may choose not to file Form 2210 and have the IRS calculate the penalty and bill them. However, a professional Form 1040 preparer who fails to complete and attach a needed Form 2210 can receive a penalty.

The IRS adjusts the underpayment penalty rate quarterly. It is the short-term federal interest rate plus three percentage points. Although the penalty looks like an interest expense deduction, it is not deductible.

Employees Should Receive a Form W-2, Wage and Tax Statement, When

1. Income or FICA taxes were withheld from wages.
2. Income taxes would have been withheld from wages if employee had not claimed more than one withholding allowance exemption from withholding.
3. Wages for services were received.
4. Advance EIC was received.
5. Supplemental unemployment compensation or third-party sick pay was received.
6. $600 or more was received from employer.
7. Under employer's Section 404 deferral compensation plan.

C H A P T E R 1 4

Questions and Problems

1. a. How does an employee claim withholding allowances?

b. If an employee does not file a Form W-4, Employee's Withholding Allowance Certificate, with his or her employer, what withholding action must the employer take?

c. If a taxpayer holds more than one job, can he or she claim withholding allowances with more than one employer?

2. a. What tax withholding action, if any, must a taxpayer take for each of the following situations:

Withholding allowances decrease?

Withholding allowances increase?

A qualifying dependent dies on July 23?

The calendar year ends?

b. For what period does an exemption from withholding apply when an employee claims the exemption on a Form W-4 filed on June 10, 1992?

c. Does an exemption from withholding that an employee claims on Form W-4 apply to both FICA taxes and federal income taxes?

3. a. Under what circumstances should an employee expect to receive copies of Form W-2, Wage and Tax Statement?

b. By what date must an employer file Copy A of an employee's Form W-2 with the Social Security Administration?

c. By what date must an employer give an employee Copies B and C of his or her Form W-2?

4. An employer in preparing Copy A of Form W-2, Wage and Tax Statement, frequently checks one of the squares in box 15. Explain the special meaning of the check when it applies to:

a. Statutory Employee:

b. Subtotal:

c. Void:

5. Assume you own the Speedy Department Store. Speedy's address is 2706 Bluff Drive, Boston, Massachusetts 02101-3214. Its Federal EIN is 04-0450523. As the owner, you are to prepare the original 1993 Form W-2, Wage and Tax Statement, for Susan R. Jenkins, a married employee with no dependents. Susan's husband does not work outside their home. Use the blank Form W-2 provided. The data below was taken from Speedy's payroll records:

Susan R. Jenkins, 214 Northrup Street, Boston, Massachusetts 02112-1415, SSN
331-06-4821, Buyer.

Total wages paid (before payroll deductions)	$45,000.00
Social security tax withheld	Calculate
Medicare tax withheld	Calculate
Federal income tax withheld	6,552.00
State income tax withheld	1,125.75
Special bonus pay (not included with total wages)	165.00
Form W-2 control number	0623
Employer's state I.D. number	25703

a Control number 22222	Void ☐	For Official Use Only ►		
b Employer's identification number		1 Wages, tips, other compensation	2 Federal income tax withheld	
c Employer's name, address, and ZIP code		3 Social security wages	4 Social security tax withheld	
		5 Medicare wages and tips	6 Medicare tax withheld	
		7 Social security tips	8 Allocated tips	
d Employee's social security number		9 Advance EIC payment	10 Dependent care benefits	
e Employee's name (first, middle initial, last)		11 Nonqualified plans	12 Benefits included in Box 1	
		13 See Instrs. for Box 13	14 Other	

15 Statutory employee ☐   Deceased ☐   Pension plan ☐   Legal rep. ☐   942 emp. ☐   Subtotal ☐   Deferred compensation ☐

f Employee's address and ZIP code					
16 State Employer's state I.D. No.	17 State wages, tips, etc.	18 State income tax	19 Locality name	20 Local wages, tips, etc.	21 Local income tax

Cat. No. 10134D   Department of the Treasury—Internal Revenue Service

Form **W-2** Wage and Tax Statement **1993**

For Paperwork Reduction Act Notice, see separate instructions.

Copy A For Social Security Administration   OMB No. 1545-0008

6. **a.** Must a taxpayer receiving annuity, pension, or deferred income payments subject to income taxes have federal income taxes withheld from the payments? Explain.

    b. If the payee of an annuity, pension, or deferred income does not direct that there be no withholding, how must payers withhold from periodic payments?

7. **a.** Should employers withhold FUTA taxes from employees? Explain.

b. When must an employer deposit FUTA taxes?

c. What is the FUTA tax rate? What is the effective FUTA tax rate for most taxpayers that are subject to it?

8. a. For 1992, Rosemary R. James, a self-employed attorney, may have to pay a self-employment tax on her net law practice earnings through the income tax payment system. If her net self-employment earnings from the law practice in 1992 were $350, how much self-employment tax does Rosemary have to pay?

b. If net earnings from self-employment in 1992 were $4,000, how much self-employment tax would be paid?

9. Based on the information given, how many withholding allowances can be claimed in 1992 by each of the following taxpayers? Identify the type of each withholding allowance claimed.

Taxpayer A: A single taxpayer, age 12, is claimed as a dependent on the parents' return. The taxpayer will earn $650 in wages during the year and will receive $50 in dividend income.

Taxpayer B: A single taxpayer, age 20, will have earned income of $18,500 and interest income of $150. Adjustments to income will total $150 and the standard deduction will be used.

Taxpayer C: A married taxpayer files jointly. The taxpayer has 4 dependents. The taxpayer has 2 jobs and the spouse has 1 job. The taxpayer's total wages will be $46,200, and the spouse's will be $3,500. Dividend income of $400 will be received. There will be no adjustments to income. Child and dependent care expenses will total $1,200, and itemized deductions are expected to be $8,000.

Taxpayer D: A single taxpayer, who has 1 dependent and is eligible to use the HOH filing status, will earn $24,600 from 1 job. Interest income of $900 is expected, and $600 will be claimed as adjustments to income. Child and dependent care expenses will total $3,200, and itemized deductions of $4,600 are expected.

Taxpayer	Number of Withholding Allowances	Type of Withholding Allowances
A	_____________	_____________
B	_____________	_____________
C	_____________	_____________
D	_____________	_____________

10. Ethel P. and Irving J. Mead, SSNs 448-47-4747 and 739-33-8990, respectively, are married and file jointly. They cannot be claimed as dependents on any other return. They reside at 1001 West Wind Plaza, Fox Lake, Wisconsin 53933-4611. Both are 42 years of age, and they have one dependent child, a daughter named Mary Jean, who is 14 years of age and has no income. Her SSN is 668-32-1184.

On December 15, 1992, the Meads became aware that their income tax for 1992 was overpaid because two withholding allowances had been claimed. They decided to file a new Form W-4, Employee's Withholding Allowance Certificate, to change the number of withholding allowances claimed for 1993 to enable more appropriate withholding. The estimates of the Meads' income and deductions for 1993 were as follows:

Wages:	Ethel:	Henry Maintenance Company	$38,000
		Arnold Corporation	12,000
		Total gross income—Ethel	$50,000
	Irving:	Readers' Specialty Store	8,500
		Total gross income	$58,500
	Dividend income—Ethel		316
	Interest income—Irving		1,034
	Total		$59,850

A preliminary estimate showed that itemized deductions for 1993 would total $12,500. In addition, "adjustments to income" and "other payments" were anticipated as follows:

Reimbursed employee business expenses (reimbursements are paid under a qualified plan)	$1,850
Fees for Mary Jean's (daughter) school textbooks	216
Television set for elderly parent	470
Total	$2,536

Complete the Form W-4 that would be filed with Ethel P. Mead's employer, Henry Maintenance Company, assuming that all withholding allowances would be claimed on one Form W-4. Ethel signs and dates the form on January 22, 1993. Also prepare the necessary Form W-4 worksheets to determine the number of withholding allowances. Use the form and worksheet provided on the following pages.

11. Indicate whether or not the following individuals are required to pay an estimated tax for individuals. (Check either the "Yes" or the "No" column.)

	Yes	No
a. Single, income derived solely from wages subject to withholding expected to amount to $6,000. Estimated unpaid tax expected to be $250	______	______
b. Married, income of taxpayer derived solely from wages subject to withholding expected to amount to $10,500. Spouse does not receive wages. Estimated unpaid tax expected to be $400	______	______
c. Qualifying widower, income derived from wages subject to withholding expected to amount to $12,500; income from other sources not subject to withholding expected to amount to $3,000. Estimated unpaid tax expected to be $600	______	______
d. Married, husband's income derived solely from wages subject to withholding expected to amount to $11,000; spouse expects to receive dividend income amounting to $2,000. Estimated unpaid tax expected to be $550	______	______

349 12-91   **1037**

19**92** Form W-4

Department of the Treasury
Internal Revenue Service

Purpose. Complete Form W-4 so that your employer can withhold the correct amount of Federal income tax from your pay.

Exemption From Withholding. Read line 7 of the certificate below to see if you can claim exempt status. If exempt, complete line 7; but do not complete lines 5 and 6. No Federal income tax will be withheld from your pay. Your exemption is good for one year only. It expires February 15, 1993.

Basic Instructions. Employees who are not exempt should complete the Personal Allowances Worksheet. Additional worksheets are provided on page 2 for employees to adjust their withholding allowances based on itemized deductions, adjustments to income, or two-earner/two-job situations. Complete all worksheets that apply to your situation. The worksheets will help you figure

the number of withholding allowances you are entitled to claim. However, you may claim fewer allowances than this.

Head of Household. Generally, you may claim head of household filing status on your tax return only if you are unmarried and pay more than 50% of the costs of keeping up a home for yourself and your dependent(s) or other qualifying individuals.

Nonwage Income. If you have a large amount of nonwage income, such as interest or dividends, you should consider making estimated tax payments using Form 1040-ES. Otherwise, you may find that you owe additional tax at the end of the year.

Two-Earner/Two-Jobs. If you have a working spouse or more than one job, figure the total number of allowances you are entitled to claim on all jobs using worksheets from only one Form

W-4. This total should be divided among all jobs. Your withholding will usually be most accurate when all allowances are claimed on the W-4 filed for the highest paying job and zero allowances are claimed for the others.

Advance Earned Income Credit. If you are eligible for this credit, you can receive it added to your paycheck throughout the year. For details, get Form W-5 from your employer.

Check Your Withholding. After your W-4 takes effect, you can use **Pub. 919,** Is My Withholding Correct for 1992?, to see how the dollar amount you are having withheld compares to your estimated total annual tax. Call 1-800-829-3676 to order this publication. Check your local telephone directory for the IRS assistance number if you need further help.

Personal Allowances Worksheet For 1992, the value of your personal exemption(s) is reduced if your income is over $105,250 ($157,900 if married filing jointly, $131,550 if head of household, or $78,950 if married filing separately). Get Pub. 919 for details.

A Enter "1" for **yourself** if no one else can claim you as a dependent . . . . **A** _____

B Enter "1" if:
 • You are single and have only one job; or
 • You are married, have only one job, and your spouse does not work; or
 • Your wages from a second job or your spouse's wages (or the total of both) are $1,000 or less. **B** _____

C Enter "1" for your **spouse.** But, you may choose to enter -0- if you are married and have either a working spouse or more than one job (this may help you avoid having too little tax withheld) . . . . **C** _____

D Enter number of **dependents** (other than your spouse or yourself) whom you will claim on your tax return . . . . . **D** _____

E Enter "1" if you will file as **head of household** on your tax return (see conditions under "Head of Household," above) . **E** _____

F Enter "1" if you have at least $1,500 of **child or dependent care expenses** for which you plan to claim a credit . . . . **F** _____

G Add lines A through F and enter total here. Note: This amount may be different from the number of exemptions you claim on your return ▶ **G** _____

For accuracy, do all worksheets that apply.
 • If you plan to **itemize or claim adjustments to income** and want to reduce your withholding, see the Deductions and Adjustments Worksheet on page 2.
 • If you are **single** and have **more than one job** and your combined earnings from all jobs exceed $29,000 OR if you are **married** and have a **working spouse or more than one job,** and the combined earnings from all jobs exceed $50,000, see the Two-Earner/Two-Job Worksheet on page 2 if you want to avoid having too little tax withheld.
 • If **neither** of the above situations applies, **stop here** and enter the number from line G on line 5 of Form W-4 below.

- - - - - - - - **Cut here and give the certificate to your employer. Keep the top portion for your records.** - - - - - - - -

Form W-4
Department of the Treasury
Internal Revenue Service

Employee's Withholding Allowance Certificate

OMB No. 1545-0010

1992

▶ **For Privacy Act and Paperwork Reduction Act Notice, see reverse.**

1 Type or print your first name and middle initial   Last name   **2** Your social security number

Home address (number and street or rural route)

3 ☐ Single ☐ Married ☐ Married, but withhold at higher Single rate.
Note: If married, but legally separated, or spouse is a nonresident alien, check the Single box.

City or town, state, and ZIP code

4 If your last name differs from that on your social security card, check here and call 1-800-772-1213 for more information . ▶ ☐

5 Total number of allowances you are claiming (from line G above or from the Worksheets on back if they apply) **5** _____

6 Additional amount, if any, you want deducted from each paycheck . . . . **6** $ _____

7 I claim exemption from withholding and I certify that I meet **ALL** of the following conditions for exemption:
 • Last year I had a right to a refund of **ALL** Federal income tax withheld because I had **NO** tax liability; **AND**
 • This year I expect a refund of **ALL** Federal income tax withheld because I expect to have **NO** tax liability; **AND**
 • This year if my income exceeds $600 and includes nonwage income, another person cannot claim me as a dependent.

If you meet all of the above conditions, enter the year effective and "EXEMPT" here . . . ▶ **7** | 19 ____

8 Are you a full-time student? (Note: Full-time students are not automatically exempt.) . . . . **8** ☐ Yes ☐ No

Under penalties of perjury, I certify that I am entitled to the number of withholding allowances claimed on this certificate or entitled to claim exempt status.

Employee's signature ▶ _______________   Date ▶ _______________ , 19 ____

9 Employer's name and address (Employer: Complete 9 and 11 only if sending to the IRS) | **10** Office code (optional) | **11** Employer identification number

Cat. No. 10220Q

1037-2

349 12-91

Form W-4 (1992) Page **2**

Deductions and Adjustments Worksheet

Note: *Use this worksheet only if you plan to itemize deductions or claim adjustments to income on your 1992 tax return.*

1   Enter an estimate of your 1992 itemized deductions. These include: qualifying home mortgage interest, charitable contributions, state and local taxes (but not sales taxes), medical expenses in excess of 7.5% of your income, and miscellaneous deductions. (For 1992, you may have to reduce your itemized deductions if your income is over $105,250 ($52,625 if married filing separately). Get Pub. 919 for details.)   **1** $ _______

2   Enter:
{
$6,000 if married filing jointly or qualifying widow(er)
$5,250 if head of household
$3,600 if single
$3,000 if married filing separately
}   **2** $ _______

3   **Subtract** line 2 from line 1. If line 2 is greater than line 1, enter -0-   **3** $ _______

4   Enter an estimate of your 1992 adjustments to income. These include alimony paid and deductible IRA contributions   **4** $ _______

5   **Add** lines 3 and 4 and enter the total   **5** $ _______

6   Enter an estimate of your 1992 nonwage income (such as dividends or interest income)   **6** $ _______

7   **Subtract** line 6 from line 5. Enter the result, but not less than -0-   **7** $ _______

8   **Divide** the amount on line 7 by $2,500 and enter the result here. Drop any fraction   **8**   _______

9   Enter the number from Personal Allowances Worksheet, line G, on page 1   **9**   _______

10   **Add** lines 8 and 9 and enter the total here. If you plan to use the Two-Earner/Two-Job Worksheet, also enter the total on line 1, below. Otherwise, **stop here** and enter this total on Form W-4, line 5, on page 1   **10**   _______

Two-Earner/Two-Job Worksheet

Note: *Use this worksheet only if the instructions for line G on page 1 direct you here.*

1   Enter the number from line G on page 1 (or from line 10 above if you used the Deductions and Adjustments Worksheet)   **1**   _______

2   Find the number in **Table 1** below that applies to the **LOWEST** paying job and enter it here   **2**   _______

3   If line 1 is **GREATER THAN OR EQUAL TO** line 2, subtract line 2 from line 1. Enter the result here (if zero, enter -0-) and on Form W-4, line 5, on page 1. **DO NOT** use the rest of this worksheet   **3**   _______

Note: *If line 1 is **LESS THAN** line 2, enter -0- on Form W-4, line 5, on page 1. Complete lines 4–9 to calculate the additional dollar withholding necessary to avoid a year-end tax bill.*

4   Enter the number from line 2 of this worksheet   **4**   _______

5   Enter the number from line 1 of this worksheet   **5**   _______

6   **Subtract** line 5 from line 4   **6**   _______

7   Find the amount in **Table 2** below that applies to the **HIGHEST** paying job and enter it here   **7** $ _______

8   **Multiply** line 7 by line 6 and enter the result here. This is the additional annual withholding amount needed   **8** $ _______

9   Divide line 8 by the number of pay periods remaining in 1992. (For example, divide by 26 if you are paid every other week and you complete this form in December of 1991.) Enter the result here and on Form W-4, line 6, page 1. This is the additional amount to be withheld from each paycheck   **9** $ _______

Table 1: Two-Earner/Two-Job Worksheet

Married Filing Jointly		All Others	
If wages from **LOWEST** paying job are—	Enter on line 2 above	If wages from **LOWEST** paying job are—	Enter on line 2 above
0 - $4,000	0	0 - $6,000	0
4,001 - 8,000	1	6,001 - 10,000	1
8,001 - 13,000	2	10,001 - 14,000	2
13,001 - 18,000	3	14,001 - 18,000	3
18,001 - 22,000	4	18,001 - 22,000	4
22,001 - 26,000	5	22,001 - 45,000	5
26,001 - 30,000	6	45,001 and over	6
30,001 - 35,000	7		
35,001 - 40,000	8		
40,001 - 60,000	9		
60,001 - 80,000	10		
80,001 and over	11		

Table 2: Two-Earner/Two-Job Worksheet

Married Filing Jointly		All Others	
If wages from **HIGHEST** paying job are—	Enter on line 7 above	If wages from **HIGHEST** paying job are—	Enter on line 7 above
0 - $50,000	$340	0 - $27,000	$340
50,001 - 100,000	640	27,001 - 58,000	640
100,001 and over	710	58,001 and over	710

12. Prepare the 1992 Estimated Tax Worksheet, reproduced on the following page, for George B. Lewis, 2111 North Second Street, Madison, Wisconsin 53705-4001. Mr. Lewis is an unmarried taxpayer who claims 1 exemption. He elects to pay the minimum amount of estimated tax required. The following data for the worksheet are available:

AGI includes: estimated salary, $25,650; estimated self-employment income, $14,000	$39,650
Itemized deductions estimated	4,000
Estimated income tax withheld (line 15)	3,216
Credit for overpayment on preceding year's final tax return, elected as a credit on the 1992 estimated tax (line 9)	250

Income taxes for 1991 as determined by the income tax return were $5,200.

13. What steps should a unmarried taxpayer with estimated AGI of $75,000 or less take to avoid a penalty for underpayment of estimated taxes?

14. What documents does an employer transmit with Form W-3 when filing it with the Social Security Administration? What is the final filing date for Form W-3?

15. During the third quarter of 1993, the Fillmore Restaurant at 244 North Second Street, Fillmore, New York 14735-0022, withheld income and social security taxes from its five employees. Income taxes of $3,117 were withheld from employees' wages and tips of $15,570. In addition, Fillmore withheld $576.60 of social security taxes on $9,300 of social security wages. It also withheld $225.77 of Medicare taxes on $15,570 of Medicare wages. During the quarter, Fillmore deposited income and social security taxes in a Federal Reserve bank as follows: August 13—$1,327.51; September 15—$1,161.32; October 15—$2,337.68. Each deposit was accompanied by a Federal Tax Deposit coupon. Fillmore's EIN is 93-0530660. Data for quarterly wages and reported tips of employees are given below:

Name	Total Wages	Social Security Wages	Taxable Tips Reported
Barker, J.R.	$ 7,025	$1,600	$315
Duwe, H.K.	3,000	3,000	180
Miller, M.M.	2,000	2,000	120
Pressman, R.M.	1,200	1,200	125
Smathers, H.H.	1,500	1,500	105
	$14,725	$9,300	$845

Prepare Form 941, Employer's Quarterly Federal Tax Return, for the Fillmore Restaurant using the blank form on page 509. The return is filed on October 25 and signed by M. L. Wright, owner.

16. a. When must employers file their Form 941 returns? How can employers extend a Form 941 due date? Can employers combine data from different quarters on one Form 941 as long as the combined period doesn't exceed three months?

1992 Estimated Tax Worksheet (keep for your records)

1	Enter amount of adjusted gross income you expect in 1992	**1**
2	• If you plan to itemize deductions, enter the estimated total of your itemized deductions. **Caution:** If line 1 above is over $105,250 ($52,625 if married filing separately), your deduction may be reduced. See Pub. 505 for details. • If you do not plan to itemize deductions, see **Standard Deduction for 1992** on page 2, and enter your standard deduction here.	**2**
3	Subtract line 2 from line 1	**3**
4	Exemptions. Multiply $2,300 by the number of personal exemptions. If you can be claimed as a dependent on another person's 1992 return, your personal exemption is not allowed. **Caution:** If line 1 above is over $157,900 ($131,550 if head of household; $105,250 if single; $78,950 if married filing separately), get Pub. 505 to figure the amount to enter . . .	**4**
5	Subtract line 4 from line 3	**5**
6	Tax. Figure your tax on the amount on line 5 by using the 1992 Tax Rate Schedules below. DO NOT use the Tax Table or the Tax Rate Schedules in the 1991 Form 1040 or Form 1040A instructions. **Caution:** If you have a net capital gain and line 5 is over $86,500 ($74,150 if head of household; $51,900 if single; $43,250 if married filing separately), get Pub. 505 to figure the tax	**6**
7	Additional taxes (see line 7 instructions)	**7**
8	Add lines 6 and 7	**8**
9	Credits (see line 9 instructions). Do not include any income tax withholding on this line	**9**
10	Subtract line 9 from line 8. Enter the result, but not less than zero	**10**
11	Self-employment tax. Estimate of 1992 net earnings from self-employment $ . . . . if **$55,500 or less,** multiply the amount by .153; if **more than $55,500,** see line 11 instructions for the amount to enter. **Caution:** If you also have wages subject to social security or Medicare tax, get Pub. 505 to figure the amount to enter .	**11**
12	Other taxes (see line 12 instructions)	**12**
13a	Add lines 10 through 12	**13a**
b	Earned income credit and credit from **Form 4136**	**13b**
c	Subtract line 13b from line 13a. Enter the result, but not less than zero. **THIS IS YOUR TOTAL 1992 ESTIMATED TAX** ▶	**13c**
14a	Multiply line 13c by 90% (66⅔% for farmers and fishermen)	**14a**
b	Enter 100% of the tax shown on your 1991 tax return	**14b**
	Caution: If 14b is **smaller** than 14a and line 1 above is over $75,000 ($37,500 if married filing separately), stop here and see **Limit on Use of Prior Year's Tax** on page 1 before continuing.	
c	Enter the **smaller** of line 14a or 14b. **THIS IS YOUR REQUIRED ANNUAL PAYMENT** . . . . . ▶ **Caution:** Generally, if you do not prepay at least the amount on line 14c, you may owe a penalty for not paying enough estimated tax. To avoid a penalty, make sure your estimate on line 13c is as accurate as possible. If you prefer, you may pay 100% of your 1992 estimated tax (line 13c). For more details, get Pub. 505.	**14c**
15	Income tax withheld and estimated to be withheld during 1992 (including income tax withholding on pensions, annuities, certain deferred income, etc.)	**15**
16	Subtract line 15 from line 14c. (**Note:** If line 13c minus line 15 is less than $500, you do not have to make estimated tax payments.) If you are applying an overpayment from 1991 to 1992 estimated tax, see **How To Complete and Use the Payment-Voucher** on page 4	**16**
17	If the first payment you are required to make is due April 15, 1992, enter ½ of line 16 (minus any 1991 overpayment that you are applying to this installment) here and on your payment-voucher(s)	**17**

1992 Tax Rate Schedules

Caution: *Do not use these Tax Rate Schedules to figure your 1991 taxes. Use only to figure your 1992 estimated taxes.*

Single—Schedule X

If line 5 is: Over—	But not over—	The tax is:	of the amount over—
$0	$21,450	. . . . 15%	$0
21,450	51,900	$3,217.50 + 28%	21,450
51,900	. . . .	11,743.50 + 31%	51,900

Head of household—Schedule Z

If line 5 is: Over—	But not over—	The tax is:	of the amount over—
$0	$28,750	. . . . 15%	$0
28,750	74,150	$4,312.50 + 28%	28,750
74,150	. . . .	17,024.50 + 31%	74,150

Married filing jointly or Qualifying widow(er)—Schedule Y-1

If line 5 is: Over—	But not over—	The tax is:	of the amount over—
$0	$35,800	. . . . 15%	$0
35,800	86,500	$5,370.00 + 28%	35,800
86,500	. . . .	19,566.00 + 31%	86,500

Married filing separately—Schedule Y-2

If line 5 is: Over—	But not over—	The tax is:	of the amount over—
$0	$17,900	. . . . 15%	$0
17,900	43,250	$2,685.00 + 28%	17,900
43,250	. . . .	9,783.00 + 31%	43,250

Form 941
(Rev. January 1993)
Department of the Treasury
Internal Revenue Service

4141

Employer's Quarterly Federal Tax Return

▶ See Circular E for more information concerning employment tax returns.

Please type or print.

OMB No. 1545-0029
Expires 5-31-93

Enter state code for state in which deposits made. ▶ (see instructions page 2).

Name (as distinguished from trade name)

Trade name, if any

Address (number and street)

Date quarter ended

Employer identification number

City, state, and ZIP code

T
FF
FD
FP
I
T

If address is different from prior return, check here ▶

IRS Use

1 1 1 1 1 1 1 1 1 1 1   2   3 3 3 3 3 3   4 4 4
5 5 5   6   7   8 8 8 8 8 8   9 9 9   10 10 10 10 10 10 10 10 10 10

If you do not have to file returns in the future, check here . ▶

Date final wages paid ▶

If you are a seasonal employer, see **Seasonal employers** on page 2 and check here ▶

1 Number of employees (except household) employed in the pay period that includes March 12th . ▶

2 Total wages and tips subject to withholding, plus other compensation . . . . . . | 2 |

3 Total income tax withheld from wages, tips, pensions, annuities, sick pay, gambling, etc. . | 3 |

4 Adjustment of withheld income tax for preceding quarters of calendar year (see instructions) . . | 4 |

5 Adjusted total of income tax withheld (line 3 as adjusted by line 4—see instructions) . . . . | 5 |

6a Taxable social security wages . . . . . $ ______ × 12.4% (.124) = | 6a |

 b Taxable social security tips . . . . . $ ______ × 12.4% (.124) = | 6b |

7 Taxable Medicare wages and tips . . . $ ______ × 2.9% (.029) = | 7 |

8 Total social security and Medicare taxes (add lines 6a, 6b, and 7) . . . . | 8 |

9 Adjustment of social security and Medicare taxes (see instructions for required explanation) . | 9 |

10 Adjusted total of social security and Medicare taxes (line 8 as adjusted by line 9—see instructions) | 10 |

11 Backup withholding (see instructions) . . . . | 11 |

12 Adjustment of backup withholding tax for preceding quarters of calendar year . . . . | 12 |

13 Adjusted total of backup withholding (line 11 as adjusted by line 12) . . . . . . | 13 |

14 **Total taxes** (add lines 5, 10, and 13) . . . . | 14 |

15 Advance earned income credit (EIC) payments made to employees, if any . . . . . | 15 |

16 Net taxes (subtract line 15 from line 14). **This should equal line 20d below or line D on Schedule B** (plus line D of Schedule A if you treated backup withholding as a separate liability) . . . | 16 |

17 **Total deposits for quarter,** including overpayment applied from a prior quarter, from your records | 17 |

18 **Balance due** (subtract line 17 from line 16). This should be less than $500. Pay to the Internal Revenue Service . . . . | 18 |

19 **Overpayment,** if line 17 is more than line 16, enter excess here ▶ $ ______ and check if to be:
☐ Applied to next return **OR** ☐ Refunded.

20 **Monthly Summary of Federal Tax Liability.** If you are a monthly depositor, summarize your monthly tax liability below. If you are a semiweekly depositor or have accumulated a liability of $100,000 or more on any day, attach Schedule B (Form 941) and check here (see instructions) . . . . ☐

	(a) First month	(b) Second month	(c) Third month	(d) Total for quarter
Liability for month				

Sign Here

Under penalties of perjury, I declare that I have examined this return, including accompanying schedules and statements, and to the best of my knowledge and belief, it is true, correct, and complete.

Signature ▶

Print Your Name and Title ▶

Date ▶

For Paperwork Reduction Act Notice, see page 2.

Cat. No. 17001Z

Form **941** Rev. 1-93

b. Certain Forms W-4 and related information are submitted with Form 941. Explain.

17. a. What is the name of Form 8109? Discuss its contents, indicate who uses it, and explain how they use it.

b. Identify the types of employment taxes that usually must be deposited with a Federal Reserve Bank or a designated depository.

18. The Golden Door Company, 1906 North Avenue, Cheyenne, Wyoming 82001-1222, withheld income and social security taxes from each of its 28 employees during 1993. In 1994, it prepared and sent to each employee a separate Form W-2. Total wages paid to employees were $475,250. Total federal income taxes withheld from employees were $80,250. Total social security wages were $469,850. Total Medicare wages were $475,250. The company's federal EIN is 39-0630726. Calculate the company's total social security tax liability for 1993 and prepare its Form W-3, Transmittal of Income and Tax Statements. Use blank Form W-3 on the following page and control number 01 to prepare the form as of January 20, 1994. If no entry applies to the box, leave it blank. Have Marsha A. Golden, President of Golden, sign the form when you have completed it.

a Control number	33333	For Official Use Only ▶ OMB No. 1545-0008		
b **Kind of Payer** ▶	941/941E ☐ Military ☐ 943 ☐ CT-1 ☐ 942 ☐ Medicare govt. emp. ☐		1 Wages, tips, other compensation	2 Federal income tax withheld
			3 Social security wages	4 Social security tax withheld
c Total number of statements	d Establishment number		5 Medicare wages and tips	6 Medicare tax withheld
	e Employer's identification number		7 Social security tips	8 Allocated tips
f Employer's name			9 Advance EIC payments	10 Dependent care benefits
			11 Nonqualified plans	12 Deferred compensation
			13 Adjusted total social security wages and tips	
			14 Adjusted total Medicare wages and tips	
g Employer's address and ZIP code				
h Other EIN used this year			15 Income tax withheld by third-party payer	
i Employer's state I.D. No.				

Under penalties of perjury, I declare that I have examined this return and accompanying documents, and, to the best of my knowledge and belief, they are true, correct, and complete.

Signature ▶   Title ▶   Date ▶

Telephone number ___________________________

Form **W-3 Transmittal of Wage and Tax Statements 1993**   Department of the Treasury
Internal Revenue Service

PARTNERSHIPS AND CORPORATIONS

➡ How to file partnership returns

➡ How to structure family partnerships for tax savings

➡ How to elect S corporation status

➡ How S corporation income is treated

➡ How to complete Form 1120S

➡ The characteristics of corporations

➡ How to file corporate returns

Partnerships

The taxation of partnerships is related to the basic view of how a partnership operates as an organization. A *partnership* is an association of individuals who conduct business in the manner of multiple proprietorships.

The Nature of a Partnership

In order for an association of individuals to be a partnership, it must meet certain conditions.

1. It must be an association of two or more persons for the purpose of conducting a business:
2. Each partner must contribute property or services to the partnership.
3. Each partner must have an ownership interest in the profits and losses.

A joint undertaking merely to share expenses is not a partnership.

EXAMPLE 1 —————————————————————

If two or more persons construct a ditch merely to drain surface water from their properties, they are not partners. If the owners of the property actively carry on a business and divide the profits, however, they are partners.

The term "partnership" is not limited to the common-law meaning of partnership, but is broader in its scope and includes some organizations not commonly called partnerships. It includes a syndicate, group, pool, joint venture, or other unincorporated organization, through or by means of which any business, financial operation, or venture is carried on, and which is not, within the meaning of the Internal Revenue Code, a trust or estate or a corporation. The term "partner" includes a member in such a syndicate, group, pool, joint venture, or organization.

Since a partnership is an aggregation of the rights and responsibilities of the individual partners, it is like a proprietorship. The rights and responsibilities of the individual partners that are characteristic of a typical partnership are these: (1) the right of each partner to act as an agent of the partnership (referred to as mutual agency); (2) the personal responsibility of each partner for the debts of the partnership, i.e., unlimited liability;

(3) the termination of the partnership by the withdrawal, death, insanity, or bankruptcy of any partner; and (4) the right to share profits equally or in some other mutually agreeable manner. These characteristics reflect the similarities with proprietorships and serve as the basis for the way partnerships are treated for tax purposes.

Partnership Returns

Since a partnership has many of the characteristics of a proprietorship, it is logical to expect that it would be taxed in a manner similar to a proprietorship. Thus, like proprietors, the individual partners, and not the partnership entity, are subject to income taxes. The income is considered to be passed through the partnership to the individual partners who pay tax on all of the partnership income whether it has been distributed to the partners or has been retained in the business. The partnership is required to file an information income tax return annually, Form 1065, U.S. Partnership Return of Income. Revenues and expenses are reported on the information return in order to determine each partner's share of the ordinary income and other special items of income and deductions. The partners then report their share of the ordinary income and special items on their individual tax returns.

Filing Partnership Returns

Every domestic partnership and foreign partnership doing business within the U. S. must file Form 1065, U.S. Partnership Return of Income, regardless of its amount of gross or net income. The return must be prepared for the taxable year of the partnership and be signed by one of the partners. The Tax Reform Act of 1986 established rules specifying the taxable year that partnerships (as well as S corporations and personal service corporations) would be required to use. For tax years beginning after 1986, the partnership must select the same taxable year as the partners owning a majority interest in the its profit and capital (principal partners). If the principal partners do not have the same taxable year as the partnership, it must adopt or change to the taxable year of its principal partners. If all of the principal partners do not have the same taxable year, a reporting year must be selected that results in the least aggregate deferral of income. The selection of the reporting year is covered by Treasury Regulations which refer to using the "least aggregate deferral method" to determine the reporting year. It is beyond the scope of this text to present the complex application of this method. The tax year selected under these rules will be referred to hereafter as the required tax year. The purpose of the required tax year is to prevent partners from deferring partnership income by selecting a year-end in an early month after the end of the individual partners' tax years in order for the partners to postpone the reporting of the partnership income for an extended period.

EXAMPLE 2 ————————————————

If the partnership tax year ends on January 31, 1993, and the partners have a calendar year as their tax year, eleven months of the partnership income was earned during the calendar year 1992, but would not be reported by the individual partners until they filed their 1993 tax returns on April 15, 1994 (or later if they requested an extension).

The Tax Reform Act of 1986 allows an exception to the rules stated above that permits the partnership to select a different tax year if a good business reason can be established, such as demonstrating that the fiscal year should coincide with the company's natural business year. The revenue section of the Omnibus Budget Reconciliation Act of 1987 (OBRA) allows an additional election. Certain partnerships may elect to use a tax year that is different from the tax year they would otherwise be required to use under the Tax Reform Act of 1986. This election is referred to as a Section 444 election. An election to have a tax year other than a required tax year can be made only if the period from the end of the new tax year to the end of the required tax year is no longer than three months. For each year that a partnership has a Section 444 election outstanding, it must make a required tax deposit earlier than normally required. The required deposit approximates the amount of tax that would have been owed by the partners if the partnership had switched to the required tax year. This required deposit is designed to eliminate the deferral advantage of having different tax years for the partnership and the partners.

To make a Section 444 election, the entity must file Form 8716, Election To Have a Tax Year Other Than a Required Tax Year. A Section 444 election remains in effect until terminated as the result of one or more specified actions enumerated in the regulations. If the election is terminated, the partnership cannot make another election to use a tax year other than a required tax year.

It is beyond the scope of this text to discuss the Section 444 election in depth, including the calculation of the required payment on a Form 8716 worksheet. Readers are referred to the government regulations and to advanced tax texts for a fuller discussion of the steps to make a Section 444 election, to meet the conditions for continuing such an election, and to calculate the required payment while the election is in effect.

A partner or partnership desiring to change its taxable year generally must apply to the IRS to make such a change. If the change is to a year other than a required tax year specified by the Tax Reform Act of 1986, the election is made on Form 8716 as indicated above. If a partnership is granted permission to change the period for calculating net income from one year to another, a separate return must be made for the period between the close of the last fiscal year for which a return was made and the following December 31.

EXAMPLE 3 ————————————————

If a change is made from a fiscal year ending March 31 to the calendar year ending December 31, a separate return must be made for the nine-month period ending December 31 following the last annual return for the fiscal year ending March 31. A return for a fractional year also must be made if a change is made from the calendar year to a fiscal year or from one fiscal year to another fiscal year.

Changes in the membership of the partnership or of the relative interests among the partners do not necessarily terminate the partnership taxable year. For taxation purposes, the partnership taxable year closes with respect to a partner whose entire interest is sold, exchanged, or liquidated. However, none of the following occurrences terminates the partnership year prior to its normal closing: death of a partner, addition of a partner, or a shift of a partial interest in the firm among partners.

However, the partnership year is closed if: (1) no part of the business of the partnership continues to be carried on by any of its partners in a partnership or (2) within a 12-month period there is a sale or exchange of 50% or more of the total interest in partnership capital and profits.

There are also special rules concerning the effect on the partnership year of the merger or consolidation of two or more partnerships into one partnership and the dividing of a partnership into two or more separate partnerships.

Penalty for Failure to File

A penalty is imposed on a partnership (not on the partners) for its failure to file a timely or complete Form 1065. The penalty is assessed each month (not exceeding five months) that the failure continues. The penalty is an amount equal to the sum of $50 times the total number of partners that are in the partnership during the taxable year.

Reporting Partnership Income and Deductions

The partnership tax return is an information return only. The individual partners report their proportionate shares of the income and deductions of the partnership on their individual tax returns, along with all of their personal income and deduction items. This passing through of income and deductions from the partnership to the partners is often referred to as an application of the *conduit principle*. The partnership serves as a conduit to pass income and deductions to the partners rather than any tax being paid by the partnership.

On first thought, the application of the conduit principle might appear to be a simple process whereby the partners report their proportionate shares of partnership net income. Generally, this simple approach will not apply because many items of income and deductions created by the partnership are subject to special tax treatment on the partners' individual tax returns and must be reported separately by them in addition to their shares of ordinary partnership income. Therefore, the partnership return calls for the calculation of partnership ordinary income, which is passed through to the partners proportionately, plus a separate identification of items of income and deductions not includ-

able in the calculation of partnership ordinary income. These separately identified items must be passed through separately on a pro rata basis to each partner. These separately identified items include net income from rental real estate activities, long-term capital gains and losses, portfolio income (dividends, interest income, and royalty income), charitable contributions, and NOLs. The process for reporting partnership income and deductions will be discussed in the following paragraphs, with the calculation of partnership ordinary income first, followed by a discussion of the items of income and deductions that must be reported separately to the partners.

Partnership Ordinary Income

The ordinary income of a partnership is computed in much the same manner as the net income from a business or profession operated by an individual proprietor. First, income is calculated for all items of income properly includable in partnership ordinary income. Then, deductions are subtracted, such as business expenses and other expenses that are properly includable, to arrive at partnership ordinary income. Thus, the difference between specified income and specified deductions is partnership ordinary income or (loss).

Total Deductions for Calculating Partnership Ordinary Income

There are specific expenses that may be deducted in calculating partnership ordinary income. Among these are guaranteed payments to the partners, salaries and wages other than to

---

Calculating Ordinary Income and Total Income for a Partnership

Gross receipts or gross sales	$XX	
Less returns and allowances	<u>XX</u>	$XX
Less cost of goods sold		<u>XX</u>
Gross profit		$XX
Ordinary income or (loss) from other partnerships and fiduciaries		XX
Net farm profit or (loss)		XX
Net gain or (loss) from Form 4797		XX
Other income or (loss)		<u>XX</u>
Partnership total income or (loss)		<u>$XX</u>

partners, rent expense, interest expense, taxes, bad debts, repairs, depreciation, and contributions to employee benefit plans.

Salaries and Wages Other Than to Partners. Salaries and wages (other than to the partners) that are not included elsewhere on the return are reported as deductions in arriving at partnership ordinary income. Salaries and wages paid to the spouse or other members of a partner's family are also deductible by the partnership, provided they are reasonably commensurate with the services rendered.

Guaranteed Payments to Partners—Salaries and Interest. Partnership agreements frequently provide that some or all of the individual partners be paid a salary as compensation for services rendered to the partnership. Compensation in the form of commissions and bonuses may also be provided in recognition of the varying skills and amounts of time devoted to partnership business. It is also not uncommon for the partnership agreement to stipulate that the partners be paid a stated rate of interest on the amount of capital that each partner has invested in the firm.

Such payments to partners are deductible in arriving at partnership ordinary income, provided they are determined without regard to partnership income and are reasonable in amount. To the extent that salaries are considered to be capital expenditures related to the construction of tangible fixed assets, they are capitalized rather than being expensed. The partners are not considered to be employees, however, and the deductible salary payments are not subject to withholding for income taxes or social security taxes. The individual partners are required, of course, to report the salary and interest received as gross income on their own individual tax returns on Schedule E, (Form 1040) Supplemental Income and Loss, Part II.

Income and Deductions Not Included in Partnership Ordinary Income

There are certain other items of income and deductions of a partnership that are not taken into consideration in calculating the ordinary income. Some of these items, together with the distributive shares allocated to each partner, must nevertheless be listed elsewhere on the partnership return, so that the partners may in turn report them on their individual tax returns. The items most frequently reported separately include net income (loss) from rental real estate activities, portfolio income (interest, dividends and royalties), capital gains and losses, tax-exempt interest, charitable contributions, NOLs, and foreign taxes paid. These items are discussed below.

Net Income or (Loss) from Rental Real Estate Activities. Since rental real estate activities may be subject to the passive loss rules, partnership rental real estate income or (loss) is not used in the calculation of partnership ordinary income. Instead, net income or (loss) from these activities is reported on Schedules K and K-1 of Form 1065 and included on the partners' own tax returns.

Portfolio Income. Portfolio income, including interest, dividends (domestic and foreign), and royalties, is subject to special tax treatment by taxpayers. Therefore, portfolio income generated by a partnership is not included in partnership ordinary income. Instead, it is reported on Schedules K and K-1 of Form 1065 and is reported separately on the partners' individual tax returns.

Capital Gains and Losses. Although gains and losses from the sale or exchange of capital assets do not enter into the determination of partnership ordinary income, they must be reported on the partnership tax return on Schedule D, Form 1065. The distributive share of the net gains and losses for each partner must also be set forth in Schedule K-1 (Form 1065). Partners are required to report their distributive shares on their own individual tax returns (using separate Schedule D, Form 1040) along with any similar gains and losses that they may have had personally.

Tax-Exempt or Tax-Free Interest Received. Excluded from partnership ordinary income is any tax-exempt interest or any interest on tax-free covenant bonds received by a partnership. This interest is reported by the taxpayer along with other tax-exempt interest income on Form 1040, page 1 (line 8b).

Charitable Contributions. Charitable contributions do not qualify as business expenses and may not be claimed as a deduction in calculating the ordinary income of a partnership. Instead, the total amount of charitable contributions is listed on Schedule K (line 8). In addition, an itemized list of the charities to which contributions have been made, including the amount given to each and whether the amount is subject to the 50%, 30%, and 20% limitation, should be attached to the partnership return. The distributive share for each partner is shown on Schedule K-1 (Form 1065). The partners then include their distributive shares with their own personal charitable contributions on Schedule A of their own individual tax returns.

Net Operating Losses (NOL). A NOL is the excess of allowable deductions over taxable gross income in any taxable year, with certain exceptions and limitations. *Individuals* incurring a NOL in a taxable year from a trade or business are permitted to elect a carryback to the 3 preceding years, applying the loss in reduction of the taxable income of those years. If the carryback exceeds the taxable income of the 3 preceding years, such excess may be carried forward and applied against taxable income of the next 15 succeeding years. However, a net loss incurred by a *partnership* is not allowed as a carryback or carryover on the partnership return, but each partner may report his or her distributive share on an individual return. Income and losses will be allocated to a partner only for that portion of the year that the partner is a member of the partnership. Allocation will not be retroactively applied to periods prior to joining the partnership.

Foreign Taxes. Partnerships that engage in business activities outside the United States may be required to pay taxes to foreign countries or to United States possessions. Such taxes are accorded special treatment in the tax return of the individual, and therefore the partnership is not permitted to deduct them in calculating its ordinary income. As is the case with other special items, the amount of foreign taxes is reported on the partnership return on Schedule K (line 17e) and the distributive share of each partner is reported on Schedule K-1, Form 1065. Individual partners report their share of these foreign taxes on their own tax returns, either as an itemized deduction on Schedule A or as a tax credit.

Deductions Not Applicable. Three types of deductions allowed to individuals that are **not** applicable to partnerships are:

1. Personal expenses
2. Standard deduction
3. Deductions for exemptions

Expenses incurred by a partnership are ordinarily of a business nature and are properly deductible from the gross income of the partnership. Medical expenses, child care expenses, and other expenses of a personal nature are not ordinarily incurred by a partnership. If personal expenses of a partner are paid directly by the partnership, the amounts paid are in the nature of withdrawals by the partner and have no bearing on the calculation of partnership income. It naturally follows that the standard deduction and itemized deductions that individuals claim on their personal tax returns are not applicable to partnerships.

Partnerships are not individuals, nor are they taxable entities; therefore, they are not entitled to any exemptions. The partners claim their deductions for personal exemptions on their individual tax returns.

Calculation of Partnership Ordinary Income

It is apparent from the foregoing discussion that, in most cases, the amount of net income as determined from the books and reported in the partnership income statement will not agree with the amount reported as ordinary income in the partnership tax return, illustrated in this example.

EXAMPLE 4 ────────────

The *income statement* of the partnership of Hosler and Rogers indicates a net income for the year of $50,000, which is shared equally by the two partners. Included in the income of the partnership are a net long-term capital gain of $1,000, dividends of $600, and $200 of interest income. Expenses include salaries of $10,000 to Hosler and $8,000 to Rogers and charitable contributions of $600. In calculating *partnership ordinary income* on the partnership tax return, only the trade and business income and expenses from the partnership's activities are included. The ordinary income to be reported in the partnership tax return would be $48,800.

Net income according to income statement*		$50,000
Deduct income items to be reported separately:		
Net long-term capital gain	$1,000	
Interest income	200	
Dividends	600	1,800
		$48,200
Add deductible items to be reported separately:		
Charitable contributions		600
Ordinary income according to tax return		$48,800

*After deducting expenses, including salaries and other guaranteed payments to partners.

The net long-term capital gain, the interest income, and the dividends are subtracted from net income for the partnership because these items are reported separately on other schedules. The charitable contributions are added back to the partnership income because contributions do not qualify as business expenses and are treated as additional charitable contributions by individual partners on their own tax returns.

Basis for Depreciation and Gain or Loss on Partnership Property Received from Partners

When property is transferred from a partner to a partnership, the basis of the property to the partnership at the date of the transfer generally is the same dollar basis that it was at that date in the hands of the partner from whom it was acquired. The partner's basis was, of course, the original cost of the property to the partner, adjusted for capital expenditures and allowable depreciation up to the date of the transfer to the partnership. This transfer basis would be the basis used by the partnership for calculating depreciation from the date of acquisition. The basis to the partnership for calculating a gain or loss on a subsequent sale would be the basis transferred from the partner, adjusted for capital expenditures made by the partnership and allowable depreciation taken by the partnership.

The application of these transfer-of-basis rules will govern how much gain or loss the partnership must report when property acquired from a partner is sold. Thus, the gain or loss is equal to the selling price less the adjusted basis of the property in the partnership hands at the date of sale.

Prior to 1984, the tax law was silent on how the partnership gain or loss on the sale of such property should be allocated among the partners. In general, it was allocated along with other profits and losses, according to the agreed-upon profit-and-loss ratio. However, the Tax Reform Act of 1984 specified the method to be used by a partnership to assign the gain or loss on the sale of partnership property contributed to the partnership by a partner. The 1984 Act required that the gain or loss should first be allocated to the partner who contributed the property to the extent of the difference between the FMV and its book value (basis) when contributed to the partnership. Any additional gain or loss occurring after it had become partner-

ship property should be allocated to the partners in their partnership profit-and-loss ratio.

EXAMPLE 5

To illustrate the allocation of gain on the sale of partnership property, assume Joyner and Wilson formed a partnership, with Joyner contributing $4,000 in cash and Wilson contributing inventory with an adjusted basis of $4,800 and a FMV of $6,000. They agreed to split profits and losses 40% to Joyner and 60% to Wilson. The partnership basis in the inventory is $4,800, the same as it was in Wilson's hands. The partnership later sells the inventory for $6,800, resulting in a gain of $2,000 to the partnership ($6,800 − $4,800). The 1984 Act requires that the first $1,200 of the gain be assigned to Wilson ($6,000 − $4,800). The remaining gain of $800, due to the inventory's appreciation since it was acquired by the partnership, is split between Joyner and Wilson in their profit-and-loss ratio, 40% ($320) to Joyner and 60% ($480) to Wilson. Thus, of the total gain of $2,000, Joyner's share is $320, and Wilson's share is $1,680 ($1,200 + $480).

For property contributed to a partnership after October 3, 1989, any distribution by the partnership, within five years of being contributed, of such property to any partner other than the partner who originally contributed the property, must be treated as a taxable sale of the property regardless of the intent of the partners. The gain (or loss) that is reported by the contributing partner is equal to the lesser of (1) the amount of built-in gain at the time of the contribution, or (2) the gain that would be recognized to the partnership if the property were sold for its FMV at the time of distribution. An exception is allowed so that there is no gain recognition to the contributing partner if other property that is like-kind property is distributed to the contributing partner within 180 days of the distribution of the contributed property by the partnership to another partner.

EXAMPLE 6

In 1991, partner Jones contributed land to a partnership consisting of three partners, Green, Jones, and Smith, who shared profits and losses equally. On the date that the partnership received title to the property, it had a basis of $12,000 to Jones, and its FMV was $15,000. During 1992, the partners decided to sell the land to partner Smith for a price of $21,000, since the partnership had no business use for the land. The total gain on the sale of the land to Smith would be $9,000 ($21,000 − $12,000). Of the $9,000 gain, the first $3,000 ($15,000 − $12,000) would be assigned to Jones who originally contributed the property. The remaining $6,000 of gain would be allocated equally among the three partners, with $2,000 assigned to each partner. Thus, partner Jones would be allocated a total of $5,000 ($3,000 + $2,000) of the profit on the sale of the land, and each of the other partners would be allocated $2,000.

Character of Property Contributed

There are two rules with respect to determining the treatment of gain or loss by a partnership on the disposition of property that was contributed by a partner. Both rules relate to whether a gain or loss is an ordinary gain or loss or a capital gain or loss. The nature of the gain or loss is determined by the character of the property in the partner's hands. The general rule is that the character of the property contributed to a partnership by a partner is determined by how the property is used by the partnership, regardless of its character in the hands of the contributing partner. Thus, if it was ordinary income property in the hands of the partnership, the gain or loss would be ordinary; and if it was capital gain property in the hands of the partnership, the gain or loss would be a capital gain or loss.

EXAMPLE 7

In Example 6, since the partnership never used the land that was contributed by Jones for business purposes, the $9,000 gain from the sale of that land would be classified as a capital gain.

A special rule was established by the Tax Reform Act of 1984 for certain assets contributed by a partner. The type of gain or loss created on the disposition of unrealized receivables, inventories, and capital loss assets is based on the character of the property when it was in the hands of the contributing partner. In other words, the gain or loss is treated in the same way by the partnership as it would have been treated if these assets had been sold by the contributing partner. The partnership gain or loss on contributed unrealized receivables will always be an ordinary gain or loss. There also will be ordinary gain or loss on the taxable disposition of contributed inventory if it is disposed of within five years after the contribution by the partner. After five years, the gain or loss on inventory is determined by the character of the inventory in the partnership's hands. However, any loss on the disposition of capital loss property within five years will be a capital loss to the extent of the contributing partner's unrealized loss potential.

Basis for Depreciation and Gain or Loss on Partnership Property Distributed to Partners

If a partnership distributes property in kind to the members of the partnership, the basis for calculating gain or loss derived from the sale or exchange of the property would be the same as the basis of the property in the hands of the partnership immediately prior to the distribution. The basis to the individual partners generally would be the proportionate part of the basis to the partnership as long as the basis distributed to the partner is no more than the partner's basis in the partnership.

EXAMPLE 8

A partnership purchased securities at a cost of $5,000. Later the securities rose in value to $23,000, at which time they were distributed in kind to the partners. A partner with a half interest in the partnership who received securities with a market value of $11,500 would have a basis in such securities of only $2,500. No gain would be realized for tax purposes until such securities were sold by the partner, at which time the basis to be used in calculating any gain or loss would be $2,500. The remaining basis of $2,500 would be distributed proportionately to the other partners in relation to their economic interest in the partnership. A partner's holding period for the property distributed to the partner by the partnership includes the period that the property was held by the partnership. If the property had been contributed to the partnership by that partner, then the period it was held by that partner before it was transferred to the partnership is also included in the holding period.

Generally, the basis of property received from the partnership cannot be more than the adjusted basis of the partner's interest in the partner reduced by any money received in the same transaction. The partnership basis distributed to a partner in the form of several properties must be divided among the properties distributed to the partner. The basis must first be allocated to unrealized receivables and inventory items that are included in the distribution. The remaining basis must then be divided among any other properties distributed to the partner in the same transaction. The division must be in proportion to their adjusted bases in the hands of the partnership before the distribution. Application of these distribution requirements is reflected in Examples 9 and 10.

EXAMPLE 9 ————————————————

Assume that a partner's adjusted basis in the partnership is $15,000. The partner receives a distribution of property from the partnership in the amount of $20,000. Of the $20,000, $6,000 is in cash, and $14,000 is property with an adjusted basis to the partnership of $14,000. The partner's basis in the property received from the partnership is limited to $9,000 ($15,000 – $6,000 cash received).

EXAMPLE 10 ————————————————

The adjusted basis of a partner's interest is $26,000. The partnership makes a partial distribution of partnership assets. A partner receives in distribution from the partnership, cash of $8,000, inventory items with a basis of $12,000, a tract of land with a partnership basis of $10,000, and a computer with a partnership basis of $5,000. First, the basis of the partner's interest in the properties is reduced to $18,000 by the $8,000 cash received ($26,000 – $8,000 = $18,000). The inventory items are assigned a basis of $12,000. The remaining basis of $6,000 ($26,000 – $8,000 – $12,000) is divided between the land and the computer

on the basis of each asset's basis to the sum of the bases of the two assets combined. The land would be assigned a basis of $4,000 ($6,000 x $10,000/$15,000), and the computer would be assigned a basis of $2,000 ($6,000 x $5,000/$15,000). Thus, the total basis assigned to the assets received in the distribution would be $26,000: Cash, $8,000; inventory, $12,000; land, $4,000; and computer, $2,000.

Other special options are available regarding adjustments for distributions of property other than cash. Likewise special rules apply to the complete liquidation of a partnership interest. Readers are referred to advanced texts for coverage of these special options.

Limitation on Losses

If a partnership incurs losses, the losses must be separately identified as either active business losses or passive losses. Partners generally may deduct their distributive shares of active business losses from other active or portfolio income. A partner's share of passive losses from the partnership must be combined with other individual passive losses and offset only against that partner's passive income. For 1991 and later years, passive losses can only be offset against other passive income with no current deduction allowed when passive losses for the year exceed passive income in that year. Any net passive losses not deductible are suspended losses which can be carried forward and utilized when passive income is earned or when the assets giving rise to the passive losses are sold.

There is another limitation as well on the deductibility of partnership losses by a partner. Partners may deduct their share of a partnership loss only up to the amount of the basis of their interest in the partnership at the end of the year in which the loss occurs, before considering any losses.

EXAMPLE 11 ————————————————

If the basis of a partner's interest in the firm is $5,000, and the share of partnership loss for the year is $6,000, the partner is allowed to deduct only $5,000 of the loss in an individual return, and the basis of the partner's interest in the firm is reduced to zero. When the partner's basis in the firm is rebuilt to $1,000 through either profitable activities of the company, increased investment by the partner, or partnership indebtedness, the partner may claim the remaining $1,000 loss on the tax return. A partner's loss deduction is further limited to the allocated loss for that portion of the partnership year during which the partner was a member of the partnership.

Credits Against Tax

Since no income tax is assessed against partnerships, they are not allowed any of the credits against the tax that are available to individuals. The benefit of such credits is passed on to the individual partners, who may claim their distributive shares of the credits on their own individual tax returns. Thus, the jobs credit can only be used by the partners on their individual tax returns. If the credit is elected by the partners, the salary expense for the partnership must be reduced by the amount of the credit.

In addition to tax credits, taxes paid by a partnership to foreign countries and possessions of the United States are not deductible from gross income by the partnership. Instead, each partner may elect to treat the distributive share of such taxes as a deduction in determining his or her taxable income or as a **credit** against income tax.

Year in Which Partnership Income Is Reported

An individual partner is required to report the distributive share of partnership items of a particular year in an individual tax return for the year within which the partnership taxable year ends.

EXAMPLE 12 —————————————————

If the taxable year of the partnership and of an individual partner is the calendar year, the distributive share of the income and other items reported by the partnership for the calendar year 1992 would be reported in the partner's individual return for the calendar year 1992. If, however, the fiscal year of the partnership should end on March 31, 1992 and the partner's individual tax return is for the calendar year, the partner's individual tax return for the calendar year 1992 would include the distributive share of income and other items of the partnership for the partnership fiscal year ended March 31, 1992.

Filled-In Form 1065

Illustrations 15-1, 15-2, and 15-3

A filled-in partnership return on Form 1065 is shown in Illustration 15-2. The primary information for the preparation of the partnership return is taken from the income statement, a departmental schedule of cost of goods sold, and a schedule of operating expenses for the calendar year ending December 31, 1992, as shown in Illustration 15-1. Schedules D and K-1 and a worksheet for net earnings from self-employment are shown in Illustrations 15-3 through 15-5. This is a return for Morton and Baker, partners engaged in the sporting goods business, who prepare Form 1065 on an accrual method. Under their partnership agreement, each draws a salary of $1,600 per month, and they share remaining income equally.

The following is a discussion of some of the items and schedules in the partnership return.

General Information. In addition to providing information at the top of Form 1065, page 1, about the partnership name and address, other information is required which includes the partnership's principal business activity, the principal product or service, the IRS business code number, the IRS EIN, the date the business was started, and the amount of total assets. Additional information required is whether this is an amended return or a final return and whether there has been a change in address. Other questions ask for the number of partners, whether it is a limited partnership, whether any partners in the partnership are also partnerships, and whether this partnership is a partner in another partnership. All of this information

Illustration 15-1
Morton and Baker Income Statement, Schedule of Cost of Goods Sold, and Schedule of Operating Expenses

Morton and Baker
Income Statement
For Year Ended December 31, 1992

	Dept. A	Dept. B	Total
Sales	$161,094.93	$55,314.57	$216,409.50
Less sales returns and allowances	2,399.10	1,102.80	3,501.90
Net sales	$158,695.83	$54,211.77	$212,907.60
Less cost of goods sold	88,490.28	18,263.34	106,753.62
Gross profit on sales	$ 70,205.55	$35,948.43	$106,153.98
Operating expenses			87,622.42
Operating income			$ 18,531.56
Other income and expenses:			
Gain on sale of securities			2,400.00
Interest income (trade or business, $145; portfolio, $100; tax-exampt, $50)			295.00
Dividend income			300.00
Interest expense			(253.04)
Charitable contributions			(425.50)
Net income			$ 20,848.02
Distribution of net income:			
R.L. Morton			$ 10,424.01
T.J. Baker			10,424.01
			$ 20,848.02

Schedule of Cost of Goods Sold
For Year Ended December 31, 1992

	Dept. A	Dept. B	Total
Inventory at beginning of year	$ 31,847.90	$ 3,121.13	$ 34,969.03
Purchases	$ 87,580.35	$18,286.62	$105,866.97
Less: Purchases returns and allowances	(739.34)	(36.35)	(775.69)
Purchase discounts	(875.80)	(126.83)	(1,002.63)
Net purchases	$ 85,965.21	$18,123.44	$104,088.65
Merchandise available for sale	$117,813.11	$21,244.57	$139,057.68
Less inventory at end of year	29,322.83	2,981.23	32,304.06
Cost of goods sold	$ 88,490.28	$18,263.34	$106,753.62

Schedule of Operating Expenses
For Year Ended December 31, 1992

Selling expenses:		General and administrative expenses:	
Sales salaries	$20,000.00	R.L. Morton, salary	$19,200.00
Advertising expenses	1,164.00	T.J. Baker, salary	19,200.00
Depreciation expense–delivery equipment	800.00	Payroll taxes	4,378.42
Depreciation expense–store equipment	600.00	Office salaries	11,250.00
Store supplies expenses	492.49	Rent expense	5,400.00
Miscellaneous selling expense	242.40	Automobile expense	998.88
Total selling expenses	$23,298.89	Utilities expense	994.65
		Bad debts expense	750.00
		Insurance expense	571.25
		Travel expense	672.50
		Office supplies expense	408.39
		Telephone expense	176.76
		Depreciation expense–office equipment	150.00
		Miscellaneous general expense	172.68
		Total general and administrative expenses	$64,323.53
		Total operating expenses	$87,622.42

Illustration 15-2
Filled-In Partnership Return, Form 1065, Page 1

Form **1065**	**U.S. Partnership Return of Income**	OMB No. 1545-0099
Department of the Treasury / Internal Revenue Service	For calendar year 1992, or tax year beginning ...., 1992, and ending ...., 19 .... . ▶ See separate instructions.	**1992**

A Principal business activity **Retail**	Use the IRS label. Otherwise, please print or type.	Name of partnership **Morton and Baker**	D Employer identification number **56-04640770**
B Principal product or service **Sporting Goods**		Number, street, and room or suite no. (If a P.O. box, see page 9 of the instructions.)	E Date business started **7-1-1965**
C Business code number **5941**		City or town, state, and ZIP code	F Total assets (see Specific Instructions) **$ 78,326.68**

G   Check applicable boxes: (1) ☐ Initial return   (2) ☐ Final return   (3) ☐ Change in address   (4) ☐ Amended return
H   Check accounting method: (1) ☐ Cash   (2) ☒ Accrual   (3) ☐ Other (specify) ▶ ....
I   Number of partners in this partnership .... ▶ ....

Caution: *Include only trade or business income and expenses on lines 1a through 22 below. See the instructions for more information.*

Income

1a	Gross receipts or sales	1a 216,409 50		
b	Minus returns and allowances	1b 3,501 90	1c	212,907 60
2	Cost of goods sold (Schedule A, line 8)		2	106,753 62
3	Gross profit. Subtract line 2 from line 1c		3	106,153 98
4	Ordinary income (loss) from other partnerships and fiduciaries (attach schedule)		4	
5	Net farm profit (loss) (attach Schedule F (Form 1040))		5	
6	Net gain (loss) from Form 4797, Part II, line 20		6	
7	Other income (loss) (see instructions) (attach schedule)		7	145 00
8	**Total income (loss).** Combine lines 3 through 7		8	106,298 98

Deductions (see instructions for limitations)

9a	Salaries and wages (other than to partners)	9a 31,250 00		
b	Minus jobs credit	9b	9c	31,250 00
10	Guaranteed payments to partners		10	38,400 00
11	Repairs		11	
12	Bad debts		12	750 00
13	Rent		13	5,400 00
14	Taxes		14	4,378 42
15	Interest		15	253 04
16a	Depreciation (see instructions)	16a 1,550 00		
b	Minus depreciation reported on Schedule A and elsewhere on return	16b	16c	1,550 00
17	Depletion (**Do not deduct oil and gas depletion.**)		17	
18	Retirement plans, etc.		18	
19	Employee benefit programs		19	
20	Other deductions (attach schedule)		20	5,894 00
21	**Total deductions.** Add the amounts shown in the far right column for lines 9c through 20		21	87,875 46
22	**Ordinary income (loss)** from trade or business activities. Subtract line 21 from line 8		22	18,423 52

Under penalties of perjury, I declare that I have examined this return, including accompanying schedules and statements, and to the best of my knowledge and belief, it is true, correct, and complete. Declaration of preparer (other than general partner) is based on all information of which preparer has any knowledge.

Please Sign Here ▶ *R. L. Morton*   Signature of general partner   ▶ April 12, 1993   Date

Paid Preparer's Use Only
Preparer's signature ▶ *Harry M. Evans*   Date 4-10-93   Check if self-employed ▶ ☒   Preparer's social security no. 371 30 1258
Firm's name (or yours if self-employed) and address ▶ Harry M. Evans, CPA   14 Pine Drive, Raleigh, NC   E.I. No. ▶ 82 0987520   ZIP code ▶ 27610-1212

For Paperwork Reduction Act Notice, see page 1 of separate instructions.   Cat. No. 11390Z   Form **1065** (1992)

Illustration 15-2
Filled-In Partnership Return, Form 1065, Page 2

Form 1065 (1992) — Page **2**

Schedule A — Cost of Goods Sold

1	Inventory at beginning of year	**1** 34,969 03
2	Purchases minus cost of items withdrawn for personal use	**2** 104,088 65
3	Cost of labor	**3**
4	Additional section 263A costs (see instructions) (attach schedule)	**4**
5	Other costs (attach schedule)	**5**
6	**Total.** Add lines 1 through 5	**6** 139,057 68
7	Inventory at end of year	**7** 32,304 06
8	**Cost of goods sold.** Subtract line 7 from line 6. Enter here and on page 1, line 2	**8** 106,753 62

9a Check all methods used for valuing closing inventory:

  (i) ☐ Cost

  (ii) ☐ Lower of cost or market as described in Regulations section 1.471-4

  (iii) ☐ Writedown of "subnormal" goods as described in Regulations section 1.471-2(c)

  (iv) ☐ Other (specify method used and attach explanation) ▶ ....

  b Check this box if the LIFO inventory method was adopted this tax year for any goods (if checked, attach Form 970) ▶ ☐

  c Do the rules of section 263A (for property produced or acquired for resale) apply to the partnership? ☐ **Yes** ☐ **No**

  d Was there any change in determining quantities, cost, or valuations between opening and closing inventory? ☐ **Yes** ☐ **No**
  If "Yes," attach explanation.

Schedule B — Other Information

		Yes	No
1	Is this partnership a limited partnership?		X
2	Are any partners in this partnership also partnerships?		X
3	Is this partnership a partner in another partnership?		X
4	Is this partnership subject to the consolidated audit procedures of sections 6221 through 6233? If "Yes," see **Designation of Tax Matters Partner** below.		X
5	Does this partnership meet **ALL THREE** of the following requirements?		
	a The partnership's total receipts for the tax year were less than $250,000;		
	b The partnership's total assets at the end of the tax year were less than $250,000; **AND**		
	c Schedules K-1 are filed with the return and furnished to the partners on or before the due date (including extensions) for the partnership return.		
	If "Yes," the partnership is not required to complete Schedules L, M-1, and M-2; Item F on page 1 of Form 1065; or Item J on Schedule K-1	X	
6	Does this partnership have any foreign partners?		X
7	Is this partnership a publicly traded partnership as defined in section 469(k)(2)?		X
8	Has this partnership filed, or is it required to file, **Form 8264,** Application for Registration of a Tax Shelter?		X
9	At any time during the calendar year 1992, did the partnership have an interest in or a signature or other authority over a financial account in a foreign country (such as a bank account, securities account, or other financial account)? (See the instructions for exceptions and filing requirements for form TD F 90-22.1.) If "Yes," enter the name of the foreign country. ▶		X
10	Was the partnership the grantor of, or transferor to, a foreign trust that existed during the current tax year, whether or not the partnership or any partner has any beneficial interest in it? If "Yes," you may have to file Forms 3520, 3520-A, or 926		X
11	Was there a distribution of property or a transfer (e.g., by sale or death) of a partnership interest during the tax year? If "Yes," you may elect to adjust the basis of the partnership's assets under section 754 by attaching the statement described under **Elections** on page 5 of the instructions		X
12	Was this partnership in operation at the end of 1992?	X	
13	How many months in 1992 was this partnership actively operated? ▶ 12		

Designation of Tax Matters Partner (See instructions.)

Enter below the general partner designated as the tax matters partner (TMP) for the tax year of this return:

Name of designated TMP ▶ R.L. Morton   Identifying number of TMP ▶ 294-65-8321

Address of designated TMP ▶ 418 N. Elm Street
Raleigh, NC 27604-1470

Illustration 15-2
Filled-In Partnership Return, Form 1065, Page 3

Form 1065 (1992) Page **3**

Schedule K	Partners' Shares of Income, Credits, Deductions, Etc.		
	(a) Distributive share items		**(b) Total amount**
Income (Loss)	1 Ordinary income (loss) from trade or business activities (page 1, line 22)	**1**	18,423 52
	2 Net income (loss) from rental real estate activities *(attach Form 8825)*	**2**	
	3a Gross income from other rental activities — **3a**		
	b Minus expenses *(attach schedule)* — **3b**		
	c Net income (loss) from other rental activities	**3c**	
	4 Portfolio income (loss) (see instructions): a Interest income	**4a**	100 00
	b Dividend income	**4b**	300 00
	c Royalty income	**4c**	
	d Net short-term capital gain (loss) *(attach Schedule D (Form 1065))*	**4d**	
	e Net long-term capital gain (loss) *(attach Schedule D (Form 1065))*	**4e**	2,400 00
	f Other portfolio income (loss) *(attach schedule)*	**4f**	
	5 Guaranteed payments to partners	**5**	38,400 00
	6 Net gain (loss) under section 1231 (other than due to casualty or theft) *(attach Form 4797)*	**6**	
	7 Other income (loss) *(attach schedule)*	**7**	
Deductions	8 Charitable contributions (see instructions) *(attach schedule)*	**8**	425 50
	9 Section 179 expense deduction *(attach Form 4562)*	**9**	
	10 Deductions related to portfolio income (see instructions) (itemize)	**10**	
	11 Other deductions *(attach schedule)*	**11**	
Investment Interest	12a Interest expense on investment debts	**12a**	
	b (1) Investment income included on lines 4a through 4f above	**12b(1)**	
	(2) Investment expenses included on line 10 above	**12b(2)**	
Credits	13a Credit for income tax withheld	**13a**	
	b Low-income housing credit (see instructions):		
	(1) From partnerships to which section 42(j)(5) applies for property placed in service before 1990	**13b(1)**	
	(2) Other than on line 13b(1) for property placed in service before 1990	**13b(2)**	
	(3) From partnerships to which section 42(j)(5) applies for property placed in service after 1989	**13b(3)**	
	(4) Other than on line 13b(3) for property placed in service after 1989	**13b(4)**	
	c Qualified rehabilitation expenditures related to rental real estate activities *(attach Form 3468)*	**13c**	
	d Credits (other than credits shown on lines 13b and 13c) related to rental real estate activities (see instructions)	**13d**	
	e Credits related to other rental activities (see instructions)	**13e**	
	14 Other credits (see instructions)	**14**	
Self-Employment	15a Net earnings (loss) from self-employment	**15a**	56,823 52
	b Gross farming or fishing income	**15b**	
	c Gross nonfarm income	**15c**	
Adjustments and Tax Preference Items	16a Depreciation adjustment on property placed in service after 1986	**16a**	
	b Adjusted gain or loss	**16b**	
	c Depletion (other than oil and gas)	**16c**	
	d (1) Gross income from oil, gas, and geothermal properties	**16d(1)**	
	(2) Deductions allocable to oil, gas, and geothermal properties	**16d(2)**	
	e Other adjustments and tax preference items *(attach schedule)*	**16e**	
Foreign Taxes	17a Type of income ▶ .... b Foreign country or U.S. possession ▶		
	c Total gross income from sources outside the United States. *(attach schedule)*	**17c**	
	d Total applicable deductions and losses *(attach schedule)*	**17d**	
	e Total foreign taxes (check one): ▶ ☐ Paid ☐ Accrued	**17e**	
	f Reduction in taxes available for credit *(attach schedule)*	**17f**	
	g Other foreign tax information *(attach schedule)*	**17g**	
Other	18a Total expenditures to which a section 59(e) election may apply	**18a**	
	b Type of expenditures ▶		
	19 Tax-exempt interest income	**19**	
	20 Other tax-exempt income	**20**	
	21 Nondeductible expenses	**21**	
	22 Other items and amounts required to be reported separately to partners (see instructions) *(attach schedule)*		
Analysis	23a Income (loss). Combine lines 1 through 7 in column (b). From the result, subtract the sum of lines 8 through 12a, 17e, and 18a	**23a**	

	b Analysis by type of partner:	(a) Corporate	(b) Individual		(c) Partnership	(d) Exempt organization	(e) Nominee/Other
			i. Active	ii. Passive			
	(1) General partners		59,198.02				
	(2) Limited partners						

Illustration 15-2
Filled-In Partnership Return, Form 1065, Page 4

Form 1065 (1992)   Page **4**

Caution: *If Question 5 of Schedule B is answered "Yes," the partnership is not required to complete Schedules L, M-1, and M-2.*

Schedule L — Balance Sheets

Assets	Beginning of tax year (a)	Beginning of tax year (b)	End of tax year (c)	End of tax year (d)
1 Cash		4,816.48		17,347.19
2a Trade notes and accounts receivable	10,415.30		11,918.65	
b Minus allowance for bad debts	600.00	9,815.30	720.00	11,198.65
3 Inventories		34,969.03		32,304.06
4 U.S. government obligations				
5 Tax-exempt securities				
6 Other current assets (attach schedule)				
7 Mortgage and real estate loans				
8 Other investments (attach schedule)		9,465.00		9,465.00
9a Buildings and other depreciable assets	11,900.00		11,900.00	
b Minus accumulated depreciation	3,850.00	8,050.00	5,400.00	6,500.00
10a Depletable assets				
b Minus accumulated depletion				
11 Land (net of any amortization)				
12a Intangible assets (amortizable only)				
b Minus accumulated amortization				
13 Other assets (attach schedule)		1,475.81		1,526.78
14 Total assets		68,576.62		78,326.68
Liabilities and Capital				
15 Accounts payable		7,624.91		8,609.17
16 Mortgages, notes, bonds payable in less than 1 year		5,000.00		
17 Other current liabilities (attach schedule)		479.65		397.43
18 All nonrecourse loans				
19 Mortgages, notes, bonds payable in 1 year or more				
20 Other liabilities (attach schedule)				
21 Partners' capital accounts		55,472.06		69,320.08
22 Total liabilities and capital		68,576.62		78,326.68

Schedule M-1 — Reconciliation of Income (Loss) per Books With Income (Loss) per Return (see instructions)

1 Net income (loss) per books	20,848.02	6 Income recorded on books this year not included on Schedule K, lines 1 through 7 (itemize):	
2 Income included on Schedule K, lines 1 through 7, not recorded on books this year (itemize):		a Tax-exempt interest $ 50.00	
			50.00
3 Guaranteed payments (other than health insurance)	38,400.00	7 Deductions included on Schedule K, lines 1 through 12a, 17e, and 18a, not charged against book income this year (itemize):	
4 Expenses recorded on books this year not included on Schedule K, lines 1 through 12a, 17e, and 18a (itemize):		a Depreciation $	
a Depreciation $			
b Travel and entertainment $		8 Total of lines 6 and 7	50.00
		9 Income (loss) (Schedule K, line 23a). Subtract line 8 from line 5	59,198.02
5 Total of lines 1 through 4	59,248.02		

Schedule M-2 — Analysis of Partners' Capital Accounts

1 Balance at beginning of year	55,472.06	6 Distributions: a Cash	7,000.00
2 Capital contributed during year		b Property	
3 Net income (loss) per books	20,848.02	7 Other decreases (itemize):	
4 Other increases (itemize):			
		8 Total of lines 6 and 7	
5 Total of lines 1 through 4	76,320.08	9 Balance at end of year. Subtract line 8 from line 5	69,320.08

Illustration 15-3
Worksheet for Net Earnings from Self-Employment

Worksheet for Figuring Net Earnings (Loss) From Self-Employment

1a	Ordinary income (loss) (Schedule K, line 1)	**1a** 18,423.52
b	Net income (loss) from **CERTAIN** rental real estate activities (see instructions)	**1b** –0–
c	Net income (loss) from other rental activities (Schedule K, line 3c)	**1c** –0–
d	Net loss from Form 4797, Part II, line 20, included on line 1a above. Enter as a positive amount	**1d** –0–
e	Combine lines 1a through 1d	**1e** 18,423.52
2	Net gain from Form 4797, Part II, line 20, included on line 1a above	**2** –0–
3a	Subtract line 2 from line 1e. If line 1e is a loss, increase the loss on line 1e by the amount on line 2	**3a** 18,423.52
b	Part of line 3a allocated to limited partners, estates, trusts, corporations, exempt organizations, and IRAs	**3b** –0–
c	Subtract line 3b from line 3a. If line 3a is a loss, reduce the loss on line 3a by the amount on line 3b. Include each individual general partner's share on line 15a of Schedule K-1	**3c** 18,423.52
4a	Guaranteed payments to partners (Schedule K, line 5) derived from a trade or business as defined in section 1402(c) (see instructions)	**4a** 38,400.00
b	Part of line 4a allocated to individual limited partners for **other than** services and to estates, trusts, corporations, exempt organizations, and IRAs	**4b** –0–
c	Subtract line 4b from line 4a. Include each individual general partner's share and each individual limited partner's share on line 15a of Schedule K-1	**4c** 38,400.00
5	Net earnings (loss) from self-employment. Combine lines 3c and 4c. Enter here and on Schedule K, line 15a	**5** 56,823.52

is helpful to the IRS in assessing the nature of the partnership in relation to the information being reported on Form 1065. It should also be noted that additional information is required through questions asked on Form 1065, page 4. These questions are discussed later in this chapter.

Designation of Tax Matters Partner. In addition to the general information described above, Form 1065, page 2, also includes space requiring the partnership to supply the name of the general partner who is designated as the "tax matters" partner. This information is designed to help improve communications between the IRS and the partnership. The partnership is asked to supply the name, address, and identifying number of the general partner who should be contacted concerning tax questions.

Description of Items and Schedules on Partnership Return

Gross receipts or sales (line 1). $216,409.50 is found on the income statement and is the total sales for both departments. Gross receipts or sales are total sales before deducting returns and allowances but after deducting sales discounts and sales taxes. The records of Morton and Baker indicate a total of $3,501.90 sales returns and allowances for both departments. Net sales (line 1c) totaled $212,907.60.

Cost of goods sold (line 2). The required information for Schedule A, top of page 2, was obtained from the schedule of cost of goods sold presented in Illustration 15-1. The opening and closing inventories are the sums of the departmental inventories. The purchases are the sums of the departmental totals for net purchases.

Other income or loss (line 7). Included are interest and dividends received by the partnership that arise from trade or business activities. Excluded would be interest exempt from tax, such as interest on tax-free covenant bonds. Taxable interest and dividends classified as portfolio income are reported on Form 1065, Schedule K, page 3, and Schedule K-1 and are included in the individual partners' tax returns as portfolio income. The interest income of $295 reported in Morton and Baker's income statement is composed of $145 of trade or business interest and $150 of investment interest, of which $100 is portfolio income and $50 is tax-exempt interest income. The $100 of portfolio income is included in Schedules K and K-1 and is not included as ordinary partnership income. The $50 of tax-exempt interest is not included as a part of ordinary partnership income, but is included on Schedule M-1 in reconciling partnership book income with partner income reported on Form 1065, page 1. Also reported on Schedules K and K-1 is the $300 of dividend income originally reported on the partnership income statement, which is also portfolio income.

Total income or loss (line 8). This amount equals $106,298.98 for Morton and Baker in 1992. It is supported by the calculation of costs of goods sold on Form 1065, Schedule A, by a Schedule F for farm income if the partnership has an interest in a farm, and by Form 4797, Sales of Business Property, if the partnership had any gains or losses from the sale of business property.

Salaries and wages (line 9a). The sum, $31,250, of the following items is taken from the schedule of operating expenses in Illustration 15-1:

Sales salaries	$20,000.00
Office salaries	11,250.00
Total	$31,250.00

These are salaries not reported elsewhere on the partnership return. If a partnership can elect a jobs credit for certain of its employees, the amount of the credit would be deducted from the salaries and wages (line 9a).

Guaranteed payments to partners (line 10). This amount is the total of the salary payments of $19,200 to each of the partners, provided all salary payments meet the requirement of deductibility. If their agreement provided for interest on capital invested, the amounts allowed would be combined with the deductible salaries and reported as one total.

Bad Debt Deduction (line 12). $750 reflects the amount of accounts receivable written off as uncollectible. The partnership follows the tax rule of deducting bad debts only when written off.

Rent (line 13). $5,400 was paid on business property. (However, rent cannot be deducted for any portion of a dwelling unit occupied by a partner for personal use.)

Taxes (line 14). $4,378.42 was deducted for payroll taxes. The taxes reported here are those that occur in carrying on a trade or business of the partnership. Property taxes also would be deductible here if they were incurred in carrying on a partnership's business. However, property taxes for income property owned by a partnership would be reported separately on Schedule K (line 10).

Interest expense (line 15). Reported is interest paid in connection with partnership trade or business operations. Interest expense on indebtedness incurred after December 16, 1969, to purchase or carry property held for investment (i.e., property held for producing taxable income or gain, but not including property used in a trade or business) is included on Schedules K and K-1 as investment interest and is passed through to the individual partners. This line also does not include any personal interest paid by the partnership that would be an itemized deduction on any of the partners' income tax returns if the interest was paid directly by the partner for the same purpose. Also excluded from this line is interest paid in connection with partnership operations that is appropriately deducted as a farm expense (line 5) or is included in Schedules K and K-1 as a rental expense. The only amount included (line 12) for the partnership of Morton and Baker is $253.04 incurred on a note payable related to the partnership's trade and business activity. Although a partnership's trade or business interest expense is treated as other expenses for financial reporting purposes, it is set out as a separate line item on Form 1065 in calculating ordinary partnership income.

Depreciation (lines 16a and 16b). $1,550 is included in a separate Schedule 4562, Depreciation and Amortization (Chapter 9). The partnership did not acquire any depreciable property during this fiscal year, and straight-line depreciation is used on the pre-1981 assets. If the partnership had been operating a manufacturing facility, factory depreciation would have been included on Schedule A as part of the computation of costs of goods sold and therefore would have been subtracted (line 16b) from the total depreciation (line 16a).

Other deductions (line 20):

Advertising expense	$1,164.00
Automobile expense	998.88
Insurance expense	571.25
Miscellaneous general expense	172.68
Miscellaneous selling expense	242.40
Office supplies expense	408.39
Store supplies expense	492.49
Telephone expense	176.76
Travel expense	672.50
Utilities expense	994.65
Total	$5,894.00

Ordinary income or loss (line 22). $18,423.52 is calculated by subtracting the total deductions, $87,875.46 (line 20) from the total income, $106,298.98 (line 8).

Schedule A. The cost of goods sold is reported in detail on Schedule A, page 2, and then reported on page 1 (line 2).

Schedule B. Schedule B, page 2, asks 13 questions about the characteristics of the partnership. Most of the questions will be answered "no" since the typical partnership is not a limited partnership, does not have foreign partners, and is not a publicly traded partnership. Question 5, however, is an important question for many partnerships to answer. Question 5 asks "Does this partnership meet **ALL THREE** of the following requirements?" Question 5 can be answered "yes" if all of the following requirements are met:

a. The parthership's total receipts were less than $250,000.
b. The partnership's total assets at the end of the tax year were less than $250,000.
c. Schedules K-1 are filed with the return and furnished to the partners on or before the due date (including extensions) for the partnership return.

If all of these requirements are met, Question 5 can be answered "yes." If Question 5 is answered "yes," the partnership is not required to complete Schedules L, M-1, and M-2. For those partnerships not meeting the requirements of Question 5, Schedules L, M-1, and M-2 must be completed. See the following paragraphs for an explanation of Schedules L, M-1, and M-2; Item F on page 1 of Form 1065; or item J on Schedule K-1.

Form 1065, page 4, includes Schedule L, Balance Sheets, for the beginning and end of the taxable year, Schedule M-1, Reconciliation of Income per Books with Income per Return, and Schedule M-2, Analysis of Partners' Capital Accounts. These schedules are discussed below and are filled in for the partnership of Morton and Baker for illustrative purposes even though Question 5 for the partnership for Morton and Baker is answered "yes."

Schedule L. Condensed balance sheets at the beginning and end of the taxable year are shown in this schedule. Some of the items must be supported by supplementary schedules, such as for other assets and other liabilities. The amounts reported in Schedule L should agree with the books of account regardless of whether the accounts have been kept in accordance with the income tax law. In case the balance sheet at the beginning of the taxable year does not agree in every respect with the balance sheet which was submitted as of the end of the previous taxable year, the difference should be explained in a statement attached to the return.

Schedule M-1. The purpose of Schedule M-1, Reconciliation of Income per Books With Income per Return, is to reconcile the net income from the income statement of the partnership with the income shown on Form 1065, which includes ordinary income from page 1 (line 22) plus separately stated income reported on Schedule K that are not recorded on the partnership's books, including income from investments (interest income, dividends, and capital gains). Likewise, income and expenses recorded on the books not included on Schedule K would need to be reported on Schedule M-1.

Applying these concepts to the Morton and Baker partnership, net income per books of $20,848.02 (as shown on the Income Statement in Illustration 15-1) is carried to Schedule M-1 (line 1). There was no income for Schedule M-1 (line 2) that was included on Schedule K and not recorded on the partnership books. Guaranteed payments to partners (line 3) is $38,400. There were no expenses for Schedule M-1 (line 4) not included in Schedule K. Thus, guaranteed payments to partners on Schedule M-1 (line 3) is added to net income per books (line 1) to determine total income (line 5). The deduction of tax-exempt interest of $50 (line 6) is also listed as a subtotal (line 8) to be subtracted from $59,248.02 (line 5), resulting in the balance of $59,198.02

(line 9). The amount reported on Schedule M-1 (line 9) must agree with the amount on Schedule K (line 23a), which includes the amounts of income and expenses on Schedule K (lines 1-8) that are not included in partnership ordinary income on Form 1065, page 1. These Schedule K items amount to a net of $2,374.50, which includes interest income, $100; dividends, $300; capital gains, $2,400; and charitable contributions, $425.50; all of which were reported on the partnership books and on Schedule K. The amount of $59,198.02 reported on Schedule M-1 (line9) and on Schedule K (line 23a) represents the total income generated by the partnership for the year, which includes $20,848.02 of partnership ordinary income, $38,400 of guaranteed payments to partners, and $2,374.50 of income and expenses described above not included in partmership ordinary income, but separately reported on Schdule K and K-1 for inclusion on the partners' personal tax returns. The $50 of tax-exempt interest is only reported on Schedule M-1 (line 6) and on Schedule K-1, page 2 (line 19).

The Schedule M-1 reconciliation of partnership book income and partnership income reported on Form 1065 was a simple matter in the case of the Morton and Baker partnership. There were no income or expense items included in ordinary income on Form 1065, page 1, or as separately stated items on Schedule K that were not also included in the calculation of partnership book income, except for the $50 of tax-exempt interest income. Other reconciling items that would be included on Schedule M-1 if they were related to the partnership's business would be warranty expenses, deducted on the books but not deducted on Form 1065, and life insurance proceeds on the death of an officer, which would be included in book income but would not be reported on Form 1065. Refer to advanced tax texts for a more comprehensive analysis of Schedule M-1 adjustments.

Schedule M-2. The purpose of Schedule M-2, Analysis of Partners' Capital Accounts, is to reconcile the balances of the individual partners' capital accounts at the beginning of the taxable year with the balances at the end of the year, as shown in the balance sheets on Schedule L (line 21). The amounts shown should agree with the partnership's books and records and the balance sheet amount. Any differences must be explained by an attached statement.

Also, the amounts on Schedule M-2 should equal the total of all the amounts reported on Item J, Analysis of Partner's Capital Account, of the partners' individual Schedules K-1 (line c).

The data needed to prepare Schedule M-2 for Morton and Baker come from the books of the partnership, such as partners' capital balances at the beginning (Schedule M-2, line 1) and end of the year (M-2, line 9) and cash distributions (M-2, line 6). In this Morton and Baker partnership example, all of the information to prepare Schedule M-2 comes from Form 1065, Schedule L, and Illustration 15-1 showing the partnership's book income information. Morton and Baker are not required to complete Schedules L and M since the total assets of the partnership do not exceed $250,000.

Calculation of Partners' Basis

When a partner makes an original contribution to a partnership, the amount of the contribution constitutes the partner's initial interest (basis) in the partnership. Each partner's basis is adjusted by further capital contributions (an increase), withdrawals (a decrease) and changes in certain liabilities. A partner's basis is increased by the partner's share of the following distributive items: (1) ordinary income of the partnership and (2) other stated income or gains of the partnership. Partnership income increases a partner's basis whether it is taxable or tax-exempt income. Each partner's basis is decreased (but not below zero) by that partner's distributive share of (1) an ordinary loss, (2) separately allocated losses and deductions of the partnership (such as charitable contributions), and (3) expenditures that are non-deductible in calculating partnership ordinary income or loss.

EXAMPLE 13 ──────────────────

Roger Booth invests in a partnership by investing cash of $25,000 and a truck with a FMV of $18,000 and a tax basis of $12,000. His share of profits and losses is 30%. During the first year after Booth becomes a partner, the partnership has ordinary income of $60,000, earns tax-exempt interest of $4,000, and had capital gains of $8,000. The partnership made charitable contributions during the first year of $6,000. Roger's withdrawals from the partnership amounted to $15,000. Based on this information, Booth's basis in the partnership at the end of the first year would be $41,800, calculated as follows:

Cash investment	$25,000
Investment of truck	12,000
Ordinary income ($60,000 x 30%)	18,000
Tax-exempt interest ($4,000 x 30%)	1,200
Capital gains ($8,000 x 30%)	2,400
Withdrawals	(15,000)
Charitable contributions ($6,000 x 30%)	(1,800)
Basis of partnership interest at the end of Year 1	$41,800

As indicated above, a partner's basis cannot be reduced below zero due to ordinary losses or other separately stated losses of the partnership. Thus, a partner may not have a negative basis in a partnership. Unused losses that would otherwise reduce a partner's basis below zero may be carried forward indefinitely and be used in subsequent years to reduce a positive partnership basis.

EXAMPLE 14 ————————————

Assume that Monroe has a partnership interest at the end of a particular year of $16,000. His share of profits and losses is 40%. Assume that the partnership had an ordinary loss of $60,000 in Year 2. Monroe's share of the loss would be $24,000 ($60,000 x 40%), but he would be allowed to deduct only $16,000 (equal to his beginning-of-the-year capital balance) which would reduce Monroe's basis in the partnership to zero. The $8,000 of the loss that is not deductible in Year 2 would be carried forward to subsequent years and be used to offset a positive partnership basis which could be achieved by partnership profits or by further contributions by Moore to the partnership.

Schedules K and K-1. Schedule K reports the total amount of the partners' shares of ordinary income (loss), special items of income, credits, net earnings from self-employment, tax preference items, investment interest, and foreign taxes. Schedule K-1 reports this information to the individual partners according to their proportionate shares. In prior years, a Schedule K only had to be completed when more than ten Schedules K-1 were attached to the partnership return. In 1988 and later years, a Schedule K

must be completed regardless of the number of Schedules K-1 attached.

The ordinary income of $18,423.52 on Schedule K (line 1) agrees with the amount reported on Form 1065, page 1 (line 22). The $38,400 of guaranteed payments to partners for salaries and interest, reported on Schedule K (line 5) agrees with the amount reported on Form 1065, page 1 (line 10).

An itemized list of the charitable contributions, which totaled $425.50, must be attached to the return to support the amount entered on Schedule K (line 8). The distributive shares of the total are assigned to the individual partners on Schedule K-1. The partnership may not deduct charitable contributions in determining taxable income. The partners combine their distributive shares with their own personal contributions to be claimed as itemized deductions on their individual income tax returns. The partnership must indicate by amount those contributions that are subject to the 50%, 30%, and 20% limitations.

The amount of $56,823.52 of net earnings from self-employment (line 15a) is the total of the partnership ordinary income ($18,423.52) plus the guaranteed payments to the partners ($38,400). The worksheet in Illustration 15-3 shows the calculation of the $56,823.52 of net earnings from self-employment.

Additional Information. Form 1065 asks for a significant amount of information about the operations of the reporting partnership, both on page 1 and page 2. Page 1 Questions A through I relate to questions regarding the current operating information, such as the partnership's principal business activity, principal product or service, business code number, EIN, date business was started, total assets, whether the current Form 1065 is an initial return or a final return and/or whether there has been a change of address, whether on the cash or accrual method, and how many partners are in the partnership.

Other information asked for on page 2, in addition to Question 5 discussed earlier, includes questions as to whether the partnership has any foreign partners, whether the partnership is subject to consolidated audit procedures, and whether the partnership is a tax shelter or a publicly-traded partnership. Several other questions ask for information regarding financial accounts in foreign countries and relationships to foreign trusts. Most of these questions would not be applicable to the typical U.S. domestic partnership and could be answered "no."

Filled-In Schedule D (Form 1065)

Illustration 15-4

Morton and Baker sold their investment in Ajax Manufacturing Company stock on February 8, 1992, for $7,300. The stock had cost $4,900 and had been held since June 8, 1985. The $2,400 gain must be reported on Schedule D (line 6). Each partner's share of the long-term gain, $1,200, is then entered on Schedule K-1, Form 1065 (line 4e), as shown for R. L. Morton in Illustration 15-5.

Filled-In Schedule K-1 (Form 1065)

Illustration 15-5

The partnership must advise each partner on Schedule K-1 (Form 1065) of each one's share of the income, deductions, credits, and tax preferences. Copy A of Schedule K-1 for each partner is filed with Form 1065. Copy B is retained by the individual partners. The partnership retains a Copy C of Schedule K-1 for each of the partners. A filled-in Form 1065, Schedule K-1 for R. L. Morton (SSN 294-65-8321) of Morton and Baker, appears in Illustration 15-5. Information regarding Morton's share of partnership income is shown on Schedule K-1 (lines 1, 4a, 4b, 4e, and 5). Charitable contributions are deductible on Morton's Schedule A, Itemized Deductions (line 8). His net earnings from self-employment must be reported on Schedule SE (line 15).

Common Items Reported on Schedule K-1 (Form 1065)

Line of K-1	Item	Form or Schedule to which Transferred
1	Ordinary income (loss)	Schedule E, Part II, Form 1040
2	Income or loss from rental real estate activities	Per instructions
4	Portfolio income	
	a. Interest	Schedule B, Part I, Line 2
	b. Dividends	Schedule B, Part II, Line 4
	c. Royalties	Schedule E, Part I, Line 5
	d. Net short-term capital gain (loss)	Schedule D, Line 5
	e. Net long-term capital gain (loss)	Schedule D, Line 12
	f. Other portfolio income (loss)	On applicable lines
5	Guaranteed payments	Per instructions
6	Other net gain (loss) under Section 1231 (other than due to casualty or theft)	Form 4797, Part I
7	Other income (attach schedule)	Schedule B, Part I, Line 2
8	Charitable contributions	Schedule A, Form 1040
13	Jobs credit	Form 5884
14a	Net earnings (loss) from self-employment	Schedule SE, Part I, Form 1040
14b	Gross farming or fishing income	Schedule E, Part IV, Form 1040

Illustration 15-4
Filled-In Schedule D, Form 1065

SCHEDULE D (Form 1065)

Department of the Treasury
Internal Revenue Service

Capital Gains and Losses

▶ Attach to Form 1065.

OMB No. 1545-0099

1992

Name of partnership: Morton and Baker

Employer identification number: 56 : 04640770

Part I   Short-Term Capital Gains and Losses—Assets Held 1 Year or Less

(a) Description of property (Example, 100 shares 7% preferred of "Z" Co.)	(b) Date acquired (month, day, year)	(c) Date sold (month, day, year)	(d) Sales price (see instructions)	(e) Cost or other basis (see instructions)	(f) Gain (loss) ((d) minus (e))
1					

2 Short-term capital gain from installment sales from Form 6252, line 26 or 37	2	
3 Short-term capital gain (loss) from like-kind exchanges from Form 8824	3	
4 Partnership's share of net short-term capital gain (loss), including specially allocated short-term capital gains (losses), from other partnerships and from fiduciaries	4	
5 Net short-term capital gain (loss). Combine lines 1 through 4. Enter here and on Form 1065, Schedule K, line 4d or 7	5	

Part II   Long-Term Capital Gains and Losses—Assets Held More Than 1 Year

(a)	(b)	(c)	(d)	(e)	(f)
6 100 Shares Ajax Mfg. Co.	6-8-85	2-8-92	7,300	4,900	2,400

7 Long-term capital gain from installment sales from Form 6252, line 26 or 37	7	
8 Long-term capital gain (loss) from like-kind exchanges from Form 8824	8	
9 Partnership's share of net long-term capital gain (loss), including specially allocated long-term capital gains (losses), from other partnerships and from fiduciaries	9	
10 Capital gain distributions	10	
11 Net long-term capital gain (loss). Combine lines 6 through 10. Enter here and on Form 1065, Schedule K, line 4e or 7	11	2,400

General Instructions

(Section references are to the Internal Revenue Code.)

Purpose of Schedule

Use Schedule D (Form 1065) to report sales or exchanges of capital assets, except capital gains (losses) that are specially allocated to any partners.

Capital gains (losses) specially allocated to the partnership as a partner in other partnerships and from fiduciaries are to be entered on Schedule D, line 4 or 9, whichever applies. Capital gains (losses) of the partnership that are specially allocated to partners should be entered directly on line 4d, 4e, or 7 of Schedules K and K-1, whichever applies. Do not include these amounts on Schedule D. See **How Income Is Shared Among Partners** in the Instructions for Form 1065 for more information.

General Information

To report sales or exchanges of property other than capital assets, including the sale or exchange of property used in a trade or business and involuntary conversions (other than casualties and thefts), see **Form 4797**, Sales of Business Property, and related instructions. If property is involuntarily converted because of a casualty or theft, use **Form 4684**, Casualties and Thefts.

For amounts received from an installment sale, the holding period rule in effect in the year of sale will determine the treatment of the amounts received as long-term or short-term capital gain.

Report every sale or exchange of property in detail, even though there is no gain or loss.

For more information, get **Pub. 544**, Sales and Other Dispositions of Assets.

What Are Capital Assets?

Each item of property the partnership held (whether or not connected with its trade or business) is a capital asset **except**:

1. Assets that can be inventoried or property held mainly for sale to customers.

2. Depreciable or real property used in the trade or business.

3. Certain copyrights; literary, musical, or artistic compositions; letters or memorandums; or similar property.

4. Accounts or notes receivable acquired in the ordinary course of trade or business for services rendered or from the sale of property described in 1 above.

5. U.S. Government publications, including the Congressional Record, that the partnership received from the government, other than by purchase at the normal sales price, or that the partnership got from another taxpayer who had received it in a similar way, if the partnership's basis is determined by reference to the previous owner.

Exchange of "Like-Kind" Property

Use **Form 8824**, Like-Kind Exchanges, to report an exchange of like-kind property. Also report the exchange on Schedule D or on Form 4797, whichever applies. Complete and attach a Form 8824 to the partnership's return for each exchange. The partnership must report an exchange of business or investment property for "like-kind" property even if no gain or loss on the property is recognized.

If Schedule D is used to report a like-kind exchange, enter the gain or loss from Form 8824, if any, on line 3 or 8. If an exchange was made with a related party, write **"Related Party Like-Kind Exchange"** in the top margin of Schedule D. See Form 8824 and its instructions for details.

Illustration 15-5
Filled-In Schedule K-1, Form 1065, Page 1

SCHEDULE K-1
(Form 1065)
Department of the Treasury
Internal Revenue Service

Partner's Share of Income, Credits, Deductions, Etc.
▶ See separate instructions.

For calendar year 1992 or tax year beginning , 1992, and ending , 19

OMB No. 1545-0099

1992

Partner's identifying number ▶ 294-65-8321 | **Partnership's identifying number** ▶ 56-04640770

Partner's name, address, and ZIP code	Partnership's name, address, and ZIP code
R.L. Morton 418 Elm Street Raleigh, NC 27640-1470	Morton and Baker 524 Southside Raleigh, NC 27610-4241

A Is this partner a general partner? . . . ☒ Yes ☐ No

B Partner's share of liabilities (see instructions):

Nonrecourse . . . . . $ ......0......

Qualified nonrecourse financing . $ ....

Other . . . . $ 4,503.20

C What type of entity is this partner? ▶ Individual

D Is this partner a ☒ domestic or a ☐ foreign partner?

E IRS Center where partnership filed return: Memphis

F Enter partner's percentage of: (i) Before change or termination (ii) End of year

Profit sharing . . . .% 50 %

Loss sharing . . . .% 50 %

Ownership of capital . . . .% 50 %

G(1) Tax shelter registration number . ▶ ....

(2) Type of tax shelter ▶ ....

H Check here if this partnership is a publicly traded partnership as defined in section 469(k)(2) . . . . ☐

I Check applicable boxes: (1) ☐ Final K-1 (2) ☐ Amended K-1

J Analysis of partner's capital account:

(a) Capital account at beginning of year	(b) Capital contributed during year	(c) Partner's share of lines 3, 4, and 7, Form 1065, Schedule M-2	(d) Withdrawals and distributions	(e) Capital account at end of year (combine columns (a) through (d))
28,236.03		10,424.01	(4,000.00)	34,660.04

	(a) Distributive share item		(b) Amount	(c) 1040 filers enter the amount in column (b) on:
Income (Loss)	**1** Ordinary income (loss) from trade or business activities .	1		⎱ See Partner's Instructions for Schedule K-1 (Form 1065).
	2 Net income (loss) from rental real estate activities .	2		
	3 Net income (loss) from other rental activities . .	3		
	4 Portfolio income (loss):			
	a Interest	4a	50.00	Sch. B, Part I, line 1
	b Dividends	4b	150.00	Sch. B, Part II, line 5
	c Royalties	4c		Sch. E, Part I, line 4
	d Net short-term capital gain (loss) . . .	4d		Sch. D, line 5, col. (f) or (g)
	e Net long-term capital gain (loss) . . .	4e	1,200.00	Sch. D, line 13, col. (f) or (g)
	f Other portfolio income (loss) (attach schedule)	4f		(Enter on applicable line of your return.)
	5 Guaranteed payments to partner	5	19,200.00	⎱ See Partner's Instructions for Schedule K-1 (Form 1065).
	6 Net gain (loss) under section 1231 (other than due to casualty or theft)	6		
	7 Other income (loss) (attach schedule) . .	7		(Enter on applicable line of your return.)
Deductions	**8** Charitable contributions (see instructions) (attach schedule) . .	8	212.75	Sch. A, line 13 or 14
	9 Section 179 expense deduction	9		⎱ See Partner's Instructions for Schedule K-1 (Form 1065).
	10 Deductions related to portfolio income (attach schedule) . . .	10		
	11 Other deductions (attach schedule)	11		
Investment Interest	**12a** Interest expense on investment debts	12a		Form 4952, line 1
	b (1) Investment income included on lines 4a through 4f above .	b(1)		⎱ See Partner's Instructions for Schedule K-1 (Form 1065).
	(2) Investment expenses included on line 10 above	b(2)		
Credits	**13a** Credit for income tax withheld	13a		⎱ See Partner's Instructions for Schedule K-1 (Form 1065).
	b Low-income housing credit:			
	(1) From section 42(j)(5) partnerships for property placed in service before 1990	b(1)		
	(2) Other than on line 13b(1) for property placed in service before 1990	b(2)		
	(3) From section 42(j)(5) partnerships for property placed in service after 1989	b(3)		Form 8586, line 5
	(4) Other than on line 13b(3) for property placed in service after 1989	b(4)		
	c Qualified rehabilitation expenditures related to rental real estate activities (see instructions)	13c		
	d Credits (other than credits shown on lines 13b and 13c) related to rental real estate activities (see instructions)	13d		⎱ See Partner's Instructions for Schedule K-1 (Form 1065).
	e Credits related to other rental activities (see instructions) . . .	13e		
	14 Other credits (see instructions)	14		

For Paperwork Reduction Act Notice, see Instructions for Form 1065.   Cat. No. 11394R   **Schedule K-1 (Form 1065) 1992**

Illustration 15-5
Filled-In Schedule K-1, Form 1065, Page 2

Schedule K-1 (Form 1065) 1992   Page **2**

	(a) Distributive share item	(b) Amount	(c) 1040 filers enter the amount in column (b) on:
Self-employment	**15a** Net earnings (loss) from self-employment	**15a** 28,411.76	Sch. SE, Section A or B
	b Gross farming or fishing income	**15b**	{ See Partner's Instructions for Schedule K-1 (Form 1065). }
	c Gross nonfarm income	**15c**	
Adjustments and Tax Preference Items	**16a** Depreciation adjustment on property placed in service after 1986	**16a**	(See Partner's Instructions for Schedule K-1 (Form 1065) and Instructions for Form 6251.)
	b Adjusted gain or loss	**16b**	
	c Depletion (other than oil and gas)	**16c**	
	d (1) Gross income from oil, gas, and geothermal properties	**d(1)**	
	(2) Deductions allocable to oil, gas, and geothermal properties	**d(2)**	
	e Other adjustments and tax preference items *(attach schedule)*	**16e**	
Foreign Taxes	**17a** Type of income ▶		Form 1116, Check boxes
	b Name of foreign country or U.S. possession ▶		
	c Total gross income from sources outside the U.S. *(attach schedule)*	**17c**	} Form 1116, Part I
	d Total applicable deductions and losses *(attach schedule)*	**17d**	
	e Total foreign taxes (check one): ▶ ☐ Paid ☐ Accrued	**17e**	Form 1116, Part II
	f Reduction in taxes available for credit *(attach schedule)*	**17f**	Form 1116, Part III
	g Other foreign tax information *(attach schedule)*	**17g**	See Instructions for Form 1116.
Other	**18a** Total expenditures to which a section 59(e) election may apply	**18a**	See Partner's Instructions for Schedule K-1 (Form 1065).
	b Type of expenditures ▶		
	19 Tax-exempt interest income	**19**	Form 1040, line 8b
	20 Other tax-exempt income	**20**	{ See Partner's Instructions for Schedule K-1 (Form 1065). }
	21 Nondeductible expenses	**21**	
	22 Recapture of low-income housing credit:		
	a From section 42(j)(5) partnerships	**22a**	} Form 8611, line 8
	b Other than on line 22a	**22b**	

23 Supplemental information required to be reported separately to each partner *(attach additional schedules if more space is needed):*

$25 Tax-Exempt Interest — Municipal Bonds

When and Where to File Returns

The returns of partnerships must be filed on or before the fifteenth day of the fourth month following the close of the taxable year.

EXAMPLE 15 ————————————————

If the accounts are kept on the calendar-year basis, the return must be filed on or before April 15 following the close of the taxable year. If the accounts are kept on a fiscal-year basis, the returns must be filed on or before the fifteenth day of the fourth month of the succeeding taxable year. Thus, if the fiscal year ended June 30, 1992, the partnership return must be filed by October 15, 1993, if no extension is granted.

Partnership returns must be filed with the regional IRS Center designated for the state in which the partnership has its principal office or principal place of business.

In the case of a foreign partnership, the returns must be filed on or before the fifteenth day of the sixth month following the close of the taxable year. If the partnership does not have any principal place of business or office or agency in the United States, the return must be filed with the IRS Center, Philadelphia, PA 19244-4444.

Signatures Required

Partnership returns contain a "declaration" which must be signed by one of the general partners. If the return is prepared by a regular full-time employee of the partnership, no additional signature is required. If the return is prepared by an independent firm or individual, the declaration must also be signed by the preparer (firm or individual). A $25 penalty may be charged a preparer who is required to sign and does not show a valid signature in the space provided.

Structuring Family Partnerships for Tax Savings

In the past, the IRS has used a number of criteria for determining whether or not a family partnership was recognized for income tax purposes. Factors considered included (1) the extent to which the alleged partner rendered services to the partnership, (2) the nature and extent of the alleged partner's participation in the control and management of the business, (3) the amount of the partner's capital interest in the firm and how it was obtained, and (4) the reasonableness of the relationship between a proportionate share in the profits and the contribution of capital and services. For example, if a son acquired an interest in his father's business as a gift, the substance of the arrangement might be open to question. If, for example, the son contributed only token services or took little part in the management of the business, these are grounds for questioning the legitimacy of the partnership. In many cases the profit distribution arrangements have not been recognized for income tax purposes, and the attempt to split income was partially or wholly ineffective.

The Internal Revenue Code provides that, for partnerships in which capital is a material income-producing factor, the means by which the partners obtained their interest is immaterial. Thus, a bona fide gift of a family partnership interest is to be respected regardless of the motives involved, and the recipient is to be recognized as a partner for federal income tax purposes. Safeguards are provided, however, against the distribution of partnership income without due regard to compensation for services rendered or amount of capital investment. If a capital interest was acquired from a member of the family by purchase or gift, a reasonable allowance must be made for the services rendered by the partners, and the balance of income must be allocated according to the amount of capital invested by the several partners. However, the distributive share of a partner need not be reduced because of absence due to military service. The "family" of an individual, as used for this purpose, includes the wife or husband, ancestors, lineal descendants, and any trust for the primary purpose of such persons.

Name _______________________________

Section _____________ Date _______________

CHAPTER 15

Questions and Problems

1. What are the characteristics of an organization that would classify it as a partnership?

2. An unmarried individual under age 65 must file a 1992 tax return if gross income is $5,900 or more. Is the filing of a partnership return determined by a similar income requirement? Explain.

3. a. Fitch and Cheng form a partnership in the current year with equal contributions of capital. They file their individual tax returns on the calendar-year basis. May the partnership adopt a fiscal year beginning July 1? Explain.

   b. Hart and Bowen, each owning a plumbing business, agree to form a joint venture to bid on the plumbing contract for a large building. They expect the plumbing work for the joint venture to take about two years. They are both on a calendar-year basis, but are uncertain how the joint venture affects their tax status. Explain what additional tax responsibilities, if any, Hart and Bowen are held accountable for by forming a joint venture.

4. Answer the following questions in the space provided:

   a. What tax form must be used by partnerships? . . . . ________________

   b. Are partnerships required to withhold income taxes on salaries paid to partners? . ________________

   c. Is each partner required to sign the partnership return? . . . . ________________

   d. A partnership return for a calendar year must be filed on or before what date? ________________

   e. A partnership return for a fiscal year ending April 30 must be filed on or before
       what date? . . . . ________________

5. If a partnership, with the approval of the IRS, changes its accounting period from a fiscal
   year ending on September 30 to a calendar year ending on December 31, for what short period must a return be filed?

6. Indicate which of the following items are applicable to the calculation of ordinary partnership income by placing a check mark in the appropriate column provided:

Item	Applicable	Not Applicable
a. Rent received from rental property	________________	________________
b. Capital sale of partnership asset	________________	________________
c. Dividend received from Canadian corporation	________________	________________
d. Contribution to Red Cross	________________	________________
e. Guaranteed salaries of partners	________________	________________
f. Personal exemption of $2,300 for each partner	________________	________________
g. Interest on partners' capital	________________	________________
h. Membership fee in local Chamber of Commerce	________________	________________
i. Interest from a municipal bond	________________	________________
j. Property taxes on partnership assets	________________	________________
k. NOL of prior year carried forward to the current year . .	________________	________________

7. Do items of partnership income and expense which cannot be included in the calculation of
   partnership ordinary income appear in any other place on the partnership return? Explain.

8. **a.** An individual taxpayer's share of partnership ordinary income is $1,500. The taxpayer has no other source of income. Is the individual required to file an income tax return? Explain.

    b. An unmarried taxpayer claiming four exemptions is a member of a partnership. The taxpayer's gross income is composed of $28,000 salary from the partnership and an undistributed ordinary partnership income of $5,500. Where, on Form 1040, should the taxpayer report the partnership salary and the undistributed partnership income?

9. How are salaries and interest paid to partners treated in calculating ordinary income on the partnership tax return, Form 1065?

10. Helen Royal is a member of a partnership that reports ordinary income for the current taxable year of $68,000. Her distributive share of the partnership income was $34,000, of which she withdrew $18,000 during the year. What amount is she required to report as income from the partnership in preparing her individual return for the year?

11. Robert Edge and Robin Barnes are partners in the law firm of Edge and Barnes, sharing profits and losses equally. The partnership adopted a fiscal year ending June 30 at the time of its organization in 1982. Edge files his individual return on the basis of the calendar year, while Barnes keeps a personal set of books and files her individual return on the basis of a fiscal year ending on June 30. The partnership ordinary income for the fiscal year ending on June 30 of the current calendar year amounted to $44,000. Edge has taxable income from other sources for the current calendar year amounting to $15,000. Barnes has income from other sources for the fiscal year ending June 30 within the current calendar year of $18,600. What amount of income should each partner report in their individual tax returns for the current taxable year?

12. Leona Mendez and Luisa Torres are engaged in a placement service as partners, sharing profits and losses equally. During the current calendar year, the partnership contributed $3,000 to the partners' alma mater, State University. This contribution was treated as an expense in the annual income statement that reported net income of $47,500.

    a. Is the partnership entitled to treat the contribution to State University as a deduction from income in the partnership return?

b. What is each partner's distributive share of the taxable income shown by the partnership return?

c. May each of the partners claim a deduction in her individual return for the partnership contribution to State University? If so, how much?

13. Samantha Burkett is entitled to 40% of the profits of a partnership. During the current year, she received a salary of $30,000 in cash as compensation for services rendered to the partnership. The other partners received no salaries. She also withdrew $20,000 of her share of income earned by the partnership during the year, and she had income from other sources for the year amounting to $4,800. On Schedule K of partnership's income tax return for the current year, the partnership reported ordinary income of $35,000, including dividends from foreign corporations of $1,000; dividends from domestic corporations of $1,400; and net long-term capital gains of $2,500. Prepare a statement showing the amounts of income, identified as to type, that Burkett should report in her individual tax return for the year, without giving effect to any exclusions to which she may be entitled.

14. John Trump and Alice Spencer are partners in a real estate agency. Trump is entitled to 70% of the profits and losses, and Spencer 30%. Trump receives a salary of $28,000, and Spencer a salary of $24,000 from the partnership. For the current calendar year, the partnership showed a profit of $32,000 after deducting partners' salaries and charitable contributions of $600 (50% type). In addition to his share of partnership contributions, Trump had itemized deductions of a personal nature as follows: mortgage interest, $855; charitable contributions, $1,350; real estate taxes, $2,500; state sales tax, $255; state income tax, $1,596. Spencer had personal itemized deductions as follows: charitable contributions, $250; interest on mortgage on home, $455; real estate taxes, $1,250; state sales tax, $255; state income tax of $820. Trump files a joint return with 3 personal exemptions. Spencer is single and has no dependents. The partners and the partnership are on a calendar-year basis.

a. What is the ordinary income of the partnership for the current calendar year?

b. Calculate the appropriate taxable income for Trump and Spencer.

c. If the partnership had incurred a loss for the year, would it have been necessary to file a partnership return?

15. Bess Hogan and Ester Perez formed a partnership to operate a clothing store. Hogan invested $47,000 in cash plus some equipment. Perez invested land and a building. They are sharing profits and losses equally. The following financial information pertained to the assets other than cash:

Item	FMV at Date of Contribution	Original Cost to Partner	Depreciation Taken by Partner
Equipment	$18,000	$25,000	$10,000
Land	20,000	12,000	0
Building	45,000	50,000	19,000

    a. What is the tax basis of (1) Hogan's interest and (2) Perez's interest in the partnership?

    b. What is the tax basis to the partnership for the purpose of depreciating the equipment and the building?

    c. Assume the partnership sold the equipment for $16,000 after taking an additional depreciation deduction of $4,000. How much gain or loss would the partnership report, and how would the gain or loss be allocated to the partners?

16. Susan Floyd invested the following assets in a partnership to operate a health center: cash, $10,000; exercise equipment, $8,000; and furniture, $15,000. The exercise equipment and furniture amounts represent Floyd's tax basis in these assets. She holds a one-third interest in the partnership, sharing profits and losses equally with two other partners. During the first year of operations the partnership had $36,000 of ordinary income and $6,000 of capital gains. Floyd withdrew $700 per month from the partnership during its first year of operations. The partnership made a charitable contribution during the year of $900. Calculate the amount of Floyd's basis in the partnership at the end of Year 1.

17. Hakan and Dyer are partners in a small management consulting firm in which they share profits and losses equally. The following information has been assembled for the purpose of completing Schedule M-2, Form 1065:

Capital accounts, January 1:
Hakan	$ 7,500
Dyer	9,000
Net income per books	39,700
Ordinary income, Form 1065, page 1	40,000
Dividends received from domestic corporations	250
Interest income from tax-exempt bonds	150
Charitable contributions (30% type)	700
Withdrawals:	
Hakan	15,000
Dyer	17,500

Prepare Schedule M-2, Form 1065, provided.

Schedule M-2	**Analysis of Partners' Capital Accounts**		
1 Balance at beginning of year		6 Distributions: **a** Cash	
2 Capital contributed during year		**b** Property	
3 Net income (loss) per books		7 Other decreases (itemize):	
4 Other increases (itemize):		. . . .	
. . . .		. . . .	
. . . .		8 Total of lines 6 and 7	
5 Total of lines 1 through 4		9 Balance at end of year. Subtract line 8 from line 5	

18. The income statement of Lopez and Dexter, a partnership, reveals a net loss for the current calendar year of $8,200. Included in the calculation of the net loss are (1) dividends received from domestic corporations amounting to $2,000, (2) dividends received from foreign corporations of $600, (3) taxable interest income (portfolio income) amounting to $300, and (4) salary payments of $28,000 and $20,000 to Lopez (60% partner) and Dexter (40% partner), respectively. Charitable contributions of $900 were treated as expenses in determining the net loss (50% type).

    a. Complete the following schedule of items to show the amount that should be reported by the partnership on Form 1065:

Line 10	Guaranteed payments to partners	$ ___________
Line 22	Ordinary income (loss)	$ ___________

    b. Using the worksheet on the following page, determine the amount of the net earnings from self-employment for the partners.

Worksheet for Figuring Net Earnings (Loss) From Self-Employment

1a Ordinary income (loss) (Schedule K, line 1)	**1a**	
b Net income (loss) from **CERTAIN** rental real estate activities (see instructions)	**1b**	
c Net income (loss) from other rental activities (Schedule K, line 3c)	**1c**	
d Net loss from Form 4797, Part II, line 20, included on line 1a above. Enter as a positive amount	**1d**	
e Combine lines 1a through 1d	**1e**	
2 Net gain from Form 4797, Part II, line 20, included on line 1a above	**2**	
3a Subtract line 2 from line 1e. If line 1e is a loss, increase the loss on line 1e by the amount on line 2	**3a**	
b Part of line 3a allocated to limited partners, estates, trusts, corporations, exempt organizations, and IRAs	**3b**	
c Subtract line 3b from line 3a. If line 3a is a loss, reduce the loss on line 3a by the amount on line 3b. Include each individual general partner's share on line 15a of Schedule K-1	**3c**	
4a Guaranteed payments to partners (Schedule K, line 5) derived from a trade or business as defined in section 1402(c) (see instructions)	**4a**	
b Part of line 4a allocated to individual limited partners for **other than** services and to estates, trusts, corporations, exempt organizations, and IRAs	**4b**	
c Subtract line 4b from line 4a. Include each individual general partner's share and each individual limited partner's share on line 15a of Schedule K-1	**4c**	
5 Net earnings (loss) from self-employment. Combine lines 3c and 4c. Enter here and on Schedule K, line 15a	**5**	

c. Based on the previous information, complete the partial Schedule K-1, Form 1065, presented on the next two pages for Dexter.

19. The income statement of Murphy and Earey, a partnership, reveals a net income of $72,500 for the current calendar year. Included in the income reported are dividends from domestic corporations amounting to $1,500; net long-term capital gains of $2,500; dividends received from foreign corporations amounting to $2,024; and taxable interest amounting to $2,500. Salary payments of $15,000 and $18,000 were paid to Murphy and Earey, respectively, and charitable contributions of $3,000 (50% type) were treated as expenses in determining net income. Complete the following schedule of items that should be reported by the partnership on Form 1065 (assuming the partnership must file Schedule K):

Line 10   Guaranteed payments to partners . . . . $ ___________

Line 22   Ordinary income . . . . $ ___________

Schedule K: . . . . $ ___________

Line 4b   Dividends income . . . . $ ___________

Line 4e   Net long-term capital gain (loss) . . . . $ ___________

Line 8   Charitable contributions . . . . $ ___________

SCHEDULE K-1
(Form 1065)
Department of the Treasury
Internal Revenue Service

Partner's Share of Income, Credits, Deductions, Etc.

▶ See separate instructions.

OMB No. 1545-0099

1992

For calendar year 1992 or tax year beginning ________ , 1992, and ending ________ , 19 ___

Partner's identifying number ▶ ________

Partnership's identifying number ▶ ________

Partner's name, address, and ZIP code

Partnership's name, address, and ZIP code

A Is this partner a general partner? . . . ☐ Yes ☐ No

B Partner's share of liabilities (see instructions):

Nonrecourse . . . . $ ________

Qualified nonrecourse financing . . $ ________

Other . . . . $ ________

C What type of entity is this partner? . ▶ ________

D Is this partner a ☐ domestic or a ☐ foreign partner?

E IRS Center where partnership filed return:

F Enter partner's percentage of:

	(i) Before change or termination	(ii) End of year
Profit sharing	________ %	________ %
Loss sharing	________ %	________ %
Ownership of capital	________ %	________ %

G(1) Tax shelter registration number . ▶ ________

(2) Type of tax shelter ▶ ________

H Check here if this partnership is a publicly traded partnership as defined in section 469(k)(2) . . . . ☐

I Check applicable boxes: **(1)** ☐ Final K-1 **(2)** ☐ Amended K-1

J Analysis of partner's capital account:

(a) Capital account at beginning of year	(b) Capital contributed during year	(c) Partner's share of lines 3, 4, and 7, Form 1065, Schedule M-2	(d) Withdrawals and distributions	(e) Capital account at end of year (combine columns (a) through (d))
			( )	

	(a) Distributive share item		(b) Amount	(c) 1040 filers enter the amount in column (b) on:
Income (Loss)	**1** Ordinary income (loss) from trade or business activities	**1**		
	2 Net income (loss) from rental real estate activities	**2**		See Partner's Instructions for Schedule K-1 (Form 1065).
	3 Net income (loss) from other rental activities	**3**		
	4 Portfolio income (loss):			
	a Interest	**4a**		Sch. B, Part I, line 1
	b Dividends	**4b**		Sch. B, Part II, line 5
	c Royalties	**4c**		Sch. E, Part I, line 4
	d Net short-term capital gain (loss)	**4d**		Sch. D, line 5, col. (f) or (g)
	e Net long-term capital gain (loss)	**4e**		Sch. D, line 13, col. (f) or (g)
	f Other portfolio income (loss) (attach schedule)	**4f**		(Enter on applicable line of your return.)
	5 Guaranteed payments to partner	**5**		See Partner's Instructions for Schedule K-1 (Form 1065).
	6 Net gain (loss) under section 1231 (other than due to casualty or theft)	**6**		
	7 Other income (loss) (attach schedule)	**7**		(Enter on applicable line of your return.)
Deductions	**8** Charitable contributions (see instructions) (attach schedule)	**8**		Sch. A, line 13 or 14
	9 Section 179 expense deduction	**9**		See Partner's Instructions for Schedule K-1 (Form 1065).
	10 Deductions related to portfolio income (attach schedule)	**10**		
	11 Other deductions (attach schedule)	**11**		
Investment Interest	**12a** Interest expense on investment debts	**12a**		Form 4952, line 1
	b (1) Investment income included on lines 4a through 4f above	**b(1)**		See Partner's Instructions for Schedule K-1 (Form 1065).
	(2) Investment expenses included on line 10 above	**b(2)**		
Credits	**13a** Credit for income tax withheld	**13a**		See Partner's Instructions for Schedule K-1 (Form 1065).
	b Low-income housing credit:			
	(1) From section 42(j)(5) partnerships for property placed in service before 1990	**b(1)**		
	(2) Other than on line 13b(1) for property placed in service before 1990	**b(2)**		Form 8586, line 5
	(3) From section 42(j)(5) partnerships for property placed in service after 1989	**b(3)**		
	(4) Other than on line 13b(3) for property placed in service after 1989	**b(4)**		
	c Qualified rehabilitation expenditures related to rental real estate activities (see instructions)	**13c**		
	d Credits (other than credits shown on lines 13b and 13c) related to rental real estate activities (see instructions)	**13d**		See Partner's Instructions for Schedule K-1 (Form 1065).
	e Credits related to other rental activities (see instructions)	**13e**		
	14 Other credits (see instructions)	**14**		

For Paperwork Reduction Act Notice, see Instructions for Form 1065.   Cat. No. 11394R   Schedule K-1 (Form 1065) 1992

Schedule K-1 (Form 1065) 1992   Page **2**

	(a) Distributive share item		(b) Amount	(c) 1040 filers enter the amount in column (b) on:
Self-employment	**15a** Net earnings (loss) from self-employment	**15a**		Sch. SE, Section A or B
	b Gross farming or fishing income	**15b**		} See Partner's Instructions for Schedule K-1 (Form 1065).)
	c Gross nonfarm income	**15c**		
Adjustments and Tax Preference Items	**16a** Depreciation adjustment on property placed in service after 1986	**16a**		(See Partner's Instructions for Schedule K-1 (Form 1065) and Instructions for Form 6251.)
	b Adjusted gain or loss	**16b**		
	c Depletion (other than oil and gas)	**16c**		
	d (1) Gross income from oil, gas, and geothermal properties	**d(1)**		
	(2) Deductions allocable to oil, gas, and geothermal properties	**d(2)**		
	e Other adjustments and tax preference items *(attach schedule)*	**16e**		
Foreign Taxes	**17a** Type of income ▶			Form 1116, Check boxes
	b Name of foreign country or U.S. possession ▶			
	c Total gross income from sources outside the U.S. *(attach schedule)*	**17c**		} Form 1116, Part I
	d Total applicable deductions and losses *(attach schedule)*	**17d**		
	e Total foreign taxes (check one): ▶ ☐ Paid ☐ Accrued	**17e**		Form 1116, Part II
	f Reduction in taxes available for credit *(attach schedule)*	**17f**		Form 1116, Part III
	g Other foreign tax information *(attach schedule)*	**17g**		See Instructions for Form 1116.
Other	**18a** Total expenditures to which a section 59(e) election may apply	**18a**		See Partner's Instructions for Schedule K-1 (Form 1065).
	b Type of expenditures ▶			
	19 Tax-exempt interest income	**19**		Form 1040, line 8b
	20 Other tax-exempt income	**20**		(See Partner's Instructions for Schedule K-1 (Form 1065).)
	21 Nondeductible expenses	**21**		
	22 Recapture of low-income housing credit:			
	a From section 42(j)(5) partnerships	**22a**		} Form 8611, line 8
	b Other than on line 22a	**22b**		

23 Supplemental information required to be reported separately to each partner *(attach additional schedules if more space is needed):*

20. George Murphy, who is entitled to one-half of the income of the partnership referred to in Problem 19, had the following income from other sources during the current calendar year:

Salary received from a corporation of which he is an officer	$25,000
Dividends from domestic corporations	300
Interest on notes receivable (portfolio income)	600

You ascertain the following additional information:

Various deductible taxes paid during year, total	$ 2,640
Interest paid on mortgage on residence	420
Contributions to charitable organizations (50% type)	1,800
Income taxes withheld from salary by corporation	5,180
Amount paid on declaration of estimated tax	10,000

Mr. Murphy is married and living with his wife who has no separate income. Both are under 65 years of age. They have two dependent children for whom they are entitled to exemptions.

Prepare a statement showing the calculation of Murphy's income tax liability for the year, assuming that a joint return is filed by him and his wife and that four exemptions are claimed.

21. On January 3, 1992, Jack Elvers and Ellen Ford formed a partnership for the purpose of operating a mercantile business at 1425 Tryon Street, Charlotte, North Carolina 28201-1301. Elvers invested $15,000 in cash as a capital contribution, and Ford contributed $8,000 in cash and $22,000 in merchandise upon which was owed accounts payable of $5,000. The firm accepted the liability and Ford received credit for $25,000. The agreement provided that Elvers was to participate in the partnership on a full-time basis and Ford on a half-time basis. It was agreed further that Elvers would receive a salary of $31,600 and Ford $18,000, and that each would receive 6% interest on their individual initial capital investment before dividing the remaining profits on the basis of 60% to Elvers and 40% to Ford.

You are employed as an accountant to prepare an income tax return for the calendar year 1992, the first year of operations. Use the Form 1065 on pages 549 through 552. Prepare Schedule K-1 for Jack Elvers on pages 553 and 554. Elvers' SSN is 299-84-1945. The partnership return is signed by Elvers on April 10, 1993.

The trial balance appearing on the next page was prepared as of December 31 after all necessary adjustments had been made except for merchandise inventory. The inventory appearing on the trial balance is the beginning inventory. The inventory at December 31 is $30,000.

The accounts for the partners entitled "Drawing" represent withdrawals in addition to their respective salaries. EIN is 31-0906034; Business Code No. is 5963.

There were no changes in the manner of determining quantities, costs, or valuations between the opening and closing inventories. (Valuation was at cost.) The appropriate Form 1096 and Form 1099 were filed for the interest paid during the year with the Internal Revenue Service Center, Memphis, TN 38110. The accounting method is the accrual method.

Worthless accounts amounting to $800 were written off directly to expense during the year.

Depreciation was calculated by MACRS on equipment costing $28,000. Cost recovery on the equipment for the year, based on MACRS with a 7-year life and a half-year convention, was $4,000. The equipment had been acquired new on January 4, 1992.

Charitable contributions are subject to the 50% limitation. Stock in ZMT Corporation was sold on October 3, 1992, for $2,900. The stock had cost $1,700 when purchased on March 29, 1990.

(For the balance sheet at the beginning of the year in Schedule L, use the data given in the original investment.)

ELVERS AND FORD
Trial Balance
December 31, 1992

Cash	$ 11,017	
Notes receivable	2,500	
Accrued interest receivable	50	
Accounts receivable	15,000	
Merchandise inventory	22,000	
Equipment (purchased January 4, 1992)	28,000	
Accumulated depreciation—equipment		$ 4,000
Prepaid insurance	500	
Supplies on hand	150	
Prepaid advertising	250	
Notes payable (to banks)		5,000
Accounts payable		8,797
Accrued liabilities		1,880
E. W. Elvers, Capital		15,000
E. W. Elvers, Drawing	2,000	
C. R. Ford, Capital		25,000
C. R. Ford, Drawing	3,200	
Sales		202,000
Sales returns and allowances	3,000	
Sales discounts	1,500	
Gain on sale of stock		1,200
Purchases	82,000	
Purchases discounts		1,300
Interest expense	300	
Partners' interest	2,400	
Partners' salaries	49,600	
Office and store salaries	14,300	
Rent expense	6,500	
Office expense	3,000	
Depreciation expense	4,000	
Property taxes (incurred in business)	383	
Payroll taxes	4,052	
Delivery expense	2,010	
Bad debts expense	800	
Store expenses	2,600	
Advertising expense	2,705	
Taxable interest income		200
Charitable contributions	560	
Total	$264,377	$264,377

Form **1065**	**U.S. Partnership Return of Income**	OMB No. 1545-0099
Department of the Treasury Internal Revenue Service	For calendar year 1992, or tax year beginning .... , 1992, and ending .... , 19 .... . ▶ See separate instructions.	**1992**

A Principal business activity	Use the IRS label. Otherwise, please print or type.	Name of partnership	D Employer identification number
B Principal product or service		Number, street, and room or suite no. (If a P.O. box, see page 9 of the instructions.)	E Date business started
C Business code number		City or town, state, and ZIP code	F Total assets (see Specific Instructions) $

G Check applicable boxes: **(1)** ☐ Initial return **(2)** ☐ Final return **(3)** ☐ Change in address **(4)** ☐ Amended return
H Check accounting method: **(1)** ☐ Cash **(2)** ☐ Accrual **(3)** ☐ Other (specify) ▶ ....
I Number of partners in this partnership . . . . ▶ ....

Caution: *Include* **only** *trade or business income and expenses on lines 1a through 22 below. See the instructions for more information.*

Income

1a	Gross receipts or sales	1a	
b	Minus returns and allowances	1b	1c
2	Cost of goods sold (Schedule A, line 8)		2
3	Gross profit. Subtract line 2 from line 1c		3
4	Ordinary income (loss) from other partnerships and fiduciaries *(attach schedule)* . . .		4
5	Net farm profit (loss) *(attach Schedule F (Form 1040))*		5
6	Net gain (loss) from Form 4797, Part II, line 20 .		6
7	Other income (loss) (see instructions) *(attach schedule)* . . .		7
8	**Total income (loss).** Combine lines 3 through 7		8

Deductions (see instructions for limitations)

9a	Salaries and wages (other than to partners) .	9a	
b	Minus jobs credit	9b	9c
10	Guaranteed payments to partners		10
11	Repairs		11
12	Bad debts		12
13	Rent		13
14	Taxes		14
15	Interest		15
16a	Depreciation (see instructions)	16a	
b	Minus depreciation reported on Schedule A and elsewhere on return	16b	16c
17	Depletion **(Do not deduct oil and gas depletion.)**		17
18	Retirement plans, etc.		18
19	Employee benefit programs		19
20	Other deductions *(attach schedule)*		20
21	**Total deductions.** Add the amounts shown in the far right column for lines 9c through 20 .		21
22	**Ordinary income (loss)** from trade or business activities. Subtract line 21 from line 8 . .		22

Please Sign Here

Under penalties of perjury, I declare that I have examined this return, including accompanying schedules and statements, and to the best of my knowledge and belief, it is true, correct, and complete. Declaration of preparer (other than general partner) is based on all information of which preparer has any knowledge.

▶ ________________ ▶ ________________
   Signature of general partner   Date

Paid Preparer's Use Only

Preparer's signature ▶	Date	Check if self-employed ▶ ☐	Preparer's social security no.
Firm's name (or yours if self-employed) and address ▶		E.I. No. ▶	
		ZIP code ▶	

For Paperwork Reduction Act Notice, see page 1 of separate instructions.   Cat. No. 11390Z   Form **1065** (1992)

Form 1065 (1992)   Page **2**

Schedule A   Cost of Goods Sold

1 Inventory at beginning of year	**1**	
2 Purchases minus cost of items withdrawn for personal use.	**2**	
3 Cost of labor	**3**	
4 Additional section 263A costs (see instructions) *(attach schedule)*	**4**	
5 Other costs *(attach schedule)*.	**5**	
6 **Total.** Add lines 1 through 5	**6**	
7 Inventory at end of year	**7**	
8 **Cost of goods sold.** Subtract line 7 from line 6. Enter here and on page 1, line 2	**8**	

9a Check all methods used for valuing closing inventory:

    (i) ☐ Cost

    (ii) ☐ Lower of cost or market as described in Regulations section 1.471-4

    (iii) ☐ Writedown of "subnormal" goods as described in Regulations section 1.471-2(c)

    (iv) ☐ Other (specify method used and attach explanation) ▶ ....

  b Check this box if the LIFO inventory method was adopted this tax year for any goods *(if checked, attach Form 970)* . ▶ ☐

  c Do the rules of section 263A (for property produced or acquired for resale) apply to the partnership? . . ☐ **Yes** ☐ **No**

  d Was there any change in determining quantities, cost, or valuations between opening and closing inventory? ☐ **Yes** ☐ **No**
    If "Yes," attach explanation.

Schedule B   Other Information

	Yes	No
1 Is this partnership a limited partnership?		
2 Are any partners in this partnership also partnerships?		
3 Is this partnership a partner in another partnership?		
4 Is this partnership subject to the consolidated audit procedures of sections 6221 through 6233? If "Yes," see **Designation of Tax Matters Partner** below.		
5 Does this partnership meet **ALL THREE** of the following requirements?		
a The partnership's total receipts for the tax year were less than $250,000;		
b The partnership's total assets at the end of the tax year were less than $250,000; **AND**		
c Schedules K-1 are filed with the return and furnished to the partners on or before the due date (including extensions) for the partnership return.		
If "Yes," the partnership is not required to complete Schedules L, M-1, and M-2; Item F on page 1 of Form 1065; or Item J on Schedule K-1		
6 Does this partnership have any foreign partners?		
7 Is this partnership a publicly traded partnership as defined in section 469(k)(2)?		
8 Has this partnership filed, or is it required to file, **Form 8264**, Application for Registration of a Tax Shelter? .		
9 At any time during the calendar year 1992, did the partnership have an interest in or a signature or other authority over a financial account in a foreign country (such as a bank account, securities account, or other financial account)? (See the instructions for exceptions and filing requirements for form TD F 90-22.1.) If "Yes," enter the name of the foreign country. ▶		
10 Was the partnership the grantor of, or transferor to, a foreign trust that existed during the current tax year, whether or not the partnership or any partner has any beneficial interest in it? If "Yes," you may have to file Forms 3520, 3520-A, or 926		
11 Was there a distribution of property or a transfer (e.g., by sale or death) of a partnership interest during the tax year? If "Yes," you may elect to adjust the basis of the partnership's assets under section 754 by attaching the statement described under **Elections** on page 5 of the instructions		
12 Was this partnership in operation at the end of 1992?		
13 How many months in 1992 was this partnership actively operated? ▶		

Designation of Tax Matters Partner (See instructions.)

Enter below the general partner designated as the tax matters partner (TMP) for the tax year of this return:

Name of
designated TMP ▶ _______________________________   Identifying
number of TMP ▶ _______________________

Address of
designated TMP ▶ ____

Form 1065 (1992)

Page **3**

Schedule K	**Partners' Shares of Income, Credits, Deductions, Etc.**		
	(a) Distributive share items		**(b) Total amount**

Income (Loss)

1	Ordinary income (loss) from trade or business activities (page 1, line 22)	**1**	
2	Net income (loss) from rental real estate activities *(attach Form 8825)*	**2**	
3a	Gross income from other rental activities **3a**		
b	Minus expenses *(attach schedule)* **3b**		
c	Net income (loss) from other rental activities	**3c**	
4	Portfolio income (loss) (see instructions): a Interest income	**4a**	
b	Dividend income	**4b**	
c	Royalty income	**4c**	
d	Net short-term capital gain (loss) *(attach Schedule D (Form 1065))*	**4d**	
e	Net long-term capital gain (loss) *(attach Schedule D (Form 1065))*	**4e**	
f	Other portfolio income (loss) *(attach schedule)*	**4f**	
5	Guaranteed payments to partners	**5**	
6	Net gain (loss) under section 1231 (other than due to casualty or theft) *(attach Form 4797)*	**6**	
7	Other income (loss) *(attach schedule)*	**7**	

Deductions

8	Charitable contributions (see instructions) *(attach schedule)*	**8**	
9	Section 179 expense deduction *(attach Form 4562)*	**9**	
10	Deductions related to portfolio income (see instructions) (itemize)	**10**	
11	Other deductions *(attach schedule)*	**11**	

Investment Interest

12a	Interest expense on investment debts	**12a**	
b	(1) Investment income included on lines 4a through 4f above	**12b(1)**	
	(2) Investment expenses included on line 10 above	**12b(2)**	

Credits

13a	Credit for income tax withheld	**13a**	
b	Low-income housing credit (see instructions):		
	(1) From partnerships to which section 42(j)(5) applies for property placed in service before 1990	**13b(1)**	
	(2) Other than on line 13b(1) for property placed in service before 1990	**13b(2)**	
	(3) From partnerships to which section 42(j)(5) applies for property placed in service after 1989	**13b(3)**	
	(4) Other than on line 13b(3) for property placed in service after 1989	**13b(4)**	
c	Qualified rehabilitation expenditures related to rental real estate activities *(attach Form 3468)*	**13c**	
d	Credits (other than credits shown on lines 13b and 13c) related to rental real estate activities (see instructions)	**13d**	
e	Credits related to other rental activities (see instructions)	**13e**	
14	Other credits (see instructions)	**14**	

Self-Employment

15a	Net earnings (loss) from self-employment	**15a**	
b	Gross farming or fishing income	**15b**	
c	Gross nonfarm income	**15c**	

Adjustments and Tax Preference Items

16a	Depreciation adjustment on property placed in service after 1986	**16a**	
b	Adjusted gain or loss	**16b**	
c	Depletion (other than oil and gas)	**16c**	
d	(1) Gross income from oil, gas, and geothermal properties	**16d(1)**	
	(2) Deductions allocable to oil, gas, and geothermal properties	**16d(2)**	
e	Other adjustments and tax preference items *(attach schedule)*	**16e**	

Foreign Taxes

17a	Type of income ▶ .... b Foreign country or U.S. possession ▶		
c	Total gross income from sources outside the United States. *(attach schedule)*	**17c**	
d	Total applicable deductions and losses *(attach schedule)*	**17d**	
e	Total foreign taxes (check one): ▶ ☐ Paid ☐ Accrued	**17e**	
f	Reduction in taxes available for credit *(attach schedule)*	**17f**	
g	Other foreign tax information *(attach schedule)*	**17g**	

Other

18a	Total expenditures to which a section 59(e) election may apply	**18a**	
b	Type of expenditures ▶		
19	Tax-exempt interest income	**19**	
20	Other tax-exempt income	**20**	
21	Nondeductible expenses	**21**	
22	Other items and amounts required to be reported separately to partners (see instructions) *(attach schedule)*		

Analysis

23a	Income (loss). Combine lines 1 through 7 in column (b). From the result, subtract the sum of lines 8 through 12a, 17e, and 18a	**23a**	

b Analysis by type of partner:	(a) Corporate	(b) Individual		(c) Partnership	(d) Exempt organization	(e) Nominee/Other
		i. Active	ii. Passive			
(1) General partners						
(2) Limited partners						

Form 1065 (1992)   Page **4**

Caution: *If Question 5 of Schedule B is answered "Yes," the partnership is not required to complete Schedules L, M-1, and M-2.*

Schedule L   Balance Sheets

Assets	Beginning of tax year		End of tax year	
	(a)	(b)	(c)	(d)
1 Cash				
2a Trade notes and accounts receivable				
b Minus allowance for bad debts				
3 Inventories				
4 U.S. government obligations				
5 Tax-exempt securities				
6 Other current assets *(attach schedule)*				
7 Mortgage and real estate loans				
8 Other investments *(attach schedule)*				
9a Buildings and other depreciable assets				
b Minus accumulated depreciation				
10a Depletable assets				
b Minus accumulated depletion				
11 Land (net of any amortization)				
12a Intangible assets (amortizable only)				
b Minus accumulated amortization				
13 Other assets *(attach schedule)*				
14 **Total** assets				
Liabilities and Capital				
15 Accounts payable				
16 Mortgages, notes, bonds payable in less than 1 year				
17 Other current liabilities *(attach schedule)*				
18 All nonrecourse loans				
19 Mortgages, notes, bonds payable in 1 year or more				
20 Other liabilities *(attach schedule)*				
21 Partners' capital accounts				
22 **Total** liabilities and capital				

Schedule M-1   Reconciliation of Income (Loss) per Books With Income (Loss) per Return (see instructions)

1 Net income (loss) per books	6 Income recorded on books this year not included on Schedule K, lines 1 through 7 (itemize):
2 Income included on Schedule K, lines 1 through 7, not recorded on books this year (itemize):	a Tax-exempt interest $ ....
3 Guaranteed payments (other than health insurance)	7 Deductions included on Schedule K, lines 1 through 12a, 17e, and 18a, not charged against book income this year (itemize):
4 Expenses recorded on books this year not included on Schedule K, lines 1 through 12a, 17e, and 18a (itemize):	a Depreciation $ ....
a Depreciation $	
b Travel and entertainment $	
	8 Total of lines 6 and 7
5 Total of lines 1 through 4	9 Income (loss) (Schedule K, line 23a). Subtract line 8 from line 5

Schedule M-2   Analysis of Partners' Capital Accounts

1 Balance at beginning of year	6 Distributions: a Cash
2 Capital contributed during year	b Property
3 Net income (loss) per books	7 Other decreases (itemize): ....
4 Other increases (itemize):	
	8 Total of lines 6 and 7
5 Total of lines 1 through 4	9 Balance at end of year. Subtract line 8 from line 5

SCHEDULE K-1
(Form 1065)
Department of the Treasury
Internal Revenue Service

Partner's Share of Income, Credits, Deductions, Etc.
▶ See separate instructions.

For calendar year 1992 or tax year beginning   , 1992, and ending   , 19

OMB No. 1545-0099

1992

Partner's identifying number ▶

Partnership's identifying number ▶

Partner's name, address, and ZIP code

Partnership's name, address, and ZIP code

A Is this partner a general partner? . . . ☐ Yes ☐ No

B Partner's share of liabilities (see instructions):

Nonrecourse . . . .$ ....

Qualified nonrecourse financing . .$ ....

Other . . . .$ ....

C What type of entity is this partner? ▶ ....

D Is this partner a ☐ domestic or a ☐ foreign partner?

E IRS Center where partnership filed return:

F Enter partner's percentage of:

	(i) Before change or termination	(ii) End of year
Profit sharing	.... %	.... %
Loss sharing	.... %	.... %
Ownership of capital	.... %	.... %

G(1) Tax shelter registration number · ▶ ....

(2) Type of tax shelter ▶ ....

H Check here if this partnership is a publicly traded partnership as defined in section 469(k)(2) . . . . ☐

I Check applicable boxes: **(1)** ☐ Final K-1 **(2)** ☐ Amended K-1

J Analysis of partner's capital account:

(a) Capital account at beginning of year	(b) Capital contributed during year	(c) Partner's share of lines 3, 4, and 7, Form 1065, Schedule M-2	(d) Withdrawals and distributions	(e) Capital account at end of year (combine columns (a) through (d))
			( )	

(a) Distributive share item	(b) Amount	(c) 1040 filers enter the amount in column (b) on:
1 Ordinary income (loss) from trade or business activities	**1**	
2 Net income (loss) from rental real estate activities	**2**	See Partner's Instructions for Schedule K-1 (Form 1065).
3 Net income (loss) from other rental activities	**3**	
4 Portfolio income (loss):		
a Interest	**4a**	Sch. B, Part I, line 1
b Dividends	**4b**	Sch. B, Part II, line 5
c Royalties	**4c**	Sch. E, Part I, line 4
d Net short-term capital gain (loss)	**4d**	Sch. D, line 5, col. (f) or (g)
e Net long-term capital gain (loss)	**4e**	Sch. D, line 13, col. (f) or (g)
f Other portfolio income (loss) *(attach schedule)*	**4f**	(Enter on applicable line of your return.)
5 Guaranteed payments to partner	**5**	See Partner's Instructions for Schedule K-1 (Form 1065).
6 Net gain (loss) under section 1231 (other than due to casualty or theft)	**6**	
7 Other income (loss) *(attach schedule)*	**7**	(Enter on applicable line of your return.)
8 Charitable contributions (see instructions) *(attach schedule)*	**8**	Sch. A, line 13 or 14
9 Section 179 expense deduction	**9**	See Partner's Instructions for Schedule K-1 (Form 1065).
10 Deductions related to portfolio income *(attach schedule)*	**10**	
11 Other deductions *(attach schedule)*	**11**	
12a Interest expense on investment debts	**12a**	Form 4952, line 1
b (1) Investment income included on lines 4a through 4f above	**b(1)**	See Partner's Instructions for Schedule K-1 (Form 1065).
(2) Investment expenses included on line 10 above	**b(2)**	
13a Credit for income tax withheld	**13a**	See Partner's Instructions for Schedule K-1 (Form 1065).
b Low-income housing credit:		
(1) From section 42(j)(5) partnerships for property placed in service before 1990	**b(1)**	
(2) Other than on line 13b(1) for property placed in service before 1990	**b(2)**	Form 8586, line 5
(3) From section 42(j)(5) partnerships for property placed in service after 1989	**b(3)**	
(4) Other than on line 13b(3) for property placed in service after 1989	**b(4)**	
c Qualified rehabilitation expenditures related to rental real estate activities (see instructions)	**13c**	
d Credits (other than credits shown on lines 13b and 13c) related to rental real estate activities (see instructions)	**13d**	See Partner's Instructions for Schedule K-1 (Form 1065).
e Credits related to other rental activities (see instructions)	**13e**	
14 Other credits (see instructions)	**14**	

Income (Loss) — *Deductions* — *Investment Interest* — *Credits*

For Paperwork Reduction Act Notice, see Instructions for Form 1065.   Cat. No. 11394R   **Schedule K-1 (Form 1065) 1992**

Proof as of August 14, 1992 (subject to change)

Schedule K-1 (Form 1065) 1992　　　　　　　　　　　　　　　　　　　　　　Page **2**

	(a) Distributive share item		(b) Amount	(c) 1040 filers enter the amount in column (b) on:
Self-employment	**15a** Net earnings (loss) from self-employment	15a		Sch. SE, Section A or B
	b Gross farming or fishing income	15b		(See Partner's Instructions for Schedule K-1 (Form 1065).)
	c Gross nonfarm income	15c		
Adjustments and Tax Preference Items	**16a** Depreciation adjustment on property placed in service after 1986	16a		(See Partner's Instructions for Schedule K-1 (Form 1065) and Instructions for Form 6251.)
	b Adjusted gain or loss	16b		
	c Depletion (other than oil and gas)	16c		
	d (1) Gross income from oil, gas, and geothermal properties	d(1)		
	(2) Deductions allocable to oil, gas, and geothermal properties	d(2)		
	e Other adjustments and tax preference items *(attach schedule)*	16e		
Foreign Taxes	**17a** Type of income ▶			Form 1116, Check boxes
	b Name of foreign country or U.S. possession ▶			
	c Total gross income from sources outside the U.S. *(attach schedule)*	17c		Form 1116, Part I
	d Total applicable deductions and losses *(attach schedule)*	17d		
	e Total foreign taxes (check one): ▶ ☐ Paid ☐ Accrued	17e		Form 1116, Part II
	f Reduction in taxes available for credit *(attach schedule)*	17f		Form 1116, Part III
	g Other foreign tax information *(attach schedule)*	17g		See Instructions for Form 1116.
Other	**18a** Total expenditures to which a section 59(e) election may apply	18a		See Partner's Instructions for Schedule K-1 (Form 1065).
	b Type of expenditures ▶			
	19 Tax-exempt interest income	19		Form 1040, line 8b
	20 Other tax-exempt income	20		(See Partner's Instructions for Schedule K-1 (Form 1065).)
	21 Nondeductible expenses	21		
	22 Recapture of low-income housing credit:			
	a From section 42(j)(5) partnerships	22a		Form 8611, line 8
	b Other than on line 22a	22b		
Supplemental Information	**23** Supplemental information required to be reported separately to each partner *(attach additional schedules if more space is needed):*			

S Corporations

Your Rights as a Taxpayer

Examination by Interview. You have the right to ask that the examination take place at a reasonable time and place that is convenient for both you and the IRS.

Source: Internal Revenue Service, Publication 1

A business organized as a sole proprietorship is not a separate taxable entity. The net income or loss of the business is reported in the tax return of the owner of the business, where it is combined with the other income, other deductions, and exemptions. Also, a business organized as a partnership is not a separate taxable entity. The partnership is required to file a return for informational purposes and the individual partners report their distributive shares in their own tax returns. In contrast to a sole proprietorship or a partnership, a business organized as a corporation is a separate taxable entity. It exists apart from its owners (shareholders) and is required to pay a tax on its income.

However, there is one significant exception to the requirement that a corporation pay a tax on its taxable income. Under the provisions in the Internal Revenue Code for *S corporations* (Subchapter S), a closely held corporation may elect not to be taxed as a corporation. Sometimes shareholders can choose to pay the tax on a corporation's income. When this treatment is elected, shareholders (individuals, estates, and certain trusts) include in their own tax returns their proportionate share of the current taxable income of the corporation, whether distributed or not, and the corporation pays no income tax. A corporation must meet the definition of a "small business corporation" to qualify as an S corporation, as described in subsequent paragraphs.

For tax years beginning in 1983 and later, the character of all items of income, deductions, losses, and credits are the same in the hands of the shareholders as they were when created in the corporation. The passing through of individual items of income, deductions, etc., is often referred to as the *conduit principle*. The conduit principle now applies to S corporations in the same manner that it applies to partnerships discussed in Chapter 15.

Like a partnership, an S corporation must file an annual tax return, Form 1120S, U.S. Income Tax Return for an S Corporation, which is due on March 15 for calendar-year corporations. This return, which usually is an information return only, shows the calculation of income taxable to shareholders and includes a Schedule K-1 to inform shareholders how individual items of income, deductions, losses, and credits must be reported on their individual tax returns.

It should be noted, however, that even though an S corporation pays no income tax, it is a corporation in all other respects under state law and must act accordingly. This means that the owners can choose the S corporation form of organization for such nontax reasons as limited liability and still have the benefit of the conduit principle for the purpose of taxing income. It also should be noted that some states do not recognize S corporation status in filing a corporation tax return under state law. In such states, the corporation must file a regular corporation tax return and pay a state corporation tax even if the corporation is not required to pay a federal corporation tax.

Election of S Corporation Status

A corporation may elect S corporation status with the consent of all shareholders at any time during the prior taxable year or on or before the fifteenth day of the third month of the current year. If the election is made after the expiration of the fifteenth day of the third month and before the fifteenth day of the third month of the next taxable year, it will be effective for the following tax year.

Each of these characteristics and other requirements to operate as an S corporation are described below:

1. An S corporation must be a domestic corporation. The corporation must either be organized in the United States or organized under federal or state law. The term "corporation" includes a joint-stock company, certain insurance companies, or an association that has the characteristics of a

corporation. Certain domestic corporations are ineligible to elect S corporation status, such as a member of an affiliated group, a DISC (Domestic International Sales Corporation), financial institutions, and certain insurance companies.

2. The corporation must have only one class of stock. One class of stock generally means that the outstanding shares of the corporation must be identical as to the rights of the holders in the distribution rights (profits) and in the liquidation rights to the assets of the corporation. Stock may have differences in voting rights and still be treated as one class of stock. Authorized but unissued stock and treasury stock are not considered in determining whether an S corporation has more than one class of stock. The existence of outstanding stock options, warrants to acquire stock, or convertible debentures will not, by themselves, be considered a second class of stock. An S corporation may execute a stock purchase agreement between itself and the shareholders that does not affect the shareholders' rights in the corporation's profits and assets and therefore does not create a second class of stock.

Whether all outstanding shares confer identical rights is determined based on the articles of incorporation, bylaws, applicable state law, and any binding agreement relating to distribution or liquidation proceeds. A commercial contract is not a governing provision unless a principal purpose of the agreement is to circumvent the one-class-of-stock requirement.

Debt obligations of a corporation that are actually contributions of equity capital may be treated as a second class of stock. However, straight debt would not be considered to be a second class of stock. Straight debt means any written unconditional promise to pay a fixed amount on demand or at a specific time if it meets the following conditions:

  a. The interest rate and interest payment dates should not be contingent on profits or be at the borrower's discretion.
  b. The debt cannot be converted directly or indirectly into stock.
  c. The creditor is an individual, an estate, or a trust, any of which are eligible to hold stock in an S corporation.

A personal financial planner recommends that a stockholder make gifts of his S corporation stock to his children to help minimize his estate tax liability at death. The stockholder agrees that this is a good idea, but does not want to pass his controlling interest in the S corporation to the children. The solution to this problem is to have the S corporation issue stock with limited or no voting rights to the stockholder who, in turn, can make gifts of such stock to his children without giving up control by retaining stock with voting rights. In this situation, the corporation will not be treated as having more than one class of stock as long as the governing provisions provide for identical distributions and liquidation rights.

3. An S corporation may have up to 35 shareholders. This requirement is designed to limit S corporation status to small, closely-held companies. S corporation shareholders must all be individuals (or an estate or eligible trust), and no shareholder may be a nonresident alien. Partnerships and corporations are not allowed to be shareholders in an S corporation since this would be an indirect way of avoiding the 35 shareholder limit. A husband and wife are counted as one shareholder, as well as their estates, for purposes of determining the number of shareholders, regardless of whether the stock is owned jointly or individually. If the stock in an S corporation is held by a trust, each owner of the trust is considered to be a shareholder, not the trust itself. Thus, other than a husband and a wife, including their estate, everyone else who owns stock in the S corporation is counted as a separate shareholder even if a shareholder's stock is owned jointly with someone else. All shareholders must be citizens or residents of the United States.

John and Mary, a married couple, each own shares in an S corporation individually. The corporation has 35 shareholders counting John and Mary as one shareholder since they are a married couple. If John and Mary obtain a divorce and each retains their respective shares in the S corporation, the corporation would now have 36 shareholders which would disqualify the corporation as an S corporation. Likewise, if John dies and his two children inherit his S corporation shares, the children would each be counted as a shareholder which would exceed the 35-shareholder limit.

4. To be treated as an S corporation, the corporation must file Form 2553, Election by a Small Business Corporation, to indicate its election of S corporation status. The corporation must meet all of the requirements of S corporation status when it files Form 2553. Form 2553 should also be used to file shareholders' consent (see Requirement 5 below) and to select a tax year.

Form 2553 should be filed with the IRS Center where the corporation intends to file its annual tax return. The election of S corporation status is effective for a particular tax year if Form 2553 is filed (1) any time during the previous tax year or (2) by the fifteenth day of the third month of the tax year designated in the election. An election becomes effective only at the beginning of the tax year.

EXAMPLE 3 ————————————————

The shareholders elect S corporation status on March 1, 1993 by filing Form 2553. The election normally would be effective for the calendar year beginning January 1, 1993. The last date an election can be made for a tax year starting with the current calendar year tax would be March 15, 1993. An election made on March 16 or later would not be effective until the beginning of the next calendar year. See Requirement 5 below for shareholder consent procedures to make the S corporation election valid.

5. All of the shareholders must consent to the election to be an S corporation. A shareholder's consent is binding and may be withdrawn only by following prescribed procedures. Shareholders execute a consent by providing all of the required information presented on Form 2553, Election by a Small Business Corporation, and appropriately signing the form. All shareholders must consent at the time Form 2553 is filed. If the consent is filed after the beginning of the tax year for which it is to be effective, all shareholders in the corporation who held stock on any day in the tax year before the date on which Form 2553 is filed must also consent.

An election made during the first 2½ months of the tax year is considered to have been made for the following tax year if one or more persons who held stock in the corporation during the current tax year before the election was made did not consent to the election. Shareholders may also consent by signing a separate consent statement which should be attached to Form 2553. The separate consent should provide the following information:

a. The name, address, and identification number of the corporation

b. The name, address, and identification number of the shareholder

c. The number of shares owned by the shareholder and the dates on which acquired

d. The day and month of the end of each shareholder's tax year

The corporation's election of S corporation status is invalid if any consent is not filed on time. Extensions of time to file a consent may be granted under certain circumstances.

Generally each **person** who is a shareholder at the time the election is made must consent.

EXAMPLE 4 ————————————————

Robert owned stock in X corporation on January 1, 1992. He sold the stock on February 10, 1992. On March 1, 1992, X corporation shareholders elected for the corporation to be an S corporation effective January 1, 1993. In order for the election to be effective, Robert must consent to the election even though he no longer was a shareholder on March 1, 1992. Robert is required to consent to the election because he will be required to report on his 1992 income tax return his share of the S corporation income components for the period January 1, 1992 to February 10, 1992 while he owned stock in X corporation. Each co-owner, tenant by the entirety, tenant in common, and joint tenant must consent. The consent of a minor must be made by the minor or by his or her legal representative. The consent of an estate must be made by an executor or administrator of the estate. The consent of a qualified trust holding stock in a newly elected S corporation must be made by each person who is treated as a shareholder.

6. Any trust receiving S corporation stock based on a decedent's will may be a shareholder for a 60-day period from the day the stock is transferred. In a voting trust, each beneficiary is considered a separate shareholder. In a grantor trust (the grantor must be a U.S. citizen or resident), the trust may be a shareholder for the 60-day period or for two years if the entire principal of the trust is included in the estate.

7. Only individuals, estates and certain trusts may be shareholders in an S corporation. Partnerships and corporations cannot be shareholders in an S corporation. The definition of eligible shareholders also includes (1) a person, other than the trust grantor, who is treated as the complete owner, and (2) a "qualified S corporation trust." A *qualified S corporation trust* is defined, in general, as one that owns stock in one or more S corporations, distributes all of its income to a U.S. citizen or resident, and has trust terms requiring only one income beneficiary.

8. An S corporation must use a permitted tax year. A **permitted tax year** is a calendar year or any other tax year for which the corporation establishes a business purpose. The permitted tax year requirement is satisfied if shareholders holding more than 50% of the stock of a corporation have the same taxable year as the corporation. An S corporation may also elect to have a tax year other than a permitted tax year under the provisions of Section 444, which generally requires certain tax payments by a specified date in the tax year.

A substantial business purpose exists if the corporation's requested tax year is a natural business year or if it satisfies an ownership tax year request. Both tax factors and nontax factors must be considered in determining whether a corporation has a substantial business purpose. Refer to IRS regulations for detailed information about what constitutes a substantial business purpose, about an ownership tax year, and the provisions for making a Section 444 election.

Termination of S Corporation Status

An S corporation may be terminated either voluntarily or automatically, as discussed in the paragraphs that follow.

Voluntary Termination

An election of S corporation status can be terminated voluntarily if shareholders holding more than one-half of the shares consent to end the status and the corporation files a statement to this effect with the IRS office where it had previously filed its election.

If the revocation specifies an effective date, the revocation will be effective on that date and the corporation will report as a regular corporation from that date forward. Thus, even though a election to become an S corporation must be effective on the first day of a tax year, a termination may be effective before the end of the regular tax year.

If no specific revocation date is designated, a revocation by the fifteenth day of the third month of the corporation's tax year is retroactive to the first day of the tax year. If the revocation is made after the fifteenth day of the third month, it is effective on the first day of the following tax year.

Automatic Termination

S corporation status terminates automatically if one of the following events occurs during the year:

1. The corporation fails to meet any of the requirements for being an S corporation, i.e., number of shareholders, type of stock, or shareholders other than individuals, estates, and certain trusts.

2. A corporation, for three consecutive years, has both accumulated earnings and profits from years when it was a regular corporation, and its passive investment income exceeds 25% of its gross receipts.

Generally the election will be considered terminated as of the date on which the disqualifying event occurred. However, if the election is terminated because of excessive passive income, it is effective beginning with the following tax year.

EXAMPLE 5 ————————————————

Assume an S corporation has been operating on a calendar-year basis for several years with 33 shareholders. On July 21, 1992, one of the shareholders dies with his 100 shares passing equally to each of four children. The status as an S corporation automatically terminates on July 21, 1992 because of the addition of the 36th shareholder. The S corporation is required to file a return for the period January 1, 1992 through July 20, 1992. On July 21, 1992, the corporation becomes a C corporation for the remainder of the year ending December 31, 1992. All income (loss) and separately identified items are prorated between the S corporation tax return and the C corporation tax return on a daily basis.

If an election has been terminated either voluntarily or automatically, the corporation may not reelect S corporation status until the fifth year after the year in which the termination was effective unless the IRS consents to an earlier election. If the S corporation election was inadvertently terminated, the IRS may waive the effect of the terminating event if the corporation makes a timely correction of the event.

Tax Treatment of S Corporation Income

While an S corporation election is in effect, the corporation generally does not pay any federal income tax. The income passes through to the stockholders and is taxed to them whether it is distributed or not. The income, deductions, losses, and credits of the corporation pass through to the shareholders in the same general manner as the similar items for a partnership pass through to the partners.

There are two exceptions to the general rule that S corporation income passes through to the shareholders and is taxed on their individual returns. Exceptions apply when an S corporation is subject to tax either on certain capital gains or on passive income. If the S corporation is subject to tax on either of these types of income, the Omnibus Reconciliation Act requires the S corporation to make estimated tax payments for tax years beginning after December 31, 1989.

Shareholders of an S corporation account separately for their proportionate shares of items of income, deductions, losses, and credits of the corporation. Shareholders report in their tax returns the corporate results for the corporation's tax year ending during the shareholder's tax year. Each shareholder's share of each item is determined on a daily basis for the number of shares held by the shareholder during each day of the corporation's tax year.

EXAMPLE 6 ————————————————

Assume an S corporation is owned equally by Smith, Jones, and Brown on November 1, 1991, the first day of a new fiscal year. Brown sells his shares to Black on August 8, 1992. The corporation's fiscal year ends on October 31, 1992. Thus, Brown held the shares for 280 days (77% of the year), and Black owned the shares for 85 days (23% of the year). The corporation earned $150,000 of ordinary taxable income and $90,000 of long-term capital gains during its fiscal year ending October 31, 1992.

Based on these facts, the corporation's income would be reported by the shareholders on their calendar-year 1992 tax returns as follows:

	Ordinary Income	Capital Gains
Smith	$ 50,000	$30,000
Jones	50,000	30,000
Brown (280 days = 77%)	38,500	23,100
Black (85 days = 23%)	11,500	6,900
Totals	$150,000	$90,000

When an S corporation shareholder sells his or her stock in the corporation during the corporation's tax year, the taxable gain or loss from the sale cannot be determined until after the end of the corporation's tax year. This is true because the shareholder who sold shares during the year is required to report his or her prorated share of the S corporation's income or loss and separately stated items on his or her individual tax return. This information will not be known until the K-1 is received from the S corporation after year-end. This unknown effect at the time of sale can be mitigated if the seller and the buyer of the stock agree to an adjustment of the selling price of the stock based on the year-end profit or loss results. As an alternative, all shareholders of interest during the year can agree to divide the tax year into two components, one from the beginning of the year to the date of sale and one from the date of sale to the end of the year. Only one tax return is filed, but the agreement to split the year limits the income or loss of the selling shareholder to the corporation's results up to the date of sale. The stockholders who remain will take the risk of sharing more heavily in losses occuring later in the year or benefit from sharing in higher profits for the remainder of the year.

Calculating the Adjusted Basis of S Corporation Stock

A shareholder in an S corporation generally has a basis in the corporation's stock (with certain special exceptions) equal to the amount paid for the stock. The basis is increased (or decreased) by ordinary income (or loss), by separately-stated items that flow through to the shareholders, by additional capital contributions, and by cash or property distributions to the shareholders.

The income reported by the shareholders increases the basis of their stock and losses decrease the basis of the stock to the extent that the losses are deductible. If the S corporation has an operating loss for the tax year, the loss is allocated proportionately among the shareholders based on the number of days in the corporation's tax year that the stock was owned.

EXAMPLE 7 ──────────────────────────

Jody acquires 100 shares of S corporation stock at the beginning of the corporation's calendar tax year at a cost of $7,500. Jody's share of income and separately stated items of the S corporation are as follows: regular income, $1,500; share of long-term capital gains, $300; and cash distributions received during the year of $1,000. Jody's basis in the S corporation stock on December 31, 1992 would be $8,300, calculated as follows:

Purchase cost of S shares	$ 7,500
Add: Share of regular income	1,500
Share of capital gains	300
Less: Distributions received	(1,000)
Jody's basis at December 31, 1992	$ 8,300

Utilizing Operating Losses in an S Corporation

Partnerships and S corporations both operate under the conduit principle in which income and separately stated items pass through to the partners or shareholders. It would be easy to jump to the conclusion that the utilization of operating losses by S corporation shareholders would be similar to the utilization of operating losses by partners in a partnership. In general, losses can be deducted by partners to the extent of their basis in the partnership, and S corporation shareholders may deduct operating losses and other separately stated losses to the extent of the shareholder's basis. Utilizing a loss deduction, however, will not necessarily be the same in an S corporation as in a partnership because a partner's basis is calculated differently than the basis is calculated for an S corporation shareholder. A partner's basis includes not only the contributed capital made by the partner adjusted for subsequent gains, losses, and distributions, but also includes his or her proportionate share of the liabilities of the partnership, such as mortgages, notes payable, accounts payable, and other accruals. On the other hand, an S corporation shareholder's basis is determined only by the shareholder's equity contributions plus any loans by the shareholder to the corporation. The S corporation's liabilities are not part of the S shareholder's basis because of the limited liability feature of corporate status. Thus, a partner has, relatively speaking, a larger basis to utilize in writing off operating losses than would an S shareholder whose basis would not include a proportionate share of an S corporation's liabilities. In essence, there are greater limitations on loss deductions by S shareholders than there are by partners of a partnership. These limitations are described below.

Reporting Loss Deductions by S Corporation Shareholders

Losses to be reported by S shareholders are determined by the amount reported by the S corporation based on its operations through the last day of the S corporation's tax year. The S corporation will allocate the ordinary loss and any separately stated losses among the shareholders based on the proportionate number of shares of stock that each S shareholder owned on each day of the S corporation's tax year. These amounts will be reported on Schedule K-1, Form 1120S as described later in this chapter.

EXAMPLE 8

Swift Corporation is an S corporation with five shareholders who each own 100 shares of the corporation's stock. Each has a basis in that stock of $25,000. During 1992, the corporation reports an operating loss of $75,000. Each shareholder's share of the loss is $15,000. Since the basis in the stock for each shareholder is $25,000, the deduction of the $15,000 loss is allowed on each shareholder's individual tax return since the deduction will not reduce any shareholder's basis below zero. After the $15,000 loss deduction by each shareholder, each shareholder's basis in the S corporation will be $10,000 ($25,000 − $15,000).

If an S corporation shareholder is required to report a loss, the amount of the loss deductible by each shareholder on the individual income tax return is limited to the sum of the shareholder's adjusted basis in the stock of the corporation plus the shareholder's adjusted basis in any indebtedness of the corporation to the shareholder. Disallowed losses may be carried forward and be deducted in any subsequent year in which the shareholder has sufficient basis in the stock and/or debt. If the operating losses and separately stated losses are larger than the stockholder's basis in the S corporation, then only a pro rata amount of the operating loss and each separately stated loss is deductible in that year. The amounts in each category not deductible in that year must be carried over to subsequent years to be deducted when operating income and separately stated incomes are available.

EXAMPLE 9

Assume that Buddy Jones owns a 30% interest in the ABC corporation which is an S corporation. At the end of 1992, Jones has a basis in ABC stock of $15,000 and a basis in loans made to the corporation of $12,000. At the end of the calendar year 1992, ABC corporation reports an operating loss of $120,000, of which Jones's share is $36,000. Jones will be allowed to deduct $27,000 of the total loss ($15,000 for the stock basis + $12,000 for the loan basis) and will have a carryover loss of $9,000 ($36,000 loss − $27,000 deductions). The 9,000 unutilized loss will be carried over to 1993 and subsequent years until it can be offset against operating income of future years.

EXAMPLE 10

Assume that a shareholder has an equity interest in an S Corporation of 20% with a basis of $20,000. The shareholder receives a K-1 at year-end indicating that the S corporation has reported that his share of the corporation's ordinary loss is $24,000 and his share of capital losses is $8,000. The shareholder is allowed to deduct $20,000 of losses, an amount equal to his basis in the S corporation. The specific losses deducted on the shareholder's tax return will be $15,000 of ordinary loss ($24,000/$32,000 x $20,000) and $5,000 of the capital loss ($8,000/$32,000 x $20,000). The taxpayer will carry forward to 1993 a total loss of $12,000, consisting of an ordinary loss deduction of $9,000 and a capital loss deduction of $3,000.

If an S corporation election is terminated, any disallowed loss will be allowed if the shareholder restores his or her basis in the stock by the later of (1) one year after the effective date of the termination or the due date of the last S corporation tax return, whichever is later, or (2) 120 days after a determination that the corporation's election had terminated for a previous year.

Distributions to Shareholders

The tax treatment of distributions by S corporations that were originally incorporated in 1983

Illustration 16-1
Filled-In Form 1120S, Page 1

Form **1120S**	**U.S. Income Tax Return for an S Corporation**	OMB No. 1545-0130

Department of the Treasury
Internal Revenue Service

For calendar year 1992, or tax year beginning ...., 1992, and ending ...., 19 .....
▶ See separate instructions.

1992

A Date of election as an S corporation **Jan. 15, 1988**

B Business code no. (see Specific Instructions) **7389**

Use IRS label. Otherwise, please print or type.

Name **Kendall Management Company**

Number, street, and room or suite no. (If a P.O. box, see page 8 of the instructions.) **731 Delhi Road**

City or town, state, and ZIP code **Atlanta, GA 30307-2062**

C Employer identification number **52-1739257**

D Date incorporated **October 1, 1987**

E Total assets (see Specific Instructions) **$ 125,650 | 00**

F Check applicable boxes: (1) ☐ Initial return (2) ☐ Final return (3) ☐ Change in address (4) ☐ Amended return

G Check this box if this S corporation is subject to the consolidated audit procedures of sections 6241 through 6245 (see instructions before checking this box) . ▶ ☐

H Enter number of shareholders in the corporation at end of the tax year . . . . ▶ **3**

Caution: *Include only trade or business income and expenses on lines 1a through 21. See the instructions for more information.*

Income

1a	Gross receipts or sales **159,150 00** b Less returns and allowances _______ c Bal ▶	1c	159,150 00
2	Cost of goods sold (Schedule A, line 8)	2	
3	Gross profit. Subtract line 2 from line 1c	3	159,150 00
4	Net gain (loss) from Form 4797, Part II, line 20 (attach Form 4797)	4	
5	Other income (loss)(see instructions) (attach schedule).	5	
6	**Total income (loss).** Combine lines 3 through 5 ▶	6	159,150 00

Deductions (See instructions for limitations.)

7	Compensation of officers	7	70,000 00
8a	Salaries and wages **21,550 00** b Less jobs credit _______ c Bal ▶	8c	21,550 00
9	Repairs	9	1,600 00
10	Bad debts	10	
11	Rents	11	
12	Taxes	12	5,000 00
13	Interest	13	
14a	Depreciation (see instructions) **14a 1,700 00**		
b	Depreciation claimed on Schedule A and elsewhere on return **14b**		
c	Subtract line 14b from line 14a	14c	1,700 00
15	Depletion **(Do not deduct oil and gas depletion.)**	15	
16	Advertising	16	7,500 00
17	Pension, profit-sharing, etc. plans	17	6,000 00
18	Employee benefit programs	18	7,500 00
19	Other deductions (see instructions) (attach schedule)	19	3,300 00
20	**Total deductions.** Add lines 7 through 19 ▶	20	124,150 00
21	Ordinary income (loss) from trade or business activities. Subtract line 20 from line 6	21	35,000 00

Tax and Payments

22	**Tax:**		
a	Excess net passive income tax (attach schedule) **22a –0–**		
b	Tax from Schedule D (Form 1120S) **22b –0–**		
c	Add lines 22a and 22b (see instructions for additional taxes)	22c	–0–
23	**Payments:**		
a	1992 estimated tax payments **23a**		
b	Tax deposited with Form 7004 **23b**		
c	Credit for Federal tax on fuels (attach Form 4136) **23c**		
d	Add lines 23a through 23c	23d	–0–
24	Estimated tax penalty (see page 3 of instructions). Check if Form 2220 is attached . ▶☐	24	
25	**Tax due.** If the total of lines 22c and 24 is larger than line 23d, enter amount owed. See instructions for depositary method of payment . . . . . ▶	25	–0–
26	**Overpayment.** If line 23d is larger than the total of lines 22c and 24, enter amount overpaid ▶	26	
27	Enter amount of line 26 you want: **Credited to 1993 estimated tax** ▶ _______ Refunded ▶	27	

Please Sign Here

Under penalties of perjury, I declare that I have examined this return, including accompanying schedules and statements, and to the best of my knowledge and belief, it is true, correct, and complete. Declaration of preparer (other than taxpayer) is based on all information of which preparer has any knowledge.

▶ *Virginia Kendell* | Signature of officer

3-12-93 | Date

▶ President | Title

Paid Preparer's Use Only

Preparer's signature ▶ *Fred C. Walker,* Date **3-10-93** Check if self-employed ▶ ☒ Preparer's social security number **202 30 6054**

Firm's name (or yours if self-employed) and address ▶ **Tax Consultants, Inc.** **12 Oak St., Atlanta, GA** E.I. No. ▶ **61 9077665** ZIP code ▶ **30307-7175**

For Paperwork Reduction Act Notice, see page 1 of separate instructions. Cat. No. 11510H Form **1120S** (1992)

Illustration 16-1
Filled-In Form 1120S, Page 2

Form 1120S (1992)   Page **2**

Schedule A Cost of Goods Sold (See instructions.)

1	Inventory at beginning of year	1
2	Purchases	2
3	Cost of labor	3
4	Additional section 263A costs (see instructions) *(attach schedule)*	4
5	Other costs *(attach schedule)*	5
6	**Total.** Add lines 1 through 5	6
7	Inventory at end of year	7
8	**Cost of goods sold.** Subtract line 7 from line 6. Enter here and on page 1, line 2	8

9a Check all methods used for valuing closing inventory:

(i) ☐ Cost

(ii) ☐ Lower of cost or market as described in Regulations section 1.471-4

(iii) ☐ Writedown of "subnormal" goods as described in Regulations section 1.471-2(c)

(iv) ☐ Other (specify method used and attach explanation) ▶ ....

b Check if the LIFO inventory method was adopted this tax year for any goods *(if checked, attach Form 970)* .... ▶ ☐

c If the LIFO inventory method was used for this tax year, enter percentage (or amounts) of closing inventory computed under LIFO 9c

d Do the rules of section 263A (for property produced or acquired for resale) apply to the corporation? ..... ☐ Yes ☐ No

e Was there any change in determining quantities, cost, or valuations between opening and closing inventory? .. ☐ Yes ☐ No
If "Yes," attach explanation.

Schedule B Other Information

		Yes	No
1	Check method of accounting: **(a)** ☐ Cash **(b)** ☐ Accrual **(c)** ☐ Other (specify) ▶		
2	Refer to the list in the instructions and state the corporation's principal: **(a)** Business activity ▶ .... **(b)** Product or service ▶		
3	Did the corporation at the end of the tax year own, directly or indirectly, 50% or more of the voting stock of a domestic corporation? (For rules of attribution, see section 267(c).) If "Yes," attach a schedule showing: **(a)** name, address, and employer identification number and **(b)** percentage owned.		X
4	Was the corporation a member of a controlled group subject to the provisions of section 1561?		X
5	At any time during calendar year 1992, did the corporation have an interest in or a signature or other authority over a financial account in a foreign country (such as a bank account, securities account, or other financial account)? (See instructions for exceptions and filing requirements for form TD F 90-22.1.) .... If "Yes," enter the name of the foreign country ▶		X
6	Was the corporation the grantor of, or transferor to, a foreign trust that existed during the current tax year, whether or not the corporation has any beneficial interest in it? If "Yes," the corporation may have to file Forms 3520, 3520-A, or 926		X
7	Check this box if the corporation has filed or is required to file **Form 8264,** Application for Registration of a Tax Shelter .... ▶ ☐		
8	Check this box if the corporation issued publicly offered debt instruments with original issue discount .. ▶ ☐ If so, the corporation may have to file **Form 8281,** Information Return for Publicly Offered Original Issue Discount Instruments.		
9	If the corporation: **(a)** filed its election to be an S corporation after 1986, **(b)** was a C corporation before it elected to be an S corporation **or** the corporation acquired an asset with a basis determined by reference to its basis (or the basis of any other property) in the hands of a C corporation, and **(c)** has net unrealized built-in gain (defined in section 1374(d)(1)) in excess of the net recognized built-in gain from prior years, enter the net unrealized built-in gain reduced by net recognized built-in gain from prior years (see instructions) .... ▶ $		
10	Check this box if the corporation had subchapter C earnings and profits at the close of the tax year (see instructions) .... ▶ ☐		
11	Was this corporation in operation at the end of 1992?		
12	How many months in 1992 was this corporation in operation?		

Designation of Tax Matters Person (See instructions.)

Enter below the shareholder designated as the tax matters person (TMP) for the tax year of this return:

Name of designated TMP ▶ Virginia Kendall

Identifying number of TMP ▶ 421-63-8045

Address of designated TMP ▶ 731 Delhi Road, Atlanta, GA 30307-2062

Illustration 16-1
Filled-In Form 1120S, Page 3

Form 1120S (1992)   Page **3**

Schedule K — Shareholders' Shares of Income, Credits, Deductions, etc.

	(a) Pro rata share items		(b) Total amount
Income (Loss)	1 Ordinary income (loss) from trade or business activities (page 1, line 21)	1	35,000 00
	2 Net income (loss) from rental real estate activities *(attach Form 8825)*	2	
	3a Gross income from other rental activities ... 3a		
	b Less expenses *(attach schedule)* ... 3b		
	c Net income (loss) from other rental activities	3c	
	4 Portfolio income (loss):		
	a Interest income	4a	1,500 00
	b Dividend income	4b	2,000 00
	c Royalty income	4c	
	d Net short-term capital gain (loss) *(attach Schedule D (Form 1120S))*	4d	
	e Net long-term capital gain (loss) *(attach Schedule D (Form 1120S))*	4e	8,600 00
	f Other portfolio income (loss) *(attach schedule)*	4f	
	5 Net gain (loss) under section 1231 (other than due to casualty or theft) *(attach Form 4797)*	5	
	6 Other income (loss) *(attach schedule)*	6	
Deductions	7 Charitable contributions (see instructions) *(attach list)*	7	7,000 00
	8 Section 179 expense deduction *(attach Form 4562)*	8	
	9 Deductions related to portfolio income (loss) (see instructions) *(itemize)*	9	
	10 Other deductions *(attach schedule)*	10	
Investment Interest	11a Interest expense on investment debts	11a	1,200 00
	b (1) Investment income included on lines 4a through 4f above	11b(1)	3,500 00
	(2) Investment expenses included on line 9 above	11b(2)	
Credits	12a Credit for alcohol used as a fuel *(attach Form 6478)*	12a	
	b Low-income housing credit (see instructions):		
	(1) From partnerships to which section 42(j)(5) applies for property placed in service before 1990	12b(1)	
	(2) Other than on line 12b(1) for property placed in service before 1990	12b(2)	
	(3) From partnerships to which section 42(j)(5) applies for property placed in service after 1989	12b(3)	
	(4) Other than on line 12b(3) for property placed in service after 1989	12b(4)	
	c Qualified rehabilitation expenditures related to rental real estate activities *(attach Form 3468)*	12c	
	d Credits (other than credits shown on lines 12b and 12c) related to rental real estate activities (see instructions)	12d	
	e Credits related to other rental activities (see instructions)	12e	
	13 Other credits (see instructions)	13	
Adjustments and Tax Preference Items	14a Depreciation adjustment on property placed in service after 1986	14a	
	b Adjusted gain or loss	14b	
	c Depletion (other than oil and gas)	14c	
	d (1) Gross income from oil, gas, or geothermal properties	14d(1)	
	(2) Deductions allocable to oil, gas, or geothermal properties	14d(2)	
	e Other adjustments and tax preference items *(attach schedule)*	14e	
Foreign Taxes	15a Type of income ▶		
	b Name of foreign country or U.S. possession ▶		
	c Total gross income from sources outside the United States *(attach schedule)*	15c	
	d Total applicable deductions and losses *(attach schedule)*	15d	
	e Total foreign taxes (check one): ▶ ☐ Paid ☐ Accrued	15e	
	f Reduction in taxes available for credit *(attach schedule)*	15f	
	g Other foreign tax information *(attach schedule)*	15g	
Other	16a Total expenditures to which a section 59(e) election may apply	16a	
	b Type of expenditures ▶		
	17 Tax-exempt interest income	17	
	18 Other tax-exempt income	18	
	19 Nondeductible expenses	19	
	20 Total property distributions (including cash) other than dividends reported on line 22 below	20	
	21 Other items and amounts required to be reported separately to shareholders (see instructions) *(attach schedule)*		
	22 Total dividend distributions paid from accumulated earnings and profits	22	26,400 00
	23 **Income (loss).** (Required only if Schedule M-1 must be completed.) Combine lines 1 through 6 in column (b). From the result, subtract the sum of lines 7 through 11a, 15e, and 16a	23	38,900 00

Illustration 16-1
Filled-In Form 1120S, Page 4

Form 1120S (1992)

Page **4**

Schedule L — Balance Sheets

Assets	Beginning of tax year (a)	(b)	End of tax year (c)	(d)
1 Cash				
2a Trade notes and accounts receivable				
b Less allowance for bad debts				
3 Inventories				
4 U.S. Government obligations				
5 Tax-exempt securities				
6 Other current assets (attach schedule)				
7 Loans to shareholders				
8 Mortgage and real estate loans				
9 Other investments (attach schedule)				
10a Buildings and other depreciable assets				
b Less accumulated depreciation				
11a Depletable assets				
b Less accumulated depletion				
12 Land (net of any amortization)				
13a Intangible assets (amortizable only)				
b Less accumulated amortization				
14 Other assets (attach schedule)				
15 Total assets				
Liabilities and Shareholders' Equity				
16 Accounts payable				
17 Mortgages, notes, bonds payable in less than 1 year				
18 Other current liabilities (attach schedule)				
19 Loans from shareholders				
20 Mortgages, notes, bonds payable in 1 year or more				
21 Other liabilities (attach schedule)				
22 Capital stock				
23 Paid-in or capital surplus				
24 Retained earnings				
25 Less cost of treasury stock		( )		( )
26 Total liabilities and shareholders' equity				

Schedule M-1 — Reconciliation of Income (Loss) per Books With Income (Loss) per Return (You are not required to complete this schedule if the total assets on line 15, column (d), of Schedule L are less than $25,000.)

1 Net income (loss) per books	47,500	5 Income recorded on books this year not included on Schedule K, lines 1 through 6 (itemize):		
2 Income included on Schedule K, lines 1 through 6, not recorded on books this year (itemize):		a Tax-exempt interest $ 7,200		7,200
3 Expenses recorded on books this year not included on Schedule K, lines 1 through 11a, 15e, and 16a (itemize):		6 Deductions included on Schedule K, lines 1 through 11a, 15e, and 16a, not charged against book income this year (itemize):		
a Depreciation $		a Depreciation $ 1,400		1,400
b Travel and entertainment $				
		7 Add lines 5 and 6		8,600
4 Add lines 1 through 3	47,500	8 Income (loss) (Schedule K, line 23). Line 4 less line 7		38,900

Schedule M-2 — Analysis of Accumulated Adjustments Account, Other Adjustments Account, and Shareholders' Undistributed Taxable Income Previously Taxed (See instructions.)

		(a) Accumulated adjustments account	(b) Other adjustments account	(c) Shareholders' undistributed taxable income previously taxed
1	Balance at beginning of tax year	22,900	1,200	
2	Ordinary income from page 1, line 21	35,000		
3	Other additions	3,500	7,200	
4	Loss from page 1, line 21	( )		
5	Other reductions	(7,000)	( )	
6	Combine lines 1 through 5	54,400	8,400	
7	Distributions other than dividend distributions			
8	Balance at end of tax year. Subtract line 7 from line 6	54,400	8,400	

company during 1992 is entered (line 3), making a total of $8,400 to be entered (lines 6 and 8) since there were no related expenses applicable to the tax-exempt interest income and there were no specific distributions of this income.

Column (c) of Schedule M-2 is for undistributed taxable income that was included in shareholders' income for tax years that began before 1990. Since the Kendall Company's first year as an S Corporation was in 1991, this column is not applicable.

Illustration 16-2
(Schedule D), Form 1120S

A filled-in Schedule D, Capital Gains and Losses and Built-In Gains, which is the reporting mechanism for the calculation of capital gains and losses, is shown in Illustration 16-2. Kendall Company sold 200 shares of Rogers Company stock acquired in 1991 for $20,800 resulting in a long-term capital gain of $8,600. Since the amount of the gain is less than $25,000, Schedule D, Part III, need not be completed. The long-term gain amount shown on Schedule D, Part II (line 6) is carried over to Form 1120S, Schedule K, shown in Illustration 16-1, page 3.

Illustration 16-3
(Schedule K-1)

The shareholders' shares of ordinary income and net long-term capital gains are shown on Form 1120S, Schedule K, page 3. Each individual shareholder's share is shown on Schedule K-1. A Schedule K-1 is shown in Illustration 16-3 for Virginia Kendall, the corporation's president, who owns 30% of the corporation's stock. Accordingly, her share of (1) ordinary income is $10,500 (30% x $35,000), (2) interest income is $450, (3) dividend income is $600, and (4) net long-term capital gain is $2,580 (30% x $8,600). Ms. Kendall will also report her $2,100 share of charitable contributions. She will report the above income amounts on her individual Form 1040, Schedule E, for ordinary income and in Form 1040, Schedule D, for her share of long-term gains. Her share of charitable contributions will be reported on Schedule A along with her personal charitable contributions and other itemized deductions.

Tax Planning Concepts for S Corporations

Tax planning is absolutely essential for S corporations if the owners desire to maintain the S corporation status to achieve their tax objectives. As this chapter indicates, S corporations must follow rather precise and complex rules to retain S Corporation status. Since automatic termination is likely if an S Corporation does not meet one or more of the requirements for being an S corporation, diligent efforts must be exercised to maintain such status.

One of the requirements for S Corporation status that is especially subject to violation is the rule requiring a maximum of 35 shareholders. The corporation should have procedures in place for monitoring sales and purchases of its stock and for dispositions of stock prescribed in shareholders' wills in order to be assured that the maximum number of 35 shareholders is not exceeded. If the maximum number of shareholders is exceeded, the S corporation status would be terminated on the date the disqualifying event occurs. In some cases, a corporation may operate for some time after the disqualifying event occurs under the assumption that it is an S Corporation and later discover that is was no longer qualified. In this interim period, management decisions may have been made that were desirable for an S corporation but not for the C corporation status it would be operating under without realizing it. Therefore, every effort must be taken to avoid violating the S corporation rules that could lead to automatic termination.

A second area for potential violation of S corporation status concerns the requirement that an S corporation have only one class of stock. Until recently there were no IRS regulations to provide guidance regarding this rule. In 1990 the IRS issued proposed regulations that would have jeopardized S corporation elections that have been in existence since 1982.

Illustration 16-2
Filled-In Form 1120S Schedule D

SCHEDULE D
(Form 1120S)

Department of the Treasury
Internal Revenue Service

Capital Gains and Losses and Built-In Gains

▶ Attach to Form 1120S.

▶ See separate instructions.

OMB No. 1545-0130

1992

Name: **Kendall Management Company**

Employer identification number: **52–1739257**

Part I — Short-Term Capital Gains and Losses—Assets Held One Year or Less

(a) Kind of property and description (Example, 100 shares of "Z" Co.)	(b) Date acquired (mo., day, yr.)	(c) Date sold (mo., day, yr.)	(d) Gross sales price	(e) Cost or other basis, plus expense of sale	(f) Gain or (loss) ((d) less (e))
1					

2	Short-term capital gain from installment sales from Form 6252, line 26 or 37	2	
3	Short-term capital gain or (loss) from like-kind exchanges from Form 8824	3	
4	Combine lines 1 through 3 and enter here	4	
5	Tax on short-term gain included on line 29 below	5	
6	**Net short-term capital gain or (loss).** Subtract line 5 from line 4. Enter here and on Form 1120S, Schedule K, line 4d or line 6	6	

Part II — Long-Term Capital Gains and Losses—Assets Held More Than One Year

(a)	(b)	(c)	(d)	(e)	(f)
7 Rogers Co. (200 shs.)	7/18/90	10/14/91	20,800	12,200	8,600

8	Long-term capital gain from installment sales from Form 6252, line 26 or 37	8	
9	Long-term capital gain or (loss) from like-kind exchanges from Form 8824	9	
10	Combine lines 7 through 9 and enter here	10	8,600
11	Tax on long-term gain included on lines 21 and 29 below	11	
12	**Net long-term capital gain or (loss).** Subtract line 11 from line 10. Enter here and on Form 1120S, Schedule K, line 4e or line 6	12	8,600

Part III — Capital Gains Tax (See instructions before completing this part.)

13	Enter section 1231 gain from Form 4797, line 11	13	
14	Net long-term capital gain or (loss)—Combine lines 10 and 13	14	

Note: If the corporation is liable for the excess net passive income tax (Form 1120S, page 1, line 22a) or the built-in gains tax (Part IV below), see the line 15 instructions before completing line 15.

15	Net capital gain. Enter excess of net long-term capital gain (line 14) over net short-term capital loss (line 4).	15	
16	Statutory minimum	16	$25,000
17	Subtract line 16 from line 15	17	
18	Enter 34% of line 17	18	
19	Taxable income (see instructions and attach computation schedule)	19	
20	Enter tax on line 19 amount (see instructions and attach computation schedule)	20	
21	**Tax.** Enter smaller of line 18 or line 20 here and on Form 1120S, page 1, line 22b	21	

Part IV — Built-In Gains Tax (See instructions before completing this part.)

22	Excess of recognized built-in gains over recognized built-in losses (see instructions and attach computation schedule)	22	
23	Taxable income (see instructions and attach computation schedule)	23	
24	Net recognized built-in gain. Enter smaller of line 22 or line 23 (see instructions)	24	
25	Section 1374(b)(2) deduction	25	
26	Subtract line 25 from line 24. (If zero or less, enter -0- here and on line 29.)	26	
27	Enter 34% of line 26	27	
28	Business credit and minimum tax credit carryforwards under section 1374(b)(3) from C corporation years	28	
29	**Tax.** Subtract line 28 from line 27 (if zero or less, enter -0-). Enter here and on Form 1120S, page 1, line 22b	29	

For Paperwork Reduction Act Notice, see page 1 of Instructions for Form 1120S.   Cat. No. 11516V   Schedule D (Form 1120S) 1992

Illustration 16-3
Filled-In Schedule K-1

SCHEDULE K-1 (Form 1120S)	Shareholder's Share of Income, Credits, Deductions, etc.	OMB No. 1545-0130

Department of the Treasury
Internal Revenue Service

▶ See separate instructions.

For calendar year 1992 or tax year beginning ____________ , 1992, and ending ____________ , 19____

1992

Shareholder's identifying number ▶	Corporation's identifying number ▶
Shareholder's name, address, and ZIP code	Corporation's name, address, and ZIP code
Virginia Kendall 4524 Peachtree Drive Atlanta, GA 30307-4250	Kendall Management Company 731 Delhi Road Atlanta, GA 30307-2062

A Shareholder's percentage of stock ownership for tax year (see Instructions for Schedule K-1) . . . . ▶ .... 30 %

B Internal Revenue Service Center where corporation filed its return ▶ Atlanta, GA 31101

C (1) Tax shelter registration number (see Instructions for Schedule K-1) . . . . ▶ ....

(2) Type of tax shelter ▶ ....

D Check applicable boxes: (1) ☐ Final K-1 (2) ☐ Amended K-1

	(a) Pro rata share items	(b) Amount	(c) Form 1040 filers enter the amount in column (b) on:
Income (Loss)	1 Ordinary income (loss) from trade or business activities	1 10,500	See Shareholder's Instructions for Schedule K-1 (Form 1120S).
	2 Net income (loss) from rental real estate activities	2	
	3 Net income (loss) from other rental activities	3	
	4 Portfolio income (loss):		
	a Interest	4a 450	Sch. B, Part I, line 1
	b Dividends	4b 600	Sch. B, Part II, line 5
	c Royalties	4c	Sch. E, Part I, line 4
	d Net short-term capital gain (loss)	4d	Sch. D, line 5, col. (f) or (g)
	e Net long-term capital gain (loss)	4e 2,580	Sch. D, line 13, col. (f) or (g)
	f Other portfolio income (loss) *(attach schedule)*	4f	(Enter on applicable line of your return.)
	5 Net gain (loss) under section 1231 (other than due to casualty or theft)	5	See Shareholder's Instructions for Schedule K-1 (Form 1120S).
	6 Other income (loss) *(attach schedule)*	6	(Enter on applicable line of your return.)
Deductions	7 Charitable contributions (see instructions) *(attach schedule)*	7 2,100	Sch. A, line 13 or 14
	8 Section 179 expense deduction	8	See Shareholder's Instructions for Schedule K-1 (Form 1120S).
	9 Deductions related to portfolio income (loss) *(attach schedule)*	9	
	10 Other deductions *(attach schedule)*	10	
Investment Interest	11a Interest expense on investment debts	11a 360	Form 4952, line 1
	b (1) Investment income included on lines 4a through 4f above	b(1) 1,050	See Shareholder's Instructions for Schedule K-1 (Form 1120S).
	(2) Investment expenses included on line 9 above	b(2)	
Credits	12a Credit for alcohol used as fuel	12a	Form 6478, line 10
	b Low-income housing credit:		
	(1) From section 42(j)(5) partnerships for property placed in service before 1990	b(1)	
	(2) Other than on line 12b(1) for property placed in service before 1990	b(2)	Form 8586, line 5
	(3) From section 42(j)(5) partnerships for property placed in service after 1989	b(3)	
	(4) Other than on line 12b(3) for property placed in service after 1989	b(4)	
	c Qualified rehabilitation expenditures related to rental real estate activities (see instructions)	12c	
	d Credits (other than credits shown on lines 12b and 12c) related to rental real estate activities (see instructions)	12d	See Shareholder's Instructions for Schedule K-1 (Form 1120S).
	e Credits related to other rental activities (see instructions)	12e	
	13 Other credits (see instructions)	13	
Adjustments and Tax Preference Items	14a Depreciation adjustment on property placed in service after 1986	14a	See Shareholder's Instructions for Schedule K-1 (Form 1120S) and Instructions for Form 6251
	b Adjusted gain or loss	14b	
	c Depletion (other than oil and gas)	14c	
	d (1) Gross income from oil, gas, or geothermal properties	d(1)	
	(2) Deductions allocable to oil, gas, or geothermal properties	d(2)	
	e Other adjustments and tax preference items *(attach schedule)*	14e	

For Paperwork Reduction Act Notice, see page 1 of Instructions for Form 1120S.   Cat. No. 11520D   **Schedule K-1 (Form 1120S) 1992**

However, with support from the accounting profession and other groups, the IRS revised its proposed regulations regarding the one-class of stock rule for S corporations. A revised proposal took the position that an S corporation has one class of stock unless deliberate actions are taken to circumvent this requirement. Under the revised regulations, facts and circumstances determine the proper tax treatment of transactions, minimizing concerns about differences in the timing and amount of distributions.

Since it is relatively easy to have distributions which could inadvertently differ in timing or amount, an S corporation's status could have been terminated for one or more years because of the existence of a second class of stock without the management and the shareholders having been aware of the terminating violation.

The crux of the problem lies in the guidelines for determining what constitutes a second class of stock. A second class of stock can exist regardless of whether the difference in rights occurs under the corporate charter, the articles of incorporation, or corporate bylaws, or by operation of state law, by administrative action, or by agreement. However, the revised regulations should provide some "safe harbors" for straight debt and disregard differences in voting rights, rights under shareholder buy-sell agreements, and restrictions on stock transferability, in determining whether a corporation has more than one class of stock. The new regulations are additional evidence that a careful interpretation and implementation of the requirements to be an S corporation must be adhered to in order to avoid inadvertent termination and insure that the tax planning policies related to S corporation status will continue to apply to the owners of the business.

A third area of potential tax planning for an S corporation relates to the taxation of capital gains. A capital gains tax is imposed on the corporation, rather than being passed through to the shareholders if the gain exceeds $25,000, the gain exceeds 50% of the corporation's taxable income, the taxable income is greater than $25,000, and the corporation is in its first three years of existence as an S Corporation. If the corporation cannot avoid the capital gains tax at the corporate level, then double taxation will apply to those gains, which defeats the benefits of a single tax when passing the gains through to the shareholders to be taxed in their individual tax brackets. Good tax planning will help an S corporation, especially those that elected S corporation status before January 1, 1989, to avoid this type of double taxation through any one of several ways:

1. Defer the gain until after the three-year period has expired. This can be achieved by selling the assets under the installment method.
2. An S corporation can revoke a Section 444 election related to using a fiscal year. The revocation will result in the creation of a short tax year when the corporation converts to a calendar year. This short tax year qualifies as one of the three tax years that must have passed before the S corporation is no longer subject to the capital gains tax.
3. Taxable income can be increased by accelerating income into the year in which the capital gains tax will apply in order to keep capital gains below 50% of taxable income.
4. Decrease taxable income below $25,000 by paying additional reasonable compensation to employees of the corporation.
5. Sell the capital gains assets to a more-than-50% shareholder. In such a case, Section 1239 of the tax law treats the sale or exchange of depreciable property between related taxpayers as ordinary income to the transferring organization. If the corporation wishes to sell a Section 1239 asset to a third party, it could avoid the capital gains tax by distributing the asset first to its shareholders, who then could sell to the third party.

All of these alternative ways of avoiding the double taxation effect on certain capital gains suggest that careful planning is necessary on a regular basis to ensure the tax benefits intended when S corporation status was elected.

C H A P T E R   1 6

Questions and Problems

1. **a.** How many shareholders may an S corporation have?

    b. What is the period during which the shareholders of a corporation may elect an S corporation status?

    c. What will either voluntarily or automatically terminate the election to be treated as an S corporation?

    d. When is the termination of S corporation status effective under voluntary termination and under automatic termination?

2. Answer each of the following questions in relation to an S corporation:
    a. What is meant by the term "conduit principle"?

    b. If a business has S corporation status, how is each shareholder's proportionate share of income determined?

c. If an S corporation has an operating loss for the tax year, how much of the loss is deductible by individual shareholders?

3. a. The Sherwin Corporation is a United States corporation owned by 12 shareholders. All of the stock outstanding is common stock. At a regular meeting of the shareholders, all except one shareholder agreed to have the corporation become an S corporation in order to have its income taxed to the shareholders directly. Can the Sherwin Corporation elect to be taxed as an S corporation? Explain.

b. What are the tax advantages for the owner of a business if the business can be operated as a corporation and yet have the right to have its income be taxed directly to the shareholders?

4. Derek Brown died on July 10, 1992. In reviewing his will, his executor determined that Brown owned 100 shares in an S corporation. The 100 shares represent a 16% interest in the corporation. In his will, Brown bequeathed the 100 shares equally to his four children. When the executor called the corporate office to work out the transfer of the shares to the children, he learned that the S corporation already had 33 shareholders including Brown and that the transfer of 25 shares to each of Brown's children increased the total shareholders to 36. Therefore, the corporation was in violation of the maximum shareholder rule and was subject to termination of its S corporation status.

a. As of what date is the S corporation status terminated as a result of having an excess of 35 shareholders?

b. In what capacity must the corporation operate after it loses its S corporation status?

c. If the corporation has been and continues to be a calendar-year corporation, how will Brown's executor and the four children report their shares of the following annual income and separately stated items: ordinary income, $73,000; long-term capital gains, $14,600; and charitable contributions, $1,046?

5. Paul Sager owns a majority interest in an S corporation. He is one of 7 shareholders. Since he is very well off financially, his financial adviser has suggested that he transfer ownership of his S corporation stock to his three children. He is reluctant to do so because he does not want to lose his voting interest in the corporation. Yet, if he does not transfer ownership of a significant portion of this major asset to his estate, he will be subject to a very large federal estate tax at his death. What advice can you give him to allow him to maintain his voting control in the S corporation and still transfer substantial ownership to his children?

6. Robert Eaves owned 200 shares of stock in a regular corporation on January 1, 1992. He held the stock until February 10, 1992 when he sold it. In early March, 1992, the remaining 20 shareholders have a meeting to consider whether they should elect S corporation status. They ask you to answer the following questions for them regarding how and when to implement this election.

a. When do they need to file the election in order to be an S corporation starting as of January 1, 1992?

b. Which shareholders are required to consent to the election to implement S corporation status as of January 1, 1992?

c. If Robert Eaves refuses to consent to the election for S corporation status as of January 1, 1992, what is the first date the corporation can begin operating as an S corporation?

d. Why might Robert Eaves be reluctant to consent to the election to be a S corporation as of January 1, 1992?

7. Indicate how the following distributions from an S corporation must be reported by a shareholder:
   a. Distributions not in excess of the shareholder's proportionate share of ordinary income and capital gains

   b. Distributions in excess of taxable income

   c. Distributions greater than the shareholder's basis

8. Richard Jordan owned a 10% interest in an S corporation for several years. The basis of his stock on January 1, 1992 is $40,000.

   On April 30, 1992 Jordan sells his entire interest in the S corporation for a price of $58,000. For the calendar year 1992, the S corporation estimated that its ordinary income for 1992 would be $80,000. No dividends had been paid for 1992 prior to the sale of Jordan's stock.

   a. On April 30, 1992, the date of sale, what would Jordan's expectation be as to how much gain he would be required to report on his 1992 tax return as the result of the sale of his interest in the S corporation?

   b. At year-end, the S corporation determines that its actual ordinary income for 1992 amounted to $100,000. Based on the year-end knowledge of what the S corporation's taxable income was for the year 1992, does this additional information affect Jordan's 1992 tax return? If so, how is the 1992 tax return affected, and if not affected, why not?

9. The Century Corporation, a calendar-year corporation, was organized as an S corporation on January 2, 1988. The corporation had no pre-1988 AEP. The corporation's taxable income for 1992 was $75,000, all of which was ordinary income. During 1992, the corporation distributed $90,000 in cash to shareholders.

   a. How do the shareholders report the $75,000 of ordinary taxable income?

   b. How do the shareholders report the $90,000 of cash distributions during 1992?

   c. What effect do the corporation's taxable income and cash distributions have on the shareholders' basis in their stock?

10. The Viking Corporation, a calendar-year corporation, elected to become an S corporation as of January 2, 1990, and continued the election in 1991 and 1992. Terry Trammel has owned 40% of the stock since the corporation's inception, with an original investment of $27,000. In 1990 and 1991, the corporation had NOLs of $45,000 and $20,000, respectively, which were appropriately deducted by the shareholders on their 1990 and 1991 individual income tax returns. During 1992, the corporation had taxable income of $60,000, all ordinary income, and made cash distributions of $40,000. The corporation had no AEP at the end of 1990.

   a. How does Terry Trammel report his share of the 1992 taxable income and cash distributions of the S corporation?

   b. What is the basis of the stock owned by Terry Trammel at December 31, 1992?

11. a. How do the shareholders of an S corporation report corporate capital gains?

   b. If an S corporation has a $42,000 net operating loss in 1992, how much of the loss is reportable by shareholder Johnson who has owned 16⅔% of the corporation's stock since September 10, 1992?

   c. If an S corporation qualifies its stock as Section 1244 stock, how are losses treated when a shareholder sells S corporation stock?

12. Under what circumstances will an S corporation lose its S corporation status if it is generating passive investment income?

13. The Siegal Management Corporation has operated as an S corporation for the years 1990, 1991, and 1992. The shareholders of the corporation are Tracy Sherman and Flora Shaw. They each own 200 shares of stock of the corporation for which each paid $25,000 at the beginning of 1990. The corporation's earnings and profits, taxable income, and cash distributions for the three years are as follows:

	1990	1991	1992
Taxable income	$10,000	$11,000	$16,000
Cash distributions:			
1990	10,000		
1991		11,000	
1992			24,000

   a. How much and in what manner do Tracy Sherman and Flora Shaw report income on their individual income tax returns for 1992?

   b. What is the basis of Sherman's and Shaw's stock at the end of 1992?

14. Melbourne Corporation is an S corporation with 10 shareholders. Bill Fox owns 200 shares of stock which represents a 15% equity in the corporation. His basis for those 100 shares is $12,000. He also has loaned the corporation $4,000 to support the purchase of a special machine to make the corporation's activities more effective. For the year 1992, the corporation reports an operating loss of $120,000. In addition, the corporation made charitable contributions for the year of $10,000.

   a. Explain how Bill Fox reports his share of the S corporation's operating loss and charitable contributions.

   b. What is Fox's basis in his S corporation stock at the end of 1992?

   c. Calculate the amount and type of carryover losses to 1993 that Fox is entitled to, if any.

15. The Prince Corporation, an S corporation, was operated as a small variety store. The company was incorporated on January 2, 1989 and elected S corporation status on the same day. John R. Prince (SSN 201-03-5064) and his wife, Joyce B. Prince (SSN 265-72-8133), who each own 30% of the corporation, manage the store. The remaining stock is owned by John's father. John is President and Designated Tax Matters person and Joyce is VP and Treasurer.

   At the end of the calendar year 1992, the income statement and balance sheet accounts and other information taken from the records were as follows:

Inventory, January 1, 1992	$ 29,500
Purchases (net)	133,800
Sales revenue	246,500
Sales returns and allowances	15,900
Inventory, December 31, 1992	32,400
Depreciation expense	5,200
Bad debts expense	1,500
Repairs and maintenance	3,300
Interest expense	2,700
Advertising	7,800
Compensation of officers	30,000
Salaries and wages	24,500
Rental of equipment	700
Long-term capital gains	3,750
Charitable contributions	1,800
Interest income	900
Travel and entertainment expenses	1,400
Dividends paid	4,000
Total assets, December 31, 1992	108,700

Based on this information, John and Joyce Prince have asked you to prepare their 1992 S corporation tax return on Form 1120S, to be signed by John Prince. You should prepare Schedule M-1 on Form 1120S, but do not prepare Schedule L or Schedule M-2. Questions 3 through 6 on page 2 should be answered "no." The method of accounting is the accrual method. Questions 7 through 10 should be left blank. On page 4, assume that the net income per books of Schedule M-1 (line 1) is $25,450. Schedule K-1 should be prepared for Joyce's share of the S corporation's income and deductions. John and Joyce live at 1074 Bright Leaf Square, College Station, TX 77841.

Form **1120S**

Department of the Treasury
Internal Revenue Service

U.S. Income Tax Return for an S Corporation

For calendar year 1992, or tax year beginning .... , 1992, and ending .... , 19 .....
▶ **See separate instructions.**

OMB No. 1545-0130

1992

A Date of election as an S corporation

B Business code no. (see Specific Instructions)

Use IRS label. Otherwise, please print or type.

Name

Number, street, and room or suite no. (If a P.O. box, see page 8 of the instructions.)

City or town, state, and ZIP code

C Employer identification number

D Date incorporated

E Total assets (see Specific Instructions)
$

F Check applicable boxes: (1) ☐ Initial return   (2) ☐ Final return   (3) ☐ Change in address   (4) ☐ Amended return

G Check this box if this S corporation is subject to the consolidated audit procedures of sections 6241 through 6245 (see instructions before checking this box) . ▶ ☐

H Enter number of shareholders in the corporation at end of the tax year . . . . ▶

Caution: *Include **only** trade or business income and expenses on lines 1a through 21. See the instructions for more information.*

Income

1a Gross receipts or sales |_______| **b** Less returns and allowances |_______| **c** Bal ▶	**1c**	
2 Cost of goods sold (Schedule A, line 8)	**2**	
3 Gross profit. Subtract line 2 from line 1c	**3**	
4 Net gain (loss) from Form 4797, Part II, line 20 *(attach Form 4797)*	**4**	
5 Other income (loss)(see instructions) *(attach schedule)*. . . .	**5**	
6 **Total income (loss).** Combine lines 3 through 5 . . . . . . ▶	**6**	

Deductions (See instructions for limitations.)

7 Compensation of officers	**7**	
8a Salaries and wages |_______| **b** Less jobs credit |_______| **c** Bal ▶	**8c**	
9 Repairs	**9**	
10 Bad debts	**10**	
11 Rents	**11**	
12 Taxes	**12**	
13 Interest	**13**	
14a Depreciation (see instructions)	**14a**	
b Depreciation claimed on Schedule A and elsewhere on return . .	**14b**	
c Subtract line 14b from line 14a	**14c**	
15 Depletion **(Do not deduct oil and gas depletion.)** . . .	**15**	
16 Advertising	**16**	
17 Pension, profit-sharing, etc. plans	**17**	
18 Employee benefit programs	**18**	
19 Other deductions (see instructions) *(attach schedule)* . .	**19**	
20 **Total deductions.** Add lines 7 through 19 . . . . . . ▶	**20**	
21 Ordinary income (loss) from trade or business activities. Subtract line 20 from line 6	**21**	

Tax and Payments

22 **Tax:**		
a Excess net passive income tax *(attach schedule)*	**22a**	
b Tax from Schedule D (Form 1120S)	**22b**	
c Add lines 22a and 22b (see instructions for additional taxes)	**22c**	
23 **Payments:**		
a 1992 estimated tax payments	**23a**	
b Tax deposited with Form 7004	**23b**	
c Credit for Federal tax on fuels *(attach Form 4136)*	**23c**	
d Add lines 23a through 23c	**23d**	
24 Estimated tax penalty (see page 3 of instructions). Check if Form 2220 is attached . . ▶☐	**24**	
25 **Tax due.** If the total of lines 22c and 24 is larger than line 23d, enter amount owed. See instructions for depositary method of payment . . . . ▶	**25**	
26 **Overpayment.** If line 23d is larger than the total of lines 22c and 24, enter amount overpaid ▶	**26**	
27 Enter amount of line 26 you want: **Credited to 1993 estimated tax** ▶ |_______| **Refunded** ▶	**27**	

Please Sign Here

Under penalties of perjury, I declare that I have examined this return, including accompanying schedules and statements, and to the best of my knowledge and belief, it is true, correct, and complete. Declaration of preparer (other than taxpayer) is based on all information of which preparer has any knowledge.

▶ _______________________________   Signature of officer   Date   ▶ Title

Paid Preparer's Use Only

Preparer's signature ▶	Date	Check if self-employed ▶ ☐ Preparer's social security number
Firm's name (or yours if self-employed) and address ▶		E.I. No. ▶ ZIP code ▶

For Paperwork Reduction Act Notice, see page 1 of separate instructions.   Cat. No. 11510H   Form **1120S** (1992)

Form 1120S (1992)   Page **2**

Schedule A   Cost of Goods Sold (See instructions.)

1 Inventory at beginning of year	**1**	
2 Purchases.	**2**	
3 Cost of labor	**3**	
4 Additional section 263A costs (see instructions) *(attach schedule)*	**4**	
5 Other costs *(attach schedule)*.	**5**	
6 **Total.** Add lines 1 through 5	**6**	
7 Inventory at end of year	**7**	
8 **Cost of goods sold.** Subtract line 7 from line 6. Enter here and on page 1, line 2	**8**	

9a Check all methods used for valuing closing inventory:

   (i) ☐ Cost

   (ii) ☐ Lower of cost or market as described in Regulations section 1.471-4

   (iii) ☐ Writedown of "subnormal" goods as described in Regulations section 1.471-2(c)

   (iv) ☐ Other (specify method used and attach explanation) ▶ ....

  b Check if the LIFO inventory method was adopted this tax year for any goods *(if checked, attach Form 970)*. . . . . . ▶ ☐

  c If the LIFO inventory method was used for this tax year, enter percentage (or amounts) of closing inventory computed under LIFO . . . . **9c** |

  d Do the rules of section 263A (for property produced or acquired for resale) apply to the corporation? . . . . ☐ Yes ☐ No

  e Was there any change in determining quantities, cost, or valuations between opening and closing inventory? . . ☐ Yes ☐ No
     If "Yes," attach explanation.

Schedule B   Other Information

	Yes	No
1 Check method of accounting: **(a)** ☐ Cash **(b)** ☐ Accrual **(c)** ☐ Other (specify) ▶		
2 Refer to the list in the instructions and state the corporation's principal: **(a)** Business activity ▶ .... **(b)** Product or service ▶		
3 Did the corporation at the end of the tax year own, directly or indirectly, 50% or more of the voting stock of a domestic corporation? (For rules of attribution, see section 267(c).) If "Yes," attach a schedule showing: **(a)** name, address, and employer identification number and **(b)** percentage owned.		
4 Was the corporation a member of a controlled group subject to the provisions of section 1561?		
5 At any time during calendar year 1992, did the corporation have an interest in or a signature or other authority over a financial account in a foreign country (such as a bank account, securities account, or other financial account)? (See instructions for exceptions and filing requirements for form TD F 90-22.1.) . . . . If "Yes," enter the name of the foreign country ▶		
6 Was the corporation the grantor of, or transferor to, a foreign trust that existed during the current tax year, whether or not the corporation has any beneficial interest in it? If "Yes," the corporation may have to file Forms 3520, 3520-A, or 926		
7 Check this box if the corporation has filed or is required to file **Form 8264,** Application for Registration of a Tax Shelter . . . . ▶ ☐		
8 Check this box if the corporation issued publicly offered debt instruments with original issue discount . . ▶ ☐ If so, the corporation may have to file **Form 8281,** Information Return for Publicly Offered Original Issue Discount Instruments.		
9 If the corporation: **(a)** filed its election to be an S corporation after 1986, **(b)** was a C corporation before it elected to be an S corporation **or** the corporation acquired an asset with a basis determined by reference to its basis (or the basis of any other property) in the hands of a C corporation, and **(c)** has net unrealized built-in gain (defined in section 1374(d)(1)) in excess of the net recognized built-in gain from prior years, enter the net unrealized built-in gain reduced by net recognized built-in gain from prior years (see instructions) . . . . ▶ $		
10 Check this box if the corporation had subchapter C earnings and profits at the close of the tax year (see instructions) . . . . ▶ ☐		
11 Was this corporation in operation at the end of 1992?		
12 How many months in 1992 was this corporation in operation?		

Designation of Tax Matters Person (See instructions.)

Enter below the shareholder designated as the tax matters person (TMP) for the tax year of this return:

Name of
designated TMP ▶ ________________________________

Identifying
number of TMP ▶ ________________________________

Address of
designated TMP ▶ ________________________________

Form 1120S (1992)   Page **3**

Schedule K   Shareholders' Shares of Income, Credits, Deductions, etc.

	(a) Pro rata share items		(b) Total amount
Income (Loss)	1 Ordinary income (loss) from trade or business activities (page 1, line 21)	1	
	2 Net income (loss) from rental real estate activities *(attach Form 8825)*	2	
	3a Gross income from other rental activities 3a		
	b Less expenses *(attach schedule)* 3b		
	c Net income (loss) from other rental activities	3c	
	4 Portfolio income (loss):		
	a Interest income	4a	
	b Dividend income	4b	
	c Royalty income	4c	
	d Net short-term capital gain (loss) *(attach Schedule D (Form 1120S))*	4d	
	e Net long-term capital gain (loss) *(attach Schedule D (Form 1120S))*	4e	
	f Other portfolio income (loss) *(attach schedule)*	4f	
	5 Net gain (loss) under section 1231 (other than due to casualty or theft) *(attach Form 4797)*	5	
	6 Other income (loss) *(attach schedule)*	6	
Deductions	7 Charitable contributions (see instructions) *(attach list)*	7	
	8 Section 179 expense deduction *(attach Form 4562)*	8	
	9 Deductions related to portfolio income (loss) (see instructions) *(itemize)*	9	
	10 Other deductions *(attach schedule)*	10	
Investment Interest	11a Interest expense on investment debts	11a	
	b (1) Investment income included on lines 4a through 4f above	11b(1)	
	(2) Investment expenses included on line 9 above	11b(2)	
Credits	12a Credit for alcohol used as a fuel *(attach Form 6478)*	12a	
	b Low-income housing credit (see instructions):		
	(1) From partnerships to which section 42(j)(5) applies for property placed in service before 1990	12b(1)	
	(2) Other than on line 12b(1) for property placed in service before 1990	12b(2)	
	(3) From partnerships to which section 42(j)(5) applies for property placed in service after 1989	12b(3)	
	(4) Other than on line 12b(3) for property placed in service after 1989	12b(4)	
	c Qualified rehabilitation expenditures related to rental real estate activities *(attach Form 3468)*	12c	
	d Credits (other than credits shown on lines 12b and 12c) related to rental real estate activities (see instructions)	12d	
	e Credits related to other rental activities (see instructions)	12e	
	13 Other credits (see instructions)	13	
Adjustments and Tax Preference Items	14a Depreciation adjustment on property placed in service after 1986	14a	
	b Adjusted gain or loss	14b	
	c Depletion (other than oil and gas)	14c	
	d (1) Gross income from oil, gas, or geothermal properties	14d(1)	
	(2) Deductions allocable to oil, gas, or geothermal properties	14d(2)	
	e Other adjustments and tax preference items *(attach schedule)*	14e	
Foreign Taxes	15a Type of income ▶		
	b Name of foreign country or U.S. possession ▶		
	c Total gross income from sources outside the United States *(attach schedule)*	15c	
	d Total applicable deductions and losses *(attach schedule)*	15d	
	e Total foreign taxes (check one): ▶ ☐ Paid ☐ Accrued	15e	
	f Reduction in taxes available for credit *(attach schedule)*	15f	
	g Other foreign tax information *(attach schedule)*	15g	
Other	16a Total expenditures to which a section 59(e) election may apply	16a	
	b Type of expenditures ▶		
	17 Tax-exempt interest income	17	
	18 Other tax-exempt income	18	
	19 Nondeductible expenses	19	
	20 Total property distributions (including cash) other than dividends reported on line 22 below	20	
	21 Other items and amounts required to be reported separately to shareholders (see instructions) *(attach schedule)*		
	22 Total dividend distributions paid from accumulated earnings and profits	22	
	23 **Income (loss).** (Required only if Schedule M-1 must be completed.) Combine lines 1 through 6 in column (b). From the result, subtract the sum of lines 7 through 11a, 15e, and 16a	23	

Form 1120S (1992)   Page **4**

Schedule L	Balance Sheets	Beginning of tax year		End of tax year	
Assets		(a)	(b)	(c)	(d)
1	Cash				
2a	Trade notes and accounts receivable				
b	Less allowance for bad debts				
3	Inventories				
4	U.S. Government obligations				
5	Tax-exempt securities				
6	Other current assets (attach schedule)				
7	Loans to shareholders				
8	Mortgage and real estate loans				
9	Other investments (attach schedule)				
10a	Buildings and other depreciable assets				
b	Less accumulated depreciation				
11a	Depletable assets				
b	Less accumulated depletion				
12	Land (net of any amortization)				
13a	Intangible assets (amortizable only)				
b	Less accumulated amortization				
14	Other assets (attach schedule)				
15	Total assets				
	Liabilities and Shareholders' Equity				
16	Accounts payable				
17	Mortgages, notes, bonds payable in less than 1 year				
18	Other current liabilities (attach schedule)				
19	Loans from shareholders				
20	Mortgages, notes, bonds payable in 1 year or more				
21	Other liabilities (attach schedule)				
22	Capital stock				
23	Paid-in or capital surplus				
24	Retained earnings				
25	Less cost of treasury stock		( )		( )
26	Total liabilities and shareholders' equity				

Schedule M-1	Reconciliation of Income (Loss) per Books With Income (Loss) per Return (You are not required to complete this schedule if the total assets on line 15, column (d), of Schedule L are less than $25,000.)

1	Net income (loss) per books		5	Income recorded on books this year not included on Schedule K, lines 1 through 6 (itemize):	
2	Income included on Schedule K, lines 1 through 6, not recorded on books this year (itemize):		a	Tax-exempt interest $	
3	Expenses recorded on books this year not included on Schedule K, lines 1 through 11a, 15e, and 16a (itemize):		6	Deductions included on Schedule K, lines 1 through 11a, 15e, and 16a, not charged against book income this year (itemize):	
a	Depreciation $		a	Depreciation $	
b	Travel and entertainment $		7	Add lines 5 and 6	
4	Add lines 1 through 3		8	Income (loss) (Schedule K, line 23). Line 4 less line 7	

Schedule M-2	Analysis of Accumulated Adjustments Account, Other Adjustments Account, and Shareholders' Undistributed Taxable Income Previously Taxed (See instructions.)

		(a) Accumulated adjustments account	(b) Other adjustments account	(c) Shareholders' undistributed taxable income previously taxed
1	Balance at beginning of tax year			
2	Ordinary income from page 1, line 21			
3	Other additions			
4	Loss from page 1, line 21	( )		
5	Other reductions	( )	( )	
6	Combine lines 1 through 5			
7	Distributions other than dividend distributions			
8	Balance at end of tax year. Subtract line 7 from line 6			

SCHEDULE K-1
(Form 1120S)

Department of the Treasury
Internal Revenue Service

Shareholder's Share of Income, Credits, Deductions, etc.

▶ See separate instructions.

For calendar year 1992 or tax year
beginning   , 1992, and ending   , 19

OMB No. 1545-0130

1992

Shareholder's identifying number ▶	Corporation's identifying number ▶
Shareholder's name, address, and ZIP code	Corporation's name, address, and ZIP code

A Shareholder's percentage of stock ownership for tax year (see Instructions for Schedule K-1) . . . . ▶ .... %

B Internal Revenue Service Center where corporation filed its return ▶ ....

C **(1)** Tax shelter registration number (see Instructions for Schedule K-1) . . . . ▶ ....

     (2) Type of tax shelter ▶ ....

D Check applicable boxes: **(1)** ☐ Final K-1   **(2)** ☐ Amended K-1

	(a) Pro rata share items		(b) Amount	(c) Form 1040 filers enter the amount in column (b) on:
Income (Loss)	**1** Ordinary income (loss) from trade or business activities	1		See Shareholder's Instructions for Schedule K-1 (Form 1120S).
	2 Net income (loss) from rental real estate activities	2		
	3 Net income (loss) from other rental activities	3		
	4 Portfolio income (loss):			
	a Interest	4a		Sch. B, Part I, line 1
	b Dividends	4b		Sch. B, Part II, line 5
	c Royalties	4c		Sch. E, Part I, line 4
	d Net short-term capital gain (loss)	4d		Sch. D, line 5, col. (f) or (g)
	e Net long-term capital gain (loss)	4e		Sch. D, line 13, col. (f) or (g)
	f Other portfolio income (loss) (attach schedule)	4f		(Enter on applicable line of your return.)
	5 Net gain (loss) under section 1231 (other than due to casualty or theft)	5		See Shareholder's Instructions for Schedule K-1 (Form 1120S).
	6 Other income (loss) (attach schedule)	6		(Enter on applicable line of your return.)
Deductions	**7** Charitable contributions (see instructions) (attach schedule)	7		Sch. A, line 13 or 14
	8 Section 179 expense deduction	8		See Shareholder's Instructions for Schedule K-1 (Form 1120S).
	9 Deductions related to portfolio income (loss) (attach schedule)	9		
	10 Other deductions (attach schedule)	10		
Investment Interest	**11a** Interest expense on investment debts	11a		Form 4952, line 1
	b **(1)** Investment income included on lines 4a through 4f above	b(1)		See Shareholder's Instructions for Schedule K-1 (Form 1120S).
	(2) Investment expenses included on line 9 above	b(2)		
Credits	**12a** Credit for alcohol used as fuel	12a		Form 6478, line 10
	b Low-income housing credit:			
	(1) From section 42(j)(5) partnerships for property placed in service before 1990	b(1)		
	(2) Other than on line 12b(1) for property placed in service before 1990.	b(2)		Form 8586, line 5
	(3) From section 42(j)(5) partnerships for property placed in service after 1989	b(3)		
	(4) Other than on line 12b(3) for property placed in service after 1989	b(4)		
	c Qualified rehabilitation expenditures related to rental real estate activities (see instructions)	12c		
	d Credits (other than credits shown on lines 12b and 12c) related to rental real estate activities (see instructions)	12d		See Shareholder's Instructions for Schedule K-1 (Form 1120S).
	e Credits related to other rental activities (see instructions) ▶	12e		
	13 Other credits (see instructions)	13		
Adjustments and Tax Preference Items	**14a** Depreciation adjustment on property placed in service after 1986	14a		See Shareholder's Instructions for Schedule K-1 (Form 1120S) and Instructions for Form 6251
	b Adjusted gain or loss	14b		
	c Depletion (other than oil and gas)	14c		
	d **(1)** Gross income from oil, gas, or geothermal properties	d(1)		
	(2) Deductions allocable to oil, gas, or geothermal properties	d(2)		
	e Other adjustments and tax preference items (attach schedule)	14e		

For Paperwork Reduction Act Notice, see page 1 of Instructions for Form 1120S.   Cat. No. 11520D   **Schedule K-1 (Form 1120S) 1992**

A business organized as a corporation is a separate taxable entity. Usually, the tax on a corporation is separate from the taxes on its shareholders. Tax professionals call these business units **C corporations**. The name comes from the location of the governing Code provisions (Subchapter C).

Some corporations qualify for tax-exempt status. These corporations include religious, charitable, scientific, educational, civic, and literary units that operate for society's general benefit. Chapter 18 discusses exempt corporations. The focus of this chapter is C corporations.

Corporate Characteristics

For federal income tax purposes, six characteristics help in identifying organizations. Two characteristics are helpful in separating trusts and corporations. These characteristics are (1) associates and (2) the goal of carrying on a business and dividing the profits. Since corporations and partnerships have both, these characteristics are of no help in distinguishing between them. The IRS and courts use the other four characteristics to distinguish between corporations and partnerships. These characteristics are: (3) continuity of life, (4) centralized management, (5) limited liability, and (6) free transfer of interests. When a business unit has more than two of the four characteristics, it is an association taxable as a corporation.

Professional Service Corporations

Today, most states authorize professional service corporations. **Professional service corporations** are corporations whose shareholders and employees supply services to the public for a fee. Doctors, dentists, lawyers, architects, certified public accountants, and others use professional corporations to get tax and other benefits.

The tax benefits include pension and profit-sharing plans, medical reimbursement plans, and group-term life insurance. As to claims for faulty service or advice, state laws govern. Here, shareholders of professional corporations are liable to patients, clients, or customers. For other claims, the corporation's limited liability protects them. Professional corporations can operate as C or S corporations.

Corporate Tax Reporting

Every corporation subject to tax must file a return, regardless of its taxable income or tax due. Form 1120, U.S. Corporation Income Tax Return, is the regular corporate tax form. Calendar-year and fiscal-year corporations can use Form 1120. When a corporation meets certain conditions, it can file Form 1120-A, U.S. Corporation Short-Form Income Tax Return. Form 1120-A is a two-page return and Form 1120 is a four-page return.

Professional corporations that qualify, and whose shareholders have not elected S status, can use Form 1120 or Form 1120-A. When corporate shareholders elect S status, the corporation files Form 1120S, U.S. Income Tax Return for an S Corporation. Regardless of the tax form a corporation uses, special filing requirements apply in some situations. These situations include returns for partial years, for corporations with no transactions, and for corporations in bankruptcy.

Period Covered by Return

Corporations, like individuals and some partnerships, can file their return on a calendar-year or fiscal-year basis. When a corporation changes its tax year, it must file a short period return. This return covers the period between the close of the last year and the start of the new fiscal year.

Some corporations use the 52-53 week year rather than the 12-month year. For these corporations, the normal year has 52 weeks of 7-days each or 364 days. For the extra day (two in a leap year), the corporation adds a week to its fiscal year every five or six years. Corporations can use the 52-53 week tax year if they use this time unit for financial reporting.

Corporations must usually get permission from the IRS to change their accounting period. Corporations request a change on Form 1128, Application to Adopt, Change, or Retain a Tax Year. To have an immediate effect, the corpora-

Form 1120-A Used by Corporations Meeting Following Conditions

1. Gross receipts, total income, and total property value are individually under $500,000
2. No ownership interests in foreign corporations
3. No foreign shareholders owning 50% or more of the corporation's stock
4. Not a personal holding company or a member of a controlled group
5. Does not file a consolidated tax return
6. Not undergoing dissolution or liquidation
7. Not the corporation's last tax return
8. Only received dividends are from domestic corporations qualifying for the 70% or 80% dividends-received deduction
9. Not eligible for nonrefundable tax credits other than the general business credit and prior year minimum tax credit
10. Not required to file any special tax returns, such as a foreign tax return or an insurance company return
11. Not subject to the environmental tax
12. No liability for interest under certain installment sales or certain installment payment plans

tion must file Form 1128 before the end of the fifteenth day of the second calendar month after the corporation's short period ends.

Reporting Method

Most corporations use the **accrual method of accounting** for tax reporting purposes. Under this method, corporations usually report all income earned in the year though some is not yet received. Also, they usually deduct all expenses incurred in the year though some are not paid.

Expenses are usually deductible when all events take place to set up and determine the offsetting debt. The process is the **all events test.** However, some expense items are not deductible in the payment year. When a corporation pays an insurance premium for more than one year, only a proportionate share is deductible in the payment year. Also, payments for depreciable property do not create a deductible expense.

Under certain conditions, a financial institution, service business, and tax shelter must use the accrual method of accounting. When a corporation's average annual gross receipts for the three prior years is more than $5 million, it must use the accrual method of accounting. A farming business and certain personal service corporations are exempt from this requirement if they were eligible to use the **cash method** of accounting under prior law.

Due Date

The due date of a domestic corporation's tax return is the fifteenth day of the third month after the corporate year ends. If the due date falls on a Saturday, Sunday, or holiday, the return is due on the next business day. This date also applies to a foreign corporation with a U.S. office or place of business. For a foreign corporation without a U.S. office or place of business, the due date is the fifteenth day of the sixth month after the corporate year ends.

Filing Place

Domestic corporations and foreign corporations with a U.S. office file their returns with the IRS Service Center stated in the instructions to the forms. Corporations with their principal place of business outside the U.S. file their returns with the IRS Service Center in Philadelphia. Corporations claiming a U.S. possessions tax credit also file there.

Signatures

A corporate officer must sign the corporation's tax return. This officer can be the president, vice-president, treasurer, chief accounting officer, or any other officer authorized to sign. When a person outside the corporation prepares the return for a fee, this person also signs the return and enters a TIN or EIN. The TIN is the *preparer's* social security number. The EIN is the identification number of the *preparer's* employer. Beneath the signature, the preparer enters the name and address of his or her place of business. If the outside person prepares the return without charging a fee, he or she does not have to sign it.

Taxable Income Calculation

Corporations calculate their taxable income somewhat like individuals calculate their profit or loss from business on Schedule C (Form 1040). Like Form 1040, Form 1120 does not have a separate gross income line. Corporate taxpayer's group their gross and net income items under one "income" heading, page 1 (left of lines 1-11). Also, while Form 1120 has only one group of deductions, page 1 (left of lines 12-29), three deduction groups exist: business deductions, NOL deduction, and special deductions. Example 1 contains an overview of the income and deduction items on Form 1120.

EXAMPLE 1 ──────────────────────────

QRM is a calender-year corporation that uses the accrual method of accounting. Nondeductible expenses are not part of the overview below since they do not enter into the calculation of taxable income.

Calculation of Corporate Taxable Income

Gross income (including dividend income of $4,000 from QST, a corp. owned 8% by QRM)	$120,500	
Less deductions (generally business expenses)	55,000	
Taxable income before NOL and special deductions	$ 65,500	
Less:		
NOL	$2,500	
Dividends received deduction ($4,000 x 70%)	2,800	5,300
Corporate taxable income		$ 60,200

────────────────────────────

Income Items

Usually, the Code provisions that govern the taxability of income items for individual taxpayers also govern them for corporations. In some cases, additional provisions apply to corporations. The discussion below covers several income items reported on Form 1120.

Gross Profit from Sales

The **gross profit from sales** is the difference between net sales and cost of goods sold. **Net sales** are gross sales less returns and allowances. Corporations can deduct *sales discounts* directly from sales, or treat the discounts as business expense.

Inventories can be a material income-producing factor in the production, manufacture, purchase, and sale of merchandise. When inventories are such a factor, corporations use them to calculate cost of goods sold. In inventory, they include raw materials, supplies, work in process, and merchandise held for sale or consumption. When a corporation manufactures products for sale, it should consider all production costs when determining cost of goods sold. These costs include direct materials, direct labor, and production overhead. The process is **full costing**.

To calculate **cost of goods sold**, a corporation adds and deducts several items. The corporation adds its (1) beginning inventory, (2) materials or merchandise bought for manufacture or sale, (3) salaries and wages of production personnel, and (4) production overhead costs. From this total, the corporation subtracts its ending inventory. To determine the cost of materials and merchandise for manufacture or sale, the corporation should deduct returns, allowances, and *trade discounts*. Sometimes, a corporation records the cost of materials before *cash discounts*. Here, a corporation deducts the discounts when they become part of income. A cash discount becomes part of income when the purchasing corporation pays an invoice within the discount period. When a corporation records material purchases net of discounts, the corporation does not take an expense deduction for the discounts.

Gross Profit from Services

In a service business (such as a commission, fee, or storage business), inventories are not a material income-producing factor. Thus, **gross profit from services** equals the gross service income. Expenses of earning this income are deductions from gross income.

Dividends

In general, a corporation includes all money and other property dividends it receives in gross income. However, corporations get a special deduction for dividends they receive. Stock dividends a corporation receives may or may not be taxable. Usually, common stock dividends to common shareholders are nontaxable. Most other stock dividends are taxable.

A corporation distributing appreciated real or personal property to shareholders usually recognizes a gain. When the market value of distributed property is below the property's cost, the corporation does not recognize a loss. To recognize a loss, the corporation must sell or exchange the property.

Interest Income

Interest on the general debts of a state, territory, or political subdivision (city, county, public school district, etc.) is wholly exempt from federal income tax. Also, interest on debts of United States possessions is exempt from tax. Corporations report this interest on Form 1120, Schedule M-1, Reconciliation of Income per Books With Income per Return. This schedule reconciles a corporation's book income with its taxable income before special deductions and NOLs.

Interest on debts of the United States and its instrumentalities is part of gross income. Corporations report taxable interest on notes, bank deposits, corporate bonds, and other debts on Form 1120.

Rents

Gross rent from property is part of gross income. A corporation separately states expenses it incurs in earning this income. Thus, a corporation can report depreciation deductions, repair expense, and taxes as business expense deductions.

Royalties

Corporations include royalties in gross income. Then, they report ordinary, necessary, and reasonable royalty expenses as a deduction from this income. These expenses include a deduction for the depletion of mines and other natural deposits.

Gains

Whether the sale or exchange of corporate property result in gain or loss, the disposing corporation must report all transaction details. A corporation reports these details on Form 4797, Sales of Business Property. First, the cor-poration determines the amount of gain or loss, if any. Then, it determines the tax treatment. Some gains and losses get ordinary treatment. Others qualify for long-term capital gain treatment through Section 1231. Chapter 12 discusses Section 1231.

A corporation must maintain a separate record of its capital gains and losses. Such a record is necessary though the rate of tax is the same on the corporation's net capital gain and other income. Corporations need this record to offset capital losses and capital gains properly. When a corporation has a net loss from capital asset transactions, it cannot deduct it against ordinary income. The corporation can carry the loss back 3 years and forward 5 years and use it to offset gains in those years. A corporation treats any capital loss carryback or carryover as a short-term capital loss. First, it uses the carryback or carryover loss to offset short-term capital gains. Then, the corporation uses the remaining loss to offset long-term capital gains. The amount offset in a year cannot create or increase an NOL.

Other Income

A corporation places income not listed separately on its return in *other income*. This income includes recoveries from bad debt deductions in a prior year when the corporation got a deduction benefit.

Assessments against shareholders are not other income. These assessments are additional contributions to capital. Also, when a shareholder cancels a debt of the corporation to itself, the corporation does not have other income. The corporation has an additional capital contribution.

Under some conditions, a corporation does not realize income when it cancels a debt through bankruptcy. The same treatment is possible through a creditor's cancellation agreement. To get this treatment, the corporation's debts at cancellation time must be more than the value of the corporation's property. Also, a corporation does not recognize income from the cancellation or reduction of debt in other situations. These situations include a reorganization, composition agreement, or real property arrangement under the Bankruptcy Act. However, a corporation may have taxable income from a reorganization when tax avoidance is one of the corporation's principal purposes.

When a corporation purchases its own bonds at a price above or below their amortized issue price, a deductible loss or taxable gain results. Also, a corporation can recognize income when it issues stock to pay the corporation's debts. The income element is the amount that the debt issue exceeds the market value of the stock.

A corporation does not recognize income when property values appreciate. When a corporation writes up the carrying value of property, the offset is usually to retained earnings or capital. The write-up amount is not part of gross income.

The gross income of foreign corporations should include only the income from sources within the United States. When a corporation sells goodwill for more than its basis, the difference is taxable.

Sometimes a corporation leases property to others with the provision that the lessee will pay any rent directly to shareholders. Here, the law treats the transaction as though the corporation received the rent and distributed it to shareholders. Thus, the corporation includes the rent in gross income and reports the shareholder payments as distributions.

Business Deductions

Many corporate deductions are similar to those proprietors and partnerships take to arrive at their profit or loss. However, within any one deduction group differences can exist.

Compensation

For personal services, compensation is deductible when it passes three tests. Test 1 examines whether the compensation is ordinary and necessary for the corporation's business. Test 2 examines whether the compensation is reasonable for the services the corporation gets. Test 3 examines whether the corporation pays or accrues the compensation during the year under its accounting method.

The deduction for salaries and wages equals the total compensation paid or accrued less any job credits. A corporation reports the net amount as a business expense. Payments to employees for something other than personal services are not deductible. Payments to corporate employees that are loans or profit distributions are not deductible. Services provided to corporate employees for the purchase of their property are not deductible. These payments are part of the acquired property's cost.

When a corporations's total receipts are $500,000 or more, it reports all compensation to officers on Form 1120, Schedule E, Compensation of Officers. Here, the reporting corporation includes each officer's name, SSN, percent of time devoted to business, and percent of stock ownership. Under the heading *amount of compensation*, a corporation includes each officer's total salary, commission, and bonus, regardless of form. A bonus is deductible if an officer's total compensation, including the bonus, is reasonable. When determining reasonableness, the IRS includes in compensation nontaxable pension and retirement plan contributions made in the officer's name. Schedule E provides the type of data the IRS can use to determine the relationship between each officer's compensation and profit distributions. This schedule also provides the data needed to test the reasonableness of an officer's compensation.

While a definite rule for determining the reasonableness of compensation does not exist, there are some guidelines. The main guideline is what other organizations, with like circumstances, ordinarily pay for like services. Other guidelines are the size of the salary, local living costs, the officer's personal ability, and degree of responsibility within the corporation.

Sometimes a corporation makes **golden parachute payments** to officers. A corporation usually makes these payments when another corporation gains control of the corporation. The usual purpose of the payments is to give the old officers more funds so they will have more time to find another job. Like a parachute, these payments let the old officers down slowly. Frequently, these payments are higher than an officer's historic compensation. The amount in excess of the officer's reasonable compensation is not deductible. Also, this officer must pay a special 20% excise tax on **excess golden parachute payments**. This tax is in addition to the officer's regular income tax.

Repairs

The cost of incidental property repairs, which does not add to a property's value or life, is usually deductible. When determining the repair deduction, corporations distinguish between capital and revenue payments. The cost of permanent improvements that increase the value or life of property, and the cost of new buildings, machinery, and equipment, are capital payments. They are not currently deductible. However, a corporation can depreciate these items (take a cost recovery deduction) over a specified life period. Payments that do not add to a property's life or value are revenue payments and usually can be deducted immediately.

Bad Debts

Under the accrual method of accounting, corporations recognize income from the sale of goods and services though they receive no cash. Later, the underlying receivable can become partially or fully uncollectible. For the part that becomes uncollectible, the accruing corporation can take a bad debt deduction. Most taxpayers, including corporations, can only use the direct write-off method for bad debts. An exception exists for certain financial institutions. Here, the reserve method of accounting (allowance for doubtful accounts) is still available.

EXAMPLE 2 ——————————————————

In August of last year, a corporation using the cash method of accounting loaned $1,000 to a supplier at 12% simple interest. On June 15 of the current year, the supplier's note became worthless. Since the interest on the loan is not recognized until collected, the corporation cannot take a deduction for the lost interest. However, the corporation can deduct $1,000 for the loss of its principal (the loan itself).

Rent Expense

Rent a corporation pays or accrues for the use of business property in which it has no equity is deductible. Amounts a corporation pays for the benefit of the landlord (property owner) is additional rent. These amounts can include tax and interest payments. The premium a corporation pays to secure a lease is deductible as rent expense. However, the corporation should prorate the premium over the rental period. Also, a corporation must prorate advance rental payments over the rental period.

Taxes

The taxes that state or local governments impose on corporations are usually deductible. One exception is a local benefit assessment that increases the value of property. **Local benefit assessments** that increase the value of property include the installation of first time items. First time items include sidewalks, storm sewers, paved roads, etc. Another exception is the sales tax on the purchase of depreciable property. Here, the sales tax is part of the property's costs. A corporation can deduct the sales taxes it pays for non-depreciable items as a business or investment expense. Taxes and carrying charges (interest) for a construction project must be capitalized under the uniform capitalization rules. Federal excise taxes, state stamp taxes, and import duties are not deductible as taxes. However, if these taxes are ordinary and necessary to the corporation's business, the corporation can deduct them. A corporation cannot deduct federal income, estate, inheritance, and gift taxes.

Taxes Included in the Cost of Property

1. Real estate taxes for unimproved and unproductive property
2. Taxes paid for work on the development of real property (such as FICA and FUTA taxes)

Interest Expense

Interest a corporation pays or accrues on business debt is usually deductible. One exception is the interest a corporation pays on money it borrows to buy or carry tax-exempt securities. Such interest is not deductible. Another exception is the interest a corporation pays on construction project loans. Such interest becomes part of the property's cost.

Charitable Contributions

Like individuals, corporations can take a limited deduction for contributions to charitable organizations. The deduction's upper limit is 10% of the corporation's taxable income before certain items. These items include any charitable contribution deductions, NOL carrybacks, special dividend deductions, and capital loss carrybacks. In addition, the giving corporation must support all non-cash property contributions with a separate contribution schedule. This schedule must show the name and address of each donee, amount of each donation, and valuation method.

Ordinarily, a corporation deducts a contribution in the year it transfers property or cash to a charity. However, a corporation using the accrual method of accounting can choose to deduct a contribution in the year it makes the accrual. To get a charitable deduction in the accrual year, the corporation must pay the contribution within the 2½ months after its year ends. Also, the corporate directors must adopt a proper authorizing resolution in the year of accrual. Then, the accruing corporation attaches a copy of the resolution to its deduction year tax return.

If a corporation donates appreciated tangible personal capital-gain property to a public charity, a special rule applies. The corporation can deduct the property's FMV when the charity uses the property for its exempt function.

When a corporation donates appreciated ordinary income property other than inventory to a public charity, there is an upper limit on the deduction. Here, the deduction usually cannot be more than the property's FMV less any ordinary income element. This market value reduction rule also applies to donations of depreciable property the corporation uses in its business.

When a corporation donates appreciated inventory items to public charities, a special rule applies. Here, the upper limit on the deduction is the inventory's adjusted basis plus one-half of the appreciation. However, the deduction cannot exceed twice the inventory's adjusted basis. Also, the charity must use the inventory in its tax-exempt charitable work.

EXAMPLE 3 ——————————————————

During 1992, a corporation made charitable contributions of $9,000. Also, the corporation's taxable income for 1992 was $75,000 before the charitable contributions, but after a special dividend received deduction. During 1992, the corporation received dividends of $5,000 and deducted $4,000 (80% x $5,000 = $4,000) as a special deduction. The

corporation's deductible contribution for 1992 is $7,900.

Taxable income (before considering charitable contributions)	$75,000
Plus special deduction	4,000
Basis for determining maximum deduction	$79,000
Charitable contributions deduction (10% of $79,000)	$ 7,900

The excess contribution of $1,100 ($9,000 – $7,900) gets a five year carryover. However, the total deduction in succeeding years is subject to the 10% of taxable income limitation.

Charitable contributions that are really payments for corporate benefits are deductible business expenses. These payments are not subject to the 10% limitation.

EXAMPLE 4 ——————————————————

XYZ corporation gives money to a hospital for a ward that the employees of XYZ will use. The corporation deducts the contribution as a business expense, not as a charitable contribution.

EXAMPLE 5 ——————————————————

Corporation RST makes yearly contributions to the local YWCA. The local YWCA operates a unit on RST property for the exclusive benefit of RST employees. RST deducts the annual contributions as business expense.

Money spent for influencing the public on specific legislation, for propaganda, and for political campaign contributions is not deductible. However, money spent testifying before a legislative group on direct interest business legislation is deductible. A portion of membership dues in an organization that engages in testifying activities on direct interest business legislation is also deductible.

Cost Recovery (Depreciation)

Corporations deduct depreciation on property placed in service before 1981 under various methods. For property placed in service between 1981-1986, corporations usually use ACRS. Usually, ACRS replaces earlier depreciation methods. For property placed in service after 1986, corporations usually use MACRS, ADS, or some authorized combination of the two.

The MACRS rules use a specific depreciation method for each class of property. Except 27½ and 31½ year real property, MACRS uses declining-balance depreciation with a switch to straight-line depreciation. The switch to straight-line depreciation gives a MACRS user a larger deduction. Technically, the switch should take place in the year a property item's straight-line depreciation exceeds its accelerated depreciation. Practically, the switch takes place in the year the straight-line depreciation equals or exceeds the property's accelerated depreciation.

For 3, 5, 7, and 10 year class property, MACRS uses the 200% declining-balance method. For 15 and 20 year class property, MACRS uses the 150% declining-balance method. MACRS rules also specify a half-year averaging convention for tangible personal property classes. In some cases, these rules specify a mid-quarter averaging convention. Corporations write-off real property in the 27½ and 31½ year classes on a straight-line basis with a mid-month averaging convention. They report the write-off deductions on Form 4562, Depreciation and Amortization.

Immediate expensing for $10,000 of tangible personal property placed in service after December 31, 1986 is available. Taxpayers who place $210,000 or more of tangible personal property in service in one year cannot take an immediate expense deduction. The expensing option phases out when the total cost of this property is between $200,000 and $210,000. The immediate expensing amount cannot be more than the taxable income from any active trade or business. For this limitation, taxable income is determined before the immediate expensing deduction.

Amortization

Corporations can take a pro rata deduction for the cost of some intangible property. This property includes franchises, trademarks, and leases; but not goodwill. Accountants call the deduction amortization. Technically, it is depreciation. Corporations calculate the deduction on Form 4562, Depreciation and Amortization.

In taxation, the term *amortization* usually refers to the write-off of bond premiums or discounts, organization costs, pollution control facilities, etc. A corporation may choose to write-off its organization costs over a period of 60 months or more, starting with the month the corporation begins business.

Depletion

Usually, a corporation can take a deduction for certain natural resources it removes from the ground. The deduction is **depletion**. It represents the cost of the wasting resource the corporation consumes in mining, quarrying, drilling, etc. activities. Two methods of calculating depletion are the *cost method* and *percentage method*. The two methods are discussed below.

Cost Method. Taxpayers determine depletion deductions by dividing a property's adjusted basis by the estimated units in the property (barrels, tons, etc.). Then, these taxpayers multiply the results by the number of units sold during the year.

EXAMPLE 6 ——————————————————————

QRM is a coal mining corporation. During the year, QRM purchases a coal mine for $240,000. The company's geologists estimate that QRM can recover 120,000 tons of coal from the mine. Assume QRM mines 40,000 tons of coal and sells 28,000 tons for $720,000 during the year. Here, QRM's cost depletion is $56,000 ($240,000/120,000 tons x 28,000 tons sold). QRM can recover its remaining $184,000 of mine cost ($240,000 − $56,000) by depletion deductions in future years.

Percentage Method. Taxpayers who use the percentage depletion method determine depletion deductions by multiplying the property's gross income by a statutory rate. Corporations can choose to use the percentage method of write-off for a variety of natural deposits. The statutory rates range from 5% to 22%. Under the percentage method, there is an upper limit on the percentage depletion deduction. The depletion cannot be more than 50% of taxable income from the property before the depletion deduction, NOL carrybacks, and capital loss carrybacks. In addition, corporations can use the percentage method only if the percentage depletion amount is more than the cost depletion amount.

EXAMPLE 7

Assume QRM in Example 6 had taxable income of $150,000 from selling 28,000 tons of coal for $720,000. The percentage depletion rate for coal is 10%. QRM can deduct percentage depletion of $72,000 (10% x $720,000). This depletion amount is less than the taxable income limit of $75,000 (50% x $150,000), and more than the $56,000 of cost depletion. After taking the depletion deduction, the remaining basis of QRM's property is $168,000 ($240,000 − $72,000). Note, percentage depletion deductions have no relationship to a property's cost. Thus, QRM can continue taking percentage depletion after it recovers all of its mine costs.

Refiners and retailers of domestic crude oil and natural gas can use the percentage depletion method. However, the percentage deduction cannot be more than a specified amount of the taxpayer's depletable oil or natural gas quantity. Taxpayers claiming percentage depletion should examine Code Sections 613 and 613A for the proper rate.

Advertising Expense

To be deductible, advertising expense must be reasonable in amount and have a reasonable relationship to the business. Advertising expenses are deductible when they are paid or accrued under the corporation's method of accounting. Though an advertising program benefits several years, the expense is still deductible in the current year. However, the IRS requires corporations to amortize the cost of catalogs that benefit more than one year.

Pension, Profit-Sharing, and Other Deferred Compensation Plans

An employer can take a limited deduction for contributions to pension, profit-sharing, or other deferred compensation plans. The contribution must be an ordinary and necessary expense of carrying on the business or profession.

Depletion Rate Examples

22%—Asbestos, bauxite, chromite, quartz crystals (radio grade), and ores of the following metals: cadmium, cobalt, lead, lithium, manganese, mercury, nickel, platinum, tin, titanium, tungsten, vanadium, and zinc

15%—Gold, silver, copper, and iron ore

14%—Metal mines (if not in the 22% or 15% rates), quartzite, rock ashphalt, and vermiculite

10%—Asbestos (if from deposits outside U.S.), coal, lignite, perlite, and sodium chloride

7½%—Clay and shale used in sewer pipe and brick

5%—Gravel, peat, pumice, sand, shale (except oil shale), and stone (except stone used as dimension or oramental stone)

The qualified plans that employers sponsor for employees fall into two major groups: defined contribution plans and defined benefit plans. Annual contributions to defined benefit plans must cover normal and past service costs to be deductible. Profit-sharing and stock-bonus plans are not subject to these minimum funding standards. However, contributions to profit-sharing plans cannot be more than 15% of compensation.

Other Benefit Plans

Employers can deduct the costs of employee benefit plans, whether or not the benefits are taxable to employees. Typical *statutory benefit plans* include group-term life insurance, accident insurance, and health-benefit plans. Like cafeteria plans, these plans are subject to comprehensive discrimination rules. The purpose of the discrimination rules is to encourage fair treatment for all employees. The rules are complex and increase an employer's record keeping costs.

An employer's benefit plan that discriminates for high-pay employees causes these employees to pay taxes on the benefits. The IRS assesses a penalty on employers who fail to report timely any discrimination benefits. However, benefits of health insurance plans are excludable from gross income even when the plans discriminate for highly-paid employees.

Nondiscriminatory Benefit Plans to be Nontaxable

1. Must be in writing
2. Must have enforceable employees' rights
3. Must require an employer to maintain the plan indefinitely
4. Must specifiy that all employees be informed of a plan's details
5. Must be for the exclusive benefit of employees

Other Deductions

A corporation enters business deductions that it does not show separately under *other deductions*. These deductions include:

1. Amortization of bond discounts over life of bonds
2. Premiums paid for fire, storm, property damage, liability, and other business insurance
3. Miscellaneous expenses related to rental and investment income
4. Premiums paid for nondiscriminatory *group-term* life insurance coverage for employees. Here, up to $50,000 of the benefits can be excluded from an employee's gross income. Employees calculate the taxes on an employer's group-term coverage above $50,000 using the Chapter 4 formula. While the premiums on the excess coverage are taxable to employees, they still are deductible to the corporation. Of course, the employee's total compensation package must be reasonable to be deductible.

   A corporation can carry life insurance policies on the lives of officers and other key personnel and name itself as the beneficiary. Premiums on such policies are not deductible by the corporation. However, the insurance proceeds the corporation receives when a person dies are not part of the corporation's gross income. Corporations can purchase regular life insurance for executives and let them name the beneficiaries. Here, the policy premiums are deductible employee compensation when the total compensation package is reasonable.

5. Research and experimental payments in the first occurrence year. If a corporation deducts these payments in this year, it does not have to get permission from the IRS for the write-off. At a later time if the corporation decides to write-off these expenses, it must ask the IRS for permission to take an immediate deduction.

6. Losses from casualties or thefts. When a corporation does not receive insurance proceeds or other compensation for the complete destruction of property by a casualty or theft, the property's adjusted basis is deductible. The corporation should explain the deduction in a separate schedule. The schedule should include a description of the property, acquisition date, cost, improvements, cost recovery deductions, and salvage value. If the corporation receives insurance proceeds or other compensation, the schedule should show this amount.

   If there are casualty and theft gains as well as losses and the corporation holds the property more than 12 months, Section 1231 applies. Chapter 12 discusses Section 1231 gains and losses.

7. Qualifying cost for safety and service awards. Corporations can deduct up to $1,600 for qualifying service or safety awards when the average annual cost of these awards for the tax year is $400 or less. To be deductible, employees can receive only tangible personal property. Also, the awards cannot discriminate for officers and high-pay employees. Regardless of the awarded item's cost, the maximum deduction for any one employee is $1,600.

   When safety awards are made to more than 10% of a corporation's eligible employees in a tax year, all such awards are deductible as additional compensation (assuming it's reasonable). When determining if safety awards are given to more than 10% of eligible employees, certain personnel are excluded from the base. Excluded employees are managers, administrators, clerical employees, and other professional personnel. Awards to excluded personnel for safety are deductible as additional compensation (assuming an employee's total compensation is reasonable).

   To be a deductible service award, an employee must have completed at least five years of company service. Also, once an employee receives a deductible service award, four intervening years must pass before this employee receives another one.

8. Miscellaneous cost associated with six non-cash benefits employees exclude from gross income. These benefits include subsidized eating facilities, de minimis (small value) items, qualifying employee discounts, working condition fringe benefits, no-additional-cost service, and athletic facilities. Chapter 4 discusses these benefits.

Net Operating Loss (NOL)

Like individuals, corporations can take a deduction for a carryback or carryover **NOL**. Chapter 18 describes the NOL calculation method. However, the deduction is not available to S corporations, mutual insurance companies (other than marine), and regulated investment companies.

A corporation subtracts all business deductions from income to arrive at taxable income *before NOL and special deductions*. Then, the corporation subtracts its NOL and special dividend deductions to arrive at taxable income. The excess of a corporation's gross income over allowable deductions corresponds roughly to a corporation's net income. It is not unusual for the two amounts to differ because of exempt income earned by the corporation, NOLs, special deductions, and nondeductible expenses or losses. Corporations use Schedule M-1 to reconcile book net income to taxable income before NOL and special deductions.

Special Deductions

Corporations subtract several special deductions from gross income to arrive at taxable income. These deductions deal primarily with dividends from other corporations. Corporations list these dividends on Form 1120, Schedule C, Dividends and Special Deductions.

Non-Affiliated Dividends

Corporations can take a special deduction for dividends from other corporations. The special deduction is usually 80% or 70% of the dividends a corporation receives from taxable domestic corporations. These percentages also apply to amounts received as dividends from foreign corporations engaged in a U.S. business. There is no special deduction for foreign companies engaged in activities exclusively outside the United States.

Unless the affiliated dividend received deduction applies, the deduction is 80% for corporations owning 20% or more of a distributing corporation. The next section covers dividends from affiliated corporations. The 20% ownership test applies to a distributing corporation's stock value and voting power. If a receiving corporation owns less than 20% of the distributing corporation, the dividend received deduction is 70% of received dividends.

Usually, the dividend received deduction cannot exceed 70% or 80% of the corporation's taxable income calculated before three items. The three items are (1) NOL deduction, (2) dividends-received deduction, and (3) capital loss carryback to the tax year. However, the taxable income limitation does not apply when the deduction for the 70% or 80% dividends result in a NOL. Thus, the corporation deducts the full dividends when calculating its NOL.

The special dividend deduction does not apply to stock a corporation holds for less than 15 days. For cumulative preferred stock held less than 91 days with dividends in arrears, the deduction does not apply.

Affiliated Dividends

Affiliated corporations that do not file consolidated returns can choose to deduct 100% of qualifying dividends from group members. The parent corporation makes the election to file a consolidated return. However, each affiliate must consent to the choice. Chapter 18 discusses affiliated groups.

Nondeductible Items

Several business payments are not deductible in determining taxable income. Some of these payments are capitalized, and then deducted in the form of depreciation (cost recovery deductions).

Nondeductible Items

1. Building and equipment purchases and replacements (capital payments)
2. Defending title to property (add to basis of property)
3. Discounts on capital stock at the time of issue (reduce corporation's capital stock accounts)
4. Fines for violation of law or police regulations (contrary to public policy and not necessary expenses)
5. Commissions on purchase or sale of real estate or securities (addition to purchase price or deduction from selling price)
6. Tax penalties (contrary to public policy and not necessary expenses)
7. Architect's fees for designing and constructing a building (addition to cost of building)
8. Advertising costs and admission fees either directly or indirectly connected with political activities (not a Code deduction)

Corporate Income Tax

The corporate rate structure is **progressive** like the one for individuals (as taxable income goes up, rates go up). At higher income levels the lower rates are subject to phase out. Once the phase out is complete, the rate is **flat** (same rate for all taxable income).

Other than professional service corporations and S corporations, all corporations calculate their tax with the same rate structure. For professional service corporations, the rate is the same on all taxable income regardless of amount. For S corporations, the law taxes each shareholder on his or her portion of corporate income.

Rate Structure and Tax Calculation

The tax rates for most corporations are shown in Table 17-1. Immediately before and after phase out of the lower rates, the marginal tax rate is 34%. For corporations with taxable income of $75,000 or less, Congress set the rates

lower than 34% to stimulate their growth. The law phases out the lower rates by a 5% additional tax on taxable income between $100,000 and $335,000. When taxable income reaches $335,000, the government recovers all lower rate benefits. The amount of these benefits is $11,750 {[(34% − 15%) x $50,000] + [(34% − 25%) x $25,000]} or [($335,000 − $100,000) x 5%]. For professional service corporations, the rate is 34% on all taxable income.

Table 17-1
Corporate Income Tax Rate Schedule

Taxable Income	1991 Corporate Tax Rate
$0–$50,000	15.0%
$50,001–75,000	25.0
$75,001–100,000	34.0
$100,001–335,000	39.0
Over $335,000	34.0

EXAMPLE 8

In 1992, XYZ corporation, a calendar-year domestic manufacturing corporation, has gross income of $900,000. The corporation also has business deductions of $750,000. XYZ's gross income includes $30,000 of domestic dividends that are eligible for the 80% dividends-received deduction. Table 17-2 shows the calculations for XYZ's taxable income of $126,000 and income tax of $32,390. If the tax on XYZ was a flat 34%,

Table 17-2
Calculation of Corporate Income Tax (Calendar-Year Corporation)

Taxable Income—1992	
Gross income	$900,000
Less: business deductions	750,000
Difference	$150,000
Less: special deductions	
Dividends received (80% x $30,000)	24,000
Taxable income	$126,000
Income Tax—1992 (Calendar-Year Corporation)	
15% x $50,000	$ 7,500
25% x $25,000	6,250
34% x $25,000	8,500
39% x $26,000	10,140
Income tax	$ 32,390

its income tax liability would have been $42,840. Thus, through the lower rates XYZ saves $10,450 ($42,840 – $32,390).

Schedule J, Tax Computation

Before discussing the elements of the total tax calculation process, an overview of the proper IRS schedule is helpful. Illustration 17-1 contains the corporate tax calculation schedule.

Illustration 17-1

This illustration shows the schedule corporations use for determining their total tax liability. After entering their income tax liability on Schedule J (line 3), corporations enter certain credits (lines 4a through 4f). They add these credits and enter a total (line 5). Then, they subtract the total (line 5) from the income tax amount (line 3) and enter the difference (line 6). Corporations enter other taxes (lines 7 through 9b), add them to the difference (line 6 less line 5), and enter their total tax liability (line 10). Corporations also enter this amount on Form 1120, page 1 (line 31).

Elements of Total Tax Calculation Process

The discussion below examines the elements corporations use to calculate their tax liability. Corporations enter a total for these items on Schedule J (line 10) and on Form 1120 (line 31).

Foreign Tax Credit. Corporations that pay taxes to a foreign country or United States' possession can claim a foreign tax credit. Corporations claiming the credit must file Form 1118, Foreign Tax Credit—Corporations. For a corporation to get the full benefit of a foreign tax credit requires careful planning. Discussion of the foreign tax credit is beyond the scope of this book.

Possessions Tax Credit. A U.S. possessions corporation claims the possessions tax credit on Form 5735, Possessions Corporation Tax Credit Under Section 936.

Orphan Drug Credit. Some corporations incur qualified clinical testing expenses for certain rare disease drugs. These corporations can claim an orphan drug credit on Form 6765, Credit for Increasing Research Activities (or for claiming the orphan drug credit). See *Highlights* (page xiv) for discussion of credit extension.

Credit for Fuel from Nonconventional Sources. Corporations that sell qualified fuels from nonconventional sources, such as oil produced from shale and tar sands, can get a fuels credit. Corporations claiming the credit must attach a schedule to Form 1120 that shows the credit calculations.

General Business Credit. Corporations also can claim a general business credit. The general business credit consists of the following items: a limited investment tax credit, jobs credit, alcohol fuel credit, research credit, and orphan drug credit. Corporations that claim two or more business credits complete Form 3800, General Business Credit. Then, these corporations enter their combined credit on Schedule J (line 4e).

With certain limitations, corporations can use the general business credit to offset their tax liability. The credit limit is $25,000 of tax liability plus 75% of the liability exceeding $25,000. To support each credit, corporations use specific tax forms. For the jobs credit, corporations use Form 5884, Jobs Credit. For the alcohol fuel credit, they use Form 6478, Credit for Alcohol Used as Fuel. For the research activity and orphan drug credit, corporations use Form 6765, Credit for Increasing Research Activities (or for claiming the orphan drug credit). See *Highlights* (page xiv) for discussion of extension of research activities and orphan drug credits.

Personal Holding Company Tax. Corporations that are personal holding companies calculate their tax on Form 1120, Sch. PH, U.S. Personal Holding Company Tax, and enter it on Schedule J. A personal holding company has 5 or fewer shareholders who own more than 50% of the outstanding stock's value. In addition, the corporation must pass certain income tests. A discussion of personal holding companies is beyond the scope of this book.

Alternative Minimum Tax (AMT). Congress offers corporations incentives to invest in organizations with certain social and economic goals. The investment incentives take the form

Illustration 17-1
Schedule J (Form 1120), Tax Computation

Form 1120 (1992)   Page **3**

Schedule J   **Tax Computation** (See instructions.)

1   Check if the corporation is a member of a controlled group (see sections 1561 and 1563) . . . . . ▶ ☐

2   If the box on line 1 is checked:

a   Enter the corporation's share of the $50,000 and $25,000 taxable income bracket amounts (in that order):
    (i) $_______________   (ii) $_______________

b   Enter the corporation's share of the additional 5% tax (not to exceed $11,750) ▶ $_______________

3   Income tax. Check this box if the corporation is a qualified personal service corporation as defined in section
    448(d)(2) (see instructions on page 14) . . . . ▶ ☐ | 3 |

4a Foreign tax credit (attach Form 1118) . . . . | 4a |
b   Possessions tax credit (attach Form 5735) . . . . | 4b |
c   Orphan drug credit (attach Form 6765) . . . . | 4c |
d   Credit for fuel produced from a nonconventional source . . . . . . | 4d |
e   General business credit. Enter here and check which forms are attached:
    ☐ Form 3800   ☐ Form 3468 ☐ Form 5884   ☐ Form 6478
    ☐ Form 6765   ☐ Form 8586 ☐ Form 8830   ☐ Form 8826 . . | 4e |
f   Credit for prior year minimum tax (attach Form 8827) . . . . . . | 4f |

5   **Total credits.** Add lines 4a through 4f . . . . | 5 |
6   Subtract line 5 from line 3 . . . . | 6 |
7   Personal holding company tax (attach Schedule PH (Form 1120)) . . | 7 |
8   Recapture taxes. Check if from: ☐ Form 4255   ☐ Form 8611 . . | 8 |
9a Alternative minimum tax (attach Form 4626) . . . . | 9a |
b   Environmental tax (attach Form 4626) . . . . | 9b |
10 **Total tax.** Add lines 6 through 9b. Enter here and on line 31, page 1 . . | 10 |

of tax credits and accelerated deductions. The Code calls them incentive tax preferences. To insure that the incentives (tax preferences) do not reduce a corporation's tax liability to zero, the law levies a minimum tax on them. Corporations subject to the minimum tax add it to their regular income tax liability.

The AMT is similar to the AMT for individual taxpayers. Corporate AMT is a second tax system that parallels the corporate income tax system. For many corporations, AMT will be the applicable tax system. This tax broadens the corporate tax base by bringing financial accounting principles into the tax system. An in-depth discussion of corporate AMT is beyond the scope of this book. However, the following comments should help in understanding the overall importance of AMT.

For many AMT items, the corporate AMT system taxes them before the income tax system taxes them. Since it is difficult to avoid most advance AMT taxes, proper planning is important. Corporations that ignore AMT taxes in their estimated tax calculation can receive an underpayment penalty. A corporation can ease some AMT impact by using AMT adjustments for regular tax purposes. However, these adjustments increase a corporation's regular taxable income. Thus, the corporation will pay income taxes on the adjustments early. A principal AMT planning goal should be to project the tax impact of AMT items accurately. By making AMT projections, a corporation can create an income tax base that optimizes the use of preference items. Reducing the impact of AMT taxes requires sophisticated tax planning. Such planning is beyond the scope of this book.

Environmental Tax. A corporation can be liable for the environmental tax if its modified alternative minimum taxable income (AMTI) exceeds $2,000,000. The rate of tax is 0.12%. Corporations subject to the environmental tax calculate it on Form 4626, Alternative Minimum Tax—Corporations. A discussion of this tax is also beyond this book's scope.

Tax and Payments Schedule

Before discussing the elements of the tax and payments schedule, an overview of this schedule is helpful. Illustration 17-2 contains the tax and payments schedule on Form 1120, bottom of page 1. Corporations use the schedule to determine the amount due to or from the government.

Illustration 17-2

On the 1992 Form 1120 tax and payments schedule, a corporation enters its 1991 tax overpayment (line 32a) and 1992 estimated tax payments (line 32b). The overpayment comes from the corporation's 1991 return (line 36). On its 1991 Form 1120, the corporation asked the IRS to credit the overpayment to its 1992 estimated tax.

On its 1992 Form 1120, a corporation that overpays its 1992 estimated tax can enter a refund request (line 32c). To support the request it uses Form 4466, Corporation Application for Quick Refund of Overpayment of Estimated Tax. Then, the corporation subtracts the refund request (line 32c) from the 1991 overpayment (line 32a) and 1992 estimated tax payment (line 32b), and enters the difference (line 32d).

On the tax and payments schedule (line 32e), a corporation enters any tax deposited with Form 7004, Application for Automatic Extension of Time To File Corporation Income Tax Return. Also on this schedule, a corporation enters any credit from a regulated investment company (line 32f) and any fuel tax credit (line 32g). The corporation adds these amounts (line 32d through 32g) and enters the total (line 32h). Then, it enters any estimated tax underpayment penalty (line 33).

The corporation adds the total tax (line 31) and underpayment penalty (line 33), and subtracts the payments and credits (line 32h). If the total (lines 31 and 33) is more than the payments and credits (line 32h), the corporation owes the government money. On the line for taxes due (line 34), it enters this amount. If the total tax and underpayment (lines 31 and 33) is less than the payments and credits (line 32h), the government owes the corporation money. The corporation enters this amount

as an overpayment (line 35). A corporation that wants to apply a portion of its 1992 overpayment to its 1993 estimated tax, enters this amount in the proper line opening (line 36). A corporation that wants to receive a portion of the 1992 overpayment, enters this amount in the blank at the right (line 36).

Elements of Tax and Payments Schedule

At the bottom of Form 1120, page 1, a corporation determines the amount due to or from the government. The starting point for the determination is the total tax (line 31). It is supported by the calculations on Schedule J, Tax Computation.

Estimated Tax Payments. When a corporation expects its estimated income taxes minus credits to be $500 or more, it must make estimated tax payments. Chapter 18 discusses estimated taxes.

Tax Deposit, Form 7004. A corporation can get an automatic six-month extension of time to file Form 1120. To get the extension, a corporation must file Form 7004. First, it must estimate the tax due. Then, it must deposit the tax before the end of the corporation's regular tax return due date. If the corporation does not deposit the tax by this date, the IRS assesses a penalty. The penalty is ½% per month, or part of a month that the tax deposit is late. The IRS does not assess the penalty when a reasonable cause for a late deposit exists.

Regulated Investment Company Credit. To claim the regulated investment companies credit, a corporation must file Form 2439, Notice to Shareholder of Undistributed Long-Term Capital Gains.

Fuels Credit. To claim the gasoline and special fuels credit, a corporation must file Form 4136, Credit for Federal Tax on Fuels.

Tax Due

Corporations do not send the tax due directly to the IRS. They deposit it with a commercial depositary or Federal Reserve bank. Corpora-

Illustration 17-3
Filled-In Corporation Return, Form 1120, Page 2

Form 1120 (1992)   Page **2**

Schedule A   Cost of Goods Sold (See instructions.)

1	Inventory at beginning of year	1 100,956 00
2	Purchases	2 207,858 00
3	Cost of labor	3 74,807 00
4	Additional section 263A costs (attach schedule)	4
5	Other costs (attach schedule)	5 30,529 00
6	**Total.** Add lines 1 through 5	6 414,150 00
7	Inventory at end of year	7 90,283 00
8	**Cost of goods sold.** Subtract line 7 from line 6. Enter here and on page 1, line 2	8 323,867 00

9a Check all methods used for valuing closing inventory:

     (i) ☒ Cost   (ii) ☐ Lower of cost or market as described in Regulations section 1.471-4

     (iii) ☐ Writedown of "subnormal" goods as described in Regulations section 1.471-2(c)

     (iv) ☐ Other (Specify method used and attach explanation.) ▶ ....

   b   Check if the LIFO inventory method was adopted this tax year for any goods (if checked, attach Form 970) . . . . . . ▶ ☐

   c   If the LIFO inventory method was used for this tax year, enter percentage (or amounts) of closing inventory computed under LIFO . . . . | 9c |

   d   Do the rules of section 263A (for property produced or acquired for resale) apply to the corporation? . . . . ☐ Yes ☒ No

   e   Was there any change in determining quantities, cost, or valuations between opening and closing inventory? If "Yes," attach explanation . . . . ☐ Yes ☒ No

Schedule C   Dividends and Special Deductions (See instructions.)

		(a) Dividends received	(b) %	(c) Special deductions: (a) × (b)
1	Dividends from less-than-20%-owned domestic corporations that are subject to the 70% deduction (other than debt-financed stock)		70	
2	Dividends from 20%-or-more-owned domestic corporations that are subject to the 80% deduction (other than debt-financed stock)	1,750	80	1,400
3	Dividends on debt-financed stock of domestic and foreign corporations (section 246A)		see instructions	
4	Dividends on certain preferred stock of less-than-20%-owned public utilities		41.176	
5	Dividends on certain preferred stock of 20%-or-more-owned public utilities		47.059	
6	Dividends from less-than-20%-owned foreign corporations and certain FSCs that are subject to the 70% deduction		70	
7	Dividends from 20%-or-more-owned foreign corporations and certain FSCs that are subject to the 80% deduction		80	
8	Dividends from wholly owned foreign subsidiaries subject to the 100% deduction (section 245(b))		100	
9	**Total.** Add lines 1 through 8. See instructions for limitation			1,400
10	Dividends from domestic corporations received by a small business investment company operating under the Small Business Investment Act of 1958		100	
11	Dividends from certain FSCs that are subject to the 100% deduction (section 245(c)(1))		100	
12	Dividends from affiliated group members subject to the 100% deduction (section 243(a)(3))		100	
13	Other dividends from foreign corporations not included on lines 3, 6, 7, 8, or 11	235		
14	Income from controlled foreign corporations under subpart F (attach Form(s) 5471)			
15	Foreign dividend gross-up (section 78)			
16	IC-DISC and former DISC dividends not included on lines 1, 2, or 3 (section 246(d))			
17	Other dividends			
18	Deduction for dividends paid on certain preferred stock of public utilities (see instructions)			
19	**Total dividends.** Add lines 1 through 17. Enter here and on line 4, page 1 ▶	1,985		
20	**Total deductions.** Add lines 9, 10, 11, 12, and 18. Enter here and on line 29b, page 1 ▶			1,400

Schedule E   Compensation of Officers (See instructions for line 12, page 1.)

Complete Schedule E only if total receipts (line 1a plus lines 4 through 10 on page 1, Form 1120) are $500,000 or more.

	(a) Name of officer	(b) Social security number	(c) Percent of time devoted to business	(d) Common	(e) Preferred	(f) Amount of compensation
1	A.T. Mason	249-36-3579	100 %	15.0 %	5 %	45,000
	A.R. Boyd	279-40-7478	100 %	7.5 %	None %	35,000
			%	%	%	
			%	%	%	
			%	%	%	
2	Total compensation of officers					80,000
3	Compensation of officers claimed on Schedule A and elsewhere on return					
4	Subtract line 3 from line 2. Enter the result here and on line 12, page 1					80,000